BANKRUPTCY CODE, RULES, AND OFFICIAL FORMS

2023 Law School Edition

ANNE LAWTON

Professor of Law Emerita
Michigan State University College of Law

WEST
ACADEMIC
PUBLISHING

© 2013 Thomson Reuters
© 2014–2022 LEG, Inc. d/b/a West Academic
© 2023 LEG, Inc. d/b/a West Academic
  860 Blue Gentian Road, Suite 350
  Eagan, MN 55121
  1-877-888-1330

Printed in the United States of America

ISBN: 979-8-88786-031-2

PREFACE

This publication contains the current Bankruptcy Code (11 U.S.C.) and related provisions of United States Code Titles 18 and 28, as amended through Pub. L. 118–7, approved June 30, 2023. Dollar amounts listed in the Code have been adjusted, pursuant to 11 U.S.C. § 104, to reflect the amounts published by the Judicial Conference of the United States on Feb. 4, 2022, 87 F.R. 6625, effective as of Apr. 1, 2022.

The current bankruptcy court fee schedule, including changes effective December 1, 2020, appears following 28 U.S.C. § 1930.

This publication also includes the 2022 amendments to the Uniform Commercial Code. The amendments appear in ~~strikeout~~/<u>underline</u> format. At the time of publication, eight states had enacted the 2022 amendments to the Uniform Commercial Code.

THE PUBLISHER

June 2023

iii

TABLE OF CONTENTS

TABLE OF CONTENTS

BANKRUPTCY CODE, RULES, AND OFFICIAL FORMS

2023 Law School Edition

THE CODE OF THE LAWS OF THE UNITED STATES OF AMERICA

TITLE 11
BANKRUPTCY CODE

Current through June 30, 2023; P.L. 118–7

For historical and amendment information see the notes following each statutory section at
http://uscode.house.gov

CHAPTER 1—GENERAL PROVISIONS

---

§ 101. Definitions

In this title the following definitions shall apply:

---

[1] So in original. Does not conform to chapter heading.

(1) The term "accountant" means accountant authorized under applicable law to practice public accounting, and includes professional accounting association, corporation, or partnership, if so authorized.

(2) The term "affiliate" means—

(A) entity that directly or indirectly owns, controls, or holds with power to vote, 20 percent or more of the outstanding voting securities of the debtor, other than an entity that holds such securities—

(i) in a fiduciary or agency capacity without sole discretionary power to vote such securities; or

(ii) solely to secure a debt, if such entity has not in fact exercised such power to vote;

(B) corporation 20 percent or more of whose outstanding voting securities are directly or indirectly owned, controlled, or held with power to vote, by the debtor, or by an entity that directly or indirectly owns, controls, or holds with power to vote, 20 percent or more of the outstanding voting securities of the debtor, other than an entity that holds such securities—

(i) in a fiduciary or agency capacity without sole discretionary power to vote such securities; or

(ii) solely to secure a debt, if such entity has not in fact exercised such power to vote;

(C) person whose business is operated under a lease or operating agreement by a debtor, or person substantially all of whose property is operated under an operating agreement with the debtor; or

(D) entity that operates the business or substantially all of the property of the debtor under a lease or operating agreement.

(3) The term "assisted person" means any person whose debts consist primarily of consumer debts and the value of whose nonexempt property is less than $226,850.

(4) The term "attorney" means attorney, professional law association, corporation, or partnership, authorized under applicable law to practice law.

(4A) The term "bankruptcy assistance" means any goods or services sold or otherwise provided to an assisted person with the express or implied purpose of providing information, advice, counsel, document preparation, or filing, or attendance at a creditors' meeting or appearing in a case or proceeding on behalf of another or providing legal representation with respect to a case or proceeding under this title.

(5) The term "claim" means—

(A) right to payment, whether or not such right is reduced to judgment, liquidated, unliquidated, fixed, contingent, matured, unmatured, disputed, undisputed, legal, equitable, secured, or unsecured; or

(B) right to an equitable remedy for breach of performance if such breach gives rise to a right to payment, whether or not such right to an equitable remedy is reduced to judgment, fixed, contingent, matured, unmatured, disputed, undisputed, secured, or unsecured.

(6) The term "commodity broker" means futures commission merchant, foreign futures commission merchant, clearing organization, leverage transaction merchant, or commodity options dealer, as defined in section 761 of this title, with respect to which there is a customer, as defined in section 761 of this title.

(7) The term "community claim" means claim that arose before the commencement of the case concerning the debtor for which property of the kind specified in section 541(a)(2) of this title is liable, whether or not there is any such property at the time of the commencement of the case.

(7A) The term "commercial fishing operation" means—

    (A) the catching or harvesting of fish, shrimp, lobsters, urchins, seaweed, shellfish, or other aquatic species or products of such species; or

    (B) for purposes of section 109 and chapter 12, aquaculture activities consisting of raising for market any species or product described in subparagraph (A).

(7B) The term "commercial fishing vessel" means a vessel used by a family fisherman to carry out a commercial fishing operation.

(8) The term "consumer debt" means debt incurred by an individual primarily for a personal, family, or household purpose.

(9) The term "corporation"—

    (A) includes—

        (i) association having a power or privilege that a private corporation, but not an individual or a partnership, possesses;

        (ii) partnership association organized under a law that makes only the capital subscribed responsible for the debts of such association;

        (iii) joint-stock company;

        (iv) unincorporated company or association; or

        (v) business trust; but

    (B) does not include limited partnership.

(10) The term "creditor" means—

    (A) entity that has a claim against the debtor that arose at the time of or before the order for relief concerning the debtor;

    (B) entity that has a claim against the estate of a kind specified in section 348(d), 502(f), 502(g), 502(h) or 502(i) of this title; or

    (C) entity that has a community claim.

(10A) The term "current monthly income"—

    (A) means the average monthly income from all sources that the debtor receives (or in a joint case the debtor and the debtor's spouse receive) without regard to whether such income is taxable income, derived during the 6-month period ending on—

        (i) the last day of the calendar month immediately preceding the date of the commencement of the case if the debtor files the schedule of current income required by section 521(a)(1)(B)(ii); or

        (ii) the date on which current income is determined by the court for purposes of this title if the debtor does not file the schedule of current income required by section 521(a)(1)(B)(ii); and

    (B)(i) includes any amount paid by any entity other than the debtor (or in a joint case the debtor and the debtor's spouse), on a regular basis for the household expenses of the debtor or the debtor's dependents (and in a joint case the debtor's spouse if not otherwise a dependent); and

        (ii) excludes—

            (I) benefits received under the Social Security Act (42 U.S.C. 301 et seq.);

            (II) payments to victims of war crimes or crimes against humanity on account of their status as victims of such crimes;

(III) payments to victims of international terrorism or domestic terrorism, as those terms are defined in section 2331 of title 18, on account of their status as victims of such terrorism; and

(IV) any monthly compensation, pension, pay, annuity, or allowance paid under title 10, 37, or 38 in connection with a disability, combat-related injury or disability, or death of a member of the uniformed services, except that any retired pay excluded under this subclause shall include retired pay paid under chapter 61 of title 10 only to the extent that such retired pay exceeds the amount of retired pay to which the debtor would otherwise be entitled if retired under any provision of title 10 other than chapter 61 of that title.

(11) The term "custodian" means—

(A) receiver or trustee of any of the property of the debtor, appointed in a case or proceeding not under this title;

(B) assignee under a general assignment for the benefit of the debtor's creditors; or

(C) trustee, receiver, or agent under applicable law, or under a contract, that is appointed or authorized to take charge of property of the debtor for the purpose of enforcing a lien against such property, or for the purpose of general administration of such property for the benefit of the debtor's creditors.

(12) The term "debt" means liability on a claim.

(12A) The term "debt relief agency" means any person who provides any bankruptcy assistance to an assisted person in return for the payment of money or other valuable consideration, or who is a bankruptcy petition preparer under section 110, but does not include—

(A) any person who is an officer, director, employee, or agent of a person who provides such assistance or of the bankruptcy petition preparer;

(B) a nonprofit organization that is exempt from taxation under section 501(c)(3) of the Internal Revenue Code of 1986;

(C) a creditor of such assisted person, to the extent that the creditor is assisting such assisted person to restructure any debt owed by such assisted person to the creditor;

(D) a depository institution (as defined in section 3 of the Federal Deposit Insurance Act) or any Federal credit union or State credit union (as those terms are defined in section 101 of the Federal Credit Union Act), or any affiliate or subsidiary of such depository institution or credit union; or

(E) an author, publisher, distributor, or seller of works subject to copyright protection under title 17, when acting in such capacity.

(13) The term "debtor" means person or municipality concerning which a case under this title has been commenced.

(13A) The term "debtor's principal residence"—

(A) means a residential structure if used as the principal residence by the debtor, including incidental property, without regard to whether that structure is attached to real property; and

(B) includes an individual condominium or cooperative unit, a mobile or manufactured home, or trailer if used as the principal residence by the debtor.

(14) The term "disinterested person" means a person that—

(A) is not a creditor, an equity security holder, or an insider;

(B) is not and was not, within 2 years before the date of the filing of the petition, a director, officer, or employee of the debtor; and

(C) does not have an interest materially adverse to the interest of the estate or of any class of creditors or equity security holders, by reason of any direct or indirect relationship to, connection with, or interest in, the debtor, or for any other reason.

(14A) The term "domestic support obligation" means a debt that accrues before, on, or after the date of the order for relief in a case under this title, including interest that accrues on that debt as provided under applicable nonbankruptcy law notwithstanding any other provision of this title, that is—

    (A) owed to or recoverable by—

        (i) a spouse, former spouse, or child of the debtor or such child's parent, legal guardian, or responsible relative; or

        (ii) a governmental unit;

    (B) in the nature of alimony, maintenance, or support (including assistance provided by a governmental unit) of such spouse, former spouse, or child of the debtor or such child's parent, without regard to whether such debt is expressly so designated;

    (C) established or subject to establishment before, on, or after the date of the order for relief in a case under this title, by reason of applicable provisions of—

        (i) a separation agreement, divorce decree, or property settlement agreement;

        (ii) an order of a court of record; or

        (iii) a determination made in accordance with applicable nonbankruptcy law by a governmental unit; and

    (D) not assigned to a nongovernmental entity, unless that obligation is assigned voluntarily by the spouse, former spouse, child of the debtor, or such child's parent, legal guardian, or responsible relative for the purpose of collecting the debt.

(15) The term "entity" includes person, estate, trust, governmental unit, and United States trustee.

(16) The term "equity security" means—

    (A) share in a corporation, whether or not transferable or denominated "stock", or similar security;

    (B) interest of a limited partner in a limited partnership; or

    (C) warrant or right, other than a right to convert, to purchase, sell, or subscribe to a share, security, or interest of a kind specified in subparagraph (A) or (B) of this paragraph.

(17) The term "equity security holder" means holder of an equity security of the debtor.

(18) The term "family farmer" means—

    (A) individual or individual and spouse engaged in a farming operation whose aggregate debts do not exceed $11,097,350 and not less than 50 percent of whose aggregate noncontingent, liquidated debts (excluding a debt for the principal residence of such individual or such individual and spouse unless such debt arises out of a farming operation), on the date the case is filed, arise out of a farming operation owned or operated by such individual or such individual and spouse, and such individual or such individual and spouse receive from such farming operation more than 50 percent of such individual's or such individual and spouse's gross income for—

        (i) the taxable year preceding; or

        (ii) each of the 2d and 3d taxable years preceding;

the taxable year in which the case concerning such individual or such individual and spouse was filed; or

(B) corporation or partnership in which more than 50 percent of the outstanding stock or equity is held by one family, or by one family and the relatives of the members of such family, and such family or such relatives conduct the farming operation, and

    (i) more than 80 percent of the value of its assets consists of assets related to the farming operation;

    (ii) its aggregate debts do not exceed $11,097,350 and not less than 50 percent of its aggregate noncontingent, liquidated debts (excluding a debt for one dwelling which is owned by such corporation or partnership and which a shareholder or partner maintains as a principal residence, unless such debt arises out of a farming operation), on the date the case is filed, arise out of the farming operation owned or operated by such corporation or such partnership; and

    (iii) if such corporation issues stock, such stock is not publicly traded.

(19) The term "family farmer with regular annual income" means family farmer whose annual income is sufficiently stable and regular to enable such family farmer to make payments under a plan under chapter 12 of this title.

(19A) The term "family fisherman" means—

(A) an individual or individual and spouse engaged in a commercial fishing operation—

    (i) whose aggregate debts do not exceed $2,268,550 and not less than 80 percent of whose aggregate noncontingent, liquidated debts (excluding a debt for the principal residence of such individual or such individual and spouse, unless such debt arises out of a commercial fishing operation), on the date the case is filed, arise out of a commercial fishing operation owned or operated by such individual or such individual and spouse; and

    (ii) who receive from such commercial fishing operation more than 50 percent of such individual's or such individual's and spouse's gross income for the taxable year preceding the taxable year in which the case concerning such individual or such individual and spouse was filed; or

(B) a corporation or partnership—

    (i) in which more than 50 percent of the outstanding stock or equity is held by—

        (I) 1 family that conducts the commercial fishing operation; or

        (II) 1 family and the relatives of the members of such family, and such family or such relatives conduct the commercial fishing operation; and

    (ii)(I) more than 80 percent of the value of its assets consists of assets related to the commercial fishing operation;

        (II) its aggregate debts do not exceed $2,268,550 and not less than 80 percent of its aggregate noncontingent, liquidated debts (excluding a debt for 1 dwelling which is owned by such corporation or partnership and which a shareholder or partner maintains as a principal residence, unless such debt arises out of a commercial fishing operation), on the date the case is filed, arise out of a commercial fishing operation owned or operated by such corporation or such partnership; and

        (III) if such corporation issues stock, such stock is not publicly traded.

(19B) The term "family fisherman with regular annual income" means a family fisherman whose annual income is sufficiently stable and regular to enable such family fisherman to make payments under a plan under chapter 12 of this title.

(20) The term "farmer" means (except when such term appears in the term "family farmer") person that received more than 80 percent of such person's gross income during the taxable year of such person immediately preceding the taxable year of such person during which the case under this title concerning such person was commenced from a farming operation owned or operated by such person.

(21) The term "farming operation" includes farming, tillage of the soil, dairy farming, ranching, production or raising of crops, poultry, or livestock, and production of poultry or livestock products in an unmanufactured state.

(21A) The term "farmout agreement" means a written agreement in which—

(A) the owner of a right to drill, produce, or operate liquid or gaseous hydrocarbons on property agrees or has agreed to transfer or assign all or a part of such right to another entity; and

(B) such other entity (either directly or through its agents or its assigns), as consideration, agrees to perform drilling, reworking, recompleting, testing, or similar or related operations, to develop or produce liquid or gaseous hydrocarbons on the property.

(21B) The term "Federal depository institutions regulatory agency" means—

(A) with respect to an insured depository institution (as defined in section 3(c)(2) of the Federal Deposit Insurance Act) for which no conservator or receiver has been appointed, the appropriate Federal banking agency (as defined in section 3(q) of such Act);

(B) with respect to an insured credit union (including an insured credit union for which the National Credit Union Administration has been appointed conservator or liquidating agent), the National Credit Union Administration;

(C) with respect to any insured depository institution for which the Resolution Trust Corporation has been appointed conservator or receiver, the Resolution Trust Corporation; and

(D) with respect to any insured depository institution for which the Federal Deposit Insurance Corporation has been appointed conservator or receiver, the Federal Deposit Insurance Corporation.

(22) The term "financial institution" means—

(A) a Federal reserve bank, or an entity that is a commercial or savings bank, industrial savings bank, savings and loan association, trust company, federally-insured credit union, or receiver, liquidating agent, or conservator for such entity and, when any such Federal reserve bank, receiver, liquidating agent, conservator or entity is acting as agent or custodian for a customer (whether or not a "customer", as defined in section 741) in connection with a securities contract (as defined in section 741) such customer; or

(B) in connection with a securities contract (as defined in section 741) an investment company registered under the Investment Company Act of 1940.

(22A) The term "financial participant" means—

(A) an entity that, at the time it enters into a securities contract, commodity contract, swap agreement, repurchase agreement, or forward contract, or at the time of the date of the filing of the petition, has one or more agreements or transactions described in paragraph (1), (2), (3), (4), (5), or (6) of section 561(a) with the debtor or any other entity (other than an affiliate) of a total gross dollar value of not less than $1,000,000,000 in notional or actual principal amount outstanding (aggregated across counterparties) at such time or on any day during the 15-month period preceding the date of the filing of the petition, or has gross mark-to-market positions of not less than $100,000,000 (aggregated across counterparties) in one or more such agreements or transactions with the debtor or any other entity (other than an affiliate) at such time or on any day during the 15-month period preceding the date of the filing of the petition; or

(B) a clearing organization (as defined in section 402 of the Federal Deposit Insurance Corporation Improvement Act of 1991).

(23) The term "foreign proceeding" means a collective judicial or administrative proceeding in a foreign country, including an interim proceeding, under a law relating to insolvency or adjustment of debt in which proceeding the assets and affairs of the debtor are subject to control or supervision by a foreign court, for the purpose of reorganization or liquidation.

(24) The term "foreign representative" means a person or body, including a person or body appointed on an interim basis, authorized in a foreign proceeding to administer the reorganization or the liquidation of the debtor's assets or affairs or to act as a representative of such foreign proceeding.

(25) The term "forward contract" means—

    (A) a contract (other than a commodity contract, as defined in section 761) for the purchase, sale, or transfer of a commodity, as defined in section 761(8) of this title, or any similar good, article, service, right, or interest which is presently or in the future becomes the subject of dealing in the forward contract trade, or product or byproduct thereof, with a maturity date more than two days after the date the contract is entered into, including, but not limited to, a repurchase or reverse repurchase transaction (whether or not such repurchase or reverse repurchase transaction is a "repurchase agreement", as defined in this section)[1] consignment, lease, swap, hedge transaction, deposit, loan, option, allocated transaction, unallocated transaction, or any other similar agreement;

    (B) any combination of agreements or transactions referred to in subparagraphs (A) and (C);

    (C) any option to enter into an agreement or transaction referred to in subparagraph (A) or (B);

    (D) a master agreement that provides for an agreement or transaction referred to in subparagraph (A), (B), or (C), together with all supplements to any such master agreement, without regard to whether such master agreement provides for an agreement or transaction that is not a forward contract under this paragraph, except that such master agreement shall be considered to be a forward contract under this paragraph only with respect to each agreement or transaction under such master agreement that is referred to in subparagraph (A), (B), or (C); or

    (E) any security agreement or arrangement, or other credit enhancement related to any agreement or transaction referred to in subparagraph (A), (B), (C), or (D), including any guarantee or reimbursement obligation by or to a forward contract merchant or financial participant in connection with any agreement or transaction referred to in any such subparagraph, but not to exceed the damages in connection with any such agreement or transaction, measured in accordance with section 562.

(26) The term "forward contract merchant" means a Federal reserve bank, or an entity the business of which consists in whole or in part of entering into forward contracts as or with merchants in a commodity (as defined in section 761) or any similar good, article, service, right, or interest which is presently or in the future becomes the subject of dealing in the forward contract trade.

(27) The term "governmental unit" means United States; State; Commonwealth; District; Territory; municipality; foreign state; department, agency, or instrumentality of the United States (but not a United States trustee while serving as a trustee in a case under this title), a State, a Commonwealth, a District, a Territory, a municipality, or a foreign state; or other foreign or domestic government.

(27A) The term "health care business"—

    (A) means any public or private entity (without regard to whether that entity is organized for profit or not for profit) that is primarily engaged in offering to the general public facilities and services for—

---

[1] So in original. Probably should be followed by a comma.

　　　　　(i)　the diagnosis or treatment of injury, deformity, or disease; and

　　　　　(ii)　surgical, drug treatment, psychiatric, or obstetric care; and

　　(B)　includes—

　　　　　(i)　any—

　　　　　　　(I)　general or specialized hospital;

　　　　　　　(II)　ancillary ambulatory, emergency, or surgical treatment facility;

　　　　　　　(III)　hospice;

　　　　　　　(IV)　home health agency; and

　　　　　　　(V)　other health care institution that is similar to an entity referred to in subclause (I), (II), (III), or (IV); and

　　　　　(ii)　any long-term care facility, including any—

　　　　　　　(I)　skilled nursing facility;

　　　　　　　(II)　intermediate care facility;

　　　　　　　(III)　assisted living facility;

　　　　　　　(IV)　home for the aged;

　　　　　　　(V)　domiciliary care facility; and

　　　　　　　(VI)　health care institution that is related to a facility referred to in subclause (I), (II), (III), (IV), or (V), if that institution is primarily engaged in offering room, board, laundry, or personal assistance with activities of daily living and incidentals to activities of daily living.

(27B) The term "incidental property" means, with respect to a debtor's principal residence—

　　(A)　property commonly conveyed with a principal residence in the area where the real property is located;

　　(B)　all easements, rights, appurtenances, fixtures, rents, royalties, mineral rights, oil or gas rights or profits, water rights, escrow funds, or insurance proceeds; and

　　(C)　all replacements or additions.

(28) The term "indenture" means mortgage, deed of trust, or indenture, under which there is outstanding a security, other than a voting-trust certificate, constituting a claim against the debtor, a claim secured by a lien on any of the debtor's property, or an equity security of the debtor.

(29) The term "indenture trustee" means trustee under an indenture.

(30) The term "individual with regular income" means individual whose income is sufficiently stable and regular to enable such individual to make payments under a plan under chapter 13 of this title, other than a stockbroker or a commodity broker.

(31) The term "insider" includes—

　　(A)　if the debtor is an individual—

　　　　　(i)　relative of the debtor or of a general partner of the debtor;

　　　　　(ii)　partnership in which the debtor is a general partner;

　　　　　(iii)　general partner of the debtor; or

　　　　　(iv)　corporation of which the debtor is a director, officer, or person in control;

　　(B)　if the debtor is a corporation—

    (i)   director of the debtor;

    (ii)   officer of the debtor;

    (iii) person in control of the debtor;

    (iv) partnership in which the debtor is a general partner;

    (v)   general partner of the debtor; or

    (vi) relative of a general partner, director, officer, or person in control of the debtor;

  (C) if the debtor is a partnership—

    (i)   general partner in the debtor;

    (ii)   relative of a general partner in, general partner of, or person in control of the debtor;

    (iii) partnership in which the debtor is a general partner;

    (iv) general partner of the debtor; or

    (v)   person in control of the debtor;

  (D) if the debtor is a municipality, elected official of the debtor or relative of an elected official of the debtor;

  (E) affiliate, or insider of an affiliate as if such affiliate were the debtor; and

  (F) managing agent of the debtor.

(32) The term "insolvent" means—

  (A) with reference to an entity other than a partnership and a municipality, financial condition such that the sum of such entity's debts is greater than all of such entity's property, at a fair valuation, exclusive of—

    (i)   property transferred, concealed, or removed with intent to hinder, delay, or defraud such entity's creditors; and

    (ii)   property that may be exempted from property of the estate under section 522 of this title;

  (B) with reference to a partnership, financial condition such that the sum of such partnership's debts is greater than the aggregate of, at a fair valuation—

    (i)   all of such partnership's property, exclusive of property of the kind specified in subparagraph (A)(i) of this paragraph; and

    (ii)   the sum of the excess of the value of each general partner's nonpartnership property, exclusive of property of the kind specified in subparagraph (A) of this paragraph, over such partner's nonpartnership debts; and

  (C) with reference to a municipality, financial condition such that the municipality is—

    (i)   generally not paying its debts as they become due unless such debts are the subject of a bona fide dispute; or

    (ii)   unable to pay its debts as they become due.

(33) The term "institution-affiliated party"—

  (A) with respect to an insured depository institution (as defined in section 3(c)(2) of the Federal Deposit Insurance Act), has the meaning given it in section 3(u) of the Federal Deposit Insurance Act; and

(B) with respect to an insured credit union, has the meaning given it in section 206(r) of the Federal Credit Union Act.

(34) The term "insured credit union" has the meaning given it in section 101(7) of the Federal Credit Union Act.

(35) The term "insured depository institution"—

    (A) has the meaning given it in section 3(c)(2) of the Federal Deposit Insurance Act; and

    (B) includes an insured credit union (except in the case of paragraphs (21B) and (33)(A) of this subsection).

(35A) The term "intellectual property" means—

    (A) trade secret;

    (B) invention, process, design, or plant protected under title 35;

    (C) patent application;

    (D) plant variety;

    (E) work of authorship protected under title 17; or

    (F) mask work protected under chapter 9 of title 17;

to the extent protected by applicable nonbankruptcy law.

(36) The term "judicial lien" means lien obtained by judgment, levy, sequestration, or other legal or equitable process or proceeding.

(37) The term "lien" means charge against or interest in property to secure payment of a debt or performance of an obligation.

(38) The term "margin payment" means, for purposes of the forward contract provisions of this title, payment or deposit of cash, a security or other property, that is commonly known in the forward contract trade as original margin, initial margin, maintenance margin, or variation margin, including mark-to-market payments, or variation payments.

(38A) The term "master netting agreement"—

    (A) means an agreement providing for the exercise of rights, including rights of netting, setoff, liquidation, termination, acceleration, or close out, under or in connection with one or more contracts that are described in any one or more of paragraphs (1) through (5) of section 561(a), or any security agreement or arrangement or other credit enhancement related to one or more of the foregoing, including any guarantee or reimbursement obligation related to 1 or more of the foregoing; and

    (B) if the agreement contains provisions relating to agreements or transactions that are not contracts described in paragraphs (1) through (5) of section 561(a), shall be deemed to be a master netting agreement only with respect to those agreements or transactions that are described in any one or more of paragraphs (1) through (5) of section 561(a).

(38B) The term "master netting agreement participant" means an entity that, at any time before the date of the filing of the petition, is a party to an outstanding master netting agreement with the debtor.

(39) The term "mask work" has the meaning given it in section 901(a)(2) of title 17.

(39A) The term "median family income" means for any year—

    (A) the median family income both calculated and reported by the Bureau of the Census in the then most recent year; and

(B) if not so calculated and reported in the then current year, adjusted annually after such most recent year until the next year in which median family income is both calculated and reported by the Bureau of the Census, to reflect the percentage change in the Consumer Price Index for All Urban Consumers during the period of years occurring after such most recent year and before such current year.

(40) The term "municipality" means political subdivision or public agency or instrumentality of a State.

(40A) The term "patient" means any individual who obtains or receives services from a health care business.

(40B) The term "patient records" means any record relating to a patient, including a written document or a record recorded in a magnetic, optical, or other form of electronic medium.

(41) The term "person" includes individual, partnership, and corporation, but does not include governmental unit, except that a governmental unit that—

    (A) acquires an asset from a person—

        (i) as a result of the operation of a loan guarantee agreement; or

        (ii) as receiver or liquidating agent of a person;

    (B) is a guarantor of a pension benefit payable by or on behalf of the debtor or an affiliate of the debtor; or

    (C) is the legal or beneficial owner of an asset of—

        (i) an employee pension benefit plan that is a governmental plan, as defined in section 414(d) of the Internal Revenue Code of 1986; or

        (ii) an eligible deferred compensation plan, as defined in section 457(b) of the Internal Revenue Code of 1986;

shall be considered, for purposes of section 1102 of this title, to be a person with respect to such asset or such benefit.

(41A) The term "personally identifiable information" means—

    (A) if provided by an individual to the debtor in connection with obtaining a product or a service from the debtor primarily for personal, family, or household purposes—

        (i) the first name (or initial) and last name of such individual, whether given at birth or time of adoption, or resulting from a lawful change of name;

        (ii) the geographical address of a physical place of residence of such individual;

        (iii) an electronic address (including an e-mail address) of such individual;

        (iv) a telephone number dedicated to contacting such individual at such physical place of residence;

        (v) a social security account number issued to such individual; or

        (vi) the account number of a credit card issued to such individual; or

    (B) if identified in connection with 1 or more of the items of information specified in subparagraph (A)—

        (i) a birth date, the number of a certificate of birth or adoption, or a place of birth; or

        (ii) any other information concerning an identified individual that, if disclosed, will result in contacting or identifying such individual physically or electronically.

(42) The term "petition" means petition filed under section 301, 302, 303 and[1] 1504 of this title, as the case may be, commencing a case under this title.

(42A) The term "production payment" means a term overriding royalty satisfiable in cash or in kind—

    (A) contingent on the production of a liquid or gaseous hydrocarbon from particular real property; and

    (B) from a specified volume, or a specified value, from the liquid or gaseous hydrocarbon produced from such property, and determined without regard to production costs.

(43) The term "purchaser" means transferee of a voluntary transfer, and includes immediate or mediate transferee of such a transferee.

(44) The term "railroad" means common carrier by railroad engaged in the transportation of individuals or property or owner of trackage facilities leased by such a common carrier.

(45) The term "relative" means individual related by affinity or consanguinity within the third degree as determined by the common law, or individual in a step or adoptive relationship within such third degree.

(46) The term "repo participant" means an entity that, at any time before the filing of the petition, has an outstanding repurchase agreement with the debtor.

(47) The term "repurchase agreement" (which definition also applies to a reverse repurchase agreement)—

    (A) means—

        (i) an agreement, including related terms, which provides for the transfer of one or more certificates of deposit, mortgage related securities (as defined in section 3 of the Securities Exchange Act of 1934), mortgage loans, interests in mortgage related securities or mortgage loans, eligible bankers' acceptances, qualified foreign government securities (defined as a security that is a direct obligation of, or that is fully guaranteed by, the central government of a member of the Organization for Economic Cooperation and Development), or securities that are direct obligations of, or that are fully guaranteed by, the United States or any agency of the United States against the transfer of funds by the transferee of such certificates of deposit, eligible bankers' acceptances, securities, mortgage loans, or interests, with a simultaneous agreement by such transferee to transfer to the transferor thereof certificates of deposit, eligible bankers' acceptance, securities, mortgage loans, or interests of the kind described in this clause, at a date certain not later than 1 year after such transfer or on demand, against the transfer of funds;

        (ii) any combination of agreements or transactions referred to in clauses (i) and (iii);

        (iii) an option to enter into an agreement or transaction referred to in clause (i) or (ii);

        (iv) a master agreement that provides for an agreement or transaction referred to in clause (i), (ii), or (iii), together with all supplements to any such master agreement, without regard to whether such master agreement provides for an agreement or transaction that is not a repurchase agreement under this paragraph, except that such master agreement shall be considered to be a repurchase agreement under this paragraph only with respect to each agreement or transaction under the master agreement that is referred to in clause (i), (ii), or (iii); or

        (v) any security agreement or arrangement or other credit enhancement related to any agreement or transaction referred to in clause (i), (ii), (iii), or (iv), including any guarantee or reimbursement obligation by or to a repo participant or financial participant in connection with any agreement or transaction referred to in any such clause, but not to

---

[1] So in original. Probably should be "or".

exceed the damages in connection with any such agreement or transaction, measured in accordance with section 562 of this title; and

(B) does not include a repurchase obligation under a participation in a commercial mortgage loan.

(48) The term "securities clearing agency" means person that is registered as a clearing agency under section 17A of the Securities Exchange Act of 1934, or exempt from such registration under such section pursuant to an order of the Securities and Exchange Commission, or whose business is confined to the performance of functions of a clearing agency with respect to exempted securities, as defined in section 3(a)(12) of such Act for the purposes of such section 17A.

(48A) The term "securities self regulatory organization" means either a securities association registered with the Securities and Exchange Commission under section 15A of the Securities Exchange Act of 1934 or a national securities exchange registered with the Securities and Exchange Commission under section 6 of the Securities Exchange Act of 1934.

(49) The term "security"—

　(A) includes—

　　(i)　note;

　　(ii)　stock;

　　(iii)　treasury stock;

　　(iv)　bond;

　　(v)　debenture;

　　(vi)　collateral trust certificate;

　　(vii)　pre-organization certificate or subscription;

　　(viii)transferable share;

　　(ix)　voting-trust certificate;

　　(x)　certificate of deposit;

　　(xi)　certificate of deposit for security;

　　(xii)　investment contract or certificate of interest or participation in a profit-sharing agreement or in an oil, gas, or mineral royalty or lease, if such contract or interest is required to be the subject of a registration statement filed with the Securities and Exchange Commission under the provisions of the Securities Act of 1933, or is exempt under section 3(b) of such Act from the requirement to file such a statement;

　　(xiii)interest of a limited partner in a limited partnership;

　　(xiv)other claim or interest commonly known as "security"; and

　　(xv)　certificate of interest or participation in, temporary or interim certificate for, receipt for, or warrant or right to subscribe to or purchase or sell, a security; but

　(B)　does not include—

　　(i)　currency, check, draft, bill of exchange, or bank letter of credit;

　　(ii)　leverage transaction, as defined in section 761 of this title;

　　(iii)　commodity futures contract or forward contract;

　　(iv)　option, warrant, or right to subscribe to or purchase or sell a commodity futures contract;

　　(v)　option to purchase or sell a commodity;

(vi) contract or certificate of a kind specified in subparagraph (A)(xii) of this paragraph that is not required to be the subject of a registration statement filed with the Securities and Exchange Commission and is not exempt under section 3(b) of the Securities Act of 1933 from the requirement to file such a statement; or

(vii) debt or evidence of indebtedness for goods sold and delivered or services rendered.

(50) The term "security agreement" means agreement that creates or provides for a security interest.

(51) The term "security interest" means lien created by an agreement.

(51A) The term "settlement payment" means, for purposes of the forward contract provisions of this title, a preliminary settlement payment, a partial settlement payment, an interim settlement payment, a settlement payment on account, a final settlement payment, a net settlement payment, or any other similar payment commonly used in the forward contract trade.

(51B) The term "single asset real estate" means real property constituting a single property or project, other than residential real property with fewer than 4 residential units, which generates substantially all of the gross income of a debtor who is not a family farmer and on which no substantial business is being conducted by a debtor other than the business of operating the real property and activities incidental thereto.

(51C) The term "small business case" means a case filed under chapter 11 of this title in which the debtor is a small business debtor and has not elected that subchapter V of chapter 11 of this title shall apply.

(51D) The term "small business debtor"—

(A) subject to subparagraph (B), means a person engaged in commercial or business activities (including any affiliate of such person that is also a debtor under this title and excluding a person whose primary activity is the business of owning single asset real estate) that has aggregate noncontingent liquidated secured and unsecured debts as of the date of the filing of the petition or the date of the order for relief in an amount not more than $3,024,725 (excluding debts owed to 1 or more affiliates or insiders) not less than 50 percent of which arose from the commercial or business activities of the debtor; and

(B) does not include—

(i) any member of a group of affiliated debtors under this title that has aggregate noncontingent liquidated secured and unsecured debts in an amount greater than $3,024,725 (excluding debt owed to 1 or more affiliates or insiders);

(ii) any debtor that is a corporation subject to the reporting requirements under section 13 or 15(d) of the Securities Exchange Act of 1934 (15 U.S.C. 78m, 78o(d)); or

(iii) any debtor that is an affiliate of a corporation described in clause (ii).

(52) The term "State" includes the District of Columbia and Puerto Rico, except for the purpose of defining who may be a debtor under chapter 9 of this title.

(53) The term "statutory lien" means lien arising solely by force of a statute on specified circumstances or conditions, or lien of distress for rent, whether or not statutory, but does not include security interest or judicial lien, whether or not such interest or lien is provided by or is dependent on a statute and whether or not such interest or lien is made fully effective by statute.

(53A) The term "stockbroker" means person—

(A) with respect to which there is a customer, as defined in section 741 of this title; and

(B) that is engaged in the business of effecting transactions in securities—

(i) for the account of others; or

(ii) with members of the general public, from or for such person's own account.

(53B) The term "swap agreement"—

(A) means—

(i) any agreement, including the terms and conditions incorporated by reference in such agreement, which is—

(I) an interest rate swap, option, future, or forward agreement, including a rate floor, rate cap, rate collar, cross-currency rate swap, and basis swap;

(II) a spot, same day-tomorrow, tomorrow-next, forward, or other foreign exchange, precious metals, or other commodity agreement;

(III) a currency swap, option, future, or forward agreement;

(IV) an equity index or equity swap, option, future, or forward agreement;

(V) a debt index or debt swap, option, future, or forward agreement;

(VI) a total return, credit spread or credit swap, option, future, or forward agreement;

(VII) a commodity index or a commodity swap, option, future, or forward agreement;

(VIII) a weather swap, option, future, or forward agreement;

(IX) an emissions swap, option, future, or forward agreement; or

(X) an inflation swap, option, future, or forward agreement;

(ii) any agreement or transaction that is similar to any other agreement or transaction referred to in this paragraph and that—

(I) is of a type that has been, is presently, or in the future becomes, the subject of recurrent dealings in the swap or other derivatives markets (including terms and conditions incorporated by reference therein); and

(II) is a forward, swap, future, option, or spot transaction on one or more rates, currencies, commodities, equity securities, or other equity instruments, debt securities or other debt instruments, quantitative measures associated with an occurrence, extent of an occurrence, or contingency associated with a financial, commercial, or economic consequence, or economic or financial indices or measures of economic or financial risk or value;

(iii) any combination of agreements or transactions referred to in this subparagraph;

(iv) any option to enter into an agreement or transaction referred to in this subparagraph;

(v) a master agreement that provides for an agreement or transaction referred to in clause (i), (ii), (iii), or (iv), together with all supplements to any such master agreement, and without regard to whether the master agreement contains an agreement or transaction that is not a swap agreement under this paragraph, except that the master agreement shall be considered to be a swap agreement under this paragraph only with respect to each agreement or transaction under the master agreement that is referred to in clause (i), (ii), (iii), or (iv); or

(vi) any security agreement or arrangement or other credit enhancement related to any agreements or transactions referred to in clause (i) through (v), including any guarantee or reimbursement obligation by or to a swap participant or financial participant in connection with any agreement or transaction referred to in any such clause, but not to exceed the damages in connection with any such agreement or transaction, measured in accordance with section 562; and

(B) is applicable for purposes of this title only, and shall not be construed or applied so as to challenge or affect the characterization, definition, or treatment of any swap agreement under any other statute, regulation, or rule, including the Gramm-Leach-Bliley Act, the Legal Certainty for Bank Products Act of 2000, the securities laws (as such term is defined in section 3(a)(47) of the Securities Exchange Act of 1934) and the Commodity Exchange Act.

(53C) The term "swap participant" means an entity that, at any time before the filing of the petition, has an outstanding swap agreement with the debtor.

(56A)[1] The term "term overriding royalty" means an interest in liquid or gaseous hydrocarbons in place or to be produced from particular real property that entitles the owner thereof to a share of production, or the value thereof, for a term limited by time, quantity, or value realized.

(53D) The term "timeshare plan" means and shall include that interest purchased in any arrangement, plan, scheme, or similar device, but not including exchange programs, whether by membership, agreement, tenancy in common, sale, lease, deed, rental agreement, license, right to use agreement, or by any other means, whereby a purchaser, in exchange for consideration, receives a right to use accommodations, facilities, or recreational sites, whether improved or unimproved, for a specific period of time less than a full year during any given year, but not necessarily for consecutive years, and which extends for a period of more than three years. A "timeshare interest" is that interest purchased in a timeshare plan which grants the purchaser the right to use and occupy accommodations, facilities, or recreational sites, whether improved or unimproved, pursuant to a timeshare plan.

(54) The term "transfer" means—

    (A) the creation of a lien;

    (B) the retention of title as a security interest;

    (C) the foreclosure of a debtor's equity of redemption; or

    (D) each mode, direct or indirect, absolute or conditional, voluntary or involuntary, of disposing of or parting with—

        (i) property; or

        (ii) an interest in property.

(54A) The term "uninsured State member bank" means a State member bank (as defined in section 3 of the Federal Deposit Insurance Act) the deposits of which are not insured by the Federal Deposit Insurance Corporation.

(55) The term "United States", when used in a geographical sense, includes all locations where the judicial jurisdiction of the United States extends, including territories and possessions of the United States.

REFERENCES IN TEXT

The Social Security Act, referred to in par. (10A)(B), is Act Aug. 14, 1935, c. 531, 49 Stat. 620, as amended, which is classified generally to chapter 7 of Title 42, 42 U.S.C.A. § 301 et seq.

Section 501(c)(3) of the Internal Revenue Code of 1986, referred to in par. (12A)(B), is classified to 26 U.S.C.A. § 501(c)(3).

Section 3 of the Federal Deposit Insurance Act, referred to in pars. (12A)(D), (21B)(A), (33)(A), (35)(A), and (54A) is Act Sept. 21, 1950, c. 967, § 2 [3], 64 Stat. 873, which is classified to 12 U.S.C.A. § 1813.

---

[1]   So in original. Par. (56A) was inserted between pars. (53C) and (53D).

Section 101 of the Federal Credit Union Act, referred to in pars. (12A)(D), (34), is Act June 26, 1934, c. 750, Title I, § 101, formerly § 2, 48 Stat. 1216, as amended, which is classified to 12 U.S.C.A. § 1752.

The Investment Company Act of 1940, referred to in par. (22)(B), is Act Aug. 22, 1940, c. 686, Title I, 54 Stat. 789, as amended, which is classified principally to subchapter 1 of chapter 2D of title 15, 15 U.S.C.A. § 80a–1 et seq. For complete classification, see Short Title set out as 15 U.S.C.A. § 80a–51 and Tables.

Section 402 of the Federal Deposit Insurance Corporation Improvement Act of 1991, referred to in par. (22A)(B), is Pub. L. 102–242, Title IV, § 402, Dec. 19, 1991, 105 Stat. 2372, which is classified to 12 U.S.C.A. § 4402.

Section 206 of the Federal Credit Union Act, referred to in par. (33)(B), is section 206 of Act June 26, 1934, c. 750, Title II, as added Oct. 19, 1970, Pub. L. 91–468, § 1(3), 84 Stat. 1003, which is classified to section 1786 of Title 12.

Sections 414(d) and 457(b) of the Internal Revenue Code of 1986, referred to in par. (41)(C), are sections 414(d) and 457(b), respectively, of Title 26, Internal Revenue Code.

Section 3 of the Securities and Exchange Act of 1934, referred to in par. (47), is Act June 6, 1934, c. 404, Title I, § 3, 48 Stat. 882, which is classified to 15 U.S.C.A. § 78c.

Section 17A of the Securities and Exchange Act of 1934, referred to in par. (48), is section 17A of Act June 6, 1934, c. 404, Title I, as added June 4, 1975, Pub. L. 94–29, § 15, 89 Stat. 141, which is classified to section 78q–1 of Title 15, Commerce and Trade.

Section 3(a)(12) of such Act, referred to in par. (48), is Section 3 of the Securities and Exchange Act of 1934, Act June 6, 1934, c. 404, Title I, 48 Stat. 882, which is classified to 15 U.S.C.A. § 78c(a)(12).

Section 15A of the Securities Exchange Act of 1934, referred to in par. (48A), is June 6, 1934, c. 404, Title I, § 15A, as added June 25, 1938, c. 677, § 1, 52 Stat. 1070, and amended which is classified to 15 U.S.C.A. § 78o–3.

Section 6 of the Securities Exchange Act of 1934, referred to in par. (48A), is June 6, 1934, c. 404, Title I, § 6, 48 Stat. 885, as amended, which is classified to 15 U.S.C.A. § 78c.

The Securities Act of 1933, referred to in par. (49)(A)(xii), is Act May 27, 1933, c. 38, Title I, 48 Stat. 74, as amended, which is classified generally to subchapter I (section 77a et seq.) of chapter 2A of Title 15, Commerce and Trade. For complete classification of this Act to the Code, see section 77a of Title 15 and Tables.

Section 3 of the Securities Act of 1933, referred to in pars. (49)(A)(xii) and (B)(vi), is section 3 of Act May 27, 1933, c. 38, Title I, 48 Stat. 75, which is classified to section 77c of Title 15.

The Securities Exchange Act of 1934, referred to in par. (53B)(B), is Act June 6, 1934, c. 404, 48 Stat. 881, as amended, which is classified principally to chapter 2B of Title 15, 15 U.S.C.A. § 78a et seq. Section 3(a)(47) of the Act, as amended, is classified to 15 U.S.C.A. § 78c(a)(47). For complete classification, see Short Title set out as 15 U.S.C.A. § 78a and Tables.

The Commodity Exchange Act, referred to in par. (53B), is Act Sept. 21, 1922, c. 369, 42 Stat. 998, as amended, which is classified principally to chapter 1 of Title 7, 7 U.S.C.A. § 1 et seq. For complete classification, see Short Title set out as 7 U.S.C.A. § 1 and Tables.

The Gramm-Leach-Bliley Act, referred to in par. (53B), is Pub. L. 106–102, Nov. 12, 1999, 113 Stat. 1338, also known as the Financial Services Modernization Act of 1999, which principally enacted chapters 93, 94 and 95 of Title 15, 15 U.S.C.A. § 6701 et seq., 15 U.S.C.A. § 6801 et seq., and 15 U.S.C.A. § 6901 et seq., respectively, and amended chapters 16 and 17 of Title 12, 12 U.S.C.A. § 1811 et seq., and 12 U.S.C.A. § 1841 et seq. For complete classification, see Tables.

The Legal Certainty for Bank Products Act of 2000, referred to in par. (53B), is Pub. L. 106–554, § 1(a)(5) [Title IV, §§ 401 to 408], Dec. 21, 2000, 114 Stat. 2763, 2763A–457, which enacted 7 U.S.C.A. §§ 27 and 27a to 27f. For complete classification, see Short Title set out as a note under 7 U.S.C.A. § 1 and Tables.

§ 102.   Rules of construction

In this title—

    (1) "after notice and a hearing", or a similar phrase—

        (A) means after such notice as is appropriate in the particular circumstances, and such opportunity for a hearing as is appropriate in the particular circumstances; but

        (B) authorizes an act without an actual hearing if such notice is given properly and if—

            (i) such a hearing is not requested timely by a party in interest; or

            (ii) there is insufficient time for a hearing to be commenced before such act must be done, and the court authorizes such act;

    (2) "claim against the debtor" includes claim against property of the debtor;

    (3) "includes" and "including" are not limiting;

    (4) "may not" is prohibitive, and not permissive;

    (5) "or" is not exclusive;

    (6) "order for relief" means entry of an order for relief;

    (7) the singular includes the plural;

    (8) a definition, contained in a section of this title that refers to another section of this title, does not, for the purpose of such reference, affect the meaning of a term used in such other section; and

    (9) "United States trustee" includes a designee of the United States trustee.

§ 103.   Applicability of chapters

    (a) Except as provided in section 1161 of this title, chapters 1, 3, and 5 of this title apply in a case under chapter 7, 11, 12, or 13 of this title, and this chapter, sections 307, 362(*o*), 555 through 557, and 559 through 562 apply in a case under chapter 15.

    (b) Subchapters I and II of chapter 7 of this title apply only in a case under such chapter.

    (c) Subchapter III of chapter 7 of this title applies only in a case under such chapter concerning a stockbroker.

    (d) Subchapter IV of chapter 7 of this title applies only in a case under such chapter concerning a commodity broker.

    (e) Scope of application.—Subchapter V of chapter 7 of this title shall apply only in a case under such chapter concerning the liquidation of an uninsured State member bank, or a corporation organized under section 25A of the Federal Reserve Act, which operates, or operates as, a multilateral clearing organization pursuant to section 409 of the Federal Deposit Insurance Corporation Improvement Act of 1991.

    (f) Except as provided in section 901 of this title, only chapters 1 and 9 of this title apply in a case under such chapter 9.

    (g) Except as provided in section 901 of this title, subchapters I, II, and III of chapter 11 of this title apply only in a case under such chapter.

    (h) Subchapter IV of chapter 11 of this title applies only in a case under such chapter concerning a railroad.

    (i) Subchapter V of chapter 11 of this title applies only in a case under chapter 11 in which a debtor (as defined in section 1182) elects that subchapter V of chapter 11 shall apply.

    (j) Chapter 13 of this title applies only in a case under such chapter.

(k) Chapter 12 of this title applies only in a case under such chapter.

(l) Chapter 15 applies only in a case under such chapter, except that—

   (1) sections 1505, 1513, and 1514 apply in all cases under this title; and

   (2) section 1509 applies whether or not a case under this title is pending.

REFERENCES IN TEXT

Section 25A of the Federal Reserve Act, referred to in subsec. (e), is Dec. 23, 1913, c. 6, § 25A, formerly § 25(a), as added Dec. 24, 1919, c. 18, 41 Stat. 378, as amended, which is classified to subchapter II of chapter 6 of Title 12, 12 U.S.C.A. § 611 et seq.

Section 409 of the Federal Deposit Insurance Corporation Improvement Act of 1991, referred to in subsec. (e), is Pub. L. 102–242, Title IV, § 409, as added by Pub. L. 106–554, § 1(a)(5) [Title I, § 112(a)(3)], Dec. 21, 2000, 114 Stat. 2763, 2763A–394, which is classified as 12 U.S.C.A. § 4422. This provision has been repealed.

CROSS REFERENCES

Applicability of other sections to Chapter 9, see 11 USCA § 901.

§ 104. Adjustment of dollar amounts

(a) On April 1, 1998, and at each 3-year interval ending on April 1 thereafter, each dollar amount in effect under sections 101(3), 101(18), 101(19A), 101(51D), 109(e), 303(b), 507(a), 522(d), 522(f)(3) and 522(f)(4), 522(n), 522(p), 522(q), 523(a)(2)(C), 541(b), 547(c)(9), 707(b), 1182(1), 1322(d), 1325(b), and 1326(b)(3) of this title and section 1409(b) of title 28 immediately before such April 1 shall be adjusted—

   (1) to reflect the change in the Consumer Price Index for All Urban Consumers, published by the Department of Labor, for the most recent 3-year period ending immediately before January 1 preceding such April 1, and

   (2) to round to the nearest $25 the dollar amount that represents such change.

(b) Not later than March 1, 1998, and at each 3-year interval ending on March 1 thereafter, the Judicial Conference of the United States shall publish in the Federal Register the dollar amounts that will become effective on such April 1 under sections 101(3), 101(18), 101(19A), 101(51D), 109(e), 303(b), 507(a), 522(d), 522(f)(3) and 522(f)(4), 522(n), 522(p), 522(q), 523(a)(2)(C), 541(b), 547(c)(9), 707(b), 1182(1), 1322(d), 1325(b), and 1326(b)(3) of this title and section 1409(b) of title 28.

(c) Adjustments made in accordance with subsection (a) shall not apply with respect to cases commenced before the date of such adjustments.

§ 105. Power of court

(a) The court may issue any order, process, or judgment that is necessary or appropriate to carry out the provisions of this title. No provision of this title providing for the raising of an issue by a party in interest shall be construed to preclude the court from, sua sponte, taking any action or making any determination necessary or appropriate to enforce or implement court orders or rules, or to prevent an abuse of process.

(b) Notwithstanding subsection (a) of this section, a court may not appoint a receiver in a case under this title.

(c) The ability of any district judge or other officer or employee of a district court to exercise any of the authority or responsibilities conferred upon the court under this title shall be determined by reference to the provisions relating to such judge, officer, or employee set forth in title 28. This subsection shall not be interpreted to exclude bankruptcy judges and other officers or employees appointed pursuant to chapter 6 of title 28 from its operation.

(d) The court, on its own motion or on the request of a party in interest—

(1) shall hold such status conferences as are necessary to further the expeditious and economical resolution of the case; and

(2) unless inconsistent with another provision of this title or with applicable Federal Rules of Bankruptcy Procedure, may issue an order at any such conference prescribing such limitations and conditions as the court deems appropriate to ensure that the case is handled expeditiously and economically, including an order that—

(A) sets the date by which the trustee must assume or reject an executory contract or unexpired lease; or

(B) in a case under chapter 11 of this title—

(i) sets a date by which the debtor, or trustee if one has been appointed, shall file a disclosure statement and plan;

(ii) sets a date by which the debtor, or trustee if one has been appointed, shall solicit acceptances of a plan;

(iii) sets the date by which a party in interest other than a debtor may file a plan;

(iv) sets a date by which a proponent of a plan, other than the debtor, shall solicit acceptances of such plan;

(v) fixes the scope and format of the notice to be provided regarding the hearing on approval of the disclosure statement; or

(vi) provides that the hearing on approval of the disclosure statement may be combined with the hearing on confirmation of the plan.

§ 106. Waiver of sovereign immunity

(a) Notwithstanding an assertion of sovereign immunity, sovereign immunity is abrogated as to a governmental unit to the extent set forth in this section with respect to the following:

(1) Sections 105, 106, 107, 108, 303, 346, 362, 363, 364, 365, 366, 502, 503, 505, 506, 510, 522, 523, 524, 525, 542, 543, 544, 545, 546, 547, 548, 549, 550, 551, 552, 553, 722, 724, 726, 744, 749, 764, 901, 922, 926, 928, 929, 944, 1107, 1141, 1142, 1143, 1146, 1201, 1203, 1205, 1206, 1227, 1231, 1301, 1303, 1305, and 1327 of this title.

(2) The court may hear and determine any issue arising with respect to the application of such sections to governmental units.

(3) The court may issue against a governmental unit an order, process, or judgment under such sections or the Federal Rules of Bankruptcy Procedure, including an order or judgment awarding a money recovery, but not including an award of punitive damages. Such order or judgment for costs or fees under this title or the Federal Rules of Bankruptcy Procedure against any governmental unit shall be consistent with the provisions and limitations of section 2412(d)(2)(A) of title 28.

(4) The enforcement of any such order, process, or judgment against any governmental unit shall be consistent with appropriate nonbankruptcy law applicable to such governmental unit and, in the case of a money judgment against the United States, shall be paid as if it is a judgment rendered by a district court of the United States.

(5) Nothing in this section shall create any substantive claim for relief or cause of action not otherwise existing under this title, the Federal Rules of Bankruptcy Procedure, or nonbankruptcy law.

(b) A governmental unit that has filed a proof of claim in the case is deemed to have waived sovereign immunity with respect to a claim against such governmental unit that is property of the estate and that arose out of the same transaction or occurrence out of which the claim of such governmental unit arose.

(c) Notwithstanding any assertion of sovereign immunity by a governmental unit, there shall be offset against a claim or interest of a governmental unit any claim against such governmental unit that is property of the estate.

§ 107. Public access to papers

(a) Except as provided in subsections (b) and (c) and subject to section 112, a paper filed in a case under this title and the dockets of a bankruptcy court are public records and open to examination by an entity at reasonable times without charge.

(b) On request of a party in interest, the bankruptcy court shall, and on the bankruptcy court's own motion, the bankruptcy court may—

    (1) protect an entity with respect to a trade secret or confidential research, development, or commercial information; or

    (2) protect a person with respect to scandalous or defamatory matter contained in a paper filed in a case under this title.

(c)(1) The bankruptcy court, for cause, may protect an individual, with respect to the following types of information to the extent the court finds that disclosure of such information would create undue risk of identity theft or other unlawful injury to the individual or the individual's property:

    (A) Any means of identification (as defined in section 1028(d) of title 18) contained in a paper filed, or to be filed, in a case under this title.

    (B) Other information contained in a paper described in subparagraph (A).

    (2) Upon ex parte application demonstrating cause, the court shall provide access to information protected pursuant to paragraph (1) to an entity acting pursuant to the police or regulatory power of a domestic governmental unit.

    (3) The United States trustee, bankruptcy administrator, trustee, and any auditor serving under section 586(f) of title 28—

    (A) shall have full access to all information contained in any paper filed or submitted in a case under this title; and

    (B) shall not disclose information specifically protected by the court under this title.

§ 108. Extension of time

(a) If applicable nonbankruptcy law, an order entered in a nonbankruptcy proceeding, or an agreement fixes a period within which the debtor may commence an action, and such period has not expired before the date of the filing of the petition, the trustee may commence such action only before the later of—

    (1) the end of such period, including any suspension of such period occurring on or after the commencement of the case; or

    (2) two years after the order for relief.

(b) Except as provided in subsection (a) of this section, if applicable nonbankruptcy law, an order entered in a nonbankruptcy proceeding, or an agreement fixes a period within which the debtor or an individual protected under section 1201 or 1301 of this title may file any pleading, demand, notice, or proof of claim or loss, cure a default, or perform any other similar act, and such period has not expired before the date of the filing of the petition, the trustee may only file, cure, or perform, as the case may be, before the later of—

(1)　the end of such period, including any suspension of such period occurring on or after the commencement of the case; or

(2)　60 days after the order for relief.

(c)　Except as provided in section 524 of this title, if applicable nonbankruptcy law, an order entered in a nonbankruptcy proceeding, or an agreement fixes a period for commencing or continuing a civil action in a court other than a bankruptcy court on a claim against the debtor, or against an individual with respect to which such individual is protected under section 1201 or 1301 of this title, and such period has not expired before the date of the filing of the petition, then such period does not expire until the later of—

(1)　the end of such period, including any suspension of such period occurring on or after the commencement of the case; or

(2)　30 days after notice of the termination or expiration of the stay under section 362, 922, 1201, or 1301 of this title, as the case may be, with respect to such claim.

§ 109.　Who may be a debtor

(a)　Notwithstanding any other provision of this section, only a person that resides or has a domicile, a place of business, or property in the United States, or a municipality, may be a debtor under this title.

(b)　A person may be a debtor under chapter 7 of this title only if such person is not—

(1)　a railroad;

(2)　a domestic insurance company, bank, savings bank, cooperative bank, savings and loan association, building and loan association, homestead association, a New Markets Venture Capital company as defined in section 351 of the Small Business Investment Act of 1958, a small business investment company licensed by the Small Business Administration under section 301 of the Small Business Investment Act of 1958, credit union, or industrial bank or similar institution which is an insured bank as defined in section 3(h) of the Federal Deposit Insurance Act, except that an uninsured State member bank, or a corporation organized under section 25A of the Federal Reserve Act, which operates, or operates as, a multilateral clearing organization pursuant to section 409 of the Federal Deposit Insurance Corporation Improvement Act of 1991 may be a debtor if a petition is filed at the direction of the Board of Governors of the Federal Reserve System; or

(3)(A)　a foreign insurance company, engaged in such business in the United States; or

(B)　a foreign bank, savings bank, cooperative bank, savings and loan association, building and loan association, or credit union, that has a branch or agency (as defined in section 1(b) of the International Banking Act of 1978) in the United States.

(c)　An entity may be a debtor under chapter 9 of this title if and only if such entity—

(1)　is a municipality;

(2)　is specifically authorized, in its capacity as a municipality or by name, to be a debtor under such chapter by State law, or by a governmental officer or organization empowered by State law to authorize such entity to be a debtor under such chapter;

(3)　is insolvent;

(4)　desires to effect a plan to adjust such debts; and

(5)(A)　has obtained the agreement of creditors holding at least a majority in amount of the claims of each class that such entity intends to impair under a plan in a case under such chapter;

(B) has negotiated in good faith with creditors and has failed to obtain the agreement of creditors holding at least a majority in amount of the claims of each class that such entity intends to impair under a plan in a case under such chapter;

(C) is unable to negotiate with creditors because such negotiation is impracticable; or

(D) reasonably believes that a creditor may attempt to obtain a transfer that is avoidable under section 547 of this title.

(d) Only a railroad, a person that may be a debtor under chapter 7 of this title (except a stockbroker or a commodity broker), and an uninsured State member bank, or a corporation organized under section 25A of the Federal Reserve Act, which operates, or operates as, a multilateral clearing organization pursuant to section 409 of the Federal Deposit Insurance Corporation Improvement Act of 1991 may be a debtor under chapter 11 of this title.

(e) Only an individual with regular income that owes, on the date of the filing of the petition, noncontingent, liquidated debts of less than $2,750,000 or an individual with regular income and such individual's spouse, except a stockbroker or a commodity broker, that owe, on the date of the filing of the petition, noncontingent, liquidated debts that aggregate less than $2,750,000 may be a debtor under chapter 13 of this title.

[*Note from West Advisor:* Congress amended § 109(e) to eliminate the separate unsecured and secured debt limits previously required for eligibility to file for chapter 13. The amendment creating a single $2.75M debt limit expires on June 21, 2024, at which point § 109(e) will read as it did on June 20, 2022. *See* 136 Stat. 1300.]

(f) Only a family farmer or family fisherman with regular annual income may be a debtor under chapter 12 of this title.

(g) Notwithstanding any other provision of this section, no individual or family farmer may be a debtor under this title who has been a debtor in a case pending under this title at any time in the preceding 180 days if—

(1) the case was dismissed by the court for willful failure of the debtor to abide by orders of the court, or to appear before the court in proper prosecution of the case; or

(2) the debtor requested and obtained the voluntary dismissal of the case following the filing of a request for relief from the automatic stay provided by section 362 of this title.

(h)(1) Subject to paragraphs (2) and (3), and notwithstanding any other provision of this section other than paragraph (4) of this subsection, an individual may not be a debtor under this title unless such individual has, during the 180-day period ending on the date of filing of the petition by such individual, received from an approved nonprofit budget and credit counseling agency described in section 111(a) an individual or group briefing (including a briefing conducted by telephone or on the Internet) that outlined the opportunities for available credit counseling and assisted such individual in performing a related budget analysis.

(2)(A) Paragraph (1) shall not apply with respect to a debtor who resides in a district for which the United States trustee (or the bankruptcy administrator, if any) determines that the approved nonprofit budget and credit counseling agencies for such district are not reasonably able to provide adequate services to the additional individuals who would otherwise seek credit counseling from such agencies by reason of the requirements of paragraph (1).

(B) The United States trustee (or the bankruptcy administrator, if any) who makes a determination described in subparagraph (A) shall review such determination not later than 1 year after the date of such determination, and not less frequently than annually thereafter. Notwithstanding the preceding sentence, a nonprofit budget and credit counseling agency may be disapproved by the United States trustee (or the bankruptcy administrator, if any) at any time.

(3)(A) Subject to subparagraph (B), the requirements of paragraph (1) shall not apply with respect to a debtor who submits to the court a certification that—

(i) describes exigent circumstances that merit a waiver of the requirements of paragraph (1);

(ii) states that the debtor requested credit counseling services from an approved nonprofit budget and credit counseling agency, but was unable to obtain the services referred to in paragraph (1) during the 7-day period beginning on the date on which the debtor made that request; and

(iii) is satisfactory to the court.

(B) With respect to a debtor, an exemption under subparagraph (A) shall cease to apply to that debtor on the date on which the debtor meets the requirements of paragraph (1), but in no case may the exemption apply to that debtor after the date that is 30 days after the debtor files a petition, except that the court, for cause, may order an additional 15 days.

(4) The requirements of paragraph (1) shall not apply with respect to a debtor whom the court determines, after notice and hearing, is unable to complete those requirements because of incapacity, disability, or active military duty in a military combat zone. For the purposes of this paragraph, incapacity means that the debtor is impaired by reason of mental illness or mental deficiency so that he is incapable of realizing and making rational decisions with respect to his financial responsibilities; and "disability" means that the debtor is so physically impaired as to be unable, after reasonable effort, to participate in an in person, telephone, or Internet briefing required under paragraph (1).

REFERENCES IN TEXT

Section 351 of the Small Business Investment Act of 1958, referred to in subsec. (b)(2), is section 351 of Pub. L. 85–699, which is classified to 15 U.S.C.A. § 689.

Subsection (c) or (d) of section 301 of the Small Business Investment Act of 1958, referred to in subsec. (b)(2), is subsection (c) or (d) of section 301 of Pub. L. 85–699, Title III, Aug. 21, 1958, which is classified to 15 U.S.C.A. § 681(c) or (d). Subsection (d) of section 301 was repealed by Pub. L. 104–208, Div. D, Title II, § 208(b)(3)(A), Sept. 30, 1996, 110 Stat. 3009–742.

Section 3 of the Federal Deposit Insurance Act, referred to in subsec. (b)(2), is section 2[3] of Act Sept. 21, 1950, c. 967, 64 Stat. 873, which is classified to 12 U.S.C.A. § 1813.

Section 25A of the Federal Reserve Act, referred to in subsecs. (b)(2) and (d), is Dec. 23, 1913, c. 6, § 25A, formerly § 25(a), as added Dec. 24, 1919, c. 18, 41 Stat. 378, as amended, which is classified to subchapter II of chapter 6 of Title 12 (12 U.S.C.A. § 611 et seq.).

Section 409 of the Federal Deposit Insurance Corporation Improvement Act of 1991, referred to in subsecs. (b)(2) and (d), is Pub. L. 102–242, Title IV, § 409, as added by Pub. L. 106–554, § 1(a)(5) [Title I, § 112(a)(3)], Dec. 21, 2000, 114 Stat. 2763, 2763A–391, which is classified as 12 U.S.C.A. § 4422.

Section 1(b) of the International Banking Act of 1978, referred to in subsec. (b)(3)(B), is Pub. L. 95–369, § 1(b), Sept. 17, 1978, 92 Stat. 607, as amended, which is classified to 12 U.S.C.A. § 3101.

CROSS REFERENCES

Filing of Chapter 9 petition by certain unincorporated tax or special assessment districts notwithstanding provisions under this section, see 11 USCA § 921.

§ 110. Penalty for persons who negligently or fraudulently prepare bankruptcy petitions

(a) In this section—

(1) "bankruptcy petition preparer" means a person, other than an attorney for the debtor or an employee of such attorney under the direct supervision of such attorney, who prepares for compensation a document for filing; and

(2) "document for filing" means a petition or any other document prepared for filing by a debtor in a United States bankruptcy court or a United States district court in connection with a case under this title.

(b)(1)   A bankruptcy petition preparer who prepares a document for filing shall sign the document and print on the document the preparer's name and address. If a bankruptcy petition preparer is not an individual, then an officer, principal, responsible person, or partner of the bankruptcy petition preparer shall be required to—

(A) sign the document for filing; and

(B) print on the document the name and address of that officer, principal, responsible person, or partner.

(2)(A)   Before preparing any document for filing or accepting any fees from or on behalf of a debtor, the bankruptcy petition preparer shall provide to the debtor a written notice which shall be on an official form prescribed by the Judicial Conference of the United States in accordance with rule 9009 of the Federal Rules of Bankruptcy Procedure.

(B) The notice under subparagraph (A)—

(i)   shall inform the debtor in simple language that a bankruptcy petition preparer is not an attorney and may not practice law or give legal advice;

(ii) may contain a description of examples of legal advice that a bankruptcy petition preparer is not authorized to give, in addition to any advice that the preparer may not give by reason of subsection (e)(2); and

(iii) shall—

(I)   be signed by the debtor and, under penalty of perjury, by the bankruptcy petition preparer; and

(II) be filed with any document for filing.

(c)(1)   A bankruptcy petition preparer who prepares a document for filing shall place on the document, after the preparer's signature, an identifying number that identifies individuals who prepared the document.

(2)(A)   Subject to subparagraph (B), for purposes of this section, the identifying number of a bankruptcy petition preparer shall be the Social Security account number of each individual who prepared the document or assisted in its preparation.

(B) If a bankruptcy petition preparer is not an individual, the identifying number of the bankruptcy petition preparer shall be the Social Security account number of the officer, principal, responsible person, or partner of the bankruptcy petition preparer.

(d) A bankruptcy petition preparer shall, not later than the time at which a document for filing is presented for the debtor's signature, furnish to the debtor a copy of the document.

(e)(1)   A bankruptcy petition preparer shall not execute any document on behalf of a debtor.

(2)(A)   A bankruptcy petition preparer may not offer a potential bankruptcy debtor any legal advice, including any legal advice described in subparagraph (B).

(B) The legal advice referred to in subparagraph (A) includes advising the debtor—

(i)   whether—

(I)   to file a petition under this title; or

(II) commencing a case under chapter 7, 11, 12, or 13 is appropriate;

(ii) whether the debtor's debts will be discharged in a case under this title;

(iii) whether the debtor will be able to retain the debtor's home, car, or other property after commencing a case under this title;

(iv) concerning—

(I) the tax consequences of a case brought under this title; or

(II) the dischargeability of tax claims;

(v) whether the debtor may or should promise to repay debts to a creditor or enter into a reaffirmation agreement with a creditor to reaffirm a debt;

(vi) concerning how to characterize the nature of the debtor's interests in property or the debtor's debts; or

(vii) concerning bankruptcy procedures and rights.

(f) A bankruptcy petition preparer shall not use the word "legal" or any similar term in any advertisements, or advertise under any category that includes the word "legal" or any similar term.

(g) A bankruptcy petition preparer shall not collect or receive any payment from the debtor or on behalf of the debtor for the court fees in connection with filing the petition.

(h)(1) The Supreme Court may promulgate rules under section 2075 of title 28, or the Judicial Conference of the United States may prescribe guidelines, for setting a maximum allowable fee chargeable by a bankruptcy petition preparer. A bankruptcy petition preparer shall notify the debtor of any such maximum amount before preparing any document for filing for the debtor or accepting any fee from or on behalf of the debtor.

(2) A declaration under penalty of perjury by the bankruptcy petition preparer shall be filed together with the petition, disclosing any fee received from or on behalf of the debtor within 12 months immediately prior to the filing of the case, and any unpaid fee charged to the debtor. If rules or guidelines setting a maximum fee for services have been promulgated or prescribed under paragraph (1), the declaration under this paragraph shall include a certification that the bankruptcy petition preparer complied with the notification requirement under paragraph (1).

(3)(A) The court shall disallow and order the immediate turnover to the bankruptcy trustee any fee referred to in paragraph (2)—

(i) found to be in excess of the value of any services rendered by the bankruptcy petition preparer during the 12-month period immediately preceding the date of the filing of the petition; or

(ii) found to be in violation of any rule or guideline promulgated or prescribed under paragraph (1).

(B) All fees charged by a bankruptcy petition preparer may be forfeited in any case in which the bankruptcy petition preparer fails to comply with this subsection or subsection (b), (c), (d), (e), (f), or (g).

(C) An individual may exempt any funds recovered under this paragraph under section 522(b).

(4) The debtor, the trustee, a creditor, the United States trustee (or the bankruptcy administrator, if any) or the court, on the initiative of the court, may file a motion for an order under paragraph (3).

(5) A bankruptcy petition preparer shall be fined not more than $500 for each failure to comply with a court order to turn over funds within 30 days of service of such order.

(i)(1) If a bankruptcy petition preparer violates this section or commits any act that the court finds to be fraudulent, unfair, or deceptive, on the motion of the debtor, trustee, United States trustee (or the bankruptcy administrator, if any), and after notice and a hearing, the court shall order the bankruptcy petition preparer to pay to the debtor—

(A) the debtor's actual damages;

(B) the greater of—

    (i) $2,000; or

    (ii) twice the amount paid by the debtor to the bankruptcy petition preparer for the preparer's services; and

(C) reasonable attorneys' fees and costs in moving for damages under this subsection.

(2) If the trustee or creditor moves for damages on behalf of the debtor under this subsection, the bankruptcy petition preparer shall be ordered to pay the movant the additional amount of $1,000 plus reasonable attorneys' fees and costs incurred.

(j)(1) A debtor for whom a bankruptcy petition preparer has prepared a document for filing, the trustee, a creditor, or the United States trustee in the district in which the bankruptcy petition preparer resides, has conducted business, or the United States trustee in any other district in which the debtor resides may bring a civil action to enjoin a bankruptcy petition preparer from engaging in any conduct in violation of this section or from further acting as a bankruptcy petition preparer.

(2)(A) In an action under paragraph (1), if the court finds that—

    (i) a bankruptcy petition preparer has—

        (I) engaged in conduct in violation of this section or of any provision of this title;

        (II) misrepresented the preparer's experience or education as a bankruptcy petition preparer; or

        (III) engaged in any other fraudulent, unfair, or deceptive conduct; and

    (ii) injunctive relief is appropriate to prevent the recurrence of such conduct,

the court may enjoin the bankruptcy petition preparer from engaging in such conduct.

(B) If the court finds that a bankruptcy petition preparer has continually engaged in conduct described in subclause (I), (II), or (III) of clause (i) and that an injunction prohibiting such conduct would not be sufficient to prevent such person's interference with the proper administration of this title, has not paid a penalty imposed under this section, or failed to disgorge all fees ordered by the court the court may enjoin the person from acting as a bankruptcy petition preparer.

(3) The court, as part of its contempt power, may enjoin a bankruptcy petition preparer that has failed to comply with a previous order issued under this section. The injunction under this paragraph may be issued on the motion of the court, the trustee, or the United States trustee (or the bankruptcy administrator, if any).

(4) The court shall award to a debtor, trustee, or creditor that brings a successful action under this subsection reasonable attorneys' fees and costs of the action, to be paid by the bankruptcy petition preparer.

(k) Nothing in this section shall be construed to permit activities that are otherwise prohibited by law, including rules and laws that prohibit the unauthorized practice of law.

(l)(1) A bankruptcy petition preparer who fails to comply with any provision of subsection (b), (c), (d), (e), (f), (g), or (h) may be fined not more than $500 for each such failure.

(2) The court shall triple the amount of a fine assessed under paragraph (1) in any case in which the court finds that a bankruptcy petition preparer—

(A) advised the debtor to exclude assets or income that should have been included on applicable schedules;

(B) advised the debtor to use a false Social Security account number;

(C) failed to inform the debtor that the debtor was filing for relief under this title; or

(D) prepared a document for filing in a manner that failed to disclose the identity of the bankruptcy petition preparer.

(3) A debtor, trustee, creditor, or United States trustee (or the bankruptcy administrator, if any) may file a motion for an order imposing a fine on the bankruptcy petition preparer for any violation of this section.

(4)(A) Fines imposed under this subsection in judicial districts served by United States trustees shall be paid to the United States trustees, who shall deposit an amount equal to such fines in the United States Trustee Fund.

(B) Fines imposed under this subsection in judicial districts served by bankruptcy administrators shall be deposited as offsetting receipts to the fund established under section 1931 of title 28, and shall remain available until expended to reimburse any appropriation for the amount paid out of such appropriation for expenses of the operation and maintenance of the courts of the United States.

§ 111. Nonprofit budget and credit counseling agencies; financial management instructional courses

(a) The clerk shall maintain a publicly available list of—

(1) nonprofit budget and credit counseling agencies that provide 1 or more services described in section 109(h) currently approved by the United States trustee (or the bankruptcy administrator, if any); and

(2) instructional courses concerning personal financial management currently approved by the United States trustee (or the bankruptcy administrator, if any), as applicable.

(b) The United States trustee (or bankruptcy administrator, if any) shall only approve a nonprofit budget and credit counseling agency or an instructional course concerning personal financial management as follows:

(1) The United States trustee (or bankruptcy administrator, if any) shall have thoroughly reviewed the qualifications of the nonprofit budget and credit counseling agency or of the provider of the instructional course under the standards set forth in this section, and the services or instructional courses that will be offered by such agency or such provider, and may require such agency or such provider that has sought approval to provide information with respect to such review.

(2) The United States trustee (or bankruptcy administrator, if any) shall have determined that such agency or such instructional course fully satisfies the applicable standards set forth in this section.

(3) If a nonprofit budget and credit counseling agency or instructional course did not appear on the approved list for the district under subsection (a) immediately before approval under this section, approval under this subsection of such agency or such instructional course shall be for a probationary period not to exceed 6 months.

(4) At the conclusion of the applicable probationary period under paragraph (3), the United States trustee (or bankruptcy administrator, if any) may only approve for an additional 1-year period, and for successive 1-year periods thereafter, an agency or instructional course that has demonstrated during the probationary or applicable subsequent period of approval that such agency or instructional course—

(A) has met the standards set forth under this section during such period; and

(B) can satisfy such standards in the future.

(5) Not later than 30 days after any final decision under paragraph (4), an interested person may seek judicial review of such decision in the appropriate district court of the United States.

(c)(1) The United States trustee (or the bankruptcy administrator, if any) shall only approve a nonprofit budget and credit counseling agency that demonstrates that it will provide qualified counselors, maintain adequate provision for safekeeping and payment of client funds, provide adequate counseling with respect to client credit problems, and deal responsibly and effectively with other matters relating to the quality, effectiveness, and financial security of the services it provides.

(2) To be approved by the United States trustee (or the bankruptcy administrator, if any), a nonprofit budget and credit counseling agency shall, at a minimum—

(A) have a board of directors the majority of which—

(i) are not employed by such agency; and

(ii) will not directly or indirectly benefit financially from the outcome of the counseling services provided by such agency;

(B) if a fee is charged for counseling services, charge a reasonable fee, and provide services without regard to ability to pay the fee;

(C) provide for safekeeping and payment of client funds, including an annual audit of the trust accounts and appropriate employee bonding;

(D) provide full disclosures to a client, including funding sources, counselor qualifications, possible impact on credit reports, and any costs of such program that will be paid by such client and how such costs will be paid;

(E) provide adequate counseling with respect to a client's credit problems that includes an analysis of such client's current financial condition, factors that caused such financial condition, and how such client can develop a plan to respond to the problems without incurring negative amortization of debt;

(F) provide trained counselors who receive no commissions or bonuses based on the outcome of the counseling services provided by such agency, and who have adequate experience, and have been adequately trained to provide counseling services to individuals in financial difficulty, including the matters described in subparagraph (E);

(G) demonstrate adequate experience and background in providing credit counseling; and

(H) have adequate financial resources to provide continuing support services for budgeting plans over the life of any repayment plan.

(d) The United States trustee (or the bankruptcy administrator, if any) shall only approve an instructional course concerning personal financial management—

(1) for an initial probationary period under subsection (b)(3) if the course will provide at a minimum—

(A) trained personnel with adequate experience and training in providing effective instruction and services;

(B) learning materials and teaching methodologies designed to assist debtors in understanding personal financial management and that are consistent with stated objectives directly related to the goals of such instructional course;

(C) adequate facilities situated in reasonably convenient locations at which such instructional course is offered, except that such facilities may include the provision of such instructional course by telephone or through the Internet, if such instructional course is effective;

(D) the preparation and retention of reasonable records (which shall include the debtor's bankruptcy case number) to permit evaluation of the effectiveness of such instructional course, including any evaluation of satisfaction of instructional course requirements for each debtor attending such instructional course, which shall be available for inspection and evaluation by the Executive Office for United States Trustees, the United States trustee (or the bankruptcy administrator, if any), or the chief bankruptcy judge for the district in which such instructional course is offered; and

(E) if a fee is charged for the instructional course, charge a reasonable fee, and provide services without regard to ability to pay the fee; and

(2) for any 1-year period if the provider thereof has demonstrated that the course meets the standards of paragraph (1) and, in addition—

(A) has been effective in assisting a substantial number of debtors to understand personal financial management; and

(B) is otherwise likely to increase substantially the debtor's understanding of personal financial management.

(e) The district court may, at any time, investigate the qualifications of a nonprofit budget and credit counseling agency referred to in subsection (a), and request production of documents to ensure the integrity and effectiveness of such agency. The district court may, at any time, remove from the approved list under subsection (a) a nonprofit budget and credit counseling agency upon finding such agency does not meet the qualifications of subsection (b).

(f) The United States trustee (or the bankruptcy administrator, if any) shall notify the clerk that a nonprofit budget and credit counseling agency or an instructional course is no longer approved, in which case the clerk shall remove it from the list maintained under subsection (a).

(g)(1) No nonprofit budget and credit counseling agency may provide to a credit reporting agency information concerning whether a debtor has received or sought instruction concerning personal financial management from such agency.

(2) A nonprofit budget and credit counseling agency that willfully or negligently fails to comply with any requirement under this title with respect to a debtor shall be liable for damages in an amount equal to the sum of—

(A) any actual damages sustained by the debtor as a result of the violation; and

(B) any court costs or reasonable attorneys' fees (as determined by the court) incurred in an action to recover those damages.

§ 112. Prohibition on disclosure of name of minor children

The debtor may be required to provide information regarding a minor child involved in matters under this title but may not be required to disclose in the public records in the case the name of such minor child. The debtor may be required to disclose the name of such minor child in a nonpublic record that is maintained by the court and made available by the court for examination by the United States trustee, the trustee, and the auditor (if any) serving under section 586(f) of title 28, in the case. The court, the United States trustee, the trustee, and such auditor shall not disclose the name of such minor child maintained in such nonpublic record.

CHAPTER 3—CASE ADMINISTRATION

SUBCHAPTER I—COMMENCEMENT OF A CASE

SUBCHAPTER II—OFFICERS

SUBCHAPTER III—ADMINISTRATION

SUBCHAPTER IV—ADMINISTRATIVE POWERS

SUBCHAPTER I—COMMENCEMENT OF A CASE

§ 301.　Voluntary cases

(a)　A voluntary case under a chapter of this title is commenced by the filing with the bankruptcy court of a petition under such chapter by an entity that may be a debtor under such chapter.

(b)　The commencement of a voluntary case under a chapter of this title constitutes an order for relief under such chapter.

CROSS REFERENCES

Applicability of this section in Chapter 9 cases, see 11 USCA § 901.

"Petition" defined, see 11 USCA § 101.

§ 302.　Joint cases

(a)　A joint case under a chapter of this title is commenced by the filing with the bankruptcy court of a single petition under such chapter by an individual that may be a debtor under such chapter and such individual's spouse. The commencement of a joint case under a chapter of this title constitutes an order for relief under such chapter.

(b)　After the commencement of a joint case, the court shall determine the extent, if any, to which the debtors' estates shall be consolidated.

CROSS REFERENCES

"Petition" defined, see 11 USCA § 101.

§ 303.　Involuntary cases

(a)　An involuntary case may be commenced only under chapter 7 or 11 of this title, and only against a person, except a farmer, family farmer, or a corporation that is not a moneyed, business, or commercial corporation, that may be a debtor under the chapter under which such case is commenced.

(b)　An involuntary case against a person is commenced by the filing with the bankruptcy court of a petition under chapter 7 or 11 of this title—

　　(1)　by three or more entities, each of which is either a holder of a claim against such person that is not contingent as to liability or the subject of a bona fide dispute as to liability or amount, or an indenture trustee representing such a holder, if such noncontingent, undisputed claims aggregate at least $18,600 more than the value of any lien on property of the debtor securing such claims held by the holders of such claims;

　　(2)　if there are fewer than 12 such holders, excluding any employee or insider of such person and any transferee of a transfer that is voidable under section 544, 545, 547, 548, 549, or 724(a) of this title, by one or more of such holders that hold in the aggregate at least $18,600 of such claims;

　　(3)　if such person is a partnership—

　　　　(A)　by fewer than all of the general partners in such partnership; or

　　　　(B)　if relief has been ordered under this title with respect to all of the general partners in such partnership, by a general partner in such partnership, the trustee of such a general partner, or a holder of a claim against such partnership; or

　　(4)　by a foreign representative of the estate in a foreign proceeding concerning such person.

(c)　After the filing of a petition under this section but before the case is dismissed or relief is ordered, a creditor holding an unsecured claim that is not contingent, other than a creditor filing under subsection (b) of this section, may join in the petition with the same effect as if such joining creditor were a petitioning creditor under subsection (b) of this section.

(d) The debtor, or a general partner in a partnership debtor that did not join in the petition, may file an answer to a petition under this section.

(e) After notice and a hearing, and for cause, the court may require the petitioners under this section to file a bond to indemnify the debtor for such amounts as the court may later allow under subsection (i) of this section.

(f) Notwithstanding section 363 of this title, except to the extent that the court orders otherwise, and until an order for relief in the case, any business of the debtor may continue to operate, and the debtor may continue to use, acquire, or dispose of property as if an involuntary case concerning the debtor had not been commenced.

(g) At any time after the commencement of an involuntary case under chapter 7 of this title but before an order for relief in the case, the court, on request of a party in interest, after notice to the debtor and a hearing, and if necessary to preserve the property of the estate or to prevent loss to the estate, may order the United States trustee to appoint an interim trustee under section 701 of this title to take possession of the property of the estate and to operate any business of the debtor. Before an order for relief, the debtor may regain possession of property in the possession of a trustee ordered appointed under this subsection if the debtor files such bond as the court requires, conditioned on the debtor's accounting for and delivering to the trustee, if there is an order for relief in the case, such property, or the value, as of the date the debtor regains possession, of such property.

(h) If the petition is not timely controverted, the court shall order relief against the debtor in an involuntary case under the chapter under which the petition was filed. Otherwise, after trial, the court shall order relief against the debtor in an involuntary case under the chapter under which the petition was filed, only if—

    (1) the debtor is generally not paying such debtor's debts as such debts become due unless such debts are the subject of a bona fide dispute as to liability or amount; or

    (2) within 120 days before the date of the filing of the petition, a custodian, other than a trustee, receiver, or agent appointed or authorized to take charge of less than substantially all of the property of the debtor for the purpose of enforcing a lien against such property, was appointed or took possession.

(i) If the court dismisses a petition under this section other than on consent of all petitioners and the debtor, and if the debtor does not waive the right to judgment under this subsection, the court may grant judgment—

    (1) against the petitioners and in favor of the debtor for—

        (A) costs; or

        (B) a reasonable attorney's fee; or

    (2) against any petitioner that filed the petition in bad faith, for—

        (A) any damages proximately caused by such filing; or

        (B) punitive damages.

(j) Only after notice to all creditors and a hearing may the court dismiss a petition filed under this section—

    (1) on the motion of a petitioner;

    (2) on consent of all petitioners and the debtor; or

    (3) for want of prosecution.

(k)(1)   If—

(A) the petition under this section is false or contains any materially false, fictitious, or fraudulent statement;

(B) the debtor is an individual; and

(C) the court dismisses such petition,

the court, upon the motion of the debtor, shall seal all the records of the court relating to such petition, and all references to such petition.

(2) If the debtor is an individual and the court dismisses a petition under this section, the court may enter an order prohibiting all consumer reporting agencies (as defined in section 603(f) of the Fair Credit Reporting Act (15 U.S.C. 1681a(f))) from making any consumer report (as defined in section 603(d) of that Act) that contains any information relating to such petition or to the case commenced by the filing of such petition.

(3) Upon the expiration of the statute of limitations described in section 3282 of title 18, for a violation of section 152 or 157 of such title, the court, upon the motion of the debtor and for good cause, may expunge any records relating to a petition filed under this section.

REFERENCES IN TEXT

Section 603 of the Fair Credit Reporting Act, referred to in subsec. (k)(2), is Pub. L. 90–321, Title VI, § 603, as added Pub. L. 91–508, Title IV, § 601, Oct. 26, 1970, 84 Stat. 1128, and amended, which is classified to 15 U.S.C.A. § 1681a.

CROSS REFERENCES

Allowance of administrative expenses incurred by creditor filing involuntary petition, see 11 USCA § 503.

"Petition" defined, see 11 USCA § 101.

[§ 304. Repealed.]

§ 305. Abstention

(a) The court, after notice and a hearing, may dismiss a case under this title, or may suspend all proceedings in a case under this title, at any time if—

(1) the interests of creditors and the debtor would be better served by such dismissal or suspension; or

(2)(A) a petition under section 1515 for recognition of a foreign proceeding has been granted; and

(B) the purposes of chapter 15 of this title would be best served by such dismissal or suspension.

(b) A foreign representative may seek dismissal or suspension under subsection (a)(2) of this section.

(c) An order under subsection (a) of this section dismissing a case or suspending all proceedings in a case, or a decision not so to dismiss or suspend, is not reviewable by appeal or otherwise by the court of appeals under section 158(d), 1291, or 1292 of title 28 or by the Supreme Court of the United States under section 1254 of title 28.

§ 306. Limited appearance

An appearance in a bankruptcy court by a foreign representative in connection with a petition or request under section 303 or 305 of this title does not submit such foreign representative to the jurisdiction of any court in the United States for any other purpose, but the bankruptcy court may condition any order under section 303 or 305 of this title on compliance by such foreign representative with the orders of such bankruptcy court.

§ 307.   United States trustee

The United States trustee may raise and may appear and be heard on any issue in any case or proceeding under this title but may not file a plan pursuant to section 1121(c) of this title.

§ 308.   Debtor reporting requirements

(a)   For purposes of this section, the term "profitability" means, with respect to a debtor, the amount of money that the debtor has earned or lost during current and recent fiscal periods.

(b)   A debtor in a small business case shall file periodic financial and other reports containing information including—

(1)   the debtor's profitability;

(2)   reasonable approximations of the debtor's projected cash receipts and cash disbursements over a reasonable period;

(3)   comparisons of actual cash receipts and disbursements with projections in prior reports;

(4)   whether the debtor is—

(A)   in compliance in all material respects with postpetition requirements imposed by this title and the Federal Rules of Bankruptcy Procedure; and

(B)   timely filing tax returns and other required government filings and paying taxes and other administrative expenses when due;

(5)   if the debtor is not in compliance with the requirements referred to in paragraph (4)(A) or filing tax returns and other required government filings and making the payments referred to in paragraph (4)(B), what the failures are and how, at what cost, and when the debtor intends to remedy such failures; and

(6)   such other matters as are in the best interests of the debtor and creditors, and in the public interest in fair and efficient procedures under chapter 11 of this title.

SUBCHAPTER II—OFFICERS

§ 321.   Eligibility to serve as trustee

(a)   A person may serve as trustee in a case under this title only if such person is—

(1)   an individual that is competent to perform the duties of trustee and, in a case under chapter 7, 12, or 13 of this title, resides or has an office in the judicial district within which the case is pending, or in any judicial district adjacent to such district; or

(2)   a corporation authorized by such corporation's charter or bylaws to act as trustee, and, in a case under chapter 7, 12, or 13 of this title, having an office in at least one of such districts.

(b)   A person that has served as an examiner in the case may not serve as trustee in the case.

(c)   The United States trustee for the judicial district in which the case is pending is eligible to serve as trustee in the case if necessary.

§ 322.   Qualification of trustee

(a)   Except as provided in subsection (b)(1), a person selected under section 701, 702, 703, 1104, 1163, 1183, 1202, or 1302 of this title to serve as trustee in a case under this title qualifies if before seven days after such selection, and before beginning official duties, such person has filed with the court a bond in favor of the United States conditioned on the faithful performance of such official duties.

(b)(1)   The United States trustee qualifies wherever such trustee serves as trustee in a case under this title.

(2)   The United States trustee shall determine—

    (A)   the amount of a bond required to be filed under subsection (a) of this section; and

    (B)   the sufficiency of the surety on such bond.

(c)   A trustee is not liable personally or on such trustee's bond in favor of the United States for any penalty or forfeiture incurred by the debtor.

(d)   A proceeding on a trustee's bond may not be commenced after two years after the date on which such trustee was discharged.

CROSS REFERENCES

Appointment of trustee or examiner upon failure to qualify, see 11 USCA § 1104.

Certain customer transactions affected before qualification of trustee, see 11 USCA § 746.

"Debtor in possession" defined as debtor except when qualified person is serving as trustee under this section, see 11 USCA § 1101.

Interim trustee, see 11 USCA § 701.

Qualification of trustee and attorney in investor protection liquidation proceedings, see 15 USCA § 78eee.

Standing trustee—

    Chapter 11 subchapter V cases, see 11 USCA § 1183.

    Chapter 12 cases, see 11 USCA § 1202.

    Chapter 13 cases, see 11 USCA § 1302.

Successor trustee, see 11 USCA § 703.

§ 323.   Role and capacity of trustee

(a)   The trustee in a case under this title is the representative of the estate.

(b)   The trustee in a case under this title has capacity to sue and be sued.

§ 324.   Removal of trustee or examiner

(a)   The court, after notice and a hearing, may remove a trustee, other than the United States trustee, or an examiner, for cause.

(b)   Whenever the court removes a trustee or examiner under subsection (a) in a case under this title, such trustee or examiner shall thereby be removed in all other cases under this title in which such trustee or examiner is then serving unless the court orders otherwise.

CROSS REFERENCES

Adverse interest and conduct of officers of estate, see 18 USCA § 154.

Appointment of trustee or examiner upon removal, see 11 USCA § 1104.

Authority of Attorney General to investigate trustees, see 28 USCA § 526.

Embezzlement by trustee, see 18 USCA § 153.

Successor trustee, see 11 USCA § 703.

§ 325. Effect of vacancy

A vacancy in the office of trustee during a case does not abate any pending action or proceeding, and the successor trustee shall be substituted as a party in such action or proceeding.

§ 326. Limitation on compensation of trustee

(a) In a case under chapter 7 or 11, other than a case under subchapter V of chapter 11, the court may allow reasonable compensation under section 330 of this title of the trustee for the trustee's services, payable after the trustee renders such services, not to exceed 25 percent on the first $5,000 or less, 10 percent on any amount in excess of $5,000 but not in excess of $50,000, 5 percent on any amount in excess of $50,000 but not in excess of $1,000,000, and reasonable compensation not to exceed 3 percent of such moneys in excess of $1,000,000, upon all moneys disbursed or turned over in the case by the trustee to parties in interest, excluding the debtor, but including holders of secured claims.

(b) In a case under subchapter V of chapter 11 or chapter 12 or 13 of this title, the court may not allow compensation for services or reimbursement of expenses of the United States trustee or of a standing trustee appointed under section 586(b) of title 28, but may allow reasonable compensation under section 330 of this title of a trustee appointed under section 1202(a) or 1302(a) of this title for the trustee's services, payable after the trustee renders such services, not to exceed five percent upon all payments under the plan.

(c) If more than one person serves as trustee in the case, the aggregate compensation of such persons for such service may not exceed the maximum compensation prescribed for a single trustee by subsection (a) or (b) of this section, as the case may be.

(d) The court may deny allowance of compensation for services or reimbursement of expenses of the trustee if the trustee failed to make diligent inquiry into facts that would permit denial of allowance under section 328(c) of this title or, with knowledge of such facts, employed a professional person under section 327 of this title.

§ 327. Employment of professional persons

(a) Except as otherwise provided in this section, the trustee, with the court's approval, may employ one or more attorneys, accountants, appraisers, auctioneers, or other professional persons, that do not hold or represent an interest adverse to the estate, and that are disinterested persons, to represent or assist the trustee in carrying out the trustee's duties under this title.

(b) If the trustee is authorized to operate the business of the debtor under section 721, 1202, or 1108 of this title, and if the debtor has regularly employed attorneys, accountants, or other professional persons on salary, the trustee may retain or replace such professional persons if necessary in the operation of such business.

(c) In a case under chapter 7, 12, or 11 of this title, a person is not disqualified for employment under this section solely because of such person's employment by or representation of a creditor, unless there is objection by another creditor or the United States trustee, in which case the court shall disapprove such employment if there is an actual conflict of interest.

(d) The court may authorize the trustee to act as attorney or accountant for the estate if such authorization is in the best interest of the estate.

(e) The trustee, with the court's approval, may employ, for a specified special purpose, other than to represent the trustee in conducting the case, an attorney that has represented the debtor, if in the best interest of the estate, and if such attorney does not represent or hold any interest adverse to the debtor or to the estate with respect to the matter on which such attorney is to be employed.

(f) The trustee may not employ a person that has served as an examiner in the case.

Duty of United States trustee to monitor applications, see 28 USCA § 586.

Qualification for employment by debtor in possession despite prior employment or representation, see 11 USCA § 1107.

§ 328. Limitation on compensation of professional persons

(a) The trustee, or a committee appointed under section 1102 of this title, with the court's approval, may employ or authorize the employment of a professional person under section 327 or 1103 of this title, as the case may be, on any reasonable terms and conditions of employment, including on a retainer, on an hourly basis, on a fixed or percentage fee basis, or on a contingent fee basis. Notwithstanding such terms and conditions, the court may allow compensation different from the compensation provided under such terms and conditions after the conclusion of such employment, if such terms and conditions prove to have been improvident in light of developments not capable of being anticipated at the time of the fixing of such terms and conditions.

(b) If the court has authorized a trustee to serve as an attorney or accountant for the estate under section 327(d) of this title, the court may allow compensation for the trustee's services as such attorney or accountant only to the extent that the trustee performed services as attorney or accountant for the estate and not for performance of any of the trustee's duties that are generally performed by a trustee without the assistance of an attorney or accountant for the estate.

(c) Except as provided in section 327(c), 327(e), or 1107(b) of this title, the court may deny allowance of compensation for services and reimbursement of expenses of a professional person employed under section 327 or 1103 of this title if, at any time during such professional person's employment under section 327 or 1103 of this title, such professional person is not a disinterested person, or represents or holds an interest adverse to the interest of the estate with respect to the matter on which such professional person is employed.

§ 329. Debtor's transactions with attorneys

(a) Any attorney representing a debtor in a case under this title, or in connection with such a case, whether or not such attorney applies for compensation under this title, shall file with the court a statement of the compensation paid or agreed to be paid, if such payment or agreement was made after one year before the date of the filing of the petition, for services rendered or to be rendered in contemplation of or in connection with the case by such attorney, and the source of such compensation.

(b) If such compensation exceeds the reasonable value of any such services, the court may cancel any such agreement, or order the return of any such payment, to the extent excessive, to—

(1) the estate, if the property transferred—

(A) would have been property of the estate; or

(B) was to be paid by or on behalf of the debtor under a plan under chapter 11, 12, or 13 of this title; or

(2) the entity that made such payment.

Disclosure of compensation of attorney for debtor, see Director's Bankruptcy Form 2030.

Fee agreements, see 18 USCA § 155.

§ 330. Compensation of officers

(a)(1) After notice to the parties in interest and the United States Trustee and a hearing, and subject to sections 326, 328, and 329, the court may award to a trustee, a consumer privacy ombudsman appointed under section 332, an examiner, an ombudsman appointed under section 333, or a professional person employed under section 327 or 1103—

    (A) reasonable compensation for actual, necessary services rendered by the trustee, examiner, ombudsman, professional person, or attorney and by any paraprofessional person employed by any such person; and

    (B) reimbursement for actual, necessary expenses.

    (2) The court may, on its own motion or on the motion of the United States Trustee, the United States Trustee for the District or Region, the trustee for the estate, or any other party in interest, award compensation that is less than the amount of compensation that is requested.

    (3) In determining the amount of reasonable compensation to be awarded to an examiner, trustee under chapter 11, or professional person, the court shall consider the nature, the extent, and the value of such services, taking into account all relevant factors, including—

    (A) the time spent on such services;

    (B) the rates charged for such services;

    (C) whether the services were necessary to the administration of, or beneficial at the time at which the service was rendered toward the completion of, a case under this title;

    (D) whether the services were performed within a reasonable amount of time commensurate with the complexity, importance, and nature of the problem, issue, or task addressed;

    (E) with respect to a professional person, whether the person is board certified or otherwise has demonstrated skill and experience in the bankruptcy field; and

    (F) whether the compensation is reasonable based on the customary compensation charged by comparably skilled practitioners in cases other than cases under this title.

    (4)(A) Except as provided in subparagraph (B), the court shall not allow compensation for—

    (i) unnecessary duplication of services; or

    (ii) services that were not—

    (I) reasonably likely to benefit the debtor's estate; or

    (II) necessary to the administration of the case.

    (B) In a chapter 12 or chapter 13 case in which the debtor is an individual, the court may allow reasonable compensation to the debtor's attorney for representing the interests of the debtor in connection with the bankruptcy case based on a consideration of the benefit and necessity of such services to the debtor and the other factors set forth in this section.

    (5) The court shall reduce the amount of compensation awarded under this section by the amount of any interim compensation awarded under section 331, and, if the amount of such interim compensation exceeds the amount of compensation awarded under this section, may order the return of the excess to the estate.

    (6) Any compensation awarded for the preparation of a fee application shall be based on the level and skill reasonably required to prepare the application.

    (7) In determining the amount of reasonable compensation to be awarded to a trustee, the court shall treat such compensation as a commission, based on section 326.

    (b)(1) There shall be paid from the filing fee in a case under chapter 7 of this title $45 to the trustee serving in such case, after such trustee's services are rendered.

    (2) The Judicial Conference of the United States—

    (A) shall prescribe additional fees of the same kind as prescribed under section 1914(b) of title 28; and

    (B) may prescribe notice of appearance fees and fees charged against distributions in cases under this title;

to pay $15 to trustees serving in cases after such trustees' services are rendered. Beginning 1 year after the date of the enactment of the Bankruptcy Reform Act of 1994, such $15 shall be paid in addition to the amount paid under paragraph (1).

    (c) Unless the court orders otherwise, in a case under chapter 12 or 13 of this title the compensation paid to the trustee serving in the case shall not be less than $5 per month from any distribution under the plan during the administration of the plan.

    (d) In a case in which the United States trustee serves as trustee, the compensation of the trustee under this section shall be paid to the clerk of the bankruptcy court and deposited by the clerk into the United States Trustee System Fund established by section 589a of title 28.

    (e)(1) There is established a fund in the Treasury of the United States, to be known as the "Chapter 7 Trustee Fund", which shall be administered by the Director of the Administrative Office of the United States Courts.

    (2) Deposits into the Chapter 7 Trustee Fund under section 589a(f)(1)(C) of title 28 shall be available until expended for the purposes described in paragraph (3).

    (3) For fiscal years 2021 through 2026, the Chapter 7 Trustee Fund shall be available to pay the trustee serving in a case that is filed under chapter 7 or a case that is converted to a chapter 7 case in the most recent fiscal year (referred to in this subsection as a "chapter 7 case") the amount described in paragraph (4) for the chapter 7 case in which the trustee has rendered services.

    (4) The amount described in this paragraph shall be the lesser of—

    (A) $60; or

    (B) a pro rata share, for each chapter 7 case, of the fees collected under section 1930(a)(6) of title 28 and deposited to the United States Trustee System Fund under section 589a(f)(1) of title 28, less the amounts specified in section 589a(f)(1)(A) and (B) of title 28.

    (5) The payment received by a trustee under paragraph (3) shall be paid in addition to the amount paid under subsection (b).

    (6) Not later than September 30, 2021, the Director of the Administrative Office of the United States Courts shall promulgate regulations for the administration of this subsection.

CROSS REFERENCES

Adverse interest and conduct of officers of estate, see 18 USCA § 154.

Allowances to trustee and trustee's attorney in investor protection liquidation proceedings, see 15 USCA § 78eee.

Approval of Securities and Exchange Commission for payment of fees, expenses and remuneration in cases involving holding companies under this title, see 15 USCA § 79k.

Debtor in possession's right of compensation—

    Chapter 11 cases, see 11 USCA § 1107.

    Chapter 12 cases, see 11 USCA § 1203.

Guidelines for reviewing applications for compensation and reimbursement of expenses, see Fed. R. Bankr. P. 2016.

Officers' compensation as administrative expense, see 11 USCA § 503.

Supervision by Attorney General, see 28 USCA § 586.

United States Trustee System Fund establishment and purpose, see 28 USCA § 589a.

§ 331. Interim compensation

A trustee, an examiner, a debtor's attorney, or any professional person employed under section 327 or 1103 of this title may apply to the court not more than once every 120 days after an order for relief in a case under this title, or more often if the court permits, for such compensation for services rendered before the date of such an application or reimbursement for expenses incurred before such date as is provided under section 330 of this title. After notice and a hearing, the court may allow and disburse to such applicant such compensation or reimbursement.

§ 332. Consumer privacy ombudsman

(a) If a hearing is required under section 363(b)(1)(B), the court shall order the United States trustee to appoint, not later than 7 days before the commencement of the hearing, 1 disinterested person (other than the United States trustee) to serve as the consumer privacy ombudsman in the case and shall require that notice of such hearing be timely given to such ombudsman.

(b) The consumer privacy ombudsman may appear and be heard at such hearing and shall provide to the court information to assist the court in its consideration of the facts, circumstances, and conditions of the proposed sale or lease of personally identifiable information under section 363(b)(1)(B). Such information may include presentation of—

(1) the debtor's privacy policy;

(2) the potential losses or gains of privacy to consumers if such sale or such lease is approved by the court;

(3) the potential costs or benefits to consumers if such sale or such lease is approved by the court; and

(4) the potential alternatives that would mitigate potential privacy losses or potential costs to consumers.

(c) A consumer privacy ombudsman shall not disclose any personally identifiable information obtained by the ombudsman under this title.

§ 333. Appointment of patient care ombudsman

(a)(1) If the debtor in a case under chapter 7, 9, or 11 is a health care business, the court shall order, not later than 30 days after the commencement of the case, the appointment of an ombudsman to monitor the quality of patient care and to represent the interests of the patients of the health care business unless the court finds that the appointment of such ombudsman is not necessary for the protection of patients under the specific facts of the case.

(2)(A) If the court orders the appointment of an ombudsman under paragraph (1), the United States trustee shall appoint 1 disinterested person (other than the United States trustee) to serve as such ombudsman.

(B) If the debtor is a health care business that provides long-term care, then the United States trustee may appoint the State Long-Term Care Ombudsman appointed under the Older Americans Act of 1965 for the State in which the case is pending to serve as the ombudsman required by paragraph (1).

(C) If the United States trustee does not appoint a State Long-Term Care Ombudsman under subparagraph (B), the court shall notify the State Long-Term Care Ombudsman appointed under the Older Americans Act of 1965 for the State in which the case is pending, of the name and address of the person who is appointed under subparagraph (A).

(b) An ombudsman appointed under subsection (a) shall—

(1) monitor the quality of patient care provided to patients of the debtor, to the extent necessary under the circumstances, including interviewing patients and physicians;

(2) not later than 60 days after the date of appointment, and not less frequently than at 60-day intervals thereafter, report to the court after notice to the parties in interest, at a hearing or in writing, regarding the quality of patient care provided to patients of the debtor; and

(3) if such ombudsman determines that the quality of patient care provided to patients of the debtor is declining significantly or is otherwise being materially compromised, file with the court a motion or a written report, with notice to the parties in interest immediately upon making such determination.

(c)(1) An ombudsman appointed under subsection (a) shall maintain any information obtained by such ombudsman under this section that relates to patients (including information relating to patient records) as confidential information. Such ombudsman may not review confidential patient records unless the court approves such review in advance and imposes restrictions on such ombudsman to protect the confidentiality of such records.

(2) An ombudsman appointed under subsection (a)(2)(B) shall have access to patient records consistent with authority of such ombudsman under the Older Americans Act of 1965 and under non-Federal laws governing the State Long-Term Care Ombudsman program.

REFERENCES IN TEXT

The Older Americans Act of 1965, referred to in subsecs. (a)(2)(B), (C) and (c)(2), is Pub. L. 89–73, July 14, 1965, 79 Stat. 218, as amended, which is classified principally to chapter 35 of Title 42, 42 U.S.C.A. § 3001 et seq. For complete classification, see Short Title note set out under 42 U.S.C.A. § 3001 and Tables.

SUBCHAPTER III—ADMINISTRATION

§ 341.   Meetings of creditors and equity security holders

(a) Within a reasonable time after the order for relief in a case under this title, the United States trustee shall convene and preside at a meeting of creditors.

(b) The United States trustee may convene a meeting of any equity security holders.

(c) The court may not preside at, and may not attend, any meeting under this section including any final meeting of creditors. Notwithstanding any local court rule, provision of a State constitution, any otherwise applicable nonbankruptcy law, or any other requirement that representation at the meeting of creditors under subsection (a) be by an attorney, a creditor holding a consumer debt or any representative of the creditor (which may include an entity or an employee of an entity and may be a representative for more than 1 creditor) shall be permitted to appear at and participate in the meeting of creditors in a case under chapter 7 or 13, either alone or in conjunction with an attorney for the creditor. Nothing in this subsection shall be construed to require any creditor to be represented by an attorney at any meeting of creditors.

(d) Prior to the conclusion of the meeting of creditors or equity security holders, the trustee shall orally examine the debtor to ensure that the debtor in a case under chapter 7 of this title is aware of—

(1) the potential consequences of seeking a discharge in bankruptcy, including the effects on credit history;

(2) the debtor's ability to file a petition under a different chapter of this title;

(3) the effect of receiving a discharge of debts under this title; and

(4) the effect of reaffirming a debt, including the debtor's knowledge of the provisions of section 524(d) of this title.

(e) Notwithstanding subsections (a) and (b), the court, on the request of a party in interest and after notice and a hearing, for cause may order that the United States trustee not convene a meeting of creditors or equity security holders if the debtor has filed a plan as to which the debtor solicited acceptances prior to the commencement of the case.

CROSS REFERENCES

Election in Chapter 7 case of—

>Creditors' committee, see 11 USCA § 705.

>Trustee, see 11 USCA § 702.

Inapplicability of this section in railroad reorganization cases, see 11 USCA § 1161.

§ 342. Notice

    (a) There shall be given such notice as is appropriate, including notice to any holder of a community claim, of an order for relief in a case under this title.

    (b) Before the commencement of a case under this title by an individual whose debts are primarily consumer debts, the clerk shall give to such individual written notice containing—

>   **(1)** a brief description of—

>>   **(A)** chapters 7, 11, 12, and 13 and the general purpose, benefits, and costs of proceeding under each of those chapters; and

>>   **(B)** the types of services available from credit counseling agencies; and

>   **(2)** statements specifying that—

>>   **(A)** a person who knowingly and fraudulently conceals assets or makes a false oath or statement under penalty of perjury in connection with a case under this title shall be subject to fine, imprisonment, or both; and

>>   **(B)** all information supplied by a debtor in connection with a case under this title is subject to examination by the Attorney General.

    (c)(1) If notice is required to be given by the debtor to a creditor under this title, any rule, any applicable law, or any order of the court, such notice shall contain the name, address, and last 4 digits of the taxpayer identification number of the debtor. If the notice concerns an amendment that adds a creditor to the schedules of assets and liabilities, the debtor shall include the full taxpayer identification number in the notice sent to that creditor, but the debtor shall include only the last 4 digits of the taxpayer identification number in the copy of the notice filed with the court.

    (2)(A) If, within the 90 days before the commencement of a voluntary case, a creditor supplies the debtor in at least 2 communications sent to the debtor with the current account number of the debtor and the address at which such creditor requests to receive correspondence, then any notice required by this title to be sent by the debtor to such creditor shall be sent to such address and shall include such account number.

    (B) If a creditor would be in violation of applicable nonbankruptcy law by sending any such communication within such 90-day period and if such creditor supplies the debtor in the last 2 communications with the current account number of the debtor and the address at which such creditor requests to receive correspondence, then any notice required by this title to be sent by the debtor to such creditor shall be sent to such address and shall include such account number.

    (d) In a case under chapter 7 of this title in which the debtor is an individual and in which the presumption of abuse arises under section 707(b), the clerk shall give written notice to all creditors not later than 10 days after the date of the filing of the petition that the presumption of abuse has arisen.

(e)(1)　　In a case under chapter 7 or 13 of this title of a debtor who is an individual, a creditor at any time may both file with the court and serve on the debtor a notice of address to be used to provide notice in such case to such creditor.

(2)　Any notice in such case required to be provided to such creditor by the debtor or the court later than 7 days after the court and the debtor receive such creditor's notice of address, shall be provided to such address.

(f)(1)　　An entity may file with any bankruptcy court a notice of address to be used by all the bankruptcy courts or by particular bankruptcy courts, as so specified by such entity at the time such notice is filed, to provide notice to such entity in all cases under chapters 7 and 13 pending in the courts with respect to which such notice is filed, in which such entity is a creditor.

(2)　In any case filed under chapter 7 or 13, any notice required to be provided by a court with respect to which a notice is filed under paragraph (1), to such entity later than 30 days after the filing of such notice under paragraph (1) shall be provided to such address unless with respect to a particular case a different address is specified in a notice filed and served in accordance with subsection (e).

(3)　A notice filed under paragraph (1) may be withdrawn by such entity.

(g)(1)　　Notice provided to a creditor by the debtor or the court other than in accordance with this section (excluding this subsection) shall not be effective notice until such notice is brought to the attention of such creditor. If such creditor designates a person or an organizational subdivision of such creditor to be responsible for receiving notices under this title and establishes reasonable procedures so that such notices receivable by such creditor are to be delivered to such person or such subdivision, then a notice provided to such creditor other than in accordance with this section (excluding this subsection) shall not be considered to have been brought to the attention of such creditor until such notice is received by such person or such subdivision.

(2)　A monetary penalty may not be imposed on a creditor for a violation of a stay in effect under section 362(a) (including a monetary penalty imposed under section 362(k)) or for failure to comply with section 542 or 543 unless the conduct that is the basis of such violation or of such failure occurs after such creditor receives notice effective under this section of the order for relief.

CROSS REFERENCES

Instructions in notice to customers, see 11 USCA § 765.

"Net equity" defined in relation to payments made by customers to trustee within 60 days after notice, see 11 USCA § 741.

Notice in—

　　　Commodity broker liquidation cases, see 11 USCA § 762.

　　　Investor protection liquidation proceedings, see 15 USCA § 78fff–2.

　　　Stockbroker liquidation cases, see 11 USCA § 743.

Notice required by 11 USC § 342(b) for individuals filing for bankruptcy, see Director's Bankruptcy Form 2010.

§ 343.　Examination of the debtor

The debtor shall appear and submit to examination under oath at the meeting of creditors under section 341(a) of this title. Creditors, any indenture trustee, any trustee or examiner in the case, or the United States trustee may examine the debtor. The United States trustee may administer the oath required under this section.

CROSS REFERENCES

Concealment of assets deemed continuing offense, see 18 USCA § 3284.

Concealment of assets; false oaths and claims, see 18 USCA § 152.

Inapplicability of this section in railroad reorganization cases, see 11 USCA § 1161.

§ 344. Self-incrimination; immunity

Immunity for persons required to submit to examination, to testify, or to provide information in a case under this title may be granted under part V of title 18.

CROSS REFERENCES

Applicability of this section in chapter 9 cases, see 11 USCA § 901.

Debtor's duty to surrender records despite grant of immunity under this section, see 11 USCA § 521.

§ 345. Money of estates

(a) A trustee in a case under this title may make such deposit or investment of the money of the estate for which such trustee serves as will yield the maximum reasonable net return on such money, taking into account the safety of such deposit or investment.

(b) Except with respect to a deposit or investment that is insured or guaranteed by the United States or by a department, agency, or instrumentality of the United States or backed by the full faith and credit of the United States, the trustee shall require from an entity with which such money is deposited or invested—

    (1) a bond—

        (A) in favor of the United States;

        (B) secured by the undertaking of a corporate surety approved by the United States trustee for the district in which the case is pending; and

        (C) conditioned on—

            (i) a proper accounting for all money so deposited or invested and for any return on such money;

            (ii) prompt repayment of such money and return; and

            (iii) faithful performance of duties as a depository; or

    (2) the deposit of securities of the kind specified in section 9303 of title 31;

unless the court for cause orders otherwise.

(c) An entity with which such moneys are deposited or invested is authorized to deposit or invest such moneys as may be required under this section.

CROSS REFERENCES

Adverse interest and conduct of officers of estate, see 18 USCA § 154.

Duty of United States trustee to deposit or invest money, see 28 USCA § 586.

Embezzlement by trustee, see 18 USCA § 153.

§ 346. Special provisions related to the treatment of State and local taxes

(a) Whenever the Internal Revenue Code of 1986 provides that a separate taxable estate or entity is created in a case concerning a debtor under this title, and the income, gain, loss, deductions, and credits of such estate shall be taxed to or claimed by the estate, a separate taxable estate is also created for purposes of any State and local law imposing a tax on or measured by income and such income, gain, loss, deductions, and credits shall be taxed to or claimed by the estate and may not be taxed to or claimed by the debtor. The preceding sentence shall not apply if the case is dismissed. The trustee shall make tax returns of income required under any such State or local law.

(b) Whenever the Internal Revenue Code of 1986 provides that no separate taxable estate shall be created in a case concerning a debtor under this title, and the income, gain, loss, deductions, and credits of an estate shall be taxed to or claimed by the debtor, such income, gain, loss, deductions, and credits shall be taxed to or claimed by the debtor under a State or local law imposing a tax on or measured by income and may not be taxed to or claimed by the estate. The trustee shall make such tax returns of income of corporations and of partnerships as are required under any State or local law, but with respect to partnerships, shall make such returns only to the extent such returns are also required to be made under such Code. The estate shall be liable for any tax imposed on such corporation or partnership, but not for any tax imposed on partners or members.

(c) With respect to a partnership or any entity treated as a partnership under a State or local law imposing a tax on or measured by income that is a debtor in a case under this title, any gain or loss resulting from a distribution of property from such partnership, or any distributive share of any income, gain, loss, deduction, or credit of a partner or member that is distributed, or considered distributed, from such partnership, after the commencement of the case, is gain, loss, income, deduction, or credit, as the case may be, of the partner or member, and if such partner or member is a debtor in a case under this title, shall be subject to tax in accordance with subsection (a) or (b).

(d) For purposes of any State or local law imposing a tax on or measured by income, the taxable period of a debtor in a case under this title shall terminate only if and to the extent that the taxable period of such debtor terminates under the Internal Revenue Code of 1986.

(e) The estate in any case described in subsection (a) shall use the same accounting method as the debtor used immediately before the commencement of the case, if such method of accounting complies with applicable nonbankruptcy tax law.

(f) For purposes of any State or local law imposing a tax on or measured by income, a transfer of property from the debtor to the estate or from the estate to the debtor shall not be treated as a disposition for purposes of any provision assigning tax consequences to a disposition, except to the extent that such transfer is treated as a disposition under the Internal Revenue Code of 1986.

(g) Whenever a tax is imposed pursuant to a State or local law imposing a tax on or measured by income pursuant to subsection (a) or (b), such tax shall be imposed at rates generally applicable to the same types of entities under such State or local law.

(h) The trustee shall withhold from any payment of claims for wages, salaries, commissions, dividends, interest, or other payments, or collect, any amount required to be withheld or collected under applicable State or local tax law, and shall pay such withheld or collected amount to the appropriate governmental unit at the time and in the manner required by such tax law, and with the same priority as the claim from which such amount was withheld or collected was paid.

(i)(1) To the extent that any State or local law imposing a tax on or measured by income provides for the carryover of any tax attribute from one taxable period to a subsequent taxable period, the estate shall succeed to such tax attribute in any case in which such estate is subject to tax under subsection (a).

(2) After such a case is closed or dismissed, the debtor shall succeed to any tax attribute to which the estate succeeded under paragraph (1) to the extent consistent with the Internal Revenue Code of 1986.

(3) The estate may carry back any loss or tax attribute to a taxable period of the debtor that ended before the date of the order for relief under this title to the extent that—

  (A) applicable State or local tax law provides for a carryback in the case of the debtor; and

  (B) the same or a similar tax attribute may be carried back by the estate to such a taxable period of the debtor under the Internal Revenue Code of 1986.

(j)(1) For purposes of any State or local law imposing a tax on or measured by income, income is not realized by the estate, the debtor, or a successor to the debtor by reason of discharge of indebtedness in a case under this title, except to the extent, if any, that such income is subject to tax under the Internal Revenue Code of 1986.

(2) Whenever the Internal Revenue Code of 1986 provides that the amount excluded from gross income in respect of the discharge of indebtedness in a case under this title shall be applied to reduce the tax attributes of the debtor or the estate, a similar reduction shall be made under any State or local law imposing a tax on or measured by income to the extent such State or local law recognizes such attributes. Such State or local law may also provide for the reduction of other attributes to the extent that the full amount of income from the discharge of indebtedness has not been applied.

(k)(1) Except as provided in this section and section 505, the time and manner of filing tax returns and the items of income, gain, loss, deduction, and credit of any taxpayer shall be determined under applicable nonbankruptcy law.

(2) For Federal tax purposes, the provisions of this section are subject to the Internal Revenue Code of 1986 and other applicable Federal nonbankruptcy law.

REFERENCES IN TEXT

The Internal Revenue Code of 1986, referred to in text, is classified to Title 26 of the Code.

CROSS REFERENCES

Request for determination of tax effects of—

Chapter 12 plan, see 11 USCA § 1231.

Reorganization plan, see 11 USCA § 1146.

§ 347. Unclaimed property

(a) Ninety days after the final distribution under section 726, 1194, 1226, or 1326 of this title in a case under chapter 7, subchapter V of chapter 11, 12, or 13 of this title, as the case may be, the trustee shall stop payment on any check remaining unpaid, and any remaining property of the estate shall be paid into the court and disposed of under chapter 129 of title 28.

(b) Any security, money, or other property remaining unclaimed at the expiration of the time allowed in a case under chapter 9, 11, or 12 of this title for the presentation of a security or the performance of any other act as a condition to participation in the distribution under any plan confirmed under section 943(b), 1129, 1173, 1191, or 1225 of this title, as the case may be, becomes the property of the debtor or of the entity acquiring the assets of the debtor under the plan, as the case may be.

CROSS REFERENCES

Applicability of this section in Chapter 9 cases, see 11 USCA § 901.

§ 348. Effect of conversion

(a) Conversion of a case from a case under one chapter of this title to a case under another chapter of this title constitutes an order for relief under the chapter to which the case is converted, but, except as provided in subsections (b) and (c) of this section, does not effect a change in the date of the filing of the petition, the commencement of the case, or the order for relief.

(b) Unless the court for cause orders otherwise, in sections 701(a), 727(a)(10), 727(b), 1102(a), 1110(a)(1), 1121(b), 1121(c), 1141(d)(4), 1201(a), 1221, 1228(a), 1301(a), and 1305(a) of this title, "the order for relief under this chapter" in a chapter to which a case has been converted under section 706, 1112, 1208, or 1307 of this title means the conversion of such case to such chapter.

(c) Sections 342 and 365(d) of this title apply in a case that has been converted under section 706, 1112, 1208, or 1307 of this title, as if the conversion order were the order for relief.

(d) A claim against the estate or the debtor that arises after the order for relief but before conversion in a case that is converted under section 1112, 1208, or 1307 of this title, other than a claim specified in section 503(b) of this title, shall be treated for all purposes as if such claim had arisen immediately before the date of the filing of the petition.

(e) Conversion of a case under section 706, 1112, 1208, or 1307 of this title terminates the service of any trustee or examiner that is serving in the case before such conversion.

(f)(1) Except as provided in paragraph (2), when a case under chapter 13 of this title is converted to a case under another chapter under this title—

    (A) property of the estate in the converted case shall consist of property of the estate, as of the date of filing of the petition, that remains in the possession of or is under the control of the debtor on the date of conversion;

    (B) valuations of property and of allowed secured claims in the chapter 13 case shall apply only in a case converted to a case under chapter 11 or 12, but not in a case converted to a case under chapter 7, with allowed secured claims in cases under chapters 11 and 12 reduced to the extent that they have been paid in accordance with the chapter 13 plan; and

    (C) with respect to cases converted from chapter 13—

        (i) the claim of any creditor holding security as of the date of the filing of the petition shall continue to be secured by that security unless the full amount of such claim determined under applicable nonbankruptcy law has been paid in full as of the date of conversion, notwithstanding any valuation or determination of the amount of an allowed secured claim made for the purposes of the case under chapter 13; and

        (ii) unless a prebankruptcy default has been fully cured under the plan at the time of conversion, in any proceeding under this title or otherwise, the default shall have the effect given under applicable nonbankruptcy law.

(2) If the debtor converts a case under chapter 13 of this title to a case under another chapter under this title in bad faith, the property of the estate in the converted case shall consist of the property of the estate as of the date of conversion.

§ 349. Effect of dismissal

(a) Unless the court, for cause, orders otherwise, the dismissal of a case under this title does not bar the discharge, in a later case under this title, of debts that were dischargeable in the case dismissed; nor does the dismissal of a case under this title prejudice the debtor with regard to the filing of a subsequent petition under this title, except as provided in section 109(g) of this title.

(b) Unless the court, for cause, orders otherwise, a dismissal of a case other than under section 742 of this title—

    (1) reinstates—

        (A) any proceeding or custodianship superseded under section 543 of this title;

        (B) any transfer avoided under section 522, 544, 545, 547, 548, 549, or 724(a) of this title, or preserved under section 510(c)(2), 522(i)(2), or 551 of this title; and

        (C) any lien voided under section 506(d) of this title;

    (2) vacates any order, judgment, or transfer ordered, under section 522(i)(1), 542, 550, or 553 of this title; and

    (3) revests the property of the estate in the entity in which such property was vested immediately before the commencement of the case under this title.

§ 350. Closing and reopening cases

(a) After an estate is fully administered and the court has discharged the trustee, the court shall close the case.

(b) A case may be reopened in the court in which such case was closed to administer assets, to accord relief to the debtor, or for other cause.

CROSS REFERENCES

Applicability of subsec. (b) of this section in Chapter 9 cases, see 11 USCA § 901.

Scheduled property deemed abandoned, see 11 USCA § 554.

Successor trustee, see 11 USCA § 703.

§ 351. Disposal of patient records

If a health care business commences a case under chapter 7, 9, or 11, and the trustee does not have a sufficient amount of funds to pay for the storage of patient records in the manner required under applicable Federal or State law, the following requirements shall apply:

    (1) The trustee shall—

        (A) promptly publish notice, in 1 or more appropriate newspapers, that if patient records are not claimed by the patient or an insurance provider (if applicable law permits the insurance provider to make that claim) by the date that is 365 days after the date of that notification, the trustee will destroy the patient records; and

        (B) during the first 180 days of the 365-day period described in subparagraph (A), promptly attempt to notify directly each patient that is the subject of the patient records and appropriate insurance carrier concerning the patient records by mailing to the most recent known address of that patient, or a family member or contact person for that patient, and to the appropriate insurance carrier an appropriate notice regarding the claiming or disposing of patient records.

    (2) If, after providing the notification under paragraph (1), patient records are not claimed during the 365-day period described under that paragraph, the trustee shall mail, by certified mail, at the end of such 365-day period a written request to each appropriate Federal agency to request permission from that agency to deposit the patient records with that agency, except that no Federal agency is required to accept patient records under this paragraph.

    (3) If, following the 365-day period described in paragraph (2) and after providing the notification under paragraph (1), patient records are not claimed by a patient or insurance provider, or request is not granted by a Federal agency to deposit such records with that agency, the trustee shall destroy those records by—

        (A) if the records are written, shredding or burning the records; or

        (B) if the records are magnetic, optical, or other electronic records, by otherwise destroying those records so that those records cannot be retrieved.

SUBCHAPTER IV—ADMINISTRATIVE POWERS

§ 361. Adequate protection

When adequate protection is required under section 362, 363, or 364 of this title of an interest of an entity in property, such adequate protection may be provided by—

    (1) requiring the trustee to make a cash payment or periodic cash payments to such entity, to the extent that the stay under section 362 of this title, use, sale, or lease under section 363 of this title, or any grant of a lien under section 364 of this title results in a decrease in the value of such entity's interest in such property;

   (2)   providing to such entity an additional or replacement lien to the extent that such stay, use, sale, lease, or grant results in a decrease in the value of such entity's interest in such property; or

   (3)   granting such other relief, other than entitling such entity to compensation allowable under section 503(b)(1) of this title as an administrative expense, as will result in the realization by such entity of the indubitable equivalent of such entity's interest in such property.

CROSS REFERENCES

Applicability of this section in Chapter 9 cases, see 11 USCA § 901.

Inapplicability of this section in Chapter 12 cases, see 11 USCA § 1205.

§ 362.   Automatic stay

   (a)   Except as provided in subsection (b) of this section, a petition filed under section 301, 302, or 303 of this title, or an application filed under section 5(a)(3) of the Securities Investor Protection Act of 1970, operates as a stay, applicable to all entities, of—

   (1)   the commencement or continuation, including the issuance or employment of process, of a judicial, administrative, or other action or proceeding against the debtor that was or could have been commenced before the commencement of the case under this title, or to recover a claim against the debtor that arose before the commencement of the case under this title;

   (2)   the enforcement, against the debtor or against property of the estate, of a judgment obtained before the commencement of the case under this title;

   (3)   any act to obtain possession of property of the estate or of property from the estate or to exercise control over property of the estate;

   (4)   any act to create, perfect, or enforce any lien against property of the estate;

   (5)   any act to create, perfect, or enforce against property of the debtor any lien to the extent that such lien secures a claim that arose before the commencement of the case under this title;

   (6)   any act to collect, assess, or recover a claim against the debtor that arose before the commencement of the case under this title;

   (7)   the setoff of any debt owing to the debtor that arose before the commencement of the case under this title against any claim against the debtor; and

   (8)   the commencement or continuation of a proceeding before the United States Tax Court concerning a tax liability of a debtor that is a corporation for a taxable period the bankruptcy court may determine or concerning the tax liability of a debtor who is an individual for a taxable period ending before the date of the order for relief under this title.

   (b)   The filing of a petition under section 301, 302, or 303 of this title, or of an application under section 5(a)(3) of the Securities Investor Protection Act of 1970, does not operate as a stay—

   (1)   under subsection (a) of this section, of the commencement or continuation of a criminal action or proceeding against the debtor;

   (2)   under subsection (a)—

      (A)   of the commencement or continuation of a civil action or proceeding—

         (i)   for the establishment of paternity;

         (ii)   for the establishment or modification of an order for domestic support obligations;

(iii) concerning child custody or visitation;

(iv) for the dissolution of a marriage, except to the extent that such proceeding seeks to determine the division of property that is property of the estate; or

(v) regarding domestic violence;

(B) of the collection of a domestic support obligation from property that is not property of the estate;

(C) with respect to the withholding of income that is property of the estate or property of the debtor for payment of a domestic support obligation under a judicial or administrative order or a statute;

(D) of the withholding, suspension, or restriction of a driver's license, a professional or occupational license, or a recreational license, under State law, as specified in section 466(a)(16) of the Social Security Act;

(E) of the reporting of overdue support owed by a parent to any consumer reporting agency as specified in section 466(a)(7) of the Social Security Act;

(F) of the interception of a tax refund, as specified in sections 464 and 466(a)(3) of the Social Security Act or under an analogous State law; or

(G) of the enforcement of a medical obligation, as specified under title IV of the Social Security Act;

(3) under subsection (a) of this section, of any act to perfect, or to maintain or continue the perfection of, an interest in property to the extent that the trustee's rights and powers are subject to such perfection under section 546(b) of this title or to the extent that such act is accomplished within the period provided under section 547(e)(2)(A) of this title;

(4) under paragraph (1), (2), (3), or (6) of subsection (a) of this section, of the commencement or continuation of an action or proceeding by a governmental unit or any organization exercising authority under the Convention on the Prohibition of the Development, Production, Stockpiling and Use of Chemical Weapons and on Their Destruction, opened for signature on January 13, 1993, to enforce such governmental unit's or organization's police and regulatory power, including the enforcement of a judgment other than a money judgment, obtained in an action or proceeding by the governmental unit to enforce such governmental unit's or organization's police or regulatory power;

[(5) Repealed.]

(6) under subsection (a) of this section, of the exercise by a commodity broker, forward contract merchant, stockbroker, financial institution, financial participant, or securities clearing agency of any contractual right (as defined in section 555 or 556) under any security agreement or arrangement or other credit enhancement forming a part of or related to any commodity contract, forward contract or securities contract, or of any contractual right (as defined in section 555 or 556) to offset or net out any termination value, payment amount, or other transfer obligation arising under or in connection with 1 or more such contracts, including any master agreement for such contracts;

(7) under subsection (a) of this section, of the exercise by a repo participant or financial participant of any contractual right (as defined in section 559) under any security agreement or arrangement or other credit enhancement forming a part of or related to any repurchase agreement, or of any contractual right (as defined in section 559) to offset or net out any termination value, payment amount, or other transfer obligation arising under or in connection with 1 or more such agreements, including any master agreement for such agreements;

(8) under subsection (a) of this section, of the commencement of any action by the Secretary of Housing and Urban Development to foreclose a mortgage or deed of trust in any case in which the mortgage or deed of trust held by the Secretary is insured or was formerly insured under the National Housing Act and covers property, or combinations of property, consisting of five or more living units;

    (9) under subsection (a), of—

        (A) an audit by a governmental unit to determine tax liability;

        (B) the issuance to the debtor by a governmental unit of a notice of tax deficiency;

        (C) a demand for tax returns; or

        (D) the making of an assessment for any tax and issuance of a notice and demand for payment of such an assessment (but any tax lien that would otherwise attach to property of the estate by reason of such an assessment shall not take effect unless such tax is a debt of the debtor that will not be discharged in the case and such property or its proceeds are transferred out of the estate to, or otherwise revested in, the debtor).

    (10) under subsection (a) of this section, of any act by a lessor to the debtor under a lease of nonresidential real property that has terminated by the expiration of the stated term of the lease before the commencement of or during a case under this title to obtain possession of such property;

    (11) under subsection (a) of this section, of the presentment of a negotiable instrument and the giving of notice of and protesting dishonor of such an instrument;

    (12) under subsection (a) of this section, after the date which is 90 days after the filing of such petition, of the commencement or continuation, and conclusion to the entry of final judgment, of an action which involves a debtor subject to reorganization pursuant to chapter 11 of this title and which was brought by the Secretary of Transportation under section 31325 of title 46 (including distribution of any proceeds of sale) to foreclose a preferred ship or fleet mortgage, or a security interest in or relating to a vessel or vessel under construction, held by the Secretary of Transportation under chapter 537 of title 46 or section 109(h) of title 49, or under applicable State law;

    (13) under subsection (a) of this section, after the date which is 90 days after the filing of such petition, of the commencement or continuation, and conclusion to the entry of final judgment, of an action which involves a debtor subject to reorganization pursuant to chapter 11 of this title and which was brought by the Secretary of Commerce under section 31325 of title 46 (including distribution of any proceeds of sale) to foreclose a preferred ship or fleet mortgage in a vessel or a mortgage, deed of trust, or other security interest in a fishing facility held by the Secretary of Commerce under chapter 537 of title 46;

    (14) under subsection (a) of this section, of any action by an accrediting agency regarding the accreditation status of the debtor as an educational institution;

    (15) under subsection (a) of this section, of any action by a State licensing body regarding the licensure of the debtor as an educational institution;

    (16) under subsection (a) of this section, of any action by a guaranty agency, as defined in section 435(j) of the Higher Education Act of 1965 or the Secretary of Education regarding the eligibility of the debtor to participate in programs authorized under such Act;

    (17) under subsection (a) of this section, of the exercise by a swap participant or financial participant of any contractual right (as defined in section 560) under any security agreement or arrangement or other credit enhancement forming a part of or related to any swap agreement, or of any contractual right (as defined in section 560) to offset or net out any termination value, payment amount, or other transfer obligation arising under or in connection with 1 or more such agreements, including any master agreement for such agreements;

(18) under subsection (a) of the creation or perfection of a statutory lien for an ad valorem property tax, or a special tax or special assessment on real property whether or not ad valorem, imposed by a governmental unit, if such tax or assessment comes due after the date of the filing of the petition;

(19) under subsection (a), of withholding of income from a debtor's wages and collection of amounts withheld, under the debtor's agreement authorizing that withholding and collection for the benefit of a pension, profit-sharing, stock bonus, or other plan established under section 401, 403, 408, 408A, 414, 457, or 501(c) of the Internal Revenue Code of 1986, that is sponsored by the employer of the debtor, or an affiliate, successor, or predecessor of such employer—

    (A) to the extent that the amounts withheld and collected are used solely for payments relating to a loan from a plan under section 408(b)(1) of the Employee Retirement Income Security Act of 1974 or is subject to section 72(p) of the Internal Revenue Code of 1986; or

    (B) a loan from a thrift savings plan permitted under subchapter III of chapter 84 of title 5, that satisfies the requirements of section 8433(g) of such title;

but nothing in this paragraph may be construed to provide that any loan made under a governmental plan under section 414(d), or a contract or account under section 403(b), of the Internal Revenue Code of 1986 constitutes a claim or a debt under this title;

(20) under subsection (a), of any act to enforce any lien against or security interest in real property following entry of the order under subsection (d)(4) as to such real property in any prior case under this title, for a period of 2 years after the date of the entry of such an order, except that the debtor, in a subsequent case under this title, may move for relief from such order based upon changed circumstances or for other good cause shown, after notice and a hearing;

(21) under subsection (a), of any act to enforce any lien against or security interest in real property—

    (A) if the debtor is ineligible under section 109(g) to be a debtor in a case under this title; or

    (B) if the case under this title was filed in violation of a bankruptcy court order in a prior case under this title prohibiting the debtor from being a debtor in another case under this title;

(22) subject to subsection (*l*), under subsection (a)(3), of the continuation of any eviction, unlawful detainer action, or similar proceeding by a lessor against a debtor involving residential property in which the debtor resides as a tenant under a lease or rental agreement and with respect to which the lessor has obtained before the date of the filing of the bankruptcy petition, a judgment for possession of such property against the debtor;

(23) subject to subsection (m), under subsection (a)(3), of an eviction action that seeks possession of the residential property in which the debtor resides as a tenant under a lease or rental agreement based on endangerment of such property or the illegal use of controlled substances on such property, but only if the lessor files with the court, and serves upon the debtor, a certification under penalty of perjury that such an eviction action has been filed, or that the debtor, during the 30-day period preceding the date of the filing of the certification, has endangered property or illegally used or allowed to be used a controlled substance on the property;

(24) under subsection (a), of any transfer that is not avoidable under section 544 and that is not avoidable under section 549;

(25) under subsection (a), of—

    (A) the commencement or continuation of an investigation or action by a securities self regulatory organization to enforce such organization's regulatory power;

(B) the enforcement of an order or decision, other than for monetary sanctions, obtained in an action by such securities self regulatory organization to enforce such organization's regulatory power; or

(C) any act taken by such securities self regulatory organization to delist, delete, or refuse to permit quotation of any stock that does not meet applicable regulatory requirements;

(26) under subsection (a), of the setoff under applicable nonbankruptcy law of an income tax refund, by a governmental unit, with respect to a taxable period that ended before the date of the order for relief against an income tax liability for a taxable period that also ended before the date of the order for relief, except that in any case in which the setoff of an income tax refund is not permitted under applicable nonbankruptcy law because of a pending action to determine the amount or legality of a tax liability, the governmental unit may hold the refund pending the resolution of the action, unless the court, on the motion of the trustee and after notice and a hearing, grants the taxing authority adequate protection (within the meaning of section 361) for the secured claim of such authority in the setoff under section 506(a);

(27) under subsection (a) of this section, of the exercise by a master netting agreement participant of any contractual right (as defined in section 555, 556, 559, or 560) under any security agreement or arrangement or other credit enhancement forming a part of or related to any master netting agreement, or of any contractual right (as defined in section 555, 556, 559, or 560) to offset or net out any termination value, payment amount, or other transfer obligation arising under or in connection with 1 or more such master netting agreements to the extent that such participant is eligible to exercise such rights under paragraph (6), (7), or (17) for each individual contract covered by the master netting agreement in issue;

(28) under subsection (a), of the exclusion by the Secretary of Health and Human Services of the debtor from participation in the medicare program or any other Federal health care program (as defined in section 1128B(f) of the Social Security Act pursuant to title XI or XVIII of such Act); and

(29) under subsection (a)(1) of this section, of any action by—

(A) an amateur sports organization, as defined in section 220501(b) of title 36, to replace a national governing body, as defined in that section, under section 220528 of that title; or

(B) the corporation, as defined in section 220501(b) of title 36, to revoke the certification of a national governing body, as defined in that section, under section 220521 of that title.

The provisions of paragraphs (12) and (13) of this subsection shall apply with respect to any such petition filed on or before December 31, 1989.

(c) Except as provided in subsections (d), (e), (f), and (h) of this section—

(1) the stay of an act against property of the estate under subsection (a) of this section continues until such property is no longer property of the estate;

(2) the stay of any other act under subsection (a) of this section continues until the earliest of—

(A) the time the case is closed;

(B) the time the case is dismissed; or

(C) if the case is a case under chapter 7 of this title concerning an individual or a case under chapter 9, 11, 12, or 13 of this title, the time a discharge is granted or denied;

(3) if a single or joint case is filed by or against a debtor who is an individual in a case under chapter 7, 11, or 13, and if a single or joint case of the debtor was pending within the preceding 1-year period but was dismissed, other than a case refiled under a chapter other than chapter 7 after dismissal under section 707(b)—

    (A) the stay under subsection (a) with respect to any action taken with respect to a debt or property securing such debt or with respect to any lease shall terminate with respect to the debtor on the 30th day after the filing of the later case;

    (B) on the motion of a party in interest for continuation of the automatic stay and upon notice and a hearing, the court may extend the stay in particular cases as to any or all creditors (subject to such conditions or limitations as the court may then impose) after notice and a hearing completed before the expiration of the 30-day period only if the party in interest demonstrates that the filing of the later case is in good faith as to the creditors to be stayed; and

    (C) for purposes of subparagraph (B), a case is presumptively filed not in good faith (but such presumption may be rebutted by clear and convincing evidence to the contrary)—

        (i) as to all creditors, if—

        (I) more than 1 previous case under any of chapters 7, 11, and 13 in which the individual was a debtor was pending within the preceding 1-year period;

        (II) a previous case under any of chapters 7, 11, and 13 in which the individual was a debtor was dismissed within such 1-year period, after the debtor failed to—

            (aa) file or amend the petition or other documents as required by this title or the court without substantial excuse (but mere inadvertence or negligence shall not be a substantial excuse unless the dismissal was caused by the negligence of the debtor's attorney);

            (bb) provide adequate protection as ordered by the court; or

            (cc) perform the terms of a plan confirmed by the court; or

        (III) there has not been a substantial change in the financial or personal affairs of the debtor since the dismissal of the next most previous case under chapter 7, 11, or 13 or any other reason to conclude that the later case will be concluded—

            (aa) if a case under chapter 7, with a discharge; or

            (bb) if a case under chapter 11 or 13, with a confirmed plan that will be fully performed; and

        (ii) as to any creditor that commenced an action under subsection (d) in a previous case in which the individual was a debtor if, as of the date of dismissal of such case, that action was still pending or had been resolved by terminating, conditioning, or limiting the stay as to actions of such creditor; and

(4)(A)(i) if a single or joint case is filed by or against a debtor who is an individual under this title, and if 2 or more single or joint cases of the debtor were pending within the previous year but were dismissed, other than a case refiled under a chapter other than chapter 7 after dismissal under section 707(b), the stay under subsection (a) shall not go into effect upon the filing of the later case; and

    (ii) on request of a party in interest, the court shall promptly enter an order confirming that no stay is in effect;

    (B) if, within 30 days after the filing of the later case, a party in interest requests the court may order the stay to take effect in the case as to any or all creditors (subject to such conditions or limitations as the court may impose), after notice and a hearing, only if the party in interest demonstrates that the filing of the later case is in good faith as to the creditors to be stayed;

    (C) a stay imposed under subparagraph (B) shall be effective on the date of the entry of the order allowing the stay to go into effect; and

    (D) for purposes of subparagraph (B), a case is presumptively filed not in good faith (but such presumption may be rebutted by clear and convincing evidence to the contrary)—

        (i) as to all creditors if—

            (I) 2 or more previous cases under this title in which the individual was a debtor were pending within the 1-year period;

            (II) a previous case under this title in which the individual was a debtor was dismissed within the time period stated in this paragraph after the debtor failed to file or amend the petition or other documents as required by this title or the court without substantial excuse (but mere inadvertence or negligence shall not be substantial excuse unless the dismissal was caused by the negligence of the debtor's attorney), failed to provide adequate protection as ordered by the court, or failed to perform the terms of a plan confirmed by the court; or

            (III) there has not been a substantial change in the financial or personal affairs of the debtor since the dismissal of the next most previous case under this title, or any other reason to conclude that the later case will not be concluded, if a case under chapter 7, with a discharge, and if a case under chapter 11 or 13, with a confirmed plan that will be fully performed; or

        (ii) as to any creditor that commenced an action under subsection (d) in a previous case in which the individual was a debtor if, as of the date of dismissal of such case, such action was still pending or had been resolved by terminating, conditioning, or limiting the stay as to such action of such creditor.

    (d) On request of a party in interest and after notice and a hearing, the court shall grant relief from the stay provided under subsection (a) of this section, such as by terminating, annulling, modifying, or conditioning such stay—

    (1) for cause, including the lack of adequate protection of an interest in property of such party in interest;

    (2) with respect to a stay of an act against property under subsection (a) of this section, if—

        (A) the debtor does not have an equity in such property; and

        (B) such property is not necessary to an effective reorganization;

    (3) with respect to a stay of an act against single asset real estate under subsection (a), by a creditor whose claim is secured by an interest in such real estate, unless, not later than the date that is 90 days after the entry of the order for relief (or such later date as the court may determine for cause by order entered within that 90-day period) or 30 days after the court determines that the debtor is subject to this paragraph, whichever is later—

        (A) the debtor has filed a plan of reorganization that has a reasonable possibility of being confirmed within a reasonable time; or

        (B) the debtor has commenced monthly payments that—

            (i) may, in the debtor's sole discretion, notwithstanding section 363(c)(2), be made from rents or other income generated before, on, or after the date of the commencement of the case by or from the property to each creditor whose claim is secured by such real estate (other than a claim secured by a judgment lien or by an unmatured statutory lien); and

    (ii) are in an amount equal to interest at the then applicable nondefault contract rate of interest on the value of the creditor's interest in the real estate; or

  (4) with respect to a stay of an act against real property under subsection (a), by a creditor whose claim is secured by an interest in such real property, if the court finds that the filing of the petition was part of a scheme to delay, hinder, or defraud creditors that involved either—

    (A) transfer of all or part ownership of, or other interest in, such real property without the consent of the secured creditor or court approval; or

    (B) multiple bankruptcy filings affecting such real property.

If recorded in compliance with applicable State laws governing notices of interests or liens in real property, an order entered under paragraph (4) shall be binding in any other case under this title purporting to affect such real property filed not later than 2 years after the date of the entry of such order by the court, except that a debtor in a subsequent case under this title may move for relief from such order based upon changed circumstances or for good cause shown, after notice and a hearing. Any Federal, State, or local governmental unit that accepts notices of interests or liens in real property shall accept any certified copy of an order described in this subsection for indexing and recording.

  (e)(1) Thirty days after a request under subsection (d) of this section for relief from the stay of any act against property of the estate under subsection (a) of this section, such stay is terminated with respect to the party in interest making such request, unless the court, after notice and a hearing, orders such stay continued in effect pending the conclusion of, or as a result of, a final hearing and determination under subsection (d) of this section. A hearing under this subsection may be a preliminary hearing, or may be consolidated with the final hearing under subsection (d) of this section. The court shall order such stay continued in effect pending the conclusion of the final hearing under subsection (d) of this section if there is a reasonable likelihood that the party opposing relief from such stay will prevail at the conclusion of such final hearing. If the hearing under this subsection is a preliminary hearing, then such final hearing shall be concluded not later than thirty days after the conclusion of such preliminary hearing, unless the 30-day period is extended with the consent of the parties in interest or for a specific time which the court finds is required by compelling circumstances.

  (2) Notwithstanding paragraph (1), in a case under chapter 7, 11, or 13 in which the debtor is an individual, the stay under subsection (a) shall terminate on the date that is 60 days after a request is made by a party in interest under subsection (d), unless—

    (A) a final decision is rendered by the court during the 60-day period beginning on the date of the request; or

    (B) such 60-day period is extended—

      (i) by agreement of all parties in interest; or

      (ii) by the court for such specific period of time as the court finds is required for good cause, as described in findings made by the court.

  (f) Upon request of a party in interest, the court, with or without a hearing, shall grant such relief from the stay provided under subsection (a) of this section as is necessary to prevent irreparable damage to the interest of an entity in property, if such interest will suffer such damage before there is an opportunity for notice and a hearing under subsection (d) or (e) of this section.

  (g) In any hearing under subsection (d) or (e) of this section concerning relief from the stay of any act under subsection (a) of this section—

  (1) the party requesting such relief has the burden of proof on the issue of the debtor's equity in property; and

  (2) the party opposing such relief has the burden of proof on all other issues.

  (h)(1) In a case in which the debtor is an individual, the stay provided by subsection (a) is terminated with respect to personal property of the estate or of the debtor securing in whole or in part a claim, or subject to an unexpired lease, and such personal property shall no longer be property of the estate if the debtor fails within the applicable time set by section 521(a)(2)—

   (A) to file timely any statement of intention required under section 521(a)(2) with respect to such personal property or to indicate in such statement that the debtor will either surrender such personal property or retain it and, if retaining such personal property, either redeem such personal property pursuant to section 722, enter into an agreement of the kind specified in section 524(c) applicable to the debt secured by such personal property, or assume such unexpired lease pursuant to section 365(p) if the trustee does not do so, as applicable; and

   (B) to take timely the action specified in such statement, as it may be amended before expiration of the period for taking action, unless such statement specifies the debtor's intention to reaffirm such debt on the original contract terms and the creditor refuses to agree to the reaffirmation on such terms.

   (2) Paragraph (1) does not apply if the court determines, on the motion of the trustee filed before the expiration of the applicable time set by section 521(a)(2), after notice and a hearing, that such personal property is of consequential value or benefit to the estate, and orders appropriate adequate protection of the creditor's interest, and orders the debtor to deliver any collateral in the debtor's possession to the trustee. If the court does not so determine, the stay provided by subsection (a) shall terminate upon the conclusion of the hearing on the motion.

   (i) If a case commenced under chapter 7, 11, or 13 is dismissed due to the creation of a debt repayment plan, for purposes of subsection (c)(3), any subsequent case commenced by the debtor under any such chapter shall not be presumed to be filed not in good faith.

   (j) On request of a party in interest, the court shall issue an order under subsection (c) confirming that the automatic stay has been terminated.

   (k)(1) Except as provided in paragraph (2), an individual injured by any willful violation of a stay provided by this section shall recover actual damages, including costs and attorneys' fees, and, in appropriate circumstances, may recover punitive damages.

   (2) If such violation is based on an action taken by an entity in the good faith belief that subsection (h) applies to the debtor, the recovery under paragraph (1) of this subsection against such entity shall be limited to actual damages.

   (*l*)(1) Except as otherwise provided in this subsection, subsection (b)(22) shall apply on the date that is 30 days after the date on which the bankruptcy petition is filed, if the debtor files with the petition and serves upon the lessor a certification under penalty of perjury that—

   (A) under nonbankruptcy law applicable in the jurisdiction, there are circumstances under which the debtor would be permitted to cure the entire monetary default that gave rise to the judgment for possession, after that judgment for possession was entered; and

   (B) the debtor (or an adult dependent of the debtor) has deposited with the clerk of the court, any rent that would become due during the 30-day period after the filing of the bankruptcy petition.

   (2) If, within the 30-day period after the filing of the bankruptcy petition, the debtor (or an adult dependent of the debtor) complies with paragraph (1) and files with the court and serves upon the lessor a further certification under penalty of perjury that the debtor (or an adult dependent of the debtor) has cured, under nonbankruptcy law applicable in the jurisdiction, the entire monetary default that gave rise to the judgment under which possession is sought by the lessor, subsection (b)(22) shall not apply, unless ordered to apply by the court under paragraph (3).

   (3)(A) If the lessor files an objection to any certification filed by the debtor under paragraph (1) or (2), and serves such objection upon the debtor, the court shall hold a hearing within 10 days after the filing and service of such objection to determine if the certification filed by the debtor under paragraph (1) or (2) is true.

(B) If the court upholds the objection of the lessor filed under subparagraph (A)—

(i) subsection (b)(22) shall apply immediately and relief from the stay provided under subsection (a)(3) shall not be required to enable the lessor to complete the process to recover full possession of the property; and

(ii) the clerk of the court shall immediately serve upon the lessor and the debtor a certified copy of the court's order upholding the lessor's objection.

(4) If a debtor, in accordance with paragraph (5), indicates on the petition that there was a judgment for possession of the residential rental property in which the debtor resides and does not file a certification under paragraph (1) or (2)—

(A) subsection (b)(22) shall apply immediately upon failure to file such certification, and relief from the stay provided under subsection (a)(3) shall not be required to enable the lessor to complete the process to recover full possession of the property; and

(B) the clerk of the court shall immediately serve upon the lessor and the debtor a certified copy of the docket indicating the absence of a filed certification and the applicability of the exception to the stay under subsection (b)(22).

(5)(A) Where a judgment for possession of residential property in which the debtor resides as a tenant under a lease or rental agreement has been obtained by the lessor, the debtor shall so indicate on the bankruptcy petition and shall provide the name and address of the lessor that obtained that pre-petition judgment on the petition and on any certification filed under this subsection.

(B) The form of certification filed with the petition, as specified in this subsection, shall provide for the debtor to certify, and the debtor shall certify—

(i) whether a judgment for possession of residential rental housing in which the debtor resides has been obtained against the debtor before the date of the filing of the petition; and

(ii) whether the debtor is claiming under paragraph (1) that under nonbankruptcy law applicable in the jurisdiction, there are circumstances under which the debtor would be permitted to cure the entire monetary default that gave rise to the judgment for possession, after that judgment of possession was entered, and has made the appropriate deposit with the court.

(C) The standard forms (electronic and otherwise) used in a bankruptcy proceeding shall be amended to reflect the requirements of this subsection.

(D) The clerk of the court shall arrange for the prompt transmittal of the rent deposited in accordance with paragraph (1)(B) to the lessor.

(m)(1) Except as otherwise provided in this subsection, subsection (b)(23) shall apply on the date that is 15 days after the date on which the lessor files and serves a certification described in subsection (b)(23).

(2)(A) If the debtor files with the court an objection to the truth or legal sufficiency of the certification described in subsection (b)(23) and serves such objection upon the lessor, subsection (b)(23) shall not apply, unless ordered to apply by the court under this subsection.

(B) If the debtor files and serves the objection under subparagraph (A), the court shall hold a hearing within 10 days after the filing and service of such objection to determine if the situation giving rise to the lessor's certification under paragraph (1) existed or has been remedied.

(C) If the debtor can demonstrate to the satisfaction of the court that the situation giving rise to the lessor's certification under paragraph (1) did not exist or has been remedied, the stay provided under subsection (a)(3) shall remain in effect until the termination of the stay under this section.

(D) If the debtor cannot demonstrate to the satisfaction of the court that the situation giving rise to the lessor's certification under paragraph (1) did not exist or has been remedied—

(i) relief from the stay provided under subsection (a)(3) shall not be required to enable the lessor to proceed with the eviction; and

(ii) the clerk of the court shall immediately serve upon the lessor and the debtor a certified copy of the court's order upholding the lessor's certification.

(3) If the debtor fails to file, within 15 days, an objection under paragraph (2)(A)—

(A) subsection (b)(23) shall apply immediately upon such failure and relief from the stay provided under subsection (a)(3) shall not be required to enable the lessor to complete the process to recover full possession of the property; and

(B) the clerk of the court shall immediately serve upon the lessor and the debtor a certified copy of the docket indicating such failure.

(n)(1) Except as provided in paragraph (2), subsection (a) does not apply in a case in which the debtor—

(A) is a debtor in a small business case pending at the time the petition is filed;

(B) was a debtor in a small business case that was dismissed for any reason by an order that became final in the 2-year period ending on the date of the order for relief entered with respect to the petition;

(C) was a debtor in a small business case in which a plan was confirmed in the 2-year period ending on the date of the order for relief entered with respect to the petition; or

(D) is an entity that has acquired substantially all of the assets or business of a small business debtor described in subparagraph (A), (B), or (C), unless such entity establishes by a preponderance of the evidence that such entity acquired substantially all of the assets or business of such small business debtor in good faith and not for the purpose of evading this paragraph.

(2) Paragraph (1) does not apply—

(A) to an involuntary case involving no collusion by the debtor with creditors; or

(B) to the filing of a petition if—

(i) the debtor proves by a preponderance of the evidence that the filing of the petition resulted from circumstances beyond the control of the debtor not foreseeable at the time the case then pending was filed; and

(ii) it is more likely than not that the court will confirm a feasible plan, but not a liquidating plan, within a reasonable period of time.

(o) The exercise of rights not subject to the stay arising under subsection (a) pursuant to paragraph (6), (7), (17), or (27) of subsection (b) shall not be stayed by any order of a court or administrative agency in any proceeding under this title.

REFERENCES IN TEXT

Section 5(a)(3) of the Securities Investor Protection Act of 1970, referred to in subsecs. (a) and (b), is section 5(a)(3) of Pub. L. 91–598, Dec. 30, 1970, 84 Stat. 1644, which is classified to section 78eee of Title 15, Commerce and Trade.

Section 466 of the Social Security Act, referred to in subsec. (b)(2)(D) to (F), is Act Aug. 14, 1935, c. 531, Title IV, § 466, as added Aug. 16, 1984, Pub. L. 98–378, § 3(b), 98 Stat. 1306, and amended, which is classified to 42 U.S.C.A. § 666.

Section 464 of the Social Security Act, referred to in subsec. (b)(2)(F), is Act Aug. 14, 1935, c. 531, Title IV, § 464, as added Aug. 13, 1981, Pub. L. 97–35, Title XXIII, § 2331(a), 95 Stat. 860, and amended, which is classified to 42 U.S.C.A. § 664.

Title IV of the Social Security Act, referred to in subsec. (b)(2)(G), is Act Aug. 14, 1935, c. 531, Title IV, § 401 et seq., as added Aug. 22, 1996, Pub. L. 104–193, Title I, § 103(a)(1), 110 Stat. 2113, and amended, which is classified principally to subchapter IV of chapter 7 of Title 42, 42 U.S.C.A. § 601 et seq. For complete classification, see Tables.

The National Housing Act, referred to in subsec. (b)(8), is Act June 27, 1934, c. 847, 48 Stat. 1246, as amended, which is classified principally to chapter 13 (section 1701 et seq.) of Title 12, Banks and Banking. For complete classification of this Act to the Code, see section 1701 of Title 12 and Tables.

Chapter 537 of title 46, referred to in subsecs. (b)(12) and (13), is Loans and Guarantees, 46 U.S.C.A. § 53701 et seq.

The Higher Education Act of 1965, including such Act, referred to in subsec. (b)(16), is Pub. L. 89–329, Nov. 8, 1965, 79 Stat. 1219, as amended, which is classified principally to chapter 28 (§ 1001 et seq.) of Title 20, Education. Section 435(j) of the Act is classified to section 1085(j) of Title 20. For complete classification of this Act to the Code, see Short Title note set out under section 1001 of Title 20 and Tables.

Section 401, 403, 408, 408A, 414, 457, or 501(c) of the Internal Revenue Code of 1986, referred to in subsec. (b)(19), is classified to 26 U.S.C.A. § 401, 403, 408, 408A, 414, 457, or 501(c).

Section 414(d) or section 403(b) of the Internal Revenue Code, referred to in subsec. (b)(19), is classified to 26 U.S.C.A. § 414(d) or 26 U.S.C.A. § 403(b).

Section 408(b)(1) of the Employee Retirement Income Security Act of 1974, referred to in subsec. (b)(19)(A), is Pub. L. 93–406, Title I, § 408(b)(1), Sept. 2, 1974, 88 Stat. 883, as amended, which is classified to 29 U.S.C.A. § 1108(b)(1).

Section 72(p) of the Internal Revenue Code of 1986, referred to in subsec. (b)(19)(A), is classified to 26 U.S.C.A. § 72(p).

Subchapter III of chapter 84 of title 5, referred to in subsec. (b)(19)(B), is 5 U.S.C.A. § 8431 et seq.

Section 1128B(f) of the Social Security Act, referred to in subsec. (b)(28), is Act Aug. 14, 1935, c. 531, Title XI, § 1128B, formerly Title XVIII, § 1877(d), and Title XIX, § 1909, as added and amended Oct. 30, 1972, Pub. L. 92–603, Title II, §§ 242(c), 278(b)(9), 86 Stat. 1419, 1454, which is classified to 42 U.S.C.A. § 1320a–7b(f).

Title XI of such Act, referred to in subsec. (b)(28), means title XI of the Social Security Act, Act Aug. 14, 1935, c. 531, Title XI, § 1101 et seq., 49 Stat. 647, as amended, which is classified principally to subchapter XI of chapter 7 of Title 42, 42 U.S.C.A. § 1301 et seq.

Title XVIII of such Act, referred to in subsec. (b)(28), means title XVIII of the Social Security Act, Act Aug. 14, 1935, c. 531, Title XVIII, § 1801 et seq., as added July 30, 1965, Pub. L. 89–97, Title I, § 102(a), 79 Stat. 291, and amended, which is classified principally to subchapter XVIII of chapter 7 of Title 42, 42 U.S.C.A. § 1395 et seq.

CROSS REFERENCES

Abstention of district court from hearing a proceeding based upon State law as cause of action, provision as not limiting applicability of stay under this section, see 28 USCA § 1334.

Adequate protection in Chapter 12 cases, method of obtaining, see 11 USCA § 1205.

Applicability of this section in Chapter 9 cases, see 11 USCA § 901.

Assessment of taxes against estate, see 11 USCA § 505.

Denial of debtor status to debtor who obtained voluntary dismissal following filing of relief from provisions of this section, see 11 USCA § 109(g).

Effect of this section on subchapter III of Chapter 7, see 11 USCA § 742.

Enforcement of claims against debtor in Chapter 9 cases, automatic stay of, see 11 USCA § 922.

Extension of time, see 11 USCA § 108.

Grain storage facility bankruptcies, expedited determinations, see 11 USCA § 557.

Right of possession of party with security interest in—

>Aircraft equipment and vessel, see 11 USCA § 1110.

>Rolling stock equipment, see 11 USCA § 1168.

Secretary of Commerce or Transportation as mortgagee, see 46 USCA § 31308.

Setoff, see 11 USCA § 553.

Turnover of property to estate, see 11 USCA § 542.

§ 363.   Use, sale, or lease of property

(a) In this section, "cash collateral" means cash, negotiable instruments, documents of title, securities, deposit accounts, or other cash equivalents whenever acquired in which the estate and an entity other than the estate have an interest and includes the proceeds, products, offspring, rents, or profits of property and the fees, charges, accounts or other payments for the use or occupancy of rooms and other public facilities in hotels, motels, or other lodging properties subject to a security interest as provided in section 552(b) of this title, whether existing before or after the commencement of a case under this title.

(b)(1)   The trustee, after notice and a hearing, may use, sell, or lease, other than in the ordinary course of business, property of the estate, except that if the debtor in connection with offering a product or a service discloses to an individual a policy prohibiting the transfer of personally identifiable information about individuals to persons that are not affiliated with the debtor and if such policy is in effect on the date of the commencement of the case, then the trustee may not sell or lease personally identifiable information to any person unless—

(A)   such sale or such lease is consistent with such policy; or

(B)   after appointment of a consumer privacy ombudsman in accordance with section 332, and after notice and a hearing, the court approves such sale or such lease—

(i)   giving due consideration to the facts, circumstances, and conditions of such sale or such lease; and

(ii)   finding that no showing was made that such sale or such lease would violate applicable nonbankruptcy law.

(2)   If notification is required under subsection (a) of section 7A of the Clayton Act in the case of a transaction under this subsection, then—

(A)   notwithstanding subsection (a) of such section, the notification required by such subsection to be given by the debtor shall be given by the trustee; and

(B)   notwithstanding subsection (b) of such section, the required waiting period shall end on the 15th day after the date of the receipt, by the Federal Trade Commission and the Assistant Attorney General in charge of the Antitrust Division of the Department of Justice, of the notification required under such subsection (a), unless such waiting period is extended—

(i)   pursuant to subsection (e)(2) of such section, in the same manner as such subsection (e)(2) applies to a cash tender offer;

(ii)   pursuant to subsection (g)(2) of such section; or

(iii)   by the court after notice and a hearing.

(c)(1)   If the business of the debtor is authorized to be operated under section 721, 1108, 1183, 1184, 1203, 1204, or 1304 of this title and unless the court orders otherwise, the trustee may enter into transactions, including the sale or lease of property of the estate, in the ordinary course of business, without notice or a hearing, and may use property of the estate in the ordinary course of business without notice or a hearing.

(2) The trustee may not use, sell, or lease cash collateral under paragraph (1) of this subsection unless—

    (A) each entity that has an interest in such cash collateral consents; or

    (B) the court, after notice and a hearing, authorizes such use, sale, or lease in accordance with the provisions of this section.

(3) Any hearing under paragraph (2)(B) of this subsection may be a preliminary hearing or may be consolidated with a hearing under subsection (e) of this section, but shall be scheduled in accordance with the needs of the debtor. If the hearing under paragraph (2)(B) of this subsection is a preliminary hearing, the court may authorize such use, sale, or lease only if there is a reasonable likelihood that the trustee will prevail at the final hearing under subsection (e) of this section. The court shall act promptly on any request for authorization under paragraph (2)(B) of this subsection.

(4) Except as provided in paragraph (2) of this subsection, the trustee shall segregate and account for any cash collateral in the trustee's possession, custody, or control.

(d) The trustee may use, sell, or lease property under subsection (b) or (c) of this section—

    (1) in the case of a debtor that is a corporation or trust that is not a moneyed business, commercial corporation, or trust, only in accordance with nonbankruptcy law applicable to the transfer of property by a debtor that is such a corporation or trust; and

    (2) only to the extent not inconsistent with any relief granted under subsection (c), (d), (e), or (f) of section 362.

(e) Notwithstanding any other provision of this section, at any time, on request of an entity that has an interest in property used, sold, or leased, or proposed to be used, sold, or leased, by the trustee, the court, with or without a hearing, shall prohibit or condition such use, sale, or lease as is necessary to provide adequate protection of such interest. This subsection also applies to property that is subject to any unexpired lease of personal property (to the exclusion of such property being subject to an order to grant relief from the stay under section 362).

(f) The trustee may sell property under subsection (b) or (c) of this section free and clear of any interest in such property of an entity other than the estate, only if—

    (1) applicable nonbankruptcy law permits sale of such property free and clear of such interest;

    (2) such entity consents;

    (3) such interest is a lien and the price at which such property is to be sold is greater than the aggregate value of all liens on such property;

    (4) such interest is in bona fide dispute; or

    (5) such entity could be compelled, in a legal or equitable proceeding, to accept a money satisfaction of such interest.

(g) Notwithstanding subsection (f) of this section, the trustee may sell property under subsection (b) or (c) of this section free and clear of any vested or contingent right in the nature of dower or curtesy.

(h) Notwithstanding subsection (f) of this section, the trustee may sell both the estate's interest, under subsection (b) or (c) of this section, and the interest of any co-owner in property in which the debtor had, at the time of the commencement of the case, an undivided interest as a tenant in common, joint tenant, or tenant by the entirety, only if—

    (1) partition in kind of such property among the estate and such co-owners is impracticable;

    (2) sale of the estate's undivided interest in such property would realize significantly less for the estate than sale of such property free of the interests of such co-owners;

(3) the benefit to the estate of a sale of such property free of the interests of co-owners outweighs the detriment, if any, to such co-owners; and

(4) such property is not used in the production, transmission, or distribution, for sale, of electric energy or of natural or synthetic gas for heat, light, or power.

(i) Before the consummation of a sale of property to which subsection (g) or (h) of this section applies, or of property of the estate that was community property of the debtor and the debtor's spouse immediately before the commencement of the case, the debtor's spouse, or a co-owner of such property, as the case may be, may purchase such property at the price at which such sale is to be consummated.

(j) After a sale of property to which subsection (g) or (h) of this section applies, the trustee shall distribute to the debtor's spouse or the co-owners of such property, as the case may be, and to the estate, the proceeds of such sale, less the costs and expenses, not including any compensation of the trustee, of such sale, according to the interests of such spouse or co-owners, and of the estate.

(k) At a sale under subsection (b) of this section of property that is subject to a lien that secures an allowed claim, unless the court for cause orders otherwise the holder of such claim may bid at such sale, and, if the holder of such claim purchases such property, such holder may offset such claim against the purchase price of such property.

(l) Subject to the provisions of section 365, the trustee may use, sell, or lease property under subsection (b) or (c) of this section, or a plan under chapter 11, 12, or 13 of this title may provide for the use, sale, or lease of property, notwithstanding any provision in a contract, a lease, or applicable law that is conditioned on the insolvency or financial condition of the debtor, on the commencement of a case under this title concerning the debtor, or on the appointment of or the taking possession by a trustee in a case under this title or a custodian, and that effects, or gives an option to effect, a forfeiture, modification, or termination of the debtor's interest in such property.

(m) The reversal or modification on appeal of an authorization under subsection (b) or (c) of this section of a sale or lease of property does not affect the validity of a sale or lease under such authorization to an entity that purchased or leased such property in good faith, whether or not such entity knew of the pendency of the appeal, unless such authorization and such sale or lease were stayed pending appeal.

(n) The trustee may avoid a sale under this section if the sale price was controlled by an agreement among potential bidders at such sale, or may recover from a party to such agreement any amount by which the value of the property sold exceeds the price at which such sale was consummated, and may recover any costs, attorneys' fees, or expenses incurred in avoiding such sale or recovering such amount. In addition to any recovery under the preceding sentence, the court may grant judgment for punitive damages in favor of the estate and against any such party that entered into such an agreement in willful disregard of this subsection.

(o) Notwithstanding subsection (f), if a person purchases any interest in a consumer credit transaction that is subject to the Truth in Lending Act or any interest in a consumer credit contract (as defined in section 433.1 of title 16 of the Code of Federal Regulations (January 1, 2004), as amended from time to time), and if such interest is purchased through a sale under this section, then such person shall remain subject to all claims and defenses that are related to such consumer credit transaction or such consumer credit contract, to the same extent as such person would be subject to such claims and defenses of the consumer had such interest been purchased at a sale not under this section.

(p) In any hearing under this section—

(1) the trustee has the burden of proof on the issue of adequate protection; and

(2) the entity asserting an interest in property has the burden of proof on the issue of the validity, priority, or extent of such interest.

REFERENCES IN TEXT

Section 7A of the Clayton Act, referred to in subsec. (b)(2), is section 7A of Act Oct. 15, 1914, c. 323, as added Sept. 30, 1976, Pub. L. 94–435, Title II, § 201, 90 Stat. 1390, which is classified to section 18a of Title 15, Commerce and Trade.

The Truth in Lending Act, referred to in subsec. (*o*), is Title I of Pub. L. 90–321, May 29, 1968, 82 Stat. 146, as amended, also known as TILA, which is classified principally to subchapter I of chapter 41 of Title 15, 15 U.S.C.A. § 1601 et seq. For complete classification, see Short Title note set out under 15 U.S.C.A. § 1601 and Tables.

CROSS REFERENCES

Adequate protection in chapter 12 cases, method of obtaining, see 11 USCA § 1205.

Adverse interest and conduct of officers of estate, see 18 USCA § 154.

Confirmation of plan, see 11 USCA § 1129.

Continuity of business operation and use, acquisition or disposition of property by debtor, see 11 USCA § 303.

Grain storage facility bankruptcies, expedited determinations, see 11 USCA § 557.

Identical rights and powers of debtor in Chapter 13 cases, see 11 USCA § 1303.

Postpetition effect of security interest, see 11 USCA § 552.

Priorities, see 11 USCA § 507.

Property of estate, see 11 USCA § 541.

Right of possession of party with security interest in—

    Aircraft equipment and vessels, see 11 USCA § 1110.

    Rolling stock equipment, see 11 USCA § 1168.

Rights and powers of debtor engaged in business, see 11 USCA § 1304.

Sale of property as affecting allowance of claim secured by lien on property of estate, see 11 USCA § 1111.

Sales free of interests, see 11 USCA § 1206.

Setoff, see 11 USCA § 553.

Turnover of property to estate, see 11 USCA § 542.

§ 364. Obtaining credit

(a) If the trustee is authorized to operate the business of the debtor under section 721, 1108, 1183, 1184, 1203, 1204, or 1304 of this title, unless the court orders otherwise, the trustee may obtain unsecured credit and incur unsecured debt in the ordinary course of business allowable under section 503(b)(1) of this title as an administrative expense.

(b) The court, after notice and a hearing, may authorize the trustee to obtain unsecured credit or to incur unsecured debt other than under subsection (a) of this section, allowable under section 503(b)(1) of this title as an administrative expense.

(c) If the trustee is unable to obtain unsecured credit allowable under section 503(b)(1) of this title as an administrative expense, the court, after notice and a hearing, may authorize the obtaining of credit or the incurring of debt—

    (1) with priority over any or all administrative expenses of the kind specified in section 503(b) or 507(b) of this title;

    (2) secured by a lien on property of the estate that is not otherwise subject to a lien; or

    (3) secured by a junior lien on property of the estate that is subject to a lien.

    (d)(1) The court, after notice and a hearing, may authorize the obtaining of credit or the incurring of debt secured by a senior or equal lien on property of the estate that is subject to a lien only if—

    (A) the trustee is unable to obtain such credit otherwise; and

    (B) there is adequate protection of the interest of the holder of the lien on the property of the estate on which such senior or equal lien is proposed to be granted.

    (2) In any hearing under this subsection, the trustee has the burden of proof on the issue of adequate protection.

    (e) The reversal or modification on appeal of an authorization under this section to obtain credit or incur debt, or of a grant under this section of a priority or a lien, does not affect the validity of any debt so incurred, or any priority or lien so granted, to an entity that extended such credit in good faith, whether or not such entity knew of the pendency of the appeal, unless such authorization and the incurring of such debt, or the granting of such priority or lien, were stayed pending appeal.

    (f) Except with respect to an entity that is an underwriter as defined in section 1145(b) of this title, section 5 of the Securities Act of 1933, the Trust Indenture Act of 1939, and any State or local law requiring registration for offer or sale of a security or registration or licensing of an issuer of, underwriter of, or broker or dealer in, a security does not apply to the offer or sale under this section of a security that is not an equity security.

    [Note from West Advisor: Pub. L. 116–260 created a temporary subsection (g) to § 364, which expired on December 27, 2022, except for any case commenced before December 27, 2022. See 134 Stat. 2015, 2016, 2017. For the text of subsection (g), see Title 11, Chapter 3, Subchapter IV, § 364 Editorial Notes, Amendments, 2020 at http://uscode.house.gov]

REFERENCES IN TEXT

    Section 5 of the Securities Act of 1933, referred to in subsec. (f), is section 5 of Act May 27, 1933, c. 38, Title I, 48 Stat. 77, which is classified to section 77e of Title 15, Commerce and Trade.

    The Trust Indenture Act of 1939, referred to in subsec. (f), is Title III of Act May 27, 1933, c. 38, as added Aug. 3, 1939, c. 411, 53 Stat. 1149, as amended, which is classified generally to subchapter III (§ 77aaa et seq.) of chapter 2A of Title 15, Commerce and Trade. For complete classification of this Act to the Code, see section 77aaa of Title 15 and Tables.

CROSS REFERENCES

Adequate protection in Chapter 12 cases, method of obtaining, see 11 USCA § 1205.

Applicability of subsecs. (c) to (f) of this section in Chapter 9 cases, see 11 USCA § 901.

Enforcement of claims against debtor in Chapter 9 cases, automatic stay of, see 11 USCA § 922.

Priorities, see 11 USCA § 507.

Reversal on appeal of finding of jurisdiction as affecting validity of debt incurred, see 11 USCA § 921.

Rights and powers of debtor engaged in business, see 11 USCA § 1304.

§ 365.   Executory contracts and unexpired leases

    (a) Except as provided in sections 765 and 766 of this title and in subsections (b), (c), and (d) of this section, the trustee, subject to the court's approval, may assume or reject any executory contract or unexpired lease of the debtor.

    (b)(1) If there has been a default in an executory contract or unexpired lease of the debtor, the trustee may not assume such contract or lease unless, at the time of assumption of such contract or lease, the trustee—

(A) cures, or provides adequate assurance that the trustee will promptly cure, such default other than a default that is a breach of a provision relating to the satisfaction of any provision (other than a penalty rate or penalty provision) relating to a default arising from any failure to perform nonmonetary obligations under an unexpired lease of real property, if it is impossible for the trustee to cure such default by performing nonmonetary acts at and after the time of assumption, except that if such default arises from a failure to operate in accordance with a nonresidential real property lease, then such default shall be cured by performance at and after the time of assumption in accordance with such lease, and pecuniary losses resulting from such default shall be compensated in accordance with the provisions of this paragraph;

(B) compensates, or provides adequate assurance that the trustee will promptly compensate, a party other than the debtor to such contract or lease, for any actual pecuniary loss to such party resulting from such default; and

(C) provides adequate assurance of future performance under such contract or lease.

(2) Paragraph (1) of this subsection does not apply to a default that is a breach of a provision relating to—

(A) the insolvency or financial condition of the debtor at any time before the closing of the case;

(B) the commencement of a case under this title;

(C) the appointment of or taking possession by a trustee in a case under this title or a custodian before such commencement; or

(D) the satisfaction of any penalty rate or penalty provision relating to a default arising from any failure by the debtor to perform nonmonetary obligations under the executory contract or unexpired lease.

(3) For the purposes of paragraph (1) of this subsection and paragraph (2)(B) of subsection (f), adequate assurance of future performance of a lease of real property in a shopping center includes adequate assurance—

(A) of the source of rent and other consideration due under such lease, and in the case of an assignment, that the financial condition and operating performance of the proposed assignee and its guarantors, if any, shall be similar to the financial condition and operating performance of the debtor and its guarantors, if any, as of the time the debtor became the lessee under the lease;

(B) that any percentage rent due under such lease will not decline substantially;

(C) that assumption or assignment of such lease is subject to all the provisions thereof, including (but not limited to) provisions such as a radius, location, use, or exclusivity provision, and will not breach any such provision contained in any other lease, financing agreement, or master agreement relating to such shopping center; and

(D) that assumption or assignment of such lease will not disrupt any tenant mix or balance in such shopping center.

(4) Notwithstanding any other provision of this section, if there has been a default in an unexpired lease of the debtor, other than a default of a kind specified in paragraph (2) of this subsection, the trustee may not require a lessor to provide services or supplies incidental to such lease before assumption of such lease unless the lessor is compensated under the terms of such lease for any services and supplies provided under such lease before assumption of such lease.

(c) The trustee may not assume or assign any executory contract or unexpired lease of the debtor, whether or not such contract or lease prohibits or restricts assignment of rights or delegation of duties, if—

(1)(A)   applicable law excuses a party, other than the debtor, to such contract or lease from accepting performance from or rendering performance to an entity other than the debtor or the debtor in possession, whether or not such contract or lease prohibits or restricts assignment of rights or delegation of duties; and

(B)   such party does not consent to such assumption or assignment; or

(2)   such contract is a contract to make a loan, or extend other debt financing or financial accommodations, to or for the benefit of the debtor, or to issue a security of the debtor; or

(3)   such lease is of nonresidential real property and has been terminated under applicable nonbankruptcy law prior to the order for relief.

(d)(1)   In a case under chapter 7 of this title, if the trustee does not assume or reject an executory contract or unexpired lease of residential real property or of personal property of the debtor within 60 days after the order for relief, or within such additional time as the court, for cause, within such 60-day period, fixes, then such contract or lease is deemed rejected.

(2)   In a case under chapter 9, 11, 12, or 13 of this title, the trustee may assume or reject an executory contract or unexpired lease of residential real property or of personal property of the debtor at any time before the confirmation of a plan but the court, on the request of any party to such contract or lease, may order the trustee to determine within a specified period of time whether to assume or reject such contract or lease.

(3)   The trustee shall timely perform all the obligations of the debtor, except those specified in section 365(b)(2), arising from and after the order for relief under any unexpired lease of nonresidential real property, until such lease is assumed or rejected, notwithstanding section 503(b)(1) of this title. The court may extend, for cause, the time for performance of any such obligation that arises within 60 days after the date of the order for relief, but the time for performance shall not be extended beyond such 60-day period. This subsection shall not be deemed to affect the trustee's obligations under the provisions of subsection (b) or (f) of this section. Acceptance of any such performance does not constitute waiver or relinquishment of the lessor's rights under such lease or under this title.

[*Note from West Advisor:* Pub. L 116–260 temporarily amended § 365(d)(3) for cases under subchapter V of chapter 11. That amendment expired on December 27, 2022, *except* for subchapter V cases commenced before December 27, 2022. *See* 134 Stat. 3219. For an explanation of § 365(d)(3)(B), (C), which expired except with respect to subchapter V cases filed before December 27, 2022, *see* Title 11, Chapter 3, Subchapter IV, § 365, Editorial Notes, Amendments, 2020 at http://uscode.house.gov]

(4)(A)   Subject to subparagraph (B), an unexpired lease of nonresidential real property under which the debtor is the lessee shall be deemed rejected, and the trustee shall immediately surrender that nonresidential real property to the lessor, if the trustee does not assume or reject the unexpired lease by the earlier of—

(i)   the date that is 120 days after the date of the order for relief; or

(ii)   the date of the entry of an order confirming a plan.

(B)(i)   The court may extend the period determined under subparagraph (A), prior to the expiration of the 120-day period, for 90 days on the motion of the trustee or lessor for cause.

(ii)   If the court grants an extension under clause (i), the court may grant a subsequent extension only upon prior written consent of the lessor in each instance.

[*Note from West Advisor:* For subchapter V cases under chapter 11 commenced before December 27, 2022, the time period in § 365(d)(4)(A)(i), (B)(i) is 210, not 120, days. *See* 134 Stat. 3219.]

(5)   The trustee shall timely perform all of the obligations of the debtor, except those specified in section 365(b)(2), first arising from or after 60 days after the order for relief in a case under chapter

11 of this title under an unexpired lease of personal property (other than personal property leased to an individual primarily for personal, family, or household purposes), until such lease is assumed or rejected notwithstanding section 503(b)(1) of this title, unless the court, after notice and a hearing and based on the equities of the case, orders otherwise with respect to the obligations or timely performance thereof. This subsection shall not be deemed to affect the trustee's obligations under the provisions of subsection (b) or (f). Acceptance of any such performance does not constitute waiver or relinquishment of the lessor's rights under such lease or under this title.

(e)(1) Notwithstanding a provision in an executory contract or unexpired lease, or in applicable law, an executory contract or unexpired lease of the debtor may not be terminated or modified, and any right or obligation under such contract or lease may not be terminated or modified, at any time after the commencement of the case solely because of a provision in such contract or lease that is conditioned on—

    (A) the insolvency or financial condition of the debtor at any time before the closing of the case;

    (B) the commencement of a case under this title; or

    (C) the appointment of or taking possession by a trustee in a case under this title or a custodian before such commencement.

(2) Paragraph (1) of this subsection does not apply to an executory contract or unexpired lease of the debtor, whether or not such contract or lease prohibits or restricts assignment of rights or delegation of duties, if—

    (A)(i) applicable law excuses a party, other than the debtor, to such contract or lease from accepting performance from or rendering performance to the trustee or to an assignee of such contract or lease, whether or not such contract or lease prohibits or restricts assignment of rights or delegation of duties; and

    (ii) such party does not consent to such assumption or assignment; or

    (B) such contract is a contract to make a loan, or extend other debt financing or financial accommodations, to or for the benefit of the debtor, or to issue a security of the debtor.

(f)(1) Except as provided in subsections (b) and (c) of this section, notwithstanding a provision in an executory contract or unexpired lease of the debtor, or in applicable law, that prohibits, restricts, or conditions the assignment of such contract or lease, the trustee may assign such contract or lease under paragraph (2) of this subsection.

(2) The trustee may assign an executory contract or unexpired lease of the debtor only if—

    (A) the trustee assumes such contract or lease in accordance with the provisions of this section; and

    (B) adequate assurance of future performance by the assignee of such contract or lease is provided, whether or not there has been a default in such contract or lease.

(3) Notwithstanding a provision in an executory contract or unexpired lease of the debtor, or in applicable law that terminates or modifies, or permits a party other than the debtor to terminate or modify, such contract or lease or a right or obligation under such contract or lease on account of an assignment of such contract or lease, such contract, lease, right, or obligation may not be terminated or modified under such provision because of the assumption or assignment of such contract or lease by the trustee.

(g) Except as provided in subsections (h)(2) and (i)(2) of this section, the rejection of an executory contract or unexpired lease of the debtor constitutes a breach of such contract or lease—

    (1) if such contract or lease has not been assumed under this section or under a plan confirmed under chapter 9, 11, 12, or 13 of this title, immediately before the date of the filing of the petition; or

(2) if such contract or lease has been assumed under this section or under a plan confirmed under chapter 9, 11, 12, or 13 of this title—

    (A) if before such rejection the case has not been converted under section 1112, 1208, or 1307 of this title, at the time of such rejection; or

    (B) if before such rejection the case has been converted under section 1112, 1208, or 1307 of this title—

        (i) immediately before the date of such conversion, if such contract or lease was assumed before such conversion; or

        (ii) at the time of such rejection, if such contract or lease was assumed after such conversion.

(h)(1)(A) If the trustee rejects an unexpired lease of real property under which the debtor is the lessor and—

    (i) if the rejection by the trustee amounts to such a breach as would entitle the lessee to treat such lease as terminated by virtue of its terms, applicable nonbankruptcy law, or any agreement made by the lessee, then the lessee under such lease may treat such lease as terminated by the rejection; or

    (ii) if the term of such lease has commenced, the lessee may retain its rights under such lease (including rights such as those relating to the amount and timing of payment of rent and other amounts payable by the lessee and any right of use, possession, quiet enjoyment, subletting, assignment, or hypothecation) that are in or appurtenant to the real property for the balance of the term of such lease and for any renewal or extension of such rights to the extent that such rights are enforceable under applicable nonbankruptcy law.

(B) If the lessee retains its rights under subparagraph (A)(ii), the lessee may offset against the rent reserved under such lease for the balance of the term after the date of the rejection of such lease and for the term of any renewal or extension of such lease, the value of any damage caused by the nonperformance after the date of such rejection, of any obligation of the debtor under such lease, but the lessee shall not have any other right against the estate or the debtor on account of any damage occurring after such date caused by such nonperformance.

(C) The rejection of a lease of real property in a shopping center with respect to which the lessee elects to retain its rights under subparagraph (A)(ii) does not affect the enforceability under applicable nonbankruptcy law of any provision in the lease pertaining to radius, location, use, exclusivity, or tenant mix or balance.

(D) In this paragraph, "lessee" includes any successor, assign, or mortgagee permitted under the terms of such lease.

(2)(A) If the trustee rejects a timeshare interest under a timeshare plan under which the debtor is the timeshare interest seller and—

    (i) if the rejection amounts to such a breach as would entitle the timeshare interest purchaser to treat the timeshare plan as terminated under its terms, applicable nonbankruptcy law, or any agreement made by timeshare interest purchaser, the timeshare interest purchaser under the timeshare plan may treat the timeshare plan as terminated by such rejection; or

    (ii) if the term of such timeshare interest has commenced, then the timeshare interest purchaser may retain its rights in such timeshare interest for the balance of such term and for any term of renewal or extension of such timeshare interest to the extent that such rights are enforceable under applicable nonbankruptcy law.

(B) If the timeshare interest purchaser retains its rights under subparagraph (A), such timeshare interest purchaser may offset against the moneys due for such timeshare interest for the balance of the term after the date of the rejection of such timeshare interest, and the term of any renewal or extension of such timeshare interest, the value of any damage caused by the nonperformance after the date of such rejection, of any obligation of the debtor under such timeshare plan, but the timeshare interest purchaser shall not have any right against the estate or the debtor on account of any damage occurring after such date caused by such nonperformance.

(i)(1) If the trustee rejects an executory contract of the debtor for the sale of real property or for the sale of a timeshare interest under a timeshare plan, under which the purchaser is in possession, such purchaser may treat such contract as terminated, or, in the alternative, may remain in possession of such real property or timeshare interest.

(2) If such purchaser remains in possession—

(A) such purchaser shall continue to make all payments due under such contract, but may,[1] offset against such payments any damages occurring after the date of the rejection of such contract caused by the nonperformance of any obligation of the debtor after such date, but such purchaser does not have any rights against the estate on account of any damages arising after such date from such rejection, other than such offset; and

(B) the trustee shall deliver title to such purchaser in accordance with the provisions of such contract, but is relieved of all other obligations to perform under such contract.

(j) A purchaser that treats an executory contract as terminated under subsection (i) of this section, or a party whose executory contract to purchase real property from the debtor is rejected and under which such party is not in possession, has a lien on the interest of the debtor in such property for the recovery of any portion of the purchase price that such purchaser or party has paid.

(k) Assignment by the trustee to an entity of a contract or lease assumed under this section relieves the trustee and the estate from any liability for any breach of such contract or lease occurring after such assignment.

(l) If an unexpired lease under which the debtor is the lessee is assigned pursuant to this section, the lessor of the property may require a deposit or other security for the performance of the debtor's obligations under the lease substantially the same as would have been required by the landlord upon the initial leasing to a similar tenant.

(m) For purposes of this section 365 and sections 541(b)(2) and 362(b)(10), leases of real property shall include any rental agreement to use real property.

(n)(1) If the trustee rejects an executory contract under which the debtor is a licensor of a right to intellectual property, the licensee under such contract may elect—

(A) to treat such contract as terminated by such rejection if such rejection by the trustee amounts to such a breach as would entitle the licensee to treat such contract as terminated by virtue of its own terms, applicable nonbankruptcy law, or an agreement made by the licensee with another entity; or

(B) to retain its rights (including a right to enforce any exclusivity provision of such contract, but excluding any other right under applicable nonbankruptcy law to specific performance of such contract) under such contract and under any agreement supplementary to such contract, to such intellectual property (including any embodiment of such intellectual property to the extent protected by applicable nonbankruptcy law), as such rights existed immediately before the case commenced, for—

(i) the duration of such contract; and

(ii) any period for which such contract may be extended by the licensee as of right under applicable nonbankruptcy law.

---

[1] So in original. The comma probably should not appear.

(2) If the licensee elects to retain its rights, as described in paragraph (1)(B) of this subsection, under such contract—

    (A) the trustee shall allow the licensee to exercise such rights;

    (B) the licensee shall make all royalty payments due under such contract for the duration of such contract and for any period described in paragraph (1)(B) of this subsection for which the licensee extends such contract; and

    (C) the licensee shall be deemed to waive—

        (i) any right of setoff it may have with respect to such contract under this title or applicable nonbankruptcy law; and

        (ii) any claim allowable under section 503(b) of this title arising from the performance of such contract.

(3) If the licensee elects to retain its rights, as described in paragraph (1)(B) of this subsection, then on the written request of the licensee the trustee shall—

    (A) to the extent provided in such contract, or any agreement supplementary to such contract, provide to the licensee any intellectual property (including such embodiment) held by the trustee; and

    (B) not interfere with the rights of the licensee as provided in such contract, or any agreement supplementary to such contract, to such intellectual property (including such embodiment) including any right to obtain such intellectual property (or such embodiment) from another entity.

(4) Unless and until the trustee rejects such contract, on the written request of the licensee the trustee shall—

    (A) to the extent provided in such contract or any agreement supplementary to such contract—

        (i) perform such contract; or

        (ii) provide to the licensee such intellectual property (including any embodiment of such intellectual property to the extent protected by applicable nonbankruptcy law) held by the trustee; and

    (B) not interfere with the rights of the licensee as provided in such contract, or any agreement supplementary to such contract, to such intellectual property (including such embodiment), including any right to obtain such intellectual property (or such embodiment) from another entity.

(o) In a case under chapter 11 of this title, the trustee shall be deemed to have assumed (consistent with the debtor's other obligations under section 507), and shall immediately cure any deficit under, any commitment by the debtor to a Federal depository institutions regulatory agency (or predecessor to such agency) to maintain the capital of an insured depository institution, and any claim for a subsequent breach of the obligations thereunder shall be entitled to priority under section 507. This subsection shall not extend any commitment that would otherwise be terminated by any act of such an agency.

(p)(1) If a lease of personal property is rejected or not timely assumed by the trustee under subsection (d), the leased property is no longer property of the estate and the stay under section 362(a) is automatically terminated.

(2)(A) If the debtor in a case under chapter 7 is an individual, the debtor may notify the creditor in writing that the debtor desires to assume the lease. Upon being so notified, the creditor may, at its option, notify the debtor that it is willing to have the lease assumed by the debtor and may condition such assumption on cure of any outstanding default on terms set by the contract.

(B) If, not later than 30 days after notice is provided under subparagraph (A), the debtor notifies the lessor in writing that the lease is assumed, the liability under the lease will be assumed by the debtor and not by the estate.

(C) The stay under section 362 and the injunction under section 524(a)(2) shall not be violated by notification of the debtor and negotiation of cure under this subsection.

(3) In a case under chapter 11 in which the debtor is an individual and in a case under chapter 13, if the debtor is the lessee with respect to personal property and the lease is not assumed in the plan confirmed by the court, the lease is deemed rejected as of the conclusion of the hearing on confirmation. If the lease is rejected, the stay under section 362 and any stay under section 1301 is automatically terminated with respect to the property subject to the lease.

CROSS REFERENCES

Allowance of claims, see 11 USCA § 502.

Applicability of this section in Chapter 9 cases, see 11 USCA § 901.

Assumption or rejection of certain executory contracts within reasonable time after order for relief, see 11 USCA § 744.

Collective bargaining agreements, see 11 USCA § 1167.

Contents of plan, see 11 USCA § 1222.

Contractual right to liquidate—

    Commodities contract or forward contract, see 11 USCA § 556.

    Repurchase agreement, see 11 USCA § 559.

    Securities contract, see 11 USCA § 555.

Contractual right to terminate a swap agreement, see 11 USCA § 560.

Effect of—

    Conversion, see 11 USCA § 348.

    Rejection of lease of railroad line, see 11 USCA § 1169.

Grain storage facility bankruptcies, expedited determinations, see 11 USCA § 557.

Impairment of claims or interests by plans which cure certain defaults, see 11 USCA § 1124.

Municipal leases, see 11 USCA § 929.

Provisions in plan for assumption or rejection of certain executory contracts or unexpired leases, see 11 USCA §§ 1123 and 1322.

Right of possession of party with security interest as affected by default—

    Aircraft equipment and vessels, see 11 USCA § 1110.

    Rolling stock equipment, see 11 USCA § 1168.

Setoff, see 11 USCA § 553.

§ 366. Utility service

(a) Except as provided in subsections (b) and (c) of this section, a utility may not alter, refuse, or discontinue service to, or discriminate against, the trustee or the debtor solely on the basis of the commencement of a case under this title or that a debt owed by the debtor to such utility for service rendered before the order for relief was not paid when due.

(b) Such utility may alter, refuse, or discontinue service if neither the trustee nor the debtor, within 20 days after the date of the order for relief, furnishes adequate assurance of payment, in the form of a deposit or other security, for service after such date. On request of a party in interest and after notice and a hearing, the court may order reasonable modification of the amount of the deposit or other security necessary to provide adequate assurance of payment.

(c)(1)(A) For purposes of this subsection, the term "assurance of payment" means—

 (i) a cash deposit;

 (ii) a letter of credit;

 (iii) a certificate of deposit;

 (iv) a surety bond;

 (v) a prepayment of utility consumption; or

 (vi) another form of security that is mutually agreed on between the utility and the debtor or the trustee.

(B) For purposes of this subsection an administrative expense priority shall not constitute an assurance of payment.

(2) Subject to paragraphs (3) and (4), with respect to a case filed under chapter 11, a utility referred to in subsection (a) may alter, refuse, or discontinue utility service, if during the 30-day period beginning on the date of the filing of the petition, the utility does not receive from the debtor or the trustee adequate assurance of payment for utility service that is satisfactory to the utility.

(3)(A) On request of a party in interest and after notice and a hearing, the court may order modification of the amount of an assurance of payment under paragraph (2).

(B) In making a determination under this paragraph whether an assurance of payment is adequate, the court may not consider—

 (i) the absence of security before the date of the filing of the petition;

 (ii) the payment by the debtor of charges for utility service in a timely manner before the date of the filing of the petition; or

 (iii) the availability of an administrative expense priority.

(4) Notwithstanding any other provision of law, with respect to a case subject to this subsection, a utility may recover or set off against a security deposit provided to the utility by the debtor before the date of the filing of the petition without notice or order of the court.

CROSS REFERENCES

Applicability of this section in Chapter 9 cases, see 11 USCA § 901.

CHAPTER 5—CREDITORS, THE DEBTOR, AND THE ESTATE

SUBCHAPTER I—CREDITORS AND CLAIMS

SUBCHAPTER II—DEBTOR'S DUTIES AND BENEFITS

SUBCHAPTER III—THE ESTATE

SUBCHAPTER I—CREDITORS AND CLAIMS

§ 501. Filing of proofs of claims or interests

(a) A creditor or an indenture trustee may file a proof of claim. An equity security holder may file a proof of interest.

(b) If a creditor does not timely file a proof of such creditor's claim, an entity that is liable to such creditor with the debtor, or that has secured such creditor, may file a proof of such claim.

(c) If a creditor does not timely file a proof of such creditor's claim, the debtor or the trustee may file a proof of such claim.

(d) A claim of a kind specified in section 502(e)(2), 502(f), 502(g), 502(h) or 502(i) of this title may be filed under subsection (a), (b), or (c) of this section the same as if such claim were a claim against the debtor and had arisen before the date of the filing of the petition.

(e) A claim arising from the liability of a debtor for fuel use tax assessed consistent with the requirements of section 31705 of title 49 may be filed by the base jurisdiction designated pursuant to the International Fuel Tax Agreement (as defined in section 31701 of title 49) and, if so filed, shall be allowed as a single claim.

CROSS REFERENCES

Applicability of this section in Chapter 9 cases, see 11 USCA § 901.

Binding effect of confirmation whether or not claim is filed or deemed filed, see 11 USCA § 944.

Distribution of property of estate, see 11 USCA § 726.

False oaths and claims, see 18 USCA § 152.

Liabilities on claims whether or not filed, see 11 USCA § 727.

Proof of claim deemed filed in—

       Chapter 9 cases, see 11 USCA § 925.

       Chapter 11 cases, see 11 USCA § 1111.

§ 502. Allowance of claims or interests

(a) A claim or interest, proof of which is filed under section 501 of this title, is deemed allowed, unless a party in interest, including a creditor of a general partner in a partnership that is a debtor in a case under chapter 7 of this title, objects.

(b) Except as provided in subsections (e)(2), (f), (g), (h) and (i) of this section, if such objection to a claim is made, the court, after notice and a hearing, shall determine the amount of such claim in lawful currency of the United States as of the date of the filing of the petition, and shall allow such claim in such amount, except to the extent that—

     (1) such claim is unenforceable against the debtor and property of the debtor, under any agreement or applicable law for a reason other than because such claim is contingent or unmatured;

     (2) such claim is for unmatured interest;

(3) if such claim is for a tax assessed against property of the estate, such claim exceeds the value of the interest of the estate in such property;

(4) if such claim is for services of an insider or attorney of the debtor, such claim exceeds the reasonable value of such services;

(5) such claim is for a debt that is unmatured on the date of the filing of the petition and that is excepted from discharge under section 523(a)(5) of this title;

(6) if such claim is the claim of a lessor for damages resulting from the termination of a lease of real property, such claim exceeds—

　　(A) the rent reserved by such lease, without acceleration, for the greater of one year, or 15 percent, not to exceed three years, of the remaining term of such lease, following the earlier of—

　　　　(i) the date of the filing of the petition; and

　　　　(ii) the date on which such lessor repossessed, or the lessee surrendered, the leased property; plus

　　(B) any unpaid rent due under such lease, without acceleration, on the earlier of such dates;

(7) if such claim is the claim of an employee for damages resulting from the termination of an employment contract, such claim exceeds—

　　(A) the compensation provided by such contract, without acceleration, for one year following the earlier of—

　　　　(i) the date of the filing of the petition; or

　　　　(ii) the date on which the employer directed the employee to terminate, or such employee terminated, performance under such contract; plus

　　(B) any unpaid compensation due under such contract, without acceleration, on the earlier of such dates;

(8) such claim results from a reduction, due to late payment, in the amount of an otherwise applicable credit available to the debtor in connection with an employment tax on wages, salaries, or commissions earned from the debtor; or

(9) proof of such claim is not timely filed, except to the extent tardily filed as permitted under paragraph (1), (2), or (3) of section 726(a) or under the Federal Rules of Bankruptcy Procedure, except that—

　　(A) a claim of a governmental unit shall be timely filed if it is filed before 180 days after the date of the order for relief or such later time as the Federal Rules of Bankruptcy Procedure may provide; and

　　(B) in a case under chapter 13, a claim of a governmental unit for a tax with respect to a return filed under section 1308 shall be timely if the claim is filed on or before the date that is 60 days after the date on which such return was filed as required.

(c) There shall be estimated for purpose of allowance under this section—

　　(1) any contingent or unliquidated claim, the fixing or liquidation of which, as the case may be, would unduly delay the administration of the case; or

　　(2) any right to payment arising from a right to an equitable remedy for breach of performance.

(d) Notwithstanding subsections (a) and (b) of this section, the court shall disallow any claim of any entity from which property is recoverable under section 542, 543, 550, or 553 of this title or that is a transferee of a transfer avoidable under section 522(f), 522(h), 544, 545, 547, 548, 549, or 724(a) of this title, unless such entity or transferee has paid the amount, or turned over any such property, for which such entity or transferee is liable under section 522(i), 542, 543, 550, or 553 of this title.

(e)(1) Notwithstanding subsections (a), (b), and (c) of this section and paragraph (2) of this subsection, the court shall disallow any claim for reimbursement or contribution of an entity that is liable with the debtor on or has secured the claim of a creditor, to the extent that—

    (A) such creditor's claim against the estate is disallowed;

    (B) such claim for reimbursement or contribution is contingent as of the time of allowance or disallowance of such claim for reimbursement or contribution; or

    (C) such entity asserts a right of subrogation to the rights of such creditor under section 509 of this title.

(2) A claim for reimbursement or contribution of such an entity that becomes fixed after the commencement of the case shall be determined, and shall be allowed under subsection (a), (b), or (c) of this section, or disallowed under subsection (d) of this section, the same as if such claim had become fixed before the date of the filing of the petition.

(f) In an involuntary case, a claim arising in the ordinary course of the debtor's business or financial affairs after the commencement of the case but before the earlier of the appointment of a trustee and the order for relief shall be determined as of the date such claim arises, and shall be allowed under subsection (a), (b), or (c) of this section or disallowed under subsection (d) or (e) of this section, the same as if such claim had arisen before the date of the filing of the petition.

(g)(1) A claim arising from the rejection, under section 365 of this title or under a plan under chapter 9, 11, 12, or 13 of this title, of an executory contract or unexpired lease of the debtor that has not been assumed shall be determined, and shall be allowed under subsection (a), (b), or (c) of this section or disallowed under subsection (d) or (e) of this section, the same as if such claim had arisen before the date of the filing of the petition.

(2) A claim for damages calculated in accordance with section 562 shall be allowed under subsection (a), (b), or (c), or disallowed under subsection (d) or (e), as if such claim had arisen before the date of the filing of the petition.

(h) A claim arising from the recovery of property under section 522, 550, or 553 of this title shall be determined, and shall be allowed under subsection (a), (b), or (c) of this section, or disallowed under subsection (d) or (e) of this section, the same as if such claim had arisen before the date of the filing of the petition.

(i) A claim that does not arise until after the commencement of the case for a tax entitled to priority under section 507(a)(8) of this title shall be determined, and shall be allowed under subsection (a), (b), or (c) of this section, or disallowed under subsection (d) or (e) of this section, the same as if such claim had arisen before the date of the filing of the petition.

(j) A claim that has been allowed or disallowed may be reconsidered for cause. A reconsidered claim may be allowed or disallowed according to the equities of the case. Reconsideration of a claim under this subsection does not affect the validity of any payment or transfer from the estate made to a holder of an allowed claim on account of such allowed claim that is not reconsidered, but if a reconsidered claim is allowed and is of the same class as such holder's claim, such holder may not receive any additional payment or transfer from the estate on account of such holder's allowed claim until the holder of such reconsidered and allowed claim receives payment on account of such claim proportionate in value to that already received by such other holder. This subsection does not alter or modify the trustee's right to recover from a creditor any excess payment or transfer made to such creditor.

(k)(1)   The court, on the motion of the debtor and after a hearing, may reduce a claim filed under this section based in whole on an unsecured consumer debt by not more than 20 percent of the claim, if—

(A) the claim was filed by a creditor who unreasonably refused to negotiate a reasonable alternative repayment schedule proposed on behalf of the debtor by an approved nonprofit budget and credit counseling agency described in section 111;

(B) the offer of the debtor under subparagraph (A)—

(i) was made at least 60 days before the date of the filing of the petition; and

(ii) provided for payment of at least 60 percent of the amount of the debt over a period not to exceed the repayment period of the loan, or a reasonable extension thereof; and

(C) no part of the debt under the alternative repayment schedule is nondischargeable.

(2) The debtor shall have the burden of proving, by clear and convincing evidence, that—

(A) the creditor unreasonably refused to consider the debtor's proposal; and

(B) the proposed alternative repayment schedule was made prior to expiration of the 60-day period specified in paragraph (1)(B)(i).

CROSS REFERENCES

Acceptance of plan by holders of claims or interests, see 11 USCA § 1126.

Applicability of this section in Chapter 9 cases, see 11 USCA § 901.

Certain claims for which partner and partnership are liable, see 11 USCA § 723.

Claims secured by lien on property of estate, see 11 USCA § 1111.

Creditor as meaning entity having certain claims specified in this section, see 11 USCA § 101.

Deductibility of allowed claim, see 11 USCA § 346.

Discharge of liabilities on claims in—

Chapter 7 cases, see 11 USCA § 727.

Chapter 12 cases, see 11 USCA § 1228.

Chapter 13 cases, see 11 USCA § 1328.

Effect of confirmation in—

Chapter 9 cases, see 11 USCA § 944.

Chapter 11 cases, see 11 USCA § 1141.

Filing and allowance of postpetition claims, see 11 USCA § 1305.

Liability of exempted property for debtor's debt, see 11 USCA § 522.

Municipal leases, see 11 USCA § 929.

Payment of insurance benefits to retired employees, see 11 USCA § 1114.

Setoff, see 11 USCA § 553.

Trustee as lien creditor and as successor to certain creditors and purchasers, see 11 USCA § 544.

§ 503. Allowance of administrative expenses

(a) An entity may timely file a request for payment of an administrative expense, or may tardily file such request if permitted by the court for cause.

(b) After notice and a hearing, there shall be allowed administrative expenses, other than claims allowed under section 502(f) of this title, including—

(1)(A) the actual, necessary costs and expenses of preserving the estate including—

(i) wages, salaries, and commissions for services rendered after the commencement of the case; and

(ii) wages and benefits awarded pursuant to a judicial proceeding or a proceeding of the National Labor Relations Board as back pay attributable to any period of time occurring after commencement of the case under this title, as a result of a violation of Federal or State law by the debtor, without regard to the time of the occurrence of unlawful conduct on which such award is based or to whether any services were rendered, if the court determines that payment of wages and benefits by reason of the operation of this clause will not substantially increase the probability of layoff or termination of current employees, or of nonpayment of domestic support obligations, during the case under this title;

(B) any tax—

(i) incurred by the estate, whether secured or unsecured, including property taxes for which liability is in rem, in personam, or both, except a tax of a kind specified in section 507(a)(8) of this title; or

(ii) attributable to an excessive allowance of a tentative carryback adjustment that the estate received, whether the taxable year to which such adjustment relates ended before or after the commencement of the case;

(C) any fine, penalty, or reduction in credit relating to a tax of a kind specified in subparagraph (B) of this paragraph; and

(D) notwithstanding the requirements of subsection (a), a governmental unit shall not be required to file a request for the payment of an expense described in subparagraph (B) or (C), as a condition of its being an allowed administrative expense;

(2) compensation and reimbursement awarded under section 330(a) of this title;

(3) the actual, necessary expenses, other than compensation and reimbursement specified in paragraph (4) of this subsection, incurred by—

(A) a creditor that files a petition under section 303 of this title;

(B) a creditor that recovers, after the court's approval, for the benefit of the estate any property transferred or concealed by the debtor;

(C) a creditor in connection with the prosecution of a criminal offense relating to the case or to the business or property of the debtor;

(D) a creditor, an indenture trustee, an equity security holder, or a committee representing creditors or equity security holders other than a committee appointed under section 1102 of this title, in making a substantial contribution in a case under chapter 9 or 11 of this title;

(E) a custodian superseded under section 543 of this title, and compensation for the services of such custodian; or

(F) a member of a committee appointed under section 1102 of this title, if such expenses are incurred in the performance of the duties of such committee;

(4) reasonable compensation for professional services rendered by an attorney or an accountant of an entity whose expense is allowable under subparagraph (A), (B), (C), (D), or (E) of paragraph (3) of this subsection, based on the time, the nature, the extent, and the value of such services, and the cost of comparable services other than in a case under this title, and reimbursement for actual, necessary expenses incurred by such attorney or accountant;

(5) reasonable compensation for services rendered by an indenture trustee in making a substantial contribution in a case under chapter 9 or 11 of this title, based on the time, the nature, the extent, and the value of such services, and the cost of comparable services other than in a case under this title;

(6) the fees and mileage payable under chapter 119 of title 28;

(7) with respect to a nonresidential real property lease previously assumed under section 365, and subsequently rejected, a sum equal to all monetary obligations due, excluding those arising from or relating to a failure to operate or a penalty provision, for the period of 2 years following the later of the rejection date or the date of actual turnover of the premises, without reduction or setoff for any reason whatsoever except for sums actually received or to be received from an entity other than the debtor, and the claim for remaining sums due for the balance of the term of the lease shall be a claim under section 502(b)(6);

(8) the actual, necessary costs and expenses of closing a health care business incurred by a trustee or by a Federal agency (as defined in section 551(1) of title 5) or a department or agency of a State or political subdivision thereof, including any cost or expense incurred—

    (A) in disposing of patient records in accordance with section 351; or

    (B) in connection with transferring patients from the health care business that is in the process of being closed to another health care business; and

(9) the value of any goods received by the debtor within 20 days before the date of commencement of a case under this title in which the goods have been sold to the debtor in the ordinary course of such debtor's business.

[*Note from West:* Pub. L. 116–260 created a temporary § 503(b)(10), which expired on December 27, 2022, *except* for cases commenced before December 27, 2022. *See* 134 Stat. 2015, 2016, 2017. For the text of temporary § 503(b)(10), *see* Title 11, Chapter 5, Subchapter I, § 503, Editorial Notes, Amendments, 2020 at http://uscode.house.gov]

(c) Notwithstanding subsection (b), there shall neither be allowed, nor paid—

(1) a transfer made to, or an obligation incurred for the benefit of, an insider of the debtor for the purpose of inducing such person to remain with the debtor's business, absent a finding by the court based on evidence in the record that—

    (A) the transfer or obligation is essential to retention of the person because the individual has a bona fide job offer from another business at the same or greater rate of compensation;

    (B) the services provided by the person are essential to the survival of the business; and

    (C) either—

        (i) the amount of the transfer made to, or obligation incurred for the benefit of, the person is not greater than an amount equal to 10 times the amount of the mean transfer or obligation of a similar kind given to nonmanagement employees for any purpose during the calendar year in which the transfer is made or the obligation is incurred; or

        (ii) if no such similar transfers were made to, or obligations were incurred for the benefit of, such nonmanagement employees during such calendar year, the amount of the transfer or obligation is not greater than an amount equal to 25 percent of the amount of any similar transfer or obligation made to or incurred for the benefit of such insider for any purpose during the calendar year before the year in which such transfer is made or obligation is incurred;

(2) a severance payment to an insider of the debtor, unless—

(A) the payment is part of a program that is generally applicable to all full-time employees; and

(B) the amount of the payment is not greater than 10 times the amount of the mean severance pay given to nonmanagement employees during the calendar year in which the payment is made; or

(3) other transfers or obligations that are outside the ordinary course of business and not justified by the facts and circumstances of the case, including transfers made to, or obligations incurred for the benefit of, officers, managers, or consultants hired after the date of the filing of the petition.

CROSS REFERENCES

Adequate protection, other than granting certain administrative expenses, see 11 USCA § 361.

Applicability of this section in Chapter 9 cases, see 11 USCA § 901.

Claims arising from automatic stay in Chapter 9 cases, see 11 USCA § 922.

Deductibility of allowed claim, see 11 USCA § 346.

Deduction of administrative expenses for income tax purposes, see 26 USCA § 1398.

Deduction of administrative expenses from payments received by trustee if plan not confirmed in—

Chapter 12 cases, see 11 USCA § 1226.

Chapter 13 cases, see 11 USCA § 1326.

Distribution of property of estate in Chapter 7 cases, see 11 USCA § 726.

Effect of conversion, see 11 USCA § 348.

Grain storage facility bankruptcies, expedited determinations, see 11 USCA § 557.

Method of obtaining adequate protection in Chapter 12 cases, see 11 USCA § 1205.

Payment of insurance benefits to retired employees, see 11 USCA § 1114.

Performance of obligations under executory contracts and unexpired leases notwithstanding subsec. (b)(1) of this section, see 11 USCA § 365.

Proof of claim, see Official Bankruptcy Form 410.

Unsecured debt as administrative expense or having priority over certain administrative expenses, see 11 USCA § 364.

§ 504. Sharing of compensation

(a) Except as provided in subsection (b) of this section, a person receiving compensation or reimbursement under section 503(b)(2) or 503(b)(4) of this title may not share or agree to share—

(1) any such compensation or reimbursement with another person; or

(2) any compensation or reimbursement received by another person under such sections.

(b)(1) A member, partner, or regular associate in a professional association, corporation, or partnership may share compensation or reimbursement received under section 503(b)(2) or 503(b)(4) of this title with another member, partner, or regular associate in such association, corporation, or partnership, and may share in any compensation or reimbursement received under such sections by another member, partner, or regular associate in such association, corporation, or partnership.

(2) An attorney for a creditor that files a petition under section 303 of this title may share compensation and reimbursement received under section 503(b)(4) of this title with any other attorney contributing to the services rendered or expenses incurred by such creditor's attorney.

(c) This section shall not apply with respect to sharing, or agreeing to share, compensation with a bona fide public service attorney referral program that operates in accordance with non-Federal law regulating attorney referral services and with rules of professional responsibility applicable to attorney acceptance of referrals.

CROSS REFERENCES

Applicability of restrictions on sharing of compensation to allowances in investor protection liquidation proceedings, see 15 USCA § 78eee.

Applicability of this section in Chapter 9 cases, see 11 USCA § 901.

§ 505. Determination of tax liability

(a)(1) Except as provided in paragraph (2) of this subsection, the court may determine the amount or legality of any tax, any fine or penalty relating to a tax, or any addition to tax, whether or not previously assessed, whether or not paid, and whether or not contested before and adjudicated by a judicial or administrative tribunal of competent jurisdiction.

(2) The court may not so determine—

(A) the amount or legality of a tax, fine, penalty, or addition to tax if such amount or legality was contested before and adjudicated by a judicial or administrative tribunal of competent jurisdiction before the commencement of the case under this title;

(B) any right of the estate to a tax refund, before the earlier of—

(i) 120 days after the trustee properly requests such refund from the governmental unit from which such refund is claimed; or

(ii) a determination by such governmental unit of such request; or

(C) the amount or legality of any amount arising in connection with an ad valorem tax on real or personal property of the estate, if the applicable period for contesting or redetermining that amount under applicable nonbankruptcy law has expired.

(b)(1)(A) The clerk shall maintain a list under which a Federal, State, or local governmental unit responsible for the collection of taxes within the district may—

(i) designate an address for service of requests under this subsection; and

(ii) describe where further information concerning additional requirements for filing such requests may be found.

(B) If such governmental unit does not designate an address and provide such address to the clerk under subparagraph (A), any request made under this subsection may be served at the address for the filing of a tax return or protest with the appropriate taxing authority of such governmental unit.

(2) A trustee may request a determination of any unpaid liability of the estate for any tax incurred during the administration of the case by submitting a tax return for such tax and a request for such a determination to the governmental unit charged with responsibility for collection or determination of such tax at the address and in the manner designated in paragraph (1). Unless such return is fraudulent, or contains a material misrepresentation, the estate, the trustee, the debtor, and any successor to the debtor are discharged from any liability for such tax—

(A) upon payment of the tax shown on such return, if—

(i) such governmental unit does not notify the trustee, within 60 days after such request, that such return has been selected for examination; or

(ii) such governmental unit does not complete such an examination and notify the trustee of any tax due, within 180 days after such request or within such additional time as the court, for cause, permits;

(B) upon payment of the tax determined by the court, after notice and a hearing, after completion by such governmental unit of such examination; or

(C) upon payment of the tax determined by such governmental unit to be due.

(c) Notwithstanding section 362 of this title, after determination by the court of a tax under this section, the governmental unit charged with responsibility for collection of such tax may assess such tax against the estate, the debtor, or a successor to the debtor, as the case may be, subject to any otherwise applicable law.

CROSS REFERENCES

Declaratory judgments, see 28 USCA § 2201.

§ 506. Determination of secured status

(a)(1) An allowed claim of a creditor secured by a lien on property in which the estate has an interest, or that is subject to setoff under section 553 of this title, is a secured claim to the extent of the value of such creditor's interest in the estate's interest in such property, or to the extent of the amount subject to setoff, as the case may be, and is an unsecured claim to the extent that the value of such creditor's interest or the amount so subject to setoff is less than the amount of such allowed claim. Such value shall be determined in light of the purpose of the valuation and of the proposed disposition or use of such property, and in conjunction with any hearing on such disposition or use or on a plan affecting such creditor's interest.

(2) If the debtor is an individual in a case under chapter 7 or 13, such value with respect to personal property securing an allowed claim shall be determined based on the replacement value of such property as of the date of the filing of the petition without deduction for costs of sale or marketing. With respect to property acquired for personal, family, or household purposes, replacement value shall mean the price a retail merchant would charge for property of that kind considering the age and condition of the property at the time value is determined.

(b) To the extent that an allowed secured claim is secured by property the value of which, after any recovery under subsection (c) of this section, is greater than the amount of such claim, there shall be allowed to the holder of such claim, interest on such claim, and any reasonable fees, costs, or charges provided for under the agreement or State statute under which such claim arose.

(c) The trustee may recover from property securing an allowed secured claim the reasonable, necessary costs and expenses of preserving, or disposing of, such property to the extent of any benefit to the holder of such claim, including the payment of all ad valorem property taxes with respect to the property.

(d) To the extent that a lien secures a claim against the debtor that is not an allowed secured claim, such lien is void, unless—

(1) such claim was disallowed only under section 502(b)(5) or 502(e) of this title; or

(2) such claim is not an allowed secured claim due only to the failure of any entity to file a proof of such claim under section 501 of this title.

CROSS REFERENCES

Applicability of this section in Chapter 9 cases, see 11 USCA § 901.

Automatic preservation of avoided transfer, see 11 USCA § 551.

Claims secured by lien on property of estate, see 11 USCA § 1111.

§ 507.   Priorities

(a)   The following expenses and claims have priority in the following order:

    (1)   First:

      (A)   Allowed unsecured claims for domestic support obligations that, as of the date of the filing of the petition in a case under this title, are owed to or recoverable by a spouse, former spouse, or child of the debtor, or such child's parent, legal guardian, or responsible relative, without regard to whether the claim is filed by such person or is filed by a governmental unit on behalf of such person, on the condition that funds received under this paragraph by a governmental unit under this title after the date of the filing of the petition shall be applied and distributed in accordance with applicable nonbankruptcy law.

      (B)   Subject to claims under subparagraph (A), allowed unsecured claims for domestic support obligations that, as of the date of the filing of the petition, are assigned by a spouse, former spouse, child of the debtor, or such child's parent, legal guardian, or responsible relative to a governmental unit (unless such obligation is assigned voluntarily by the spouse, former spouse, child, parent, legal guardian, or responsible relative of the child for the purpose of collecting the debt) or are owed directly to or recoverable by a governmental unit under applicable nonbankruptcy law, on the condition that funds received under this paragraph by a governmental unit under this title after the date of the filing of the petition be applied and distributed in accordance with applicable nonbankruptcy law.

      (C)   If a trustee is appointed or elected under section 701, 702, 703, 1104, 1202, or 1302, the administrative expenses of the trustee allowed under paragraphs (1)(A), (2), and (6) of section 503(b) shall be paid before payment of claims under subparagraphs (A) and (B), to the extent that the trustee administers assets that are otherwise available for the payment of such claims.

    (2)   Second, administrative expenses allowed under section 503(b) of this title, unsecured claims of any Federal reserve bank related to loans made through programs or facilities authorized under section 13(3) of the Federal Reserve Act (12 U.S.C. 343), and any fees and charges assessed against the estate under chapter 123 of title 28.

    (3)   Third, unsecured claims allowed under section 502(f) of this title.

    (4)   Fourth, allowed unsecured claims, but only to the extent of $15,150 for each individual or corporation, as the case may be, earned within 180 days before the date of the filing of the petition or the date of the cessation of the debtor's business, whichever occurs first, for—

      (A)   wages, salaries, or commissions, including vacation, severance, and sick leave pay earned by an individual; or

      (B)   sales commissions earned by an individual or by a corporation with only 1 employee, acting as an independent contractor in the sale of goods or services for the debtor in the ordinary course of the debtor's business if, and only if, during the 12 months preceding that date, at least 75 percent of the amount that the individual or corporation earned by acting as an independent contractor in the sale of goods or services was earned from the debtor.

    (5)   Fifth, allowed unsecured claims for contributions to an employee benefit plan—

    (A) arising from services rendered within 180 days before the date of the filing of the petition or the date of the cessation of the debtor's business, whichever occurs first; but only

    (B) for each such plan, to the extent of—

        (i) the number of employees covered by each such plan multiplied by $15,150; less

        (ii) the aggregate amount paid to such employees under paragraph (4) of this subsection, plus the aggregate amount paid by the estate on behalf of such employees to any other employee benefit plan.

(6) Sixth, allowed unsecured claims of persons—

    (A) engaged in the production or raising of grain, as defined in section 557(b) of this title, against a debtor who owns or operates a grain storage facility, as defined in section 557(b) of this title, for grain or the proceeds of grain, or

    (B) engaged as a United States fisherman against a debtor who has acquired fish or fish produce from a fisherman through a sale or conversion, and who is engaged in operating a fish produce storage or processing facility—

but only to the extent of $7,475 for each such individual.

(7) Seventh, allowed unsecured claims of individuals, to the extent of $3,350 for each such individual, arising from the deposit, before the commencement of the case, of money in connection with the purchase, lease, or rental of property, or the purchase of services, for the personal, family, or household use of such individuals, that were not delivered or provided.

(8) Eighth, allowed unsecured claims of governmental units, only to the extent that such claims are for—

    (A) a tax on or measured by income or gross receipts for a taxable year ending on or before the date of the filing of the petition—

        (i) for which a return, if required, is last due, including extensions, after three years before the date of the filing of the petition;

        (ii) assessed within 240 days before the date of the filing of the petition, exclusive of—

            (I) any time during which an offer in compromise with respect to that tax was pending or in effect during that 240-day period, plus 30 days; and

            (II) any time during which a stay of proceedings against collections was in effect in a prior case under this title during that 240-day period, plus 90 days; or

        (iii) other than a tax of a kind specified in section 523(a)(1)(B) or 523(a)(1)(C) of this title, not assessed before, but assessable, under applicable law or by agreement, after, the commencement of the case;

    (B) a property tax incurred before the commencement of the case and last payable without penalty after one year before the date of the filing of the petition;

    (C) a tax required to be collected or withheld and for which the debtor is liable in whatever capacity;

    (D) an employment tax on a wage, salary, or commission of a kind specified in paragraph (4) of this subsection earned from the debtor before the date of the filing of the petition, whether or not actually paid before such date, for which a return is last due, under applicable law or under any extension, after three years before the date of the filing of the petition;

    (E) an excise tax on—

(i) a transaction occurring before the date of the filing of the petition for which a return, if required, is last due, under applicable law or under any extension, after three years before the date of the filing of the petition; or

(ii) if a return is not required, a transaction occurring during the three years immediately preceding the date of the filing of the petition;

(F) a customs duty arising out of the importation of merchandise—

(i) entered for consumption within one year before the date of the filing of the petition;

(ii) covered by an entry liquidated or reliquidated within one year before the date of the filing of the petition; or

(iii) entered for consumption within four years before the date of the filing of the petition but unliquidated on such date, if the Secretary of the Treasury certifies that failure to liquidate such entry was due to an investigation pending on such date into assessment of antidumping or countervailing duties or fraud, or if information needed for the proper appraisement or classification of such merchandise was not available to the appropriate customs officer before such date; or

(G) a penalty related to a claim of a kind specified in this paragraph and in compensation for actual pecuniary loss.

An otherwise applicable time period specified in this paragraph shall be suspended for any period during which a governmental unit is prohibited under applicable nonbankruptcy law from collecting a tax as a result of a request by the debtor for a hearing and an appeal of any collection action taken or proposed against the debtor, plus 90 days; plus any time during which the stay of proceedings was in effect in a prior case under this title or during which collection was precluded by the existence of 1 or more confirmed plans under this title, plus 90 days.

(9) Ninth, allowed unsecured claims based upon any commitment by the debtor to a Federal depository institutions regulatory agency (or predecessor to such agency) to maintain the capital of an insured depository institution.

(10) Tenth, allowed claims for death or personal injury resulting from the operation of a motor vehicle or vessel if such operation was unlawful because the debtor was intoxicated from using alcohol, a drug, or another substance.

(b) If the trustee, under section 362, 363, or 364 of this title, provides adequate protection of the interest of a holder of a claim secured by a lien on property of the debtor and if, notwithstanding such protection, such creditor has a claim allowable under subsection (a)(2) of this section arising from the stay of action against such property under section 362 of this title, from the use, sale, or lease of such property under section 363 of this title, or from the granting of a lien under section 364(d) of this title, then such creditor's claim under such subsection shall have priority over every other claim allowable under such subsection.

(c) For the purpose of subsection (a) of this section, a claim of a governmental unit arising from an erroneous refund or credit of a tax has the same priority as a claim for the tax to which such refund or credit relates.

(d) An entity that is subrogated to the rights of a holder of a claim of a kind specified in subsection (a)(1), (a)(4), (a)(5), (a)(6), (a)(7), (a)(8), or (a)(9) of this section is not subrogated to the right of the holder of such claim to priority under such subsection.

REFERENCES IN TEXT

The Federal Reserve Act, referred to in subsec. (a)(2), is Act Dec. 23, 1913, c. 6, 38 Stat. 251, as amended, which is classified principally to chapter 3 of Title 12, 12 U.S.C.A. § 221 et seq. Section 13(3) of such Act is classified to 12 U.S.C.A. § 343. For complete classification, see References in Text note set out under 12 U.S.C.A. § 226 and Tables.

CROSS REFERENCES

Applicability of subsec. (a)(1) of this section in Chapter 9 cases, see 11 USCA § 901.

Confirmation in Chapter 9 cases upon payment of administrative expenses, fees, and charges, see 11 USCA § 943.

Contents of plan in—

> Chapter 12 cases, see 11 USCA § 1222.

> Chapter 13 cases, see 11 USCA § 1322.

Designation by plan of classes of claims, see 11 USCA § 1123.

Distribution of—

> Certain estate property subject to liens, see 11 USCA § 724.

> Customer property in commodity broker liquidation cases, see 11 USCA § 766.

> Customer property in stockbroker liquidation cases, see 11 USCA § 752.

> Property of estate, see 11 USCA § 726.

Executory contracts and unexpired leases, see 11 USCA § 365.

Involuntary cases future adjustments, see 11 USCA § 104.

Proof of claim, see Official Bankruptcy Form 410.

Recoupment of funds advanced by Securities Investor Protection Corporation as priority administrative expense, see 15 USCA § 78fff.

Tax or customs duty excepted from discharge, see 11 USCA § 523.

Time of payment of administrative expenses, fees and charges in—

> Chapter 12 cases, see 11 USCA § 1226.

> Chapter 13 cases, see 11 USCA § 1326.

Treatment of certain claims as affecting confirmation of plan in Chapter 11 cases, see 11 USCA § 1129.

Unsecured debt having priority over certain administrative expenses, see 11 USCA § 364.

§ 508. Effect of distribution other than under this title

If a creditor of a partnership debtor receives, from a general partner that is not a debtor in a case under chapter 7 of this title, payment of, or a transfer of property on account of, a claim that is allowed under this title and that is not secured by a lien on property of such partner, such creditor may not receive any payment under this title on account of such claim until each of the other holders of claims on account of which such holders are entitled to share equally with such creditor under this title has received payment under this title equal in value to the consideration received by such creditor from such general partner.

§ 509. Claims of codebtors

(a) Except as provided in subsection (b) or (c) of this section, an entity that is liable with the debtor on, or that has secured, a claim of a creditor against the debtor, and that pays such claim, is subrogated to the rights of such creditor to the extent of such payment.

(b) Such entity is not subrogated to the rights of such creditor to the extent that—

(1) a claim of such entity for reimbursement or contribution on account of such payment of such creditor's claim is—

    (A) allowed under section 502 of this title;

    (B) disallowed other than under section 502(e) of this title; or

    (C) subordinated under section 510 of this title; or

(2) as between the debtor and such entity, such entity received the consideration for the claim held by such creditor.

(c) The court shall subordinate to the claim of a creditor and for the benefit of such creditor an allowed claim, by way of subrogation under this section, or for reimbursement or contribution, of an entity that is liable with the debtor on, or that has secured, such creditor's claim, until such creditor's claim is paid in full, either through payments under this title or otherwise.

CROSS REFERENCES

Applicability of this section in Chapter 9 cases, see 11 USCA § 901.

§ 510. Subordination

(a) A subordination agreement is enforceable in a case under this title to the same extent that such agreement is enforceable under applicable nonbankruptcy law.

(b) For the purpose of distribution under this title, a claim arising from rescission of a purchase or sale of a security of the debtor or of an affiliate of the debtor, for damages arising from the purchase or sale of such a security, or for reimbursement or contribution allowed under section 502 on account of such a claim, shall be subordinated to all claims or interests that are senior to or equal the claim or interest represented by such security, except that if such security is common stock, such claim has the same priority as common stock.

(c) Notwithstanding subsections (a) and (b) of this section, after notice and a hearing, the court may—

    (1) under principles of equitable subordination, subordinate for purposes of distribution all or part of an allowed claim to all or part of another allowed claim or all or part of an allowed interest to all or part of another allowed interest; or

    (2) order that any lien securing such a subordinated claim be transferred to the estate.

CROSS REFERENCES

Applicability of this section in Chapter 9 cases, see 11 USCA § 901.

Certain customer claims in stockbroker liquidation proceedings, see 11 USCA § 747.

Confirmation of plan in Chapter 11 cases, see 11 USCA §§ 1129, 1191.

Distribution of—

    Customer property, see 11 USCA § 752.

    Property of estate, see 11 USCA § 726.

Effect of dismissal, see 11 USCA § 349.

Property of estate, see 11 USCA § 541.

Property recoverable by trustee as exempt, see 11 USCA § 522.

Unpaid portion of certain claims as entitled to distribution, see 11 USCA § 766.

§ 511. Rate of interest on tax claims

(a) If any provision of this title requires the payment of interest on a tax claim or on an administrative expense tax, or the payment of interest to enable a creditor to receive the present value of the allowed amount of a tax claim, the rate of interest shall be the rate determined under applicable nonbankruptcy law.

(b) In the case of taxes paid under a confirmed plan under this title, the rate of interest shall be determined as of the calendar month in which the plan is confirmed.

SUBCHAPTER II—DEBTOR'S DUTIES AND BENEFITS

§ 521. Debtor's duties

(a) The debtor shall—

    (1) file—

        (A) a list of creditors; and

        (B) unless the court orders otherwise—

            (i) a schedule of assets and liabilities;

            (ii) a schedule of current income and current expenditures;

            (iii) a statement of the debtor's financial affairs and, if section 342(b) applies, a certificate—

                (I) of an attorney whose name is indicated on the petition as the attorney for the debtor, or a bankruptcy petition preparer signing the petition under section 110(b)(1), indicating that such attorney or the bankruptcy petition preparer delivered to the debtor the notice required by section 342(b); or

                (II) if no attorney is so indicated, and no bankruptcy petition preparer signed the petition, of the debtor that such notice was received and read by the debtor;

            (iv) copies of all payment advices or other evidence of payment received within 60 days before the date of the filing of the petition, by the debtor from any employer of the debtor;

            (v) a statement of the amount of monthly net income, itemized to show how the amount is calculated; and

            (vi) a statement disclosing any reasonably anticipated increase in income or expenditures over the 12-month period following the date of the filing of the petition;

    (2) if an individual debtor's schedule of assets and liabilities includes debts which are secured by property of the estate—

        (A) within thirty days after the date of the filing of a petition under chapter 7 of this title or on or before the date of the meeting of creditors, whichever is earlier, or within such additional time as the court, for cause, within such period fixes, file with the clerk a statement of his intention with respect to the retention or surrender of such property and, if applicable, specifying that such property is claimed as exempt, that the debtor intends to redeem such property, or that the debtor intends to reaffirm debts secured by such property; and

        (B) within 30 days after the first date set for the meeting of creditors under section 341(a), or within such additional time as the court, for cause, within such 30-day period fixes, perform his intention with respect to such property, as specified by subparagraph (A) of this paragraph;

except that nothing in subparagraphs (A) and (B) of this paragraph shall alter the debtor's or the trustee's rights with regard to such property under this title, except as provided in section 362(h);

(3)   if a trustee is serving in the case or an auditor is serving under section 586(f) of title 28, cooperate with the trustee as necessary to enable the trustee to perform the trustee's duties under this title;

(4)   if a trustee is serving in the case or an auditor is serving under section 586(f) of title 28, surrender to the trustee all property of the estate and any recorded information, including books, documents, records, and papers, relating to property of the estate, whether or not immunity is granted under section 344 of this title;

(5)   appear at the hearing required under section 524(d) of this title;

(6)   in a case under chapter 7 of this title in which the debtor is an individual, not retain possession of personal property as to which a creditor has an allowed claim for the purchase price secured in whole or in part by an interest in such personal property unless the debtor, not later than 45 days after the first meeting of creditors under section 341(a), either—

(A)   enters into an agreement with the creditor pursuant to section 524(c) with respect to the claim secured by such property; or

(B)   redeems such property from the security interest pursuant to section 722; and

(7)   unless a trustee is serving in the case, continue to perform the obligations required of the administrator (as defined in section 3 of the Employee Retirement Income Security Act of 1974) of an employee benefit plan if at the time of the commencement of the case the debtor (or any entity designated by the debtor) served as such administrator.

If the debtor fails to so act within the 45-day period referred to in paragraph (6), the stay under section 362(a) is terminated with respect to the personal property of the estate or of the debtor which is affected, such property shall no longer be property of the estate, and the creditor may take whatever action as to such property as is permitted by applicable nonbankruptcy law, unless the court determines on the motion of the trustee filed before the expiration of such 45-day period, and after notice and a hearing, that such property is of consequential value or benefit to the estate, orders appropriate adequate protection of the creditor's interest, and orders the debtor to deliver any collateral in the debtor's possession to the trustee.

(b)   In addition to the requirements under subsection (a), a debtor who is an individual shall file with the court—

(1)   a certificate from the approved nonprofit budget and credit counseling agency that provided the debtor services under section 109(h) describing the services provided to the debtor; and

(2)   a copy of the debt repayment plan, if any, developed under section 109(h) through the approved nonprofit budget and credit counseling agency referred to in paragraph (1).

(c)   In addition to meeting the requirements under subsection (a), a debtor shall file with the court a record of any interest that a debtor has in an education individual retirement account (as defined in section 530(b)(1) of the Internal Revenue Code of 1986,[4] an interest in an account in a qualified ABLE program (as defined in section 529A(b) of such Code, or under a qualified State tuition program (as defined in section 529(b)(1) of such Code).

(d)   If the debtor fails timely to take the action specified in subsection (a)(6) of this section, or in paragraphs (1) and (2) of section 362(h), with respect to property which a lessor or bailor owns and has leased, rented, or bailed to the debtor or as to which a creditor holds a security interest not otherwise voidable under section 522(f), 544, 545, 547, 548, or 549, nothing in this title shall prevent or limit the operation of a provision in the underlying lease or agreement that has the effect of placing the debtor

---

[4]   So in original. A closing parenthesis probably should precede the comma.

in default under such lease or agreement by reason of the occurrence, pendency, or existence of a proceeding under this title or the insolvency of the debtor. Nothing in this subsection shall be deemed to justify limiting such a provision in any other circumstance.

(e)(1) If the debtor in a case under chapter 7 or 13 is an individual and if a creditor files with the court at any time a request to receive a copy of the petition, schedules, and statement of financial affairs filed by the debtor, then the court shall make such petition, such schedules, and such statement available to such creditor.

(2)(A) The debtor shall provide—

(i) not later than 7 days before the date first set for the first meeting of creditors, to the trustee a copy of the Federal income tax return required under applicable law (or at the election of the debtor, a transcript of such return) for the most recent tax year ending immediately before the commencement of the case and for which a Federal income tax return was filed; and

(ii) at the same time the debtor complies with clause (i), a copy of such return (or if elected under clause (i), such transcript) to any creditor that timely requests such copy.

(B) If the debtor fails to comply with clause (i) or (ii) of subparagraph (A), the court shall dismiss the case unless the debtor demonstrates that the failure to so comply is due to circumstances beyond the control of the debtor.

(C) If a creditor requests a copy of such tax return or such transcript and if the debtor fails to provide a copy of such tax return or such transcript to such creditor at the time the debtor provides such tax return or such transcript to the trustee, then the court shall dismiss the case unless the debtor demonstrates that the failure to provide a copy of such tax return or such transcript is due to circumstances beyond the control of the debtor.

(3) If a creditor in a case under chapter 13 files with the court at any time a request to receive a copy of the plan filed by the debtor, then the court shall make available to such creditor a copy of the plan—

(A) at a reasonable cost; and

(B) not later than 7 days after such request is filed.

(f) At the request of the court, the United States trustee, or any party in interest in a case under chapter 7, 11, or 13, a debtor who is an individual shall file with the court—

(1) at the same time filed with the taxing authority, a copy of each Federal income tax return required under applicable law (or at the election of the debtor, a transcript of such tax return) with respect to each tax year of the debtor ending while the case is pending under such chapter;

(2) at the same time filed with the taxing authority, each Federal income tax return required under applicable law (or at the election of the debtor, a transcript of such tax return) that had not been filed with such authority as of the date of the commencement of the case and that was subsequently filed for any tax year of the debtor ending in the 3-year period ending on the date of the commencement of the case;

(3) a copy of each amendment to any Federal income tax return or transcript filed with the court under paragraph (1) or (2); and

(4) in a case under chapter 13—

(A) on the date that is either 90 days after the end of such tax year or 1 year after the date of the commencement of the case, whichever is later, if a plan is not confirmed before such later date; and

(B) annually after the plan is confirmed and until the case is closed, not later than the date that is 45 days before the anniversary of the confirmation of the plan;

a statement, under penalty of perjury, of the income and expenditures of the debtor during the tax year of the debtor most recently concluded before such statement is filed under this paragraph, and of the monthly income of the debtor, that shows how income, expenditures, and monthly income are calculated.

(g)(1)   A statement referred to in subsection (f)(4) shall disclose—

    (A) the amount and sources of the income of the debtor;

    (B) the identity of any person responsible with the debtor for the support of any dependent of the debtor; and

    (C) the identity of any person who contributed, and the amount contributed, to the household in which the debtor resides.

(2)   The tax returns, amendments, and statement of income and expenditures described in subsections (e)(2)(A) and (f) shall be available to the United States trustee (or the bankruptcy administrator, if any), the trustee, and any party in interest for inspection and copying, subject to the requirements of section 315(c) of the Bankruptcy Abuse Prevention and Consumer Protection Act of 2005.

(h)   If requested by the United States trustee or by the trustee, the debtor shall provide—

    (1) a document that establishes the identity of the debtor, including a driver's license, passport, or other document that contains a photograph of the debtor; or

    (2) such other personal identifying information relating to the debtor that establishes the identity of the debtor.

(i)(1)   Subject to paragraphs (2) and (4) and notwithstanding section 707(a), if an individual debtor in a voluntary case under chapter 7 or 13 fails to file all of the information required under subsection (a)(1) within 45 days after the date of the filing of the petition, the case shall be automatically dismissed effective on the 46th day after the date of the filing of the petition.

(2)   Subject to paragraph (4) and with respect to a case described in paragraph (1), any party in interest may request the court to enter an order dismissing the case. If requested, the court shall enter an order of dismissal not later than 7 days after such request.

(3)   Subject to paragraph (4) and upon request of the debtor made within 45 days after the date of the filing of the petition described in paragraph (1), the court may allow the debtor an additional period of not to exceed 45 days to file the information required under subsection (a)(1) if the court finds justification for extending the period for the filing.

(4)   Notwithstanding any other provision of this subsection, on the motion of the trustee filed before the expiration of the applicable period of time specified in paragraph (1), (2), or (3), and after notice and a hearing, the court may decline to dismiss the case if the court finds that the debtor attempted in good faith to file all the information required by subsection (a)(1)(B)(iv) and that the best interests of creditors would be served by administration of the case.

(j)(1)   Notwithstanding any other provision of this title, if the debtor fails to file a tax return that becomes due after the commencement of the case or to properly obtain an extension of the due date for filing such return, the taxing authority may request that the court enter an order converting or dismissing the case.

(2)   If the debtor does not file the required return or obtain the extension referred to in paragraph (1) within 90 days after a request is filed by the taxing authority under that paragraph, the court shall convert or dismiss the case, whichever is in the best interests of creditors and the estate.

REFERENCES IN TEXT

Section 3 of the Employee Retirement Income Security Act of 1974, referred to in subsec. (a)(7), is Pub. L. 93–406, Title I, § 3, Sept. 2, 1974, 88 Stat. 833, which is classified to 29 U.S.C.A. § 1002.

Section 530(b)(1) of the Internal Revenue Code of 1986, referred to in subsec. (c), is classified to 26 U.S.C.A. § 530(b)(1).

Section 529(b)(1) of such Code, referred to in subsec. (c), is classified to 26 U.S.C.A. § 529(b)(1).

Section 315(c) of the Bankruptcy Abuse Prevention and Consumer Protection Act of 2005, referred to in subsec. (g)(2), is Pub. L. 109–8, Title III, § 315(c), Apr. 20, 2005, 119 Stat. 91, which is set out as a note under this section.

CROSS REFERENCES

Conversion or dismissal of—

> Chapter 11 case, see 11 USCA § 1112.

> Chapter 13 case, see 11 USCA § 1307.

Debtor's statement of intention, see Official Bankruptcy Form 108.

Dismissal of Chapter 7 case, see 11 USCA § 707.

Filing of list, schedule and statement by trustee, see 11 USCA § 1106.

Penalty for persons who negligently or fraudulently prepare bankruptcy petitions or failure to file bankruptcy papers, see 11 USCA § 110.

Proof of claim or interest deemed filed if scheduled in Chapter 11 cases, see 11 USCA § 1111.

Property scheduled but unadministered before close of case deemed abandoned, see 11 USCA § 554.

Required lists, schedules, statements, and fees, see Director's Bankruptcy Form 2000.

Trustee's duty to ensure performance of debtor's intention as specified in subsec. (2)(B) of this section, see 11 USCA § 704.

§ 522. Exemptions

(a) In this section—

(1) "dependent" includes spouse, whether or not actually dependent; and

(2) "value" means fair market value as of the date of the filing of the petition or, with respect to property that becomes property of the estate after such date, as of the date such property becomes property of the estate.

(b)(1) Notwithstanding section 541 of this title, an individual debtor may exempt from property of the estate the property listed in either paragraph (2) or, in the alternative, paragraph (3) of this subsection. In joint cases filed under section 302 of this title and individual cases filed under section 301 or 303 of this title by or against debtors who are husband and wife, and whose estates are ordered to be jointly administered under Rule 1015(b) of the Federal Rules of Bankruptcy Procedure, one debtor may not elect to exempt property listed in paragraph (2) and the other debtor elect to exempt property listed in paragraph (3) of this subsection. If the parties cannot agree on the alternative to be elected, they shall be deemed to elect paragraph (2), where such election is permitted under the law of the jurisdiction where the case is filed.

(2) Property listed in this paragraph is property that is specified under subsection (d), unless the State law that is applicable to the debtor under paragraph (3)(A) specifically does not so authorize.

(3) Property listed in this paragraph is—

(A) subject to subsections (*o*) and (p), any property that is exempt under Federal law, other than subsection (d) of this section, or State or local law that is applicable on the date of the filing of the petition to the place in which the debtor's domicile has been located for the 730 days immediately preceding the date of the filing of the petition or if the debtor's domicile has not been located in a single State for such 730-day period, the place in which the debtor's domicile was located for 180 days immediately preceding the 730-day period or for a longer portion of such 180-day period than in any other place;

(B) any interest in property in which the debtor had, immediately before the commencement of the case, an interest as a tenant by the entirety or joint tenant to the extent that such interest as a tenant by the entirety or joint tenant is exempt from process under applicable nonbankruptcy law; and

(C) retirement funds to the extent that those funds are in a fund or account that is exempt from taxation under section 401, 403, 408, 408A, 414, 457, or 501(a) of the Internal Revenue Code of 1986.

If the effect of the domiciliary requirement under subparagraph (A) is to render the debtor ineligible for any exemption, the debtor may elect to exempt property that is specified under subsection (d).

(4) For purposes of paragraph (3)(C) and subsection (d)(12), the following shall apply:

(A) If the retirement funds are in a retirement fund that has received a favorable determination under section 7805 of the Internal Revenue Code of 1986, and that determination is in effect as of the date of the filing of the petition in a case under this title, those funds shall be presumed to be exempt from the estate.

(B) If the retirement funds are in a retirement fund that has not received a favorable determination under such section 7805, those funds are exempt from the estate if the debtor demonstrates that—

(i) no prior determination to the contrary has been made by a court or the Internal Revenue Service; and

(ii)(I) the retirement fund is in substantial compliance with the applicable requirements of the Internal Revenue Code of 1986; or

(II) the retirement fund fails to be in substantial compliance with the applicable requirements of the Internal Revenue Code of 1986 and the debtor is not materially responsible for that failure.

(C) A direct transfer of retirement funds from 1 fund or account that is exempt from taxation under section 401, 403, 408, 408A, 414, 457, or 501(a) of the Internal Revenue Code of 1986, under section 401(a)(31) of the Internal Revenue Code of 1986, or otherwise, shall not cease to qualify for exemption under paragraph (3)(C) or subsection (d)(12) by reason of such direct transfer.

(D)(i) Any distribution that qualifies as an eligible rollover distribution within the meaning of section 402(c) of the Internal Revenue Code of 1986 or that is described in clause (ii) shall not cease to qualify for exemption under paragraph (3)(C) or subsection (d)(12) by reason of such distribution.

(ii) A distribution described in this clause is an amount that—

(I) has been distributed from a fund or account that is exempt from taxation under section 401, 403, 408, 408A, 414, 457, or 501(a) of the Internal Revenue Code of 1986; and

(II) to the extent allowed by law, is deposited in such a fund or account not later than 60 days after the distribution of such amount.

(c) Unless the case is dismissed, property exempted under this section is not liable during or after the case for any debt of the debtor that arose, or that is determined under section 502 of this title as if such debt had arisen, before the commencement of the case, except—

(1) a debt of a kind specified in paragraph (1) or (5) of section 523(a) (in which case, notwithstanding any provision of applicable nonbankruptcy law to the contrary, such property shall be liable for a debt of a kind specified in such paragraph);

(2)　a debt secured by a lien that is—

(A)(i)　　not avoided under subsection (f) or (g) of this section or under section 544, 545, 547, 548, 549, or 724(a) of this title; and

(ii)　not void under section 506(d) of this title; or

(B)　a tax lien, notice of which is properly filed;

(3)　a debt of a kind specified in section 523(a)(4) or 523(a)(6) of this title owed by an institution-affiliated party of an insured depository institution to a Federal depository institutions regulatory agency acting in its capacity as conservator, receiver, or liquidating agent for such institution; or

(4)　a debt in connection with fraud in the obtaining or providing of any scholarship, grant, loan, tuition, discount, award, or other financial assistance for purposes of financing an education at an institution of higher education (as that term is defined in section 101 of the Higher Education Act of 1965 (20 U.S.C. 1001)).

(d)　The following property may be exempted under subsection (b)(2) of this section:

(1)　The debtor's aggregate interest, not to exceed $27,900 in value, in real property or personal property that the debtor or a dependent of the debtor uses as a residence, in a cooperative that owns property that the debtor or a dependent of the debtor uses as a residence, or in a burial plot for the debtor or a dependent of the debtor.

(2)　The debtor's interest, not to exceed $4,450 in value, in one motor vehicle.

(3)　The debtor's interest, not to exceed $700 in value in any particular item or $14,875 in aggregate value, in household furnishings, household goods, wearing apparel, appliances, books, animals, crops, or musical instruments, that are held primarily for the personal, family, or household use of the debtor or a dependent of the debtor.

(4)　The debtor's aggregate interest, not to exceed $1,875 in value, in jewelry held primarily for the personal, family, or household use of the debtor or a dependent of the debtor.

(5)　The debtor's aggregate interest in any property, not to exceed in value $1,475 plus up to $13,950 of any unused amount of the exemption provided under paragraph (1) of this subsection.

(6)　The debtor's aggregate interest, not to exceed $2,800 in value, in any implements, professional books, or tools, of the trade of the debtor or the trade of a dependent of the debtor.

(7)　Any unmatured life insurance contract owned by the debtor, other than a credit life insurance contract.

(8)　The debtor's aggregate interest, not to exceed in value $14,875 less any amount of property of the estate transferred in the manner specified in section 542(d) of this title, in any accrued dividend or interest under, or loan value of, any unmatured life insurance contract owned by the debtor under which the insured is the debtor or an individual of whom the debtor is a dependent.

(9)　Professionally prescribed health aids for the debtor or a dependent of the debtor.

(10)　The debtor's right to receive—

(A)　a social security benefit, unemployment compensation, or a local public assistance benefit;

(B)　a veterans' benefit;

(C)　a disability, illness, or unemployment benefit;

(D) alimony, support, or separate maintenance, to the extent reasonably necessary for the support of the debtor and any dependent of the debtor;

(E) a payment under a stock bonus, pension, profitsharing, annuity, or similar plan or contract on account of illness, disability, death, age, or length of service, to the extent reasonably necessary for the support of the debtor and any dependent of the debtor, unless—

　(i) such plan or contract was established by or under the auspices of an insider that employed the debtor at the time the debtor's rights under such plan or contract arose;

　(ii) such payment is on account of age or length of service; and

　(iii) such plan or contract does not qualify under section 401(a), 403(a), 403(b), or 408 of the Internal Revenue Code of 1986.

(11) The debtor's right to receive, or property that is traceable to—

(A) an award under a crime victim's reparation law;

(B) a payment on account of the wrongful death of an individual of whom the debtor was a dependent, to the extent reasonably necessary for the support of the debtor and any dependent of the debtor;

(C) a payment under a life insurance contract that insured the life of an individual of whom the debtor was a dependent on the date of such individual's death, to the extent reasonably necessary for the support of the debtor and any dependent of the debtor;

(D) a payment, not to exceed $27,900, on account of personal bodily injury, not including pain and suffering or compensation for actual pecuniary loss, of the debtor or an individual of whom the debtor is a dependent; or

(E) a payment in compensation of loss of future earnings of the debtor or an individual of whom the debtor is or was a dependent, to the extent reasonably necessary for the support of the debtor and any dependent of the debtor.

(12) Retirement funds to the extent that those funds are in a fund or account that is exempt from taxation under section 401, 403, 408, 408A, 414, 457, or 501(a) of the Internal Revenue Code of 1986.

(e) A waiver of an exemption executed in favor of a creditor that holds an unsecured claim against the debtor is unenforceable in a case under this title with respect to such claim against property that the debtor may exempt under subsection (b) of this section. A waiver by the debtor of a power under subsection (f) or (h) of this section to avoid a transfer, under subsection (g) or (i) of this section to exempt property, or under subsection (i) of this section to recover property or to preserve a transfer, is unenforceable in a case under this title.

(f)(1)　　Notwithstanding any waiver of exemptions but subject to paragraph (3), the debtor may avoid the fixing of a lien on an interest of the debtor in property to the extent that such lien impairs an exemption to which the debtor would have been entitled under subsection (b) of this section, if such lien is—

(A) a judicial lien, other than a judicial lien that secures a debt of a kind that is specified in section 523(a)(5); or

(B) a nonpossessory, nonpurchase-money security interest in any—

　(i) household furnishings, household goods, wearing apparel, appliances, books, animals, crops, musical instruments, or jewelry that are held primarily for the personal, family, or household use of the debtor or a dependent of the debtor;

　(ii) implements, professional books, or tools, of the trade of the debtor or the trade of a dependent of the debtor; or

(iii) professionally prescribed health aids for the debtor or a dependent of the debtor.

(2)(A)   For the purposes of this subsection, a lien shall be considered to impair an exemption to the extent that the sum of—

(i)   the lien;

(ii)   all other liens on the property; and

(iii) the amount of the exemption that the debtor could claim if there were no liens on the property;

exceeds the value that the debtor's interest in the property would have in the absence of any liens.

(B) In the case of a property subject to more than 1 lien, a lien that has been avoided shall not be considered in making the calculation under subparagraph (A) with respect to other liens.

(C) This paragraph shall not apply with respect to a judgment arising out of a mortgage foreclosure.

(3) In a case in which State law that is applicable to the debtor—

(A) permits a person to voluntarily waive a right to claim exemptions under subsection (d) or prohibits a debtor from claiming exemptions under subsection (d); and

(B) either permits the debtor to claim exemptions under State law without limitation in amount, except to the extent that the debtor has permitted the fixing of a consensual lien on any property or prohibits avoidance of a consensual lien on property otherwise eligible to be claimed as exempt property;

the debtor may not avoid the fixing of a lien on an interest of the debtor or a dependent of the debtor in property if the lien is a nonpossessory, nonpurchase-money security interest in implements, professional books, or tools of the trade of the debtor or a dependent of the debtor or farm animals or crops of the debtor or a dependent of the debtor to the extent the value of such implements, professional books, tools of the trade, animals, and crops exceeds $7,575.

(4)(A)   Subject to subparagraph (B), for purposes of paragraph (1)(B), the term "household goods" means—

(i)   clothing;

(ii)   furniture;

(iii)   appliances;

(iv)   1 radio;

(v)   1 television;

(vi)   1 VCR;

(vii)   linens;

(viii) china;

(ix)   crockery;

(x)   kitchenware;

(xi)   educational materials and educational equipment primarily for the use of minor dependent children of the debtor;

(xii)   medical equipment and supplies;

(xiii) furniture exclusively for the use of minor children, or elderly or disabled dependents of the debtor;

(xiv) personal effects (including the toys and hobby equipment of minor dependent children and wedding rings) of the debtor and the dependents of the debtor; and

(xv) 1 personal computer and related equipment.

(B) The term "household goods" does not include—

(i) works of art (unless by or of the debtor, or any relative of the debtor);

(ii) electronic entertainment equipment with a fair market value of more than $800 in the aggregate (except 1 television, 1 radio, and 1 VCR);

(iii) items acquired as antiques with a fair market value of more than $800 in the aggregate;

(iv) jewelry with a fair market value of more than $800 in the aggregate (except wedding rings); and

(v) a computer (except as otherwise provided for in this section), motor vehicle (including a tractor or lawn tractor), boat, or a motorized recreational device, conveyance, vehicle, watercraft, or aircraft.

(g) Notwithstanding sections 550 and 551 of this title, the debtor may exempt under subsection (b) of this section property that the trustee recovers under section 510(c)(2), 542, 543, 550, 551, or 553 of this title, to the extent that the debtor could have exempted such property under subsection (b) of this section if such property had not been transferred, if—

(1)(A) such transfer was not a voluntary transfer of such property by the debtor; and

(B) the debtor did not conceal such property; or

(2) the debtor could have avoided such transfer under subsection (f)(1)(B) of this section.

(h) The debtor may avoid a transfer of property of the debtor or recover a setoff to the extent that the debtor could have exempted such property under subsection (g)(1) of this section if the trustee had avoided such transfer, if—

(1) such transfer is avoidable by the trustee under section 544, 545, 547, 548, 549, or 724(a) of this title or recoverable by the trustee under section 553 of this title; and

(2) the trustee does not attempt to avoid such transfer.

(i)(1) If the debtor avoids a transfer or recovers a setoff under subsection (f) or (h) of this section, the debtor may recover in the manner prescribed by, and subject to the limitations of, section 550 of this title, the same as if the trustee had avoided such transfer, and may exempt any property so recovered under subsection (b) of this section.

(2) Notwithstanding section 551 of this title, a transfer avoided under section 544, 545, 547, 548, 549, or 724(a) of this title, under subsection (f) or (h) of this section, or property recovered under section 553 of this title, may be preserved for the benefit of the debtor to the extent that the debtor may exempt such property under subsection (g) of this section or paragraph (1) of this subsection.

(j) Notwithstanding subsections (g) and (i) of this section, the debtor may exempt a particular kind of property under subsections (g) and (i) of this section only to the extent that the debtor has exempted less property in value of such kind than that to which the debtor is entitled under subsection (b) of this section.

(k) Property that the debtor exempts under this section is not liable for payment of any administrative expense except—

(1) the aliquot share of the costs and expenses of avoiding a transfer of property that the debtor exempts under subsection (g) of this section, or of recovery of such property, that is attributable to the value of the portion of such property exempted in relation to the value of the property recovered; and

(2) any costs and expenses of avoiding a transfer under subsection (f) or (h) of this section, or of recovery of property under subsection (i)(1) of this section, that the debtor has not paid.

(*l*) The debtor shall file a list of property that the debtor claims as exempt under subsection (b) of this section. If the debtor does not file such a list, a dependent of the debtor may file such a list, or may claim property as exempt from property of the estate on behalf of the debtor. Unless a party in interest objects, the property claimed as exempt on such list is exempt.

(m) Subject to the limitation in subsection (b), this section shall apply separately with respect to each debtor in a joint case.

(n) For assets in individual retirement accounts described in section 408 or 408A of the Internal Revenue Code of 1986, other than a simplified employee pension under section 408(k) of such Code or a simple retirement account under section 408(p) of such Code, the aggregate value of such assets exempted under this section, without regard to amounts attributable to rollover contributions under section 402(c), 402(e)(6), 403(a)(4), 403(a)(5), and 403(b)(8) of the Internal Revenue Code of 1986, and earnings thereon, shall not exceed $1,512,350 in a case filed by a debtor who is an individual, except that such amount may be increased if the interests of justice so require.

(o) For purposes of subsection (b)(3)(A), and notwithstanding subsection (a), the value of an interest in—

(1) real or personal property that the debtor or a dependent of the debtor uses as a residence;

(2) a cooperative that owns property that the debtor or a dependent of the debtor uses as a residence;

(3) a burial plot for the debtor or a dependent of the debtor; or

(4) real or personal property that the debtor or a dependent of the debtor claims as a homestead;

shall be reduced to the extent that such value is attributable to any portion of any property that the debtor disposed of in the 10-year period ending on the date of the filing of the petition with the intent to hinder, delay, or defraud a creditor and that the debtor could not exempt, or that portion that the debtor could not exempt, under subsection (b), if on such date the debtor had held the property so disposed of.

(p)(1) Except as provided in paragraph (2) of this subsection and sections 544 and 548, as a result of electing under subsection (b)(3)(A) to exempt property under State or local law, a debtor may not exempt any amount of interest that was acquired by the debtor during the 1215-day period preceding the date of the filing of the petition that exceeds in the aggregate $189,050 in value in—

(A) real or personal property that the debtor or a dependent of the debtor uses as a residence;

(B) a cooperative that owns property that the debtor or a dependent of the debtor uses as a residence;

(C) a burial plot for the debtor or a dependent of the debtor; or

(D) real or personal property that the debtor or dependent of the debtor claims as a homestead.

(2)(A) The limitation under paragraph (1) shall not apply to an exemption claimed under subsection (b)(3)(A) by a family farmer for the principal residence of such farmer.

(B) For purposes of paragraph (1), any amount of such interest does not include any interest transferred from a debtor's previous principal residence (which was acquired prior to the beginning of such 1215-day period) into the debtor's current principal residence, if the debtor's previous and current residences are located in the same State.

(q)(1)   As a result of electing under subsection (b)(3)(A) to exempt property under State or local law, a debtor may not exempt any amount of an interest in property described in subparagraphs (A), (B), (C), and (D) of subsection (p)(1) which exceeds in the aggregate $189,050 if—

(A) the court determines, after notice and a hearing, that the debtor has been convicted of a felony (as defined in section 3156 of title 18), which under the circumstances, demonstrates that the filing of the case was an abuse of the provisions of this title; or

(B) the debtor owes a debt arising from—

(i) any violation of the Federal securities laws (as defined in section 3(a)(47) of the Securities Exchange Act of 1934), any State securities laws, or any regulation or order issued under Federal securities laws or State securities laws;

(ii) fraud, deceit, or manipulation in a fiduciary capacity or in connection with the purchase or sale of any security registered under section 12 or 15(d) of the Securities Exchange Act of 1934 or under section 6 of the Securities Act of 1933;

(iii) any civil remedy under section 1964 of title 18; or

(iv) any criminal act, intentional tort, or willful or reckless misconduct that caused serious physical injury or death to another individual in the preceding 5 years.

(2) Paragraph (1) shall not apply to the extent the amount of an interest in property described in subparagraphs (A), (B), (C), and (D) of subsection (p)(1) is reasonably necessary for the support of the debtor and any dependent of the debtor.

REFERENCES IN TEXT

Section 401, 403, 408, 408A, 414, 457, or 501(a) of the Internal Revenue Code of 1986, referred to in subsecs. (b)(3)(C), (4)(C), (D)(ii)(I), (d)(12), is classified to 26 U.S.C.A. § 401, 403, 408, 408A, 414, 457, or 501(a).

Section 7805 of the Internal Revenue Code of 1986, referred to in subsec. (b)(4)(A), (B), is 26 U.S.C.A. § 7805.

The Internal Revenue Code of 1986, referred to in subsec. (b)(4)(B)(ii)(I), (II), is classified to Title 26 of the Code.

Section 402(c) of the Internal Revenue Code of 1986, referred to in subsec. (b)(4)(D)(i), is 26 U.S.C.A. § 402(c).

Section 401(a), 403(a), 403(b), or 408, of the Internal Revenue Code of 1986, referred to in subsec. (d)(10)(E)(iii), is classified to 26 U.S.C.A. § 401(a), 403(a), 403(b), or 408.

Section 408 or 408A of the Internal Revenue Code of 1986, referred to in subsec. (n), is classified to 26 U.S.C.A. § 408 or 408A.

Section 402(c), 402(e)(6), 403(a)(4), 403(a)(5), and 403(b)(8) of the Internal Revenue Code of 1986, referred to in subsec. (n), are classified to 26 U.S.C.A. §§ 402(c), 402(e)(6), 403(a)(4), 403(a)(5), and 403(b)(8).

Section 3(a)(47) of the Securities Exchange Act of 1934, referred to in subsec. (q)(1)(B)(i), is June 6, 1934, c. 404, Title I, § 3(a)(47), 48 Stat. 882, as amended, which is classified to 15 U.S.C.A. § 78c(a)(47).

Section 12 or 15(d) of the Securities Exchange Act of 1934, referred to in subsec. (q)(1)(B)(ii), is June 6, 1934, c. 404, Title I, § 12 or 15, 48 Stat. 892 or 895, as amended, which is classified to 15 U.S.C.A. § 78l or 15 U.S.C.A. § 78o.

Section 6 of the Securities Act of 1933, referred to in subsec. (q)(1)(B)(ii), is Act May 27, 1933, c. 38, Title I, § 6, 48 Stat. 78, which is classified to 15 U.S.C.A. § 77f.

CROSS REFERENCES

Allowance of claims or interests, see 11 USCA § 502.

Automatic preservation of avoided transfer, see 11 USCA § 551.

Effect of dismissal, see 11 USCA § 349.

Election to terminate debtor's taxable year for purposes of Internal Revenue Code not available to debtor with no assets other than property treated as exempt under this section, see 26 USCA § 1398.

Exempt property as including property treated as exempt under this section for purposes of Federal Debt Collection Act, see 28 USCA § 3014.

Insolvent as meaning financial condition wherein entity's debts are greater than entity's property exclusive of property that may be exempted under this section, see 11 USCA § 101.

Involuntary cases and future adjustments, see 11 USCA § 104.

Penalty for persons who negligently or fraudulently prepare bankruptcy petitions and exempt funds, see 11 USCA § 110.

Postpetition effect of security interest, see 11 USCA § 552.

Property claimed as exempt, see Official Bankruptcy Form 106C.

Property exempt under this section not subject to enforcement of withdrawal liability for purposes of Employee Retirement Income Security Act Program, see 29 USCA § 1405.

Provisions in plan for use, sale or lease of exempt property in individual non-subchapter V cases, see 11 USCA § 1123.

Redemption, see 11 USCA § 722.

Reduction in basis not allowed for property exempt under this section for purposes of Internal Revenue Code, see 26 USCA § 1017.

Turnover of property to estate, see 11 USCA § 542.

§ 523.　Exceptions to discharge

(a)　A discharge under section 727, 1141, 1192, 1228(a), 1228(b), or 1328(b) of this title does not discharge an individual debtor from any debt—

　(1)　for a tax or a customs duty—

　　(A)　of the kind and for the periods specified in section 507(a)(3) or 507(a)(8) of this title, whether or not a claim for such tax was filed or allowed;

　　(B)　with respect to which a return, or equivalent report or notice, if required—

　　　(i)　was not filed or given; or

　　　(ii)　was filed or given after the date on which such return, report, or notice was last due, under applicable law or under any extension, and after two years before the date of the filing of the petition; or

　　(C)　with respect to which the debtor made a fraudulent return or willfully attempted in any manner to evade or defeat such tax;

　(2)　for money, property, services, or an extension, renewal, or refinancing of credit, to the extent obtained by—

　　(A)　false pretenses, a false representation, or actual fraud, other than a statement respecting the debtor's or an insider's financial condition;

　　(B)　use of a statement in writing—

　　　(i)　that is materially false;

　　　(ii)　respecting the debtor's or an insider's financial condition;

　　　(iii)　on which the creditor to whom the debtor is liable for such money, property, services, or credit reasonably relied; and

    (iv) that the debtor caused to be made or published with intent to deceive; or

(C)(i)   for purposes of subparagraph (A)—

    (I) consumer debts owed to a single creditor and aggregating more than $800 for luxury goods or services incurred by an individual debtor on or within 90 days before the order for relief under this title are presumed to be nondischargeable; and

    (II) cash advances aggregating more than $1,100 that are extensions of consumer credit under an open end credit plan obtained by an individual debtor on or within 70 days before the order for relief under this title, are presumed to be nondischargeable; and

    (ii) for purposes of this subparagraph—

    (I) the terms "consumer", "credit", and "open end credit plan" have the same meanings as in section 103 of the Truth in Lending Act; and

    (II) the term "luxury goods or services" does not include goods or services reasonably necessary for the support or maintenance of the debtor or a dependent of the debtor;

    (3) neither listed nor scheduled under section 521(a)(1) of this title, with the name, if known to the debtor, of the creditor to whom such debt is owed, in time to permit—

    (A) if such debt is not of a kind specified in paragraph (2), (4), or (6) of this subsection, timely filing of a proof of claim, unless such creditor had notice or actual knowledge of the case in time for such timely filing; or

    (B) if such debt is of a kind specified in paragraph (2), (4), or (6) of this subsection, timely filing of a proof of claim and timely request for a determination of dischargeability of such debt under one of such paragraphs, unless such creditor had notice or actual knowledge of the case in time for such timely filing and request;

    (4) for fraud or defalcation while acting in a fiduciary capacity, embezzlement, or larceny;

    (5) for a domestic support obligation;

    (6) for willful and malicious injury by the debtor to another entity or to the property of another entity;

    (7) to the extent such debt is for a fine, penalty, or forfeiture payable to and for the benefit of a governmental unit, and is not compensation for actual pecuniary loss, other than a tax penalty—

    (A) relating to a tax of a kind not specified in paragraph (1) of this subsection; or

    (B) imposed with respect to a transaction or event that occurred before three years before the date of the filing of the petition;

    (8) unless excepting such debt from discharge under this paragraph would impose an undue hardship on the debtor and the debtor's dependents, for—

    (A)(i) an educational benefit overpayment or loan made, insured, or guaranteed by a governmental unit, or made under any program funded in whole or in part by a governmental unit or nonprofit institution; or

    (ii) an obligation to repay funds received as an educational benefit, scholarship, or stipend; or

    (B) any other educational loan that is a qualified education loan, as defined in section 221(d)(1) of the Internal Revenue Code of 1986, incurred by a debtor who is an individual;

(9) for death or personal injury caused by the debtor's operation of a motor vehicle, vessel, or aircraft if such operation was unlawful because the debtor was intoxicated from using alcohol, a drug, or another substance;

(10) that was or could have been listed or scheduled by the debtor in a prior case concerning the debtor under this title or under the Bankruptcy Act in which the debtor waived discharge, or was denied a discharge under section 727(a)(2), (3), (4), (5), (6), or (7) of this title, or under section 14c(1), (2), (3), (4), (6), or (7) of such Act;

(11) provided in any final judgment, unreviewable order, or consent order or decree entered in any court of the United States or of any State, issued by a Federal depository institutions regulatory agency, or contained in any settlement agreement entered into by the debtor, arising from any act of fraud or defalcation while acting in a fiduciary capacity committed with respect to any depository institution or insured credit union;

(12) for malicious or reckless failure to fulfill any commitment by the debtor to a Federal depository institutions regulatory agency to maintain the capital of an insured depository institution, except that this paragraph shall not extend any such commitment which would otherwise be terminated due to any act of such agency;

(13) for any payment of an order of restitution issued under title 18, United States Code;

(14) incurred to pay a tax to the United States that would be nondischargeable pursuant to paragraph (1);

(14A) incurred to pay a tax to a governmental unit, other than the United States, that would be nondischargeable under paragraph (1);

(14B) incurred to pay fines or penalties imposed under Federal election law;

(15) to a spouse, former spouse, or child of the debtor and not of the kind described in paragraph (5) that is incurred by the debtor in the course of a divorce or separation or in connection with a separation agreement, divorce decree or other order of a court of record, or a determination made in accordance with State or territorial law by a governmental unit;

(16) for a fee or assessment that becomes due and payable after the order for relief to a membership association with respect to the debtor's interest in a unit that has condominium ownership, in a share of a cooperative corporation, or a lot in a homeowners association, for as long as the debtor or the trustee has a legal, equitable, or possessory ownership interest in such unit, such corporation, or such lot, but nothing in this paragraph shall except from discharge the debt of a debtor for a membership association fee or assessment for a period arising before entry of the order for relief in a pending or subsequent bankruptcy case;

(17) for a fee imposed on a prisoner by any court for the filing of a case, motion, complaint, or appeal, or for other costs and expenses assessed with respect to such filing, regardless of an assertion of poverty by the debtor under subsection (b) or (f)(2) of section 1915 of title 28 (or a similar non-Federal law), or the debtor's status as a prisoner, as defined in section 1915(h) of title 28 (or a similar non-Federal law);

(18) owed to a pension, profit-sharing, stock bonus, or other plan established under section 401, 403, 408, 408A, 414, 457, or 501(c) of the Internal Revenue Code of 1986, under—

    (A) a loan permitted under section 408(b)(1) of the Employee Retirement Income Security Act of 1974, or subject to section 72(p) of the Internal Revenue Code of 1986; or

    (B) a loan from a thrift savings plan permitted under subchapter III of chapter 84 of title 5, that satisfies the requirements of section 8433(g) of such title;

but nothing in this paragraph may be construed to provide that any loan made under a governmental plan under section 414(d), or a contract or account under section 403(b), of the Internal Revenue Code of 1986 constitutes a claim or a debt under this title; or

(19) that—

(A) is for—

(i) the violation of any of the Federal securities laws (as that term is defined in section 3(a)(47) of the Securities Exchange Act of 1934), any of the State securities laws, or any regulation or order issued under such Federal or State securities laws; or

(ii) common law fraud, deceit, or manipulation in connection with the purchase or sale of any security; and

(B) results, before, on, or after the date on which the petition was filed, from—

(i) any judgment, order, consent order, or decree entered in any Federal or State judicial or administrative proceeding;

(ii) any settlement agreement entered into by the debtor; or

(iii) any court or administrative order for any damages, fine, penalty, citation, restitutionary payment, disgorgement payment, attorney fee, cost, or other payment owed by the debtor.

For purposes of this subsection, the term "return" means a return that satisfies the requirements of applicable nonbankruptcy law (including applicable filing requirements). Such term includes a return prepared pursuant to section 6020(a) of the Internal Revenue Code of 1986, or similar State or local law, or a written stipulation to a judgment or a final order entered by a nonbankruptcy tribunal, but does not include a return made pursuant to section 6020(b) of the Internal Revenue Code of 1986, or a similar State or local law.

(b) Notwithstanding subsection (a) of this section, a debt that was excepted from discharge under subsection (a)(1), (a)(3), or (a)(8) of this section, under section 17a(1), 17a(3), or 17a(5) of the Bankruptcy Act, under section 439A of the Higher Education Act of 1965, or under section 733(g) of the Public Health Service Act in a prior case concerning the debtor under this title, or under the Bankruptcy Act, is dischargeable in a case under this title unless, by the terms of subsection (a) of this section, such debt is not dischargeable in the case under this title.

(c)(1) Except as provided in subsection (a)(3)(B) of this section, the debtor shall be discharged from a debt of a kind specified in paragraph (2), (4), or (6) of subsection (a) of this section, unless, on request of the creditor to whom such debt is owed, and after notice and a hearing, the court determines such debt to be excepted from discharge under paragraph (2), (4), or (6), as the case may be, of subsection (a) of this section.

(2) Paragraph (1) shall not apply in the case of a Federal depository institutions regulatory agency seeking, in its capacity as conservator, receiver, or liquidating agent for an insured depository institution, to recover a debt described in subsection (a)(2), (a)(4), (a)(6), or (a)(11) owed to such institution by an institution-affiliated party unless the receiver, conservator, or liquidating agent was appointed in time to reasonably comply, or for a Federal depository institutions regulatory agency acting in its corporate capacity as a successor to such receiver, conservator, or liquidating agent to reasonably comply, with subsection (a)(3)(B) as a creditor of such institution-affiliated party with respect to such debt.

(d) If a creditor requests a determination of dischargeability of a consumer debt under subsection (a)(2) of this section, and such debt is discharged, the court shall grant judgment in favor of the debtor for the costs of, and a reasonable attorney's fee for, the proceeding if the court finds that the position of the creditor was not substantially justified, except that the court shall not award such costs and fees if special circumstances would make the award unjust.

(e) Any institution-affiliated party of an insured depository institution shall be considered to be acting in a fiduciary capacity with respect to the purposes of subsection (a)(4) or (11).

REFERENCES IN TEXT

Section 6020(a) of the Internal Revenue Code of 1986, referred to in subsec. (a), is classified to 26 U.S.C.A. § 6020(a).

Section 6020(b) of the Internal Revenue Code of 1986, referred to in subsec. (a), is classified to 26 U.S.C.A. § 6020(b).

The Consumer Credit Protection Act, referred to in subsec. (a)(2)(C), is Pub. L. 90–321, May 29, 1968, 82 Stat. 146, as amended, which is classified principally to chapter 41 (section 1601 et seq.) of Title 15, Commerce and Trade. For complete classification of this Act to the Code, see Short Title note set out under section 1601 of Title 15 and Tables.

Section 103 of the Truth in Lending Act, referred to in subsec. (a)(2)(C)(ii)(I), is Pub. L. 90–321, Title I, § 103, May 29, 1968, 82 Stat. 147, as amended, which is classified to 15 U.S.C.A. § 1602.

The Social Security Act, referred to in subsec. (a)(5)(A), (18)(B), is Act Aug. 14, 1935, c. 531, 49 Stat. 620, as amended. Section 408(a)(3) of that Act is classified to section 608(a)(3) of Title 42, The Public Health and Welfare. Part D of Title IV of such Act is classified generally to part D (section 651 et seq.) of subchapter IV of chapter 7 of Title 42. For complete classification of this Act to the Code, see section 1305 of Title 42 and Tables.

Section 221(d)(1) of the Internal Revenue Code of 1986, referred to in subsec. (a)(8)(B), is classified to 26 U.S.C.A. § 221(d)(1).

The Bankruptcy Act, referred to in subsecs. (a)(10) and (b), is Act July 1, 1898, c. 541, 30 Stat. 544, as amended, which was classified generally to former Title 11. Sections 14c and 17a of the Bankruptcy Act were classified to sections 32(c) and 35(a) of former Title 11.

Section 401, 403, 408, 408A, 414, 457, or 501(c) of the Internal Revenue Code of 1986, referred to in subsec. (a)(18), is classified to 26 U.S.C.A. § 401, 403, 408, 408A, 414, 457, or 501(c).

Section 408(b)(1) of the Employee Retirement Income Security Act of 1974, referred to in subsec. (a)(18)(A), is Pub. L. 93–406, Title I, § 408(b)(1), Sept. 2, 1974, 88 Stat. 883, as amended, which is classified to 29 U.S.C.A. § 1108(b)(1).

Section 72(p) of the Internal Revenue Code of 1986, referred to in subsec. (a)(18)(A), is classified to 26 U.S.C.A. § 72(p).

Subchapter III of chapter 84 of title 5, referred to in subsec. (a)(18)(B), is 5 U.S.C.A. § 8431 et seq.

Section 414(d) or section 403(b) of the Internal Revenue Code, referred to in the undesignated paragraph following subsec. (a)(18), is classified to 26 U.S.C.A. § 414(d) or 26 U.S.C.A. § 403(b).

Section 3(a)(47) of the Securities Exchange Act of 1934, referred to in subsec. (a)(19)(A)(i), is section 3(a)(47) of Act June 6, 1934, c. 404, Title I, 48 Stat. 882, as amended, which is classified to 15 U.S.C.A. § 78c(a)(47).

Section 439A of the Higher Education Act of 1965, referred to in subsec. (b), is section 439A of Pub. L. 89–329, Title IV, as added Pub. L. 94–482, Title I, § 127(a), Oct. 12, 1976, 90 Stat. 2141, which was classified to section 1087–3 of Title 20, Education, and was repealed by Pub. L. 95–598, Title III, § 317, Nov. 6, 1978, 92 Stat. 2678.

Section 733 of the Public Health Service Act, referred to in subsec. (b), is section 733 of Act July 1, 1944, c. 373, Title VII as added Oct. 12, 1976, Pub. L. 94–484, Title IV, § 401(b)(3), 90 Stat. 2262, which was classified to section 294f of Title 42, The Public Health and Welfare, and which was repealed by Pub. L. 95–598, Title III, § 327, Nov. 6, 1978, 92 Stat. 2679. A subsec. (g), containing similar provisions, was added to section 733 by Pub. L. 97–35, Title XXVII, § 2730, Aug. 13, 1981, 95 Stat. 919. Section 733 was subsequently omitted in the general revision of subchapter V of chapter 6A of Title 42 by Pub. L. 102–408, Title I, § 102, Oct. 13, 1992, 106 Stat. 1992.

CROSS REFERENCES

Disallowance of claim to extent claim is for unmatured debt and excepted from discharge as debt for alimony, maintenance or support, see 11 USCA § 502.

Discharge of debtor—

    Chapter 7 cases, see 11 USCA § 727.

    Chapter 12 cases, see 11 USCA § 1228.

    Chapter 13 cases, see 11 USCA § 1328.

Effect of confirmation, see 11 USCA § 1141.

Extent of priorities for unsecured claims of governmental units, see 11 USCA § 507.

Involuntary cases and future adjustments, see 11 USCA § 104.

§ 524. Effect of discharge

(a) A discharge in a case under this title—

(1) voids any judgment at any time obtained, to the extent that such judgment is a determination of the personal liability of the debtor with respect to any debt discharged under section 727, 944, 1141, 1192, 1228, or 1328 of this title, whether or not discharge of such debt is waived;

(2) operates as an injunction against the commencement or continuation of an action, the employment of process, or an act, to collect, recover or offset any such debt as a personal liability of the debtor, whether or not discharge of such debt is waived; and

(3) operates as an injunction against the commencement or continuation of an action, the employment of process, or an act, to collect or recover from, or offset against, property of the debtor of the kind specified in section 541(a)(2) of this title that is acquired after the commencement of the case, on account of any allowable community claim, except a community claim that is excepted from discharge under section 523, 1192, 1228(a)(1), or 1328(a)(1), or that would be so excepted, determined in accordance with the provisions of sections 523(c) and 523(d) of this title, in a case concerning the debtor's spouse commenced on the date of the filing of the petition in the case concerning the debtor, whether or not discharge of the debt based on such community claim is waived.

(b) Subsection (a)(3) of this section does not apply if—

(1)(A) the debtor's spouse is a debtor in a case under this title, or a bankrupt or a debtor in a case under the Bankruptcy Act, commenced within six years of the date of the filing of the petition in the case concerning the debtor; and

(B) the court does not grant the debtor's spouse a discharge in such case concerning the debtor's spouse; or

(2)(A) the court would not grant the debtor's spouse a discharge in a case under chapter 7 of this title concerning such spouse commenced on the date of the filing of the petition in the case concerning the debtor; and

(B) a determination that the court would not so grant such discharge is made by the bankruptcy court within the time and in the manner provided for a determination under section 727 of this title of whether a debtor is granted a discharge.

(c) An agreement between a holder of a claim and the debtor, the consideration for which, in whole or in part, is based on a debt that is dischargeable in a case under this title is enforceable only to any extent enforceable under applicable nonbankruptcy law, whether or not discharge of such debt is waived, only if—

(1)   such agreement was made before the granting of the discharge under section 727, 1141, 1192, 1228, or 1328 of this title;

(2)   the debtor received the disclosures described in subsection (k) at or before the time at which the debtor signed the agreement;

(3)   such agreement has been filed with the court and, if applicable, accompanied by a declaration or an affidavit of the attorney that represented the debtor during the course of negotiating an agreement under this subsection, which states that—

(A)   such agreement represents a fully informed and voluntary agreement by the debtor;

(B)   such agreement does not impose an undue hardship on the debtor or a dependent of the debtor; and

(C)   the attorney fully advised the debtor of the legal effect and consequences of—

(i)   an agreement of the kind specified in this subsection; and

(ii)   any default under such an agreement;

(4)   the debtor has not rescinded such agreement at any time prior to discharge or within sixty days after such agreement is filed with the court, whichever occurs later, by giving notice of rescission to the holder of such claim;

(5)   the provisions of subsection (d) of this section have been complied with; and

(6)(A)   in a case concerning an individual who was not represented by an attorney during the course of negotiating an agreement under this subsection, the court approves such agreement as—

(i)   not imposing an undue hardship on the debtor or a dependent of the debtor; and

(ii)   in the best interest of the debtor.

(B)   Subparagraph (A) shall not apply to the extent that such debt is a consumer debt secured by real property.

(d)   In a case concerning an individual, when the court has determined whether to grant or not to grant a discharge under section 727, 1141, 1192, 1228, or 1328 of this title, the court may hold a hearing at which the debtor shall appear in person. At any such hearing, the court shall inform the debtor that a discharge has been granted or the reason why a discharge has not been granted. If a discharge has been granted and if the debtor desires to make an agreement of the kind specified in subsection (c) of this section and was not represented by an attorney during the course of negotiating such agreement, then the court shall hold a hearing at which the debtor shall appear in person and at such hearing the court shall—

(1)   inform the debtor—

(A)   that such an agreement is not required under this title, under nonbankruptcy law, or under any agreement not made in accordance with the provisions of subsection (c) of this section; and

(B)   of the legal effect and consequences of—

(i)   an agreement of the kind specified in subsection (c) of this section; and

(ii)   a default under such an agreement; and

(2)   determine whether the agreement that the debtor desires to make complies with the requirements of subsection (c)(6) of this section, if the consideration for such agreement is based in whole or in part on a consumer debt that is not secured by real property of the debtor.

(e) Except as provided in subsection (a)(3) of this section, discharge of a debt of the debtor does not affect the liability of any other entity on, or the property of any other entity for, such debt.

(f) Nothing contained in subsection (c) or (d) of this section prevents a debtor from voluntarily repaying any debt.

(g)(1)(A) After notice and hearing, a court that enters an order confirming a plan of reorganization under chapter 11 may issue, in connection with such order, an injunction in accordance with this subsection to supplement the injunctive effect of a discharge under this section.

(B) An injunction may be issued under subparagraph (A) to enjoin entities from taking legal action for the purpose of directly or indirectly collecting, recovering, or receiving payment or recovery with respect to any claim or demand that, under a plan of reorganization, is to be paid in whole or in part by a trust described in paragraph (2)(B)(i), except such legal actions as are expressly allowed by the injunction, the confirmation order, or the plan of reorganization.

(2)(A) Subject to subsection (h), if the requirements of subparagraph (B) are met at the time an injunction described in paragraph (1) is entered, then after entry of such injunction, any proceeding that involves the validity, application, construction, or modification of such injunction, or of this subsection with respect to such injunction, may be commenced only in the district court in which such injunction was entered, and such court shall have exclusive jurisdiction over any such proceeding without regard to the amount in controversy.

(B) The requirements of this subparagraph are that—

(i) the injunction is to be implemented in connection with a trust that, pursuant to the plan of reorganization—

(I) is to assume the liabilities of a debtor which at the time of entry of the order for relief has been named as a defendant in personal injury, wrongful death, or property-damage actions seeking recovery for damages allegedly caused by the presence of, or exposure to, asbestos or asbestos-containing products;

(II) is to be funded in whole or in part by the securities of 1 or more debtors involved in such plan and by the obligation of such debtor or debtors to make future payments, including dividends;

(III) is to own, or by the exercise of rights granted under such plan would be entitled to own if specified contingencies occur, a majority of the voting shares of—

(aa) each such debtor;

(bb) the parent corporation of each such debtor; or

(cc) a subsidiary of each such debtor that is also a debtor; and

(IV) is to use its assets or income to pay claims and demands; and

(ii) subject to subsection (h), the court determines that—

(I) the debtor is likely to be subject to substantial future demands for payment arising out of the same or similar conduct or events that gave rise to the claims that are addressed by the injunction;

(II) the actual amounts, numbers, and timing of such future demands cannot be determined;

(III) pursuit of such demands outside the procedures prescribed by such plan is likely to threaten the plan's purpose to deal equitably with claims and future demands;

(IV) as part of the process of seeking confirmation of such plan—

(aa) the terms of the injunction proposed to be issued under paragraph (1)(A), including any provisions barring actions against third parties pursuant to paragraph

(4)(A), are set out in such plan and in any disclosure statement supporting the plan; and

    (bb) a separate class or classes of the claimants whose claims are to be addressed by a trust described in clause (i) is established and votes, by at least 75 percent of those voting, in favor of the plan; and

    (V) subject to subsection (h), pursuant to court orders or otherwise, the trust will operate through mechanisms such as structured, periodic, or supplemental payments, pro rata distributions, matrices, or periodic review of estimates of the numbers and values of present claims and future demands, or other comparable mechanisms, that provide reasonable assurance that the trust will value, and be in a financial position to pay, present claims and future demands that involve similar claims in substantially the same manner.

(3)(A)   If the requirements of paragraph (2)(B) are met and the order confirming the plan of reorganization was issued or affirmed by the district court that has jurisdiction over the reorganization case, then after the time for appeal of the order that issues or affirms the plan—

    (i) the injunction shall be valid and enforceable and may not be revoked or modified by any court except through appeal in accordance with paragraph (6);

    (ii) no entity that pursuant to such plan or thereafter becomes a direct or indirect transferee of, or successor to any assets of, a debtor or trust that is the subject of the injunction shall be liable with respect to any claim or demand made against such entity by reason of its becoming such a transferee or successor; and

    (iii) no entity that pursuant to such plan or thereafter makes a loan to such a debtor or trust or to such a successor or transferee shall, by reason of making the loan, be liable with respect to any claim or demand made against such entity, nor shall any pledge of assets made in connection with such a loan be upset or impaired for that reason;

(B) Subparagraph (A) shall not be construed to—

    (i) imply that an entity described in subparagraph (A)(ii) or (iii) would, if this paragraph were not applicable, necessarily be liable to any entity by reason of any of the acts described in subparagraph (A);

    (ii) relieve any such entity of the duty to comply with, or of liability under, any Federal or State law regarding the making of a fraudulent conveyance in a transaction described in subparagraph (A)(ii) or (iii); or

    (iii) relieve a debtor of the debtor's obligation to comply with the terms of the plan of reorganization, or affect the power of the court to exercise its authority under sections 1141 and 1142 to compel the debtor to do so.

(4)(A)(i) Subject to subparagraph (B), an injunction described in paragraph (1) shall be valid and enforceable against all entities that it addresses.

(ii) Notwithstanding the provisions of section 524(e), such an injunction may bar any action directed against a third party who is identifiable from the terms of such injunction (by name or as part of an identifiable group) and is alleged to be directly or indirectly liable for the conduct of, claims against, or demands on the debtor to the extent such alleged liability of such third party arises by reason of—

    (I) the third party's ownership of a financial interest in the debtor, a past or present affiliate of the debtor, or a predecessor in interest of the debtor;

    (II) the third party's involvement in the management of the debtor or a predecessor in interest of the debtor, or service as an officer, director or employee of the debtor or a related party;

    (III) the third party's provision of insurance to the debtor or a related party; or

(IV) the third party's involvement in a transaction changing the corporate structure, or in a loan or other financial transaction affecting the financial condition, of the debtor or a related party, including but not limited to—

(aa) involvement in providing financing (debt or equity), or advice to an entity involved in such a transaction; or

(bb) acquiring or selling a financial interest in an entity as part of such a transaction.

(iii) As used in this subparagraph, the term "related party" means—

(I) a past or present affiliate of the debtor;

(II) a predecessor in interest of the debtor; or

(III) any entity that owned a financial interest in—

(aa) the debtor;

(bb) a past or present affiliate of the debtor; or

(cc) a predecessor in interest of the debtor.

(B) Subject to subsection (h), if, under a plan of reorganization, a kind of demand described in such plan is to be paid in whole or in part by a trust described in paragraph (2)(B)(i) in connection with which an injunction described in paragraph (1) is to be implemented, then such injunction shall be valid and enforceable with respect to a demand of such kind made, after such plan is confirmed, against the debtor or debtors involved, or against a third party described in subparagraph (A)(ii), if—

(i) as part of the proceedings leading to issuance of such injunction, the court appoints a legal representative for the purpose of protecting the rights of persons that might subsequently assert demands of such kind, and

(ii) the court determines, before entering the order confirming such plan, that identifying such debtor or debtors, or such third party (by name or as part of an identifiable group), in such injunction with respect to such demands for purposes of this subparagraph is fair and equitable with respect to the persons that might subsequently assert such demands, in light of the benefits provided, or to be provided, to such trust on behalf of such debtor or debtors or such third party.

(5) In this subsection, the term "demand" means a demand for payment, present or future, that—

(A) was not a claim during the proceedings leading to the confirmation of a plan of reorganization;

(B) arises out of the same or similar conduct or events that gave rise to the claims addressed by the injunction issued under paragraph (1); and

(C) pursuant to the plan, is to be paid by a trust described in paragraph (2)(B)(i).

(6) Paragraph (3)(A)(i) does not bar an action taken by or at the direction of an appellate court on appeal of an injunction issued under paragraph (1) or of the order of confirmation that relates to the injunction.

(7) This subsection does not affect the operation of section 1144 or the power of the district court to refer a proceeding under section 157 of title 28 or any reference of a proceeding made prior to the date of the enactment of this subsection.

(h) Application to existing injunctions.—For purposes of subsection (g)—

(1) subject to paragraph (2), if an injunction of the kind described in subsection (g)(1)(B) was issued before the date of the enactment of this Act, as part of a plan of reorganization confirmed by an order entered before such date, then the injunction shall be considered to meet the requirements of subsection (g)(2)(B) for purposes of subsection (g)(2)(A), and to satisfy subsection (g)(4)(A)(ii), if—

 (A) the court determined at the time the plan was confirmed that the plan was fair and equitable in accordance with the requirements of section 1129(b);

 (B) as part of the proceedings leading to issuance of such injunction and confirmation of such plan, the court had appointed a legal representative for the purpose of protecting the rights of persons that might subsequently assert demands described in subsection (g)(4)(B) with respect to such plan; and

 (C) such legal representative did not object to confirmation of such plan or issuance of such injunction; and

 (2) for purposes of paragraph (1), if a trust described in subsection (g)(2)(B)(i) is subject to a court order on the date of the enactment of this Act staying such trust from settling or paying further claims—

 (A) the requirements of subsection (g)(2)(B)(ii)(V) shall not apply with respect to such trust until such stay is lifted or dissolved; and

 (B) if such trust meets such requirements on the date such stay is lifted or dissolved, such trust shall be considered to have met such requirements continuously from the date of the enactment of this Act.

 (i) The willful failure of a creditor to credit payments received under a plan confirmed under this title, unless the order confirming the plan is revoked, the plan is in default, or the creditor has not received payments required to be made under the plan in the manner required by the plan (including crediting the amounts required under the plan), shall constitute a violation of an injunction under subsection (a)(2) if the act of the creditor to collect and failure to credit payments in the manner required by the plan caused material injury to the debtor.

 (j) Subsection (a)(2) does not operate as an injunction against an act by a creditor that is the holder of a secured claim, if—

 (1) such creditor retains a security interest in real property that is the principal residence of the debtor;

 (2) such act is in the ordinary course of business between the creditor and the debtor; and

 (3) such act is limited to seeking or obtaining periodic payments associated with a valid security interest in lieu of pursuit of in rem relief to enforce the lien.

 (k)(1) The disclosures required under subsection (c)(2) shall consist of the disclosure statement described in paragraph (3), completed as required in that paragraph, together with the agreement specified in subsection (c), statement, declaration, motion and order described, respectively, in paragraphs (4) through (8), and shall be the only disclosures required in connection with entering into such agreement.

 (2) Disclosures made under paragraph (1) shall be made clearly and conspicuously and in writing. The terms "Amount Reaffirmed" and "Annual Percentage Rate" shall be disclosed more conspicuously than other terms, data or information provided in connection with this disclosure, except that the phrases "Before agreeing to reaffirm a debt, review these important disclosures" and "Summary of Reaffirmation Agreement" may be equally conspicuous. Disclosures may be made in a different order and may use terminology different from that set forth in paragraphs (2) through (8), except that the terms "Amount Reaffirmed" and "Annual Percentage Rate" must be used where indicated.

 (3) The disclosure statement required under this paragraph shall consist of the following:

 (A) The statement: "Part A: Before agreeing to reaffirm a debt, review these important disclosures:";

(B) Under the heading "Summary of Reaffirmation Agreement", the statement: "This Summary is made pursuant to the requirements of the Bankruptcy Code";

(C) The "Amount Reaffirmed", using that term, which shall be—

(i) the total amount of debt that the debtor agrees to reaffirm by entering into an agreement of the kind specified in subsection (c), and

(ii) the total of any fees and costs accrued as of the date of the disclosure statement, related to such total amount.

(D) In conjunction with the disclosure of the "Amount Reaffirmed", the statements—

(i) "The amount of debt you have agreed to reaffirm"; and

(ii) "Your credit agreement may obligate you to pay additional amounts which may come due after the date of this disclosure. Consult your credit agreement.".

(E) The "Annual Percentage Rate", using that term, which shall be disclosed as—

(i) if, at the time the petition is filed, the debt is an extension of credit under an open end credit plan, as the terms "credit" and "open end credit plan" are defined in section 103 of the Truth in Lending Act, then—

(I) the annual percentage rate determined under paragraphs (5) and (6) of section 127(b) of the Truth in Lending Act, as applicable, as disclosed to the debtor in the most recent periodic statement prior to entering into an agreement of the kind specified in subsection (c) or, if no such periodic statement has been given to the debtor during the prior 6 months, the annual percentage rate as it would have been so disclosed at the time the disclosure statement is given to the debtor, or to the extent this annual percentage rate is not readily available or not applicable, then

(II) the simple interest rate applicable to the amount reaffirmed as of the date the disclosure statement is given to the debtor, or if different simple interest rates apply to different balances, the simple interest rate applicable to each such balance, identifying the amount of each such balance included in the amount reaffirmed, or

(III) if the entity making the disclosure elects, to disclose the annual percentage rate under subclause (I) and the simple interest rate under subclause (II); or

(ii) if, at the time the petition is filed, the debt is an extension of credit other than under an open end credit plan, as the terms "credit" and "open end credit plan" are defined in section 103 of the Truth in Lending Act, then—

(I) the annual percentage rate under section 128(a)(4) of the Truth in Lending Act, as disclosed to the debtor in the most recent disclosure statement given to the debtor prior to the entering into an agreement of the kind specified in subsection (c) with respect to the debt, or, if no such disclosure statement was given to the debtor, the annual percentage rate as it would have been so disclosed at the time the disclosure statement is given to the debtor, or to the extent this annual percentage rate is not readily available or not applicable, then

(II) the simple interest rate applicable to the amount reaffirmed as of the date the disclosure statement is given to the debtor, or if different simple interest rates apply to different balances, the simple interest rate applicable to each such balance, identifying the amount of such balance included in the amount reaffirmed, or

(III) if the entity making the disclosure elects, to disclose the annual percentage rate under (I) and the simple interest rate under (II).

(F) If the underlying debt transaction was disclosed as a variable rate transaction on the most recent disclosure given under the Truth in Lending Act, by stating "The interest rate on your loan may be a variable interest rate which changes from time to time, so that the annual percentage rate disclosed here may be higher or lower."

(G) If the debt is secured by a security interest which has not been waived in whole or in part or determined to be void by a final order of the court at the time of the disclosure, by disclosing that a security interest or lien in goods or property is asserted over some or all of the debts the debtor is reaffirming and listing the items and their original purchase price that are subject to the asserted security interest, or if not a purchase-money security interest then listing by items or types and the original amount of the loan.

(H) At the election of the creditor, a statement of the repayment schedule using 1 or a combination of the following—

   (i) by making the statement: "Your first payment in the amount of $___ is due on ___ but the future payment amount may be different. Consult your reaffirmation agreement or credit agreement, as applicable.", and stating the amount of the first payment and the due date of that payment in the places provided;

   (ii) by making the statement: "Your payment schedule will be:", and describing the repayment schedule with the number, amount, and due dates or period of payments scheduled to repay the debts reaffirmed to the extent then known by the disclosing party; or

   (iii) by describing the debtor's repayment obligations with reasonable specificity to the extent then known by the disclosing party.

(I) The following statement: "Note: When this disclosure refers to what a creditor 'may' do, it does not use the word 'may' to give the creditor specific permission. The word 'may' is used to tell you what might occur if the law permits the creditor to take the action. If you have questions about your reaffirming a debt or what the law requires, consult with the attorney who helped you negotiate this agreement reaffirming a debt. If you don't have an attorney helping you, the judge will explain the effect of your reaffirming a debt when the hearing on the reaffirmation agreement is held.".

(J)(i) The following additional statements:

"Reaffirming a debt is a serious financial decision. The law requires you to take certain steps to make sure the decision is in your best interest. If these steps are not completed, the reaffirmation agreement is not effective, even though you have signed it.

"1.   Read the disclosures in this Part A carefully. Consider the decision to reaffirm carefully. Then, if you want to reaffirm, sign the reaffirmation agreement in Part B (or you may use a separate agreement you and your creditor agree on).

"2.   Complete and sign Part D and be sure you can afford to make the payments you are agreeing to make and have received a copy of the disclosure statement and a completed and signed reaffirmation agreement.

"3.   If you were represented by an attorney during the negotiation of your reaffirmation agreement, the attorney must have signed the certification in Part C.

"4.   If you were not represented by an attorney during the negotiation of your reaffirmation agreement, you must have completed and signed Part E.

"5.   The original of this disclosure must be filed with the court by you or your creditor. If a separate reaffirmation agreement (other than the one in Part B) has been signed, it must be attached.

"6.   If you were represented by an attorney during the negotiation of your reaffirmation agreement, your reaffirmation agreement becomes effective upon filing with the court unless the reaffirmation is presumed to be an undue hardship as explained in Part D.

"7.   If you were not represented by an attorney during the negotiation of your reaffirmation agreement, it will not be effective unless the court approves it. The court will notify you of the hearing on your reaffirmation agreement. You must attend this hearing in bankruptcy court where the judge will review your reaffirmation agreement. The bankruptcy court must approve your reaffirmation agreement as consistent with your best interests, except that no court approval is required if your reaffirmation agreement is for a consumer debt secured by a mortgage, deed of trust, security deed, or other lien on your real property, like your home.

"Your right to rescind (cancel) your reaffirmation agreement. You may rescind (cancel) your reaffirmation agreement at any time before the bankruptcy court enters a discharge order, or before the expiration of the 60-day period that begins on the date your reaffirmation agreement is filed with the court, whichever occurs later. To rescind (cancel) your reaffirmation agreement, you must notify the creditor that your reaffirmation agreement is rescinded (or canceled).

"What are your obligations if you reaffirm the debt? A reaffirmed debt remains your personal legal obligation. It is not discharged in your bankruptcy case. That means that if you default on your reaffirmed debt after your bankruptcy case is over, your creditor may be able to take your property or your wages. Otherwise, your obligations will be determined by the reaffirmation agreement which may have changed the terms of the original agreement. For example, if you are reaffirming an open end credit agreement, the creditor may be permitted by that agreement or applicable law to change the terms of that agreement in the future under certain conditions.

"Are you required to enter into a reaffirmation agreement by any law? No, you are not required to reaffirm a debt by any law. Only agree to reaffirm a debt if it is in your best interest. Be sure you can afford the payments you agree to make.

"What if your creditor has a security interest or lien? Your bankruptcy discharge does not eliminate any lien on your property. A 'lien' is often referred to as a security interest, deed of trust, mortgage or security deed. Even if you do not reaffirm and your personal liability on the debt is discharged, because of the lien your creditor may still have the right to take the property securing the lien if you do not pay the debt or default on it. If the lien is on an item of personal property that is exempt under your State's law or that the trustee has abandoned, you may be able to redeem the item rather than reaffirm the debt. To redeem, you must make a single payment to the creditor equal to the amount of the allowed secured claim, as agreed by the parties or determined by the court.".

(ii)   In the case of a reaffirmation under subsection (m)(2), numbered paragraph 6 in the disclosures required by clause (i) of this subparagraph shall read as follows:

"6.   If you were represented by an attorney during the negotiation of your reaffirmation agreement, your reaffirmation agreement becomes effective upon filing with the court.".

(4)   The form of such agreement required under this paragraph shall consist of the following:

"Part B: Reaffirmation Agreement. I (we) agree to reaffirm the debts arising under the credit agreement described below.

"Brief description of credit agreement:

"Description of any changes to the credit agreement made as part of this reaffirmation agreement:

"Signature: Date:

"Borrower:

"Co-borrower, if also reaffirming these debts:

"Accepted by creditor:

"Date of creditor acceptance:".

(5)   The declaration shall consist of the following:

(A)   The following certification:

"Part C: Certification by Debtor's Attorney (If Any).

"I hereby certify that (1) this agreement represents a fully informed and voluntary agreement by the debtor; (2) this agreement does not impose an undue hardship on the debtor or any dependent of the debtor; and (3) I have fully advised the debtor of the legal effect and consequences of this agreement and any default under this agreement.

"Signature of Debtor's Attorney: Date:".

(B) If a presumption of undue hardship has been established with respect to such agreement, such certification shall state that, in the opinion of the attorney, the debtor is able to make the payment.

(C) In the case of a reaffirmation agreement under subsection (m)(2), subparagraph (B) is not applicable.

(6)(A) The statement in support of such agreement, which the debtor shall sign and date prior to filing with the court, shall consist of the following:

"Part D: Debtor's Statement in Support of Reaffirmation Agreement.

"1. I believe this reaffirmation agreement will not impose an undue hardship on my dependents or me. I can afford to make the payments on the reaffirmed debt because my monthly income (take home pay plus any other income received) is $___, and my actual current monthly expenses including monthly payments on post-bankruptcy debt and other reaffirmation agreements total $___, leaving $___ to make the required payments on this reaffirmed debt. I understand that if my income less my monthly expenses does not leave enough to make the payments, this reaffirmation agreement is presumed to be an undue hardship on me and must be reviewed by the court. However, this presumption may be overcome if I explain to the satisfaction of the court how I can afford to make the payments here: ___.

"2. I received a copy of the Reaffirmation Disclosure Statement in Part A and a completed and signed reaffirmation agreement.".

(B) Where the debtor is represented by an attorney and is reaffirming a debt owed to a creditor defined in section 19(b)(1)(A)(iv) of the Federal Reserve Act, the statement of support of the reaffirmation agreement, which the debtor shall sign and date prior to filing with the court, shall consist of the following:

"I believe this reaffirmation agreement is in my financial interest. I can afford to make the payments on the reaffirmed debt. I received a copy of the Reaffirmation Disclosure Statement in Part A and a completed and signed reaffirmation agreement.".

(7) The motion that may be used if approval of such agreement by the court is required in order for it to be effective, shall be signed and dated by the movant and shall consist of the following:

"Part E: Motion for Court Approval (To be completed only if the debtor is not represented by an attorney.). I (we), the debtor(s), affirm the following to be true and correct:

"I am not represented by an attorney in connection with this reaffirmation agreement.

"I believe this reaffirmation agreement is in my best interest based on the income and expenses I have disclosed in my Statement in Support of this reaffirmation agreement, and because (provide any additional relevant reasons the court should consider):

"Therefore, I ask the court for an order approving this reaffirmation agreement."

(8) The court order, which may be used to approve such agreement, shall consist of the following:

"Court Order: The court grants the debtor's motion and approves the reaffirmation agreement described above.".

(*l*)   Notwithstanding any other provision of this title the following shall apply:

(1)   A creditor may accept payments from a debtor before and after the filing of an agreement of the kind specified in subsection (c) with the court.

(2)   A creditor may accept payments from a debtor under such agreement that the creditor believes in good faith to be effective.

(3)   The requirements of subsections (c)(2) and (k) shall be satisfied if disclosures required under those subsections are given in good faith.

(m)(1)   Until 60 days after an agreement of the kind specified in subsection (c) is filed with the court (or such additional period as the court, after notice and a hearing and for cause, orders before the expiration of such period), it shall be presumed that such agreement is an undue hardship on the debtor if the debtor's monthly income less the debtor's monthly expenses as shown on the debtor's completed and signed statement in support of such agreement required under subsection (k)(6)(A) is less than the scheduled payments on the reaffirmed debt. This presumption shall be reviewed by the court. The presumption may be rebutted in writing by the debtor if the statement includes an explanation that identifies additional sources of funds to make the payments as agreed upon under the terms of such agreement. If the presumption is not rebutted to the satisfaction of the court, the court may disapprove such agreement. No agreement shall be disapproved without notice and a hearing to the debtor and creditor, and such hearing shall be concluded before the entry of the debtor's discharge.

(2)   This subsection does not apply to reaffirmation agreements where the creditor is a credit union, as defined in section 19(b)(1)(A)(iv) of the Federal Reserve Act.

REFERENCES IN TEXT

The Bankruptcy Act, referred to in subsec. (b)(1), is Act July 1, 1898, c. 541, 30 Stat. 544, as amended, which was classified generally to former Title 11.

The date of enactment of this subsection, referred to in subsec. (g), is the date of enactment of section 111(a) of Pub. L. 103–394, which enacted subsec. (g) of this section and which was approved Oct. 22, 1994.

The date of enactment of this Act, referred to in subsec. (h), probably means the date of enactment of Pub. L. 103–394, known as the Bankruptcy Reform Act of 1994, which was approved Oct. 22, 1994.

Section 103 of the Truth in Lending Act, referred to in subsec. (k)(3)(E)(i), (ii), is Pub. L. 90–321, Title I, § 103, May 29, 1968, 82 Stat. 147, as amended, which is classified to 15 U.S.C.A. § 1602.

Section 127(b) of the Truth in Lending Act, referred to in subsec. (k)(3)(E)(i)(I), is Pub. L. 90–321, Title I, § 127(b), May 29, 1968, 82 Stat. 153, as amended, which is classified to 15 U.S.C.A. § 1637(b).

Section 128(a)(4) of the Truth in Lending Act, referred to in subsec. (k)(3)(E)(ii)(I), is Pub. L. 90–321, Title I, § 128(a)(4), May 29, 1968, 82 Stat. 155, as amended, which is classified to 15 U.S.C.A. § 1638(a)(4).

The Truth in Lending Act, referred to in subsec. (k)(3)(F), is Title I of Pub. L. 90–321, May 29, 1968, 82 Stat. 146, as amended, also known as TILA, which is classified principally to subchapter I of chapter 41 of Title 15, 15 U.S.C.A. § 1601 et seq. For complete classification, see Short Title note set out under 15 U.S.C.A. § 1601 and Tables.

Section 19(b)(1)(A)(iv) of the Federal Reserve Act, referred to in subsecs. (k)(6)(B), (m)(2), is Act Dec. 23, 1913, c. 6, § 19(b)(1)(A)(iv), 38 Stat. 270, as amended, which is classified to 12 U.S.C.A. § 461(b)(1)(A)(iv).

CROSS REFERENCES

Applicability of subsec. (a)(1), (2) of this section in Chapter 9 cases, see 11 USCA § 901.

Cancellation of indebtedness from discharged farm loans, see 12 USCA § 1150.

Cover sheet for reaffirmation agreement, see Official Bankruptcy Form 427.

Extension of time generally, see 11 USCA § 108.

Meetings of creditors and equity security holders reaffirming a debt, see 11 USCA § 341.

Statement of intention for individuals filing under Chapter 7, see Official Bankruptcy Form 108.

§ 525. Protection against discriminatory treatment

(a) Except as provided in the Perishable Agricultural Commodities Act, 1930, the Packers and Stockyards Act, 1921, and section 1 of the Act entitled "An Act making appropriations for the Department of Agriculture for the fiscal year ending June 30, 1944, and for other purposes," approved July 12, 1943, a governmental unit may not deny, revoke, suspend, or refuse to renew a license, permit, charter, franchise, or other similar grant to, condition such a grant to, discriminate with respect to such a grant against, deny employment to, terminate the employment of, or discriminate with respect to employment against, a person that is or has been a debtor under this title or a bankrupt or a debtor under the Bankruptcy Act, or another person with whom such bankrupt or debtor has been associated, solely because such bankrupt or debtor is or has been a debtor under this title or a bankrupt or debtor under the Bankruptcy Act, has been insolvent before the commencement of the case under this title, or during the case but before the debtor is granted or denied a discharge, or has not paid a debt that is dischargeable in the case under this title or that was discharged under the Bankruptcy Act.

(b) No private employer may terminate the employment of, or discriminate with respect to employment against, an individual who is or has been a debtor under this title, a debtor or bankrupt under the Bankruptcy Act, or an individual associated with such debtor or bankrupt, solely because such debtor or bankrupt—

(1) is or has been a debtor under this title or a debtor or bankrupt under the Bankruptcy Act;

(2) has been insolvent before the commencement of a case under this title or during the case but before the grant or denial of a discharge; or

(3) has not paid a debt that is dischargeable in a case under this title or that was discharged under the Bankruptcy Act.

(c)(1) A governmental unit that operates a student grant or loan program and a person engaged in a business that includes the making of loans guaranteed or insured under a student loan program may not deny a student grant, loan, loan guarantee, or loan insurance to a person that is or has been a debtor under this title or a bankrupt or debtor under the Bankruptcy Act, or another person with whom the debtor or bankrupt has been associated, because the debtor or bankrupt is or has been a debtor under this title or a bankrupt or debtor under the Bankruptcy Act, has been insolvent before the commencement of a case under this title or during the pendency of the case but before the debtor is granted or denied a discharge, or has not paid a debt that is dischargeable in the case under this title or that was discharged under the Bankruptcy Act.

(2) In this section, "student loan program" means any program operated under title IV of the Higher Education Act of 1965 or a similar program operated under State or local law.

REFERENCES IN TEXT

The Perishable Agricultural Commodities Act, 1930, referred to in subsec. (a), is Act June 10, 1930, c. 436, 46 Stat. 531, as amended, which is classified principally to chapter 20A (section 499a et seq.) of Title 7, Agriculture. For complete classification of this Act to the Code, see section 499a of Title 7 and Tables.

The Packers and Stockyards Act, 1921, referred to in subsec. (a), is Act Aug. 15, 1921, c. 64, 42 Stat. 159, which is classified principally to chapter 9 (section 181 et seq.) of Title 7, Agriculture. For complete classification of this Act to the Code, see section 181 of Title 7 and Tables.

Section 1 of an Act entitled "An Act making appropriations for the Department of Agriculture for the fiscal year ending June 30, 1944, and for other purposes," approved July 12, 1943, referred to in subsec. (a), is section 1 of Act July 12, 1943, c. 215, 57 Stat. 422, which is classified to section 204 of Title 7, Agriculture.

The Bankruptcy Act, referred to in subsecs. (a), (b), and (c)(1), is Act July 1, 1898, c. 541, 30 Stat. 544, as amended, which was classified generally to former Title 11.

The Higher Education Act of 1965, referred to in subsec. (c)(2), is Pub. L. 89–329, Nov. 8, 1965, 79 Stat. 1219, as amended. Title IV of the Act is classified generally to subchapter IV of chapter 28 of Title 20, 20 U.S.C.A. § 1070 et seq., and part C of subchapter I of chapter 34 of Title 42, 42 U.S.C.A. § 2751 et seq. For complete classification, see Short Title note set out under 20 U.S.C.A. § 1001 and Tables.

CROSS REFERENCES

Reporting of obsolete information prohibited, see 15 USCA § 1681c.

§ 526. Restrictions on debt relief agencies

(a) A debt relief agency shall not—

(1) fail to perform any service that such agency informed an assisted person or prospective assisted person it would provide in connection with a case or proceeding under this title;

(2) make any statement, or counsel or advise any assisted person or prospective assisted person to make a statement in a document filed in a case or proceeding under this title, that is untrue or misleading, or that upon the exercise of reasonable care, should have been known by such agency to be untrue or misleading;

(3) misrepresent to any assisted person or prospective assisted person, directly or indirectly, affirmatively or by material omission, with respect to—

(A) the services that such agency will provide to such person; or

(B) the benefits and risks that may result if such person becomes a debtor in a case under this title; or

(4) advise an assisted person or prospective assisted person to incur more debt in contemplation of such person filing a case under this title or to pay an attorney or bankruptcy petition preparer a fee or charge for services performed as part of preparing for or representing a debtor in a case under this title.

(b) Any waiver by any assisted person of any protection or right provided under this section shall not be enforceable against the debtor by any Federal or State court or any other person, but may be enforced against a debt relief agency.

(c)(1) Any contract for bankruptcy assistance between a debt relief agency and an assisted person that does not comply with the material requirements of this section, section 527, or section 528 shall be void and may not be enforced by any Federal or State court or by any other person, other than such assisted person.

(2) Any debt relief agency shall be liable to an assisted person in the amount of any fees or charges in connection with providing bankruptcy assistance to such person that such debt relief agency has received, for actual damages, and for reasonable attorneys' fees and costs if such agency is found, after notice and a hearing, to have—

(A) intentionally or negligently failed to comply with any provision of this section, section 527, or section 528 with respect to a case or proceeding under this title for such assisted person;

(B) provided bankruptcy assistance to an assisted person in a case or proceeding under this title that is dismissed or converted to a case under another chapter of this title because of such agency's intentional or negligent failure to file any required document including those specified in section 521; or

(C) intentionally or negligently disregarded the material requirements of this title or the Federal Rules of Bankruptcy Procedure applicable to such agency.

(3) In addition to such other remedies as are provided under State law, whenever the chief law enforcement officer of a State, or an official or agency designated by a State, has reason to believe that any person has violated or is violating this section, the State—

(A) may bring an action to enjoin such violation;

(B) may bring an action on behalf of its residents to recover the actual damages of assisted persons arising from such violation, including any liability under paragraph (2); and

(C) in the case of any successful action under subparagraph (A) or (B), shall be awarded the costs of the action and reasonable attorneys' fees as determined by the court.

(4) The district courts of the United States for districts located in the State shall have concurrent jurisdiction of any action under subparagraph (A) or (B) of paragraph (3).

(5) Notwithstanding any other provision of Federal law and in addition to any other remedy provided under Federal or State law, if the court, on its own motion or on the motion of the United States trustee or the debtor, finds that a person intentionally violated this section, or engaged in a clear and consistent pattern or practice of violating this section, the court may—

(A) enjoin the violation of such section; or

(B) impose an appropriate civil penalty against such person.

(d) No provision of this section, section 527, or section 528 shall—

(1) annul, alter, affect, or exempt any person subject to such sections from complying with any law of any State except to the extent that such law is inconsistent with those sections, and then only to the extent of the inconsistency; or

(2) be deemed to limit or curtail the authority or ability—

(A) of a State or subdivision or instrumentality thereof, to determine and enforce qualifications for the practice of law under the laws of that State; or

(B) of a Federal court to determine and enforce the qualifications for the practice of law before that court.

§ 527. Disclosures

(a) A debt relief agency providing bankruptcy assistance to an assisted person shall provide—

(1) the written notice required under section 342(b)(1); and

(2) to the extent not covered in the written notice described in paragraph (1), and not later than 3 business days after the first date on which a debt relief agency first offers to provide any bankruptcy assistance services to an assisted person, a clear and conspicuous written notice advising assisted persons that—

(A) all information that the assisted person is required to provide with a petition and thereafter during a case under this title is required to be complete, accurate, and truthful;

(B) all assets and all liabilities are required to be completely and accurately disclosed in the documents filed to commence the case, and the replacement value of each asset as defined in section 506 must be stated in those documents where requested after reasonable inquiry to establish such value;

(C) current monthly income, the amounts specified in section 707(b)(2), and, in a case under chapter 13 of this title, disposable income (determined in accordance with section 707(b)(2)), are required to be stated after reasonable inquiry; and

           (D) information that an assisted person provides during their case may be audited pursuant to this title, and that failure to provide such information may result in dismissal of the case under this title or other sanction, including a criminal sanction.

     (b) A debt relief agency providing bankruptcy assistance to an assisted person shall provide each assisted person at the same time as the notices required under subsection (a)(1) the following statement, to the extent applicable, or one substantially similar. The statement shall be clear and conspicuous and shall be in a single document separate from other documents or notices provided to the assisted person:

"IMPORTANT INFORMATION ABOUT BANKRUPTCY ASSISTANCE SERVICES FROM AN ATTORNEY OR BANKRUPTCY PETITION PREPARER.

"If you decide to seek bankruptcy relief, you can represent yourself, you can hire an attorney to represent you, or you can get help in some localities from a bankruptcy petition preparer who is not an attorney. THE LAW REQUIRES AN ATTORNEY OR BANKRUPTCY PETITION PREPARER TO GIVE YOU A WRITTEN CONTRACT SPECIFYING WHAT THE ATTORNEY OR BANKRUPTCY PETITION PREPARER WILL DO FOR YOU AND HOW MUCH IT WILL COST. Ask to see the contract before you hire anyone.

"The following information helps you understand what must be done in a routine bankruptcy case to help you evaluate how much service you need. Although bankruptcy can be complex, many cases are routine.

"Before filing a bankruptcy case, either you or your attorney should analyze your eligibility for different forms of debt relief available under the Bankruptcy Code and which form of relief is most likely to be beneficial for you. Be sure you understand the relief you can obtain and its limitations. To file a bankruptcy case, documents called a Petition, Schedules, and Statement of Financial Affairs, and in some cases a Statement of Intention, need to be prepared correctly and filed with the bankruptcy court. You will have to pay a filing fee to the bankruptcy court. Once your case starts, you will have to attend the required first meeting of creditors where you may be questioned by a court official called a 'trustee' and by creditors.

"If you choose to file a chapter 7 case, you may be asked by a creditor to reaffirm a debt. You may want help deciding whether to do so. A creditor is not permitted to coerce you into reaffirming your debts.

"If you choose to file a chapter 13 case in which you repay your creditors what you can afford over 3 to 5 years, you may also want help with preparing your chapter 13 plan and with the confirmation hearing on your plan which will be before a bankruptcy judge.

"If you select another type of relief under the Bankruptcy Code other than chapter 7 or chapter 13, you will want to find out what should be done from someone familiar with that type of relief.

"Your bankruptcy case may also involve litigation. You are generally permitted to represent yourself in litigation in bankruptcy court, but only attorneys, not bankruptcy petition preparers, can give you legal advice.".

     (c) Except to the extent the debt relief agency provides the required information itself after reasonably diligent inquiry of the assisted person or others so as to obtain such information reasonably accurately for inclusion on the petition, schedules or statement of financial affairs, a debt relief agency providing bankruptcy assistance to an assisted person, to the extent permitted by nonbankruptcy law, shall provide each assisted person at the time required for the notice required under subsection (a)(1) reasonably sufficient information (which shall be provided in a clear and conspicuous writing) to the assisted person on how to provide all the information the assisted person is required to provide under this title pursuant to section 521, including—

(1)   how to value assets at replacement value, determine current monthly income, the amounts specified in section 707(b)(2) and, in a chapter 13 case, how to determine disposable income in accordance with section 707(b)(2) and related calculations;

(2)   how to complete the list of creditors, including how to determine what amount is owed and what address for the creditor should be shown; and

(3)   how to determine what property is exempt and how to value exempt property at replacement value as defined in section 506.

(d)   A debt relief agency shall maintain a copy of the notices required under subsection (a) of this section for 2 years after the date on which the notice is given the assisted person.

§ 528.   Requirements for debt relief agencies

(a)   A debt relief agency shall—

(1)   not later than 5 business days after the first date on which such agency provides any bankruptcy assistance services to an assisted person, but prior to such assisted person's petition under this title being filed, execute a written contract with such assisted person that explains clearly and conspicuously—

(A)   the services such agency will provide to such assisted person; and

(B)   the fees or charges for such services, and the terms of payment;

(2)   provide the assisted person with a copy of the fully executed and completed contract;

(3)   clearly and conspicuously disclose in any advertisement of bankruptcy assistance services or of the benefits of bankruptcy directed to the general public (whether in general media, seminars or specific mailings, telephonic or electronic messages, or otherwise) that the services or benefits are with respect to bankruptcy relief under this title; and

(4)   clearly and conspicuously use the following statement in such advertisement: "We are a debt relief agency. We help people file for bankruptcy relief under the Bankruptcy Code." or a substantially similar statement.

(b)(1)   An advertisement of bankruptcy assistance services or of the benefits of bankruptcy directed to the general public includes—

(A)   descriptions of bankruptcy assistance in connection with a chapter 13 plan whether or not chapter 13 is specifically mentioned in such advertisement; and

(B)   statements such as "federally supervised repayment plan" or "Federal debt restructuring help" or other similar statements that could lead a reasonable consumer to believe that debt counseling was being offered when in fact the services were directed to providing bankruptcy assistance with a chapter 13 plan or other form of bankruptcy relief under this title.

(2)   An advertisement, directed to the general public, indicating that the debt relief agency provides assistance with respect to credit defaults, mortgage foreclosures, eviction proceedings, excessive debt, debt collection pressure, or inability to pay any consumer debt shall—

(A)   disclose clearly and conspicuously in such advertisement that the assistance may involve bankruptcy relief under this title; and

(B)   include the following statement: "We are a debt relief agency. We help people file for bankruptcy relief under the Bankruptcy Code." or a substantially similar statement.

SUBCHAPTER III—THE ESTATE

§ 541. Property of the estate

(a) The commencement of a case under section 301, 302, or 303 of this title creates an estate. Such estate is comprised of all the following property, wherever located and by whomever held:

(1) Except as provided in subsections (b) and (c)(2) of this section, all legal or equitable interests of the debtor in property as of the commencement of the case.

(2) All interests of the debtor and the debtor's spouse in community property as of the commencement of the case that is—

(A) under the sole, equal, or joint management and control of the debtor; or

(B) liable for an allowable claim against the debtor, or for both an allowable claim against the debtor and an allowable claim against the debtor's spouse, to the extent that such interest is so liable.

(3) Any interest in property that the trustee recovers under section 329(b), 363(n), 543, 550, 553, or 723 of this title.

(4) Any interest in property preserved for the benefit of or ordered transferred to the estate under section 510(c) or 551 of this title.

(5) Any interest in property that would have been property of the estate if such interest had been an interest of the debtor on the date of the filing of the petition, and that the debtor acquires or becomes entitled to acquire within 180 days after such date—

(A) by bequest, devise, or inheritance;

(B) as a result of a property settlement agreement with the debtor's spouse, or of an interlocutory or final divorce decree; or

(C) as a beneficiary of a life insurance policy or of a death benefit plan.

(6) Proceeds, product, offspring, rents, or profits of or from property of the estate, except such as are earnings from services performed by an individual debtor after the commencement of the case.

(7) Any interest in property that the estate acquires after the commencement of the case.

(b) Property of the estate does not include—

(1) any power that the debtor may exercise solely for the benefit of an entity other than the debtor;

(2) any interest of the debtor as a lessee under a lease of nonresidential real property that has terminated at the expiration of the stated term of such lease before the commencement of the case under this title, and ceases to include any interest of the debtor as a lessee under a lease of nonresidential real property that has terminated at the expiration of the stated term of such lease during the case;

(3) any eligibility of the debtor to participate in programs authorized under the Higher Education Act of 1965 (20 U.S.C. 1001 et seq.; 42 U.S.C. 2751 et seq.), or any accreditation status or State licensure of the debtor as an educational institution;

(4) any interest of the debtor in liquid or gaseous hydrocarbons to the extent that—

(A)(i) the debtor has transferred or has agreed to transfer such interest pursuant to a farmout agreement or any written agreement directly related to a farmout agreement; and

(ii) but for the operation of this paragraph, the estate could include the interest referred to in clause (i) only by virtue of section 365 or 544(a)(3) of this title; or

(B)(i) the debtor has transferred such interest pursuant to a written conveyance of a production payment to an entity that does not participate in the operation of the property from which such production payment is transferred; and

(ii) but for the operation of this paragraph, the estate could include the interest referred to in clause (i) only by virtue of section 365 or 542 of this title;

(5) funds placed in an education individual retirement account (as defined in section 530(b)(1) of the Internal Revenue Code of 1986) not later than 365 days before the date of the filing of the petition in a case under this title, but—

(A) only if the designated beneficiary of such account was a child, stepchild, grandchild, or stepgrandchild of the debtor for the taxable year for which funds were placed in such account;

(B) only to the extent that such funds—

(i) are not pledged or promised to any entity in connection with any extension of credit; and

(ii) are not excess contributions (as described in section 4973(e) of the Internal Revenue Code of 1986); and

(C) in the case of funds placed in all such accounts having the same designated beneficiary not earlier than 720 days nor later than 365 days before such date, only so much of such funds as does not exceed $7,575;

(6) funds used to purchase a tuition credit or certificate or contributed to an account in accordance with section 529(b)(1)(A) of the Internal Revenue Code of 1986 under a qualified State tuition program (as defined in section 529(b)(1) of such Code) not later than 365 days before the date of the filing of the petition in a case under this title, but—

(A) only if the designated beneficiary of the amounts paid or contributed to such tuition program was a child, stepchild, grandchild, or stepgrandchild of the debtor for the taxable year for which funds were paid or contributed;

(B) with respect to the aggregate amount paid or contributed to such program having the same designated beneficiary, only so much of such amount as does not exceed the total contributions permitted under section 529(b)(6) of such Code with respect to such beneficiary, as adjusted beginning on the date of the filing of the petition in a case under this title by the annual increase or decrease (rounded to the nearest tenth of 1 percent) in the education expenditure category of the Consumer Price Index prepared by the Department of Labor; and

(C) in the case of funds paid or contributed to such program having the same designated beneficiary not earlier than 720 days nor later than 365 days before such date, only so much of such funds as does not exceed $7,575;

(7) any amount—

(A) withheld by an employer from the wages of employees for payment as contributions—

(i) to—

(I) an employee benefit plan that is subject to title I of the Employee Retirement Income Security Act of 1974 or under an employee benefit plan which is a governmental plan under section 414(d) of the Internal Revenue Code of 1986;

    (II) a deferred compensation plan under section 457 of the Internal Revenue Code of 1986; or

    (III) a tax-deferred annuity under section 403(b) of the Internal Revenue Code of 1986;

except that such amount under this subparagraph shall not constitute disposable income as defined in section 1325(b)(2); or

    (ii) to a health insurance plan regulated by State law whether or not subject to such title; or

  (B) received by an employer from employees for payment as contributions—

    (i) to—

    (I) an employee benefit plan that is subject to title I of the Employee Retirement Income Security Act of 1974 or under an employee benefit plan which is a governmental plan under section 414(d) of the Internal Revenue Code of 1986;

    (II) a deferred compensation plan under section 457 of the Internal Revenue Code of 1986; or

    (III) a tax-deferred annuity under section 403(b) of the Internal Revenue Code of 1986;

except that such amount under this subparagraph shall not constitute disposable income, as defined in section 1325(b)(2); or

    (ii) to a health insurance plan regulated by State law whether or not subject to such title;

  (8) subject to subchapter III of chapter 5, any interest of the debtor in property where the debtor pledged or sold tangible personal property (other than securities or written or printed evidences of indebtedness or title) as collateral for a loan or advance of money given by a person licensed under law to make such loans or advances, where—

  (A) the tangible personal property is in the possession of the pledgee or transferee;

  (B) the debtor has no obligation to repay the money, redeem the collateral, or buy back the property at a stipulated price; and

  (C) neither the debtor nor the trustee have exercised any right to redeem provided under the contract or State law, in a timely manner as provided under State law and section 108(b);

  (9) any interest in cash or cash equivalents that constitute proceeds of a sale by the debtor of a money order that is made—

  (A) on or after the date that is 14 days prior to the date on which the petition is filed; and

  (B) under an agreement with a money order issuer that prohibits the commingling of such proceeds with property of the debtor (notwithstanding that, contrary to the agreement, the proceeds may have been commingled with property of the debtor),

unless the money order issuer had not taken action, prior to the filing of the petition, to require compliance with the prohibition.

Paragraph (4) shall not be construed to exclude from the estate any consideration the debtor retains, receives, or is entitled to receive for transferring an interest in liquid or gaseous hydrocarbons pursuant to a farmout agreement; or

(10) funds placed in an account of a qualified ABLE program (as defined in section 529A(b) of the Internal Revenue Code of 1986) not later than 365 days before the date of the filing of the petition in a case under this title, but—

    (A) only if the designated beneficiary of such account was a child, stepchild, grandchild, or stepgrandchild of the debtor for the taxable year for which funds were placed in such account;

    (B) only to the extent that such funds—

        (i) are not pledged or promised to any entity in connection with any extension of credit; and

        (ii) are not excess contributions (as described in section 4973(h) of the Internal Revenue Code of 1986); and

    (C) in the case of funds placed in all such accounts having the same designated beneficiary not earlier than 720 days nor later than 365 days before such date, only so much of such funds as does not exceed $7,575.

(c)(1) Except as provided in paragraph (2) of this subsection, an interest of the debtor in property becomes property of the estate under subsection (a)(1), (a)(2), or (a)(5) of this section notwithstanding any provision in an agreement, transfer instrument, or applicable nonbankruptcy law—

    (A) that restricts or conditions transfer of such interest by the debtor; or

    (B) that is conditioned on the insolvency or financial condition of the debtor, on the commencement of a case under this title, or on the appointment of or taking possession by a trustee in a case under this title or a custodian before such commencement, and that effects or gives an option to effect a forfeiture, modification, or termination of the debtor's interest in property.

    (2) A restriction on the transfer of a beneficial interest of the debtor in a trust that is enforceable under applicable nonbankruptcy law is enforceable in a case under this title.

(d) Property in which the debtor holds, as of the commencement of the case, only legal title and not an equitable interest, such as a mortgage secured by real property, or an interest in such a mortgage, sold by the debtor but as to which the debtor retains legal title to service or supervise the servicing of such mortgage or interest, becomes property of the estate under subsection (a)(1) or (2) of this section only to the extent of the debtor's legal title to such property, but not to the extent of any equitable interest in such property that the debtor does not hold.

(e) In determining whether any of the relationships specified in paragraph (5)(A) or (6)(A) of subsection (b) exists, a legally adopted child of an individual (and a child who is a member of an individual's household, if placed with such individual by an authorized placement agency for legal adoption by such individual), or a foster child of an individual (if such child has as the child's principal place of abode the home of the debtor and is a member of the debtor's household) shall be treated as a child of such individual by blood.

(f) Notwithstanding any other provision of this title, property that is held by a debtor that is a corporation described in section 501(c)(3) of the Internal Revenue Code of 1986 and exempt from tax under section 501(a) of such Code may be transferred to an entity that is not such a corporation, but only under the same conditions as would apply if the debtor had not filed a case under this title.

REFERENCES IN TEXT

The Higher Education Act of 1965, referred to in subsec. (b)(3), is Pub. L. 89–329, Nov. 8, 1965, 79 Stat. 1219, as amended, which is classified principally to chapter 28 (§ 1001 et seq.) of Title 20, Education. For complete classification of this Act to the Code, see Short Title note set out under section 1001 of Title 20 and Tables.

Section 530(b)(1) of the Internal Revenue Code of 1986, referred to in subsec. (b)(5), is classified to 26 U.S.C.A. § 530(b)(1).

Section 4973(e) of the Internal Revenue Code of 1986, referred to in subsec. (b)(5)(B)(ii), is classified to 26 U.S.C.A. § 4973(e).

"Section 529(b)(1) of such Code" and "section 529(b)(6) of such Code", referred to in subsec. (b)(6), are classified to 26 U.S.C.A. § 529(b)(1) and to 26 U.S.C.A. § 529(b)(6), respectively.

Title I of the Employee Retirement Income Security Act of 1974, referred to in subsec. (b)(7)(A)(i)(I), (B)(i)(I), means Pub. L. 93–406, Title I, Sept. 2, 1974, 88 Stat. 829, which principally enacted subchapter I of chapter 18 of Title 29, 29 U.S.C.A. § 1001 et seq.; see Tables for complete classification.

Section 414(d) of the Internal Revenue Code of 1986, referred to in subsec. (b)(7)(A)(i)(I), (B)(i)(I), is 26 U.S.C.A. § 414(d).

Section 457 of the Internal Revenue Code of 1986, referred to in subsec. (b)(7)(A)(i)(II), (B)(i)(II), is 26 U.S.C.A. § 457.

Section 403(b) of the Internal Revenue Code of 1986, referred to in subsec. (b)(7)(A)(i)(III), (B)(i)(III), is 26 U.S.C.A. § 403(b).

CROSS REFERENCES

Community claim defined, see 11 USCA § 101.

Distribution of property of estate, see 11 USCA § 726.

Effect of discharge, see 11 USCA § 524.

Executory contracts and unexpired leases, see 11 USCA § 365.

Exemptions, see 11 USCA § 522.

Ownership of copyright, see 17 USCA § 201.

Property of estate in—

> Chapter 11 non-subchapter V cases, see 11 USCA § 1115.
>
> Chapter 11 subchapter V cases, see 11 USCA § 1186.
>
> Chapter 12 cases, see 11 USCA § 1207.
>
> Chapter 13 cases, see 11 USCA § 1306.

Special tax provisions concerning estates of partners and partnerships, see 11 USCA § 728.

Trustee considered consignee of merchandise consigned to deceased or insolvent persons, see 19 USCA § 1485.

Venue of action brought under this title by trustee as statutory successor under this section to debtor, see 28 USCA § 1409.

§ 542. Turnover of property to the estate

(a) Except as provided in subsection (c) or (d) of this section, an entity, other than a custodian, in possession, custody, or control, during the case, of property that the trustee may use, sell, or lease under section 363 of this title, or that the debtor may exempt under section 522 of this title, shall deliver to the trustee, and account for, such property or the value of such property, unless such property is of inconsequential value or benefit to the estate.

(b) Except as provided in subsection (c) or (d) of this section, an entity that owes a debt that is property of the estate and that is matured, payable on demand, or payable on order, shall pay such debt to, or on the order of, the trustee, except to the extent that such debt may be offset under section 553 of this title against a claim against the debtor.

(c) Except as provided in section 362(a)(7) of this title, an entity that has neither actual notice nor actual knowledge of the commencement of the case concerning the debtor may transfer property of the estate, or pay a debt owing to the debtor, in good faith and other than in the manner specified in subsection (d) of this section, to an entity other than the trustee, with the same effect as to the entity making such transfer or payment as if the case under this title concerning the debtor had not been commenced.

(d) A life insurance company may transfer property of the estate or property of the debtor to such company in good faith, with the same effect with respect to such company as if the case under this title concerning the debtor had not been commenced, if such transfer is to pay a premium or to carry out a nonforfeiture insurance option, and is required to be made automatically, under a life insurance contract with such company that was entered into before the date of the filing of the petition and that is property of the estate.

(e) Subject to any applicable privilege, after notice and a hearing, the court may order an attorney, accountant, or other person that holds recorded information, including books, documents, records, and papers, relating to the debtor's property or financial affairs, to turn over or disclose such recorded information to the trustee.

CROSS REFERENCES

Assignability or accrual to third persons of farm loan agreements respecting credits or principal and interest, see 42 USCA § 1473.

Concealment of assets, see 18 USCA § 152.

Disallowance of claims of entity from which property is recoverable, see 11 USCA § 502.

Effect of dismissal, see 11 USCA § 349.

Exemptions, see 11 USCA § 522.

§ 543.   Turnover of property by a custodian

(a) A custodian with knowledge of the commencement of a case under this title concerning the debtor may not make any disbursement from, or take any action in the administration of, property of the debtor, proceeds, product, offspring, rents, or profits of such property, or property of the estate, in the possession, custody, or control of such custodian, except such action as is necessary to preserve such property.

(b) A custodian shall—

(1) deliver to the trustee any property of the debtor held by or transferred to such custodian, or proceeds, product, offspring, rents, or profits of such property, that is in such custodian's possession, custody, or control on the date that such custodian acquires knowledge of the commencement of the case; and

(2) file an accounting of any property of the debtor, or proceeds, product, offspring, rents, or profits of such property, that, at any time, came into the possession, custody, or control of such custodian.

(c) The court, after notice and a hearing, shall—

(1) protect all entities to which a custodian has become obligated with respect to such property or proceeds, product, offspring, rents, or profits of such property;

(2) provide for the payment of reasonable compensation for services rendered and costs and expenses incurred by such custodian; and

(3) surcharge such custodian, other than an assignee for the benefit of the debtor's creditors that was appointed or took possession more than 120 days before the date of the filing of the petition, for any improper or excessive disbursement, other than a disbursement that has been made in accordance with applicable law or that has been approved, after notice and a hearing, by a court of competent jurisdiction before the commencement of the case under this title.

(d) After notice and hearing, the bankruptcy court—

(1) may excuse compliance with subsection (a), (b), or (c) of this section if the interests of creditors and, if the debtor is not insolvent, of equity security holders would be better served by permitting a custodian to continue in possession, custody, or control of such property, and

(2) shall excuse compliance with subsections (a) and (b)(1) of this section if the custodian is an assignee for the benefit of the debtor's creditors that was appointed or took possession more than 120 days before the date of the filing of the petition, unless compliance with such subsections is necessary to prevent fraud or injustice.

CROSS REFERENCES

Administrative expenses of superseded custodians, see 11 USCA § 503.

Concealment of assets, see 18 USCA § 152.

Disallowance of claim of entity from which property is recoverable, see 11 USCA § 502.

Effect of dismissal, see 11 USCA § 349.

Order of payment on claims for expenses of superseded custodians, see 11 USCA § 726.

Property recoverable by trustee as exempt, see 11 USCA § 522.

§ 544. Trustee as lien creditor and as successor to certain creditors and purchasers

(a) The trustee shall have, as of the commencement of the case, and without regard to any knowledge of the trustee or of any creditor, the rights and powers of, or may avoid any transfer of property of the debtor or any obligation incurred by the debtor that is voidable by—

(1) a creditor that extends credit to the debtor at the time of the commencement of the case, and that obtains, at such time and with respect to such credit, a judicial lien on all property on which a creditor on a simple contract could have obtained such a judicial lien, whether or not such a creditor exists;

(2) a creditor that extends credit to the debtor at the time of the commencement of the case, and obtains, at such time and with respect to such credit, an execution against the debtor that is returned unsatisfied at such time, whether or not such a creditor exists; or

(3) a bona fide purchaser of real property, other than fixtures, from the debtor, against whom applicable law permits such transfer to be perfected, that obtains the status of a bona fide purchaser and has perfected such transfer at the time of the commencement of the case, whether or not such a purchaser exists.

(b)(1) Except as provided in paragraph (2), the trustee may avoid any transfer of an interest of the debtor in property or any obligation incurred by the debtor that is voidable under applicable law by a creditor holding an unsecured claim that is allowable under section 502 of this title or that is not allowable only under section 502(e) of this title.

(2) Paragraph (1) shall not apply to a transfer of a charitable contribution (as that term is defined in section 548(d)(3)) that is not covered under section 548(a)(1)(B), by reason of section 548(a)(2). Any claim by any person to recover a transferred contribution described in the preceding sentence under Federal or State law in a Federal or State court shall be preempted by the commencement of the case.

CROSS REFERENCES

Applicability of this section in Chapter 9 cases, see 11 USCA § 901.

Appointment of trustee upon Chapter 9 debtor's refusal to pursue cause of action under this section, see 11 USCA § 926.

Commencement of involuntary cases by transferees of voidable transfer, see 11 USCA § 303.

Disallowance of claims of entity that is transferee of avoidable transfer, see 11 USCA § 502.

Effect of dismissal, see 11 USCA § 349.

Exemptions, see 11 USCA § 522.

Recovery of voidable transfers in investor protection liquidation proceedings, see 15 USCA § 78fff–2.

Venue of action brought under this title by trustee as statutory successor under this section to creditors, see 28 USCA § 1409.

Voidable transfers in—

    Commodity broker liquidation cases, see 11 USCA § 764.

    Stockbroker liquidation proceedings, see 11 USCA § 749.

§ 545. Statutory liens

The trustee may avoid the fixing of a statutory lien on property of the debtor to the extent that such lien—

    (1) first becomes effective against the debtor—

        (A) when a case under this title concerning the debtor is commenced;

        (B) when an insolvency proceeding other than under this title concerning the debtor is commenced;

        (C) when a custodian is appointed or authorized to take or takes possession;

        (D) when the debtor becomes insolvent;

        (E) when the debtor's financial condition fails to meet a specified standard; or

        (F) at the time of an execution against property of the debtor levied at the instance of an entity other than the holder of such statutory lien;

    (2) is not perfected or enforceable at the time of the commencement of the case against a bona fide purchaser that purchases such property at the time of the commencement of the case, whether or not such a purchaser exists, except in any case in which a purchaser is a purchaser described in section 6323 of the Internal Revenue Code of 1986, or in any other similar provision of State or local law;

    (3) is for rent; or

    (4) is a lien of distress for rent.

REFERENCES IN TEXT

Section 6323 of the Internal Revenue Code of 1986, referred to in par. (2), is classified to 26 U.S.C.A. § 6323.

CROSS REFERENCES

Applicability of this section in Chapter 9 cases, see 11 USCA § 901.

Appointment of trustee upon Chapter 9 debtor's refusal to pursue cause of action under this section, see 11 USCA § 926.

Commencement of involuntary cases by transferees of voidable transfers, see 11 USCA § 303.

Disallowance of claims of entity that is a transferee of an avoidable transfer, see 11 USCA § 502.

Effect of dismissal, see 11 USCA § 349.

Exemptions, see 11 USCA § 522.

Recovery of voidable transfers in investor protection liquidation proceedings, see 15 USCA § 78fff–2.

Voidable transfers in—

Commodity broker liquidation cases, see 11 USCA § 764.

Stockbroker liquidation cases, see 11 USCA § 749.

§ 546. Limitations on avoiding powers

(a) An action or proceeding under section 544, 545, 547, 548, or 553 of this title may not be commenced after the earlier of—

(1) the later of—

(A) 2 years after the entry of the order for relief; or

(B) 1 year after the appointment or election of the first trustee under section 702, 1104, 1163, 1202, or 1302 of this title if such appointment or such election occurs before the expiration of the period specified in subparagraph (A); or

(2) the time the case is closed or dismissed.

(b)(1) The rights and powers of a trustee under sections 544, 545, and 549 of this title are subject to any generally applicable law that—

(A) permits perfection of an interest in property to be effective against an entity that acquires rights in such property before the date of perfection; or

(B) provides for the maintenance or continuation of perfection of an interest in property to be effective against an entity that acquires rights in such property before the date on which action is taken to effect such maintenance or continuation.

(2) If—

(A) a law described in paragraph (1) requires seizure of such property or commencement of an action to accomplish such perfection, or maintenance or continuation of perfection of an interest in property; and

(B) such property has not been seized or such an action has not been commenced before the date of the filing of the petition;

such interest in such property shall be perfected, or perfection of such interest shall be maintained or continued, by giving notice within the time fixed by such law for such seizure or such commencement.

(c)(1) Except as provided in subsection (d) of this section and in section 507(c), and subject to the prior rights of a holder of a security interest in such goods or the proceeds thereof, the rights and powers of the trustee under sections 544(a), 545, 547, and 549 are subject to the right of a seller of goods that has sold goods to the debtor, in the ordinary course of such seller's business, to reclaim such goods if the debtor has received such goods while insolvent, within 45 days before the date of the commencement of a case under this title, but such seller may not reclaim such goods unless such seller demands in writing reclamation of such goods—

(A) not later than 45 days after the date of receipt of such goods by the debtor; or

(B) not later than 20 days after the date of commencement of the case, if the 45-day period expires after the commencement of the case.

(2) If a seller of goods fails to provide notice in the manner described in paragraph (1), the seller still may assert the rights contained in section 503(b)(9).

(d) In the case of a seller who is a producer of grain sold to a grain storage facility, owned or operated by the debtor, in the ordinary course of such seller's business (as such terms are defined in section 557 of this title) or in the case of a United States fisherman who has caught fish sold to a fish processing facility owned or operated by the debtor in the ordinary course of such fisherman's business, the rights and powers of the trustee under sections 544(a), 545, 547, and 549 of this title are subject to any statutory or common law right of such producer or fisherman to reclaim such grain or fish if the debtor has received such grain or fish while insolvent, but—

    (1) such producer or fisherman may not reclaim any grain or fish unless such producer or fisherman demands, in writing, reclamation of such grain or fish before ten days after receipt thereof by the debtor; and

    (2) the court may deny reclamation to such a producer or fisherman with a right of reclamation that has made such a demand only if the court secures such claim by a lien.

(e) Notwithstanding sections 544, 545, 547, 548(a)(1)(B), and 548(b) of this title, the trustee may not avoid a transfer that is a margin payment, as defined in section 101, 741, or 761 of this title, or settlement payment, as defined in section 101 or 741 of this title, made by or to (or for the benefit of) a commodity broker, forward contract merchant, stockbroker, financial institution, financial participant, or securities clearing agency, or that is a transfer made by or to (or for the benefit of) a commodity broker, forward contract merchant, stockbroker, financial institution, financial participant, or securities clearing agency, in connection with a securities contract, as defined in section 741(7), commodity contract, as defined in section 761(4), or forward contract, that is made before the commencement of the case, except under section 548(a)(1)(A) of this title.

(f) Notwithstanding sections 544, 545, 547, 548(a)(1)(B), and 548(b) of this title, the trustee may not avoid a transfer made by or to (or for the benefit of) a repo participant or financial participant, in connection with a repurchase agreement and that is made before the commencement of the case, except under section 548(a)(1)(A) of this title.

(g) Notwithstanding sections 544, 545, 547, 548(a)(1)(B) and 548(b) of this title, the trustee may not avoid a transfer, made by or to (or for the benefit of) a swap participant or financial participant, under or in connection with any swap agreement and that is made before the commencement of the case, except under section 548(a)(1)(A) of this title.

(h) Notwithstanding the rights and powers of a trustee under sections 544(a), 545, 547, 549, and 553, if the court determines on a motion by the trustee made not later than 120 days after the date of the order for relief in a case under chapter 11 of this title and after notice and a hearing, that a return is in the best interests of the estate, the debtor, with the consent of a creditor and subject to the prior rights of holders of security interests in such goods or the proceeds of such goods, may return goods shipped to the debtor by the creditor before the commencement of the case, and the creditor may offset the purchase price of such goods against any claim of the creditor against the debtor that arose before the commencement of the case.

(i)(1) Notwithstanding paragraphs (2) and (3) of section 545, the trustee may not avoid a warehouseman's lien for storage, transportation, or other costs incidental to the storage and handling of goods.

    (2) The prohibition under paragraph (1) shall be applied in a manner consistent with any State statute applicable to such lien that is similar to section 7–209 of the Uniform Commercial Code, as in effect on the date of enactment of the Bankruptcy Abuse Prevention and Consumer Protection Act of 2005, or any successor to such section 7–209.

(j) Notwithstanding sections 544, 545, 547, 548(a)(1)(B), and 548(b) the trustee may not avoid a transfer made by or to (or for the benefit of) a master netting agreement participant under or in connection with any master netting agreement or any individual contract covered thereby that is made before the commencement of the case, except under section 548(a)(1)(A) and except to the extent that the trustee could otherwise avoid such a transfer made under an individual contract covered by such master netting agreement.

REFERENCES IN TEXT

The date of enactment of the Bankruptcy Abuse Prevention and Consumer Protection Act of 2005, referred to in subsec. (i)(2), is April 20, 2005, the approval date of Pub. L. 109–8, 119 Stat. 23.

CROSS REFERENCES

Applicability of this section in Chapter 9 cases, see 11 USCA § 901.

Automatic stay, see 11 USCA § 362.

Concealment of debtor's assets deemed continuing offense, see 18 USCA § 3284.

§ 547. Preferences

(a) In this section—

(1) "inventory" means personal property leased or furnished, held for sale or lease, or to be furnished under a contract for service, raw materials, work in process, or materials used or consumed in a business, including farm products such as crops or livestock, held for sale or lease;

(2) "new value" means money or money's worth in goods, services, or new credit, or release by a transferee of property previously transferred to such transferee in a transaction that is neither void nor voidable by the debtor or the trustee under any applicable law, including proceeds of such property, but does not include an obligation substituted for an existing obligation;

(3) "receivable" means right to payment, whether or not such right has been earned by performance; and

(4) a debt for a tax is incurred on the day when such tax is last payable without penalty, including any extension.

(b) Except as provided in subsections (c) and (i) of this section, the trustee may, based on reasonable due diligence in the circumstances of the case and taking into account a party's known or reasonably knowable affirmative defenses under subsection (c), avoid any transfer of an interest of the debtor in property—

(1) to or for the benefit of a creditor;

(2) for or on account of an antecedent debt owed by the debtor before such transfer was made;

(3) made while the debtor was insolvent;

(4) made—

    (A) on or within 90 days before the date of the filing of the petition; or

    (B) between ninety days and one year before the date of the filing of the petition, if such creditor at the time of such transfer was an insider; and

(5) that enables such creditor to receive more than such creditor would receive if—

    (A) the case were a case under chapter 7 of this title;

    (B) the transfer had not been made; and

    (C) such creditor received payment of such debt to the extent provided by the provisions of this title.

(c) The trustee may not avoid under this section a transfer—

(1) to the extent that such transfer was—

(A) intended by the debtor and the creditor to or for whose benefit such transfer was made to be a contemporaneous exchange for new value given to the debtor; and

(B) in fact a substantially contemporaneous exchange;

(2) to the extent that such transfer was in payment of a debt incurred by the debtor in the ordinary course of business or financial affairs of the debtor and the transferee, and such transfer was—

(A) made in the ordinary course of business or financial affairs of the debtor and the transferee; or

(B) made according to ordinary business terms;

(3) that creates a security interest in property acquired by the debtor—

(A) to the extent such security interest secures new value that was—

(i) given at or after the signing of a security agreement that contains a description of such property as collateral;

(ii) given by or on behalf of the secured party under such agreement;

(iii) given to enable the debtor to acquire such property; and

(iv) in fact used by the debtor to acquire such property; and

(B) that is perfected on or before 30 days after the debtor receives possession of such property;

(4) to or for the benefit of a creditor, to the extent that, after such transfer, such creditor gave new value to or for the benefit of the debtor—

(A) not secured by an otherwise unavoidable security interest; and

(B) on account of which new value the debtor did not make an otherwise unavoidable transfer to or for the benefit of such creditor;

(5) that creates a perfected security interest in inventory or a receivable or the proceeds of either, except to the extent that the aggregate of all such transfers to the transferee caused a reduction, as of the date of the filing of the petition and to the prejudice of other creditors holding unsecured claims, of any amount by which the debt secured by such security interest exceeded the value of all security interests for such debt on the later of—

(A)(i) with respect to a transfer to which subsection (b)(4)(A) of this section applies, 90 days before the date of the filing of the petition; or

(ii) with respect to a transfer to which subsection (b)(4)(B) of this section applies, one year before the date of the filing of the petition; or

(B) the date on which new value was first given under the security agreement creating such security interest;

(6) that is the fixing of a statutory lien that is not avoidable under section 545 of this title;

(7) to the extent such transfer was a bona fide payment of a debt for a domestic support obligation;

(8) if, in a case filed by an individual debtor whose debts are primarily consumer debts, the aggregate value of all property that constitutes or is affected by such transfer is less than $600; or

(9) if, in a case filed by a debtor whose debts are not primarily consumer debts, the aggregate value of all property that constitutes or is affected by such transfer is less than $7,575.

(d) The trustee may avoid a transfer of an interest in property of the debtor transferred to or for the benefit of a surety to secure reimbursement of such a surety that furnished a bond or other obligation to dissolve a judicial lien that would have been avoidable by the trustee under subsection (b) of this section. The liability of such surety under such bond or obligation shall be discharged to the extent of the value of such property recovered by the trustee or the amount paid to the trustee.

(e)(1) For the purposes of this section—

(A) a transfer of real property other than fixtures, but including the interest of a seller or purchaser under a contract for the sale of real property, is perfected when a bona fide purchaser of such property from the debtor against whom applicable law permits such transfer to be perfected cannot acquire an interest that is superior to the interest of the transferee; and

(B) a transfer of a fixture or property other than real property is perfected when a creditor on a simple contract cannot acquire a judicial lien that is superior to the interest of the transferee.

(2) For the purposes of this section, except as provided in paragraph (3) of this subsection, a transfer is made—

(A) at the time such transfer takes effect between the transferor and the transferee, if such transfer is perfected at, or within 30 days after, such time, except as provided in subsection (c)(3)(B);

(B) at the time such transfer is perfected, if such transfer is perfected after such 30 days; or

(C) immediately before the date of the filing of the petition, if such transfer is not perfected at the later of—

(i) the commencement of the case; or

(ii) 30 days after such transfer takes effect between the transferor and the transferee.

(3) For the purposes of this section, a transfer is not made until the debtor has acquired rights in the property transferred.

(f) For the purposes of this section, the debtor is presumed to have been insolvent on and during the 90 days immediately preceding the date of the filing of the petition.

(g) For the purposes of this section, the trustee has the burden of proving the avoidability of a transfer under subsection (b) of this section, and the creditor or party in interest against whom recovery or avoidance is sought has the burden of proving the nonavoidability of a transfer under subsection (c) of this section.

(h) The trustee may not avoid a transfer if such transfer was made as a part of an alternative repayment schedule between the debtor and any creditor of the debtor created by an approved nonprofit budget and credit counseling agency.

(i) If the trustee avoids under subsection (b) a transfer made between 90 days and 1 year before the date of the filing of the petition, by the debtor to an entity that is not an insider for the benefit of a creditor that is an insider, such transfer shall be considered to be avoided under this section only with respect to the creditor that is an insider.

[*Note from West:* Pub. L. 116–260 created a temporary § 547(j), which expired on December 27, 2022, *except* for cases commenced before December 27, 2022. *See* 134 Stat. 3219, 3220, 3221. For an explanation of what this temporary amendment covered, *see* Title 11, Chapter 5, Subchapter III, § 547, Editorial Notes, Amendments, 2020 at http://uscode.house.gov]

CROSS REFERENCES

Applicability of this section in Chapter 9 cases, see 11 USCA § 901.

Appointment of trustee upon Chapter 9 debtor's refusal to pursue cause of action under this section, see 11 USCA § 926.

Automatic stay, see 11 USCA § 362.

Commencement of involuntary cases by transferees of voidable transfers, see 11 USCA § 303.

Disallowance of claims of entity that is transferee of avoidable transfer, see 11 USCA § 502.

Effect of dismissal, see 11 USCA § 349.

Exemptions, see 11 USCA § 522.

Recovery of voidable transfers in investor protection liquidation proceedings, see 15 USCA § 78fff–2.

Transfers to defeat cases under this title, see 18 USCA § 152.

Voidable transfers in—

 Commodity broker liquidation cases, see 11 USCA § 764.

 Stockbroker liquidation cases, see 11 USCA § 749.

§ 548. Fraudulent transfers and obligations

(a)(1) The trustee may avoid any transfer (including any transfer to or for the benefit of an insider under an employment contract) of an interest of the debtor in property, or any obligation (including any obligation to or for the benefit of an insider under an employment contract) incurred by the debtor, that was made or incurred on or within 2 years before the date of the filing of the petition, if the debtor voluntarily or involuntarily—

(A) made such transfer or incurred such obligation with actual intent to hinder, delay, or defraud any entity to which the debtor was or became, on or after the date that such transfer was made or such obligation was incurred, indebted; or

(B)(i) received less than a reasonably equivalent value in exchange for such transfer or obligation; and

(ii)(I) was insolvent on the date that such transfer was made or such obligation was incurred, or became insolvent as a result of such transfer or obligation;

(II) was engaged in business or a transaction, or was about to engage in business or a transaction, for which any property remaining with the debtor was an unreasonably small capital;

(III) intended to incur, or believed that the debtor would incur, debts that would be beyond the debtor's ability to pay as such debts matured; or

(IV) made such transfer to or for the benefit of an insider, or incurred such obligation to or for the benefit of an insider, under an employment contract and not in the ordinary course of business.

(2) A transfer of a charitable contribution to a qualified religious or charitable entity or organization shall not be considered to be a transfer covered under paragraph (1)(B) in any case in which—

(A) the amount of that contribution does not exceed 15 percent of the gross annual income of the debtor for the year in which the transfer of the contribution is made; or

(B) the contribution made by a debtor exceeded the percentage amount of gross annual income specified in subparagraph (A), if the transfer was consistent with the practices of the debtor in making charitable contributions.

(b) The trustee of a partnership debtor may avoid any transfer of an interest of the debtor in property, or any obligation incurred by the debtor, that was made or incurred on or within 2 years before the date of the filing of the petition, to a general partner in the debtor, if the debtor was insolvent on the date such transfer was made or such obligation was incurred, or became insolvent as a result of such transfer or obligation.

(c)   Except to the extent that a transfer or obligation voidable under this section is voidable under section 544, 545, or 547 of this title, a transferee or obligee of such a transfer or obligation that takes for value and in good faith has a lien on or may retain any interest transferred or may enforce any obligation incurred, as the case may be, to the extent that such transferee or obligee gave value to the debtor in exchange for such transfer or obligation.

(d)(1)   For the purposes of this section, a transfer is made when such transfer is so perfected that a bona fide purchaser from the debtor against whom applicable law permits such transfer to be perfected cannot acquire an interest in the property transferred that is superior to the interest in such property of the transferee, but if such transfer is not so perfected before the commencement of the case, such transfer is made immediately before the date of the filing of the petition.

(2)   In this section—

(A)   "value" means property, or satisfaction or securing of a present or antecedent debt of the debtor, but does not include an unperformed promise to furnish support to the debtor or to a relative of the debtor;

(B)   a commodity broker, forward contract merchant, stockbroker, financial institution, financial participant, or securities clearing agency that receives a margin payment, as defined in section 101, 741, or 761 of this title, or settlement payment, as defined in section 101 or 741 of this title, takes for value to the extent of such payment;

(C)   a repo participant or financial participant that receives a margin payment, as defined in section 741 or 761 of this title, or settlement payment, as defined in section 741 of this title, in connection with a repurchase agreement, takes for value to the extent of such payment;

(D)   a swap participant or financial participant that receives a transfer in connection with a swap agreement takes for value to the extent of such transfer; and

(E)   a master netting agreement participant that receives a transfer in connection with a master netting agreement or any individual contract covered thereby takes for value to the extent of such transfer, except that, with respect to a transfer under any individual contract covered thereby, to the extent that such master netting agreement participant otherwise did not take (or is otherwise not deemed to have taken) such transfer for value.

(3)   In this section, the term "charitable contribution" means a charitable contribution, as that term is defined in section 170(c) of the Internal Revenue Code of 1986, if that contribution—

(A)   is made by a natural person; and

(B)   consists of—

(i)   a financial instrument (as that term is defined in section 731(c)(2)(C) of the Internal Revenue Code of 1986); or

(ii)   cash.

(4)   In this section, the term "qualified religious or charitable entity or organization" means—

(A)   an entity described in section 170(c)(1) of the Internal Revenue Code of 1986; or

(B)   an entity or organization described in section 170(c)(2) of the Internal Revenue Code of 1986.

(e)(1)   In addition to any transfer that the trustee may otherwise avoid, the trustee may avoid any transfer of an interest of the debtor in property that was made on or within 10 years before the date of the filing of the petition, if—

(A) such transfer was made to a self-settled trust or similar device;

(B) such transfer was by the debtor;

(C) the debtor is a beneficiary of such trust or similar device; and

(D) the debtor made such transfer with actual intent to hinder, delay, or defraud any entity to which the debtor was or became, on or after the date that such transfer was made, indebted.

(2) For the purposes of this subsection, a transfer includes a transfer made in anticipation of any money judgment, settlement, civil penalty, equitable order, or criminal fine incurred by, or which the debtor believed would be incurred by—

(A) any violation of the securities laws (as defined in section 3(a)(47) of the Securities Exchange Act of 1934 (15 U.S.C. 78c(a)(47))), any State securities laws, or any regulation or order issued under Federal securities laws or State securities laws; or

(B) fraud, deceit, or manipulation in a fiduciary capacity or in connection with the purchase or sale of any security registered under section 12 or 15(d) of the Securities Exchange Act of 1934 (15 U.S.C. 78*l* and 78*o*(d)) or under section 6 of the Securities Act of 1933 (15 U.S.C. 77f).

REFERENCES IN TEXT

The Internal Revenue Code of 1986, referred to in subsec. (d)(3) and (4), is classified generally to Title 26.

Section 3(a)(47) of the Securities Exchange Act of 1934, referred to in subsec. (e)(2)(A), is June 6, 1934, c. 404, Title I, § 3(a)(47), 48 Stat. 882, as amended, which is classified to 15 U.S.C.A. § 78c(a)(47).

Section 12 of the Securities Exchange Act of 1934, referred to in subsec. (e)(2)(B), is June 6, 1934, c. 404, Title I, § 12, 48 Stat. 892, as amended, which is classified to 15 U.S.C.A. § 78*l*.

Section 15(d) of the Securities Exchange Act of 1934, referred to in subsec. (e)(2)(B), is June 6, 1934, c. 404, Title I, § 15(d), 48 Stat. 895, as amended, which is classified to 15 U.S.C.A. § 78*o*.

Section 6 of the Securities Act of 1933, referred to in subsec. (e)(2)(B), is Act May 27, 1933, c. 38, Title I, § 6, 48 Stat. 78, as amended, which is classified to 15 U.S.C.A. § 77f.

CROSS REFERENCES

Applicability of this section in Chapter 9 cases, see 11 USCA § 901.

Appointment of trustee upon Chapter 9 debtor's refusal to pursue cause of action under this section, see 11 USCA § 926.

Commencement of involuntary cases by transferees of voidable transfers, see 11 USCA § 303.

Disallowance of claims of entity that is transferee of avoidable transfer, see 11 USCA § 502.

Effect of dismissal, see 11 USCA § 349.

Exemptions, see 11 USCA § 522.

Inappropriate transfers included in determining net worth of employer, see 29 USCA § 1362.

Recovery of voidable transfers in investor protection liquidation proceedings, see 15 USCA § 78fff–2.

Transfers to defeat cases under this title, see 18 USCA § 152.

Voidable transfers in—

Commodity broker liquidation cases, see 11 USCA § 764.

Stockbroker liquidation cases, see 11 USCA § 749.

§ 549. Postpetition transactions

(a) Except as provided in subsection (b) or (c) of this section, the trustee may avoid a transfer of property of the estate—

(1) that occurs after the commencement of the case; and

(2)(A) that is authorized only under section 303(f) or 542(c) of this title; or

(B) that is not authorized under this title or by the court.

(b) In an involuntary case, the trustee may not avoid under subsection (a) of this section a transfer made after the commencement of such case but before the order for relief to the extent any value, including services, but not including satisfaction or securing of a debt that arose before the commencement of the case, is given after the commencement of the case in exchange for such transfer, notwithstanding any notice or knowledge of the case that the transferee has.

(c) The trustee may not avoid under subsection (a) of this section a transfer of an interest in real property to a good faith purchaser without knowledge of the commencement of the case and for present fair equivalent value unless a copy or notice of the petition was filed, where a transfer of an interest in such real property may be recorded to perfect such transfer, before such transfer is so perfected that a bona fide purchaser of such real property, against whom applicable law permits such transfer to be perfected, could not acquire an interest that is superior to such interest of such good faith purchaser. A good faith purchaser without knowledge of the commencement of the case and for less than present fair equivalent value has a lien on the property transferred to the extent of any present value given, unless a copy or notice of the petition was so filed before such transfer was so perfected.

(d) An action or proceeding under this section may not be commenced after the earlier of—

(1) two years after the date of the transfer sought to be avoided; or

(2) the time the case is closed or dismissed.

CROSS REFERENCES

Applicability of subsecs. (a), (c) and (d) of this section in Chapter 9 cases, see 11 USCA § 901.

Appointment of trustee upon Chapter 9 debtor's refusal to pursue cause of action under this section, see 11 USCA § 926.

Commencement of involuntary cases by transferees of voidable transfers, see 11 USCA § 303.

Disallowance of claims of entity that is transferee of avoidable transfer, see 11 USCA § 502.

Effect of dismissal, see 11 USCA § 349.

Exemptions, see 11 USCA § 522.

Inappropriate transfers included in determining net worth of employer, see 29 USCA § 1362.

Recovery of voidable transfers in investor liquidation proceedings, see 15 USCA § 78fff–2.

Voidable transfers in—

Commodity broker liquidation cases, see 11 USCA § 764.

Stockbroker liquidation cases, see 11 USCA § 749.

§ 550. Liability of transferee of avoided transfer

(a) Except as otherwise provided in this section, to the extent that a transfer is avoided under section 544, 545, 547, 548, 549, 553(b), or 724(a) of this title, the trustee may recover, for the benefit of the estate, the property transferred, or, if the court so orders, the value of such property, from—

    (1) the initial transferee of such transfer or the entity for whose benefit such transfer was made; or

    (2) any immediate or mediate transferee of such initial transferee.

(b) The trustee may not recover under section[1] (a)(2) of this section from—

    (1) a transferee that takes for value, including satisfaction or securing of a present or antecedent debt, in good faith, and without knowledge of the voidability of the transfer avoided; or

    (2) any immediate or mediate good faith transferee of such transferee.

(c) If a transfer made between 90 days and one year before the filing of the petition—

    (1) is avoided under section 547(b) of this title; and

    (2) was made for the benefit of a creditor that at the time of such transfer was an insider;

the trustee may not recover under subsection (a) from a transferee that is not an insider.

(d) The trustee is entitled to only a single satisfaction under subsection (a) of this section.

(e)(1) A good faith transferee from whom the trustee may recover under subsection (a) of this section has a lien on the property recovered to secure the lesser of—

    (A) the cost, to such transferee, of any improvement made after the transfer, less the amount of any profit realized by or accruing to such transferee from such property; and

    (B) any increase in the value of such property as a result of such improvement, of the property transferred.

    (2) In this subsection, "improvement" includes—

    (A) physical additions or changes to the property transferred;

    (B) repairs to such property;

    (C) payment of any tax on such property;

    (D) payment of any debt secured by a lien on such property that is superior or equal to the rights of the trustee; and

    (E) preservation of such property.

(f) An action or proceeding under this section may not be commenced after the earlier of—

    (1) one year after the avoidance of the transfer on account of which recovery under this section is sought; or

    (2) the time the case is closed or dismissed.

CROSS REFERENCES

Allowance of claims or interests, see 11 USCA § 502.

Applicability of this section in Chapter 9 cases, see 11 USCA § 901.

Appointment of trustee upon Chapter 9 debtor's refusal to pursue cause of action under this section, see 11 USCA § 926.

Effect of dismissal, see 11 USCA § 349.

Exemptions, see 11 USCA § 522.

---

[1] So in original. Probably should be "subsection".

§ 551. Automatic preservation of avoided transfer

Any transfer avoided under section 522, 544, 545, 547, 548, 549, or 724(a) of this title, or any lien void under section 506(d) of this title, is preserved for the benefit of the estate but only with respect to property of the estate.

CROSS REFERENCES

Applicability of this section in Chapter 9 cases, see 11 USCA § 901.

Effect of dismissal, see 11 USCA § 349.

Exemptions, see 11 USCA § 522.

§ 552. Postpetition effect of security interest

(a) Except as provided in subsection (b) of this section, property acquired by the estate or by the debtor after the commencement of the case is not subject to any lien resulting from any security agreement entered into by the debtor before the commencement of the case.

(b)(1) Except as provided in sections 363, 506(c), 522, 544, 545, 547, and 548 of this title, if the debtor and an entity entered into a security agreement before the commencement of the case and if the security interest created by such security agreement extends to property of the debtor acquired before the commencement of the case and to proceeds, products, offspring, or profits of such property, then such security interest extends to such proceeds, products, offspring, or profits acquired by the estate after the commencement of the case to the extent provided by such security agreement and by applicable nonbankruptcy law, except to any extent that the court, after notice and a hearing and based on the equities of the case, orders otherwise.

(2) Except as provided in sections 363, 506(c), 522, 544, 545, 547, and 548 of this title, and notwithstanding section 546(b) of this title, if the debtor and an entity entered into a security agreement before the commencement of the case and if the security interest created by such security agreement extends to property of the debtor acquired before the commencement of the case and to amounts paid as rents of such property or the fees, charges, accounts, or other payments for the use or occupancy of rooms and other public facilities in hotels, motels, or other lodging properties, then such security interest extends to such rents and such fees, charges, accounts, or other payments acquired by the estate after the commencement of the case to the extent provided in such security agreement, except to any extent that the court, after notice and a hearing and based on the equities of the case, orders otherwise.

CROSS REFERENCES

Applicability of this section in Chapter 9 cases, see 11 USCA § 901.

"Cash collateral" as including proceeds, products, offspring, rents or profits of property subject to security interest as provided in this section, see 11 USCA § 363.

Special revenues acquired by debtor after commencement of Chapter 9 case subject to security interest, see 11 USCA § 928.

§ 553. Setoff

(a) Except as otherwise provided in this section and in sections 362 and 363 of this title, this title does not affect any right of a creditor to offset a mutual debt owing by such creditor to the debtor that arose before the commencement of the case under this title against a claim of such creditor against the debtor that arose before the commencement of the case, except to the extent that—

    (1) the claim of such creditor against the debtor is disallowed;

    (2) such claim was transferred, by an entity other than the debtor, to such creditor—

(A) after the commencement of the case; or

(B)(i)   after 90 days before the date of the filing of the petition; and

(ii) while the debtor was insolvent (except for a setoff of a kind described in section 362(b)(6), 362(b)(7), 362(b)(17), 362(b)(27), 555, 556, 559, 560, or 561); or

(3) the debt owed to the debtor by such creditor was incurred by such creditor—

(A) after 90 days before the date of the filing of the petition;

(B) while the debtor was insolvent; and

(C) for the purpose of obtaining a right of setoff against the debtor (except for a setoff of a kind described in section 362(b)(6), 362(b)(7), 362(b)(17), 362(b)(27), 555, 556, 559, 560, or 561).

(b)(1)   Except with respect to a setoff of a kind described in section 362(b)(6), 362(b)(7), 362(b)(17), 362(b)(27), 555, 556, 559, 560, 561, 365(h), 546(h), or 365(i)(2) of this title, if a creditor offsets a mutual debt owing to the debtor against a claim against the debtor on or within 90 days before the date of the filing of the petition, then the trustee may recover from such creditor the amount so offset to the extent that any insufficiency on the date of such setoff is less than the insufficiency on the later of—

(A) 90 days before the date of the filing of the petition; and

(B) the first date during the 90 days immediately preceding the date of the filing of the petition on which there is an insufficiency.

(2) In this subsection, "insufficiency" means amount, if any, by which a claim against the debtor exceeds a mutual debt owing to the debtor by the holder of such claim.

(c) For the purposes of this section, the debtor is presumed to have been insolvent on and during the 90 days immediately preceding the date of the filing of the petition.

CROSS REFERENCES

Allowance of claims or interests, see 11 USCA § 502.

Applicability of this section in Chapter 9 cases, see 11 USCA § 901.

Determination of secured status, see 11 USCA § 506.

Effect of dismissal, see 11 USCA § 349.

Recovered property as exempt, see 11 USCA § 522.

Stay of pending actions in investor protection liquidation proceedings, see 15 USCA § 78eee.

§ 554. Abandonment of property of the estate

(a) After notice and a hearing, the trustee may abandon any property of the estate that is burdensome to the estate or that is of inconsequential value and benefit to the estate.

(b) On request of a party in interest and after notice and a hearing, the court may order the trustee to abandon any property of the estate that is burdensome to the estate or that is of inconsequential value and benefit to the estate.

(c) Unless the court orders otherwise, any property scheduled under section 521(a)(1) of this title not otherwise administered at the time of the closing of a case is abandoned to the debtor and administered for purposes of section 350 of this title.

(d) Unless the court orders otherwise, property of the estate that is not abandoned under this section and that is not administered in the case remains property of the estate.

§ 555. Contractual right to liquidate, terminate, or accelerate a securities contract

The exercise of a contractual right of a stockbroker, financial institution, financial participant, or securities clearing agency to cause the liquidation, termination, or acceleration of a securities contract, as defined in section 741 of this title, because of a condition of the kind specified in section 365(e)(1) of this title shall not be stayed, avoided, or otherwise limited by operation of any provision of this title or by order of a court or administrative agency in any proceeding under this title unless such order is authorized under the provisions of the Securities Investor Protection Act of 1970 or any statute administered by the Securities and Exchange Commission. As used in this section, the term "contractual right" includes a right set forth in a rule or bylaw of a derivatives clearing organization (as defined in the Commodity Exchange Act), a multilateral clearing organization (as defined in the Federal Deposit Insurance Corporation Improvement Act of 1991), a national securities exchange, a national securities association, a securities clearing agency, a contract market designated under the Commodity Exchange Act, a derivatives transaction execution facility registered under the Commodity Exchange Act, or a board of trade (as defined in the Commodity Exchange Act), or in a resolution of the governing board thereof, and a right, whether or not in writing, arising under common law, under law merchant, or by reason of normal business practice.

REFERENCES IN TEXT

The Securities Investor Protection Act of 1970, referred to in text, is Pub. L. 91–598, Dec. 30, 1970, 84 Stat. 1636, as amended, which is classified generally to chapter 2B-1 (section 78aaa et seq.) of Title 15, Commerce and Trade. For complete classification of this Act to the Code, see section 78aaa of Title 15 and Tables.

The Commodity Exchange Act, referred to in text, is Act Sept. 21, 1922, c. 369, 42 Stat. 998, as amended, which is classified principally to chapter 1 of Title 7, 7 U.S.C.A. § 1 et seq. For complete classification, see Short Title set out as 7 U.S.C.A. § 1 and Tables.

The Federal Deposit Insurance Corporation Improvement Act of 1991, referred to in text, is Pub. L. 102–242, Dec. 19, 1991, 105 Stat. 2236. See Tables for classification.

§ 556. Contractual right to liquidate, terminate, or accelerate a commodities contract or forward contract

The contractual right of a commodity broker, financial participant, or forward contract merchant to cause the liquidation, termination, or acceleration of a commodity contract, as defined in section 761 of this title, or forward contract because of a condition of the kind specified in section 365(e)(1) of this title, and the right to a variation or maintenance margin payment received from a trustee with respect to open commodity contracts or forward contracts, shall not be stayed, avoided, or otherwise limited by operation of any provision of this title or by the order of a court in any proceeding under this title. As used in this section, the term "contractual right" includes a right set forth in a rule or bylaw of a derivatives clearing organization (as defined in the Commodity Exchange Act), a multilateral clearing organization (as defined in the Federal Deposit Insurance Corporation Improvement Act of 1991), a national securities exchange, a national securities association, a securities clearing agency, a contract market designated under the Commodity Exchange Act, a derivatives transaction execution facility registered under the Commodity Exchange Act, or a board of trade (as defined in the Commodity Exchange Act) or in a resolution of the governing board thereof and a right, whether or not evidenced in writing, arising under common law, under law merchant or by reason of normal business practice.

REFERENCES IN TEXT

The Commodity Exchange Act, referred to in text, is Act Sept. 21, 1922, c. 369, 42 Stat. 998, as amended, which is classified principally to chapter 1 of Title 7, 7 U.S.C.A. § 1. For complete classification, see Short Title set out as 7 U.S.C.A. § 1 and Tables.

The Federal Deposit Insurance Corporation Improvement Act of 1991, referred to in text, is Pub. L. 102–242, Dec. 19, 1991, 105 Stat. 2236. See Tables for classification.

§ 557. Expedited determination of interests in, and abandonment or other disposition of grain assets

(a) This section applies only in a case concerning a debtor that owns or operates a grain storage facility and only with respect to grain and the proceeds of grain. This section does not affect the application of any other section of this title to property other than grain and proceeds of grain.

(b) In this section—

(1) "grain" means wheat, corn, flaxseed, grain sorghum, barley, oats, rye, soybeans, other dry edible beans, or rice;

(2) "grain storage facility" means a site or physical structure regularly used to store grain for producers, or to store grain acquired from producers for resale; and

(3) "producer" means an entity which engages in the growing of grain.

(c)(1) Notwithstanding sections 362, 363, 365, and 554 of this title, on the court's own motion the court may, and on the request of the trustee or an entity that claims an interest in grain or the proceeds of grain the court shall, expedite the procedures for the determination of interests in and the disposition of grain and the proceeds of grain, by shortening to the greatest extent feasible such time periods as are otherwise applicable for such procedures and by establishing, by order, a timetable having a duration of not to exceed 120 days for the completion of the applicable procedure specified in subsection (d) of this section. Such time periods and such timetable may be modified by the court, for cause, in accordance with subsection (f) of this section.

(2) The court shall determine the extent to which such time periods shall be shortened, based upon—

(A) any need of an entity claiming an interest in such grain or the proceeds of grain for a prompt determination of such interest;

(B) any need of such entity for a prompt disposition of such grain;

(C) the market for such grain;

(D) the conditions under which such grain is stored;

(E) the costs of continued storage or disposition of such grain;

(F) the orderly administration of the estate;

(G) the appropriate opportunity for an entity to assert an interest in such grain; and

(H) such other considerations as are relevant to the need to expedite such procedures in the case.

(d) The procedures that may be expedited under subsection (c) of this section include—

(1) the filing of and response to—

(A) a claim of ownership;

(B) a proof of claim;

(C) a request for abandonment;

      (D) a request for relief from the stay of action against property under section 362(a) of this title;

      (E) a request for determination of secured status;

      (F) a request for determination of whether such grain or the proceeds of grain—

          (i) is property of the estate;

          (ii) must be turned over to the estate; or

          (iii) may be used, sold, or leased; and

      (G) any other request for determination of an interest in such grain or the proceeds of grain;

    (2) the disposition of such grain or the proceeds of grain, before or after determination of interests in such grain or the proceeds of grain, by way of—

      (A) sale of such grain;

      (B) abandonment;

      (C) distribution; or

      (D) such other method as is equitable in the case;

    (3) subject to sections 701, 702, 703, 1104, 1183, 1202, and 1302 of this title, the appointment of a trustee or examiner and the retention and compensation of any professional person required to assist with respect to matters relevant to the determination of interests in or disposition of such grain or the proceeds of grain; and

    (4) the determination of any dispute concerning a matter specified in paragraph (1), (2), or (3) of this subsection.

    (e)(1) Any governmental unit that has regulatory jurisdiction over the operation or liquidation of the debtor or the debtor's business shall be given notice of any request made or order entered under subsection (c) of this section.

    (2) Any such governmental unit may raise, and may appear and be heard on, any issue relating to grain or the proceeds of grain in a case in which a request is made, or an order is entered, under subsection (c) of this section.

    (3) The trustee shall consult with such governmental unit before taking any action relating to the disposition of grain in the possession, custody, or control of the debtor or the estate.

    (f) The court may extend the period for final disposition of grain or the proceeds of grain under this section beyond 120 days if the court finds that—

    (1) the interests of justice so require in light of the complexity of the case; and

    (2) the interests of those claimants entitled to distribution of grain or the proceeds of grain will not be materially injured by such additional delay.

    (g) Unless an order establishing an expedited procedure under subsection (c) of this section, or determining any interest in or approving any disposition of grain or the proceeds of grain, is stayed pending appeal—

    (1) the reversal or modification of such order on appeal does not affect the validity of any procedure, determination, or disposition that occurs before such reversal or modification, whether or not any entity knew of the pendency of the appeal; and

    (2) neither the court nor the trustee may delay, due to the appeal of such order, any proceeding in the case in which such order is issued.

(h)(1) The trustee may recover from grain and the proceeds of grain the reasonable and necessary costs and expenses allowable under section 503(b) of this title attributable to preserving or disposing of grain or the proceeds of grain, but may not recover from such grain or the proceeds of grain any other costs or expenses.

(2) Notwithstanding section 326(a) of this title, the dollar amounts of money specified in such section include the value, as of the date of disposition, of any grain that the trustee distributes in kind.

(i) In all cases where the quantity of a specific type of grain held by a debtor operating a grain storage facility exceeds ten thousand bushels, such grain shall be sold by the trustee and the assets thereof distributed in accordance with the provisions of this section.

CROSS REFERENCES

Applicability of this section in Chapter 9 cases, see 11 USCA § 901.

Priorities, see 11 USCA § 507.

Rights and powers of trustee subject to right of seller who is "producer" of "grain" sold to "grain storage facility" owned or operated by debtor, as such terms are defined under this section, see 11 USCA § 546.

§ 558. Defenses of the estate

The estate shall have the benefit of any defense available to the debtor as against any entity other than the estate, including statutes of limitation, statutes of frauds, usury, and other personal defenses. A waiver of any such defense by the debtor after the commencement of the case does not bind the estate.

§ 559. Contractual right to liquidate, terminate, or accelerate a repurchase agreement

The exercise of a contractual right of a repo participant or financial participant to cause the liquidation, termination, or acceleration of a repurchase agreement because of a condition of the kind specified in section 365(e)(1) of this title shall not be stayed, avoided, or otherwise limited by operation of any provision of this title or by order of a court or administrative agency in any proceeding under this title, unless, where the debtor is a stockbroker or securities clearing agency, such order is authorized under the provisions of the Securities Investor Protection Act of 1970 or any statute administered by the Securities and Exchange Commission. In the event that a repo participant or financial participant liquidates one or more repurchase agreements with a debtor and under the terms of one or more such agreements has agreed to deliver assets subject to repurchase agreements to the debtor, any excess of the market prices received on liquidation of such assets (or if any such assets are not disposed of on the date of liquidation of such repurchase agreements, at the prices available at the time of liquidation of such repurchase agreements from a generally recognized source or the most recent closing bid quotation from such a source) over the sum of the stated repurchase prices and all expenses in connection with the liquidation of such repurchase agreements shall be deemed property of the estate, subject to the available rights of setoff. As used in this section, the term "contractual right" includes a right set forth in a rule or bylaw of a derivatives clearing organization (as defined in the Commodity Exchange Act), a multilateral clearing organization (as defined in the Federal Deposit Insurance Corporation Improvement Act of 1991), a national securities exchange, a national securities association, a securities clearing agency, a contract market designated under the Commodity Exchange Act, a derivatives transaction execution facility registered under the Commodity Exchange Act, or a board of trade (as defined in the Commodity Exchange Act) or in a resolution of the governing board thereof and a right, whether or not evidenced in writing, arising under common law, under law merchant or by reason of normal business practice.

REFERENCES IN TEXT

The Securities Investor Protection Act of 1970, referred to in text, is Pub. L. 91–598, Dec. 30, 1970, 84 Stat. 1636, as amended, which is classified generally to chapter 2B-1 (section 78aaa et seq.) of Title 15,

Commerce and Trade. For complete classification of this Act to the Code, see section 78aaa of Title 15 and Tables.

The Commodity Exchange Act, referred to in text, is Act Sept. 21, 1922, c. 369, 42 Stat. 998, as amended, which is classified principally to chapter 1 of Title 7, 7 U.S.C.A. § 1. For complete classification, see Short Title set out as 7 U.S.C.A. § 1 and Tables.

The Federal Deposit Insurance Corporation Improvement Act of 1991, referred to in text, is Pub. L. 102–242, Dec. 19, 1991, 105 Stat. 2236. See Tables for classification.

§ 560. Contractual right to liquidate, terminate, or accelerate a swap agreement

The exercise of any contractual right of any swap participant or financial participant to cause the liquidation, termination, or acceleration of one or more swap agreements because of a condition of the kind specified in section 365(e)(1) of this title or to offset or net out any termination values or payment amounts arising under or in connection with the termination, liquidation, or acceleration of one or more swap agreements shall not be stayed, avoided, or otherwise limited by operation of any provision of this title or by order of a court or administrative agency in any proceeding under this title. As used in this section, the term "contractual right" includes a right set forth in a rule or bylaw of a derivatives clearing organization (as defined in the Commodity Exchange Act), a multilateral clearing organization (as defined in the Federal Deposit Insurance Corporation Improvement Act of 1991), a national securities exchange, a national securities association, a securities clearing agency, a contract market designated under the Commodity Exchange Act, a derivatives transaction execution facility registered under the Commodity Exchange Act, or a board of trade (as defined in the Commodity Exchange Act) or in a resolution of the governing board thereof and a right, whether or not evidenced in writing, arising under common law, under law merchant, or by reason of normal business practice.

REFERENCES IN TEXT

The Commodity Exchange Act, referred to in text, is Act Sept. 21, 1922, c. 369, 42 Stat. 998, as amended, which is classified principally to chapter 1 of Title 7, 7 U.S.C.A. § 1. For complete classification, see Short Title set out as 7 U.S.C.A. § 1 and Tables.

The Federal Deposit Insurance Corporation Improvement Act of 1991, referred to in text, is Pub. L. 102–242, Dec. 19, 1991, 105 Stat. 2236. See Tables for classification.

§ 561. Contractual right to terminate, liquidate, accelerate, or offset under a master netting agreement and across contracts; proceedings under chapter 15

(a) Subject to subsection (b), the exercise of any contractual right, because of a condition of the kind specified in section 365(e)(1), to cause the termination, liquidation, or acceleration of or to offset or net termination values, payment amounts, or other transfer obligations arising under or in connection with one or more (or the termination, liquidation, or acceleration of one or more)—

(1) securities contracts, as defined in section 741(7);

(2) commodity contracts, as defined in section 761(4);

(3) forward contracts;

(4) repurchase agreements;

(5) swap agreements; or

(6) master netting agreements,

shall not be stayed, avoided, or otherwise limited by operation of any provision of this title or by any order of a court or administrative agency in any proceeding under this title.

(b)(1) A party may exercise a contractual right described in subsection (a) to terminate, liquidate, or accelerate only to the extent that such party could exercise such a right under section 555, 556, 559, or 560 for each individual contract covered by the master netting agreement in issue.

(2) If a debtor is a commodity broker subject to subchapter IV of chapter 7—

(A) a party may not net or offset an obligation to the debtor arising under, or in connection with, a commodity contract traded on or subject to the rules of a contract market designated under the Commodity Exchange Act or a derivatives transaction execution facility registered under the Commodity Exchange Act against any claim arising under, or in connection with, other instruments, contracts, or agreements listed in subsection (a) except to the extent that the party has positive net equity in the commodity accounts at the debtor, as calculated under such subchapter; and

(B) another commodity broker may not net or offset an obligation to the debtor arising under, or in connection with, a commodity contract entered into or held on behalf of a customer of the debtor and traded on or subject to the rules of a contract market designated under the Commodity Exchange Act or a derivatives transaction execution facility registered under the Commodity Exchange Act against any claim arising under, or in connection with, other instruments, contracts, or agreements listed in subsection (a).

(3) No provision of subparagraph (A) or (B) of paragraph (2) shall prohibit the offset of claims and obligations that arise under—

(A) a cross-margining agreement or similar arrangement that has been approved by the Commodity Futures Trading Commission or submitted to the Commodity Futures Trading Commission under paragraph (1) or (2) of section 5c(c) of the Commodity Exchange Act and has not been abrogated or rendered ineffective by the Commodity Futures Trading Commission; or

(B) any other netting agreement between a clearing organization (as defined in section 761) and another entity that has been approved by the Commodity Futures Trading Commission.

(c) As used in this section, the term "contractual right" includes a right set forth in a rule or bylaw of a derivatives clearing organization (as defined in the Commodity Exchange Act), a multilateral clearing organization (as defined in the Federal Deposit Insurance Corporation Improvement Act of 1991), a national securities exchange, a national securities association, a securities clearing agency, a contract market designated under the Commodity Exchange Act, a derivatives transaction execution facility registered under the Commodity Exchange Act, or a board of trade (as defined in the Commodity Exchange Act) or in a resolution of the governing board thereof, and a right, whether or not evidenced in writing, arising under common law, under law merchant, or by reason of normal business practice.

(d) Any provisions of this title relating to securities contracts, commodity contracts, forward contracts, repurchase agreements, swap agreements, or master netting agreements shall apply in a case under chapter 15, so that enforcement of contractual provisions of such contracts and agreements in accordance with their terms will not be stayed or otherwise limited by operation of any provision of this title or by order of a court in any case under this title, and to limit avoidance powers to the same extent as in a proceeding under chapter 7 or 11 of this title (such enforcement not to be limited based on the presence or absence of assets of the debtor in the United States).

REFERENCES IN TEXT

The Commodity Exchange Act, referred to in subsecs. (b)(2)(A) and (c), is Act Sept. 21, 1922, c. 369, 42 Stat. 998, as amended, which is classified principally to chapter 1 of Title 7, 7 U.S.C.A. § 1 et seq. For complete classification, see Short Title set out as 7 U.S.C.A. § 1 and Tables.

Section 5c(c) of the Commodity Exchange Act, referred to in subsec. (b)(2)(A), is Act Sept. 21, 1922, c. 369, § 5c, as added and amended Dec. 21, 2000, Pub. L. 106–554, § 1(a)(5) [Title I, § 113, Title II, § 251(h)], 114 Stat. 2763, 2763A–399, 2763a–444, which is classified to 7 U.S.C.A. § 7a–2.

The Federal Deposit Insurance Corporation Improvement Act of 1991, referred to in subsec. (c), is Pub. L. 102–242, Dec. 19, 1991, 105 Stat. 2236. See Tables for classification.

§ 562. Timing of damage measurement in connection with swap agreements, securities contracts, forward contracts, commodity contracts, repurchase agreements, and master netting agreements

(a) If the trustee rejects a swap agreement, securities contract (as defined in section 741), forward contract, commodity contract (as defined in section 761), repurchase agreement, or master netting agreement pursuant to section 365(a), or if a forward contract merchant, stockbroker, financial institution, securities clearing agency, repo participant, financial participant, master netting agreement participant, or swap participant liquidates, terminates, or accelerates such contract or agreement, damages shall be measured as of the earlier of—

    (1) the date of such rejection; or

    (2) the date or dates of such liquidation, termination, or acceleration.

(b) If there are not any commercially reasonable determinants of value as of any date referred to in paragraph (1) or (2) of subsection (a), damages shall be measured as of the earliest subsequent date or dates on which there are commercially reasonable determinants of value.

(c) For the purposes of subsection (b), if damages are not measured as of the date or dates of rejection, liquidation, termination, or acceleration, and the forward contract merchant, stockbroker, financial institution, securities clearing agency, repo participant, financial participant, master netting agreement participant, or swap participant or the trustee objects to the timing of the measurement of damages—

    (1) the trustee, in the case of an objection by a forward contract merchant, stockbroker, financial institution, securities clearing agency, repo participant, financial participant, master netting agreement participant, or swap participant; or

    (2) the forward contract merchant, stockbroker, financial institution, securities clearing agency, repo participant, financial participant, master netting agreement participant, or swap participant, in the case of an objection by the trustee,

has the burden of proving that there were no commercially reasonable determinants of value as of such date or dates.

CHAPTER 7—LIQUIDATION

SUBCHAPTER I—OFFICERS AND ADMINISTRATION

SUBCHAPTER II—COLLECTION, LIQUIDATION, AND DISTRIBUTION OF THE ESTATE

SUBCHAPTER III—STOCKBROKER LIQUIDATION

SUBCHAPTER IV—COMMODITY BROKER LIQUIDATION

SUBCHAPTER V—CLEARING BANK LIQUIDATION

SUBCHAPTER I—OFFICERS AND ADMINISTRATION

§ 701.   Interim trustee

(a)(1)   Promptly after the order for relief under this chapter, the United States trustee shall appoint one disinterested person that is a member of the panel of private trustees established under section 586(a)(1) of title 28 or that is serving as trustee in the case immediately before the order for relief under this chapter to serve as interim trustee in the case.

(2)   If none of the members of such panel is willing to serve as interim trustee in the case, then the United States trustee may serve as interim trustee in the case.

(b)   The service of an interim trustee under this section terminates when a trustee elected or designated under section 702 of this title to serve as trustee in the case qualifies under section 322 of this title.

(c)   An interim trustee serving under this section is a trustee in a case under this title.

CROSS REFERENCES

Appointment of interim trustee after commencement of involuntary case, see 11 USCA § 303.

Effect of conversion, see 11 USCA § 348.

Grain storage facility bankruptcies, expedited appointment of trustee, see 11 USCA § 557.

Qualification of trustee, see 11 USCA § 322.

§ 702.   Election of trustee

(a)   A creditor may vote for a candidate for trustee only if such creditor—

(1)   holds an allowable, undisputed, fixed, liquidated, unsecured claim of a kind entitled to distribution under section 726(a)(2), 726(a)(3), 726(a)(4), 752(a), 766(h), or 766(i) of this title;

(2)   does not have an interest materially adverse, other than an equity interest that is not substantial in relation to such creditor's interest as a creditor, to the interest of creditors entitled to such distribution; and

(3)   is not an insider.

(b)   At the meeting of creditors held under section 341 of this title, creditors may elect one person to serve as trustee in the case if election of a trustee is requested by creditors that may vote under subsection (a) of this section, and that hold at least 20 percent in amount of the claims specified in subsection (a)(1) of this section that are held by creditors that may vote under subsection (a) of this section.

(c)   A candidate for trustee is elected trustee if—

(1)   creditors holding at least 20 percent in amount of the claims of a kind specified in subsection (a)(1) of this section that are held by creditors that may vote under subsection (a) of this section vote; and

(2) such candidate receives the votes of creditors holding a majority in amount of claims specified in subsection (a)(1) of this section that are held by creditors that vote for a trustee.

(d) If a trustee is not elected under this section, then the interim trustee shall serve as trustee in the case.

CROSS REFERENCES

Compensation of officers, see 11 USCA § 330.

Eligibility to serve as trustee, see 11 USCA § 321.

Employment of professional persons, see 11 USCA § 327.

Grain storage facility bankruptcies, expedited appointment of trustee, see 11 USCA § 557.

Limitation on compensation of trustee, see 11 USCA § 326.

Qualification of trustee, see 11 USCA § 322.

Time for bringing action, see 11 USCA § 546.

§ 703. Successor trustee

(a) If a trustee dies or resigns during a case, fails to qualify under section 322 of this title, or is removed under section 324 of this title, creditors may elect, in the manner specified in section 702 of this title, a person to fill the vacancy in the office of trustee.

(b) Pending election of a trustee under subsection (a) of this section, if necessary to preserve or prevent loss to the estate, the United States trustee may appoint an interim trustee in the manner specified in section 701(a).

(c) If creditors do not elect a successor trustee under subsection (a) of this section or if a trustee is needed in a case reopened under section 350 of this title, then the United States trustee—

(1) shall appoint one disinterested person that is a member of the panel of private trustees established under section 586(a)(1) of title 28 to serve as trustee in the case; or

(2) may, if none of the disinterested members of such panel is willing to serve as trustee, serve as trustee in the case.

CROSS REFERENCES

Effect of vacancy in office of trustee, see 11 USCA § 325.

Grain storage facility bankruptcies, expedited appointment of trustee, see 11 USCA § 557.

Qualification of trustee, see 11 USCA § 322.

§ 704. Duties of trustee

(a) The trustee shall—

(1) collect and reduce to money the property of the estate for which such trustee serves, and close such estate as expeditiously as is compatible with the best interests of parties in interest;

(2) be accountable for all property received;

(3) ensure that the debtor shall perform his intention as specified in section 521(a)(2)(B) of this title;

(4) investigate the financial affairs of the debtor;

(5) if a purpose would be served, examine proofs of claims and object to the allowance of any claim that is improper;

(6) if advisable, oppose the discharge of the debtor;

(7) unless the court orders otherwise, furnish such information concerning the estate and the estate's administration as is requested by a party in interest;

(8) if the business of the debtor is authorized to be operated, file with the court, with the United States trustee, and with any governmental unit charged with responsibility for collection or determination of any tax arising out of such operation, periodic reports and summaries of the operation of such business, including a statement of receipts and disbursements, and such other information as the United States trustee or the court requires;

(9) make a final report and file a final account of the administration of the estate with the court and with the United States trustee;

(10) if with respect to the debtor there is a claim for a domestic support obligation, provide the applicable notice specified in subsection (c);

(11) if, at the time of the commencement of the case, the debtor (or any entity designated by the debtor) served as the administrator (as defined in section 3 of the Employee Retirement Income Security Act of 1974) of an employee benefit plan, continue to perform the obligations required of the administrator; and

(12) use all reasonable and best efforts to transfer patients from a health care business that is in the process of being closed to an appropriate health care business that—

(A) is in the vicinity of the health care business that is closing;

(B) provides the patient with services that are substantially similar to those provided by the health care business that is in the process of being closed; and

(C) maintains a reasonable quality of care.

(b)(1) With respect to a debtor who is an individual in a case under this chapter—

(A) the United States trustee (or the bankruptcy administrator, if any) shall review all materials filed by the debtor and, not later than 10 days after the date of the first meeting of creditors, file with the court a statement as to whether the debtor's case would be presumed to be an abuse under section 707(b); and

(B) not later than 7 days after receiving a statement under subparagraph (A), the court shall provide a copy of the statement to all creditors.

(2) The United States trustee (or bankruptcy administrator, if any) shall, not later than 30 days after the date of filing a statement under paragraph (1), either file a motion to dismiss or convert under section 707(b) or file a statement setting forth the reasons the United States trustee (or the bankruptcy administrator, if any) does not consider such a motion to be appropriate, if the United States trustee (or the bankruptcy administrator, if any) determines that the debtor's case should be presumed to be an abuse under section 707(b) and the product of the debtor's current monthly income, multiplied by 12 is not less than—

(A) in the case of a debtor in a household of 1 person, the median family income of the applicable State for 1 earner; or

(B) in the case of a debtor in a household of 2 or more individuals, the highest median family income of the applicable State for a family of the same number or fewer individuals.

(c)(1) In a case described in subsection (a)(10) to which subsection (a)(10) applies, the trustee shall—

(A)(i) provide written notice to the holder of the claim described in subsection (a)(10) of such claim and of the right of such holder to use the services of the State child support enforcement agency established under sections 464 and 466 of the Social Security Act for the

State in which such holder resides, for assistance in collecting child support during and after the case under this title;

    (ii) include in the notice provided under clause (i) the address and telephone number of such State child support enforcement agency; and

    (iii) include in the notice provided under clause (i) an explanation of the rights of such holder to payment of such claim under this chapter;

    (B)(i) provide written notice to such State child support enforcement agency of such claim; and

    (ii) include in the notice provided under clause (i) the name, address, and telephone number of such holder; and

    (C) at such time as the debtor is granted a discharge under section 727, provide written notice to such holder and to such State child support enforcement agency of—

        (i) the granting of the discharge;

        (ii) the last recent known address of the debtor;

        (iii) the last recent known name and address of the debtor's employer; and

        (iv) the name of each creditor that holds a claim that—

            (I) is not discharged under paragraph (2), (4), or (14A) of section 523(a); or

            (II) was reaffirmed by the debtor under section 524(c).

    (2)(A) The holder of a claim described in subsection (a)(10) or the State child support enforcement agency of the State in which such holder resides may request from a creditor described in paragraph (1)(C)(iv) the last known address of the debtor.

    (B) Notwithstanding any other provision of law, a creditor that makes a disclosure of a last known address of a debtor in connection with a request made under subparagraph (A) shall not be liable by reason of making such disclosure.

REFERENCES IN TEXT

Section 3 of the Employee Retirement Income Security Act of 1974, referred to in subsec. (a)(11), is Pub. L. 93–406, Title I, § 3, Sept. 2, 1974, 88 Stat. 833, which is classified to 29 U.S.C.A. § 1002.

Section 464 of the Social Security Act, referred to in subsec. (c)(1)(A)(i), is Act Aug. 14, 1935, c. 531, Title IV, § 464, as added Aug. 13, 1981, Pub. L. 97–35, Title XXIII, § 2331(a), 95 Stat. 860, and amended, which is classified to 42 U.S.C.A. § 664.

Section 466 of the Social Security Act, referred to in subsec. (c)(1)(A)(i), is Act Aug. 14, 1935, c. 531, Title IV, § 466, as added Aug. 16, 1984, Pub. L. 98–378, § 3(b), 98 Stat. 1306, and amended, which is classified to 42 U.S.C.A. § 666.

CROSS REFERENCES

Duties of trustee in—

    Chapter 11 non-subchapter V cases, see 11 USCA § 1106.

    Chapter 11 subchapter V cases, see 11 USCA § 1183.

    Chapter 12 cases, see 11 USCA § 1202.

    Chapter 13 cases, see 11 USCA § 1302.

Multiemployer plan termination proceedings, see 29 USCA § 1342.

Filing of reports and summaries by Chapter 13 debtor engaged in business, see 11 USCA § 1304.

Powers and duties of trustee in investor protection liquidation proceedings, see 15 USCA § 78fff–1.

§ 705. Creditors' committee

(a) At the meeting under section 341(a) of this title, creditors that may vote for a trustee under section 702(a) of this title may elect a committee of not fewer than three, and not more than eleven, creditors, each of whom holds an allowable unsecured claim of a kind entitled to distribution under section 726(a)(2) of this title.

(b) A committee elected under subsection (a) of this section may consult with the trustee or the United States trustee in connection with the administration of the estate, make recommendations to the trustee or the United States trustee respecting the performance of the trustee's duties, and submit to the court or the United States trustee any question affecting the administration of the estate.

CROSS REFERENCES

Appointment of creditors' committees in chapter 11 non-small business cases and non-subchapter V cases, see 11 USCA § 1102.

Powers and duties of committees in chapter 11 cases, see 11 USCA § 1103.

§ 706. Conversion

(a) The debtor may convert a case under this chapter to a case under chapter 11, 12, or 13 of this title at any time, if the case has not been converted under section 1112, 1208, or 1307 of this title. Any waiver of the right to convert a case under this subsection is unenforceable.

(b) On request of a party in interest and after notice and a hearing, the court may convert a case under this chapter to a case under chapter 11 of this title at any time.

(c) The court may not convert a case under this chapter to a case under chapter 12 or 13 of this title unless the debtor requests or consents to such conversion.

(d) Notwithstanding any other provision of this section, a case may not be converted to a case under another chapter of this title unless the debtor may be a debtor under such chapter.

CROSS REFERENCES

Conversion or dismissal of—

    Chapter 11 cases, see 11 USCA § 1112.

    Chapter 12 cases, see 11 USCA § 1208.

    Chapter 13 cases, see 11 USCA § 1307.

Effect of conversion, see 11 USCA § 348.

Termination of debtor's taxable period in—

    Chapter 11 cases, see 11 USCA § 1146.

    Chapter 12 cases, see 11 USCA § 1231.

§ 707. Dismissal of a case or conversion to a case under chapter 11 or 13

(a) The court may dismiss a case under this chapter only after notice and a hearing and only for cause, including—

    (1) unreasonable delay by the debtor that is prejudicial to creditors;

    (2) nonpayment of any fees or charges required under chapter 123 of title 28; and

    (3) failure of the debtor in a voluntary case to file, within fifteen days or such additional time as the court may allow after the filing of the petition commencing such case, the information required by paragraph (1) of section 521(a), but only on a motion by the United States trustee.

(b)(1)   After notice and a hearing, the court, on its own motion or on a motion by the United States trustee, trustee (or bankruptcy administrator, if any), or any party in interest, may dismiss a case filed by an individual debtor under this chapter whose debts are primarily consumer debts, or, with the debtor's consent, convert such a case to a case under chapter 11 or 13 of this title, if it finds that the granting of relief would be an abuse of the provisions of this chapter. In making a determination whether to dismiss a case under this section, the court may not take into consideration whether a debtor has made, or continues to make, charitable contributions (that meet the definition of "charitable contribution" under section 548(d)(3)) to any qualified religious or charitable entity or organization (as that term is defined in section 548(d)(4)).

(2)(A)(i) In considering under paragraph (1) whether the granting of relief would be an abuse of the provisions of this chapter, the court shall presume abuse exists if the debtor's current monthly income reduced by the amounts determined under clauses (ii), (iii), and (iv), and multiplied by 60 is not less than the lesser of—

       (I)   25 percent of the debtor's nonpriority unsecured claims in the case, or $9,075, whichever is greater; or

       (II) $15,150.

(ii)(I) The debtor's monthly expenses shall be the debtor's applicable monthly expense amounts specified under the National Standards and Local Standards, and the debtor's actual monthly expenses for the categories specified as Other Necessary Expenses issued by the Internal Revenue Service for the area in which the debtor resides, as in effect on the date of the order for relief, for the debtor, the dependents of the debtor, and the spouse of the debtor in a joint case, if the spouse is not otherwise a dependent. Such expenses shall include reasonably necessary health insurance, disability insurance, and health savings account expenses for the debtor, the spouse of the debtor, or the dependents of the debtor. Notwithstanding any other provision of this clause, the monthly expenses of the debtor shall not include any payments for debts. In addition, the debtor's monthly expenses shall include the debtor's reasonably necessary expenses incurred to maintain the safety of the debtor and the family of the debtor from family violence as identified under section 302 of the Family Violence Prevention and Services Act, or other applicable Federal law. The expenses included in the debtor's monthly expenses described in the preceding sentence shall be kept confidential by the court. In addition, if it is demonstrated that it is reasonable and necessary, the debtor's monthly expenses may also include an additional allowance for food and clothing of up to 5 percent of the food and clothing categories as specified by the National Standards issued by the Internal Revenue Service.

       (II) In addition, the debtor's monthly expenses may include, if applicable, the continuation of actual expenses paid by the debtor that are reasonable and necessary for care and support of an elderly, chronically ill, or disabled household member or member of the debtor's immediate family (including parents, grandparents, siblings, children, and grandchildren of the debtor, the dependents of the debtor, and the spouse of the debtor in a joint case who is not a dependent) and who is unable to pay for such reasonable and necessary expenses. Such monthly expenses may include, if applicable, contributions to an account of a qualified ABLE program to the extent such contributions are not excess contributions (as described in section 4973(h) of the Internal Revenue Code of 1986) and if the designated beneficiary of such account is a child, stepchild, grandchild, or stepgrandchild of the debtor.

       (III) In addition, for a debtor eligible for chapter 13, the debtor's monthly expenses may include the actual administrative expenses of administering a chapter 13 plan for the district in which the debtor resides, up to an amount of 10 percent of the projected plan payments, as determined under schedules issued by the Executive Office for United States Trustees.

       (IV) In addition, the debtor's monthly expenses may include the actual expenses for each dependent child less than 18 years of age, not to exceed $2,275 per year per child, to attend a private or public elementary or secondary school if the debtor provides documentation of such expenses and a detailed explanation of why such expenses are reasonable and necessary, and why such expenses are not already accounted for in the National Standards, Local Standards, or Other Necessary Expenses referred to in subclause (I).

(V) In addition, the debtor's monthly expenses may include an allowance for housing and utilities, in excess of the allowance specified by the Local Standards for housing and utilities issued by the Internal Revenue Service, based on the actual expenses for home energy costs if the debtor provides documentation of such actual expenses and demonstrates that such actual expenses are reasonable and necessary.

(iii) The debtor's average monthly payments on account of secured debts shall be calculated as the sum of—

(I) the total of all amounts scheduled as contractually due to secured creditors in each month of the 60 months following the date of the filing of the petition; and

(II) any additional payments to secured creditors necessary for the debtor, in filing a plan under chapter 13 of this title, to maintain possession of the debtor's primary residence, motor vehicle, or other property necessary for the support of the debtor and the debtor's dependents, that serves as collateral for secured debts;

divided by 60.

(iv) The debtor's expenses for payment of all priority claims (including priority child support and alimony claims) shall be calculated as the total amount of debts entitled to priority, divided by 60.

(B)(i) In any proceeding brought under this subsection, the presumption of abuse may only be rebutted by demonstrating special circumstances, such as a serious medical condition or a call or order to active duty in the Armed Forces, to the extent such special circumstances that justify additional expenses or adjustments of current monthly income for which there is no reasonable alternative.

(ii) In order to establish special circumstances, the debtor shall be required to itemize each additional expense or adjustment of income and to provide—

(I) documentation for such expense or adjustment to income; and

(II) a detailed explanation of the special circumstances that make such expenses or adjustment to income necessary and reasonable.

(iii) The debtor shall attest under oath to the accuracy of any information provided to demonstrate that additional expenses or adjustments to income are required.

(iv) The presumption of abuse may only be rebutted if the additional expenses or adjustments to income referred to in clause (i) cause the product of the debtor's current monthly income reduced by the amounts determined under clauses (ii), (iii), and (iv) of subparagraph (A) when multiplied by 60 to be less than the lesser of—

(I) 25 percent of the debtor's nonpriority unsecured claims, or $9,075, whichever is greater; or

(II) $15,150.

(C) As part of the schedule of current income and expenditures required under section 521, the debtor shall include a statement of the debtor's current monthly income, and the calculations that determine whether a presumption arises under subparagraph (A)(i), that show how each such amount is calculated.

(D) Subparagraphs (A) through (C) shall not apply, and the court may not dismiss or convert a case based on any form of means testing—

(i) if the debtor is a disabled veteran (as defined in section 3741(1) of title 38), and the indebtedness occurred primarily during a period during which he or she was—

(I) on active duty (as defined in section 101(d)(1) of title 10); or

(II) performing a homeland defense activity (as defined in section 901(1) of title 32); or

(ii) with respect to the debtor, while the debtor is—

(I) on, and during the 540-day period beginning immediately after the debtor is released from, a period of active duty (as defined in section 101(d)(1) of title 10) of not less than 90 days; or

(II) performing, and during the 540-day period beginning immediately after the debtor is no longer performing, a homeland defense activity (as defined in section 901(1) of title 32) performed for a period of not less than 90 days;

if after September 11, 2001, the debtor while a member of a reserve component of the Armed Forces or a member of the National Guard, was called to such active duty or performed such homeland defense activity.

(3) In considering under paragraph (1) whether the granting of relief would be an abuse of the provisions of this chapter in a case in which the presumption in paragraph (2)(A)(i) does not arise or is rebutted, the court shall consider—

(A) whether the debtor filed the petition in bad faith; or

(B) the totality of the circumstances (including whether the debtor seeks to reject a personal services contract and the financial need for such rejection as sought by the debtor) of the debtor's financial situation demonstrates abuse.

(4)(A) The court, on its own initiative or on the motion of a party in interest, in accordance with the procedures described in rule 9011 of the Federal Rules of Bankruptcy Procedure, may order the attorney for the debtor to reimburse the trustee for all reasonable costs in prosecuting a motion filed under section 707(b), including reasonable attorneys' fees, if—

(i) a trustee files a motion for dismissal or conversion under this subsection; and

(ii) the court—

(I) grants such motion; and

(II) finds that the action of the attorney for the debtor in filing a case under this chapter violated rule 9011 of the Federal Rules of Bankruptcy Procedure.

(B) If the court finds that the attorney for the debtor violated rule 9011 of the Federal Rules of Bankruptcy Procedure, the court, on its own initiative or on the motion of a party in interest, in accordance with such procedures, may order—

(i) the assessment of an appropriate civil penalty against the attorney for the debtor; and

(ii) the payment of such civil penalty to the trustee, the United States trustee (or the bankruptcy administrator, if any).

(C) The signature of an attorney on a petition, pleading, or written motion shall constitute a certification that the attorney has—

(i) performed a reasonable investigation into the circumstances that gave rise to the petition, pleading, or written motion; and

(ii) determined that the petition, pleading, or written motion—

(I) is well grounded in fact; and

(II) is warranted by existing law or a good faith argument for the extension, modification, or reversal of existing law and does not constitute an abuse under paragraph (1).

(D) The signature of an attorney on the petition shall constitute a certification that the attorney has no knowledge after an inquiry that the information in the schedules filed with such petition is incorrect.

(5)(A) Except as provided in subparagraph (B) and subject to paragraph (6), the court, on its own initiative or on the motion of a party in interest, in accordance with the procedures described in rule 9011 of the Federal Rules of Bankruptcy Procedure, may award a debtor all reasonable costs (including reasonable attorneys' fees) in contesting a motion filed by a party in interest (other than a trustee or United States trustee (or bankruptcy administrator, if any)) under this subsection if—

    (i) the court does not grant the motion; and

    (ii) the court finds that—

        (I) the position of the party that filed the motion violated rule 9011 of the Federal Rules of Bankruptcy Procedure; or

        (II) the attorney (if any) who filed the motion did not comply with the requirements of clauses (i) and (ii) of paragraph (4)(C), and the motion was made solely for the purpose of coercing a debtor into waiving a right guaranteed to the debtor under this title.

(B) A small business that has a claim of an aggregate amount less than $1,525 shall not be subject to subparagraph (A)(ii)(I).

(C) For purposes of this paragraph—

    (i) the term "small business" means an unincorporated business, partnership, corporation, association, or organization that—

        (I) has fewer than 25 full-time employees as determined on the date on which the motion is filed; and

        (II) is engaged in commercial or business activity; and

    (ii) the number of employees of a wholly owned subsidiary of a corporation includes the employees of—

        (I) a parent corporation; and

        (II) any other subsidiary corporation of the parent corporation.

(6) Only the judge or United States trustee (or bankruptcy administrator, if any) may file a motion under section 707(b), if the current monthly income of the debtor, or in a joint case, the debtor and the debtor's spouse, as of the date of the order for relief, when multiplied by 12, is equal to or less than—

    (A) in the case of a debtor in a household of 1 person, the median family income of the applicable State for 1 earner;

    (B) in the case of a debtor in a household of 2, 3, or 4 individuals, the highest median family income of the applicable State for a family of the same number or fewer individuals; or

    (C) in the case of a debtor in a household exceeding 4 individuals, the highest median family income of the applicable State for a family of 4 or fewer individuals, plus $825 per month for each individual in excess of 4.

(7)(A) No judge, United States trustee (or bankruptcy administrator, if any), trustee, or other party in interest may file a motion under paragraph (2) if the current monthly income of the debtor, including a veteran (as that term is defined in section 101 of title 38), and the debtor's spouse combined, as of the date of the order for relief when multiplied by 12, is equal to or less than—

    (i)   in the case of a debtor in a household of 1 person, the median family income of the applicable State for 1 earner;

    (ii)   in the case of a debtor in a household of 2, 3, or 4 individuals, the highest median family income of the applicable State for a family of the same number or fewer individuals; or

    (iii)   in the case of a debtor in a household exceeding 4 individuals, the highest median family income of the applicable State for a family of 4 or fewer individuals, plus \$825 per month for each individual in excess of 4.

(B)   In a case that is not a joint case, current monthly income of the debtor's spouse shall not be considered for purposes of subparagraph (A) if—

    (i)(I)   the debtor and the debtor's spouse are separated under applicable nonbankruptcy law; or

    (II)   the debtor and the debtor's spouse are living separate and apart, other than for the purpose of evading subparagraph (A); and

    (ii)   the debtor files a statement under penalty of perjury—

        (I)   specifying that the debtor meets the requirement of subclause (I) or (II) of clause (i); and

        (II)   disclosing the aggregate, or best estimate of the aggregate, amount of any cash or money payments received from the debtor's spouse attributed to the debtor's current monthly income.

(c)(1)   In this subsection—

    (A)   the term "crime of violence" has the meaning given such term in section 16 of title 18; and

    (B)   the term "drug trafficking crime" has the meaning given such term in section 924(c)(2) of title 18.

(2)   Except as provided in paragraph (3), after notice and a hearing, the court, on a motion by the victim of a crime of violence or a drug trafficking crime, may when it is in the best interest of the victim dismiss a voluntary case filed under this chapter by a debtor who is an individual if such individual was convicted of such crime.

(3)   The court may not dismiss a case under paragraph (2) if the debtor establishes by a preponderance of the evidence that the filing of a case under this chapter is necessary to satisfy a claim for a domestic support obligation.

REFERENCES IN TEXT

     The Family Violence Prevention and Services Act, referred to in subsec. (b)(2)(A)(ii)(I), is Pub. L. 98–457, Title III, § 301 et seq., as revised by Pub. L. 111–320, § 201, Dec. 20, 2010, 124 Stat. 3484, which is classified principally to chapter 110 of Title 42, 42 U.S.C.A. § 10401 et seq. Section 302 of the Act is classified to 42 U.S.C.A. § 10402.

CROSS REFERENCES

Chapter 7 means test calculation, see Official Bankruptcy Form 122A-2.

Chapter 7 statement of your current monthly income, see Official Bankruptcy Form 122A-1.

Conversion or dismissal of—

     Chapter 11 cases, see 11 USCA § 1112.

     Chapter 13 cases, see 11 USCA § 1307.

Crime victims' rights, rights afforded and best efforts to accord rights, procedures to promote compliance, see 18 U.S.C.A. § 3771.

Dismissal of Chapter 9 cases, see 11 USCA § 930.

Effect of dismissal, see 11 USCA § 349.

Statement of exemption from presumption of abuse under § 707(b)(2), see Official Bankruptcy Form 122A-1 Supp.

SUBCHAPTER II—COLLECTION, LIQUIDATION, AND DISTRIBUTION OF THE ESTATE

§ 721. Authorization to operate business

The court may authorize the trustee to operate the business of the debtor for a limited period, if such operation is in the best interest of the estate and consistent with the orderly liquidation of the estate.

CROSS REFERENCES

Authorization to operate business in Chapter 11 cases, see 11 USCA § 1108.

Debtor engaged in business in Chapter 13 cases, see 11 USCA § 1304.

Executory contracts and unexpired leases, see 11 USCA § 365.

Executory contracts in stockbroker liquidation cases, see 11 USCA § 744.

Obtaining credit, see 11 USCA § 364.

Retention or replacement of professional persons, see 11 USCA § 327.

Treatment of accounts in—

    Commodity broker liquidation cases, see 11 USCA § 763.

    Stockbroker liquidation cases, see 11 USCA § 745.

Use, sale or lease of property, see 11 USCA § 363.

Utility service, see 11 USCA § 366.

§ 722. Redemption

An individual debtor may, whether or not the debtor has waived the right to redeem under this section, redeem tangible personal property intended primarily for personal, family, or household use, from a lien securing a dischargeable consumer debt, if such property is exempted under section 522 of this title or has been abandoned under section 554 of this title, by paying the holder of such lien the amount of the allowed secured claim of such holder that is secured by such lien in full at the time of redemption.

§ 723. Rights of partnership trustee against general partners

(a) If there is a deficiency of property of the estate to pay in full all claims which are allowed in a case under this chapter concerning a partnership and with respect to which a general partner of the partnership is personally liable, the trustee shall have a claim against such general partner to the extent that under applicable nonbankruptcy law such general partner is personally liable for such deficiency.

(b) To the extent practicable, the trustee shall first seek recovery of such deficiency from any general partner in such partnership that is not a debtor in a case under this title. Pending determination of such deficiency, the court may order any such partner to provide the estate with indemnity for, or assurance of payment of, any deficiency recoverable from such partner, or not to dispose of property.

(c) The trustee has a claim against the estate of each general partner in such partnership that is a debtor in a case under this title for the full amount of all claims of creditors allowed in the case concerning such partnership. Notwithstanding section 502 of this title, there shall not be allowed in such partner's case a claim against such partner on which both such partner and such partnership are liable, except to any extent that such claim is secured only by property of such partner and not by property of such partnership. The claim of the trustee under this subsection is entitled to distribution in such partner's case under section 726(a) of this title the same as any other claim of a kind specified in such section.

(d) If the aggregate that the trustee recovers from the estates of general partners under subsection (c) of this section is greater than any deficiency not recovered under subsection (b) of this section, the court, after notice and a hearing, shall determine an equitable distribution of the surplus so recovered, and the trustee shall distribute such surplus to the estates of the general partners in such partnership according to such determination.

REFERENCES IN TEXT

Section 728(a), (b) of this title, referred to in subsec. (b), is subsecs. (a) and (b) of 11 U.S.C.A. § 728, which was repealed by Pub. L. 109–8, Title VII, § 719(b)(1), Apr. 20, 2005, 119 Stat. 133.

CROSS REFERENCES

Property of estate, see 11 USCA § 541.

§ 724. Treatment of certain liens

(a) The trustee may avoid a lien that secures a claim of a kind specified in section 726(a)(4) of this title.

(b) Property in which the estate has an interest and that is subject to a lien that is not avoidable under this title (other than to the extent that there is a properly perfected unavoidable tax lien arising in connection with an ad valorem tax on real or personal property of the estate) and that secures an allowed claim for a tax, or proceeds of such property, shall be distributed—

    (1) first, to any holder of an allowed claim secured by a lien on such property that is not avoidable under this title and that is senior to such tax lien;

    (2) second, to any holder of a claim of a kind specified in section 507(a)(1)(C) or 507(a)(2) (except that such expenses under each such section, other than claims for wages, salaries, or commissions that arise after the date of the filing of the petition, shall be limited to expenses incurred under this chapter and shall not include expenses incurred under chapter 11 of this title), 507(a)(1)(A), 507(a)(1)(B), 507(a)(3), 507(a)(4), 507(a)(5), 507(a)(6), or 507(a)(7) of this title, to the extent of the amount of such allowed tax claim that is secured by such tax lien;

    (3) third, to the holder of such tax lien, to any extent that such holder's allowed tax claim that is secured by such tax lien exceeds any amount distributed under paragraph (2) of this subsection;

    (4) fourth, to any holder of an allowed claim secured by a lien on such property that is not avoidable under this title and that is junior to such tax lien;

    (5) fifth, to the holder of such tax lien, to the extent that such holder's allowed claim secured by such tax lien is not paid under paragraph (3) of this subsection; and

    (6) sixth, to the estate.

(c) If more than one holder of a claim is entitled to distribution under a particular paragraph of subsection (b) of this section, distribution to such holders under such paragraph shall be in the same order as distribution to such holders would have been other than under this section.

(d) A statutory lien the priority of which is determined in the same manner as the priority of a tax lien under section 6323 of the Internal Revenue Code of 1986 shall be treated under subsection (b) of this section the same as if such lien were a tax lien.

(e) Before subordinating a tax lien on real or personal property of the estate, the trustee shall—

    (1) exhaust the unencumbered assets of the estate; and

    (2) in a manner consistent with section 506(c), recover from property securing an allowed secured claim the reasonable, necessary costs and expenses of preserving or disposing of such property.

(f) Notwithstanding the exclusion of ad valorem tax liens under this section and subject to the requirements of subsection (e), the following may be paid from property of the estate which secures a tax lien, or the proceeds of such property:

    (1) Claims for wages, salaries, and commissions that are entitled to priority under section 507(a)(4).

    (2) Claims for contributions to an employee benefit plan entitled to priority under section 507(a)(5).

REFERENCES IN TEXT

Section 6323 of the Internal Revenue Code of 1986, referred to in subsec. (d), is classified to section 6323 of Title 26, Internal Revenue Code.

CROSS REFERENCES

Automatic preservation of avoided transfer, see 11 USCA § 551.

Commencement of involuntary cases by transferees of voidable transfers, see 11 USCA § 303.

Disallowance of claims of entity that is transferee of avoidable transfer, see 11 USCA § 502.

Effect of dismissal, see 11 USCA § 349.

Exemptions, see 11 USCA § 522.

Liability of transferee of avoided transfer, see 11 USCA § 550.

Recovery of voidable transfers in investor protection liquidation proceedings, see 15 USCA § 78fff–2.

Voidable transfers in commodity broker liquidation cases, see 11 USCA § 764.

§ 725. Disposition of certain property

After the commencement of a case under this chapter, but before final distribution of property of the estate under section 726 of this title, the trustee, after notice and a hearing, shall dispose of any property in which an entity other than the estate has an interest, such as a lien, and that has not been disposed of under another section of this title.

§ 726. Distribution of property of the estate

(a) Except as provided in section 510 of this title, property of the estate shall be distributed—

    (1) first, in payment of claims of the kind specified in, and in the order specified in, section 507 of this title, proof of which is timely filed under section 501 of this title or tardily filed on or before the earlier of—

        (A) the date that is 10 days after the mailing to creditors of the summary of the trustee's final report; or

        (B) the date on which the trustee commences final distribution under this section;

(2) second, in payment of any allowed unsecured claim, other than a claim of a kind specified in paragraph (1), (3), or (4) of this subsection, proof of which is—

(A) timely filed under section 501(a) of this title;

(B) timely filed under section 501(b) or 501(c) of this title; or

(C) tardily filed under section 501(a) of this title, if—

(i) the creditor that holds such claim did not have notice or actual knowledge of the case in time for timely filing of a proof of such claim under section 501(a) of this title; and

(ii) proof of such claim is filed in time to permit payment of such claim;

(3) third, in payment of any allowed unsecured claim proof of which is tardily filed under section 501(a) of this title, other than a claim of the kind specified in paragraph (2)(C) of this subsection;

(4) fourth, in payment of any allowed claim, whether secured or unsecured, for any fine, penalty, or forfeiture, or for multiple, exemplary, or punitive damages, arising before the earlier of the order for relief or the appointment of a trustee, to the extent that such fine, penalty, forfeiture, or damages are not compensation for actual pecuniary loss suffered by the holder of such claim;

(5) fifth, in payment of interest at the legal rate from the date of the filing of the petition, on any claim paid under paragraph (1), (2), (3), or (4) of this subsection; and

(6) sixth, to the debtor.

(b) Payment on claims of a kind specified in paragraph (1), (2), (3), (4), (5), (6), (7), (8), (9), or (10) of section 507(a) of this title, or in paragraph (2), (3), (4), or (5) of subsection (a) of this section, shall be made pro rata among claims of the kind specified in each such particular paragraph, except that in a case that has been converted to this chapter under section 1112, 1208, or 1307 of this title, a claim allowed under section 503(b) of this title incurred under this chapter after such conversion has priority over a claim allowed under section 503(b) of this title incurred under any other chapter of this title or under this chapter before such conversion and over any expenses of a custodian superseded under section 543 of this title.

(c) Notwithstanding subsections (a) and (b) of this section, if there is property of the kind specified in section 541(a)(2) of this title, or proceeds of such property, in the estate, such property or proceeds shall be segregated from other property of the estate, and such property or proceeds and other property of the estate shall be distributed as follows:

(1) Claims allowed under section 503 of this title shall be paid either from property of the kind specified in section 541(a)(2) of this title, or from other property of the estate, as the interest of justice requires.

(2) Allowed claims, other than claims allowed under section 503 of this title, shall be paid in the order specified in subsection (a) of this section, and, with respect to claims of a kind specified in a particular paragraph of section 507 of this title or subsection (a) of this section, in the following order and manner:

(A) First, community claims against the debtor or the debtor's spouse shall be paid from property of the kind specified in section 541(a)(2) of this title, except to the extent that such property is solely liable for debts of the debtor.

(B) Second, to the extent that community claims against the debtor are not paid under subparagraph (A) of this paragraph, such community claims shall be paid from property of the kind specified in section 541(a)(2) of this title that is solely liable for debts of the debtor.

(C) Third, to the extent that all claims against the debtor including community claims against the debtor are not paid under subparagraph (A) or (B) of this paragraph such claims shall be paid from property of the estate other than property of the kind specified in section 541(a)(2) of this title.

(D) Fourth, to the extent that community claims against the debtor or the debtor's spouse are not paid under subparagraph (A), (B), or (C) of this paragraph, such claims shall be paid from all remaining property of the estate.

CROSS REFERENCES

Customer property, distribution in—

    Commodity broker liquidation cases, see 11 USCA § 766.

    Stockbroker liquidation cases, see 11 USCA § 752.

Distribution in Chapter 11 cases, see 11 USCA § 1143.

Distribution of securities in stockbroker liquidation cases, see 11 USCA § 750.

Election of creditors holding certain claims entitled to distribution to creditors' committee, see 11 USCA § 705.

Election of trustee by creditors holding claims entitled to distribution, see 11 USCA § 702.

Impairment of claims and interests and objection to claims filed untimely, see 11 USCA § 502.

Ownership of copyright, see 17 USCA § 201.

Payment stopped on checks remaining unpaid 90 days after final distribution, see 11 USCA § 347.

Priorities of distribution in investor liquidation proceedings, see 15 USCA § 78fff.

Student Loan Marketing Association of the Robert T. Stafford Student Loan Program deemed person within meaning of this title for purposes of distribution of its property pursuant to this section, see 20 USCA § 1087–2.

§ 727. Discharge

(a) The court shall grant the debtor a discharge, unless—

    (1) the debtor is not an individual;

    (2) the debtor, with intent to hinder, delay, or defraud a creditor or an officer of the estate charged with custody of property under this title, has transferred, removed, destroyed, mutilated, or concealed, or has permitted to be transferred, removed, destroyed, mutilated, or concealed—

        (A) property of the debtor, within one year before the date of the filing of the petition; or

        (B) property of the estate, after the date of the filing of the petition;

    (3) the debtor has concealed, destroyed, mutilated, falsified, or failed to keep or preserve any recorded information, including books, documents, records, and papers, from which the debtor's financial condition or business transactions might be ascertained, unless such act or failure to act was justified under all of the circumstances of the case;

    (4) the debtor knowingly and fraudulently, in or in connection with the case—

        (A) made a false oath or account;

        (B) presented or used a false claim;

        (C) gave, offered, received, or attempted to obtain money, property, or advantage, or a promise of money, property, or advantage, for acting or forbearing to act; or

(D) withheld from an officer of the estate entitled to possession under this title, any recorded information, including books, documents, records, and papers, relating to the debtor's property or financial affairs;

(5) the debtor has failed to explain satisfactorily, before determination of denial of discharge under this paragraph, any loss of assets or deficiency of assets to meet the debtor's liabilities;

(6) the debtor has refused, in the case—

(A) to obey any lawful order of the court, other than an order to respond to a material question or to testify;

(B) on the ground of privilege against self-incrimination, to respond to a material question approved by the court or to testify, after the debtor has been granted immunity with respect to the matter concerning which such privilege was invoked; or

(C) on a ground other than the properly invoked privilege against self-incrimination, to respond to a material question approved by the court or to testify;

(7) the debtor has committed any act specified in paragraph (2), (3), (4), (5), or (6) of this subsection, on or within one year before the date of the filing of the petition, or during the case, in connection with another case, under this title or under the Bankruptcy Act, concerning an insider;

(8) the debtor has been granted a discharge under this section, under section 1141 of this title, or under section 14, 371, or 476 of the Bankruptcy Act, in a case commenced within 8 years before the date of the filing of the petition;

(9) the debtor has been granted a discharge under section 1228 or 1328 of this title, or under section 660 or 661 of the Bankruptcy Act, in a case commenced within six years before the date of the filing of the petition, unless payments under the plan in such case totaled at least—

(A) 100 percent of the allowed unsecured claims in such case; or

(B)(i) 70 percent of such claims; and

(ii) the plan was proposed by the debtor in good faith, and was the debtor's best effort;

(10) the court approves a written waiver of discharge executed by the debtor after the order for relief under this chapter;

(11) after filing the petition, the debtor failed to complete an instructional course concerning personal financial management described in section 111, except that this paragraph shall not apply with respect to a debtor who is a person described in section 109(h)(4) or who resides in a district for which the United States trustee (or the bankruptcy administrator, if any) determines that the approved instructional courses are not adequate to service the additional individuals who would otherwise be required to complete such instructional courses under this section (The United States trustee (or the bankruptcy administrator, if any) who makes a determination described in this paragraph shall review such determination not later than 1 year after the date of such determination, and not less frequently than annually thereafter.); or

(12) the court after notice and a hearing held not more than 10 days before the date of the entry of the order granting the discharge finds that there is reasonable cause to believe that—

(A) section 522(q)(1) may be applicable to the debtor; and

(B) there is pending any proceeding in which the debtor may be found guilty of a felony of the kind described in section 522(q)(1)(A) or liable for a debt of the kind described in section 522(q)(1)(B).

(b) Except as provided in section 523 of this title, a discharge under subsection (a) of this section discharges the debtor from all debts that arose before the date of the order for relief under this chapter, and any liability on a claim that is determined under section 502 of this title as if such claim had arisen before the commencement of the case, whether or not a proof of claim based on any such debt or liability is filed under section 501 of this title, and whether or not a claim based on any such debt or liability is allowed under section 502 of this title.

(c)(1) The trustee, a creditor, or the United States trustee may object to the granting of a discharge under subsection (a) of this section.

(2) On request of a party in interest, the court may order the trustee to examine the acts and conduct of the debtor to determine whether a ground exists for denial of discharge.

(d) On request of the trustee, a creditor, or the United States trustee, and after notice and a hearing, the court shall revoke a discharge granted under subsection (a) of this section if—

(1) such discharge was obtained through the fraud of the debtor, and the requesting party did not know of such fraud until after the granting of such discharge;

(2) the debtor acquired property that is property of the estate, or became entitled to acquire property that would be property of the estate, and knowingly and fraudulently failed to report the acquisition of or entitlement to such property, or to deliver or surrender such property to the trustee;

(3) the debtor committed an act specified in subsection (a)(6) of this section; or

(4) the debtor has failed to explain satisfactorily—

(A) a material misstatement in an audit referred to in section 586(f) of title 28; or

(B) a failure to make available for inspection all necessary accounts, papers, documents, financial records, files, and all other papers, things, or property belonging to the debtor that are requested for an audit referred to in section 586(f) of title 28.

(e) The trustee, a creditor, or the United States trustee may request a revocation of a discharge—

(1) under subsection (d)(1) of this section within one year after such discharge is granted; or

(2) under subsection (d)(2) or (d)(3) of this section before the later of—

(A) one year after the granting of such discharge; and

(B) the date the case is closed.

REFERENCES IN TEXT

The Bankruptcy Act, referred to in subsec. (a)(7), is Act July 1, 1898, c. 541, 30 Stat. 544, as amended, which was classified generally to former Title 11, prior to repeal of such Act by Pub. L. 95–598, Title IV, § 401(a), Nov. 6, 1978, 92 Stat. 2692.

Sections 14, 371, and 476 of the Bankruptcy Act, referred to in subsec. (a)(8), are section 14 of Act July 1, 1898, c. 541, 30 Stat. 550, and sections 371 and 476 of Act July 1, 1898, c. 541, as added June 22, 1938, c. 575, § 1, 52 Stat. 912, 924, which were classified to sections 32, 771, and 876 of former Title 11, respectively.

Sections 660 and 661 of the Bankruptcy Act, referred to in subsec. (a)(9), are sections 660 and 661 of Act July 1, 1898, c. 541, as added June 22, 1938, c. 575, § 1, 52 Stat. 935, 936, which were classified, respectively, to sections 1060 and 1061 of former Title 11.

CROSS REFERENCES

Cancellation of indebtedness from discharged farm loans, see 12 USCA § 1150.

Concealment of assets; false oaths and claims, see 18 USCA § 152.

Confirmation of plan as affecting discharge in—

Chapter 9 cases, see 11 USCA § 944.

Chapter 11 cases, see 11 USCA § 1141.

Discharge in Chapter 13 cases, see 11 USCA § 1328.

Duty of trustee to oppose discharge, see 11 USCA § 704.

Effect of—

Conversion, see 11 USCA § 348.

Discharge, see 11 USCA § 524.

Exceptions to discharge, see 11 USCA § 523.

Nondischargeability of capital improvement loans for multifamily housing projects in proceedings under this section, see 12 USCA § 1715z–1a.

SUBCHAPTER III—STOCKBROKER LIQUIDATION

§ 741. Definitions for this subchapter

In this subchapter—

(1) "Commission" means Securities and Exchange Commission;

(2) "customer" includes—

(A) entity with whom a person deals as principal or agent and that has a claim against such person on account of a security received, acquired, or held by such person in the ordinary course of such person's business as a stockbroker, from or for the securities account or accounts of such entity—

(i) for safekeeping;

(ii) with a view to sale;

(iii) to cover a consummated sale;

(iv) pursuant to a purchase;

(v) as collateral under a security agreement; or

(vi) for the purpose of effecting registration of transfer; and

(B) entity that has a claim against a person arising out of—

(i) a sale or conversion of a security received, acquired, or held as specified in subparagraph (A) of this paragraph; or

(ii) a deposit of cash, a security, or other property with such person for the purpose of purchasing or selling a security;

(3) "customer name security" means security—

(A) held for the account of a customer on the date of the filing of the petition by or on behalf of the debtor;

(B) registered in such customer's name on such date or in the process of being so registered under instructions from the debtor; and

(C) not in a form transferable by delivery on such date;

(4) "customer property" means cash, security, or other property, and proceeds of such cash, security, or property, received, acquired, or held by or for the account of the debtor, from or for the securities account of a customer—

(A) including—

(i) property that was unlawfully converted from and that is the lawful property of the estate;

(ii) a security held as property of the debtor to the extent such security is necessary to meet a net equity claim of a customer based on a security of the same class and series of an issuer;

(iii) resources provided through the use or realization of a customer's debit cash balance or a debit item includible in the Formula for Determination of Reserve Requirement for Brokers and Dealers as promulgated by the Commission under the Securities Exchange Act of 1934; and

(iv) other property of the debtor that any applicable law, rule, or regulation requires to be set aside or held for the benefit of a customer, unless including such property as customer property would not significantly increase customer property; but

(B) not including—

(i) a customer name security delivered to or reclaimed by a customer under section 751 of this title; or

(ii) property to the extent that a customer does not have a claim against the debtor based on such property;

(5) "margin payment" means payment or deposit of cash, a security, or other property, that is commonly known to the securities trade as original margin, initial margin, maintenance margin, or variation margin, or as a mark-to-market payment, or that secures an obligation of a participant in a securities clearing agency;

(6) "net equity" means, with respect to all accounts of a customer that such customer has in the same capacity—

(A)(i) aggregate dollar balance that would remain in such accounts after the liquidation, by sale or purchase, at the time of the filing of the petition, of all securities positions in all such accounts, except any customer name securities of such customer; minus

(ii) any claim of the debtor against such customer in such capacity that would have been owing immediately after such liquidation; plus

(B) any payment by such customer to the trustee, within 60 days after notice under section 342 of this title, of any business related claim of the debtor against such customer in such capacity;

(7) "securities contract"—

(A) means—

(i) a contract for the purchase, sale, or loan of a security, a certificate of deposit, a mortgage loan, any interest in a mortgage loan, a group or index of securities, certificates of deposit, or mortgage loans or interests therein (including an interest therein or based on the value thereof), or option on any of the foregoing, including an option to purchase or sell any such security, certificate of deposit, mortgage loan, interest, group or index, or option, and including any repurchase or reverse repurchase transaction on any such security, certificate of deposit, mortgage loan, interest, group or index, or option (whether or not such repurchase or reverse repurchase transaction is a "repurchase agreement", as defined in section 101);

(ii) any option entered into on a national securities exchange relating to foreign currencies;

    (iii) the guarantee (including by novation) by or to any securities clearing agency of a settlement of cash, securities, certificates of deposit, mortgage loans or interests therein, group or index of securities, or mortgage loans or interests therein (including any interest therein or based on the value thereof), or option on any of the foregoing, including an option to purchase or sell any such security, certificate of deposit, mortgage loan, interest, group or index, or option (whether or not such settlement is in connection with any agreement or transaction referred to in clauses (i) through (xi));

    (iv) any margin loan;

    (v) any extension of credit for the clearance or settlement of securities transactions;

    (vi) any loan transaction coupled with a securities collar transaction, any prepaid forward securities transaction, or any total return swap transaction coupled with a securities sale transaction;

    (vii) any other agreement or transaction that is similar to an agreement or transaction referred to in this subparagraph;

    (viii) any combination of the agreements or transactions referred to in this subparagraph;

    (ix) any option to enter into any agreement or transaction referred to in this subparagraph;

    (x) a master agreement that provides for an agreement or transaction referred to in clause (i), (ii), (iii), (iv), (v), (vi), (vii), (viii), or (ix), together with all supplements to any such master agreement, without regard to whether the master agreement provides for an agreement or transaction that is not a securities contract under this subparagraph, except that such master agreement shall be considered to be a securities contract under this subparagraph only with respect to each agreement or transaction under such master agreement that is referred to in clause (i), (ii), (iii), (iv), (v), (vi), (vii), (viii), or (ix); or

    (xi) any security agreement or arrangement or other credit enhancement related to any agreement or transaction referred to in this subparagraph, including any guarantee or reimbursement obligation by or to a stockbroker, securities clearing agency, financial institution, or financial participant in connection with any agreement or transaction referred to in this subparagraph, but not to exceed the damages in connection with any such agreement or transaction, measured in accordance with section 562; and

    (B) does not include any purchase, sale, or repurchase obligation under a participation in a commercial mortgage loan;

  (8) "settlement payment" means a preliminary settlement payment, a partial settlement payment, an interim settlement payment, a settlement payment on account, a final settlement payment, or any other similar payment commonly used in the securities trade; and

  (9) "SIPC" means Securities Investor Protection Corporation.

REFERENCES IN TEXT

The Securities Exchange Act of 1934, referred to in par. (4)(A)(iii), is Act June 6, 1934, c. 404, 48 Stat. 881, as amended, which is classified principally to chapter 2B (section 78a et seq.) of Title 15, Commerce and Trade. For complete classification of this Act to the Code, see section 78l of Title 15 and Tables.

CROSS REFERENCES

Certain persons acting as agent or custodian for customer in connection with "securities contract" as defined under this section considered a financial institution for purposes of this title, see 11 USCA § 101.

Contractual right to liquidate "securities contract" as defined under this section not stayed, avoided or limited by operation of any provision of this title, see 11 USCA § 555.

"Customer" defined under this section as determining who is a stockbroker for purposes of this title, see 11 USCA § 101.

Definitions applicable in—

> Chapter 9 cases, see 11 USCA § 902.
>
> Chapter 11 cases, see 11 USCA § 1101.
>
> Commodity broker liquidation cases, see 11 USCA § 761.
>
> Railroad reorganization cases, see 11 USCA § 1162.

Limitation on power of trustee to avoid transfer of "margin payment" and "settlement payment" as defined under this section, see 11 USCA § 546.

Receipt of "margin payment" or "settlement payment" as defined under this section is taking for value for purposes of avoidance of fraudulent transfers and obligations, see 11 USCA § 548.

"Securities contract" as defined under this section as having same meaning for purposes of—

> Federal credit union insurance, see 12 USCA § 1787.
>
> Federal deposit insurance corporation, see 12 USCA § 1821.

Setoff of mutual debt in connection with "securities contract", "margin payment" or "settlement payment", not stayed by filing of petitions for voluntary cases, joint cases or involuntary cases or protective decrees in investor protection liquidation proceedings, see 11 USCA § 362.

§ 742. Effect of section 362 of this title in this subchapter

Notwithstanding section 362 of this title, SIPC may file an application for a protective decree under the Securities Investor Protection Act of 1970. The filing of such application stays all proceedings in the case under this title unless and until such application is dismissed. If SIPC completes the liquidation of the debtor, then the court shall dismiss the case.

REFERENCES IN TEXT

The Securities Investor Protection Act of 1970, referred to in text, is Pub. L. 91–598, Dec. 30, 1970, 84 Stat. 1636, as amended, which is classified generally to chapter 2B-1 (section 78aaa et seq.) of Title 15, Commerce and Trade. For complete classification of this Act to the Code, see section 78aaa of Title 15 and Tables.

CROSS REFERENCES

Automatic stay of enforcement of claims against debtor in Chapter 9 cases, see 11 USCA § 922.

Effect of dismissal, see 11 USCA § 349.

Stay of action against codebtor in Chapter 13 cases, see 11 USCA § 1301.

§ 743. Notice

The clerk shall give the notice required by section 342 of this title to SIPC and to the Commission.

CROSS REFERENCES

Notice in Chapter 9 cases, see 11 USCA § 923.

Notice to the Commodity Futures Trading Commission, see 11 USCA § 762.

§ 744. Executory contracts

Notwithstanding section 365(d)(1) of this title, the trustee shall assume or reject, under section 365 of this title, any executory contract of the debtor for the purchase or sale of a security in the ordinary course of the debtor's business, within a reasonable time after the date of the order for relief, but not to exceed 30 days. If the trustee does not assume such a contract within such time, such contract is rejected.

CROSS REFERENCES

Effect of rejection of lease of railroad line, see 11 USCA § 1169.

§ 745. Treatment of accounts

(a) Accounts held by the debtor for a particular customer in separate capacities shall be treated as accounts of separate customers.

(b) If a stockbroker or a bank holds a customer net equity claim against the debtor that arose out of a transaction for a customer of such stockbroker or bank, each such customer of such stockbroker or bank shall be treated as a separate customer of the debtor.

(c) Each trustee's account specified as such on the debtor's books, and supported by a trust deed filed with, and qualified as such by, the Internal Revenue Service, and under the Internal Revenue Code of 1986, shall be treated as a separate customer account for each beneficiary under such trustee account.

REFERENCES IN TEXT

The Internal Revenue Code of 1986, referred to in subsec. (c), is classified to Title 26, Internal Revenue Code.

CROSS REFERENCES

Stockbroker defined, see 11 USCA § 101.

Treatment of accounts in commodity broker liquidation cases, see 11 USCA § 763.

§ 746. Extent of customer claims

(a) If, after the date of the filing of the petition, an entity enters into a transaction with the debtor, in a manner that would have made such entity a customer had such transaction occurred before the date of the filing of the petition, and such transaction was entered into by such entity in good faith and before the qualification under section 322 of this title of a trustee, such entity shall be deemed a customer, and the date of such transaction shall be deemed to be the date of the filing of the petition for the purpose of determining such entity's net equity.

(b) An entity does not have a claim as a customer to the extent that such entity transferred to the debtor cash or a security that, by contract, agreement, understanding, or operation of law, is—

(1) part of the capital of the debtor; or

(2) subordinated to the claims of any or all creditors.

CROSS REFERENCES

Allowance of claims or interests, see 11 USCA § 502.

§ 747. Subordination of certain customer claims

Except as provided in section 510 of this title, unless all other customer net equity claims have been paid in full, the trustee may not pay in full or pay in part, directly or indirectly, any net equity claim of a customer that was, on the date the transaction giving rise to such claim occurred—

  (1) an insider;

  (2) a beneficial owner of at least five percent of any class of equity securities of the debtor, other than—

    (A) nonconvertible stock having fixed preferential dividend and liquidation rights; or

    (B) interests of limited partners in a limited partnership;

  (3) a limited partner with a participation of at least five percent in the net assets or net profits of the debtor; or

  (4) an entity that, directly or indirectly, through agreement or otherwise, exercised or had the power to exercise control over the management or policies of the debtor.

CROSS REFERENCES

Insider defined, see 11 USCA § 101.

§ 748. Reduction of securities to money

  As soon as practicable after the date of the order for relief, the trustee shall reduce to money, consistent with good market practice, all securities held as property of the estate, except for customer name securities delivered or reclaimed under section 751 of this title.

CROSS REFERENCES

Reduction of certain securities and property to money in commodity broker liquidation cases, see 11 USCA § 766.

§ 749. Voidable transfers

  (a) Except as otherwise provided in this section, any transfer of property that, but for such transfer, would have been customer property, may be avoided by the trustee, and such property shall be treated as customer property, if and to the extent that the trustee avoids such transfer under section 544, 545, 547, 548, or 549 of this title. For the purpose of such sections, the property so transferred shall be deemed to have been property of the debtor and, if such transfer was made to a customer or for a customer's benefit, such customer shall be deemed, for the purposes of this section, to have been a creditor.

  (b) Notwithstanding sections 544, 545, 547, 548, and 549 of this title, the trustee may not avoid a transfer made before seven days after the order for relief if such transfer is approved by the Commission by rule or order, either before or after such transfer, and if such transfer is—

  (1) a transfer of a securities contract entered into or carried by or through the debtor on behalf of a customer, and of any cash, security, or other property margining or securing such securities contract; or

  (2) the liquidation of a securities contract entered into or carried by or through the debtor on behalf of a customer.

CROSS REFERENCES

Voidable transfers in commodity broker liquidation cases, see 11 USCA § 764.

§ 750. Distribution of securities

  The trustee may not distribute a security except under section 751 of this title.

CROSS REFERENCES

Distribution in Chapter 11 cases, see 11 USCA § 1143.

Distribution of property of estate, see 11 USCA § 726.

§ 751. Customer name securities

The trustee shall deliver any customer name security to or on behalf of the customer entitled to such security, unless such customer has a negative net equity. With the approval of the trustee, a customer may reclaim a customer name security after payment to the trustee, within such period as the trustee allows, of any claim of the debtor against such customer to the extent that such customer will not have a negative net equity after such payment.

§ 752. Customer property

(a) The trustee shall distribute customer property ratably to customers on the basis and to the extent of such customers' allowed net equity claims and in priority to all other claims, except claims of the kind specified in section 507(a)(2) of this title that are attributable to the administration of such customer property.

(b)(1) The trustee shall distribute customer property in excess of that distributed under subsection (a) of this section in accordance with section 726 of this title.

(2) Except as provided in section 510 of this title, if a customer is not paid the full amount of such customer's allowed net equity claim from customer property, the unpaid portion of such claim is a claim entitled to distribution under section 726 of this title.

(c) Any cash or security remaining after the liquidation of a security interest created under a security agreement made by the debtor, excluding property excluded under section 741(4)(B) of this title, shall be apportioned between the general estate and customer property in the same proportion as the general estate of the debtor and customer property were subject to such security interest.

CROSS REFERENCES

Distribution in Chapter 11 cases, see 11 USCA § 1143.

Distribution of—

    Customer property in commodity broker liquidation cases, see 11 USCA § 766.

    Property of the estate, see 11 USCA § 726.

Election of trustee by creditors holding claims entitled to distribution, see 11 USCA § 702.

Priorities, see 11 USCA § 507.

§ 753. Stockbroker liquidation and forward contract merchants, commodity brokers, stockbrokers, financial institutions, financial participants, securities clearing agencies, swap participants, repo participants, and master netting agreement participants

Notwithstanding any other provision of this title, the exercise of rights by a forward contract merchant, commodity broker, stockbroker, financial institution, financial participant, securities clearing agency, swap participant, repo participant, or master netting agreement participant under this title shall not affect the priority of any unsecured claim it may have after the exercise of such rights.

SUBCHAPTER IV—COMMODITY BROKER LIQUIDATION

§ 761. Definitions for this subchapter

In this subchapter—

(1) "Act" means Commodity Exchange Act;

(2) "clearing organization" means a derivatives clearing organization registered under the Act;

(3) "Commission" means Commodity Futures Trading Commission;

(4) "commodity contract" means—

(A) with respect to a futures commission merchant, contract for the purchase or sale of a commodity for future delivery on, or subject to the rules of, a contract market or board of trade;

(B) with respect to a foreign futures commission merchant, foreign future;

(C) with respect to a leverage transaction merchant, leverage transaction;

(D) with respect to a clearing organization, contract for the purchase or sale of a commodity for future delivery on, or subject to the rules of, a contract market or board of trade that is cleared by such clearing organization, or commodity option traded on, or subject to the rules of, a contract market or board of trade that is cleared by such clearing organization;

(E) with respect to a commodity options dealer, commodity option;

(F)(i) any other contract, option, agreement, or transaction that is similar to a contract, option, agreement, or transaction referred to in this paragraph; and

(ii) with respect to a futures commission merchant or a clearing organization, any other contract, option, agreement, or transaction, in each case, that is cleared by a clearing organization;

(G) any combination of the agreements or transactions referred to in this paragraph;

(H) any option to enter into an agreement or transaction referred to in this paragraph;

(I) a master agreement that provides for an agreement or transaction referred to in subparagraph (A), (B), (C), (D), (E), (F), (G), or (H), together with all supplements to such master agreement, without regard to whether the master agreement provides for an agreement or transaction that is not a commodity contract under this paragraph, except that the master agreement shall be considered to be a commodity contract under this paragraph only with respect to each agreement or transaction under the master agreement that is referred to in subparagraph (A), (B), (C), (D), (E), (F), (G), or (H); or

(J) any security agreement or arrangement or other credit enhancement related to any agreement or transaction referred to in this paragraph, including any guarantee or reimbursement obligation by or to a commodity broker or financial participant in connection with any agreement or transaction referred to in this paragraph, but not to exceed the damages in connection with any such agreement or transaction, measured in accordance with section 562;

(5) "commodity option" means agreement or transaction subject to regulation under section 4c(b) of the Act;

(6) "commodity options dealer" means person that extends credit to, or that accepts cash, a security, or other property from, a customer of such person for the purchase or sale of an interest in a commodity option;

(7) "contract market" means a registered entity;

(8) "contract of sale", "commodity", "derivatives clearing organization", "future delivery", "board of trade", "registered entity", and "futures commission merchant" have the meanings assigned to those terms in the Act;

(9) "customer" means—

(A) with respect to a futures commission merchant—

(i) entity for or with whom such futures commission merchant deals and that holds a claim against such futures commission merchant on account of a commodity contract made, received, acquired, or held by or through such futures commission merchant in the ordinary course of such futures commission merchant's business as a futures commission merchant from or for a commodity contract account of such entity; or

(ii) entity that holds a claim against such futures commission merchant arising out of—

(I) the making, liquidation, or change in the value of a commodity contract of a kind specified in clause (i) of this subparagraph;

(II) a deposit or payment of cash, a security, or other property with such futures commission merchant for the purpose of making or margining such a commodity contract; or

(III) the making or taking of delivery on such a commodity contract;

(B) with respect to a foreign futures commission merchant—

(i) entity for or with whom such foreign futures commission merchant deals and that holds a claim against such foreign futures commission merchant on account of a commodity contract made, received, acquired, or held by or through such foreign futures commission merchant in the ordinary course of such foreign futures commission merchant's business as a foreign futures commission merchant from or for the foreign futures account of such entity; or

(ii) entity that holds a claim against such foreign futures commission merchant arising out of—

(I) the making, liquidation, or change in value of a commodity contract of a kind specified in clause (i) of this subparagraph;

(II) a deposit or payment of cash, a security, or other property with such foreign futures commission merchant for the purpose of making or margining such a commodity contract; or

(III) the making or taking of delivery on such a commodity contract;

(C) with respect to a leverage transaction merchant—

(i) entity for or with whom such leverage transaction merchant deals and that holds a claim against such leverage transaction merchant on account of a commodity contract engaged in by or with such leverage transaction merchant in the ordinary course of such leverage transaction merchant's business as a leverage transaction merchant from or for the leverage account of such entity; or

(ii) entity that holds a claim against such leverage transaction merchant arising out of—

(I) the making, liquidation, or change in value of a commodity contract of a kind specified in clause (i) of this subparagraph;

(II) a deposit or payment of cash, a security, or other property with such leverage transaction merchant for the purpose of entering into or margining such a commodity contract; or

(III) the making or taking of delivery on such a commodity contract;

(D) with respect to a clearing organization, clearing member of such clearing organization with whom such clearing organization deals and that holds a claim against such clearing organization on account of cash, a security, or other property received by such clearing organization to margin, guarantee, or secure a commodity contract in such clearing member's proprietary account or customers' account; or

(E) with respect to a commodity options dealer—

(i) entity for or with whom such commodity options dealer deals and that holds a claim on account of a commodity contract made, received, acquired, or held by or through such commodity options dealer in the ordinary course of such commodity options dealer's business as a commodity options dealer from or for the commodity options account of such entity; or

(ii) entity that holds a claim against such commodity options dealer arising out of—

(I) the making of, liquidation of, exercise of, or a change in value of, a commodity contract of a kind specified in clause (i) of this subparagraph; or

(II) a deposit or payment of cash, a security, or other property with such commodity options dealer for the purpose of making, exercising, or margining such a commodity contract;

(10) "customer property" means cash, a security, or other property, or proceeds of such cash, security, or property, received, acquired, or held by or for the account of the debtor, from or for the account of a customer—

(A) including—

(i) property received, acquired, or held to margin, guarantee, secure, purchase, or sell a commodity contract;

(ii) profits or contractual or other rights accruing to a customer as a result of a commodity contract;

(iii) an open commodity contract;

(iv) specifically identifiable customer property;

(v) warehouse receipt or other document held by the debtor evidencing ownership of or title to property to be delivered to fulfill a commodity contract from or for the account of a customer;

(vi) cash, a security, or other property received by the debtor as payment for a commodity to be delivered to fulfill a commodity contract from or for the account of a customer;

(vii) a security held as property of the debtor to the extent such security is necessary to meet a net equity claim based on a security of the same class and series of an issuer;

(viii) property that was unlawfully converted from and that is the lawful property of the estate; and

(ix) other property of the debtor that any applicable law, rule, or regulation requires to be set aside or held for the benefit of a customer, unless including such property as customer property would not significantly increase customer property; but

(B) not including property to the extent that a customer does not have a claim against the debtor based on such property;

(11) foreign future" means contract for the purchase or sale of a commodity for future delivery on, or subject to the rules of, a board of trade outside the United States;

(12) "foreign futures commission merchant" means entity engaged in soliciting or accepting orders for the purchase or sale of a foreign future or that, in connection with such a solicitation or acceptance, accepts cash, a security, or other property, or extends credit to margin, guarantee, or secure any trade or contract that results from such a solicitation or acceptance;

(13) "leverage transaction" means agreement that is subject to regulation under section 19 of the Commodity Exchange Act, and that is commonly known to the commodities trade as a margin account, margin contract, leverage account, or leverage contract;

(14) "leverage transaction merchant" means person in the business of engaging in leverage transactions;

(15) "margin payment" means payment or deposit of cash, a security, or other property, that is commonly known to the commodities trade as original margin, initial margin, maintenance margin, or variation margin, including mark-to-market payments, settlement payments, variation payments, daily settlement payments, and final settlement payments made as adjustments to settlement prices;

(16) "member property" means customer property received, acquired, or held by or for the account of a debtor that is a clearing organization, from or for the proprietary account of a customer that is a clearing member of the debtor; and

(17) "net equity" means, subject to such rules and regulations as the Commission promulgates under the Act, with respect to the aggregate of all of a customer's accounts that such customer has in the same capacity—

(A) the balance remaining in such customer's accounts immediately after—

(i) all commodity contracts of such customer have been transferred, liquidated, or become identified for delivery; and

(ii) all obligations of such customer in such capacity to the debtor have been offset; plus

(B) the value, as of the date of return under section 766 of this title, of any specifically identifiable customer property actually returned to such customer before the date specified in subparagraph (A) of this paragraph; plus

(C) the value, as of the date of transfer, of—

(i) any commodity contract to which such customer is entitled that is transferred to another person under section 766 of this title; and

(ii) any cash, security, or other property of such customer transferred to such other person under section 766 of this title to margin or secure such transferred commodity contract.

REFERENCES IN TEXT

The Commodity Exchange Act or the Act, referred to in pars. (1), (8), and (17), is Act Sept. 21, 1922, c. 369, 42 Stat. 998, as amended, which is classified generally to chapter 1 (section 1 et seq.) of Title 7, Agriculture. For complete classification of this Act to the Code, see section 1 of Title 7 and Tables.

Section 4c of the Commodity Exchange Act, referred to in par. (5), is section 4c of Act Sept. 21, 1922, c. 369, as added June 15, 1936, c. 545, § 5, 49 Stat. 1494, which is classified to section 6c of Title 7, Agriculture.

Section 19 of the Commodity Exchange Act, referred to in par. (13), is section 19 of Act Sept. 21, 1922, c. 369, as added Sept. 30, 1978, Pub. L. 95–405, § 23, 92 Stat. 876, which is classified to section 23 of Title 7.

CROSS REFERENCES

Certain terms having same meanings as under this section, see 7 USCA § 24.

Commodity broker defined, see 11 USCA § 101.

"Commodity contract" defined under this section as having same meaning for purposes of Federal deposit insurance corporation, see 12 USCA § 1821.

Contractual right to liquidate "commodity contract" as defined under this section not stayed, avoided or limited by operation of any provision of this title, see 11 USCA § 556.

Definitions applicable in—

> Chapter 9 cases, see 11 USCA § 902.
>
> Chapter 11 cases, see 11 USCA § 1101.
>
> Railroad reorganization cases, see 11 USCA § 1162.
>
> Stockbroker liquidation cases, see 11 USCA § 741.

Limitation on power of trustee to avoid transfer of "margin payment" as defined in this section, see 11 USCA § 546.

Reception of margin payments by commodity brokers or forward contract merchants as taking for value, see 11 USCA § 548.

Setoff of mutual debt in connection with "commodity contracts" or "margin payment" not stayed by filing of petitions for voluntary cases, joint cases or involuntary cases or protective decrees in investor protection liquidation proceedings, see 11 USCA § 362.

§ 762. Notice to the Commission and right to be heard

(a) The clerk shall give the notice required by section 342 of this title to the Commission.

(b) The Commission may raise and may appear and be heard on any issue in a case under this chapter.

CROSS REFERENCES

Notice in—

> Chapter 9 cases, see 11 USCA § 923.
>
> Stockbroker liquidation proceedings, see 11 USCA § 743.

§ 763. Treatment of accounts

(a) Accounts held by the debtor for a particular customer in separate capacities shall be treated as accounts of separate customers.

(b) A member of a clearing organization shall be deemed to hold such member's proprietary account in a separate capacity from such member's customers' account.

(c) The net equity in a customer's account may not be offset against the net equity in the account of any other customer.

CROSS REFERENCES

Treatment of accounts in stockbroker liquidation cases, see 11 USCA § 745.

§ 764. Voidable transfers

(a) Except as otherwise provided in this section, any transfer by the debtor of property that, but for such transfer, would have been customer property, may be avoided by the trustee, and such property shall be treated as customer property, if and to the extent that the trustee avoids such transfer under section 544, 545, 547, 548, 549, or 724(a) of this title. For the purpose of such sections, the property so transferred shall be deemed to have been property of the debtor, and, if such transfer was made to a customer or for a customer's benefit, such customer shall be deemed, for the purposes of this section, to have been a creditor.

(b) Notwithstanding sections 544, 545, 547, 548, 549, and 724(a) of this title, the trustee may not avoid a transfer made before seven days after the order for relief, if such transfer is approved by the Commission by rule or order, either before or after such transfer, and if such transfer is—

    (1) a transfer of a commodity contract entered into or carried by or through the debtor on behalf of a customer, and of any cash, securities, or other property margining or securing such commodity contract; or

    (2) the liquidation of a commodity contract entered into or carried by or through the debtor on behalf of a customer.

CROSS REFERENCES

Voidable transfers in stockbroker liquidation cases, see 11 USCA § 749.

§ 765. Customer instructions

(a) The notice required by section 342 of this title to customers shall instruct each customer—

    (1) to file a proof of such customer's claim promptly, and to specify in such claim any specifically identifiable security, property, or commodity contract; and

    (2) to instruct the trustee of such customer's desired disposition, including transfer under section 766 of this title or liquidation, of any commodity contract specifically identified to such customer.

(b) The trustee shall comply, to the extent practicable, with any instruction received from a customer regarding such customer's desired disposition of any commodity contract specifically identified to such customer. If the trustee has transferred, under section 766 of this title, such a commodity contract, the trustee shall transmit any such instruction to the commodity broker to whom such commodity contract was so transferred.

CROSS REFERENCES

Executory contracts and unexpired leases, see 11 USCA § 365.

§ 766. Treatment of customer property

(a) The trustee shall answer all margin calls with respect to a specifically identifiable commodity contract of a customer until such time as the trustee returns or transfers such commodity contract, but the trustee may not make a margin payment that has the effect of a distribution to such customer of more than that to which such customer is entitled under subsection (h) or (i) of this section.

(b) The trustee shall prevent any open commodity contract from remaining open after the last day of trading in such commodity contract, or into the first day on which notice of intent to deliver on such commodity contract may be tendered, whichever occurs first. With respect to any commodity contract that has remained open after the last day of trading in such commodity contract or with respect to which delivery must be made or accepted under the rules of the contract market on which such commodity contract was made, the trustee may operate the business of the debtor for the purpose of—

    (1) accepting or making tender of notice of intent to deliver the physical commodity underlying such commodity contract;

    (2) facilitating delivery of such commodity; or

    (3) disposing of such commodity if a party to such commodity contract defaults.

    (c) The trustee shall return promptly to a customer any specifically identifiable security, property, or commodity contract to which such customer is entitled, or shall transfer, on such customer's behalf, such security, property, or commodity contract to a commodity broker that is not a debtor under this title, subject to such rules or regulations as the Commission may prescribe, to the extent that the value of such security, property, or commodity contract does not exceed the amount to which such customer would be entitled under subsection (h) or (i) of this section if such security, property, or commodity contract were not returned or transferred under this subsection.

    (d) If the value of a specifically identifiable security, property, or commodity contract exceeds the amount to which the customer of the debtor is entitled under subsection (h) or (i) of this section, then such customer to whom such security, property, or commodity contract is specifically identified may deposit cash with the trustee equal to the difference between the value of such security, property, or commodity contract and such amount, and the trustee then shall—

    (1) return promptly such security, property, or commodity contract to such customer; or

    (2) transfer, on such customer's behalf, such security, property, or commodity contract to a commodity broker that is not a debtor under this title, subject to such rules or regulations as the Commission may prescribe.

    (e) Subject to subsection (b) of this section, the trustee shall liquidate any commodity contract that—

    (1) is identified to a particular customer and with respect to which such customer has not timely instructed the trustee as to the desired disposition of such commodity contract;

    (2) cannot be transferred under subsection (c) of this section; or

    (3) cannot be identified to a particular customer.

    (f) As soon as practicable after the commencement of the case, the trustee shall reduce to money, consistent with good market practice, all securities and other property, other than commodity contracts, held as property of the estate, except for specifically identifiable securities or property distributable under subsection (h) or (i) of this section.

    (g) The trustee may not distribute a security or other property except under subsection (h) or (i) of this section.

    (h) Except as provided in subsection (b) of this section, the trustee shall distribute customer property ratably to customers on the basis and to the extent of such customers' allowed net equity claims, and in priority to all other claims, except claims of a kind specified in section 507(a)(2) of this title that are attributable to the administration of customer property. Such distribution shall be in the form of—

    (1) cash;

    (2) the return or transfer, under subsection (c) or (d) of this section, of specifically identifiable customer securities, property, or commodity contracts; or

    (3) payment of margin calls under subsection (a) of this section.

Notwithstanding any other provision of this subsection, a customer net equity claim based on a proprietary account, as defined by Commission rule, regulation, or order, may not be paid either in whole or in part, directly or indirectly, out of customer property unless all other customer net equity claims have been paid in full.

  (i)   If the debtor is a clearing organization, the trustee shall distribute—

    (1)   customer property, other than member property, ratably to customers on the basis and to the extent of such customers' allowed net equity claims based on such customers' accounts other than proprietary accounts, and in priority to all other claims, except claims of a kind specified in section 507(a)(2) of this title that are attributable to the administration of such customer property; and

    (2)   member property ratably to customers on the basis and to the extent of such customers' allowed net equity claims based on such customers' proprietary accounts, and in priority to all other claims, except claims of a kind specified in section 507(a)(2) of this title that are attributable to the administration of member property or customer property.

  (j)(1)   The trustee shall distribute customer property in excess of that distributed under subsection (h) or (i) of this section in accordance with section 726 of this title.

  (2)   Except as provided in section 510 of this title, if a customer is not paid the full amount of such customer's allowed net equity claim from customer property, the unpaid portion of such claim is a claim entitled to distribution under section 726 of this title.

CROSS REFERENCES

Distribution in Chapter 11 cases, see 11 USCA § 1143.

Distribution of—

    Customer property in stockbroker liquidation cases, see 11 USCA § 752.

    Property of estate, see 11 USCA § 726.

Election of trustee by creditors holding claims entitled to distribution, see 11 USCA § 702.

Executory contracts and unexpired leases, see 11 USCA § 365.

Provisions relating to transferability of customer property and commodity contracts, see 7 USCA § 24.

§ 767. Commodity broker liquidation and forward contract merchants, commodity brokers, stockbrokers, financial institutions, financial participants, securities clearing agencies, swap participants, repo participants, and master netting agreement participants

Notwithstanding any other provision of this title, the exercise of rights by a forward contract merchant, commodity broker, stockbroker, financial institution, financial participant, securities clearing agency, swap participant, repo participant, or master netting agreement participant under this title shall not affect the priority of any unsecured claim it may have after the exercise of such rights.

SUBCHAPTER V—CLEARING BANK LIQUIDATION

§ 781. Definitions

For purposes of this subchapter, the following definitions shall apply:

    (1) **Board.**—The term "Board" means the Board of Governors of the Federal Reserve System.

(2) **Depository institution.**—The term "depository institution" has the same meaning as in section 3 of the Federal Deposit Insurance Act.

(3) **Clearing bank.**—The term "clearing bank" means an uninsured State member bank, or a corporation organized under section 25A of the Federal Reserve Act, which operates, or operates as, a multilateral clearing organization pursuant to section 409 of the Federal Deposit Insurance Corporation Improvement Act of 1991.

REFERENCES IN TEXT

Section 3 of the Federal Deposit Insurance Act, referred to in par. (2), is Act Sept. 21, 1950, c. 967, § 2[3], 64 Stat. 873, which is classified to 12 U.S.C.A. § 1813.

Section 25A of the Federal Reserve Act, referred to in par. (3), is Dec. 23, 1913, c. 6, § 25A, formerly § 25(a), as added Dec. 24, 1919, c. 18, 41 Stat. 378, as amended, which is classified to subchapter II of chapter 6 of Title 12, 12 U.S.C.A. § 611 et seq.

Section 409 of the Federal Deposit Insurance Corporation Improvement Act of 1991, referred to in par. (3), is Pub. L. 102–242, Title IV, § 409, as added by Pub. L. 106–554, § 1(a)(5) [Title I, § 112(a)(3)], Dec. 21, 2000, 114 Stat. 2763, 2763A–392, which is classified as 12 U.S.C.A. § 4422.

§ 782. Selection of trustee

(a) **In general.**—

(1) **Appointment.**—Notwithstanding any other provision of this title, the conservator or receiver who files the petition shall be the trustee under this chapter, unless the Board designates an alternative trustee.

(2) **Successor.**—The Board may designate a successor trustee if required.

(b) **Authority of trustee.**—Whenever the Board appoints or designates a trustee, chapter 3 and sections 704 and 705 of this title shall apply to the Board in the same way and to the same extent that they apply to a United States trustee.

§ 783. Additional powers of trustee

(a) **Distribution of property not of the estate.**—The trustee under this subchapter has power to distribute property not of the estate, including distributions to customers that are mandated by subchapters III and IV of this chapter.

(b) **Disposition of institution.**—The trustee under this subchapter may, after notice and a hearing—

(1) sell the clearing bank to a depository institution or consortium of depository institutions (which consortium may agree on the allocation of the clearing bank among the consortium);

(2) merge the clearing bank with a depository institution;

(3) transfer contracts to the same extent as could a receiver for a depository institution under paragraphs (9) and (10) of section 11(e) of the Federal Deposit Insurance Act;

(4) transfer assets or liabilities to a depository institution; and

(5) transfer assets and liabilities to a bridge depository institution as provided in paragraphs (1), (3)(A), (5), and (6) of section 11(n) of the Federal Deposit Insurance Act, paragraphs (9) through (13) of such section, and subparagraphs (A) through (H) and subparagraph (K) of paragraph (4) of such section 11(n), except that—

(A) the bridge depository institution to which such assets or liabilities are transferred shall be treated as a clearing bank for the purpose of this subsection; and

(B) any references in any such provision of law to the Federal Deposit Insurance Corporation shall be construed to be references to the appointing agency and that references to deposit insurance shall be omitted.

(c) Certain transfers included.—Any reference in this section to transfers of liabilities includes a ratable transfer of liabilities within a priority class.

REFERENCES IN TEXT

Subchapters III and IV of this chapter, referred to in subsec. (a), are 11 U.S.C.A. §§ 741 et seq. and 761 et seq.

Paragraphs (9) and (10) of section 11(e) of the Federal Deposit Insurance Act, referred to in subsec. (b)(3), are classified to 12 U.S.C.A. § 1821(e)(9), (10).

Paragraphs (1), (3)(A), (5), and (6) of section 11(n) of the Federal Deposit Insurance Act, paragraphs (9) through (13) of such section, and subparagraphs (A) through (H) and subparagraph (K) of paragraph (4) of such section 11(n), referred to in subsec. (b)(5), are classified to 12 U.S.C.A. § 1821(n)(1), (3)(A), (5), (6), and (4)(A) to (K).

§ 784. Right to be heard

The Board or a Federal reserve bank (in the case of a clearing bank that is a member of that bank) may raise and may appear and be heard on any issue in a case under this subchapter.

CHAPTER 9—ADJUSTMENT OF DEBTS OF A MUNICIPALITY

SUBCHAPTER I—GENERAL PROVISIONS

SUBCHAPTER I—GENERAL PROVISIONS

§ 901. Applicability of other sections of this title

(a) Sections 301, 333, 344, 347(b), 349, 350(b) 351,,[1] 361, 362, 364(c), 364(d), 364(e), 364(f), 365, 366, 501, 502, 503, 504, 506, 507(a)(2), 509, 510, 524(a)(1), 524(a)(2), 544, 545, 546, 547, 548, 549(a), 549(c), 549(d), 550, 551, 552, 553, 555, 556, 557, 559, 560, 561, 562, 1102, 1103, 1109, 1111(b), 1122, 1123(a)(1), 1123(a)(2), 1123(a)(3), 1123(a)(4), 1123(a)(5), 1123(b), 1123(d), 1124, 1125, 1126(a), 1126(b), 1126(c), 1126(e), 1126(f), 1126(g), 1127(d), 1128, 1129(a)(2), 1129(a)(3), 1129(a)(6), 1129(a)(8), 1129(a)(10), 1129(b)(1), 1129(b)(2)(A), 1129(b)(2)(B), 1142(b), 1143, 1144, and 1145 of this title apply in a case under this chapter.

(b) A term used in a section of this title made applicable in a case under this chapter by subsection (a) of this section or section 103(e) of this title has the meaning defined for such term for the purpose of such applicable section, unless such term is otherwise defined in section 902 of this title.

(c) A section made applicable in a case under this chapter by subsection (a) of this section that is operative if the business of the debtor is authorized to be operated is operative in a case under this chapter.

---

[1] So in original. The second comma should probably follow "350(b)".

REFERENCES IN TEXT

Section 103(e) of this title, referred to in subsec. (b), was redesignated subsec. (f) and a new subsec. (e) was added by Pub. L. 106–554, § 1(a)(5) [Title I, § 112(c)(5)(A)], Dec. 21, 2000, 114 Stat. 2763, 2763A–394.

CROSS REFERENCES

Chapters 1 and 9 of this title solely applicable in cases under Chapter 9 except as provided in this section, see 11 USCA § 103(f).

Confirmation in Chapter 9 cases upon compliance with provisions of this title made applicable by this section, see 11 USCA § 943.

Entities which may be debtors under this chapter, see 11 USCA § 109(c).

Filing fees, see 28 USCA § 1930.

§ 902.　Definitions for this chapter

In this chapter—

(1)　"property of the estate", when used in a section that is made applicable in a case under this chapter by section 103(e) or 901 of this title, means property of the debtor;

(2)　"special revenues" means—

(A)　receipts derived from the ownership, operation, or disposition of projects or systems of the debtor that are primarily used or intended to be used primarily to provide transportation, utility, or other services, including the proceeds of borrowings to finance the projects or systems;

(B)　special excise taxes imposed on particular activities or transactions;

(C)　incremental tax receipts from the benefited area in the case of tax-increment financing;

(D)　other revenues or receipts derived from particular functions of the debtor, whether or not the debtor has other functions; or

(E)　taxes specifically levied to finance one or more projects or systems, excluding receipts from general property, sales, or income taxes (other than tax-increment financing) levied to finance the general purposes of the debtor;

(3)　"special tax payer" means record owner or holder of legal or equitable title to real property against which a special assessment or special tax has been levied the proceeds of which are the sole source of payment of an obligation issued by the debtor to defray the cost of an improvement relating to such real property;

(4)　"special tax payer affected by the plan" means special tax payer with respect to whose real property the plan proposes to increase the proportion of special assessments or special taxes referred to in paragraph (2) of this section assessed against such real property; and

(5)　"trustee", when used in a section that is made applicable in a case under this chapter by section 103(e) or 901 of this title, means debtor, except as provided in section 926 of this title.

REFERENCES IN TEXT

Section 103(e) of this title, referred to in pars. (1) and (5), was redesignated section 103(f) and a new section 103(e) was added by Pub. L. 106–554, § 1(a)(5) [Title I, § 112(c)(5)(A)], Dec. 21, 2000, 114 Stat. 2763, 2763A–394.

CROSS REFERENCES

Definition of municipality, see 11 USCA § 101(40).

Limitation on recourse, see 11 USCA § 927.

Post petition effect of security interest, see 11 USCA § 928.

§ 903. Reservation of State power to control municipalities

This chapter does not limit or impair the power of a State to control, by legislation or otherwise, a municipality of or in such State in the exercise of the political or governmental powers of such municipality, including expenditures for such exercise, but—

(1) a State law prescribing a method of composition of indebtedness of such municipality may not bind any creditor that does not consent to such composition; and

(2) a judgment entered under such a law may not bind a creditor that does not consent to such composition.

CROSS REFERENCES

Authorization by state to be debtor under this chapter, see 11 USCA § 109(c).

§ 904. Limitation on jurisdiction and powers of court

Notwithstanding any power of the court, unless the debtor consents or the plan so provides, the court may not, by any stay, order, or decree, in the case or otherwise, interfere with—

(1) any of the political or governmental powers of the debtor;

(2) any of the property or revenues of the debtor; or

(3) the debtor's use or enjoyment of any income-producing property.

CROSS REFERENCES

Power of court, see 11 USCA § 105.

SUBCHAPTER II—ADMINISTRATION

§ 921. Petition and proceedings relating to petition

(a) Notwithstanding sections 109(d) and 301 of this title, a case under this chapter concerning an unincorporated tax or special assessment district that does not have such district's own officials is commenced by the filing under section 301 of this title of a petition under this chapter by such district's governing authority or the board or body having authority to levy taxes or assessments to meet the obligations of such district.

(b) The chief judge of the court of appeals for the circuit embracing the district in which the case is commenced shall designate the bankruptcy judge to conduct the case.

(c) After any objection to the petition, the court, after notice and a hearing, may dismiss the petition if the debtor did not file the petition in good faith or if the petition does not meet the requirements of this title.

(d) If the petition is not dismissed under subsection (c) of this section, the court shall order relief under this chapter notwithstanding section 301(b).

(e) The court may not, on account of an appeal from an order for relief, delay any proceeding under this chapter in the case in which the appeal is being taken; nor shall any court order a stay of such proceeding pending such appeal. The reversal on appeal of a finding of jurisdiction does not affect the validity of any debt incurred that is authorized by the court under section 364(c) or 364(d) of this title.

§ 922. Automatic stay of enforcement of claims against the debtor

(a) A petition filed under this chapter operates as a stay, in addition to the stay provided by section 362 of this title, applicable to all entities, of—

 (1) the commencement or continuation, including the issuance or employment of process, of a judicial, administrative, or other action or proceeding against an officer or inhabitant of the debtor that seeks to enforce a claim against the debtor; and

 (2) the enforcement of a lien on or arising out of taxes or assessments owed to the debtor.

(b) Subsections (c), (d), (e), (f), and (g) of section 362 of this title apply to a stay under subsection (a) of this section the same as such subsections apply to a stay under section 362(a) of this title.

(c) If the debtor provides, under section 362, 364, or 922 of this title, adequate protection of the interest of the holder of a claim secured by a lien on property of the debtor and if, notwithstanding such protection such creditor has a claim arising from the stay of action against such property under section 362 or 922 of this title or from the granting of a lien under section 364(d) of this title, then such claim shall be allowable as an administrative expense under section 503(b) of this title.

(d) Notwithstanding section 362 of this title and subsection (a) of this section, a petition filed under this chapter does not operate as a stay of application of pledged special revenues in a manner consistent with section 927 of this title to payment of indebtedness secured by such revenues.

CROSS REFERENCES

Adequate protection, see 11 USCA § 361.

Extension of time generally, see 11 USCA § 108.

§ 923. Notice

There shall be given notice of the commencement of a case under this chapter, notice of an order for relief under this chapter, and notice of the dismissal of a case under this chapter. Such notice shall also be published at least once a week for three successive weeks in at least one newspaper of general circulation published within the district in which the case is commenced, and in such other newspaper having a general circulation among bond dealers and bondholders as the court designates.

CROSS REFERENCES

Notice of order for relief, see 11 USCA § 342.

§ 924. List of creditors

The debtor shall file a list of creditors.

CROSS REFERENCES

Duty of debtor to file list of creditors, see 11 USCA § 521.

Time to file list of creditors, see Fed. R. Bankr. P. 1007(e).

§ 925. Effect of list of claims

A proof of claim is deemed filed under section 501 of this title for any claim that appears in the list filed under section 924 of this title, except a claim that is listed as disputed, contingent, or unliquidated.

CROSS REFERENCES

Filing proof of claim in Chapter 9 cases, see Fed. R. Bankr. P. 3003.

§ 926. Avoiding powers

(a) If the debtor refuses to pursue a cause of action under section 544, 545, 547, 548, 549(a), or 550 of this title, then on request of a creditor, the court may appoint a trustee to pursue such cause of action.

(b) A transfer of property of the debtor to or for the benefit of any holder of a bond or note, on account of such bond or note, may not be avoided under section 547 of this title.

CROSS REFERENCES

Trustee defined when used in sections made applicable to cases under this chapter, see 11 USCA § 902(5).

§ 927. Limitation on recourse

The holder of a claim payable solely from special revenues of the debtor under applicable nonbankruptcy law shall not be treated as having recourse against the debtor on account of such claim pursuant to section 1111(b) of this title.

CROSS REFERENCES

Definition of special revenues, see 11 USCA § 902(2).

§ 928. Post petition effect of security interest

(a) Notwithstanding section 552(a) of this title and subject to subsection (b) of this section, special revenues acquired by the debtor after the commencement of the case shall remain subject to any lien resulting from any security agreement entered into by the debtor before the commencement of the case.

(b) Any such lien on special revenues, other than municipal betterment assessments, derived from a project or system shall be subject to the necessary operating expenses of such project or system, as the case may be.

§ 929. Municipal leases

A lease to a municipality shall not be treated as an executory contract or unexpired lease for the purposes of section 365 or 502(b)(6) of this title solely by reason of its being subject to termination in the event the debtor fails to appropriate rent.

§ 930. Dismissal

(a) After notice and a hearing, the court may dismiss a case under this chapter for cause, including—

   (1) want of prosecution;

   (2) unreasonable delay by the debtor that is prejudicial to creditors;

   (3) failure to propose a plan within the time fixed under section 941 of this title;

   (4) if a plan is not accepted within any time fixed by the court;

   (5) denial of confirmation of a plan under section 943(b) of this title and denial of additional time for filing another plan or a modification of a plan; or

   (6) if the court has retained jurisdiction after confirmation of a plan—

      (A) material default by the debtor with respect to a term of such plan; or

(B) termination of such plan by reason of the occurrence of a condition specified in such plan.

(b) The court shall dismiss a case under this chapter if confirmation of a plan under this chapter is refused.

CROSS REFERENCES

Effect of dismissal, see 11 USCA § 349.

SUBCHAPTER III—THE PLAN

§ 941. Filing of plan

The debtor shall file a plan for the adjustment of the debtor's debts. If such a plan is not filed with the petition, the debtor shall file such a plan at such later time as the court fixes.

CROSS REFERENCES

Acceptance or rejection of plan in Chapter 9 cases, see Fed. R. Bankr. P. 3018.

Dismissal for failure to timely propose plan, see 11 USCA § 930.

Filing of plan and disclosure statement in Chapter 9 cases, see Fed. R. Bankr. P. 3016.

§ 942. Modification of plan

The debtor may modify the plan at any time before confirmation, but may not modify the plan so that the plan as modified fails to meet the requirements of this chapter. After the debtor files a modification, the plan as modified becomes the plan.

CROSS REFERENCES

Modification of accepted plan in Chapter 9 cases, see Fed. R. Bankr. P. 3019.

§ 943. Confirmation

(a) A special tax payer may object to confirmation of a plan.

(b) The court shall confirm the plan if—

    (1) the plan complies with the provisions of this title made applicable by sections 103(e) and 901 of this title;

    (2) the plan complies with the provisions of this chapter;

    (3) all amounts to be paid by the debtor or by any person for services or expenses in the case or incident to the plan have been fully disclosed and are reasonable;

    (4) the debtor is not prohibited by law from taking any action necessary to carry out the plan;

    (5) except to the extent that the holder of a particular claim has agreed to a different treatment of such claim, the plan provides that on the effective date of the plan each holder of a claim of a kind specified in section 507(a)(2) of this title will receive on account of such claim cash equal to the allowed amount of such claim;

    (6) any regulatory or electoral approval necessary under applicable nonbankruptcy law in order to carry out any provision of the plan has been obtained, or such provision is expressly conditioned on such approval; and

    (7) the plan is in the best interests of creditors and is feasible.

REFERENCES IN TEXT

Section 103(e) of this title, referred to in subsec. (b), was redesignated subsec. (f) and a new subsec. (e) was added by Pub. L. 106–554, § 1(a)(5) [Title I, § 112(c)(5)(A)], Dec. 21, 2000, 114 Stat. 2763, 2763A–394.

CROSS REFERENCES

Confirmation of plan in Chapter 9 cases, see Fed. R. Bankr. P. 3020.

Definition of special tax payer, see 11 USCA § 902(3).

Definition of special tax payer affected by the plan, see 11 USCA § 902(4).

Dismissal for denial of confirmation of plan, see 11 USCA § 930.

Unclaimed property, see 11 USCA § 347.

§ 944. Effect of confirmation

(a) The provisions of a confirmed plan bind the debtor and any creditor, whether or not—

    (1) a proof of such creditor's claim is filed or deemed filed under section 501 of this title;

    (2) such claim is allowed under section 502 of this title; or

    (3) such creditor has accepted the plan.

(b) Except as provided in subsection (c) of this section, the debtor is discharged from all debts as of the time when—

    (1) the plan is confirmed;

    (2) the debtor deposits any consideration to be distributed under the plan with a disbursing agent appointed by the court; and

    (3) the court has determined—

        (A) that any security so deposited will constitute, after distribution, a valid legal obligation of the debtor; and

        (B) that any provision made to pay or secure payment of such obligation is valid.

(c) The debtor is not discharged under subsection (b) of this section from any debt—

    (1) excepted from discharge by the plan or order confirming the plan; or

    (2) owed to an entity that, before confirmation of the plan, had neither notice nor actual knowledge of the case.

CROSS REFERENCES

Effect of discharge, see 11 USCA § 524(a)(1) & (2).

§ 945. Continuing jurisdiction and closing of the case

(a) The court may retain jurisdiction over the case for such period of time as is necessary for the successful implementation of the plan.

(b) Except as provided in subsection (a) of this section, the court shall close the case when administration of the case has been completed.

CROSS REFERENCES

Closing and reopening cases, see 11 USCA § 350(b).

§ 946.   Effect of exchange of securities before the date of the filing of the petition

The exchange of a new security under the plan for a claim covered by the plan, whether such exchange occurred before or after the date of the filing of the petition, does not limit or impair the effectiveness of the plan or of any provision of this chapter. The amount and number specified in section 1126(c) of this title include the amount and number of claims formerly held by a creditor that has participated in any such exchange.

CHAPTER 11—REORGANIZATION

SUBCHAPTER I—OFFICERS AND ADMINISTRATION

SUBCHAPTER II—THE PLAN

SUBCHAPTER III—POSTCONFIRMATION MATTERS

SUBCHAPTER IV—RAILROAD REORGANIZATION

SUBCHAPTER I—OFFICERS AND ADMINISTRATION

§ 1101. Definitions for this chapter

In this chapter—

(1) "debtor in possession" means debtor except when a person that has qualified under section 322 of this title is serving as trustee in the case;

(2) "substantial consummation" means—

(A) transfer of all or substantially all of the property proposed by the plan to be transferred;

(B) assumption by the debtor or by the successor to the debtor under the plan of the business or of the management of all or substantially all of the property dealt with by the plan; and

(C) commencement of distribution under the plan.

CROSS REFERENCES

Chapters 1, 3, and 5 of this title applicable in cases under this chapter except as provided in § 1161 or § 1181 of this title, see 11 USCA § 103(a).

Conversion to this chapter from—

Chapter 7, see 11 USCA § 706.

Chapter 13, see 11 USCA § 1307.

Definitions applicable in cases under this title, see 11 USCA § 101.

Filing fees, see 28 USCA § 1930.

Persons who may be debtors under this chapter, see 11 USCA § 109(d).

§ 1102. Creditors' and equity security holders' committees

(a)(1)   Except as provided in paragraph (3), as soon as practicable after the order for relief under chapter 11 of this title, the United States trustee shall appoint a committee of creditors holding unsecured claims and may appoint additional committees of creditors or of equity security holders as the United States trustee deems appropriate.

(2)   On request of a party in interest, the court may order the appointment of additional committees of creditors or of equity security holders if necessary to assure adequate representation of creditors or of equity security holders. The United States trustee shall appoint any such committee.

(3)   Unless the court for cause orders otherwise, a committee of creditors may not be appointed in a small business case or a case under subchapter V of this chapter.

(4)   On request of a party in interest and after notice and a hearing, the court may order the United States trustee to change the membership of a committee appointed under this subsection, if the court determines that the change is necessary to ensure adequate representation of creditors or equity security holders. The court may order the United States trustee to increase the number of members of a committee to include a creditor that is a small business concern (as described in section 3(a)(1) of the Small Business Act), if the court determines that the creditor holds claims (of the kind represented by the committee) the aggregate amount of which, in comparison to the annual gross revenue of that creditor, is disproportionately large.

(b)(1)   A committee of creditors appointed under subsection (a) of this section shall ordinarily consist of the persons, willing to serve, that hold the seven largest claims against the debtor of the kinds represented on such committee, or of the members of a committee organized by creditors before the commencement of the case under this chapter, if such committee was fairly chosen and is representative of the different kinds of claims to be represented.

(2)   A committee of equity security holders appointed under subsection (a)(2) of this section shall ordinarily consist of the persons, willing to serve, that hold the seven largest amounts of equity securities of the debtor of the kinds represented on such committee.

(3)   A committee appointed under subsection (a) shall—

(A)   provide access to information for creditors who—

(i)   hold claims of the kind represented by that committee; and

(ii)   are not appointed to the committee;

(B)   solicit and receive comments from the creditors described in subparagraph (A); and

(C)   be subject to a court order that compels any additional report or disclosure to be made to the creditors described in subparagraph (A).

REFERENCES IN TEXT

Section 3(a)(1) of the Small Business Act, referred to in subsec. (a)(4), is section 3(a)(1) of Pub. L. 85–536 § 2[3], July 18, 1958, 72 Stat. 384, as amended, which is classified to 15 U.S.C.A. § 632(a)(1). For complete classification, see Short Title note under 15 U.S.C.A. § 631 and Tables.

CROSS REFERENCES

Actual, necessary expenses of creditors' committee, see 11 USCA § 503(b)(3).

Applicability of this section in Chapter 9 cases, see 11 USCA § 901.

Creditors' committees in Chapter 7 cases, see 11 USCA § 705.

Effect of conversion, see 11 USCA § 348(b).

Inapplicability of subsec. (a)(1) of this section to railroad reorganization cases, see 11 USCA § 1161.

Limitation on compensation of professional persons, see 11 USCA § 328.

"Person" defined for purposes of this section, see 11 USCA § 101(41).

Unless the court for cause orders otherwise, subsecs. (a)(1), (2), and (4) and subsec. (b) of this section do not apply in Chapter 11 subchapter V cases, see 11 USCA § 1181(b).

§ 1103. Powers and duties of committees

(a) At a scheduled meeting of a committee appointed under section 1102 of this title, at which a majority of the members of such committee are present, and with the court's approval, such committee may select and authorize the employment by such committee of one or more attorneys, accountants, or other agents, to represent or perform services for such committee.

(b) An attorney or accountant employed to represent a committee appointed under section 1102 of this title may not, while employed by such committee, represent any other entity having an adverse interest in connection with the case. Representation of one or more creditors of the same class as represented by the committee shall not per se constitute the representation of an adverse interest.

(c) A committee appointed under section 1102 of this title may—

   (1) consult with the trustee or debtor in possession concerning the administration of the case;

   (2) investigate the acts, conduct, assets, liabilities, and financial condition of the debtor, the operation of the debtor's business and the desirability of the continuance of such business, and any other matter relevant to the case or to the formulation of a plan;

   (3) participate in the formulation of a plan, advise those represented by such committee of such committee's determinations as to any plan formulated, and collect and file with the court acceptances or rejections of a plan;

   (4) request the appointment of a trustee or examiner under section 1104 of this title; and

   (5) perform such other services as are in the interest of those represented.

(d) As soon as practicable after the appointment of a committee under section 1102 of this title, the trustee shall meet with such committee to transact such business as may be necessary and proper.

CROSS REFERENCES

Applicability of this section in Chapter 9 cases, see 11 USCA § 901.

Compensation of officers, see 11 USCA § 330.

Creditors' committees in Chapter 7 cases, see 11 USCA § 705.

Interim compensation for professional persons, see 11 USCA § 331.

Limitation on compensation of professional persons, see 11 USCA § 328.

Unless the court for cause orders otherwise, this section does not apply in Chapter 11 subchapter V cases, see 11 USCA § 1181(b).

§ 1104. Appointment of trustee or examiner

(a) At any time after the commencement of the case but before confirmation of a plan, on request of a party in interest or the United States trustee, and after notice and a hearing, the court shall order the appointment of a trustee—

(1) for cause, including fraud, dishonesty, incompetence, or gross mismanagement of the affairs of the debtor by current management, either before or after the commencement of the case, or similar cause, but not including the number of holders of securities of the debtor or the amount of assets or liabilities of the debtor; or

(2) if such appointment is in the interests of creditors, any equity security holders, and other interests of the estate, without regard to the number of holders of securities of the debtor or the amount of assets or liabilities of the debtor.

(b)(1) Except as provided in section 1163 of this title, on the request of a party in interest made not later than 30 days after the court orders the appointment of a trustee under subsection (a), the United States trustee shall convene a meeting of creditors for the purpose of electing one disinterested person to serve as trustee in the case. The election of a trustee shall be conducted in the manner provided in subsections (a), (b), and (c) of section 702 of this title.

(2)(A) If an eligible, disinterested trustee is elected at a meeting of creditors under paragraph (1), the United States trustee shall file a report certifying that election.

(B) Upon the filing of a report under subparagraph (A)—

(i) the trustee elected under paragraph (1) shall be considered to have been selected and appointed for purposes of this section; and

(ii) the service of any trustee appointed under subsection (a) shall terminate.

(C) The court shall resolve any dispute arising out of an election described in subparagraph (A).

(c) If the court does not order the appointment of a trustee under this section, then at any time before the confirmation of a plan, on request of a party in interest or the United States trustee, and after notice and a hearing, the court shall order the appointment of an examiner to conduct such an investigation of the debtor as is appropriate, including an investigation of any allegations of fraud, dishonesty, incompetence, misconduct, mismanagement, or irregularity in the management of the affairs of the debtor of or by current or former management of the debtor, if—

(1) such appointment is in the interests of creditors, any equity security holders, and other interests of the estate; or

(2) the debtor's fixed, liquidated, unsecured debts, other than debts for goods, services, or taxes, or owing to an insider, exceed $5,000,000.

(d) If the court orders the appointment of a trustee or an examiner, if a trustee or an examiner dies or resigns during the case or is removed under section 324 of this title, or if a trustee fails to qualify under section 322 of this title, then the United States trustee, after consultation with parties in interest, shall appoint, subject to the court's approval, one disinterested person other than the United States trustee to serve as trustee or examiner, as the case may be, in the case.

(e) The United States trustee shall move for the appointment of a trustee under subsection (a) if there are reasonable grounds to suspect that current members of the governing body of the debtor, the debtor's chief executive or chief financial officer, or members of the governing body who selected the debtor's chief executive or chief financial officer, participated in actual fraud, dishonesty, or criminal conduct in the management of the debtor or the debtor's public financial reporting.

CROSS REFERENCES

Appointment of Secretary of Transportation as sole trustee, see 46 USCA § 50305.

Appointment of trustee in—

    Chapter 11 subchapter V cases, see 11 USCA § 1183.

    Chapter 12 cases, see 11 USCA § 1202.

    Chapter 13 cases, see 11 USCA § 1302.

Railroad reorganization cases, see 11 USCA § 1163.

Election of trustee in Chapter 7 cases, see 11 USCA § 702.

Eligibility to serve as trustee, see 11 USCA § 321.

Grain storage facility bankruptcies, expedited appointment of trustee or examiner, see 11 USCA § 557.

Inapplicability of this section to railroad reorganization cases, see 11 USCA § 1161.

Inapplicability of this section to Chapter 11 subchapter V cases, see 11 USCA § 1181(a).

Limitation on compensation of trustee, see 11 USCA § 326.

Qualification of trustee, see 11 USCA § 322.

Removal of trustee or examiner, see 11 USCA § 324.

Time for bringing avoidance action, see 11 USCA § 546.

§ 1105. Termination of trustee's appointment

At any time before confirmation of a plan, on request of a party in interest or the United States trustee, and after notice and a hearing, the court may terminate the trustee's appointment and restore the debtor to possession and management of the property of the estate and of the operation of the debtor's business.

CROSS REFERENCES

Effect of vacancy in office of trustee, see 11 USCA § 325.

Inapplicability of this section to railroad reorganization cases, see 11 USCA § 1161.

Inapplicability of this section to Chapter 11 subchapter V cases, see 11 USCA § 1181(a).

Removal of trustee, see 11 USCA § 324.

§ 1106. Duties of trustee and examiner

(a) A trustee shall—

    (1) perform the duties of the trustee, as specified in paragraphs (2), (5), (7), (8), (9), (10), (11), and (12) of section 704(a);

    (2) if the debtor has not done so, file the list, schedule, and statement required under section 521(a)(1) of this title;

    (3) except to the extent that the court orders otherwise, investigate the acts, conduct, assets, liabilities, and financial condition of the debtor, the operation of the debtor's business and the desirability of the continuance of such business, and any other matter relevant to the case or to the formulation of a plan;

    (4) as soon as practicable—

        (A) file a statement of any investigation conducted under paragraph (3) of this subsection, including any fact ascertained pertaining to fraud, dishonesty, incompetence, misconduct, mismanagement, or irregularity in the management of the affairs of the debtor, or to a cause of action available to the estate; and

(B) transmit a copy or a summary of any such statement to any creditors' committee or equity security holders' committee, to any indenture trustee, and to such other entity as the court designates;

(5) as soon as practicable, file a plan under section 1121 of this title, file a report of why the trustee will not file a plan, or recommend conversion of the case to a case under chapter 7, 12, or 13 of this title or dismissal of the case;

(6) for any year for which the debtor has not filed a tax return required by law, furnish, without personal liability, such information as may be required by the governmental unit with which such tax return was to be filed, in light of the condition of the debtor's books and records and the availability of such information;

(7) after confirmation of a plan, file such reports as are necessary or as the court orders; and

(8) if with respect to the debtor there is a claim for a domestic support obligation, provide the applicable notice specified in subsection (c).

(b) An examiner appointed under section 1104(d) of this title shall perform the duties specified in paragraphs (3) and (4) of subsection (a) of this section, and, except to the extent that the court orders otherwise, any other duties of the trustee that the court orders the debtor in possession not to perform.

(c)(1) In a case described in subsection (a)(8) to which subsection (a)(8) applies, the trustee shall—

(A)(i) provide written notice to the holder of the claim described in subsection (a)(8) of such claim and of the right of such holder to use the services of the State child support enforcement agency established under sections 464 and 466 of the Social Security Act for the State in which such holder resides, for assistance in collecting child support during and after the case under this title; and

(ii) include in the notice required by clause (i) the address and telephone number of such State child support enforcement agency;

(B)(i) provide written notice to such State child support enforcement agency of such claim; and

(ii) include in the notice required by clause (i) the name, address, and telephone number of such holder; and

(C) at such time as the debtor is granted a discharge under section 1141, provide written notice to such holder and to such State child support enforcement agency of—

(i) the granting of the discharge;

(ii) the last recent known address of the debtor;

(iii) the last recent known name and address of the debtor's employer; and

(iv) the name of each creditor that holds a claim that—

(I) is not discharged under paragraph (2), (4), or (14A) of section 523(a); or

(II) was reaffirmed by the debtor under section 524(c).

(2)(A) The holder of a claim described in subsection (a)(8) or the State child enforcement support agency of the State in which such holder resides may request from a creditor described in paragraph (1)(C)(iv) the last known address of the debtor.

(B) Notwithstanding any other provision of law, a creditor that makes a disclosure of a last known address of a debtor in connection with a request made under subparagraph (A) shall not be liable by reason of making such disclosure.

REFERENCES IN TEXT

Section 464 of the Social Security Act, referred to in subsec. (c)(1)(A)(i), is Act Aug. 14, 1935, c. 531, Title IV, § 464, as added Aug. 13, 1981, Pub. L. 97–35, Title XXIII, § 2331(a), 95 Stat. 860, and amended, which is classified to 42 U.S.C.A. § 664.

Section 466 of the Social Security Act, referred to in subsec. (c)(1)(A)(i), is Act Aug. 14, 1935, c. 531, Title IV, § 466, as added Aug. 16, 1984, Pub. L. 98–378, § 3(b), 98 Stat. 1306, and amended, which is classified to 42 U.S.C.A. § 666.

CROSS REFERENCES

Duties of trustees in—

>> Chapter 12 cases, see 11 USCA § 1202.

>> Chapter 13 cases, see 11 USCA § 1302.

Inapplicability of this section to Chapter 11 subchapter V cases, see 11 USCA § 1181(a).

Powers and duties of trustee in investor protection liquidation proceedings, see 15 USCA § 78fff–1.

Rights and powers of debtor in Chapter 12 case do not include duties specified in subsec. (a)(3) and (4) of this section, see 11 USCA § 1203.

§ 1107. Rights, powers, and duties of debtor in possession

(a) Subject to any limitations on a trustee serving in a case under this chapter, and to such limitations or conditions as the court prescribes, a debtor in possession shall have all the rights, other than the right to compensation under section 330 of this title, and powers, and shall perform all the functions and duties, except the duties specified in sections 1106(a)(2), (3), and (4) of this title, of a trustee serving in a case under this chapter.

(b) Notwithstanding section 327(a) of this title, a person is not disqualified for employment under section 327 of this title by a debtor in possession solely because of such person's employment by or representation of the debtor before the commencement of the case.

CROSS REFERENCES

Debtor's duties, see 11 USCA § 521.

Inapplicability of this section in railroad reorganization cases, see 11 USCA § 1161.

Inapplicability of this section to Chapter 11 subchapter V cases, see 11 USCA § 1181(a).

Limitation on compensation of professional persons, see 11 USCA § 328.

Rights and powers of debtor in—

>> Chapter 12 cases, see 11 USCA § 1203.

>> Chapter 13 cases, see 11 USCA § 1303.

§ 1108. Authorization to operate business

Unless the court, on request of a party in interest and after notice and a hearing, orders otherwise, the trustee may operate the debtor's business.

CROSS REFERENCES

Executory contracts and unexpired leases, see 11 USCA § 365.

Inapplicability of this section to Chapter 11 subchapter V cases, see 11 USCA § 1181(a).

Obtaining credit, see 11 USCA § 364.

Retention or replacement of professional persons, see 11 USCA § 327.

Use, sale or lease of property, see 11 USCA § 363.

Utility service, see 11 USCA § 366.

§ 1109. Right to be heard

(a) The Securities and Exchange Commission may raise and may appear and be heard on any issue in a case under this chapter, but the Securities and Exchange Commission may not appeal from any judgment, order, or decree entered in the case.

(b) A party in interest, including the debtor, the trustee, a creditors' committee, an equity security holders' committee, a creditor, an equity security holder, or any indenture trustee, may raise and may appear and be heard on any issue in a case under this chapter.

CROSS REFERENCES

Applicability of this section in Chapter 9 cases, see 11 USCA § 901.

Right of Commodity Futures Trading Commission to be heard in commodity broker liquidation cases, see 11 USCA § 762.

Right of Interstate Commerce Commission, Department of Transportation, and State or local regulatory commission to be heard in railroad reorganization, see 11 USCA § 1164.

§ 1110. Aircraft equipment and vessels

(a)(1) Except as provided in paragraph (2) and subject to subsection (b), the right of a secured party with a security interest in equipment described in paragraph (3), or of a lessor or conditional vendor of such equipment, to take possession of such equipment in compliance with a security agreement, lease, or conditional sale contract, and to enforce any of its other rights or remedies, under such security agreement, lease, or conditional sale contract, to sell, lease, or otherwise retain or dispose of such equipment, is not limited or otherwise affected by any other provision of this title or by any power of the court.

(2) The right to take possession and to enforce the other rights and remedies described in paragraph (1) shall be subject to section 362 if—

(A) before the date that is 60 days after the date of the order for relief under this chapter, the trustee, subject to the approval of the court, agrees to perform all obligations of the debtor under such security agreement, lease, or conditional sale contract; and

(B) any default, other than a default of a kind specified in section 365(b)(2), under such security agreement, lease, or conditional sale contract—

    (i) that occurs before the date of the order is cured before the expiration of such 60-day period;

    (ii) that occurs after the date of the order and before the expiration of such 60-day period is cured before the later of—

        (I) the date that is 30 days after the date of the default; or

        (II) the expiration of such 60-day period; and

    (iii) that occurs on or after the expiration of such 60-day period is cured in compliance with the terms of such security agreement, lease, or conditional sale contract, if a cure is permitted under that agreement, lease, or contract.

(3) The equipment described in this paragraph—

    (A) is—

(i)　an aircraft, aircraft engine, propeller, appliance, or spare part (as defined in section 40102 of title 49) that is subject to a security interest granted by, leased to, or conditionally sold to a debtor that, at the time such transaction is entered into, holds an air carrier operating certificate issued pursuant to chapter 447 of title 49 for aircraft capable of carrying 10 or more individuals or 6,000 pounds or more of cargo; or

(ii)　a vessel documented under chapter 121 of title 46 that is subject to a security interest granted by, leased to, or conditionally sold to a debtor that is a water carrier that, at the time such transaction is entered into, holds a certificate of public convenience and necessity or permit issued by the Department of Transportation; and

(B)　includes all records and documents relating to such equipment that are required, under the terms of the security agreement, lease, or conditional sale contract, to be surrendered or returned by the debtor in connection with the surrender or return of such equipment.

(4)　Paragraph (1) applies to a secured party, lessor, or conditional vendor acting in its own behalf or acting as trustee or otherwise in behalf of another party.

(b)　The trustee and the secured party, lessor, or conditional vendor whose right to take possession is protected under subsection (a) may agree, subject to the approval of the court, to extend the 60-day period specified in subsection (a)(1).

(c)(1)　In any case under this chapter, the trustee shall immediately surrender and return to a secured party, lessor, or conditional vendor, described in subsection (a)(1), equipment described in subsection (a)(3), if at any time after the date of the order for relief under this chapter such secured party, lessor, or conditional vendor is entitled pursuant to subsection (a)(1) to take possession of such equipment and makes a written demand for such possession to the trustee.

(2)　At such time as the trustee is required under paragraph (1) to surrender and return equipment described in subsection (a)(3), any lease of such equipment, and any security agreement or conditional sale contract relating to such equipment, if such security agreement or conditional sale contract is an executory contract, shall be deemed rejected.

(d)　With respect to equipment first placed in service on or before October 22, 1994, for purposes of this section—

(1)　the term 'lease' includes any written agreement with respect to which the lessor and the debtor, as lessee, have expressed in the agreement or in a substantially contemporaneous writing that the agreement is to be treated as a lease for Federal income tax purposes; and

(2)　the term "security interest" means a purchase-money equipment security interest.

REFERENCES IN TEXT

Chapter 447 of Title 49, referred to in subsec. (a)(3)(A)(i), is classified to 49 U.S.C.A. § 44701 et seq.

Chapter 121 of this title, referred to in subsec. (a)(3)(A)(ii), is Documentation of Vessels, 46 U.S.C.A. § 12101 et seq.

CROSS REFERENCES

Effect of conversion, see 11 USCA § 348.

Rights of certain secured parties in rolling stock equipment, see 11 USCA § 1168.

§ 1111. Claims and interests

(a)　A proof of claim or interest is deemed filed under section 501 of this title for any claim or interest that appears in the schedules filed under section 521(a)(1) or 1106(a)(2) of this title, except a claim or interest that is scheduled as disputed, contingent, or unliquidated.

(b)(1)(A) A claim secured by a lien on property of the estate shall be allowed or disallowed under section 502 of this title the same as if the holder of such claim had recourse against the debtor on account of such claim, whether or not such holder has such recourse, unless—

    (i) the class of which such claim is a part elects, by at least two-thirds in amount and more than half in number of allowed claims of such class, application of paragraph (2) of this subsection; or

    (ii) such holder does not have such recourse and such property is sold under section 363 of this title or is to be sold under the plan.

(B) A class of claims may not elect application of paragraph (2) of this subsection if—

    (i) the interest on account of such claims of the holders of such claims in such property is of inconsequential value; or

    (ii) the holder of a claim of such class has recourse against the debtor on account of such claim and such property is sold under section 363 of this title or is to be sold under the plan.

(2) If such an election is made, then notwithstanding section 506(a) of this title, such claim is a secured claim to the extent that such claim is allowed.

CROSS REFERENCES

Applicability of subsec. (b) of this section in Chapter 9 cases, see 11 USCA § 901.

Election as affecting confirmation of plan, see 11 USCA § 1129(a)(7).

Election under § 1111(b) by secured creditor in Chapter 9 or Chapter 11 cases, see Fed. R. Bankr. P. 3014.

Filing proof of claim in Chapter 11 cases, see Fed. R. Bankr. P. 3003.

Limitation on recourse of claim payable solely from special revenues of debtor, see 11 USCA § 927.

§ 1112. Conversion or dismissal

(a) The debtor may convert a case under this chapter to a case under chapter 7 of this title unless—

    (1) the debtor is not a debtor in possession;

    (2) the case originally was commenced as an involuntary case under this chapter; or

    (3) the case was converted to a case under this chapter other than on the debtor's request.

(b)(1) Except as provided in paragraph (2) and subsection (c), on request of a party in interest, and after notice and a hearing, the court shall convert a case under this chapter to a case under chapter 7 or dismiss a case under this chapter, whichever is in the best interests of creditors and the estate, for cause unless the court determines that the appointment under section 1104(a) of a trustee or an examiner is in the best interests of creditors and the estate.

(2) The court may not convert a case under this chapter to a case under chapter 7 or dismiss a case under this chapter if the court finds and specifically identifies unusual circumstances establishing that converting or dismissing the case is not in the best interests of creditors and the estate, and the debtor or any other party in interest establishes that—

    (A) there is a reasonable likelihood that a plan will be confirmed within the timeframes established in sections 1121(e) and 1129(e) of this title, or if such sections do not apply, within a reasonable period of time; and

    (B) the grounds for converting or dismissing the case include an act or omission of the debtor other than under paragraph (4)(A)—

        (i) for which there exists a reasonable justification for the act or omission; and

(ii) that will be cured within a reasonable period of time fixed by the court.

(3) The court shall commence the hearing on a motion under this subsection not later than 30 days after filing of the motion, and shall decide the motion not later than 15 days after commencement of such hearing, unless the movant expressly consents to a continuance for a specific period of time or compelling circumstances prevent the court from meeting the time limits established by this paragraph.

(4) For purposes of this subsection, the term 'cause' includes—

(A) substantial or continuing loss to or diminution of the estate and the absence of a reasonable likelihood of rehabilitation;

(B) gross mismanagement of the estate;

(C) failure to maintain appropriate insurance that poses a risk to the estate or to the public;

(D) unauthorized use of cash collateral substantially harmful to 1 or more creditors;

(E) failure to comply with an order of the court;

(F) unexcused failure to satisfy timely any filing or reporting requirement established by this title or by any rule applicable to a case under this chapter;

(G) failure to attend the meeting of creditors convened under section 341(a) or an examination ordered under rule 2004 of the Federal Rules of Bankruptcy Procedure without good cause shown by the debtor;

(H) failure timely to provide information or attend meetings reasonably requested by the United States trustee (or the bankruptcy administrator, if any);

(I) failure timely to pay taxes owed after the date of the order for relief or to file tax returns due after the date of the order for relief;

(J) failure to file a disclosure statement, or to file or confirm a plan, within the time fixed by this title or by order of the court;

(K) failure to pay any fees or charges required under chapter 123 of title 28;

(L) revocation of an order of confirmation under section 1144;

(M) inability to effectuate substantial consummation of a confirmed plan;

(N) material default by the debtor with respect to a confirmed plan;

(O) termination of a confirmed plan by reason of the occurrence of a condition specified in the plan; and

(P) failure of the debtor to pay any domestic support obligation that first becomes payable after the date of the filing of the petition.

(c) The court may not convert a case under this chapter to a case under chapter 7 of this title if the debtor is a farmer or a corporation that is not a moneyed, business, or commercial corporation, unless the debtor requests such conversion.

(d) The court may convert a case under this chapter to a case under chapter 12 or 13 of this title only if—

(1) the debtor requests such conversion;

(2) the debtor has not been discharged under section 1141(d) of this title; and

(3) if the debtor requests conversion to chapter 12 of this title, such conversion is equitable.

(e) Except as provided in subsections (c) and (f), the court, on request of the United States trustee, may convert a case under this chapter to a case under chapter 7 of this title or may dismiss a case under this chapter, whichever is in the best interest of creditors and the estate if the debtor in a voluntary case fails to file, within fifteen days after the filing of the petition commencing such case or such additional time as the court may allow, the information required by paragraph (1) of section 521(a), including a list containing the names and addresses of the holders of the twenty largest unsecured claims (or of all unsecured claims if there are fewer than twenty unsecured claims), and the approximate dollar amounts of each of such claims.

(f) Notwithstanding any other provision of this section, a case may not be converted to a case under another chapter of this title unless the debtor may be a debtor under such chapter.

REFERENCES IN TEXT

Chapter 123 of title 28, referred to in subsec. (b)(4)(K), is 28 U.S.C.A. § 1911 et seq.

CROSS REFERENCES

Conversion of Chapter 11 case to Chapter 7 case, see Fed. R. Bankr. P. 1019.

Conversion of—

> Chapter 7 cases, see 11 USCA § 706.

> Chapter 12 cases, see 11 USCA § 1208.

> Chapter13 cases, see 11 USCA § 1307.

Dismissal of—

> Chapter 7 cases, see 11 USCA § 707.

> Chapter 9 cases, see 11 USCA § 930.

Distribution of property of estate converted to Chapter 7, see 11 USCA § 726.

Effect of conversion, see 11 USCA § 348.

Effect of dismissal, see 11 USCA § 349.

Executory contracts and unexpired leases, see 11 USCA § 365.

Liquidation of estate in railroad reorganization cases, see 11 USCA § 1174.

Procedure for dismissal or conversion of Chapter 11 cases, see Fed. R. Bankr. P. 1017(f).

Termination of debtor's taxable period for cases converted to Chapter 7, see 11 USCA § 728.

§ 1113. Rejection of collective bargaining agreements

(a) The debtor in possession, or the trustee if one has been appointed under the provisions of this chapter, other than a trustee in a case covered by subchapter IV of this chapter and by title I of the Railway Labor Act, may assume or reject a collective bargaining agreement only in accordance with the provisions of this section.

(b)(1) Subsequent to filing a petition and prior to filing an application seeking rejection of a collective bargaining agreement, the debtor in possession or trustee (hereinafter in this section "trustee" shall include a debtor in possession), shall—

> **(A)** make a proposal to the authorized representative of the employees covered by such agreement, based on the most complete and reliable information available at the time of such proposal, which provides for those necessary modifications in the employees benefits and protections that are necessary to permit the reorganization of the debtor and assures that all creditors, the debtor and all of the affected parties are treated fairly and equitably; and

> **(B)** provide, subject to subsection (d)(3), the representative of the employees with such relevant information as is necessary to evaluate the proposal.

(2) During the period beginning on the date of the making of a proposal provided for in paragraph (1) and ending on the date of the hearing provided for in subsection (d)(1), the trustee shall meet, at reasonable times, with the authorized representative to confer in good faith in attempting to reach mutually satisfactory modifications of such agreement.

(c) The court shall approve an application for rejection of a collective bargaining agreement only if the court finds that—

(1) the trustee has, prior to the hearing, made a proposal that fulfills the requirements of subsection (b)(1);

(2) the authorized representative of the employees has refused to accept such proposal without good cause; and

(3) the balance of the equities clearly favors rejection of such agreement.

(d)(1) Upon the filing of an application for rejection the court shall schedule a hearing to be held not later than fourteen days after the date of the filing of such application. All interested parties may appear and be heard at such hearing. Adequate notice shall be provided to such parties at least ten days before the date of such hearing. The court may extend the time for the commencement of such hearing for a period not exceeding seven days where the circumstances of the case, and the interests of justice require such extension, or for additional periods of time to which the trustee and representative agree.

(2) The court shall rule on such application for rejection within thirty days after the date of the commencement of the hearing. In the interests of justice, the court may extend such time for ruling for such additional period as the trustee and the employees' representative may agree to. If the court does not rule on such application within thirty days after the date of the commencement of the hearing, or within such additional time as the trustee and the employees' representative may agree to, the trustee may terminate or alter any provisions of the collective bargaining agreement pending the ruling of the court on such application.

(3) The court may enter such protective orders, consistent with the need of the authorized representative of the employee to evaluate the trustee's proposal and the application for rejection, as may be necessary to prevent disclosure of information provided to such representative where such disclosure could compromise the position of the debtor with respect to its competitors in the industry in which it is engaged.

(e) If during a period when the collective bargaining agreement continues in effect, and if essential to the continuation of the debtor's business, or in order to avoid irreparable damage to the estate, the court, after notice and a hearing, may authorize the trustee to implement interim changes in the terms, conditions, wages, benefits, or work rules provided by a collective bargaining agreement. Any hearing under this paragraph shall be scheduled in accordance with the needs of the trustee. The implementation of such interim changes shall not render the application for rejection moot.

(f) No provision of this title shall be construed to permit a trustee to unilaterally terminate or alter any provisions of a collective bargaining agreement prior to compliance with the provisions of this section.

REFERENCES IN TEXT

The Railway Labor Act, referred to in subsec. (a), is Act May 20, 1926, c. 347, 44 Stat. 577, as amended. Title I of the Railway Labor Act is classified principally to subchapter I (section 151 et seq.) of chapter 8 of Title 45, Railroads. For complete classification of this Act to the Code, see section 151 of Title 45 and Tables.

CROSS REFERENCES

Collective bargaining agreements, railroad reorganizations, see 11 USCA § 1167.

§ 1114. Payment of insurance benefits to retired employees

(a) For purposes of this section, the term "retiree benefits" means payments to any entity or person for the purpose of providing or reimbursing payments for retired employees and their spouses and dependents, for medical, surgical, or hospital care benefits, or benefits in the event of sickness, accident, disability, or death under any plan, fund, or program (through the purchase of insurance or otherwise) maintained or established in whole or in part by the debtor prior to filing a petition commencing a case under this title.

(b)(1) For purposes of this section, the term "authorized representative" means the authorized representative designated pursuant to subsection (c) for persons receiving any retiree benefits covered by a collective bargaining agreement or subsection (d) in the case of persons receiving retiree benefits not covered by such an agreement.

(2) Committees of retired employees appointed by the court pursuant to this section shall have the same rights, powers, and duties as committees appointed under sections 1102 and 1103 of this title for the purpose of carrying out the purposes of sections 1114 and 1129(a)(13) and, as permitted by the court, shall have the power to enforce the rights of persons under this title as they relate to retiree benefits.

(c)(1) A labor organization shall be, for purposes of this section, the authorized representative of those persons receiving any retiree benefits covered by any collective bargaining agreement to which that labor organization is signatory, unless (A) such labor organization elects not to serve as the authorized representative of such persons, or (B) the court, upon a motion by any party in interest, after notice and hearing, determines that different representation of such persons is appropriate.

(2) In cases where the labor organization referred to in paragraph (1) elects not to serve as the authorized representative of those persons receiving any retiree benefits covered by any collective bargaining agreement to which that labor organization is signatory, or in cases where the court, pursuant to paragraph (1) finds different representation of such persons appropriate, the court, upon a motion by any party in interest, and after notice and a hearing, shall appoint a committee of retired employees if the debtor seeks to modify or not pay the retiree benefits or if the court otherwise determines that it is appropriate, from among such persons, to serve as the authorized representative of such persons under this section.

(d) The court, upon a motion by any party in interest, and after notice and a hearing, shall order the appointment of a committee of retired employees if the debtor seeks to modify or not pay the retiree benefits or if the court otherwise determines that it is appropriate, to serve as the authorized representative, under this section, of those persons receiving any retiree benefits not covered by a collective bargaining agreement. The United States trustee shall appoint any such committee.

(e)(1) Notwithstanding any other provision of this title, the debtor in possession, or the trustee if one has been appointed under the provisions of this chapter (hereinafter in this section "trustee" shall include a debtor in possession), shall timely pay and shall not modify any retiree benefits, except that—

    (A) the court, on motion of the trustee or authorized representative, and after notice and a hearing, may order modification of such payments, pursuant to the provisions of subsections (g) and (h) of this section, or

    (B) the trustee and the authorized representative of the recipients of those benefits may agree to modification of such payments,

after which such benefits as modified shall continue to be paid by the trustee.

(2) Any payment for retiree benefits required to be made before a plan confirmed under section 1129 of this title is effective has the status of an allowed administrative expense as provided in section 503 of this title.

(f)(1) Subsequent to filing a petition and prior to filing an application seeking modification of the retiree benefits, the trustee shall—

    (A) make a proposal to the authorized representative of the retirees, based on the most complete and reliable information available at the time of such proposal, which provides for those necessary modifications in the retiree benefits that are necessary to permit the reorganization of the debtor and assures that all creditors, the debtor and all of the affected parties are treated fairly and equitably; and

(B) provide, subject to subsection (k)(3), the representative of the retirees with such relevant information as is necessary to evaluate the proposal.

(2) During the period beginning on the date of the making of a proposal provided for in paragraph (1), and ending on the date of the hearing provided for in subsection (k)(1), the trustee shall meet, at reasonable times, with the authorized representative to confer in good faith in attempting to reach mutually satisfactory modifications of such retiree benefits.

(g) The court shall enter an order providing for modification in the payment of retiree benefits if the court finds that—

(1) the trustee has, prior to the hearing, made a proposal that fulfills the requirements of subsection (f);

(2) the authorized representative of the retirees has refused to accept such proposal without good cause; and

(3) such modification is necessary to permit the reorganization of the debtor and assures that all creditors, the debtor, and all of the affected parties are treated fairly and equitably, and is clearly favored by the balance of the equities;

except that in no case shall the court enter an order providing for such modification which provides for a modification to a level lower than that proposed by the trustee in the proposal found by the court to have complied with the requirements of this subsection and subsection (f): *Provided, however,* That at any time after an order is entered providing for modification in the payment of retiree benefits, or at any time after an agreement modifying such benefits is made between the trustee and the authorized representative of the recipients of such benefits, the authorized representative may apply to the court for an order increasing those benefits which order shall be granted if the increase in retiree benefits sought is consistent with the standard set forth in paragraph (3): *Provided further,* That neither the trustee nor the authorized representative is precluded from making more than one motion for a modification order governed by this subsection.

(h)(1) Prior to a court issuing a final order under subsection (g) of this section, if essential to the continuation of the debtor's business, or in order to avoid irreparable damage to the estate, the court, after notice and a hearing, may authorize the trustee to implement interim modifications in retiree benefits.

(2) Any hearing under this subsection shall be scheduled in accordance with the needs of the trustee.

(3) The implementation of such interim changes does not render the motion for modification moot.

(i) No retiree benefits paid between the filing of the petition and the time a plan confirmed under section 1129 of this title becomes effective shall be deducted or offset from the amounts allowed as claims for any benefits which remain unpaid, or from the amounts to be paid under the plan with respect to such claims for unpaid benefits, whether such claims for unpaid benefits are based upon or arise from a right to future unpaid benefits or from any benefits not paid as a result of modifications allowed pursuant to this section.

(j) No claim for retiree benefits shall be limited by section 502(b)(7) of this title.

(k)(1) Upon the filing of an application for modifying retiree benefits, the court shall schedule a hearing to be held not later than fourteen days after the date of the filing of such application. All interested parties may appear and be heard at such hearing. Adequate notice shall be provided to such parties at least ten days before the date of such hearing. The court may extend the time for the commencement of such hearing for a period not exceeding seven days where the circumstances of the case, and the interests of justice require such extension, or for additional periods of time to which the trustee and the authorized representative agree.

(2) The court shall rule on such application for modification within ninety days after the date of the commencement of the hearing. In the interests of justice, the court may extend such time for ruling for such additional period as the trustee and the authorized representative may agree to. If the court does not rule on such application within ninety days after the date of the commencement of the hearing, or within such additional time as the trustee and the authorized representative may agree to, the trustee may implement the proposed modifications pending the ruling of the court on such application.

(3) The court may enter such protective orders, consistent with the need of the authorized representative of the retirees to evaluate the trustee's proposal and the application for modification, as may be necessary to prevent disclosure of information provided to such representative where such disclosure could compromise the position of the debtor with respect to its competitors in the industry in which it is engaged.

(l) If the debtor, during the 180-day period ending on the date of the filing of the petition—

(1) modified retiree benefits; and

(2) was insolvent on the date such benefits were modified;

the court, on motion of a party in interest, and after notice and a hearing, shall issue an order reinstating as of the date the modification was made, such benefits as in effect immediately before such date unless the court finds that the balance of the equities clearly favors such modification.

(m) This section shall not apply to any retiree, or the spouse or dependents of such retiree, if such retiree's gross income for the twelve months preceding the filing of the bankruptcy petition equals or exceeds $250,000, unless such retiree can demonstrate to the satisfaction of the court that he is unable to obtain health, medical, life, and disability coverage for himself, his spouse, and his dependents who would otherwise be covered by the employer's insurance plan, comparable to the coverage provided by the employer on the day before the filing of a petition under this title.

CROSS REFERENCES

Confirmation of plan if plan provides for continuation of "retiree benefits" as defined under this section, see 11 USCA § 1129(a)(13).

§ 1115. Property of the estate

(a) In a case in which the debtor is an individual, property of the estate includes, in addition to the property specified in section 541—

(1) all property of the kind specified in section 541 that the debtor acquires after the commencement of the case but before the case is closed, dismissed, or converted to a case under chapter 7, 12, or 13, whichever occurs first; and

(2) earnings from services performed by the debtor after the commencement of the case but before the case is closed, dismissed, or converted to a case under chapter 7, 12, or 13, whichever occurs first.

(b) Except as provided in section 1104 or a confirmed plan or order confirming a plan, the debtor shall remain in possession of all property of the estate.

REFERENCES IN TEXT

Chapter 7, 12, or 13, referred to in subsec. (a)(1), (2), is chapter 7, 12, or 13 of this title, 11 U.S.C.A. § 701 et seq., 11 U.S.C.A. § 1201 et seq., or 11 U.S.C.A. § 1301 et seq., respectively.

§ 1116. Duties of trustee or debtor in possession in small business cases

In a small business case, a trustee or the debtor in possession, in addition to the duties provided in this title and as otherwise required by law, shall—

    (1) append to the voluntary petition or, in an involuntary case, file not later than 7 days after the date of the order for relief—

        (A) its most recent balance sheet, statement of operations, cash-flow statement, and Federal income tax return; or

        (B) a statement made under penalty of perjury that no balance sheet, statement of operations, or cash-flow statement has been prepared and no Federal tax return has been filed;

    (2) attend, through its senior management personnel and counsel, meetings scheduled by the court or the United States trustee, including initial debtor interviews, scheduling conferences, and meetings of creditors convened under section 341 unless the court, after notice and a hearing, waives that requirement upon a finding of extraordinary and compelling circumstances;

    (3) timely file all schedules and statements of financial affairs, unless the court, after notice and a hearing, grants an extension, which shall not extend such time period to a date later than 30 days after the date of the order for relief, absent extraordinary and compelling circumstances;

    (4) file all postpetition financial and other reports required by the Federal Rules of Bankruptcy Procedure or by local rule of the district court;

    (5) subject to section 363(c)(2), maintain insurance customary and appropriate to the industry;

    (6)(A) timely file tax returns and other required government filings; and

    (B) subject to section 363(c)(2), timely pay all taxes entitled to administrative expense priority except those being contested by appropriate proceedings being diligently prosecuted; and

    (7) allow the United States trustee, or a designated representative of the United States trustee, to inspect the debtor's business premises, books, and records at reasonable times, after reasonable prior written notice, unless notice is waived by the debtor.

SUBCHAPTER II—THE PLAN

§ 1121. Who may file a plan

    (a) The debtor may file a plan with a petition commencing a voluntary case, or at any time in a voluntary case or an involuntary case.

    (b) Except as otherwise provided in this section, only the debtor may file a plan until after 120 days after the date of the order for relief under this chapter.

    (c) Any party in interest, including the debtor, the trustee, a creditors' committee, an equity security holders' committee, a creditor, an equity security holder, or any indenture trustee, may file a plan if and only if—

        (1) a trustee has been appointed under this chapter;

(2) the debtor has not filed a plan before 120 days after the date of the order for relief under this chapter; or

(3) the debtor has not filed a plan that has been accepted, before 180 days after the date of the order for relief under this chapter, by each class of claims or interests that is impaired under the plan.

(d)(1) Subject to paragraph (2), on request of a party in interest made within the respective periods specified in subsections (b) and (c) of this section and after notice and a hearing, the court may for cause reduce or increase the 120-day period or the 180-day period referred to in this section.

(2)(A) The 120-day period specified in paragraph (1) may not be extended beyond a date that is 18 months after the date of the order for relief under this chapter.

(B) The 180-day period specified in paragraph (1) may not be extended beyond a date that is 20 months after the date of the order for relief under this chapter.

(e) In a small business case—

(1) only the debtor may file a plan until after 180 days after the date of the order for relief, unless that period is—

(A) extended as provided by this subsection, after notice and a hearing; or

(B) the court, for cause, orders otherwise;

(2) the plan and a disclosure statement (if any) shall be filed not later than 300 days after the date of the order for relief; and

(3) the time periods specified in paragraphs (1) and (2), and the time fixed in section 1129(e) within which the plan shall be confirmed, may be extended only if—

(A) the debtor, after providing notice to parties in interest (including the United States trustee), demonstrates by a preponderance of the evidence that it is more likely than not that the court will confirm a plan within a reasonable period of time;

(B) a new deadline is imposed at the time the extension is granted; and

(C) the order extending time is signed before the existing deadline has expired.

CROSS REFERENCES

Effect of conversion, see 11 USCA § 348.

Failure to propose plan as cause for conversion or dismissal, see 11 USCA § 1112.

Filing of plan by trustee, see 11 USCA § 1106.

Filing of plan in—

Chapter 9 cases, see 11 USCA § 941.

Chapter 11 subchapter V cases, see 11 USCA § 1189.

Chapter 12 cases, see 11 USCA § 1221.

Chapter 13 cases, see 11 USCA § 1321.

Inapplicability of this section in Chapter 11 subchapter V cases, see 11 USCA § 1181(a).

United States trustee not permitted to file plan, see 11 USCA § 307.

§ 1122. Classification of claims or interests

(a) Except as provided in subsection (b) of this section, a plan may place a claim or an interest in a particular class only if such claim or interest is substantially similar to the other claims or interests of such class.

(b) A plan may designate a separate class of claims consisting only of every unsecured claim that is less than or reduced to an amount that the court approves as reasonable and necessary for administrative convenience.

CROSS REFERENCES

Applicability of this section in Chapter 9 cases, see 11 USCA § 901.

Filing of proofs of claims or interests, see 11 USCA § 501.

§ 1123. Contents of plan

(a) Notwithstanding any otherwise applicable nonbankruptcy law, a plan shall—

(1) designate, subject to section 1122 of this title, classes of claims, other than claims of a kind specified in section 507(a)(2), 507(a)(3), or 507(a)(8) of this title, and classes of interests;

(2) specify any class of claims or interests that is not impaired under the plan;

(3) specify the treatment of any class of claims or interests that is impaired under the plan;

(4) provide the same treatment for each claim or interest of a particular class, unless the holder of a particular claim or interest agrees to a less favorable treatment of such particular claim or interest;

(5) provide adequate means for the plan's implementation, such as—

(A) retention by the debtor of all or any part of the property of the estate;

(B) transfer of all or any part of the property of the estate to one or more entities, whether organized before or after the confirmation of such plan;

(C) merger or consolidation of the debtor with one or more persons;

(D) sale of all or any part of the property of the estate, either subject to or free of any lien, or the distribution of all or any part of the property of the estate among those having an interest in such property of the estate;

(E) satisfaction or modification of any lien;

(F) cancellation or modification of any indenture or similar instrument;

(G) curing or waiving of any default;

(H) extension of a maturity date or a change in an interest rate or other term of outstanding securities;

(I) amendment of the debtor's charter; or

(J) issuance of securities of the debtor, or of any entity referred to in subparagraph (B) or (C) of this paragraph, for cash, for property, for existing securities, or in exchange for claims or interests, or for any other appropriate purpose;

(6) provide for the inclusion in the charter of the debtor, if the debtor is a corporation, or of any corporation referred to in paragraph (5)(B) or (5)(C) of this subsection, of a provision prohibiting the issuance of nonvoting equity securities, and providing, as to the several classes of securities possessing voting power, an appropriate distribution of such power among such classes, including, in the case of any class of equity securities having a preference over another class of equity securities with respect to dividends, adequate provisions for the election of directors representing such preferred class in the event of default in the payment of such dividends;

(7) contain only provisions that are consistent with the interests of creditors and equity security holders and with public policy with respect to the manner of selection of any officer, director, or trustee under the plan and any successor to such officer, director, or trustee; and

(8) in a case in which the debtor is an individual, provide for the payment to creditors under the plan of all or such portion of earnings from personal services performed by the debtor after the commencement of the case or other future income of the debtor as is necessary for the execution of the plan.

(b) Subject to subsection (a) of this section, a plan may—

(1) impair or leave unimpaired any class of claims, secured or unsecured, or of interests;

(2) subject to section 365 of this title, provide for the assumption, rejection, or assignment of any executory contract or unexpired lease of the debtor not previously rejected under such section;

(3) provide for—

(A) the settlement or adjustment of any claim or interest belonging to the debtor or to the estate; or

(B) the retention and enforcement by the debtor, by the trustee, or by a representative of the estate appointed for such purpose, of any such claim or interest;

(4) provide for the sale of all or substantially all of the property of the estate, and the distribution of the proceeds of such sale among holders of claims or interests;

(5) modify the rights of holders of secured claims, other than a claim secured only by a security interest in real property that is the debtor's principal residence, or of holders of unsecured claims, or leave unaffected the rights of holders of any class of claims; and

(6) include any other appropriate provision not inconsistent with the applicable provisions of this title.

(c) In a case concerning an individual, a plan proposed by an entity other than the debtor may not provide for the use, sale, or lease of property exempted under section 522 of this title, unless the debtor consents to such use, sale, or lease.

(d) Notwithstanding subsection (a) of this section and sections 506(b), 1129(a)(7), and 1129(b) of this title, if it is proposed in a plan to cure a default the amount necessary to cure the default shall be determined in accordance with the underlying agreement and applicable nonbankruptcy law.

CROSS REFERENCES

Applicability of subsecs. (a)(1) to (5), and (b) and (d) of this section in Chapter 9 cases, see 11 USCA § 901.

Contents of plan filed in—

Chapter 11 subchapter V cases, see 11 USCA § 1190.

Chapter 12 cases, see 11 USCA § 1222.

Chapter 13 cases, see 11 USCA § 1322.

Railroad reorganization cases, see 11 USCA § 1172.

Inapplicability of subsecs.(a)(8) and (c) of this section in Chapter 11 subchapter V cases, see 11 USCA § 1181(a).

Plan of reorganization for small business under Chapter 11, see Official Bankruptcy Form 425A.

§ 1124. Impairment of claims or interests

Except as provided in section 1123(a)(4) of this title, a class of claims or interests is impaired under a plan unless, with respect to each claim or interest of such class, the plan—

(1) leaves unaltered the legal, equitable, and contractual rights to which such claim or interest entitles the holder of such claim or interest; or

(2) notwithstanding any contractual provision or applicable law that entitles the holder of such claim or interest to demand or receive accelerated payment of such claim or interest after the occurrence of a default—

    (A) cures any such default that occurred before or after the commencement of the case under this title, other than a default of a kind specified in section 365(b)(2) of this title or of a kind that section 365(b)(2) expressly does not require to be cured;

    (B) reinstates the maturity of such claim or interest as such maturity existed before such default;

    (C) compensates the holder of such claim or interest for any damages incurred as a result of any reasonable reliance by such holder on such contractual provision or such applicable law;

    (D) if such claim or such interest arises from any failure to perform a nonmonetary obligation, other than a default arising from failure to operate a nonresidential real property lease subject to section 365(b)(1)(A), compensates the holder of such claim or such interest (other than the debtor or an insider) for any actual pecuniary loss incurred by such holder as a result of such failure; and

    (E) does not otherwise alter the legal, equitable, or contractual rights to which such claim or interest entitles the holder of such claim or interest.

CROSS REFERENCES

Allowance of claims or interests, see 11 USCA § 502.

Applicability of this section in Chapter 9 cases, see 11 USCA § 901.

Claims and interests generally, see 11 USCA § 1111.

Filing of proofs of claims or interests, see 11 USCA § 501.

§ 1125. Postpetition disclosure and solicitation

(a) In this section—

(1) "adequate information" means information of a kind, and in sufficient detail, as far as is reasonably practicable in light of the nature and history of the debtor and the condition of the debtor's books and records, including a discussion of the potential material Federal tax consequences of the plan to the debtor, any successor to the debtor, and a hypothetical investor typical of the holders of claims or interests in the case, that would enable such a hypothetical investor of the relevant class to make an informed judgment about the plan, but adequate information need not include such information about any other possible or proposed plan and in determining whether a disclosure statement provides adequate information, the court shall consider the complexity of the case, the benefit of additional information to creditors and other parties in interest, and the cost of providing additional information; and

(2) "investor typical of holders of claims or interests of the relevant class" means investor having—

    (A) a claim or interest of the relevant class;

    (B) such a relationship with the debtor as the holders of other claims or interests of such class generally have; and

    (C) such ability to obtain such information from sources other than the disclosure required by this section as holders of claims or interests in such class generally have.

(b) An acceptance or rejection of a plan may not be solicited after the commencement of the case under this title from a holder of a claim or interest with respect to such claim or interest, unless, at the time of or before such solicitation, there is transmitted to such holder the plan or a summary of the plan, and a written disclosure statement approved, after notice and a hearing, by the court as containing adequate information. The court may approve a disclosure statement without a valuation of the debtor or an appraisal of the debtor's assets.

(c) The same disclosure statement shall be transmitted to each holder of a claim or interest of a particular class, but there may be transmitted different disclosure statements, differing in amount, detail, or kind of information, as between classes.

(d) Whether a disclosure statement required under subsection (b) of this section contains adequate information is not governed by any otherwise applicable nonbankruptcy law, rule, or regulation, but an agency or official whose duty is to administer or enforce such a law, rule, or regulation may be heard on the issue of whether a disclosure statement contains adequate information. Such an agency or official may not appeal from, or otherwise seek review of, an order approving a disclosure statement.

(e) A person that solicits acceptance or rejection of a plan, in good faith and in compliance with the applicable provisions of this title, or that participates, in good faith and in compliance with the applicable provisions of this title, in the offer, issuance, sale, or purchase of a security, offered or sold under the plan, of the debtor, of an affiliate participating in a joint plan with the debtor, or of a newly organized successor to the debtor under the plan, is not liable, on account of such solicitation or participation, for violation of any applicable law, rule, or regulation governing solicitation of acceptance or rejection of a plan or the offer, issuance, sale, or purchase of securities.

(f) Notwithstanding subsection (b), in a small business case—

    (1) the court may determine that the plan itself provides adequate information and that a separate disclosure statement is not necessary;

    (2) the court may approve a disclosure statement submitted on standard forms approved by the court or adopted under section 2075 of title 28; and

    (3)(A) the court may conditionally approve a disclosure statement subject to final approval after notice and a hearing;

    (B) acceptances and rejections of a plan may be solicited based on a conditionally approved disclosure statement if the debtor provides adequate information to each holder of a claim or interest that is solicited, but a conditionally approved disclosure statement shall be mailed not later than 25 days before the date of the hearing on confirmation of the plan; and

    (C) the hearing on the disclosure statement may be combined with the hearing on confirmation of a plan.

(g) Notwithstanding subsection (b), an acceptance or rejection of the plan may be solicited from a holder of a claim or interest if such solicitation complies with applicable nonbankruptcy law and if such holder was solicited before the commencement of the case in a manner complying with applicable nonbankruptcy law.

CROSS REFERENCES

Applicability of this section in Chapter 9 cases, see 11 USCA § 901.

Court consideration of disclosure statement in Chapter 9 or Chapter 11 cases, see Fed. R. Bankr. P. 3017.

Court consideration of disclosure statement in small business or subchapter V cases, see Fed. R. Bankr. P. 3017.1.

Disclosure statement for small business under Chapter 11, see Official Bankruptcy Form 425B.

Duty of United States trustee to file comments with respect to plans and disclosure statements filed in connection with hearings under this section, see 28 USCA § 586.

Exemption from securities laws of certain transactions in which disclosure statements are provided, see 11 USCA § 1145.

Unless the court for cause orders otherwise, this section does not apply in Chapter 11 subchapter V cases, see 11 USCA § 1181(b).

§ 1126. Acceptance of plan

(a) The holder of a claim or interest allowed under section 502 of this title may accept or reject a plan. If the United States is a creditor or equity security holder, the Secretary of the Treasury may accept or reject the plan on behalf of the United States.

(b) For the purposes of subsections (c) and (d) of this section, a holder of a claim or interest that has accepted or rejected the plan before the commencement of the case under this title is deemed to have accepted or rejected such plan, as the case may be, if—

(1) the solicitation of such acceptance or rejection was in compliance with any applicable nonbankruptcy law, rule, or regulation governing the adequacy of disclosure in connection with such solicitation; or

(2) if there is not any such law, rule, or regulation, such acceptance or rejection was solicited after disclosure to such holder of adequate information, as defined in section 1125(a) of this title.

(c) A class of claims has accepted a plan if such plan has been accepted by creditors, other than any entity designated under subsection (e) of this section, that hold at least two-thirds in amount and more than one-half in number of the allowed claims of such class held by creditors, other than any entity designated under subsection (e) of this section, that have accepted or rejected such plan.

(d) A class of interests has accepted a plan if such plan has been accepted by holders of such interests, other than any entity designated under subsection (e) of this section, that hold at least two-thirds in amount of the allowed interests of such class held by holders of such interests, other than any entity designated under subsection (e) of this section, that have accepted or rejected such plan.

(e) On request of a party in interest, and after notice and a hearing, the court may designate any entity whose acceptance or rejection of such plan was not in good faith, or was not solicited or procured in good faith or in accordance with the provisions of this title.

(f) Notwithstanding any other provision of this section, a class that is not impaired under a plan, and each holder of a claim or interest of such class, are conclusively presumed to have accepted the plan, and solicitation of acceptances with respect to such class from the holders of claims or interests of such class is not required.

(g) Notwithstanding any other provision of this section, a class is deemed not to have accepted a plan if such plan provides that the claims or interests of such class do not entitle the holders of such claims or interests to receive or retain any property under the plan on account of such claims or interests.

CROSS REFERENCES

Acceptance or rejection of plan in Chapter 9 or Chapter 11 cases, see Fed. R. Bankr. P. 3018.

Amount and number of claims within class as including claims formerly held by creditors that participated in exchange of securities in Chapter 9 cases, see 11 USCA § 946.

Applicability of subsecs. (a) to (c) and (e) to (g) of this section in Chapter 9 cases, see 11 USCA § 901.

§ 1127. Modification of plan

(a) The proponent of a plan may modify such plan at any time before confirmation, but may not modify such plan so that such plan as modified fails to meet the requirements of sections 1122 and 1123 of this title. After the proponent of a plan files a modification of such plan with the court, the plan as modified becomes the plan.

(b) The proponent of a plan or the reorganized debtor may modify such plan at any time after confirmation of such plan and before substantial consummation of such plan, but may not modify such plan so that such plan as modified fails to meet the requirements of sections 1122 and 1123 of this title. Such plan as modified under this subsection becomes the plan only if circumstances warrant such modification and the court, after notice and a hearing, confirms such plan as modified, under section 1129 of this title.

(c) The proponent of a modification shall comply with section 1125 of this title with respect to the plan as modified.

(d) Any holder of a claim or interest that has accepted or rejected a plan is deemed to have accepted or rejected, as the case may be, such plan as modified, unless, within the time fixed by the court, such holder changes such holder's previous acceptance or rejection.

(e) If the debtor is an individual, the plan may be modified at any time after confirmation of the plan but before the completion of payments under the plan, whether or not the plan has been substantially consummated, upon request of the debtor, the trustee, the United States trustee, or the holder of an allowed unsecured claim, to—

    (1) increase or reduce the amount of payments on claims of a particular class provided for by the plan;

    (2) extend or reduce the time period for such payments; or

    (3) alter the amount of the distribution to a creditor whose claim is provided for by the plan to the extent necessary to take account of any payment of such claim made other than under the plan.

(f)(1) Sections 1121 through 1128 and the requirements of section 1129 apply to any modification under subsection (e).

(2) The plan, as modified, shall become the plan only after there has been disclosure under section 1125 as the court may direct, notice and a hearing, and such modification is approved.

CROSS REFERENCES

Applicability of subsec. (d) of this section in Chapter 9 cases, see 11 USCA § 901.

Inapplicability of this section to Chapter 11 subchapter V cases, see 11 USCA § 1181(a).

Modification in Chapter 11 subchapter V cases, see 11 USCA § 1193.

Modification of accepted plan in Chapter 9 or Chapter 11 cases, see Fed. R. Bankr. P. 3019.

Modification of plan after confirmation in—

    Chapter 12 cases, see 11 USCA § 1229.

    Chapter 13 cases, see 11 USCA § 1329.

Modification of plan before confirmation in—

    Chapter 12 cases, see 11 USCA § 1223.

    Chapter 13 cases, see 11 USCA § 1323.

Modification of plan in Chapter 9 cases, see 11 USCA § 942.

§ 1128. Confirmation hearing

(a)　After notice, the court shall hold a hearing on confirmation of a plan.

(b)　A party in interest may object to confirmation of a plan.

CROSS REFERENCES

Applicability of this section in Chapter 9 cases, see 11 USCA § 901.

Confirmation hearing in—

　　Chapter 12 cases, see 11 USCA § 1224.

　　Chapter 13 cases, see 11 USCA § 1324.

Duty of United States trustee to file comments with respect to plans and disclosure statements filed in connection with hearings under this section, see 28 USCA § 586.

Right to be heard in cases under this chapter, see 11 USCA § 1109.

§ 1129. Confirmation of plan

(a)　The court shall confirm a plan only if all of the following requirements are met:

(1)　The plan complies with the applicable provisions of this title.

(2)　The proponent of the plan complies with the applicable provisions of this title.

(3)　The plan has been proposed in good faith and not by any means forbidden by law.

(4)　Any payment made or to be made by the proponent, by the debtor, or by a person issuing securities or acquiring property under the plan, for services or for costs and expenses in or in connection with the case, or in connection with the plan and incident to the case, has been approved by, or is subject to the approval of, the court as reasonable.

(5)(A)(i)　The proponent of the plan has disclosed the identity and affiliations of any individual proposed to serve, after confirmation of the plan, as a director, officer, or voting trustee of the debtor, an affiliate of the debtor participating in a joint plan with the debtor, or a successor to the debtor under the plan; and

(ii)　the appointment to, or continuance in, such office of such individual, is consistent with the interests of creditors and equity security holders and with public policy; and

(B)　the proponent of the plan has disclosed the identity of any insider that will be employed or retained by the reorganized debtor, and the nature of any compensation for such insider.

(6)　Any governmental regulatory commission with jurisdiction, after confirmation of the plan, over the rates of the debtor has approved any rate change provided for in the plan, or such rate change is expressly conditioned on such approval.

(7)　With respect to each impaired class of claims or interests—

(A)　each holder of a claim or interest of such class—

(i)　has accepted the plan; or

(ii)　will receive or retain under the plan on account of such claim or interest property of a value, as of the effective date of the plan, that is not less than the amount that such holder would so receive or retain if the debtor were liquidated under chapter 7 of this title on such date; or

(B)　if section 1111(b)(2) of this title applies to the claims of such class, each holder of a claim of such class will receive or retain under the plan on account of such claim property of a value, as of the effective date of the plan, that is not less than the value of such holder's interest in the estate's interest in the property that secures such claims.

(8) With respect to each class of claims or interests—

    (A) such class has accepted the plan; or

    (B) such class is not impaired under the plan.

(9) Except to the extent that the holder of a particular claim has agreed to a different treatment of such claim, the plan provides that—

    (A) with respect to a claim of a kind specified in section 507(a)(2) or 507(a)(3) of this title, on the effective date of the plan, the holder of such claim will receive on account of such claim cash equal to the allowed amount of such claim;

    (B) with respect to a class of claims of a kind specified in section 507(a)(1), 507(a)(4), 507(a)(5), 507(a)(6), or 507(a)(7) of this title, each holder of a claim of such class will receive—

        (i) if such class has accepted the plan, deferred cash payments of a value, as of the effective date of the plan, equal to the allowed amount of such claim; or

        (ii) if such class has not accepted the plan, cash on the effective date of the plan equal to the allowed amount of such claim;

    (C) with respect to a claim of a kind specified in section 507(a)(8) of this title, the holder of such claim will receive on account of such claim regular installment payments in cash—

        (i) of a total value, as of the effective date of the plan, equal to the allowed amount of such claim;

        (ii) over a period ending not later than 5 years after the date of the order for relief under section 301, 302, or 303; and

        (iii) in a manner not less favorable than the most favored nonpriority unsecured claim provided for by the plan (other than cash payments made to a class of creditors under section 1122(b)); and

    (D) with respect to a secured claim which would otherwise meet the description of an unsecured claim of a governmental unit under section 507(a)(8), but for the secured status of that claim, the holder of that claim will receive on account of that claim, cash payments, in the same manner and over the same period, as prescribed in subparagraph (C).

(10) If a class of claims is impaired under the plan, at least one class of claims that is impaired under the plan has accepted the plan, determined without including any acceptance of the plan by any insider.

(11) Confirmation of the plan is not likely to be followed by the liquidation, or the need for further financial reorganization, of the debtor or any successor to the debtor under the plan, unless such liquidation or reorganization is proposed in the plan.

(12) All fees payable under section 1930 of title 28, as determined by the court at the hearing on confirmation of the plan, have been paid or the plan provides for the payment of all such fees on the effective date of the plan.

(13) The plan provides for the continuation after its effective date of payment of all retiree benefits, as that term is defined in section 1114 of this title, at the level established pursuant to subsection (e)(1)(B) or (g) of section 1114 of this title, at any time prior to confirmation of the plan, for the duration of the period the debtor has obligated itself to provide such benefits.

(14) If the debtor is required by a judicial or administrative order, or by statute, to pay a domestic support obligation, the debtor has paid all amounts payable under such order or such statute for such obligation that first become payable after the date of the filing of the petition.

(15) In a case in which the debtor is an individual and in which the holder of an allowed unsecured claim objects to the confirmation of the plan—

(A) the value, as of the effective date of the plan, of the property to be distributed under the plan on account of such claim is not less than the amount of such claim; or

(B) the value of the property to be distributed under the plan is not less than the projected disposable income of the debtor (as defined in section 1325(b)(2)) to be received during the 5-year period beginning on the date that the first payment is due under the plan, or during the period for which the plan provides payments, whichever is longer.

(16) All transfers of property under the plan shall be made in accordance with any applicable provisions of nonbankruptcy law that govern the transfer of property by a corporation or trust that is not a moneyed, business, or commercial corporation or trust.

(b)(1) Notwithstanding section 510(a) of this title, if all of the applicable requirements of subsection (a) of this section other than paragraph (8) are met with respect to a plan, the court, on request of the proponent of the plan, shall confirm the plan notwithstanding the requirements of such paragraph if the plan does not discriminate unfairly, and is fair and equitable, with respect to each class of claims or interests that is impaired under, and has not accepted, the plan.

(2) For the purpose of this subsection, the condition that a plan be fair and equitable with respect to a class includes the following requirements:

(A) With respect to a class of secured claims, the plan provides—

(i)(I) that the holders of such claims retain the liens securing such claims, whether the property subject to such liens is retained by the debtor or transferred to another entity, to the extent of the allowed amount of such claims; and

(II) that each holder of a claim of such class receive on account of such claim deferred cash payments totaling at least the allowed amount of such claim, of a value, as of the effective date of the plan, of at least the value of such holder's interest in the estate's interest in such property;

(ii) for the sale, subject to section 363(k) of this title, of any property that is subject to the liens securing such claims, free and clear of such liens, with such liens to attach to the proceeds of such sale, and the treatment of such liens on proceeds under clause (i) or (iii) of this subparagraph; or

(iii) for the realization by such holders of the indubitable equivalent of such claims.

(B) With respect to a class of unsecured claims—

(i) the plan provides that each holder of a claim of such class receive or retain on account of such claim property of a value, as of the effective date of the plan, equal to the allowed amount of such claim; or

(ii) the holder of any claim or interest that is junior to the claims of such class will not receive or retain under the plan on account of such junior claim or interest any property, except that in a case in which the debtor is an individual, the debtor may retain property included in the estate under section 1115, subject to the requirements of subsection (a)(14) of this section.

(C) With respect to a class of interests—

(i) the plan provides that each holder of an interest of such class receive or retain on account of such interest property of a value, as of the effective date of the plan, equal to the greatest of the allowed amount of any fixed liquidation preference to which such holder is entitled, any fixed redemption price to which such holder is entitled, or the value of such interest; or

(ii) the holder of any interest that is junior to the interests of such class will not receive or retain under the plan on account of such junior interest any property.

(c) Notwithstanding subsections (a) and (b) of this section and except as provided in section 1127(b) of this title, the court may confirm only one plan, unless the order of confirmation in the case has been revoked under section 1144 of this title. If the requirements of subsections (a) and (b) of this section are met with respect to more than one plan, the court shall consider the preferences of creditors and equity security holders in determining which plan to confirm.

(d) Notwithstanding any other provision of this section, on request of a party in interest that is a governmental unit, the court may not confirm a plan if the principal purpose of the plan is the avoidance of taxes or the avoidance of the application of section 5 of the Securities Act of 1933. In any hearing under this subsection, the governmental unit has the burden of proof on the issue of avoidance.

(e) In a small business case, the court shall confirm a plan that complies with the applicable provisions of this title and that is filed in accordance with section 1121(e) not later than 45 days after the plan is filed unless the time for confirmation is extended in accordance with section 1121(e)(3).

REFERENCES IN TEXT

Section 5 of the Securities Act of 1933, referred to in subsec. (d), is section 5 of Act May 27, 1933, c. 38, Title I, 48 Stat. 77, which is classified to section 77e of Title 15, Commerce and Trade.

CROSS REFERENCES

Applicability of subsecs. (a)(2), (3), (6), (8), (10) and (b)(1), (2)(A), (2)(B) of this section in Chapter 9 cases, see 11 USCA § 901.

Confirmation of plan in Chapter 9 or Chapter 11 cases, see Fed. R. Bankr. P. 3020.

Confirmation of plan in—

Chapter 9 cases, see 11 USCA § 943.

Chapter 11 subchapter V cases, see 11 USCA § 1191.

Chapter 12 cases, see 11 USCA § 1225.

Chapter 13 cases, see 11 USCA § 1325.

Railroad reorganization cases, see 11 USCA § 1173.

Denial of confirmation of plan as cause for conversion or dismissal, see 11 USCA § 1112.

Effect of confirmation in cases under this chapter, see 11 USCA § 1141.

Inapplicability of subsecs. (a)(7) and (c) of this section in railroad reorganization cases, see 11 USCA § 1161.

Inapplicability of subsecs. (a)(15), (b), (c), and (e) of this section in Chapter 11 subchapter V cases, see 11 USCA § 1181(a).

Payment of insurance benefits to retired employees, see 11 USCA § 1114.

Revocation of order of confirmation in cases under this chapter, see 11 USCA § 1144.

Special tax provisions for certain dispositions of securities or instruments under confirmed plan, see 11 USCA § 1146.

Supplemental injunctions and plan fair and equitable, see 11 USCA § 524.

Unclaimed property, see 11 USCA § 347.

SUBCHAPTER III—POSTCONFIRMATION MATTERS

§ 1141. Effect of confirmation

(a) Except as provided in subsections (d)(2) and (d)(3) of this section, the provisions of a confirmed plan bind the debtor, any entity issuing securities under the plan, any entity acquiring property under the plan, and any creditor, equity security holder, or general partner in the debtor, whether or not the claim or interest of such creditor, equity security holder, or general partner is impaired under the plan and whether or not such creditor, equity security holder, or general partner has accepted the plan.

(b) Except as otherwise provided in the plan or the order confirming the plan, the confirmation of a plan vests all of the property of the estate in the debtor.

(c) Except as provided in subsections (d)(2) and (d)(3) of this section and except as otherwise provided in the plan or in the order confirming the plan, after confirmation of a plan, the property dealt with by the plan is free and clear of all claims and interests of creditors, equity security holders, and of general partners in the debtor.

(d)(1) Except as otherwise provided in this subsection, in the plan, or in the order confirming the plan, the confirmation of a plan—

    (A) discharges the debtor from any debt that arose before the date of such confirmation, and any debt of a kind specified in section 502(g), 502(h), or 502(i) of this title, whether or not—

        (i) a proof of the claim based on such debt is filed or deemed filed under section 501 of this title;

        (ii) such claim is allowed under section 502 of this title; or

        (iii) the holder of such claim has accepted the plan; and

    (B) terminates all rights and interests of equity security holders and general partners provided for by the plan.

(2) A discharge under this chapter does not discharge a debtor who is an individual from any debt excepted from discharge under section 523 of this title.

(3) The confirmation of a plan does not discharge a debtor if—

    (A) the plan provides for the liquidation of all or substantially all of the property of the estate;

    (B) the debtor does not engage in business after consummation of the plan; and

    (C) the debtor would be denied a discharge under section 727(a) of this title if the case were a case under chapter 7 of this title.

(4) The court may approve a written waiver of discharge executed by the debtor after the order for relief under this chapter.

(5) In a case in which the debtor is an individual—

    (A) unless after notice and a hearing the court orders otherwise for cause, confirmation of the plan does not discharge any debt provided for in the plan until the court grants a discharge on completion of all payments under the plan;

    (B) at any time after the confirmation of the plan, and after notice and a hearing, the court may grant a discharge to the debtor who has not completed payments under the plan if—

        (i) the value, as of the effective date of the plan, of property actually distributed under the plan on account of each allowed unsecured claim is not less than the amount that would have been paid on such claim if the estate of the debtor had been liquidated under chapter 7 on such date;

    (ii) modification of the plan under section 1127 is not practicable; and

    (iii) subparagraph (C) permits the court to grant a discharge; and

  (C) the court may grant a discharge if, after notice and a hearing held not more than 10 days before the date of the entry of the order granting the discharge, the court finds that there is no reasonable cause to believe that—

    (i) section 522(q)(1) may be applicable to the debtor; and

    (ii) there is pending any proceeding in which the debtor may be found guilty of a felony of the kind described in section 522(q)(1)(A) or liable for a debt of the kind described in section 522(q)(1)(B);

and if the requirements of subparagraph (A) or (B) are met.

(6) Notwithstanding paragraph (1), the confirmation of a plan does not discharge a debtor that is a corporation from any debt—

  (A) of a kind specified in paragraph (2)(A) or (2)(B) of section 523(a) that is owed to a domestic governmental unit, or owed to a person as the result of an action filed under subchapter III of chapter 37 of title 31 or any similar State statute; or

  (B) for a tax or customs duty with respect to which the debtor—

    (i) made a fraudulent return; or

    (ii) willfully attempted in any manner to evade or to defeat such tax or such customs duty.

REFERENCES IN TEXT

Subchapter III of chapter 37 of title 31, referred to in subsec. (d)(6)(A), is 31 U.S.C.A. § 3721 et seq.

CROSS REFERENCES

Confirmation of plan filed under this chapter, see 11 USCA § 1129.

Effect of confirmation of plans filed in—

    Chapter 9 cases, see 11 USCA § 944.

    Chapter 12 cases, see 11 USCA § 1227.

    Chapter 13 cases, see 11 USCA § 1327.

Effect of conversion, see 11 USCA § 348.

Effect of discharge, see 11 USCA § 524.

Exceptions to discharge, see 11 USCA § 523.

Failure of discharge as cause for conversion, see 11 USCA § 1112.

Inapplicability of subsec. (d) of this section to Chapter 11 subchapter V plans confirmed under § 1191(b), see 11 USCA § 1181(c).

Inapplicability of subsec. (d)(5) of this section to Chapter 11 subchapter V cases, see 11 USCA § 1181(a).

Individual Chapter 11 discharge, see Director's Bankruptcy Form 3180RI.

Nondischargeability of capital improvement loans for multifamily housing projects in proceedings under this section, see 12 USCA § 1715z–1a.

Supplemental injunctions, debtor and plan of reorganization, see 11 USCA § 524.

§ 1142. Implementation of plan

(a) Notwithstanding any otherwise applicable nonbankruptcy law, rule, or regulation relating to financial condition, the debtor and any entity organized or to be organized for the purpose of carrying out the plan shall carry out the plan and shall comply with any orders of the court.

(b) The court may direct the debtor and any other necessary party to execute or deliver or to join in the execution or delivery of any instrument required to effect a transfer of property dealt with by a confirmed plan, and to perform any other act, including the satisfaction of any lien, that is necessary for the consummation of the plan.

CROSS REFERENCES

Applicability of subsec. (b) of this section in Chapter 9 cases, see 11 USCA § 901.

Supplemental injunctions, debtor and plan of reorganization, see 11 USCA § 524.

§ 1143. Distribution

If a plan requires presentment or surrender of a security or the performance of any other act as a condition to participation in distribution under the plan, such action shall be taken not later than five years after the date of the entry of the order of confirmation. Any entity that has not within such time presented or surrendered such entity's security or taken any such other action that the plan requires may not participate in distribution under the plan.

CROSS REFERENCES

Applicability of this section in Chapter 9 cases, see 11 USCA § 901.

Distribution under plan, see Fed. R. Bankr. P. 3021.

§ 1144. Revocation of an order of confirmation

On request of a party in interest at any time before 180 days after the date of the entry of the order of confirmation, and after notice and a hearing, the court may revoke such order if and only if such order was procured by fraud. An order under this section revoking an order of confirmation shall—

(1) contain such provisions as are necessary to protect any entity acquiring rights in good faith reliance on the order of confirmation; and

(2) revoke the discharge of the debtor.

CROSS REFERENCES

Applicability of this section in Chapter 9 cases, see 11 USCA § 901.

Confirmation of one plan as affected by revocation, see 11 USCA § 1129.

Revocation of confirmation order as cause for conversion or dismissal, see 11 USCA § 1112.

Revocation of order of confirmation in—

Chapter 12 cases, see 11 USCA § 1230.

Chapter 13 cases, see 11 USCA § 1330.

Supplemental injunctions, see 11 USCA § 524.

§ 1145. Exemption from securities laws

(a) Except with respect to an entity that is an underwriter as defined in subsection (b) of this section, section 5 of the Securities Act of 1933 and any State or local law requiring registration for offer or sale of a security or registration or licensing of an issuer of, underwriter of, or broker or dealer in, a security do not apply to—

  (1) the offer or sale under a plan of a security of the debtor, of an affiliate participating in a joint plan with the debtor, or of a successor to the debtor under the plan—

    (A) in exchange for a claim against, an interest in, or a claim for an administrative expense in the case concerning, the debtor or such affiliate; or

    (B) principally in such exchange and partly for cash or property;

  (2) the offer of a security through any warrant, option, right to subscribe, or conversion privilege that was sold in the manner specified in paragraph (1) of this subsection, or the sale of a security upon the exercise of such a warrant, option, right, or privilege;

  (3) the offer or sale, other than under a plan, of a security of an issuer other than the debtor or an affiliate, if—

    (A) such security was owned by the debtor on the date of the filing of the petition;

    (B) the issuer of such security is—

      (i) required to file reports under section 13 or 15(d) of the Securities Exchange Act of 1934; and

      (ii) in compliance with the disclosure and reporting provision of such applicable section; and

    (C) such offer or sale is of securities that do not exceed—

      (i) during the two-year period immediately following the date of the filing of the petition, four percent of the securities of such class outstanding on such date; and

      (ii) during any 180-day period following such two-year period, one percent of the securities outstanding at the beginning of such 180-day period; or

  (4) a transaction by a stockbroker in a security that is executed after a transaction of a kind specified in paragraph (1) or (2) of this subsection in such security and before the expiration of 40 days after the first date on which such security was bona fide offered to the public by the issuer or by or through an underwriter, if such stockbroker provides, at the time of or before such transaction by such stockbroker, a disclosure statement approved under section 1125 of this title, and, if the court orders, information supplementing such disclosure statement.

  (b)(1) Except as provided in paragraph (2) of this subsection and except with respect to ordinary trading transactions of an entity that is not an issuer, an entity is an underwriter under section 2(a)(11) of the Securities Act of 1933, if such entity—

    (A) purchases a claim against, interest in, or claim for an administrative expense in the case concerning, the debtor, if such purchase is with a view to distribution of any security received or to be received in exchange for such a claim or interest;

    (B) offers to sell securities offered or sold under the plan for the holders of such securities;

    (C) offers to buy securities offered or sold under the plan from the holders of such securities, if such offer to buy is—

      (i) with a view to distribution of such securities; and

      (ii) under an agreement made in connection with the plan, with the consummation of the plan, or with the offer or sale of securities under the plan; or

    (D) is an issuer, as used in such section 2(a)(11), with respect to such securities.

  (2) An entity is not an underwriter under section 2(a)(11) of the Securities Act of 1933 or under paragraph (1) of this subsection with respect to an agreement that provides only for—

(A)(i) the matching or combining of fractional interests in securities offered or sold under the plan into whole interests; or

(ii) the purchase or sale of such fractional interests from or to entities receiving such fractional interests under the plan; or

(B) the purchase or sale for such entities of such fractional or whole interests as are necessary to adjust for any remaining fractional interests after such matching.

(3) An entity other than an entity of the kind specified in paragraph (1) of this subsection is not an underwriter under section 2(a)(11) of the Securities Act of 1933 with respect to any securities offered or sold to such entity in the manner specified in subsection (a)(1) of this section.

(c) An offer or sale of securities of the kind and in the manner specified under subsection (a)(1) of this section is deemed to be a public offering.

(d) The Trust Indenture Act of 1939 does not apply to a note issued under the plan that matures not later than one year after the effective date of the plan.

REFERENCES IN TEXT

Section 5 of the Securities Act of 1933, referred to in subsec. (a), is section 5 of Act May 27, 1933, c. 38, Title I, 48 Stat. 77, which is classified to section 77e of Title 15, Commerce and Trade.

Section 13 or 15 of the Securities Exchange Act of 1934, referred to in subsec. (a)(3)(B)(i), are section 13 and 15 of Act June 6, 1934, c. 404, Title I, 48 Stat. 894, 895, which are classified to sections 78m and 78o, respectively, of Title 15.

Section 2(a)(11) of the Securities Act of 1933, referred to in subsec. (b), is subsec. (a)(11) of section 2 of Act May 27, 1933, c. 38, Title I, 48 Stat. 74, as amended, which is classified to 15 U.S.C.A. § 77b(a)(11).

The Trust Indenture Act of 1939, referred to in subsec. (d), is Title III of Act May 27, 1933, ch. 38, as added Aug. 3, 1939, ch. 411, 53 Stat. 1149, as amended, which is classified generally to subchapter III (section 77aaa et seq.) of chapter 2A of Title 15. For complete classification of this Act to the Code, see section 77aaa of Title 15 and Tables.

CROSS REFERENCES

Applicability of term "security" to offers or sales under § 364 of this title to underwriters, see 11 USCA § 364(f).

Applicability of this section in Chapter 9 cases, see 11 USCA § 901.

Protection of securities customers, see 15 USCA § 78eee.

Racketeering activity defined as offense involving fraud in sale of securities in case under this title, see 18 USCA § 1961.

Securities exempted from Securities Act of 1933, see 15 USCA § 77c.

§ 1146. Special tax provisions

(a) The issuance, transfer, or exchange of a security, or the making or delivery of an instrument of transfer under a plan confirmed under section 1129 or 1191 of this title, may not be taxed under any law imposing a stamp tax or similar tax.

(b) The court may authorize the proponent of a plan to request a determination, limited to questions of law, by a State or local governmental unit charged with responsibility for collection or determination of a tax on or measured by income, of the tax effects, under section 346 of this title and under the law imposing such tax, of the plan. In the event of an actual controversy, the court may declare such effects after the earlier of—

(1) the date on which such governmental unit responds to the request under this subsection; or

(2) 270 days after such request.

CROSS REFERENCES

Declaratory judgments, see 28 USCA § 2201.

Determination of—

　　Number of taxable periods during which debtor may use loss carryover or carryback, see 11 USCA § 346.

　　Tax liability, see 11 USCA § 505.

Effect of conversion, see 11 USCA § 348.

Special tax provisions in Chapter 7 cases, see 11 USCA § 728.

SUBCHAPTER IV—RAILROAD REORGANIZATION

§ 1161. Inapplicability of other sections

Sections 341, 343, 1102(a)(1), 1104, 1105, 1107, 1129(a)(7), and 1129(c) of this title do not apply in a case concerning a railroad.

§ 1162. Definition

In this subchapter, "Board" means the "Surface Transportation Board".

§ 1163. Appointment of trustee

As soon as practicable after the order for relief the Secretary of Transportation shall submit a list of five disinterested persons that are qualified and willing to serve as trustees in the case. The United States trustee shall appoint one of such persons to serve as trustee in the case.

CROSS REFERENCES

Appointment of trustee in—

　　Cases under subchapter V of this chapter, see 11 USCA § 1183.

　　Cases under this chapter, see 11 USCA § 1104.

　　Chapter 12 cases, see 11 USCA § 1202.

　　Chapter 13 cases, see 11 USCA § 1302.

Collective bargaining agreement, manner of assumption or rejection by trustee other than a trustee in a case covered by this subchapter, see 11 USCA § 1113.

Election of trustee in Chapter 7 cases, see 11 USCA § 702.

Guarantees of certificates, see 45 USCA § 662.

Qualification of trustee, see 11 USCA § 322.

Time for bringing action, see 11 USCA § 546.

§ 1164. Right to be heard

The Board, the Department of Transportation, and any State or local commission having regulatory jurisdiction over the debtor may raise and may appear and be heard on any issue in a case under this chapter, but may not appeal from any judgment, order, or decree entered in the case.

CROSS REFERENCES

Right of Commodity Futures Trading Commission to be heard in Chapter 7 cases, see 11 USCA § 762.

231

Right of Securities and Exchange Commission and party in interest to be heard in case under this chapter, see 11 USCA § 1109.

§ 1165. Protection of the public interest

In applying sections 1166, 1167, 1169, 1170, 1171, 1172, 1173, and 1174 of this title, the court and the trustee shall consider the public interest in addition to the interests of the debtor, creditors, and equity security holders.

§ 1166. Effect of subtitle IV of title 49 and of Federal, State, or local regulations

Except with respect to abandonment under section 1170 of this title, or merger, modification of the financial structure of the debtor, or issuance or sale of securities under a plan, the trustee and the debtor are subject to the provisions of subtitle IV of title 49 that are applicable to railroads, and the trustee is subject to orders of any Federal, State, or local regulatory body to the same extent as the debtor would be if a petition commencing the case under this chapter had not been filed, but—

   (1) any such order that would require the expenditure, or the incurring of an obligation for the expenditure, of money from the estate is not effective unless approved by the court; and

   (2) the provisions of this chapter are subject to section 601(b) of the Regional Rail Reorganization Act of 1973.

REFERENCES IN TEXT

Section 601(b) of Regional Rail Reorganization Act of 1973, referred to in par. (2), is section 601(b) of Pub. L. 93–236, Title VI, Jan. 2, 1974, 87 Stat. 1021, which is classified to section 791(b) of Title 45, Railroads.

§ 1167. Collective bargaining agreements

Notwithstanding section 365 of this title, neither the court nor the trustee may change the wages or working conditions of employees of the debtor established by a collective bargaining agreement that is subject to the Railway Labor Act except in accordance with section 6 of such Act.

REFERENCES IN TEXT

The Railway Labor Act, referred to in text, is Act May 20, 1926, c. 347, 44 Stat. 577, as amended, which is classified principally to chapter 8 (section 151 et seq.) of Title 45, Railroads. Section 6 of such Act is classified to section 156 of Title 15. For complete classification of this Act to the Code, see section 151 of Title 45 and Tables.

CROSS REFERENCES

Authorization of trustee to operate business, see 11 USCA § 1108.

§ 1168. Rolling stock equipment

   (a)(1) The right of a secured party with a security interest in or of a lessor or conditional vendor of equipment described in paragraph (2) to take possession of such equipment in compliance with an equipment security agreement, lease, or conditional sale contract, and to enforce any of its other rights or remedies under such security agreement, lease, or conditional sale contract, to sell, lease, or otherwise retain or dispose of such equipment, is not limited or otherwise affected by any other provision of this title or by any power of the court, except that right to take possession and enforce those other rights and remedies shall be subject to section 362, if—

   (A) before the date that is 60 days after the date of commencement of a case under this chapter, the trustee, subject to the court's approval, agrees to perform all obligations of the debtor under such security agreement, lease, or conditional sale contract; and

(B) any default, other than a default of a kind described in section 365(b)(2), under such security agreement, lease, or conditional sale contract—

    (i) that occurs before the date of commencement of the case and is an event of default therewith is cured before the expiration of such 60-day period;

    (ii) that occurs or becomes an event of default after the date of commencement of the case and before the expiration of such 60-day period is cured before the later of—

        (I) the date that is 30 days after the date of the default or event of the default; or

        (II) the expiration of such 60-day period; and

    (iii) that occurs on or after the expiration of such 60-day period is cured in accordance with the terms of such security agreement, lease, or conditional sale contract, if cure is permitted under that agreement, lease, or conditional sale contract.

(2) The equipment described in this paragraph—

    (A) is rolling stock equipment or accessories used on rolling stock equipment, including superstructures or racks, that is subject to a security interest granted by, leased to, or conditionally sold to a debtor; and

    (B) includes all records and documents relating to such equipment that are required, under the terms of the security agreement, lease, or conditional sale contract, that is to be surrendered or returned by the debtor in connection with the surrender or return of such equipment.

(3) Paragraph (1) applies to a secured party, lessor, or conditional vendor acting in its own behalf or acting as trustee or otherwise in behalf of another party.

(b) The trustee and the secured party, lessor, or conditional vendor whose right to take possession is protected under subsection (a) may agree, subject to the court's approval, to extend the 60-day period specified in subsection (a)(1).

(c)(1) In any case under this chapter, the trustee shall immediately surrender and return to a secured party, lessor, or conditional vendor, described in subsection (a)(1), equipment described in subsection (a)(2), if at any time after the date of commencement of the case under this chapter such secured party, lessor, or conditional vendor is entitled pursuant to subsection (a)(1) to take possession of such equipment and makes a written demand for such possession of the trustee.

(2) At such time as the trustee is required under paragraph (1) to surrender and return equipment described in subsection (a)(2), any lease of such equipment, and any security agreement or conditional sale contract relating to such equipment, if such security agreement or conditional sale contract is an executory contract, shall be deemed rejected.

(d) With respect to equipment first placed in service on or prior to October 22, 1994, for purposes of this section—

    (1) the term "lease" includes any written agreement with respect to which the lessor and the debtor, as lessee, have expressed in the agreement or in a substantially contemporaneous writing that the agreement is to be treated as a lease for Federal income tax purposes; and

    (2) the term "security interest" means a purchase-money equipment security interest.

(e) With respect to equipment first placed in service after October 22, 1994, for purposes of this section, the term "rolling stock equipment" includes rolling stock equipment that is substantially rebuilt and accessories used on such equipment.

CROSS REFERENCES

Rights of certain secured parties in aircraft equipment and vessels, see 11 USCA § 1110.

§ 1169. Effect of rejection of lease of railroad line

(a) Except as provided in subsection (b) of this section, if a lease of a line of railroad under which the debtor is the lessee is rejected under section 365 of this title, and if the trustee, within such time as the court fixes, and with the court's approval, elects not to operate the leased line, the lessor under such lease, after such approval, shall operate the line.

(b) If operation of such line by such lessor is impracticable or contrary to the public interest, the court, on request of such lessor, and after notice and a hearing, shall order the trustee to continue operation of such line for the account of such lessor until abandonment is ordered under section 1170 of this title, or until such operation is otherwise lawfully terminated, whichever occurs first.

(c) During any such operation, such lessor is deemed a carrier subject to the provisions of subtitle IV of title 49 that are applicable to railroads.

§ 1170. Abandonment of railroad line

(a) The court, after notice and a hearing, may authorize the abandonment of all or a portion of a railroad line if such abandonment is—

    (1)(A) in the best interest of the estate; or

    (B) essential to the formulation of a plan; and

    (2) consistent with the public interest.

(b) If, except for the pendency of the case under this chapter, such abandonment would require approval by the Board under a law of the United States, the trustee shall initiate an appropriate application for such abandonment with the Board. The court may fix a time within which the Board shall report to the court on such application.

(c) After the court receives the report of the Board, or the expiration of the time fixed under subsection (b) of this section, whichever occurs first, the court may authorize such abandonment, after notice to the Board, the Secretary of Transportation, the trustee, any party in interest that has requested notice, any affected shipper or community, and any other entity prescribed by the court, and a hearing.

(d)(1) Enforcement of an order authorizing such abandonment shall be stayed until the time for taking an appeal has expired, or, if an appeal is timely taken, until such order has become final.

(2) If an order authorizing such abandonment is appealed, the court, on request of a party in interest, may authorize suspension of service on a line or a portion of a line pending the determination of such appeal, after notice to the Board, the Secretary of Transportation, the trustee, any party in interest that has requested notice, any affected shipper or community, and any other entity prescribed by the court, and a hearing. An appellant may not obtain a stay of the enforcement of an order authorizing such suspension by the giving of a supersedeas bond or otherwise, during the pendency of such appeal.

(e)(1) In authorizing any abandonment of a railroad line under this section, the court shall require the rail carrier to provide a fair arrangement at least as protective of the interests of employees as that established under section 11326(a) of title 49.

(2) Nothing in this subsection shall be deemed to affect the priorities or timing of payment of employee protection which might have existed in the absence of this subsection.

CROSS REFERENCES

Abandonment of lines of Milwaukee Railroad in cases pending under § 77 of Bankruptcy Act on November 4, 1979, see 45 USCA § 915.

Abandonment of lines of Milwaukee Railroad under this section, see 45 USCA § 904.

Abandonment of property of estate, see 11 USCA § 554.

§ 1171. Priority claims

(a) There shall be paid as an administrative expense any claim of an individual or of the personal representative of a deceased individual against the debtor or the estate, for personal injury to or death of such individual arising out of the operation of the debtor or the estate, whether such claim arose before or after the commencement of the case.

(b) Any unsecured claim against the debtor that would have been entitled to priority if a receiver in equity of the property of the debtor had been appointed by a Federal court on the date of the order for relief under this title shall be entitled to the same priority in the case under this chapter.

CROSS REFERENCES

Allowance of administrative expenses, see 11 USCA § 503.

Priorities, see 11 USCA § 507.

§ 1172. Contents of plan

(a) In addition to the provisions required or permitted under section 1123 of this title, a plan—

(1) shall specify the extent to and the means by which the debtor's rail service is proposed to be continued, and the extent to which any of the debtor's rail service is proposed to be terminated; and

(2) may include a provision for—

(A) the transfer of any or all of the operating railroad lines of the debtor to another operating railroad; or

(B) abandonment of any railroad line in accordance with section 1170 of this title.

(b) If, except for the pendency of the case under this chapter, transfer of, or operation of or over, any of the debtor's rail lines by an entity other than the debtor or a successor to the debtor under the plan would require approval by the Board under a law of the United States, then a plan may not propose such a transfer or such operation unless the proponent of the plan initiates an appropriate application for such a transfer or such operation with the Board and, within such time as the court may fix, not exceeding 180 days, the Board, with or without a hearing, as the Board may determine, and with or without modification or condition, approves such application, or does not act on such application. Any action or order of the Board approving, modifying, conditioning, or disapproving such application is subject to review by the court only under sections 706(2)(A), 706(2)(B), 706(2)(C), and 706(2)(D) of title 5.

(c)(1) In approving an application under subsection (b) of this section, the Board shall require the rail carrier to provide a fair arrangement at least as protective of the interests of employees as that established under section 11326(a) of title 49.

(2) Nothing in this subsection shall be deemed to affect the priorities or timing of payment of employee protection which might have existed in the absence of this subsection.

§ 1173. Confirmation of plan

(a) The court shall confirm a plan if—

(1) the applicable requirements of section 1129 of this title have been met;

(2) each creditor or equity security holder will receive or retain under the plan property of a value, as of the effective date of the plan, that is not less than the value of property that each such creditor or equity security holder would so receive or retain if all of the operating railroad lines of the debtor were sold, and the proceeds of such sale, and the other property of the estate, were distributed under chapter 7 of this title on such date;

　(3)　in light of the debtor's past earnings and the probable prospective earnings of the reorganized debtor, there will be adequate coverage by such prospective earnings of any fixed charges, such as interest on debt, amortization of funded debt, and rent for leased railroads, provided for by the plan; and

　(4)　the plan is consistent with the public interest.

　(b)　If the requirements of subsection (a) of this section are met with respect to more than one plan, the court shall confirm the plan that is most likely to maintain adequate rail service in the public interest.

CROSS REFERENCES

Effect of confirmation in cases under this chapter, see 11 USCA § 1141.

Inapplicability of § 1129(a)(7) and (c) to confirmed plans under this subchapter, see 11 USCA § 1161.

Nonrecognition of gain or loss for income tax purposes of exchanges of stock and securities in reorganizations confirmed under this section, see 26 USCA § 354.

Revocation of order of confirmation in cases under this chapter, see 11 USCA § 1144.

Unclaimed property, see 11 USCA § 347.

§ 1174. Liquidation

On request of a party in interest and after notice and a hearing, the court may, or, if a plan has not been confirmed under section 1173 of this title before five years after the date of the order for relief, the court shall, order the trustee to cease the debtor's operation and to collect and reduce to money all of the property of the estate in the same manner as if the case were a case under chapter 7 of this title.

SUBCHAPTER V—SMALL BUSINESS DEBTOR REORGANIZATION

§ 1181. Inapplicability of other sections

　(a)　**In General.**—Sections 105(d), 1101(1), 1104, 1105, 1106, 1107, 1108, 1115, 1116, 1121, 1123(a)(8), 1123(c), 1127, 1129(a)(15), 1129(b), 1129(c), 1129(e), and 1141(d)(5) of this title do not apply in a case under this subchapter.

　(b)　**Court Authority.**—Unless the court for cause orders otherwise, paragraphs (1), (2), and (4) of section 1102(a) and sections 1102(b), 1103, and 1125 of this title do not apply in a case under this subchapter.

　(c)　**Special Rule for Discharge.**—If a plan is confirmed under section 1191(b) of this title, section 1141(d) of this title shall not apply, except as provided in section 1192 of this title.

§ 1182. Definitions

In this subchapter:

　(1)　**Debtor.**—The term 'debtor'—

　　(A)　subject to subparagraph (B), means a person engaged in commercial or business activities (including any affiliate of such person that is also a debtor under this title and excluding a person whose primary activity is the business of owning single asset real estate) that has aggregate noncontingent liquidated secured and unsecured debts as of the date of the filing of the petition or the date of the order for relief in an amount not more than $7,500,000 (excluding debts owed to 1 or more affiliates or insiders) not less than 50 percent of which arose from the commercial or business activities of the debtor; and

(B) does not include—

(i) any member of a group of affiliated debtors that has aggregate noncontingent liquidated secured and unsecured debts in an amount greater than $7,500,000 (excluding debt owed to 1 or more affiliates or insiders);

(ii) any debtor that is a corporation subject to the reporting requirements under section 13 or 15(d) of the Securities Exchange Act of 1934 (15 U.S.C. 78m, 78o(d)); or

(iii) any debtor that is an affiliate of a corporation described in clause (ii).

(2) **Debtor in possession.**—The term 'debtor in possession' means the debtor, unless removed as debtor in possession under section 1185(a) of this title.

[*Note from West Advisor:* Congress amended § 1182(1) to increase the debt limit for subchapter V to $7.5M. The amendment expires on June 21, 2024, at which point the term "debtor" in § 1182(1) will mean a small business debtor. *See* 136 Stat. 1298, 1299, 1300.]

§ 1183. Trustee

(a) **In General.**—If the United States trustee has appointed an individual under section 586(b) of title 28 to serve as standing trustee in cases under this subchapter, and if such individual qualifies as a trustee under section 322 of this title, then that individual shall serve as trustee in any case under this subchapter. Otherwise, the United States trustee shall appoint one disinterested person to serve as trustee in the case or the United States trustee may serve as trustee in the case, as necessary.

(b) **Duties.**—The trustee shall—

(1) perform the duties specified in paragraphs (2), (5), (6), (7), and (9) of section 704(a) of this title;

(2) perform the duties specified in paragraphs (3), (4), and (7) of section 1106(a) of this title, if the court, for cause and on request of a party in interest, the trustee, or the United States trustee, so orders;

(3) appear and be heard at the status conference under section 1188 of this title and any hearing that concerns—

(A) the value of property subject to a lien;

(B) confirmation of a plan filed under this subchapter;

(C) modification of the plan after confirmation; or

(D) the sale of property of the estate;

(4) ensure that the debtor commences making timely payments required by a plan confirmed under this subchapter;

(5) if the debtor ceases to be a debtor in possession—

(A) perform the duties specified in section 704(a)(8) and paragraphs (1), (2), and (6) of section 1106(a) of this title; and

(B) be authorized to operate the business of the debtor.

(6) if there is a claim for a domestic support obligation with respect to the debtor, perform the duties specified in section 704(c) of this title; and

(7) facilitate the development of a consensual plan of reorganization.

(c) **Termination of Trustee Service.**—

(1) **In general.**—If the plan of the debtor is confirmed under section 1191(a) of this title, the service of the trustee in the case shall terminate when the plan has been substantially consummated, except that the United States trustee may reappoint a trustee as needed for performance of duties under subsection (b)(3)(C) of this section and section 1185(a) of this title.

(2) Service of notice of substantial consummation.—Not later than 14 days after the plan of the debtor is substantially consummated, the debtor shall file with the court and serve on the trustee, the United States trustee, and all parties in interest notice of such substantial consummation.

CROSS REFERENCES

Inapplicability of §§ 1104–1106 (trustee appointment, termination, and duties) to cases under this subchapter, see 11 USCA § 1181(a).

§ 1184. Rights and powers of a debtor in possession

Subject to such limitations or conditions as the court may prescribe, a debtor in possession shall have all the rights, other than the right to compensation under section 330 of this title, and powers, and shall perform all functions and duties, except the duties specified in paragraphs (2), (3), and (4) of section 1106(a) of this title, of a trustee serving in a case under this chapter, including operating the business of the debtor.

CROSS REFERENCES

Inapplicability of § 1107 (rights, powers, and duties of debtor in possession) to cases under this subchapter, see 11 USCA § 1181(a).

Inapplicability of § 1108 (trustee's authorization to operate business) to cases under this subchapter, see 11 USCA § 1181(a).

§ 1185. Removal of debtor in possession

(a) In General.—On request of a party in interest, and after notice and a hearing, the court shall order that the debtor shall not be a debtor in possession for cause, including fraud, dishonesty, incompetence, or gross mismanagement of the affairs of the debtor, either before or after the date of commencement of the case, or for failure to perform the obligations of the debtor under a plan confirmed under this subchapter.

(b) Reinstatement.—On request of a party in interest, and after notice and a hearing, the court may reinstate the debtor in possession.

§ 1186. Property of the estate

(a) Inclusions.—If a plan is confirmed under section 1191(b) of this title, property of the estate includes, in addition to the property specified in section 541 of this title—

(1) all property of the kind specified in that section that the debtor acquires after the date of commencement of the case but before the case is closed, dismissed, or converted to a case under chapter 7, 12, or 13 of this title, whichever occurs first; and

(2) earnings from services performed by the debtor after the date of commencement of the case but before the case is closed, dismissed, or converted to a case under chapter 7, 12, or 13 of this title, whichever occurs first.

(b) Debtor Remaining in Possession.—Except as provided in section 1185 of this title, a plan confirmed under this subchapter, or an order confirming a plan under this subchapter, the debtor shall remain in possession of all property of the estate.

CROSS REFERENCES

Inapplicability of § 1115 (property of the estate) to cases under this subchapter, see 11 USCA § 1181(a).

§ 1187. Duties and reporting requirements of debtors

(a) **Filing Requirements.**—Upon electing to be a debtor under this subchapter, the debtor shall file the documents required by subparagraphs (A) and (B) of section 1116(1) of this title.

(b) **Other Applicable Provisions.**—A debtor, in addition to the duties provided in this title and as otherwise required by law, shall comply with the requirements of section 308 and paragraphs (2), (3), (4), (5), (6), and (7) of section 1116 of this title.

(c) **Separate Disclosure Statement Exemption.**—If the court orders under section 1181(b) of this title that section 1125 of this title applies, section 1125(f) of this title shall apply.

CROSS REFERENCES

Court consideration of disclosure statement in Chapter 11 subchapter V cases in which the court has ordered that § 1125 applies, see Fed. R. Bankr. P. 3017.1(a).

Fixing of dates by the court in Chapter 11 subchapter V cases in which there is no disclosure statement, see Fed. R. Bankr. P. 3017.2.

§ 1188. Status conference

(a) **In General.**—Except as provided in subsection (b), not later than 60 days after the entry of the order for relief under this chapter, the court shall hold a status conference to further the expeditious and economical resolution of a case under this subchapter.

(b) **Exception.**—The court may extend the period of time for holding a status conference under subsection (a) if the need for an extension is attributable to circumstances for which the debtor should not justly be held accountable.

(c) **Report.**—Not later than 14 days before the date of the status conference under subsection (a), the debtor shall file with the court and serve on the trustee and all parties in interest a report that details the efforts the debtor has undertaken and will undertake to attain a consensual plan of reorganization.

§ 1189. Filing of the plan

(a) **Who May File a Plan.**—Only the debtor may file a plan under this subchapter.

(b) **Deadline.**—The debtor shall file a plan not later than 90 days after the order for relief under this chapter, except that the court may extend the period if the need for the extension is attributable to circumstances for which the debtor should not justly be held accountable.

CROSS REFERENCES

Who may file a plan and time periods for filing a plan in non-subchapter V Chapter 11 cases, see 11 USCA § 1121.

§ 1190. Contents of plan

A plan filed under this subchapter—

(1) shall include—

(A) a brief history of the business operations of the debtor;

(B) a liquidation analysis; and

(C) projections with respect to the ability of the debtor to make payments under the proposed plan of reorganization;

(2) shall provide for the submission of all or such portion of the future earnings or other future income of the debtor to the supervision and control of the trustee as is necessary for the execution of the plan; and

(3) notwithstanding section 1123(b)(5) of this title, may modify the rights of the holder of a claim secured only by a security interest in real property that is the principal residence of the debtor if the new value received in connection with the granting of the security interest was—

    (A) not used primarily to acquire the real property; and

    (B) used primarily in connection with the small business of the debtor.

CROSS REFERENCES

Contents of the plan in non-subchapter V Chapter 11 cases, see 11 USCA § 1123.

§ 1191. Confirmation of plan

    (a) Terms.—The court shall confirm a plan under this subchapter only if all of the requirements of section 1129(a), other than paragraph (15) of that section, of this title are met.

    (b) Exception.—Notwithstanding section 510(a) of this title, if all of the applicable requirements of section 1129(a) of this title, other than paragraphs (8), (10), and (15) of that section, are met with respect to a plan, the court, on request of the debtor, shall confirm the plan notwithstanding the requirements of such paragraphs if the plan does not discriminate unfairly, and is fair and equitable, with respect to each class of claims or interests that is impaired under, and has not accepted, the plan.

    (c) Rule of Construction.—For purposes of this section, the condition that a plan be fair and equitable with respect to each class of claims or interests includes the following requirements:

    (1) With respect to a class of secured claims, the plan meets the requirements of section 1129(b)(2)(A) of this title.

    (2) As of the effective date of the plan—

        (A) the plan provides that all of the projected disposable income of the debtor to be received in the 3-year period, or such longer period not to exceed 5 years as the court may fix, beginning on the date that the first payment is due under the plan will be applied to make payments under the plan; or

        (B) the value of the property to be distributed under the plan in the 3-year period, or such longer period not to exceed 5 years as the court may fix, beginning on the date on which the first distribution is due under the plan is not less than the projected disposable income of the debtor.

    (3)(A) The debtor will be able to make all payments under the plan; or

    (B)(i) there is a reasonable likelihood that the debtor will be able to make all payments under the plan; and

        (ii) the plan provides appropriate remedies, which may include the liquidation of nonexempt assets, to protect the holders of claims or interests in the event that the payments are not made.

    (d) Disposable Income.—For purposes of this section, the term 'disposable income' means the income that is received by the debtor and that is not reasonably necessary to be expended—

    (1) for—

        (A) the maintenance or support of the debtor or a dependent of the debtor; or

(B) a domestic support obligation that first becomes payable after the date of the filing of the petition; or

(2) for the payment of expenditures necessary for the continuation, preservation, or operation of the business of the debtor.

(e) **Special Rule.**—Notwithstanding section 1129(a)(9)(A) of this title, a plan that provides for the payment through the plan of a claim of a kind specified in paragraph (2) or (3) of section 507(a) of this title may be confirmed under subsection (b) of this section.

[*Note from West Advisor.* Pub. L. 116–260 created a temporary § 1191(f), which expired on December 27, 2022, *except* for cases commenced before December 27, 2022. *See* 134 Stat. 2015, 2016, 2017. For the text of temporary § 1191(f), *see* Title 11, Chapter 11, Subchapter V, § 1191, Editorial Notes, Amendments, 2020 at http://uscode.house.gov]

CROSS REFERENCES

Chapter 11 discharge for individual whose plan was confirmed under § 1191(a), see Director's Bankruptcy Form 3180RV1.

Chapter 11 discharge for individual whose plan was confirmed under § 1191(b), see Director's Bankruptcy Form 3180RV2.

Fixing of confirmation hearing date by court in Chapter 11 subchapter V cases in which there is no disclosure statement, see Fed. R. Bankr. P. 3017.2.

For cases confirmed under § 1191(b), § 1141(d) does not apply, except as provided in § 1192, see 11 USCA § 1181(c).

For corporation or partnership whose plan was confirmed under § 1191(b), see Director's Bankruptcy Form 3180RV3.

Inapplicability of § 1129(a)(15), (b), (c), and (e) to cases under this subchapter, see § 1181(a).

§ 1192. Discharge

If the plan of the debtor is confirmed under section 1191(b) of this title, as soon as practicable after completion by the debtor of all payments due within the first 3 years of the plan, or such longer period not to exceed 5 years as the court may fix, unless the court approves a written waiver of discharge executed by the debtor after the order for relief under this chapter, the court shall grant the debtor a discharge of all debts provided in section 1141(d)(1)(A) of this title, and all other debts allowed under section 503 of this title and provided for in the plan, except any debt—

(1) on which the last payment is due after the first 3 years of the plan, or such other time not to exceed 5 years fixed by the court; or

(2) of the kind specified in section 523(a) of this title.

CROSS REFERENCES

Inapplicability of § 1141(d)(5) (discharge of individual debtor) to cases under this subchapter, see 11 USCA § 1181(a).

§ 1193. Modification of plan

(a) **Modification Before Confirmation.**—The debtor may modify a plan at any time before confirmation, but may not modify the plan so that the plan as modified fails to meet the requirements of sections 1122 and 1123 of this title, with the exception of subsection (a)(8) of such section 1123. After the modification is filed with the court, the plan as modified becomes the plan.

(b) **Modification After Confirmation.**—If a plan has been confirmed under section 1191(a) of this title, the debtor may modify the plan at any time after confirmation of the plan and before substantial consummation of the plan, but may not modify the plan so that the plan as modified fails to meet the requirements of sections 1122 and 1123 of this title, with the exception of subsection (a)(8) of such section 1123. The plan, as modified under this subsection, becomes the plan only if circumstances warrant the modification and the court, after notice and a hearing, confirms the plan as modified under section 1191(a) of this title.

(c) **Certain Other Modifications.**—If a plan has been confirmed under section 1191(b) of this title, the debtor may modify the plan at any time within 3 years, or such longer time not to exceed 5 years, as fixed by the court, but may not modify the plan so that the plan as modified fails to meet the requirements of section 1191(b) of this title. The plan as modified under this subsection becomes the plan only if circumstances warrant such modification and the court, after notice and a hearing, confirms such plan, as modified, under section 1191(b) of this title.

(d) **Holders of a Claim or Interest.**—If a plan has been confirmed under section 1191(a) of this title, any holder of a claim or interest that has accepted or rejected the plan is deemed to have accepted or rejected, as the case may be, the plan as modified, unless, within the time fixed by the court, such holder changes the previous acceptance or rejection of the holder.

CROSS REFERENCES

Inapplicability of § 1127 (modification of plan) to cases under this subchapter, see 11 USCA § 1181(a).

§ 1194. Payments

(a) **Retention and Distribution by Trustee.**—Payments and funds received by the trustee shall be retained by the trustee until confirmation or denial of confirmation of a plan. If a plan is confirmed, the trustee shall distribute any such payment in accordance with the plan. If a plan is not confirmed, the trustee shall return any such payments to the debtor after deducting—

(1) any unpaid claim allowed under section 503(b) of this title;

(2) any payment made for the purpose of providing adequate protection of an interest in property due to the holder of a secured claim; and

(3) any fee owing to the trustee.

(b) **Other Plans.**—If a plan is confirmed under section 1191(b) of this title, except as otherwise provided in the plan or in the order confirming the plan, the trustee shall make payments to creditors under the plan.

(c) **Payments Prior to Confirmation.**—Prior to confirmation of a plan, the court, after notice and a hearing, may authorize the trustee to make payments to the holder of a secured claim for the purpose of providing adequate protection of an interest in property.

§ 1195. Transactions with professionals

Notwithstanding section 327(a) of this title, a person is not disqualified for employment under section 327 of this title, by a debtor solely because that person holds a claim of less than $10,000 that arose prior to commencement of the case.

CHAPTER 12—ADJUSTMENT OF DEBTS OF A FAMILY FARMER OR FISHERMAN WITH REGULAR ANNUAL INCOME

SUBCHAPTER I—OFFICERS, ADMINISTRATION, AND THE ESTATE

SUBCHAPTER II—THE PLAN

SUBCHAPTER I—OFFICERS, ADMINISTRATION, AND THE ESTATE

§ 1201. Stay of action against codebtor

(a) Except as provided in subsections (b) and (c) of this section, after the order for relief under this chapter, a creditor may not act, or commence or continue any civil action, to collect all or any part of a consumer debt of the debtor from any individual that is liable on such debt with the debtor, or that secured such debt, unless—

(1) such individual became liable on or secured such debt in the ordinary course of such individual's business; or

(2) the case is closed, dismissed, or converted to a case under chapter 7 of this title.

(b) A creditor may present a negotiable instrument, and may give notice of dishonor of such an instrument.

(c) On request of a party in interest and after notice and a hearing, the court shall grant relief from the stay provided by subsection (a) of this section with respect to a creditor, to the extent that—

(1) as between the debtor and the individual protected under subsection (a) of this section, such individual received the consideration for the claim held by such creditor;

(2) the plan filed by the debtor proposes not to pay such claim; or

(3) such creditor's interest would be irreparably harmed by continuation of such stay.

(d) Twenty days after the filing of a request under subsection (c)(2) of this section for relief from the stay provided by subsection (a) of this section, such stay is terminated with respect to the party in interest making such request, unless the debtor or any individual that is liable on such debt with the debtor files and serves upon such party in interest a written objection to the taking of the proposed action.

CROSS REFERENCES

Automatic stay, see 11 USCA § 362.

Automatic stay of enforcement of claims against debtor in Chapter 9 cases, see 11 USCA § 922.

Claims of codebtors, see 11 USCA § 509.

Effect of conversion, see 11 USCA § 348.

Extension of time generally, see 11 USCA § 108.

§ 1202. Trustee

(a) If the United States trustee has appointed an individual under section 586(b) of title 28 to serve as standing trustee in cases under this chapter and if such individual qualifies as a trustee under section 322 of this title, then such individual shall serve as trustee in any case filed under this chapter. Otherwise, the United States trustee shall appoint one disinterested person to serve as trustee in the case or the United States trustee may serve as trustee in the case if necessary.

(b) The trustee shall—

(1) perform the duties specified in sections 704(a)(2), 704(a)(3), 704(a)(5), 704(a)(6), 704(a)(7), and 704(a)(9) of this title;

(2) perform the duties specified in section 1106(a)(3) and 1106(a)(4) of this title if the court, for cause and on request of a party in interest, the trustee, or the United States trustee, so orders;

(3) appear and be heard at any hearing that concerns—

(A) the value of property subject to a lien;

(B) confirmation of a plan;

(C) modification of the plan after confirmation; or

(D) the sale of property of the estate;

(4) ensure that the debtor commences making timely payments required by a confirmed plan;

(5) if the debtor ceases to be a debtor in possession, perform the duties specified in sections 704(a)(8), 1106(a)(1), 1106(a)(2), 1106(a)(6), 1106(a)(7), and 1203; and

(6) if with respect to the debtor there is a claim for a domestic support obligation, provide the applicable notice specified in subsection (c).

(c)(1) In a case described in subsection (b)(6) to which subsection (b)(6) applies, the trustee shall—

(A)(i) provide written notice to the holder of the claim described in subsection (b)(6) of such claim and of the right of such holder to use the services of the State child support enforcement agency established under sections 464 and 466 of the Social Security Act for the State in which such holder resides, for assistance in collecting child support during and after the case under this title; and

(ii) include in the notice provided under clause (i) the address and telephone number of such State child support enforcement agency;

(B)(i) provide written notice to such State child support enforcement agency of such claim; and

(ii) include in the notice provided under clause (i) the name, address, and telephone number of such holder; and

(C) at such time as the debtor is granted a discharge under section 1228, provide written notice to such holder and to such State child support enforcement agency of—

    (i) the granting of the discharge;

    (ii) the last recent known address of the debtor;

    (iii) the last recent known name and address of the debtor's employer; and

    (iv) the name of each creditor that holds a claim that—

        (I) is not discharged under paragraph (2), (4), or (14A) of section 523(a); or

        (II) was reaffirmed by the debtor under section 524(c).

(2)(A) The holder of a claim described in subsection (b)(6) or the State child support enforcement agency of the State in which such holder resides may request from a creditor described in paragraph (1)(C)(iv) the last known address of the debtor.

(B) Notwithstanding any other provision of law, a creditor that makes a disclosure of a last known address of a debtor in connection with a request made under subparagraph (A) shall not be liable by reason of making that disclosure.

REFERENCES IN TEXT

Section 464 of the Social Security Act, referred to in subsec. (c)(1)(A)(i), is Act Aug. 14, 1935, c. 531, Title IV, § 464, as added Aug. 13, 1981, Pub. L. 97–35, Title XXIII, § 2331(a), 95 Stat. 860, and amended, which is classified to 42 U.S.C.A. § 664.

Section 466 of the Social Security Act, referred to in subsec. (c)(1)(A)(i), is Act Aug. 14, 1935, c. 531, Title IV, § 466, as added Aug. 16, 1984, Pub. L. 98–378, § 3(b), 98 Stat. 1306, and amended, which is classified to 42 U.S.C.A. § 666.

CROSS REFERENCES

Appointment of standing trustee, see 28 USCA § 586(b).

Appointment of trustee in—

    Chapter 11 cases, see 11 USCA § 1104.

    Chapter 11 subchapter V cases, see 11 USCA § 1183(a).

    Chapter 13 cases, see 11 USCA § 1302.

    Railroad reorganization cases, see 11 USCA § 1163.

Compensation of officers, see 11 USCA § 330.

Election of trustee in Chapter 7 cases, see 11 USCA § 702.

Eligibility to serve as trustee, see 11 USCA § 321.

Grain storage facility bankruptcies, expedited appointment of trustee or examiner, see 11 USCA § 557.

Limitation on compensation of trustee, see 11 USCA § 326.

Qualification of trustee, see 11 USCA § 322.

Removal of trustee, see 11 USCA § 324.

Retention or replacement of professional persons, see 11 USCA § 327.

Role and capacity of trustee, see 11 USCA § 323.

Time of bringing action, see 11 USCA § 546.

Time of payment of percentage fee fixed for standing trustee, see 11 USCA § 1226(b).

§ 1203. Rights and powers of debtor

Subject to such limitations as the court may prescribe, a debtor in possession shall have all the rights, other than the right to compensation under section 330, and powers, and shall perform all the functions and duties, except the duties specified in paragraphs (3) and (4) of section 1106(a), of a trustee serving in a case under chapter 11, including operating the debtor's farm or commercial fishing operation.

CROSS REFERENCES

Obtaining credit, see 11 USCA § 364.

Rights and powers of debtor in—

Chapter 11 cases, see 11 USCA § 1107.

Chapter 11 subchapter V cases, see 11 USCA § 1184.

Chapter 13 cases, see 11 USCA § 1303.

Use, sale or lease of property, see 11 USCA § 363.

§ 1204. Removal of debtor as debtor in possession

(a) On request of a party in interest, and after notice and a hearing, the court shall order that the debtor shall not be a debtor in possession for cause, including fraud, dishonesty, incompetence, or gross mismanagement of the affairs of the debtor, either before or after the commencement of the case.

(b) On request of a party in interest, and after notice and a hearing, the court may reinstate the debtor in possession.

CROSS REFERENCES

Obtaining credit, see 11 USCA § 364.

Removal of a debtor in possession in Chapter 11 subchapter V cases, see 11 USCA § 1185.

Revocation of an order of confirmation, see 11 USCA § 1230.

Use, sale or lease of property, see 11 USCA § 363.

§ 1205. Adequate protection

(a) Section 361 does not apply in a case under this chapter.

(b) In a case under this chapter, when adequate protection is required under section 362, 363, or 364 of this title of an interest of an entity in property, such adequate protection may be provided by—

(1) requiring the trustee to make a cash payment or periodic cash payments to such entity, to the extent that the stay under section 362 of this title, use, sale, or lease under section 363 of this title, or any grant of a lien under section 364 of this title results in a decrease in the value of property securing a claim or of an entity's ownership interest in property;

(2) providing to such entity an additional or replacement lien to the extent that such stay, use, sale, lease, or grant results in a decrease in the value of property securing a claim or of an entity's ownership interest in property;

(3) paying to such entity for the use of farmland the reasonable rent customary in the community where the property is located, based upon the rental value, net income, and earning capacity of the property; or

(4) granting such other relief, other than entitling such entity to compensation allowable under section 503(b)(1) of this title as an administrative expense, as will adequately protect the value of property securing a claim or of such entity's ownership interest in property.

§ 1206. Sales free of interests

After notice and a hearing, in addition to the authorization contained in section 363(f), the trustee in a case under this chapter may sell property under section 363(b) and (c) free and clear of any interest in such property of an entity other than the estate if the property is farmland, farm equipment, or property used to carry out a commercial fishing operation (including a commercial fishing vessel), except that the proceeds of such sale shall be subject to such interest.

§ 1207. Property of the estate

(a) Property of the estate includes, in addition to the property specified in section 541 of this title—

(1) all property of the kind specified in such section that the debtor acquires after the commencement of the case but before the case is closed, dismissed, or converted to a case under chapter 7 of this title, whichever occurs first; and

(2) earnings from services performed by the debtor after the commencement of the case but before the case is closed, dismissed, or converted to a case under chapter 7 of this title, whichever occurs first.

(b) Except as provided in section 1204, a confirmed plan, or an order confirming a plan, the debtor shall remain in possession of all property of the estate.

CROSS REFERENCES

Property of the estate in—

Chapter 11 cases, see 11 USCA § 1115.

Chapter 11 subchapter V cases, see 11 USCA § 1186.

Chapter 13 cases, see 11 USCA § 1306.

§ 1208. Conversion or dismissal

(a) The debtor may convert a case under this chapter to a case under chapter 7 of this title at any time. Any waiver of the right to convert under this subsection is unenforceable.

(b) On request of the debtor at any time, if the case has not been converted under section 706 or 1112 of this title, the court shall dismiss a case under this chapter. Any waiver of the right to dismiss under this subsection is unenforceable.

(c) On request of a party in interest, and after notice and a hearing, the court may dismiss a case under this chapter for cause, including—

(1) unreasonable delay, or gross mismanagement, by the debtor that is prejudicial to creditors;

(2) nonpayment of any fees and charges required under chapter 123 of title 28;

(3) failure to file a plan timely under section 1221 of this title;

(4) failure to commence making timely payments required by a confirmed plan;

(5) denial of confirmation of a plan under section 1225 of this title and denial of a request made for additional time for filing another plan or a modification of a plan;

(6) material default by the debtor with respect to a term of a confirmed plan;

(7) revocation of the order of confirmation under section 1230 of this title, and denial of confirmation of a modified plan under section 1229 of this title;

(8) termination of a confirmed plan by reason of the occurrence of a condition specified in the plan;

(9) continuing loss to or diminution of the estate and absence of a reasonable likelihood of rehabilitation; and

(10) failure of the debtor to pay any domestic support obligation that first becomes payable after the date of the filing of the petition.

(d) On request of a party in interest, and after notice and a hearing, the court may dismiss a case under this chapter or convert a case under this chapter to a case under chapter 7 of this title upon a showing that the debtor has committed fraud in connection with the case.

(e) Notwithstanding any other provision of this section, a case may not be converted to a case under another chapter of this title unless the debtor may be a debtor under such chapter.

CROSS REFERENCES

Conversion from Chapter 7, see 11 USCA § 706.

Dismissal of Chapter 13 cases where not converted under this section, see 11 USCA § 1307(b).

Distribution of property of estate converted to Chapter 7, see 11 USCA § 726.

Effect of—

    Conversion, see 11 USCA § 348.

    Dismissal, see 11 USCA § 349.

Executory contracts and unexpired leases, see 11 USCA § 365.

SUBCHAPTER II—THE PLAN

§ 1221. Filing of plan

The debtor shall file a plan not later than 90 days after the order for relief under this chapter, except that the court may extend such period if the need for an extension is attributable to circumstances for which the debtor should not justly be held accountable.

CROSS REFERENCES

Conversion or dismissal for failure to timely file plan, see 11 USCA § 1208(c)(3).

Effect of conversion, see 11 USCA § 348.

Filing of plan in—

    Chapter 9 cases, see 11 USCA § 941.

    Chapter 11 cases, see 11 USCA § 1121.

    Chapter 11 subchapter V cases, see 11 USCA § 1189.

    Chapter 13 cases, see 11 USCA § 1321.

§ 1222. Contents of plan

(a) The plan shall—

(1) provide for the submission of all or such portion of future earnings or other future income of the debtor to the supervision and control of the trustee as is necessary for the execution of the plan;

(2) provide for the full payment, in deferred cash payments, of all claims entitled to priority under section 507, unless the holder of a particular claim agrees to a different treatment of that claim;

(3) if the plan classifies claims and interests, provide the same treatment for each claim or interest within a particular class unless the holder of a particular claim or interest agrees to less favorable treatment;

(4) notwithstanding any other provision of this section, a plan may provide for less than full payment of all amounts owed for a claim entitled to priority under section 507(a)(1)(B) only if the plan provides that all of the debtor's projected disposable income for a 5-year period beginning on the date that the first payment is due under the plan will be applied to make payments under the plan; and

(5) subject to section 1232, provide for the treatment of any claim by a governmental unit of a kind described in section 1232(a).

(b) Subject to subsections (a) and (c) of this section, the plan may—

(1) designate a class or classes of unsecured claims, as provided in section 1122 of this title, but may not discriminate unfairly against any class so designated; however, such plan may treat claims for a consumer debt of the debtor if an individual is liable on such consumer debt with the debtor differently than other unsecured claims;

(2) modify the rights of holders of secured claims, or of holders of unsecured claims, or leave unaffected the rights of holders of any class of claims;

(3) provide for the curing or waiving of any default;

(4) provide for payments on any unsecured claim to be made concurrently with payments on any secured claim or any other unsecured claim;

(5) provide for the curing of any default within a reasonable time and maintenance of payments while the case is pending on any unsecured claim or secured claim on which the last payment is due after the date on which the final payment under the plan is due;

(6) subject to section 365 of this title, provide for the assumption, rejection, or assignment of any executory contract or unexpired lease of the debtor not previously rejected under such section;

(7) provide for the payment of all or part of a claim against the debtor from property of the estate or property of the debtor;

(8) provide for the sale of all or any part of the property of the estate or the distribution of all or any part of the property of the estate among those having an interest in such property;

(9) provide for payment of allowed secured claims consistent with section 1225(a)(5) of this title, over a period exceeding the period permitted under section 1222(c);

(10) provide for the vesting of property of the estate, on confirmation of the plan or at a later time, in the debtor or in any other entity;

(11) provide for the payment of interest accruing after the date of the filing of the petition on unsecured claims that are nondischargeable under section 1228(a), except that such interest may be paid only to the extent that the debtor has disposable income available to pay such interest after making provision for full payment of all allowed claims; and

(12) include any other appropriate provision not inconsistent with this title.

(c) Except as provided in subsections (b)(5) and (b)(9), the plan may not provide for payments over a period that is longer than three years unless the court for cause approves a longer period, but the court may not approve a period that is longer than five years.

(d) Notwithstanding subsection (b)(2) of this section and sections 506(b) and 1225(a)(5) of this title, if it is proposed in a plan to cure a default, the amount necessary to cure the default, shall be determined in accordance with the underlying agreement and applicable nonbankruptcy law.

CROSS REFERENCES

Contents of plan filed in—

  Chapter 11 cases, see 11 USCA § 1123.

  Chapter 11 subchapter V cases, see 11 USCA § 1190.

  Chapter 13 cases, see 11 USCA § 1322.

  Railroad reorganization cases, see 11 USCA § 1172.

§ 1223. Modification of plan before confirmation

(a) The debtor may modify the plan at any time before confirmation, but may not modify the plan so that the plan as modified fails to meet the requirements of section 1222 of this title.

(b) After the debtor files a modification under this section, the plan as modified becomes the plan.

(c) Any holder of a secured claim that has accepted or rejected the plan is deemed to have accepted or rejected, as the case may be, the plan as modified, unless the modification provides for a change in the rights of such holder from what such rights were under the plan before modification, and such holder changes such holder's previous acceptance or rejection.

CROSS REFERENCES

Modification of plan filed in—

  Chapter 9 cases, see 11 USCA § 942.

  Chapter 11 cases, see 11 USCA § 1127(a).

  Chapter 11 subchapter V cases, see 11 USCA § 1193(a).

  Chapter 13 cases, see 11 USCA § 1323.

§ 1224. Confirmation hearing

After expedited notice, the court shall hold a hearing on confirmation of the plan. A party in interest, the trustee, or the United States trustee may object to the confirmation of the plan. Except for cause, the hearing shall be concluded not later than 45 days after the filing of the plan.

CROSS REFERENCES

Confirmation hearing in—

  Chapter 11 cases, see 11 USCA § 1128.

  Chapter 13 cases, see 11 USCA § 1324.

Duties of United States trustee, see 28 USCA § 586.

§ 1225. Confirmation of plan

(a) Except as provided in subsection (b), the court shall confirm a plan if—

(1) the plan complies with the provisions of this chapter and with the other applicable provisions of this title;

(2) any fee, charge, or amount required under chapter 123 of title 28, or by the plan, to be paid before confirmation, has been paid;

(3) the plan has been proposed in good faith and not by any means forbidden by law;

(4) the value, as of the effective date of the plan, of property to be distributed under the plan on account of each allowed unsecured claim is not less than the amount that would be paid on such claim if the estate of the debtor were liquidated under chapter 7 of this title on such date;

(5) with respect to each allowed secured claim provided for by the plan—

(A) the holder of such claim has accepted the plan;

(B)(i)   the plan provides that the holder of such claim retain the lien securing such claim; and

(ii) the value, as of the effective date of the plan, of property to be distributed by the trustee or the debtor under the plan on account of such claim is not less than the allowed amount of such claim; or

(C) the debtor surrenders the property securing such claim to such holder;

(6) the debtor will be able to make all payments under the plan and to comply with the plan; and

(7) the debtor has paid all amounts that are required to be paid under a domestic support obligation and that first become payable after the date of the filing of the petition if the debtor is required by a judicial or administrative order, or by statute, to pay such domestic support obligation.

(b)(1)   If the trustee or the holder of an allowed unsecured claim objects to the confirmation of the plan, then the court may not approve the plan unless, as of the effective date of the plan—

(A) the value of the property to be distributed under the plan on account of such claim is not less than the amount of such claim;

(B) the plan provides that all of the debtor's projected disposable income to be received in the three-year period, or such longer period as the court may approve under section 1222(c), beginning on the date that the first payment is due under the plan will be applied to make payments under the plan; or

(C) the value of the property to be distributed under the plan in the 3-year period, or such longer period as the court may approve under section 1222(c), beginning on the date that the first distribution is due under the plan is not less than the debtor's projected disposable income for such period.

(2) For purposes of this subsection, "disposable income" means income which is received by the debtor and which is not reasonably necessary to be expended—

(A) for the maintenance or support of the debtor or a dependent of the debtor or for a domestic support obligation that first becomes payable after the date of the filing of the petition; or

(B) for the payment of expenditures necessary for the continuation, preservation, and operation of the debtor's business.

(c) After confirmation of a plan, the court may order any entity from whom the debtor receives income to pay all or any part of such income to the trustee.

[*Note from West Advisor.* Pub. L. 116–260 created a temporary § 1225(d), which expired on December 27, 2022, *except* for cases commenced before December 27, 2022. *See* 134 Stat. 2016, 2017. For the text of temporary § 1225(d), *see* Title 11, Chapter 12, Subchapter II, § 1225, Editorial Notes, Amendments, 2020 at http://uscode.house.gov]

CROSS REFERENCES

Confirmation of plan in—

    Chapter 9 cases, see 11 USCA § 943.

    Chapter 11 cases, see 11 USCA § 1129.

    Chapter 11 subchapter V cases, see 11 USCA § 1191.

    Chapter 13 cases, see 11 USCA § 1325.

    Railroad reorganization cases, see 11 USCA § 1173.

Conversion or dismissal, see 11 USCA § 1208.

Order confirming Chapter 12 plan, see Director's Bankruptcy Form 2300A.

Unclaimed property, see 11 USCA § 347.

§ 1226. Payments

(a) Payments and funds received by the trustee shall be retained by the trustee until confirmation or denial of confirmation of a plan. If a plan is confirmed, the trustee shall distribute any such payment in accordance with the plan. If a plan is not confirmed, the trustee shall return any such payments to the debtor, after deducting—

    (1) any unpaid claim allowed under section 503(b) of this title; and

    (2) if a standing trustee is serving in the case, the percentage fee fixed for such standing trustee.

(b) Before or at the time of each payment to creditors under the plan, there shall be paid—

    (1) any unpaid claim of the kind specified in section 507(a)(2) of this title; and

    (2) if a standing trustee appointed under section 1202(c) of this title is serving in the case, the percentage fee fixed for such standing trustee under section 1202(d) of this title.

(c) Except as otherwise provided in the plan or in the order confirming the plan, the trustee shall make payments to creditors under the plan.

REFERENCES IN TEXT

Section 1202(c) and (d) of this title, referred to in subsec. (b)(2), were repealed by section 227 of Pub. L. 99–554, and provisions relating to appointment of and fixing percentage fees for standing trustees are contained in section 586(b) and (e) of Title 28, Judiciary and Judicial Procedure, as amended by section 113(b) and (c) of Pub. L. 99–554.

CROSS REFERENCES

Payment stopped on checks remaining unpaid 90 days after final distribution, see 11 USCA § 347.

Payments in—

    Chapter 11 subchapter V cases, see 11 USCA § 1194.

    Chapter 13 cases, see 11 USCA § 1326.

§ 1227. Effect of confirmation

(a) Except as provided in section 1228(a) of this title, the provisions of a confirmed plan bind the debtor, each creditor, each equity security holder, and each general partner in the debtor, whether or not the claim of such creditor, such equity security holder, or such general partner in the debtor is provided for by the plan, and whether or not such creditor, such equity security holder, or such general partner in the debtor has objected to, has accepted, or has rejected the plan.

(b) Except as otherwise provided in the plan or the order confirming the plan, the confirmation of a plan vests all of the property of the estate in the debtor.

(c) Except as provided in section 1228(a) of this title and except as otherwise provided in the plan or in the order confirming the plan, the property vesting in the debtor under subsection (b) of this section is free and clear of any claim or interest of any creditor provided for by the plan.

CROSS REFERENCES

Effect of confirmation in—

Chapter 9 cases, see 11 USCA § 944.

Chapter 11 cases, see 11 USCA § 1141.

Chapter 13 cases, see 11 USCA § 1327.

§ 1228. Discharge

(a) Subject to subsection (d), as soon as practicable after completion by the debtor of all payments under the plan, and in the case of a debtor who is required by a judicial or administrative order, or by statute, to pay a domestic support obligation, after such debtor certifies that all amounts payable under such order or such statute that are due on or before the date of the certification (including amounts due before the petition was filed, but only to the extent provided for by the plan) have been paid, other than payments to holders of allowed claims provided for under section 1222(b)(5) or 1222(b)(9) of this title, unless the court approves a written waiver of discharge executed by the debtor after the order for relief under this chapter, the court shall grant the debtor a discharge of all debts provided for by the plan, allowed under section 503 of this title, or disallowed under section 502 of this title, except any debt—

    (1) provided for under section 1222(b)(5) or 1222(b)(9) of this title; or

    (2) of a kind specified in section 523(a) of this title, except as provided in section 1232(c).

(b) Subject to subsection (d), at any time after the confirmation of the plan and after notice and a hearing, the court may grant a discharge to a debtor that has not completed payments under the plan only if—

    (1) the debtor's failure to complete such payments is due to circumstances for which the debtor should not justly be held accountable;

    (2) the value, as of the effective date of the plan, of property actually distributed under the plan on account of each allowed unsecured claim is not less than the amount that would have been paid on such claim if the estate of the debtor had been liquidated under chapter 7 of this title on such date; and

    (3) modification of the plan under section 1229 of this title is not practicable.

(c) A discharge granted under subsection (b) of this section discharges the debtor from all unsecured debts provided for by the plan or disallowed under section 502 of this title, except any debt—

    (1) provided for under section 1222(b)(5) or 1222(b)(9) of this title; or

    (2) of a kind specified in section 523(a) of this title, except as provided in section 1232(c).

(d) On request of a party in interest before one year after a discharge under this section is granted, and after notice and a hearing, the court may revoke such discharge only if—

(1) such discharge was obtained by the debtor through fraud; and

(2) the requesting party did not know of such fraud until after such discharge was granted.

(e) After the debtor is granted a discharge, the court shall terminate the services of any trustee serving in the case.

(f) The court may not grant a discharge under this chapter unless the court after notice and a hearing held not more than 10 days before the date of the entry of the order granting the discharge finds that there is no reasonable cause to believe that—

(1) section 522(q)(1) may be applicable to the debtor; and

(2) there is pending any proceeding in which the debtor may be found guilty of a felony of the kind described in section 522(q)(1)(A) or liable for a debt of the kind described in section 522(q)(1)(B).

CROSS REFERENCES

Cancellation of indebtedness from discharged farm loans, see 12 USCA § 1150.

Chapter 12 discharge, see Director's Bankruptcy Form 3180F.

Chapter 12 hardship discharge, see Director's Bankruptcy Form 3180FH.

Discharge in—

> Chapter 7 cases, see 11 USCA § 727.
>
> Chapter 11 cases, see 11 USCA § 1141(d).
>
> Chapter 11 subchapter V cases, see 11 USCA § 1192.
>
> Chapter 13 cases, see 11 USCA § 1328.

Effect of—

> Conversion, see 11 USCA § 348.
>
> Discharge, see 11 USCA § 524.

Exceptions to discharge, see 11 USCA § 523.

§ 1229. Modification of plan after confirmation

(a) At any time after confirmation of the plan but before the completion of payments under such plan, the plan may be modified, on request of the debtor, the trustee, or the holder of an allowed unsecured claim, to—

(1) increase or reduce the amount of payments on claims of a particular class provided for by the plan;

(2) extend or reduce the time for such payments;

(3) alter the amount of the distribution to a creditor whose claim is provided for by the plan to the extent necessary to take account of any payment of such claim other than under the plan; or

(4) provide for the payment of a claim described in section 1232(a) that arose after the date on which the petition was filed.

(b)(1) Sections 1222(a), 1222(b), and 1223(c) of this title and the requirements of section 1225(a) of this title apply to any modification under subsection (a) of this section.

(2) The plan as modified becomes the plan unless, after notice and a hearing, such modification is disapproved.

(c) A plan modified under this section may not provide for payments over a period that expires after three years after the time that the first payment under the original confirmed plan was due, unless the court, for cause, approves a longer period, but the court may not approve a period that expires after five years after such time.

(d) A plan may not be modified under this section—

(1) to increase the amount of any payment due before the plan as modified becomes the plan;

(2) by anyone except the debtor, based on an increase in the debtor's disposable income, to increase the amount of payments to unsecured creditors required for a particular month so that the aggregate of such payments exceeds the debtor's disposable income for such month; or

(3) in the last year of the plan by anyone except the debtor, to require payments that would leave the debtor with insufficient funds to carry on the farming operation after the plan is completed.

CROSS REFERENCES

Conversion or dismissal upon denial of confirmation and denial of additional time to file a modified plan, see 11 USCA § 1208(c)(5).

Duties of United States trustee, see 28 USCA § 586.

Modification of Chapter 12 plan after confirmation, see Fed. R. Bankr. P. 3015(h).

Modification of plan after confirmation in—

Chapter 11 cases, see 11 USCA § 1127(b), (e), (f).

Chapter 11 subchapter V cases, see 11 USCA § 1193(b)–(d).

Chapter 13 cases, see 11 USCA § 1329.

Order fixing time to object to proposed modification of confirmed Chapter 13 plan, see Director's Bankruptcy Form 2310A.

§ 1230. Revocation of an order of confirmation

(a) On request of a party in interest at any time within 180 days after the date of the entry of an order of confirmation under section 1225 of this title, and after notice and a hearing, the court may revoke such order if such order was procured by fraud.

(b) If the court revokes an order of confirmation under subsection (a) of this section, the court shall dispose of the case under section 1207 of this title, unless, within the time fixed by the court, the debtor proposes and the court confirms a modification of the plan under section 1229 of this title.

CROSS REFERENCES

Conversion or dismissal upon revocation of confirmation order and denial of confirmation of modified plan, see 11 USCA § 1208(c)(7).

Revocation of order of confirmation in—

Chapter 11 cases, see 11 USCA § 1144.

Chapter 13 cases, see 11 USCA § 1330.

§ 1231. Special tax provisions

(a) The issuance, transfer, or exchange of a security, or the making or delivery of an instrument of transfer under a plan confirmed under section 1225 of this title, may not be taxed under any law imposing a stamp tax or similar tax.

(b) The court may authorize the proponent of a plan to request a determination, limited to questions of law, by any governmental unit charged with responsibility for collection or determination of a tax on or measured by income, of the tax effects, under section 346 of this title and under the law imposing such tax, of the plan. In the event of an actual controversy, the court may declare such effects after the earlier of—

    (1) the date on which such governmental unit responds to the request under this subsection; or

    (2) 270 days after such request.

§ 1232. Claim by a governmental unit based on the disposition of property used in a farming operation

(a) Any unsecured claim of a governmental unit against the debtor or the estate that arises before the filing of the petition, or that arises after the filing of the petition and before the debtor's discharge under section 1228, as a result of the sale, transfer, exchange, or other disposition of any property used in the debtor's farming operation—

    (1) shall be treated as an unsecured claim arising before the date on which the petition is filed;

    (2) shall not be entitled to priority under section 507;

    (3) shall be provided for under a plan; and

    (4) shall be discharged in accordance with section 1228.

(b) For purposes of applying sections 1225(a)(4), 1228(b)(2), and 1229(b)(1) to a claim described in subsection (a) of this section, the amount that would be paid on such claim if the estate of the debtor were liquidated in a case under chapter 7 of this title shall be the amount that would be paid by the estate in a chapter 7 case if the claim were an unsecured claim arising before the date on which the petition was filed and were not entitled to priority under section 507.

(c) For purposes of applying sections 523(a), 1228(a)(2), and 1228(c)(2) to a claim described in subsection (a) of this section, the claim shall not be treated as a claim of a kind specified in subparagraph (A) or (B) of section 523(a)(1).

(d)(1) A governmental unit may file a proof of claim for a claim described in subsection (a) that arises after the date on which the petition is filed.

    (2) If a debtor files a tax return after the filing of the petition for a period in which a claim described in subsection (a) arises, and the claim relates to the tax return, the debtor shall serve notice of the claim on the governmental unit charged with the responsibility for the collection of the tax at the address and in the manner designated in section 505(b)(1). Notice under this paragraph shall state that the debtor has filed a petition under this chapter, state the name and location of the court in which the case under this chapter is pending, state the amount of the claim, and include a copy of the filed tax return and documentation supporting the calculation of the claim.

    (3) If notice of a claim has been served on the governmental unit in accordance with paragraph (2), the governmental unit may file a proof of claim not later than 180 days after the date on which such notice was served. If the governmental unit has not filed a timely proof of the claim, the debtor or trustee may file proof of the claim that is consistent with the notice served under paragraph (2). If a proof of claim is filed by the debtor or trustee under this paragraph, the governmental unit may not amend the proof of claim.

(4) A claim filed under this subsection shall be determined and shall be allowed under subsection (a), (b), or (c) of section 502, or disallowed under subsection (d) or (e) of section 502, in the same manner as if the claim had arisen immediately before the date of the filing of the petition.

CHAPTER 13—ADJUSTMENT OF DEBTS OF AN INDIVIDUAL WITH REGULAR INCOME

SUBCHAPTER I—OFFICERS, ADMINISTRATION, AND THE ESTATE

SUBCHAPTER I—OFFICERS, ADMINISTRATION, AND THE ESTATE

§ 1301. Stay of action against codebtor

(a) Except as provided in subsections (b) and (c) of this section, after the order for relief under this chapter, a creditor may not act, or commence or continue any civil action, to collect all or any part of a consumer debt of the debtor from any individual that is liable on such debt with the debtor, or that secured such debt, unless—

    (1) such individual became liable on or secured such debt in the ordinary course of such individual's business; or

    (2) the case is closed, dismissed, or converted to a case under chapter 7 or 11 of this title.

(b) A creditor may present a negotiable instrument, and may give notice of dishonor of such an instrument.

(c) On request of a party in interest and after notice and a hearing, the court shall grant relief from the stay provided by subsection (a) of this section with respect to a creditor, to the extent that—

    (1) as between the debtor and the individual protected under subsection (a) of this section, such individual received the consideration for the claim held by such creditor;

    (2) the plan filed by the debtor proposes not to pay such claim; or

    (3) such creditor's interest would be irreparably harmed by continuation of such stay.

(d) Twenty days after the filing of a request under subsection (c)(2) of this section for relief from the stay provided by subsection (a) of this section, such stay is terminated with respect to the party in interest making such request, unless the debtor or any individual that is liable on such debt with the debtor files and serves upon such party in interest a written objection to the taking of the proposed action.

CROSS REFERENCES

Automatic stay, see 11 USCA § 362.

Automatic stay of enforcement of claims against debtor in Chapter 9 cases, see 11 USCA § 922.

Claims of codebtors, see 11 USCA § 509.

Effect of conversion, see 11 USCA § 348.

Extension of time generally, see 11 USCA § 108.

Stay of action against codebtor in Chapter 12 cases, see 11 USCA § 1201.

§ 1302. Trustee

(a) If the United States trustee appoints an individual under section 586(b) of title 28 to serve as standing trustee in cases under this chapter and if such individual qualifies under section 322 of this title, then such individual shall serve as trustee in the case. Otherwise, the United States trustee shall appoint one disinterested person to serve as trustee in the case or the United States trustee may serve as a trustee in the case.

(b) The trustee shall—

(1) perform the duties specified in sections 704(a)(2), 704(a)(3), 704(a)(4), 704(a)(5), 704(a)(6), 704(a)(7), and 704(a)(9) of this title;

(2) appear and be heard at any hearing that concerns—

(A) the value of property subject to a lien;

(B) confirmation of a plan; or

(C) modification of the plan after confirmation;

(3) dispose of, under regulations issued by the Director of the Administrative Office of the United States Courts, moneys received or to be received in a case under chapter XIII of the Bankruptcy Act;

(4) advise, other than on legal matters, and assist the debtor in performance under the plan;

(5) ensure that the debtor commences making timely payments under section 1326 of this title; and

(6) if with respect to the debtor there is a claim for a domestic support obligation, provide the applicable notice specified in subsection (d).

(c) If the debtor is engaged in business, then in addition to the duties specified in subsection (b) of this section, the trustee shall perform the duties specified in sections 1106(a)(3) and 1106(a)(4) of this title.

(d)(1) In a case described in subsection (b)(6) to which subsection (b)(6) applies, the trustee shall—

(A)(i) provide written notice to the holder of the claim described in subsection (b)(6) of such claim and of the right of such holder to use the services of the State child support enforcement agency established under sections 464 and 466 of the Social Security Act for the State in which such holder resides, for assistance in collecting child support during and after the case under this title; and

(ii) include in the notice provided under clause (i) the address and telephone number of such State child support enforcement agency;

(B)(i) provide written notice to such State child support enforcement agency of such claim; and

(ii) include in the notice provided under clause (i) the name, address, and telephone number of such holder; and

(C) at such time as the debtor is granted a discharge under section 1328, provide written notice to such holder and to such State child support enforcement agency of—

(i) the granting of the discharge;

(ii) the last recent known address of the debtor;

(iii) the last recent known name and address of the debtor's employer; and

(iv) the name of each creditor that holds a claim that—

(I) is not discharged under paragraph (2) or (4) of section 523(a); or

(II) was reaffirmed by the debtor under section 524(c).

(2)(A) The holder of a claim described in subsection (b)(6) or the State child support enforcement agency of the State in which such holder resides may request from a creditor described in paragraph (1)(C)(iv) the last known address of the debtor.

(B) Notwithstanding any other provision of law, a creditor that makes a disclosure of a last known address of a debtor in connection with a request made under subparagraph (A) shall not be liable by reason of making that disclosure.

REFERENCES IN TEXT

Chapter XIII of the Bankruptcy Act, referred to in subsec. (b)(3), is chapter XIII of Act July 1, 1898, c. 541, as added June 22, 1938, c. 575, § 1, 52 Stat. 930, which was classified to chapter 13 (section 1001 et seq.) of former Title 11.

Section 464 of the Social Security Act, referred to in subsec. (d)(1)(A)(i), is Act Aug. 14, 1935, c. 531, Title IV, § 464, as added Aug. 13, 1981, Pub. L. 97–35, Title XXIII, § 2331(a), 95 Stat. 860, and amended, which is classified to 42 U.S.C.A. § 664.

Section 466 of the Social Security Act, referred to in subsec. (d)(1)(A)(i), is Act Aug. 14, 1935, c. 531, Title IV, § 466, as added Aug. 16, 1984, Pub. L. 98–378, § 3(b), 98 Stat. 1306, and amended, which is classified to 42 U.S.C.A. § 666.

CROSS REFERENCES

Appointment of standing trustee, see 28 USCA § 586(b).

Appointment of trustee in—

Chapter 11 cases, see 11 USCA § 1104.

Chapter 11 subchapter V cases, see 11 USCA § 1183(a).

Chapter 12 cases, see 11 USCA § 1202.

Railroad reorganization cases, see 11 USCA § 1163.

Compensation of officers, see 11 USCA § 330.

Election of trustee, see 11 USCA § 702.

Eligibility to serve as trustee, see 11 USCA § 321.

Grain storage facility bankruptcies, expedited appointment of trustee or examiner, see 11 USCA § 557.

Limitation on compensation of trustee, see 11 USCA § 326.

Qualification of trustee, see 11 USCA § 322.

Removal of trustee, see 11 USCA § 324.

Role and capacity of trustee, see 11 USCA § 323.

Time of bringing action, see 11 USCA § 546.

§ 1303. Rights and powers of debtor

Subject to any limitations on a trustee under this chapter, the debtor shall have, exclusive of the trustee, the rights and powers of a trustee under sections 363(b), 363(d), 363(e), 363(f), and 363(*l*), of this title.

CROSS REFERENCES

Rights and powers of debtor in—

      Chapter 11 cases, see 11 USCA § 1107.

      Chapter 11 subchapter V cases, see 11 USCA § 1184.

      Chapter 12 cases, see 11 USCA § 1203.

§ 1304. Debtor engaged in business

(a) A debtor that is self-employed and incurs trade credit in the production of income from such employment is engaged in business.

(b) Unless the court orders otherwise, a debtor engaged in business may operate the business of the debtor and, subject to any limitations on a trustee under sections 363(c) and 364 of this title and to such limitations or conditions as the court prescribes, shall have, exclusive of the trustee, the rights and powers of the trustee under such sections.

(c) A debtor engaged in business shall perform the duties of the trustee specified in section 704(a)(8) of this title.

CROSS REFERENCES

Authorization of trustee to operate business in—

      Chapter 7 cases, see 11 USCA § 721.

      Chapter 11 cases, see 11 USCA § 1108.

      Chapter 11 subchapter V cases in which debtor ceases to be debtor in possession, see 11 USCA § 1183(b)(5).

Obtaining credit, see 11 USCA § 364.

Rights, powers and duties of debtor in possession in Chapter 11 cases, see 11 USCA § 1107.

Use, sale or lease of property, see 11 USCA § 363.

§ 1305. Filing and allowance of postpetition claims

(a) A proof of claim may be filed by any entity that holds a claim against the debtor—

    (1) for taxes that become payable to a governmental unit while the case is pending; or

    (2) that is a consumer debt, that arises after the date of the order for relief under this chapter, and that is for property or services necessary for the debtor's performance under the plan.

(b) Except as provided in subsection (c) of this section, a claim filed under subsection (a) of this section shall be allowed or disallowed under section 502 of this title, but shall be determined as of the date such claim arises, and shall be allowed under section 502(a), 502(b), or 502(c) of this title, or disallowed under section 502(d) or 502(e) of this title, the same as if such claim had arisen before the date of the filing of the petition.

(c) A claim filed under subsection (a)(2) of this section shall be disallowed if the holder of such claim knew or should have known that prior approval by the trustee of the debtor's incurring the obligation was practicable and was not obtained.

CROSS REFERENCES

Discharge of certain consumer debts, see 11 USCA § 1328.

Effect of conversion, see 11 USCA § 348.

Filing of proofs of claims or interests, see 11 USCA § 501.

Provisions in plans for payment of claims, see 11 USCA § 1322.

§ 1306. Property of the estate

(a) Property of the estate includes, in addition to the property specified in section 541 of this title—

(1) all property of the kind specified in such section that the debtor acquires after the commencement of the case but before the case is closed, dismissed, or converted to a case under chapter 7, 11, or 12 of this title, whichever occurs first; and

(2) earnings from services performed by the debtor after the commencement of the case but before the case is closed, dismissed, or converted to a case under chapter 7, 11, or 12 of this title, whichever occurs first.

(b) Except as provided in a confirmed plan or order confirming a plan, the debtor shall remain in possession of all property of the estate.

CROSS REFERENCES

Property of the estate in—

Chapter 11 cases, see 11 USCA § 1115.

Chapter 11 subchapter V cases, see 11 USCA § 1186.

Chapter 12 cases, see 11 USCA § 1207.

§ 1307. Conversion or dismissal

(a) The debtor may convert a case under this chapter to a case under chapter 7 of this title at any time. Any waiver of the right to convert under this subsection is unenforceable.

(b) On request of the debtor at any time, if the case has not been converted under section 706, 1112, or 1208 of this title, the court shall dismiss a case under this chapter. Any waiver of the right to dismiss under this subsection is unenforceable.

(c) Except as provided in subsection (f) of this section, on request of a party in interest or the United States trustee and after notice and a hearing, the court may convert a case under this chapter to a case under chapter 7 of this title, or may dismiss a case under this chapter, whichever is in the best interests of creditors and the estate, for cause, including—

(1) unreasonable delay by the debtor that is prejudicial to creditors;

(2) nonpayment of any fees and charges required under chapter 123 of title 28;

(3) failure to file a plan timely under section 1321 of this title;

(4) failure to commence making timely payments under section 1326 of this title;

(5) denial of confirmation of a plan under section 1325 of this title and denial of a request made for additional time for filing another plan or a modification of a plan;

(6) material default by the debtor with respect to a term of a confirmed plan;

(7) revocation of the order of confirmation under section 1330 of this title, and denial of confirmation of a modified plan under section 1329 of this title;

(8) termination of a confirmed plan by reason of the occurrence of a condition specified in the plan other than completion of payments under the plan;

(9) only on request of the United States trustee, failure of the debtor to file, within fifteen days, or such additional time as the court may allow, after the filing of the petition commencing such case, the information required by paragraph (1) of section 521(a);

(10) only on request of the United States trustee, failure to timely file the information required by paragraph (2) of section 521(a); or

(11) failure of the debtor to pay any domestic support obligation that first becomes payable after the date of the filing of the petition.

(d) Except as provided in subsection (f) of this section, at any time before the confirmation of a plan under section 1325 of this title, on request of a party in interest or the United States trustee and after notice and a hearing, the court may convert a case under this chapter to a case under chapter 11 or 12 of this title.

(e) Upon the failure of the debtor to file a tax return under section 1308, on request of a party in interest or the United States trustee and after notice and a hearing, the court shall dismiss a case or convert a case under this chapter to a case under chapter 7 of this title, whichever is in the best interest of the creditors and the estate.

(f) The court may not convert a case under this chapter to a case under chapter 7, 11, or 12 of this title if the debtor is a farmer, unless the debtor requests such conversion.

(g) Notwithstanding any other provision of this section, a case may not be converted to a case under another chapter of this title unless the debtor may be a debtor under such chapter.

CROSS REFERENCES

Conversion from Chapter 7, see 11 USCA § 706.

Conversion or dismissal upon revocation of order of confirmation, see 11 USCA § 1330.

Dismissal of—

> Chapter 7 case, see 11 USCA § 707.

> Chapter 9 cases, see 11 USCA § 930.

Distribution of property of estate converted to Chapter 7, see 11 USCA § 726.

Effect of—

> Conversion, see 11 USCA § 348.

> Dismissal, see 11 USCA § 349.

Executory contracts and unexpired leases, see 11 USCA § 365.

§ 1308. Filing of prepetition tax returns

(a) Not later than the day before the date on which the meeting of the creditors is first scheduled to be held under section 341(a), if the debtor was required to file a tax return under applicable nonbankruptcy law, the debtor shall file with appropriate tax authorities all tax returns for all taxable periods ending during the 4-year period ending on the date of the filing of the petition.

(b)(1)   Subject to paragraph (2), if the tax returns required by subsection (a) have not been filed by the date on which the meeting of creditors is first scheduled to be held under section 341(a), the trustee may hold open that meeting for a reasonable period of time to allow the debtor an additional period of time to file any unfiled returns, but such additional period of time shall not extend beyond—

(A)   for any return that is past due as of the date of the filing of the petition, the date that is 120 days after the date of that meeting; or

(B)   for any return that is not past due as of the date of the filing of the petition, the later of—

  (i)   the date that is 120 days after the date of that meeting; or

  (ii)   the date on which the return is due under the last automatic extension of time for filing that return to which the debtor is entitled, and for which request is timely made, in accordance with applicable nonbankruptcy law.

(2)   After notice and a hearing, and order entered before the tolling of any applicable filing period determined under paragraph (1), if the debtor demonstrates by a preponderance of the evidence that the failure to file a return as required under paragraph (1) is attributable to circumstances beyond the control of the debtor, the court may extend the filing period established by the trustee under paragraph (1) for—

(A)   a period of not more than 30 days for returns described in paragraph (1)(A); and

(B)   a period not to extend after the applicable extended due date for a return described in paragraph (1)(B).

(c)   For purposes of this section, the term "return" includes a return prepared pursuant to subsection (a) or (b) of section 6020 of the Internal Revenue Code of 1986, or a similar State or local law, or a written stipulation to a judgment or a final order entered by a nonbankruptcy tribunal.

REFERENCES IN TEXT

Subsection (a) or (b) of section 6020 of the Internal Revenue Code of 1986, referred to in subsec. (c), is classified to 26 U.S.C.A. § 6020(a) or (b).

SUBCHAPTER II—THE PLAN

§ 1321. Filing of plan

The debtor shall file a plan.

CROSS REFERENCES

Chapter 13 plan, Official Bankruptcy Form 113.

Conversion or dismissal for failure to timely file plan, see 11 USCA § 1307.

Filing and form of Chapter 13 plan, see Fed. R. Bankr. P. 3015(b), (c).

Filing of plan in—

  Chapter 9 cases, see 11 USCA § 941.

  Chapter 11 cases, see 11 USCA § 1121.

  Chapter 11 subchapter V cases, see 11 USCA § 1189.

  Chapter 12 cases, see 11 USCA § 1221.

Requirements for a local form for plans filed in a Chapter 13 case, see Fed. R. Bankr. P. 3015.1.

§ 1322. Contents of plan

(a) The plan—

(1) shall provide for the submission of all or such portion of future earnings or other future income of the debtor to the supervision and control of the trustee as is necessary for the execution of the plan;

(2) shall provide for the full payment, in deferred cash payments, of all claims entitled to priority under section 507 of this title, unless the holder of a particular claim agrees to a different treatment of such claim;

(3) if the plan classifies claims, shall provide the same treatment for each claim within a particular class; and

(4) notwithstanding any other provision of this section, may provide for less than full payment of all amounts owed for a claim entitled to priority under section 507(a)(1)(B) only if the plan provides that all of the debtor's projected disposable income for a 5-year period beginning on the date that the first payment is due under the plan will be applied to make payments under the plan.

(b) Subject to subsections (a) and (c) of this section, the plan may—

(1) designate a class or classes of unsecured claims, as provided in section 1122 of this title, but may not discriminate unfairly against any class so designated; however, such plan may treat claims for a consumer debt of the debtor if an individual is liable on such consumer debt with the debtor differently than other unsecured claims;

(2) modify the rights of holders of secured claims, other than a claim secured only by a security interest in real property that is the debtor's principal residence, or of holders of unsecured claims, or leave unaffected the rights of holders of any class of claims;

(3) provide for the curing or waiving of any default;

(4) provide for payments on any unsecured claim to be made concurrently with payments on any secured claim or any other unsecured claim;

(5) notwithstanding paragraph (2) of this subsection, provide for the curing of any default within a reasonable time and maintenance of payments while the case is pending on any unsecured claim or secured claim on which the last payment is due after the date on which the final payment under the plan is due;

(6) provide for the payment of all or any part of any claim allowed under section 1305 of this title;

(7) subject to section 365 of this title, provide for the assumption, rejection, or assignment of any executory contract or unexpired lease of the debtor not previously rejected under such section;

(8) provide for the payment of all or part of a claim against the debtor from property of the estate or property of the debtor;

(9) provide for the vesting of property of the estate, on confirmation of the plan or at a later time, in the debtor or in any other entity;

(10) provide for the payment of interest accruing after the date of the filing of the petition on unsecured claims that are nondischargeable under section 1328(a), except that such interest may be paid only to the extent that the debtor has disposable income available to pay such interest after making provision for full payment of all allowed claims; and

(11) include any other appropriate provision not inconsistent with this title.

(c) Notwithstanding subsection (b)(2) and applicable nonbankruptcy law—

(1) a default with respect to, or that gave rise to, a lien on the debtor's principal residence may be cured under paragraph (3) or (5) of subsection (b) until such residence is sold at a foreclosure sale that is conducted in accordance with applicable nonbankruptcy law; and

(2) in a case in which the last payment on the original payment schedule for a claim secured only by a security interest in real property that is the debtor's principal residence is due before the date on which the final payment under the plan is due, the plan may provide for the payment of the claim as modified pursuant to section 1325(a)(5) of this title.

(d)(1) If the current monthly income of the debtor and the debtor's spouse combined, when multiplied by 12, is not less than—

(A) in the case of a debtor in a household of 1 person, the median family income of the applicable State for 1 earner;

(B) in the case of a debtor in a household of 2, 3, or 4 individuals, the highest median family income of the applicable State for a family of the same number or fewer individuals; or

(C) in the case of a debtor in a household exceeding 4 individuals, the highest median family income of the applicable State for a family of 4 or fewer individuals, plus $825 per month for each individual in excess of 4,

the plan may not provide for payments over a period that is longer than 5 years.

(2) If the current monthly income of the debtor and the debtor's spouse combined, when multiplied by 12, is less than—

(A) in the case of a debtor in a household of 1 person, the median family income of the applicable State for 1 earner;

(B) in the case of a debtor in a household of 2, 3, or 4 individuals, the highest median family income of the applicable State for a family of the same number or fewer individuals; or

(C) in the case of a debtor in a household exceeding 4 individuals, the highest median family income of the applicable State for a family of 4 or fewer individuals, plus $825 per month for each individual in excess of 4,

the plan may not provide for payments over a period that is longer than 3 years, unless the court, for cause, approves a longer period, but the court may not approve a period that is longer than 5 years.

(e) Notwithstanding subsection (b)(2) of this section and sections 506(b) and 1325(a)(5) of this title, if it is proposed in a plan to cure a default, the amount necessary to cure the default, shall be determined in accordance with the underlying agreement and applicable nonbankruptcy law.

(f) A plan may not materially alter the terms of a loan described in section 362(b)(19) and any amounts required to repay such loan shall not constitute "disposable income" under section 1325.

CROSS REFERENCES

Chapter 13 plan, Official Bankruptcy Form 113.

Contents of plan filed in—

Requirements for a local form for plans filed in a Chapter 13 case, see Fed. R. Bankr. P. 3015.1.

§ 1323. Modification of plan before confirmation

(a) The debtor may modify the plan at any time before confirmation, but may not modify the plan so that the plan as modified fails to meet the requirements of section 1322 of this title.

(b) After the debtor files a modification under this section, the plan as modified becomes the plan.

(c) Any holder of a secured claim that has accepted or rejected the plan is deemed to have accepted or rejected, as the case may be, the plan as modified, unless the modification provides for a change in the rights of such holder from what such rights were under the plan before modification, and such holder changes such holder's previous acceptance or rejection.

CROSS REFERENCES

Modification of plan filed in—

    Chapter 9 cases, see 11 USCA § 942.

    Chapter 11 cases, see 11 USCA § 1127(a).

    Chapter 11 subchapter V cases, see 11 USCA § 1193(a).

    Chapter 12 cases, see 11 USCA § 1223.

§ 1324. Confirmation hearing

(a) Except as provided in subsection (b) and after notice, the court shall hold a hearing on confirmation of the plan. A party in interest may object to confirmation of the plan.

(b) The hearing on confirmation of the plan may be held not earlier than 20 days and not later than 45 days after the date of the meeting of creditors under section 341(a), unless the court determines that it would be in the best interests of the creditors and the estate to hold such hearing at an earlier date and there is no objection to such earlier date.

CROSS REFERENCES

Confirmation hearing in—

    Chapter 11 cases, see 11 USCA § 1128.

    Chapter 12 cases, see 11 USCA § 1224.

Duties of United States trustee, see 28 USCA § 586.

§ 1325. Confirmation of plan

(a) Except as provided in subsection (b), the court shall confirm a plan if—

    (1) the plan complies with the provisions of this chapter and with the other applicable provisions of this title;

    (2) any fee, charge, or amount required under chapter 123 of title 28, or by the plan, to be paid before confirmation, has been paid;

    (3) the plan has been proposed in good faith and not by any means forbidden by law;

    (4) the value, as of the effective date of the plan, of property to be distributed under the plan on account of each allowed unsecured claim is not less than the amount that would be paid on such claim if the estate of the debtor were liquidated under chapter 7 of this title on such date;

    (5) with respect to each allowed secured claim provided for by the plan—

        (A) the holder of such claim has accepted the plan;

        (B)(i) the plan provides that—

        (I)   the holder of such claim retain the lien securing such claim until the earlier of—

           (aa) the payment of the underlying debt determined under nonbankruptcy law; or

           (bb) discharge under section 1328; and

        (II) if the case under this chapter is dismissed or converted without completion of the plan, such lien shall also be retained by such holder to the extent recognized by applicable nonbankruptcy law;

    (ii) the value, as of the effective date of the plan, of property to be distributed under the plan on account of such claim is not less than the allowed amount of such claim; and

    (iii) if—

        (I) property to be distributed pursuant to this subsection is in the form of periodic payments, such payments shall be in equal monthly amounts; and

        (II) the holder of the claim is secured by personal property, the amount of such payments shall not be less than an amount sufficient to provide to the holder of such claim adequate protection during the period of the plan; or

    (C) the debtor surrenders the property securing such claim to such holder;

  (6) the debtor will be able to make all payments under the plan and to comply with the plan;

  (7) the action of the debtor in filing the petition was in good faith;

  (8) the debtor has paid all amounts that are required to be paid under a domestic support obligation and that first become payable after the date of the filing of the petition if the debtor is required by a judicial or administrative order, or by statute, to pay such domestic support obligation; and

  (9) the debtor has filed all applicable Federal, State, and local tax returns as required by section 1308.

For purposes of paragraph (5), section 506 shall not apply to a claim described in that paragraph if the creditor has a purchase money security interest securing the debt that is the subject of the claim, the debt was incurred within the 910-day period preceding the date of the filing of the petition, and the collateral for that debt consists of a motor vehicle (as defined in section 30102 of title 49) acquired for the personal use of the debtor, or if collateral for that debt consists of any other thing of value, if the debt was incurred during the 1-year period preceding that filing.

  (b)(1) If the trustee or the holder of an allowed unsecured claim objects to the confirmation of the plan, then the court may not approve the plan unless, as of the effective date of the plan—

    (A) the value of the property to be distributed under the plan on account of such claim is not less than the amount of such claim; or

    (B) the plan provides that all of the debtor's projected disposable income to be received in the applicable commitment period beginning on the date that the first payment is due under the plan will be applied to make payments to unsecured creditors under the plan.

  (2) For purposes of this subsection, the term "disposable income" means current monthly income received by the debtor (other than child support payments, foster care payments, or disability payments for a dependent child made in accordance with applicable nonbankruptcy law to the extent reasonably necessary to be expended for such child) less amounts reasonably necessary to be expended—

(A)(i) for the maintenance or support of the debtor or a dependent of the debtor, or for a domestic support obligation, that first becomes payable after the date the petition is filed; and

(ii) for charitable contributions (that meet the definition of "charitable contribution" under section 548(d)(3)) to a qualified religious or charitable entity or organization (as defined in section 548(d)(4)) in an amount not to exceed 15 percent of gross income of the debtor for the year in which the contributions are made; and

(B) if the debtor is engaged in business, for the payment of expenditures necessary for the continuation, preservation, and operation of such business.

(3) Amounts reasonably necessary to be expended under paragraph (2), other than subparagraph (A)(ii) of paragraph (2), shall be determined in accordance with subparagraphs (A) and (B) of section 707(b)(2), if the debtor has current monthly income, when multiplied by 12, greater than—

(A) in the case of a debtor in a household of 1 person, the median family income of the applicable State for 1 earner;

(B) in the case of a debtor in a household of 2, 3, or 4 individuals, the highest median family income of the applicable State for a family of the same number or fewer individuals; or

(C) in the case of a debtor in a household exceeding 4 individuals, the highest median family income of the applicable State for a family of 4 or fewer individuals, plus $825 per month for each individual in excess of 4.

(4) For purposes of this subsection, the "applicable commitment period"—

(A) subject to subparagraph (B), shall be—

(i) 3 years; or

(ii) not less than 5 years, if the current monthly income of the debtor and the debtor's spouse combined, when multiplied by 12, is not less than—

(I) in the case of a debtor in a household of 1 person, the median family income of the applicable State for 1 earner;

(II) in the case of a debtor in a household of 2, 3, or 4 individuals, the highest median family income of the applicable State for a family of the same number or fewer individuals; or

(III) in the case of a debtor in a household exceeding 4 individuals, the highest median family income of the applicable State for a family of 4 or fewer individuals, plus $825 per month for each individual in excess of 4; and

(B) may be less than 3 or 5 years, whichever is applicable under subparagraph (A), but only if the plan provides for payment in full of all allowed unsecured claims over a shorter period.

(c) After confirmation of a plan, the court may order any entity from whom the debtor receives income to pay all or any part of such income to the trustee.

[*Note from West Advisory Panel.* Pub. L. 116–260 created a temporary § 1325(d), which expired on December 27, 2022, *except* for cases commenced before December 27, 2022. *See* 134 Stat. 2016, 2017. For the text of temporary § 1325(d), *see* Title 11, Chapter 13, Subchapter II, § 1325, Editorial Notes, Amendments, 2020 at http://uscode.house.gov]

CROSS REFERENCES

Confirmation of plan in—

Chapter 9 cases, see 11 USCA § 943.

Chapter 11 cases, see 11 USCA § 1129.

§ 1326. Payments

(a)(1) Unless the court orders otherwise, the debtor shall commence making payments not later than 30 days after the date of the filing of the plan or the order for relief, whichever is earlier, in the amount—

(A) proposed by the plan to the trustee;

(B) scheduled in a lease of personal property directly to the lessor for that portion of the obligation that becomes due after the order for relief, reducing the payments under subparagraph (A) by the amount so paid and providing the trustee with evidence of such payment, including the amount and date of payment; and

(C) that provides adequate protection directly to a creditor holding an allowed claim secured by personal property to the extent the claim is attributable to the purchase of such property by the debtor for that portion of the obligation that becomes due after the order for relief, reducing the payments under subparagraph (A) by the amount so paid and providing the trustee with evidence of such payment, including the amount and date of payment.

(2) A payment made under paragraph (1)(A) shall be retained by the trustee until confirmation or denial of confirmation. If a plan is confirmed, the trustee shall distribute any such payment in accordance with the plan as soon as is practicable. If a plan is not confirmed, the trustee shall return any such payments not previously paid and not yet due and owing to creditors pursuant to paragraph (3) to the debtor, after deducting any unpaid claim allowed under section 503(b).

(3) Subject to section 363, the court may, upon notice and a hearing, modify, increase, or reduce the payments required under this subsection pending confirmation of a plan.

(4) Not later than 60 days after the date of filing of a case under this chapter, a debtor retaining possession of personal property subject to a lease or securing a claim attributable in whole or in part to the purchase price of such property shall provide the lessor or secured creditor reasonable evidence of the maintenance of any required insurance coverage with respect to the use or ownership of such property and continue to do so for so long as the debtor retains possession of such property.

(b) Before or at the time of each payment to creditors under the plan, there shall be paid—

(1) any unpaid claim of the kind specified in section 507(a)(2) of this title;

(2) if a standing trustee appointed under section 586(b) of title 28 is serving in the case, the percentage fee fixed for such standing trustee under section 586(e)(1)(B) of title 28; and

(3) if a chapter 7 trustee has been allowed compensation due to the conversion or dismissal of the debtor's prior case pursuant to section 707(b), and some portion of that compensation remains unpaid in a case converted to this chapter or in the case dismissed under section 707(b) and refiled under this chapter, the amount of any such unpaid compensation, which shall be paid monthly—

(A) by prorating such amount over the remaining duration of the plan; and

(B) by monthly payments not to exceed the greater of—

(i) $25; or

(ii) the amount payable to unsecured nonpriority creditors, as provided by the plan, multiplied by 5 percent, and the result divided by the number of months in the plan.

(c) Except as otherwise provided in the plan or in the order confirming the plan, the trustee shall make payments to creditors under the plan.

(d) Notwithstanding any other provision of this title—

(1) compensation referred to in subsection (b)(3) is payable and may be collected by the trustee under that paragraph, even if such amount has been discharged in a prior case under this title; and

(2) such compensation is payable in a case under this chapter only to the extent permitted by subsection (b)(3).

CROSS REFERENCES

Conversion or dismissal for failure to commence making timely payments under this section, see 11 USCA § 1307(c)(4).

Duty of trustee to ensure that debtor commences making timely payments under this section, see 11 USCA § 1302(b)(5).

Payment stopped on checks remaining unpaid 90 days after final distribution, see 11 USCA § 347.

§ 1327. Effect of confirmation

(a) The provisions of a confirmed plan bind the debtor and each creditor, whether or not the claim of such creditor is provided for by the plan, and whether or not such creditor has objected to, has accepted, or has rejected the plan.

(b) Except as otherwise provided in the plan or the order confirming the plan, the confirmation of a plan vests all of the property of the estate in the debtor.

(c) Except as otherwise provided in the plan or in the order confirming the plan, the property vesting in the debtor under subsection (b) of this section is free and clear of any claim or interest of any creditor provided for by the plan.

CROSS REFERENCES

Effect of confirmation, see Fed. R. Bankr. P. 3015(g).

Effect of confirmation in—

Chapter 9 cases, see 11 USCA § 944.

Chapter 11 cases, see 11 USCA § 1141.

Chapter 12 cases, see 11 USCA § 1227.

§ 1328. Discharge

(a) Subject to subsection (d), as soon as practicable after completion by the debtor of all payments under the plan, and in the case of a debtor who is required by a judicial or administrative order, or by statute, to pay a domestic support obligation, after such debtor certifies that all amounts payable under such order or such statute that are due on or before the date of the certification (including amounts due before the petition was filed, but only to the extent provided for by the plan) have been paid, unless the court approves a written waiver of discharge executed by the debtor after the order for relief under this chapter, the court shall grant the debtor a discharge of all debts provided for by the plan or disallowed under section 502 of this title, except any debt—

(1) provided for under section 1322(b)(5);

(2) of the kind specified in section 507(a)(8)(C) or in paragraph (1)(B), (1)(C), (2), (3), (4), (5), (8), or (9) of section 523(a);

(3) for restitution, or a criminal fine, included in a sentence on the debtor's conviction of a crime; or

(4) for restitution, or damages, awarded in a civil action against the debtor as a result of willful or malicious injury by the debtor that caused personal injury to an individual or the death of an individual.

(b) Subject to subsection (d), at any time after the confirmation of the plan and after notice and a hearing, the court may grant a discharge to a debtor that has not completed payments under the plan only if—

(1) the debtor's failure to complete such payments is due to circumstances for which the debtor should not justly be held accountable;

(2) the value, as of the effective date of the plan, of property actually distributed under the plan on account of each allowed unsecured claim is not less than the amount that would have been paid on such claim if the estate of the debtor had been liquidated under chapter 7 of this title on such date; and

(3) modification of the plan under section 1329 of this title is not practicable.

(c) A discharge granted under subsection (b) of this section discharges the debtor from all unsecured debts provided for by the plan or disallowed under section 502 of this title, except any debt—

(1) provided for under section 1322(b)(5) of this title; or

(2) of a kind specified in section 523(a) of this title.

(d) Notwithstanding any other provision of this section, a discharge granted under this section does not discharge the debtor from any debt based on an allowed claim filed under section 1305(a)(2) of this title if prior approval by the trustee of the debtor's incurring such debt was practicable and was not obtained.

(e) On request of a party in interest before one year after a discharge under this section is granted, and after notice and a hearing, the court may revoke such discharge only if—

(1) such discharge was obtained by the debtor through fraud; and

(2) the requesting party did not know of such fraud until after such discharge was granted.

(f) Notwithstanding subsections (a) and (b), the court shall not grant a discharge of all debts provided for in the plan or disallowed under section 502, if the debtor has received a discharge—

(1) in a case filed under chapter 7, 11, or 12 of this title during the 4-year period preceding the date of the order for relief under this chapter, or

(2) in a case filed under chapter 13 of this title during the 2-year period preceding the date of such order.

(g)(1) The court shall not grant a discharge under this section to a debtor unless after filing a petition the debtor has completed an instructional course concerning personal financial management described in section 111.

(2) Paragraph (1) shall not apply with respect to a debtor who is a person described in section 109(h)(4) or who resides in a district for which the United States trustee (or the bankruptcy administrator, if any) determines that the approved instructional courses are not adequate to service the additional individuals who would otherwise be required to complete such instructional course by reason of the requirements of paragraph (1).

(3) The United States trustee (or the bankruptcy administrator, if any) who makes a determination described in paragraph (2) shall review such determination not later than 1 year after the date of such determination, and not less frequently than annually thereafter.

(h) The court may not grant a discharge under this chapter unless the court after notice and a hearing held not more than 10 days before the date of the entry of the order granting the discharge finds that there is no reasonable cause to believe that—

    (1) section 522(q)(1) may be applicable to the debtor; and

    (2) there is pending any proceeding in which the debtor may be found guilty of a felony of the kind described in section 522(q)(1)(A) or liable for a debt of the kind described in section 522(q)(1)(B).

CROSS REFERENCES

Chapter 13 discharge, see Director's Bankruptcy Form 3180W.

Chapter 13 hardship discharge, see Director's Bankruptcy Form 3180WH.

Discharge in—

    Chapter 7 cases, see 11 USCA § 727.

    Chapter 11 cases, see 11 USCA § 1141(d).

    Chapter 11 subchapter V cases, see 11 USCA § 1192.

    Chapter 12 cases, see 11 USCA § 1228.

Effect of discharge, see 11 USCA § 524.

Exceptions to discharge, see 11 USCA § 523.

Nondischargeability of capital improvement loans for multifamily housing projects in proceedings under this section, see 12 USCA § 1715z–1a.

§ 1329. Modification of plan after confirmation

(a) At any time after confirmation of the plan but before the completion of payments under such plan, the plan may be modified, upon request of the debtor, the trustee, or the holder of an allowed unsecured claim, to—

    (1) increase or reduce the amount of payments on claims of a particular class provided for by the plan;

    (2) extend or reduce the time for such payments;

    (3) alter the amount of the distribution to a creditor whose claim is provided for by the plan to the extent necessary to take account of any payment of such claim other than under the plan; or

    (4) reduce amounts to be paid under the plan by the actual amount expended by the debtor to purchase health insurance for the debtor (and for any dependent of the debtor if such dependent does not otherwise have health insurance coverage) if the debtor documents the cost of such insurance and demonstrates that—

        (A) such expenses are reasonable and necessary;

        (B)(i) if the debtor previously paid for health insurance, the amount is not materially larger than the cost the debtor previously paid or the cost necessary to maintain the lapsed policy; or

        (ii) if the debtor did not have health insurance, the amount is not materially larger than the reasonable cost that would be incurred by a debtor who purchases health insurance, who has similar income, expenses, age, and health status, and who lives in the same geographical location with the same number of dependents who do not otherwise have health insurance coverage; and

      (C) the amount is not otherwise allowed for purposes of determining disposable income under section 1325(b) of this title;

and upon request of any party in interest, files proof that a health insurance policy was purchased.

(b)(1)   Sections 1322(a), 1322(b), and 1323(c) of this title and the requirements of section 1325(a) of this title apply to any modification under subsection (a) of this section.

(2)   The plan as modified becomes the plan unless, after notice and a hearing, such modification is disapproved.

(c)   A plan modified under this section may not provide for payments over a period that expires after the applicable commitment period under section 1325(b)(1)(B) after the time that the first payment under the original confirmed plan was due, unless the court, for cause, approves a longer period, but the court may not approve a period that expires after five years after such time.

CROSS REFERENCES

Conversion or dismissal upon denial of confirmation and denial of request for additional time to file a modified plan, see 11 USCA § 1307(c)(5).

Duties of United States trustee, see 28 USCA § 586.

Modification of Chapter 13 plan after confirmation, see Fed. R. Bankr. P. 3015(h).

Modification of plan after confirmation in—

    Chapter 11 cases, see 11 USCA § 1127(b), (e), (f).

    Chapter 11 subchapter V cases, see 11 USCA § 1193(b)–(d).

    Chapter 12 cases, see 11 USCA § 1229.

Order fixing time to object to proposed modification of confirmed Chapter 13 plan, see Director's Bankruptcy Form 2310B.

§ 1330. Revocation of an order of confirmation

(a)   On request of a party in interest at any time within 180 days after the date of the entry of an order of confirmation under section 1325 of this title, and after notice and a hearing, the court may revoke such order if such order was procured by fraud.

(b)   If the court revokes an order of confirmation under subsection (a) of this section, the court shall dispose of the case under section 1307 of this title, unless, within the time fixed by the court, the debtor proposes and the court confirms a modification of the plan under section 1329 of this title.

CROSS REFERENCES

Conversion or dismissal upon revocation of order of confirmation and denial confirmation of a modified plan, see 11 USCA § 1307(c)(7).

Revocation of order of confirmation in—

    Chapter 11 cases, see 11 USCA § 1144.

    Chapter 12 cases, see 11 USCA § 1230.

CHAPTER 15—ANCILLARY AND OTHER CROSS-BORDER CASES

§ 1501. Purpose and scope of application

(a) The purpose of this chapter is to incorporate the Model Law on Cross-Border Insolvency so as to provide effective mechanisms for dealing with cases of cross-border insolvency with the objectives of—

  (1) cooperation between—

  (A) courts of the United States, United States trustees, trustees, examiners, debtors, and debtors in possession; and

  (B) the courts and other competent authorities of foreign countries involved in cross-border insolvency cases;

  (2) greater legal certainty for trade and investment;

  (3) fair and efficient administration of cross-border insolvencies that protects the interests of all creditors, and other interested entities, including the debtor;

  (4) protection and maximization of the value of the debtor's assets; and

  (5) facilitation of the rescue of financially troubled businesses, thereby protecting investment and preserving employment.

(b) This chapter applies where—

  (1) assistance is sought in the United States by a foreign court or a foreign representative in connection with a foreign proceeding;

  (2) assistance is sought in a foreign country in connection with a case under this title;

  (3) a foreign proceeding and a case under this title with respect to the same debtor are pending concurrently; or

  (4) creditors or other interested persons in a foreign country have an interest in requesting the commencement of, or participating in, a case or proceeding under this title.

(c) This chapter does not apply to—

  (1) a proceeding concerning an entity, other than a foreign insurance company, identified by exclusion in section 109(b);

  (2) an individual, or to an individual and such individual's spouse, who have debts within the limits specified in section 109(e) and who are citizens of the United States or aliens lawfully admitted for permanent residence in the United States; or

  (3) an entity subject to a proceeding under the Securities Investor Protection Act of 1970, a stockbroker subject to subchapter III of chapter 7 of this title, or a commodity broker subject to subchapter IV of chapter 7 of this title.

(d) The court may not grant relief under this chapter with respect to any deposit, escrow, trust fund, or other security required or permitted under any applicable State insurance law or regulation for the benefit of claim holders in the United States.

REFERENCES IN TEXT

The Securities Investor Protection Act of 1970, referred to in subsec. (c)(3), is Pub. L. 91–598, Dec. 30, 1970, 84 Stat. 1636, also known as SIPA, which is classified principally to chapter 2B–1 of Title 15, 15 U.S.C.A. § 78aaa et seq.

SUBCHAPTER I—GENERAL PROVISIONS

§ 1502. Definitions

For the purposes of this chapter, the term—

(1)   "debtor" means an entity that is the subject of a foreign proceeding;

(2)   "establishment" means any place of operations where the debtor carries out a nontransitory economic activity;

(3)   "foreign court" means a judicial or other authority competent to control or supervise a foreign proceeding;

(4)   "foreign main proceeding" means a foreign proceeding pending in the country where the debtor has the center of its main interests;

(5)   "foreign nonmain proceeding" means a foreign proceeding, other than a foreign main proceeding, pending in a country where the debtor has an establishment;

(6)   "trustee" includes a trustee, a debtor in possession in a case under any chapter of this title, or a debtor under chapter 9 of this title;

(7)   "recognition" means the entry of an order granting recognition of a foreign main proceeding or foreign nonmain proceeding under this chapter; and

(8)   "within the territorial jurisdiction of the United States", when used with reference to property of a debtor, refers to tangible property located within the territory of the United States and intangible property deemed under applicable nonbankruptcy law to be located within that territory, including any property subject to attachment or garnishment that may properly be seized or garnished by an action in a Federal or State court in the United States.

§ 1503. International obligations of the United States

To the extent that this chapter conflicts with an obligation of the United States arising out of any treaty or other form of agreement to which it is a party with one or more other countries, the requirements of the treaty or agreement prevail.

§ 1504. Commencement of ancillary case

A case under this chapter is commenced by the filing of a petition for recognition of a foreign proceeding under section 1515.

§ 1505. Authorization to act in a foreign country

A trustee or another entity (including an examiner) may be authorized by the court to act in a foreign country on behalf of an estate created under section 541. An entity authorized to act under this section may act in any way permitted by the applicable foreign law.

§ 1506. Public policy exception

Nothing in this chapter prevents the court from refusing to take an action governed by this chapter if the action would be manifestly contrary to the public policy of the United States.

§ 1507. Additional assistance

(a)   Subject to the specific limitations stated elsewhere in this chapter the court, if recognition is granted, may provide additional assistance to a foreign representative under this title or under other laws of the United States.

(b)   In determining whether to provide additional assistance under this title or under other laws of the United States, the court shall consider whether such additional assistance, consistent with the principles of comity, will reasonably assure—

(1)   just treatment of all holders of claims against or interests in the debtor's property;

(2) protection of claim holders in the United States against prejudice and inconvenience in the processing of claims in such foreign proceeding;

(3) prevention of preferential or fraudulent dispositions of property of the debtor;

(4) distribution of proceeds of the debtor's property substantially in accordance with the order prescribed by this title; and

(5) if appropriate, the provision of an opportunity for a fresh start for the individual that such foreign proceeding concerns.

§ 1508. Interpretation

In interpreting this chapter, the court shall consider its international origin, and the need to promote an application of this chapter that is consistent with the application of similar statutes adopted by foreign jurisdictions.

SUBCHAPTER II—ACCESS OF FOREIGN REPRESENTATIVES AND CREDITORS TO THE COURT

§ 1509. Right of direct access

(a) A foreign representative may commence a case under section 1504 by filing directly with the court a petition for recognition of a foreign proceeding under section 1515.

(b) If the court grants recognition under section 1517, and subject to any limitations that the court may impose consistent with the policy of this chapter—

(1) the foreign representative has the capacity to sue and be sued in a court in the United States;

(2) the foreign representative may apply directly to a court in the United States for appropriate relief in that court; and

(3) a court in the United States shall grant comity or cooperation to the foreign representative.

(c) A request for comity or cooperation by a foreign representative in a court in the United States other than the court which granted recognition shall be accompanied by a certified copy of an order granting recognition under section 1517.

(d) If the court denies recognition under this chapter, the court may issue any appropriate order necessary to prevent the foreign representative from obtaining comity or cooperation from courts in the United States.

(e) Whether or not the court grants recognition, and subject to sections 306 and 1510, a foreign representative is subject to applicable nonbankruptcy law.

(f) Notwithstanding any other provision of this section, the failure of a foreign representative to commence a case or to obtain recognition under this chapter does not affect any right the foreign representative may have to sue in a court in the United States to collect or recover a claim which is the property of the debtor.

§ 1510. Limited jurisdiction

The sole fact that a foreign representative files a petition under section 1515 does not subject the foreign representative to the jurisdiction of any court in the United States for any other purpose.

§ 1511. Commencement of case under section 301, 302, or 303

(a) Upon recognition, a foreign representative may commence—

(1) an involuntary case under section 303; or

(2) a voluntary case under section 301 or 302, if the foreign proceeding is a foreign main proceeding.

(b) The petition commencing a case under subsection (a) must be accompanied by a certified copy of an order granting recognition. The court where the petition for recognition has been filed must be advised of the foreign representative's intent to commence a case under subsection (a) prior to such commencement.

§ 1512. Participation of a foreign representative in a case under this title

Upon recognition of a foreign proceeding, the foreign representative in the recognized proceeding is entitled to participate as a party in interest in a case regarding the debtor under this title.

§ 1513. Access of foreign creditors to a case under this title

(a) Foreign creditors have the same rights regarding the commencement of, and participation in, a case under this title as domestic creditors.

(b)(1) Subsection (a) does not change or codify present law as to the priority of claims under section 507 or 726, except that the claim of a foreign creditor under those sections shall not be given a lower priority than that of general unsecured claims without priority solely because the holder of such claim is a foreign creditor.

(2)(A) Subsection (a) and paragraph (1) do not change or codify present law as to the allowability of foreign revenue claims or other foreign public law claims in a proceeding under this title.

(B) Allowance and priority as to a foreign tax claim or other foreign public law claim shall be governed by any applicable tax treaty of the United States, under the conditions and circumstances specified therein.

§ 1514. Notification to foreign creditors concerning a case under this title

(a) Whenever in a case under this title notice is to be given to creditors generally or to any class or category of creditors, such notice shall also be given to the known creditors generally, or to creditors in the notified class or category, that do not have addresses in the United States. The court may order that appropriate steps be taken with a view to notifying any creditor whose address is not yet known.

(b) Such notification to creditors with foreign addresses described in subsection (a) shall be given individually, unless the court considers that, under the circumstances, some other form of notification would be more appropriate. No letter or other formality is required.

(c) When a notification of commencement of a case is to be given to foreign creditors, such notification shall—

(1) indicate the time period for filing proofs of claim and specify the place for filing such proofs of claim;

(2) indicate whether secured creditors need to file proofs of claim; and

(3) contain any other information required to be included in such notification to creditors under this title and the orders of the court.

(d) Any rule of procedure or order of the court as to notice or the filing of a proof of claim shall provide such additional time to creditors with foreign addresses as is reasonable under the circumstances.

SUBCHAPTER III—RECOGNITION OF A FOREIGN PROCEEDING AND RELIEF

§ 1515. Application for recognition

(a) A foreign representative applies to the court for recognition of a foreign proceeding in which the foreign representative has been appointed by filing a petition for recognition.

(b) A petition for recognition shall be accompanied by—

(1) a certified copy of the decision commencing such foreign proceeding and appointing the foreign representative;

(2) a certificate from the foreign court affirming the existence of such foreign proceeding and of the appointment of the foreign representative; or

(3) in the absence of evidence referred to in paragraphs (1) and (2), any other evidence acceptable to the court of the existence of such foreign proceeding and of the appointment of the foreign representative.

(c) A petition for recognition shall also be accompanied by a statement identifying all foreign proceedings with respect to the debtor that are known to the foreign representative.

(d) The documents referred to in paragraphs (1) and (2) of subsection (b) shall be translated into English. The court may require a translation into English of additional documents.

§ 1516. Presumptions concerning recognition

(a) If the decision or certificate referred to in section 1515(b) indicates that the foreign proceeding is a foreign proceeding and that the person or body is a foreign representative, the court is entitled to so presume.

(b) The court is entitled to presume that documents submitted in support of the petition for recognition are authentic, whether or not they have been legalized.

(c) In the absence of evidence to the contrary, the debtor's registered office, or habitual residence in the case of an individual, is presumed to be the center of the debtor's main interests.

§ 1517. Order granting recognition

(a) Subject to section 1506, after notice and a hearing, an order recognizing a foreign proceeding shall be entered if—

(1) such foreign proceeding for which recognition is sought is a foreign main proceeding or foreign nonmain proceeding within the meaning of section 1502;

(2) the foreign representative applying for recognition is a person or body; and

(3) the petition meets the requirements of section 1515.

(b) Such foreign proceeding shall be recognized—

(1) as a foreign main proceeding if it is pending in the country where the debtor has the center of its main interests; or

(2) as a foreign nonmain proceeding if the debtor has an establishment within the meaning of section 1502 in the foreign country where the proceeding is pending.

(c) A petition for recognition of a foreign proceeding shall be decided upon at the earliest possible time. Entry of an order recognizing a foreign proceeding constitutes recognition under this chapter.

(d) The provisions of this subchapter do not prevent modification or termination of recognition if it is shown that the grounds for granting it were fully or partially lacking or have ceased to exist, but in considering such action the court shall give due weight to possible prejudice to parties that have relied upon the order granting recognition. A case under this chapter may be closed in the manner prescribed under section 350.

§ 1518. Subsequent information

From the time of filing the petition for recognition of a foreign proceeding, the foreign representative shall file with the court promptly a notice of change of status concerning—

> **(1)** any substantial change in the status of such foreign proceeding or the status of the foreign representative's appointment; and

> **(2)** any other foreign proceeding regarding the debtor that becomes known to the foreign representative.

§ 1519. Relief that may be granted upon filing petition for recognition

(a) From the time of filing a petition for recognition until the court rules on the petition, the court may, at the request of the foreign representative, where relief is urgently needed to protect the assets of the debtor or the interests of the creditors, grant relief of a provisional nature, including—

> **(1)** staying execution against the debtor's assets;

> **(2)** entrusting the administration or realization of all or part of the debtor's assets located in the United States to the foreign representative or another person authorized by the court, including an examiner, in order to protect and preserve the value of assets that, by their nature or because of other circumstances, are perishable, susceptible to devaluation or otherwise in jeopardy; and

> **(3)** any relief referred to in paragraph (3), (4), or (7) of section 1521(a).

(b) Unless extended under section 1521(a)(6), the relief granted under this section terminates when the petition for recognition is granted.

(c) It is a ground for denial of relief under this section that such relief would interfere with the administration of a foreign main proceeding.

(d) The court may not enjoin a police or regulatory act of a governmental unit, including a criminal action or proceeding, under this section.

(e) The standards, procedures, and limitations applicable to an injunction shall apply to relief under this section.

(f) The exercise of rights not subject to the stay arising under section 362(a) pursuant to paragraph (6), (7), (17), or (27) of section 362(b) or pursuant to section 362(*o*) shall not be stayed by any order of a court or administrative agency in any proceeding under this chapter.

§ 1520. Effects of recognition of a foreign main proceeding

(a) Upon recognition of a foreign proceeding that is a foreign main proceeding—

> **(1)** sections 361 and 362 apply with respect to the debtor and the property of the debtor that is within the territorial jurisdiction of the United States;

> **(2)** sections 363, 549, and 552 apply to a transfer of an interest of the debtor in property that is within the territorial jurisdiction of the United States to the same extent that the sections would apply to property of an estate;

> **(3)** unless the court orders otherwise, the foreign representative may operate the debtor's business and may exercise the rights and powers of a trustee under and to the extent provided by sections 363 and 552; and

(4)   section 552 applies to property of the debtor that is within the territorial jurisdiction of the United States.

(b)   Subsection (a) does not affect the right to commence an individual action or proceeding in a foreign country to the extent necessary to preserve a claim against the debtor.

(c)   Subsection (a) does not affect the right of a foreign representative or an entity to file a petition commencing a case under this title or the right of any party to file claims or take other proper actions in such a case.

§ 1521. Relief that may be granted upon recognition

(a)   Upon recognition of a foreign proceeding, whether main or nonmain, where necessary to effectuate the purpose of this chapter and to protect the assets of the debtor or the interests of the creditors, the court may, at the request of the foreign representative, grant any appropriate relief, including—

(1)   staying the commencement or continuation of an individual action or proceeding concerning the debtor's assets, rights, obligations or liabilities to the extent they have not been stayed under section 1520(a);

(2)   staying execution against the debtor's assets to the extent it has not been stayed under section 1520(a);

(3)   suspending the right to transfer, encumber or otherwise dispose of any assets of the debtor to the extent this right has not been suspended under section 1520(a);

(4)   providing for the examination of witnesses, the taking of evidence or the delivery of information concerning the debtor's assets, affairs, rights, obligations or liabilities;

(5)   entrusting the administration or realization of all or part of the debtor's assets within the territorial jurisdiction of the United States to the foreign representative or another person, including an examiner, authorized by the court;

(6)   extending relief granted under section 1519(a); and

(7)   granting any additional relief that may be available to a trustee, except for relief available under sections 522, 544, 545, 547, 548, 550, and 724(a).

(b)   Upon recognition of a foreign proceeding, whether main or nonmain, the court may, at the request of the foreign representative, entrust the distribution of all or part of the debtor's assets located in the United States to the foreign representative or another person, including an examiner, authorized by the court, provided that the court is satisfied that the interests of creditors in the United States are sufficiently protected.

(c)   In granting relief under this section to a representative of a foreign nonmain proceeding, the court must be satisfied that the relief relates to assets that, under the law of the United States, should be administered in the foreign nonmain proceeding or concerns information required in that proceeding.

(d)   The court may not enjoin a police or regulatory act of a governmental unit, including a criminal action or proceeding, under this section.

(e)   The standards, procedures, and limitations applicable to an injunction shall apply to relief under paragraphs (1), (2), (3), and (6) of subsection (a).

(f)   The exercise of rights not subject to the stay arising under section 362(a) pursuant to paragraph (6), (7), (17), or (27) of section 362(b) or pursuant to section 362(o) shall not be stayed by any order of a court or administrative agency in any proceeding under this chapter.

§ 1522. Protection of creditors and other interested persons

(a) The court may grant relief under section 1519 or 1521, or may modify or terminate relief under subsection (c), only if the interests of the creditors and other interested entities, including the debtor, are sufficiently protected.

(b) The court may subject relief granted under section 1519 or 1521, or the operation of the debtor's business under section 1520(a)(3), to conditions it considers appropriate, including the giving of security or the filing of a bond.

(c) The court may, at the request of the foreign representative or an entity affected by relief granted under section 1519 or 1521, or at its own motion, modify or terminate such relief.

(d) Section 1104(d) shall apply to the appointment of an examiner under this chapter. Any examiner shall comply with the qualification requirements imposed on a trustee by section 322.

§ 1523. Actions to avoid acts detrimental to creditors

(a) Upon recognition of a foreign proceeding, the foreign representative has standing in a case concerning the debtor pending under another chapter of this title to initiate actions under sections 522, 544, 545, 547, 548, 550, 553, and 724(a).

(b) When a foreign proceeding is a foreign nonmain proceeding, the court must be satisfied that an action under subsection (a) relates to assets that, under United States law, should be administered in the foreign nonmain proceeding.

§ 1524. Intervention by a foreign representative

Upon recognition of a foreign proceeding, the foreign representative may intervene in any proceedings in a State or Federal court in the United States in which the debtor is a party.

SUBCHAPTER IV—COOPERATION WITH FOREIGN
COURTS AND FOREIGN REPRESENTATIVES

§ 1525. Cooperation and direct communication between the court and foreign courts or foreign representatives

(a) Consistent with section 1501, the court shall cooperate to the maximum extent possible with a foreign court or a foreign representative, either directly or through the trustee.

(b) The court is entitled to communicate directly with, or to request information or assistance directly from, a foreign court or a foreign representative, subject to the rights of a party in interest to notice and participation.

§ 1526. Cooperation and direct communication between the trustee and foreign courts or foreign representatives

(a) Consistent with section 1501, the trustee or other person, including an examiner, authorized by the court, shall, subject to the supervision of the court, cooperate to the maximum extent possible with a foreign court or a foreign representative.

(b) The trustee or other person, including an examiner, authorized by the court is entitled, subject to the supervision of the court, to communicate directly with a foreign court or a foreign representative.

§ 1527. Forms of cooperation

Cooperation referred to in sections 1525 and 1526 may be implemented by any appropriate means, including—

(1) appointment of a person or body, including an examiner, to act at the direction of the court;

(2) communication of information by any means considered appropriate by the court;

(3) coordination of the administration and supervision of the debtor's assets and affairs;

(4) approval or implementation of agreements concerning the coordination of proceedings; and

(5) coordination of concurrent proceedings regarding the same debtor.

SUBCHAPTER V—CONCURRENT PROCEEDINGS

§ 1528. Commencement of a case under this title after recognition of a foreign main proceeding

After recognition of a foreign main proceeding, a case under another chapter of this title may be commenced only if the debtor has assets in the United States. The effects of such case shall be restricted to the assets of the debtor that are within the territorial jurisdiction of the United States and, to the extent necessary to implement cooperation and coordination under sections 1525, 1526, and 1527, to other assets of the debtor that are within the jurisdiction of the court under sections 541(a) of this title, and 1334(e) of title 28, to the extent that such other assets are not subject to the jurisdiction and control of a foreign proceeding that has been recognized under this chapter.

§ 1529. Coordination of a case under this title and a foreign proceeding

If a foreign proceeding and a case under another chapter of this title are pending concurrently regarding the same debtor, the court shall seek cooperation and coordination under sections 1525, 1526, and 1527, and the following shall apply:

(1) If the case in the United States is pending at the time the petition for recognition of such foreign proceeding is filed—

(A) any relief granted under section 1519 or 1521 must be consistent with the relief granted in the case in the United States; and

(B) section 1520 does not apply even if such foreign proceeding is recognized as a foreign main proceeding.

(2) If a case in the United States under this title commences after recognition, or after the date of the filing of the petition for recognition, of such foreign proceeding—

(A) any relief in effect under section 1519 or 1521 shall be reviewed by the court and shall be modified or terminated if inconsistent with the case in the United States; and

(B) if such foreign proceeding is a foreign main proceeding, the stay and suspension referred to in section 1520(a) shall be modified or terminated if inconsistent with the relief granted in the case in the United States.

(3) In granting, extending, or modifying relief granted to a representative of a foreign nonmain proceeding, the court must be satisfied that the relief relates to assets that, under the laws of the United States, should be administered in the foreign nonmain proceeding or concerns information required in that proceeding.

(4) In achieving cooperation and coordination under sections 1528 and 1529, the court may grant any of the relief authorized under section 305.

§ 1530. Coordination of more than 1 foreign proceeding

In matters referred to in section 1501, with respect to more than 1 foreign proceeding regarding the debtor, the court shall seek cooperation and coordination under sections 1525, 1526, and 1527, and the following shall apply:

    (1) Any relief granted under section 1519 or 1521 to a representative of a foreign nonmain proceeding after recognition of a foreign main proceeding must be consistent with the foreign main proceeding.

    (2) If a foreign main proceeding is recognized after recognition, or after the filing of a petition for recognition, of a foreign nonmain proceeding, any relief in effect under section 1519 or 1521 shall be reviewed by the court and shall be modified or terminated if inconsistent with the foreign main proceeding.

    (3) If, after recognition of a foreign nonmain proceeding, another foreign nonmain proceeding is recognized, the court shall grant, modify, or terminate relief for the purpose of facilitating coordination of the proceedings.

§ 1531. Presumption of insolvency based on recognition of a foreign main proceeding

In the absence of evidence to the contrary, recognition of a foreign main proceeding is, for the purpose of commencing a proceeding under section 303, proof that the debtor is generally not paying its debts as such debts become due.

§ 1532. Rule of payment in concurrent proceedings

Without prejudice to secured claims or rights in rem, a creditor who has received payment with respect to its claim in a foreign proceeding pursuant to a law relating to insolvency may not receive a payment for the same claim in a case under any other chapter of this title regarding the debtor, so long as the payment to other creditors of the same class is proportionately less than the payment the creditor has already received.

RELATED PROVISIONS
OF
U.S. CODE TITLES 18 AND 28

TITLE 18—CRIMES AND CRIMINAL PROCEDURE

PART I—CRIMES

Chapter 9—Bankruptcy

Chapter 47—Fraud and False Statements

Chapter 73—Obstruction of Justice

PART II—CRIMINAL PROCEDURE

Chapter 203—Arrest and Commitment

Chapter 213—Limitations

PART V—IMMUNITY OF WITNESSES

Chapter 601—Immunity of Witnesses

TITLE 28—JUDICIARY AND JUDICIAL PROCEDURE

PART I—ORGANIZATION OF COURTS

Chapter 6—Bankruptcy Judges

RELATED PROVISIONS

Chapter 21—General Provisions Applicable to Courts and Judges

PART II—DEPARTMENT OF JUSTICE

Chapter 39—United States Trustees

PART III—COURT OFFICERS AND EMPLOYEES

Chapter 41—Administrative Office of United States Courts

Chapter 44—Alternative Dispute Resolution

Chapter 57—General Provisions Applicable to Court Officers and Employees

PART IV—JURISDICTION AND VENUE

Chapter 83—Courts of Appeals

U.S. CODE TITLES

Chapter 85—District Courts; Jurisdiction

Chapter 87—District Courts; Venue

Chapter 89—District Courts; Removal of Cases from State Courts

PART V—PROCEDURE

Chapter 123—Fees and Costs

Chapter 131—Rules of Courts

TITLE 18

CRIMES AND CRIMINAL PROCEDURE

Current through June 30, 2023; P.L.118–7

For the enactment history of a statutory section, consult the notes following the statutory section at *http://uscode.house.gov*

PART I—CRIMES

Chapter 9—Bankruptcy

§ 151. Definition

As used in this chapter, the term "debtor" means a debtor concerning whom a petition has been filed under Title 11.

§ 152. Concealment of assets; false oaths and claims; bribery

A person who—

(1)   knowingly and fraudulently conceals from a custodian, trustee, marshal, or other officer of the court charged with the control or custody of property, or, in connection with a case under title 11, from creditors or the United States Trustee, any property belonging to the estate of a debtor;

(2)   knowingly and fraudulently makes a false oath or account in or in relation to any case under title 11;

(3)   knowingly and fraudulently makes a false declaration, certificate, verification, or statement under penalty of perjury as permitted under section 1746 of title 28, in or in relation to any case under title 11;

(4)   knowingly and fraudulently presents any false claim for proof against the estate of a debtor, or uses any such claim in any case under title 11, in a personal capacity or as or through an agent, proxy, or attorney;

(5)   knowingly and fraudulently receives any material amount of property from a debtor after the filing of a case under title 11, with intent to defeat the provisions of title 11;

(6)   knowingly and fraudulently gives, offers, receives, or attempts to obtain any money or property, remuneration, compensation, reward, advantage, or promise thereof for acting or forbearing to act in any case under title 11;

(7)   in a personal capacity or as an agent or officer of any person or corporation, in contemplation of a case under title 11 by or against the person or any other person or corporation, or with intent to defeat the provisions of title 11, knowingly and fraudulently transfers or conceals any of his property or the property of such other person or corporation;

(8)   after the filing of a case under title 11 or in contemplation thereof, knowingly and fraudulently conceals, destroys, mutilates, falsifies, or makes a false entry in any recorded information (including books, documents, records, and papers) relating to the property or financial affairs of a debtor; or

(9)   after the filing of a case under title 11, knowingly and fraudulently withholds from a custodian, trustee, marshal, or other officer of the court or a United States Trustee entitled to its

possession, any recorded information (including books, documents, records, and papers) relating to the property or financial affairs of a debtor,

shall be fined under this title, imprisoned not more than 5 years, or both.

CROSS REFERENCES

Bankruptcy investigations; duties of United States attorney, see 18 USCA § 3057.

Concealment of bankrupt's assets, see 18 USCA § 3284.

Discharges, refusal to grant when offense committed under this section, see 11 USCA § 727.

§ 153. Embezzlement against estate

(a) Offense.—A person described in subsection (b) who knowingly and fraudulently appropriates to the person's own use, embezzles, spends, or transfers any property or secretes or destroys any document belonging to the estate of a debtor shall be fined under this title, imprisoned not more than 5 years, or both.

(b) Person to whom section applies.—A person described in this subsection is one who has access to property or documents belonging to an estate by virtue of the person's participation in the administration of the estate as a trustee, custodian, marshal, attorney, or other officer of the court or as an agent, employee, or other person engaged by such an officer to perform a service with respect to the estate.

CROSS REFERENCES

Debts of bankrupt created by fraud, embezzlement, misappropriation or defalcation while acting as an officer or in any fiduciary capacity as not affected by a discharge, see 11 USCA § 523.

Embezzlement by court officers, generally, see 18 USCA § 645.

§ 154. Adverse interest and conduct of officers

A person who, being a custodian, trustee, marshal, or other officer of the court—

    (1) knowingly purchases, directly or indirectly, any property of the estate of which the person is such an officer in a case under title 11;

    (2) knowingly refuses to permit a reasonable opportunity for the inspection by parties in interest of the documents and accounts relating to the affairs of estates in the person's charge by parties when directed by the court to do so; or

    (3) knowingly refuses to permit a reasonable opportunity for the inspection by the United States Trustee of the documents and accounts relating to the affairs of an estate in the person's charge,

shall be fined under this title and shall forfeit the person's office, which shall thereupon become vacant.

§ 155. Fee agreements in cases under title 11 and receiverships

Whoever, being a party in interest, whether as a debtor, creditor, receiver, trustee or representative of any of them, or attorney for any such party in interest, in any receivership or case under title 11 in any United States court or under its supervision, knowingly and fraudulently enters into any agreement, express or implied, with another such party in interest or attorney for another such party in interest, for the purpose of fixing the fees or other compensation to be paid to any party in interest or to any attorney for any party in interest for services rendered in connection therewith, from the assets of the estate, shall be fined under this title or imprisoned not more than one year, or both.

§ 156. Knowing disregard of bankruptcy law or rule

(a) Definitions.—In this section—

(1) the term "bankruptcy petition preparer" means a person, other than the debtor's attorney or an employee of such an attorney, who prepares for compensation a document for filing; and

(2) the term "document for filing" means a petition or any other document prepared for filing by a debtor in a United States bankruptcy court or a United States district court in connection with a case under title 11.

(b) Offense.—If a bankruptcy case or related proceeding is dismissed because of a knowing attempt by a bankruptcy petition preparer in any manner to disregard the requirements of title 11, United States Code, or the Federal Rules of Bankruptcy Procedure, the bankruptcy petition preparer shall be fined under this title, imprisoned not more than 1 year, or both.

§ 157. Bankruptcy fraud

A person who, having devised or intending to devise a scheme or artifice to defraud and for the purpose of executing or concealing such a scheme or artifice or attempting to do so—

(1) files a petition under title 11, including a fraudulent involuntary petition under section 303 of such title;

(2) files a document in a proceeding under title 11; or

(3) makes a false or fraudulent representation, claim, or promise concerning or in relation to a proceeding under title 11, at any time before or after the filing of the petition, or in relation to a proceeding falsely asserted to be pending under such title,

shall be fined under this title, imprisoned not more than 5 years, or both.

§ 158. Designation of United States attorneys and agents of the Federal Bureau of Investigation to address abusive reaffirmations of debt and materially fraudulent statements in bankruptcy schedules

(a) In general.—The Attorney General of the United States shall designate the individuals described in subsection (b) to have primary responsibility in carrying out enforcement activities in addressing violations of section 152 or 157 relating to abusive reaffirmations of debt. In addition to addressing the violations referred to in the preceding sentence, the individuals described under subsection (b) shall address violations of section 152 or 157 relating to materially fraudulent statements in bankruptcy schedules that are intentionally false or intentionally misleading.

(b) United States attorneys and agents of the Federal Bureau of Investigation.—The individuals referred to in subsection (a) are—

(1) the United States attorney for each judicial district of the United States; and

(2) an agent of the Federal Bureau of Investigation for each field office of the Federal Bureau of Investigation.

(c) Bankruptcy investigations.—Each United States attorney designated under this section shall, in addition to any other responsibilities, have primary responsibility for carrying out the duties of a United States attorney under section 3057.

(d) Bankruptcy procedures.—The bankruptcy courts shall establish procedures for referring any case that may contain a materially fraudulent statement in a bankruptcy schedule to the individuals designated under this section.

Chapter 47—Fraud and False Statements

§ 1032 .Concealment of assets from conservator, receiver, or liquidating agent.

Whoever—

(1) knowingly conceals or endeavors to conceal an asset or property from the Federal Deposit Insurance Corporation, acting as conservator or receiver or in the Corporation's corporate capacity with respect to any asset acquired or liability assumed by the Corporation under section 11, 12, or 13 of the Federal Deposit Insurance Act, any conservator appointed by the Comptroller of the Currency, the Federal Deposit Insurance Corporation acting as receiver for a covered financial company, in accordance with title II of the Dodd-Frank Wall Street Reform and Consumer Protection Act, or the National Credit Union Administration Board, acting as conservator or liquidating agent;

(2) corruptly impedes or endeavors to impede the functions of such Corporation, Board, or conservator; or

(3) corruptly places or endeavors to place an asset or property beyond the reach of such Corporation, Board, or conservator,

shall be fined under this title or imprisoned not more than 5 years, or both.

Chapter 73—Obstruction of Justice

§ 1519.　　Destruction, alteration, or falsification of records in Federal investigations and bankruptcy

Whoever knowingly alters, destroys, mutilates, conceals, covers up, falsifies, or makes a false entry in any record, document, or tangible object with the intent to impede, obstruct, or influence the investigation or proper administration of any matter within the jurisdiction of any department or agency of the United States or any case filed under title 11, or in relation to or contemplation of any such matter or case, shall be fined under this title, imprisoned not more than 20 years, or both.

PART II—CRIMINAL PROCEDURE

Chapter 203—Arrest and Commitment

§ 3057. Bankruptcy investigations

(a) Any judge, receiver, or trustee having reasonable grounds for believing that any violation under chapter 9 of this title or other laws of the United States relating to insolvent debtors, receiverships or reorganization plans has been committed, or that an investigation should be had in connection therewith, shall report to the appropriate United States attorney all the facts and circumstances of the case, the names of the witnesses and the offense or offenses believed to have been committed. Where one of such officers has made such report, the others need not do so.

(b) The United States attorney thereupon shall inquire into the facts and report thereon to the judge, and if it appears probable that any such offense has been committed, shall without delay, present the matter to the grand jury, unless upon inquiry and examination he decides that the ends of public justice do not require investigation or prosecution, in which case he shall report the facts to the Attorney General for his direction.

Chapter 213—Limitations

§ 3284. Concealment of bankrupt's assets

The concealment of assets of a debtor in a case under title 11 shall be deemed to be a continuing offense until the debtor shall have been finally discharged or a discharge denied, and the period of limitations shall not begin to run until such final discharge or denial of discharge.

CROSS REFERENCES

Bankruptcy investigations, see 18 USCA § 3057.

Five year limitation on offenses relating to bankruptcy, see 18 USCA § 3282.

Offenses relating to bankruptcy, see 18 USCA § 151 et seq.

PART V—IMMUNITY OF WITNESSES

Chapter 601—Immunity of Witnesses

§ 6001. Definitions

As used in this chapter—

(1) "agency of the United States" means any executive department as defined in section 101 of title 5, United States Code, a military department as defined in section 102 of title 5, United States Code, the Nuclear Regulatory Commission, the Board of Governors of the Federal Reserve System, the China Trade Act registrar appointed under 53 Stat. 1432 (15 U.S.C. sec. 143), the Commodity Futures Trading Commission, the Federal Communications Commission, the Federal Deposit Insurance Corporation, the Federal Maritime Commission, the Federal Power Commission, the Federal Trade Commission, the Surface Transportation Board, the National Labor Relations Board, the National Transportation Safety Board, the Railroad Retirement Board, an arbitration board established under 48 Stat. 1193 (45 U.S.C. sec. 157), the Securities and Exchange Commission, or a board established under 49 Stat. 31 (15 U.S.C. sec. 715d);

(2) "other information" includes any book, paper, document, record, recording, or other material;

(3) "proceeding before an agency of the United States" means any proceeding before such an agency with respect to which it is authorized to issue subpenas[1] and to take testimony or receive other information from witnesses under oath; and

(4) "court of the United States" means any of the following courts: the Supreme Court of the United States, a United States court of appeals, a United States district court established under chapter 5, title 28, United States Code, a United States bankruptcy court established under chapter 6, title 28, United States Code, the District of Columbia Court of Appeals, the Superior Court of the District of Columbia, the District Court of Guam, the District Court of the Virgin Islands, the United States Court of Federal Claims, the Tax Court of the United States, the Court of International Trade, and the Court of Appeals for the Armed Forces.

§ 6002. Immunity generally

Whenever a witness refuses, on the basis of his privilege against self-incrimination, to testify or provide other information in a proceeding before or ancillary to-

(1) a court or grand jury of the United States,

---

[1] So in original. Probably should be subpoenas.

(2)　an agency of the United States, or

(3)　either House of Congress, a joint committee of the two Houses, or a committee or a subcommittee of either House,

and the person presiding over the proceeding communicates to the witness an order issued under this title, the witness may not refuse to comply with the order on the basis of his privilege against self-incrimination; but no testimony or other information compelled under the order (or any information directly or indirectly derived from such testimony or other information) may be used against the witness in any criminal case, except a prosecution for perjury, giving a false statement, or otherwise failing to comply with the order.

§ 6003. Court and grand jury proceedings

(a)　In the case of any individual who has been or may be called to testify or provide other information at any proceeding before or ancillary to a court of the United States or a grand jury of the United States, the United States district court for the judicial district in which the proceeding is or may be held shall issue, in accordance with subsection (b) of this section, upon the request of the United States attorney for such district, an order requiring such individual to give testimony or provide other information which he refuses to give or provide on the basis of his privilege against self-incrimination, such order to become effective as provided in section 6002 of this title.

(b)　A United States attorney may, with the approval of the Attorney General, the Deputy Attorney General, the Associate Attorney General, or any designated Assistant Attorney General or Deputy Assistant Attorney General, request an order under subsection (a) of this section when in his judgment—

(1)　the testimony or other information from such individual may be necessary to the public interest; and

(2)　such individual has refused or is likely to refuse to testify or provide other information on the basis of his privilege against self-incrimination.

TITLE 28

JUDICIARY AND JUDICIAL PROCEDURE

Current through June 30, 2023; P.L.118–7

For the enactment history of a statutory section, consult the notes following the statutory section at *http://uscode.house.gov*

PART I—ORGANIZATION OF COURTS
Chapter 6—Bankruptcy Judges

§ 151. Designation of bankruptcy courts

In each judicial district, the bankruptcy judges in regular active service shall constitute a unit of the district court to be known as the bankruptcy court for that district. Each bankruptcy judge, as a judicial officer of the district court, may exercise the authority conferred under this chapter with respect to any action, suit, or proceeding and may preside alone and hold a regular or special session of the court, except as otherwise provided by law or by rule or order of the district court.

CROSS REFERENCES

Court of the United States defined as including bankruptcy court established under this chapter for purposes of immunity of witnesses, see 18 USCA § 6001.

Power of Bankruptcy Court, see 11 USCA § 105.

§ 152. Appointment of bankruptcy judges

(a)(1)   Each bankruptcy judge to be appointed for a judicial district, as provided in paragraph (2), shall be appointed by the court of appeals of the United States for the circuit in which such district is located. Such appointments shall be made after considering the recommendations of the Judicial Conference submitted pursuant to subsection (b). Each bankruptcy judge shall be appointed for a term of fourteen years, subject to the provisions of subsection (e). However, upon the expiration of the term, a bankruptcy judge may, with the approval of the judicial council of the circuit, continue to perform the duties of the office until the earlier of the date which is 180 days after the expiration of the term or the date of the appointment of a successor. Bankruptcy judges shall serve as judicial officers of the United States district court established under Article III of the Constitution.

(2)   The bankruptcy judges appointed pursuant to this section shall be appointed for the several judicial districts as follows:

Districts	Judges
Alabama:	
Northern	5
Middle	2
Southern	2
Alaska	2
Arizona	7
Arkansas:	
Eastern and Western	3

(3) Whenever a majority of the judges of any court of appeals cannot agree upon the appointment of a bankruptcy judge, the chief judge of such court shall make such appointment.

(4) The judges of the district courts for the territories shall serve as the bankruptcy judges for such courts. The United States court of appeals for the circuit within which such a territorial district court is located may appoint bankruptcy judges under this chapter for such district if authorized to do so by the Congress of the United States under this section.

(b)(1) The Judicial Conference of the United States shall, from time to time, and after considering the recommendations submitted by the Director of the Administrative Office of the United States Courts after such Director has consulted with the judicial council of the circuit involved, determine the official duty stations of bankruptcy judges and places of holding court.

(2) The Judicial Conference shall, from time to time, submit recommendations to the Congress regarding the number of bankruptcy judges needed and the districts in which such judges are needed.

(3) Not later than December 31, 1994, and not later than the end of each 2-year period thereafter, the Judicial Conference of the United States shall conduct a comprehensive review of all judicial districts to assess the continuing need for the bankruptcy judges authorized by this section, and shall report to the Congress its findings and any recommendations for the elimination of any

authorized position which can be eliminated when a vacancy exists by reason of resignation, retirement, removal, or death.

(c)(1) Each bankruptcy judge may hold court at such places within the judicial district, in addition to the official duty station of such judge, as the business of the court may require.

(2)(A) Bankruptcy judges may hold court at such places within the United States outside the judicial district as the nature of the business of the court may require, and upon such notice as the court orders, upon a finding by either the chief judge of the bankruptcy court (or, if the chief judge is unavailable, the most senior available bankruptcy judge) or by the judicial council of the circuit that, because of emergency conditions, no location within the district is reasonably available where the bankruptcy judges could hold court.

(B) Bankruptcy judges may transact any business at special sessions of court held outside the district pursuant to this paragraph that might be transacted at a regular session.

(C) If a bankruptcy court issues an order exercising its authority under subparagraph (A), the court—

  (i) through the Administrative Office of the United States Courts, shall—

  (I) send notice of such order, including the reasons for the issuance of such order, to the Committee on the Judiciary of the Senate and the Committee on the Judiciary of the House of Representatives; and

  (II) not later than 180 days after the expiration of such court order submit a brief report to the Committee on the Judiciary of the Senate and the Committee on the Judiciary of the House of Representatives describing the impact of such order, including—

   (aa) the reasons for the issuance of such order;

   (bb) the duration of such order;

   (cc) the impact of such order on litigants; and

   (dd) the costs to the judiciary resulting from such order; and

  (ii) shall provide reasonable notice to the United States Marshals Service before the commencement of any special session held pursuant to such order.

(d) With the approval of the Judicial Conference and of each of the judicial councils involved, a bankruptcy judge may be designated to serve in any district adjacent to or near the district for which such bankruptcy judge was appointed.

(e) A bankruptcy judge may be removed during the term for which such bankruptcy judge is appointed, only for incompetence, misconduct, neglect of duty, or physical or mental disability and only by the judicial council of the circuit in which the judge's official duty station is located. Removal may not occur unless a majority of all of the judges of such council concur in the order of removal. Before any order of removal may be entered, a full specification of charges shall be furnished to such bankruptcy judge who shall be accorded an opportunity to be heard on such charges.

CROSS REFERENCES

Appeals, hearing of, see 28 USCA § 158.

Definition of Bankruptcy judge as including a judge appointed under this section for purposes of civil service retirement, see 5 USCA § 8331.

Recall of judges and magistrates, see 28 USCA § 375.

Removal of judges for disability to be in accordance with provisions of this section, see 28 USCA § 372.

Retirement of bankruptcy judges and magistrates, see 28 USCA § 377.

§ 153. Salaries; character of service

(a) Each bankruptcy judge shall serve on a full-time basis and shall receive as full compensation for his services, a salary at an annual rate that is equal to 92 percent of the salary of a judge of the district court of the United States as determined pursuant to section 135, to be paid at such times as the Judicial Conference of the United States determines.

(b) A bankruptcy judge may not engage in the practice of law and may not engage in any other practice, business, occupation, or employment inconsistent with the expeditious, proper, and impartial performance of such bankruptcy judge's duties as a judicial officer. The Conference may promulgate appropriate rules and regulations to implement this subsection.

(c) Each individual appointed under this chapter shall take the oath or affirmation prescribed by section 453 of this title before performing the duties of the office of bankruptcy judge.

(d) A bankruptcy judge appointed under this chapter shall be exempt from the provisions of subchapter I of chapter 63 of title 5.

§ 154. Division of businesses[1]; chief judge

(a) Each bankruptcy court for a district having more than one bankruptcy judge shall by majority vote promulgate rules for the division of business among the bankruptcy judges to the extent that the division of business is not otherwise provided for by the rules of the district court.

(b) In each district court having more than one bankruptcy judge the district court shall designate one judge to serve as chief judge of such bankruptcy court. Whenever a majority of the judges of such district court cannot agree upon the designation as chief judge, the chief judge of such district court shall make such designation. The chief judge of the bankruptcy court shall ensure that the rules of the bankruptcy court and of the district court are observed and that the business of the bankruptcy court is handled effectively and expeditiously.

§ 155. Temporary transfer of bankruptcy judges

(a) A bankruptcy judge may be transferred to serve temporarily as a bankruptcy judge in any judicial district other than the judicial district for which such bankruptcy judge was appointed upon the approval of the judicial council of each of the circuits involved.

(b) A bankruptcy judge who has retired may, upon consent, be recalled to serve as a bankruptcy judge in any judicial district by the judicial council of the circuit within which such district is located. Upon recall, a bankruptcy judge may receive a salary for such service in accordance with regulations promulgated by the Judicial Conference of the United States, subject to the restrictions on the payment of an annuity in section 377 of this title or in subchapter III of chapter 83, and chapter 84, of title 5 which are applicable to such judge.

CROSS REFERENCES

Recall of retired judges—

    Generally, see 28 USCA § 375.

    Actual abode deemed official station for purposes of residency, see 28 USCA § 374.

    Practicing attorney not eligible for recall, see 28 USCA § 377.

§ 156. Staff; expenses

(a) Each bankruptcy judge may appoint a secretary, a law clerk, and such additional assistants as the Director of the Administrative Office of the United States Courts determines to be necessary. A

---

[1] So in original. Probably should be "business" and not "businesses."

law clerk appointed under this section shall be exempt from the provisions of subchapter I of chapter 63 of title 5, unless specifically included by the appointing judge or by local rule of court.

(b) Upon certification to the judicial council of the circuit involved and to the Director of the Administrative Office of the United States Courts that the number of cases and proceedings pending within the jurisdiction under section 1334 of this title within a judicial district so warrants, the bankruptcy judges for such district may appoint an individual to serve as clerk of such bankruptcy court. The clerk may appoint, with the approval of such bankruptcy judges, and in such number as may be approved by the Director, necessary deputies, and may remove such deputies with the approval of such bankruptcy judges.

(c) Any court may utilize facilities or services, either on or off the court's premises, which pertain to the provision of notices, dockets, calendars, and other administrative information to parties in cases filed under the provisions of title 11, United States Code, where the costs of such facilities or services are paid for out of the assets of the estate and are not charged to the United States. The utilization of such facilities or services shall be subject to such conditions and limitations as the pertinent circuit council may prescribe.

(d) No office of the bankruptcy clerk of court may be consolidated with the district clerk of court office without the prior approval of the Judicial Conference and the Congress.

(e) In a judicial district where a bankruptcy clerk has been appointed pursuant to subsection (b), the bankruptcy clerk shall be the official custodian of the records and dockets of the bankruptcy court.

(f) For purposes of financial accountability in a district where a bankruptcy clerk has been certified, such clerk shall be accountable for and pay into the Treasury all fees, costs, and other monies collected by such clerk except uncollected fees not required by an Act of Congress to be prepaid. Such clerk shall make returns thereof to the Director of the Administrative Office of the United States Courts and the Director of the Executive Office For United States Trustees, under regulations prescribed by such Directors.

CROSS REFERENCES

Conversion fees in bankruptcy, see 28 USCA § 1930.

§ 157. Procedures

(a) Each district court may provide that any or all cases under title 11 and any or all proceedings arising under title 11 or arising in or related to a case under title 11 shall be referred to the bankruptcy judges for the district.

(b)(1) Bankruptcy judges may hear and determine all cases under title 11 and all core proceedings arising under title 11, or arising in a case under title 11, referred under subsection (a) of this section, and may enter appropriate orders and judgments, subject to review under section 158 of this title.

(2) Core proceedings include, but are not limited to—

    (A) matters concerning the administration of the estate;

    (B) allowance or disallowance of claims against the estate or exemptions from property of the estate, and estimation of claims or interests for the purposes of confirming a plan under chapter 11, 12, or 13 of title 11 but not the liquidation or estimation of contingent or unliquidated personal injury tort or wrongful death claims against the estate for purposes of distribution in a case under title 11;

    (C) counterclaims by the estate against persons filing claims against the estate;

    (D) orders in respect to obtaining credit;

(E) orders to turn over property of the estate;

(F) proceedings to determine, avoid, or recover preferences;

(G) motions to terminate, annul, or modify the automatic stay;

(H) proceedings to determine, avoid, or recover fraudulent conveyances;

(I) determinations as to the dischargeability of particular debts;

(J) objections to discharges;

(K) determinations of the validity, extent, or priority of liens;

(L) confirmations of plans;

(M) orders approving the use or lease of property, including the use of cash collateral;

(N) orders approving the sale of property other than property resulting from claims brought by the estate against persons who have not filed claims against the estate;

(O) other proceedings affecting the liquidation of the assets of the estate or the adjustment of the debtor-creditor or the equity security holder relationship, except personal injury tort or wrongful death claims; and

(P) recognition of foreign proceedings and other matters under chapter 15 of title 11.

(3) The bankruptcy judge shall determine, on the judge's own motion or on timely motion of a party, whether a proceeding is a core proceeding under this subsection or is a proceeding that is otherwise related to a case under title 11. A determination that a proceeding is not a core proceeding shall not be made solely on the basis that its resolution may be affected by State law.

(4) Non-core proceedings under section 157(b)(2)(B) of title 28, United States Code, shall not be subject to the mandatory abstention provisions of section 1334(c)(2).

(5) The district court shall order that personal injury tort and wrongful death claims shall be tried in the district court in which the bankruptcy case is pending, or in the district court in the district in which the claim arose, as determined by the district court in which the bankruptcy case is pending.

(c)(1) A bankruptcy judge may hear a proceeding that is not a core proceeding but that is otherwise related to a case under title 11. In such proceeding, the bankruptcy judge shall submit proposed findings of fact and conclusions of law to the district court, and any final order or judgment shall be entered by the district judge after considering the bankruptcy judge's proposed findings and conclusions and after reviewing de novo those matters to which any party has timely and specifically objected.

(2) Notwithstanding the provisions of paragraph (1) of this subsection, the district court, with the consent of all the parties to the proceeding, may refer a proceeding related to a case under title 11 to a bankruptcy judge to hear and determine and to enter appropriate orders and judgments, subject to review under section 158 of this title.

(d) The district court may withdraw, in whole or in part, any case or proceeding referred under this section, on its own motion or on timely motion of any party, for cause shown. The district court shall, on timely motion of a party, so withdraw a proceeding if the court determines that resolution of the proceeding requires consideration of both title 11 and other laws of the United States regulating organizations or activities affecting interstate commerce.

(e) If the right to a jury trial applies in a proceeding that may be heard under this section by a bankruptcy judge, the bankruptcy judge may conduct the jury trial if specially designated to exercise such jurisdiction by the district court and with the express consent of all the parties.

REFERENCES IN TEXT

Chapter 11, 12, or 13 of title 11, referred to in subsec. (b)(2)(B), is 11 U.S.C.A. § 1101 et seq., 11 U.S.C.A. § 1201 et seq., or 11 U.S.C.A. § 1301 et seq., respectively.

Chapter 15 of title 11, referred to in subsec. (b)(2)(P), is 11 U.S.C.A. § 1501 et seq.

CROSS REFERENCES

Supplemental injunctions and power of district court to refer proceedings, see 11 USCA § 524.

§ 158. Appeals

(a) The district courts of the United States shall have jurisdiction to hear appeals[1]

    (1) from final judgments, orders, and decrees;

    (2) from interlocutory orders and decrees issued under section 1121(d) of title 11 increasing or reducing the time periods referred to in section 1121 of such title; and

    (3) with leave of the court, from other interlocutory orders and decrees;

and, with leave of the court, from interlocutory orders and decrees, of bankruptcy judges entered in cases and proceedings referred to the bankruptcy judges under section 157 of this title. An appeal under this subsection shall be taken only to the district court for the judicial district in which the bankruptcy judge is serving.

(b)(1) The judicial council of a circuit shall establish a bankruptcy appellate panel service composed of bankruptcy judges of the districts in the circuit who are appointed by the judicial council in accordance with paragraph (3), to hear and determine, with the consent of all the parties, appeals under subsection (a) unless the judicial council finds that—

    (A) there are insufficient judicial resources available in the circuit; or

    (B) establishment of such service would result in undue delay or increased cost to parties in cases under title 11.

Not later than 90 days after making the finding, the judicial council shall submit to the Judicial Conference of the United States a report containing the factual basis of such finding.

    (2)(A) A judicial council may reconsider, at any time, the finding described in paragraph (1).

    (B) On the request of a majority of the district judges in a circuit for which a bankruptcy appellate panel service is established under paragraph (1), made after the expiration of the 1-year period beginning on the date such service is established, the judicial council of the circuit shall determine whether a circumstance specified in subparagraph (A) or (B) of such paragraph exists.

    (C) On its own motion, after the expiration of the 3-year period beginning on the date a bankruptcy appellate panel service is established under paragraph (1), the judicial council of the circuit may determine whether a circumstance specified in subparagraph (A) or (B) of such paragraph exists.

    (D) If the judicial council finds that either of such circumstances exists, the judicial council may provide for the completion of the appeals then pending before such service and the orderly termination of such service.

    (3) Bankruptcy judges appointed under paragraph (1) shall be appointed and may be reappointed under such paragraph.

    (4) If authorized by the Judicial Conference of the United States, the judicial councils of 2 or more circuits may establish a joint bankruptcy appellate panel comprised of bankruptcy judges from the districts within the circuits for which such panel is established, to hear and determine, upon the consent of all the parties, appeals under subsection (a) of this section.

    (5) An appeal to be heard under this subsection shall be heard by a panel of 3 members of the bankruptcy appellate panel service, except that a member of such service may not hear an appeal

---

[1] So in original.

originating in the district for which such member is appointed or designated under section 152 of this title.

(6) Appeals may not be heard under this subsection by a panel of the bankruptcy appellate panel service unless the district judges for the district in which the appeals occur, by majority vote, have authorized such service to hear and determine appeals originating in such district.

(c)(1) Subject to subsections (b) and (d)(2), each appeal under subsection (a) shall be heard by a 3-judge panel of the bankruptcy appellate panel service established under subsection (b)(1) unless—

    (A) the appellant elects at the time of filing the appeal; or

    (B) any other party elects, not later than 30 days after service of notice of the appeal;

to have such appeal heard by the district court.

(2) An appeal under subsections (a) and (b) of this section shall be taken in the same manner as appeals in civil proceedings generally are taken to the courts of appeals from the district courts and in the time provided by Rule 8002 of the Bankruptcy Rules.

(d)(1) The courts of appeals shall have jurisdiction of appeals from all final decisions, judgments, orders, and decrees entered under subsections (a) and (b) of this section.

(2)(A) The appropriate court of appeals shall have jurisdiction of appeals described in the first sentence of subsection (a) if the bankruptcy court, the district court, or the bankruptcy appellate panel involved, acting on its own motion or on the request of a party to the judgment, order, or decree described in such first sentence, or all the appellants and appellees (if any) acting jointly, certify that—

    (i) the judgment, order, or decree involves a question of law as to which there is no controlling decision of the court of appeals for the circuit or of the Supreme Court of the United States, or involves a matter of public importance;

    (ii) the judgment, order, or decree involves a question of law requiring resolution of conflicting decisions; or

    (iii) an immediate appeal from the judgment, order, or decree may materially advance the progress of the case or proceeding in which the appeal is taken;

and if the court of appeals authorizes the direct appeal of the judgment, order, or decree.

(B) If the bankruptcy court, the district court, or the bankruptcy appellate panel—

    (i) on its own motion or on the request of a party, determines that a circumstance specified in clause (i), (ii), or (iii) of subparagraph (A) exists; or

    (ii) receives a request made by a majority of the appellants and a majority of appellees (if any) to make the certification described in subparagraph (A);

then the bankruptcy court, the district court, or the bankruptcy appellate panel shall make the certification described in subparagraph (A).

(C) The parties may supplement the certification with a short statement of the basis for the certification.

(D) An appeal under this paragraph does not stay any proceeding of the bankruptcy court, the district court, or the bankruptcy appellate panel from which the appeal is taken, unless the respective bankruptcy court, district court, or bankruptcy appellate panel, or the court of appeals in which the appeal is pending, issues a stay of such proceeding pending the appeal.

(E) Any request under subparagraph (B) for certification shall be made not later than 60 days after the entry of the judgment, order, or decree.

CROSS REFERENCES

Orders and decisions not reviewable under this section—

Abstention from exercising jurisdiction generally, see 28 USCA § 1334.

Dismissal or suspension of bankruptcy case on abstention grounds, see 11 USCA § 305.

Remand orders, see 28 USCA § 1452.

§ 159. Bankruptcy statistics

(a)   The clerk of the district court, or the clerk of the bankruptcy court if one is certified pursuant to section 156(b) of this title, shall collect statistics regarding debtors who are individuals with primarily consumer debts seeking relief under chapters 7, 11, and 13 of title 11. Those statistics shall be in a standardized format prescribed by the Director of the Administrative Office of the United States Courts (referred to in this section as the "Director").

(b)   The Director shall—

    (1)   compile the statistics referred to in subsection (a);

    (2)   make the statistics available to the public; and

    (3)   not later than July 1, 2008, and annually thereafter, prepare, and submit to Congress a report concerning the information collected under subsection (a) that contains an analysis of the information.

(c)   The compilation required under subsection (b) shall—

    (1)   be itemized, by chapter, with respect to title 11;

    (2)   be presented in the aggregate and for each district; and

    (3)   include information concerning—

        (A)   the total assets and total liabilities of the debtors described in subsection (a), and in each category of assets and liabilities, as reported in the schedules prescribed pursuant to section 2075 of this title and filed by debtors;

        (B)   the current monthly income, average income, and average expenses of debtors as reported on the schedules and statements that each such debtor files under sections 521 and 1322 of title 11;

        (C)   the aggregate amount of debt discharged in cases filed during the reporting period, determined as the difference between the total amount of debt and obligations of a debtor reported on the schedules and the amount of such debt reported in categories which are predominantly nondischargeable;

        (D)   the average period of time between the date of the filing of the petition and the closing of the case for cases closed during the reporting period;

        (E)   for cases closed during the reporting period—

            (i)   the number of cases in which a reaffirmation agreement was filed; and

            (ii)(I) the total number of reaffirmation agreements filed;

            (II)   of those cases in which a reaffirmation agreement was filed, the number of cases in which the debtor was not represented by an attorney; and

            (III) of those cases in which a reaffirmation agreement was filed, the number of cases in which the reaffirmation agreement was approved by the court;

        (F)   with respect to cases filed under chapter 13 of title 11, for the reporting period—

            (i)(I)   the number of cases in which a final order was entered determining the value of property securing a claim in an amount less than the amount of the claim; and

(II) the number of final orders entered determining the value of property securing a claim;

(ii) the number of cases dismissed, the number of cases dismissed for failure to make payments under the plan, the number of cases refiled after dismissal, and the number of cases in which the plan was completed, separately itemized with respect to the number of modifications made before completion of the plan, if any; and

(iii) the number of cases in which the debtor filed another case during the 6-year period preceding the filing;

(G) the number of cases in which creditors were fined for misconduct and any amount of punitive damages awarded by the court for creditor misconduct; and

(H) the number of cases in which sanctions under rule 9011 of the Federal Rules of Bankruptcy Procedure were imposed against the debtor's attorney or damages awarded under such Rule.

Chapter 21—General Provisions Applicable to Courts and Judges

§ 455. Disqualification of justice, judge, or magistrate judge

(a) Any justice, judge, or magistrate judge of the United States shall disqualify himself in any proceeding in which his impartiality might reasonably be questioned.

(b) He shall also disqualify himself in the following circumstances:

(1) Where he has a personal bias or prejudice concerning a party, or personal knowledge of disputed evidentiary facts concerning the proceeding;

(2) Where in private practice he served as lawyer in the matter in controversy, or a lawyer with whom he previously practiced law served during such association as a lawyer concerning the matter, or the judge or such lawyer has been a material witness concerning it;

(3) Where he has served in governmental employment and in such capacity participated as counsel, adviser or material witness concerning the proceeding or expressed an opinion concerning the merits of the particular case in controversy;

(4) He knows that he, individually or as a fiduciary, or his spouse or minor child residing in his household, has a financial interest in the subject matter in controversy or in a party to the proceeding, or any other interest that could be substantially affected by the outcome of the proceeding;

(5) He or his spouse, or a person within the third degree of relationship to either of them, or the spouse of such a person:

(i) Is a party to the proceeding, or an officer, director, or trustee of a party;

(ii) Is acting as a lawyer in the proceeding;

(iii) Is known by the judge to have an interest that could be substantially affected by the outcome of the proceeding;

(iv) Is to the judge's knowledge likely to be a material witness in the proceeding.

(c) A judge should inform himself about his personal and fiduciary financial interests, and make a reasonable effort to inform himself about the personal financial interests of his spouse and minor children residing in his household.

(d) For the purposes of this section the following words or phrases shall have the meaning indicated:

(1) "proceeding" includes pretrial, trial, appellate review, or other stages of litigation;

(2) the degree of relationship is calculated according to the civil law system;

(3) "fiduciary" includes such relationships as executor, administrator, trustee, and guardian;

(4) "financial interest" means ownership of a legal or equitable interest, however small, or a relationship as director, adviser, or other active participant in the affairs of a party, except that:

(i) Ownership in a mutual or common investment fund that holds securities is not a "financial interest" in such securities unless the judge participates in the management of the fund;

(ii) An office in an educational, religious, charitable, fraternal, or civic organization is not a "financial interest" in securities held by the organization;

(iii) The proprietary interest of a policyholder in a mutual insurance company, of a depositor in a mutual savings association, or a similar proprietary interest, is a "financial interest" in the organization only if the outcome of the proceeding could substantially affect the value of the interest;

(iv) Ownership of government securities is a "financial interest" in the issuer only if the outcome of the proceeding could substantially affect the value of the securities.

(e) No justice, judge, or magistrate judge shall accept from the parties to the proceeding a waiver of any ground for disqualification enumerated in subsection (b). Where the ground for disqualification arises only under subsection (a), waiver may be accepted provided it is preceded by a full disclosure on the record of the basis for disqualification.

(f) Notwithstanding the preceding provisions of this section, if any justice, judge, magistrate judge, or bankruptcy judge to whom a matter has been assigned would be disqualified, after substantial judicial time has been devoted to the matter, because of the appearance or discovery, after the matter was assigned to him or her, that he or she individually or as a fiduciary, or his or her spouse or minor child residing in his or her household, has a financial interest in a party (other than an interest that could be substantially affected by the outcome), disqualification is not required if the justice, judge, magistrate judge, bankruptcy judge, spouse or minor child, as the case may be, divests himself or herself of the interest that provides the grounds for the disqualification.

CROSS REFERENCES

Application to other courts, see 28 USCA § 460.

Arbitrators subject to disqualification rules under this section, see 28 USCA § 656.

Bias or prejudice of judge, see 28 USCA § 144.

Disqualification of trial judge to hear appeal, see 28 USCA § 47.

United States Court of Veterans affairs, judges and proceedings of subject to this section, see 38 USCA § 7264.

PART II—DEPARTMENT OF JUSTICE

Chapter 39—United States Trustees

§ 581. United States trustees

(a) The Attorney General shall appoint one United States trustee for each of the following regions composed of Federal judicial districts (without regard to section 451):

(1) The judicial districts established for the States of Maine, Massachusetts, New Hampshire, and Rhode Island.

(2) The judicial districts established for the States of Connecticut, New York, and Vermont.

(3) The judicial districts established for the States of Delaware, New Jersey, and Pennsylvania.

(4) The judicial districts established for the States of Maryland, North Carolina, South Carolina, Virginia, and West Virginia and for the District of Columbia.

(5) The judicial districts established for the States of Louisiana and Mississippi.

(6) The Northern District of Texas and the Eastern District of Texas.

(7) The Southern District of Texas and the Western District of Texas.

(8) The judicial districts established for the States of Kentucky and Tennessee.

(9) The judicial districts established for the States of Michigan and Ohio.

(10) The Central District of Illinois and the Southern District of Illinois; and the judicial districts established for the State of Indiana.

(11) The Northern District of Illinois; and the judicial districts established for the State of Wisconsin.

(12) The judicial districts established for the States of Minnesota, Iowa, North Dakota, and South Dakota.

(13) The judicial districts established for the States of Arkansas, Nebraska, and Missouri.

(14) The District of Arizona.

(15) The Southern District of California; and the judicial districts established for the State of Hawaii, and for Guam and the Commonwealth of the Northern Mariana Islands.

(16) The Central District of California.

(17) The Eastern District of California and the Northern District of California; and the judicial district established for the State of Nevada.

(18) The judicial districts established for the States of Alaska, Idaho (exclusive of Yellowstone National Park), Montana (exclusive of Yellowstone National Park), Oregon, and Washington.

(19) The judicial districts established for the States of Colorado, Utah, and Wyoming (including those portions of Yellowstone National Park situated in the States of Montana and Idaho).

(20) he judicial districts established for the States of Kansas, New Mexico, and Oklahoma.

(21) The judicial districts established for the States of Alabama, Florida, and Georgia and for the Commonwealth of Puerto Rico and the Virgin Islands of the United States.

(b) Each United States trustee shall be appointed for a term of five years. On the expiration of his term, a United States trustee shall continue to perform the duties of his office until his successor is appointed and qualifies.

(c) Each United States trustee is subject to removal by the Attorney General.

CROSS REFERENCES

Appointment of acting United States trustee by Attorney General to serve until vacancy is filled by appointment under this section, see 28 USCA § 585.

§ 582.   Assistant United States trustees

(a) The Attorney General may appoint one or more assistant United States trustees in any region when the public interest so requires.

(b) Each assistant United States trustee is subject to removal by the Attorney General.

§ 583.   Oath of office

Each United States trustee and assistant United States trustee, before taking office, shall take an oath to execute faithfully his duties.

§ 584.   Official stations

The Attorney General may determine the official stations of the United States trustees and assistant United States trustees within the regions for which they were appointed.

§ 585.   Vacancies

(a) The Attorney General may appoint an acting United States trustee for a region in which the office of the United States trustee is vacant. The individual so appointed may serve until the date on which the vacancy is filled by appointment under section 581 of this title or by designation under subsection (b) of this section.

(b) The Attorney General may designate a United States trustee to serve in not more than two regions for such time as the public interest requires.

§ 586.   Duties; supervision by Attorney General

(a) Each United States trustee, within the region for which such United States trustee is appointed, shall—

(1) establish, maintain, and supervise a panel of private trustees that are eligible and available to serve as trustees in cases under chapter 7 of title 11;

(2) serve as and perform the duties of a trustee in a case under title 11 when required under title 11 to serve as trustee in such a case;

(3) supervise the administration of cases and trustees in cases under chapter 7, 11 (including subchapter V of chapter 11), 12, 13, or 15 of title 11 by, whenever the United States trustee considers it to be appropriate—

(A)(i) reviewing, in accordance with procedural guidelines adopted by the Executive Office of the United States Trustee (which guidelines shall be applied uniformly by the United States trustee except when circumstances warrant different treatment), applications filed for compensation and reimbursement under section 330 of title 11; and

(ii) filing with the court comments with respect to such application and, if the United States Trustee considers it to be appropriate, objections to such application;

(B) monitoring plans and disclosure statements filed in cases under chapter 11 of title 11 and filing with the court, in connection with hearings under sections 1125 and 1128 of such title, comments with respect to such plans and disclosure statements;

(C) monitoring plans filed under chapters 12 and 13 of title 11 and filing with the court, in connection with hearings under sections 1224, 1229, 1324, and 1329 of such title, comments with respect to such plans;

(D) taking such action as the United States trustee deems to be appropriate to ensure that all reports, schedules, and fees required to be filed under title 11 and this title by the debtor are properly and timely filed;

(E) monitoring creditors' committees appointed under title 11;

(F) notifying the appropriate United States attorney of matters which relate to the occurrence of any action which may constitute a crime under the laws of the United States and, on the request of the United States attorney, assisting the United States attorney in carrying out prosecutions based on such action;

(G) monitoring the progress of cases under title 11 and taking such actions as the United States trustee deems to be appropriate to prevent undue delay in such progress;

(H) in small business cases (as defined in section 101 of title 11), performing the additional duties specified in title 11 pertaining to such cases; and

(I) monitoring applications filed under section 327 of title 11 and, whenever the United States trustee deems it to be appropriate, filing with the court comments with respect to the approval of such applications;

(4) deposit or invest under section 345 of title 11 money received as trustee in cases under title 11;

(5) perform the duties prescribed for the United States trustee under title 11 and this title, and such duties consistent with title 11 and this title as the Attorney General may prescribe;

(6) make such reports as the Attorney General directs, including the results of audits performed under section 603(a) of the Bankruptcy Abuse Prevention and Consumer Protection Act of 2005;

(7) in each of such small business cases—

(A) conduct an initial debtor interview as soon as practicable after the date of the order for relief but before the first meeting scheduled under section 341(a) of title 11, at which time the United States trustee shall—

(i) begin to investigate the debtor's viability;

(ii) inquire about the debtor's business plan;

(iii) explain the debtor's obligations to file monthly operating reports and other required reports;

(iv) attempt to develop an agreed scheduling order; and

(v) inform the debtor of other obligations;

(B) if determined to be appropriate and advisable, visit the appropriate business premises of the debtor, ascertain the state of the debtor's books and records, and verify that the debtor has filed its tax returns; and

(C) review and monitor diligently the debtor's activities, to determine as promptly as possible whether the debtor will be unable to confirm a plan; and

(8) in any case in which the United States trustee finds material grounds for any relief under section 1112 of title 11, apply promptly after making that finding to the court for relief.

(b) If the number of cases under subchapter V of chapter 11 or chapter 12 or 13 of title 11 commenced in a particular region so warrants, the United States trustee for such region may, subject to the approval of the Attorney General, appoint one or more individuals to serve as standing trustee, or designate one or more assistant United States trustees to serve in cases under such chapter. The United States trustee for such region shall supervise any such individual appointed as standing trustee in the performance of the duties of standing trustee.

(c) Each United States trustee shall be under the general supervision of the Attorney General, who shall provide general coordination and assistance to the United States trustees.

(d)(1) The Attorney General shall prescribe by rule qualifications for membership on the panels established by United States trustees under paragraph (a)(1) of this section, and qualifications for appointment under subsection (b) of this section to serve as standing trustee in cases under subchapter V of chapter 11 or chapter 12 or 13 of title 11. The Attorney General may not require that an individual be an attorney in order to qualify for appointment under subsection (b) of this section to serve as standing trustee in cases under subchapter V of chapter 11 or chapter 12 or 13 of title 11.

(2) A trustee whose appointment under subsection (a)(1) or under subsection (b) is terminated or who ceases to be assigned to cases filed under title 11, United States Code, may obtain judicial review of the final agency decision by commencing an action in the district court of the United States for the district for which the panel to which the trustee is appointed under subsection (a)(1), or in the district court of the United States for the district in which the trustee is appointed under subsection (b) resides, after first exhausting all available administrative remedies, which if the trustee so elects, shall also include an administrative hearing on the record. Unless the trustee elects to have an administrative hearing on the record, the trustee shall be deemed to have exhausted all administrative remedies for purposes of this paragraph if the agency fails to make a final agency decision within 90 days after the trustee requests administrative remedies. The Attorney General shall prescribe procedures to implement this paragraph. The decision of the agency shall be affirmed by the district court unless it is unreasonable and without cause based on the administrative record before the agency.

(e)(1) The Attorney General, after consultation with a United States trustee that has appointed an individual under subsection (b) of this section to serve as standing trustee in cases under subchapter V of chapter 11 or chapter 12 or 13 of title 11, shall fix—

    (A) a maximum annual compensation for such individual consisting of—

        (i) an amount not to exceed the highest annual rate of basic pay in effect for level V of the Executive Schedule; and

        (ii) the cash value of employment benefits comparable to the employment benefits provided by the United States to individuals who are employed by the United States at the same rate of basic pay to perform similar services during the same period of time; and

    (B) a percentage fee not to exceed—

        (i) in the case of a debtor who is not a family farmer, ten percent; or

        (ii) in the case of a debtor who is a family farmer, the sum of—

            (I) not to exceed ten percent of the payments made under the plan of such debtor, with respect to payments in an aggregate amount not to exceed $450,000; and

            (II) three percent of payments made under the plan of such debtor, with respect to payments made after the aggregate amount of payments made under the plan exceeds $450,000;

based on such maximum annual compensation and the actual, necessary expenses incurred by such individual as standing trustee.

(2) Such individual shall collect such percentage fee from all payments received by such individual under plans in the cases under subchapter V of chapter 11 or chapter 12 or 13 of title 11 for which such individual serves as standing trustee. Such individual shall pay to the United States trustee, and the United States trustee shall deposit in the United States Trustee System Fund—

    (A) any amount by which the actual compensation of such individual exceeds 5 per centum upon all payments received under plans in cases under subchapter V of chapter 11 or chapter 12 or 13 of title 11 for which such individual serves as standing trustee; and

    (B) any amount by which the percentage for all such cases exceeds—

(i) such individual's actual compensation for such cases, as adjusted under subparagraph (A) of paragraph (1); plus

(ii) the actual, necessary expenses incurred by such individual as standing trustee in such cases. Subject to the approval of the Attorney General, any or all of the interest earned from the deposit of payments under plans by such individual may be utilized to pay actual, necessary expenses without regard to the percentage limitation contained in subparagraph (d)(1)(B) of this section.

(3) After first exhausting all available administrative remedies, an individual appointed under subsection (b) may obtain judicial review of final agency action to deny a claim of actual, necessary expenses under this subsection by commencing an action in the district court of the United States for the district where the individual resides. The decision of the agency shall be affirmed by the district court unless it is unreasonable and without cause based upon the administrative record before the agency.

(4) The Attorney General shall prescribe procedures to implement this subsection.

(5) In the event that the services of the trustee in a case under subchapter V of chapter 11 of title 11 are terminated by dismissal or conversion of the case, or upon substantial consummation of a plan under section 1183(c)(1) of that title, the court shall award compensation to the trustee consistent with services performed by the trustee and the limits on the compensation of the trustee established pursuant to paragraph (1) of this subsection.

(f)(1) The United States trustee for each district is authorized to contract with auditors to perform audits in cases designated by the United States trustee, in accordance with the procedures established under section 603(a) of the Bankruptcy Abuse Prevention and Consumer Protection Act of 2005.

(2)(A) The report of each audit referred to in paragraph (1) shall be filed with the court and transmitted to the United States trustee. Each report shall clearly and conspicuously specify any material misstatement of income or expenditures or of assets identified by the person performing the audit. In any case in which a material misstatement of income or expenditures or of assets has been reported, the clerk of the district court (or the clerk of the bankruptcy court if one is certified under section 156(b) of this title) shall give notice of the misstatement to the creditors in the case.

(B) If a material misstatement of income or expenditures or of assets is reported, the United States trustee shall—

(i) report the material misstatement, if appropriate, to the United States Attorney pursuant to section 3057 of title 18; and

(ii) if advisable, take appropriate action, including but not limited to commencing an adversary proceeding to revoke the debtor's discharge pursuant to section 727(d) of title 11.

REFERENCES IN TEXT

Chapter 12 or 13 of title 11, referred to in text, is 11 U.S.C.A. § 1201 et seq. or 11 U.S.C.A. § 1301 et seq., respectively.

Chapter 7, 11, 12, 13, or 15 of title 11, referred to in subsec. (a)(3), is 11 U.S.C.A. § 701 et seq., 11 U.S.C.A. § 1101 et seq., 11 U.S.C.A. § 1201 et seq., 11 U.S.C.A. § 1301 et seq., or 11 U.S.C.A. § 1501 et seq., respectively.

Level V of the Executive Schedule, referred to in subsec. (e)(1)(A)(i), is set out in section 5316 of Title 5, Government Organization and Employees.

Section 603(a) of the Bankruptcy Abuse Prevention and Consumer Protection Act of 2005, referred to in subsecs. (a)(6) and (f)(1), is Pub. L. 109–8, Title VII, § 603(a), Apr. 20, 2005, 119 Stat. 122, which is set out as a note under this section.

CROSS REFERENCES

Appointment of disinterested person from panel of private trustees established under this section to serve as—

> Interim trustee, see 11 USCA § 701.

> Successor trustee, see 11 USCA § 703.

Appointment of standing trustee to serve in cases under—

> Chapter 12, see 11 USCA § 1202.

> Chapter 13, see 11 USCA § 1302.

Compensation for services or reimbursement of expenses not allowable for standing trustee appointed under this section, see 11 USCA § 326.

Payments to standing trustee; percentage fee fixed under this section, see 11 USCA § 1326.

§ 587. Salaries

Subject to sections 5315 through 5317 of title 5, the Attorney General shall fix the annual salaries of United States trustees and assistant United States trustees at rates of compensation not in excess of the rate of basic compensation provided for Executive Level IV of the Executive Schedule set forth in section 5315 of title 5, United States Code.

§ 588. Expenses

Necessary office expenses of the United States trustee shall be allowed when authorized by the Attorney General.

§ 589. Staff and other employees

The United States trustee may employ staff and other employees on approval of the Attorney General.

§ 589a. United States Trustee System Fund

(a) There is hereby established in the Treasury of the United States a special fund to be known as the "United States Trustee System Fund" (hereinafter in this section referred to as the "Fund"). Monies in the Fund shall be available to the Attorney General without fiscal year limitation in such amounts as may be specified in appropriations Acts for the following purposes in connection with the operations of United States trustees—

(1) salaries and related employee benefits;

(2) travel and transportation;

(3) rental of space;

(4) communication, utilities, and miscellaneous computer charges;

(5) security investigations and audits;

(6) supplies, books, and other materials for legal research;

(7) furniture and equipment;

(8) miscellaneous services, including those obtained by contract; and

(9) printing.

(b) For the purpose of recovering the cost of services of the United States Trustee System, there shall be deposited as offsetting collections to the appropriation "United States Trustee System Fund", to remain available until expended, the following—

    (1)(A)   40.46 percent of the fees collected under section 1930(a)(1)(A); and

    (B)   28.33 percent of the fees collected under section 1930(a)(1)(B);

    (2)   48.89 percent of the fees collected under section 1930(a)(3) of this title;

    (3)   one-half of the fees collected under section 1930(a)(4) of this title;

    (4)   one-half of the fees collected under section 1930(a)(5) of this title;

    (5)   100 percent of the fees collected under section 1930(a)(6) of this title;

    (6)   three-fourths of the fees collected under the last sentence of section 1930(a) of this title;

    (7)   the compensation of trustees received under section 330(d) of title 11 by the clerks of the bankruptcy courts;

    (8)   excess fees collected under section 586(e)(2) of this title;

    (9)   interest earned on Fund investment; and

    (10) fines imposed under section 110(*l*) of title 11, United States Code.

(c) Amounts in the Fund which are not currently needed for the purposes specified in subsections (a) and (f) shall be kept on deposit or invested in obligations of, or guaranteed by, the United States.

(d) The Attorney General shall transmit to the Congress, not later than 120 days after the end of each fiscal year, a detailed report on the amounts deposited in the Fund and a description of expenditures made under this section.

(e) There are authorized to be appropriated to the Fund for any fiscal year such sums as may be necessary to supplement amounts deposited under subsection (b) for the purposes specified in subsection (a).

(f)(1)   During each of fiscal years 2021 through 2026 and notwithstanding subsection (b)(5), the fees collected under section 1930(a)(6), less the amount specified in paragraph (2), shall be deposited as follows, in the following order:

    (A) First, the amounts needed to offset the amount specified in the Department of Justice appropriations for that fiscal year, shall be deposited as discretionary offsetting collections to the "United States Trustee System Fund", pursuant to subsection (a), to remain available until expended.

    (B) Second, the amounts determined annually by the Director of the Administrative Office of the United States Courts that are necessary to reimburse the judiciary for the costs of administering payments under section 330(e) of title 11, shall be deposited as mandatory offsetting collections to the "United States Trustee System Fund", and transferred and deposited into the special fund established under section 1931(a), and notwithstanding subsection (a), shall be available for expenditure without further appropriation.

    (C) Third, the amounts determined annually by the Director of the Administrative Office of the United States Courts that are necessary to pay trustee compensation authorized by section 330(e)(2) of title 11, shall be deposited as mandatory offsetting collections to the "United States Trustee System Fund", and transferred and deposited into the Chapter 7 Trustee Fund established under section 330(e) of title 11 for payment to trustees serving in cases under chapter 7 of title 11 (in addition to the amounts paid under section 330(b) of title 11), in accordance with that section, and notwithstanding subsection (a), shall be available for expenditure without further appropriation.

(D) Fourth, any remaining amounts shall be deposited as discretionary offsetting collections to the "United States Trustee System Fund", to remain available until expended.

(2) Notwithstanding subsection (b), for each of fiscal years 2021 through 2026, $5,400,000 of the fees collected under section 1930(a)(6) shall be deposited in the general fund of the Treasury.

CROSS REFERENCES

Compensation of bankruptcy trustee to be deposited by clerk of bankruptcy court into Fund established by this section, see 11 USCA § 330.

§ 589b. Bankruptcy data

(a) Rules.—The Attorney General shall, within a reasonable time after the effective date of this section, issue rules requiring uniform forms for (and from time to time thereafter to appropriately modify and approve)—

(1) final reports by trustees in cases under subchapter V of chapter 11 and chapters 7, 12, and 13 of title 11; and

(2) periodic reports by debtors in possession or trustees in cases under chapter 11 of title 11.

(b) Reports.—Each report referred to in subsection (a) shall be designed (and the requirements as to place and manner of filing shall be established) so as to facilitate compilation of data and maximum possible access of the public, both by physical inspection at one or more central filing locations, and by electronic access through the Internet or other appropriate media.

(c) Required information.—The information required to be filed in the reports referred to in subsection (b) shall be that which is in the best interests of debtors and creditors, and in the public interest in reasonable and adequate information to evaluate the efficiency and practicality of the Federal bankruptcy system. In issuing rules proposing the forms referred to in subsection (a), the Attorney General shall strike the best achievable practical balance between—

(1) the reasonable needs of the public for information about the operational results of the Federal bankruptcy system;

(2) economy, simplicity, and lack of undue burden on persons with a duty to file reports; and

(3) appropriate privacy concerns and safeguards.

(d) Final reports.—The uniform forms for final reports required under subsection (a) for use by trustees under subchapter V of chapter 11 and chapters 7, 12, and 13 of title 11 shall, in addition to such other matters as are required by law or as the Attorney General in the discretion of the Attorney General shall propose, include with respect to a case under such title—

(1) information about the length of time the case was pending;

(2) assets abandoned;

(3) assets exempted;

(4) receipts and disbursements of the estate;

(5) expenses of administration, including for use under section 707(b), actual costs of administering cases under chapter 13 of title 11;

(6) claims asserted;

(7) claims allowed; and

(8) distributions to claimants and claims discharged without payment, in each case by appropriate category and, in cases under subchapter V of chapter 11 and chapters 12 and 13 of title 11, date of confirmation of the plan, each modification thereto, and defaults by the debtor in performance under the plan.

(e) **Periodic reports.**—The uniform forms for periodic reports required under subsection (a) for use by trustees or debtors in possession under chapter 11 of title 11 shall, in addition to such other matters as are required by law or as the Attorney General in the discretion of the Attorney General shall propose, include—

(1) information about the industry classification, published by the Department of Commerce, for the businesses conducted by the debtor;

(2) length of time the case has been pending;

(3) number of full-time employees as of the date of the order for relief and at the end of each reporting period since the case was filed;

(4) cash receipts, cash disbursements and profitability of the debtor for the most recent period and cumulatively since the date of the order for relief;

(5) compliance with title 11, whether or not tax returns and tax payments since the date of the order for relief have been timely filed and made;

(6) all professional fees approved by the court in the case for the most recent period and cumulatively since the date of the order for relief (separately reported, for the professional fees incurred by or on behalf of the debtor, between those that would have been incurred absent a bankruptcy case and those not); and

(7) plans of reorganization filed and confirmed and, with respect thereto, by class, the recoveries of the holders, expressed in aggregate dollar values and, in the case of claims, as a percentage of total claims of the class allowed.

REFERENCES IN TEXT

The effective date of this section, referred to in subsec. (a), means 180 days after April 20, 2005. See Pub. L. 109–8, § 1501, set out as an Effective and Applicability Provisions note for 2005 Acts under 11 U.S.C.A. § 101.

Chapters 7, 12, and 13 of title 11, referred to in subsecs. (a)(1) and (d), are 11 U.S.C.A. § 701 et seq., 11 U.S.C.A. § 1201 et seq., and 11 U.S.C.A. § 1301 et seq., respectively.

Chapter 11 of title 11, referred to in subsecs. (a)(2) and (e), is 11 U.S.C.A. § 1101 et seq.

PART III—COURT OFFICERS AND EMPLOYEES

Chapter 41—Administrative Office of United States Courts

§ 604. Duties of Director generally

(a) The Director shall be the administrative officer of the courts, and under the supervision and direction of the Judicial Conference of the United States, shall:

(1) Supervise all administrative matters relating to the offices of clerks and other clerical and administrative personnel of the courts;

(2) Examine the state of the dockets of the courts; secure information as to the courts' need of assistance; prepare and transmit semiannually to the chief judges of the circuits, statistical data and reports as to the business of the courts;

(3) Submit to the annual meeting of the Judicial Conference of the United States, at least two weeks prior thereto, a report of the activities of the Administrative Office and the state of the business of the courts, together with the statistical data submitted to the chief judges of the

circuits under paragraph (a)(2) of this section, and the Director's recommendations, which report, data and recommendations shall be public documents.

(4) Submit to Congress and the Attorney General copies of the report, data and recommendations required by paragraph (a)(3) of this section;

(5) Fix the compensation of clerks of court, deputies, librarians, criers, messengers, law clerks, secretaries, stenographers, clerical assistants, and other employees of the courts whose compensation is not otherwise fixed by law, and, notwithstanding any other provision of law, pay on behalf of Justices and judges of the United States appointed to hold office during good behavior, United States magistrate judges, bankruptcy judges appointed under chapter 6 of this title, judges of the District Court of Guam, judges of the District Court for the Northern Mariana Islands, judges of the District Court of the Virgin Islands, bankruptcy judges and magistrate judges retired under section 377 of this title, and judges retired under section 373 of this title, who are,[1] aged 65 or over, any increases in the cost of Federal Employees' Group Life Insurance imposed after April 24, 1999, including any expenses generated by such payments, as authorized by the Judicial Conference of the United States;

(6) Determine and pay necessary office expenses of courts, judges, and those court officials whose expenses are by law allowable, and the lawful fees of United States magistrate judges;

(7) Regulate and pay annuities to widows and surviving dependent children of justices and judges of the United States, judges of the United States Court of Federal Claims, bankruptcy judges, United States magistrate judges, Directors of the Federal Judicial Center, and Directors of the Administrative Office, and necessary travel and subsistence expenses incurred by judges, court officers and employees, and officers and employees of the Administrative Office, and the Federal Judicial Center, while absent from their official stations on official business, without regard to the per diem allowances and amounts for reimbursement of actual and necessary expenses established by the Administrator of General Services under section 5702 of title 5, except that the reimbursement of subsistence expenses may not exceed that authorized by the Director for judges of the United States under section 456 of this title;

(8) Disburse appropriations and other funds for the maintenance and operation of the courts;

(9) Establish pretrial services pursuant to section 3152 of title 18, United States Code;

(10) (A) Purchase, exchange, transfer, distribute, and assign the custody of lawbooks, equipment, supplies, and other personal property for the judicial branch of Government (except the Supreme Court unless otherwise provided pursuant to paragraph (17)); (B) provide or make available readily to each court appropriate equipment for the interpretation of proceedings in accordance with section 1828 of this title; and (C) enter into and perform contracts and other transactions upon such terms as the Director may deem appropriate as may be necessary to the conduct of the work of the judicial branch of Government (except the Supreme Court unless otherwise provided pursuant to paragraph (17)), and contracts for nonpersonal services providing pretrial services, agencies for the interpretation of proceedings, and for the provision of special interpretation services pursuant to section 1828 of this title may be awarded without regard to section 6101(b) to (d) of title 41;

(11) Audit vouchers and accounts of the courts, the Federal Judicial Center, the offices providing pretrial services, and their clerical and administrative personnel;

(12) Provide accommodations for the courts, the Federal Judicial Center, the offices providing pretrial services and their clerical and administrative personnel;

---

[1]   So in original. The comma probably should not appear.

(13) Lay before Congress, annually, statistical tables that will accurately reflect the business transacted by the several bankruptcy courts, and all other pertinent data relating to such courts;

(14) Pursuant to section 1827 of this title, establish a program for the certification and utilization of interpreters in courts of the United States;

(15) Pursuant to section 1828 of this title, establish a program for the provision of special interpretation services in courts of the United States;

(16) (A) In those districts where the Director considers it advisable based on the need for interpreters, authorize the full-time or part-time employment by the court of certified interpreters; (B) where the Director considers it advisable based on the need for interpreters, appoint certified interpreters on a full-time or part-time basis, for services in various courts when he determines that such appointments will result in the economical provision of interpretation services; and (C) pay out of moneys appropriated for the judiciary interpreters' salaries, fees, and expenses, and other costs which may accrue in accordance with the provisions of sections 1827 and 1828 of this title;

(17) In the Director's discretion, (A) accept and utilize voluntary and uncompensated (gratuitous) services, including services as authorized by section 3102(b) of title 5, United States Code; and (B) accept, hold, administer, and utilize gifts and bequests of personal property for the purpose of aiding or facilitating the work of the judicial branch of Government, but gifts or bequests of money shall be covered into the Treasury;

(18) Establish procedures and mechanisms within the judicial branch for processing fines, restitution, forfeitures of bail bonds or collateral, and assessments;

(19) Regulate and pay annuities to bankruptcy judges and United States magistrate judges in accordance with section 377 of this title and paragraphs (1)(B) and (2) of section 2(c) of the Retirement and Survivors' Annuities for Bankruptcy Judges and Magistrates Act of 1988;

(20) Periodically compile—

    (A) the rules which are prescribed under section 2071 of this title by courts other than the Supreme Court;

    (B) the rules which are prescribed under section 358 of this title; and

    (C) the orders which are required to be publicly available under section 360(b) of this title;

so as to provide a current record of such rules and orders;

(21) Establish a program of incentive awards for employees of the judicial branch of the United States Government, other than any judge who is entitled to hold office during good behavior;

(22) Receive and expend, either directly or by transfer to the United States Marshals Service or other Government agency, funds appropriated for the procurement, installation, and maintenance of security equipment and protective services for the United States Courts in courtrooms and adjacent areas, including building ingress/egress control, inspection of packages, directed security patrols, and other similar activities;

(23) Regulate and pay annuities to judges of the United States Court of Federal Claims in accordance with section 178 of this title;

(24) Establish and administer a vulnerability management program in the judicial branch; and

(25) Perform such other duties as may be assigned to the Director by the Supreme Court or the Judicial Conference of the United States.

(b) The clerical and administrative personnel of the courts shall comply with all requests by the Director for information or statistical data as to the state of court dockets.

(c) Inspection of court dockets outside the continental United States may be made through United States officials residing within the jurisdiction where the inspection is made.

(d) The Director, under the supervision and direction of the conference, shall:

(1) supervise all administrative matters relating to the offices of the United States magistrate judges;

(2) gather, compile, and evaluate all statistical and other information required for the performance of his duties and the duties of the conference with respect to such officers;

(3) lay before Congress annually statistical tables and other information which will accurately reflect the business which has come before the various United States magistrate judges, including (A) the number of matters in which the parties consented to the exercise of jurisdiction by a magistrate judge, (B) the number of appeals taken pursuant to the decisions of magistrate judges and the disposition of such appeals, and (C) the professional background and qualifications of individuals appointed under section 631 of this title to serve as magistrate judges;

(4) prepare and distribute a manual, with annual supplements and periodic revisions, for the use of such officers, which shall set forth their powers and duties, describe all categories of proceedings that may arise before them, and contain such other information as may be required to enable them to discharge their powers and duties promptly, effectively, and impartially.

(e) The Director may promulgate appropriate rules and regulations approved by the conference and not inconsistent with any provision of law, to assist him in the performance of the duties conferred upon him by subsection (d) of this section. Magistrate judges shall keep such records and make such reports as are specified in such rules and regulations.

(f) The Director may make, promulgate, issue, rescind, and amend rules and regulations (including regulations prescribing standards of conduct for Administrative Office employees) as may be necessary to carry out the Director's functions, powers, duties, and authority. The Director may publish in the Federal Register such rules, regulations, and notices for the judicial branch of Government as the Director determines to be of public interest; and the Director of the Federal Register hereby is authorized to accept and shall publish such materials.

(g)(1) When authorized to exchange personal property, the Director may exchange or sell similar items and may apply the exchange allowance or proceeds of sale in such cases in whole or in part payment for the property acquired, but any transaction carried out under the authority of this subsection shall be evidenced in writing.

(2) The Director hereby is authorized to enter into contracts for public utility services and related terminal equipment for periods not exceeding ten years.

(3)(A) In order to promote the recycling and reuse of recyclable materials, the Director may provide for the sale or disposal of recyclable scrap materials from paper products and other consumable office supplies held by an entity within the judicial branch.

(B) The sale or disposal of recyclable materials under subparagraph (A) shall be consistent with the procedures provided in sections 541–555 of title 40 for the sale of surplus property.

(C) Proceeds from the sale of recyclable materials under subparagraph (A) shall be deposited as offsetting collections to the fund established under section 1931 of this title and shall remain available until expended to reimburse any appropriations for the operation and maintenance of the judicial branch.

(4) The Director is hereby authorized:

(A) to enter into contracts for the acquisition of severable services for a period that begins in one fiscal year and ends in the next fiscal year to the same extent as the head of an executive agency under the authority of section 253*l* of Title 41, United States Code;

(B) to enter into contracts for multiple years for the acquisition of property and services to the same extent as executive agencies under the authority of section 254c of Title 41, United States Code; and

(C) to make advance, partial, progress or other payments under contracts for property or services to the same extent as executive agencies under the authority of section 255 of title 41, United States Code.

(h)(1) The Director shall, out of funds appropriated for the operation and maintenance of the courts, provide facilities and pay necessary expenses incurred by the judicial councils of the circuits and the Judicial Conference under chapter 16 of this title, including mileage allowance and witness fees, at the same rate as provided in section 1821 of this title. Administrative and professional assistance from the Administrative Office of the United States Courts may be requested by each judicial council and the Judicial Conference for purposes of discharging their duties under chapter 16 of this title.

(2) The Director of the Administrative Office of the United States Courts shall include in his annual report filed with the Congress under this section a summary of the number of complaints filed with each judicial council under chapter 16 of this title, indicating the general nature of such complaints and the disposition of those complaints in which action has been taken.

(i)   Restrictions on criminal history inquiries.—

(1)   Definitions.—In this subsection—

(A) the terms "agency" and "criminal history record information" have the meanings given those terms in section 9201 of title 5;

(B) the term "covered employee" means an employee of the judicial branch of the United States Government, other than—

(i) any judge or justice who is entitled to hold office during good behavior;

(ii) a United States magistrate judge; or

(iii) a bankruptcy judge; and

(C) the term "employing office" means any office or entity of the judicial branch of the United States Government that employs covered employees.

(2)   Restriction.—A covered employee may not request that an applicant for employment as a covered employee disclose criminal history record information if the request would be prohibited under section 9202 of title 5 if made by an employee of an agency.

(3)   Employing office policies; complaint procedure.—The provisions of sections 9203 and 9206 of title 5 shall apply to employing offices and to applicants for employment as covered employees, consistent with regulations issued by the Director to implement this subsection.

(4)   Adverse action.—

(A)   Adverse action.—The Director may take such adverse action with respect to a covered employee who violates paragraph (2) as would be appropriate under section 9204 of title 5 if the violation had been committed by an employee of an agency.

(B)   Appeals.—The Director shall by rule establish procedures providing for an appeal from any adverse action taken under subparagraph (A) by not later than 30 days after the date of the action.

(C) **Applicability of other laws.**—Except as provided in subparagraph (B), an adverse action taken under subparagraph (A) (including a determination in an appeal from such an action under subparagraph (B)) shall not be subject to appeal or judicial review.

(5) **Regulations to be issued.**—

(A) **In general.**—Not later than 18 months after the date of enactment of the Fair Chance to Compete for Jobs Act of 2019, the Director shall issue regulations to implement this subsection.

(B) **Parallel with agency regulations.**—The regulations issued under subparagraph (A) shall be the same as substantive regulations promulgated by the Director of the Office of Personnel Management under section 2(b)(1) of the Fair Chance to Compete for Jobs Act of 2019 except to the extent that the Director of the Administrative Office of the United States Courts may determine, for good cause shown and stated together with the regulation, that a modification of such regulations would be more effective for the implementation of the rights and protections under this subsection.

(6) **Effective date.**—Paragraphs (1) through (4) shall take effect on the date on which section 9202 of title 5 applies with respect to agencies.

REFERENCES IN TEXT

Chapter 6 of this title, referred to in subsec. (a)(5), is chapter 6 of part I of this title, which is classified to 28 U.S.C.A. § 151 et seq.

Section 2(c) of the Retirement and Survivors' Annuities for Bankruptcy Judges and Magistrates Act of 1988, referred to in subsec. (a)(19), is section 2(c) of Pub. L. 100–659, Nov. 15, 1988, 102 Stat. 3916, which is set out as a note under section 377 of this title.

Section 253*l* of Title 41, United States Code, referred to in subsec. (g)(4)(A), probably means section 303L of Act June 30, 1949, c. 288, which was classified to section 253*l* of former Title 41, Public Contracts, and was repealed and restated as section 3902 of Title 41, Public Contracts, by Pub. L. 111–350, §§ 3, 7(b), Jan. 4, 2011, 124 Stat. 3677, 3855.

Section 254c of Title 41, United States Code, referred to in subsec. (g)(4)(B), probably means section 304B of Act June 30, 1949, c. 288, which was classified to section 254c of former Title 41, Public Contracts, and was repealed and restated as section 3903 of Title 41, Public Contracts, by Pub. L. 111–350, §§ 3, 7(b), Jan. 4, 2011, 124 Stat. 3677, 3855.

Section 255 of Title 41, referred to in subsec. (g)(4)(C), probably means section 305 of Act June 30, 1949, c. 288, which was classified to section 255 of former Title 41, Public Contracts, and was repealed and restated as chapter 45 (§ 4501 et seq.) of Title 41, Public Contracts, by Pub. L. 111–350, §§ 3, 7(b), Jan. 4, 2011, 124 Stat. 3677, 3855.

CROSS REFERENCES

Actual abode of recalled judge or magistrate deemed official station for purposes of this section, see 28 USCA § 374.

Annual report to Judicial Conference under this section to include administration and operation of pretrial services for previous year, see 18 USCA § 3155.

Classification and general schedule pay rates, see 5 USCA §§ 5101 et seq. and 5331 et seq.

Duties of Supreme Court Marshal, see 28 USCA § 672.

Expenses of judges and United States attorneys, see 28 USCA §§ 456, 460, 549, and 566.

Juror travel allowance not to exceed maximum rate per mile that Director prescribes pursuant to this section, see 28 USCA § 1871.

Notification to Attorney General of receipt of payment of unpaid fines, see 18 USCA § 3612.

Office expenses of clerks of court, see 28 USCA § 961.

Overtime pay, see 5 USCA § 5541 et seq.

Specification by Director in payment of fine as provided under this section, see 18 USCA § 3611.

Supreme Court officers and employees; compensation and disbursement, see 28 USCA § 671 et seq.

Chapter 44—Alternative Dispute Resolution

§ 651. Authorization of alternative dispute resolution

(a) **Definition.**—For purposes of this chapter, an alternative dispute resolution process includes any process or procedure, other than an adjudication by a presiding judge, in which a neutral third party participates to assist in the resolution of issues in controversy, through processes such as early neutral evaluation, mediation, minitrial, and arbitration as provided in sections 654 through 658.

(b) **Authority.**—Each United States district court shall authorize, by local rule adopted under section 2071(a), the use of alternative dispute resolution processes in all civil actions, including adversary proceedings in bankruptcy, in accordance with this chapter, except that the use of arbitration may be authorized only as provided in section 654. Each United States district court shall devise and implement its own alternative dispute resolution program, by local rule adopted under section 2071(a), to encourage and promote the use of alternative dispute resolution in its district.

(c) **Existing alternative dispute resolution programs.**—In those courts where an alternative dispute resolution program is in place on the date of the enactment of the Alternative Dispute Resolution Act of 1998, the court shall examine the effectiveness of that program and adopt such improvements to the program as are consistent with the provisions and purposes of this chapter [28 U.S.C.A. § 651 et seq.].

(d) **Administration of alternative dispute resolution programs.**—Each United States district court shall designate an employee, or a judicial officer, who is knowledgeable in alternative dispute resolution practices and processes to implement, administer, oversee, and evaluate the court's alternative dispute resolution program. Such person may also be responsible for recruiting, screening, and training attorneys to serve as neutrals and arbitrators in the court's alternative dispute resolution program.

(e) **Title 9 not affected.**—This chapter [28 U.S.C.A. § 651 et seq.] shall not affect title 9, United States Code.

(f) **Program support.**—The Federal Judicial Center and the Administrative Office of the United States Courts are authorized to assist the district courts in the establishment and improvement of alternative dispute resolution programs by identifying particular practices employed in successful programs and providing additional assistance as needed and appropriate.

REFERENCES IN TEXT

The enactment of the Alternative Dispute Resolution Act of 1998, referred to in subsec. (c), is the enactment of Pub. L. 105–315, 112 Stat. 2993, which was approved Oct. 30, 1998.

§ 652. Jurisdiction

(a) **Consideration of alternative dispute resolution in appropriate cases.**— Notwithstanding any provision of law to the contrary and except as provided in subsections (b) and (c), each district court shall, by local rule adopted under section 2071(a), require that litigants in all civil cases consider the use of an alternative dispute resolution process at an appropriate stage in the litigation. Each district court shall provide litigants in all civil cases with at least one alternative dispute resolution process, including, but not limited to, mediation, early neutral evaluation, minitrial, and arbitration as authorized in sections 654 through 658. Any district court that elects to require the use of alternative dispute resolution in certain cases may do so only with respect to mediation, early neutral evaluation, and, if the parties consent, arbitration.

(b) Actions exempted from consideration of alternative dispute resolution.—Each district court may exempt from the requirements of this section specific cases or categories of cases in which use of alternative dispute resolution would not be appropriate. In defining these exemptions, each district court shall consult with members of the bar, including the United States Attorney for that district.

(c) Authority of the Attorney General.—Nothing in this section shall alter or conflict with the authority of the Attorney General to conduct litigation on behalf of the United States, with the authority of any Federal agency authorized to conduct litigation in the United States courts, or with any delegation of litigation authority by the Attorney General.

(d) Confidentiality provisions.—Until such time as rules are adopted under chapter 131 of this title [28 U.S.C.A. § 2071 et seq.] providing for the confidentiality of alternative dispute resolution processes under this chapter [28 U.S.C.A. § 651 et seq.], each district court shall, by local rule adopted under section 2071(a), provide for the confidentiality of the alternative dispute resolution processes and to prohibit disclosure of confidential dispute resolution communications.

§ 653. Neutrals

(a) Panel of neutrals.—Each district court that authorizes the use of alternative dispute resolution processes shall adopt appropriate processes for making neutrals available for use by the parties for each category of process offered. Each district court shall promulgate its own procedures and criteria for the selection of neutrals on its panels.

(b) Qualifications and training.—Each person serving as a neutral in an alternative dispute resolution process should be qualified and trained to serve as a neutral in the appropriate alternative dispute resolution process. For this purpose, the district court may use, among others, magistrate judges who have been trained to serve as neutrals in alternative dispute resolution processes, professional neutrals from the private sector, and persons who have been trained to serve as neutrals in alternative dispute resolution processes. Until such time as rules are adopted under chapter 131 of this title [28 U.S.C.A. § 2071 et seq.] relating to the disqualification of neutrals, each district court shall issue rules under section 2071(a) relating to the disqualification of neutrals (including, where appropriate, disqualification under section 455 of this title, other applicable law, and professional responsibility standards).

§ 654. Arbitration

(a) Referral of actions to arbitration.—Notwithstanding any provision of law to the contrary and except as provided in subsections (a), (b), and (c) of section 652 and subsection (d) of this section, a district court may allow the referral to arbitration of any civil action (including any adversary proceeding in bankruptcy) pending before it when the parties consent, except that referral to arbitration may not be made where—

    (1) the action is based on an alleged violation of a right secured by the Constitution of the United States;

    (2) jurisdiction is based in whole or in part on section 1343 of this title; or

    (3) the relief sought consists of money damages in an amount greater than $150,000.

(b) Safeguards in consent cases.—Until such time as rules are adopted under chapter 131 of this title relating to procedures described in this subsection, the district court shall, by local rule adopted under section 2071(a), establish procedures to ensure that any civil action in which arbitration by consent is allowed under subsection (a)—

    (1) consent to arbitration is freely and knowingly obtained; and

    (2) no party or attorney is prejudiced for refusing to participate in arbitration.

(c) **Presumptions.**—For purposes of subsection (a)(3), a district court may presume damages are not in excess of $150,000 unless counsel certifies that damages exceed such amount.

(d) **Existing programs.**—Nothing in this chapter is deemed to affect any program in which arbitration is conducted pursuant to section[1] title IX of the Judicial Improvements and Access to Justice Act (Public Law 100–702), as amended by section 1 of Public Law 105–53.

REFERENCES IN TEXT

Title IX of the Judicial Improvements and Access to Justice Act, referred to in subsec. (d), is Pub. L. 100–702, Title IX, Nov. 19, 1988, 102 Stat. 4663. See Codifications note under this section.

§ 655. Arbitrators

(a) **Powers of arbitrators.**—An arbitrator to whom an action is referred under section 654 shall have the power, within the judicial district of the district court which referred the action to arbitration—

    (1) to conduct arbitration hearings;

    (2) to administer oaths and affirmations; and

    (3) to make awards.

(b) **Standards for certification.**—Each district court that authorizes arbitration shall establish standards for the certification of arbitrators and shall certify arbitrators to perform services in accordance with such standards and this chapter. The standards shall include provisions requiring that any arbitrator—

    (1) shall take the oath or affirmation described in section 453; and

    (2) shall be subject to the disqualification rules under section 455.

(c) **Immunity.**—All individuals serving as arbitrators in an alternative dispute resolution program under this chapter are performing quasi-judicial functions and are entitled to the immunities and protections that the law accords to persons serving in such capacity.

§ 656. Subpoenas

Rule 45 of the Federal Rules of Civil Procedure (relating to subpoenas) applies to subpoenas for the attendance of witnesses and the production of documentary evidence at an arbitration hearing under this chapter.

§ 657. Arbitration award and judgment

(a) **Filing and effect of arbitration award.**—An arbitration award made by an arbitrator under this chapter, along with proof of service of such award on the other party by the prevailing party or by the plaintiff, shall be filed promptly after the arbitration hearing is concluded with the clerk of the district court that referred the case to arbitration. Such award shall be entered as the judgment of the court after the time has expired for requesting a trial de novo. The judgment so entered shall be subject to the same provisions of law and shall have the same force and effect as a judgment of the court in a civil action, except that the judgment shall not be subject to review in any other court by appeal or otherwise.

(b) **Sealing of arbitration award.**—The district court shall provide, by local rule adopted under section 2071(a), that the contents of any arbitration award made under this chapter shall not be made known to any judge who might be assigned to the case until the district court has entered final judgment in the action or the action has otherwise terminated.

---

[1] So in original. The word "section" probably should not appear.

(c) Trial de novo of arbitration awards.—

(1) Time for filing demand.—Within 30 days after the filing of an arbitration award with a district court under subsection (a), any party may file a written demand for a trial de novo in the district court.

(2) Action restored to court docket.—Upon a demand for a trial de novo, the action shall be restored to the docket of the court and treated for all purposes as if it had not been referred to arbitration.

(3) Exclusion of evidence of arbitration.—The court shall not admit at the trial de novo any evidence that there has been an arbitration proceeding, the nature or amount of any award, or any other matter concerning the conduct of the arbitration proceeding, unless—

    (A) the evidence would otherwise be admissible in the court under the Federal Rules of Evidence; or

    (B) the parties have otherwise stipulated.

§ 658. Compensation of arbitrators and neutrals

(a) Compensation.—The district court shall, subject to regulations approved by the Judicial Conference of the United States, establish the amount of compensation, if any, that each arbitrator or neutral shall receive for services rendered in each case under this chapter.

(b) Transportation allowances.—Under regulations prescribed by the Director of the Administrative Office of the United States Courts, a district court may reimburse arbitrators and other neutrals for actual transportation expenses necessarily incurred in the performance of duties under this chapter.

Chapter 57—General Provisions Applicable to Court Officers and Employees

§ 959. Trustees and receivers suable; management; State laws

(a) Trustees, receivers or managers of any property, including debtors in possession, may be sued, without leave of the court appointing them, with respect to any of their acts or transactions in carrying on business connected with such property. Such actions shall be subject to the general equity power of such court so far as the same may be necessary to the ends of justice, but this shall not deprive a litigant of his right to trial by jury.

(b) Except as provided in section 1166 of title 11, a trustee, receiver or manager appointed in any cause pending in any court of the United States, including a debtor in possession, shall manage and operate the property in his possession as such trustee, receiver or manager according to the requirements of the valid laws of the State in which such property is situated, in the same manner that the owner or possessor thereof would be bound to do if in possession thereof.

CROSS REFERENCES

Capacity to sue or be sued, see Fed. R. Civ. Proc. 17.

Mismanagement of property by receiver, criminal penalty, see 18 USCA § 1911.

Process and orders affecting property in different districts, see 28 USCA § 1692.

Receivers of property in different districts; jurisdiction, see 28 USCA § 754.

§ 960. Tax liability

(a) Any officers and agents conducting any business under authority of a United States court shall be subject to all Federal, State and local taxes applicable to such business to the same extent as if it were conducted by an individual or corporation.

(b) A tax under subsection (a) shall be paid on or before the due date of the tax under applicable nonbankruptcy law, unless—

(1) the tax is a property tax secured by a lien against property that is abandoned under section 554 of title 11, within a reasonable period of time after the lien attaches, by the trustee in a case under title 11; or

(2) payment of the tax is excused under a specific provision of title 11.

(c) In a case pending under chapter 7 of title 11, payment of a tax may be deferred until final distribution is made under section 726 of title 11, if—

(1) the tax was not incurred by a trustee duly appointed or elected under chapter 7 of title 11; or

(2) before the due date of the tax, an order of the court makes a finding of probable insufficiency of funds of the estate to pay in full the administrative expenses allowed under section 503(b) of title 11 that have the same priority in distribution under section 726(b) of title 11 as the priority of that tax.

PART IV—JURISDICTION AND VENUE
Chapter 83—Courts of Appeals

§ 1291.   Final decisions of district courts

The courts of appeals (other than the United States Court of Appeals for the Federal Circuit) shall have jurisdiction of appeals from all final decisions of the district courts of the United States, the United States District Court for the District of the Canal Zone, the District Court of Guam, and the District Court of the Virgin Islands, except where a direct review may be had in the Supreme Court. The jurisdiction of the United States Court of Appeals for the Federal Circuit shall be limited to the jurisdiction described in sections 1292(c) and (d) and 1295 of this title.

§ 1292.   Interlocutory decisions

(a) Except as provided in subsections (c) and (d) of this section, the courts of appeals shall have jurisdiction of appeals from:

(1) Interlocutory orders of the district courts of the United States, the United States District Court for the District of the Canal Zone, the District Court of Guam, and the District Court of the Virgin Islands, or of the judges thereof, granting, continuing, modifying, refusing or dissolving injunctions, or refusing to dissolve or modify injunctions, except where a direct review may be had in the Supreme Court;

(2) Interlocutory orders appointing receivers, or refusing orders to wind up receiverships or to take steps to accomplish the purposes thereof, such as directing sales or other disposals of property;

(3) Interlocutory decrees of such district courts or the judges thereof determining the rights and liabilities of the parties to admiralty cases in which appeals from final decrees are allowed.

(b) When a district judge, in making in a civil action an order not otherwise appealable under this section, shall be of the opinion that such order involves a controlling question of law as to which there is substantial ground for difference of opinion and that an immediate appeal from the order may materially advance the ultimate termination of the litigation, he shall so state in writing in such order. The Court of Appeals which would have jurisdiction of an appeal of such action may thereupon, in its discretion, permit an appeal to be taken from such order, if application is made to it within ten days after the entry of the order: *Provided, however,* That application for an appeal hereunder shall not stay proceedings in the district court unless the district judge or the Court of Appeals or a judge thereof shall so order.

(c) The United States Court of Appeals for the Federal Circuit shall have exclusive jurisdiction—

(1) of an appeal from an interlocutory order or decree described in subsection (a) or (b) of this section in any case over which the court would have jurisdiction of an appeal under section 1295 of this title; and

(2) of an appeal from a judgment in a civil action for patent infringement which would otherwise be appealable to the United States Court of Appeals for the Federal Circuit and is final except for an accounting.

(d)(1) When the chief judge of the Court of International Trade issues an order under the provisions of section 256(b) of this title, or when any judge of the Court of International Trade, in issuing any other interlocutory order, includes in the order a statement that a controlling question of law is involved with respect to which there is a substantial ground for difference of opinion and that an immediate appeal from that order may materially advance the ultimate termination of the litigation, the United States Court of Appeals for the Federal Circuit may, in its discretion, permit an appeal to be taken from such order, if application is made to that Court within ten days after the entry of such order.

(2) When the chief judge of the United States Court of Federal Claims issues an order under section 798(b) of this title, or when any judge of the United States Court of Federal Claims, in issuing an interlocutory order, includes in the order a statement that a controlling question of law is involved with respect to which there is a substantial ground for difference of opinion and that an immediate appeal from that order may materially advance the ultimate termination of the litigation, the United States Court of Appeals for the Federal Circuit may, in its discretion, permit an appeal to be taken from such order, if application is made to that Court within ten days after the entry of such order.

(3) Neither the application for nor the granting of an appeal under this subsection shall stay proceedings in the Court of International Trade or in the Court of Federal Claims, as the case may be, unless a stay is ordered by a judge of the Court of International Trade or of the Court of Federal Claims or by the United States Court of Appeals for the Federal Circuit or a judge of that court.

(4)(A) The United States Court of Appeals for the Federal Circuit shall have exclusive jurisdiction of an appeal from an interlocutory order of a district court of the United States, the District Court of Guam, the District Court of the Virgin Islands, or the District Court for the Northern Mariana Islands, granting or denying, in whole or in part, a motion to transfer an action to the United States Court of Federal Claims under section 1631 of this title.

(B) When a motion to transfer an action to the Court of Federal Claims is filed in a district court, no further proceedings shall be taken in the district court until 60 days after the court has ruled upon the motion. If an appeal is taken from the district court's grant or denial of the motion, proceedings shall be further stayed until the appeal has been decided by the Court of Appeals for the Federal Circuit. The stay of proceedings in the district court shall not bar the granting of preliminary or injunctive relief, where appropriate and where expedition is reasonably necessary. However, during the period in which proceedings are stayed as provided in this subparagraph, no transfer to the Court of Federal Claims pursuant to the motion shall be carried out.

(e) The Supreme Court may prescribe rules, in accordance with section 2072 of this title, to provide for an appeal of an interlocutory decision to the courts of appeals that is not otherwise provided for under subsection (a), (b), (c), or (d).

Chapter 85—District Courts; Jurisdiction

§ 1334. Bankruptcy cases and proceedings

(a) Except as provided in subsection (b) of this section, the district courts shall have original and exclusive jurisdiction of all cases under title 11.

(b) Except as provided in subsection (e)(2), and notwithstanding any Act of Congress that confers exclusive jurisdiction on a court or courts other than the district courts, the district courts shall have original but not exclusive jurisdiction of all civil proceedings arising under title 11, or arising in or related to cases under title 11.

(c)(1) Except with respect to a case under chapter 15 of title 11, nothing in this section prevents a district court in the interest of justice, or in the interest of comity with State courts or respect for State law, from abstaining from hearing a particular proceeding arising under title 11 or arising in or related to a case under title 11.

(2) Upon timely motion of a party in a proceeding based upon a State law claim or State law cause of action, related to a case under title 11 but not arising under title 11 or arising in a case under title 11, with respect to which an action could not have been commenced in a court of the United States absent jurisdiction under this section, the district court shall abstain from hearing such proceeding if an action is commenced, and can be timely adjudicated, in a State forum of appropriate jurisdiction.

(d) Any decision to abstain or not to abstain made under subsection (c) (other than a decision not to abstain in a proceeding described in subsection (c)(2)) is not reviewable by appeal or otherwise by the court of appeals under section 158(d), 1291, or 1292 of this title or by the Supreme Court of the United States under section 1254 of this title. Subsection (c) and this subsection shall not be construed to limit the applicability of the stay provided for by section 362 of title 11, United States Code, as such section applies to an action affecting the property of the estate in bankruptcy.

(e) The district court in which a case under title 11 is commenced or is pending shall have exclusive jurisdiction—

(1) of all the property, wherever located, of the debtor as of the commencement of such case, and of property of the estate; and

(2) over all claims or causes of action that involve construction of section 327 of title 11, United States Code, or rules relating to disclosure requirements under section 327.

REFERENCES IN TEXT

Chapter 15 of title 11, referred to in subsec. (c), is 11 U.S.C.A. § 1501 et seq.

CROSS REFERENCES

Appointment of clerk for bankruptcy court where warranted by number of cases and proceedings pending, see 28 USCA § 156.

Non-core proceedings not subject to mandatory abstention provisions, see 28 USCA § 157.

Removal of claims related to bankruptcy cases, see 28 USCA § 1452.

Venue, see 28 USCA §§ 1408 and 1409.

Chapter 87—District Courts; Venue

§ 1408. Venue of cases under title 11

Except as provided in section 1410 of this title, a case under title 11 may be commenced in the district court for the district—

(1) in which the domicile, residence, principal place of business in the United States, or principal assets in the United States, of the person or entity that is the subject of such case have been located for the one hundred and eighty days immediately preceding such commencement, or for a longer portion of such one-hundred-and-eighty-day period than the domicile, residence, or principal place of business, in the United States, or principal assets in the United States, of such person were located in any other district; or

(2) in which there is pending a case under title 11 concerning such person's affiliate, general partner, or partnership.

§ 1409. Venue of proceedings arising under title 11 or arising in or related to cases under title 11

(a) Except as otherwise provided in subsections (b) and (d), a proceeding arising under title 11 or arising in or related to a case under title 11 may be commenced in the district court in which such case is pending.

(b) Except as provided in subsection (d) of this section, a trustee in a case under title 11 may commence a proceeding arising in or related to such case to recover a money judgment of or property worth less than $1,525 or a consumer debt of less than $22,700, or a debt (excluding a consumer debt) against a noninsider of less than $27,750, only in the district court for the district in which the defendant resides.

(c) Except as provided in subsection (b) of this section, a trustee in a case under title 11 may commence a proceeding arising in or related to such case as statutory successor to the debtor or creditors under section 541 or 544(b) of title 11 in the district court for the district where the State or Federal court sits in which, under applicable nonbankruptcy venue provisions, the debtor or creditors, as the case may be, may have commenced an action on which such proceeding is based if the case under title 11 had not been commenced.

(d) A trustee may commence a proceeding arising under title 11 or arising in or related to a case under title 11 based on a claim arising after the commencement of such case from the operation of the business of the debtor only in the district court for the district where a State or Federal court sits in which, under applicable nonbankruptcy venue provisions, an action on such claim may have been brought.

(e) A proceeding arising under title 11 or arising in or related to a case under title 11, based on a claim arising after the commencement of such case from the operation of the business of the debtor, may be commenced against the representative of the estate in such case in the district court for the district where the State or Federal court sits in which the party commencing such proceeding may, under applicable nonbankruptcy venue provisions, have brought an action on such claim, or in the district court in which such case is pending.

§ 1410. Venue of cases ancillary to foreign proceedings

A case under chapter 15 of title 11 may be commenced in the district court of the United States for the district—

(1) in which the debtor has its principal place of business or principal assets in the United States;

(2) if the debtor does not have a place of business or assets in the United States, in which there is pending against the debtor an action or proceeding in a Federal or State court; or

(3) in a case other than those specified in paragraph (1) or (2), in which venue will be consistent with the interests of justice and the convenience of the parties, having regard to the relief sought by the foreign representative.

CROSS REFERENCES

Commencement of bankruptcy cases in district courts having venue except as provided by this section, see 28 USCA § 1408.

§ 1411. Jury trials

(a) Except as provided in subsection (b) of this section, this chapter and title 11 do not affect any right to trial by jury that an individual has under applicable nonbankruptcy law with regard to a personal injury or wrongful death tort claim.

(b) The district court may order the issues arising under section 303 of title 11 to be tried without a jury.

§ 1412. Change of venue

A district court may transfer a case or proceeding under title 11 to a district court for another district, in the interest of justice or for the convenience of the parties.

§ 1413. Venue of cases under chapter 5 of title 3

Notwithstanding the preceding provisions of this chapter, a civil action under section 1346(g) may be brought in the United States district court for the district in which the employee is employed or in the United States District Court for the District of Columbia.

Chapter 89—District Courts; Removal of Cases from State Courts

§ 1452. Removal of claims related to bankruptcy cases

(a) A party may remove any claim or cause of action in a civil action other than a proceeding before the United States Tax Court or a civil action by a governmental unit to enforce such governmental unit's police or regulatory power, to the district court for the district where such civil action is pending, if such district court has jurisdiction of such claim or cause of action under section 1334 of this title.

(b) The court to which such claim or cause of action is removed may remand such claim or cause of action on any equitable ground. An order entered under this subsection remanding a claim or cause of action, or a decision to not remand, is not reviewable by appeal or otherwise by the court of appeals under section 158(d), 1291, or 1292 of this title or by the Supreme Court of the United States under section 1254 of this title.

PART V—PROCEDURE

Chapter 123—Fees and Costs

§ 1930. Bankruptcy fees

(a) The parties commencing a case under title 11 shall pay to the clerk of the district court or the clerk of the bankruptcy court, if one has been certified pursuant to section 156(b) of this title, the following filing fees:

    (1) For a case commenced under—

        (A) chapter 7 of title 11, $245, and

        (B) chapter 13 of title 11, $235.

    (2) For a case commenced under chapter 9 of title 11, equal to the fee specified in paragraph (3) for filing a case under chapter 11 of title 11. The amount by which the fee payable under this paragraph exceeds $300 shall be deposited in the fund established under section 1931 of this title.

    (3) For a case commenced under chapter 11 of title 11 that does not concern a railroad, as defined in section 101 of title 11, $1,167.

(4)   For a case commenced under chapter 11 of title 11 concerning a railroad, as so defined, $1,000.

(5)   For a case commenced under chapter 12 of title 11, $200.

(6)(A)   Except as provided in subparagraph (B), in addition to the filing fee paid to the clerk, a quarterly fee shall be paid to the United States trustee, for deposit in the Treasury, in each case under chapter 11 of title 11, other than under subchapter V, for each quarter (including any fraction thereof) until the case is converted or dismissed, whichever occurs first. The fee shall be $325 for each quarter in which disbursements total less than $15,000; $650 for each quarter in which disbursements total $15,000 or more but less than $75,000; $975 for each quarter in which disbursements total $75,000 or more but less than $150,000; $1,625 for each quarter in which disbursements total $150,000 or more but less than $225,000; $1,950 for each quarter in which disbursements total $225,000 or more but less than $300,000; $4,875 for each quarter in which disbursements total $300,000 or more but less than $1,000,000; $6,500 for each quarter in which disbursements total $1,000,000 or more but less than $2,000,000; $9,750 for each quarter in which disbursements total $2,000,000 or more but less than $3,000,000; $10,400 for each quarter in which disbursements total $3,000,000 or more but less than $5,000,000; $13,000 for each quarter in which disbursements total $5,000,000 or more but less than $15,000,000; $20,000 for each quarter in which disbursements total $15,000,000 or more but less than $30,000,000; $30,000 for each quarter in which disbursements total more than $30,000,000. The fee shall be payable on the last day of the calendar month following the calendar quarter for which the fee is owed.

(B)(i)   During the 5-year period beginning on January 1, 2021, in addition to the filing fee paid to the clerk, a quarterly fee shall be paid to the United States trustee, for deposit in the Treasury, in each open and reopened case under chapter 11 of title 11, other than under subchapter V, for each quarter (including any fraction thereof) until the case is closed, converted, or dismissed, whichever occurs first.

(ii)   The fee shall be the greater of—

(I)   0.4 percent of disbursements or $250 for each quarter in which disbursements total less than $1,000,000; and

(II)   0.8 percent of disbursements but not more than $250,000 for each quarter in which disbursements total at least $1,000,000.

(iii) The fee shall be payable on the last day of the calendar month following the calendar quarter for which the fee is owed.

(7)   In districts that are not part of a United States trustee region as defined in section 581 of this title, the Judicial Conference of the United States shall require the debtor in a case under chapter 11 of title 11 to pay fees equal to those imposed by paragraph (6) of this subsection. Such fees shall be deposited as offsetting receipts to the fund established under section 1931 of this title and shall remain available until expended.

An individual commencing a voluntary case or a joint case under title 11 may pay such fee in installments. For converting, on request of the debtor, a case under chapter 7, or 13 of title 11, to a case under chapter 11 of title 11, the debtor shall pay to the clerk of the district court or the clerk of the bankruptcy court, if one has been certified pursuant to section 156(b) of this title, a fee of the amount equal to the difference between the fee specified in paragraph (3) and the fee specified in paragraph (1).

(b)   The Judicial Conference of the United States may prescribe additional fees in cases under title 11 of the same kind as the Judicial Conference prescribes under section 1914(b) of this title.

(c)   Upon the filing of any separate or joint notice of appeal or application for appeal or upon the receipt of any order allowing, or notice of the allowance of, an appeal or a writ of certiorari $5 shall be paid to the clerk of the court, by the appellant or petitioner.

(d)   Whenever any case or proceeding is dismissed in any bankruptcy court for want of jurisdiction, such court may order the payment of just costs.

(e)   The clerk of the court may collect only the fees prescribed under this section.

(f)(1)   Under the procedures prescribed by the Judicial Conference of the United States, the district court or the bankruptcy court may waive the filing fee in a case under chapter 7 of title 11 for an individual if the court determines that such individual has income less than 150 percent of the income official poverty line (as defined by the Office of Management and Budget, and revised annually in accordance with section 673(2) of the Omnibus Budget Reconciliation Act of 1981) applicable to a family of the size involved and is unable to pay that fee in installments. For purposes of this paragraph, the term "filing fee" means the filing fee required by subsection (a), or any other fee prescribed by the Judicial Conference under subsections (b) and (c) that is payable to the clerk upon the commencement of a case under chapter 7.

(2)   The district court or the bankruptcy court may waive for such debtors other fees prescribed under subsections (b) and (c).

(3)   This subsection does not restrict the district court or the bankruptcy court from waiving, in accordance with Judicial Conference policy, fees prescribed under this section for other debtors and creditors.

REFERENCES IN TEXT

Chapter 7, 11, 12, or 13 of title 11, referred to in text, is 11 U.S.C.A. § 701 et seq., 11 U.S.C.A. § 1101 et seq., 11 U.S.C.A. § 1201 et seq., or 11 U.S.C.A. § 1301 et seq., respectively.

Section 673(2) of the Omnibus Budget Reconciliation Act of 1981, referred to in subsec. (f)(1), is Pub. L. 97–35, Title VI, § 673(2), Aug. 13, 1981, as added Pub. L. 105–285, Title II, § 201, Oct. 27, 1998, 112 Stat. 2729, which is classified to 42 U.S.C.A. § 9902(2).

CROSS REFERENCES

Confirmation of reorganization plan contingent on payment of fees, see 11 USCA § 1129.

Recommendation for adjustment of dollar amounts of fees, see 11 USCA § 104.

United States Trustee System Fund, depositing of bankruptcy fees into Fund, see 28 USCA § 589a.

Bankruptcy Court Miscellaneous Fee Schedule (28 U.S.C. § 1930)

(Effective December 1, 2020)

The fees included in the Bankruptcy Court Miscellaneous Fee Schedule are to be charged for services provided by the bankruptcy courts.

- The United States should not be charged fees under this schedule, with the exception of those specifically prescribed in Items 1, 3 and 5 when the information requested is available through remote electronic access.

- Federal agencies or programs that are funded from judiciary appropriations (agencies, organizations, and individuals providing services authorized by the Criminal Justice Act, 18 U.S.C. § 3006A, and bankruptcy administrators) should not be charged any fees under this schedule.

(1)   a. For reproducing any document and providing a copy in paper form, $.50 per page. This fee applies to services rendered on behalf of the United States if the document requested is available through electronic access.

b.   For reproducing and transmitting in any manner a copy of an electronic record stored outside of the court's electronic case management system, including but not limited to, document files, audio recordings, and video recordings, $31 per record provided. Audio recordings of court proceedings continue to be governed by a separate fee under item 3 of this schedule.

(2) For certification of any document, $11.

For exemplification of any document, $23.

(3) For reproduction of an audio recording of a court proceeding, $32. This fee applies to services rendered on behalf of the United States if the recording is available electronically.

(4) For filing an amendment to the debtor's schedules of creditors, lists of creditors, or mailing list, $32, except:

- The bankruptcy judge may, for good cause, waive the charge in any case.

- This fee must not be charged if—

  o the amendment is to change the address of a creditor or an attorney for a creditor listed on the schedules; or

  o the amendment is to add the name and address of an attorney for a creditor listed on the schedules.

(5) For conducting a search of the bankruptcy court records, $32 per name or item searched. This fee applies to services rendered on behalf of the United States if the information requested is available through electronic access.

(6) For filing a complaint, $350, except:

- If the trustee or debtor-in-possession files the complaint, the fee must be paid only by the estate, to the extent there is an estate.

- This fee must not be charged if—

  o the debtor is the plaintiff; or

  o a child support creditor or representative files the complaint and submits the form required by § 304(g) of the Bankruptcy Reform Act of 1994.

(7) For filing any document that is not related to a pending case or proceeding, $49.

(8) Administrative fee:

- For filing a petition under Chapter 7, 12, or 13, $78.

- For filing a petition under Chapter 9, 11, or 15, $571.

- When a motion to divide a joint case under Chapter 7, 12, or 13 is filed, $78.

- When a motion to divide a joint case under Chapter 11 is filed, $571.

(9) For payment to trustees pursuant to 11 U.S.C. § 330(b)(2), a $15 fee applies in the following circumstances:

- For filing a petition under Chapter 7.

- For filing a notice of conversion to a Chapter 7 case.

- For filing a motion to convert a case to a Chapter 7 case.

- For filing a motion to divide a joint Chapter 7 case.

- For filing a motion to reopen a Chapter 7 case.

(10) In addition to any fees imposed under Item 9, above, the following fees must be collected:

- For filing a motion to convert a Chapter 12 case to a Chapter 7 case or a notice of conversion pursuant to 11 U.S.C. § 1208(a), $45.

- For filing a motion to convert a Chapter 13 case to a Chapter 7 case or a notice of conversion pursuant to 11 U.S.C. § 1307(a), $10.

The fee amounts in this item are derived from the fees prescribed in 28 U.S.C. § 1930(a).

If the trustee files the motion to convert, the fee is payable only from the estate that exists prior to conversion.

If the filing fee for the chapter to which the case is requested to be converted is less than the fee paid at the commencement of the case, no refund may be provided.

(11) For filing a motion to reopen, the following fees apply:

- For filing a motion to reopen a Chapter 7 case, $245.
- For filing a motion to reopen a Chapter 9 case, $1167.
- For filing a motion to reopen a Chapter 11 case, $1167.
- For filing a motion to reopen a Chapter 12 case, $200.
- For filing a motion to reopen a Chapter 13 case, $235.
- For filing a motion to reopen a Chapter 15 case, $1167.

The fee amounts in this item are derived from the fees prescribed in 28 U.S.C. § 1930(a).

The reopening fee must be charged when a case has been closed without a discharge being entered.

The court may waive this fee under appropriate circumstances or may defer payment of the fee from trustees pending discovery of additional assets. If payment is deferred, the fee should be waived if no additional assets are discovered.

The reopening fee must not be charged in the following situations:

- to permit a party to file a complaint to obtain a determination under Rule 4007(b); or
- when a debtor files a motion to reopen a case based upon an alleged violation of the terms of the discharge under 11 U.S.C. § 524; or
- when the reopening is to correct an administrative error; or
- to redact a record already filed in a case, pursuant to Fed. R. Bankr. P. 9037, if redaction is the only reason for reopening; or
- when a party files a motion to reopen a case to request to withdraw unclaimed funds, unless the court orders otherwise.

(12) For retrieval of one box of records from a Federal Records Center, National Archives, or other storage location removed from the place of business of the court, $64. For retrievals involving multiple boxes, $39 for each additional box. For electronic retrievals, $10 plus any charges assessed by the Federal Records Center, National Archives, or other storage location removed from the place of business of the courts.

(13) For any payment returned or denied for insufficient funds, or reversed due to a chargeback, $53.

(14) For filing an appeal or cross appeal from a judgment, order, or decree, $293.

This fee is collected in addition to the statutory fee of $5 that is collected under 28 U.S.C. § 1930(c) when a notice of appeal is filed.

Parties filing a joint notice of appeal should pay only one fee.

If a trustee or debtor-in-possession is the appellant, the fee must be paid only by the estate, to the extent there is an estate.

Upon notice from the court of appeals that a direct appeal or direct cross-appeal has been authorized, an additional fee of $207 must be collected.

(15) For filing a case under Chapter 15 of the Bankruptcy Code, $1167.

This fee is derived from and equal to the fee prescribed in 28 U.S.C. § 1930(a)(3) for filing a case commenced under Chapter 11 of Title 11.

(16) The court may charge and collect fees commensurate with the cost of providing copies of the local rules of court. The court may also distribute copies of the local rules without charge.

(17)

- For handling registry funds deposited with and held by the court, the clerk shall assess a charge from interest earnings, in accordance with the detailed fee schedule issued by the Director of the Administrative Office of the United States Courts.

- For management of registry funds invested through the Court Registry Investment System, a fee at an annual rate of 10 basis points of assets on deposit shall be assessed from interest earnings, excluding registry funds from disputed ownership interpleader cases deposited under 28 U.S.C. § 1335 and held in a Court Registry Investment System Disputed Ownership Fund.

- For management of funds deposited under 28 U.S.C. § 1335 and invested in a Disputed Ownership Fund through the Court Registry Investment System, a fee at an annual rate of 20 basis points of assets on deposit shall be assessed from interest earnings.

- The Director of the Administrative Office has the authority to waive these fees for cause.

(18) For a motion filed by the debtor to divide a joint case filed under 11 U.S.C. § 302, the following fees apply:

- For filing a motion to divide a joint Chapter 7 case, $245.

- For filing a motion to divide a joint Chapter 11 case, $1167.

- For filing a motion to divide a joint Chapter 12 case, $200.

- For filing a motion to divide a joint Chapter 13 case, $235.

These fees are derived from and equal to the filing fees prescribed in 28 U.S.C. § 1930(a).

(19) For filing the following motions, $188:

- To terminate, annul, modify or condition the automatic stay;

- To compel abandonment of property of the estate pursuant to Rule 6007(b) of the Federal Rules of Bankruptcy Procedure;

- To withdraw the reference of a case or proceeding under 28 U.S.C. § 157(d); or

- To sell property of the estate free and clear of liens under 11 U.S.C. § 363(f).

This fee must not be collected in the following situations:

- For a motion for relief from the co-debtor stay;

- For a stipulation for court approval of an agreement for relief from a stay; or

- For a motion filed by a child support creditor or its representative, if the form required by § 304(g) of the Bankruptcy Reform Act of 1994 is filed.

(20) For filing a transfer of claim, $26 per claim transferred.

(21) For filing a motion to redact a record, $26 per affected case. The court may waive this fee under appropriate circumstances.

Electronic Public Access Fee Schedule (Eff. 1/1/2020)

(Issued in Accordance with 28 U.S.C. §§ 1913, 1914, 1926, 1930, 1932)

The fees included in the Electronic Public Access Fee Schedule are to be charged for providing electronic public access to court records.

Fees for Public Access to Court Electronic Records (PACER)

(1) Except as provided below, for electronic access to any case document, docket sheet, or case-specific report via PACER: $0.10 per page, not to exceed the fee for thirty pages.

(2) For electronic access to transcripts and non-case specific reports via PACER (such as reports obtained from the PACER Case Locator or docket activity reports): $0.10 per page.

(3) For electronic access to an audio file of a court hearing via PACER: $2.40 per audio file.

Fees for Courthouse Electronic Access

(4) For printing copies of any record or document accessed electronically at a public terminal in a courthouse: $0.10 per page.

PACER Service Center Fees

(5) For every search of court records conducted by the PACER Service Center, $30 per name or item searched.

(6) For the PACER Service Center to reproduce on paper any record pertaining to a PACER account, if this information is remotely available through electronic access: $0.50 per page.

(7) For any payment returned or denied for insufficient funds, $53.

Free Access and Exemptions

(8) Automatic Fee Exemptions:

- No fee is owed for electronic access to court data or audio files via PACER until an account holder accrues charges of more than $30.00 in a quarterly billing cycle.

- Parties in a case (including *pro se* litigants) and attorneys of record receive one free electronic copy, via the notice of electronic filing or notice of docket activity, of all documents filed electronically, if receipt is required by law or directed by the filer.

- No fee is charged for access to judicial opinions.

- No fee is charged for viewing case information or documents at courthouse public access terminals.

- No fee is charged for Chapter 13 bankruptcy trustees to download quarterly (i.e., once every 90 days) a list of the trustee's cases from the PACER Case Locator.

(9) Discretionary Fee Exemptions:

- Courts may exempt certain persons or classes of persons from payment of the user access fee. Examples of individuals and groups that a court may consider exempting include: indigents, bankruptcy case trustees, *pro bono* attorneys, *pro bono* alternative dispute resolution neutrals, Section 501(c)(3) not-for-profit organizations, and individual researchers associated with educational institutions. Courts should not, however, exempt individuals or groups that have the ability to pay the statutorily established access fee. Examples of individuals and groups that a court should not exempt include: local, state or federal government agencies, members of the media, privately paid attorneys or others who have the ability to pay the fee.

- In considering granting an exemption, courts must find:

  - that those seeking an exemption have demonstrated that an exemption is necessary in order to avoid unreasonable burdens and to promote public access to information.

  - that individual researchers requesting an exemption have shown that the defined research project is intended for scholarly research, that it is limited in scope, and that it is not intended for redistribution on the internet or for commercial purposes. A request is limited in scope if the amount of exempt access requested is narrowly tailored to meet the needs of the defined research project.

- If the court grants an exemption:

  - the user receiving the exemption must agree not to sell the data obtained as a result, and must not transfer any data obtained as the result of a fee exemption, unless expressly authorized by the court; and

- o   the exemption should be granted for a definite period of time, should be limited in scope, and may be revoked at the discretion of the court granting the exemption.

- Courts may provide local court information at no cost (e.g., local rules, court forms, news items, court calendars, and other information) to benefit the public.

Applicability to the United States and State and Local Governments

(10) Unless otherwise authorized by the Judicial Conference, these fees must be charged to the United States, except to federal agencies or programs that are funded from judiciary appropriations (including, but not limited to, agencies, organizations, and individuals providing services authorized by the Criminal Justice Act [18 U.S.C. § 3006A], and bankruptcy administrators).

(11) The fee for printing copies of any record or document accessed electronically at a public terminal ($0.10 per page) described in (4) above does not apply to services rendered on behalf of the United States if the record requested is not remotely available through electronic access.

(12) The fee for local, state, and federal government entities, shall be $0.08 per page until April 1, 2015, after which time, the fee shall be $0.10 per page.

Judicial Conference Policy Notes

The Electronic Public Access (EPA) fee and its exemptions are directly related to the requirement that the judiciary charge user-based fees for the development and maintenance of electronic public access services. The fee schedule provides examples of users that may not be able to afford reasonable user fees (such as indigents, bankruptcy case trustees, individual researchers associated with educational institutions, 501(c)(3) not-for-profit organizations, and court-appointed pro bono attorneys), but requires those seeking an exemption to demonstrate that an exemption is limited in scope and is necessary in order to avoid an unreasonable burden. In addition, the fee schedule includes examples of other entities that courts should not exempt from the fee (such as local, state or federal government agencies, members of the media, and attorneys). The goal is to provide courts with guidance in evaluating a requestor's ability to pay the fee.

Judicial Conference policy also limits exemptions in other ways. First, it requires exempted users to agree not to sell the data they receive through an exemption (unless expressly authorized by the court). This prohibition is not intended to bar a quote or reference to information received as a result of a fee exemption in a scholarly or other similar work. Second, it permits courts to grant exemptions for a definite period of time, to limit the scope of the exemptions, and to revoke exemptions. Third, it cautions that exemptions should be granted as the exception, not the rule, and prohibits courts from exempting all users from EPA fees.

Chapter 131—Rules of Courts

§ 2075. Bankruptcy rules

The Supreme Court shall have the power to prescribe by general rules, the forms of process, writs, pleadings, and motions, and the practice and procedure in cases under title 11.

Such rules shall not abridge, enlarge, or modify any substantive right.

The Supreme Court shall transmit to Congress not later than May 1 of the year in which a rule prescribed under this section is to become effective a copy of the proposed rule. The rule shall take effect no earlier than December 1 of the year in which it is transmitted to Congress unless otherwise provided by law.

The bankruptcy rules promulgated under this section shall prescribe a form for the statement required under section 707(b)(2)(C) of title 11 and may provide general rules on the content of such statement.

BANKRUPTCY RULES

Last Amended December 1, 2022

For the adoption and amendment history of a rule, consult **Notes of Advisory Committee on Rules**, which follows the rule's text at *https://www.uscourts.gov/rules-policies/current-rules-practice-procedure/federal-rules-bankruptcy-procedure*

Rule 1001. Scope of Rules and Forms; Short Title

The Bankruptcy Rules and Forms govern procedure in cases under title 11 of the United States Code. The rules shall be cited as the Federal Rules of Bankruptcy Procedure and the forms as the Official Bankruptcy Forms. These rules shall be construed, administered, and employed by the court and the parties to secure the just, speedy, and inexpensive determination of every case and proceeding.

CROSS REFERENCES

Promulgation of bankruptcy rules by Supreme Court, see 28 USCA § 2075.

Applicability of rules, see Fed. R. Civ. P. 81.

Scope of rules, see Fed. R. Civ. P. 1.

Applicability of rules, see Fed. R. Evid. 1101.

Scope of rules, see Fed. R. Evid. 101.

PART I

COMMENCEMENT OF CASE: PROCEEDINGS RELATING TO PETITION AND ORDER FOR RELIEF

Rule 1002. Commencement of Case

(a) Petition

A petition commencing a case under the Code shall be filed with the clerk.

(b) Transmission to United States trustee

The clerk shall forthwith transmit to the United States trustee a copy of the petition filed pursuant to subdivision (a) of this rule.

CROSS REFERENCES

Commencement of voluntary cases, see 11 USCA § 301.

Debtors for whom relief available, see 11 USCA § 109.

Joint cases, see 11 USCA § 302.

Number of copies—

    Involuntary petition, see Fed. R. Bankr. P. 1003.

    Schedules, statements, and lists, see Fed. R. Bankr. P. 1007.

Signing and verification of petitions, see Fed. R. Bankr. P. 1008 and 9011.

Stay of acts and proceedings against debtor and estate property, see 11 USCA § 362.

Rule 1003. Involuntary Petition

(a) Transferor or transferee of claim

A transferor or transferee of a claim shall annex to the original and each copy of the petition a copy of all documents evidencing the transfer, whether transferred unconditionally, for security, or otherwise, and a signed statement that the claim was not transferred for the purpose of commencing the case and setting forth the consideration for and terms of the transfer. An entity that has transferred or acquired a claim for the purpose of commencing a case for liquidation under chapter 7 or for reorganization under chapter 11 shall not be a qualified petitioner.

(b) Joinder of petitioners after filing

If the answer to an involuntary petition filed by fewer than three creditors avers the existence of 12 or more creditors, the debtor shall file with the answer a list of all creditors with their addresses, a brief statement of the nature of their claims, and the amounts thereof. If it appears that there are 12 or more creditors as provided in § 303(b) of the Code, the court shall afford a reasonable opportunity for other creditors to join in the petition before a hearing is held thereon.

CROSS REFERENCES

Case ancillary to foreign proceeding, foreign proceeding and foreign representative defined, see 11 USCA § 101(23), (24).

Debtors for whom relief available, see 11 USCA § 109.

Number of copies, voluntary petition, see Fed. R. Bankr. P. 1002.

Requisite allegations and joinder of parties, see 11 USCA § 303.

Signing and verification of petitions, see Fed. R. Bankr. P. 1008 and 9011.

Stay of acts and proceedings against debtor and estate property, see 11 USCA § 362.

Rule 1004. Involuntary Petition Against a Partnership

After filing of an involuntary petition under § 303(b)(3) of the Code, (1) the petitioning partners or other petitioners shall promptly send to or serve on each general partner who is not a petitioner a copy of the petition; and (2) the clerk shall promptly issue a summons for service on each general partner who is not a petitioner. Rule 1010 applies to the form and service of the summons.

CROSS REFERENCES

Commencement of—

> Involuntary cases, see 11 USCA § 303.

> Voluntary cases, see 11 USCA § 301.

Contested petition by general partners, see Fed. R. Bankr. P. 1011.

No change in status for purposes of state or local income tax law, see 11 USCA § 346.

Person defined to include partnership, see 11 USCA § 101.

Rule 1004.1. Petition for an Infant or Incompetent Person

If an infant or incompetent person has a representative, including a general guardian, committee, conservator, or similar fiduciary, the representative may file a voluntary petition on behalf of the infant or incompetent person. An infant or incompetent person who does not have a duly appointed representative may file a voluntary petition by next friend or guardian ad litem. The court shall appoint a guardian ad litem for an infant or incompetent person who is a debtor and is not otherwise represented or shall make any other order to protect the infant or incompetent debtor.

Rule 1004.2. Petition in Chapter 15 Cases

(a) Designating center of main interests

A petition for recognition of a foreign proceeding under chapter 15 of the Code shall state the country where the debtor has its center of main interests. The petition shall also identify each country in which a foreign proceeding by, regarding, or against the debtor is pending.

(b) Challenging designation

The United States trustee or a party in interest may file a motion for a determination that the debtor's center of main interests is other than as stated in the petition for recognition commencing the chapter 15 case. Unless the court orders otherwise, the motion shall be filed no later than seven days before the date set for the hearing on the petition. The motion shall be transmitted to the United States trustee and served on the debtor, all persons or bodies authorized to administer foreign proceedings of the debtor, all entities against whom provisional relief is being sought under § 1519 of the Code, all parties to litigation pending in the United States in which the debtor was a party as of the time the petition was filed, and such other entities as the court may direct.

Rule 1005. Caption of Petition

The caption of a petition commencing a case under the Code shall contain the name of the court, the title of the case, and the docket number. The title of the case shall include the following information about the debtor: name, employer identification number, last four digits of the social-security number or individual debtor's taxpayer-identification number, any other federal taxpayer-identification number, and all other names used within eight years before filing the petition. If the petition is not filed by the debtor, it shall include all names used by the debtor which are known to the petitioners.

CROSS REFERENCES

Conformance of captions of creditor notices with this rule, see Fed. R. Bankr. P. 2002.

General requirements of form for petition, see Fed. R. Bankr. P. 9004.

Rule 1006. Filing Fee

(a) General requirement

Every petition shall be accompanied by the filing fee except as provided in subdivisions (b) and (c) of this rule. For the purpose of this rule, "filing fee" means the filing fee prescribed by 28 U.S.C. § 1930(a)(1)–(a)(5) and any other fee prescribed by the Judicial Conference of the United States under 28 U.S.C. § 1930(b) that is payable to the clerk upon the commencement of a case under the Code.

(b) Payment of filing fee in installments

(1) Application to pay filing fee in installments

A voluntary petition by an individual shall be accepted for filing, regardless of whether any portion of the filing fee is paid, if accompanied by the debtor's signed application, prepared as prescribed by the appropriate Official Form, stating that the debtor is unable to pay the filing fee except in installments.

(2) Action on application

Prior to the meeting of creditors, the court may order the filing fee paid to the clerk or grant leave to pay in installments and fix the number, amount and dates of payment. The number of installments shall not exceed four, and the final installment shall be payable not later than 120 days after filing the petition. For cause shown, the court may extend the time of any installment, provided the last installment is paid not later than 180 days after filing the petition.

(3) Postponement of attorney's fees

All installments of the filing fee must be paid in full before the debtor or chapter 13 trustee may make further payments to an attorney or any other person who renders services to the debtor in connection with the case.

(c) Waiver of filing fee

A voluntary chapter 7 petition filed by an individual shall be accepted for filing if accompanied by the debtor's application requesting a waiver under 28 U.S.C. § 1930(f), prepared as prescribed by the appropriate Official Form.

CROSS REFERENCES

District court; filing and miscellaneous fees; rules of court, see 28 USCA § 1914.

Enlargement of time for payment of filing fee installments permitted as limited under this rule, see Fed. R. Bankr. P. Rule 9006.

Specific amount of fee, see 28 USCA § 1930.

Rule 1007. Lists, Schedules, Statements, and Other Documents; Time Limits

(a) Corporate ownership statement, list of creditors and equity security holders, and other lists

(1) Voluntary case

In a voluntary case, the debtor shall file with the petition a list containing the name and address of each entity included or to be included on Schedules D, E/F, G, and H as prescribed by the Official Forms. If the debtor is a corporation, other than a governmental unit, the debtor shall file with the petition a corporate ownership statement containing the information described in Rule 7007.1. The debtor shall file a supplemental statement promptly upon any change in circumstances that renders the corporate ownership statement inaccurate.

(2) Involuntary case

In an involuntary case, the debtor shall file, within seven days after entry of the order for relief, a list containing the name and address of each entity included or to be included on Schedules D, E/F, G, and H as prescribed by the Official Forms.

(3) Equity security holders

In a chapter 11 reorganization case, unless the court orders otherwise, the debtor shall file within 14 days after entry of the order for relief a list of the debtor's equity security holders of each class showing the number and kind of interests registered in the name of each holder, and the last known address or place of business of each holder.

(4) Chapter 15 case

In addition to the documents required under § 1515 of the Code, a foreign representative filing a petition for recognition under chapter 15 shall file with the petition: (A) a corporate ownership statement containing the information described in Rule 7007.1; and (B) unless the court orders otherwise, a list containing the names and addresses of all persons or bodies authorized to administer foreign proceedings of the debtor, all parties to litigation pending in the United States in which the debtor is a party at the time of the filing of the petition, and all entities against whom provisional relief is being sought under § 1519 of the Code.

(5) Extension of time

Any extension of time for the filing of the lists required by this subdivision may be granted only on motion for cause shown and on notice to the United States trustee and to any trustee, committee elected under § 705 or appointed under § 1102 of the Code, or other party as the court may direct.

(b) Schedules, statements, and other documents required

(1) Except in a chapter 9 municipality case, the debtor, unless the court orders otherwise, shall file the following schedules, statements, and other documents, prepared as prescribed by the appropriate Official Forms, if any:

(A) schedules of assets and liabilities;

(B) a schedule of current income and expenditures;

(C) a schedule of executory contracts and unexpired leases;

(D) a statement of financial affairs;

(E) copies of all payment advices or other evidence of payment, if any, received by the debtor from an employer within 60 days before the filing of the petition, with redaction of all but the last four digits of the debtor's social-security number or individual taxpayer-identification number; and

(F) a record of any interest that the debtor has in an account or program of the type specified in § 521(c) of the Code.

(2) An individual debtor in a chapter 7 case shall file a statement of intention as required by § 521(a) of the Code, prepared as prescribed by the appropriate Official Form. A copy of the statement of intention shall be served on the trustee and the creditors named in the statement on or before the filing of the statement.

(3) Unless the United States trustee has determined that the credit counseling requirement of § 109(h) does not apply in the district, an individual debtor must file a statement of compliance with the credit counseling requirement, prepared as prescribed by the appropriate Official Form which must include one of the following:

(A) an attached certificate and debt repayment plan, if any, required by § 521(b);

(B) a statement that the debtor has received the credit counseling briefing required by § 109(h)(1) but does not have the certificate required by § 521(b);

(C) a certification under § 109(h)(3); or

(D) a request for a determination by the court under § 109(h)(4).

(4) Unless § 707(b)(2)(D) applies, an individual debtor in a chapter 7 case shall file a statement of current monthly income prepared as prescribed by the appropriate Official Form, and, if the current monthly income exceeds the median family income for the applicable state and household size, the information, including calculations, required by § 707(b), prepared as prescribed by the appropriate Official Form.

(5) An individual debtor in a chapter 11 case (unless under subchapter V) shall file a statement of current monthly income, prepared as prescribed by the appropriate Official Form.

(6) A debtor in a chapter 13 case shall file a statement of current monthly income, prepared as prescribed by the appropriate Official Form, and, if the current monthly income exceeds the median family income for the applicable state and household size, a calculation of disposable income made in accordance with § 1325(b)(3), prepared as prescribed by the appropriate Official Form.

(7) Unless an approved provider of an instructional course concerning personal financial management has notified the court that a debtor has completed the course after filing the petition:

(A) An individual debtor in a chapter 7 or chapter 13 case shall file a statement of completion of the course, prepared as prescribed by the appropriate Official Form; and

(B) An individual debtor in a chapter 11 case shall file the statement if § 1141(d)(3) applies.

(8) If an individual debtor in a chapter 11, 12, or 13 case has claimed an exemption under § 522(b)(3)(A) in property of the kind described in § 522(p)(1) with a value in excess of the amount set out in § 522(q)(1), the debtor shall file a statement as to whether there is any proceeding pending in which the debtor may be found guilty of a felony of a kind described in § 522(q)(1)(A) or found liable for a debt of the kind described in § 522(q)(1)(B).

(c) Time limits

In a voluntary case, the schedules, statements, and other documents required by subdivision (b)(1), (4), (5), and (6) shall be filed with the petition or within 14 days thereafter, except as otherwise provided in subdivisions (d), (e), (f), and (h) of this rule. In an involuntary case, the schedules, statements, and other documents required by subdivision (b)(1) shall be filed by the debtor within 14 days after the entry of the order for relief. In a voluntary case, the documents required by paragraphs (A), (C), and (D) of subdivision (b)(3) shall be filed with the petition. Unless the court orders otherwise, a debtor who has filed a statement under subdivision (b)(3)(B), shall file the documents required by subdivision (b)(3)(A) within 14 days of the order for relief. In a chapter 7 case, the debtor shall file the statement required by subdivision (b)(7) within 60 days after the first date set for the meeting of creditors under § 341 of the Code, and in a chapter 11 or 13 case no later than the date when the last payment was made by the debtor as required by the plan or the filing of a motion for a discharge under § 1141(d)(5)(B) or § 1328(b) of the Code. The court may, at any time and in its discretion, enlarge the time to file the statement required by subdivision (b)(7). The debtor shall file the statement required by subdivision (b)(8) no earlier than the date of the last payment made under the plan or the date of the filing of a motion for a discharge under §§[1] 1141(d)(5)(B), 1228(b), or 1328(b) of the Code. Lists, schedules, statements, and other documents filed prior to the conversion of a case to another chapter shall be deemed filed in the converted case unless the court directs otherwise. Except as provided in § 1116(3), any extension of time to file schedules, statements, and other documents required under this rule may be granted only on motion for cause shown and on notice to the United States trustee, any committee elected under § 705 or appointed under § 1102 of the Code, trustee, examiner, or other party as the court may direct. Notice of an extension shall be given to the United States trustee and to any committee, trustee, or other party as the court may direct.

(d) List of 20 largest creditors in chapter 9 municipality case or chapter 11 reorganization case

In addition to the list required by subdivision (a) of this rule, a debtor in a chapter 9 municipality case or a debtor in a voluntary chapter 11 reorganization case shall file with the petition a list containing the name, address and claim of the creditors that hold the 20 largest unsecured claims, excluding insiders, as prescribed by the appropriate Official Form. In an involuntary chapter 11 reorganization case, such list shall be filed by the debtor within 2 days after entry of the order for relief under § 303(h) of the Code.

(e) List in chapter 9 municipality cases

The list required by subdivision (a) of this rule shall be filed by the debtor in a chapter 9 municipality case within such time as the court shall fix. If a proposed plan requires a revision of assessments so that the proportion of special assessments or special taxes to be assessed against some real property will be different from the proportion in effect at the date the petition is filed, the debtor shall also file a list showing the name and address of each known holder of title, legal or equitable, to

---

[1] So in original. Probably should be only one section symbol.

real property adversely affected. On motion for cause shown, the court may modify the requirements of this subdivision and subdivision (a) of this rule.

(f) Statement of social security number

An individual debtor shall submit a verified statement that sets out the debtor's social security number, or states that the debtor does not have a social security number. In a voluntary case, the debtor shall submit the statement with the petition. In an involuntary case, the debtor shall submit the statement within 14 days after the entry of the order for relief.

(g) Partnership and partners

The general partners of a debtor partnership shall prepare and file the list required under subdivision (a), the schedules of the assets and liabilities, schedule of current income and expenditures, schedule of executory contracts and unexpired leases, and statement of financial affairs of the partnership. The court may order any general partner to file a statement of personal assets and liabilities within such time as the court may fix.

(h) Interests acquired or arising after petition

If, as provided by § 541(a)(5) of the Code, the debtor acquires or becomes entitled to acquire any interest in property, the debtor shall within 14 days after the information comes to the debtor's knowledge or within such further time the court may allow, file a supplemental schedule in the chapter 7 liquidation case, chapter 11 reorganization case, chapter 12 family farmer's debt adjustment case, or chapter 13 individual debt adjustment case. If any of the property required to be reported under this subdivision is claimed by the debtor as exempt, the debtor shall claim the exemptions in the supplemental schedule. This duty to file a supplemental schedule continues even after the case is closed, except for property acquired after an order is entered:

(1) confirming a chapter 11 plan (other than one confirmed under § 1191(b)); or

(2) discharging the debtor in a chapter 12 case, a chapter 13 case, or a case under subchapter V of chapter 11 in which the plan is confirmed under § 1191(b).

(i) Disclosure of list of security holders

After notice and hearing and for cause shown, the court may direct an entity other than the debtor or trustee to disclose any list of security holders of the debtor in its possession or under its control, indicating the name, address and security held by any of them. The entity possessing this list may be required either to produce the list or a true copy thereof, or permit inspection or copying, or otherwise disclose the information contained on the list.

(j) Impounding of lists

On motion of a party in interest and for cause shown the court may direct the impounding of the lists filed under this rule, and may refuse to permit inspection by any entity. The court may permit inspection or use of the lists, however, by any party in interest on terms prescribed by the court.

(k) Preparation of list, schedules, or statements on default of debtor

If a list, schedule, or statement, other than a statement of intention, is not prepared and filed as required by this rule, the court may order the trustee, a petitioning creditor, committee, or other party to prepare and file any of these papers within a time fixed by the court. The court may approve reimbursement of the cost incurred in complying with such an order as an administrative expense.

(*l*) Transmission to United States trustee

The clerk shall forthwith transmit to the United States trustee a copy of every list, schedule, and statement filed pursuant to subdivision (a)(1), (a)(2), (b), (d), or (h) of this rule.

(m) Infants and incompetent persons

If the debtor knows that a person on the list of creditors or schedules is an infant or incompetent person, the debtor also shall include the name, address, and legal relationship of any person upon whom process would be served in an adversary proceeding against the infant or incompetent person in accordance with Rule 7004(b)(2).

CROSS REFERENCES

Committee of seven unsecured creditors appointed in reorganization case, see 11 USCA § 1102.

Compliance with this rule upon conversion to liquidation case, see Fed. R. Bankr. P. 1019.

Duty of debtor to—

> Inform trustee as to property location and name and address of money and property obligors, see Fed. R. Bankr. P. 4002.

> Prepare and file schedule and statement, see 11 USCA § 521.

Enlargement of time for filing list of twenty largest unsecured creditors not permitted, see Fed. R. Bankr. P. 9006.

Filing of proof of interest by equity security holder obviated by list filed by debtor, see Fed. R. Bankr. P. 3003.

Immunity from self-incrimination, see 11 USCA § 344.

Insider for purposes of list of 20 unsecured claims defined, see 11 USCA § 101.

List of exempt property to be filed—

> By dependent of debtor, see Fed. R. Bankr. P. 4003.

> With schedule of assets, see Fed. R. Bankr. P. 4003.

Motions; form and service, see Fed. R. Bankr. P. 9013.

Notice required for—

> Creditors' meetings, see Fed. R. Bankr. P. 2002.

> Order for relief, see 11 USCA § 342.

Rule 1008. Verification of Petitions and Accompanying Papers

All petitions, lists, schedules, statements and amendments thereto shall be verified or contain an unsworn declaration as provided in 28 U.S.C. § 1746.

CROSS REFERENCES

Signing and verification of papers, see Fed. R. Bankr. P. 9011.

Rule 1009. Amendments of Voluntary Petitions, Lists, Schedules and Statements

(a) General right to amend

A voluntary petition, list, schedule, or statement may be amended by the debtor as a matter of course at any time before the case is closed. The debtor shall give notice of the amendment to the trustee and to any entity affected thereby. On motion of a party in interest, after notice and a hearing, the court may order any voluntary petition, list, schedule, or statement to be amended and the clerk shall give notice of the amendment to entities designated by the court.

(b) Statement of intention

The statement of intention may be amended by the debtor at any time before the expiration of the period provided in § 521(a) of the Code. The debtor shall give notice of the amendment to the trustee and to any entity affected thereby.

(c) Statement of social security number

If a debtor becomes aware that the statement of social security number submitted under Rule 1007(f) is incorrect, the debtor shall promptly submit an amended verified statement setting forth the correct social security number. The debtor shall give notice of the amendment to all of the entities required to be included on the list filed under Rule 1007(a)(1) or (a)(2).

(d) Transmission to United States trustee

The clerk shall promptly transmit to the United States trustee a copy of every amendment filed or submitted under subdivision (a), (b), or (c) of this rule.

CROSS REFERENCES

Dischargeability of debts added to list or schedule, see 11 USCA § 523.

Motions; form and service, see Fed. R. Bankr. P. 9013.

Amended and supplemental pleadings, see Fed. R. Civ. P. 15.

Rule 1010. Service of Involuntary Petition and Summons

(a) Service of involuntary petition and summons

On the filing of an involuntary petition, the clerk shall forthwith issue a summons for service. When an involuntary petition is filed, service shall be made on the debtor. The summons shall be served with a copy of the petition in the manner provided for service of a summons and complaint by Rule 7004(a) or (b). If service cannot be so made, the court may order that the summons and petition be served by mailing copies to the party's last known address, and by at least one publication in a manner and form directed by the court. The summons and petition may be served on the party anywhere. Rule 7004(e) and Rule 4(*l*) F.R.Civ.P. apply when service is made or attempted under this rule.

(b) Corporate ownership statement

Each petitioner that is a corporation shall file with the involuntary petition a corporate ownership statement containing the information described in Rule 7007.1.

CROSS REFERENCES

Applicability of this rule to involuntary partnership petitions, see Fed. R. Bankr. P. 1004.

Form and manner of service by publication, see Fed. R. Bankr. P. 9007 and 9008.

Jurisdictional basis for service, see 11 USCA § 109.

Process, see Fed. R. Civ. P. 4.

Rule 1011. Responsive Pleading or Motion in Involuntary Cases

(a) Who may contest petition

The debtor named in an involuntary petition may contest the petition. In the case of a petition against a partnership under Rule 1004, a nonpetitioning general partner, or a person who is alleged to be a general partner but denies the allegation, may contest the petition.

(b) Defenses and objections; when presented

Defenses and objections to the petition shall be presented in the manner prescribed by Rule 12 F.R.Civ.P. and shall be filed and served within 21 days after service of the summons, except that if service is made by publication on a party or partner not residing or found within the state in which the court sits, the court shall prescribe the time for filing and serving the response.

(c) Effect of motion

353

Service of a motion under Rule 12(b) F.R.Civ.P. shall extend the time for filing and serving a responsive pleading as permitted by Rule 12(a) F.R.Civ.P.

(d) Claims against petitioners

A claim against a petitioning creditor may not be asserted in the answer except for the purpose of defeating the petition.

(e) Other pleadings

No other pleadings shall be permitted, except that the court may order a reply to an answer and prescribe the time for filing and service.

(f) Corporate ownership statement

If the entity responding to the involuntary petition is a corporation, the entity shall file with its first appearance, pleading, motion, response, or other request addressed to the court a corporate ownership statement containing the information described in Rule 7007.1.

CROSS REFERENCES

Entry of default upon failure to plead within time, see Fed. R. Bankr. P. 1013.

Motions; form and service, see Fed. R. Bankr. P. 9013.

Responsive pleadings, see 11 USCA § 303.

Pleadings—

    Amended and supplemental, see Fed. R. Civ. P. 15.

    Capacity, fraud, and other special matters, see Fed. R. Civ. P. 9.

    General rules, see Fed. R. Civ. P. 8.

    Service and filing, see Fed. R. Civ. P. 5.

Summary judgment, see Fed. R. Civ. P. 56.

Rule 1012. Responsive Pleading in Cross-Border Cases

(a) Who may contest petition

The debtor or any party in interest may contest a petition for recognition of a foreign proceeding.

(b) Objections and responses; when presented

Objections and other responses to the petition shall be presented no later than seven days before the date set for the hearing on the petition, unless the court prescribes some other time or manner for responses.

(c) Corporate ownership statement

If the entity responding to the petition is a corporation, then the entity shall file a corporate ownership statement containing the information described in Rule 7007.1 with its first appearance, pleading, motion, response, or other request addressed to the court.

Rule 1013. Hearing and Disposition of a Petition in an Involuntary Case

(a) Contested petition

The court shall determine the issues of a contested petition at the earliest practicable time and forthwith enter an order for relief, dismiss the petition, or enter any other appropriate order.

(b) Default

If no pleading or other defense to a petition is filed within the time provided by Rule 1011, the court, on the next day, or as soon thereafter as practicable, shall enter an order for the relief requested in the petition.

CROSS REFERENCES

Costs, counsel fees, expenses and damages upon dismissal of petition, see 11 USCA § 303.

Power of court to render judgments, see 11 USCA § 105.

Setting aside default for cause, see Fed. R. Bankr. P. 9024.

Instructions to jury; objection, see Fed. R. Civ. P. 51.

Juries of less than twelve; majority verdict, see Fed. R. Civ. P. 48.

Jurors, see Fed. R. Civ. P. 47.

Jury trial of right, see Fed. R. Civ. P. 38.

Motion for directed verdict and for judgment notwithstanding verdict, see Fed. R. Civ. P. 50.

Special verdicts and interrogatories, see Fed. R. Civ. P. 49.

Trial by jury or by court, see Fed. R. Civ. P. 39.

Rule 1014. Dismissal and Change of Venue

(a) Dismissal and transfer of cases

(1) Cases filed in proper district

If a petition is filed in the proper district, the court, on the timely motion of a party in interest or on its own motion, and after hearing on notice to the petitioners, the United States trustee, and other entities as directed by the court, may transfer the case to any other district if the court determines that the transfer is in the interest of justice or for the convenience of the parties.

(2) Cases filed in improper district

If a petition is filed in an improper district, the court, on the timely motion of a party in interest or on its own motion, and after hearing on notice to the petitioners, the United States trustee, and other entities as directed by the court, may dismiss the case or transfer it to any other district if the court determines that transfer is in the interest of justice or for the convenience of the parties.

(b) Procedure when petitions involving the same debtor or related debtors are filed in different courts

If petitions commencing cases under the Code or seeking recognition under chapter 15 are filed in different districts by, regarding, or against (1) the same debtor, (2) a partnership and one or more of its general partners, (3) two or more general partners, or (4) a debtor and an affiliate, the court in the district in which the first-filed petition is pending may determine, in the interest of justice or for the convenience of the parties, the district or districts in which any of the cases should proceed. The court may so determine on motion and after a hearing, with notice to the following entities in the affected cases: the United States trustee, entities entitled to notice under Rule 2002(a), and other entities as the court directs. The court may order the parties to the later-filed cases not to proceed further until it makes the determination.

CROSS REFERENCES

Change of venue, see 28 USCA § 1404.

Motions; form and service, see Fed. R. Bankr. P. 9013.

Transfer of adversary proceeding, see Fed. R. Bankr. P. 7087.

Rule 1015. Consolidation or Joint Administration of Cases Pending in Same Court

(a) Cases involving same debtor

If two or more petitions by, regarding, or against the same debtor are pending in the same court, the court may order consolidation of the cases.

(b) Cases involving two or more related debtors

If a joint petition or two or more petitions are pending in the same court by or against (1) spouses, or (2) a partnership and one or more of its general partners, or (3) two or more general partners, or (4) a debtor and an affiliate, the court may order a joint administration of the estates. Prior to entering an order the court shall give consideration to protecting creditors of different estates against potential conflicts of interest. An order directing joint administration of individual cases of spouses shall, if one spouse has elected the exemptions under § 522(b)(2) of the Code and the other has elected the exemptions under § 522(b)(3), fix a reasonable time within which either may amend the election so that both shall have elected the same exemptions. The order shall notify the debtors that unless they elect the same exemptions within the time fixed by the court, they will be deemed to have elected the exemptions provided by § 522(b)(2).

(c) Expediting and protective orders

When an order for consolidation or joint administration of a joint case or two or more cases is entered pursuant to this rule, while protecting the rights of the parties under the Code, the court may enter orders as may tend to avoid unnecessary costs and delay.

CROSS REFERENCES

Election of trustees in liquidation cases when joint administration ordered, see Fed. R. Bankr. P. 2009.

Joint cases, see 11 USCA § 302.

Consolidation, see Fed. R. Civ. P. 42.

Rule 1016. Death or Incompetency of Debtor

Death or incompetency of the debtor shall not abate a liquidation case under chapter 7 of the Code. In such event the estate shall be administered and the case concluded in the same manner, so far as possible, as though the death or incompetency had not occurred. If a reorganization, family farmer's debt adjustment, or individual's debt adjustment case is pending under chapter 11, chapter 12, or chapter 13, the case may be dismissed; or if further administration is possible and in the best interest of the parties, the case may proceed and be concluded in the same manner, so far as possible, as though the death or incompetency had not occurred.

CROSS REFERENCES

Exemptions, see 11 USCA § 522.

Property of estate, see 11 USCA § 541.

Rule 1017. Dismissal or Conversion of Case; Suspension

(a) Voluntary dismissal; dismissal for want of prosecution or other cause

Except as provided in §§ 707(a)(3), 707(b), 1208(b), and 1307(b) of the Code, and in Rule 1017(b), (c), and (e), a case shall not be dismissed on motion of the petitioner, for want of prosecution or other cause, or by consent of the parties, before a hearing on notice as provided in Rule 2002. For the purpose of the notice, the debtor shall file a list of creditors with their addresses within the time fixed by the court unless the list was previously filed. If the debtor fails to file the list, the court may order the debtor or another entity to prepare and file it.

(b) Dismissal for failure to pay filing fee

(1) If any installment of the filing fee has not been paid, the court may, after a hearing on notice to the debtor and the trustee, dismiss the case.

(2) If the case is dismissed or closed without full payment of the filing fee, the installments collected shall be distributed in the same manner and proportions as if the filing fee had been paid in full.

(c) Dismissal of voluntary chapter 7 or chapter 13 case for failure to timely file list of creditors, schedules, and statement of financial affairs

The court may dismiss a voluntary chapter 7 or chapter 13 case under § 707(a)(3) or § 1307(c)(9) after a hearing on notice served by the United States trustee on the debtor, the trustee, and any other entities as the court directs.

(d) Suspension

The court shall not dismiss a case or suspend proceedings under § 305 before a hearing on notice as provided in Rule 2002(a).

(e) Dismissal of an individual debtor's chapter 7 case, or conversion to a case under chapter 11 or 13, for abuse

The court may dismiss or, with the debtor's consent, convert an individual debtor's case for abuse under § 707(b) only on motion and after a hearing on notice to the debtor, the trustee, the United States trustee, and any other entity as the court directs.

(1) Except as otherwise provided in § 704(b)(2), a motion to dismiss a case for abuse under § 707(b) or (c) may be filed only within 60 days after the first date set for the meeting of creditors under § 341(a), unless, on request filed before the time has expired, the court for cause extends the time for filing the motion to dismiss. The party filing the motion shall set forth in the motion all matters to be considered at the hearing. In addition, a motion to dismiss under § 707(b)(1) and (3) shall state with particularity the circumstances alleged to constitute abuse.

(2) If the hearing is set on the court's own motion, notice of the hearing shall be served on the debtor no later than 60 days after the first date set for the meeting of creditors under § 341(a). The notice shall set forth all matters to be considered by the court at the hearing.

(f) Procedure for dismissal, conversion, or suspension

(1) Rule 9014 governs a proceeding to dismiss or suspend a case, or to convert a case to another chapter, except under §§ 706(a), 1112(a), 1208(a) or (b), or 1307(a) or (b).

(2) Conversion or dismissal under §§ 706(a), 1112(a), 1208(b), or 1307(b) shall be on motion filed and served as required by Rule 9013.

(3) A chapter 12 or chapter 13 case shall be converted without court order when the debtor files a notice of conversion under §§ 1208(a) or 1307(a). The filing date of the notice becomes the date of the conversion order for the purposes of applying § 348(c) and Rule 1019. The clerk shall promptly transmit a copy of the notice to the United States trustee.

CROSS REFERENCES

Conversion of—

> Individual debt adjustment case, see 11 USCA § 1307.

> Liquidation case, see 11 USCA § 706.

> Reorganization case, see 11 USCA § 1112.

Dismissal of—

> Individual debt adjustment case, see 11 USCA § 1307.

Involuntary petition, see 11 USCA § 303.

Liquidation case, see 11 USCA § 707.

Reorganization case, see 11 USCA § 1112.

Enlargement of thirty-day period for notice of dismissal for failure to pay filing fee not permitted, see Fed. R. Bankr. P. 9006.

Motions; form and service, see Fed. R. Bankr. P. 9013.

Rule 1018. Contested Involuntary Petitions; Contested Petitions Commencing Chapter 15 Cases; Proceedings to Vacate Order for Relief; Applicability of Rules in Part VII Governing Adversary Proceedings

Unless the court otherwise directs and except as otherwise prescribed in Part I of these rules, the following rules in Part VII apply to all proceedings contesting an involuntary petition or a chapter 15 petition for recognition, and to all proceedings to vacate an order for relief: Rules 7005, 7008–7010, 7015, 7016, 7024–7026, 7028–7037, 7052, 7054, 7056, and 7062. The court may direct that other rules in Part VII shall also apply. For the purposes of this rule a reference in the Part VII rules to adversary proceedings shall be read as a reference to proceedings contesting an involuntary petition or a chapter 15 petition for recognition, or proceedings to vacate an order for relief. Reference in the Federal Rules of Civil Procedure to the complaint shall be read as a reference to the petition.

CROSS REFERENCES

Effect of amendment of Federal Rules of Civil Procedure, see Fed. R. Bankr. P. 9032.

Rule 1019. Conversion of a Chapter 11 Reorganization Case, Chapter 12 Family Farmer's Debt Adjustment Case, or Chapter 13 Individual's Debt Adjustment Case to a Chapter 7 Liquidation Case

When a chapter 11, chapter 12, or chapter 13 case has been converted or reconverted to a chapter 7 case:

(1) Filing of lists, inventories, schedules, statements

(A) Lists, inventories, schedules, and statements of financial affairs theretofore filed shall be deemed to be filed in the chapter 7 case, unless the court directs otherwise. If they have not been previously filed, the debtor shall comply with Rule 1007 as if an order for relief had been entered on an involuntary petition on the date of the entry of the order directing that the case continue under chapter 7.

(B) If a statement of intention is required, it shall be filed within 30 days after entry of the order of conversion or before the first date set for the meeting of creditors, whichever is earlier. The court may grant an extension of time for cause only on written motion filed, or oral request made during a hearing, before the time has expired. Notice of an extension shall be given to the United States trustee and to any committee, trustee, or other party as the court may direct.

(2) New filing periods

(A) A new time period for filing a motion under § 707(b) or (c), a claim, a complaint objecting to discharge, or a complaint to obtain a determination of dischargeability of any debt shall commence under Rules[1] 1017, 3002, 4004, or 4007, but a new time period shall not commence if a chapter 7 case had been converted to a chapter 11, 12, or 13 case and thereafter reconverted to a chapter 7 case and the time for filing a motion under § 707(b) or (c), a claim, a complaint objecting to discharge, or a complaint to obtain a determination of the dischargeability of any debt, or any extension thereof, expired in the original chapter 7 case.

---

[1]   So in original. Probably should be "Rule".

(B) A new time period for filing an objection to a claim of exemptions shall commence under Rule 4003(b) after conversion of a case to chapter 7 unless:

    (i) the case was converted to chapter 7 more than one year after the entry of the first order confirming a plan under chapter 11, 12, or 13; or

    (ii) the case was previously pending in chapter 7 and the time to object to a claimed exemption had expired in the original chapter 7 case.

(3) Claims filed before conversion

All claims actually filed by a creditor before conversion of the case are deemed filed in the chapter 7 case.

(4) Turnover of records and property

After qualification of, or assumption of duties by the chapter 7 trustee, any debtor in possession or trustee previously acting in the chapter 11, 12, or 13 case shall, forthwith, unless otherwise ordered, turn over to the chapter 7 trustee all records and property of the estate in the possession or control of the debtor in possession or trustee.

(5) Filing final report and schedule of postpetition debts

(A) Conversion of chapter 11 or chapter 12 case

Unless the court directs otherwise, if a chapter 11 or chapter 12 case is converted to chapter 7, the debtor in possession or, if the debtor is not a debtor in possession, the trustee serving at the time of conversion, shall:

    (i) not later than 14 days after conversion of the case, file a schedule of unpaid debts incurred after the filing of the petition and before conversion of the case, including the name and address of each holder of a claim; and

    (ii) not later than 30 days after conversion of the case, file and transmit to the United States trustee a final report and account;

(B) Conversion of chapter 13 case

Unless the court directs otherwise, if a chapter 13 case is converted to chapter 7,

    (i) the debtor, not later than 14 days after conversion of the case, shall file a schedule of unpaid debts incurred after the filing of the petition and before conversion of the case, including the name and address of each holder of a claim; and

    (ii) the trustee, not later than 30 days after conversion of the case, shall file and transmit to the United States trustee a final report and account;

(C) Conversion after confirmation of a plan

Unless the court orders otherwise, if a chapter 11, chapter 12, or chapter 13 case is converted to chapter 7 after confirmation of a plan, the debtor shall file:

    (i) a schedule of property not listed in the final report and account acquired after the filing of the petition but before conversion, except if the case is converted from chapter 13 to chapter 7 and § 348(f)(2) does not apply;

    (ii) a schedule of unpaid debts not listed in the final report and account incurred after confirmation but before the conversion; and

    (iii) a schedule of executory contracts and unexpired leases entered into or assumed after the filing of the petition but before conversion.

(D) Transmission to United States trustee

The clerk shall forthwith transmit to the United States trustee a copy of every schedule filed pursuant to Rule 1019(5).

(6) Postpetition claims; preconversion administrative expenses; notice

A request for payment of an administrative expense incurred before conversion of the case is timely filed under § 503(a) of the Code if it is filed before conversion or a time fixed by the court. If the request is filed by a governmental unit, it is timely if it is filed before conversion or within the later of a time fixed by the court or 180 days after the date of the conversion. A claim of a kind specified in § 348(d) may be filed in accordance with Rules 3001(a)–(d) and 3002. Upon the filing of the schedule of unpaid debts incurred after commencement of the case and before conversion, the clerk, or some other person as the court may direct, shall give notice to those entities listed on the schedule of the time for filing a request for payment of an administrative expense and, unless a notice of insufficient assets to pay a dividend is mailed in accordance with Rule 2002(e), the time for filing a claim of a kind specified in § 348(d).

CROSS REFERENCES

Appointment of interim trustee, see Fed. R. Bankr. P. 2001.

Election of trustee, see 11 USCA § 702.

Failure to effect plan or substantial consummation of confirmed plan, see 11 USCA § 1112.

Meeting of creditors or equity security holders, see Fed. R. Bankr. P. 2003.

Rule 1020. Chapter 11 Reorganization Case for Small Business Debtors

(a) Small business debtor designation

In a voluntary chapter 11 case, the debtor shall state in the petition whether the debtor is a small business debtor and, if so, whether the debtor elects to have subchapter V of chapter 11 apply. In an involuntary chapter 11 case, the debtor shall file within 14 days after entry of the order for relief a statement as to whether the debtor is a small business debtor and, if so, whether the debtor elects to have subchapter V of chapter 11 apply. The status of the case as a small business case or a case under subchapter V of chapter 11 shall be in accordance with the debtor's statement under this subdivision, unless and until the court enters an order finding that the debtor's statement is incorrect.

(b) Objecting to designation

The United States trustee or a party in interest may file an objection to the debtor's statement under subdivision (a) no later than 30 days after the conclusion of the meeting of creditors held under § 341(a) of the Code, or within 30 days after any amendment to the statement, whichever is later.

(c) Procedure for objection or determination

Any objection or request for a determination under this rule shall be governed by Rule 9014 and served on: the debtor; the debtor's attorney; the United States trustee; the trustee; the creditors included on the list filed under Rule 1007(d) or, if a committee has been appointed under § 1102(a)(3), the committee or its authorized agent; and any other entity as the court directs.

Rule 1021. Health Care Business Case

(a) Health care business designation

Unless the court orders otherwise, if a petition in a case under Chapter 7, chapter 9, or chapter 11 states that the debtor is a health care business, the case shall proceed as a case in which the debtor is a health care business.

(b) Motion

The United States trustee or a party in interest may file a motion to determine whether the debtor is a health care business. The motion shall be transmitted to the United States trustee and served on: the debtor; the trustee; any committee elected under § 705 or appointed under § 1102 of the Code or its authorized agent, or, if the case is a chapter 9 municipality case or a chapter 11 reorganization case and no committee of unsecured creditors has been appointed under § 1102, the creditors included on the list filed under Rule 1007(d); and any other entity as the court directs. The motion shall be governed by Rule 9014.

PART II

OFFICERS AND ADMINISTRATION; NOTICES; MEETINGS; EXAMINATIONS; ELECTIONS; ATTORNEYS AND ACCOUNTANTS

Rule 2001.　Appointment of Interim Trustee Before Order for Relief in a Chapter 7 Liquidation Case

(a)　Appointment

At any time following the commencement of an involuntary liquidation case and before an order for relief, the court on written motion of a party in interest may order the appointment of an interim trustee under § 303(g) of the Code. The motion shall set forth the necessity for the appointment and may be granted only after hearing on notice to the debtor, the petitioning creditors, the United States trustee, and other parties in interest as the court may designate.

(b)　Bond of movant

An interim trustee may not be appointed under this rule unless the movant furnishes a bond in an amount approved by the court, conditioned to indemnify the debtor for costs, attorney's fee, expenses, and damages allowable under § 303(i) of the Code.

(c)　Order of Appointment

The order directing the appointment of an interim trustee shall state the reason the appointment is necessary and shall specify the trustee's duties.

(d) Turnover and report

Following qualification of the trustee selected under § 702 of the Code, the interim trustee, unless otherwise ordered, shall (1) forthwith deliver to the trustee all the records and property of the estate in possession or subject to control of the interim trustee and, (2) within 30 days thereafter file a final report and account.

CROSS REFERENCES

Duty to keep and file records and reports, see Fed. R. Bankr. P. 2015.

Interim trustee, see 11 USCA § 701.

Motions; form and service, see Fed. R. Bankr. P. 9013.

Security; proceedings against sureties, see Fed. R. Bankr. P. 9025.

Rule 2002. Notices to Creditors, Equity Security Holders, Administrators in Foreign Proceedings, Persons Against Whom Provisional Relief Is Sought in Ancillary and Other Cross-Border Cases, United States, and United States Trustee

(a) Twenty-one-day notices to parties in interest

Except as provided in subdivisions (h), (i), (*l*), (p), and (q) of this rule, the clerk, or some other person as the court may direct, shall give the debtor, the trustee, all creditors and indenture trustees at least 21 days' notice by mail of:

   (1) the meeting of creditors under § 341 or § 1104(b) of the Code, which notice, unless the court orders otherwise, shall include the debtor's employer identification number, social security number, and any other federal taxpayer identification number;

   (2) a proposed use, sale, or lease of property of the estate other than in the ordinary course of business, unless the court for cause shown shortens the time or directs another method of giving notice;

   (3) the hearing on approval of a compromise or settlement of a controversy other than approval of an agreement pursuant to Rule 4001(d), unless the court for cause shown directs that notice not be sent;

   (4) in a chapter 7 liquidation, a chapter 11 reorganization case, or a chapter 12 family farmer debt adjustment case, the hearing on the dismissal of the case or the conversion of the case to another chapter, unless the hearing is under § 707(a)(3) or § 707(b) or is on dismissal of the case for failure to pay the filing fee;

   (5) the time fixed to accept or reject a proposed modification of a plan;

   (6) a hearing on any entity's request for compensation or reimbursement of expenses if the request exceeds $1,000;

   (7) the time fixed for filing proofs of claims pursuant to Rule 3003(c);

   (8) the time fixed for filing objections and the hearing to consider confirmation of a chapter 12 plan; and

   (9) the time fixed for filing objections to confirmation of a chapter 13 plan.

(b) Twenty-eight-day notices to parties in interest

Except as provided in subdivision (*l*) of this rule, the clerk, or some other person as the court may direct, shall give the debtor, the trustee, all creditors and indenture trustees not less than 28 days' notice by mail of the time fixed (1) for filing objections and the hearing to consider approval of a disclosure statement or, under § 1125(f), to make a final determination whether the plan provides adequate information so that a separate disclosure statement is not necessary; (2) for filing objections and the hearing to consider confirmation of a chapter 9 or chapter 11 plan; and (3) for the hearing to consider confirmation of a chapter 13 plan.

(c) Content of notice

(1) Proposed Use, Sale, or Lease of Property

Subject to Rule 6004, the notice of a proposed use, sale, or lease of property required by subdivision (a)(2) of this rule shall include the time and place of any public sale, the terms and conditions of any private sale and the time fixed for filing objections. The notice of a proposed use, sale, or lease of property, including real estate, is sufficient if it generally describes the property. The notice of a proposed sale or lease of personally identifiable information under § 363(b)(1) of the Code shall state whether the sale is consistent with any policy prohibiting the transfer of the information.

(2) Notice of hearing on compensation

The notice of a hearing on an application for compensation or reimbursement of expenses required by subdivision (a)(6) of this rule shall identify the applicant and the amounts requested.

(3) Notice of hearing on confirmation when plan provides for an injunction

If a plan provides for an injunction against conduct not otherwise enjoined under the Code, the notice required under Rule 2002(b)(2) shall:

(A) include in conspicuous language (bold, italic, or underlined text) a statement that the plan proposes an injunction;

(B) describe briefly the nature of the injunction; and

(C) identify the entities that would be subject to the injunction.

(d) Notice to equity security holders

In a chapter 11 reorganization case, unless otherwise ordered by the court, the clerk, or some other person as the court may direct, shall in the manner and form directed by the court give notice to all equity security holders of (1) the order for relief; (2) any meeting of equity security holders held pursuant to § 341 of the Code; (3) the hearing on the proposed sale of all or substantially all of the debtor's assets; (4) the hearing on the dismissal or conversion of a case to another chapter; (5) the time fixed for filing objections to and the hearing to consider approval of a disclosure statement; (6) the time fixed for filing objections to and the hearing to consider confirmation of a plan; and (7) the time fixed to accept or reject a proposed modification of a plan.

(e) Notice of no dividend

In a chapter 7 liquidation case, if it appears from the schedules that there are no assets from which a dividend can be paid, the notice of the meeting of creditors may include a statement to that effect; that it is unnecessary to file claims; and that if sufficient assets become available for the payment of a dividend, further notice will be given for the filing of claims.

(f) Other notices

Except as provided in subdivision (*l*) of this rule, the clerk, or some other person as the court may direct, shall give the debtor, all creditors, and indenture trustees notice by mail of:

(1) the order for relief;

(2) the dismissal or the conversion of the case to another chapter, or the suspension of proceedings under § 305;

(3) the time allowed for filing claims pursuant to Rule 3002;

(4) the time fixed for filing a complaint objecting to the debtor's discharge pursuant to § 727 of the Code as provided in Rule 4004;

(5) the time fixed for filing a complaint to determine the dischargeability of a debt pursuant to § 523 of the Code as provided in Rule 4007;

(6) the waiver, denial, or revocation of a discharge as provided in Rule 4006;

(7) entry of an order confirming a chapter 9, 11, 12, or 13 plan;

(8) a summary of the trustee's final report in a chapter 7 case if the net proceeds realized exceed $1,500;

(9) a notice under Rule 5008 regarding the presumption of abuse;

(10) a statement under § 704(b)(1) as to whether the debtor's case would be presumed to be an abuse under § 707(b); and

(11) the time to request a delay in the entry of the discharge under §§ 1141(d)(5)(C), 1228(f), and 1328(h). Notice of the time fixed for accepting or rejecting a plan pursuant to Rule 3017(c) shall be given in accordance with Rule 3017(d).

(g) Addressing notices

(1) Notices required to be mailed under Rule 2002 to a creditor, indenture trustee, or equity security holder shall be addressed as such entity or an authorized agent has directed in its last request filed in the particular case. For the purposes of this subdivision—

(A) a proof of claim filed by a creditor or indenture trustee that designates a mailing address constitutes a filed request to mail notices to that address, unless a notice of no dividend has been given under Rule 2002(e) and a later notice of possible dividend under Rule 3002(c)(5) has not been given; and

(B) a proof of interest filed by an equity security holder that designates a mailing address constitutes a filed request to mail notices to that address.

(2) Except as provided in § 342(f) of the Code, if a creditor or indenture trustee has not filed a request designating a mailing address under Rule 2002(g)(1) or Rule 5003(e), the notices shall be mailed to the address shown on the list of creditors or schedule of liabilities, whichever is filed later. If an equity security holder has not filed a request designating a mailing address under Rule 2002(g)(1) or Rule 5003(e), the notices shall be mailed to the address shown on the list of equity security holders.

(3) If a list or schedule filed under Rule 1007 includes the name and address of a legal representative of an infant or incompetent person, and a person other than that representative files a request or proof of claim designating a name and mailing address that differs from the name and address of the representative included in the list or schedule, unless the court orders otherwise, notices under Rule 2002 shall be mailed to the representative included in the list or schedules and to the name and address designated in the request or proof of claim.

(4) Notwithstanding Rule 2002(g)(1)–(3), an entity and a notice provider may agree that when the notice provider is directed by the court to give a notice, the notice provider shall give the notice to the entity in the manner agreed to and at the address or addresses the entity supplies to the notice provider. That address is conclusively presumed to be a proper address for the notice. The notice provider's failure to use the supplied address does not invalidate any notice that is otherwise effective under applicable law.

(5) A creditor may treat a notice as not having been brought to the creditor's attention under § 342(g)(1) only if, prior to issuance of the notice, the creditor has filed a statement that designates the name and address of the person or organizational subdivision of the creditor responsible for receiving notices under the Code, and that describes the procedures established by the creditor to cause such notices to be delivered to the designated person or subdivision.

(h) Notices to creditors whose claims are filed

(1) Voluntary Case

In a voluntary chapter 7 case, chapter 12 case, or chapter 13 case, after 70 days following the order for relief under that chapter or the date of the order converting the case to chapter 12 or chapter 13, the court may direct that all notices required by subdivision (a) of this rule be mailed only to:

- the debtor;
- the trustee;
- all indenture trustees;
- creditors that hold claims for which proofs of claim have been filed; and
- creditors, if any, that are still permitted to file claims because an extension was granted under Rule 3002(c)(1) or (c)(2).

(2) Involuntary Case

In an involuntary chapter 7 case, after 90 days following the order for relief under that chapter, the court may direct that all notices required by subdivision (a) of this rule be mailed only to:

- the debtor;
- the trustee;
- all indenture trustees;
- creditors that hold claims for which proofs of claim have been filed; and
- creditors, if any, that are still permitted to file claims because an extension was granted under Rule 3002(c)(1) or (c)(2).

(3) Insufficient Assets

In a case where notice of insufficient assets to pay a dividend has been given to creditors under subdivision (e) of this rule, after 90 days following the mailing of a notice of the time for filing claims under Rule 3002(c)(5), the court may direct that notices be mailed only to the entities specified in the preceding sentence.

(i) Notices to committees

Copies of all notices required to be mailed pursuant to this rule shall be mailed to the committees elected under § 705 or appointed under § 1102 of the Code or to their authorized agents. Notwithstanding the foregoing subdivisions, the court may order that notices required by subdivision (a)(2), (3) and (6) of this rule be transmitted to the United States trustee and be mailed only to the committees elected under § 705 or appointed under § 1102 of the Code or to their authorized agents and to the creditors and equity security holders who serve on the trustee or debtor in possession and file a request that all notices be mailed to them. A committee appointed under § 1114 shall receive copies of all notices required by subdivisions (a)(1), (a)(5), (b), (f)(2), and (f)(7), and such other notices as the court may direct.

(j) Notices to the United States

Copies of notices required to be mailed to all creditors under this rule shall be mailed (1) in a chapter 11 reorganization case, to the Securities and Exchange Commission at any place the Commission designates, if the Commission has filed either a notice of appearance in the case or a written request to receive notices; (2) in a commodity broker case, to the Commodity Futures Trading Commission at Washington, D.C.; (3) in a chapter 11 case, to the Internal Revenue Service at its address set out in the register maintained under Rule 5003(e) for the district in which the case is pending; (4) if the papers in the case disclose a debt to the United States other than for taxes, to the United States attorney for the district in which the case is pending and to the department, agency, or instrumentality of the United States through which the debtor became indebted; or (5) if the filed papers disclose a stock interest of the United States, to the Secretary of the Treasury at Washington, D.C.

(k) Notices to United States trustee

Unless the case is a chapter 9 municipality case or unless the United States trustee requests otherwise, the clerk, or some other person as the court may direct, shall transmit to the United States trustee notice of the matters described in subdivisions (a)(2), (a)(3), (a)(4), (a)(8), (a)(9), (b), (f)(1), (f)(2), (f)(4), (f)(6), (f)(7), (f)(8), and (q) of this rule and notice of hearings on all applications for compensation or reimbursement of expenses. Notices to the United States trustee shall be transmitted within the time prescribed in subdivision (a) or (b) of this rule. The United States trustee shall also receive notice of any other matter if such notice is requested by the United States trustee or ordered by the court. Nothing in these rules requires the clerk or any other person to transmit to the United States trustee any notice, schedule, report, application or other document in a case under the Securities Investor Protection Act, 15 U.S.C. § 78aaa et.[1] seq.

(*l*) Notice by publication

The court may order notice by publication if it finds that notice by mail is impracticable or that it is desirable to supplement the notice.

(m) Orders designating matter of notices

The court may from time to time enter orders designating the matters in respect to which, the entity to whom, and the form and manner in which notices shall be sent except as otherwise provided by these rules.

(n) Caption

The caption of every notice given under this rule shall comply with Rule 1005. The caption of every notice required to be given by the debtor to a creditor shall include the information required to be in the notice by § 342(c) of the Code.

(o) Notice of order for relief in consumer case

In a voluntary case commenced by an individual debtor whose debts are primarily consumer debts, the clerk or some other person as the court may direct shall give the trustee and all creditors notice by mail of the order for relief within 21 days from the date thereof.

(p) Notice to a creditor with a foreign address

(1) If, at the request of the United States trustee or a party in interest, or on its own initiative, the court finds that a notice mailed within the time prescribed by these rules would not be sufficient to give a creditor with a foreign address to which notices under these rules are mailed reasonable notice under the circumstances, the court may order that the notice be supplemented with notice by other means or that the time prescribed for the notice by mail be enlarged.

(2) Unless the court for cause orders otherwise, a creditor with a foreign address to which notices under this rule are mailed shall be given at least 30 days' notice of the time fixed for filing a proof of claim under Rule 3002(c) or Rule 3003(c).

(3) Unless the court for cause orders otherwise, the mailing address of a creditor with a foreign address shall be determined under Rule 2002(g).

---

[1]   So in original. Period probably should not appear.

(q) Notice of petition for recognition of foreign proceeding and of court's intention to communicate with foreign courts and foreign representatives

(1) Notice of petition for recognition

After the filing of a petition for recognition of a foreign proceeding, the court shall promptly schedule and hold a hearing on the petition. The clerk, or some other person as the court may direct, shall forthwith give the debtor, all persons or bodies authorized to administer foreign proceedings of the debtor, all entities against whom provisional relief is being sought under § 1519 of the Code, all parties to litigation pending in the United States in which the debtor is a party at the time of the filing of the petition, and such other entities as the court may direct, at least 21 days' notice by mail of the hearing. The notice shall state whether the petition seeks recognition as a foreign main proceeding or foreign nonmain proceeding and shall include the petition and any other document the court may require. If the court consolidates the hearing on the petition with the hearing on a request for provisional relief, the court may set a shorter notice period, with notice to the entities listed in this subdivision.

(2) Notice of court's intention to communicate with foreign courts and foreign representatives

The clerk, or some other person as the court may direct, shall give the debtor, all persons or bodies authorized to administer foreign proceedings of the debtor, all entities against whom provisional relief is being sought under § 1519 of the Code, all parties to litigation pending in the United States in which the debtor is a party at the time of the filing of the petition, and such other entities as the court may direct, notice by mail of the court's intention to communicate with a foreign court or foreign representative.

CROSS REFERENCES

Form and manner of publication of notices, see Fed. R. Bankr. P. 9008.

General requirements of form for creditors' notices, see Fed. R. Bankr. P. 9004.

Hearing on disclosure statement in municipality debt adjustment and reorganization cases, see Fed. R. Bankr. P. 3017.

Notice by mail complete on mailing, see Fed. R. Bankr. P. 9006.

Notice of—

Dismissal for failure to pay filing fees, see Fed. R. Bankr. P. 1017.

Dividend and of time to file proof of claim in liquidation case, see Fed. R. Bankr. P. 3002.

Hearing on compromise or settlement to creditors, debtor, indenture trustees, and others designated by court, see Fed. R. Bankr. P. 9019.

Hearing on confirmation of individual debt adjustment plan to include plan or summary, see Fed. R. Bankr. P. 3015.

Hearing on dismissal of case, see Fed. R. Bankr. P. 1017.

Order of conversion to liquidation case, see Fed. R. Bankr. P. 1019.

Time extended to file claims against surplus in converted liquidation case, see Fed. R. Bankr. P. 1019.

Time fixed for filing complaint objecting to discharge in reorganization case, see Fed. R. Bankr. P. case, see Fed. R. Bankr. P. 4004.

Time fixed for filing complaint to determine debt's dischargeability, see Fed. R. Bankr. P. 4007.

Use, sale, or lease of property other than in ordinary course, see Fed. R. Bankr. P. 6004.

Waiver, denial, or revocation of discharge, see Fed. R. Bankr. P. 4006.

Reduction in time periods generally, see Fed. R. Bankr. P. 9006.

Review by court on plan's confirmation after notice and hearing pursuant to, see Fed. R. Bankr. P. 3020.

Rule 2003. Meeting of Creditors or Equity Security Holders

(a) Date and place

Except as otherwise provided in § 341(e) of the Code, in a chapter 7 liquidation or a chapter 11 reorganization case, the United States trustee shall call a meeting of creditors to be held no fewer than 21 and no more than 40 days after the order for relief. In a chapter 12 family farmer debt adjustment case, the United States trustee shall call a meeting of creditors to be held no fewer than 21 and no more than 35 days after the order for relief. In a chapter 13 individual's debt adjustment case, the United States trustee shall call a meeting of creditors to be held no fewer than 21 and no more than 50 days after the order for relief. If there is an appeal from or a motion to vacate the order for relief, or if there is a motion to dismiss the case, the United States trustee may set a later date for the meeting. The meeting may be held at a regular place for holding court or at any other place designated by the United States trustee within the district convenient for the parties in interest. If the United States trustee designates a place for the meeting which is not regularly staffed by the United States trustee or an assistant who may preside at the meeting, the meeting may be held not more than 60 days after the order for relief.

(b) Order of meeting

(1) Meeting of creditors

The United States trustee shall preside at the meeting of creditors. The business of the meeting shall include the examination of the debtor under oath and, in a chapter 7 liquidation case, may include the election of a creditors' committee and, if the case is not under subchapter V of chapter 7, the election of a trustee. The presiding officer shall have the authority to administer oaths.

(2) Meeting of equity security holders

If the United States trustee convenes a meeting of equity security holders pursuant to § 341(b) of the Code, the United States trustee shall fix a date for the meeting and shall preside.

(3) Right to vote

In a chapter 7 liquidation case, a creditor is entitled to vote at a meeting if, at or before the meeting, the creditor has filed a proof of claim or a writing setting forth facts evidencing a right to vote pursuant to § 702(a) of the Code unless objection is made to the claim or the proof of claim is insufficient on its face. A creditor of a partnership may file a proof of claim or writing evidencing a right to vote for the trustee for the estate of a general partner notwithstanding that a trustee for the estate of the partnership has previously qualified. In the event of an objection to the amount or allowability of a claim for the purpose of voting, unless the court orders otherwise, the United States trustee shall tabulate the votes for each alternative presented by the dispute and, if resolution of such dispute is necessary to determine the result of the election, the tabulations for each alternative shall be reported to the court.

(c) Record of meeting

Any examination under oath at the meeting of creditors held pursuant to § 341(a) of the Code shall be recorded verbatim by the United States trustee using electronic sound recording equipment or other means of recording, and such record shall be preserved by the United States trustee and available for public access until two years after the conclusion of the meeting of creditors. Upon request of any entity, the United States trustee shall certify and provide a copy or transcript of such recording at the entity's expense.

(d) Report of election and resolution of disputes in a chapter 7 case

(1) Report of undisputed election

In a chapter 7 case, if the election of a trustee or a member of a creditors' committee is not disputed, the United States trustee shall promptly file a report of the election, including the name and address of the person or entity elected and a statement that the election is undisputed.

(2) Disputed election

If the election is disputed, the United States trustee shall promptly file a report stating that the election is disputed, informing the court of the nature of the dispute, and listing the name and address of any candidate elected under any alternative presented by the dispute. No later than the date on which the report is filed, the United States trustee shall mail a copy of the report to any party in interest that has made a request to receive a copy of the report. Pending disposition by the court of a disputed election for trustee, the interim trustee shall continue in office. Unless a motion for the resolution of the dispute is filed no later than 14 days after the United States trustee files a report of a disputed election for trustee, the interim trustee shall serve as trustee in the case.

(e) Adjournment

The meeting may be adjourned from time to time by announcement at the meeting of the adjourned date and time. The presiding official shall promptly file a statement specifying the date and time to which the meeting is adjourned.

(f) Special meetings

The United States trustee may call a special meeting of creditors on request of a party in interest or on the United States trustee's own initiative.

(g) Final meeting

If the United States trustee calls a final meeting of creditors in a case in which the net proceeds realized exceed $1,500, the clerk shall mail a summary of the trustee's final account to the creditors with a notice of the meeting, together with a statement of the amount of the claims allowed. The trustee shall attend the final meeting and shall, if requested, report on the administration of the estate.

CROSS REFERENCES

Affirmations, see Fed. R. Bankr. P. 9012.

Election of creditors' committee in liquidation case, see 11 USCA § 705.

Eligibility to serve as and qualification of trustee, see 11 USCA §§ 321 and 322.

Enlargement of time not permitted—

　　Date of meeting of creditors, see Fed. R. Bankr. P. 9006.

　　Motion for resolution of trustee election dispute, see Fed. R. Bankr. P. 9006.

Holders of multiple proxies to file list of proxies to be voted, see Fed. R. Bankr. P. 2006.

Inapplicability of this rule to—

　　Municipality debt adjustment case, see 11 USCA § 901.

　　Railroad reorganization case, see 11 USCA § 1161.

Interim trustee in liquidation case, see Fed. R. Bankr. P. 2001, and 11 USCA § 701.

Motions; form and service, see Fed. R. Bankr. P. 9013.

Reduction of twenty-day period for date of meeting of creditors not permitted, see Fed. R. Bankr. P. 9006.

Selection and substitution of trustees, see Fed. R. Bankr. P. 2008 and 2012.

Time for objections to property claimed to be exempt, see Fed. R. Bankr. P. 4003.

Rule 2004. Examination

(a) Examination on motion

On motion of any party in interest, the court may order the examination of any entity.

(b) Scope of examination

The examination of an entity under this rule or of the debtor under § 343 of the Code may relate only to the acts, conduct, or property or to the liabilities and financial condition of the debtor, or to any matter which may affect the administration of the debtor's estate, or to the debtor's right to a discharge. In a family farmer's debt adjustment case under chapter 12, an individual's debt adjustment case under chapter 13, or a reorganization case under chapter 11 of the Code, other than for the reorganization of a railroad, the examination may also relate to the operation of any business and the desirability of its continuance, the source of any money or property acquired or to be acquired by the debtor for purposes of consummating a plan and the consideration given or offered therefor, and any other matter relevant to the case or to the formulation of a plan.

(c) Compelling attendance and production of documents or electronically stored information

The attendance of an entity for examination and for the production of documents or electronically stored information, whether the examination is to be conducted within or without the district in which the case is pending, may be compelled as provided in Rule 9016 for the attendance of a witness at a hearing or trial. As an officer of the court, an attorney may issue and sign a subpoena on behalf of the court where the case is pending if the attorney is admitted to practice in that court.

(d) Time and place of examination of debtor

The court may for cause shown and on terms as it may impose order the debtor to be examined under this rule at any time or place it designates, whether within or without the district wherein the case is pending.

(e) Mileage

An entity other than a debtor shall not be required to attend as a witness unless lawful mileage and witness fee for one day's attendance shall be first tendered. If the debtor resides more than 100 miles from the place of examination when required to appear for an examination under this rule, the mileage allowed by law to a witness shall be tendered for any distance more than 100 miles from the debtor's residence at the date of the filing of the first petition commencing a case under the Code or the residence at the time the debtor is required to appear for the examination, whichever is the lesser.

CROSS REFERENCES

Allowances and travel expenses of witnesses, see 28 USCA § 1821.

Apprehension and removal of debtor to compel attendance for examination, see Fed. R. Bankr. P. 2005.

Debtor as corporation or partnership for purposes of this rule, see Fed. R. Bankr. P. 9001.

Duty of bankrupt to—

> Attend hearing on right to discharge, see 11 USCA § 524.

> Submit to examination, see Fed. R. Bankr. P. 4002.

Duty of trustee to investigate debtor—

> Individual debt adjustment case, see 11 USCA § 1302.

> Liquidation case, see 11 USCA § 704.

Examination of debtor concerning compensation agreements with attorney, see Fed. R. Bankr. P. 2017.

Immunity from self-incrimination, see 11 USCA § 344.

Motions; form and service, see Fed. R. Bankr. P. 9013.

Subpoena, see Fed. R. Civ. P. 45.

Privileges, see Fed. R. Evid. 501.

Rule 2005. Apprehension and Removal of Debtor to Compel Attendance for Examination

(a) Order to compel attendance for examination

On motion of any party in interest supported by an affidavit alleging (1) that the examination of the debtor is necessary for the proper administration of the estate and that there is reasonable cause to believe that the debtor is about to leave or has left the debtor's residence or principal place of business to avoid examination, or (2) that the debtor has evaded service of a subpoena or of an order to attend for examination, or (3) that the debtor has willfully disobeyed a subpoena or order to attend for examination, duly served, the court may issue to the marshal, or some other officer authorized by law, an order directing the officer to bring the debtor before the court without unnecessary delay. If, after hearing, the court finds the allegations to be true, the court shall thereupon cause the debtor to be examined forthwith. If necessary, the court shall fix conditions for further examination and for the debtor's obedience to all orders made in reference thereto.

(b) Removal

Whenever any order to bring the debtor before the court is issued under this rule and the debtor is found in a district other than that of the court issuing the order, the debtor may be taken into custody under the order and removed in accordance with the following rules:

> **(1)** If the debtor is taken into custody under the order at a place less than 100 miles from the place of issue of the order, the debtor shall be brought forthwith before the court that issued the order.

> **(2)** If the debtor is taken into custody under the order at a place 100 miles or more from the place of issue of the order, the debtor shall be brought without unnecessary delay before the nearest available United States magistrate judge, bankruptcy judge, or district judge. If, after hearing, the magistrate judge, bankruptcy judge, or district judge finds that an order has issued under this rule and that the person in custody is the debtor, or if the person in custody waives a hearing, the magistrate judge, bankruptcy judge, or district judge shall order removal, and the person in custody shall be released on conditions ensuring prompt appearance before the court that issued the order to compel the attendance.

(c) Conditions of release

In determining what conditions will reasonably assure attendance or obedience under subdivision (a) of this rule or appearance under subdivision (b) of this rule, the court shall be governed by the relevant provisions and policies of title 18 U.S.C. § 3142.

CROSS REFERENCES

Debtor as corporation or partnership for purposes of this rule, see Fed. R. Bankr. P. 9001.

Motions; form and service, see Fed. R. Bankr. P. 9013.

Commitment to another district; removal, see Fed. R. Crim. P. Rule 40.

Rule 2006. Solicitation and Voting of Proxies in Chapter 7 Liquidation Cases

(a) Applicability

This rule applies only in a liquidation case pending under chapter 7 of the Code.

(b) Definitions

(1) Proxy

A proxy is a written power of attorney authorizing any entity to vote the claim or otherwise act as the owner's attorney in fact in connection with the administration of the estate.

(2) Solicitation of proxy

The solicitation of a proxy is any communication, other than one from an attorney to a regular client who owns a claim or from an attorney to the owner of a claim who has requested the attorney to represent the owner, by which a creditor is asked, directly or indirectly, to give a proxy after or in contemplation of the filing of a petition by or against the debtor.

(c) Authorized solicitation

(1) A proxy may be solicited only by (A) a creditor owning an allowable unsecured claim against the estate on the date of the filing of the petition; (B) a committee elected pursuant to § 705 of the Code; (C) a committee of creditors selected by a majority in number and amount of claims of creditors (i) whose claims are not contingent or unliquidated, (ii) who are not disqualified from voting under § 702(a) of the Code and (iii) who were present or represented at a meeting of which all creditors having claims of over $500 or the 100 creditors having the largest claims had at least seven days' notice in writing and of which meeting written minutes were kept and are available reporting the names of the creditors present or represented and voting and the amounts of their claims; or (D) a bona fide trade or credit association, but such association may solicit only creditors who were its members or subscribers in good standing and had allowable unsecured claims on the date of the filing of the petition.

(2) A proxy may be solicited only in writing.

(d) Solicitation not authorized

This rule does not permit solicitation (1) in any interest other than that of general creditors; (2) by or on behalf of any custodian; (3) by the interim trustee or by or on behalf of any entity not qualified to vote under § 702(a) of the Code; (4) by or on behalf of an attorney at law; or (5) by or on behalf of a transferee of a claim for collection only.

(e) Data required from holders of multiple proxies

At any time before the voting commences at any meeting of creditors pursuant to § 341(a) of the Code, or at any other time as the court may direct, a holder of two or more proxies shall file and transmit to the United States trustee a verified list of the proxies to be voted and a verified statement of the pertinent facts and circumstances in connection with the execution and delivery of each proxy, including:

(1) a copy of the solicitation;

(2) identification of the solicitor, the forwarder, if the forwarder is neither the solicitor nor the owner of the claim, and the proxyholder, including their connections with the debtor and with each other. If the solicitor, forwarder, or proxyholder is an association, there shall also be included a statement that the creditors whose claims have been solicited and the creditors whose claims are to be voted were members or subscribers in good standing and had allowable unsecured claims on the date of the filing of the petition. If the solicitor, forwarder, or proxyholder is a committee of creditors, the statement shall also set forth the date and place the committee was organized, that the committee was organized in accordance with clause (B) or (C) of paragraph (c)(1) of this rule, the members of the committee, the amounts of their claims, when the claims were acquired,

the amounts paid therefor, and the extent to which the claims of the committee members are secured or entitled to priority;

(3) a statement that no consideration has been paid or promised by the proxyholder for the proxy;

(4) a statement as to whether there is any agreement and, if so, the particulars thereof, between the proxyholder and any other entity for the payment of any consideration in connection with voting the proxy, or for the sharing of compensation with any entity, other than a member or regular associate of the proxyholder's law firm, which may be allowed the trustee or any entity for services rendered in the case, or for the employment of any person as attorney, accountant, appraiser, auctioneer, or other employee for the estate;

(5) if the proxy was solicited by an entity other than the proxyholder, or forwarded to the holder by an entity who is neither a solicitor of the proxy nor the owner of the claim, a statement signed and verified by the solicitor or forwarder that no consideration has been paid or promised for the proxy, and whether there is any agreement, and, if so, the particulars thereof, between the solicitor or forwarder and any other entity for the payment of any consideration in connection with voting the proxy, or for sharing compensation with any entity, other than a member or regular associate of the solicitor's or forwarder's law firm which may be allowed the trustee or any entity for services rendered in the case, or for the employment of any person as attorney, accountant, appraiser, auctioneer, or other employee for the estate;

(6) if the solicitor, forwarder, or proxyholder is a committee, a statement signed and verified by each member as to the amount and source of any consideration paid or to be paid to such member in connection with the case other than by way of dividend on the member's claim.

(f) Enforcement of restrictions on solicitation

On motion of any party in interest or on its own initiative, the court may determine whether there has been a failure to comply with the provisions of this rule or any other impropriety in connection with the solicitation or voting of a proxy. After notice and a hearing the court may reject any proxy for cause, vacate any order entered in consequence of the voting of any proxy which should have been rejected, or take any other appropriate action.

CROSS REFERENCES

Committee of unsecured creditors selected before order for relief, solicitation pursuant to this rule, see Fed. R. Bankr. P. 2007.

Motions; form and service, see Fed. R. Bankr. P. 9013.

Signing and verification of papers, see Fed. R. Bankr. P. 9011.

Rule 2007. Review of Appointment of Creditors' Committee Organized Before Commencement of the Case

(a) Motion to review appointment

If a committee appointed by the United States trustee pursuant to § 1102(a) of the Code consists of the members of a committee organized by creditors before the commencement of a chapter 9 or chapter 11 case, on motion of a party in interest and after a hearing on notice to the United States trustee and other entities as the court may direct, the court may determine whether the appointment of the committee satisfies the requirements of § 1102(b)(1) of the Code.

(b) Selection of members of committee

The court may find that a committee organized by unsecured creditors before the commencement of a chapter 9 or chapter 11 case was fairly chosen if:

(1) it was selected by a majority in number and amount of claims of unsecured creditors who may vote under § 702(a) of the Code and were present in person or represented at a meeting of which all creditors having unsecured claims of over $1,000 or the 100 unsecured creditors having the largest claims had at least seven days' notice in writing, and of which meeting written minutes reporting the names of the creditors present or represented and voting and the amounts of their claims were kept and are available for inspection;

(2) all proxies voted at the meeting for the elected committee were solicited pursuant to Rule 2006 and the lists and statements required by subdivision (e) thereof have been transmitted to the United States trustee; and

(3) the organization of the committee was in all other respects fair and proper.

(c) Failure to comply with requirements for appointment

After a hearing on notice pursuant to subdivision (a) of this rule, the court shall direct the United States trustee to vacate the appointment of the committee and may order other appropriate action if the court finds that such appointment failed to satisfy the requirements of § 1102(b)(1) of the Code.

CROSS REFERENCES

Representation of creditors and equity security holders in municipality debt adjustment and reorganization cases, see Fed. R. Bankr. P. 2019.

Rule 2007.1. Appointment of Trustee or Examiner in a Chapter 11 Reorganization Case

(a) Order to appoint trustee or examiner

In a chapter 11 reorganization case, a motion for an order to appoint a trustee or an examiner under § 1104(a) or § 1104(c) of the Code shall be made in accordance with Rule 9014.

(b) Election of trustee

(1) Request for an election

A request to convene a meeting of creditors for the purpose of electing a trustee in a chapter 11 reorganization case shall be filed and transmitted to the United States trustee in accordance with Rule 5005 within the time prescribed by § 1104(b) of the Code. Pending court approval of the person elected, any person appointed by the United States trustee under § 1104(d) and approved in accordance with subdivision (c) of this rule shall serve as trustee.

(2) Manner of election and notice

An election of a trustee under § 1104(b) of the Code shall be conducted in the manner provided in Rules 2003(b)(3) and 2006. Notice of the meeting of creditors convened under § 1104(b) shall be given as provided in Rule 2002. The United States trustee shall preside at the meeting. A proxy for the purpose of voting in the election may be solicited only by a committee of creditors appointed under § 1102 of the Code or by any other party entitled to solicit a proxy pursuant to Rule 2006.

(3) Report of election and resolution of disputes.

(A) Report of undisputed election

If no dispute arises out of the election, the United States trustee shall promptly file a report certifying the election, including the name and address of the person elected and a statement that the election is undisputed. The report shall be accompanied by a verified statement of the person elected setting forth that person's connections with the debtor, creditors, any other party in interest, their respective attorneys and accountants, the United States trustee, or any person employed in the office of the United States trustee.

(B) Dispute arising out of an election

If a dispute arises out of an election, the United States trustee shall promptly file a report stating that the election is disputed, informing the court of the nature of the dispute, and listing the name and address of any candidate elected under any alternative presented by the dispute. The report shall be accompanied by a verified statement by each candidate elected under each alternative presented by the dispute, setting forth the person's connections with the debtor, creditors, any other party in interest, their respective attorneys and accountants, the United States trustee, or any person employed in the office of the United States trustee. Not later than the date on which the report of the disputed election is filed, the United States trustee shall mail a copy of the report and each verified statement to any party in interest that has made a request to convene a meeting under § 1104(b) or to receive a copy of the report, and to any committee appointed under § 1102 of the Code.

(c) Approval of appointment

An order approving the appointment of a trustee or an examiner under § 1104(d) of the Code shall be made on application of the United States trustee. The application shall state the name of the person appointed and, to the best of the applicant's knowledge, all the person's connections with the debtor, creditors, any other parties in interest, their respective attorneys and accountants, the United States trustee, or persons employed in the office of the United States trustee. The application shall state the names of the parties in interest with whom the United States trustee consulted regarding the appointment. The application shall be accompanied by a verified statement of the person appointed setting forth the person's connections with the debtor, creditors, any other party in interest, their respective attorneys and accountants, the United States trustee, or any person employed in the office of the United States trustee.

Rule 2007.2. Appointment of Patient Care Ombudsman in a Health Care Business Case

(a) Order to appoint patient care ombudsman

In a chapter 7, chapter 9, or chapter 11 case in which the debtor is a health care business, the court shall order the appointment of a patient care ombudsman under § 333 of the Code, unless the court, on motion of the United States trustee or a party in interest filed no later than 21 days after the commencement of the case or within another time fixed by the court, finds that the appointment of a patient care ombudsman is not necessary under the specific circumstances of the case for the protection of patients.

(b) Motion for order to appoint ombudsman

If the court has found that the appointment of an ombudsman is not necessary, or has terminated the appointment, the court, on motion of the United States trustee or a party in interest, may order the appointment at a later time if it finds that the appointment has become necessary to protect patients.

(c) Notice of appointment

If a patient care ombudsman is appointed under § 333, the United States trustee shall promptly file a notice of the appointment, including the name and address of the person appointed. Unless the person appointed is a State Long-Term Care Ombudsman, the notice shall be accompanied by a verified statement of the person appointed setting forth the person's connections with the debtor, creditors, patients, any other party in interest, their respective attorneys and accountants, the United States trustee, and any person employed in the office of the United States trustee.

(d) Termination of appointment

On motion of the United States trustee or a party in interest, the court may terminate the appointment of a patient care ombudsman if the court finds that the appointment is not necessary to protect patients.

(e) Motion

A motion under this rule shall be governed by Rule 9014. The motion shall be transmitted to the United States trustee and served on: the debtor; the trustee; any committee elected under § 705 or appointed under § 1102 of the Code or its authorized agent, or, if the case is a chapter 9 municipality case or a chapter 11 reorganization case and no committee of unsecured creditors has been appointed under § 1102, on the creditors included on the list filed under Rule 1007(d); and such other entities as the court may direct.

Rule 2008. Notice to Trustee of Selection

The United States trustee shall immediately notify the person selected as trustee how to qualify and, if applicable, the amount of the trustee's bond. A trustee that has filed a blanket bond pursuant to Rule 2010 and has been selected as trustee in a chapter 7, chapter 12, or chapter 13 case that does not notify the court and the United States trustee in writing of rejection of the office within seven days after receipt of notice of selection shall be deemed to have accepted the office. Any other person selected as trustee shall notify the court and the United States trustee in writing of acceptance of the office within seven days after receipt of notice of selection or shall be deemed to have rejected the office.

CROSS REFERENCES

Appointment of trustees—

    Individual debt adjustment case, see 11 USCA § 1302.

    Railroad reorganization case, see 11 USCA § 1163.

    Reorganization case, see 11 USCA § 1104.

Bonds of trustees, see 11 USCA § 322.

Election of trustee in liquidation case, see 11 USCA § 702.

Eligibility to serve as trustee, see 11 USCA § 321.

Limited purpose of trustee appointed in municipality debt adjustment case, see 11 USCA § 926.

Representation of creditors and equity security holders in municipality debt adjustment and reorganization cases, see Fed. R. Bankr. P. 2019.

Right of creditors to elect single trustee when joint administration ordered, see Fed. R. Bankr. P. 2009.

Rule 2009. Trustees for Estates When Joint Administration Ordered

(a) Election of single trustee for estates being jointly administered

If the court orders a joint administration of two or more estates under Rule 1015(b), creditors may elect a single trustee for the estates being jointly administered, unless the case is under subchapter V of chapter 7 or subchapter V of chapter 11 of the Code.

(b) Right of creditors to elect separate trustee

Notwithstanding entry of an order for joint administration under Rule 1015(b), the creditors of any debtor may elect a separate trustee for the estate of the debtor as provided in § 702 of the Code, unless the case is under subchapter V of chapter 7 or subchapter V of chapter 11 of the Code.

(c)   Appointment of trustees for estates being jointly administered

(1)   Chapter 7 liquidation cases

Except in a case governed by subchapter V of chapter 7, the United States trustee may appoint one or more interim trustees for estates being jointly administered in chapter 7 cases.

(2)   Chapter 11 reorganization cases

If the appointment of a trustee is ordered or is required by the Code, the United States trustee may appoint one or more trustees for estates being jointly administered in chapter 11 cases.

(3)   Chapter 12 family farmer's debt adjustment cases

The United States trustee may appoint one or more trustees for estates being jointly administered in chapter 12 cases.

(4)   Chapter 13 individual's debt adjustment cases

The United States trustee may appoint one or more trustees for estates being jointly administered in chapter 13 cases.

(d)   Potential conflicts of interest

On a showing that creditors or equity security holders of the different estates will be prejudiced by conflicts of interest of a common trustee who has been elected or appointed, the court shall order the selection of separate trustees for estates being jointly administered.

(e)   Separate accounts

The trustee or trustees of estates being jointly administered shall keep separate accounts of the property and distribution of each estate.

CROSS REFERENCES

Partnerships—

Commencement of involuntary cases, see 11 USCA § 303.

Person defined to include partnerships, see 11 USCA § 101.

Representation of creditors and equity security holders in municipality debt adjustment and reorganization cases, see Fed. R. Bankr. P. 2019.

Rule 2010.   Qualification by Trustee; Proceeding on Bond

(a)   Blanket bond

The United States trustee may authorize a blanket bond in favor of the United States conditioned on the faithful performance of official duties by the trustee or trustees to cover (1) a person who qualifies as trustee in a number of cases, and (2) a number of trustees each of whom qualifies in a different case.

(b)   Proceeding on bond

A proceeding on the trustee's bond may be brought by any party in interest in the name of the United States for the use of the entity injured by the breach of the condition.

CROSS REFERENCES

Proceeding on trustee's bond as exception to procedural rule of prosecution in name of real party in interest, see Fed. R. Bankr. P. 7017.

Security; proceedings against sureties, see Fed. R. Bankr. P. 9025.

Two-year limitations period on bond proceeding, see 11 USCA § 322.

Parties plaintiff and defendant; capacity, see Fed. R. Civ. P. 17.

Security; proceedings against sureties, see Fed. R. Civ. P. 65.1.

Rule 2011. Evidence of Debtor in Possession or Qualification of Trustee

(a) Whenever evidence is required that a debtor is a debtor in possession or that a trustee has qualified, the clerk may so certify and the certificate shall constitute conclusive evidence of that fact.

(b) If a person elected or appointed as trustee does not qualify within the time prescribed by § 322(a) of the Code, the clerk shall so notify the court and the United States trustee.

CROSS REFERENCES

Debtor in possession for purposes of non-subchapter V reorganization case defined as debtor except when trustee is serving, see 11 USCA § 1101.

Rule 2012. Substitution of Trustee or Successor Trustee; Accounting

(a) Trustee

If a trustee is appointed in a chapter 11 case (other than under subchapter V), or the debtor is removed as debtor in possession in a chapter 12 case or in a case under subchapter V of chapter 11, the trustee is substituted automatically for the debtor in possession as a party in any pending action, proceeding, or matter.

(b) Successor trustee

When a trustee dies, resigns, is removed, or otherwise ceases to hold office during the pendency of a case under the Code (1) the successor is automatically substituted as a party in any pending action, proceeding, or matter; and (2) the successor trustee shall prepare, file, and transmit to the United States trustee an accounting of the prior administration of the estate.

CROSS REFERENCES

Abatement of suit or proceeding upon death or removal of trustee, see 11 USCA § 325.

Election by creditors of successor trustee in liquidation case, see 11 USCA § 703.

Exception to procedural rule for substitution of parties, see Fed. R. Bankr. P. 7025.

Power of court to remove trustee, see 11 USCA § 324.

Substitution of public officer on death or separation from office, see Fed. R. Civ. P. 25.

Rule 2013. Public Record of Compensation Awarded to Trustees, Examiners, and Professionals

(a) Record to be kept

The clerk shall maintain a public record listing fees awarded by the court (1) to trustees and attorneys, accountants, appraisers, auctioneers and other professionals employed by trustees, and (2) to examiners. The record shall include the name and docket number of the case, the name of the individual or firm receiving the fee and the amount of the fee awarded. The record shall be maintained chronologically and shall be kept current and open to examination by the public without charge. "Trustees," as used in this rule, does not include debtors in possession.

(b) Summary of record

At the close of each annual period, the clerk shall prepare a summary of the public record by individual or firm name, to reflect total fees awarded during the preceding year. The summary shall be open to examination by the public without charge. The clerk shall transmit a copy of the summary to the United States trustee.

Rule 2014. Employment of Professional Persons

(a) Application for an order of employment

An order approving the employment of attorneys, accountants, appraisers, auctioneers, agents, or other professionals pursuant to § 327, § 1103, or § 1114 of the Code shall be made only on application of the trustee or committee. The application shall be filed and, unless the case is a chapter 9 municipality case, a copy of the application shall be transmitted by the applicant to the United States trustee. The application shall state the specific facts showing the necessity for the employment, the name of the person to be employed, the reasons for the selection, the professional services to be rendered, any proposed arrangement for compensation, and, to the best of the applicant's knowledge, all of the person's connections with the debtor, creditors, any other party in interest, their respective attorneys and accountants, the United States trustee, or any person employed in the office of the United States trustee. The application shall be accompanied by a verified statement of the person to be employed setting forth the person's connections with the debtor, creditors, any other party in interest, their respective attorneys and accountants, the United States trustee, or any person employed in the office of the United States trustee.

(b) Services rendered by member or associate of firm of attorneys or accountants

If, under the Code and this rule, a law partnership or corporation is employed as an attorney, or an accounting partnership or corporation is employed as an accountant, or if a named attorney or accountant is employed, any partner, member, or regular associate of the partnership, corporation or individual may act as attorney or accountant so employed, without further order of the court.

Rule 2015. Duty to Keep Records, Make Reports, and Give Notice of Case or Change of Status

(a) Trustee or debtor in possession

A trustee or debtor in possession shall:

(1) in a chapter 7 liquidation case and, if the court directs, in a chapter 11 reorganization case (other than under subchapter V), file and transmit to the United States trustee a complete inventory of the property of the debtor within 30 days after qualifying as a trustee or debtor in possession, unless such an inventory has already been filed;

(2) keep a record of receipts and the disposition of money and property received;

(3) file the reports and summaries required by § 704(a)(8) of the Code, which shall include a statement, if payments are made to employees, of the amounts of deductions for all taxes required to be withheld or paid for and in behalf of employees and the place where these amounts are deposited;

(4) as soon as possible after the commencement of the case, give notice of the case to every entity known to be holding money or property subject to withdrawal or order of the debtor, including every bank, savings or building and loan association, public utility company, and landlord with whom the debtor has a deposit, and to every insurance company which has issued a policy having a cash surrender value payable to the debtor, except that notice need not be given to any entity who has knowledge or has previously been notified of the case;

(5) in a chapter 11 reorganization case (other than under subchapter V), on or before the last day of the month after each calendar quarter during which there is a duty to pay fees under 28 U.S.C. § 1930(a)(6), file and transmit to the United States trustee a statement of any disbursements made during that quarter and of any fees payable under 28 U.S.C. § 1930(a)(6) for that quarter; and

(6) in a chapter 11 small business case, unless the court, for cause, sets another reporting interval, file and transmit to the United States trustee for each calendar month after the order for relief, on the appropriate Official Form, the report required by § 308. If the order for relief is within the first 15 days of a calendar month, a report shall be filed for the portion of the month that follows the order for relief. If the order for relief is after the 15th day of a calendar month, the period for the remainder of the month shall be included in the report for the next calendar month. Each report shall be filed no later than 21 days after the last day of the calendar month following the month covered by the report. The obligation to file reports under this subparagraph terminates on the effective date of the plan, or conversion or dismissal of the case.

(b) Trustee, Debtor in Possession, and Debtor in a Case Under Subchapter V of Chapter 11

In a case under subchapter V of chapter 11, the debtor in possession shall perform the duties prescribed in (a)(2)–(4) and, if the court directs, shall file and transmit to the United States trustee a complete inventory of the debtor's property within the time fixed by the court. If the debtor is removed as debtor in possession, the trustee shall perform the duties of the debtor in possession prescribed in this subdivision (b). The debtor shall perform the duties prescribed in (a)(6).

(c) Chapter 12 trustee and debtor in possession

In a chapter 12 family farmer's debt adjustment case, the debtor in possession shall perform the duties prescribed in clauses (2)–(4) of subdivision (a) of this rule and, if the court directs, shall file and transmit to the United States trustee a complete inventory of the property of the debtor within the time fixed by the court. If the debtor is removed as debtor in possession, the trustee shall perform the duties of the debtor in possession prescribed in this subdivision (c).

(d) Chapter 13 trustee and debtor

(1) Business cases

In a chapter 13 individual's debt adjustment case, when the debtor is engaged in business, the debtor shall perform the duties prescribed by clauses (2)–(4) of subdivision (a) of this rule and, if the court directs, shall file and transmit to the United States trustee a complete inventory of the property of the debtor within the time fixed by the court.

(2) Nonbusiness cases

In a chapter 13 individual's debt adjustment case, when the debtor is not engaged in business, the trustee shall perform the duties prescribed by clause (2) of subdivision (a) of this rule.

(e) Foreign representative

In a case in which the court has granted recognition of a foreign proceeding under chapter 15, the foreign representative shall file any notice required under § 1518 of the Code within 14 days after the date when the representative becomes aware of the subsequent information.

(f) Transmission of reports

In a chapter 11 case the court may direct that copies or summaries of annual reports and copies or summaries of other reports shall be mailed to the creditors, equity security holders, and indenture trustees. The court may also direct the publication of summaries of any such reports. A copy of every report or summary mailed or published pursuant to this subdivision shall be transmitted to the United States trustee.

CROSS REFERENCES

Duties of trustee—

Individual debt adjustment case, see 11 USCA § 1302.

Reorganization case, see 11 USCA § 1106.

Operation of business by debtor, see 11 USCA § 1304.

Public access to papers filed in case under this title, see 11 USCA § 107.

Rule 2015.1. Patient Care Ombudsman

(a) Reports

A patient care ombudsman, at least 14 days before making a report under § 333(b)(2) of the Code, shall give notice that the report will be made to the court, unless the court orders otherwise. The notice shall be transmitted to the United States trustee, posted conspicuously at the health care facility that is the subject of the report, and served on: the debtor; the trustee; all patients; and any committee elected under § 705 or appointed under § 1102 of the Code or its authorized agent, or, if the case is a chapter 9 municipality case or a chapter 11 reorganization case and no committee of unsecured creditors has been appointed under § 1102, on the creditors included on the list filed under Rule 1007(d); and such other entities as the court may direct. The notice shall state the date and time when the report will be made, the manner in which the report will be made, and, if the report is in writing, the name, address, telephone number, email address, and website, if any, of the person from whom a copy of the report may be obtained at the debtor's expense.

(b) Authorization to review confidential patient records

A motion by a patient care ombudsman under § 333(c) to review confidential patient records shall be governed by Rule 9014, served on the patient and any family member or other contact person whose name and address have been given to the trustee or the debtor for the purpose of providing information regarding the patient's health care, and transmitted to the United States trustee subject to applicable nonbankruptcy law relating to patient privacy. Unless the court orders otherwise, a hearing on the motion may not be commenced earlier than 14 days after service of the motion.

Rule 2015.2. Transfer of Patient in Health Care Business Case

Unless the court orders otherwise, if the debtor is a health care business, the trustee may not transfer a patient to another health care business under § 704(a)(12) of the Code unless the trustee gives at least 14 days' notice of the transfer to the patient care ombudsman, if any, the patient, and any family member or other contact person whose name and address has been given to the trustee or the debtor for the purpose of providing information regarding the patient's health care. The notice is subject to applicable nonbankruptcy law relating to patient privacy.

Rule 2015.3. Reports of Financial Information on Entities in Which a Chapter 11 Estate Holds a Controlling or Substantial Interest

(a) Reporting requirement

In a chapter 11 case, the trustee or debtor in possession shall file periodic financial reports of the value, operations, and profitability of each entity that is not a publicly traded corporation or a debtor in a case under title 11, and in which the estate holds a substantial or controlling interest. The reports shall be prepared as prescribed by the appropriate Official Form, and shall be based upon the most recent information reasonably available to the trustee or debtor in possession.

(b) Time for filing; service

The first report required by this rule shall be filed no later than seven days before the first date set for the meeting of creditors under § 341 of the Code. Subsequent reports shall be filed no less frequently than every six months thereafter, until the effective date of a plan or the case is dismissed or converted. Copies of the report shall be served on the United States trustee, any committee appointed under § 1102 of the Code, and any other party in interest that has filed a request therefor.

(c) Presumption of substantial or controlling interest; judicial determination

For purposes of this rule, an entity of which the estate controls or owns at least a 20 percent interest, shall be presumed to be an entity in which the estate has a substantial or controlling interest. An entity in which the estate controls or owns less than a 20 percent interest shall be presumed not to be an entity in which the estate has a substantial or controlling interest. Upon motion, the entity, any holder of an interest therein, the United States trustee, or any other party in interest may seek to rebut either presumption, and the court shall, after notice and a hearing, determine whether the estate's interest in the entity is substantial or controlling.

(d) Modification of reporting requirement

The court may, after notice and a hearing, vary the reporting requirement established by subdivision (a) of this rule for cause, including that the trustee or debtor in possession is not able, after a good faith effort, to comply with those reporting requirements, or that the information required by subdivision (a) is publicly available.

(e) Notice and protective orders

No later than 14 days before filing the first report required by this rule, the trustee or debtor in possession shall send notice to the entity in which the estate has a substantial or controlling interest, and to all holders—known to the trustee or debtor in possession—of an interest in that entity, that the trustee or debtor in possession expects to file and serve financial information relating to the entity in accordance with this rule. The entity in which the estate has a substantial or controlling interest, or a person holding an interest in that entity, may request protection of the information under § 107 of the Code.

(f) Effect of request

Unless the court orders otherwise, the pendency of a request under subdivisions (c), (d), or (e) of this rule shall not alter or stay the requirements of subdivision (a).

Rule 2016. Compensation for Services Rendered and Reimbursement of Expenses

(a) Application for compensation or reimbursement

An entity seeking interim or final compensation for services, or reimbursement of necessary expenses, from the estate shall file an application setting forth a detailed statement of (1) the services rendered, time expended and expenses incurred, and (2) the amounts requested. An application for compensation shall include a statement as to what payments have theretofore been made or promised to the applicant for services rendered or to be rendered in any capacity whatsoever in connection with the case, the source of the compensation so paid or promised, whether any compensation previously received has been shared and whether an agreement or understanding exists between the applicant and any other entity for the sharing of compensation received or to be received for services rendered in or in connection with the case, and the particulars of any sharing of compensation or agreement or understanding therefor, except that details of any agreement by the applicant for the sharing of compensation as a member or regular associate of a firm of lawyers or accountants shall not be required. The requirements of this subdivision shall apply to an application for compensation for services rendered by an attorney or accountant even though the application is filed by a creditor or other entity. Unless the case is a chapter 9 municipality case, the applicant shall transmit to the United States trustee a copy of the application.

(b) Disclosure of compensation paid or promised to attorney for debtor

Every attorney for a debtor, whether or not the attorney applies for compensation, shall file and transmit to the United States trustee within 14 days after the order for relief, or at another time as the court may direct, the statement required by § 329 of the Code including whether the attorney has shared or agreed to share the compensation with any other entity. The statement shall include the particulars of any such sharing or agreement to share by the attorney, but the details of any agreement for the sharing of the compensation with a member or regular associate of the attorney's law firm shall not be required. A supplemental statement shall be filed and transmitted to the United States trustee within 14 days after any payment or agreement not previously disclosed.

(c) Disclosure of compensation paid or promised to bankruptcy petition preparer

Before a petition is filed, every bankruptcy petition preparer for a debtor shall deliver to the debtor, the declaration under penalty of perjury required by § 110(h)(2). The declaration shall disclose any fee, and the source of any fee, received from or on behalf of the debtor within 12 months of the filing of the case and all unpaid fees charged to the debtor. The declaration shall also describe the services performed and documents prepared or caused to be prepared by the bankruptcy petition preparer. The declaration shall be filed with the petition. The petition preparer shall file a supplemental statement within 14 days after any payment or agreement not previously disclosed.

CROSS REFERENCES

Compensation of professional persons—

    Actual, necessary services, see 11 USCA § 330.

    Limitation on, see 11 USCA § 328.

    Sharing of, see 11 USCA § 504.

Definition of—

    Firm to include partnership or professional corporation, see Fed. R. Bankr. P. 9001.

    Regular associate to mean attorney employed by, associated with, as counsel to firm or individual, see Fed. R. Bankr. P. 9001.

Employment of professional persons, see Fed. R. Bankr. P. 2014.

Rule 2017. Examination of Debtor's Transactions With Debtor's Attorney

(a) Payment or transfer to attorney before order for relief

On motion by any party in interest or on the court's own initiative, the court after notice and a hearing may determine whether any payment of money or any transfer of property by the debtor, made directly or indirectly and in contemplation of the filing of a petition under the Code by or against the debtor or before entry of the order for relief in an involuntary case, to an attorney for services rendered or to be rendered is excessive.

(b) Payment or transfer to attorney after order for relief

On motion by the debtor, the United States trustee, or on the court's own initiative, the court after notice and a hearing may determine whether any payment of money or any transfer of property, or any agreement therefor, by the debtor to an attorney after entry of an order for relief in a case under the Code is excessive, whether the payment or transfer is made or is to be made directly or indirectly, if the payment, transfer, or agreement therefor is for services in any way related to the case.

CROSS REFERENCES

Court filing of compensation paid or agreed to be paid, see 11 USCA § 329.

Motions; form and service, see Fed. R. Bankr. P. 9013.

Proceedings under this rule as nonadversarial proceedings, see Fed. R. Bankr. P. 7001.

Process; service of summons, complaint, see Fed. R. Bankr. P. 7004.

Rule 2018. Intervention; Right to Be Heard

(a) Permissive intervention

In a case under the Code, after hearing on such notice as the court directs and for cause shown, the court may permit any interested entity to intervene generally or with respect to any specified matter.

(b) Intervention by Attorney General of a State

In a chapter 7, 11, 12, or 13 case, the Attorney General of a State may appear and be heard on behalf of consumer creditors if the court determines the appearance is in the public interest, but the Attorney General may not appeal from any judgment, order, or decree in the case.

(c) Chapter 9 municipality case

The Secretary of the Treasury of the United States may, or if requested by the court shall, intervene in a chapter 9 case. Representatives of the state in which the debtor is located may intervene in a chapter 9 case with respect to matters specified by the court.

(d) Labor unions

In a chapter 9, 11, or 12 case, a labor union or employees' association, representative of employees of the debtor, shall have the right to be heard on the economic soundness of a plan affecting the interests of the employees. A labor union or employees' association which exercises its right to be heard under this subdivision shall not be entitled to appeal any judgment, order, or decree relating to the plan, unless otherwise permitted by law.

(e) Service on entities covered by this rule

The court may enter orders governing the service of notice and papers on entities permitted to intervene or be heard pursuant to this rule.

CROSS REFERENCES

Consumer debt defined as debt primarily for personal, family, or household purpose, see 11 USCA § 101(8).

Definitions for purposes of this rule of—

Entity, see 11 USCA § 101(15).

Governmental unit, see 11 USCA § 101(27).

Person, see 11 USCA § 101(41).

Intervention of—

Department of Transportation, see 11 USCA § 1164.

Party in interest, see 11 USCA § 1109.

Securities and Exchange Commission, see 11 USCA § 1109.

State or local regulatory commission, see 11 USCA § 1164.

Intervention in adversary proceedings, see Fed. R. Bankr. P. 7024.

Rule 2019. Disclosure Regarding Creditors and Equity Security Holders in Chapter 9 and Chapter 11 Cases

(a) Definitions

In this rule the following terms have the meanings indicated:

(1) "Disclosable economic interest" means any claim, interest, pledge, lien, option, participation, derivative instrument, or any other right or derivative right granting the holder an economic interest that is affected by the value, acquisition, or disposition of a claim or interest.

(2) "Represent" or "represents" means to take a position before the court or to solicit votes regarding the confirmation of a plan on behalf of another.

(b) Disclosure by groups, committees, and entities

(1) In a chapter 9 or 11 case, a verified statement setting forth the information specified in subdivision (c) of this rule shall be filed by every group or committee that consists of or represents, and every entity that represents, multiple creditors or equity security holders that are (A) acting in concert to advance their common interests, and (B) not composed entirely of affiliates or insiders of one another.

(2) Unless the court orders otherwise, an entity is not required to file the verified statement described in paragraph (1) of this subdivision solely because of its status as:

(A) an indenture trustee;

(B) an agent for one or more other entities under an agreement for the extension of credit;

(C) a class action representative; or

(D) a governmental unit that is not a person.

(c) Information required

The verified statement shall include:

(1) the pertinent facts and circumstances concerning:

(A) with respect to a group or committee, other than a committee appointed under § 1102 or § 1114 of the Code, the formation of the group or committee, including the name of each entity at whose instance the group or committee was formed or for whom the group or committee has agreed to act; or

(B) with respect to an entity, the employment of the entity, including the name of each creditor or equity security holder at whose instance the employment was arranged;

(2) if not disclosed under subdivision (c)(1), with respect to an entity, and with respect to each member of a group or committee:

(A) name and address;

(B) the nature and amount of each disclosable economic interest held in relation to the debtor as of the date the entity was employed or the group or committee was formed; and

(C) with respect to each member of a group or committee that claims to represent any entity in addition to the members of the group or committee, other than a committee appointed under § 1102 or § 1114 of the Code, the date of acquisition by quarter and year of each disclosable economic interest, unless acquired more than one year before the petition was filed;

(3) if not disclosed under subdivision (c)(1) or (c)(2), with respect to each creditor or equity security holder represented by an entity, group, or committee, other than a committee appointed under § 1102 or § 1114 of the Code:

(A) name and address; and

(B) the nature and amount of each disclosable economic interest held in relation to the debtor as of the date of the statement; and

(4) a copy of the instrument, if any, authorizing the entity, group, or committee to act on behalf of creditors or equity security holders.

(d) Supplemental statements

If any fact disclosed in its most recently filed statement has changed materially, an entity, group, or committee shall file a verified supplemental statement whenever it takes a position before the court or solicits votes on the confirmation of a plan. The supplemental statement shall set forth the material changes in the facts required by subdivision (c) to be disclosed.

(e) Determination of failure to comply; sanctions

(1) On motion of any party in interest, or on its own motion, the court may determine whether there has been a failure to comply with any provision of this rule.

(2) If the court finds such a failure to comply, it may:

(A) refuse to permit the entity, group, or committee to be heard or to intervene in the case;

(B) hold invalid any authority, acceptance, rejection, or objection given, procured, or received by the entity, group, or committee; or

(C) grant other appropriate relief.

CROSS REFERENCES

Appointment of creditors' committee organized before order for relief, see Fed. R. Bankr. P. 2007.

Motions; form and service, see Fed. R. Bankr. P. 9013.

Trustees for estates when joint administration ordered, see Fed. R. Bankr. P. 2009.

Rule 2020. Review of Acts by United States Trustee

A proceeding to contest any act or failure to act by the United States trustee is governed by Rule 9014.

PART III

CLAIMS AND DISTRIBUTION TO CREDITORS AND EQUITY INTEREST HOLDERS; PLANS

Rule 3001. Proof of Claim

(a) Form and content

A proof of claim is a written statement setting forth a creditor's claim. A proof of claim shall conform substantially to the appropriate Official Form.

(b) Who may execute

A proof of claim shall be executed by the creditor or the creditor's authorized agent except as provided in Rules 3004 and 3005.

(c) Supporting information

(1) Claim based on a writing

Except for a claim governed by paragraph (3) of this subdivision, when a claim, or an interest in property of the debtor securing the claim, is based on a writing, a copy of the writing shall be filed with the proof of claim. If the writing has been lost or destroyed, a statement of the circumstances of the loss or destruction shall be filed with the claim.

(2) Additional requirements in an individual debtor case: sanctions for failure to comply

In a case in which the debtor is an individual:

(A) If, in addition to its principal amount, a claim includes interest, fees, expenses, or other charges incurred before the petition was filed, an itemized statement of the interest, fees, expenses, or charges shall be filed with the proof of claim.

(B) If a security interest is claimed in the debtor's property, a statement of the amount necessary to cure any default as of the date of the petition shall be filed with the proof of claim.

(C) If a security interest is claimed in property that is the debtor's principal residence, the attachment prescribed by the appropriate Official Form shall be filed with the proof of claim. If an escrow account has been established in connection with the claim, an escrow account statement prepared as of the date the petition was filed and in a form consistent with applicable nonbankruptcy law shall be filed with the attachment to the proof of claim.

(D) If the holder of a claim fails to provide any information required by this subdivision (c), the court may, after notice and hearing, take either or both of the following actions:

(i) preclude the holder from presenting the omitted information, in any form, as evidence in any contested matter or adversary proceeding in the case, unless the court determines that the failure was substantially justified or is harmless; or

(ii) award other appropriate relief, including reasonable expenses and attorney's fees caused by the failure.

(3) Claim based on an open-end or revolving consumer credit agreement

(A) When a claim is based on an open-end or revolving consumer credit agreement— except one for which a security interest is claimed in the debtor's real property—a statement shall be filed with the proof of claim, including all of the following information that applies to the account:

(i) the name of the entity from whom the creditor purchased the account;

(ii) the name of the entity to whom the debt was owed at the time of an account holder's last transaction on the account;

(iii) the date of an account holder's last transaction;

(iv) the date of the last payment on the account; and

(v) the date on which the account was charged to profit and loss.

(B) On written request by a party in interest, the holder of a claim based on an open-end or revolving consumer credit agreement shall, within 30 days after the request is sent, provide the requesting party a copy of the writing specified in paragraph (1) of this subdivision.

(d) Evidence of perfection of security interest

If a security interest in property of the debtor is claimed, the proof of claim shall be accompanied by evidence that the security interest has been perfected.

(e) Transferred claim

(1) Transfer of claim other than for security before proof filed

If a claim has been transferred other than for security before proof of the claim has been filed, the proof of claim may be filed only by the transferee or an indenture trustee.

(2) Transfer of claim other than for security after proof filed

If a claim other than one based on a publicly traded note, bond, or debenture has been transferred other than for security after the proof of claim has been filed, evidence of the transfer shall be filed by the transferee. The clerk shall immediately notify the alleged transferor by mail of the filing of the evidence of transfer and that objection thereto, if any, must be filed within 21 days of the mailing of the notice or within any additional time allowed by the court. If the alleged transferor files a timely objection and the court finds, after notice and a hearing, that the claim has been transferred other than for security, it shall enter an order substituting the transferee for the transferor. If a timely objection is not filed by the alleged transferor, the transferee shall be substituted for the transferor.

(3) Transfer of claim for security before proof filed

If a claim other than one based on a publicly traded note, bond, or debenture has been transferred for security before proof of the claim has been filed, the transferor or transferee or both may file a proof of claim for the full amount. The proof shall be supported by a statement setting forth the terms of the transfer. If either the transferor or the transferee files a proof of claim, the clerk shall immediately notify the other by mail of the right to join in the filed claim. If both transferor and transferee file proofs of the same claim, the proofs shall be consolidated. If the transferor or transferee does not file an agreement regarding its relative rights respecting voting of the claim, payment of dividends thereon, or participation in the administration of the estate, on motion by a party in interest and after notice and a hearing, the court shall enter such orders respecting these matters as may be appropriate.

(4) Transfer of claim for security after proof filed

If a claim other than one based on a publicly traded note, bond, or debenture has been transferred for security after the proof of claim has been filed, evidence of the terms of the transfer shall be filed by the transferee. The clerk shall immediately notify the alleged transferor by mail of the filing of the evidence of transfer and that objection thereto, if any, must be filed within 21 days of the mailing of the notice or within any additional time allowed by the court. If a timely objection is filed by the alleged transferor, the court, after notice and a hearing, shall determine whether the claim has been transferred for security. If the transferor or transferee does not file an agreement regarding its relative rights respecting voting of the claim, payment of dividends thereon, or participation in the administration of the estate, on motion by a party in interest and after notice and a hearing, the court shall enter such orders respecting these matters as may be appropriate.

(5) Service of objection or motion; notice of hearing

A copy of an objection filed pursuant to paragraph (2) or (4) or a motion filed pursuant to paragraph (3) or (4) of this subdivision together with a notice of a hearing shall be mailed or otherwise delivered to the transferor or transferee, whichever is appropriate, at least 30 days prior to the hearing.

(f) Evidentiary effect

A proof of claim executed and filed in accordance with these rules shall constitute prima facie evidence of the validity and amount of the claim.

(g)[1] To the extent not inconsistent with the United States Warehouse Act or applicable State law, a warehouse receipt, scale ticket, or similar document of the type routinely issued as evidence of title by a grain storage facility, as defined in section 557 of title 11, shall constitute prima facie evidence of the validity and amount of a claim of ownership of a quantity of grain.

CROSS REFERENCES

Filed claims or interests deemed allowed, see 11 USCA § 502.

Filing of proofs of claims or interests, see 11 USCA § 501.

Notice to claimants in converted liquidation case, see Fed. R. Bankr. P. 1019.

Admissibility of duplicates, see Fed. R. Evid. 1003.

Rule 3002. Filing Proof of Claim or Interest

(a) Necessity for filing

A secured creditor, unsecured creditor, or equity security holder must file a proof of claim or interest for the claim or interest to be allowed, except as provided in Rules 1019(3), 3003, 3004, and 3005. A lien that secures a claim against the debtor is not void due only to the failure of any entity to file a proof of claim.

(b) Place of filing

A proof of claim or interest shall be filed in accordance with Rule 5005.

(c) Time for filing

In a voluntary chapter 7 case, chapter 12 case, or chapter 13 case, a proof of claim is timely filed if it is filed not later than 70 days after the order for relief under that chapter or the date of the order of conversion to a case under chapter 12 or 13. In an involuntary chapter 7 case, a proof of claim is timely filed if it is filed not later than 90 days after the order for relief under that chapter is entered. But in all these cases, the following exceptions apply:

(1) A proof of claim filed by a governmental unit, other than for a claim resulting from a tax return filed under § 1308, is timely filed if it is filed not later than 180 days after the date of the order for relief. A proof of claim filed by a governmental unit for a claim resulting from a tax return filed under § 1308 is timely filed if it is filed no later than 180 days after the date of the order for relief or 60 days after the date of the filing of the tax return. The court may, for cause, enlarge the time for a governmental unit to file a proof of claim only upon motion of the governmental unit made before expiration of the period for filing a timely proof of claim.

(2) In the interest of justice and if it will not unduly delay the administration of the case, the court may extend the time for filing a proof of claim by an infant or incompetent person or the representative of either.

(3) An unsecured claim which arises in favor of an entity or becomes allowable as a result of a judgment may be filed within 30 days after the judgment becomes final if the judgment is for the recovery of money or property from that entity or denies or avoids the entity's interest in property. If the judgment imposes a liability which is not satisfied, or a duty which is not performed within such period or such further time as the court may permit, the claim shall not be allowed.

(4) A claim arising from the rejection of an executory contract or unexpired lease of the debtor may be filed within such time as the court may direct.

(5) If notice of insufficient assets to pay a dividend was given to creditors under Rule 2002(e), and subsequently the trustee notifies the court that payment of a dividend appears

---

[1] So in original. Subsec. (g) was enacted without a catchline.

possible, the clerk shall give at least **90** days' notice by mail to creditors of that fact and of the date by which proofs of claim must be filed.

(6) On motion filed by a creditor before or after the expiration of the time to file a proof of claim, the court may extend the time by not more than **60** days from the date of the order granting the motion. The motion may be granted if the court finds that the notice was insufficient under the circumstances to give the creditor a reasonable time to file a proof of claim.

(7) A proof of claim filed by the holder of a claim that is secured by a security interest in the debtor's principal residence is timely filed if:

(A) the proof of claim, together with the attachments required by Rule 3001(c)(2)(C), is filed not later than 70 days after the order for relief is entered; and

(B) any attachments required by Rule 3001(c)(1) and (d) are filed as a supplement to the holder's claim not later than 120 days after the order for relief is entered.

CROSS REFERENCES

Filed claims or interests deemed allowed, see 11 USCA § 502.

Filing of—

> Claims by debtor or trustee, see Fed. R. Bankr. P. 3004.

> Claims by guarantor, surety, indorser, or other codebtor, see Fed. R. Bankr. P. 3005.

> Proofs of claims or interests, see 11 USCA § 501.

Filing proof of claim in liquidation or individual debt adjustment case—

> Enlargement permitted as limited in this rule, see Fed. R. Bankr. P. 9006.

> Reduction not permitted, see Fed. R. Bankr. P. 9006.

Motions; form and service, see Fed. R. Bankr. P. 9013.

Notice by mail of time allowed to file claims, see Fed. R. Bankr. P. 2002.

Rule 3002.1.   Notice Relating to Claims Secured by Security Interest in the Debtor's Principal Residence

(a) In General

This rule applies in a chapter 13 case to claims (1) that are secured by a security interest in the debtor's principal residence, and (2) for which the plan provides that either the trustee or the debtor will make contractual installment payments. Unless the court orders otherwise, the notice requirements of this rule cease to apply when an order terminating or annulling the automatic stay becomes effective with respect to the residence that secures the claim.

(b) Notice of payment changes; objection

(1) Notice

The holder of the claim shall file and serve on the debtor, debtor's counsel, and the trustee a notice of any change in the payment amount, including any change that results from an interest rate or escrow account adjustment, no later than 21 days before a payment in the new amount is due. If the claim arises from a home-equity line of credit, this requirement may be modified by court order.

(2) Objection

A party in interest who objects to the payment change may file a motion to determine whether the change is required to maintain payments in accordance with § 1322(b)(5) of the Code.

If no motion is filed by the day before the new amount is due, the change goes into effect, unless the court orders otherwise.

(c) Notice of fees, expenses, and charges

The holder of the claim shall file and serve on the debtor, debtor's counsel, and the trustee a notice itemizing all fees, expenses, or charges (1) that were incurred in connection with the claim after the bankruptcy case was filed, and (2) that the holder asserts are recoverable against the debtor or against the debtor's principal residence. The notice shall be served within 180 days after the date on which the fees, expenses, or charges are incurred.

(d) Form and content

A notice filed and served under subdivision (b) or (c) of this rule shall be prepared as prescribed by the appropriate Official Form, and filed as a supplement to the holder's proof of claim. The notice is not subject to Rule 3001(f).

(e) Determination of fees, expenses, or charges

On motion of a party in interest filed within one year after service of a notice under subdivision (c) of this rule, the court shall, after notice and hearing, determine whether payment of any claimed fee, expense, or charge is required by the underlying agreement and applicable nonbankruptcy law to cure a default or maintain payments in accordance with § 1322(b)(5) of the Code.

(f) Notice of final cure payment

Within 30 days after the debtor completes all payments under the plan, the trustee shall file and serve on the holder of the claim, the debtor, and debtor's counsel a notice stating that the debtor has paid in full the amount required to cure any default on the claim. The notice shall also inform the holder of its obligation to file and serve a response under subdivision (g). If the debtor contends that final cure payment has been made and all plan payments have been completed, and the trustee does not timely file and serve the notice required by this subdivision, the debtor may file and serve the notice.

(g) Response to notice of final cure payment

Within 21 days after service of the notice under subdivision (f) of this rule, the holder shall file and serve on the debtor, debtor's counsel, and the trustee a statement indicating (1) whether it agrees that the debtor has paid in full the amount required to cure the default on the claim, and (2) whether the debtor is otherwise current on all payments consistent with § 1322(b)(5) of the Code. The statement shall itemize the required cure or postpetition amounts, if any, that the holder contends remain unpaid as of the date of the statement. The statement shall be filed as a supplement to the holder's proof of claim and is not subject to Rule 3001(f).

(h) Determination of final cure and payment

On motion of the debtor or trustee filed within 21 days after service of the statement under subdivision (g) of this rule, the court shall, after notice and hearing, determine whether the debtor has cured the default and paid all required postpetition amounts.

(i) Failure to notify

If the holder of a claim fails to provide any information as required by subdivision (b), (c), or (g) of this rule, the court may, after notice and hearing, take either or both of the following actions:

    (1) preclude the holder from presenting the omitted information, in any form, as evidence in any contested matter or adversary proceeding in the case, unless the court determines that the failure was substantially justified or is harmless; or

    (2) award other appropriate relief, including reasonable expenses and attorney's fees caused by the failure.

Rule 3003. Filing Proof of Claim or Equity Security Interest in Chapter 9 Municipality or Chapter 11 Reorganization Cases

(a) Applicability of rule

This rule applies in chapter 9 and 11 cases.

(b) Schedule of liabilities and list of equity security holders

(1) Schedule of liabilities

The schedule of liabilities filed pursuant to § 521(1) of the Code shall constitute prima facie evidence of the validity and amount of the claims of creditors, unless they are scheduled as disputed, contingent, or unliquidated. It shall not be necessary for a creditor or equity security holder to file a proof of claim or interest except as provided in subdivision (c)(2) of this rule.

(2) List of equity security holders

The list of equity security holders filed pursuant to Rule 1007(a)(3) shall constitute prima facie evidence of the validity and amount of the equity security interests and it shall not be necessary for the holders of such interests to file a proof of interest.

(c) Filing of proof of claim

(1) Who may file

Any creditor or indenture trustee may file a proof of claim within the time prescribed by subdivision (c)(3) of this rule.

(2) Who must file

Any creditor or equity security holder whose claim or interest is not scheduled or scheduled as disputed, contingent, or unliquidated shall file a proof of claim or interest within the time prescribed by subdivision (c)(3) of this rule; any creditor who fails to do so shall not be treated as a creditor with respect to such claim for the purposes of voting and distribution.

(3) Time for filing

The court shall fix and for cause shown may extend the time within which proofs of claim or interest may be filed. Notwithstanding the expiration of such time, a proof of claim may be filed to the extent and under the conditions stated in Rule 3002(c)(2), (c)(3), (c)(4), and (c)(6).

(4) Effect of filing claim or interest

A proof of claim or interest executed and filed in accordance with this subdivision shall supersede any scheduling of that claim or interest pursuant to § 521(a)(1) of the Code.

(5) Filing by indenture trustee

An indenture trustee may file a claim on behalf of all known or unknown holders of securities issued pursuant to the trust instrument under which it is trustee.

(d) Proof of right to record status

For the purposes of Rules 3017, 3018 and 3021 and for receiving notices, an entity who is not the record holder of a security may file a statement setting forth facts which entitle that entity to be treated as the record holder. An objection to the statement may be filed by any party in interest.

CROSS REFERENCES

Acceptance or rejection of municipality debt adjustment or reorganization plan by obligor filing creditor's claim, see Fed. R. Bankr. P. 3005.

Distribution under confirmed plan to indenture trustee filing under this rule, see Fed. R. Bankr. P. 3021.

Exception to filing requirement for—

    Municipality debt adjustment case, see 11 USCA § 925.

    Reorganization case, see 11 USCA § 1111.

Filing of claims by—

    Debtor or trustee, see Fed. R. Bankr. P. 3004.

    Guarantor, surety, indorser, or other codebtor, see Fed. R. Bankr. P. 3005.

Rule 3004. Filing of Claims by Debtor or Trustee

If a creditor does not timely file a proof of claim under Rule 3002(c) or 3003(c), the debtor or trustee may file a proof of the claim within 30 days after the expiration of the time for filing claims prescribed by Rule 3002(c) or 3003(c), whichever is applicable. The clerk shall forthwith give notice of the filing to the creditor, the debtor and the trustee.

CROSS REFERENCES

Exception to execution of proof of claim by creditor or agent, see Fed. R. Bankr. P. 3001.

Filing of claims by debtor or trustee, see 11 USCA § 501.

Rule 3005. Filing of Claim, Acceptance, or Rejection by Guarantor, Surety, Indorser, or Other Codebtor

(a) Filing of claim

If a creditor does not timely file a proof of claim under Rule 3002(c) or 3003(c), any entity that is or may be liable with the debtor to that creditor, or who has secured that creditor, may file a proof of the claim within 30 days after the expiration of the time for filing claims prescribed by Rule 3002(c) or Rule 3003(c) whichever is applicable. No distribution shall be made on the claim except on satisfactory proof that the original debt will be diminished by the amount of distribution.

(b) Filing of acceptance or rejection; substitution of creditor

An entity which has filed a claim pursuant to the first sentence of subdivision (a) of this rule may file an acceptance or rejection of a plan in the name of the creditor, if known, or if unknown, in the entity's own name but if the creditor files a proof of claim within the time permitted by Rule 3003(c) or files a notice prior to confirmation of a plan of the creditor's intention to act in the creditor's own behalf, the creditor shall be substituted for the obligor with respect to that claim.

CROSS REFERENCES

Exception to execution of proof of claim by creditor or agent, see Fed. R. Bankr. P. 3001.

Rule 3006. Withdrawal of Claim; Effect on Acceptance or Rejection of Plan

A creditor may withdraw a claim as of right by filing a notice of withdrawal, except as provided in this rule. If after a creditor has filed a proof of claim an objection is filed thereto or a complaint is filed against that creditor in an adversary proceeding, or the creditor has accepted or rejected the plan or otherwise has participated significantly in the case, the creditor may not withdraw the claim except on order of the court after a hearing on notice to the trustee or debtor in possession, and any creditors' committee elected pursuant to § 705(a) or appointed pursuant to § 1102 of the Code. The order of the court shall contain such terms and conditions as the court deems proper. Unless the court orders otherwise, an authorized withdrawal of a claim shall constitute withdrawal of any related acceptance or rejection of a plan.

Dismissal of actions, see Fed. R. Civ. P. 41.

Rule 3007. Objections to Claims

(a) Time and manner of service

(1) Time of Service. An objection to the allowance of a claim and a notice of objection that substantially conforms to the appropriate Official Form shall be filed and served at least 30 days before any scheduled hearing on the objection or any deadline for the claimant to request a hearing.

(2) Manner of service

(A) The objection and notice shall be served on a claimant by first-class mail to the person most recently designated on the claimant's original or amended proof of claim as the person to receive notices, at the address so indicated; and

(i) if the objection is to a claim of the United States, or any of its officers or agencies, in the manner provided for service of a summons and complaint by Rule 7004(b)(4) or (5); or

(ii) if the objection is to a claim of an insured depository institution as defined in section 3 of the Federal Deposit Insurance Act, in the manner provided in Rule 7004(h).

(B) Service of the objection and notice shall also be made by first-class mail or other permitted means on the debtor or debtor in possession, the trustee, and, if applicable, the entity filing the proof of claim under Rule 3005.

(b) Demand for relief requiring an adversary proceeding

A party in interest shall not include a demand for relief of a kind specified in Rule 7001 in an objection to the allowance of a claim, but may include the objection in an adversary proceeding.

(c) Limitation on joinder of claims objections

Unless otherwise ordered by the court or permitted by subdivision (d), objections to more than one claim shall not be joined in a single objection.

(d) Omnibus objection

Subject to subdivision (e), objections to more than one claim may be joined in an omnibus objection if all the claims were filed by the same entity, or the objections are based solely on the grounds that the claims should be disallowed, in whole or in part, because:

(1) they duplicate other claims;

(2) they have been filed in the wrong case;

(3) they have been amended by subsequently filed proofs of claim;

(4) they were not timely filed;

(5) they have been satisfied or released during the case in accordance with the Code, applicable rules, or a court order;

(6) they were presented in a form that does not comply with applicable rules, and the objection states that the objector is unable to determine the validity of the claim because of the noncompliance;

(7) they are interests, rather than claims; or

(8) they assert priority in an amount that exceeds the maximum amount under § 507 of the Code.

(e) Requirements for omnibus objection

An omnibus objection shall:

(1) state in a conspicuous place that claimants receiving the objection should locate their names and claims in the objection;

(2) list claimants alphabetically, provide a cross-reference to claim numbers, and, if appropriate, list claimants by category of claims;

(3) state the grounds of the objection to each claim and provide a cross-reference to the pages in the omnibus objection pertinent to the stated grounds;

(4) state in the title the identity of the objector and the grounds for the objections;

(5) be numbered consecutively with other omnibus objections filed by the same objector; and

(6) contain objections to no more than 100 claims.

(f) Finality of objection

The finality of any order regarding a claim objection included in an omnibus objection shall be determined as though the claim had been subject to an individual objection.

CROSS REFERENCES

Allowance of claims or interests after objection, see 11 USCA § 502.

Contested matters, see Fed. R. Bankr. P. 9014.

Duty of trustee to examine proofs of claims and to object to improper claims—

Individual debt adjustment case, see 11 USCA § 1302.

Liquidation case, see 11 USCA § 704.

Reorganization case, see 11 USCA § 1106.

Objection to claim for purpose of voting for trustee or creditors' committee in liquidation case, see Fed. R. Bankr. P. 2003.

Rule 3008. Reconsideration of Claims

A party in interest may move for reconsideration of an order allowing or disallowing a claim against the estate. The court after a hearing on notice shall enter an appropriate order.

CROSS REFERENCES

Closing and reopening cases, see 11 USCA § 350.

Exception to procedural rule on new trials and amendment of judgments, see Fed. R. Bankr. P. 9023.

Motions; form and service, see Fed. R. Bankr. P. 9013.

Reconsideration of claim prior to closing of case, see 11 USCA § 502.

Rule 3009. Declaration and Payment of Dividends in a Chapter 7 Liquidation Case

In a chapter 7 case, dividends to creditors shall be paid as promptly as practicable. Dividend checks shall be made payable to and mailed to each creditor whose claim has been allowed, unless a power of attorney authorizing another entity to receive dividends has been executed and filed in accordance with Rule 9010. In that event, dividend checks shall be made payable to the creditor and to the other entity and shall be mailed to the other entity.

CROSS REFERENCES

Dividend records kept by clerk, see Fed. R. Bankr. P. 5003.

Unclaimed dividends, see 11 USCA § 347.

Rule 3010. Small Dividends and Payments in Cases under Chapter 7, Subchapter V of Chapter 11, Chapter 12, and Chapter 13

(a) Chapter 7 cases

In a chapter 7 case no dividend in an amount less than $5 shall be distributed by the trustee to any creditor unless authorized by local rule or order of the court. Any dividend not distributed to a creditor shall be treated in the same manner as unclaimed funds as provided in § 347 of the Code.

(b) Cases Under Subchapter V of Chapter 11, Chapter 12, and Chapter 13

In a case under subchapter V of chapter 11, chapter 12, or chapter 13, no payment in an amount less than $15 shall be distributed by the trustee to any creditor unless authorized by local rule or order of the court. Funds not distributed because of this subdivision shall accumulate and shall be paid whenever the accumulation aggregates $15. Any funds remaining shall be distributed with the final payment.

Rule 3011. Unclaimed Funds in Cases Under Chapter 7, Subchapter V of Chapter 11, Chapter 12, and Chapter 13

The trustee shall file a list of all known names and addresses of the entities and the amounts which they are entitled to be paid from remaining property of the estate that is paid into court pursuant to § 347(a) of the Code.

CROSS REFERENCES

Treatment of small dividends as unclaimed funds, see Fed. R. Bankr. P. 3010.

Unclaimed property, see 11 USCA § 347.

Rule 3012. Determining the Amount of Secured and Priority Claims

(a) Determination of Amount of Claim

On request by a party in interest and after notice—to the holder of the claim and any other entity the court designates—and a hearing, the court may determine:

(1) the amount of a secured claim under § 506(a) of the Code; or

(2) the amount of a claim entitled to priority under § 507 of the Code.

(b) Request for Determination; How Made

Except as provided in subdivision (c), a request to determine the amount of a secured claim may be made by motion, in a claim objection, or in a plan filed in a chapter 12 or chapter 13 case. When the request is made in a chapter 12 or chapter 13 plan, the plan shall be served on the holder of the claim and any other entity the court designates in the manner provided for service of a summons and complaint by Rule 7004. A request to determine the amount of a claim entitled to priority may be made only by motion after a claim is filed or in a claim objection.

(c) Claims of Governmental Units

A request to determine the amount of a secured claim of a governmental unit may be made only by motion or in a claim objection after the governmental unit files a proof of claim or after the time for filing one under Rule 3002(c)(1) has expired.

CROSS REFERENCES

Definition of—

Lien, see 11 USCA § 101(37).

Security, see 11 USCA § 101(49).

Security interest, see 11 USCA § 101(51).

Determination of secured status, see 11 USCA § 506.

Motions; form and service, see Fed. R. Bankr. P. 9013.

Rule 3013. Classification of Claims and Interests

For the purposes of the plan and its acceptance, the court may, on motion after hearing on notice as the court may direct, determine classes of creditors and equity security holders pursuant to §§ 1122, 1222(b)(1), and 1322(b)(1) of the Code.

CROSS REFERENCES

Motions; form and service, see Fed. R. Bankr. P. 9013.

Rule 3014. Election Under § 1111(b) by Secured Creditor in Chapter 9 Municipality or Chapter 11 Reorganization Case

An election of application of § 1111(b)(2) of the Code by a class of secured creditors in a chapter 9 or 11 case may be made at any time prior to the conclusion of the hearing on the disclosure statement or within such later time as the court may fix. If the disclosure statement is conditionally approved pursuant to Rule 3017.1, and a final hearing on the disclosure statement is not held, the election of application of § 1111(b)(2) may be made not later than the date fixed pursuant to Rule 3017.1(a)(2) or another date the court may fix. In a case under subchapter V of chapter 11 in which § 1125 of the Code does not apply, the election may be made not later than a date the court may fix. The election shall be in writing and signed unless made at the hearing on the disclosure statement. The election, if made by the majorities required by § 1111(b)(1)(A)(i), shall be binding on all members of the class with respect to the plan.

CROSS REFERENCES

Hearing on disclosure statement, see Fed. R. Bankr. P. 3017.

Reduction of time for election pursuant to § 1111(b) not permitted, see Fed. R. Bankr. P. 9006.

Rule 3015. Filing, Objection to Confirmation, Effect of Confirmation, and Modification of a Plan in a Chapter 12 or a Chapter 13 Case

(a) Filing a Chapter 12 plan

The debtor may file a chapter 12 plan with the petition. If a plan is not filed with the petition, it shall be filed within the time prescribed by § 1221 of the Code.

(b) Filing a Chapter 13 plan

The debtor may file a chapter 13 plan with the petition. If a plan is not filed with the petition, it shall be filed within 14 days thereafter, and such time may not be further extended except for cause shown and on notice as the court may direct. If a case is converted to chapter 13, a plan shall be filed within 14 days thereafter, and such time may not be further extended except for cause shown and on notice as the court may direct.

(c) Form of Chapter 13 plan

If there is an Official Form for a plan filed in a chapter 13 case, that form must be used unless a Local Form has been adopted in compliance with Rule 3015.1. With either the Official Form or a Local Form, a nonstandard provision is effective only if it is included in a section of the form designated for nonstandard provisions and is also identified in accordance with any other requirements of the form. As used in this rule and the Official Form or a Local Form, "nonstandard provision" means a provision not otherwise included in the Official or Local Form or deviating from it.

(d) Notice

If the plan is not included with the notice of the hearing on confirmation mailed under Rule 2002, the debtor shall serve the plan on the trustee and all creditors when it is filed with the court.

(e) Transmission to United States trustee

The clerk shall forthwith transmit to the United States trustee a copy of the plan and any modification thereof filed under to subdivision (a) or (b) of this rule.

(f) Objection to confirmation; determination of good faith in the absence of an objection

An objection to confirmation of a plan shall be filed and served on the debtor, the trustee, and any other entity designated by the court, and shall be transmitted to the United States trustee, at least seven days before the date set for the hearing on confirmation, unless the court orders otherwise. An objection to confirmation is governed by Rule 9014. If no objection is timely filed, the court may determine that the plan has been proposed in good faith and not by any means forbidden by law without receiving evidence on such issues.

(g) Effect of confirmation

Upon the confirmation of a chapter 12 or chapter 13 plan:

(1) any determination in the plan made under Rule 3012 about the amount of a secured claim is binding on the holder of the claim, even if the holder files a contrary proof of claim or the debtor schedules that claim, and regardless of whether an objection to the claim has been filed; and

(2) any request in the plan to terminate the stay imposed by § 362(a), § 1201(a), or § 1301(a) is granted.

(h) Modification of plan after confirmation

A request to modify a plan pursuant to § 1229 or § 1329 of the Code shall identify the proponent and shall be filed together with the proposed modification. The clerk, or some other person as the court may direct, shall give the debtor, the trustee, and all creditors not less than 21 days' notice by mail of the time fixed for filing objections and, if an objection is filed, the hearing to consider the proposed modification, unless the court orders otherwise with respect to creditors who are not affected by the proposed modification. A copy of the notice shall be transmitted to the United States trustee. A copy of the proposed modification, or a summary thereof, shall be included with the notice. Any objection to the proposed modification shall be filed and served on the debtor, the trustee, and any other entity designated by the court, and shall be transmitted to the United States trustee. An objection to a proposed modification is governed by Rule 9014.

CROSS REFERENCES

Acceptance or rejection of plans, see Fed. R. Bankr. P. 3018.

Deposit; confirmation of plan, see Fed. R. Bankr. P. 3020.

Reduction of time for filing plan not permitted, see Fed. R. Bankr. P. 9006.

Rule 3015.1.   Requirements for a Local Form for Plans Filed in a Chapter 13 Case

Notwithstanding Rule 9029(a)(1), a district may require that a Local Form for a plan filed in a chapter 13 case be used instead of an Official Form adopted for that purpose if the following conditions are satisfied:

(a) a single Local Form is adopted for the district after public notice and an opportunity for public comment;

(b) each paragraph is numbered and labeled in boldface with a heading stating the general subject matter of the paragraph;

(c) the Local Form includes an initial paragraph for the debtor to indicate that the plan does or does not:

    (1) contain any nonstandard provision;

    (2) limit the amount of a secured claim based on a valuation of the collateral for the claim; or

    (3) avoid a security interest or lien;

(d) the Local Form contains separate paragraphs for:

    (1) curing any default and maintaining payments on a claim secured by the debtor's principal residence;

    (2) paying a domestic-support obligation;

    (3) paying a claim described in the final paragraph of § 1325(a) of the Bankruptcy Code; and

    (4) surrendering property that secures a claim with a request that the stay under §§ 363(a) and 1301(a) be terminated as to the surrendered collateral; and

(e) the Local Form contains a final paragraph for:

    (1) the placement of nonstandard provisions, as defined in Rule 3015(c), along with a statement that any nonstandard provision placed elsewhere in the plan is void; and

    (2) certification by the debtor's attorney or by an unrepresented debtor that the plan contains no nonstandard provision other than those set out in the final paragraph.

Rule 3016. Filing of Plan and Disclosure Statement in a Chapter 9 Municipality or Chapter 11 Reorganization Case

(a) Identification of plan

Every proposed plan and any modification thereof shall be dated and, in a chapter 11 case, identified with the name of the entity or entities submitting or filing it.

(b) Disclosure statement

In a chapter 9 or 11 case, a disclosure statement, if required under § 1125 of the Code, or evidence showing compliance with § 1126(b) shall be filed with the plan or within a time fixed by the court, unless the plan is intended to provide adequate information under § 1125(f)(1). If the plan is intended to provide adequate information under § 1125(f)(1), it shall be so designated and Rule 3017.1 shall apply as if the plan is a disclosure statement.

(c) Injunction under a plan

If a plan provides for an injunction against conduct not otherwise enjoined under the Code, the plan and disclosure statement shall describe in specific and conspicuous language (bold, italic, or underlined text) all acts to be enjoined and identify the entities that would be subject to the injunction.

(d) Standard form small business disclosure statement and plan

In a small business case or a case under subchapter V of chapter 11, the court may approve a disclosure statement and may confirm a plan that conform substantially to the appropriate Official Forms or other standard forms approved by the court.

CROSS REFERENCES

Filing of municipality debt adjustment plan, see 11 USCA § 941.

Hearing on disclosure statement, see Fed. R. Bankr. P. 3017.

Rule 3017. **Court Consideration of Disclosure Statement in a Chapter 9 Municipality or Chapter 11 Reorganization Case**

(a) Hearing on disclosure statement and objections

Except as provided in Rule 3017.1, after a disclosure statement is filed in accordance with Rule 3016(b), the court shall hold a hearing on at least 28 days' notice to the debtor, creditors, equity security holders and other parties in interest as provided in Rule 2002 to consider the disclosure statement and any objections or modifications thereto. The plan and the disclosure statement shall be mailed with the notice of the hearing only to the debtor, any trustee or committee appointed under the Code, the Securities and Exchange Commission and any party in interest who requests in writing a copy of the statement or plan. Objections to the disclosure statement shall be filed and served on the debtor, the trustee, any committee appointed under the Code, and any other entity designated by the court, at any time before the disclosure statement is approved or by an earlier date as the court may fix. In a chapter 11 reorganization case, every notice, plan, disclosure statement, and objection required to be served or mailed pursuant to this subdivision shall be transmitted to the United States trustee within the time provided in this subdivision.

(b) Determination on disclosure statement

Following the hearing the court shall determine whether the disclosure statement should be approved.

(c) Dates fixed for voting on plan and confirmation

On or before approval of the disclosure statement, the court shall fix a time within which the holders of claims and interests may accept or reject the plan and may fix a date for the hearing on confirmation.

(d) Transmission and notice to United States trustee, creditors and equity security holders

Upon approval of a disclosure statement,[1]—except to the extent that the court orders otherwise with respect to one or more unimpaired classes of creditors or equity security holders—the debtor in possession, trustee, proponent of the plan, or clerk as the court orders shall mail to all creditors and equity security holders, and in a chapter 11 reorganization case shall transmit to the United States trustee,

    (1) the plan or a court-approved summary of the plan;

    (2) the disclosure statement approved by the court;

    (3) notice of the time within which acceptances and rejections of the plan may be filed; and

    (4) any other information as the court may direct, including any court opinion approving the disclosure statement or a court-approved summary of the opinion.

In addition, notice of the time fixed for filing objections and the hearing on confirmation shall be mailed to all creditors and equity security holders in accordance with Rule 2002(b), and a form of ballot conforming to the appropriate Official Form shall be mailed to creditors and equity security holders entitled to vote on the plan. If the court opinion is not transmitted or only a summary of the plan is transmitted, the court opinion or the plan shall be provided on request of a party in interest at the plan proponent's expense. If the court orders that the disclosure statement and the plan or a summary of the plan shall not be mailed to any unimpaired class, notice that the class is designated in the plan as unimpaired and notice of the name and address of the person from whom the plan or summary of the plan and disclosure statement may be obtained upon request and at the plan proponent's expense, shall be mailed to members of the unimpaired class together with the notice of the time fixed for filing objections to and the hearing on confirmation. For the purposes of this subdivision, creditors and

---

[1] So in original. The comma probably should not appear.

equity security holders shall include holders of stock, bonds, debentures, notes, and other securities of record on the date the order approving the disclosure statement is entered or another date fixed by the court, for cause, after notice and a hearing.

(e) Transmission to beneficial holders of securities

At the hearing held pursuant to subdivision (a) of this rule, the court shall consider the procedures for transmitting the documents and information required by subdivision (d) of this rule to beneficial holders of stock, bonds, debentures, notes, and other securities, determine the adequacy of the procedures, and enter any orders the court deems appropriate.

(f) Notice and transmission of documents to entities subject to an injunction under a plan

If a plan provides for an injunction against conduct not otherwise enjoined under the Code and an entity that would be subject to the injunction is not a creditor or equity security holder, at the hearing held under Rule 3017(a), the court shall consider procedures for providing the entity with:

(1) at least 28 days' notice of the time fixed for filing objections and the hearing on confirmation of the plan containing the information described in Rule 2002(c)(3); and

(2) to the extent feasible, a copy of the plan and disclosure statement.

CROSS REFERENCES

Acceptance or rejection of plan—

Eligible persons, see Fed. R. Bankr. P. 3018(a).

Preference when more than one plan accepted, see Fed. R. Bankr. P. 3018(c).

Disclosure statement—

Different statements as between different classes of claims, see 11 USCA § 1125(c).

Right to be heard on adequacy of information, see 11 USCA § 1125.

Solicitation of plan's acceptance, see 11 USCA § 1125.

Notice of time fixed for plan's acceptance or rejection in accord with this rule, see Fed. R. Bankr. P. 2002.

Proof of right to record status filed by security holder, see Fed. R. Bankr. P. 3003.

Rule 3017.1. Court Consideration of Disclosure Statement in a Small Business Case or in a Case Under Subchapter V of Chapter 11

(a) Conditional approval of disclosure statement

In a small business case or in a case under subchapter V of chapter 11 in which the court has ordered that § 1125 applies, the court may, on application of the plan proponent or on its own initiative, conditionally approve a disclosure statement filed in accordance with Rule 3016. On or before conditional approval of the disclosure statement, the court shall:

(1) fix a time within which the holders of claims and interests may accept or reject the plan;

(2) fix a time for filing objections to the disclosure statement;

(3) fix a date for the hearing on final approval of the disclosure statement to be held if a timely objection is filed; and

(4) fix a date for the hearing on confirmation.

(b) Application of Rule 3017

Rule 3017(a), (b), (c), and (e) do not apply to a conditionally approved disclosure statement. Rule 3017(d) applies to a conditionally approved disclosure statement, except that conditional approval is considered approval of the disclosure statement for the purpose of applying Rule 3017(d).

(c) Final approval

(1) Notice

Notice of the time fixed for filing objections and the hearing to consider final approval of the disclosure statement shall be given in accordance with Rule 2002 and may be combined with notice of the hearing on confirmation of the plan.

(2) Objections

Objections to the disclosure statement shall be filed, transmitted to the United States trustee, and served on the debtor, the trustee, any committee appointed under the Code and any other entity designated by the court at any time before final approval of the disclosure statement or by an earlier date as the court may fix.

(3) Hearing

If a timely objection to the disclosure statement is filed, the court shall hold a hearing to consider final approval before or combined with the hearing on confirmation of the plan.

Rule 3017.2.   Fixing of Dates by the Court in Subchapter V Cases in Which There Is No Disclosure Statement

In a case under subchapter V of chapter 11 in which § 1125 does not apply, the court shall:

(a)   fix a time within which the holders of claims and interests may accept or reject the plan;

(b)   fix a date on which an equity security holder or creditor whose claim is based on a security must be the holder of record of the security in order to be eligible to accept or reject the plan;

(c)   fix a date for the hearing on confirmation; and

(d)   fix a date for transmitting the plan, notice of the time within which the holders of claims and interests may accept or reject it, and notice of the date for the hearing on confirmation.

CROSS REFERENCES

General rule on applicability of disclosure statement requirement in a subchapter V case, see 11 USCA § 1181.

Rule 3018. Acceptance or Rejection of Plan in a Chapter 9 Municipality or a Chapter 11 Reorganization Case

(a) Entities entitled to accept or reject plan; time for acceptance or rejection

A plan may be accepted or rejected in accordance with § 1126 of the Code within the time fixed by the court pursuant to Rule 3017, 3017.1, or 3017.2. Subject to subdivision (b) of this rule, an equity security holder or creditor whose claim is based on a security of record shall not be entitled to accept or reject a plan unless the equity security holder or creditor is the holder of record of the security on the date the order approving the disclosure statement is entered or on another date fixed by the court under Rule 3017.2, or fixed for cause after notice and a hearing. For cause shown, the court after notice and hearing may permit a creditor or equity security holder to change or withdraw an acceptance or rejection. Notwithstanding objection to a claim or interest, the court after notice and hearing may temporarily allow the claim or interest in an amount which the court deems proper for the purpose of accepting or rejecting a plan.

(b) Acceptances or rejections obtained before petition

An equity security holder or creditor whose claim is based on a security of record who accepted or rejected the plan before the commencement of the case shall not be deemed to have accepted or rejected the plan pursuant to § 1126(b) of the Code unless the equity security holder or creditor was the holder of record of the security on the date specified in the solicitation of such acceptance or rejection for the purposes of such solicitation. A holder of a claim or interest who has accepted or rejected a plan before the commencement of the case under the Code shall not be deemed to have accepted or rejected the plan if the court finds after notice and hearing that the plan was not transmitted to substantially all creditors and equity security holders of the same class, that an unreasonably short time was prescribed for such creditors and equity security holders to accept or reject the plan, or that the solicitation was not in compliance with § 1126(b) of the Code.

(c) Form of acceptance or rejection

An acceptance or rejection shall be in writing, identify the plan or plans accepted or rejected, be signed by the creditor or equity security holder or an authorized agent, and conform to the appropriate Official Form. If more than one plan is transmitted pursuant to Rule 3017, an acceptance or rejection may be filed by each creditor or equity security holder for any number of plans transmitted and if acceptances are filed for more than one plan, the creditor or equity security holder may indicate a preference or preferences among the plans so accepted.

(d) Acceptance or rejection by partially secured creditor

A creditor whose claim has been allowed in part as a secured claim and in part as an unsecured claim shall be entitled to accept or reject a plan in both capacities.

CROSS REFERENCES

Acceptance of altered or modified plan, see 11 USCA § 1127.

Disqualification of votes on acceptance in absence of good faith, see 11 USCA § 1126.

Filing of plan in—

Individual debt adjustment case, see Fed. R. Bankr. P. 3015.

Municipality debt adjustment and reorganization cases, with disclosure statement, see Fed. R. Bankr. P. 3016.

Proof of right to record status filed by security holder, see Fed. R. Bankr. P. 3003.

Rule 3019. Modification of Accepted Plan in a Chapter 9 Municipality or a Chapter 11 Reorganization Case

(a) Modification of plan before confirmation

In a chapter 9 or chapter 11 case, after a plan has been accepted and before its confirmation, the proponent may file a modification of the plan. If the court finds after hearing on notice to the trustee, any committee appointed under the Code, and any other entity designated by the court that the proposed modification does not adversely change the treatment of the claim of any creditor or the interest of any equity security holder who has not accepted in writing the modification, it shall be deemed accepted by all creditors and equity security holders who have previously accepted the plan.

(b) Modification of plan after confirmation in individual debtor case

If the debtor is an individual, a request to modify the plan under § 1127(e) of the Code is governed by Rule 9014. The request shall identify the proponent and shall be filed together with the proposed modification. The clerk, or some other person as the court may direct, shall give the debtor, the trustee, and all creditors not less than 21 days' notice by mail of the time fixed to file objections and, if an objection is filed, the hearing to consider the proposed modification, unless the court orders otherwise with respect to creditors who are not affected by the proposed modification. A copy of the notice shall be transmitted to the United States trustee, together with a copy of the proposed modification. Any objection to the proposed modification shall be filed and served on the debtor, the proponent of the modification, the trustee, and any other entity designated by the court, and shall be transmitted to the United States trustee.

(c) Modification of plan after confirmation in a subchapter V case.

In a case under subchapter V of chapter 11, a request to modify the plan under § 1193(b) or (c) of the Code is governed by Rule 9014, and the provisions of this Rule 3019(b) apply.

CROSS REFERENCES

Acceptance or rejection of plans, see Fed. R. Bankr. P. 3018.

Modification of plan in—

Individual debt adjustment case, see 11 USCA §§ 1323, 1329.

Municipality debt adjustment case, see 11 USCA § 942.

Reorganization case, see 11 USCA § 1127.

Subchapter V case, see 11 USCA § 1193.

Rule 3020. Deposit; Confirmation of Plan in a Chapter 9 Municipality or Chapter 11 Reorganization Case

(a) Deposit

In a chapter 11 case, prior to entry of the order confirming the plan, the court may order the deposit with the trustee or debtor in possession of the consideration required by the plan to be distributed on confirmation. Any money deposited shall be kept in a special account established for the exclusive purpose of making the distribution.

(b) Objection to and hearing on confirmation in a Chapter 9 or Chapter 11 case

(1) Objection

An objection to confirmation of the plan shall be filed and served on the debtor, the trustee, the proponent of the plan, any committee appointed under the Code, and any other entity designated by the court, within a time fixed by the court. Unless the case is a chapter 9 municipality case, a copy of every objection to confirmation shall be transmitted by the objecting party to the United States trustee within the time fixed for filing objections. An objection to confirmation is governed by Rule 9014.

(2) Hearing

The court shall rule on confirmation of the plan after notice and hearing as provided in Rule 2002. If no objection is timely filed, the court may determine that the plan has been proposed in good faith and not by any means forbidden by law without receiving evidence on such issues.

(c) Order of confirmation

(1) The order of confirmation shall conform to the appropriate Official Form. If the plan provides for an injunction against conduct not otherwise enjoined under the Code, the order of confirmation shall (1) describe in reasonable detail all acts enjoined; (2) be specific in its terms regarding the injunction; and (3) identify the entities subject to the injunction.

(2) Notice of entry of the order of confirmation shall be mailed promptly to the debtor, the trustee, creditors, equity security holders, other parties in interest, and, if known, to any identified entity subject to an injunction provided for in the plan against conduct not otherwise enjoined under the Code.

(3) Except in a chapter 9 municipality case, notice of entry of the order of confirmation shall be transmitted to the United States trustee as provided in Rule 2002(k).

(d) Retained power

Notwithstanding the entry of the order of confirmation, the court may issue any other order necessary to administer the estate.

(e) Stay of confirmation order

An order confirming a plan is stayed until the expiration of 14 days after the entry of the order, unless the court orders otherwise.

CROSS REFERENCES

Modification of accepted plan before confirmation, see Fed. R. Bankr. P. 3019.

Rule 3021. Distribution Under Plan

Except as provided in Rule 3020(e), after a plan is confirmed, distribution shall be made to creditors whose claims have been allowed, to interest holders whose interests have not been disallowed, and to indenture trustees who have filed claims under Rule 3003(c)(5) that have been allowed. For purposes of this rule, creditors include holders of bonds, debentures, notes, and other debt securities, and interest holders include the holders of stock and other equity securities, of record at the time of commencement of distribution, unless a different time is fixed by the plan or the order confirming the plan.

CROSS REFERENCES

Disposition of unclaimed property, see 11 USCA § 347.

Implementation of plan, see 11 USCA § 1142.

Proof of right to record status filed by security holder, see Fed. R. Bankr. P. 3003.

Time for surrender of security or performance of required act under reorganization plan, see 11 USCA § 1143.

Rule 3022. Final Decree in Chapter 11 Reorganization Case

After an estate is fully administered in a chapter 11 reorganization case, the court, on its own motion or on motion of a party in interest, shall enter a final decree closing the case.

CROSS REFERENCES

Close of case after trustee's discharge, see 11 USCA § 350.

Surrender of security or performance of required act under reorganization plan, denial of distribution, see 11 USCA § 1143.

PART IV

THE DEBTOR: DUTIES AND BENEFITS

Rule 4001. Relief From Automatic Stay; Prohibiting or Conditioning the Use, Sale, or Lease of Property; Use of Cash Collateral; Obtaining Credit; Agreements

(a) Relief from stay; prohibiting or conditioning the use, sale, or lease of property

(1) Motion

A motion for relief from an automatic stay provided by the Code or a motion to prohibit or condition the use, sale, or lease of property pursuant to § 363(e) shall be made in accordance with Rule 9014 and shall be served on any committee elected pursuant to § 705 or appointed pursuant to § 1102 of the Code or its authorized agent, or, if the case is a chapter 9 municipality case or a chapter 11 reorganization case and no committee of unsecured creditors has been appointed pursuant to § 1102, on the creditors included on the list filed pursuant to Rule 1007(d), and on such other entities as the court may direct.

(2) Ex parte relief

Relief from a stay under § 362(a) or a request to prohibit or condition the use, sale, or lease of property pursuant to § 363(e) may be granted without prior notice only if (A) it clearly appears from specific facts shown by affidavit or by a verified motion that immediate and irreparable injury, loss, or damage will result to the movant before the adverse party or the attorney for the adverse party can be heard in opposition, and (B) the movant's attorney certifies to the court in writing the efforts, if any, which have been made to give notice and the reasons why notice should not be required. The party obtaining relief under this subdivision and § 362(f) or § 363(e) shall immediately give oral notice thereof to the trustee or debtor in possession and to the debtor and forthwith mail or otherwise transmit to such adverse party or parties a copy of the order granting relief. On two days notice to the party who obtained relief from the stay without notice or on shorter notice to that party as the court may prescribe, the adverse party may appear and move reinstatement of the stay or reconsideration of the order prohibiting or conditioning the use, sale, or lease of property. In that event, the court shall proceed expeditiously to hear and determine the motion.

(3) Stay of order

An order granting a motion for relief from an automatic stay made in accordance with Rule 4001(a)(1) is stayed until the expiration of 14 days after the entry of the order, unless the court orders otherwise.

409

(b) Use of cash collateral

(1) Motion; service

(A) Motion

A motion for authority to use cash collateral shall be made in accordance with Rule 9014 and shall be accompanied by a proposed form of order.

(B) Contents

The motion shall consist of or (if the motion is more than five pages in length) begin with a concise statement of the relief requested, not to exceed five pages, that lists or summarizes, and sets out the location within the relevant documents of, all material provisions, including:

    (i) the name of each entity with an interest in the cash collateral;

    (ii) the purposes for the use of the cash collateral;

    (iii) the material terms, including duration, of the use of the cash collateral; and

    (iv) any liens, cash payments, or other adequate protection that will be provided to each entity with an interest in the cash collateral or, if no additional adequate protection is proposed, an explanation of why each entity's interest is adequately protected.

(C) Service

The motion shall be served on: (1) any entity with an interest in the cash collateral; (2) any committee elected under § 705 or appointed under § 1102 of the Code, or its authorized agent, or, if the case is a chapter 9 municipality case or a chapter 11 reorganization case and no committee of unsecured creditors has been appointed under § 1102, the creditors included on the list filed under Rule 1007(d); and (3) any other entity that the court directs.

(2) Hearing

The court may commence a final hearing on a motion for authorization to use cash collateral no earlier than 14 days after service of the motion. If the motion so requests, the court may conduct a preliminary hearing before such 14-day period expires, but the court may authorize the use of only that amount of cash collateral as is necessary to avoid immediate and irreparable harm to the estate pending a final hearing.

(3) Notice

Notice of hearing pursuant to this subdivision shall be given to the parties on whom service of the motion is required by paragraph (1) of this subdivision and to such other entities as the court may direct.

(4) Inapplicability in a Chapter 13 case

This subdivision (c) does not apply in a chapter 13 case.

(c) Obtaining credit

(1) Motion; service

(A) Motion

A motion for authority to obtain credit shall be made in accordance with Rule 9014 and shall be accompanied by a copy of the credit agreement and a proposed form of order.

(B) Contents

The motion shall consist of or (if the motion is more than five pages in length) begin with a concise statement of the relief requested, not to exceed five pages, that lists or summarizes, and sets out the location within the relevant documents of, all material provisions of the proposed credit agreement and form of order, including interest rate, maturity, events of default, liens, borrowing limits, and borrowing conditions. If the proposed credit agreement or form of order includes any of the provisions listed below, the concise statement shall also: briefly list or summarize each one; identify its specific location in the proposed agreement and form of order; and identify any such provision that is proposed to remain in effect if interim approval is granted, but final relief is denied, as provided under Rule 4001(c)(2). In addition, the motion shall describe the nature and extent of each provision listed below:

    (i)   a grant of priority or a lien on property of the estate under § 364(c) or (d);

    (ii)   the providing of adequate protection or priority for a claim that arose before the commencement of the case, including the granting of a lien on property of the estate to secure the claim, or the use of property of the estate or credit obtained under § 364 to make cash payments on account of the claim;

    (iii)   a determination of the validity, enforceability, priority, or amount of a claim that arose before the commencement of the case, or of any lien securing the claim;

    (iv)   a waiver or modification of Code provisions or applicable rules relating to the automatic stay;

    (v)   a waiver or modification of any entity's authority or right to file a plan, seek an extension of time in which the debtor has the exclusive right to file a plan, request the use of cash collateral under § 363(c), or request authority to obtain credit under § 364;

    (vi)   the establishment of deadlines for filing a plan of reorganization, for approval of a disclosure statement, for a hearing on confirmation, or for entry of a confirmation order;

    (vii)   a waiver or modification of the applicability of nonbankruptcy law relating to the perfection of a lien on property of the estate, or on the foreclosure or other enforcement of the lien;

    (viii)a release, waiver, or limitation on any claim or other cause of action belonging to the estate or the trustee, including any modification of the statute of limitations or other deadline to commence an action;

    (ix)   the indemnification of any entity;

    (x)   a release, waiver, or limitation of any right under § 506(c); or

    (xi)   the granting of a lien on any claim or cause of action arising under §§[1] 544, 545, 547, 548, 549, 553(b), 723(a), or 724(a).

(C) Service

The motion shall be served on: (1) any committee elected under § 705 or appointed under § 1102 of the Code, or its authorized agent, or, if the case is a chapter 9 municipality case or a chapter 11 reorganization case and no committee of unsecured creditors has been appointed under § 1102, on the creditors included on the list filed under Rule 1007(d); and (2) on any other entity that the court directs.

(2) Hearing

The court may commence a final hearing on a motion for authority to obtain credit no earlier than 14 days after service of the motion. If the motion so requests, the court may conduct a hearing before such 14-day period expires, but the court may authorize the obtaining of credit

---

[1]   So in original. Probably should be only one section symbol.

only to the extent necessary to avoid immediate and irreparable harm to the estate pending a final hearing.

(3) Notice

Notice of hearing pursuant to this subdivision shall be given to the parties on whom service of the motion is required by paragraph (1) of this subdivision and to such other entities as the court may direct.

(d) Agreement relating to relief from the automatic stay, prohibiting or conditioning the use, sale, or lease of property, providing adequate protection, use of cash collateral, and obtaining credit

(1) Motion; service

(A) Motion

A motion for approval of any of the following shall be accompanied by a copy of the agreement and a proposed form of order:

(i) an agreement to provide adequate protection;

(ii) an agreement to prohibit or condition the use, sale, or lease of property;

(iii) an agreement to modify or terminate the stay provided for in § 362;

(iv) an agreement to use cash collateral; or

(v) an agreement between the debtor and an entity that has a lien or interest in property of the estate pursuant to which the entity consents to the creation of a lien senior or equal to the entity's lien or interest in such property.

(B) Contents

The motion shall consist of or (if the motion is more than five pages in length) begin with a concise statement of the relief requested, not to exceed five pages, that lists or summarizes, and sets out the location within the relevant documents of, all material provisions of the agreement. In addition, the concise statement shall briefly list or summarize, and identify the specific location of, each provision in the proposed form of order, agreement, or other document of the type listed in subdivision (c)(1)(B). The motion shall also describe the nature and extent of each such provision.

(C) Service

The motion shall be served on: (1) any committee elected under § 705 or appointed under § 1102 of the Code, or its authorized agent, or, if the case is a chapter 9 municipality case or a chapter 11 reorganization case and no committee of unsecured creditors has been appointed under § 1102, on the creditors included on the list filed under Rule 1007(d); and (2) on any other entity the court directs.

(2) Objection

Notice of the motion and the time within which objections may be filed and served on the debtor in possession or trustee shall be mailed to the parties on whom service is required by paragraph (1) of this subdivision and to such other entities as the court may direct. Unless the court fixes a different time, objections may be filed within 14 days of the mailing of the notice.

(3) Disposition; hearing

If no objection is filed, the court may enter an order approving or disapproving the agreement without conducting a hearing. If an objection is filed or if the court determines a hearing is appropriate, the court shall hold a hearing on no less than seven days' notice to the objector, the movant, the parties on whom service is required by paragraph (1) of this subdivision and such other entities as the court may direct.

(4) Agreement in settlement of motion

The court may direct that the procedures prescribed in paragraphs (1), (2), and (3) of this subdivision shall not apply and the agreement may be approved without further notice if the court determines that a motion made pursuant to subdivisions (a), (b), or (c) of this rule was sufficient to afford reasonable notice of the material provisions of the agreement and opportunity for a hearing.

CROSS REFERENCES

Extension of time for trustee to redeem debtor's property, see 11 USCA § 108.

Methods for providing adequate protection, see 11 USCA § 361.

Motions—

For relief from stay filed with court in which case is pending, see Fed. R. Bankr. P. 5005.

Form and service, see Fed. R. Bankr. P. 9013.

Signing and verification of papers, see Fed. R. Bankr. P. 9011.

Stay of actions on claims against codebtor in individual debt adjustment case, see 11 USCA § 1301.

Rule 4002. Duties of Debtor

(a) In general

In addition to performing other duties prescribed by the Code and rules, the debtor shall:

(1) attend and submit to an examination at the times ordered by the court;

(2) attend the hearing on a complaint objecting to discharge and testify, if called as a witness;

(3) inform the trustee immediately in writing as to the location of real property in which the debtor has an interest and the name and address of every person holding money or property subject to the debtor's withdrawal or order if a schedule of property has not yet been filed pursuant to Rule 1007;

(4) cooperate with the trustee in the preparation of an inventory, the examination of proofs of claim, and the administration of the estate; and

(5) file a statement of any change of the debtor's address.

(b) Individual debtor's duty to provide documentation

(1) Personal identification

Every individual debtor shall bring to the meeting of creditors under § 341:

(A) a picture identification issued by a governmental unit, or other personal identifying information that establishes the debtor's identity; and

(B) evidence of social-security number(s), or a written statement that such documentation does not exist.

(2) Financial information

Every individual debtor shall bring to the meeting of creditors under § 341, and make available to the trustee, the following documents or copies of them, or provide a written statement that the documentation does not exist or is not in the debtor's possession:

(A) evidence of current income such as the most recent payment advice;

(B) unless the trustee or the United States trustee instructs otherwise, statements for each of the debtor's depository and investment accounts, including checking, savings, and money market accounts, mutual funds and brokerage accounts for the time period that includes the date of the filing of the petition; and

(C) documentation of monthly expenses claimed by the debtor if required by § 707(b)(2)(A) or (B).

(3) Tax return

At least 7 days before the first date set for the meeting of creditors under § 341, the debtor shall provide to the trustee a copy of the debtor's federal income tax return for the most recent tax year ending immediately before the commencement of the case and for which a return was filed, including any attachments, or a transcript of the tax return, or provide a written statement that the documentation does not exist.

(4) Tax returns provided to creditors

If a creditor, at least 14 days before the first date set for the meeting of creditors under § 341, requests a copy of the debtor's tax return that is to be provided to the trustee under subdivision (b)(3), the debtor, at least 7 days before the first date set for the meeting of creditors under § 341, shall provide to the requesting creditor a copy of the return, including any attachments, or a transcript of the tax return, or provide a written statement that the documentation does not exist.

(5) Confidentiality of tax information

The debtor's obligation to provide tax returns under Rule 4002(b)(3) and (b)(4) is subject to procedures for safeguarding the confidentiality of tax information established by the Director of the Administrative Office of the United States Courts.

CROSS REFERENCES

Debtor's duties to—

Appear at meeting of creditors, see 11 USCA § 343.

File list of creditors and assets, cooperate with trustee, and appear at discharge hearing, see 11 USCA § 521.

File lists, schedules, and statements, see Fed. R. Bankr. P. 1007.

Keep records, make reports, and give notice, see Fed. R. Bankr. P. 2015.

Immunity from self-incrimination, see 11 USCA § 344.

Rule 4003. Exemptions

(a) Claim of exemptions

A debtor shall list the property claimed as exempt under § 522 of the Code on the schedule of assets required to be filed by Rule 1007. If the debtor fails to claim exemptions or file the schedule within the time specified in Rule 1007, a dependent of the debtor may file the list within 30 days thereafter.

(b) Objecting to a claim of exemptions

(1) Except as provided in paragraphs (2) and (3), a party in interest may file an objection to the list of property claimed as exempt within 30 days after the meeting of creditors held under § 341(a) is concluded or within 30 days after any amendment to the list or supplemental schedules is filed, whichever is later. The court may, for cause, extend the time for filing objections if, before the time to object expires, a party in interest files a request for an extension.

(2) The trustee may file an objection to a claim of exemption at any time prior to one year after the closing of the case if the debtor fraudulently asserted the claim of exemption. The trustee shall deliver or mail the objection to the debtor and the debtor's attorney, and to any person filing the list of exempt property and that person's attorney.

(3) An objection to a claim of exemption based on § 522(q) shall be filed before the closing of the case. If an exemption is first claimed after a case is reopened, an objection shall be filed before the reopened case is closed.

(4) A copy of any objection shall be delivered or mailed to the trustee, the debtor and the debtor's attorney, and the person filing the list and that person's attorney.

(c) Burden of proof

In any hearing under this rule, the objecting party has the burden of proving that the exemptions are not properly claimed. After hearing on notice, the court shall determine the issues presented by the objections.

(d) Avoidance by debtor of transfers of exempt property

A proceeding under § 522(f) to avoid a lien or other transfer of property exempt under the Code shall be commenced by motion in the manner provided by Rule 9014, or by serving a chapter 12 or chapter 13 plan on the affected creditors in the manner provided by Rule 7004 for service of a summons and complaint. Notwithstanding the provisions of subdivision (b), a creditor may object to a request under § 522(f) by challenging the validity of the exemption asserted to be impaired by the lien.

CROSS REFERENCES

Automatic preservation of avoided property transfers for benefit of estate, see 11 USCA § 551.

Enlargement of thirty-day period for filing objections to property claimed as exempt permitted as limited in this rule, see Fed. R. Bankr. P. 9006.

Motions; form and service, see Fed. R. Bankr. P. 9013.

Proceedings to avoid transfers of exempt property as nonadversarial proceedings, see Fed. R. Bankr. P. 7001.

Reduction of time to claim property as exempt by dependent not permitted, see Fed. R. Bankr. P. 9006.

Right of debtor's redemption of personal property from lien securing dischargeable consumer debt, see 11 USCA § 722.

Rule 4004. Grant or Denial of Discharge

(a) Time for objecting to discharge; notice of time fixed

In a chapter 7 case, a complaint, or a motion under § 727(a)(8) or (a)(9) of the Code, objecting to the debtor's discharge shall be filed no later than 60 days after the first date set for the meeting of creditors under § 341(a). In a chapter 11 case, the complaint shall be filed no later than the first date set for the hearing on confirmation. In a chapter 13 case, a motion objecting to the debtor's discharge under § 1328(f) shall be filed no later than 60 days after the first date set for the meeting of creditors under § 341(a). At least 28 days' notice of the time so fixed shall be given to the United States trustee and all creditors as provided in Rule 2002(f) and (k) and to the trustee and the trustee's attorney.

(b) Extension of time

(1) On motion of any party in interest, after notice and hearing, the court may for cause extend the time to object to discharge. Except as provided in subdivision (b)(2), the motion shall be filed before the time has expired.

(2) A motion to extend the time to object to discharge may be filed after the time for objection has expired and before discharge is granted if (A) the objection is based on facts that, if learned after the discharge, would provide a basis for revocation under § 727(d) of the Code, and

(B) the movant did not have knowledge of those facts in time to permit an objection. The motion shall be filed promptly after the movant discovers the facts on which the objection is based.

(c) Grant of discharge

(1) In a chapter 7 case, on expiration of the times fixed for objecting to discharge and for filing a motion to dismiss the case under Rule 1017(e), the court shall forthwith grant the discharge, except that the court shall not grant the discharge if:

(A) the debtor is not an individual;

(B) a complaint, or a motion under § 727(a)(8) or (a)(9), objecting to the discharge has been filed and not decided in the debtor's favor;

(C) the debtor has filed a waiver under § 727(a)(10);

(D) a motion to dismiss the case under § 707 is pending;

(E) a motion to extend the time for filing a complaint objecting to the discharge is pending;

(F) a motion to extend the time for filing a motion to dismiss the case under Rule 1017(e)(1) is pending;

(G) the debtor has not paid in full the filing fee prescribed by 28 U.S.C. § 1930(a) and any other fee prescribed by the Judicial Conference of the United States under 28 U.S.C. § 1930(b) that is payable to the clerk upon the commencement of a case under the Code, unless the court has waived the fees under 28 U.S.C. § 1930(f);

(H) the debtor has not filed with the court a statement of completion of a course concerning personal financial management if required by Rule 1007(b)(7);

(I) a motion to delay or postpone discharge under § 727(a)(12) is pending;

(J) a motion to enlarge the time to file a reaffirmation agreement under Rule 4008(a) is pending;

(K) a presumption is in effect under § 524(m) that a reaffirmation agreement is an undue hardship and the court has not concluded a hearing on the presumption; or

(L) a motion is pending to delay discharge because the debtor has not filed with the court all tax documents required to be filed under § 521(f).

(2) Notwithstanding Rule 4004(c)(1), on motion of the debtor, the court may defer the entry of an order granting a discharge for 30 days and, on motion within that period, the court may defer entry of the order to a date certain.

(3) If the debtor is required to file a statement under Rule 1007(b)(8), the court shall not grant a discharge earlier than 30 days after the statement is filed.

(4) In a chapter 11 case in which the debtor is an individual, or a chapter 13 case, the court shall not grant a discharge if the debtor has not filed any statement required by Rule 1007(b)(7).

(d) Applicability of rules in Part VII and Rule 9014

An objection to discharge is governed by Part VII of these rules, except that an objection to discharge under §§[1] 727(a)(8), (a)(9), or 1328(f) is commenced by motion and governed by Rule 9014.

(e) Order of discharge

An order of discharge shall conform to the appropriate Official Form.

---

[1] So in original. Probably should be only one section symbol.

(f)   Registration in other districts

An order of discharge that has become final may be registered in any other district by filing a certified copy of the order in the office of the clerk of that district. When so registered the order of discharge shall have the same effect as an order of the court of the district where registered.

(g)   Notice of discharge

The clerk shall promptly mail a copy of the final order of discharge to those specified in subdivision (a) of this rule.

CROSS REFERENCES

Discharge—

> Effect of, see 11 USCA § 524.

> Exceptions to, see 11 USCA § 523.

Filing complaint to object to discharge, sixty-day period—

> Enlargement permitted as limited in this rule, see Fed. R. Bankr. P. 9006.

> Reduction not permitted, see Fed. R. Bankr. P. 9006.

Motions; form and service, see Fed. R. Bankr. P. 9013.

Notice by mail—

> Order of discharge, see Fed. R. Bankr. P. 2002.

> Time fixed to file complaint objecting to discharge, see Fed. R. Bankr. P. 2002.

Time for filing complaint in reconverted liquidation case revived or extended as under this rule, see Fed. R. Bankr. P. 1019.

Transfer of claim before or after proof of claim filed, see Fed. R. Bankr. P. 3001.

Rule 4005.   Burden of Proof in Objecting to Discharge

At the trial on a complaint objecting to a discharge, the plaintiff has the burden of proving the objection.

Rule 4006.   Notice of No Discharge

If an order is entered: denying a discharge; revoking a discharge; approving a waiver of discharge; or, in the case of an individual debtor, closing the case without the entry of a discharge, the clerk shall promptly notify all parties in interest in the manner provided by Rule 2002.

CROSS REFERENCES

Notice by mail, see Fed. R. Bankr. P. 2002.

Suspension of statute of limitations on debts of debtor, see 11 USCA § 108.

Rule 4007.   Determination of Dischargeability of a Debt

(a)   Persons entitled to file complaint

A debtor or any creditor may file a complaint to obtain a determination of the dischargeability of any debt.

(b) Time for commencing proceeding other than under § 523(c) of the Code

A complaint other than under § 523(c) may be filed at any time. A case may be reopened without payment of an additional filing fee for the purpose of filing a complaint to obtain a determination under this rule.

(c) Time for filing complaint under § 523(c) in a chapter 7 liquidation, chapter 11 reorganization, chapter 12 family farmer's debt adjustment case, or chapter 13 individual's debt adjustment case; notice of time fixed

Except as otherwise provided in subdivision (d), a complaint to determine the dischargeability of a debt under § 523(c) shall be filed no later than 60 days after the first date set for the meeting of creditors under § 341(a). The court shall give all creditors no less than 30 days' notice of the time so fixed in the manner provided in Rule 2002. On motion of a party in interest, after hearing on notice, the court may for cause extend the time fixed under this subdivision. The motion shall be filed before the time has expired.

(d) Time for filing complaint under § 523(a)(6) in a chapter 13 individual's debt adjustment case; notice of time fixed

On motion by a debtor for a discharge under § 1328(b), the court shall enter an order fixing the time to file a complaint to determine the dischargeability of any debt under § 523(a)(6) and shall give no less than 30 days' notice of the time fixed to all creditors in the manner provided in Rule 2002. On motion of any party in interest, after hearing on notice, the court may for cause extend the time fixed under this subdivision. The motion shall be filed before the time has expired.

(e) Applicability of Rules in Part VII

A proceeding commenced by a complaint filed under this rule is governed by Part VII of these rules.

CROSS REFERENCES

Costs and attorney fees to consumer debtor upon discharge of debt, see 11 USCA § 523.

Effect of dismissal on dischargeability of debt, see 11 USCA § 349.

Filing complaint to determine dischargeability of debt, sixty-day period—

     Enlargement permitted as limited in this rule, see Fed. R. Bankr. P. 9006.

     Reduction not permitted, see Fed. R. Bankr. P. 9006.

Motions; form and service, see Fed. R. Bankr. P. 9013.

Notice by mail of time fixed to file complaint, see Fed. R. Bankr. P. 2002.

Time for filing complaint in reconverted liquidation case revived or extended as under this rule, see Fed. R. Bankr. P. 1019.

Rule 4008. Filing of Reaffirmation Agreement; Statement in Support of Reaffirmation Agreement

(a) Filing of reaffirmation agreement

A reaffirmation agreement shall be filed no later than 60 days after the first date set for the meeting of creditors under § 341(a) of the Code. The reaffirmation agreement shall be accompanied by a cover sheet, prepared as prescribed by the appropriate Official Form. The court may, at any time and in its discretion, enlarge the time to file a reaffirmation agreement.

(b) Statement in support of reaffirmation agreement

The debtor's statement required under § 524(k)(6)(A) of the Code shall be accompanied by a statement of the total income and expenses stated on schedules I and J. If there is a difference between the total income and expenses stated on those schedules and the statement required under § 524(k)(6)(A), the statement required by this subdivision shall include an explanation of the difference.

CROSS REFERENCES

Motions; form and service, see Fed. R. Bankr. P. 9013.

PART V

COURTS AND CLERKS

Rule 5001. Courts and Clerks' Offices

(a) Courts always open

The courts shall be deemed always open for the purpose of filing any pleading or other proper paper, issuing and returning process, and filing, making, or entering motions, orders and rules.

(b) Trials and hearings; orders in chambers

All trials and hearings shall be conducted in open court and so far as convenient in a regular court room. Except as otherwise provided in 28 U.S.C. § 152(c), all other acts or proceedings may be done or conducted by a judge in chambers and at any place either within or without the district; but no hearing, other than one ex parte, shall be conducted outside the district without the consent of all parties affected thereby.

(c) Clerk's office

The clerk's office with the clerk or a deputy in attendance shall be open during business hours on all days except Saturdays, Sundays and the legal holidays listed in Rule 9006(a).

CROSS REFERENCES

Legal holiday defined, see Fed. R. Bankr. P. 9006.

Rule 5002. Restrictions on Approval of Appointments

(a) Approval of appointment of relatives prohibited

The appointment of an individual as a trustee or examiner pursuant to § 1104 of the Code shall not be approved by the court if the individual is a relative of the bankruptcy judge approving the appointment or the United States trustee in the region in which the case is pending. The employment of an individual as attorney, accountant, appraiser, auctioneer, or other professional person pursuant to §§ 327, 1103, or 1114 shall not be approved by the court if the individual is a relative of the bankruptcy judge approving the employment. The employment of an individual as attorney, accountant, appraiser, auctioneer, or other professional person pursuant to §§ 327, 1103, or 1114 may be approved by the court if the individual is a relative of the United States trustee in the region in which the case is pending, unless the court finds that the relationship with the United States trustee renders the employment improper under the circumstances of the case. Whenever under this subdivision an individual may not be approved for appointment or employment, the individual's firm, partnership, corporation, or any other form of business association or relationship, and all members, associates and professional employees thereof also may not be approved for appointment or employment.

(b) Judicial determination that approval of appointment or employment is improper

A bankruptcy judge may not approve the appointment of a person as a trustee or examiner pursuant to § 1104 of the Code or approve the employment of a person as an attorney, accountant, appraiser, auctioneer, or other professional person pursuant to §§ 327, 1103, or 1114 of the Code if that person is or has been so connected with such judge or the United States trustee as to render the appointment or employment improper.

CROSS REFERENCES

Appointment of trustee or examiner, see 11 USCA § 1104.

Definition of relative, see 11 USCA § 101.

Nepotism in appointment of receiver or trustee, see 18 USCA § 1910.

Relative of justice or judge ineligible to appointment, see 28 USCA § 458.

Rule 5003. Records Kept by the Clerk

(a) Bankruptcy dockets

The clerk shall keep a docket in each case under the Code and shall enter thereon each judgment, order, and activity in that case as prescribed by the Director of the Administrative Office of the United States Courts. The entry of a judgment or order in a docket shall show the date the entry is made.

(b) Claims register

The clerk shall keep in a claims register a list of claims filed in a case when it appears that there will be a distribution to unsecured creditors.

(c) Judgments and orders

The clerk shall keep, in the form and manner as the Director of the Administrative Office of the United States Courts may prescribe, a correct copy of every final judgment or order affecting title to or lien on real property or for the recovery of money or property, and any other order which the court may direct to be kept. On request of the prevailing party, a correct copy of every judgment or order affecting title to or lien upon real or personal property or for the recovery of money or property shall be kept and indexed with the civil judgments of the district court.

(d) Index of cases; certificate of search

The clerk shall keep indices of all cases and adversary proceedings as prescribed by the Director of the Administrative Office of the United States Courts. On request, the clerk shall make a search of any index and papers in the clerk's custody and certify whether a case or proceeding has been filed in or transferred to the court or if a discharge has been entered in its records.

(e) Register of mailing addresses of federal and state governmental units and certain taxing authorities

The United States or the state or territory in which the court is located may file a statement designating its mailing address. The United States, state, territory, or local governmental unit responsible for collecting taxes within the district in which the case is pending may also file a statement designating an address for service of requests under § 505(b) of the Code, and the designation shall describe where further information concerning additional requirements for filing such requests may be found. The clerk shall keep, in the form and manner as the Director of the Administrative Office of the United States Courts may prescribe, a register that includes the mailing addresses designated under the first sentence of this subdivision, and a separate register of the addresses designated for the service of requests under § 505(b) of the Code. The clerk is not required to include in any single register more than one mailing address for each department, agency, or instrumentality of the United States or the state or territory. If more than one address for a department, agency, or instrumentality is included in the register, the clerk shall also include information that would enable a user of the register to determine the circumstances when each address is applicable, and mailing notice to only one applicable address is sufficient to provide effective notice. The clerk shall update the register annually, effective January 2 of each year. The mailing address in the register is conclusively presumed to be a proper address for the governmental unit, but the failure to use that mailing address does not invalidate any notice that is otherwise effective under applicable law.

(f) Other books and records of the clerk

The clerk shall keep any other books and records required by the Director of the Administrative Office of the United States Courts.

CROSS REFERENCES

Books and records kept by Clerk and entries therein, see Fed. R. Civ. P. 79.

Judgment effective when entered as provided in this rule, see Fed. R. Bankr. P. 9021.

Public access to case dockets, see 11 USCA § 107.

Public record of estate fees to be kept by clerk, see Fed. R. Bankr. P. 2013.

Rule 5004. Disqualification

(a) Disqualification of judge

A bankruptcy judge shall be governed by 28 U.S.C. § 455, and disqualified from presiding over the proceeding or contested matter in which the disqualifying circumstances[1] arises or, if appropriate, shall be disqualified from presiding over the case.

(b) Disqualification of judge from allowing compensation

A bankruptcy judge shall be disqualified from allowing compensation to a person who is a relative of the bankruptcy judge or with whom the judge is so connected as to render it improper for the judge to authorize such compensation.

CROSS REFERENCES

Definition of relative, see 11 USCA § 101.

Prohibited appointments, see Fed. R. Bankr. P. 5002.

Rule 5005. Filing and Transmittal of Papers

(a) Filing

(1) Place of filing

The lists, schedules, statements, proofs of claim or interest, complaints, motions, applications, objections and other papers required to be filed by these rules, except as provided in 28 U.S.C. § 1409, shall be filed with the clerk in the district where the case under the Code is pending. The judge of that court may permit the papers to be filed with the judge, in which event the filing date shall be noted thereon, and they shall be forthwith transmitted to the clerk. The clerk shall not refuse to accept for filing any petition or other paper presented for the purpose of

---

[1]   So in original. Probably should be "circumstance".

filing solely because it is not presented in proper form as required by these rules or any local rules or practices.

(2) Electronic filing and signing

(A) By a represented entity—generally required; exceptions

An entity represented by an attorney shall file electronically, unless nonelectronic filing is allowed by the court for good cause or is allowed by local rule.

(B) By an unrepresented individual—when allowed or required

An individual not represented by an attorney:

(i) may file electronically only if allowed by court order or by local rule; and

(ii) may be required to file electronically only by court order, or by a local rule that includes reasonable exceptions.

(C) Signing

A filing made through a person's electronic-filing account and authorized by that person, together with that person's name on a signature block, constitutes the person's signature.

(D) Same as a written paper

A paper filed electronically is a written paper for purposes of these rules, the Federal Rules of Civil Procedure made applicable by these rules, and § 107 of the Code.

(b) Transmittal to the United States trustee

(1) The complaints, notices, motions, applications, objections and other papers required to be transmitted to the United States trustee may be sent by filing with the court's electronic-filing system in accordance with Rule 9036, unless a court order or local rule provides otherwise.

(2) The entity, other than the clerk, transmitting a paper to the United States trustee other than through the court's electronic-filing system shall promptly file as proof of such transmittal a statement identifying the paper and stating the manner by which and the date on which it was transmitted to the United States trustee.

(3) Nothing in these rules shall require the clerk to transmit any paper to the United States trustee if the United States trustee requests in writing that the paper not be transmitted.

(c) Error in filing or transmittal

A paper intended to be filed with the clerk but erroneously delivered to the United States trustee, the trustee, the attorney for the trustee, a bankruptcy judge, a district judge, the clerk of the bankruptcy appellate panel, or the clerk of the district court shall, after the date of its receipt has been noted thereon, be transmitted forthwith to the clerk of the bankruptcy court. A paper intended to be transmitted to the United States trustee but erroneously delivered to the clerk, the trustee, the attorney for the trustee, a bankruptcy judge, a district judge, the clerk of the bankruptcy appellate panel, or the clerk of the district court shall, after the date of its receipt has been noted thereon, be transmitted forthwith to the United States trustee. In the interest of justice, the court may order that a paper erroneously delivered shall be deemed filed with the clerk or transmitted to the United States trustee as of the date of its original delivery.

CROSS REFERENCES

Filing of pleadings and other papers with court, see Fed. R. Civ. P. 5.

Notice and Service by Electronic Transmission, see Fed. R. Bankr. P. 9036.

Rule 5006. Certification of Copies of Papers

The clerk shall issue a certified copy of the record of any proceeding in a case under the Code or of any paper filed with the clerk on payment of any prescribed fee.

CROSS REFERENCES

Public records, see Fed. R. Evid. 1005.

Rule 5007. Record of Proceedings and Transcripts

(a) Filing of record or transcript

The reporter or operator of a recording device shall certify the original notes of testimony, tape recording, or other original record of the proceeding and promptly file them with the clerk. The person preparing any transcript shall promptly file a certified copy.

(b) Transcript fees

The fees for copies of transcripts shall be charged at rates prescribed by the Judicial Conference of the United States. No fee may be charged for the certified copy filed with the clerk.

(c) Admissibility of record in evidence

A certified sound recording or a transcript of a proceeding shall be admissible as prima facie evidence to establish the record.

CROSS REFERENCES

Reporters, see 28 USCA § 753.

Stenographer; stenographic report or transcript as evidence, see Fed. R. Civ. P. 80.

Rule 5008. Notice Regarding Presumption of Abuse in Chapter 7 Cases of Individual Debtors

If a presumption of abuse has arisen under § 707(b) in a chapter 7 case of an individual with primarily consumer debts, the clerk shall within 10 days after the date of the filing of the petition notify creditors of the presumption of abuse in accordance with Rule 2002. If the debtor has not filed a statement indicating whether a presumption of abuse has arisen, the clerk shall within 10 days after the date of the filing of the petition notify creditors that the debtor has not filed the statement and that further notice will be given if a later filed statement indicates that a presumption of abuse has arisen. If a debtor later files a statement indicating that a presumption of abuse has arisen, the clerk shall notify creditors of the presumption of abuse as promptly as practicable.

Rule 5009. Closing Chapter 7, Chapter 12, Chapter 13, and Chapter 15 Cases; Order Declaring Lien Satisfied

(a) Closing of cases under chapters 7, 12, and 13

If in a chapter 7, chapter 12, or chapter 13 case the trustee has filed a final report and final account and has certified that the estate has been fully administered, and if within 30 days no objection has been filed by the United States trustee or a party in interest, there shall be a presumption that the estate has been fully administered.

(b) Notice of failure to file Rule 1007(b)(7) statement

If an individual debtor in a chapter 7 or 13 case is required to file a statement under Rule 1007(b)(7) and fails to do so within 45 days after the first date set for the meeting of creditors under § 341(a) of the Code, the clerk shall promptly notify the debtor that the case will be closed without entry of a discharge unless the required statement is filed within the applicable time limit under Rule 1007(c).

(c) Cases under chapter 15

A foreign representative in a proceeding recognized under § 1517 of the Code shall file a final report when the purpose of the representative's appearance in the court is completed. The report shall describe the nature and results of the representative's activities in the court. The foreign representative shall transmit the report to the United States trustee, and give notice of its filing to the debtor, all persons or bodies authorized to administer foreign proceedings of the debtor, all parties to litigation pending in the United States in which the debtor was a party at the time of the filing of the petition, and such other entities as the court may direct. The foreign representative shall file a certificate with the court that notice has been given. If no objection has been filed by the United States trustee or a party in interest within 30 days after the certificate is filed, there shall be a presumption that the case has been fully administered.

(d) Order declaring lien satisfied

In a chapter 12 or chapter 13 case, if a claim that was secured by property of the estate is subject to a lien under applicable nonbankruptcy law, the debtor may request entry of an order declaring that the secured claim has been satisfied and the lien has been released under the terms of a confirmed plan. The request shall be made by motion and shall be served on the holder of the claim and any other entity the court designates in the manner provided by Rule 7004 for service of a summons and complaint.

CROSS REFERENCES

Debtor to succeed to any tax attributes of estate, see 11 USCA § 346.

Dismissal of case; suspension, see Fed. R. Bankr. P. 1017.

Final decree, see Fed. R. Bankr. P. 3022.

Postpetition transfers of estate property not avoidable by trustee after case closed, see 11 USCA § 549.

Scheduled property not administered before case closed deemed abandoned, see 11 USCA § 554.

Rule 5010. Reopening Cases

A case may be reopened on motion of the debtor or other party in interest pursuant to § 350(b) of the Code. In a chapter 7, 12, or 13 case a trustee shall not be appointed by the United States trustee unless the court determines that a trustee is necessary to protect the interests of creditors and the debtor or to insure efficient administration of the case.

CROSS REFERENCES

Motions; form and service, see Fed. R. Bankr. P. 9013.

Relief from judgment or order, see Fed. R. Bankr. P. 9024.

Rule 5011. Withdrawal and Abstention From Hearing a Proceeding

(a) Withdrawal

A motion for withdrawal of a case or proceeding shall be heard by a district judge.

(b) Abstention from hearing a proceeding

A motion for abstention pursuant to 28 U.S.C. § 1334(c) shall be governed by Rule 9014 and shall be served on the parties to the proceeding.

(c) Effect of filing of motion for withdrawal or abstention

The filing of a motion for withdrawal of a case or proceeding or for abstention pursuant to 28 U.S.C. § 1334(c) shall not stay the administration of the case or any proceeding therein before the bankruptcy judge except that the bankruptcy judge may stay, on such terms and conditions as are proper, proceedings pending disposition of the motion. A motion for a stay ordinarily shall be presented first to the bankruptcy judge. A motion for a stay or relief from a stay filed in the district court shall state why it has not been presented to or obtained from the bankruptcy judge. Relief granted by the district judge shall be on such terms and conditions as the judge deems proper.

Rule 5012. Agreements Concerning Coordination of Proceedings in Chapter 15 Cases

Approval of an agreement under § 1527(4) of the Code shall be sought by motion. The movant shall attach to the motion a copy of the proposed agreement or protocol and, unless the court directs otherwise, give at least 30 days' notice of any hearing on the motion by transmitting the motion to the United States trustee, and serving it on the debtor, all persons or bodies authorized to administer foreign proceedings of the debtor, all entities against whom provisional relief is being sought under § 1519, all parties to litigation pending in the United States in which the debtor was a party at the time of the filing of the petition, and such other entities as the court may direct.

PART VI

COLLECTION AND LIQUIDATION OF THE ESTATE

Rule 6001. Burden of Proof as to Validity of Postpetition Transfer

Any entity asserting the validity of a transfer under § 549 of the Code shall have the burden of proof.

Rule 6002. Accounting by Prior Custodian of Property of the Estate

(a) Accounting required

Any custodian required by the Code to deliver property in the custodian's possession or control to the trustee shall promptly file and transmit to the United States trustee a report and account with respect to the property of the estate and the administration thereof.

(b) Examination of administration

On the filing and transmittal of the report and account required by subdivision (a) of this rule and after an examination has been made into the superseded administration, after notice and a hearing, the court shall determine the propriety of the administration, including the reasonableness of all disbursements.

CROSS REFERENCES

Accountability of prior custodians for estate property, see 11 USCA § 543.

Definition of custodian, see 11 USCA § 101.

Proceedings under this rule as nonadversarial proceedings, see Fed. R. Bankr. P. 7001.

Property of estate, see 11 USCA § 541.

Rule 6003. Interim and Final Relief Immediately Following the Commencement of the Case—Applications for Employment; Motions for Use, Sale, or Lease of Property; and Motions for Assumption or Assignment of Executory Contracts

Except to the extent that relief is necessary to avoid immediate and irreparable harm, the court shall not, within 21 days after the filing of the petition, issue an order granting the following:

(a) an application under Rule 2014;

(b) a motion to use, sell, lease, or otherwise incur an obligation regarding property of the estate, including a motion to pay all or part of a claim that arose before the filing of the petition, but not a motion under Rule 4001; or

(c) a motion to assume or assign an executory contract or unexpired lease in accordance with § 365.

Rule 6004. Use, Sale, or Lease of Property

(a) Notice of proposed use, sale, or lease of property

Notice of a proposed use, sale, or lease of property, other than cash collateral, not in the ordinary course of business shall be given pursuant to Rule 2002(a)(2), (c)(1), (i), and (k) and, if applicable, in accordance with § 363(b)(2) of the Code.

(b) Objection to proposal

Except as provided in subdivisions (c) and (d) of this rule, an objection to a proposed use, sale, or lease of property shall be filed and served not less than seven days before the date set for the proposed action or within the time fixed by the court. An objection to the proposed use, sale, or lease of property is governed by Rule 9014.

(c) Sale free and clear of liens and other interests

A motion for authority to sell property free and clear of liens or other interests shall be made in accordance with Rule 9014 and shall be served on the parties who have liens or other interests in the property to be sold. The notice required by subdivision (a) of this rule shall include the date of the hearing on the motion and the time within which objections may be filed and served on the debtor in possession or trustee.

(d) Sale of property under $2,500

Notwithstanding subdivision (a) of this rule, when all of the nonexempt property of the estate has an aggregate gross value less than $2,500, it shall be sufficient to give a general notice of intent to sell such property other than in the ordinary course of business to all creditors, indenture trustees, committees appointed or elected pursuant to the Code, the United States trustee and other persons as the court may direct. An objection to any such sale may be filed and served by a party in interest within 14 days of the mailing of the notice, or within the time fixed by the court. An objection is governed by Rule 9014.

(e) Hearing

If a timely objection is made pursuant to subdivision (b) or (d) of this rule, the date of the hearing thereon may be set in the notice given pursuant to subdivision (a) of this rule.

(f) Conduct of sale not in the ordinary course of business

(1) Public or private sale

All sales not in the ordinary course of business may be by private sale or by public auction. Unless it is impracticable, an itemized statement of the property sold, the name of each purchaser, and the price received for each item or lot or for the property as a whole if sold in bulk shall be filed on completion of a sale. If the property is sold by an auctioneer, the auctioneer shall file the statement, transmit a copy thereof to the United States trustee, and furnish a copy to the trustee, debtor in possession, or chapter 13 debtor. If the property is not sold by an auctioneer, the trustee, debtor in possession, or chapter 13 debtor shall file the statement and transmit a copy thereof to the United States trustee.

(2) Execution of instruments

After a sale in accordance with this rule the debtor, the trustee, or debtor in possession, as the case may be, shall execute any instrument necessary or ordered by the court to effectuate the transfer to the purchaser.

(g) Sale of personally identifiable information

(1) Motion

A motion for authority to sell or lease personally identifiable information under § 363(b)(1)(B) shall include a request for an order directing the United States trustee to appoint a consumer privacy ombudsman under § 332. Rule 9014 governs the motion which shall be served on: any committee elected under § 705 or appointed under § 1102 of the Code, or if the case is a chapter 11 reorganization case and no committee of unsecured creditors has been appointed under § 1102, on the creditors included on the list of creditors filed under Rule 1007(d); and on such other entities as the court may direct. The motion shall be transmitted to the United States trustee.

(2) Appointment

If a consumer privacy ombudsman is appointed under § 332, no later than seven days before the hearing on the motion under § 363(b)(1)(B), the United States trustee shall file a notice of the appointment, including the name and address of the person appointed. The United States trustee's notice shall be accompanied by a verified statement of the person appointed setting forth the person's connections with the debtor, creditors, any other party in interest, their respective attorneys and accountants, the United States trustee, or any person employed in the office of the United States trustee.

(h) Stay of order authorizing use, sale, or lease of property

An order authorizing the use, sale, or lease of property other than cash collateral is stayed until the expiration of 14 days after entry of the order, unless the court orders otherwise.

CROSS REFERENCES

Appraisers and auctioneers, see Fed. R. Bankr. P. 6005.

Authorization to operate debtor's business—

> Individual debt adjustment case, see 11 USCA § 1304.

> Liquidation case, see 11 USCA § 721.

> Reorganization case, see 11 USCA § 1108.

Notice of property disposition to include certain information, see Fed. R. Bankr. P. 2002.

Rule 6005. Appraisers and Auctioneers

The order of the court approving the employment of an appraiser or auctioneer shall fix the amount or rate of compensation. No officer or employee of the Judicial Branch of the United States or the United States Department of Justice shall be eligible to act as appraiser or auctioneer. No residence or licensing requirement shall disqualify an appraiser or auctioneer from employment.

CROSS REFERENCES

Employment—

> Application for, see Fed. R. Bankr. P. 2014.

> Professional persons, see 11 USCA § 327.

Sharing of compensation prohibited, see 11 USCA § 504.

Rule 6006. Assumption, Rejection or Assignment of an Executory Contract or Unexpired Lease

(a) Proceeding to assume, reject, or assign

A proceeding to assume, reject, or assign an executory contract or unexpired lease, other than as part of a plan, is governed by Rule 9014.

(b) Proceeding to require trustee to act

A proceeding by a party to an executory contract or unexpired lease in a chapter 9 municipality case, chapter 11 reorganization case, chapter 12 family farmer's debt adjustment case, or chapter 13 individual's debt adjustment case, to require the trustee, debtor in possession, or debtor to determine whether to assume or reject the contract or lease is governed by Rule 9014.

(c) Notice

Notice of a motion made pursuant to subdivision (a) or (b) of this rule shall be given to the other party to the contract or lease, to other parties in interest as the court may direct, and, except in a chapter 9 municipality case, to the United States trustee.

(d) Stay of order authorizing assignment

An order authorizing the trustee to assign an executory contract or unexpired lease under § 365(f) is stayed until the expiration of 14 days after the entry of the order, unless the court orders otherwise.

(e) Limitations

The trustee shall not seek authority to assume or assign multiple executory contracts or unexpired leases in one motion unless: (1) all executory contracts or unexpired leases to be assumed or assigned are between the same parties or are to be assigned to the same assignee; (2) the trustee seeks to assume, but not assign to more than one assignee, unexpired leases of real property; or (3) the court otherwise authorizes the motion to be filed. Subject to subdivision (f), the trustee may join requests for authority to reject multiple executory contracts or unexpired leases in one motion.

(f) Omnibus Motions

A motion to reject or, if permitted under subdivision (e), a motion to assume or assign multiple executory contracts or unexpired leases that are not between the same parties shall:

(1) state in a conspicuous place that parties receiving the omnibus motion should locate their names and their contracts or leases listed in the motion;

(2) list parties alphabetically and identify the corresponding contract or lease;

(3) specify the terms, including the curing of defaults, for each requested assumption or assignment;

(4) specify the terms, including the identity of each assignee and the adequate assurance of future performance by each assignee, for each requested assignment;

(5) be numbered consecutively with other omnibus motions to assume, assign, or reject executory contracts or unexpired leases; and

(6) be limited to no more than 100 executory contracts or unexpired leases.

(g) Finality of Determination

The finality of any order respecting an executory contract or unexpired lease included in an omnibus motion shall be determined as though such contract or lease had been the subject of a separate motion.

CROSS REFERENCES

Assumption or rejection of executory contracts by trustee, see 11 USCA § 365.

Commodity contracts—

Compliance by trustee with customer's instructions, see 11 USCA § 765.

Definition of, see 11 USCA § 761.

Treatment of customer property, see 11 USCA § 766.

Motions; form and service, see Fed. R. Bankr. P. 9013.

Provisions in plan for assumption or rejection of certain executory contracts or unexpired leases, see 11 USCA §§ 1123 and 1322.

Rule 6007. Abandonment or Disposition of Property

(a) Notice of proposed abandonment or disposition; objections; hearing

Unless otherwise directed by the court, the trustee or debtor in possession shall give notice of a proposed abandonment or disposition of property to the United States trustee, all creditors, indenture trustees, and committees elected pursuant to § 705 or appointed pursuant to § 1102 of the Code. A party in interest may file and serve an objection within 14 days of the mailing of the notice, or within the time fixed by the court. If a timely objection is made, the court shall set a hearing on notice to the United States trustee and to other entities as the court may direct.

(b) Motion by party in interest

A party in interest may file and serve a motion requiring the trustee or debtor in possession to abandon property of the estate. Unless otherwise directed by the court, the party filing the motion shall serve the motion and any notice of the motion on the trustee or debtor in possession, the United States trustee, all creditors, indenture trustees, and committees elected pursuant to § 705 or appointed pursuant to § 1102 of the Code. A party in interest may file and serve an objection within 14 days of service, or within the time fixed by the court. If a timely objection is made, the court shall set a hearing on notice to the United States trustee and to other entities as the court may direct. If the court grants the motion, the order effects the trustee's or debtor in possession's abandonment without further notice, unless otherwise directed by the court.

CROSS REFERENCES

Abandonment of property burdensome or of little value to estate, see 11 USCA § 554.

Abandonment of railroad line—

Authorization by court, see 11 USCA § 1170.

Provision of plan, see 11 USCA § 1172.

Disposition of property with lien in liquidation case, see 11 USCA § 725.

Motions; form and service, see Fed. R. Bankr. P. 9013.

Rule 6008. Redemption of Property From Lien or Sale

On motion by the debtor, trustee, or debtor in possession and after hearing on notice as the court may direct, the court may authorize the redemption of property from a lien or from a sale to enforce a lien in accordance with applicable law.

CROSS REFERENCES

Motions; form and service, see Fed. R. Bankr. P. 9013.

Tangible personal property—

Enforceability of agreement between holder of claim and debtor having consideration based on dischargeable debt, see 11 USCA § 524.

Redemption of exempt or abandoned property from lien securing dischargeable consumer debt, see 11 USCA § 722.

Rule 6009. Prosecution and Defense of Proceedings by Trustee or Debtor in Possession

With or without court approval, the trustee or debtor in possession may prosecute or may enter an appearance and defend any pending action or proceeding by or against the debtor, or commence and prosecute any action or proceeding in behalf of the estate before any tribunal.

CROSS REFERENCES

Suspension of statutes of limitations, see 11 USCA § 108.

Voluntary or involuntary petition filed to operate as automatic stay on other proceedings, see 11 USCA § 362.

Rule 6010. Proceeding to Avoid Indemnifying Lien or Transfer to Surety

If a lien voidable under § 547 of the Code has been dissolved by the furnishing of a bond or other obligation and the surety thereon has been indemnified by the transfer of, or the creation of a lien upon, nonexempt property of the debtor, the surety shall be joined as a defendant in any proceeding to avoid the indemnifying transfer or lien. Such proceeding is governed by the rules in Part VII.

CROSS REFERENCES

Motions; form and service, see Fed. R. Bankr. P. 9013.

Rule 6011. Disposal of Patient Records in Health Care Business Case

(a) Notice by publication under § 351(1)(A)

A notice regarding the claiming or disposing of patient records under § 351(1)(A) shall not identify any patient by name or other identifying information, but shall:

(1) identify with particularity the health care facility whose patient records the trustee proposes to destroy;

(2) state the name, address, telephone number, email address, and website, if any, of a person from whom information about the patient records may be obtained;

(3) state how to claim the patient records; and

(4) state the date by which patient records must be claimed, and that if they are not so claimed the records will be destroyed.

(b) Notice by mail under § 351(1)(B)

Subject to applicable nonbankruptcy law relating to patient privacy, a notice regarding the claiming or disposing of patient records under § 351(1)(B) shall, in addition to including the information in subdivision (a), direct that a patient's family member or other representative who receives the notice inform the patient of the notice. Any notice under this subdivision shall be mailed to the patient and any family member or other contact person whose name and address have been given to the trustee or the debtor for the purpose of providing information regarding the patient's health care, to the Attorney General of the State where the health care facility is located, and to any insurance company known to have provided health care insurance to the patient.

(c) Proof of compliance with notice requirement

Unless the court orders the trustee to file proof of compliance with § 351(1)(B) under seal, the trustee shall not file, but shall maintain, the proof of compliance for a reasonable time.

(d) Report of destruction of records

The trustee shall file, no later than 30 days after the destruction of patient records under § 351(3), a report certifying that the unclaimed records have been destroyed and explaining the method used to effect the destruction. The report shall not identify any patient by name or other identifying information.

PART VII

ADVERSARY PROCEEDINGS

437

Rule 7001.   Scope of Rules of Part VII

An adversary proceeding is governed by the rules of this Part VII. The following are adversary proceedings:

(1) a proceeding to recover money or property, other than a proceeding to compel the debtor to deliver property to the trustee, or a proceeding under § 554(b) or § 725 of the Code, Rule 2017, or Rule 6002;

(2) a proceeding to determine the validity, priority, or extent of a lien or other interest in property, but not a proceeding under Rule 3012 or Rule 4003(d);

(3) a proceeding to obtain approval under § 363(h) for the sale of both the interest of the estate and of a co-owner in property;

(4) a proceeding to object to or revoke a discharge, other than an objection to discharge under §§[1] 727(a)(8), (a)(9), or 1328(f);

(5) a proceeding to revoke an order of confirmation of a chapter 11, chapter 12, or chapter 13 plan;

(6) a proceeding to determine the dischargeability of a debt;

(7) a proceeding to obtain an injunction or other equitable relief, except when a chapter 9, chapter 11, chapter 12, or chapter 13 plan provides for the relief;

(8) a proceeding to subordinate any allowed claim or interest, except when a chapter 9, chapter 11, chapter 12, or chapter 13 plan provides for subordination;

(9) a proceeding to obtain a declaratory judgment relating to any of the foregoing; or

(10) a proceeding to determine a claim or cause of action removed under 28 U.S.C. § 1452.

CROSS REFERENCES

Adversarial nature of proceeding—

Avoidance of indemnifying lien or transfer to surety, see Fed. R. Bankr. P. 6010.

Commenced by complaint objecting to discharge, see Fed. R. Bankr. P. 4004.

Commenced by complaint to obtain determination of debt's dischargeability, see Fed. R. Bankr. P. 4007.

Joinder of objection to claim with demand for relief, see Fed. R. Bankr. P. 3007.

Liability of sureties on bond or stipulation or other undertaking, see Fed. R. Bankr. P. 9025.

Applicability of rules of this part to removed claim or cause of action, see Fed. R. Bankr. P. 9027.

---

[1] So in original. Probably should be only one section symbol.

Contested matters, applicability of and notice to parties of applicability of rules of this part, see Fed. R. Bankr. P. 9014.

Effect of amendment of Federal Rules of Civil Procedure, see Fed. R. Bankr. P. 9032.

Meanings of words in Federal Rules of Civil Procedure when applicable, see Fed. R. Bankr. P. 9002.

Rule 7002. References to Federal Rules of Civil Procedure

Whenever a Federal Rule of Civil Procedure applicable to adversary proceedings makes reference to another Federal Rule of Civil Procedure, the reference shall be read as a reference to the Federal Rule of Civil Procedure as modified in this Part VII..

Rule 7003. Commencement of Adversary Proceeding

Rule 3 F.R.Civ.P. applies in adversary proceedings.

CROSS REFERENCES

Complaint filed with court in which case is pending, see Fed. R. Bankr. P. 5005.

Rule 7004. Process; Service of Summons, Complaint

(a) Summons; service; proof of service

(1) Except as provided in Rule 7004(a)(2), Rule 4(a), (b), (c)(1), (d)(5), (e)–(j), (*l*), and (m) F.R.Civ.P. applies in adversary proceedings. Personal service under Rule 4(e)–(j) F.R.Civ.P. may be made by any person at least 18 years of age who is not a party, and the summons may be delivered by the clerk to any such person.

(2) The clerk may sign, seal, and issue a summons electronically by putting an "s/" before the clerk's name and including the court's seal on the summons.

(b) Service by first class mail

Except as provided in subdivision (h), in addition to the methods of service authorized by Rule 4(e)–(j) F.R.Civ.P., service may be made within the United States by first class mail postage prepaid as follows:

(1) Upon an individual other than an infant or incompetent, by mailing a copy of the summons and complaint to the individual's dwelling house or usual place of abode or to the place where the individual regularly conducts a business or profession.

(2) Upon an infant or an incompetent person, by mailing a copy of the summons and complaint to the person upon whom process is prescribed to be served by the law of the state in which service is made when an action is brought against such a defendant in the courts of general jurisdiction of that state. The summons and complaint in that case shall be addressed to the person required to be served at that person's dwelling house or usual place of abode or at the place where the person regularly conducts a business or profession.

(3) Upon a domestic or foreign corporation or upon a partnership or other unincorporated association, by mailing a copy of the summons and complaint to the attention of an officer, a managing or general agent, or to any other agent authorized by appointment or by law to receive service of process and, if the agent is one authorized by statute to receive service and the statute so requires, by also mailing a copy to the defendant.

(4) Upon the United States, by mailing a copy of the summons and complaint addressed to the civil process clerk at the office of the United States attorney for the district in which the action is brought and by mailing a copy of the summons and complaint to the Attorney General of the United States at Washington, District of Columbia, and in any action attacking the validity of an order of an officer or an agency of the United States not made a party, by also mailing a copy of

the summons and complaint to that officer or agency. The court shall allow a reasonable time for service pursuant to this subdivision for the purpose of curing the failure to mail a copy of the summons and complaint to multiple officers, agencies, or corporations of the United States if the plaintiff has mailed a copy of the summons and complaint either to the civil process clerk at the office of the United States attorney or to the Attorney General of the United States.

(5) Upon any officer or agency of the United States, by mailing a copy of the summons and complaint to the United States as prescribed in paragraph (4) of this subdivision and also to the officer or agency. If the agency is a corporation, the mailing shall be as prescribed in paragraph (3) of this subdivision of this rule. The court shall allow a reasonable time for service pursuant to this subdivision for the purpose of curing the failure to mail a copy of the summons and complaint to multiple officers, agencies, or corporations of the United States if the plaintiff has mailed a copy of the summons and complaint either to the civil process clerk at the office of the United States attorney or to the Attorney General of the United States. If the United States trustee is the trustee in the case and service is made upon the United States trustee solely as trustee, service may be made as prescribed in paragraph (10) of this subdivision of this rule.

(6) Upon a state or municipal corporation or other governmental organization thereof subject to suit, by mailing a copy of the summons and complaint to the person or office upon whom process is prescribed to be served by the law of the state in which service is made when an action is brought against such a defendant in the courts of general jurisdiction of that state, or in the absence of the designation of any such person or office by state law, then to the chief executive officer thereof.

(7) Upon a defendant of any class referred to in paragraph (1) or (3) of this subdivision of this rule, it is also sufficient if a copy of the summons and complaint is mailed to the entity upon whom service is prescribed to be served by any statute of the United States or by the law of the state in which service is made when an action is brought against such a defendant in the court of general jurisdiction of that state.

(8) Upon any defendant, it is also sufficient if a copy of the summons and complaint is mailed to an agent of such defendant authorized by appointment or by law to receive service of process, at the agent's dwelling house or usual place of abode or at the place where the agent regularly carries on a business or profession and, if the authorization so requires, by mailing also a copy of the summons and complaint to the defendant as provided in this subdivision.

(9) Upon the debtor, after a petition has been filed by or served upon the debtor and until the case is dismissed or closed, by mailing a copy of the summons and complaint to the debtor at the address shown in the petition or to such other address as the debtor may designate in a filed writing.

(10) Upon the United States trustee, when the United States trustee is the trustee in the case and service is made upon the United States trustee solely as trustee, by mailing a copy of the summons and complaint to an office of the United States trustee or another place designated by the United States trustee in the district where the case under the Code is pending.

(c) Service by publication

If a party to an adversary proceeding to determine or protect rights in property in the custody of the court cannot be served as provided in Rule 4(e)–(j) F.R.Civ.P. or subdivision (b) of this rule, the court may order the summons and complaint to be served by mailing copies thereof by first class mail, postage prepaid, to the party's last known address, and by at least one publication in such manner and form as the court may direct.

(d) Nationwide service of process

The summons and complaint and all other process except a subpoena may be served anywhere in the United States.

(e) Summons: time limit for service within the United States

Service made under Rule 4(e), (g), (h)(1), (i), or (j)(2) F.R.Civ.P. shall be by delivery of the summons and complaint within 7 days after the summons is issued. If service is by any authorized form of mail, the summons and complaint shall be deposited in the mail within 7 days after the summons is issued. If a summons is not timely delivered or mailed, another summons will be issued for service. This subdivision does not apply to service in a foreign country.

(f) Personal jurisdiction

If the exercise of jurisdiction is consistent with the Constitution and laws of the United States, serving a summons or filing a waiver of service in accordance with this rule or the subdivisions of Rule 4 F.R.Civ.P. made applicable by these rules is effective to establish personal jurisdiction over the person of any defendant with respect to a case under the Code or a civil proceeding arising under the Code, or arising in or related to a case under the Code.

(g) Service on debtor's attorney

If the debtor is represented by an attorney, whenever service is made upon the debtor under this Rule, service shall also be made upon the debtor's attorney by any means authorized under Rule 5(b) F.R.Civ.P.

(h) Service of process on an insured depository institution

Service on an insured depository institution (as defined in section 3 of the Federal Deposit Insurance Act) in a contested matter or adversary proceeding shall be made by certified mail addressed to an officer of the institution unless—

    (1) the institution has appeared by its attorney, in which case the attorney shall be served by first class mail;

    (2) the court orders otherwise after service upon the institution by certified mail of notice of an application to permit service on the institution by first class mail sent to an officer of the institution designated by the institution; or

    (3) the institution has waived in writing its entitlement to service by certified mail by designating an officer to receive service.

(i) Service of process by title

This subdivision (i) applies to service on a domestic or foreign corporation or partnership or other unincorporated association under Rule 7004(b)(3) or on an officer of an insured depository institution under Rule 7004(h). The defendant's officer or agent need not be correctly named in the address—or even be named—if the envelope is addressed to the defendant's proper address and directed to the attention of the officer's or agent's position or title.

CROSS REFERENCES

Contested matters, request for relief by motion served in manner provided in this rule, see Fed. R. Bankr. P. 9014.

Form of pleadings, see Fed. R. Bankr. P. 7010.

Service of—

    Motion for substitution of parties, see Fed. R. Bankr. P. 7025.

    Notice of depositions before adversary proceedings or pending appeal, see Fed. R. Bankr. P. 7027.

    Pleadings and other papers, see Fed. R. Bankr. P. 7005.

Summons and involuntary petition, manner of service, see Fed. R. Bankr. P. 1010.

Rule 7005. Service and Filing of Pleadings and Other Papers

Rule 5 F.R.Civ.P. applies in adversary proceedings.

CROSS REFERENCES

Applicability of this rule in proceedings on contested involuntary petition and to vacate order for relief, see Fed. R. Bankr. P. 1018.

Form of pleadings, see Fed. R. Bankr. P. 7010.

Service of—

> Motion for substitution, see Fed. R. Bankr. P. 7025.

> Motion to intervene, see Fed. R. Bankr. P. 7024.

> Notice of judgment or order, see Fed. R. Bankr. P. 9022.

> Requests for depositions and discovery, see Fed. R. Bankr. P. 7027 et seq.

Rule 7007. Pleadings Allowed

Rule 7 F.R.Civ.P. applies in adversary proceedings.

CROSS REFERENCES

Amended and supplemental pleadings, see Fed. R. Bankr. P. 7015.

Counterclaim and cross-claim, see Fed. R. Bankr. P. 7013.

Form of pleadings, see Fed. R. Bankr. P. 7010.

Service and filing of pleadings and other papers, see Fed. R. Bankr. P. 7005.

Third-party practice, see Fed. R. Bankr. P. 7014.

Rule 7007.1. Corporate Ownership Statement

(a) Required disclosure

Any nongovernmental corporation that is a party to an adversary proceeding, other than the debtor, shall file a statement that identifies any parent corporation and any publicly held corporation that owns 10% or more of its stock or states that there is no such corporation. The same requirement applies to a nongovernmental corporation that seeks to intervene.

(b) Time for filing; supplemental filing

The corporate ownership statement shall:

> **(1)** be filed with the corporation's first appearance, pleading, motion, response, or other request addressed to the court; and

> **(2)** be supplemented whenever the information required by this rule changes.

Rule 7008. General Rules of Pleading

Rule 8 F.R.Civ.P. applies in adversary proceedings. The allegation of jurisdiction required by Rule 8(a) shall also contain a reference to the name, number, and chapter of the case under the Code to which the adversary proceeding relates and to the district and division where the case under the Code is pending. In an adversary proceeding before a bankruptcy court, the complaint, counterclaim, cross-claim, or third-party complaint shall contain a statement that the proceeding is core or non-core and, if non-core, that the pleader does or does not consent to entry of final orders or judgment by the bankruptcy court.

CROSS REFERENCES

Amended and supplemental pleadings, see Fed. R. Bankr. P. 7015.

Applicability of this rule in proceedings on contested involuntary petition and to vacate order for relief, see Fed. R. Bankr. P. 1018.

Defenses and objections, see Fed. R. Bankr. P. 7012.

Joinder of claims and remedies, see Fed. R. Bankr. P. 7013.

Rule 7009. Pleading Special Matters

Rule 9 F.R.Civ.P. applies in adversary proceedings.

CROSS REFERENCES

Applicability of this rule in proceedings on contested involuntary petition and to vacate order for relief, see Fed. R. Bankr. P. 1018.

Parties plaintiff and defendant; capacity, see Fed. R. Bankr. P. 7017.

Pleading affirmative defenses, see Fed. R. Bankr. P. 7008.

Rule 7010. Form of Pleadings

Rule 10 F.R.Civ.P. applies in adversary proceedings, except that the caption of each pleading in such a proceeding shall conform substantially to the appropriate Official Form.

CROSS REFERENCES

Applicability of this rule in proceedings on contested involuntary petition and to vacate order for relief, see Fed. R. Bankr. P. 1018.

General requirements of form for adversarial pleading or paper, see Fed. R. Bankr. P. 9004.

Rule 7012. Defenses and Objections—When and How Presented—By Pleading or Motion—Motion for Judgment on the Pleadings

(a) When presented

If a complaint is duly served, the defendant shall serve an answer within 30 days after the issuance of the summons, except when a different time is prescribed by the court. The court shall prescribe the time for service of the answer when service of a complaint is made by publication or upon a party in a foreign country. A party served with a pleading stating a cross-claim shall serve an answer thereto within 21 days after service. The plaintiff shall serve a reply to a counterclaim in the answer within 21 days after service of the answer or, if a reply is ordered by the court, within 21 days after service of the order, unless the order otherwise directs. The United States or an officer or agency thereof shall serve an answer to a complaint within 35 days after the issuance of the summons, and shall serve an answer to a cross-claim, or a reply to a counterclaim, within 35 days after service upon the United States attorney of the pleading in which the claim is asserted. The service of a motion permitted under this rule alters these periods of time as follows, unless a different time is fixed by order of the court: (1) if the court denies the motion or postpones its disposition until the trial on the merits, the responsive pleading shall be served within 14 days after notice of the court's action; (2) if the court grants a motion for a more definite statement, the responsive pleading shall be served within 14 days after the service of a more definite statement.

(b) Applicability of Rule 12(b)–(i) F.R.Civ.P.

Rule 12(b)–(i) F.R.Civ.P. applies in adversary proceedings. A responsive pleading shall include a statement that the party does or does not consent to entry of final orders or judgment by the bankruptcy court.

CROSS REFERENCES

Averments of defense in separate statements, see Fed. R. Bankr. P. 7010.

Counterclaim and cross-claim, see Fed. R. Bankr. P. 7013.

Defenses of third-party defendant, see Fed. R. Bankr. P. 7014.

Pleadings allowed, see Fed. R. Bankr. P. 7007.

Removed actions, see Fed. R. Bankr. P. 9027.

Waiver of sovereign immunity, see 11 USCA § 106.

Rule 7013. Counterclaim and Cross-Claim

Rule 13 F.R.Civ.P. applies in adversary proceedings, except that a party sued by a trustee or debtor in possession need not state as a counterclaim any claim that the party has against the debtor, the debtor's property, or the estate, unless the claim arose after the entry of an order for relief. A trustee or debtor in possession who fails to plead a counterclaim through oversight, inadvertence, or excusable neglect, or when justice so requires, may by leave of court amend the pleading, or commence a new adversary proceeding or separate action.

CROSS REFERENCES

Amended and supplemental pleadings, see Fed. R. Bankr. P. 7015.

Counterclaims and cross-claims of third-party defendant, see Fed. R. Bankr. P. 7014.

Default judgment against counterclaimants and cross-claimants, see Fed. R. Bankr. P. 7055.

Dismissal of counterclaims and cross-claims, see Fed. R. Bankr. P. 7041.

Separate trial of counterclaims and cross-claims, see Fed. R. Bankr. P. 7042.

Rule 7014. Third-Party Practice

Rule 14 F.R.Civ.P. applies in adversary proceedings.

CROSS REFERENCES

Default judgment against third-party plaintiff, see Fed. R. Bankr. P. 7055.

Joinder of claims, see Fed. R. Bankr. P. 7018.

Requisites of pleading, see Fed. R. Bankr. P. 7008.

Separate trial of third-party claim, see Fed. R. Bankr. P. 7042.

Rule 7015. Amended and Supplemental Pleadings

Rule 15 F.R.Civ.P. applies in adversary proceedings.

CROSS REFERENCES

Amendments to pleadings considered at pre-trial conference, see Fed. R. Bankr. P. 7016.

Applicability of this rule in proceedings on contested involuntary petition and to vacate order for relief, see Fed. R. Bankr. P. 1018.

Substitution of parties, see Fed. R. Bankr. P. 7025.

Rule 7016. Pre-Trial Procedures

(a) **Pretrial conferences; scheduling; management**

Rule 16 F.R.Civ.P. applies in adversary proceedings.

(b) **Determining procedure**

The bankruptcy court shall decide, on its own motion or a party's timely motion, whether:

(1) to hear and determine the proceeding;

(2) to hear the proceeding and issue proposed findings of fact and conclusions of law; or

(3) to take some other action.

CROSS REFERENCES

Amended and supplemental pleadings, see Fed. R. Bankr. P. 7015.

Applicability of this rule in proceedings on contested involuntary petition and to vacate order for relief, see Fed. R. Bankr. P. 1018.

Preliminary hearing before trial to determine merit of defenses, see Fed. R. Bankr. P. 7012.

Rule 7017. Parties Plaintiff and Defendant; Capacity

Rule 17 F.R.Civ.P. applies in adversary proceedings, except as provided in Rule 2010(b).

CROSS REFERENCES

Bond requirement for deposit or investment by trustee of estate money, see 11 USCA § 345.

Filing by trustee of bond in favor of United States as qualification to serve, see 11 USCA § 322.

Service upon infants or incompetent persons of—

Notice of application for depositions before adversary proceedings or pending appeal, see Fed. R. Bankr. P. 7027.

Summons and complaint, see Fed. R. Bankr. P. 7004.

Rule 7018. Joinder of Claims and Remedies

Rule 18 F.R.Civ.P. applies in adversary proceedings.

CROSS REFERENCES

Joinder of parties—

Misjoinder and non-joinder, see Fed. R. Bankr. P. 7021.

Permissive joinder, see Fed. R. Bankr. P. 7020.

Persons needed for just determination, see Fed. R. Bankr. P. 7019.

Rule 7019. Joinder of Persons Needed for Just Determination

Rule 19 F.R.Civ.P. applies in adversary proceedings, except that (1) if an entity joined as a party raises the defense that the court lacks jurisdiction over the subject matter and the defense is sustained, the court shall dismiss such entity from the adversary proceeding and (2) if an entity joined as a party properly and timely raises the defense of improper venue, the court shall determine, as provided in 28 U.S.C. § 1412, whether that part of the proceeding involving the joined party shall be transferred to another district, or whether the entire adversary proceeding shall be transferred to another district.

CROSS REFERENCES

Additional parties for determination of counterclaim or cross-claim, see Fed. R. Bankr. P. 7013.

Exception to procedural rule on transfer by court of adversary proceeding, see Fed. R. Bankr. P. 7087.

Parties—

> Permissive joinder, see Fed. R. Bankr. P. 7020.
>
> Substitution of, see Fed. R. Bankr. P. 7025.

Rule 7020. Permissive Joinder of Parties

Rule 20 F.R.Civ.P. applies in adversary proceedings.

CROSS REFERENCES

Additional parties for determination of counterclaim or cross-claim, see Fed. R. Bankr. P. 7013.

Parties—

> Joinder of persons needed for just determination, see Fed. R. Bankr. P. 7019.
>
> Substitution of, see Fed. R. Bankr. P. 7025.

Rule 7021. Misjoinder and Non-Joinder of Parties

Rule 21 F.R.Civ.P. applies in adversary proceedings.

CROSS REFERENCES

Applicability of this rule in contested matters not otherwise provided for, see Fed. R. Bankr. P. 9014.

Judgment on counterclaim or cross-claim rendered in separate trials, see Fed. R. Bankr. P. 7013.

Separate trials—

> In furtherance of convenience or to avoid prejudice, see Fed. R. Bankr. P. 7042.
>
> Of parties joined permissively, see Fed. R. Bankr. P. 7020.

Rule 7022. Interpleader

Rule 22(a) F.R.Civ.P. applies in adversary proceedings. This rule supplements—and does not limit—the joinder of parties allowed by Rule 7020.

CROSS REFERENCES

Preliminary injunction in interpleader actions, see Fed. R. Bankr. P. 7065.

Rule 7023. Class Proceedings

Rule 23 F.R.Civ.P. applies in adversary proceedings.

CROSS REFERENCES

Exception of class actions from procedural rule of necessary joinder of parties, see Fed. R. Bankr. P. 7019.

Rule 7023.1. Derivative Actions

Rule 23.1 F.R.Civ.P. applies in adversary proceedings.

Rule 7023.2. Adversary Proceedings Relating to Unincorporated Associations

Rule 23.2 F.R.Civ.P. applies in adversary proceedings.

CROSS REFERENCES

Capacity of unincorporated association to sue or be sued, see Fed. R. Bankr. P. 7017.

Derivative actions by shareholders, see Fed. R. Bankr. P. 7023.1.

Rule 7024. Intervention

Rule 24 F.R.Civ.P. applies in adversary proceedings.

CROSS REFERENCES

Applicability of this rule in proceedings on contested involuntary petition and to vacate order for relief, see Fed. R. Bankr. P. 1018.

Intervention in case under this title, see Fed. R. Bankr. P. 2018.

Rule 7025. Substitution of Parties

Subject to the provisions of Rule 2012, Rule 25 F.R.Civ.P. applies in adversary proceedings.

CROSS REFERENCES

Applicability of this rule in—

Contested matters not otherwise provided for, see Fed. R. Bankr. P. 9014.

Proceedings on contested involuntary petition and to vacate order for relief, see Fed. R. Bankr. P. 1018.

Right to use depositions previously taken, see Fed. R. Bankr. P. 7026.

Rule 7026. General Provisions Governing Discovery

Rule 26 F.R.Civ.P. applies in adversary proceedings.

CROSS REFERENCES

Applicability of this rule in—

Contested matters not otherwise provided for, see Fed. R. Bankr. P. 9014.

Proceedings on contested involuntary petition and to vacate order for relief, see Fed. R. Bankr. P. 1018.

Failure to make discovery; sanctions, see Fed. R. Bankr. P. 7037.

Subpoena for taking depositions; place of examination, see Fed. R. Bankr. P. 9016.

Rule 7027. Depositions Before Adversary Proceedings or Pending Appeal

Rule 27 F.R.Civ.P. applies to adversary proceedings.

CROSS REFERENCES

Applicability of this rule in contested matters not otherwise provided for, see Fed. R. Bankr. P. 9014.

Rule 7028. Persons Before Whom Depositions May Be Taken

Rule 28 F.R.Civ.P. applies in adversary proceedings.

CROSS REFERENCES

Affirmations, see Fed. R. Bankr. P. 9012.

Applicability of this rule in—

    Contested matters not otherwise provided for, see Fed. R. Bankr. P. 9014.

    Proceedings on contested involuntary petition and to vacate order for relief, see Fed. R. Bankr. P. 1018, 11 USCA.

Rule 7029.   Stipulations Regarding Discovery Procedure

Rule 29 F.R.Civ.P. applies in adversary proceedings.

CROSS REFERENCES

Applicability of this rule in—

    Contested matters not otherwise provided for, see Fed. R. Bankr. P. 9014.

    Proceedings on contested involuntary petition and to vacate order for relief, see Fed. R. Bankr. P. 1018.

Rule 7030.   Depositions Upon Oral Examination

Rule 30 F.R.Civ.P. applies in adversary proceedings.

CROSS REFERENCES

Applicability of this rule in—

    Contested matters not otherwise provided for, see Fed. R. Bankr. P. 9014.

    Proceedings on contested involuntary petition and to vacate order for relief, see Fed. R. Bankr. P. 1018.

Failure to make discovery; sanctions, see Fed. R. Bankr. P. 7037.

Subpoena for taking depositions; place of examination, see Fed. R. Bankr. P. 9016.

Rule 7031.   Deposition Upon Written Questions

Rule 31 F.R.Civ.P. applies in adversary proceedings.

CROSS REFERENCES

Applicability of this rule in—

    Contested matters not otherwise provided for, see Fed. R. Bankr. P. 9014, 11 USCA.

    Proceedings on contested involuntary petition and to vacate order for relief, see Fed. R. Bankr. P. 1018, 11 USCA.

Failure to make discovery; sanctions, see Fed. R. Bankr. P. 7037, 11 USCA.

Rule 7032.   Use of Depositions in Adversary Proceedings

Rule 32 F.R.Civ.P. applies in adversary proceedings.

CROSS REFERENCES

Applicability of this rule in—

    Contested matters not otherwise provided for, see Fed. R. Bankr. P. 9014.

Proceedings on contested involuntary petition and to vacate order for relief, see Fed. R. Bankr. P. 1018.

Rule 7033. Interrogatories to Parties

Rule 33 F.R.Civ.P. applies in adversary proceedings.

CROSS REFERENCES

Applicability of this rule in—

> Contested matters not otherwise provided for, see Fed. R. Bankr. P. 9014.

> Proceedings on contested involuntary petition and to vacate order for relief, see Fed. R. Bankr. P. 1018.

Failure to make discovery; sanctions, see Fed. R. Bankr. P. 7037.

Rule 7034. Production of Documents and Things and Entry Upon Land for Inspection and Other Purposes

Rule 34 F.R.Civ.P. applies in adversary proceedings.

CROSS REFERENCES

Applicability of this rule in—

> Contested matters not otherwise provided for, see Fed. R. Bankr. P. 9014.

> Proceedings on contested involuntary petition and to vacate order for relief, see Fed. R. Bankr. P. 1018.

Failure to make discovery; sanctions, see Fed. R. Bankr. P. 7037.

Subpoena for production of documentary evidence, see Fed. R. Bankr. P. 9016.

Rule 7035. Physical and Mental Examination of Persons

Rule 35 F.R.Civ.P. applies in adversary proceedings.

CROSS REFERENCES

Applicability of this rule in—

> Contested matters not otherwise provided for, see Fed. R. Bankr. P. 9014.

> Proceedings on contested involuntary petition and to vacate order for relief, see Fed. R. Bankr. P. 1018.

Failure to make discovery; sanctions, see Fed. R. Bankr. P. 7037.

Rule 7036. Requests for Admission

Rule 36 F.R.Civ.P. applies in adversary proceedings.

CROSS REFERENCES

Applicability of this rule in—

> Contested matters not otherwise provided for, see Fed. R. Bankr. P. 9014.

> Proceedings on contested involuntary petition and to vacate order for relief, see Fed. R. Bankr. P. 1018.

Pre-trial conference to obtain admissions of facts and documents, see Fed. R. Bankr. P. 7016.

Rule 7037. Failure to Make Discovery: Sanctions

Rule 37 F.R.Civ.P. applies in adversary proceedings.

CROSS REFERENCES

Applicability of this rule in—

     Contested matters not otherwise provided for, see Fed. R. Bankr. P. 9014.

     Proceedings on contested involuntary petition and to vacate order for relief, see Fed. R. Bankr. P. 1018.

Rule 7040. Assignment of Cases for Trial

Rule 40 F.R.Civ.P. applies in adversary proceedings.

CROSS REFERENCES

Local bankruptcy rules on practice and procedure not inconsistent with these rules, see Fed. R. Bankr. P. 9029.

Rule 7041. Dismissal of Adversary Proceedings

Rule 41 F.R.Civ.P. applies in adversary proceedings, except that a complaint objecting to the debtor's discharge shall not be dismissed at the plaintiff's instance without notice to the trustee, the United States trustee, and such other persons as the court may direct, and only on order of the court containing terms and conditions which the court deems proper.

CROSS REFERENCES

Applicability of this rule in contested matters not otherwise provided for, see Fed. R. Bankr. P. 9014.

Findings by court necessary when judgment rendered on merits of motion to dismiss after trial on facts, see Fed. R. Bankr. P. 7052.

Sanction for failure to attend deposition, to answer interrogatories, or to respond to inspection request, see Fed. R. Bankr. P. 7037.

Rule 7042. Consolidation of Adversary Proceedings; Separate Trials

Rule 42 F.R.Civ.P. applies in adversary proceedings.

CROSS REFERENCES

Applicability of this rule in contested matters not otherwise provided for, see Fed. R. Bankr. P. 9014.

Separate trials—

     Joinder of party against whom no claim exists, see Fed. R. Bankr. P. 7020.

     Separate judgments rendered on counterclaim or cross-claim, see Fed. R. Bankr. P. 7013.

Rule 7052. Findings by the Court

Rule 52 F.R.Civ.P. applies in adversary proceedings, except that any motion under subdivision (b) of that rule for amended or additional findings shall be filed no later than 14 days after entry of judgment. In these proceedings, the reference in Rule 52 F.R.Civ.P. to the entry of judgment under Rule 58 F.R.Civ.P. shall be read as a reference to the entry of a judgment or order under Rule 5003(a).

Amendment of findings—

> On motion for new trial, see Fed. R. Bankr. P. 9023.

> Stay of proceedings to enforce judgment pending disposition of motion to amend, see Fed. R. Bankr. P. 7062.

Applicability of this rule in—

> Contested matters not otherwise provided for, see Fed. R. Bankr. P. 9014.

> Proceedings on contested involuntary petition and to vacate order for relief, see Fed. R. Bankr. P. 1018.

Effect of motion to amend or to add fact findings on time for appeal, see Fed. R. Bankr. P. 8002.

Enlargement of time for motion to amend findings of court not permitted, see Fed. R. Bankr. P. 9006.

Rule 7054. Judgments; Costs

(a) Judgments

Rule 54(a)–(c) F.R.Civ.P. applies in adversary proceedings.

(b) Costs; Attorney's Fees

(1) Costs Other Than Attorney's Fees. The court may allow costs to the prevailing party except when a statute of the United States or these rules otherwise provides. Costs against the United States, its officers and agencies shall be imposed only to the extent permitted by law. Costs may be taxed by the clerk on 14 days' notice; on motion served within seven days thereafter, the action of the clerk may be reviewed by the court.

(2) Attorney's Fees.

(A) Rule 54(d)(2)(A)–(C) and (E) F.R.Civ.P. applies in adversary proceedings except for the reference in Rule 54(d)(2)(C) to Rule 78.

(B) By local rule, the court may establish special procedures to resolve fee-related issues without extensive evidentiary hearings.

Amendment or alteration—

> Stay of proceedings pending disposition of motion for, see Fed. R. Bankr. P. 7062.

> Time for service of motion, see Fed. R. Bankr. P. 9023.

Applicability of this rule in—

> Contested matters not otherwise provided for, see Fed. R. Bankr. P. 9014.

> Proceedings on contested involuntary petition and to vacate order for relief, see Fed. R. Bankr. P. 1018.

Entry of judgment, district court record of judgment, see Fed. R. Bankr. P. 9021.

Relief from judgment or order, see Fed. R. Bankr. P. 9024.

Rule 7055. Default

Rule 55 F.R.Civ.P. applies in adversary proceedings.

Applicability of this rule in contested matters not otherwise provided for, see Fed. R. Bankr. P. 9014.

Demand for judgment, see Fed. R. Bankr. P. 7054.

Rule 7056.　Summary Judgment

Rule 56 F.R.Civ.P. applies in adversary proceedings, except that any motion for summary judgment must be made at least 30 days before the initial date set for an evidentiary hearing on any issue for which summary judgment is sought, unless a different time is set by local rule or the court orders otherwise.

CROSS REFERENCES

Applicability of this rule in—

Contested matters, not otherwise provided for, see Fed. R. Bankr. P. 9014.

Proceedings on contested involuntary petition and to vacate order for relief, see Fed. R. Bankr. P. 1018.

Rule 7058.　Entering Judgment in Adversary Proceeding

Rule 58 F.R.Civ.P. applies in adversary proceedings. In these proceedings, the reference in Rule 58 F.R.Civ.P. to the civil docket shall be read as a reference to the docket maintained by the clerk under Rule 5003(a).

Rule 7062.　Stay of Proceedings to Enforce a Judgment

Rule 62 F.R.Civ.P. applies in adversary proceedings, except that proceedings to enforce a judgment are stayed for 14 days after its entry.

CROSS REFERENCES

Applicability of this rule in—

Contested matters not otherwise provided for, see Fed. R. Bankr. P. 9014.

Proceedings on contested involuntary petition and to vacate order for relief, see Fed. R. Bankr. P. 1018.

Effect of entry of judgment on availability of relief under this rule, see Fed. R. Bankr. P. 9021.

Power of court to suspend or to order continuation of other proceedings pending appeal, see Fed. R. Bankr. P. 8007.

Security; proceedings against sureties, see Fed. R. Bankr. P. 9025.

Stay of new proceedings until payment of costs of previously dismissed action, see Fed. R. Bankr. P. 7041.

Rule 7064.　Seizure of Person or Property

Rule 64 F.R.Civ.P. applies in adversary proceedings.

CROSS REFERENCES

Applicability of this rule in contested matters not otherwise provided for, see Fed. R. Bankr. P. 9014.

Writ of attachment or sequestration issued against property ordered by judgment to be conveyed, see Fed. R. Bankr. P. 7070.

Rule 7065. Injunctions

Rule 65 F.R.Civ.P. applies in adversary proceedings, except that a temporary restraining order or preliminary injunction may be issued on application of a debtor, trustee, or debtor in possession without compliance with Rule 65(c).

CROSS REFERENCES

Security; proceedings against sureties, see Fed. R. Bankr. P. 9025.

Signing and verification of papers, see Fed. R. Bankr. P. 9011.

Rule 7067. Deposit in Court

Rule 67 F.R.Civ.P. applies in adversary proceedings.

Rule 7068. Offer of Judgment

Rule 68 F.R.Civ.P. applies in adversary proceedings.

Rule 7069. Execution

Rule 69 F.R.Civ.P. applies in adversary proceedings.

CROSS REFERENCES

Applicability of this rule in contested matters not otherwise provided for, see Fed. R. Bankr. P. 9014.

Effect of entry of judgment on availability of process to enforce judgment, see Fed. R. Bankr. P. 9021.

Writ of execution to enforce judgment to deliver possession of property, see Fed. R. Bankr. P. 7070.

Rule 7070. Judgment for Specific Acts; Vesting Title

Rule 70 F.R.Civ.P. applies in adversary proceedings and the court may enter a judgment divesting the title of any party and vesting title in others whenever the real or personal property involved is within the jurisdiction of the court.

CROSS REFERENCES

Effect of entry of judgment on availability of relief under this rule, see Fed. R. Bankr. P. 9021.

Rule 7071. Process in Behalf of and Against Persons Not Parties

Rule 71 F.R.Civ.P. applies in adversary proceedings.

CROSS REFERENCES

Applicability of this rule in contested matters not otherwise provided for, see Fed. R. Bankr. P. 9014.

Rule 7087. Transfer of Adversary Proceeding

On motion and after a hearing, the court may transfer an adversary proceeding or any part thereof to another district pursuant to 28 U.S.C. § 1412, except as provided in Rule 7019(2).

PART VIII

APPEALS TO DISTRICT COURT
OR BANKRUPTCY APPELLATE PANEL[1]

Rule

Rule 8001.   Scope of Part VIII Rules; Definition of "BAP"; Method of Transmission

(a) General Scope

These Part VIII rules govern the procedure in a United States district court and a bankruptcy appellate panel on appeal from a judgment, order, or decree of a bankruptcy court. They also govern certain procedures on appeal to a United States court of appeals under 28 U.S.C. § 158(d).

(b) Definition of "BAP"

"BAP" means a bankruptcy appellate panel established by a circuit's judicial council and authorized to hear appeals from a bankruptcy court under 28 U.S.C. § 158.

---

[1]   The 2014 amendments to Part VIII of the Bankruptcy Rules are comprehensive. Proposed amendment of the heading, "Part VIII. Bankruptcy Appeals", was not transmitted for Congressional review.

(c) Method of Transmitting Documents

A document must be sent electronically under these Part VIII rules, unless it is being sent by or to an individual who is not represented by counsel or the court's governing rules permit or require mailing or other means of delivery.

Rule 8002. Time for Filing Notice of Appeal

(a) In General.

(1) Fourteen-Day Period

Except as provided in subdivisions (b) and (c), a notice of appeal must be filed with the bankruptcy clerk within 14 days after entry of the judgment, order, or decree being appealed.

(2) Filing Before the Entry of Judgment

A notice of appeal filed after the bankruptcy court announces a decision or order—but before entry of the judgment, order, or decree—is treated as filed on the date of and after the entry.

(3) Multiple Appeals

If one party files a timely notice of appeal, any other party may file a notice of appeal within 14 days after the date when the first notice was filed, or within the time otherwise allowed by this rule, whichever period ends later.

(4) Mistaken Filing in Another Court

If a notice of appeal is mistakenly filed in a district court, BAP, or court of appeals, the clerk of that court must state on the notice the date on which it was received and transmit it to the bankruptcy clerk. The notice of appeal is then considered filed in the bankruptcy court on the date so stated.

(5) Entry Defined

(A) A judgment, order, or decree is entered for purposes of this Rule 8002(a):

(i) when it is entered in the docket under Rule 5003(a), or

(ii) if Rule 7058 applies and Rule 58(a) F.R.Civ.P. requires a separate document, when the judgment, order, or decree is entered in the docket under Rule 5003(a) and when the earlier of these events occurs:

- The judgment, order, or decree is set out in a separate document; or

- 150 days have run from entry of the judgment, order, or decree in the docket under Rule 5003(a).

(B) A failure to set out a judgment, order, or decree in a separate document when required by Rule 58(a) F.R.Civ.P. does not affect the validity of an appeal from that judgment, order, or decree.

(b) Effect of a Motion on the Time to Appeal.

(1) In General

If a party files in the bankruptcy court any of the following motions and does so within the time allowed by these rules, the time to file an appeal runs for all parties from the entry of the order disposing of the last such remaining motion:

(A) to amend or make additional findings under Rule 7052, whether or not granting the motion would alter the judgment;

(B) to alter or amend the judgment under Rule 9023;

(C) for a new trial under Rule 9023; or

(D) for relief under Rule 9024 if the motion is filed within 14 days after the judgment is entered.

(2) Filing an Appeal Before the Motion is Decided

If a party files a notice of appeal after the court announces or enters a judgment, order, or decree—but before it disposes of any motion listed in subdivision (b)(1)—the notice becomes effective when the order disposing of the last such remaining motion is entered.

(3) Appealing the Ruling on the Motion

If a party intends to challenge an order disposing of any motion listed in subdivision (b)(1)— or the alteration or amendment of a judgment, order, or decree upon the motion—the party must file a notice of appeal or an amended notice of appeal. The notice or amended notice must comply with Rule 8003 or 8004 and be filed within the time prescribed by this rule, measured from the entry of the order disposing of the last such remaining motion.

(4) No Additional Fee

No additional fee is required to file an amended notice of appeal.

(c) Appeal by an Inmate Confined in an Institution

(1) In General

If an institution has a system designed for legal mail, an inmate confined there must use that system to receive the benefit of this Rule 8002(c)(1). If an inmate files a notice of appeal from a judgment, order, or decree of a bankruptcy court, the notice is timely if it is deposited in the institution's internal mail system on or before the last day for filing and:

(A) it is accomplished by:

(i) a declaration in compliance with 28 U.S.C. § 1746—or a notarized statement— setting out the date of deposit and stating that first-class postage is being prepaid; or

(ii) evidence (such as a postmark or date stamp) showing that the notice was so deposited and that postage was prepaid; or

(B) the appellate court exercises its discretion to permit the later filing of a declaration or notarized statement that satisfies Rule 8002(c)(1)(A)(i).

(2) Multiple Appeals

If an inmate files under this subdivision the first notice of appeal, the 14-day period provided in subdivision (a)(3) for another party to file a notice of appeal runs from the date when the bankruptcy clerk dockets the first notice.

(d) Extending the Time to Appeal

(1) When the Time May be Extended

Except as provided in subdivision (d)(2), the bankruptcy court may extend the time to file a notice of appeal upon a party's motion that is filed:

(A) within the time prescribed by this rule; or

(B) within 21 days after that time, if the party shows excusable neglect.

(2) When the Time May Not be Extended

The bankruptcy court may not extend the time to file a notice of appeal if the judgment, order, or decree appealed from:

(A) grants relief from an automatic stay under § 362, 922, 1201, or 1301 of the Code;

(B) authorizes the sale or lease of property or the use of cash collateral under § 363 of the Code;

(C) authorizes the obtaining of credit under § 364 of the Code;

(D) authorizes the assumption or assignment of an executory contract or unexpired lease under § 365 of the Code;

(E) approves a disclosure statement under § 1125 of the Code; or

(F) confirms a plan under § 943, 1129, 1225, or 1325 of the Code.

(3) Time Limits on an Extension

No extension of time may exceed 21 days after the time prescribed by this rule, or 14 days after the order granting the motion to extend time is entered, whichever is later.

Rule 8003. Appeal as of Right—How Taken; Docketing the Appeal

(a) Filing the Notice of Appeal

(1) In General

An appeal from a judgment, order, or decree of a bankruptcy court to a district court or BAP under 28 U.S.C. § 158(a)(1) or (a)(2) may be taken only by filing a notice of appeal with the bankruptcy clerk within the time allowed by Rule 8002.

(2) Effect of Not Taking Other Steps

An appellant's failure to take any step other than the timely filing of a notice of appeal does not affect the validity of the appeal, but is ground only for the district court or BAP to act as it considers appropriate, including dismissing the appeal.

(3) Contents

The notice of appeal must:

(A) conform substantially to the appropriate Official Form;

(B) be accompanied by the judgment, order, or decree, or the part of it, being appealed; and

(C) be accompanied by the prescribed fee.

(4) Additional Copies

If requested to do so, the appellant must furnish the bankruptcy clerk with enough copies of the notice to enable the clerk to comply with subdivision (c).

(b) Joint or Consolidated Appeals.

(1) Joint Notice of Appeal

When two or more parties are entitled to appeal from a judgment, order, or decree of a bankruptcy court and their interests make joinder practicable, they may file a joint notice of appeal. They may then proceed on appeal as a single appellant.

(2) Consolidating Appeals

When parties have separately filed timely notices of appeal, the district court or BAP may join or consolidate the appeals.

(c) Serving the Notice of Appeal.

(1) Serving Parties and Transmitting to the United States Trustee

The bankruptcy clerk must serve the notice of appeal on counsel of record for each party to the appeal, excluding the appellant, and transmit it to the United States trustee. If a party is proceeding pro se, the clerk must send the notice of appeal to the party's last known address. The clerk must note, on each copy, the date when the notice of appeal was filed.

(2) Effect of Failing to Serve or Transmit Notice

The bankruptcy clerk's failure to serve notice on a party or transmit notice to the United States trustee does not affect the validity of the appeal.

(3) Noting Service on the Docket

The clerk must note on the docket the names of the parties served and the date and method of the service.

(d) Transmitting the Notice of Appeal to the District Court or BAP; Docketing the Appeal.

(1) Transmitting the Notice

The bankruptcy clerk must promptly transmit the notice of appeal to the BAP clerk if a BAP has been established for appeals from that district and the appellant has not elected to have the district court hear the appeal. Otherwise, the bankruptcy clerk must promptly transmit the notice to the district clerk.

(2) Docketing in the District Court or BAP

Upon receiving the notice of appeal, the district or BAP clerk must docket the appeal under the title of the bankruptcy case and the title of any adversary proceeding, and must identify the appellant, adding the appellant's name if necessary.

Rule 8004. Appeal by Leave—How Taken; Docketing the Appeal

(a) Notice of Appeal and Motion for Leave to Appeal

To appeal from an interlocutory order or decree of a bankruptcy court under 28 U.S.C. § 158(a)(3), a party must file with the bankruptcy clerk a notice of appeal as prescribed by Rule 8003(a). The notice must:

(1) be filed within the time allowed by Rule 8002;

(2) be accompanied by a motion for leave to appeal prepared in accordance with subdivision (b); and

(3) unless served electronically using the court's transmission equipment, include proof of service in accordance with Rule 8011(d).

(b) Contents of the Motion; Response

(1) Contents

A motion for leave to appeal under 28 U.S.C. § 158(a)(3) must include the following:

(A) the facts necessary to understand the question presented;

(B) the question itself;

(C) the relief sought;

(D) the reasons why leave to appeal should be granted; and

(E) a copy of the interlocutory order or decree and any related opinion or memorandum.

(2) Response

A party may file with the district or BAP clerk a response in opposition or a cross-motion within 14 days after the motion is served.

(c) Transmitting the Notice of Appeal and the Motion; Docketing the Appeal; Determining the Motion

(1) Transmitting to the District Court or BAP

The bankruptcy clerk must promptly transmit the notice of appeal and the motion for leave to the BAP clerk if a BAP has been established for appeals from that district and the appellant has not elected to have the district court hear the appeal. Otherwise, the bankruptcy clerk must promptly transmit the notice and motion to the district clerk.

(2) Docketing in the District Court or BAP

Upon receiving the notice and motion, the district or BAP clerk must docket the appeal under the title of the bankruptcy case and the title of any adversary proceeding, and must identify the appellant, adding the appellant's name if necessary.

(3) Oral Argument Not Required

The motion and any response or cross-motion are submitted without oral argument unless the district court or BAP orders otherwise.

(d) Failure to File a Motion With a Notice of Appeal

If an appellant timely files a notice of appeal under this rule but does not include a motion for leave, the district court or BAP may order the appellant to file a motion for leave, or treat the notice of appeal as a motion for leave and either grant or deny it. If the court orders that a motion for leave be filed, the appellant must do so within 14 days after the order is entered, unless the order provides otherwise.

(e) Direct Appeal to a Court of Appeals

If leave to appeal an interlocutory order or decree is required under 28 U.S.C. § 158(a)(3), an authorization of a direct appeal by the court of appeals under 28 U.S.C. § 158(d)(2) satisfies the requirement.

Rule 8005. Election to Have an Appeal Heard by the District Court Instead of the BAP

(a) Filing of a Statement of Election

To elect to have an appeal heard by the district court, a party must:

(1) file a statement of election that conforms substantially to the appropriate Official Form; and

(2) do so within the time prescribed by 28 U.S.C. § 158(c)(1).

(b) Transmitting the Documents Related to the Appeal

Upon receiving an appellant's timely statement of election, the bankruptcy clerk must transmit to the district clerk all documents related to the appeal. Upon receiving a timely statement of election by a party other than the appellant, the BAP clerk must transmit to the district clerk all documents related to the appeal and notify the bankruptcy clerk of the transmission.

(c) Determining the Validity of an Election

A party seeking a determination of the validity of an election must file a motion in the court where the appeal is then pending. The motion must be filed within 14 days after the statement of election is filed.

(d) Motion for Leave Without a Notice of Appeal—Effect on the Timing of an Election

If an appellant moves for leave to appeal under Rule 8004 but fails to file a separate notice of appeal with the motion, the motion must be treated as a notice of appeal for purposes of determining the timeliness of a statement of election.

Rule 8006. Certifying a Direct Appeal to the Court of Appeals

(a) Effective Date of a Certification

A certification of a judgment, order, or decree of a bankruptcy court for direct review in a court of appeals under 28 U.S.C. § 158(d)(2) is effective when:

> **(1)**   the certification has been filed;
>
> **(2)**   a timely appeal has been taken under Rule 8003 or 8004; and
>
> **(3)**   the notice of appeal has become effective under Rule 8002.

(b) Filing The Certification

The certification must be filed with the clerk of the court where the matter is pending. For purposes of this rule, a matter remains pending in the bankruptcy court for 30 days after the effective date under Rule 8002 of the first notice of appeal from the judgment, order, or decree for which direct review is sought. A matter is pending in the district court or BAP thereafter.

(c) Joint Certification By All Appellants And Appellees

(1) How Accomplished

A joint certification by all the appellants and appellees under 28 U.S.C. § 158(d)(2)(A) must be made by using the appropriate Official Form. The parties may supplement the certification with a short statement of the basis for the certification, which may include the information listed in subdivision (f)(2).

(2) Supplemental Statement by the Court

Within 14 days after the parties' certification, the bankruptcy court or the court in which the matter is then pending may file a short supplemental statement about the merits of the certification.

(d) The Court That May Make the Certification

Only the court where the matter is pending, as provided in subdivision (b), may certify a direct review on request of parties or on its own motion.

(e) Certification on the Court's Own Motion.

(1) How Accomplished

A certification on the court's own motion must be set forth in a separate document. The clerk of the certifying court must serve it on the parties to the appeal in the manner required for service of a notice of appeal under Rule 8003(c)(1). The certification must be accompanied by an opinion or memorandum that contains the information required by subdivision (f)(2)(A)–(D).

(2) Supplemental Statement by a Party

Within 14 days after the court's certification, a party may file with the clerk of the certifying court a short supplemental statement regarding the merits of certification.

(f) Certification by the Court on Request

(1) How Requested

A request by a party for certification that a circumstance specified in 28 U.S.C. § 158(d)(2)(A)(i)–(iii) applies—or a request by a majority of the appellants and a majority of the appellees—must be filed with the clerk of the court where the matter is pending within 60 days after the entry of the judgment, order, or decree.

(2) Service and Contents

The request must be served on all parties to the appeal in the manner required for service of a notice of appeal under Rule 8003(c)(1), and it must include the following:

    (A) the facts necessary to understand the question presented;

    (B) the question itself;

    (C) the relief sought;

    (D) the reasons why the direct appeal should be allowed, including which circumstance specified in 28 U.S.C. § 158(d)(2)(A)(i)–(iii) applies; and

    (E) a copy of the judgment, order, or decree and any related opinion or memorandum.

(3) Time to File a Response or a Cross-Request

A party may file a response to the request within 14 days after the request is served, or such other time as the court where the matter is pending allows. A party may file a cross-request for certification within 14 days after the request is served, or within 60 days after the entry of the judgment, order, or decree, whichever occurs first.

(4) Oral Argument Not Required

The request, cross-request, and any response are submitted without oral argument unless the court where the matter is pending orders otherwise.

(5) Form and Service of the Certification

If the court certifies a direct appeal in response to the request, it must do so in a separate document. The certification must be served on the parties to the appeal in the manner required for service of a notice of appeal under Rule 8003(c)(1).

(g) Proceeding in the Court of Appeals Following a Certification

Within 30 days after the date the certification becomes effective under subdivision (a), a request for permission to take a direct appeal to the court of appeals must be filed with the circuit clerk in accordance with Fed. R. App. P. 6(c).

Rule 8007. Stay Pending Appeal; Bonds; Suspension of Proceedings

(a) Initial Motion in the Bankruptcy Court

    (1) In General

Ordinarily, a party must move first in the bankruptcy court for the following relief:

    (A) a stay of a judgment, order, or decree of the bankruptcy court pending appeal;

    (B) the approval of a bond or other security provided to obtain a stay of judgment;

    (C) an order suspending, modifying, restoring, or granting an injunction while an appeal is pending; or

    (D) the suspension or continuation of proceedings in a case or other relief permitted by subdivision (e).

    (2) Time to File

The motion may be made either before or after the notice of appeal is filed.

(b) Motion in the District Court, the BAP, or the Court of Appeals on Direct Appeal

(1) Request for Relief

A motion for the relief specified in subdivision (a)(1)—or to vacate or modify a bankruptcy court's order granting such relief—may be made in the court where the appeal is pending.

(2) Showing or Statement Required

The motion must:

(A) show that moving first in the bankruptcy court would be impracticable; or

(B) if a motion was made in the bankruptcy court, either state that the court has not yet ruled on the motion, or state that the court has ruled and set out any reasons given for the ruling.

(3) Additional Content

The motion must also include:

(A) the reasons for granting the relief requested and the facts relied upon;

(B) affidavits or other sworn statements supporting facts subject to dispute; and

(C) relevant parts of the record.

(4) Serving Notice

The movant must give reasonable notice of the motion to all parties.

(c) Filing a Bond or Other Security

The district court, BAP, or court of appeals may condition relief on filing a bond or other security with the bankruptcy court.

(d) Bond or Other Security for a Trustee or the United States

The court may require a trustee to file a bond or other security when the trustee appeals. A bond or other security is not required when an appeal is taken by the United States, its officer, or its agency or by direction of any department of the federal government.

(e) Continuation of Proceedings in the Bankruptcy Court

Despite Rule 7062 and subject to the authority of the district court, BAP, or court of appeals, the bankruptcy court may:

(1) suspend or order the continuation of other proceedings in the case; or

(2) issue any other appropriate orders during the pendency of an appeal to protect the rights of all parties in interest.

Rule 8008. Indicative Rulings

(a) Relief Pending Appeal

If a party files a timely motion in the bankruptcy court for relief that the court lacks authority to grant because of an appeal that has been docketed and is pending, the bankruptcy court may:

(1) defer considering the motion;

(2) deny the motion; or

(3) state that the court would grant the motion if the court where the appeal is pending remands for that purpose, or state that the motion raises a substantial issue.

(b) Notice to the Court Where the Appeal Is Pending

The movant must promptly notify the clerk of the court where the appeal is pending if the bankruptcy court states that it would grant the motion or that the motion raises a substantial issue.

(c) Remand After An Indicative Ruling

If the bankruptcy court states that it would grant the motion or that the motion raises a substantial issue, the district court or BAP may remand for further proceedings, but it retains jurisdiction unless it expressly dismisses the appeal. If the district court or BAP remands but retains jurisdiction, the parties must promptly notify the clerk of that court when the bankruptcy court has decided the motion on remand.

Rule 8009. Record on Appeal; Sealed Documents

(a) Designating the Record on Appeal; Statement of the Issues

(1) Appellant

(A) The appellant must file with the bankruptcy clerk and serve on the appellee a designation of the items to be included in the record on appeal and a statement of the issues to be presented.

(B) The appellant must file and serve the designation and statement within 14 days after:

(i) the appellant's notice of appeal as of right becomes effective under Rule 8002; or

(ii) an order granting leave to appeal is entered. A designation and statement served prematurely must be treated as served on the first day on which filing is timely.

(2) Appellee and Cross-Appellant

Within 14 days after being served, the appellee may file with the bankruptcy clerk and serve on the appellant a designation of additional items to be included in the record. An appellee who files a cross-appeal must file and serve a designation of additional items to be included in the record and a statement of the issues to be presented on the cross-appeal.

(3) Cross-Appellee

Within 14 days after service of the cross-appellant's designation and statement, a cross-appellee may file with the bankruptcy clerk and serve on the cross-appellant a designation of additional items to be included in the record.

(4) Record on Appeal

The record on appeal must include the following:

- docket entries kept by the bankruptcy clerk;
- items designated by the parties;
- the notice of appeal;
- the judgment, order, or decree being appealed;
- any order granting leave to appeal;
- any certification required for a direct appeal to the court of appeals;
- any opinion, findings of fact, and conclusions of law relating to the issues on appeal, including transcripts of all oral rulings;
- any transcript ordered under subdivision (b);
- any statement required by subdivision (c); and

- any additional items from the record that the court where the appeal is pending orders.

(5) Copies for the Bankruptcy Clerk

If paper copies are needed, a party filing a designation of items must provide a copy of any of those items that the bankruptcy clerk requests. If the party fails to do so, the bankruptcy clerk must prepare the copy at the party's expense.

(b) Transcript of Proceedings

(1) Appellant's Duty to Order

Within the time period prescribed by subdivision (a)(1), the appellant must:

(A) order in writing from the reporter, as defined in Rule 8010(a)(1), a transcript of such parts of the proceedings not already on file as the appellant considers necessary for the appeal, and file a copy of the order with the bankruptcy clerk; or

(B) file with the bankruptcy clerk a certificate stating that the appellant is not ordering a transcript.

(2) Cross-Appellant's Duty to Order

Within 14 days after the appellant files a copy of the transcript order or a certificate of not ordering a transcript, the appellee as cross-appellant must:

(A) order in writing from the reporter, as defined in Rule 8010(a)(1), a transcript of such additional parts of the proceedings as the cross-appellant considers necessary for the appeal, and file a copy of the order with the bankruptcy clerk; or

(B) file with the bankruptcy clerk a certificate stating that the cross-appellant is not ordering a transcript.

(3) Appellee's or Cross-Appellee's Right to Order

Within 14 days after the appellant or cross-appellant files a copy of a transcript order or certificate of not ordering a transcript, the appellee or cross-appellee may order in writing from the reporter a transcript of such additional parts of the proceedings as the appellee or cross-appellee considers necessary for the appeal. A copy of the order must be filed with the bankruptcy clerk.

(4) Payment

At the time of ordering, a party must make satisfactory arrangements with the reporter for paying the cost of the transcript.

(5) Unsupported Finding or Conclusion

If the appellant intends to argue on appeal that a finding or conclusion is unsupported by the evidence or is contrary to the evidence, the appellant must include in the record a transcript of all relevant testimony and copies of all relevant exhibits.

(c) Statement of the Evidence When a Transcript Is Unavailable

If a transcript of a hearing or trial is unavailable, the appellant may prepare a statement of the evidence or proceedings from the best available means, including the appellant's recollection. The statement must be filed within the time prescribed by subdivision (a)(1) and served on the appellee, who may serve objections or proposed amendments within 14 days after being served. The statement and any objections or proposed amendments must then be submitted to the bankruptcy court for settlement and approval. As settled and approved, the statement must be included by the bankruptcy clerk in the record on appeal.

(d) Agreed Statement as the Record on Appeal

Instead of the record on appeal as defined in subdivision (a), the parties may prepare, sign, and submit to the bankruptcy court a statement of the case showing how the issues presented by the appeal arose and were decided in the bankruptcy court. The statement must set forth only those facts alleged and proved or sought to be proved that are essential to the court's resolution of the issues. If the statement is accurate, it—together with any additions that the bankruptcy court may consider necessary to a full presentation of the issues on appeal—must be approved by the bankruptcy court and must then be certified to the court where the appeal is pending as the record on appeal. The bankruptcy clerk must then transmit it to the clerk of that court within the time provided by Rule 8010. A copy of the agreed statement may be filed in place of the appendix required by Rule 8018(b) or, in the case of a direct appeal to the court of appeals, by Fed. R. App. P. 30.

(e) Correcting or Modifying the Record.

(1) Submitting to the Bankruptcy Court

If any difference arises about whether the record accurately discloses what occurred in the bankruptcy court, the difference must be submitted to and settled by the bankruptcy court and the record conformed accordingly. If an item has been improperly designated as part of the record on appeal, a party may move to strike that item.

(2) Correcting in Other Ways

If anything material to either party is omitted from or misstated in the record by error or accident, the omission or misstatement may be corrected, and a supplemental record may be certified and transmitted:

    (A) on stipulation of the parties;

    (B) by the bankruptcy court before or after the record has been forwarded; or

    (C) by the court where the appeal is pending.

(3) Remaining Questions

All other questions as to the form and content of the record must be presented to the court where the appeal is pending.

(f) Sealed Documents

A document placed under seal by the bankruptcy court may be designated as part of the record on appeal. In doing so, a party must identify it without revealing confidential or secret information, but the bankruptcy clerk must not transmit it to the clerk of the court where the appeal is pending as part of the record. Instead, a party must file a motion with the court where the appeal is pending to accept the document under seal. If the motion is granted, the movant must notify the bankruptcy court of the ruling, and the bankruptcy clerk must promptly transmit the sealed document to the clerk of the court where the appeal is pending.

(g) Other Necessary Actions

All parties to an appeal must take any other action necessary to enable the bankruptcy clerk to assemble and transmit the record.

Rule 8010. Completing and Transmitting the Record

(a) Reporter's Duties

(1) Proceedings Recorded Without a Reporter Present

If proceedings were recorded without a reporter being present, the person or service selected under bankruptcy court procedures to transcribe the recording is the reporter for purposes of this rule.

(2) Preparing and Filing the Transcript

The reporter must prepare and file a transcript as follows:

(A) Upon receiving an order for a transcript in accordance with Rule 8009(b), the reporter must file in the bankruptcy court an acknowledgment of the request that shows when it was received, and when the reporter expects to have the transcript completed.

(B) After completing the transcript, the reporter must file it with the bankruptcy clerk, who will notify the district, BAP, or circuit clerk of its filing.

(C) If the transcript cannot be completed within 30 days after receiving the order, the reporter must request an extension of time from the bankruptcy clerk. The clerk must enter on the docket and notify the parties whether the extension is granted.

(D) If the reporter does not file the transcript on time, the bankruptcy clerk must notify the bankruptcy judge.

(b) Clerk's Duties

(1) Transmitting the Record—In General

Subject to Rule 8009(f) and subdivision (b)(5) of this rule, when the record is complete, the bankruptcy clerk must transmit to the clerk of the court where the appeal is pending either the record or a notice that the record is available electronically.

(2) Multiple Appeals

If there are multiple appeals from a judgment, order, or decree, the bankruptcy clerk must transmit a single record.

(3) Receiving the Record

Upon receiving the record or notice that it is available electronically, the district, BAP, or circuit clerk must enter that information on the docket and promptly notify all parties to the appeal.

(4) If Paper Copies Are Ordered

If the court where the appeal is pending directs that paper copies of the record be provided, the clerk of that court must so notify the appellant. If the appellant fails to provide them, the bankruptcy clerk must prepare them at the appellant's expense.

(5) When Leave to Appeal is Requested

Subject to subdivision (c), if a motion for leave to appeal has been filed under Rule 8004, the bankruptcy clerk must prepare and transmit the record only after the district court, BAP, or court of appeals grants leave.

(c) Record for a Preliminary Motion in the District Court, BAP, or Court of Appeals

This subdivision (c) applies if, before the record is transmitted, a party moves in the district court, BAP, or court of appeals for any of the following relief:

- leave to appeal;
- dismissal;
- stay pending appeal;
- approval of a bond or other security provided to obtain a stay of judgment; or
- any other intermediate order.

The bankruptcy clerk must then transmit to the clerk of the court where the relief is sought any parts of the record designated by a party to the appeal or a notice that those parts are available electronically.

Rule 8011. Filing and Service; Signature

(a) Filing

(1) With the Clerk

A document required or permitted to be filed in a district court or BAP must be filed with the clerk of that court.

(2) Method and Timeliness

(A) Nonelectronic Filing

(i) In General

For a document not filed electronically, filing may be accomplished by mail addressed to the clerk of the district court or BAP. Except as provided in subdivision (a)(2)(A)(ii) and (iii), filing is timely only if the clerk receives the document within the time fixed for filing.

(ii) Brief or Appendix

A brief or appendix not filed electronically is also timely filed if, on or before the last day for filing, it is:

- mailed to the clerk by first-class mail—or other class of mail that is at least expeditious—postage prepaid; or

- dispatched to a third-party commercial carrier for delivery within 3 days to the clerk.

(iii) Inmate Filing

If an institution has a system designed for legal mail, an inmate confined there must use that system to receive the benefit of this Rule 8011(a)(2)(A)(iii). A document not filed electronically by an inmate confined in an institution is timely if it is deposited in the institution's internal mailing system on or before the last day for filing and:

- it is accompanied by a declaration in compliance with 28 U.S.C. § 1746—or notarized statement—setting out the date of deposit and stating that first-class postage is being prepaid; or evidence (such as a postmark or date stamp) showing that the notice was so deposited and that postage was prepaid; or

- the appellate court exercises its discretion to permit the later filing of a declaration or notarized statement that satisfies this Rule 8011(a)(2)(A)(iii).

(B) Electronic Filing

(i) By a Represented Person—Generally Required; Exceptions

An entity represented by an attorney must file electronically, unless nonelectronic filing is allowed by the court for good cause or is allowed or required by local rule.

(ii) By an Unrepresented Individual—When Allowed or Required

An individual not represented by an attorney:

- may file electronically only if allowed by court order or by local rule; and

- may be required to file electronically only by court order, or by a local rule that includes reasonable exceptions.

(iii) Same as a Written Paper

A document filed electronically is a written paper for purposes of these rules.

(C) Copies

If a document is filed electronically, no paper copy is required. If a document is filed by mail or delivery to the district court or BAP, no additional copies are required. But the district court or BAP may require by local rule or by order in a particular case the filing or furnishing of a specified number of paper copies.

(3) Clerk's Refusal of Documents.

The court's clerk must not refuse to accept for filing any document transmitted for that purpose solely because it is not presented in proper form as required by these rules or by any local rule or practice.

(b) Service of All Documents Required

Unless a rule requires service by the clerk, a party must, at or before the time of the filing of a document, serve it on the other parties to the appeal. Service on a party represented by counsel must be made on the party's counsel.

(c) Manner of Service

(1) Nonelectronic Service

Nonelectronic service may be by any of the following methods:

(A) personal delivery;

(B) mail; or

(C) third-party commercial carrier for delivery within 3 days.

(2) Electronic Service

Electronic service may be made by sending a document to a registered user by filing it with the court's electronic-filing system or by using other electronic means that the person served consented to in writing.

(3) When Service Is Complete

Service by electronic means is complete on filing or sending, unless the person making service receives notice that the document was not received by the person served. Service by mail or by commercial carrier is complete on mailing or delivery to the carrier.

(d) Proof of Service.

(1) What Is Required

A document presented for filing must contain either of the following if it was served other than through the court's electronic-filing system:

(A) an acknowledgment of service by the person served; or

(B) proof of service consisting of a statement by the person who made service certifying:

(i) the date and manner of service;

(ii) the names of the persons served; and

(iii) the mail or electronic address, the fax number, or the address of the place of delivery, as appropriate for the manner of service, for each person served.

(2) Delayed Proof

The district or BAP clerk may permit documents to be filed without acknowledgment or proof of service, but must require the acknowledgment or proof to be filed promptly thereafter.

(3) Brief or Appendix

When a brief or appendix is filed, the proof of service must also state the date and manner by which it was filed.

(e) Signature

Every document filed electronically must include the electronic signature of the person filing it or, if the person is represented, the electronic signature of counsel. A filing made through a person's electronic-filing account and authorized by that person, together with that person's name on a signature block, constitutes the person's signature. Every document filed in paper form must be signed by the person filing the document or, if the person is represented, by counsel.

Rule 8012. Disclosure Statement

(a) Nongovernmental Corporations

Any nongovernmental corporation that is a party to a proceeding in the district court or BAP must file a statement that identifies any parent corporation and any publicly held corporation that owns 10% or more of its stock or states that there is no such corporation. The same requirement applies to a nongovernmental corporation that seeks to intervene.

(b) Disclosure About the Debtor.

The 11 debtor, the trustee, or, if neither is a party, the appellant must file a statement that:

(1) identifies each debtor not named in the caption; and

(2) for each debtor that is a corporation, discloses the information required by Rule 8012(a).

(c) Time to File; Supplemental Filing

A Rule 8012 statement must:

(1) be filed with the principal brief or upon filing a motion, response, petition, or answer in the district court or BAP, whichever occurs first, unless a local rule requires earlier filing;

(2) be included before the table of contents in the principal brief; and

(3) be supplemented whenever the information required by Rule 8012 changes.

Rule 8013. Motions; Intervention

(a) Contents of a Motion; Response; Reply

(1) Request for Relief

A request for an order or other relief is made by filing a motion with the district or BAP clerk.

(2) Contents of a Motion

(A) Grounds and the Relief Sought

A motion must state with particularity the grounds for the motion, the relief sought, and the legal argument necessary to support it.

(B) Motion to Expedite an Appeal

A motion to expedite an appeal must explain what justifies considering the appeal ahead of other matters. If the district court or BAP grants the motion, it may accelerate the time to transmit the record, the deadline for filing briefs and other documents, oral argument, and the resolution of the appeal. A motion to expedite an appeal may be filed as an emergency motion under subdivision (d).

(C) Accompanying Documents

(i) Any affidavit or other document necessary to support a motion must be served and filed with the motion.

(ii) An affidavit must contain only factual information, not legal argument.

(iii) A motion seeking substantive relief must include a copy of the bankruptcy court's judgment, order, or decree, and any accompanying opinion as a separate exhibit.

(D) Documents Barred or Not Required

(i) A separate brief supporting or responding to a motion must not be filed.

(ii) Unless the court orders otherwise, a notice of motion or a proposed order is not required.

(3) Response and Reply; Time to File

Unless the district court or BAP orders otherwise,

(A) any party to the appeal may file a response to the motion within 7 days after service of the motion; and

(B) the movant may file a reply to a response within 7 days after service of the response, but may only address matters raised in the response.

(b) Disposition of a Motion for a Procedural Order

The district court or BAP may rule on a motion for a procedural order—including a motion under Rule 9006(b) or (c)—at any time without awaiting a response. A party adversely affected by the ruling may move to reconsider, vacate, or modify it within 7 days after the procedural order is served.

(c) Oral Argument

A motion will be decided without oral argument unless the district court or BAP orders otherwise.

(d) Emergency Motion

(1) Noting the Emergency

When a movant requests expedited action on a motion because irreparable harm would occur during the time needed to consider a response, the movant must insert the word "Emergency" before the title of the motion.

(2) Contents of the Motion

The emergency motion must

(A) be accompanied by an affidavit setting out the nature of the emergency;

(B) state whether all grounds for it were submitted to the bankruptcy court and, if not, why the motion should not be remanded for the bankruptcy court to consider;

(C) include the e-mail addresses, office addresses, and telephone numbers of moving counsel and, when known, of opposing counsel and any unrepresented parties to the appeal; and

(D) be served as prescribed by Rule 8011.

(3) Notifying Opposing Parties

Before filing an emergency motion, the movant must make every practicable effort to notify opposing counsel and any unrepresented parties in time for them to respond. The affidavit accompanying the emergency motion must state when and how notice was given or state why giving it was impracticable.

(e) Power of a Single BAP Judge to Entertain a Motion

(1) Single Judge's Authority

A BAP judge may act alone on any motion, but may not dismiss or otherwise determine an appeal, deny a motion for leave to appeal, or deny a motion for a stay pending appeal if denial would make the appeal moot.

(2) Reviewing a Single Judge's Action

The BAP may review a single judge's action, either on its own motion or on a party's motion.

(f) Form of Documents; Page Length; Number of Copies

(1) Format of a Paper Document

Rule 27(d)(1) Fed. R. App. P. applies in the district court or BAP to a paper version of a motion, response, or reply.

(2) Format of an Electronically Filed Document

A motion, response, or reply filed electronically must comply with the requirements for a paper version regarding covers, line spacing, margins, typeface, and type style. It must also comply with the page length under paragraph (3).

(3) Length Limits

Except by the district court's or BAP's permission, and excluding the accompanying documents authorized by subdivision (a)(2)(C):

> **(A)** a motion or a response to a motion produced using a computer must include a certificate under Rule 8015(h) and not exceed 5,200 words;

> **(B)** a handwritten or typewritten motion or a response to a motion must not exceed 20 pages;

> **(C)** a reply produced using a computer must include a certificate under Rule 8015(h) and not exceed 2,600 words; and

> **(D)** a handwritten or typewritten reply must not exceed 10 pages.

(4) Paper Copies

Paper copies must be provided only if required by local rule or by an order in a particular case.

(g) Intervening in an Appeal

Unless a statute provides otherwise, an entity that seeks to intervene in an appeal pending in the district court or BAP must move for leave to intervene and serve a copy of the motion on the parties to the appeal. The motion or other notice of intervention authorized by statute must be filed within 30 days after the appeal is docketed. It must concisely state the movant's interest, the grounds for intervention, whether intervention was sought in the bankruptcy court, why intervention is being sought at this stage of the proceeding, and why participating as an amicus curiae would not be adequate.

Rule 8014. Briefs

(a) Appellant's Brief

The appellant's brief must contain the following under appropriate headings and in the order indicated:

> **(1)** a corporate disclosure statement, if required by Rule 8012;

> **(2)** a table of contents, with page references;

(3) a table of authorities—cases (alphabetically arranged), statutes, and other authorities—with references to the pages of the brief where they are cited;

(4) a jurisdictional statement, including:

(A) the basis for the bankruptcy court's subject-matter jurisdiction, with citations to applicable statutory provisions and stating relevant facts establishing jurisdiction;

(B) the basis for the district court's or BAP's jurisdiction, with citations to applicable statutory provisions and stating relevant facts establishing jurisdiction;

(C) the filing dates establishing the timeliness of the appeal; and

(D) an assertion that the appeal is from a final judgment, order, or decree, or information establishing the district court's or BAP's jurisdiction on another basis;

(5) a statement of the issues presented and, for each one, a concise statement of the applicable standard of appellate review;

(6) a concise statement of the case setting out the facts relevant to the issues submitted for review, describing the relevant procedural history, and identifying the rulings presented for review, with appropriate references to the record;

(7) a summary of the argument, which must contain a succinct, clear, and accurate statement of the arguments made in the body of the brief, and which must not merely repeat the argument headings;

(8) the argument, which must contain the appellant's contentions and the reasons for them, with citations to the authorities and parts of the record on which the appellant relies;

(9) a short conclusion stating the precise relief sought; and

(10) the certificate of compliance, if required by Rule 8015(a)(7) or (b).

(b) Appellee's Brief

The appellee's brief must conform to the requirements of subdivision (a)(1)–(8) and (10), except that none of the following need appear unless the appellee is dissatisfied with the appellant's statement:

(1) the jurisdictional statement;

(2) the statement of the issues and the applicable standard of appellate review; and

(3) the statement of the case.

(c) Reply Brief

The appellant may file a brief in reply to the appellee's brief. A reply brief must comply with the requirements of subdivision (a)(2)–(3).

(d) Statutes, Rules, Regulations, or Similar Authority

If the court's determination of the issues presented requires the study of the Code or other statutes, rules, regulations, or similar authority, the relevant parts must be set out in the brief or in an addendum.

(e) Briefs in a Case Involving Multiple Appellants or Appellees

In a case involving more than one appellant or appellee, including consolidated cases, any number of appellants or appellees may join in a brief, and any party may adopt by reference a part of another's brief. Parties may also join in reply briefs.

(f) Citation of Supplemental Authorities

If pertinent and significant authorities come to a party's attention after the party's brief has been filed—or after oral argument but before a decision—a party may promptly advise the district or BAP clerk by a signed submission setting forth the citations. The submission, which must be served on the other parties to the appeal, must state the reasons for the supplemental citations, referring either to the pertinent page of a brief or to a point argued orally. The body of the submission must not exceed 350 words. Any response must be made within 7 days after the party is served, unless the court orders otherwise, and must be similarly limited.

Rule 8015. Form and Length of Briefs; Form of Appendices and Other Papers

(a) Paper Copies of a Brief

If a paper copy of a brief may or must be filed, the following provisions apply:

(1) Reproduction

(A) A brief may be reproduced by any process that yields a clear black image on light paper. The paper must be opaque and unglazed. Only one side of the paper may be used.

(B) Text must be reproduced with a clarity that equals or exceeds the output of a laser printer.

(C) Photographs, illustrations, and tables may be reproduced by any method that results in a good copy of the original. A glossy finish is acceptable if the original is glossy.

(2) Cover

The front cover of a brief must contain:

(A) the number of the case centered at the top;

(B) the name of the court;

(C) the title of the case as prescribed by Rule 8003(d)(2) or 8004(c)(2);

(D) the nature of the proceeding and the name of the court below;

(E) the title of the brief, identifying the party or parties for whom the brief is filed; and

(F) the name, office address, telephone number, and e-mail address of counsel representing the party for whom the brief is filed.

(3) Binding

The brief must be bound in any manner that is secure, does not obscure the text, and permits the brief to lie reasonably flat when open.

(4) Paper Size, Line Spacing, and Margins

The brief must be on 8½-by-11 inch paper. The text must be double-spaced, but quotations more than two lines long may be indented and single-spaced. Headings and footnotes may be single-spaced. Margins must be at least one inch on all four sides. Page numbers may be placed in the margins, but no text may appear there.

(5) Typeface

Either a proportionally spaced or monospaced face may be used.

(A) A proportionally spaced face must include serifs, but sans-serif type may be used in headings and captions. A proportionally spaced face must be 14-point or larger.

(B) A monospaced face may not contain more than 10½ characters per inch.

(6) Type Styles

A brief must be set in plain, roman style, although italics or boldface may be used for emphasis. Case names must be italicized or underlined.

(7) Length

(A) Page Limitation

A principal brief must not exceed 30 pages, or a reply brief 15 pages, unless it complies with subparagraph (B).

(B) Type-volume Limitation

(i) A principal brief is acceptable if it contains a certificate under Rule 8015(h) and:

- contains no more than 13,000 words; or

- uses a monospaced face and contains no more than 1,300 lines of text.

(ii) A reply brief is acceptable if it includes a certificate under Rule 8015(h) and contains no more than half of the type volume specified in item (i).

(b) Electronically Filed Briefs

A brief filed electronically must comply with subdivision (a), except for (a)(1), (a)(3), and the paper requirement of (a)(4).

(c) Paper Copies of Appendices

A paper copy of an appendix must comply with subdivision (a)(1), (2), (3), and (4), with the following exceptions:

(1) An appendix may include a legible photocopy of any document found in the record or of a printed decision.

(2) When necessary to facilitate inclusion of odd-sized documents such as technical drawings, an appendix may be a size other than 8½-by-11 inches, and need not lie reasonably flat when opened.

(d) Electronically Filed Appendices

An appendix filed electronically must comply with subdivision (a)(2) and (4), except for the paper requirement of (a)(4).

(e) Other Documents

(1) Motion

Rule 8013(f) governs the form of a motion, response, or reply.

(2) Paper Copies of Other Documents

A paper copy of any other document, other than a submission under Rule 8014(f), must comply with subdivision (a), with the following exceptions:

(A) A cover is not necessary if the caption and signature page together contain the information required by subdivision (a)(2).

(B) Subdivision (a)(7) does not apply.

(3) Other Documents Filed Electronically

Any other document filed electronically, other than a submission under Rule 8014(f), must comply with the appearance requirements of paragraph (2).

(f) Local Variation

A district court or BAP must accept documents that comply with the form requirements of this rule and the length limits set by Part VIII of these rules. By local rule or order in a particular case, a district court or BAP may accept documents that do not meet all the form requirements of this rule or the length limits set by Part VIII of these rules.

(g) Items Excluded from Length

In computing any length limit, headings, footnotes, and quotations count toward the limit, but the following items do not:

- cover page;
- disclosure statement under Rule 8012;
- table of contents;
- table of citations;
- statement regarding oral argument;
- addendum containing statutes, rules, or regulations;
- certificates of counsel;
- signature block;
- proof of service; and
- any item specifically excluded by these rules or local rule.

(h) Certificate of Compliance

(1) Briefs and Documents that Require a Certificate

A brief submitted under Rule 8015(a)(7)(B), 8016(d)(2), or 8017(b)(4)—and a document submitted under Rule 8013(f)(3)(A), 8013(f)(3)(C), or 8022(b)(1)—must include a certificate by the attorney, or an unrepresented party, that the document complies with the type-volume limitation. The individual preparing the certificate may rely on the word or line count of the word-processing system used to prepare the document. The certificate must state the number of words—or the number of lines of monospaced type—in the document.

(2) Acceptable Form

The certificate requirement is satisfied by a certificate of compliance that conforms substantially to the appropriate Official Form.

Rule 8016. Cross-Appeals

(a) Applicability

This rule applies to a case in which a cross-appeal is filed. Rules 8014(a)–(c), 8015(a)(7)(A)–(B), and 8018(a)(1)–(3) do not apply to such a case, except as otherwise provided in this rule.

(b) Designation of Appellant

The party who files a notice of appeal first is the appellant for purposes of this rule and Rule 8018(a)(4) and (b) and Rule 8019. If notices are filed on the same day, the plaintiff, petitioner, applicant, or movant in the proceeding below is the appellant. These designations may be modified by the parties' agreement or by court order.

(c) Briefs. In a case involving a cross-appeal:

(1) Appellant's Principal Brief

The appellant must file a principal brief in the appeal. That brief must comply with Rule 8014(a).

(2) Appellee's Principal and Response Brief

The appellee must file a principal brief in the cross-appeal and must, in the same brief, respond to the principal brief in the appeal. That brief must comply with Rule 8014(a), except that the brief need not include a statement of the case unless the appellee is dissatisfied with the appellant's statement.

(3) Appellant's Response and Reply Brief

The appellant must file a brief that responds to the principal brief in the cross-appeal and may, in the same brief, reply to the response in the appeal. That brief must comply with Rule 8014(a)(2)–(8) and (10), except that none of the following need appear unless the appellant is dissatisfied with the appellee's statement in the cross-appeal:

    (A) the jurisdictional statement;

    (B) the statement of the issues and the applicable standard of appellate review; and

    (C) the statement of the case.

(4) Appellee's Reply Brief

The appellee may file a brief in reply to the response in the cross-appeal. That brief must comply with Rule 8014(a)(2)–(3) and (10) and must be limited to the issues presented by the cross-appeal.

(d) Length

(1) Page Limitation

Unless it complies with paragraph (2), the appellant's principal brief must not exceed 30 pages; the appellee's principal and response brief, 35 pages; the appellant's response and reply brief, 30 pages; and the appellee's reply brief, 15 pages.

(2) Type-volume Limitation

    (A) The appellant's principal brief or the appellant's response and reply brief is acceptable if it includes a certificate under Rule 8015(h) and:

        (i) contains no more than 13,000 words; or

        (ii) uses a monospaced face and contains no more than 1,300 lines of text.

    (B) The appellee's principal and response brief is acceptable if it includes a certificate under Rule 8015(h) and:

        (i) contains no more than 15,300 words; or

        (ii) uses a monospaced face and contains no more than 1,500 lines of text.

    (C) The appellee's reply brief is acceptable if it includes a certificate under Rule 8015(h) and contains no more than half of the type volume specified in subparagraph (A).

(e) Time to Serve and File a Brief

Briefs must be served and filed as follows, unless the district court or BAP by order in a particular case excuses the filing of briefs or specifies different time limits:

    (1) the appellant's principal brief, within 30 days after the docketing of notice that the record has been transmitted or is available electronically;

    (2) the appellee's principal and response brief, within 30 days after the appellant's principal brief is served;

    (3) the appellant's response and reply brief, within 30 days after the appellee's principal and response brief is served; and

    (4) the appellee's reply brief, within 14 days after the appellant's response and reply brief is served, but at least 7 days before scheduled argument unless the district court or BAP, for good cause, allows a later filing.

Rule 8017. Brief of an Amicus Curiae

(a) During Initial Consideration of a Case on the Merits

(1) Applicability

This Rule 8017(a) governs amicus filings during a court's initial consideration of a case on the merits.

(2) When Permitted

The United States or its officer or agency or a state may file an amicus brief without the consent of the parties or leave of court. Any other amicus curiae may file a brief only by leave of court or if the brief states that all parties have consented to its filing, but a district court or BAP may prohibit the filing of or may strike an amicus brief that would result in a judge's disqualification. On its own motion, and with notice to all parties to an appeal, the district court or BAP may request a brief by an amicus curiae.

(3) Motion for Leave to File

The motion must be accompanied by the proposed brief and state:

(A) the movant's interest; and

(B) the reason why an amicus brief is desirable and why the matters asserted are relevant to the disposition of the appeal.

(4) Contents and Form

An amicus brief must comply with Rule 8015. In addition to the requirements of Rule 8015, the cover must identify the party or parties supported and indicate whether the brief supports affirmance or reversal. If an amicus curiae is a corporation, the brief must include a disclosure statement like that required of parties by Rule 8012. An amicus brief need not comply with Rule 8014, but must include the following:

(A) a table of contents, with page references;

(B) a table of authorities—cases (alphabetically arranged), statutes, and other authorities—with references to the pages of the brief where they are cited;

(C) a concise statement of the identity of the amicus curiae, its interest in the case, and the source of its authority to file;

(D) unless the amicus curiae is one listed in the first sentence of subdivision (a)(2), a statement that indicates whether:

(i) a party's counsel authored the brief in whole or in part;

(ii) a party or a party's counsel contributed money that was intended to fund preparing or submitting the brief; and

(iii) a person—other than the amicus curiae, its members, or its counsel—contributed money that was intended to fund preparing or submitting the brief and, if so, identifies each such person;

(E) an argument, which may be preceded by a summary and need not include a statement of the applicable standard of review; and

(F) a certificate of compliance, if required by Rule 8015.

(5) Length

Except by the district court's or BAP's permission, an amicus brief must be no more than one-half the maximum length authorized by these rules for a party's principal brief. If the court grants a party permission to file a longer brief, that extension does not affect the length of an amicus brief.

(6) Time for Filing

An amicus curiae must file its brief, accompanied by a motion for filing when necessary, no later than 7 days after the principal brief of the party being supported is filed. An amicus curiae that does not support either party must file its brief no later than 7 days after the appellant's principal brief is filed. The district court or BAP may grant leave for later filing, specifying the time within which an opposing party may answer.

(7) Reply Brief

Except by the district court's or BAP's permission, an amicus curiae may not file a reply brief.

(8) Oral Argument

An amicus curiae may participate in oral argument only with the district court's or BAP's permission.

(b) During Consideration of Whether to Grant Rehearing

(1) Applicability

This Rule 8017(b) governs amicus filings during a district court's or BAP's consideration of whether to grant rehearing, unless a local rule or order in a case provides otherwise.

(2) When Permitted

The United States or its officer or agency or a state may file an amicus brief without the consent of the parties or leave of court. Any other amicus curiae may file a brief only by leave of court.

(3) Motion for Leave to File

Rule 8017(a)(3) applies to a motion for leave.

(4) Contents, For, and Length

Rule 8017(a)(4) applies to the amicus brief. The brief must include a certificate under Rule 8015(h) and not exceed 2,600 words.

(5) Time for Filing

An amicus curiae supporting the motion for rehearing or supporting neither party must file its brief, accompanied by a motion for filing when necessary, no later than 7 days after the motion is filed. An amicus curiae opposing the motion for rehearing must file its brief, accompanied by a motion for filing when necessary, no later than the date set by the court for the response.

Rule 8018. Serving and Filing Briefs; Appendices

(a) Time to Serve and File a Brief

The following rules apply unless the district court or BAP by order in a particular case excuses the filing of briefs or specifies different time limits:

(1) The appellant must serve and file a brief within 30 days after the docketing of notice that the record has been transmitted or is available electronically.

(2) The appellee must serve and file a brief within 30 days after service of the appellant's brief.

(3) The appellant may serve and file a reply brief within 14 days after service of the appellee's brief, but a reply brief must be filed at least 7 days before scheduled argument unless the district court or BAP, for good cause, allows a later filing.

(4) If an appellant fails to file a brief on time or within an extended time authorized by the district court or BAP, an appellee may move to dismiss the appeal—or the district court or BAP, after notice, may dismiss the appeal on its own motion. An appellee who fails to file a brief will not be heard at oral argument unless the district court or BAP grants permission.

(b) Duty to Serve and File an Appendix to the Brief

(1) Appellant

Subject to subdivision (e) and Rule 8009(d), the appellant must serve and file with its principal brief excerpts of the record as an appendix. It must contain the following:

(A) the relevant entries in the bankruptcy docket;

(B) the complaint and answer, or other equivalent filings;

(C) the judgment, order, or decree from which the appeal is taken;

(D) any other orders, pleadings, jury instructions, findings, conclusions, or opinions relevant to the appeal;

(E) the notice of appeal; and

(F) any relevant transcript or portion of it.

(2) Appellee

The appellee may also serve and file with its brief an appendix that contains material required to be included by the appellant or relevant to the appeal or cross-appeal, but omitted by the appellant.

(3) Cross-Appellee

The appellant as cross-appellee may also serve and file with its response an appendix that contains material relevant to matters raised initially by the principal brief in the cross-appeal, but omitted by the cross-appellant.

(c) Format of the Appendix

The appendix must begin with a table of contents identifying the page at which each part begins. The relevant docket entries must follow the table of contents. Other parts of the record must follow chronologically. When pages from the transcript of proceedings are placed in the appendix, the transcript page numbers must be shown in brackets immediately before the included pages. Omissions in the text of documents or of the transcript must be indicated by asterisks. Immaterial formal matters (captions, subscriptions, acknowledgments, and the like) should be omitted.

(d) Exhibits

Exhibits designated for inclusion in the appendix may be reproduced in a separate volume or volumes, suitably indexed.

(e) Appeal on the Original Record Without an Appendix

The district court or BAP may, either by rule for all cases or classes of cases or by order in a particular case, dispense with the appendix and permit an appeal to proceed on the original record, with the submission of any relevant parts of the record that the district court or BAP orders the parties to file.

Rule 8018.1. District-Court Review of a Judgment that the Bankruptcy Court Lacked the Constitutional Authority to Enter

If, on appeal, a district court determines that the bankruptcy court did not have the power under Article III of the Constitution to enter the judgment, order, or decree appealed from, the district court may treat it as proposed findings of fact and conclusions of law.

Rule 8019. Oral Argument

(a) Party's Statement

Any party may file, or a district court or BAP may require, a statement explaining why oral argument should, or need not, be permitted.

(b) Presumption of Oral Argument and Exceptions

Oral argument must be allowed in every case unless the district judge—or all the BAP judges assigned to hear the appeal—examine the briefs and record and determine that oral argument is unnecessary because

> **(1)** the appeal is frivolous;
>
> **(2)** the dispositive issue or issues have been authoritatively decided; or
>
> **(3)** the facts and legal arguments are adequately presented in the briefs and record, and the decisional process would not be significantly aided by oral argument.

(c) Notice of Argument; Postponement

The district court or BAP must advise all parties of the date, time, and place for oral argument, and the time allowed for each side. A motion to postpone the argument or to allow longer argument must be filed reasonably in advance of the hearing date.

(d) Order and Contents of Argument

The appellant opens and concludes the argument. Counsel must not read at length from briefs, the record, or authorities.

(e) Cross-Appeals and Separate Appeals

If there is a cross-appeal, Rule 8016(b) determines which party is the appellant and which is the appellee for the purposes of oral argument. Unless the district court or BAP directs otherwise, a cross-appeal or separate appeal must be argued when the initial appeal is argued. Separate parties should avoid duplicative argument.

(f) Nonappearance of a Party

If the appellee fails to appear for argument, the district court or BAP may hear the appellant's argument. If the appellant fails to appear for argument, the district court or BAP may hear the appellee's argument. If neither party appears, the case will be decided on the briefs unless the district court or BAP orders otherwise.

(g) Submission on Briefs

The parties may agree to submit a case for decision on the briefs, but the district court or BAP may direct that the case be argued.

(h) Use of Physical Exhibits at Argument; Removal

Counsel intending to use physical exhibits other than documents at the argument must arrange to place them in the courtroom on the day of the argument before the court convenes. After the argument, counsel must remove the exhibits from the courtroom unless the district court or BAP directs otherwise. The clerk may destroy or dispose of the exhibits if counsel does not reclaim them within a reasonable time after the clerk gives notice to remove them.

Rule 8020. Frivolous Appeal and Other Misconduct

(a) Frivolous Appeal—Damages and Costs

If the district court or BAP determines that an appeal is frivolous, it may, after a separately filed motion or notice from the court and reasonable opportunity to respond, award just damages and single or double costs to the appellee.

(b) Other Misconduct

The district court or BAP may discipline or sanction an attorney or party appearing before it for other misconduct, including failure to comply with any court order. First, however, the court must afford the attorney or party reasonable notice, an opportunity to show cause to the contrary, and, if requested, a hearing.

Rule 8021. Costs

(a) Against Whom Assessed

The following rules apply unless the law provides or the district court or BAP orders otherwise:

    (1) if an appeal is dismissed, costs are taxed against the appellant, unless the parties agree otherwise;

    (2) if a judgment, order, or decree is affirmed, costs are taxed against the appellant;

    (3) if a judgment, order, or decree is reversed, costs are taxed against the appellee;

    (4) if a judgment, order, or decree is affirmed or reversed in part, modified, or vacated, costs are taxed only as the district court or BAP orders.

(b) Costs for and Against the United States

Costs for or against the United States, its agency, or its officer may be assessed under subdivision (a) only if authorized by law.

(c) Costs on Appeal Taxable in the Bankruptcy Court

The following costs on appeal are taxable in the bankruptcy court for the benefit of the party entitled to costs under this rule:

    (1) the production of any required copies of a brief, appendix, exhibit, or the record;

    (2) the preparation and transmission of the record;

    (3) the reporter's transcript, if needed to determine the appeal;

    (4) premiums paid for a bond or other security to preserve rights pending appeal; and

    (5) the fee for filing the notice of appeal.

(d) Bill of Costs; Objections

A party who wants costs taxed must, within 14 days after entry of judgment on appeal, file with the bankruptcy clerk and serve an itemized and verified bill of costs. Objections must be filed within 14 days after service of the bill of costs, unless the bankruptcy court extends the time.

Rule 8022. Motion for Rehearing

(a) Time to File; Contents; Response; Action by the District Court or BAP if Granted

    (1) Time

    Unless the time is shortened or extended by order or local rule, any motion for rehearing by the district court or BAP must be filed within 14 days after entry of judgment on appeal.

    (2) Contents

    The motion must state with particularity each point of law or fact that the movant believes the district court or BAP has overlooked or misapprehended and must argue in support of the motion. Oral argument is not permitted.

(3) Response

Unless the district court or BAP requests, no response to a motion for rehearing is permitted. But ordinarily, rehearing will not be granted in the absence of such a request.

(4) Action by the District Court or BAP

If a motion for rehearing is granted, the district court or BAP may do any of the following:

    (A) make a final disposition of the appeal without re-argument;

    (B) restore the case to the calendar for reargument or re-submission; or

    (C) issue any other appropriate order.

(b) Form of the Motion; Length

The motion must comply in form with Rule 8013(f)(1) and (2). Copies must be served and filed as provided by Rule 8011. Except by the district court's or BAP's permission:

    (1) a motion for rehearing produced using a computer must include a certificate under Rule 8015(h) and not exceed 3,900 words; and

    (2) a handwritten or typewritten motion must not exceed 15 pages.

Rule 8023. Voluntary Dismissal

(a) Stipulated Dismissal

The clerk of the district court or BAP must dismiss an appeal if the parties file a signed dismissal agreement specifying how costs are to be paid and pay any fees that are due.

(b) Appellant's Motion to Dismiss

An appeal may be dismissed on the appellant's motion on terms agreed to by the parties or fixed by the district court or BAP.

(c) Other Relief

A court order is required for any relief under Rule 8023(a) or (b) beyond the dismissal of an appeal—including approving a settlement, vacating an action of the bankruptcy court, or remanding the case to it.

(d) Court Approval

This rule does not alter the legal requirements governing court approval of a settlement, payment, or other consideration.

Rule 8024. Clerk's Duties on Disposition of the Appeal

(a) Judgment on Appeal

The district or BAP clerk must prepare, sign, and enter the judgment after receiving the court's opinion or, if there is no opinion, as the court instructs. Noting the judgment on the docket constitutes entry of judgment.

(b) Notice of a Judgment

Immediately upon the entry of a judgment, the district or BAP clerk must:

    (1) transmit a notice of the entry to each party to the appeal, to the United States trustee, and to the bankruptcy clerk, together with a copy of any opinion; and

    (2) note the date of the transmission on the docket.

(c) Returning Physical Items

If any physical items were transmitted as the record on appeal, they must be returned to the bankruptcy clerk on disposition of the appeal.

Rule 8025. Stay of a District Court or BAP Judgment

(a) Automatic Stay of Judgment on Appeal

Unless the district court or BAP orders otherwise, its judgment is stayed for 14 days after entry.

(b) Stay Pending Appeal to the Court of Appeals

(1) In General

On a party's motion and notice to all other parties to the appeal, the district court or BAP may stay its judgment pending an appeal to the court of appeals.

(2) Time Limit

The stay must not exceed 30 days after the judgment is entered, except for cause shown.

(3) Stay Continued

If, before a stay expires, the party who obtained the stay appeals to the court of appeals, the stay continues until final disposition by the court of appeals.

(4) Bond or Other Security

A bond or other security may be required as a condition for granting or continuing a stay of the judgment. A bond or other security may be required if a trustee obtains a stay, but not if a stay is obtained by the United States or its officer or agency or at the direction of any department of the United States government.

(c) Automatic Stay of an Order, Judgment, or Decree of a Bankruptcy Court

If the district court or BAP enters a judgment affirming an order, judgment, or decree of the bankruptcy court, a stay of the district court's or BAP's judgment automatically stays the bankruptcy court's order, judgment, or decree for the duration of the appellate stay.

(d) Power of a Court of Appeals Not Limited

This rule does not limit the power of a court of appeals or any of its judges to do the following:

(1) stay a judgment pending appeal;

(2) stay proceedings while an appeal is pending;

(3) suspend, modify, restore, vacate, or grant a stay or an injunction while an appeal is pending; or

(4) issue any order appropriate to preserve the status quo or the effectiveness of any judgment to be entered.

Rule 8026. Rules by Circuit Councils and District Courts; Procedure When There is No Controlling Law

(a) Local Rules by Circuit Councils and District Courts

(1) Adopting Local Rules

A circuit council that has authorized a BAP under 28 U.S.C. § 158(b) may make and amend rules governing the practice and procedure on appeal from a judgment, order, or decree of a bankruptcy court to the BAP. A district court may make and amend rules governing the practice and procedure on appeal from a judgment, order, or decree of a bankruptcy court to the district court. Local rules must be consistent with, but not duplicative of, Acts of Congress and these Part

VIII rules. Rule 83 F.R.Civ.P. governs the procedure for making and amending rules to govern appeals.

(2) Numbering

Local rules must conform to any uniform numbering system prescribed by the Judicial Conference of the United States.

(3) Limitation on Imposing Requirements of Form

A local rule imposing a requirement of form must not be enforced in a way that causes a party to lose any right because of a nonwillful failure to comply.

(b) Procedure When There Is No Controlling Law

(1) In General

A district court or BAP may regulate practice in any manner consistent with federal law, applicable federal rules, the Official Forms, and local rules.

(2) Limitation on Sanctions

No sanction or other disadvantage may be imposed for noncompliance with any requirement not in federal law, applicable federal rules, the Official Forms, or local rules unless the alleged violator has been furnished in the particular case with actual notice of the requirement.

Rule 8027. Notice of a Mediation Procedure

If the district court or BAP has a mediation procedure applicable to bankruptcy appeals, the clerk must notify the parties promptly after docketing the appeal of:

(a) the requirements of the mediation procedure; and

(b) any effect the mediation procedure has on the time to file briefs.

Rule 8028. Suspension of Rules in Part VIII

In the interest of expediting decision or for other cause in a particular case, the district court or BAP, or where appropriate the court of appeals, may suspend the requirements or provisions of the rules in Part VIII, except Rules 8001, 8002, 8003, 8004, 8005, 8006, 8007, 8012, 8020, 8024, 8025, 8026, and 8028.

PART IX

GENERAL PROVISIONS

Rule 9001. General Definitions

The definitions of words and phrases in §§ 101, 902, 1101, and 1502 of the Code, and the rules of construction in § 102, govern their use in these rules. In addition, the following words and phrases used in these rules have the meanings indicated:

   (1) "Bankruptcy clerk" means a clerk appointed pursuant to 28 U.S.C. § 156(b).

(2) "Bankruptcy Code" or "Code" means title 11 of the United States Code.

(3) "Clerk" means bankruptcy clerk, if one has been appointed, otherwise clerk of the district court.

(4) "Court" or "judge" means the judicial officer before whom a case or proceeding is pending.

(5) "Debtor." When any act is required by these rules to be performed by a debtor or when it is necessary to compel attendance of a debtor for examination and the debtor is not a natural person: (A) if the debtor is a corporation, "debtor" includes, if designated by the court, any or all of its officers, members of its board of directors or trustees or of a similar controlling body, a controlling stockholder or member, or any other person in control; (B) if the debtor is a partnership, "debtor" includes any or all of its general partners or, if designated by the court, any other person in control.

(6) "Firm" includes a partnership or professional corporation of attorneys or accountants.

(7) "Judgment" means any appealable order.

(8) "Mail" means first class, postage prepaid.

(9) "Notice provider" means any entity approved by the Administrative Office of the United States Courts to give notice to creditors under Rule 2002(g)(4).

(10) "Regular associate" means any attorney regularly employed by, associated with, or counsel to an individual or firm.

(11) "Trustee" includes a debtor in possession in a chapter 11 case.

(12) "United States trustee" includes an assistant United States trustee and any designee of the United States trustee.

CROSS REFERENCES

Clerk defined, see Fed. R. Bankr. P. 9002.

Judgment defined, see Fed. R. Bankr. P. 7054 and 9002.

Rule 9002. Meanings of Words in the Federal Rules of Civil Procedure When Applicable to Cases Under the Code

The following words and phrases used in the Federal Rules of Civil Procedure made applicable to cases under the Code by these rules have the meanings indicated unless they are inconsistent with the context:

(1) "Action" or "civil action" means an adversary proceeding or, when appropriate, a contested petition, or proceedings to vacate an order for relief or to determine any other contested matter.

(2) "Appeal" means an appeal as provided by 28 U.S.C. § 158.

(3) "Clerk" or "clerk of the district court" means the court officer responsible for the bankruptcy records in the district.

(4) "District court," "trial court," "court," "district judge," or "judge" means bankruptcy judge if the case or proceeding is pending before a bankruptcy judge.

(5) "Judgment" includes any order appealable to an appellate court.

CROSS REFERENCES

Contested matters, see Fed. R. Bankr. P. 9014.

Judgment defined, see Fed. R. Civ. P. 54.

One form of action, see Fed. R. Civ. P. 2.

Procedural rules which govern adversary proceedings, see Fed. R. Bankr. P. 7001 et seq..

Rule 9003. Prohibition of Ex Parte Contacts

(a) General prohibition

Except as otherwise permitted by applicable law, any examiner, any party in interest, and any attorney, accountant, or employee of a party in interest shall refrain from ex parte meetings and communications with the court concerning matters affecting a particular case or proceeding.

(b) United States trustee

Except as otherwise permitted by applicable law, the United States trustee and assistants to and employees or agents of the United States trustee shall refrain from ex parte meetings and communications with the court concerning matters affecting a particular case or proceeding. This rule does not preclude communications with the court to discuss general problems of administration and improvement of bankruptcy administration, including the operation of the United States trustee system.

CROSS REFERENCES

Disqualification of judge, see Fed. R. Bankr. P. 5004.

Rule 9004. General Requirements of Form

(a) Legibility; abbreviations

All petitions, pleadings, schedules and other papers shall be clearly legible. Abbreviations in common use in the English language may be used.

(b) Caption

Each paper filed shall contain a caption setting forth the name of the court, the title of the case, the bankruptcy docket number, and a brief designation of the character of the paper.

Rule 9005. Harmless Error

Rule 61 F.R.Civ.P. applies in cases under the Code. When appropriate, the court may order the correction of any error or defect or the cure of any omission which does not affect substantial rights.

Rule 9005.1. Constitutional Challenge to a Statute—Notice, Certification, and Intervention

Rule 5.1 F.R.Civ.P. applies in cases under the Code.

Rule 9006. Computing and Extending Time; Time for Motion Papers

(a) Computing time

The following rules apply in computing any time period specified in these rules, in the Federal Rules of Civil Procedure, in any local rule or court order, or in any statute that does not specify a method of computing time.

(1) Period stated in days or a longer unit

When the period is stated in days or a longer unit of time:

(A) exclude the day of the event that triggers the period;

(B) count every day, including intermediate Saturdays, Sundays, and legal holidays; and

(C) include the last day of the period, but if the last day is a Saturday, Sunday, or legal holiday, the period continues to run until the end of the next day that is not a Saturday, Sunday, or legal holiday.

(2) Period stated in hours

When the period is stated in hours:

(A) begin counting immediately on the occurrence of the event that triggers the period;

(B) count every hour, including hours during intermediate Saturdays, Sundays, and legal holidays; and

(C) if the period would end on a Saturday, Sunday, or legal holiday, then continue the period until the same time on the next day that is not a Saturday, Sunday, or legal holiday.

(3) Inaccessibility of clerk's office

Unless the court orders otherwise, if the clerk's office is inaccessible:

(A) on the last day for filing under Rule 9006(a)(1), then the time for filing is extended to the first accessible day that is not a Saturday, Sunday, or legal holiday; or

(B) during the last hour for filing under Rule 9006(a)(2), then the time for filing is extended to the same time on the first accessible day that is not a Saturday, Sunday, or legal holiday.

(4) "Last day" defined

Unless a different time is set by a statute, local rule, or order in the case, the last day ends:

(A) for electronic filing, at midnight in the court's time zone; and

(B) for filing by other means, when the clerk's office is scheduled to close.

(5) "Next day" defined

The "next day" is determined by continuing to count forward when the period is measured after an event and backward when measured before an event.

(6) "Legal holiday" defined

"Legal holiday" means:

(A) the day set aside by statute for observing New Year's Day, Martin Luther King Jr.'s Birthday, Washington's Birthday, Memorial Day, Independence Day, Labor Day, Columbus Day, Veterans' Day, Thanksgiving Day, or Christmas Day;

(B) any day declared a holiday by the President or Congress; and

(C) for periods that are measured after an event, any other day declared a holiday by the state where the district court is located. (In this rule, "state" includes the District of Columbia and any United States commonwealth or territory.)

(b) Enlargement

(1) In general

Except as provided in paragraphs (2) and (3) of this subdivision, when an act is required or allowed to be done at or within a specified period by these rules or by a notice given thereunder or by order of court, the court for cause shown may at any time in its discretion (1) with or without motion or notice order the period enlarged if the request therefor is made before the expiration of the period originally prescribed or as extended by a previous order or (2) on motion made after the expiration of the specified period permit the act to be done where the failure to act was the result of excusable neglect.

(2) Enlargement not permitted

The court may not enlarge the time for taking action under Rules 1007(d), 2003(a) and (d), 7052, 9023, and 9024.

(3) Enlargement governed by other rules

The court may enlarge the time for taking action under Rules 1006(b)(2), 1017(e), 3002(c), 4003(b), 4004(a), 4007(c), 4008(a), 8002, and 9033, only to the extent and under the conditions stated in those rules. In addition, the court may enlarge the time to file the statement required under Rule 1007(b)(7), and to file schedules and statements in a small business case under § 1116(3) of the Code, only to the extent and under the conditions stated in Rule 1007(c).

(c) Reduction

(1) In general

Except as provided in paragraph (2) of this subdivision, when an act is required or allowed to be done at or within a specified time by these rules or by a notice given thereunder or by order of court, the court for cause shown may in its discretion with or without motion or notice order the period reduced.

(2) Reduction not permitted

The court may not reduce the time for taking action under Rules 2002(a)(7), 2003(a), 3002(c), 3014, 3015, 4001(b)(2), (c)(2), 4003(a), 4004(a), 4007(c), 4008(a), 8002, and 9033(b). In addition, the court may not reduce the time under Rule 1007(c) to file the statement required by Rule 1007(b)(7).

(d) Motions papers

A written motion, other than one which may be heard ex parte, and notice of any hearing shall be served not later than seven days before the time specified for such hearing, unless a different period is fixed by these rules or by order of the court. Such an order may for cause shown be made on ex parte application. When a motion is supported by affidavit, the affidavit shall be served with the motion. Except as otherwise provided in Rule 9023, any written response shall be served not later than one day before the hearing, unless the court permits otherwise.

(e) Time of service

Service of process and service of any paper other than process or of notice by mail is complete on mailing.

(f) Additional time after service by mail or under Rule 5(b)(2)(D), (E), or (F) F.R.Civ.P.

When there is a right or requirement to act or undertake some proceedings within a prescribed period after being served and that service is by mail or under Rule 5(b)(2)(D) (leaving with the clerk) or (F) (other means consented to) F.R.Civ.P., three days are added after the prescribed period would otherwise expire under Rule 9006(a).

(g) Grain storage facility cases

This rule shall not limit the court's authority under § 557 of the Code to enter orders governing procedures in cases in which the debtor is an owner or operator of a grain storage facility.

CROSS REFERENCES

Completion of service by mail upon mailing, see Fed. R. Civ. P. 5.

Motions, form and service, see Fed. R. Bankr. P. 9013.

Time, see Fed. R. Civ. P. 6.

Rule 9007. General Authority to Regulate Notices

When notice is to be given under these rules, the court shall designate, if not otherwise specified herein, the time within which, the entities to whom, and the form and manner in which the notice shall be given. When feasible, the court may order any notices under these rules to be combined.

CROSS REFERENCES

Construction of phrase "after notice and a hearing", see 11 USCA § 102.

Notice as is appropriate of order for relief, see 11 USCA § 342.

Rule 9008. Service or Notice by Publication

Whenever these rules require or authorize service or notice by publication, the court shall, to the extent not otherwise specified in these rules, determine the form and manner thereof, including the newspaper or other medium to be used and the number of publications.

CROSS REFERENCES

Construction of phrase "after notice and a hearing", see 11 USCA § 102.

Notice as is appropriate of order for relief, see 11 USCA § 342.

Rule 9009. Forms

(a) Official Forms

The Official Forms prescribed by the Judicial Conference of the United States shall be used without alteration, except as otherwise provided in these rules, in a particular Official Form, or in the national instructions for a particular Official Form. Official Forms may be modified to permit minor changes not affecting wording or the order of presenting information, including changes that:

(1) expand the prescribed areas for responses in order to permit complete responses;

(2) delete space not needed for responses; or

(3) delete items requiring detail in a question or category if the filer indicates—either by checking "no" or "none" or by stating in words—that there is nothing to report on that question or category.

(b) Director's Forms

The Director of the Administrative Office of the United States Courts may issue additional forms for use under the Code.

(c) Construction

The forms shall be construed to be consistent with these rules and the Code.

CROSS REFERENCES

Correction of harmless errors or cure of harmless omissions, see Fed. R. Bankr. P. 9005.

Rule 9010. Representation and Appearances; Powers of Attorney

(a) Authority to act personally or by attorney

A debtor, creditor, equity security holder, indenture trustee, committee or other party may (1) appear in a case under the Code and act either in the entity's own behalf or by an attorney authorized to practice in the court, and (2) perform any act not constituting the practice of law, by an authorized agent, attorney in fact, or proxy.

(b) Notice of appearance

An attorney appearing for a party in a case under the Code shall file a notice of appearance with the attorney's name, office address and telephone number, unless the attorney's appearance is otherwise noted in the record.

(c) Power of attorney

The authority of any agent, attorney in fact, or proxy to represent a creditor for any purpose other than the execution and filing of a proof of claim or the acceptance or rejection of a plan shall be evidenced by a power of attorney conforming substantially to the appropriate Official Form. The execution of any such power of attorney shall be acknowledged before one of the officers enumerated in 28 U.S.C. § 459, § 953, Rule 9012, or a person authorized to administer oaths under the laws of the state where the oath is administered.

CROSS REFERENCES

Ex parte relief from automatic stay, see Fed. R. Bankr. P. 4001.

Payment of dividends to persons authorized to receive them by power of attorney executed and filed in accordance with this rule, see Fed. R. Bankr. P. 3009.

Rule 9011. Signing of Papers; Representations to the Court; Sanctions; Verification and Copies of Papers

(a) Signing of papers

Every petition, pleading, written motion, and other paper, except a list, schedule, or statement, or amendments thereto, shall be signed by at least one attorney of record in the attorney's individual name. A party who is not represented by an attorney shall sign all papers. Each paper shall state the signer's address and telephone number, if any. An unsigned paper shall be stricken unless omission of the signature is corrected promptly after being called to the attention of the attorney or party.

(b) Representations to the court

By presenting to the court (whether by signing, filing, submitting, or later advocating) a petition, pleading, written motion, or other paper, an attorney or unrepresented party is certifying that to the best of the person's knowledge, information, and belief, formed after an inquiry reasonable under the circumstances,[1]—

 (1) it is not being presented for any improper purpose, such as to harass or to cause unnecessary delay or needless increase in the cost of litigation;

 (2) the claims, defenses, and other legal contentions therein are warranted by existing law or by a nonfrivolous argument for the extension, modification, or reversal of existing law or the establishment of new law;

 (3) the allegations and other factual contentions have evidentiary support or, if specifically so identified, are likely to have evidentiary support after a reasonable opportunity for further investigation or discovery; and

 (4) the denials of factual contentions are warranted on the evidence or, if specifically so identified, are reasonably based on a lack of information or belief.

(c) Sanctions

If, after notice and a reasonable opportunity to respond, the court determines that subdivision (b) has been violated, the court may, subject to the conditions stated below, impose an appropriate

---

[1] So in original. The comma probably should not appear.

sanction upon the attorneys, law firms, or parties that have violated subdivision (b) or are responsible for the violation.

(1) How initiated

(A) By motion

A motion for sanctions under this rule shall be made separately from other motions or requests and shall describe the specific conduct alleged to violate subdivision (b). It shall be served as provided in Rule 7004. The motion for sanctions may not be filed with or presented to the court unless, within 21 days after service of the motion (or such other period as the court may prescribe), the challenged paper, claim, defense, contention, allegation, or denial is not withdrawn or appropriately corrected, except that this limitation shall not apply if the conduct alleged is the filing of a petition in violation of subdivision (b). If warranted, the court may award to the party prevailing on the motion the reasonable expenses and attorney's fees incurred in presenting or opposing the motion. Absent exceptional circumstances, a law firm shall be held jointly responsible for violations committed by its partners, associates, and employees.

(B) On court's initiative

On its own initiative, the court may enter an order describing the specific conduct that appears to violate subdivision (b) and directing an attorney, law firm, or party to show cause why it has not violated subdivision (b) with respect thereto.

(2) Nature of sanction; limitations

A sanction imposed for violation of this rule shall be limited to what is sufficient to deter repetition of such conduct or comparable conduct by others similarly situated. Subject to the limitations in subparagraphs (A) and (B), the sanction may consist of, or include, directives of a nonmonetary nature, an order to pay a penalty into court, or, if imposed on motion and warranted for effective deterrence, an order directing payment to the movant of some or all of the reasonable attorneys' fees and other expenses incurred as a direct result of the violation.

> **(A)** Monetary sanctions may not be awarded against a represented party for a violation of subdivision (b)(2).

> **(B)** Monetary sanctions may not be awarded on the court's initiative unless the court issues its order to show cause before a voluntary dismissal or settlement of the claims made by or against the party which is, or whose attorneys are, to be sanctioned.

(3) Order

When imposing sanctions, the court shall describe the conduct determined to constitute a violation of this rule and explain the basis for the sanction imposed.

(d) Inapplicability to discovery

Subdivisions (a) through (c) of this rule do not apply to disclosures and discovery requests, responses, objections, and motions that are subject to the provisions of Rules 7026 through 7037.

(e) Verification

Except as otherwise specifically provided by these rules, papers filed in a case under the Code need not be verified. Whenever verification is required by these rules, an unsworn declaration as provided in 28 U.S.C. § 1746 satisfies the requirement of verification.

(f) Copies of signed or verified papers

When these rules require copies of a signed or verified paper, it shall suffice if the original is signed or verified and the copies are conformed to the original.

Affidavit in support of—

> Complaint seeking temporary restraining order, see Fed. R. Bankr. P. 7065.

> Motion for ex parte relief from stay, see Fed. R. Bankr. P. 4001.

Verification of—

> Complaint seeking temporary restraining order, see Fed. R. Bankr. P. 7065.

> List of multiple proxies and acquisition statement, see Fed. R. Bankr. P. 2006.

> Motions for ex parte relief from stay, see Fed. R. Bankr. P. 4001.

> Petitions and accompanying papers, see Fed. R. Bankr. P. 1008.

Pleadings allowed; form of motions, see Fed. R. Civ. P. 7.

Signing of pleadings, see Fed. R. Civ. P. 11.

Statements in pleadings subject to obligations set forth in rule 11, see Fed. R. Civ. P. 8.

Rule 9012. Oaths and Affirmations

(a) Persons authorized to administer oaths

The following persons may administer oaths and affirmations and take acknowledgments: a bankruptcy judge, clerk, deputy clerk, United States trustee, officer authorized to administer oaths in proceedings before the courts of the United States or under the laws of the state where the oath is to be taken, or a diplomatic or consular officer of the United States in any foreign country.

(b) Affirmation in lieu of oath

When in a case under the Code an oath is required to be taken, a solemn affirmation may be accepted in lieu thereof.

Acknowledgment of power of attorney, see Fed. R. Bankr. P. 9010.

Administration of oaths and acknowledgments by—

> Clerks of court, see 28 USCA § 953.

> Justices or judges, see 28 USCA § 459.

Affirmation in lieu of oath, see Fed. R. Civ. P. 43.

Oath defined to include affirmation, see 1 USCA § 1.

Oath or affirmation of witnesses, see Fed. R. Evid. 603.

Rule 9013. Motions: Form and Service

A request for an order, except when an application is authorized by the rules, shall be by written motion, unless made during a hearing. The motion shall state with particularity the grounds therefor, and shall set forth the relief or order sought. Every written motion, other than one which may be considered ex parte, shall be served by the moving party within the time determined under Rule 9006(d). The moving party shall serve the motion on:

(a) the trustee or debtor in possession and on those entities specified by these rules; or

(b) the entities the court directs if these rules do not require service or specify the entities to be served.

Rule 9014. Contested Matters

(a) Motion. In a contested matter not otherwise governed by these rules, relief shall be requested by motion, and reasonable notice and opportunity for hearing shall be afforded the party against whom relief is sought. No response is required under this rule unless the court directs otherwise.

(b) Service. The motion shall be served in the manner provided for service of a summons and complaint by Rule 7004 and within the time determined under Rule 9006(d). Any written response to the motion shall be served within the time determined under Rule 9006(d). Any paper served after the motion shall be served in the manner provided by Rule 5(b) F. R. Civ. P.

(c) Application of Part VII rules. Except as otherwise provided in this rule, and unless the court directs otherwise, the following rules shall apply: 7009, 7017, 7021, 7025, 7026, 7028–7037, 7041, 7042, 7052, 7054–7056, 7064, 7069, and 7071. The following subdivisions of Fed. R. Civ. P. 26, as incorporated by Rule 7026, shall not apply in a contested matter unless the court directs otherwise: 26(a)(1) (mandatory disclosure), 26(a)(2) (disclosures regarding expert testimony) and 26(a)(3) (additional pre-trial disclosure), and 26(f) (mandatory meeting before scheduling conference/ discovery plan). An entity that desires to perpetuate testimony may proceed in the same manner as provided in Rule 7027 for the taking of a deposition before an adversary proceeding. The court may at any stage in a particular matter direct that one or more of the other rules in Part VII shall apply. The court shall give the parties notice of any order issued under this paragraph to afford them a reasonable opportunity to comply with the procedures prescribed by the order.

(d) Testimony of witnesses. Testimony of witnesses with respect to disputed material factual issues shall be taken in the same manner as testimony in an adversary proceeding.

(e) Attendance of witnesses. The court shall provide procedures that enable parties to ascertain at a reasonable time before any scheduled hearing whether the hearing will be an evidentiary hearing at which witnesses may testify.

CROSS REFERENCES

Contested matters—

> Assumption, rejection, or assignment of executory contract or unexpired lease, or proceeding to require trustee to act, see Fed. R. Bankr. P. 6006.

> Avoidance by debtor of transfers of exempt property, see Fed. R. Bankr. P. 4003.

> Dismissal or conversion to another chapter, see Fed. R. Bankr. P. 1017.

> Objection to confirmation of plan, see Fed. R. Bankr. P. 3020.

> Relief from automatic stay, see Fed. R. Bankr. P. 4001.

> Request for use of cash collateral, see Fed. R. Bankr. P. 4001.

Effect of amendment of Federal Rules of Civil Procedure, see Fed. R. Bankr. P. 9032.

Meanings of words in Federal Rules of Civil Procedure when applicable, see Fed. R. Bankr. P. 9002.

Motions; form and service, see Fed. R. Bankr. P. 9013.

Rule 9015. Jury Trials

(a) Applicability of certain Federal Rules of Civil Procedure

Rules 38, 39, 47–49, and 51, F.R.Civ.P., and Rule 81(c) F.R.Civ.P. insofar as it applies to jury trials, apply in cases and proceedings, except that a demand made under Rule 38(b) F.R.Civ.P. shall be filed in accordance with Rule 5005.

(b) Consent to have trial conducted by bankruptcy judge

If the right to a jury trial applies, a timely demand has been filed pursuant to Rule 38(b) F.R.Civ.P., and the bankruptcy judge has been specially designated to conduct the jury trial, the parties may consent to have a jury trial conducted by a bankruptcy judge under 28 U.S.C. § 157(e) by jointly or separately filing a statement of consent within any applicable time limits specified by local rule.

(c) Applicability of Rule 50 F.R.Civ.P.

Rule 50 F.R.Civ.P. applies in cases and proceedings, except that any renewed motion for judgment or request for a new trial shall be filed no later than 14 days after the entry of judgment.

Rule 9016.   Subpoena

Rule 45 F.R.Civ.P. applies in cases under the Code.

CROSS REFERENCES

Compelling attendance of witnesses by use of subpoena—

Deposition upon oral examination, see Fed. R. Bankr. P. 7030.

Deposition upon written questions, see Fed. R. Bankr. P. 7031.

Examination of debtor—

Apprehension and removal of debtor to compel attendance, see Fed. R. Bankr. P. 2005.

Compelling attendance for examination and production of documentary evidence, see Fed. R. Bankr. P. 2004.

Rule 9017.   Evidence

The Federal Rules of Evidence and Rules 43, 44 and 44.1 F.R.Civ.P. apply in cases under the Code.

CROSS REFERENCES

Applicability of rules to proceedings and cases under this title, see Fed. R. Evid. 1101.

Rule 9018.   Secret, Confidential, Scandalous, or Defamatory Matter

On motion or on its own initiative, with or without notice, the court may make any order which justice requires (1) to protect the estate or any entity in respect of a trade secret or other confidential research, development, or commercial information, (2) to protect any entity against scandalous or defamatory matter contained in any paper filed in a case under the Code, or (3) to protect governmental matters that are made confidential by statute or regulation. If an order is entered under this rule without notice, any entity affected thereby may move to vacate or modify the order, and after a hearing on notice the court shall determine the motion.

CROSS REFERENCES

Motion to strike scandalous matter, see Fed. R. Civ. P. 12.

Motions; form and service, see Fed. R. Bankr. P. 9013.

Protective orders, see Fed. R. Civ. P. 26.

Rule 9019. Compromise and Arbitration

(a) Compromise

On motion by the trustee and after notice and a hearing, the court may approve a compromise or settlement. Notice shall be given to creditors, the United States trustee, the debtor, and indenture trustees as provided in Rule 2002 and to any other entity as the court may direct.

(b) Authority to compromise or settle controversies within classes

After a hearing on such notice as the court may direct, the court may fix a class or classes of controversies and authorize the trustee to compromise or settle controversies within such class or classes without further hearing or notice.

(c) Arbitration

On stipulation of the parties to any controversy affecting the estate the court may authorize the matter to be submitted to final and binding arbitration.

CROSS REFERENCES

Motions; form and service, see Fed. R. Bankr. P. 9013.

Rule 9020. Contempt Proceedings

Rule 9014 governs a motion for an order of contempt made by the United States trustee or a party in interest.

CROSS REFERENCES

Contempt, see 18 USCA §§ 401 et seq. and 3691 et seq.

Criminal contempt, see Fed. R. Crim. P. 42.

Power of court to punish persons for contempt, see 11 USCA § 105.

Rule 9021. Entry of Judgment

A judgment or order is effective when entered under Rule 5003.

CROSS REFERENCES

Entry of judgment, see Fed. R. Civ. P. 58.

Findings by court, see Fed. R. Bankr. P. 7052.

Judgments rendered by district court—

    Effect as lien on local property, see 28 USCA § 1962.

    Interest allowed on money judgment, see 28 USCA § 1961.

    Registration of final judgments in other districts, see 28 USCA § 1963.

Rule 9022. Notice of Judgment or Order

(a) Judgment or order of bankruptcy judge

Immediately on the entry of a judgment or order the clerk shall serve a notice of entry in the manner provided in Rule 5(b) F.R.Civ.P. on the contesting parties and on other entities as the court directs. Unless the case is a chapter 9 municipality case, the clerk shall forthwith transmit to the United States trustee a copy of the judgment or order. Service of the notice shall be noted in the docket. Lack of notice of the entry does not affect the time to appeal or relieve or authorize the court to relieve a party for failure to appeal within the time allowed, except as permitted in Rule 8002.

(b) Judgment or order of district judge

Notice of a judgment or order entered by a district judge is governed by Rule 77(d) F.R.Civ.P. Unless the case is a chapter 9 municipality case, the clerk shall forthwith transmit to the United States trustee a copy of a judgment or order entered by a district judge.

CROSS REFERENCES

Entry of judgment; district court record of judgment, see Fed. R. Bankr. P. 9021.

Rule 9023. New Trials; Amendment of Judgments

Except as provided in this rule and Rule 3008, Rule 59 F.R.Civ.P. applies in cases under the Code. A motion for a new trial or to alter or amend a judgment shall be filed, and a court may on its own order a new trial, no later than 14 days after entry of judgment. In some circumstances, Rule 8008 governs post-judgment motion practice after an appeal has been docketed and is pending.

CROSS REFERENCES

Amendment of findings by court, see Fed. R. Bankr. P. 7052.

Effect of motion under this rule on time for appeal, see Fed. R. Bankr. P. 8002.

Enlargement of time for motion for new trial not permitted, see Fed. R. Bankr. P. 9006.

Time for service of opposing affidavits to motion for new trial, see Fed. R. Bankr. P. 9006.

Rule 9024. Relief From Judgment or Order

Rule 60 F.R.Civ.P. applies in cases under the Code except that (1) a motion to reopen a case under the Code or for the reconsideration of an order allowing or disallowing a claim against the estate entered without a contest is not subject to the one year limitation prescribed in Rule 60(c), (2) a complaint to revoke a discharge in a chapter 7 liquidation case may be filed only within the time allowed by § 727(e) of the Code, and (3) a complaint to revoke an order confirming a plan may be filed only within the time allowed by § 1144, § 1230, or § 1330. In some circumstances, Rule 8008 governs post-judgment motion practice after an appeal has been docketed and is pending.

CROSS REFERENCES

Enlargement of time for motion for relief from judgment or order not permitted, see Fed. R. Bankr. P. 9006.

Motions; form and service, see Fed. R. Bankr. P. 9013.

Reconsideration of allowance or disallowance of claims, see Fed. R. Bankr. P. 3008.

Reopening cases, see Fed. R. Bankr. P. 5010.

Revocation of discharge under individual debt adjustment plan, see 11 USCA § 1328.

Setting aside judgment by default, see Fed. R. Bankr. P. 7055.

Rule 9025. Security: Proceedings Against Security Providers

Whenever the Code or these rules require or permit a party to give security, and security is given with one or more security providers, each provider submits to the jurisdiction of the court, and liability may be determined in an adversary proceeding governed by the rules in Part VII.

CROSS REFERENCES

Bonds—

Deposit or investment by trustee of money of estates, see 11 USCA § 345.

Indemnification bond in involuntary cases, see 11 USCA § 303.

Qualification to serve as trustee, see 11 USCA § 322.

Enforcement of bond or undertaking on injunction against surety, see Fed. R. Bankr. P. 7065.

Security; proceedings against sureties, see Fed. R. Civ. P. 65.1.

Security defined, see 11 USCA § 101(49).

Rule 9026. Exceptions Unnecessary

Rule 46 F.R.Civ.P. applies in cases under the Code.

Rule 9027. Removal

(a) Notice of removal

(1) Where filed; form and content

A notice of removal shall be filed with the clerk for the district and division within which is located the state or federal court where the civil action is pending. The notice shall be signed pursuant to Rule 9011 and contain a short and plain statement of the facts which entitle the party filing the notice to remove, contain a statement that upon removal of the claim or cause of action, the party filing the notice does or does not consent to entry of final orders or judgment by the bankruptcy court, and be accompanied by a copy of all process and pleadings.

(2) Time for filing; civil action initiated before commencement of the case under the Code

If the claim or cause of action in a civil action is pending when a case under the Code is commenced, a notice of removal may be filed only within the longest of (A) 90 days after the order for relief in the case under the Code, (B) 30 days after entry of an order terminating a stay, if the claim or cause of action in a civil action has been stayed under § 362 of the Code, or (C) 30 days after a trustee qualifies in a chapter 11 reorganization case but not later than 180 days after the order for relief.

(3) Time for filing; civil action initiated after commencement of the case under the Code

If a claim or cause of action is asserted in another court after the commencement of a case under the Code, a notice of removal may be filed with the clerk only within the shorter of (A) 30 days after receipt, through service or otherwise, of a copy of the initial pleading setting forth the claim or cause of action sought to be removed, or (B) 30 days after receipt of the summons if the initial pleading has been filed with the court but not served with the summons.

(b) Notice

Promptly after filing the notice of removal, the party filing the notice shall serve a copy of it on all parties to the removed claim or cause of action.

(c) Filing in non-bankruptcy court

Promptly after filing the notice of removal, the party filing the notice shall file a copy of it with the clerk of the court from which the claim or cause of action is removed. Removal of the claim or cause of action is effected on such filing of a copy of the notice of removal. The parties shall proceed no further in that court unless and until the claim or cause of action is remanded.

(d) Remand

A motion for remand of the removed claim or cause of action shall be governed by Rule 9014 and served on the parties to the removed claim or cause of action.

(e) Procedure after removal

(1)   After removal of a claim or cause of action to a district court the district court or, if the case under the Code has been referred to a bankruptcy judge of the district, the bankruptcy judge, may issue all necessary orders and process to bring before it all proper parties whether served by process issued by the court from which the claim or cause of action was removed or otherwise.

(2)   The district court or, if the case under the Code has been referred to a bankruptcy judge of the district, the bankruptcy judge, may require the party filing the notice of removal to file with the clerk copies of all records and proceedings relating to the claim or cause of action in the court from which the claim or cause of action was removed.

(3)   Any party who has filed a pleading in connection with the removed claim or cause of action, other than the party filing the notice of removal, shall file a statement that the party does or does not consent to entry of final orders or judgment by the bankruptcy court. A statement required by this paragraph shall be signed pursuant to Rule 9011 and shall be filed not later than 14 days after the filing of the notice of removal. Any party who files a statement pursuant to this paragraph shall mail a copy to every other party to the removed claim or cause of action.

(f) Process after removal

If one or more of the defendants has not been served with process, the service has not been perfected prior to removal, or the process served proves to be defective, such process or service may be completed or new process issued pursuant to Part VII of these rules. This subdivision shall not deprive any defendant on whom process is served after removal of the defendant's right to move to remand the case.

(g) Applicability of Part VII

The rules of Part VII apply to a claim or cause of action removed to a district court from a federal or state court and govern procedure after removal. Repleading is not necessary unless the court so orders. In a removed action in which the defendant has not answered, the defendant shall answer or present the other defenses or objections available under the rules of Part VII within 21 days following the receipt through service or otherwise of a copy of the initial pleading setting forth the claim for relief on which the action or proceeding is based, or within 21 days following the service of summons on such initial pleading, or within seven days following the filing of the notice of removal, whichever period is longest.

(h) Record supplied

When a party is entitled to copies of the records and proceedings in any civil action or proceeding in a federal or a state court, to be used in the removed civil action or proceeding, and the clerk of the federal or state court, on demand accompanied by payment or tender of the lawful fees, fails to deliver certified copies, the court may, on affidavit reciting the facts, direct such record to be supplied by affidavit or otherwise. Thereupon the proceedings, trial and judgment may be had in the court, and all process awarded, as if certified copies had been filed.

(i) Attachment or sequestration; securities

When a claim or cause of action is removed to a district court, any attachment or sequestration of property in the court from which the claim or cause of action was removed shall hold the property to answer the final judgment or decree in the same manner as the property would have been held to answer final judgment or decree had it been rendered by the court from which the claim or cause of action was removed. All bonds, undertakings, or security given by either party to the claim or cause of action prior to its removal shall remain valid and effectual notwithstanding such removal. All injunctions issued, orders entered and other proceedings had prior to removal shall remain in full force and effect until dissolved or modified by the court.

CROSS REFERENCES

Removed actions, see Fed. R. Civ. P. 81.

Removal of actions, see 28 USCA §§ 1446 to 1452.

Rule 9028. Disability of a Judge

Rule 63 F.R.Civ.P. applies in cases under the Code.

CROSS REFERENCES

Disability of judge, see Fed. R. Civ. P. 63.

Rule 9029. Local Bankruptcy Rules; Procedure When There Is No Controlling Law

(a) Local bankruptcy rules

(1) Each district court acting by a majority of its district judges may make and amend rules governing practice and procedure in all cases and proceedings within the district court's bankruptcy jurisdiction which are consistent with—but not duplicative of—Acts of Congress and these rules and which do not prohibit or limit the use of the Official Forms. Rule 83 F.R.Civ.P. governs the procedure for making local rules. A district court may authorize the bankruptcy judges of the district, subject to any limitation or condition it may prescribe and the requirements of 83 F.R.Civ.P., to make and amend rules of practice and procedure which are consistent with—but not duplicative of—Acts of Congress and these rules and which do not prohibit or limit the use of the Official Forms. Local rules shall conform to any uniform numbering system prescribed by the Judicial Conference of the United States.

(2) A local rule imposing a requirement of form shall not be enforced in a manner that causes a party to lose rights because of a nonwillful failure to comply with the requirement.

(b) Procedure when there is no controlling law. A judge may regulate practice in any manner consistent with federal law, these rules, Official Forms, and local rules of the district. No sanction or other disadvantage may be imposed for noncompliance with any requirement not in federal law, federal rules, Official Forms, or the local rules of the district unless the alleged violator has been furnished in the particular case with actual notice of the requirement.

CROSS REFERENCES

Rules by district courts, see Fed. R. Civ. P. 83.

Rules by district courts, see Fed. R. Crim. P. 57.

Rule 9030. Jurisdiction and Venue Unaffected

These rules shall not be construed to extend or limit the jurisdiction of the courts or the venue of any matters therein.

CROSS REFERENCES

Jurisdiction and venue unaffected, see Fed. R. Civ. P. 82.

Power of Supreme Court to prescribe bankruptcy rules, see 28 USCA § 2075.

Rule 9031. Masters Not Authorized

Rule 53 F.R.Civ.P. does not apply in cases under the Code.

Rule 9032. Effect of Amendment of Federal Rules of Civil Procedure

The Federal Rules of Civil Procedure which are incorporated by reference and made applicable by these rules shall be the Federal Rules of Civil Procedure in effect on the effective date of these rules and as thereafter amended, unless otherwise provided by such amendment or by these rules.

Rule 9033. Proposed Findings of Fact and Conclusions of Law

(a) Service

In a proceeding in which the bankruptcy court has issued proposed findings of fact and conclusions of law, the clerk shall serve forthwith copies on all parties by mail and note the date of mailing on the docket.

(b) Objections: time for filing

Within 14 days after being served with a copy of the proposed findings of fact and conclusions of law a party may serve and file with the clerk written objections which identify the specific proposed findings or conclusions objected to and state the grounds for such objection. A party may respond to another party's objections within 14 days after being served with a copy thereof. A party objecting to the bankruptcy judge's proposed findings or conclusions shall arrange promptly for the transcription of the record, or such portions of it as all parties may agree upon or the bankruptcy judge deems sufficient, unless the district judge otherwise directs.

(c) Extension of time

The bankruptcy judge may for cause extend the time for filing objections by any party for a period not to exceed 21 days from the expiration of the time otherwise prescribed by this rule. A request to extend the time for filing objections must be made before the time for filing objections has expired, except that a request made no more than 21 days after the expiration of the time for filing objections may be granted upon a showing of excusable neglect.

(d) Standard of review

The district judge shall make a de novo review upon the record or, after additional evidence, of any portion of the bankruptcy judge's findings of fact or conclusions of law to which specific written objection has been made in accordance with this rule. The district judge may accept, reject, or modify the proposed findings of fact or conclusions of law, receive further evidence, or recommit the matter to the bankruptcy judge with instructions.

Rule 9034. Transmittal of Pleadings, Motion Papers, Objections, and Other Papers to the United States Trustee

Unless the United States trustee requests otherwise or the case is a chapter 9 municipality case, any entity that files a pleading, motion, objection, or similar paper relating to any of the following matters shall transmit a copy thereof to the United States trustee within the time required by these rules for service of the paper:

    (a) a proposed use, sale, or lease of property of the estate other than in the ordinary course of business;

    (b) the approval of a compromise or settlement of a controversy;

    (c) the dismissal or conversion of a case to another chapter;

    (d) the employment of professional persons;

    (e) an application for compensation or reimbursement of expenses;

    (f) a motion for, or approval of an agreement relating to, the use of cash collateral or authority to obtain credit;

(g) the appointment of a trustee or examiner in a chapter 11 reorganization case;

(h) the approval of a disclosure statement;

(i) the confirmation of a plan;

(j) an objection to, or waiver or revocation of, the debtor's discharge;

(k) any other matter in which the United States trustee requests copies of filed papers or the court orders copies transmitted to the United States trustee.

Rule 9035. Applicability of Rules in Judicial Districts in Alabama and North Carolina

In any case under the Code that is filed in or transferred to a district in the State of Alabama or the State of North Carolina and in which a United States trustee is not authorized to act, these rules apply to the extent that they are not inconsistent with any federal statute effective in the case.

Rule 9036. Notice and Service by Electronic Transmission

(a) In general

This rule applies whenever these rules require or permit sending a notice or serving a paper by mail or other means.

(b) Notices from and service by the court

(1) Registered users

The clerk may send notice to or serve a registered user by filing the notice or paper with the court's electronic-filing system.

(2) All recipients

For any recipient, the clerk may send notice or serve a paper by electronic means that the recipient consented to in writing, including by designating an electronic address for receipt of notices. But these exceptions apply:

(A) if the recipient has registered an electronic address with the Administrative Office of the United States Courts' bankruptcy-noticing program, the clerk shall send the notice to or serve the paper at that address; and

(B) if an entity has been designated by the Director of the Administrative Office of the United States Courts as a high-volume paper-notice recipient, the clerk may send the notice to or serve the paper electronically at an address designated by the Director, unless the entity has designated an address under § 342(e) or (f) of the Code.

(c) Notices from and service by an entity

An entity may send notice or serve a paper in the same manner that the clerk does under (b), excluding (b)(2)(A) and (B).

(d) Completing notice or service

Electronic notice or service is complete upon filing or sending but is not effective if the filer or sender receives notice that it did not reach the person to be served. It is the recipient's responsibility to keep its electronic address current with the clerk.

(e) Inapplicability

This rule does not apply to any paper required to be served in accordance with Rule 7004.

Rule 9037. Privacy Protection for Filings Made With the Court

(a) Redacted filings

Unless the court orders otherwise, in an electronic or paper filing made with the court that contains an individual's social-security number, taxpayer-identification number, or birth date, the name of an individual, other than the debtor, known to be and identified as a minor, or a financial-account number, a party or nonparty making the filing may include only:

(1) the last four digits of the social-security number and taxpayer-identification number;

(2) the year of the individual's birth;

(3) the minor's initials; and

(4) the last four digits of the financial-account number.

(b) Exemptions from the redaction requirement

The redaction requirement does not apply to the following:

(1) a financial-account number that identifies the property allegedly subject to forfeiture in a forfeiture proceeding;

(2) the record of an administrative or agency proceeding unless filed with a proof of claim;

(3) the official record of a state-court proceeding;

(4) the record of a court or tribunal, if that record was not subject to the redaction requirement when originally filed;

(5) a filing covered by subdivision (c) of this rule; and

(6) a filing that is subject to § 110 of the Code.

(c) Filings made under seal

The court may order that a filing be made under seal without redaction. The court may later unseal the filing or order the entity that made the filing to file a redacted version for the public record.

(d) Protective orders

For cause, the court may by order in a case under the Code:

(1) require redaction of additional information; or

(2) limit or prohibit a nonparty's remote electronic access to a document filed with the court.

(e) Option for additional unredacted filing under seal

An entity making a redacted filing may also file an unredacted copy under seal. The court must retain the unredacted copy as part of the record.

(f) Option for filing a reference list

A filing that contains redacted information may be filed together with a reference list that identifies each item of redacted information and specifies an appropriate identifier that uniquely corresponds to each item listed. The list must be filed under seal and may be amended as of right. Any reference in the case to a listed identifier will be construed to refer to the corresponding item of information.

(g) Waiver of protection of identifiers

An entity waives the protection of subdivision (a) as to the entity's own information by filing it without redaction and not under seal.

(h) Motion to redact a previously filed document

(1) Content of the Motion; Service. Unless the court orders otherwise, if an entity seeks to redact from a previously filed document information that is protected under subdivision (a), the entity must:

(A) file a motion to redact identifying the proposed redactions;

(B) attach to the motion the proposed redacted document;

(C) include in the motion the docket or proof-of-claim number of the previously filed document; and

(D) serve the motion and attachment on the debtor, debtor's attorney, trustee (if any), United States trustee, filer of the unredacted document, and any individual whose personal identifying information is to be redacted.

(2) Restricting Public Access to the Unredacted Document; Docketing the Redacted Document. The court must promptly restrict public access to the motion and the unredacted document pending its ruling on the motion. If the court grants it, the court must docket the redacted document. The restrictions on public access to the motion and unredacted document remain in effect until a further court order. If the court denies it, the restrictions must be lifted, unless the court orders otherwise.

SELECTED OFFICIAL FORMS

SELECTED OFFICIAL FORMS

Director's Bankruptcy Forms

For a complete list of Director's Bankruptcy Forms, see https://www.uscourts.gov/forms/bankruptcy-forms

SELECTED OFFICIAL FORMS

3180FH	Chapter 12 Hardship Discharge
3180R1	Individual Chapter 11 Discharge
3180RV1	Chapter 11 Discharge for Individual Whose Plan was Confirmed under § 1191(a)
3180RV2	Chapter 11 Discharge for Individual Whose Plan was Confirmed under § 1191(b)
3180RV3	For Corporation or Partnership Whose Plan was Confirmed under § 1191(b)
3180W	Chapter 13 Discharge
3180WH	Chapter 13 Hardship Discharge

INTRODUCTION

Rule 9009 of the Federal Rules of Bankruptcy Procedure states that the Official Forms prescribed by the Judicial Conference of the United States "shall be used without alteration, except as otherwise provided in these rules, in a particular Official Form, or in the national instructions for a particular Official Form." The Official Forms, accordingly, are obligatory in character.

Rule 9009 expressly permits the user of the Official Forms to make "minor changes not affecting wording or the order of presenting information." For example, the user may "expand the prescribed areas for responses in order to permit complete responses" or delete spaces [that are] not needed for responses. The use of the Official Forms has been held to be subject to a "rule of substantial compliance." Some rules, for example Fed. R. Bankr. P. 3001(a), specifically state that the filed document need only "conform substantially" to the Official Form. A document for which an Official Form is prescribed generally will meet the standard of substantial compliance if the document contains the complete substance, that is, all of the information required by the Official Form.

Official Forms in the 100 series are designed for individuals and married couples filing for bankruptcy relief. Those forms also apply to sole proprietorships. Official Forms in the 200 series are designed for nonindividuals seeking bankruptcy protection, such as corporations, partnerships, and limited liability companies. The Official Forms in the remaining series are for courts, pleadings, and other special uses.

In addition, there are more than sixty Director's Bankruptcy Forms, starting with Form 1040. Director's Bankruptcy Forms are issued under Bankruptcy Rule 9009 by the Director of the Administrative Office of the United States Courts and may be required by local court rule, but otherwise exist for the convenience of the parties.

All of the Official Forms, Director's Bankruptcy Forms, and instructions on how to use the forms are available in pdf format on a web site maintained by the U.S. Courts:

http://www.uscourts.gov/forms/bankruptcy-forms

Fill in this information to identify your case:

United States Bankruptcy Court for the:

_____ District of _____

Case number (if known) _____

Chapter you are filing under:
- ☐ Chapter 7
- ☐ Chapter 11
- ☐ Chapter 12
- ☐ Chapter 13

☐ Check if this is an amended filing

Official Form 101

Voluntary Petition for Individuals Filing for Bankruptcy 12/22

The bankruptcy forms use *you* and *Debtor 1* to refer to a debtor filing alone. A married couple may file a bankruptcy case together—called a *joint case*—and in joint cases, these forms use *you* to ask for information from both debtors. For example, if a form asks, "Do you own a car," the answer would be *yes* if either debtor owns a car. When information is needed about the spouses separately, the form uses *Debtor 1* and *Debtor 2* to distinguish between them. In joint cases, one of the spouses must report information as *Debtor 1* and the other as *Debtor 2*. The same person must be *Debtor 1* in all of the forms.

Be as complete and accurate as possible. If two married people are filing together, both are equally responsible for supplying correct information. If more space is needed, attach a separate sheet to this form. On the top of any additional pages, write your name and case number (if known). Answer every question.

Part 1: Identify Yourself

	About Debtor 1:	About Debtor 2 (Spouse Only in a Joint Case):
1. Your full name Write the name that is on your government-issued picture identification (for example, your driver's license or passport). Bring your picture identification to your meeting with the trustee.	First name Middle name Last name Suffix (Sr., Jr., II, III)	First name Middle name Last name Suffix (Sr., Jr., II, III)
2. All other names you have used in the last 8 years Include your married or maiden names and any assumed, trade names and *doing business as* names. Do NOT list the name of any separate legal entity such as a corporation, partnership, or LLC that is not filing this petition.	First name Middle name Last name First name Middle name Last name Business name (if applicable) Business name (if applicable)	First name Middle name Last name First name Middle name Last name Business name (if applicable) Business name (if applicable)
3. Only the last 4 digits of your Social Security number or federal Individual Taxpayer Identification number (ITIN)	XXX – XX – ____ ____ ____ ____ OR **9** XX – XX – ____ ____ ____ ____	XXX – XX – ____ ____ ____ ____ OR **9** XX – XX – ____ ____ ____ ____

Official Form 101   Voluntary Petition for Individuals Filing for Bankruptcy   page 1

Debtor 1 _____ Case number (if known)_____
　　　　　First Name　　Middle Name　　　Last Name

	About Debtor 1:	About Debtor 2 (Spouse Only in a Joint Case):
4. Your Employer Identification Number (EIN), if any.	EIN __ __ - __ __ __ __ __ __ __ EIN __ __ - __ __ __ __ __ __ __	EIN __ __ - __ __ __ __ __ __ __ EIN __ __ - __ __ __ __ __ __ __
5. Where you live		If Debtor 2 lives at a different address:
	_____ Number　　Street _____ _____ City　　　　　　State　ZIP Code _____ County **If your mailing address is different from the one above, fill it in here.** Note that the court will send any notices to you at this mailing address. _____ Number　　Street _____ P.O. Box _____ City　　　　　　State　ZIP Code	_____ Number　　Street _____ _____ City　　　　　　State　ZIP Code _____ County **If Debtor 2's mailing address is different from yours, fill it in here.** Note that the court will send any notices to this mailing address. _____ Number　　Street _____ P.O. Box _____ City　　　　　　State　ZIP Code
6. Why you are choosing *this district* to file for bankruptcy	*Check one:* ☐ Over the last 180 days before filing this petition, I have lived in this district longer than in any other district. ☐ I have another reason. Explain. (See 28 U.S.C. § 1408.) _____ _____ _____ _____	*Check one:* ☐ Over the last 180 days before filing this petition, I have lived in this district longer than in any other district. ☐ I have another reason. Explain. (See 28 U.S.C. § 1408.) _____ _____ _____ _____

Debtor 1			Case number (if known)
	First Name	Middle Name	Last Name

Part 2: **Tell the Court About Your Bankruptcy Case**

---

7. The chapter of the Bankruptcy Code you are choosing to file under

Check one. (For a brief description of each, see *Notice Required by 11 U.S.C. § 342(b) for Individuals Filing for Bankruptcy* (Form 2010)). Also, go to the top of page 1 and check the appropriate box.

❑ Chapter 7

❑ Chapter 11

❑ Chapter 12

❑ Chapter 13

---

8. How you will pay the fee

❑ **I will pay the entire fee when I file my petition.** Please check with the clerk's office in your local court for more details about how you may pay. Typically, if you are paying the fee yourself, you may pay with cash, cashier's check, or money order. If your attorney is submitting your payment on your behalf, your attorney may pay with a credit card or check with a pre-printed address.

❑ **I need to pay the fee in installments.** If you choose this option, sign and attach the *Application for Individuals to Pay The Filing Fee in Installments* (Official Form 103A).

❑ **I request that my fee be waived** (You may request this option only if you are filing for Chapter 7. By law, a judge may, but is not required to, waive your fee, and may do so only if your income is less than 150% of the official poverty line that applies to your family size and you are unable to pay the fee in installments). If you choose this option, you must fill out the *Application to Have the Chapter 7 Filing Fee Waived* (Official Form 103B) and file it with your petition.

---

9. Have you filed for bankruptcy within the last 8 years?

❑ No

❑ Yes. District _____ When _____ Case number _____
      MM / DD / YYYY

District _____ When _____ Case number _____
      MM / DD / YYYY

District _____ When _____ Case number _____
      MM / DD / YYYY

---

10. Are any bankruptcy cases pending or being filed by a spouse who is not filing this case with you, or by a business partner, or by an affiliate?

❑ No

❑ Yes. Debtor _____ Relationship to you _____

District _____ When _____ Case number, if known _____
      MM / DD / YYYY

Debtor _____ Relationship to you _____

District _____ When _____ Case number, if known _____
      MM / DD / YYYY

---

11. Do you rent your residence?

❑ No. Go to line 12.

❑ Yes. Has your landlord obtained an eviction judgment against you?

  ❑ No. Go to line 12.

  ❑ Yes. Fill out *Initial Statement About an Eviction Judgment Against You* (Form 101A) and file it as part of this bankruptcy petition.

SELECTED OFFICIAL FORMS

Debtor 1 _____   Case number *(if known)*_____
         First Name   Middle Name   Last Name

Part 4:	Report if You Own or Have Any Hazardous Property or Any Property That Needs Immediate Attention

14. **Do you own or have any property that poses or is alleged to pose a threat of imminent and identifiable hazard to public health or safety? Or do you own any property that needs immediate attention?**

    For example, do you own perishable goods, or livestock that must be fed, or a building that needs urgent repairs?

    ☐ No

    ☐ Yes. What is the hazard? _____

                                        _____

        If immediate attention is needed, why is it needed? _____

                                          _____

        Where is the property? _____
                                    Number   Street

                                          _____

                                        City   State   ZIP Code

Debtor 1 _____   Case number *(if known)* _____
       First Name   Middle Name   Last Name

Part 5:   **Explain Your Efforts to Receive a Briefing About Credit Counseling**

15. Tell the court whether you have received a briefing about credit counseling.	**About Debtor 1:**	**About Debtor 2 (Spouse Only in a Joint Case):**

The law requires that you receive a briefing about credit counseling before you file for bankruptcy. You must truthfully check one of the following choices. If you cannot do so, you are not eligible to file.
 	
If you file anyway, the court can dismiss your case, you will lose whatever filing fee you paid, and your creditors can begin collection activities again.
	You must check one:
	
	❏ I received a briefing from an approved credit counseling agency within the 180 days before I filed this bankruptcy petition, and I received a certificate of completion.
	Attach a copy of the certificate and the payment plan, if any, that you developed with the agency.
	
	❏ I received a briefing from an approved credit counseling agency within the 180 days before I filed this bankruptcy petition, but I do not have a certificate of completion.
	Within 14 days after you file this bankruptcy petition, you MUST file a copy of the certificate and payment plan, if any.
	
	❏ I certify that I asked for credit counseling services from an approved agency, but was unable to obtain those services during the 7 days after I made my request, and exigent circumstances merit a 30-day temporary waiver of the requirement.
	To ask for a 30-day temporary waiver of the requirement, attach a separate sheet explaining what efforts you made to obtain the briefing, why you were unable to obtain it before you filed for bankruptcy, and what exigent circumstances required you to file this case.
	Your case may be dismissed if the court is dissatisfied with your reasons for not receiving a briefing before you filed for bankruptcy.
	If the court is satisfied with your reasons, you must still receive a briefing within 30 days after you file. You must file a certificate from the approved agency, along with a copy of the payment plan you developed, if any. If you do not do so, your case may be dismissed.
	Any extension of the 30-day deadline is granted only for cause and is limited to a maximum of 15 days.
	
	❏ I am not required to receive a briefing about credit counseling because of:
	
	   ❏ **Incapacity.** I have a mental illness or a mental deficiency that makes me incapable of realizing or making rational decisions about finances.
	
	   ❏ **Disability.** My physical disability causes me to be unable to participate in a briefing in person, by phone, or through the internet, even after I reasonably tried to do so.
	
	   ❏ **Active duty.** I am currently on active military duty in a military combat zone.
	
	If you believe you are not required to receive a briefing about credit counseling, you must file a motion for waiver of credit counseling with the court.
		You must check one:
		
		❏ I received a briefing from an approved credit counseling agency within the 180 days before I filed this bankruptcy petition, and I received a certificate of completion.
		Attach a copy of the certificate and the payment plan, if any, that you developed with the agency.
		
		❏ I received a briefing from an approved credit counseling agency within the 180 days before I filed this bankruptcy petition, but I do not have a certificate of completion.
		Within 14 days after you file this bankruptcy petition, you MUST file a copy of the certificate and payment plan, if any.
		
		❏ I certify that I asked for credit counseling services from an approved agency, but was unable to obtain those services during the 7 days after I made my request, and exigent circumstances merit a 30-day temporary waiver of the requirement.
		To ask for a 30-day temporary waiver of the requirement, attach a separate sheet explaining what efforts you made to obtain the briefing, why you were unable to obtain it before you filed for bankruptcy, and what exigent circumstances required you to file this case.
		Your case may be dismissed if the court is dissatisfied with your reasons for not receiving a briefing before you filed for bankruptcy.
		If the court is satisfied with your reasons, you must still receive a briefing within 30 days after you file. You must file a certificate from the approved agency, along with a copy of the payment plan you developed, if any. If you do not do so, your case may be dismissed.
		Any extension of the 30-day deadline is granted only for cause and is limited to a maximum of 15 days.
		
		❏ I am not required to receive a briefing about credit counseling because of:
		
		   ❏ **Incapacity.** I have a mental illness or a mental deficiency that makes me incapable of realizing or making rational decisions about finances.
		
		   ❏ **Disability.** My physical disability causes me to be unable to participate in a briefing in person, by phone, or through the internet, even after I reasonably tried to do so.
		
		   ❏ **Active duty.** I am currently on active military duty in a military combat zone.
		
		If you believe you are not required to receive a briefing about credit counseling, you must file a motion for waiver of credit counseling with the court.

Debtor 1				Case number (if known)	
	First Name	Middle Name	Last Name		

Part 6: **Answer These Questions for Reporting Purposes**

16. What kind of debts do you have?

16a. **Are your debts primarily consumer debts?** *Consumer debts* are defined in 11 U.S.C. § 101(8) as "incurred by an individual primarily for a personal, family, or household purpose."

  ☐ No. Go to line 16b.
  ☐ Yes. Go to line 17.

16b. **Are your debts primarily business debts?** *Business debts* are debts that you incurred to obtain money for a business or investment or through the operation of the business or investment.

  ☐ No. Go to line 16c.
  ☐ Yes. Go to line 17.

16c. State the type of debts you owe that are not consumer debts or business debts.

_____

17. Are you filing under Chapter 7?

Do you estimate that after any exempt property is excluded and administrative expenses are paid that funds will be available for distribution to unsecured creditors?

☐ No. I am not filing under Chapter 7. Go to line 18.

☐ Yes. I am filing under Chapter 7. Do you estimate that after any exempt property is excluded and administrative expenses are paid that funds will be available to distribute to unsecured creditors?

  ☐ No
  ☐ Yes

18. How many creditors do you estimate that you owe?

☐ 1-49	☐ 1,000-5,000	☐ 25,001-50,000
☐ 50-99	☐ 5,001-10,000	☐ 50,001-100,000
☐ 100-199	☐ 10,001-25,000	☐ More than 100,000
☐ 200-999		

19. How much do you estimate your assets to be worth?

☐ $0-$50,000	☐ $1,000,001-$10 million	☐ $500,000,001-$1 billion
☐ $50,001-$100,000	☐ $10,000,001-$50 million	☐ $1,000,000,001-$10 billion
☐ $100,001-$500,000	☐ $50,000,001-$100 million	☐ $10,000,000,001-$50 billion
☐ $500,001-$1 million	☐ $100,000,001-$500 million	☐ More than $50 billion

20. How much do you estimate your liabilities to be?

☐ $0-$50,000	☐ $1,000,001-$10 million	☐ $500,000,001-$1 billion
☐ $50,001-$100,000	☐ $10,000,001-$50 million	☐ $1,000,000,001-$10 billion
☐ $100,001-$500,000	☐ $50,000,001-$100 million	☐ $10,000,000,001-$50 billion
☐ $500,001-$1 million	☐ $100,000,001-$500 million	☐ More than $50 billion

Part 7: **Sign Below**

For you

I have examined this petition, and I declare under penalty of perjury that the information provided is true and correct.

If I have chosen to file under Chapter 7, I am aware that I may proceed, if eligible, under Chapter 7, 11,12, or 13 of title 11, United States Code. I understand the relief available under each chapter, and I choose to proceed under Chapter 7.

If no attorney represents me and I did not pay or agree to pay someone who is not an attorney to help me fill out this document, I have obtained and read the notice required by 11 U.S.C. § 342(b).

I request relief in accordance with the chapter of title 11, United States Code, specified in this petition.

I understand making a false statement, concealing property, or obtaining money or property by fraud in connection with a bankruptcy case can result in fines up to $250,000, or imprisonment for up to 20 years, or both. 18 U.S.C. §§ 152, 1341, 1519, and 3571.

✗ _____   ✗ _____
  Signature of Debtor 1   Signature of Debtor 2

  Executed on _____   Executed on _____
            MM / DD /YYYY   MM / DD /YYYY

SELECTED OFFICIAL FORMS

Debtor 1 _____   Case number *(if known)*_____
    First Name   Middle Name   Last Name

For your attorney, if you are represented by one

If you are not represented by an attorney, you do not need to file this page.

I, the attorney for the debtor(s) named in this petition, declare that I have informed the debtor(s) about eligibility to proceed under Chapter 7, 11, 12, or 13 of title 11, United States Code, and have explained the relief available under each chapter for which the person is eligible. I also certify that I have delivered to the debtor(s) the notice required by 11 U.S.C. § 342(b) and, in a case in which § 707(b)(4)(D) applies, certify that I have no knowledge after an inquiry that the information in the schedules filed with the petition is incorrect.

✗ _____   Date _____
Signature of Attorney for Debtor   MM / DD /YYYY

_____
Printed name

_____
Firm name

_____
Number   Street

_____

_____
City   State   ZIP Code

Contact phone _____   Email address _____

_____
Bar number   State

SELECTED OFFICIAL FORMS

Debtor 1 _____ Case number (if known)_____
First Name   Middle Name   Last Name

For you if you are filing this bankruptcy without an attorney

If you are represented by an attorney, you do not need to file this page.

The law allows you, as an individual, to represent yourself in bankruptcy court, but **you should understand that many people find it extremely difficult to represent themselves successfully. Because bankruptcy has long-term financial and legal consequences, you are strongly urged to hire a qualified attorney.**

To be successful, you must correctly file and handle your bankruptcy case. The rules are very technical, and a mistake or inaction may affect your rights. For example, your case may be dismissed because you did not file a required document, pay a fee on time, attend a meeting or hearing, or cooperate with the court, case trustee, U.S. trustee, bankruptcy administrator, or audit firm if your case is selected for audit. If that happens, you could lose your right to file another case, or you may lose protections, including the benefit of the automatic stay.

You must list all your property and debts in the schedules that you are required to file with the court. Even if you plan to pay a particular debt outside of your bankruptcy, you must list that debt in your schedules. If you do not list a debt, the debt may not be discharged. If you do not list property or properly claim it as exempt, you may not be able to keep the property. The judge can also deny you a discharge of all your debts if you do something dishonest in your bankruptcy case, such as destroying or hiding property, falsifying records, or lying. Individual bankruptcy cases are randomly audited to determine if debtors have been accurate, truthful, and complete. **Bankruptcy fraud is a serious crime; you could be fined and imprisoned.**

If you decide to file without an attorney, the court expects you to follow the rules as if you had hired an attorney. The court will not treat you differently because you are filing for yourself. To be successful, you must be familiar with the United States Bankruptcy Code, the Federal Rules of Bankruptcy Procedure, and the local rules of the court in which your case is filed. You must also be familiar with any state exemption laws that apply.

Are you aware that filing for bankruptcy is a serious action with long-term financial and legal consequences?

☐ No
☐ Yes

Are you aware that bankruptcy fraud is a serious crime and that if your bankruptcy forms are inaccurate or incomplete, you could be fined or imprisoned?

☐ No
☐ Yes

Did you pay or agree to pay someone who is not an attorney to help you fill out your bankruptcy forms?
☐ No
☐ Yes. Name of Person_____.
Attach *Bankruptcy Petition Preparer's Notice, Declaration, and Signature* (Official Form 119).

By signing here, I acknowledge that I understand the risks involved in filing without an attorney. I have read and understood this notice, and I am aware that filing a bankruptcy case without an attorney may cause me to lose my rights or property if I do not properly handle the case.

✗ _____   ✗ _____
Signature of Debtor 1   Signature of Debtor 2

Date _____   Date _____
MM / DD / YYYY   MM / DD / YYYY

Contact phone _____   Contact phone _____

Cell phone _____   Cell phone _____

Email address _____   Email address _____

Official Form 101   Voluntary Petition for Individuals Filing for Bankruptcy   page 9

| Print | Save As... | Add Attachment | | Reset |

Official Form 101 (Committee Note) (12/22)

Committee Note

Form 101 is amended to eliminate language in former Part 1, Question 4, which asked for "any business names . . . you have used in the last 8 years." Instead, Part 1, Question 2, is modified to add to the direction with respect to "other names you have used in the last 8 years" – which currently directs the debtor to "Include your married and maiden names" – to ask the debtor to include "any assumed, trade names, or *doing business as* names," and to direct that the debtor should not include the names of separate legal entities that are not filing the petition. Many individual debtors erroneously believed that Question 4 was asking for the names of corporations or Limited Liability Corporations in which they held any interest in the past 8 years, and any names listed in response were then treated as additional debtors for purposes of noticing and reporting. By asking for the information in Question 2, the form now makes it clearer that the only names to be listed are names that were used by the debtor personally in conducting business, not names used by other legal entities. This amendment also conforms Form 101 to Forms 105, 201 and 205 with respect to the same information.

Fill in this information to identify your case:

Debtor 1 _____
First Name   Middle Name   Last Name

Debtor 2 _____
(Spouse, if filing) First Name   Middle Name   Last Name

United States Bankruptcy Court for the: _____ District of _____

Case number _____
(If known)

☐ Check if this is an amended filing

Official Form 103A

Application for Individuals to Pay the Filing Fee in Installments   12/15

Be as complete and accurate as possible. If two married people are filing together, both are equally responsible for supplying correct information.

Part 1:   Specify Your Proposed Payment Timetable

1. Which chapter of the Bankruptcy Code are you choosing to file under?

   ☐ Chapter 7
   ☐ Chapter 11
   ☐ Chapter 12
   ☐ Chapter 13

2. You may apply to pay the filing fee in up to four installments. Fill in the amounts you propose to pay and the dates you plan to pay them. Be sure all dates are business days. Then add the payments you propose to pay.

   You must propose to pay the entire fee no later than 120 days after you file this bankruptcy case. If the court approves your application, the court will set your final payment timetable.

   You propose to pay...

   $_____   ☐ With the filing of the petition
                  ☐ On or before this date .... MM / DD / YYYY

   $_____   On or before this date .... MM / DD / YYYY

   $_____   On or before this date .... MM / DD / YYYY

   + $_____ On or before this date .... MM / DD / YYYY

   Total $_____   ◀ Your total must equal the entire fee for the chapter you checked in line 1.

Part 2:   Sign Below

By signing here, you state that you are unable to pay the full filing fee at once, that you want to pay the fee in installments, and that you understand that:

▪ You must pay your entire filing fee before you make any more payments or transfer any more property to an attorney, bankruptcy petition preparer, or anyone else for services in connection with your bankruptcy case.

▪ You must pay the entire fee no later than 120 days after you first file for bankruptcy, unless the court later extends your deadline. Your debts will not be discharged until your entire fee is paid.

▪ If you do not make any payment when it is due, your bankruptcy case may be dismissed, and your rights in other bankruptcy proceedings may be affected.

x _____   x _____   x _____
Signature of Debtor 1   Signature of Debtor 2   Your attorney's name and signature, if you used one

Date _____   Date _____   Date _____
MM / DD / YYYY   MM / DD / YYYY   MM / DD / YYYY

Official Form 103A   Application for Individuals to Pay the Filing Fee in Installments

Fill in this information to identify the case:

Debtor 1 _____
First Name   Middle Name   Last Name

Debtor 2 _____
(Spouse, if filing) First Name   Middle Name   Last Name

United States Bankruptcy Court for the: _____ District of

Case number _____
(If known)

Chapter filing under:

☐ Chapter 7
☐ Chapter 11
☐ Chapter 12
☐ Chapter 13

Order Approving Payment of Filing Fee in Installments

After considering the *Application for Individuals to Pay the Filing Fee in Installments* (Official Form 103A), the court orders that:

[ ] The debtor(s) may pay the filing fee in installments on the terms proposed in the application.

[ ] The debtor(s) must pay the filing fee according to the following terms:

You must pay...	On or before this date...
$_____	_____ Month / day / year
$_____	_____ Month / day / year
$_____	_____ Month / day / year
+ $_____	_____ Month / day / year

Total $_____

Until the filing fee is paid in full, the debtor(s) must not make any additional payment or transfer any additional property to an attorney or to anyone else for services in connection with this case.

_____   **By the court:** _____
Month / day / year   United States Bankruptcy Judge

| Print | Save As... | Add Attachment | | Reset |

Fill in this information to identify your case:

Debtor 1 _____
First Name   Middle Name   Last Name

Debtor 2 _____
(Spouse, if filing) First Name   Middle Name   Last Name

United States Bankruptcy Court for the: _____ District of _____

Case number _____
(If known)

☐ Check if this is an
amended filing

Official Form 103B

Application to Have the Chapter 7 Filing Fee Waived   12/15

Be as complete and accurate as possible. If two married people are filing together, both are equally responsible for supplying correct information. If more space is needed, attach a separate sheet to this form. On the top of any additional pages, write your name and case number (if known).

Part 1:	Tell the Court About Your Family and Your Family's Income

1. What is the size of your family?

Your family includes you, your spouse, and any dependents listed on Schedule J: Your Expenses (Official Form 106J).

Check all that apply:

☐ You
☐ Your spouse
☐ Your dependents   _____   _____
                     How many dependents?   Total number of people

2. Fill in your family's average monthly income.

Include your spouse's income if your spouse is living with you, even if your spouse is not filing.

Do not include your spouse's income if you are separated and your spouse is not filing with you.

Add your income and your spouse's income. Include the value (if known) of any non-cash governmental assistance that you receive, such as food stamps (benefits under the Supplemental Nutrition Assistance Program) or housing subsidies.

If you have already filled out Schedule I: Your Income, see line 10 of that schedule.

Subtract any non-cash governmental assistance that you included above.

Your family's average monthly net income

That person's average monthly net income (take-home pay)

You .... $_____

Your spouse .... + $_____

Subtotal............ $_____

— $_____

Total .... $_____

3. Do you receive non-cash governmental assistance?

☐ No
☐ Yes. Describe...........

Type of assistance
_____

4. Do you expect your family's average monthly net income to increase or decrease by more than 10% during the next 6 months?

☐ No
☐ Yes. Explain. ....
_____

5. Tell the court why you are unable to pay the filing fee in installments within 120 days. If you have some additional circumstances that cause you to not be able to pay your filing fee in installments, explain them.

_____

Official Form 103B   Application to Have the Chapter 7 Filing Fee Waived   page 1

Debtor 1 _____   Case number *(if known)* _____
First Name   Middle Name   Last Name

Part 2: Tell the Court About Your Monthly Expenses

6. **Estimate your average monthly expenses.**

   Include amounts paid by any government assistance that you reported on line 2. $ _____

   If you have already filled out *Schedule J, Your Expenses,* copy line 22 from that form.

7. Do these expenses cover anyone who is not included in your family as reported in line 1?

   ☐ No
   ☐ Yes. Identify who........ _____

8. Does anyone other than you regularly pay any of these expenses?

   If you have already filled out *Schedule I: Your Income,* copy the total from line 11.

   ☐ No
   ☐ Yes. How much do you regularly receive as contributions? $ _____ monthly

9. Do you expect your average monthly expenses to increase or decrease by more than 10% during the next 6 months?

   ☐ No
   ☐ Yes. Explain .... _____

Part 3: Tell the Court About Your Property

If you have already filled out *Schedule A/B: Property (Official Form 106A/B)* attach copies to this application and go to Part 4.

10. **How much cash do you have?**

    Examples: Money you have in your wallet, in your home, and on hand when you file this application

    Cash: $ _____

11. **Bank accounts and other deposits of money?**

    Examples: Checking, savings, money market, or other financial accounts; certificates of deposit; shares in banks, credit unions, brokerage houses, and other similar institutions. If you have more than one account with the same institution, list each. Do not include 401(k) and IRA accounts.

	Institution name:	Amount:
Checking account:	_____	$ _____
Savings account:	_____	$ _____
Other financial accounts:	_____	$ _____
Other financial accounts:	_____	$ _____

12. **Your home?** (if you own it outright or are purchasing it)

    Examples: House, condominium, manufactured home, or mobile home

    Number   Street   _____
    City   State   ZIP Code

    Current value: $ _____
    Amount you owe on mortgage and liens: $ _____

13. **Other real estate?**

    Number   Street   _____
    City   State   ZIP Code

    Current value: $ _____
    Amount you owe on mortgage and liens: $ _____

14. **The vehicles you own?**

    Examples: Cars, vans, trucks, sports utility vehicles, motorcycles, tractors, boats

    Make: _____
    Model: _____
    Year: _____
    Mileage _____

    Current value: $ _____
    Amount you owe on liens: $ _____

    Make: _____
    Model: _____
    Year: _____
    Mileage _____

    Current value: $ _____
    Amount you owe on liens: $ _____

Official Form 103B   Application to Have the Chapter 7 Filing Fee Waived   page 2

Debtor 1 _____   Case number *(if known)* _____
First Name   Middle Name   Last Name

15. Other assets?	Describe the other assets:		
Do not include household items and clothing.		Current value:	$_____
		Amount you owe on liens:	$_____

16. Money or property due you?

Examples: Tax refunds, past due or lump sum alimony, spousal support, child support, maintenance, divorce or property settlements, Social Security benefits, workers' compensation, personal injury recovery

Who owes you the money or property?

_____
_____

How much is owed?

$_____
$_____

Do you believe you will likely receive payment in the next 180 days?

☐ No
☐ Yes. Explain:

```
┌──────────────┐
│              │
│              │
└──────────────┘
```

Part 4:   Answer These Additional Questions

17. Have you paid anyone for services for this case, including filling out this application, the bankruptcy filing package, or the schedules?

☐ No
☐ Yes. Whom did you pay? *Check all that apply:*
  ☐ An attorney
  ☐ A bankruptcy petition preparer, paralegal, or typing service
  ☐ Someone else _____

How much did you pay?

$_____

18. Have you promised to pay or do you expect to pay someone for services for your bankruptcy case?

☐ No
☐ Yes. Whom do you expect to pay? *Check all that apply:*
  ☐ An attorney
  ☐ A bankruptcy petition preparer, paralegal, or typing service
  ☐ Someone else _____

How much do you expect to pay?

$_____

19. Has anyone paid someone on your behalf for services for this case?

☐ No
☐ Yes. Who was paid on your behalf? *Check all that apply:*
  ☐ An attorney
  ☐ A bankruptcy petition preparer, paralegal, or typing service
  ☐ Someone else _____

Who paid? *Check all that apply:*
  ☐ Parent
  ☐ Brother or sister
  ☐ Friend
  ☐ Pastor or clergy
  ☐ Someone else _____

How much did someone else pay?

$_____

20. Have you filed for bankruptcy within the last 8 years?

☐ No
☐ Yes. District _____ When _____ Case number _____
                                    MM/ DD/ YYYY

District _____ When _____ Case number _____
                          MM/ DD/ YYYY

District _____ When _____ Case number _____
                          MM/ DD/ YYYY

Part 5:   Sign Below

By signing here under penalty of perjury, I declare that I cannot afford to pay the filing fee either in full or in installments. I also declare that the information I provided in this application is true and correct.

✗ _____   ✗ _____
Signature of Debtor 1   Signature of Debtor 2

Date _____   Date _____
     MM / DD / YYYY   MM / DD / YYYY

Fill in this information to identify the case:

Debtor 1 _____
First Name   Middle Name   Last Name

Debtor 2 _____
(Spouse, if filing) First Name   Middle Name   Last Name

United States Bankruptcy Court for the: _____ District of .

Case number _____
(if known)

Order on the Application to Have the Chapter 7 Filing Fee Waived

After considering the debtor's *Application to Have the Chapter 7 Filing Fee Waived* (Official Form 103B), the court orders that the application is:

[ ] Granted. However, the court may order the debtor to pay the fee in the future if developments in administering the bankruptcy case show that the waiver was unwarranted.

[ ] Denied. The debtor must pay the filing fee according to the following terms:

	You must pay...	On or before this date...
	$_____	Month / day / year
	$_____	Month / day / year
	$_____	Month / day / year
+	$_____	Month / day / year
Total	[_____]	

If the debtor would like to propose a different payment timetable, the debtor must file a motion promptly with a payment proposal. The debtor may use *Application for Individuals to Pay the Filing Fee in Installments* (Official Form 103A) for this purpose. The court will consider it.

The debtor must pay the entire filing fee before making any more payments or transferring any more property to an attorney, bankruptcy petition preparer, or anyone else in connection with the bankruptcy case. The debtor must also pay the entire filing fee to receive a discharge. If the debtor does not make any payment when it is due, the bankruptcy case may be dismissed and the debtor's rights in future bankruptcy cases may be affected.

[ ] Scheduled for hearing.

A hearing to consider the debtor's application will be held

on _____ at _____ AM / PM at _____.
Month / day / year   Address of courthouse

If the debtor does not appear at this hearing, the court may deny the application.

_____   By the court: _____
Month / day / year   United States Bankruptcy Judge

Print	Save As...	Add Attachment		Reset

Fill in this information to identify your case:

Debtor 1 _____
First Name   Middle Name   Last Name

Debtor 2 _____
(Spouse, if filing) First Name   Middle Name   Last Name

United States Bankruptcy Court for the: _____ District of _____

Case number _____
(if known)

☐ Check if this is an amended filing

Official Form 104

For Individual Chapter 11 Cases: List of Creditors Who Have the 20 Largest Unsecured Claims Against You and Are Not Insiders

12/15

If you are an individual filing for bankruptcy under Chapter 11, you must fill out this form. If you are filing under Chapter 7, Chapter 12, or Chapter 13, do not fill out this form. Do not include claims by anyone who is an *insider*. Insiders include your relatives; any general partners; relatives of any general partners; partnerships of which you are a general partner; corporations of which you are an officer, director, person in control, or owner of 20 percent or more of their voting securities; and any managing agent, including one for a business you operate as a sole proprietor. 11 U.S.C. § 101. Also, do not include claims by secured creditors unless the unsecured claim resulting from inadequate collateral value places the creditor among the holders of the 20 largest unsecured claims.

Be as complete and accurate as possible. If two married people are filing together, both are equally responsible for supplying correct information.

Part 1: List the 20 Unsecured Claims in Order from Largest to Smallest. Do Not Include Claims by Insiders.

Unsecured claim

1

Creditor's Name

Number   Street

City   State   ZIP Code

Contact

Contact phone

What is the nature of the claim? _____ $_____

As of the date you file, the claim is: Check all that apply.
☐ Contingent
☐ Unliquidated
☐ Disputed
☐ None of the above apply

Does the creditor have a lien on your property?
☐ No
☐ Yes. Total claim (secured and unsecured): $_____
       Value of security: − $_____
       Unsecured claim $_____

2

Creditor's Name

Number   Street

City   State   ZIP Code

Contact

Contact phone

What is the nature of the claim? _____ $_____

As of the date you file, the claim is: Check all that apply.
☐ Contingent
☐ Unliquidated
☐ Disputed
☐ None of the above apply

Does the creditor have a lien on your property?
☐ No
☐ Yes. Total claim (secured and unsecured): $_____
       Value of security: − $_____
       Unsecured claim $_____

Official Form 104   For Individual Chapter 11 Cases: List of Creditors Who Have the 20 Largest Unsecured Claims   page 1

SELECTED OFFICIAL FORMS

Debtor 1 _____ Case number *(if known)* _____
     First Name   Middle Name   Last Name

	Unsecured claim

3

Creditor's Name _____

Number _____ Street _____

_____

City _____ State ____ ZIP Code ____

Contact _____

Contact phone _____

What is the nature of the claim? _____ $ _____

As of the date you file, the claim is: Check all that apply.
- ❑ Contingent
- ❑ Unliquidated
- ❑ Disputed
- ❑ None of the above apply

Does the creditor have a lien on your property?
- ❑ No
- ❑ Yes. Total claim (secured and unsecured): $ _____
  - Value of security: − $ _____
  - Unsecured claim $ _____

4

Creditor's Name _____

Number _____ Street _____

_____

City _____ State ____ ZIP Code ____

Contact _____

Contact phone _____

What is the nature of the claim? _____ $ _____

As of the date you file, the claim is: Check all that apply.
- ❑ Contingent
- ❑ Unliquidated
- ❑ Disputed
- ❑ None of the above apply

Does the creditor have a lien on your property?
- ❑ No
- ❑ Yes. Total claim (secured and unsecured): $ _____
  - Value of security: − $ _____
  - Unsecured claim $ _____

5

Creditor's Name _____

Number _____ Street _____

_____

City _____ State ____ ZIP Code ____

Contact _____

Contact phone _____

What is the nature of the claim? _____ $ _____

As of the date you file, the claim is: Check all that apply.
- ❑ Contingent
- ❑ Unliquidated
- ❑ Disputed
- ❑ None of the above apply

Does the creditor have a lien on your property?
- ❑ No
- ❑ Yes. Total claim (secured and unsecured): $ _____
  - Value of security: − $ _____
  - Unsecured claim $ _____

6

Creditor's Name _____

Number _____ Street _____

_____

City _____ State ____ ZIP Code ____

Contact _____

Contact phone _____

What is the nature of the claim? _____ $ _____

As of the date you file, the claim is: Check all that apply.
- ❑ Contingent
- ❑ Unliquidated
- ❑ Disputed
- ❑ None of the above apply

Does the creditor have a lien on your property?
- ❑ No
- ❑ Yes. Total claim (secured and unsecured): $ _____
  - Value of security: − $ _____
  - Unsecured claim $ _____

7

Creditor's Name _____

Number _____ Street _____

_____

City _____ State ____ ZIP Code ____

Contact _____

Contact phone _____

What is the nature of the claim? _____ $ _____

As of the date you file, the claim is: Check all that apply.
- ❑ Contingent
- ❑ Unliquidated
- ❑ Disputed
- ❑ None of the above apply

Does the creditor have a lien on your property?
- ❑ No
- ❑ Yes. Total claim (secured and unsecured): $ _____
  - Value of security: − $ _____
  - Unsecured claim $ _____

Official Form 104   **For Individual Chapter 11 Cases: List of Creditors Who Have the 20 Largest Unsecured Claims**   page 2

526

Debtor 1 _____ Case number (if known)_____

First Name   Middle Name   Last Name

	Unsecured claim

8

Creditor's Name _____

Number   Street _____

_____

City   State   ZIP Code

Contact _____

Contact phone _____

What is the nature of the claim? _____ $_____

As of the date you file, the claim is: Check all that apply.
- ❏ Contingent
- ❏ Unliquidated
- ❏ Disputed
- ❏ None of the above apply

Does the creditor have a lien on your property?
- ❏ No
- ❏ Yes. Total claim (secured and unsecured): $_____
  - Value of security: − $_____
  - Unsecured claim $_____

9

Creditor's Name _____

Number   Street _____

_____

City   State   ZIP Code

Contact _____

Contact phone _____

What is the nature of the claim? _____ $_____

As of the date you file, the claim is: Check all that apply.
- ❏ Contingent
- ❏ Unliquidated
- ❏ Disputed
- ❏ None of the above apply

Does the creditor have a lien on your property?
- ❏ No
- ❏ Yes. Total claim (secured and unsecured): $_____
  - Value of security: − $_____
  - Unsecured claim $_____

10

Creditor's Name _____

Number   Street _____

_____

City   State   ZIP Code

Contact _____

Contact phone _____

What is the nature of the claim? _____ $_____

As of the date you file, the claim is: Check all that apply.
- ❏ Contingent
- ❏ Unliquidated
- ❏ Disputed
- ❏ None of the above apply

Does the creditor have a lien on your property?
- ❏ No
- ❏ Yes. Total claim (secured and unsecured): $_____
  - Value of security: − $_____
  - Unsecured claim $_____

11

Creditor's Name _____

Number   Street _____

_____

City   State   ZIP Code

Contact _____

Contact phone _____

What is the nature of the claim? _____ $_____

As of the date you file, the claim is: Check all that apply.
- ❏ Contingent
- ❏ Unliquidated
- ❏ Disputed
- ❏ None of the above apply

Does the creditor have a lien on your property?
- ❏ No
- ❏ Yes. Total claim (secured and unsecured): $_____
  - Value of security: − $_____
  - Unsecured claim $_____

12

Creditor's Name _____

Number   Street _____

_____

City   State   ZIP Code

Contact _____

Contact phone _____

What is the nature of the claim? _____ $_____

As of the date you file, the claim is: Check all that apply.
- ❏ Contingent
- ❏ Unliquidated
- ❏ Disputed
- ❏ None of the above apply

Does the creditor have a lien on your property?
- ❏ No
- ❏ Yes. Total claim (secured and unsecured): $_____
  - Value of security: − $_____
  - Unsecured claim $_____

Debtor 1 _____   Case number (if known)_____
         First Name   Middle Name   Last Name

		Unsecured claim

13

Creditor's Name _____

Number _____ Street _____

_____

City _____ State ____ ZIP Code

Contact _____

Contact phone _____

What is the nature of the claim? _____ $_____

As of the date you file, the claim is: Check all that apply.
- ☐ Contingent
- ☐ Unliquidated
- ☐ Disputed
- ☐ None of the above apply

Does the creditor have a lien on your property?
- ☐ No
- ☐ Yes. Total claim (secured and unsecured): $_____
      Value of security: – $_____
      Unsecured claim $_____

14

Creditor's Name _____

Number _____ Street _____

_____

City _____ State ____ ZIP Code

Contact _____

Contact phone _____

What is the nature of the claim? _____ $_____

As of the date you file, the claim is: Check all that apply.
- ☐ Contingent
- ☐ Unliquidated
- ☐ Disputed
- ☐ None of the above apply

Does the creditor have a lien on your property?
- ☐ No
- ☐ Yes. Total claim (secured and unsecured): $_____
      Value of security: – $_____
      Unsecured claim $_____

15

Creditor's Name _____

Number _____ Street _____

_____

City _____ State ____ ZIP Code

Contact _____

Contact phone _____

What is the nature of the claim? _____ $_____

As of the date you file, the claim is: Check all that apply.
- ☐ Contingent
- ☐ Unliquidated
- ☐ Disputed
- ☐ None of the above apply

Does the creditor have a lien on your property?
- ☐ No
- ☐ Yes. Total claim (secured and unsecured): $_____
      Value of security: – $_____
      Unsecured claim $_____

16

Creditor's Name _____

Number _____ Street _____

_____

City _____ State ____ ZIP Code

Contact _____

Contact phone _____

What is the nature of the claim? _____ $_____

As of the date you file, the claim is: Check all that apply.
- ☐ Contingent
- ☐ Unliquidated
- ☐ Disputed
- ☐ None of the above apply

Does the creditor have a lien on your property?
- ☐ No
- ☐ Yes. Total claim (secured and unsecured): $_____
      Value of security: – $_____
      Unsecured claim $_____

17

Creditor's Name _____

Number _____ Street _____

_____

City _____ State ____ ZIP Code

Contact _____

Contact phone _____

What is the nature of the claim? _____ $_____

As of the date you file, the claim is: Check all that apply.
- ☐ Contingent
- ☐ Unliquidated
- ☐ Disputed
- ☐ None of the above apply

Does the creditor have a lien on your property?
- ☐ No
- ☐ Yes. Total claim (secured and unsecured): $_____
      Value of security: – $_____
      Unsecured claim $_____

Official Form 104   For Individual Chapter 11 Cases: List of Creditors Who Have the 20 Largest Unsecured Claims   page 4

Debtor 1 _____   Case number (if known)_____
First Name   Middle Name   Last Name

		Unsecured claim

18 _____   What is the nature of the claim? _____ $_____
Creditor's Name

_____   **As of the date you file, the claim is:** Check all that apply.
Number   Street   ☐ Contingent
_____   ☐ Unliquidated
                              ☐ Disputed
City   State   ZIP Code   ☐ None of the above apply

_____   **Does the creditor have a lien on your property?**
Contact   ☐ No
                              ☐ Yes. Total claim (secured and unsecured): $_____
Contact phone _____   Value of security: − $_____
                                   Unsecured claim $_____

19 _____   What is the nature of the claim? _____ $_____
Creditor's Name

_____   **As of the date you file, the claim is:** Check all that apply.
Number   Street   ☐ Contingent
_____   ☐ Unliquidated
                              ☐ Disputed
City   State   ZIP Code   ☐ None of the above apply

_____   **Does the creditor have a lien on your property?**
Contact   ☐ No
                              ☐ Yes. Total claim (secured and unsecured): $_____
Contact phone   Value of security: − $_____
                                   Unsecured claim $_____

20 _____   What is the nature of the claim? _____ $_____

                            As of the date you file, the claim is: Check all that apply.
                              ☐ Contingent
Creditor's Name   ☐ Unliquidated
_____   ☐ Disputed
Number   Street   ☐ None of the above apply

_____   **Does the creditor have a lien on your property?**
City   State   ZIP Code   ☐ No
                              ☐ Yes. Total claim (secured and unsecured): $_____
_____   Value of security: − $_____
Contact   Unsecured claim $_____

Contact phone

Part 2:   Sign Below

Under penalty of perjury, I declare that the information provided in this form is true and correct.

✗ _____   ✗ _____
Signature of Debtor 1   Signature of Debtor 2

Date _____   Date _____
      MM / DD / YYYY   MM / DD / YYYY

Official Form 104   For Individual Chapter 11 Cases: List of Creditors Who Have the 20 Largest Unsecured Claims   page 5

Print	Save As...	Reset

☐ Check if this is an
amended filing

Official Form 105

Involuntary Petition Against an Individual   12/15

Use this form to begin a bankruptcy case against an individual you allege to be a debtor subject to an involuntary case. If you want to begin a case against a non-individual, use the *Involuntary Petition Against a Non-individual* (Official Form 205). Be as complete and accurate as possible. If more space is needed, attach a separate sheet to this form. On the top of any additional pages, write name and case number (if known).

Part 1: Identify the Chapter of the Bankruptcy Code Under Which Petition Is Filed

1. **Chapter of the Bankruptcy Code**

    Check one:

    ☐ Chapter 7
    ☐ Chapter 11

Part 2: Identify the Debtor

2. **Debtor's full name**

    _____
    First name

    _____
    Middle name

    _____
    Last name

    _____
    Suffix (Sr., Jr., II, III)

3. **Other names you know the debtor has used in the last 8 years**

    Include any assumed, married, maiden, or trade names, or *doing business as* names.

    _____
    _____
    _____

4. **Only the last 4 digits of debtor's Social Security Number or federal Individual Taxpayer Identification Number (ITIN)**

    ☐ Unknown

    xxx – xx – ___ ___ ___ ___   OR   **9** xx – xx – ___ ___ ___ ___

5. **Any Employer Identification Numbers (EINs) used in the last 8 years**

    ☐ Unknown

    ___ ___ – ___ ___ ___ ___ ___ ___ ___
    EIN

    ___ ___ – ___ ___ ___ ___ ___ ___ ___
    EIN

Official Form 105   Involuntary Petition Against an Individual   page **1**

Debtor _____

Case number *(if known)* _____

6. Debtor's address	**Principal residence**	**Mailing address, if different from residence**

Principal residence

_____
Number   Street

_____

_____
City   State   ZIP Code

_____
County

Principal place of business

_____
Number   Street

_____

_____
City   State   ZIP Code

_____
County

Mailing address, if different from residence

_____
Number   Street

_____

_____
City   State   ZIP Code

---

7. Type of business

❑ Debtor does not operate a business

Check one if the debtor operates a business:

❑ Health Care Business (as defined in 11 U.S.C. § 101(27A))
❑ Single Asset Real Estate (as defined in 11 U.S.C. § 101(51B))
❑ Stockbroker (as defined in 11 U.S.C. § 101(53A))
❑ Commodity Broker (as defined in 11 U.S.C. § 101(6))
❑ None of the above

---

8. Type of debt

Each petitioner believes:

❑ **Debts are primarily consumer debts.** *Consumer debts* are defined in 11 U.S.C. § 101(8) as "incurred by an individual primarily for a personal, family, or household purpose."

❑ **Debts are primarily business debts.** *Business debts* are debts that were incurred to obtain money for a business or investment or through the operation of the business or investment.

---

9. Do you know of any bankruptcy cases pending by or against any partner, spouse, or affiliate of this debtor?

❑ No

❑ Yes. Debtor _____   Relationship _____

District _____ Date filed _____   Case number, if known _____
                                   MM / DD / YYYY

Debtor _____   Relationship _____

District _____ Date filed _____   Case number, if known _____
                                   MM / DD / YYYY

Debtor _____   Case number *(if known)*_____

Part 3:	Report About the Case

10. Venue

Reason for filing in this court.

Check one:

❑ Over the last 180 days before the filing of this bankruptcy, the debtor has resided, had the principal place of business, or had principal assets in this district longer than in any other district.

❑ A bankruptcy case concerning debtor's affiliates, general partner, or partnership is pending in this district.

❑ Other reason. Explain. (See 28 U.S.C. § 1408.) _____

11. Allegations

Each petitioner is eligible to file this petition under 11 U.S.C. § 303(b).

The debtor may be the subject of an involuntary case under 11 U.S.C. § 303(a).

At least one box must be checked:

❑ The debtor is generally not paying such debtor's debts as they become due, unless they are the subject of a bona fide dispute as to liability or amount.

❑ Within 120 days before the filing of this petition, a custodian, other than a trustee, receiver, or agent appointed or authorized to take charge of less than substantially all of the property of the debtor for the purpose of enforcing a lien against such property, was appointed or took possession.

12. Has there been a transfer of any claim against the debtor by or to any petitioner?

❑ No

❑ Yes. Attach all documents that evidence the transfer and any statements required under Bankruptcy Rule 1003(a).

13. Each petitioner's claim

Name of petitioner	Nature of petitioner's claim	Amount of the claim above the value of any lien
		$ _____
		$ _____
		$ _____
	Total	$ _____

If more than 3 petitioners, attach additional sheets with the statement under penalty of perjury, each petitioner's (or representative's) signature under the statement, along with the signature of the petitioner's attorney, and the information on the petitioning creditor, the petitioner's claim, the petitioner's representative, and the attorney following the format on this form.

Debtor _____	Case number (if known) _____

Part 4: Request for Relief

Petitioners request that an order for relief be entered against the debtor under the chapter specified in Part 1 of this petition. If a petitioning creditor is a corporation, attach the corporate ownership statement required by Bankruptcy Rule 1010(b). If any petitioner is a foreign representative appointed in a foreign proceeding, a certified copy of the order of the court granting recognition is attached.

Petitioners declare under penalty of perjury that the information provided in this petition is true and correct. Petitioners understand that if they make a false statement, they could be fined up to $250,000 or imprisoned for up to 5 years, or both.
18 U.S.C. §§ 152 and 3571. If relief is not ordered, the court may award attorneys' fees, costs, damages, and punitive damages. 11 U.S.C. § 303(i).

Petitioners or Petitioners' Representative	Attorneys
✘ _____	✘ _____
Signature of petitioner or representative, including representative's title	Signature of attorney
Printed name of petitioner	Printed name
Date signed _____	Firm name, if any
MM / DD / YYYY	
	Number Street
Mailing address of petitioner	
	City State ZIP Code
Number Street	
	Date signed _____
City State ZIP Code	MM / DD / YYYY
	Contact phone _____ Email _____
If petitioner is an individual and is not represented by an attorney:	
Contact phone _____	
Email _____	
Name and mailing address of petitioner's representative, if any	
Name	
Number Street	
City State ZIP Code	

Debtor _____   Case number (if known)_____

✖ _____

Signature of petitioner or representative, including representative's title

Printed name of petitioner

Date signed _____
MM / DD / YYYY

Mailing address of petitioner

_____
Number   Street

_____
City   State   ZIP Code

Name and mailing address of petitioner's representative, if any

_____
Name

_____
Number   Street

_____
City   State ZIP Code

✖ _____

Signature of Attorney

Printed name

Firm name, if any

_____
Number   Street

_____
City   State   ZIP Code

Date signed _____
MM / DD / YYYY

Contact phone _____ Email _____

✖ _____

Signature of petitioner or representative, including representative's title

Printed name of petitioner

Date signed _____
MM / DD / YYYY

Mailing address of petitioner

_____
Number   Street

_____
City   State   ZIP Code

Name and mailing address of petitioner's representative, if any

_____
Name

_____
Number   Street

_____
City   State   ZIP Code

✖ _____

Signature of Attorney

Printed name

Firm name, if any

_____
Number   Street

_____
City   State   ZIP Code

Date signed _____
MM / DD / YYYY

Contact phone _____ Email _____

Official Form 105   Involuntary Petition Against an Individual   page **5**

| Print | Save As... | Add Attachment | Reset |

Fill in this information to identify your case:

Debtor 1 _____
        First Name   Middle Name   Last Name

Debtor 2 _____
(Spouse, if filing) First Name   Middle Name   Last Name

United States Bankruptcy Court for the: _____ District of _____

Case number _____
        (If known)

☐ Check if this is an amended filing

Official Form 106Sum

Summary of Your Assets and Liabilities and Certain Statistical Information   12/15

Be as complete and accurate as possible. If two married people are filing together, both are equally responsible for supplying correct information. Fill out all of your schedules first; then complete the information on this form. If you are filing amended schedules after you file your original forms, you must fill out a new *Summary* and check the box at the top of this page.

Part 1:   **Summarize Your Assets**

	Your assets Value of what you own
1. *Schedule A/B: Property* (Official Form 106A/B)	
1a. Copy line 55, Total real estate, from *Schedule A/B*	$ _____
1b. Copy line 62, Total personal property, from *Schedule A/B*	$ _____
1c. Copy line 63, Total of all property on *Schedule A/B*	$ _____

Part 2:   **Summarize Your Liabilities**

	Your liabilities Amount you owe
2. *Schedule D: Creditors Who Have Claims Secured by Property* (Official Form 106D)	
2a. Copy the total you listed in Column A, *Amount of claim*, at the bottom of the last page of Part 1 of *Schedule D*	$ _____
3. *Schedule E/F: Creditors Who Have Unsecured Claims* (Official Form 106E/F)	
3a. Copy the total claims from Part 1 (priority unsecured claims) from line 6e of *Schedule E/F*	$ _____
3b. Copy the total claims from Part 2 (nonpriority unsecured claims) from line 6j of *Schedule E/F*	+ $ _____
Your total liabilities	$ _____

Part 3:   **Summarize Your Income and Expenses**

4. *Schedule I: Your Income* (Official Form 106I)	
Copy your combined monthly income from line 12 of *Schedule I*	$ _____
5. *Schedule J: Your Expenses* (Official Form 106J)	
Copy your monthly expenses from line 22c of *Schedule J*	$ _____

Debtor 1 _____   Case number (if known)_____
         First Name   Middle Name   Last Name

Part 4:	Answer These Questions for Administrative and Statistical Records

6. **Are you filing for bankruptcy under Chapters 7, 11, or 13?**

   ☐ No. You have nothing to report on this part of the form. Check this box and submit this form to the court with your other schedules.
   ☐ Yes

7. **What kind of debt do you have?**

   ☐ **Your debts are primarily consumer debts.** *Consumer debts* are those "incurred by an individual primarily for a personal, family, or household purpose." 11 U.S.C. § 101(8). Fill out lines 8-9g for statistical purposes. 28 U.S.C. § 159.

   ☐ **Your debts are not primarily consumer debts.** You have nothing to report on this part of the form. Check this box and submit this form to the court with your other schedules.

8. From the *Statement of Your Current Monthly Income*: Copy your total current monthly income from Official Form 122A-1 Line 11; **OR**, Form 122B Line 11; **OR**, Form 122C-1 Line 14.

   $ _____

9. Copy the following special categories of claims from Part 4, line 6 of *Schedule E/F*:

	Total claim
From Part 4 on *Schedule E/F*, copy the following:	
9a. Domestic support obligations (Copy line 6a.)	$_____
9b. Taxes and certain other debts you owe the government. (Copy line 6b.)	$_____
9c. Claims for death or personal injury while you were intoxicated. (Copy line 6c.)	$_____
9d. Student loans. (Copy line 6f.)	$_____
9e. Obligations arising out of a separation agreement or divorce that you did not report as priority claims. (Copy line 6g.)	$_____
9f. Debts to pension or profit-sharing plans, and other similar debts. (Copy line 6h.)	+ $_____
9g. **Total.** Add lines 9a through 9f.	$_____

Print	Save As...	Add Attachment	Reset

Fill in this information to identify your case and this filing:

Debtor 1 _____
         First Name   Middle Name   Last Name

Debtor 2 _____
(Spouse, if filing) First Name   Middle Name   Last Name

United States Bankruptcy Court for the: _____ District of _____

Case number _____

☐ Check if this is an
amended filing

Official Form 106A/B

Schedule A/B: Property

12/15

In each category, separately list and describe items. List an asset only once. If an asset fits in more than one category, list the asset in the category where you think it fits best. Be as complete and accurate as possible. If two married people are filing together, both are equally responsible for supplying correct information. If more space is needed, attach a separate sheet to this form. On the top of any additional pages, write your name and case number (if known). Answer every question.

Part 1: **Describe Each Residence, Building, Land, or Other Real Estate You Own or Have an Interest In**

1. Do you own or have any legal or equitable interest in any residence, building, land, or similar property?

   ☐ No. Go to Part 2.
   ☐ Yes. Where is the property?

1.1. _____
Street address, if available, or other description

_____

_____
City   State   ZIP Code

_____
County

What is the property? Check all that apply.
☐ Single-family home
☐ Duplex or multi-unit building
☐ Condominium or cooperative
☐ Manufactured or mobile home
☐ Land
☐ Investment property
☐ Timeshare
☐ Other _____

Who has an interest in the property? Check one.
☐ Debtor 1 only
☐ Debtor 2 only
☐ Debtor 1 and Debtor 2 only
☐ At least one of the debtors and another

Other information you wish to add about this item, such as local property identification number: _____

Do not deduct secured claims or exemptions. Put the amount of any secured claims on *Schedule D: Creditors Who Have Claims Secured by Property.*

Current value of the   Current value of the
entire property?   portion you own?
$_____ $_____

Describe the nature of your ownership interest (such as fee simple, tenancy by the entireties, or a life estate), if known.

_____

☐ Check if this is community property
(see instructions)

If you own or have more than one, list here:

1.2. _____
Street address, if available, or other description

_____

_____
City   State   ZIP Code

_____
County

What is the property? Check all that apply.
☐ Single-family home
☐ Duplex or multi-unit building
☐ Condominium or cooperative
☐ Manufactured or mobile home
☐ Land
☐ Investment property
☐ Timeshare
☐ Other _____

Who has an interest in the property? Check one.
☐ Debtor 1 only
☐ Debtor 2 only
☐ Debtor 1 and Debtor 2 only
☐ At least one of the debtors and another

Other information you wish to add about this item, such as local property identification number: _____

Do not deduct secured claims or exemptions. Put the amount of any secured claims on *Schedule D: Creditors Who Have Claims Secured by Property.*

Current value of the   Current value of the
entire property?   portion you own?
$_____ $_____

Describe the nature of your ownership interest (such as fee simple, tenancy by the entireties, or a life estate), if known.

_____

☐ Check if this is community property
(see instructions)

SELECTED OFFICIAL FORMS

Debtor 1 _____   Case number (if known) _____
First Name   Middle Name   Last Name

| 1.3. _____
Street address, if available, or other description

_____

_____
City   State   ZIP Code

_____
County | **What is the property?** Check all that apply.
☐ Single-family home
☐ Duplex or multi-unit building
☐ Condominium or cooperative
☐ Manufactured or mobile home
☐ Land
☐ Investment property
☐ Timeshare
☐ Other _____

Who has an interest in the property? Check one.
☐ Debtor 1 only
☐ Debtor 2 only
☐ Debtor 1 and Debtor 2 only
☐ At least one of the debtors and another

Other information you wish to add about this item, such as local property identification number: _____ | Do not deduct secured claims or exemptions. Put the amount of any secured claims on *Schedule D: Creditors Who Have Claims Secured by Property.*

Current value of the entire property?   Current value of the portion you own?
$_____ $_____

Describe the nature of your ownership interest (such as fee simple, tenancy by the entireties, or a life estate), if known.
_____

☐ **Check if this is community property** (see instructions) |

2. Add the dollar value of the portion you own for all of your entries from Part 1, including any entries for pages you have attached for Part 1. Write that number here. ....→ $_____

Part 2: Describe Your Vehicles

Do you own, lease, or have legal or equitable interest in any vehicles, whether they are registered or not? Include any vehicles you own that someone else drives. If you lease a vehicle, also report it on *Schedule G: Executory Contracts and Unexpired Leases.*

3. Cars, vans, trucks, tractors, sport utility vehicles, motorcycles
☐ No
☐ Yes

| 3.1. Make: _____
Model: _____
Year: _____
Approximate mileage: _____
Other information:
[_____] | **Who has an interest in the property?** Check one.
☐ Debtor 1 only
☐ Debtor 2 only
☐ Debtor 1 and Debtor 2 only
☐ At least one of the debtors and another

☐ **Check if this is community property** (see instructions) | Do not deduct secured claims or exemptions. Put the amount of any secured claims on *Schedule D: Creditors Who Have Claims Secured by Property.*

Current value of the entire property?   Current value of the portion you own?
$_____ $_____ |

If you own or have more than one, describe here:

| 3.2. Make: _____
Model: _____
Year: _____
Approximate mileage: _____
Other information:
[_____] | **Who has an interest in the property?** Check one.
☐ Debtor 1 only
☐ Debtor 2 only
☐ Debtor 1 and Debtor 2 only
☐ At least one of the debtors and another

☐ **Check if this is community property** (see instructions) | Do not deduct secured claims or exemptions. Put the amount of any secured claims on *Schedule D: Creditors Who Have Claims Secured by Property.*

Current value of the entire property?   Current value of the portion you own?
$_____ $_____ |

Official Form 106A/B   Schedule A/B: Property   page 2

Debtor 1 _____   Case number *(if known)*_____
First Name   Middle Name   Last Name

3.3. Make: _____

Model: _____

Year: _____

Approximate mileage: _____

Other information:

[ ]

Who has an interest in the property? Check one.
- [ ] Debtor 1 only
- [ ] Debtor 2 only
- [ ] Debtor 1 and Debtor 2 only
- [ ] At least one of the debtors and another

- [ ] Check if this is community property (see instructions)

Do not deduct secured claims or exemptions. Put the amount of any secured claims on *Schedule D: Creditors Who Have Claims Secured by Property.*

Current value of the entire property?	Current value of the portion you own?
$_____	$_____

3.4. Make: _____

Model: _____

Year: _____

Approximate mileage: _____

Other information:

[ ]

Who has an interest in the property? Check one.
- [ ] Debtor 1 only
- [ ] Debtor 2 only
- [ ] Debtor 1 and Debtor 2 only
- [ ] At least one of the debtors and another

- [ ] Check if this is community property (see instructions)

Do not deduct secured claims or exemptions. Put the amount of any secured claims on *Schedule D: Creditors Who Have Claims Secured by Property.*

Current value of the entire property?	Current value of the portion you own?
$_____	$_____

---

4. Watercraft, aircraft, motor homes, ATVs and other recreational vehicles, other vehicles, and accessories

Examples: Boats, trailers, motors, personal watercraft, fishing vessels, snowmobiles, motorcycle accessories

- [ ] No
- [ ] Yes

4.1. Make: _____

Model: _____

Year: _____

Other information:

[ ]

Who has an interest in the property? Check one.
- [ ] Debtor 1 only
- [ ] Debtor 2 only
- [ ] Debtor 1 and Debtor 2 only
- [ ] At least one of the debtors and another

- [ ] Check if this is community property (see instructions)

Do not deduct secured claims or exemptions. Put the amount of any secured claims on *Schedule D: Creditors Who Have Claims Secured by Property.*

Current value of the entire property?	Current value of the portion you own?
$_____	$_____

If you own or have more than one, list here:

4.2. Make: _____

Model: _____

Year: _____

Other information:

[ ]

Who has an interest in the property? Check one.
- [ ] Debtor 1 only
- [ ] Debtor 2 only
- [ ] Debtor 1 and Debtor 2 only
- [ ] At least one of the debtors and another

- [ ] Check if this is community property (see instructions)

Do not deduct secured claims or exemptions. Put the amount of any secured claims on *Schedule D: Creditors Who Have Claims Secured by Property.*

Current value of the entire property?	Current value of the portion you own?
$_____	$_____

---

5. Add the dollar value of the portion you own for all of your entries from Part 2, including any entries for pages you have attached for Part 2. Write that number here .... → | $_____ |

SELECTED OFFICIAL FORMS

Debtor 1 _____   Case number *(if known)*_____

First Name   Middle Name   Last Name

Part 3:	Describe Your Personal and Household Items

Do you own or have any legal or equitable interest in any of the following items?	Current value of the portion you own? Do not deduct secured claims or exemptions.

6. Household goods and furnishings

Examples: Major appliances, furniture, linens, china, kitchenware

❑ No

❑ Yes. Describe......... [_____] $_____

7. Electronics

Examples: Televisions and radios; audio, video, stereo, and digital equipment; computers, printers, scanners; music collections; electronic devices including cell phones, cameras, media players, games

❑ No

❑ Yes. Describe......... [_____] $_____

8. Collectibles of value

Examples: Antiques and figurines; paintings, prints, or other artwork; books, pictures, or other art objects; stamp, coin, or baseball card collections; other collections, memorabilia, collectibles

❑ No

❑ Yes. Describe......... [_____] $_____

9. Equipment for sports and hobbies

Examples: Sports, photographic, exercise, and other hobby equipment; bicycles, pool tables, golf clubs, skis; canoes and kayaks; carpentry tools; musical instruments

❑ No

❑ Yes. Describe......... [_____] $_____

10. Firearms

Examples: Pistols, rifles, shotguns, ammunition, and related equipment

❑ No

❑ Yes. Describe......... [_____] $_____

11. Clothes

Examples: Everyday clothes, furs, leather coats, designer wear, shoes, accessories

❑ No

❑ Yes. Describe......... [_____] $_____

12. Jewelry

Examples: Everyday jewelry, costume jewelry, engagement rings, wedding rings, heirloom jewelry, watches, gems, gold, silver

❑ No

❑ Yes. Describe......... [_____] $_____

13. Non-farm animals

Examples: Dogs, cats, birds, horses

❑ No

❑ Yes. Describe......... [_____] $_____

14. Any other personal and household items you did not already list, including any health aids you did not list

❑ No

❑ Yes. Give specific information. .... [_____] $_____

15. Add the dollar value of all of your entries from Part 3, including any entries for pages you have attached for Part 3. Write that number here .... ➔ $_____

SELECTED OFFICIAL FORMS

Debtor 1 _____   Case number (if known)_____
         First Name   Middle Name   Last Name

Part 4:   Describe Your Financial Assets

Do you own or have any legal or equitable interest in any of the following?	Current value of the portion you own? Do not deduct secured claims or exemptions.

16. Cash

Examples: Money you have in your wallet, in your home, in a safe deposit box, and on hand when you file your petition

❏ No
❏ Yes ....   Cash: .... $_____

17. Deposits of money

Examples: Checking, savings, or other financial accounts; certificates of deposit; shares in credit unions, brokerage houses, and other similar institutions. If you have multiple accounts with the same institution, list each.

❏ No
❏ Yes ....   Institution name:

17.1. Checking account:	_____	$_____
17.2. Checking account:	_____	$_____
17.3. Savings account:	_____	$_____
17.4. Savings account:	_____	$_____
17.5. Certificates of deposit:	_____	$_____
17.6. Other financial account:	_____	$_____
17.7. Other financial account:	_____	$_____
17.8. Other financial account:	_____	$_____
17.9. Other financial account:	_____	$_____

18. Bonds, mutual funds, or publicly traded stocks

Examples: Bond funds, investment accounts with brokerage firms, money market accounts

❏ No
❏ Yes ....   Institution or issuer name:

_____ $_____
_____ $_____
_____ $_____

19. Non-publicly traded stock and interests in incorporated and unincorporated businesses, including an interest in an LLC, partnership, and joint venture

❏ No   Name of entity: % of ownership:
❏ Yes. Give specific   0%____% $_____
   information about   _____   0%____% $_____
   them..................... _____   0%____% $_____
                        _____

Debtor 1 _____   Case number *(if known)*_____
                First Name   Middle Name   Last Name

20. **Government and corporate bonds and other negotiable and non-negotiable instruments**

   Negotiable instruments include personal checks, cashiers' checks, promissory notes, and money orders.
   Non-negotiable instruments are those you cannot transfer to someone by signing or delivering them.

   ❑ No
   ❑ Yes. Give specific   Issuer name:
       information about
       them......................   _____ $_____
                                      _____ $_____
                                      _____ $_____

21. **Retirement or pension accounts**

   Examples: Interests in IRA, ERISA, Keogh, 401(k), 403(b), thrift savings accounts, or other pension or profit-sharing plans

   ❑ No
   ❑ Yes. List each
       account separately.   Type of account: Institution name:

                             401(k) or similar plan: _____ $_____

                             Pension plan: _____ $_____

                             IRA: _____ $_____

                             Retirement account: _____ $_____

                             Keogh: _____ $_____

                             Additional account: _____ $_____

                             Additional account: _____ $_____

22. **Security deposits and prepayments**

   Your share of all unused deposits you have made so that you may continue service or use from a company
   Examples: Agreements with landlords, prepaid rent, public utilities (electric, gas, water), telecommunications
   companies, or others

   ❑ No
   ❑ Yes ....   Institution name or individual:

                             Electric: _____ $_____

                             Gas: _____ $_____

                             Heating oil: _____ $_____

                             Security deposit on rental unit: _____ $_____

                             Prepaid rent: _____ $_____

                             Telephone: _____ $_____

                             Water: _____ $_____

                             Rented furniture: _____ $_____

                             Other: _____ $_____

23. **Annuities** (A contract for a periodic payment of money to you, either for life or for a number of years)

   ❑ No
   ❑ Yes ....   Issuer name and description:

                             _____ $_____
                             _____ $_____
                             _____ $_____

Official Form 106A/B   **Schedule A/B: Property**   page 6

Debtor 1 _____ Case number (if known)_____
              First Name   Middle Name   Last Name

24. Interests in an education IRA, in an account in a qualified ABLE program, or under a qualified state tuition program.
    26 U.S.C. §§ 530(b)(1), 529A(b), and 529(b)(1).

☐ No
☐ Yes .... Institution name and description. Separately file the records of any interests.11 U.S.C. § 521(c):

_____ $_____
_____ $_____
_____ $_____

25. Trusts, equitable or future interests in property (other than anything listed in line 1), and rights or powers
    exercisable for your benefit

☐ No
☐ Yes. Give specific
    information about them.... [   ] $_____

26. Patents, copyrights, trademarks, trade secrets, and other intellectual property
    Examples: Internet domain names, websites, proceeds from royalties and licensing agreements

☐ No
☐ Yes. Give specific
    information about them.... [   ] $_____

27. Licenses, franchises, and other general intangibles
    Examples: Building permits, exclusive licenses, cooperative association holdings, liquor licenses, professional licenses

☐ No
☐ Yes. Give specific
    information about them.... [   ] $_____

Money or property owed to you?	Current value of the portion you own? Do not deduct secured claims or exemptions.

28. Tax refunds owed to you

☐ No
☐ Yes. Give specific information
    about them, including whether
    you already filed the returns
    and the tax years. ....

Federal: $_____
State: $_____
Local: $_____

29. Family support
    Examples: Past due or lump sum alimony, spousal support, child support, maintenance, divorce settlement, property settlement

☐ No
☐ Yes. Give specific information.............

Alimony: $_____
Maintenance: $_____
Support: $_____
Divorce settlement: $_____
Property settlement: $_____

30. Other amounts someone owes you
    Examples: Unpaid wages, disability insurance payments, disability benefits, sick pay, vacation pay, workers' compensation,
              Social Security benefits; unpaid loans you made to someone else

☐ No
☐ Yes. Give specific information............. [   ] $_____

Official Form 106A/B   Schedule A/B: Property   page 7

Debtor 1 _____ Case number (if known)_____
         First Name   Middle Name   Last Name

31. Interests in insurance policies

Examples: Health, disability, or life insurance; health savings account (HSA); credit, homeowner's, or renter's insurance

☐ No

☐ Yes. Name the insurance company   Company name: Beneficiary: Surrender or refund value:
      of each policy and list its value. ...

                                           _____   _____ $_____

                                         _____   _____ $_____

                                         _____   _____ $_____

32. Any interest in property that is due you from someone who has died

If you are the beneficiary of a living trust, expect proceeds from a life insurance policy, or are currently entitled to receive property because someone has died.

☐ No

☐ Yes. Give specific information.............

                                     $_____

33. Claims against third parties, whether or not you have filed a lawsuit or made a demand for payment

Examples: Accidents, employment disputes, insurance claims, or rights to sue

☐ No

☐ Yes. Describe each claim. ....

                                     $_____

34. Other contingent and unliquidated claims of every nature, including counterclaims of the debtor and rights to set off claims

☐ No

☐ Yes. Describe each claim. ....

                                     $_____

35. Any financial assets you did not already list

☐ No

☐ Yes. Give specific information............

                                     $_____

36. Add the dollar value of all of your entries from Part 4, including any entries for pages you have attached for Part 4. Write that number here .... → $_____

Part 5:   **Describe Any Business-Related Property You Own or Have an Interest In. List any real estate in Part 1.**

37. Do you own or have any legal or equitable interest in any business-related property?

☐ No. Go to Part 6.

☐ Yes. Go to line 38.

                                            Current value of the portion you own?

                                            Do not deduct secured claims or exemptions.

38. Accounts receivable or commissions you already earned

☐ No

☐ Yes. Describe......

                                     $_____

39. Office equipment, furnishings, and supplies

Examples: Business-related computers, software, modems, printers, copiers, fax machines, rugs, telephones, desks, chairs, electronic devices

☐ No

☐ Yes. Describe......

                                     $_____

Official Form 106A/B   Schedule A/B: Property   page 8

Debtor 1 _____   Case number (if known)_____
First Name   Middle Name   Last Name

40. **Machinery, fixtures, equipment, supplies you use in business, and tools of your trade**

☐ No
☐ Yes. Describe........ [_____] $_____

41. **Inventory**

☐ No
☐ Yes. Describe........ [_____] $_____

42. **Interests in partnerships or joint ventures**

☐ No
☐ Yes. Describe .... Name of entity: % of ownership:

_____   _____ % $_____
_____   _____ % $_____
_____   _____ % $_____

43. **Customer lists, mailing lists, or other compilations**

☐ No
☐ Yes. Do your lists include personally identifiable information (as defined in 11 U.S.C. § 101(41A))?

   ☐ No
   ☐ Yes. Describe........ [_____] $_____

44. **Any business-related property you did not already list**

☐ No
☐ Yes. Give specific   _____ $_____
information ....   _____ $_____
                         _____ $_____
                         _____ $_____
                         _____ $_____
                         _____ $_____

45. **Add the dollar value of all of your entries from Part 5, including any entries for pages you have attached
for Part 5. Write that number here** .... → $_____

Part 6:   Describe Any Farm- and Commercial Fishing-Related Property You Own or Have an Interest In.
If you own or have an interest in farmland, list it in Part 1.

46. **Do you own or have any legal or equitable interest in any farm- or commercial fishing-related property?**

☐ No. Go to Part 7.
☐ Yes. Go to line 47.

> Current value of the portion you own?
> Do not deduct secured claims or exemptions.

47. **Farm animals**
Examples: Livestock, poultry, farm-raised fish

☐ No
☐ Yes .... [_____] $_____

Official Form 106A/B   Schedule A/B: Property   page 9

545

Debtor 1 _____ Case number (if known)_____
First Name   Middle Name   Last Name

48. **Crops—either growing or harvested**
☐ No
☐ Yes. Give specific
   information. ....

   $_____

49. **Farm and fishing equipment, implements, machinery, fixtures, and tools of trade**
☐ No
☐ Yes......................

   $_____

50. **Farm and fishing supplies, chemicals, and feed**
☐ No
☐ Yes......................

   $_____

51. **Any farm- and commercial fishing-related property you did not already list**
☐ No
☐ Yes. Give specific
   information. ....

   $_____

52. Add the dollar value of all of your entries from Part 6, including any entries for pages you have attached
    for Part 6. Write that number here ....➔ $_____

Part 7: Describe All Property You Own or Have an Interest in That You Did Not List Above

53. **Do you have other property of any kind you did not already list?**
    Examples: Season tickets, country club membership
☐ No
☐ Yes. Give specific
   information. ....

   $_____
   $_____
   $_____

54. Add the dollar value of all of your entries from Part 7. Write that number here ....➔ $_____

Part 8: List the Totals of Each Part of this Form

55. Part 1: Total real estate, line 2 ....➔ $_____

56. Part 2: Total vehicles, line 5 $_____

57. Part 3: Total personal and household items, line 15 $_____

58. Part 4: Total financial assets, line 36 $_____

59. Part 5: Total business-related property, line 45 $_____

60. Part 6: Total farm- and fishing-related property, line 52 $_____

61. Part 7: Total other property not listed, line 54   + $_____

62. Total personal property. Add lines 56 through 61. .... $_____   Copy personal property total ➔ + $_____

63. Total of all property on Schedule A/B. Add line 55 + line 62..................................... $_____

Official Form 106A/B   Schedule A/B: Property   page 10

| Print | Save As... | Add Attachment | | Reset |

SELECTED OFFICIAL FORMS

Fill in this information to identify your case:

Debtor 1 _____
First Name   Middle Name   Last Name

Debtor 2
(Spouse, if filing) First Name   Middle Name   Last Name

United States Bankruptcy Court for the: _____ District of _____

Case number _____
(If known)

☐ Check if this is an amended filing

Official Form 106C

Schedule C: The Property You Claim as Exempt   04/22

Be as complete and accurate as possible. If two married people are filing together, both are equally responsible for supplying correct information. Using the property you listed on *Schedule A/B: Property* (Official Form 106A/B) as your source, list the property that you claim as exempt. If more space is needed, fill out and attach to this page as many copies of *Part 2: Additional Page* as necessary. On the top of any additional pages, write your name and case number (if known).

For each item of property you claim as exempt, you must specify the amount of the exemption you claim. One way of doing so is to state a specific dollar amount as exempt. Alternatively, you may claim the full fair market value of the property being exempted up to the amount of any applicable statutory limit. Some exemptions—such as those for health aids, rights to receive certain benefits, and tax-exempt retirement funds—may be unlimited in dollar amount. However, if you claim an exemption of 100% of fair market value under a law that limits the exemption to a particular dollar amount and the value of the property is determined to exceed that amount, your exemption would be limited to the applicable statutory amount.

Part 1:   Identify the Property You Claim as Exempt

1. Which set of exemptions are you claiming? *Check one only, even if your spouse is filing with you.*

   ☐ You are claiming state and federal nonbankruptcy exemptions. 11 U.S.C. § 522(b)(3)
   ☐ You are claiming federal exemptions. 11 U.S.C. § 522(b)(2)

2. For any property you list on *Schedule A/B* that you claim as exempt, fill in the information below.

Brief description of the property and line on *Schedule A/B* that lists this property	Current value of the portion you own Copy the value from *Schedule A/B*	Amount of the exemption you claim *Check only one box for each exemption.*	Specific laws that allow exemption
Brief description: _____ Line from *Schedule A/B*: ____	$_____	☐ $_____ ☐ 100% of fair market value, up to any applicable statutory limit	_____
Brief description: _____ Line from *Schedule A/B*: ____	$_____	☐ $_____ ☐ 100% of fair market value, up to any applicable statutory limit	_____
Brief description: _____ Line from *Schedule A/B*: ____	$_____	☐ $_____ ☐ 100% of fair market value, up to any applicable statutory limit	_____

3. Are you claiming a homestead exemption of more than $189,050?
   (Subject to adjustment on 4/01/25 and every 3 years after that for cases filed on or after the date of adjustment.)

   ☐ No
   ☐ Yes. Did you acquire the property covered by the exemption within 1,215 days before you filed this case?
      ☐ No
      ☐ Yes

SELECTED OFFICIAL FORMS

Debtor 1 _____ Case number (if known)_____
First Name   Middle Name   Last Name

Part 2:   Additional Page

Brief description of the property and line on *Schedule A/B* that lists this property	Current value of the portion you own Copy the value from *Schedule A/B*	Amount of the exemption you claim *Check only one box for each exemption*	Specific laws that allow exemption
Brief description: _____ Line from *Schedule A/B*: _____	$_____	☐ $ _____ ☐ 100% of fair market value, up to any applicable statutory limit	_____
Brief description: _____ Line from *Schedule A/B*: _____	$_____	☐ $ _____ ☐ 100% of fair market value, up to any applicable statutory limit	_____
Brief description: _____ Line from *Schedule A/B*: _____	$_____	☐ $ _____ ☐ 100% of fair market value, up to any applicable statutory limit	_____
Brief description: _____ Line from *Schedule A/B*: _____	$_____	☐ $ _____ ☐ 100% of fair market value, up to any applicable statutory limit	_____
Brief description: _____ Line from *Schedule A/B*: _____	$_____	☐ $ _____ ☐ 100% of fair market value, up to any applicable statutory limit	_____
Brief description: _____ Line from *Schedule A/B*: _____	$_____	☐ $ _____ ☐ 100% of fair market value, up to any applicable statutory limit	_____
Brief description: _____ Line from *Schedule A/B*: _____	$_____	☐ $ _____ ☐ 100% of fair market value, up to any applicable statutory limit	_____
Brief description: _____ Line from *Schedule A/B*: _____	$_____	☐ $ _____ ☐ 100% of fair market value, up to any applicable statutory limit	_____
Brief description: _____ Line from *Schedule A/B*: _____	$_____	☐ $ _____ ☐ 100% of fair market value, up to any applicable statutory limit	_____
Brief description: _____ Line from *Schedule A/B*: _____	$_____	☐ $ _____ ☐ 100% of fair market value, up to any applicable statutory limit	_____
Brief description: _____ Line from *Schedule A/B*: _____	$_____	☐ $ _____ ☐ 100% of fair market value, up to any applicable statutory limit	_____
Brief description: _____ Line from *Schedule A/B*: _____	$_____	☐ $ _____ ☐ 100% of fair market value, up to any applicable statutory limit	_____

Official Form 106C   Schedule C: The Property You Claim as Exempt   page 2 of __

[Print]   [Save As...]   [Add Attachment]   [Reset]

SELECTED OFFICIAL FORMS

<table>
<tr><td colspan="3">Fill in this information to identify your case:</td></tr>
<tr><td>Debtor 1</td><td>First Name</td><td>Middle Name</td><td>Last Name</td></tr>
<tr><td>Debtor 2
(Spouse, if filing)</td><td>First Name</td><td>Middle Name</td><td>Last Name</td></tr>
<tr><td colspan="4">United States Bankruptcy Court for the: _____ District of _____</td></tr>
<tr><td colspan="4">Case number
(If known) _____</td></tr>
</table>

☐ Check if this is an amended filing

Official Form 106D

Schedule D: Creditors Who Have Claims Secured by Property   12/15

Be as complete and accurate as possible. If two married people are filing together, both are equally responsible for supplying correct information. If more space is needed, copy the Additional Page, fill it out, number the entries, and attach it to this form. On the top of any additional pages, write your name and case number (if known).

1. Do any creditors have claims secured by your property?
   ☐ No. Check this box and submit this form to the court with your other schedules. You have nothing else to report on this form.
   ☐ Yes. Fill in all of the information below.

Part 1:   List All Secured Claims

2. List all secured claims. If a creditor has more than one secured claim, list the creditor separately for each claim. If more than one creditor has a particular claim, list the other creditors in Part 2. As much as possible, list the claims in alphabetical order according to the creditor's name.

	Column A Amount of claim Do not deduct the value of collateral.	Column B Value of collateral that supports this claim	Column C Unsecured portion If any

2.1

Creditor's Name

Number   Street

City   State   ZIP Code

Describe the property that secures the claim:

$_____ $_____ $_____

As of the date you file, the claim is: Check all that apply.
☐ Contingent
☐ Unliquidated
☐ Disputed

Who owes the debt? Check one.
☐ Debtor 1 only
☐ Debtor 2 only
☐ Debtor 1 and Debtor 2 only
☐ At least one of the debtors and another

☐ Check if this claim relates to a community debt

Date debt was incurred _____

Nature of lien. Check all that apply.
☐ An agreement you made (such as mortgage or secured car loan)
☐ Statutory lien (such as tax lien, mechanic's lien)
☐ Judgment lien from a lawsuit
☐ Other (including a right to offset) _____

Last 4 digits of account number ___ ___ ___ ___

2.2

Creditor's Name

Number   Street

City   State   ZIP Code

Describe the property that secures the claim:

$_____ $_____ $_____

As of the date you file, the claim is: Check all that apply.
☐ Contingent
☐ Unliquidated
☐ Disputed

Who owes the debt? Check one.
☐ Debtor 1 only
☐ Debtor 2 only
☐ Debtor 1 and Debtor 2 only
☐ At least one of the debtors and another

☐ Check if this claim relates to a community debt

Date debt was incurred _____

Nature of lien. Check all that apply.
☐ An agreement you made (such as mortgage or secured car loan)
☐ Statutory lien (such as tax lien, mechanic's lien)
☐ Judgment lien from a lawsuit
☐ Other (including a right to offset) _____

Last 4 digits of account number ___ ___ ___ ___

Add the dollar value of your entries in Column A on this page. Write that number here: $_____

Official Form 106D   Schedule D: Creditors Who Have Claims Secured by Property   page 1 of ___

Debtor 1 _____   Case number (if known)_____
First Name   Middle Name   Last Name

Part 1: **Additional Page** After listing any entries on this page, number them beginning with 2.3, followed by 2.4, and so forth.	Column A Amount of claim Do not deduct the value of collateral.	Column B Value of collateral that supports this claim	Column C Unsecured portion If any

_____
Creditor's Name

_____
Number   Street

_____

_____
City   State   ZIP Code

Who owes the debt? Check one.
- ☐ Debtor 1 only
- ☐ Debtor 2 only
- ☐ Debtor 1 and Debtor 2 only
- ☐ At least one of the debtors and another

☐ Check if this claim relates to a community debt

Date debt was incurred _____

Describe the property that secures the claim:

[ ]

As of the date you file, the claim is: Check all that apply.
- ☐ Contingent
- ☐ Unliquidated
- ☐ Disputed

Nature of lien. Check all that apply.
- ☐ An agreement you made (such as mortgage or secured car loan)
- ☐ Statutory lien (such as tax lien, mechanic's lien)
- ☐ Judgment lien from a lawsuit
- ☐ Other (including a right to offset) _____

Last 4 digits of account number ___ ___ ___ ___

$_____ $_____ $_____

_____
Creditor's Name

_____
Number   Street

_____

_____
City   State   ZIP Code

Who owes the debt? Check one.
- ☐ Debtor 1 only
- ☐ Debtor 2 only
- ☐ Debtor 1 and Debtor 2 only
- ☐ At least one of the debtors and another

☐ Check if this claim relates to a community debt

Date debt was incurred _____

Describe the property that secures the claim:

[ ]

As of the date you file, the claim is: Check all that apply.
- ☐ Contingent
- ☐ Unliquidated
- ☐ Disputed

Nature of lien. Check all that apply.
- ☐ An agreement you made (such as mortgage or secured car loan)
- ☐ Statutory lien (such as tax lien, mechanic's lien)
- ☐ Judgment lien from a lawsuit
- ☐ Other (including a right to offset) _____

Last 4 digits of account number ___ ___ ___ ___

$_____ $_____ $_____

_____
Creditor's Name

_____
Number   Street

_____

_____
City   State   ZIP Code

Who owes the debt? Check one.
- ☐ Debtor 1 only
- ☐ Debtor 2 only
- ☐ Debtor 1 and Debtor 2 only
- ☐ At least one of the debtors and another

☐ Check if this claim relates to a community debt

Date debt was incurred _____

Describe the property that secures the claim:

[ ]

As of the date you file, the claim is: Check all that apply.
- ☐ Contingent
- ☐ Unliquidated
- ☐ Disputed

Nature of lien. Check all that apply.
- ☐ An agreement you made (such as mortgage or secured car loan)
- ☐ Statutory lien (such as tax lien, mechanic's lien)
- ☐ Judgment lien from a lawsuit
- ☐ Other (including a right to offset) _____

Last 4 digits of account number ___ ___ ___ ___

$_____ $_____ $_____

Add the dollar value of your entries in Column A on this page. Write that number here:	$_____
If this is the last page of your form, add the dollar value totals from all pages. Write that number here:	$_____

Official Form 106D   Additional Page of **Schedule D: Creditors Who Have Claims Secured by Property**   page ___ of ___

Debtor 1 _____ _____ _____   Case number (if known)_____
            First Name   Middle Name   Last Name

Part 2:	List Others to Be Notified for a Debt That You Already Listed

Use this page only if you have others to be notified about your bankruptcy for a debt that you already listed in Part 1. For example, if a collection agency is trying to collect from you for a debt you owe to someone else, list the creditor in Part 1, and then list the collection agency here. Similarly, if you have more than one creditor for any of the debts that you listed in Part 1, list the additional creditors here. If you do not have additional persons to be notified for any debts in Part 1, do not fill out or submit this page.

▢
Name _____

Number   Street _____

_____

City _____ State _____ ZIP Code _____

On which line in Part 1 did you enter the creditor? _____

Last 4 digits of account number ___ ___ ___ ___

▢
Name _____

Number   Street _____

_____

City _____ State _____ ZIP Code _____

On which line in Part 1 did you enter the creditor? _____

Last 4 digits of account number ___ ___ ___ ___

▢
Name _____

Number   Street _____

_____

City _____ State _____ ZIP Code _____

On which line in Part 1 did you enter the creditor? _____

Last 4 digits of account number ___ ___ ___ ___

▢
Name _____

Number   Street _____

_____

City _____ State _____ ZIP Code _____

On which line in Part 1 did you enter the creditor? _____

Last 4 digits of account number ___ ___ ___ ___

▢
Name _____

Number   Street _____

_____

City _____ State _____ ZIP Code _____

On which line in Part 1 did you enter the creditor? _____

Last 4 digits of account number ___ ___ ___ ___

▢
Name _____

Number   Street _____

_____

City _____ State _____ ZIP Code _____

On which line in Part 1 did you enter the creditor? _____

Last 4 digits of account number ___ ___ ___ ___

Print	Save As...	Add Attachment		Reset

Official Form 106D   Part 2 of Schedule D: Creditors Who Have Claims Secured by Property   page ___ of ___

Fill in this information to identify your case:

Debtor 1 _____
          First Name   Middle Name   Last Name

Debtor 2 _____
(Spouse, if filing) First Name   Middle Name   Last Name

United States Bankruptcy Court for the: _____ District of _____

Case number _____
(If known)

☐ Check if this is an amended filing

Official Form 106E/F

Schedule E/F: Creditors Who Have Unsecured Claims

12/15

Be as complete and accurate as possible. Use Part 1 for creditors with PRIORITY claims and Part 2 for creditors with NONPRIORITY claims. List the other party to any executory contracts or unexpired leases that could result in a claim. Also list executory contracts on *Schedule A/B: Property* (Official Form 106A/B) and on *Schedule G: Executory Contracts and Unexpired Leases* (Official Form 106G). Do not include any creditors with partially secured claims that are listed in *Schedule D: Creditors Who Have Claims Secured by Property*. If more space is needed, copy the Part you need, fill it out, number the entries in the boxes on the left. Attach the Continuation Page to this page. On the top of any additional pages, write your name and case number (if known).

Part 1:   List All of Your PRIORITY Unsecured Claims

1. Do any creditors have priority unsecured claims against you?
   ☐ No. Go to Part 2.
   ☐ Yes.

2. List all of your priority unsecured claims. If a creditor has more than one priority unsecured claim, list the creditor separately for each claim. For each claim listed, identify what type of claim it is. If a claim has both priority and nonpriority amounts, list that claim here and show both priority and nonpriority amounts. As much as possible, list the claims in alphabetical order according to the creditor's name. If you have more than two priority unsecured claims, fill out the Continuation Page of Part 1. If more than one creditor holds a particular claim, list the other creditors in Part 3.

   (For an explanation of each type of claim, see the instructions for this form in the instruction booklet.)

		Total claim	Priority amount	Nonpriority amount

2.1
_____
Priority Creditor's Name

_____
Number   Street

_____

_____
City   State   ZIP Code

Who incurred the debt? Check one.
☐ Debtor 1 only
☐ Debtor 2 only
☐ Debtor 1 and Debtor 2 only
☐ At least one of the debtors and another
☐ Check if this claim is for a community debt

Is the claim subject to offset?
☐ No
☐ Yes

Last 4 digits of account number __ __ __ __

When was the debt incurred? _____

As of the date you file, the claim is: Check all that apply.
☐ Contingent
☐ Unliquidated
☐ Disputed

Type of PRIORITY unsecured claim:
☐ Domestic support obligations
☐ Taxes and certain other debts you owe the government
☐ Claims for death or personal injury while you were intoxicated
☐ Other. Specify _____

$_____ $_____ $_____

2.2
_____
Priority Creditor's Name

_____
Number   Street

_____

_____
City   State   ZIP Code

Who incurred the debt? Check one.
☐ Debtor 1 only
☐ Debtor 2 only
☐ Debtor 1 and Debtor 2 only
☐ At least one of the debtors and another
☐ Check if this claim is for a community debt

Is the claim subject to offset?
☐ No
☐ Yes

Last 4 digits of account number __ __ __ __

When was the debt incurred? _____

As of the date you file, the claim is: Check all that apply.
☐ Contingent
☐ Unliquidated
☐ Disputed

Type of PRIORITY unsecured claim:
☐ Domestic support obligations
☐ Taxes and certain other debts you owe the government
☐ Claims for death or personal injury while you were intoxicated
☐ Other. Specify _____

$_____ $_____ $_____

SELECTED OFFICIAL FORMS

Debtor 1 _____ Case number (if known)_____
First Name   Middle Name   Last Name

| Part 1: | Your PRIORITY Unsecured Claims — Continuation Page | | | | |

After listing any entries on this page, number them beginning with 2.3, followed by 2.4, and so forth.

		Total claim	Priority amount	Nonpriority amount

_____
Priority Creditor's Name

_____
Number   Street

_____

_____
City   State   ZIP Code

Who incurred the debt? Check one.

- ☐ Debtor 1 only
- ☐ Debtor 2 only
- ☐ Debtor 1 and Debtor 2 only
- ☐ At least one of the debtors and another

- ☐ **Check if this claim is for a community debt**

Is the claim subject to offset?

- ☐ No
- ☐ Yes

Last 4 digits of account number ___ ___ ___ ___ $_____ $_____ $_____

When was the debt incurred?   _____

As of the date you file, the claim is: Check all that apply.

- ☐ Contingent
- ☐ Unliquidated
- ☐ Disputed

Type of PRIORITY unsecured claim:

- ☐ Domestic support obligations
- ☐ Taxes and certain other debts you owe the government
- ☐ Claims for death or personal injury while you were intoxicated
- ☐ Other. Specify _____

_____
Priority Creditor's Name

_____
Number   Street

_____

_____
City   State   ZIP Code

Who incurred the debt? Check one.

- ☐ Debtor 1 only
- ☐ Debtor 2 only
- ☐ Debtor 1 and Debtor 2 only
- ☐ At least one of the debtors and another

- ☐ **Check if this claim is for a community debt**

Is the claim subject to offset?

- ☐ No
- ☐ Yes

Last 4 digits of account number ___ ___ ___ ___ $_____ $_____ $_____

When was the debt incurred?   _____

As of the date you file, the claim is: Check all that apply.

- ☐ Contingent
- ☐ Unliquidated
- ☐ Disputed

Type of PRIORITY unsecured claim:

- ☐ Domestic support obligations
- ☐ Taxes and certain other debts you owe the government
- ☐ Claims for death or personal injury while you were intoxicated
- ☐ Other. Specify _____

_____
Priority Creditor's Name

_____
Number   Street

_____

_____
City   State   ZIP Code

Who incurred the debt? Check one.

- ☐ Debtor 1 only
- ☐ Debtor 2 only
- ☐ Debtor 1 and Debtor 2 only
- ☐ At least one of the debtors and another

- ☐ **Check if this claim is for a community debt**

Is the claim subject to offset?

- ☐ No
- ☐ Yes

Last 4 digits of account number ___ ___ ___ ___ $_____ $_____ $_____

When was the debt incurred?   _____

As of the date you file, the claim is: Check all that apply.

- ☐ Contingent
- ☐ Unliquidated
- ☐ Disputed

Type of PRIORITY unsecured claim:

- ☐ Domestic support obligations
- ☐ Taxes and certain other debts you owe the government
- ☐ Claims for death or personal injury while you were intoxicated
- ☐ Other. Specify _____

Debtor 1 _____   Case number (if known)_____
             First Name   Middle Name   Last Name

Part 2:   List All of Your NONPRIORITY Unsecured Claims

3. Do any creditors have nonpriority unsecured claims against you?

☐ No. You have nothing to report in this part. Submit this form to the court with your other schedules.
☐ Yes

4. List all of your nonpriority unsecured claims in the alphabetical order of the creditor who holds each claim. If a creditor has more than one
    nonpriority unsecured claim, list the creditor separately for each claim. For each claim listed, identify what type of claim it is. Do not list claims already
    included in Part 1. If more than one creditor holds a particular claim, list the other creditors in Part 3. If you have more than three nonpriority unsecured
    claims fill out the Continuation Page of Part 2.

		Total claim

4.1 _____   Last 4 digits of account number __ __ __ __ $_____
        Nonpriority Creditor's Name
                                                When was the debt incurred?   _____
        _____
        Number   Street

        _____   As of the date you file, the claim is: Check all that apply.
        City   State   ZIP Code
                                                ☐ Contingent
        Who incurred the debt? Check one.   ☐ Unliquidated
                                                ☐ Disputed
        ☐ Debtor 1 only
        ☐ Debtor 2 only
        ☐ Debtor 1 and Debtor 2 only   Type of NONPRIORITY unsecured claim:
        ☐ At least one of the debtors and another
                                                ☐ Student loans
        ☐ Check if this claim is for a community debt   ☐ Obligations arising out of a separation agreement or divorce
                                                   that you did not report as priority claims
        Is the claim subject to offset?   ☐ Debts to pension or profit-sharing plans, and other similar debts
        ☐ No   ☐ Other. Specify _____
        ☐ Yes

4.2 _____   Last 4 digits of account number __ __ __ __ $_____
        Nonpriority Creditor's Name
                                                When was the debt incurred?   _____
        _____
        Number   Street

        _____   As of the date you file, the claim is: Check all that apply.
        City   State   ZIP Code
                                                ☐ Contingent
        Who incurred the debt? Check one.   ☐ Unliquidated
                                                ☐ Disputed
        ☐ Debtor 1 only
        ☐ Debtor 2 only
        ☐ Debtor 1 and Debtor 2 only   Type of NONPRIORITY unsecured claim:
        ☐ At least one of the debtors and another
                                                ☐ Student loans
        ☐ Check if this claim is for a community debt   ☐ Obligations arising out of a separation agreement or divorce
                                                   that you did not report as priority claims
        Is the claim subject to offset?   ☐ Debts to pension or profit-sharing plans, and other similar debts
        ☐ No   ☐ Other. Specify _____
        ☐ Yes

4.3 _____   Last 4 digits of account number __ __ __ __ $_____
        Nonpriority Creditor's Name
                                                When was the debt incurred?   _____
        _____
        Number   Street

        _____   As of the date you file, the claim is: Check all that apply.
        City   State   ZIP Code
                                                ☐ Contingent
        Who incurred the debt? Check one.   ☐ Unliquidated
                                                ☐ Disputed
        ☐ Debtor 1 only
        ☐ Debtor 2 only
        ☐ Debtor 1 and Debtor 2 only   Type of NONPRIORITY unsecured claim:
        ☐ At least one of the debtors and another
                                                ☐ Student loans
        ☐ Check if this claim is for a community debt   ☐ Obligations arising out of a separation agreement or divorce
                                                   that you did not report as priority claims
        Is the claim subject to offset?   ☐ Debts to pension or profit-sharing plans, and other similar debts
        ☐ No   ☐ Other. Specify _____
        ☐ Yes

Official Form 106E/F   Schedule E/F: Creditors Who Have Unsecured Claims   page __ of ___

Debtor 1 _____ Case number (if known)_____
First Name   Middle Name   Last Name

Part 2: **Your NONPRIORITY Unsecured Claims — Continuation Page**

After listing any entries on this page, number them beginning with 4.4, followed by 4.5, and so forth.	Total claim

_____

Nonpriority Creditor's Name

Number   Street

City   State   ZIP Code

Who incurred the debt? Check one.

❑ Debtor 1 only
❑ Debtor 2 only
❑ Debtor 1 and Debtor 2 only
❑ At least one of the debtors and another

❑ Check if this claim is for a community debt

Is the claim subject to offset?

❑ No
❑ Yes

Last 4 digits of account number ___ ___ ___ ___ $_____

When was the debt incurred? _____

As of the date you file, the claim is: Check all that apply.

❑ Contingent
❑ Unliquidated
❑ Disputed

Type of NONPRIORITY unsecured claim:

❑ Student loans
❑ Obligations arising out of a separation agreement or divorce that you did not report as priority claims
❑ Debts to pension or profit-sharing plans, and other similar debts
❑ Other. Specify_____

_____

Nonpriority Creditor's Name

Number   Street

City   State   ZIP Code

Who incurred the debt? Check one.

❑ Debtor 1 only
❑ Debtor 2 only
❑ Debtor 1 and Debtor 2 only
❑ At least one of the debtors and another

❑ Check if this claim is for a community debt

Is the claim subject to offset?

❑ No
❑ Yes

Last 4 digits of account number ___ ___ ___ ___ $_____

When was the debt incurred? _____

As of the date you file, the claim is: Check all that apply.

❑ Contingent
❑ Unliquidated
❑ Disputed

Type of NONPRIORITY unsecured claim:

❑ Student loans
❑ Obligations arising out of a separation agreement or divorce that you did not report as priority claims
❑ Debts to pension or profit-sharing plans, and other similar debts
❑ Other. Specify_____

_____

Nonpriority Creditor's Name

Number   Street

City   State   ZIP Code

Who incurred the debt? Check one.

❑ Debtor 1 only
❑ Debtor 2 only
❑ Debtor 1 and Debtor 2 only
❑ At least one of the debtors and another

❑ Check if this claim is for a community debt

Is the claim subject to offset?

❑ No
❑ Yes

$_____

Last 4 digits of account number ___ ___ ___ ___

When was the debt incurred? _____

As of the date you file, the claim is: Check all that apply.

❑ Contingent
❑ Unliquidated
❑ Disputed

Type of NONPRIORITY unsecured claim:

❑ Student loans
❑ Obligations arising out of a separation agreement or divorce that you did not report as priority claims
❑ Debts to pension or profit-sharing plans, and other similar debts
❑ Other. Specify_____

Official Form 106E/F   Schedule E/F: Creditors Who Have Unsecured Claims   page __ of ___

Debtor 1 _____   Case number (if known)_____
          First Name   Middle Name   Last Name

Part 3:   List Others to Be Notified About a Debt That You Already Listed

5. Use this page only if you have others to be notified about your bankruptcy, for a debt that you already listed in Parts 1 or 2. For
    example, if a collection agency is trying to collect from you for a debt you owe to someone else, list the original creditor in Parts 1 or
    2, then list the collection agency here. Similarly, if you have more than one creditor for any of the debts that you listed in Parts 1 or 2, list the
    additional creditors here. If you do not have additional persons to be notified for any debts in Parts 1 or 2, do not fill out or submit this page.

_____   On which entry in Part 1 or Part 2 did you list the original creditor?
Name

_____   Line _____ of (Check one): ❏ Part 1: Creditors with Priority Unsecured Claims
Number   Street   ❏ Part 2: Creditors with Nonpriority Unsecured Claims

_____   Last 4 digits of account number ___ ___ ___ ___
City   State   ZIP Code

_____   On which entry in Part 1 or Part 2 did you list the original creditor?
Name

_____   Line _____ of (Check one): ❏ Part 1: Creditors with Priority Unsecured Claims
Number   Street   ❏ Part 2: Creditors with Nonpriority Unsecured
                                              Claims

_____   Last 4 digits of account number ___ ___ ___ ___
City   State   ZIP Code

_____   On which entry in Part 1 or Part 2 did you list the original creditor?
Name

_____   Line _____ of (Check one): ❏ Part 1: Creditors with Priority Unsecured Claims
Number   Street   ❏ Part 2: Creditors with Nonpriority Unsecured
                                              Claims

_____   Last 4 digits of account number ___ ___ ___ ___
City   State   ZIP Code

_____   On which entry in Part 1 or Part 2 did you list the original creditor?
Name

_____   Line _____ of (Check one): ❏ Part 1: Creditors with Priority Unsecured Claims
Number   Street   ❏ Part 2: Creditors with Nonpriority Unsecured
                                              Claims

_____   Last 4 digits of account number ___ ___ ___ ___
City   State   ZIP Code

_____   On which entry in Part 1 or Part 2 did you list the original creditor?
Name

_____   Line _____ of (Check one): ❏ Part 1: Creditors with Priority Unsecured Claims
Number   Street   ❏ Part 2: Creditors with Nonpriority Unsecured
                                              Claims

_____   Last 4 digits of account number ___ ___ ___ ___
City   State   ZIP Code

_____   On which entry in Part 1 or Part 2 did you list the original creditor?
Name

_____   Line _____ of (Check one): ❏ Part 1: Creditors with Priority Unsecured Claims
Number   Street   ❏ Part 2: Creditors with Nonpriority Unsecured
                                              Claims

_____   Last 4 digits of account number ___ ___ ___ ___
City   State   ZIP Code

_____   On which entry in Part 1 or Part 2 did you list the original creditor?
Name

_____   Line _____ of (Check one): ❏ Part 1: Creditors with Priority Unsecured Claims
Number   Street   ❏ Part 2: Creditors with Nonpriority Unsecured
                                              Claims

_____   Last 4 digits of account number ___ ___ ___ ___
City   State   ZIP Code

Official Form 106E/F   Schedule E/F: Creditors Who Have Unsecured Claims   page ___ of ___

Debtor 1 _____   Case number *(if known)* _____
　　　　First Name　　Middle Name　　Last Name

Part 4:	Add the Amounts for Each Type of Unsecured Claim

6. Total the amounts of certain types of unsecured claims. This information is for statistical reporting purposes only. 28 U.S.C. § 159.
Add the amounts for each type of unsecured claim.

			Total claim
Total claims from Part 1	6a. **Domestic support obligations**	6a.	$_____
	6b. **Taxes and certain other debts you owe the government**	6b.	$_____
	6c. **Claims for death or personal injury while you were intoxicated**	6c.	$_____
	6d. **Other.** Add all other priority unsecured claims. Write that amount here.	6d.	+ $_____
	6e. **Total.** Add lines 6a through 6d.	6e.	$_____

			Total claim
Total claims from Part 2	6f. **Student loans**	6f.	$_____
	6g. **Obligations arising out of a separation agreement or divorce that you did not report as priority claims**	6g.	$_____
	6h. **Debts to pension or profit-sharing plans, and other similar debts**	6h.	$_____
	6i. **Other.** Add all other nonpriority unsecured claims. Write that amount here.	6i.	+ $_____
	6j. **Total.** Add lines 6f through 6i.	6j.	$_____

Print	Save As...	Add Attachment		Reset

Official Form 106E/F   Schedule E/F: Creditors Who Have Unsecured Claims   page ___ of ___

Fill in this information to identify your case:

Debtor _____
First Name   Middle Name   Last Name

Debtor 2 _____
(Spouse if filing) First Name   Middle Name   Last Name

United States Bankruptcy Court for the: _____ District of _____

Case number _____
(If known)

☐ Check if this is an
amended filing

Official Form 106G

Schedule G: Executory Contracts and Unexpired Leases

12/15

Be as complete and accurate as possible. If two married people are filing together, both are equally responsible for supplying correct information. If more space is needed, copy the additional page, fill it out, number the entries, and attach it to this page. On the top of any additional pages, write your name and case number (if known).

1. Do you have any executory contracts or unexpired leases?

☐ No. Check this box and file this form with the court with your other schedules. You have nothing else to report on this form.

☐ Yes. Fill in all of the information below even if the contracts or leases are listed on *Schedule A/B: Property* (Official Form 106A/B).

2. **List separately each person or company with whom you have the contract or lease. Then state what each contract or lease is for (for example, rent, vehicle lease, cell phone).** See the instructions for this form in the instruction booklet for more examples of executory contracts and unexpired leases.

Person or company with whom you have the contract or lease	State what the contract or lease is for
2.1	
Name	
Number Street	
City State ZIP Code	
2.2	
Name	
Number Street	
City State ZIP Code	
2.3	
Name	
Number Street	
City State ZIP Code	
2.4	
Name	
Number Street	
City State ZIP Code	
2.5	
Name	
Number Street	
City State ZIP Code	

Official Form 106G   Schedule G: Executory Contracts and Unexpired Leases   page 1 of ___

Debtor 1 _____   Case number *(if known)* _____
         First Name   Middle Name   Last Name

Additional Page if You Have More Contracts or Leases

Person or company with whom you have the contract or lease	What the contract or lease is for

2.2
Name _____

Number   Street _____

City _____ State ____ ZIP Code ____

2._
Name _____

Number   Street _____

City _____ State ____ ZIP Code ____

2._
Name _____

Number   Street _____

City _____ State ____ ZIP Code ____

2._
Name _____

Number   Street _____

City _____ State ____ ZIP Code ____

2._
Name _____

Number   Street _____

City _____ State ____ ZIP Code ____

2._
Name _____

Number   Street _____

City _____ State ____ ZIP Code ____

2._
Name _____

Number   Street _____

City _____ State ____ ZIP Code ____

2._
Name _____

Number   Street _____

City _____ State ____ ZIP Code ____

Print	Save As...	Add Attachment		Reset

Official Form 106G   Schedule G: Executory Contracts and Unexpired Leases   page ___ of ___

Fill in this information to identify your case:

Debtor 1 _____
First Name   Middle Name   Last Name

Debtor 2 _____
(Spouse, if filing) First Name   Middle Name   Last Name

United States Bankruptcy Court for the: _____ District of _____

Case number _____
(If known)

☐ Check if this is an
amended filing

Official Form 106H

Schedule H: Your Codebtors

12/15

Codebtors are people or entities who are also liable for any debts you may have. Be as complete and accurate as possible. If two married people are filing together, both are equally responsible for supplying correct information. If more space is needed, copy the Additional Page, fill it out, and number the entries in the boxes on the left. Attach the Additional Page to this page. On the top of any Additional Pages, write your name and case number (if known). Answer every question.

1. **Do you have any codebtors?** (If you are filing a joint case, do not list either spouse as a codebtor.)

   ☐ No

   ☐ Yes

2. **Within the last 8 years, have you lived in a community property state or territory?** (*Community property states and territories* include Arizona, California, Idaho, Louisiana, Nevada, New Mexico, Puerto Rico, Texas, Washington, and Wisconsin.)

   ☐ No. Go to line 3.

   ☐ Yes. Did your spouse, former spouse, or legal equivalent live with you at the time?

      ☐ No

      ☐ Yes. In which community state or territory did you live? _____. Fill in the name and current address of that person.

      _____
      Name of your spouse, former spouse, or legal equivalent

      _____
      Number   Street

      _____
      City   State   ZIP Code

3. **In Column 1, list all of your codebtors. Do not include your spouse as a codebtor if your spouse is filing with you. List the person shown in line 2 again as a codebtor only if that person is a guarantor or cosigner. Make sure you have listed the creditor on *Schedule D* (Official Form 106D), *Schedule E/F* (Official Form 106E/F), or *Schedule G* (Official Form 106G). Use *Schedule D, Schedule E/F, or Schedule G* to fill out Column 2.**

Column 1: Your codebtor	Column 2: The creditor to whom you owe the debt
	Check all schedules that apply:

3.1

_____
Name

_____
Number   Street

_____
City   State   ZIP Code

☐ Schedule D, line _____
☐ Schedule E/F, line _____
☐ Schedule G, line _____

3.2

_____
Name

_____
Number   Street

_____
City   State   ZIP Code

☐ Schedule D, line _____
☐ Schedule E/F, line _____
☐ Schedule G, line _____

3.3

_____
Name

_____
Number   Street

_____
City   State   ZIP Code

☐ Schedule D, line _____
☐ Schedule E/F, line _____
☐ Schedule G, line _____

Official Form 106H   Schedule H: Your Codebtors   page 1 of ___

Debtor 1 _____ Case number (if known)_____
First Name   Middle Name   Last Name

Additional Page to List More Codebtors

Column 1: Your codebtor	*Column 2:* The creditor to whom you owe the debt
	Check all schedules that apply:

3.__

Name _____
Number   Street _____
City _____ State _____ ZIP Code _____

❑ Schedule D, line _____
❑ Schedule E/F, line _____
❑ Schedule G, line _____

3.__

Name _____
Number   Street _____
City _____ State _____ ZIP Code _____

❑ Schedule D, line _____
❑ Schedule E/F, line _____
❑ Schedule G, line _____

3.__

Name _____
Number   Street _____
City _____ State _____ ZIP Code _____

❑ Schedule D, line _____
❑ Schedule E/F, line _____
❑ Schedule G, line _____

3.__

Name _____
Number   Street _____
City _____ State _____ ZIP Code _____

❑ Schedule D, line _____
❑ Schedule E/F, line _____
❑ Schedule G, line _____

3.__

Name _____
Number   Street _____
City _____ State _____ ZIP Code _____

❑ Schedule D, line _____
❑ Schedule E/F, line _____
❑ Schedule G, line _____

3.__

Name _____
Number   Street _____
City _____ State _____ ZIP Code _____

❑ Schedule D, line _____
❑ Schedule E/F, line _____
❑ Schedule G, line _____

3.__

Name _____
Number   Street _____
City _____ State _____ ZIP Code _____

❑ Schedule D, line _____
❑ Schedule E/F, line _____
❑ Schedule G, line _____

3.__

Name _____
Number   Street _____
City _____ State _____ ZIP Code _____

❑ Schedule D, line _____
❑ Schedule E/F, line _____
❑ Schedule G, line _____

Print	Save As...	Add Attachment		Reset

Official Form 106H   Schedule H: Your Codebtors   page ___ of ___

Fill in this information to identify your case:

Debtor 1 _____
First Name   Middle Name   Last Name

Debtor 2 _____
(Spouse, if filing) First Name   Middle Name   Last Name

United States Bankruptcy Court for the: _____ District of _____

Case number _____
(if known)

Check if this is:

☐ An amended filing

☐ A supplement showing postpetition chapter 13 income as of the following date:

_____
MM / DD / YYYY

Official Form 106I

Schedule I: Your Income

12/15

Be as complete and accurate as possible. If two married people are filing together (Debtor 1 and Debtor 2), both are equally responsible for supplying correct information. If you are married and not filing jointly, and your spouse is living with you, include information about your spouse. If you are separated and your spouse is not filing with you, do not include information about your spouse. If more space is needed, attach a separate sheet to this form. On the top of any additional pages, write your name and case number (if known). Answer every question.

Part 1:	Describe Employment

1. Fill in your employment information.		Debtor 1	Debtor 2 or non-filing spouse
If you have more than one job, attach a separate page with information about additional employers.	Employment status	☐ Employed ☐ Not employed	☐ Employed ☐ Not employed
Include part-time, seasonal, or self-employed work.			
Occupation may include student or homemaker, if it applies.	Occupation	_____	_____
	Employer's name	_____	_____
	Employer's address	_____ Number Street	_____ Number Street
		_____ _____	_____ _____
		_____ City State ZIP Code	_____ City State ZIP Code
	How long employed there?	_____	_____

Part 2:	Give Details About Monthly Income

Estimate monthly income as of the date you file this form. If you have nothing to report for any line, write $0 in the space. Include your non-filing spouse unless you are separated.

If you or your non-filing spouse have more than one employer, combine the information for all employers for that person on the lines below. If you need more space, attach a separate sheet to this form.

		For Debtor 1	For Debtor 2 or non-filing spouse
2. List monthly gross wages, salary, and commissions (before all payroll deductions). If not paid monthly, calculate what the monthly wage would be.	2.	$_____	$_____
3. Estimate and list monthly overtime pay.	3.	+ $_____	+ $_____
4. Calculate gross income. Add line 2 + line 3.	4.	$_____	$_____

Debtor 1 _____ Case number (if known)_____
First Name   Middle Name   Last Name

	For Debtor 1	For Debtor 2 or non-filing spouse
Copy line 4 here.. → 4.	$_____	$_____

5. List all payroll deductions:

5a. Tax, Medicare, and Social Security deductions	5a.	$_____	$_____
5b. Mandatory contributions for retirement plans	5b.	$_____	$_____
5c. Voluntary contributions for retirement plans	5c.	$_____	$_____
5d. Required repayments of retirement fund loans	5d.	$_____	$_____
5e. Insurance	5e.	$_____	$_____
5f. Domestic support obligations	5f.	$_____	$_____
5g. Union dues	5g.	$_____	$_____
5h. Other deductions. Specify: _____	5h.	+ $_____	+ $_____

6. Add the payroll deductions. Add lines 5a + 5b + 5c + 5d + 5e +5f + 5g + 5h. 6. $_____ $_____

7. Calculate total monthly take-home pay. Subtract line 6 from line 4. 7. $_____ $_____

8. List all other income regularly received:

8a. Net income from rental property and from operating a business, profession, or farm

Attach a statement for each property and business showing gross receipts, ordinary and necessary business expenses, and the total monthly net income. 8a. $_____ $_____

8b. Interest and dividends 8b. $_____ $_____

8c. Family support payments that you, a non-filing spouse, or a dependent regularly receive

Include alimony, spousal support, child support, maintenance, divorce settlement, and property settlement. 8c. $_____ $_____

8d. Unemployment compensation 8d. $_____ $_____

8e. Social Security 8e. $_____ $_____

8f. Other government assistance that you regularly receive

Include cash assistance and the value (if known) of any non-cash assistance that you receive, such as food stamps (benefits under the Supplemental Nutrition Assistance Program) or housing subsidies.
Specify: _____ 8f. $_____ $_____

8g. Pension or retirement income 8g. $_____ $_____

8h. Other monthly income. Specify: _____ 8h. + $_____   + $_____

9. Add all other income. Add lines 8a + 8b + 8c + 8d + 8e + 8f +8g + 8h. 9. $_____ $_____

10. Calculate monthly income. Add line 7 + line 9.
Add the entries in line 10 for Debtor 1 and Debtor 2 or non-filing spouse. 10. $_____ + $_____ = $_____

11. State all other regular contributions to the expenses that you list in *Schedule J.*

Include contributions from an unmarried partner, members of your household, your dependents, your roommates, and other friends or relatives.

Do not include any amounts already included in lines 2-10 or amounts that are not available to pay expenses listed in *Schedule J.*

Specify: _____ 11. + $_____

12. Add the amount in the last column of line 10 to the amount in line 11. The result is the combined monthly income.
Write that amount on the *Summary of Your Assets and Liabilities and Certain Statistical Information*, if it applies 12. $_____

Combined monthly income

13. Do you expect an increase or decrease within the year after you file this form?
☐ No.
☐ Yes. Explain: _____

Print	Save As...	Add Attachment		Reset

Fill in this information to identify your case:

Debtor 1 _____
        First Name   Middle Name   Last Name

Debtor 2 _____
(Spouse, if filing) First Name   Middle Name   Last Name

United States Bankruptcy Court for the: _____ District of _____

Case number _____
(if known)

Check if this is:

☐ An amended filing

☐ A supplement showing postpetition chapter 13
    expenses as of the following date:

    _____
    MM / DD / YYYY

Official Form 106J

Schedule J: Your Expenses

12/15

Be as complete and accurate as possible. If two married people are filing together, both are equally responsible for supplying correct information. If more space is needed, attach another sheet to this form. On the top of any additional pages, write your name and case number (if known). Answer every question.

Part 1: Describe Your Household

1. **Is this a joint case?**

  ☐ No. Go to line 2.
  ☐ Yes. **Does Debtor 2 live in a separate household?**

      ☐ No
      ☐ Yes. Debtor 2 must file Official Form 106J-2, *Expenses for Separate Household of Debtor 2.*

2. **Do you have dependents?**

  Do not list Debtor 1 and Debtor 2.

  Do not state the dependents' names.

  ☐ No
  ☐ Yes. Fill out this information for each dependent ....

Dependent's relationship to Debtor 1 or Debtor 2	Dependent's age	Does dependent live with you?
_____	_____	☐ No ☐ Yes
_____	_____	☐ No ☐ Yes
_____	_____	☐ No ☐ Yes
_____	_____	☐ No ☐ Yes
_____	_____	☐ No ☐ Yes

3. **Do your expenses include expenses of people other than yourself and your dependents?**

  ☐ No
  ☐ Yes

Part 2: Estimate Your Ongoing Monthly Expenses

Estimate your expenses as of your bankruptcy filing date unless you are using this form as a supplement in a Chapter 13 case to report expenses as of a date after the bankruptcy is filed. If this is a supplemental *Schedule J*, check the box at the top of the form and fill in the applicable date.

Include expenses paid for with non-cash government assistance if you know the value of such assistance and have included it on *Schedule I: Your Income* (Official Form 106I.)

Your expenses

4. The rental or home ownership expenses for your residence. Include first mortgage payments and any rent for the ground or lot.   **4.** $_____

  If not included in line 4:

  4a. Real estate taxes   **4a.** $_____

  4b. Property, homeowner's, or renter's insurance   **4b.** $_____

  4c. Home maintenance, repair, and upkeep expenses   **4c.** $_____

  4d. Homeowner's association or condominium dues   **4d.** $_____

Debtor 1 _____   Case number (if known)_____
　　　　　First Name　　Middle Name　　　Last Name

	Your expenses

5. Additional mortgage payments for your residence, such as home equity loans   5. $_____

6. Utilities:

   6a.　Electricity, heat, natural gas   6a. $_____

   6b.　Water, sewer, garbage collection   6b. $_____

   6c.　Telephone, cell phone, Internet, satellite, and cable services   6c. $_____

   6d.　Other. Specify: _____   6d. $_____

7. Food and housekeeping supplies   7. $_____

8. Childcare and children's education costs   8. $_____

9. Clothing, laundry, and dry cleaning   9. $_____

10. Personal care products and services   10. $_____

11. Medical and dental expenses   11. $_____

12. Transportation. Include gas, maintenance, bus or train fare.
Do not include car payments.   12. $_____

13. Entertainment, clubs, recreation, newspapers, magazines, and books   13. $_____

14. Charitable contributions and religious donations   14. $_____

15. Insurance.
Do not include insurance deducted from your pay or included in lines 4 or 20.

   15a.　Life insurance   15a. $_____

   15b.　Health insurance   15b. $_____

   15c.　Vehicle insurance   15c. $_____

   15d.　Other insurance. Specify:_____   15d. $_____

16. Taxes. Do not include taxes deducted from your pay or included in lines 4 or 20.
Specify: _____   16. $_____

17. Installment or lease payments:

   17a.　Car payments for Vehicle 1   17a. $_____

   17b.　Car payments for Vehicle 2   17b. $_____

   17c.　Other. Specify:_____   17c. $_____

   17d.　Other. Specify:_____   17d. $_____

18. Your payments of alimony, maintenance, and support that you did not report as deducted from
your pay on line 5, *Schedule I, Your Income* (Official Form 106I).   18. $_____

19. Other payments you make to support others who do not live with you.
Specify:_____   19. $_____

20. Other real property expenses not included in lines 4 or 5 of this form or on *Schedule I: Your Income.*

   20a. Mortgages on other property   20a. $_____

   20b. Real estate taxes   20b. $_____

   20c. Property, homeowner's, or renter's insurance   20c. $_____

   20d. Maintenance, repair, and upkeep expenses   20d. $_____

   20e. Homeowner's association or condominium dues   20e. $_____

Official Form 106J　　　　　Schedule J: Your Expenses　　　　　page 2

Debtor 1 _____ Case number (if known)_____
         First Name   Middle Name   Last Name

21. **Other.** Specify: _____ 21. **+**$_____

22. **Calculate your monthly expenses.**

    22a. Add lines 4 through 21. 22a. $_____

    22b. Copy line 22 (monthly expenses for Debtor 2), if any, from Official Form 106J-2 22b. $_____

    22c. Add line 22a and 22b. The result is your monthly expenses. 22c. $_____

23. **Calculate your monthly net income.**

    23a. Copy line 12 (*your combined monthly income*) from *Schedule I*. 23a. $_____

    23b. Copy your monthly expenses from line 22c above. 23b. **−**$_____

    23c. Subtract your monthly expenses from your monthly income.
         The result is your *monthly net income*. 23c. $_____

24. **Do you expect an increase or decrease in your expenses within the year after you file this form?**

    For example, do you expect to finish paying for your car loan within the year or do you expect your
    mortgage payment to increase or decrease because of a modification to the terms of your mortgage?

    ❏ No.
    ❏ Yes.   Explain here:

Print   Save As...   Add Attachment   Reset

Fill in this information to identify your case:

Debtor 1 _____
        First Name   Middle Name   Last Name

Debtor 2 _____
(Spouse, if filing) First Name   Middle Name   Last Name

United States Bankruptcy Court for the: _____ District of _____

Case number _____
(If known)

☐ Check if this is an amended filing

Official Form 107

Statement of Financial Affairs for Individuals Filing for Bankruptcy   04/22

Be as complete and accurate as possible. If two married people are filing together, both are equally responsible for supplying correct information. If more space is needed, attach a separate sheet to this form. On the top of any additional pages, write your name and case number (if known). Answer every question.

Part 1: Give Details About Your Marital Status and Where You Lived Before

1. What is your current marital status?

   ☐ Married
   ☐ Not married

2. During the last 3 years, have you lived anywhere other than where you live now?

   ☐ No
   ☐ Yes. List all of the places you lived in the last 3 years. Do not include where you live now.

Debtor 1:	Dates Debtor 1 lived there	Debtor 2:	Dates Debtor 2 lived there
		☐ Same as Debtor 1	☐ Same as Debtor 1
_____ Number Street	From _____ To _____	_____ Number Street	From _____ To _____
_____ City State ZIP Code		_____ City State ZIP Code	
		☐ Same as Debtor 1	☐ Same as Debtor 1
_____ Number Street	From _____ To _____	_____ Number Street	From _____ To _____
_____ City State ZIP Code		_____ City State ZIP Code	

3. Within the last 8 years, did you ever live with a spouse or legal equivalent in a community property state or territory? (*Community property states and territories* include Arizona, California, Idaho, Louisiana, Nevada, New Mexico, Puerto Rico, Texas, Washington, and Wisconsin.)

   ☐ No
   ☐ Yes. Make sure you fill out *Schedule H: Your Codebtors* (Official Form 106H).

Part 2: Explain the Sources of Your Income

Debtor 1 _____ Case number (if known)_____
First Name   Middle Name   Last Name

4. **Did you have any income from employment or from operating a business during this year or the two previous calendar years?**
Fill in the total amount of income you received from all jobs and all businesses, including part-time activities.
If you are filing a joint case and you have income that you receive together, list it only once under Debtor 1.

☐ No
☐ Yes. Fill in the details.

	Debtor 1		Debtor 2	
	Sources of income Check all that apply.	**Gross income** (before deductions and exclusions)	**Sources of income** Check all that apply.	**Gross income** (before deductions and exclusions)
From January 1 of current year until the date you filed for bankruptcy:	☐ Wages, commissions, bonuses, tips ☐ Operating a business	$_____	☐ Wages, commissions, bonuses, tips ☐ Operating a business	$_____
For last calendar year: (January 1 to December 31, _____) YYYY	☐ Wages, commissions, bonuses, tips ☐ Operating a business	$_____	☐ Wages, commissions, bonuses, tips ☐ Operating a business	$_____
For the calendar year before that: (January 1 to December 31, _____) YYYY	☐ Wages, commissions, bonuses, tips ☐ Operating a business	$_____	☐ Wages, commissions, bonuses, tips ☐ Operating a business	$_____

5. **Did you receive any other income during this year or the two previous calendar years?**
Include income regardless of whether that income is taxable. Examples of *other income* are alimony; child support; Social Security, unemployment, and other public benefit payments; pensions; rental income; interest; dividends; money collected from lawsuits; royalties; and gambling and lottery winnings. If you are filing a joint case and you have income that you received together, list it only once under Debtor 1.

List each source and the gross income from each source separately. Do not include income that you listed in line 4.

☐ No
☐ Yes. Fill in the details.

	Debtor 1		Debtor 2	
	Sources of income Describe below.	**Gross income from each source** (before deductions and exclusions)	**Sources of income** Describe below.	**Gross income from each source** (before deductions and exclusions)
From January 1 of current year until the date you filed for bankruptcy:	_____ _____ _____	$_____ $_____ $_____	_____ _____ _____	$_____ $_____ $_____
For last calendar year: (January 1 to December 31, _____) YYYY	_____ _____ _____	$_____ $_____ $_____	_____ _____ _____	$_____ $_____ $_____
For the calendar year before that: (January 1 to December 31, _____) YYYY	_____ _____ _____	$_____ $_____ $_____	_____ _____ _____	$_____ $_____ $_____

Debtor 1 _____ Case number (if known)_____
         First Name   Middle Name   Last Name

Part 3: **List Certain Payments You Made Before You Filed for Bankruptcy**

6. Are either Debtor 1's or Debtor 2's debts primarily consumer debts?

☐ No. **Neither Debtor 1 nor Debtor 2 has primarily consumer debts.** *Consumer debts* are defined in 11 U.S.C. § 101(8) as "incurred by an individual primarily for a personal, family, or household purpose."

During the 90 days before you filed for bankruptcy, did you pay any creditor a total of $7,575* or more?

☐ No. Go to line 7.

☐ Yes. List below each creditor to whom you paid a total of $7,575* or more in one or more payments and the total amount you paid that creditor. Do not include payments for domestic support obligations, such as child support and alimony. Also, do not include payments to an attorney for this bankruptcy case.

* Subject to adjustment on 4/01/25 and every 3 years after that for cases filed on or after the date of adjustment.

☐ Yes. **Debtor 1 or Debtor 2 or both have primarily consumer debts.**

During the 90 days before you filed for bankruptcy, did you pay any creditor a total of $600 or more?

☐ No. Go to line 7.

☐ Yes. List below each creditor to whom you paid a total of $600 or more and the total amount you paid that creditor. Do not include payments for domestic support obligations, such as child support and alimony. Also, do not include payments to an attorney for this bankruptcy case.

	Dates of payment	Total amount paid	Amount you still owe	Was this payment for...
_____ Creditor's Name _____ Number Street _____ _____ City State ZIP Code	_____ _____ _____	$_____	$_____	☐ Mortgage ☐ Car ☐ Credit card ☐ Loan repayment ☐ Suppliers or vendors ☐ Other _____
_____ Creditor's Name _____ Number Street _____ _____ City State ZIP Code	_____ _____ _____	$_____	$_____	☐ Mortgage ☐ Car ☐ Credit card ☐ Loan repayment ☐ Suppliers or vendors ☐ Other _____
_____ Creditor's Name _____ Number Street _____ _____ City State ZIP Code	_____ _____ _____	$_____	$_____	☐ Mortgage ☐ Car ☐ Credit card ☐ Loan repayment ☐ Suppliers or vendors ☐ Other _____

Official Form 107   Statement of Financial Affairs for Individuals Filing for Bankruptcy   page 3

SELECTED OFFICIAL FORMS

Debtor 1 _____ Case number (if known)_____
          First Name   Middle Name   Last Name

7. **Within 1 year before you filed for bankruptcy, did you make a payment on a debt you owed anyone who was an insider?**
   Insiders include your relatives; any general partners; relatives of any general partners; partnerships of which you are a general partner; corporations of which you are an officer, director, person in control, or owner of 20% or more of their voting securities; and any managing agent, including one for a business you operate as a sole proprietor. 11 U.S.C. § 101. Include payments for domestic support obligations, such as child support and alimony.

   ❏ No
   ❏ Yes. List all payments to an insider.

	Dates of payment	Total amount paid	Amount you still owe	Reason for this payment
Insider's Name _____	_____	$_____	$_____	
Number Street _____	_____			
_____	_____			
City State ZIP Code				
Insider's Name _____	_____	$_____	$_____	
Number Street _____	_____			
_____	_____			
City State ZIP Code				

8. **Within 1 year before you filed for bankruptcy, did you make any payments or transfer any property on account of a debt that benefited an insider?**
   Include payments on debts guaranteed or cosigned by an insider.

   ❏ No
   ❏ Yes. List all payments that benefited an insider.

	Dates of payment	Total amount paid	Amount you still owe	Reason for this payment Include creditor's name
Insider's Name _____	_____	$_____	$_____	
Number Street _____	_____			
_____	_____			
City State ZIP Code				
Insider's Name _____	_____	$_____	$_____	
Number Street _____	_____			
_____	_____			
City State ZIP Code				

Debtor 1 _____   Case number *(if known)*_____
First Name   Middle Name   Last Name

Part 4: **Identify Legal Actions, Repossessions, and Foreclosures**

9. Within 1 year before you filed for bankruptcy, were you a party in any lawsuit, court action, or administrative proceeding?
List all such matters, including personal injury cases, small claims actions, divorces, collection suits, paternity actions, support or custody modifications, and contract disputes.

❑ No
❑ Yes. Fill in the details.

	Nature of the case	Court or agency	Status of the case
Case title_____ _____ Case number _____		Court Name_____ Number Street_____ City State ZIP Code	❑ Pending ❑ On appeal ❑ Concluded
Case title_____ _____ Case number _____		Court Name_____ Number Street_____ City State ZIP Code	❑ Pending ❑ On appeal ❑ Concluded

10. Within 1 year before you filed for bankruptcy, was any of your property repossessed, foreclosed, garnished, attached, seized, or levied?
Check all that apply and fill in the details below.

❑ No. Go to line 11.
❑ Yes. Fill in the information below.

	Describe the property	Date	Value of the property
_____ Creditor's Name _____ Number Street _____ _____ City State ZIP Code		_____	$_____
	Explain what happened ❑ Property was repossessed. ❑ Property was foreclosed. ❑ Property was garnished. ❑ Property was attached, seized, or levied.		
_____ Creditor's Name _____ Number Street _____ _____ City State ZIP Code		_____	$_____
	Explain what happened ❑ Property was repossessed. ❑ Property was foreclosed. ❑ Property was garnished. ❑ Property was attached, seized, or levied.		

Debtor 1 _____   Case number (if known)_____
    First Name   Middle Name   Last Name

11. Within 90 days before you filed for bankruptcy, did any creditor, including a bank or financial institution, set off any amounts from your accounts or refuse to make a payment because you owed a debt?

☐ No

☐ Yes. Fill in the details.

	Describe the action the creditor took	Date action was taken	Amount
_____ Creditor's Name			
_____ Number Street		_____	$_____
_____			
_____ City State ZIP Code	Last 4 digits of account number: XXXX–___ ___ ___ ___		

12. Within 1 year before you filed for bankruptcy, was any of your property in the possession of an assignee for the benefit of creditors, a court-appointed receiver, a custodian, or another official?

☐ No

☐ Yes

Part 5: List Certain Gifts and Contributions

13. Within 2 years before you filed for bankruptcy, did you give any gifts with a total value of more than $600 per person?

☐ No

☐ Yes. Fill in the details for each gift.

Gifts with a total value of more than $600 per person	Describe the gifts	Dates you gave the gifts	Value
_____ Person to Whom You Gave the Gift		_____	$_____
_____		_____	$_____
_____ Number Street			
_____ City State ZIP Code			
Person's relationship to you _____			

Gifts with a total value of more than $600 per person	Describe the gifts	Dates you gave the gifts	Value
_____ Person to Whom You Gave the Gift		_____	$_____
_____		_____	$_____
_____ Number Street			
_____ City State ZIP Code			
Person's relationship to you _____			

Debtor 1 _____ Case number (if known)_____
First Name   Middle Name   Last Name

14. Within 2 years before you filed for bankruptcy, did you give any gifts or contributions with a total value of more than $600 to any charity?

☐ No
☐ Yes. Fill in the details for each gift or contribution.

Gifts or contributions to charities that total more than $600	Describe what you contributed	Date you contributed	Value
_____ Charity's Name		_____	$_____
_____		_____	$_____
_____ Number Street			
_____ City State ZIP Code			

Part 6:   List Certain Losses

15. Within 1 year before you filed for bankruptcy or since you filed for bankruptcy, did you lose anything because of theft, fire, other disaster, or gambling?

☐ No
☐ Yes. Fill in the details.

Describe the property you lost and how the loss occurred	Describe any insurance coverage for the loss Include the amount that insurance has paid. List pending insurance claims on line 33 of *Schedule A/B: Property*.	Date of your loss	Value of property lost
		_____	$_____

Part 7:   List Certain Payments or Transfers

16. Within 1 year before you filed for bankruptcy, did you or anyone else acting on your behalf pay or transfer any property to anyone you consulted about seeking bankruptcy or preparing a bankruptcy petition?
Include any attorneys, bankruptcy petition preparers, or credit counseling agencies for services required in your bankruptcy.

☐ No
☐ Yes. Fill in the details.

	Description and value of any property transferred	Date payment or transfer was made	Amount of payment
_____ Person Who Was Paid			
_____ Number Street		_____	$_____
_____		_____	$_____
_____ City State ZIP Code			
_____ Email or website address			
_____ Person Who Made the Payment, if Not You			

Official Form 107   Statement of Financial Affairs for Individuals Filing for Bankruptcy   page 7

Debtor 1 _____ Case number *(if known)*_____

First Name   Middle Name   Last Name

	Description and value of any property transferred	Date payment or transfer was made	Amount of payment
Person Who Was Paid _____			
Number Street _____		_____	$_____
_____		_____	$_____
City State ZIP Code			
Email or website address _____			
Person Who Made the Payment, if Not You _____			

17. Within 1 year before you filed for bankruptcy, did you or anyone else acting on your behalf pay or transfer any property to anyone who promised to help you deal with your creditors or to make payments to your creditors?
Do not include any payment or transfer that you listed on line 16.

❏ No
❏ Yes. Fill in the details.

	Description and value of any property transferred	Date payment or transfer was made	Amount of payment
Person Who Was Paid _____			
Number Street _____		_____	$_____
_____		_____	$_____
City State ZIP Code			

18. Within 2 years before you filed for bankruptcy, did you sell, trade, or otherwise transfer any property to anyone, other than property transferred in the ordinary course of your business or financial affairs?
Include both outright transfers and transfers made as security (such as the granting of a security interest or mortgage on your property).
Do not include gifts and transfers that you have already listed on this statement.

❏ No
❏ Yes. Fill in the details.

	Description and value of property transferred	Describe any property or payments received or debts paid in exchange	Date transfer was made
Person Who Received Transfer _____			
Number Street _____			_____
_____			
City State ZIP Code			
Person's relationship to you _____			
Person Who Received Transfer _____			
Number Street _____			_____
_____			
City State ZIP Code			
Person's relationship to you _____			

Official Form 107   Statement of Financial Affairs for Individuals Filing for Bankruptcy   page 8

Debtor 1 _____   Case number (if known)_____
      First Name   Middle Name   Last Name

19. Within 10 years before you filed for bankruptcy, did you transfer any property to a self-settled trust or similar device of which you are a beneficiary? (These are often called *asset-protection devices*.)

❑ No
❑ Yes. Fill in the details.

	Description and value of the property transferred	Date transfer was made
Name of trust _____		_____
_____		

Part 8: List Certain Financial Accounts, Instruments, Safe Deposit Boxes, and Storage Units

20. Within 1 year before you filed for bankruptcy, were any financial accounts or instruments held in your name, or for your benefit, closed, sold, moved, or transferred?
Include checking, savings, money market, or other financial accounts; certificates of deposit; shares in banks, credit unions, brokerage houses, pension funds, cooperatives, associations, and other financial institutions.

❑ No
❑ Yes. Fill in the details.

	Last 4 digits of account number	Type of account or instrument	Date account was closed, sold, moved, or transferred	Last balance before closing or transfer
Name of Financial Institution _____ Number Street _____ _____ City State ZIP Code	XXXX–___ ___ ___ ___	❑ Checking ❑ Savings ❑ Money market ❑ Brokerage ❑ Other_____	_____	$_____
Name of Financial Institution _____ Number Street _____ _____ City State ZIP Code	XXXX–___ ___ ___ ___	❑ Checking ❑ Savings ❑ Money market ❑ Brokerage ❑ Other_____	_____	$_____

21. Do you now have, or did you have within 1 year before you filed for bankruptcy, any safe deposit box or other depository for securities, cash, or other valuables?

❑ No
❑ Yes. Fill in the details.

	Who else had access to it?	Describe the contents	Do you still have it?
Name of Financial Institution _____ Number Street _____ _____ City State ZIP Code	Name _____ Number Street _____ _____ City State ZIP Code		❑ No ❑ Yes

Debtor 1 _____   Case number (if known)_____
         First Name   Middle Name   Last Name

22. Have you stored property in a storage unit or place other than your home within 1 year before you filed for bankruptcy?

☐ No
☐ Yes. Fill in the details.

	Who else has or had access to it?	Describe the contents	Do you still have it?
			☐ No ☐ Yes
_____ Name of Storage Facility	_____ Name		
_____ Number Street	_____ Number Street		
	_____ City State ZIP Code		
_____ City State ZIP Code			

Part 9:   Identify Property You Hold or Control for Someone Else

23. Do you hold or control any property that someone else owns? Include any property you borrowed from, are storing for, or hold in trust for someone.

☐ No
☐ Yes. Fill in the details.

	Where is the property?	Describe the property	Value
_____ Owner's Name			$_____
_____ Number Street	_____ Number Street		
	_____		
_____ City State ZIP Code	City State ZIP Code		

Part 10:   Give Details About Environmental Information

For the purpose of Part 10, the following definitions apply:

- *Environmental law* means any federal, state, or local statute or regulation concerning pollution, contamination, releases of hazardous or toxic substances, wastes, or material into the air, land, soil, surface water, groundwater, or other medium, including statutes or regulations controlling the cleanup of these substances, wastes, or material.

- *Site* means any location, facility, or property as defined under any environmental law, whether you now own, operate, or utilize it or used to own, operate, or utilize it, including disposal sites.

- *Hazardous material* means anything an environmental law defines as a hazardous waste, hazardous substance, toxic substance, hazardous material, pollutant, contaminant, or similar term.

Report all notices, releases, and proceedings that you know about, regardless of when they occurred.

24. Has any governmental unit notified you that you may be liable or potentially liable under or in violation of an environmental law?

☐ No
☐ Yes. Fill in the details.

	Governmental unit	Environmental law, if you know it	Date of notice
_____ Name of site	_____ Governmental unit		_____
_____ Number Street	_____ Number Street		
_____ City State ZIP Code	_____ City State ZIP Code		

Debtor 1 _____   Case number (if known)_____
First Name   Middle Name   Last Name

25. Have you notified any governmental unit of any release of hazardous material?

❑ No
❑ Yes. Fill in the details.

	Governmental unit	Environmental law, if you know it	Date of notice
_____ Name of site	_____ Governmental unit		_____
_____ Number Street	_____ Number Street		
_____ City State ZIP Code	_____ City State ZIP Code		

26. Have you been a party in any judicial or administrative proceeding under any environmental law? Include settlements and orders.

❑ No
❑ Yes. Fill in the details.

	Court or agency	Nature of the case	Status of the case
Case title_____	_____ Court Name		❑ Pending
_____	_____ Number Street		❑ On appeal
_____ Case number	_____ City State ZIP Code		❑ Concluded

Part 11:   Give Details About Your Business or Connections to Any Business

27. Within 4 years before you filed for bankruptcy, did you own a business or have any of the following connections to any business?

❑ A sole proprietor or self-employed in a trade, profession, or other activity, either full-time or part-time
❑ A member of a limited liability company (LLC) or limited liability partnership (LLP)
❑ A partner in a partnership
❑ An officer, director, or managing executive of a corporation
❑ An owner of at least 5% of the voting or equity securities of a corporation

❑ No. None of the above applies. Go to Part 12.
❑ Yes. Check all that apply above and fill in the details below for each business.

	Describe the nature of the business	Employer Identification number Do not include Social Security number or ITIN.
_____ Business Name		EIN: __ __ - __ __ __ __ __ __ __
_____ Number Street	Name of accountant or bookkeeper	Dates business existed
_____ City State ZIP Code		From _____ To _____
_____ Business Name	Describe the nature of the business	Employer Identification number Do not include Social Security number or ITIN.
_____ Number Street		EIN: __ __ - __ __ __ __ __ __ __
_____ City State ZIP Code	Name of accountant or bookkeeper	Dates business existed
		From _____ To _____

Official Form 107   Statement of Financial Affairs for Individuals Filing for Bankruptcy   page 11

Debtor 1 _____   Case number *(if known)*_____
          First Name   Middle Name   Last Name

Business Name _____	Describe the nature of the business	Employer Identification number
		Do not include Social Security number or ITIN.
		EIN: __ __ - __ __ __ __ __ __ __
Number Street _____	Name of accountant or bookkeeper	Dates business existed
_____		
City State ZIP Code		From _____ To _____

28. Within 2 years before you filed for bankruptcy, did you give a financial statement to anyone about your business? Include all financial institutions, creditors, or other parties.

☐ No
☐ Yes. Fill in the details below.

Date issued

Name _____   _____
                                 MM / DD / YYYY

Number   Street _____

_____

City   State   ZIP Code

Part 12:   Sign Below

I have read the answers on this *Statement of Financial Affairs* and any attachments, and I declare under penalty of perjury that the answers are true and correct. I understand that making a false statement, concealing property, or obtaining money or property by fraud in connection with a bankruptcy case can result in fines up to $250,000, or imprisonment for up to 20 years, or both. 18 U.S.C. §§ 152, 1341, 1519, and 3571.

✗ _____   ✗ _____
Signature of Debtor 1   Signature of Debtor 2

Date _____   Date _____

Did you attach additional pages to *Your Statement of Financial Affairs for Individuals Filing for Bankruptcy* (Official Form 107)?

☐ No
☐ Yes

Did you pay or agree to pay someone who is not an attorney to help you fill out bankruptcy forms?

☐ No
☐ Yes. Name of person_____.   Attach the *Bankruptcy Petition Preparer's Notice, Declaration, and Signature* (Official Form 119).

[Print]   [Save As...]   [Add Attachment]   [Reset]

Fill in this information to identify your case:

Debtor 1 _____
First Name   Middle Name   Last Name

Debtor 2 _____
(Spouse, if filing) First Name   Middle Name   Last Name

United States Bankruptcy Court for the: _____ District of _____

Case number _____
(If known)

☐ Check if this is an
amended filing

Official Form 108

Statement of Intention for Individuals Filing Under Chapter 7   12/15

If you are an individual filing under chapter 7, you must fill out this form if:
- creditors have claims secured by your property, or
- you have leased personal property and the lease has not expired.

You must file this form with the court within 30 days after you file your bankruptcy petition or by the date set for the meeting of creditors, whichever is earlier, unless the court extends the time for cause. You must also send copies to the creditors and lessors you list on the form.

If two married people are filing together in a joint case, both are equally responsible for supplying correct information. Both debtors must sign and date the form.

Be as complete and accurate as possible. If more space is needed, attach a separate sheet to this form. On the top of any additional pages, write your name and case number (if known).

Part 1:   List Your Creditors Who Have Secured Claims

1. For any creditors that you listed in Part 1 of *Schedule D: Creditors Who Have Claims Secured by Property* (Official Form 106D), fill in the information below.

Identify the creditor and the property that is collateral	What do you intend to do with the property that secures a debt?	Did you claim the property as exempt on Schedule C?
Creditor's name: _____ Description of property securing debt:	☐ Surrender the property. ☐ Retain the property and redeem it. ☐ Retain the property and enter into a *Reaffirmation Agreement.* ☐ Retain the property and [explain]: _____	☐ No ☐ Yes
Creditor's name: _____ Description of property securing debt:	☐ Surrender the property. ☐ Retain the property and redeem it. ☐ Retain the property and enter into a *Reaffirmation Agreement.* ☐ Retain the property and [explain]: _____	☐ No ☐ Yes
Creditor's name: _____ Description of property securing debt:	☐ Surrender the property. ☐ Retain the property and redeem it. ☐ Retain the property and enter into a *Reaffirmation Agreement.* ☐ Retain the property and [explain]: _____	☐ No ☐ Yes
Creditor's name: _____ Description of property securing debt:	☐ Surrender the property. ☐ Retain the property and redeem it. ☐ Retain the property and enter into a *Reaffirmation Agreement.* ☐ Retain the property and [explain]: _____	☐ No ☐ Yes

Official Form 108   Statement of Intention for Individuals Filing Under Chapter 7   page 1

Debtor 1 _____ Case number *(if known)*_____
First Name Middle Name Last Name

Part 2: **List Your Unexpired Personal Property Leases**

For any unexpired personal property lease that you listed in *Schedule G: Executory Contracts and Unexpired Leases* (Official Form 106G), fill in the information below. Do not list real estate leases. *Unexpired leases* are leases that are still in effect; the lease period has not yet ended. You may assume an unexpired personal property lease if the trustee does not assume it. 11 U.S.C. § 365(p)(2).

Describe your unexpired personal property leases	Will the lease be assumed?
Lessor's name:	❑ No
Description of leased property:	❑ Yes
Lessor's name:	❑ No
Description of leased property:	❑ Yes
Lessor's name:	❑ No
Description of leased property:	❑ Yes
Lessor's name:	❑ No
Description of leased property:	❑ Yes
Lessor's name:	❑ No
Description of leased property:	❑ Yes
Lessor's name:	❑ No
Description of leased property:	❑ Yes
Lessor's name:	❑ No
Description of leased property:	❑ Yes

Part 3: **Sign Below**

Under penalty of perjury, I declare that I have indicated my intention about any property of my estate that secures a debt and any personal property that is subject to an unexpired lease.

✗ _____   ✗ _____
Signature of Debtor 1   Signature of Debtor 2

Date _____   Date _____
MM / DD / YYYY   MM / DD / YYYY

Official Form 108   Statement of Intention for Individuals Filing Under Chapter 7   page 2

| Print | Save As... | Add Attachment | | Reset |

SELECTED OFFICIAL FORMS

Official Form 113

Chapter 13 Plan

12/17

Part 1: Notices

To Debtors: This form sets out options that may be appropriate in some cases, but the presence of an option on the form does not indicate that the option is appropriate in your circumstances or that it is permissible in your judicial district. Plans that do not comply with local rules and judicial rulings may not be confirmable.

In the following notice to creditors, you must check each box that applies.

To Creditors: Your rights may be affected by this plan. Your claim may be reduced, modified, or eliminated.

You should read this plan carefully and discuss it with your attorney if you have one in this bankruptcy case. If you do not have an attorney, you may wish to consult one.

If you oppose the plan's treatment of your claim or any provision of this plan, you or your attorney must file an objection to confirmation at least 7 days before the date set for the hearing on confirmation, unless otherwise ordered by the Bankruptcy Court. The Bankruptcy Court may confirm this plan without further notice if no objection to confirmation is filed. See Bankruptcy Rule 3015. In addition, you may need to file a timely proof of claim in order to be paid under any plan.

The following matters may be of particular importance. *Debtors must check one box on each line to state whether or not the plan includes each of the following items. If an item is checked as "Not included" or if both boxes are checked, the provision will be ineffective if set out later in the plan.*

1.1	A limit on the amount of a secured claim, set out in Section 3.2, which may result in a partial payment or no payment at all to the secured creditor	☐ Included	☐ Not included
1.2	Avoidance of a judicial lien or nonpossessory, nonpurchase-money security interest, set out in Section 3.4	☐ Included	☐ Not included
1.3	Nonstandard provisions, set out in Part 8	☐ Included	☐ Not included

---

Part 2: Plan Payments and Length of Plan

2.1 Debtor(s) will make regular payments to the trustee as follows:

$ _____ per_____ for _____ months

[and $ _____ per_____ for _____ months.] *Insert additional lines if needed.*

If fewer than 60 months of payments are specified, additional monthly payments will be made to the extent necessary to make the payments to creditors specified in this plan.

SELECTED OFFICIAL FORMS

Debtor _____   Case number _____

2.2 Regular payments to the trustee will be made from future income in the following manner:

Check all that apply.

❑ Debtor(s) will make payments pursuant to a payroll deduction order.

❑ Debtor(s) will make payments directly to the trustee.

❑ Other (specify method of payment):_____.

2.3 Income tax refunds.

Check one.

❑ Debtor(s) will retain any income tax refunds received during the plan term.

❑ Debtor(s) will supply the trustee with a copy of each income tax return filed during the plan term within 14 days of filing the return and will turn over to the trustee all income tax refunds received during the plan term.

❑ Debtor(s) will treat income tax refunds as follows:

_____

_____

2.4 Additional payments.

Check one.

❑ None. *If "None" is checked, the rest of § 2.4 need not be completed or reproduced.*

❑ Debtor(s) will make additional payment(s) to the trustee from other sources, as specified below. Describe the source, estimated amount, and date of each anticipated payment.

_____

_____

2.5 The total amount of estimated payments to the trustee provided for in §§ 2.1 and 2.4 is $ _____.

Part 3:   Treatment of Secured Claims

3.1 Maintenance of payments and cure of default, if any.

Check one.

❑ None. *If "None" is checked, the rest of § 3.1 need not be completed or reproduced.*

❑ The debtor(s) will maintain the current contractual installment payments on the secured claims listed below, with any changes required by the applicable contract and noticed in conformity with any applicable rules. These payments will be disbursed either by the trustee or directly by the debtor(s), as specified below. Any existing arrearage on a listed claim will be paid in full through disbursements by the trustee, with interest, if any, at the rate stated. Unless otherwise ordered by the court, the amounts listed on a proof of claim filed before the filing deadline under Bankruptcy Rule 3002(c) control over any contrary amounts listed below as to the current installment payment and arrearage. In the absence of a contrary timely filed proof of claim, the amounts stated below are controlling. If relief from the automatic stay is ordered as to any item of collateral listed in this paragraph, then, unless otherwise ordered by the court, all payments under this paragraph as to that collateral will cease, and all secured claims based on that collateral will no longer be treated by the plan. The final column includes only payments disbursed by the trustee rather than by the debtor(s).

Name of creditor	Collateral	Current installment payment (including escrow)	Amount of arrearage (if any)	Interest rate on arrearage (if applicable)	Monthly plan payment on arrearage	Estimated total payments by trustee
_____	_____	$_____ Disbursed by: ❑ Trustee ❑ Debtor(s)	$_____	_____%	$_____	$_____
_____	_____	$_____ Disbursed by: ❑ Trustee ❑ Debtor(s)	$_____	_____%	$_____	$_____

Insert additional claims as needed.

SELECTED OFFICIAL FORMS

Debtor _____   Case number _____

3.2 Request for valuation of security, payment of fully secured claims, and modification of undersecured claims. *Check one.*

❏ **None.** *If "None" is checked, the rest of § 3.2 need not be completed or reproduced.*

The remainder of this paragraph will be effective only if the applicable box in Part 1 of this plan is checked.

❏ The debtor(s) request that the court determine the value of the secured claims listed below. For each non-governmental secured claim listed below, the debtor(s) state that the value of the secured claim should be as set out in the column headed *Amount of secured claim.* For secured claims of governmental units, unless otherwise ordered by the court, the value of a secured claim listed in a proof of claim filed in accordance with the Bankruptcy Rules controls over any contrary amount listed below. For each listed claim, the value of the secured claim will be paid in full with interest at the rate stated below.

The portion of any allowed claim that exceeds the amount of the secured claim will be treated as an unsecured claim under Part 5 of this plan. If the amount of a creditor's secured claim is listed below as having no value, the creditor's allowed claim will be treated in its entirety as an unsecured claim under Part 5 of this plan. Unless otherwise ordered by the court, the amount of the creditor's total claim listed on the proof of claim controls over any contrary amounts listed in this paragraph.

The holder of any claim listed below as having value in the column headed *Amount of secured claim* will retain the lien on the property interest of the debtor(s) or the estate(s) until the earlier of:

(a) payment of the underlying debt determined under nonbankruptcy law, or

(b) discharge of the underlying debt under 11 U.S.C. § 1328, at which time the lien will terminate and be released by the creditor.

Name of creditor	Estimated amount of creditor's total claim	Collateral	Value of collateral	Amount of claims senior to creditor's claim	Amount of secured claim	Interest rate	Monthly payment to creditor	Estimated total of monthly payments
_____	$_____	_____	$_____	$_____	$_____	___%	$_____	$_____
_____	$_____	_____	$_____	$_____	$_____	___%	$_____	$_____

Insert additional claims as needed.

3.3 Secured claims excluded from 11 U.S.C. § 506.

Check one.

❏ **None.** *If "None" is checked, the rest of § 3.3 need not be completed or reproduced.*

❏ The claims listed below were either:

(1) incurred within 910 days before the petition date and secured by a purchase money security interest in a motor vehicle acquired for the personal use of the debtor(s), or

(2) incurred within 1 year of the petition date and secured by a purchase money security interest in any other thing of value.

These claims will be paid in full under the plan with interest at the rate stated below. These payments will be disbursed either by the trustee or directly by the debtor(s), as specified below. Unless otherwise ordered by the court, the claim amount stated on a proof of claim filed before the filing deadline under Bankruptcy Rule 3002(c) controls over any contrary amount listed below. In the absence of a contrary timely filed proof of claim, the amounts stated below are controlling. The final column includes only payments disbursed by the trustee rather than by the debtor(s).

Name of creditor	Collateral	Amount of claim	Interest rate	Monthly plan payment	Estimated total payments by trustee
_____	_____	$_____	____%	$_____ Disbursed by: ❏ Trustee ❏ Debtor(s)	$_____
_____	_____	$_____	____%	$_____ Disbursed by: ❏ Trustee ❏ Debtor(s)	$_____

Insert additional claims as needed.

Official Form 113   Chapter 13 Plan   Page 3

Debtor _____   Case number _____

3.4 Lien avoidance.

Check one.

❑ **None.** *If "None" is checked, the rest of § 3.4 need not be completed or reproduced.*
The remainder of this paragraph will be effective only if the applicable box in Part 1 of this plan is checked.

❑ The judicial liens or nonpossessory, nonpurchase money security interests securing the claims listed below impair exemptions to which the debtor(s) would have been entitled under 11 U.S.C. § 522(b). Unless otherwise ordered by the court, a judicial lien or security interest securing a claim listed below will be avoided to the extent that it impairs such exemptions upon entry of the order confirming the plan. The amount of the judicial lien or security interest that is avoided will be treated as an unsecured claim in Part 5 to the extent allowed. The amount, if any, of the judicial lien or security interest that is not avoided will be paid in full as a secured claim under the plan. See 11 U.S.C. § 522(f) and Bankruptcy Rule 4003(d). *If more than one lien is to be avoided, provide the information separately for each lien.*

Information regarding judicial lien or security interest	Calculation of lien avoidance		Treatment of remaining secured claim
Name of creditor _____	a. Amount of lien	$_____	Amount of secured claim after avoidance (line a minus line f) $_____
	b. Amount of all other liens	$_____	
Collateral _____	c. Value of claimed exemptions	+ $_____	Interest rate (if applicable) _____ %
	d. Total of adding lines a, b, and c	$_____	
Lien identification (such as judgment date, date of lien recording, book and page number) _____ _____	e. Value of debtor(s)' interest in property	– $_____	Monthly payment on secured claim $_____
	f. Subtract line e from line d.	$_____	Estimated total payments on secured claim $_____
	Extent of exemption impairment *(Check applicable box):* ❑ **Line f is equal to or greater than line a.** The entire lien is avoided. *(Do not complete the next column.)* ❑ **Line f is less than line a.** A portion of the lien is avoided. *(Complete the next column.)*		

Insert additional claims as needed.

3.5 Surrender of collateral.

Check one.

❑ **None.** *If "None" is checked, the rest of § 3.5 need not be completed or reproduced.*

❑ The debtor(s) elect to surrender to each creditor listed below the collateral that secures the creditor's claim. The debtor(s) request that upon confirmation of this plan the stay under 11 U.S.C. § 362(a) be terminated as to the collateral only and that the stay under § 1301 be terminated in all respects. Any allowed unsecured claim resulting from the disposition of the collateral will be treated in Part 5 below.

Name of creditor	Collateral
_____	_____
_____	_____

Insert additional claims as needed.

SELECTED OFFICIAL FORMS

Debtor _____   Case number _____

Part 4:   Treatment of Fees and Priority Claims

4.1   General

Trustee's fees and all allowed priority claims, including domestic support obligations other than those treated in § 4.5, will be paid in full without postpetition interest.

4.2   Trustee's fees

Trustee's fees are governed by statute and may change during the course of the case but are estimated to be _____% of plan payments; and during the plan term, they are estimated to total $_____.

4.3   Attorney's fees

The balance of the fees owed to the attorney for the debtor(s) is estimated to be $_____.

4.4   Priority claims other than attorney's fees and those treated in § 4.5.

Check one.

❑ **None.** *If "None" is checked, the rest of § 4.4 need not be completed or reproduced.*

❑ The debtor(s) estimate the total amount of other priority claims to be _____.

4.5   Domestic support obligations assigned or owed to a governmental unit and paid less than full amount.

Check one.

❑ **None.** *If "None" is checked, the rest of § 4.5 need not be completed or reproduced.*

❑ The allowed priority claims listed below are based on a domestic support obligation that has been assigned to or is owed to a governmental unit and will be paid less than the full amount of the claim under 11 U.S.C. § 1322(a)(4). *This plan provision requires that payments in § 2.1 be for a term of 60 months; see 11 U.S.C. § 1322(a)(4).*

Name of creditor	Amount of claim to be paid
_____	$_____
_____	$_____

Insert additional claims as needed.

Part 5:   Treatment of Nonpriority Unsecured Claims

5.1   Nonpriority unsecured claims not separately classified.

Allowed nonpriority unsecured claims that are not separately classified will be paid, pro rata. If more than one option is checked, the option providing the largest payment will be effective. *Check all that apply.*

❑ The sum of $_____.

❑ _____% of the total amount of these claims, an estimated payment of $_____.

❑ The funds remaining after disbursements have been made to all other creditors provided for in this plan.

If the estate of the debtor(s) were liquidated under chapter 7, nonpriority unsecured claims would be paid approximately $_____. Regardless of the options checked above, payments on allowed nonpriority unsecured claims will be made in at least this amount.

Debtor _____   Case number _____

5.2 Maintenance of payments and cure of any default on nonpriority unsecured claims. *Check one.*

☐ **None.** *If "None" is checked, the rest of § 5.2 need not be completed or reproduced.*

☐ The debtor(s) will maintain the contractual installment payments and cure any default in payments on the unsecured claims listed below on which the last payment is due after the final plan payment. These payments will be disbursed either by the trustee or directly by the debtor(s), as specified below. The claim for the arrearage amount will be paid in full as specified below and disbursed by the trustee. The final column includes only payments disbursed by the trustee rather than by the debtor(s).

Name of creditor	Current installment payment	Amount of arrearage to be paid	Estimated total payments by trustee
_____	$_____ Disbursed by: ☐ Trustee ☐ Debtor(s)	$_____	$_____
_____	$_____ Disbursed by: ☐ Trustee ☐ Debtor(s)	$_____	$_____

Insert additional claims as needed.

5.3 Other separately classified nonpriority unsecured claims. *Check one.*

☐ **None.** *If "None" is checked, the rest of § 5.3 need not be completed or reproduced.*

☐ The nonpriority unsecured allowed claims listed below are separately classified and will be treated as follows

Name of creditor	Basis for separate classification and treatment	Amount to be paid on the claim	Interest rate (if applicable)	Estimated total amount of payments
_____	_____	$_____	_____%	$_____
_____	_____	$_____	_____%	$_____

Insert additional claims as needed.

Part 6: Executory Contracts and Unexpired Leases

6.1 The executory contracts and unexpired leases listed below are assumed and will be treated as specified. All other executory contracts and unexpired leases are rejected. *Check one.*

☐ **None.** *If "None" is checked, the rest of § 6.1 need not be completed or reproduced.*

☐ **Assumed items.** Current installment payments will be disbursed either by the trustee or directly by the debtor(s), as specified below, subject to any contrary court order or rule. Arrearage payments will be disbursed by the trustee. The final column includes only payments disbursed by the trustee rather than by the debtor(s).

Debtor _____   Case number _____

Name of creditor	Description of leased property or executory contract	Current installment payment	Amount of arrearage to be paid	Treatment of arrearage (Refer to other plan section if applicable)	Estimated total payments by trustee
_____	_____	$_____ Disbursed by: ❑ Trustee ❑ Debtor(s)	$_____	_____ _____	$_____
_____	_____	$_____ Disbursed by: ❑ Trustee ❑ Debtor(s)	$_____	_____ _____	$_____

Insert additional contracts or leases as needed.

Part 7: Vesting of Property of the Estate

7.1 Property of the estate will vest in the debtor(s) upon

Check the applicable box:

❑ plan confirmation.

❑ entry of discharge.

❑ other: _____.

Part 8: Nonstandard Plan Provisions

8.1 Check "None" or List Nonstandard Plan Provisions

❑ None. *If "None" is checked, the rest of Part 8 need not be completed or reproduced.*

Under Bankruptcy Rule 3015(c), nonstandard provisions must be set forth below. A nonstandard provision is a provision not otherwise included in the Official Form or deviating from it. Nonstandard provisions set out elsewhere in this plan are ineffective.

The following plan provisions will be effective only if there is a check in the box "Included" in § 1.3.

_____
_____
_____
_____
_____

Debtor _____   Case number _____

Part 9:   Signature(s):

9.1 Signatures of Debtor(s) and Debtor(s)' Attorney

If the Debtor(s) do not have an attorney, the Debtor(s) must sign below; otherwise the Debtor(s) signatures are optional. The attorney for the Debtor(s), if any, must sign below.

✘ _____   ✘ _____
  Signature of Debtor 1   Signature of Debtor 2

  Executed on _____   Executed on _____
              MM / DD / YYYY   MM / DD / YYYY

✘ _____   Date _____
  Signature of Attorney for Debtor(s)   MM / DD / YYYY

By filing this document, the Debtor(s), if not represented by an attorney, or the Attorney for Debtor(s) also certify(ies) that the wording and order of the provisions in this Chapter 13 plan are identical to those contained in Official Form 113, other than any nonstandard provisions included in Part 8.

Exhibit: Total Amount of Estimated Trustee Payments

The following are the estimated payments that the plan requires the trustee to disburse. If there is any difference between the amounts set out below and the actual plan terms, the plan terms control.

a. **Maintenance and cure payments on secured claims** *(Part 3, Section 3.1 total)* $_____

b. **Modified secured claims** *(Part 3, Section 3.2 total)* $_____

c. **Secured claims excluded from 11 U.S.C. § 506** *(Part 3, Section 3.3 total)* $_____

d. **Judicial liens or security interests partially avoided** *(Part 3, Section 3.4 total)* $_____

e. **Fees and priority claims** *(Part 4 total)* $_____

f. **Nonpriority unsecured claims** *(Part 5, Section 5.1, highest stated amount)* $_____

g. **Maintenance and cure payments on unsecured claims** *(Part 5, Section 5.2 total)* $_____

h. **Separately classified unsecured claims** *(Part 5, Section 5.3 total)* $_____

i. **Trustee payments on executory contracts and unexpired leases** *(Part 6, Section 6.1 total)* $_____

j. **Nonstandard payments** *(Part 8, total)*   + $_____

    Total of lines a through j $_____

Fill in this information to identify your case:

Debtor 1 _____
First Name   Middle Name   Last Name

Debtor 2 _____
(Spouse, if filing) First Name   Middle Name   Last Name

United States Bankruptcy Court for the: _____ District of _____

Case number _____
(If known)

Check one box only as directed in this form and in Form 122A-1Supp:

☐ 1. There is no presumption of abuse.

☐ 2. The calculation to determine if a presumption of abuse applies will be made under *Chapter 7 Means Test Calculation* (Official Form 122A–2).

☐ 3. The Means Test does not apply now because of qualified military service but it could apply later.

☐ Check if this is an amended filing

Official Form 122A—1

Chapter 7 Statement of Your Current Monthly Income

12/19

Be as complete and accurate as possible. If two married people are filing together, both are equally responsible for being accurate. If more space is needed, attach a separate sheet to this form. Include the line number to which the additional information applies. On the top of any additional pages, write your name and case number (if known). If you believe that you are exempted from a presumption of abuse because you do not have primarily consumer debts or because of qualifying military service, complete and file *Statement of Exemption from Presumption of Abuse Under § 707(b)(2)* (Official Form 122A-1Supp) with this form.

Part 1: Calculate Your Current Monthly Income

1. **What is your marital and filing status?** Check one only.

   ☐ **Not married.** Fill out Column A, lines 2-11.
   ☐ **Married and your spouse is filing with you.** Fill out both Columns A and B, lines 2-11.
   ☐ **Married and your spouse is NOT filing with you.** You and your spouse are:

   ☐ **Living in the same household and are not legally separated.** Fill out both Columns A and B, lines 2-11.
   ☐ **Living separately or are legally separated.** Fill out Column A, lines 2-11; do not fill out Column B. By checking this box, you declare under penalty of perjury that you and your spouse are legally separated under nonbankruptcy law that applies or that you and your spouse are living apart for reasons that do not include evading the Means Test requirements. 11 U.S.C. § 707(b)(7)(B).

   Fill in the average monthly income that you received from all sources, derived during the 6 full months before you file this bankruptcy case. 11 U.S.C. § 101(10A). For example, if you are filing on September 15, the 6-month period would be March 1 through August 31. If the amount of your monthly income varied during the 6 months, add the income for all 6 months and divide the total by 6. Fill in the result. Do not include any income amount more than once. For example, if both spouses own the same rental property, put the income from that property in one column only. If you have nothing to report for any line, write $0 in the space.

	Column A Debtor 1	Column B Debtor 2 or non-filing spouse
2. **Your gross wages, salary, tips, bonuses, overtime, and commissions** (before all payroll deductions).	$_____	$_____
3. **Alimony and maintenance payments.** Do not include payments from a spouse if Column B is filled in.	$_____	$_____
4. **All amounts from any source which are regularly paid for household expenses of you or your dependents, including child support.** Include regular contributions from an unmarried partner, members of your household, your dependents, parents, and roommates. Include regular contributions from a spouse only if Column B is not filled in. Do not include payments you listed on line 3.	$_____	$_____

5. **Net income from operating a business, profession, or farm**

	Debtor 1	Debtor 2			
Gross receipts (before all deductions)	$_____	$_____			
Ordinary and necessary operating expenses	– $_____	– $_____			
Net monthly income from a business, profession, or farm	$_____	$_____	Copy here ➔	$_____	$_____

6. **Net income from rental and other real property**

	Debtor 1	Debtor 2			
Gross receipts (before all deductions)	$_____	$_____			
Ordinary and necessary operating expenses	– $_____	– $_____			
Net monthly income from rental or other real property	$_____	$_____	Copy here ➔	$_____	$_____

7. **Interest, dividends, and royalties**	$_____	$_____

Debtor 1 _____ Case number (if known)_____

First Name   Middle Name   Last Name

	Column A Debtor 1	Column B Debtor 2 or non-filing spouse
8. **Unemployment compensation**	$_____	$_____

Do not enter the amount if you contend that the amount received was a benefit under the Social Security Act. Instead, list it here: ....↓

For you .... $_____

For your spouse .... $_____

9. **Pension or retirement income.** Do not include any amount received that was a benefit under the Social Security Act. Also, except as stated in the next sentence, do not include any compensation, pension, pay, annuity, or allowance paid by the United States Government in connection with a disability, combat-related injury or disability, or death of a member of the uniformed services. If you received any retired pay paid under chapter 61 of title 10, then include that pay only to the extent that it does not exceed the amount of retired pay to which you would otherwise be entitled if retired under any provision of title 10 other than chapter 61 of that title.

$_____ $_____

10. **Income from all other sources not listed above.** Specify the source and amount. Do not include any benefits received under the Social Security Act; payments received as a victim of a war crime, a crime against humanity, or international or domestic terrorism; or compensation, pension, pay, annuity, or allowance paid by the United States Government in connection with a disability, combat-related injury or disability, or death of a member of the uniformed services. If necessary, list other sources on a separate page and put the total below.

_____ $_____ $_____

_____ $_____ $_____

Total amounts from separate pages, if any.   + $_____   + $_____

11. **Calculate your total current monthly income.** Add lines 2 through 10 for each column. Then add the total for Column A to the total for Column B.

$_____ + $_____ = $_____

Total current monthly income

Part 2:   Determine Whether the Means Test Applies to You

12. **Calculate your current monthly income for the year.** Follow these steps:

12a.   Copy your total current monthly income from line 11. .... Copy line 11 here → $_____

Multiply by 12 (the number of months in a year).   x 12

12b.   The result is your annual income for this part of the form.   12b. $_____

13. **Calculate the median family income that applies to you.** Follow these steps:

Fill in the state in which you live.   [   ]

Fill in the number of people in your household.   [   ]

Fill in the median family income for your state and size of household. ....13. $_____

To find a list of applicable median income amounts, go online using the link specified in the separate instructions for this form. This list may also be available at the bankruptcy clerk's office.

14. **How do the lines compare?**

14a. ☐ Line 12b is less than or equal to line 13. On the top of page 1, check box 1, *There is no presumption of abuse.* Go to Part 3. Do NOT fill out or file Official Form 122A-2

14b. ☐ Line 12b is more than line 13. On the top of page 1, check box 2, *The presumption of abuse is determined by Form 122A-2.* Go to Part 3 and fill out Form 122A–2.

Debtor 1 _____   Case number (if known)_____
         First Name   Middle Name   Last Name

Part 3:	Sign Below

By signing here, I declare under penalty of perjury that the information on this statement and in any attachments is true and correct.

✗ _____   ✗ _____
Signature of Debtor 1   Signature of Debtor 2

Date _____   Date _____
     MM / DD / YYYY   MM / DD / YYYY

If you checked line 14a, do NOT fill out or file Form 122A–2.

If you checked line 14b, fill out Form 122A–2 and file it with this form.

[Print]   [Save As...]   [Add Attachment]   [Reset]

Fill in this information to identify your case:

Debtor 1 _____
 First Name   Middle Name   Last Name

Debtor 2 _____
(Spouse, if filing) First Name   Middle Name   Last Name

United States Bankruptcy Court for the: _____ District of _____

Case number _____
(If known)

☐ Check if this is an amended filing

Official Form 122A—1Supp

Statement of Exemption from Presumption of Abuse Under § 707(b)(2)   12/15

File this supplement together with *Chapter 7 Statement of Your Current Monthly Income* (Official Form 122A-1), if you believe that you are exempted from a presumption of abuse. Be as complete and accurate as possible. If two married people are filing together, and any of the exclusions in this statement applies to only one of you, the other person should complete a separate Form 122A-1 if you believe that this is required by 11 U.S.C. § 707(b)(2)(C).

Part 1:   Identify the Kind of Debts You Have

1. **Are your debts primarily consumer debts?** *Consumer debts* are defined in 11 U.S.C. § 101(8) as "incurred by an individual primarily for a personal, family, or household purpose." Make sure that your answer is consistent with the answer you gave at line 16 of the *Voluntary Petition for Individuals Filing for Bankruptcy* (Official Form 101).

   ☐ No. Go to Form 122A-1; on the top of page 1 of that form, check box 1, *There is no presumption of abuse*, and sign Part 3. Then submit this supplement with the signed Form 122A-1.

   ☐ Yes. Go to Part 2.

Part 2:   Determine Whether Military Service Provisions Apply to You

2. **Are you a disabled veteran** (as defined in 38 U.S.C. § 3741(1))?

   ☐ No. Go to line 3.

   ☐ Yes. Did you incur debts mostly while you were on active duty or while you were performing a homeland defense activity?
      10 U.S.C. § 101(d)(1); 32 U.S.C. § 901(1).

      ☐ No. Go to line 3.

      ☐ Yes. Go to Form 122A-1; on the top of page 1 of that form, check box 1, *There is no presumption of abuse*, and sign Part 3. Then submit this supplement with the signed Form 122A-1.

3. **Are you or have you been a Reservist or member of the National Guard?**

   ☐ No. Complete Form 122A-1. Do not submit this supplement.

   ☐ Yes. Were you called to active duty or did you perform a homeland defense activity? 10 U.S.C. § 101(d)(1); 32 U.S.C. § 901(1).

      ☐ No. Complete Form 122A-1. Do not submit this supplement.

      ☐ Yes. Check any one of the following categories that applies:

         ☐ I was called to active duty after September 11, 2001, for at least 90 days and remain on active duty.

         ☐ I was called to active duty after September 11, 2001, for at least 90 days and was released from active duty on _____, which is fewer than 540 days before I file this bankruptcy case.

         ☐ I am performing a homeland defense activity for at least 90 days.

         ☐ I performed a homeland defense activity for at least 90 days, ending on _____, which is fewer than 540 days before I file this bankruptcy case.

      If you checked one of the categories to the left, go to Form 122A-1. On the top of page 1 of Form 122A-1, check box 3, *The Means Test does not apply now*, and sign Part 3. Then submit this supplement with the signed Form 122A-1. You are not required to fill out the rest of Official Form 122A-1 during the exclusion period. The *exclusion period* means the time you are on active duty or are performing a homeland defense activity, and for 540 days afterward. 11 U.S.C. § 707(b)(2)(D)(ii).

      If your exclusion period ends before your case is closed, you may have to file an amended form later.

Official Form 122A-1Supp   Statement of Exemption from Presumption of Abuse Under § 707(b)(2)

| Print | Save As... | Add Attachment | | Reset |

Fill in this information to identify your case:

Debtor 1 _____
First Name   Middle Name   Last Name

Debtor 2 _____
(Spouse, if filing) First Name   Middle Name   Last Name

United States Bankruptcy Court for the: _____ District of _____

Case number _____
(If known)

Check the appropriate box as directed in lines 40 or 42:

According to the calculations required by this Statement:

❏ 1. There is no presumption of abuse.

❏ 2. There is a presumption of abuse.

❏ Check if this is an amended filing

Official Form 122A–2

Chapter 7 Means Test Calculation

04/22

To fill out this form, you will need your completed copy of *Chapter 7 Statement of Your Current Monthly Income* (Official Form 122A-1).

Be as complete and accurate as possible. If two married people are filing together, both are equally responsible for being accurate. If more space is needed, attach a separate sheet to this form. Include the line number to which the additional information applies. On the top of any additional pages, write your name and case number (if known).

Part 1:   Determine Your Adjusted Income

1. Copy your total current monthly income. .... Copy line 11 from Official Form 122A-1 here ➡ .... $_____

2. Did you fill out Column B in Part 1 of Form 122A–1?

   ❏ No. Fill in $0 for the total on line 3.

   ❏ Yes. Is your spouse filing with you?

      ❏ No. Go to line 3.

      ❏ Yes. Fill in $0 for the total on line 3.

3. **Adjust your current monthly income by subtracting any part of your spouse's income not used to pay for the household expenses of you or your dependents.** Follow these steps:

   On line 11, Column of Form 122A–1, was any amount of the income you reported for your spouse NOT regularly used for the household expenses of you or your dependents?

   ❏ No. Fill in 0 for the total on line 3.

   ❏ Yes. Fill in the information below:

State each purpose for which the income was used For example, the income is used to pay your spouse's tax debt or to support people other than you or your dependents	Fill in the amount you are subtracting from your spouse's income
_____	$_____
_____	$_____
_____	+ $_____
Total.	$_____ Copy total here .... ➡ − $_____

4. **Adjust your current monthly income.** Subtract the total on line 3 from line 1.

   $_____

Debtor 1 _____ Case number (if known)_____
First Name   Middle Name   Last Name

Part 2:   Calculate Your Deductions from Your Income

The Internal Revenue Service (IRS) issues National and Local Standards for certain expense amounts. Use these amounts to answer the questions in lines 6-15. To find the IRS standards, go online using the link specified in the separate instructions for this form. This information may also be available at the bankruptcy clerk's office.

Deduct the expense amounts set out in lines 6-15 regardless of your actual expense. In later parts of the form, you will use some of your actual expenses if they are higher than the standards. Do not deduct any amounts that you subtracted from your spouse's income in line 3 and do not deduct any operating expenses that you subtracted from income in lines 5 and 6 of Form 122A–1.

If your expenses differ from month to month, enter the average expense.

Whenever this part of the form refers to *you*, it means both you and your spouse if Column B of Form 122A–1 is filled in.

5. **The number of people used in determining your deductions from income**

   Fill in the number of people who could be claimed as exemptions on your federal income tax return, plus the number of any additional dependents whom you support. This number may be different from the number of people in your household.

   _____

National Standards   You must use the IRS National Standards to answer the questions in lines 6-7.

6. **Food, clothing, and other items:** Using the number of people you entered in line 5 and the IRS National Standards, fill in the dollar amount for food, clothing, and other items. $_____

7. **Out-of-pocket health care allowance:** Using the number of people you entered in line 5 and the IRS National Standards, fill in the dollar amount for out-of-pocket health care. The number of people is split into two categories—people who are under 65 and people who are 65 or older—because older people have a higher IRS allowance for health care costs. If your actual expenses are higher than this IRS amount, you may deduct the additional amount on line 22.

   People who are under 65 years of age

   7a. Out-of-pocket health care allowance per person $_____

   7b. Number of people who are under 65   X _____

   7c. **Subtotal.** Multiply line 7a by line 7b. $_____   Copy here ➔ $_____

   People who are 65 years of age or older

   7d. Out-of-pocket health care allowance per person $_____

   7e. Number of people who are 65 or older   X _____

   7f. **Subtotal.** Multiply line 7d by line 7e. $_____   Copy here ➔ + $_____

   7g. **Total.** Add lines 7c and 7f.. $_____   Copy total here ➔ $_____

Official Form 122A–2   Chapter 7 Means Test Calculation   page 2

Debtor 1 _____   Case number (if known)_____
      First Name   Middle Name   Last Name

Local Standards   You must use the IRS Local Standards to answer the questions in lines 8-15.

Based on information from the IRS, the U.S. Trustee Program has divided the IRS Local Standard for housing for bankruptcy purposes into two parts:

■ Housing and utilities – Insurance and operating expenses
■ Housing and utilities – Mortgage or rent expenses

To answer the questions in lines 8-9, use the U.S. Trustee Program chart.

To find the chart, go online using the link specified in the separate instructions for this form. This chart may also be available at the bankruptcy clerk's office.

8. **Housing and utilities – Insurance and operating expenses:** Using the number of people you entered in line 5, fill in the dollar amount listed for your county for insurance and operating expenses. .... $_____

9. **Housing and utilities – Mortgage or rent expenses:**

    9a. Using the number of people you entered in line 5, fill in the dollar amount listed for your county for mortgage or rent expenses... $_____

    9b. Total average monthly payment for all mortgages and other debts secured by your home.

        To calculate the total average monthly payment, add all amounts that are contractually due to each secured creditor in the 60 months after you file for bankruptcy. Then divide by 60.

Name of the creditor	Average monthly payment		
_____	$_____		
_____	$_____		
_____	+ $_____		
Total average monthly payment	$_____	Copy here ➜ – $_____	Repeat this amount on line 33a.

    9c. Net mortgage or rent expense.
        Subtract line 9b (*total average monthly payment*) from line 9a (*mortgage or rent expense*). If this amount is less than $0, enter $0. .... $_____ Copy here ➜ $_____

10. If you claim that the U.S. Trustee Program's division of the IRS Local Standard for housing is incorrect and affects the calculation of your monthly expenses, fill in any additional amount you claim. $_____

    Explain why: _____
    _____

11. **Local transportation expenses:** Check the number of vehicles for which you claim an ownership or operating expense.

    ❑ 0. Go to line 14.
    ❑ 1. Go to line 12.
    ❑ 2 or more. Go to line 12.

12. **Vehicle operation expense:** Using the IRS Local Standards and the number of vehicles for which you claim the operating expenses, fill in the *Operating Costs* that apply for your Census region or metropolitan statistical area. $_____

Official Form 122A–2   Chapter 7 Means Test Calculation   page 3

Debtor 1 _____   Case number (if known)_____
         First Name   Middle Name   Last Name

13. **Vehicle ownership or lease expense:** Using the IRS Local Standards, calculate the net ownership or lease expense for each vehicle below. You may not claim the expense if you do not make any loan or lease payments on the vehicle. In addition, you may not claim the expense for more than two vehicles.

   Vehicle 1   **Describe Vehicle 1:** _____

   _____

   13a. Ownership or leasing costs using IRS Local Standard. .... $_____

   13b. Average monthly payment for all debts secured by Vehicle 1.
        Do not include costs for leased vehicles.

        To calculate the average monthly payment here and on line 13e, add all amounts that are contractually due to each secured creditor in the 60 months after you filed for bankruptcy. Then divide by 60.

Name of each creditor for Vehicle 1	Average monthly payment
_____	$_____
_____	+ $_____

   Total average monthly payment | $_____ | Copy here ➡   — $_____   Repeat this amount on line 33b.

   13c. Net Vehicle 1 ownership or lease expense
        Subtract line 13b from line 13a. If this amount is less than $0, enter $0. .... | $_____ | Copy net Vehicle 1 expense here ..... ➡ $_____

   Vehicle 2   **Describe Vehicle 2:** _____

   _____

   13d. Ownership or leasing costs using IRS Local Standard. .... $_____

   13e. Average monthly payment for all debts secured by Vehicle 2.
        Do not include costs for leased vehicles.

Name of each creditor for Vehicle 2	Average monthly payment
_____	$_____
_____	+ $_____

   Total average monthly payment | $_____ | Copy here ➡   — $_____   Repeat this amount on line 33c.

   13f. Net Vehicle 2 ownership or lease expense
        Subtract line 13e from 13d. If this amount is less than $0, enter $0. .... | $_____ | Copy net Vehicle 2 expense here ... ➡ $_____

14. **Public transportation expense:** If you claimed 0 vehicles in line 11, using the IRS Local Standards, fill in the *Public Transportation* expense allowance regardless of whether you use public transportation. $_____

15. **Additional public transportation expense:** If you claimed 1 or more vehicles in line 11 and if you claim that you may also deduct a public transportation expense, you may fill in what you believe is the appropriate expense, but you may not claim more than the IRS Local Standard for *Public Transportation*. $_____

Debtor 1 _____   Case number *(if known)*_____
First Name   Middle Name   Last Name

Other Necessary Expenses In addition to the expense deductions listed above, you are allowed your monthly expenses for the following IRS categories.

16. **Taxes:** The total monthly amount that you will actually owe for federal, state and local taxes, such as income taxes, self-employment taxes, Social Security taxes, and Medicare taxes. You may include the monthly amount withheld from your pay for these taxes. However, if you expect to receive a tax refund, you must divide the expected refund by 12 and subtract that number from the total monthly amount that is withheld to pay for taxes. $_____

Do not include real estate, sales, or use taxes.

17. **Involuntary deductions:** The total monthly payroll deductions that your job requires, such as retirement contributions, union dues, and uniform costs. $_____

Do not include amounts that are not required by your job, such as voluntary 401(k) contributions or payroll savings.

18. **Life insurance:** The total monthly premiums that you pay for your own term life insurance. If two married people are filing together, include payments that you make for your spouse's term life insurance. Do not include premiums for life insurance on your dependents, for a non-filing spouse's life insurance, or for any form of life insurance other than term. $_____

19. **Court-ordered payments:** The total monthly amount that you pay as required by the order of a court or administrative agency, such as spousal or child support payments. $_____

Do not include payments on past due obligations for spousal or child support. You will list these obligations in line 35.

20. **Education:** The total monthly amount that you pay for education that is either required:
   ■ as a condition for your job, or
   ■ for your physically or mentally challenged dependent child if no public education is available for similar services. $_____

21. **Childcare:** The total monthly amount that you pay for childcare, such as babysitting, daycare, nursery, and preschool. $_____

Do not include payments for any elementary or secondary school education.

22. **Additional health care expenses, excluding insurance costs:** The monthly amount that you pay for health care that is required for the health and welfare of you or your dependents and that is not reimbursed by insurance or paid by a health savings account. Include only the amount that is more than the total entered in line 7.
Payments for health insurance or health savings accounts should be listed only in line 25. $_____

23. **Optional telephones and telephone services:** The total monthly amount that you pay for telecommunication services for you and your dependents, such as pagers, call waiting, caller identification, special long distance, or business cell phone service, to the extent necessary for your health and welfare or that of your dependents or for the production of income, if it is not reimbursed by your employer.   + $_____

Do not include payments for basic home telephone, internet and cell phone service. Do not include self-employment expenses, such as those reported on line 5 of Official Form 122A-1, or any amount you previously deducted.

24. **Add all of the expenses allowed under the IRS expense allowances.**
Add lines 6 through 23. $_____

SELECTED OFFICIAL FORMS

Debtor 1 _____   Case number *(if known)*_____

First Name   Middle Name   Last Name

25. **Health insurance, disability insurance, and health savings account expenses.** The monthly expenses for health insurance, disability insurance, and health savings accounts that are reasonably necessary for yourself, your spouse, or your dependents.

Health insurance	$_____
Disability insurance	$_____
Health savings account	+ $_____
Total	$_____

Copy total here ➔ .... $_____

Do you actually spend this total amount?

☐ No. How much do you actually spend? $_____
☐ Yes

26. **Continuing contributions to the care of household or family members.** The actual monthly expenses that you will continue to pay for the reasonable and necessary care and support of an elderly, chronically ill, or disabled member of your household or member of your immediate family who is unable to pay for such expenses. These expenses may include contributions to an account of a qualified ABLE program. 26 U.S.C. § 529A(b). $_____

27. **Protection against family violence.** The reasonably necessary monthly expenses that you incur to maintain the safety of you and your family under the Family Violence Prevention and Services Act or other federal laws that apply. $_____

By law, the court must keep the nature of these expenses confidential.

28. **Additional home energy costs.** Your home energy costs are included in your insurance and operating expenses on line 8.

If you believe that you have home energy costs that are more than the home energy costs included in expenses on line 8, then fill in the excess amount of home energy costs.

You must give your case trustee documentation of your actual expenses, and you must show that the additional amount claimed is reasonable and necessary. $_____

29. **Education expenses for dependent children who are younger than 18.** The monthly expenses (not more than $189.58* per child) that you pay for your dependent children who are younger than 18 years old to attend a private or public elementary or secondary school.

You must give your case trustee documentation of your actual expenses, and you must explain why the amount claimed is reasonable and necessary and not already accounted for in lines 6-23. $_____

 * Subject to adjustment on 4/01/25, and every 3 years after that for cases begun on or after the date of adjustment.

30. **Additional food and clothing expense.** The monthly amount by which your actual food and clothing expenses are higher than the combined food and clothing allowances in the IRS National Standards. That amount cannot be more than 5% of the food and clothing allowances in the IRS National Standards.

To find a chart showing the maximum additional allowance, go online using the link specified in the separate instructions for this form. This chart may also be available at the bankruptcy clerk's office.

You must show that the additional amount claimed is reasonable and necessary. $_____

31. **Continuing charitable contributions.** The amount that you will continue to contribute in the form of cash or financial instruments to a religious or charitable organization. 26 U.S.C. § 170(c)(1)-(2).   + $_____

32. **Add all of the additional expense deductions.** $_____

Add lines 25 through 31.

Debtor 1 _____   Case number (if known)_____
          First Name   Middle Name   Last Name

Deductions for Debt Payment

33. **For debts that are secured by an interest in property that you own, including home mortgages, vehicle loans, and other secured debt, fill in lines 33a through 33e.**

To calculate the total average monthly payment, add all amounts that are contractually due to each secured creditor in the 60 months after you file for bankruptcy. Then divide by 60.

		Average monthly payment
Mortgages on your home:		
33a. Copy line 9b here .... ➔		$_____
Loans on your first two vehicles:		
33b. Copy line 13b here. .... ➔		$_____
33c. Copy line 13e here. .... ➔		$_____

33d. List other secured debts:

Name of each creditor for other secured debt	Identify property that secures the debt	Does payment include taxes or insurance?	
_____	_____	❑ No ❑ Yes	$_____
_____	_____	❑ No ❑ Yes	$_____
_____	_____	❑ No ❑ Yes	+ $_____

33e. Total average monthly payment. Add lines 33a through 33d. .... | $_____ | **Copy total here ➔** | $_____

34. **Are any debts that you listed in line 33 secured by your primary residence, a vehicle, or other property necessary for your support or the support of your dependents?**

❑ No. Go to line 35.
❑ Yes. State any amount that you must pay to a creditor, in addition to the payments listed in line 33, to keep possession of your property (called the *cure amount*). Next, divide by 60 and fill in the information below.

Name of the creditor	Identify property that secures the debt	Total cure amount		Monthly cure amount
_____	_____	$_____	÷ 60 =	$_____
_____	_____	$_____	÷ 60 =	$_____
_____	_____	$_____	÷ 60 =	+ $_____
		Total	$_____	**Copy total here ➔** $_____

35. **Do you owe any priority claims such as a priority tax, child support, or alimony — that are past due as of the filing date of your bankruptcy case?** 11 U.S.C. § 507.

❑ No. Go to line 36.
❑ Yes. Fill in the total amount of all of these priority claims. Do not include current or ongoing priority claims, such as those you listed in line 19.

Total amount of all past-due priority claims .... $_____ ÷ 60 = $_____

Debtor 1 _____   Case number (if known)_____
First Name   Middle Name   Last Name

36. **Are you eligible to file a case under Chapter 13?** 11 U.S.C. § 109(e).
    For more information, go online using the link for *Bankruptcy Basics* specified in the separate
    instructions for this form. *Bankruptcy Basics* may also be available at the bankruptcy clerk's office.

    ☐ No. Go to line 37.

    ☐ Yes. Fill in the following information.

    Projected monthly plan payment if you were filing under Chapter 13 $_____

    Current multiplier for your district as stated on the list issued by the
    Administrative Office of the United States Courts (for districts in Alabama and
    North Carolina) or by the Executive Office for United States Trustees (for all
    other districts).   X _____

    To find a list of district multipliers that includes your district, go online using the
    link specified in the separate instructions for this form. This list may also be
    available at the bankruptcy clerk's office.

    Average monthly administrative expense if you were filing under Chapter 13 $_____ | Copy total here ➡ $_____

37. **Add all of the deductions for debt payment.**
    Add lines 33e through 36. .... $_____

Total Deductions from Income

38. **Add all of the allowed deductions.**

    Copy line 24, *All of the expenses allowed under IRS*
    expense allowances .... $_____

    Copy line 32, *All of the additional expense deductions* .... $_____

    Copy line 37, *All of the deductions for debt payment* .... + $_____

    Total deductions $_____   Copy total here .... ➡ $_____

Part 3:   Determine Whether There Is a Presumption of Abuse

39. **Calculate monthly disposable income for 60 months**

    39a. Copy line 4, *adjusted current monthly income* ..... $_____

    39b. Copy line 38, *Total deductions*.........   − $_____

    39c. Monthly disposable income. 11 U.S.C. § 707(b)(2). $_____   Copy here ➡ $_____
         Subtract line 39b from line 39a.

         For the next 60 months (5 years)...   x 60

    39d. **Total.** Multiply line 39c by 60. .... $_____   Copy here ➡ $_____

40. **Find out whether there is a presumption of abuse.** Check the box that applies:

    ☐ **The line 39d is less than $9,075*.** On the top of page 1 of this form, check box 1, *There is no presumption of abuse.* Go to
      Part 5.

    ☐ **The line 39d is more than $15,150*.** On the top of page 1 of this form, check box 2, *There is a presumption of abuse.* You
      may fill out Part 4 if you claim special circumstances. Then go to Part 5.

    ☐ **The line 39d is at least $9,075*, but not more than $15,150*.** Go to line 41.

      * Subject to adjustment on 4/01/25, and every 3 years after that for cases filed on or after the date of adjustment.

Official Form 122A–2   Chapter 7 Means Test Calculation   page 8

SELECTED OFFICIAL FORMS

Debtor 1 _____   Case number (if known)_____

First Name   Middle Name   Last Name

---

41. 41a. **Fill in the amount of your total nonpriority unsecured debt.** If you filled out *A Summary of Your Assets and Liabilities and Certain Statistical Information Schedules* (Official Form 106Sum), you may refer to line 3b on that form.. $_____

    x .25

    41b. **25% of your total nonpriority unsecured debt.** 11 U.S.C. § 707(b)(2)(A)(i)(I).
    Multiply line 41a by 0.25. .... $_____   Copy here→ $_____

42. **Determine whether the income you have left over after subtracting all allowed deductions is enough to pay 25% of your unsecured, nonpriority debt.**
    Check the box that applies:

    ☐ **Line 39d is less than line 41b.** On the top of page 1 of this form, check box 1, *There is no presumption of abuse.* Go to Part 5.

    ☐ **Line 39d is equal to or more than line 41b.** On the top of page 1 of this form, check box 2, *There is a presumption of abuse.* You may fill out Part 4 if you claim special circumstances. Then go to Part 5.

Part 4: Give Details About Special Circumstances

43. **Do you have any special circumstances that justify additional expenses or adjustments of current monthly income for which there is no reasonable alternative?** 11 U.S.C. § 707(b)(2)(B).

    ☐ No. Go to Part 5.

    ☐ Yes. Fill in the following information. All figures should reflect your average monthly expense or income adjustment for each item. You may include expenses you listed in line 25.

    You must give a detailed explanation of the special circumstances that make the expenses or income adjustments necessary and reasonable. You must also give your case trustee documentation of your actual expenses or income adjustments.

Give a detailed explanation of the special circumstances	Average monthly expense or income adjustment
_____	$_____
_____	$_____
_____	$_____
_____	$_____

Part 5: Sign Below

By signing here, I declare under penalty of perjury that the information on this statement and in any attachments is true and correct.

✗ _____   ✗ _____
Signature of Debtor 1   Signature of Debtor 2

Date _____   Date _____
MM / DD / YYYY   MM / DD / YYYY

Official Form 122A–2   Chapter 7 Means Test Calculation   page 9

| Print | Save As... | Add Attachment | | Reset |

SELECTED OFFICIAL FORMS

2022-04 STAFF NOTATION

The CARES Act changes Official Forms 122A-1, 122B, and 122C-1 described in the 2020-04 Committee Note lapsed on March 27, 2022. The three forms have reverted to their pre-CARES Act versions (December 2019 in the case of 122A-1, October 2019 as amended in December 2021 in the case of 122B, and October 2019 in the case of 122C-1).

In addition, the dollar amounts listed in lines 29 and 40 of 122A-2, and line 29 of 122C-2 are adjusted effective April 1, 2022, as part of the tri-annual dollar adjustments required by 11 U.S.C. § 104.

Fill in this information to identify your case:

Debtor 1 _____
First Name   Middle Name   Last Name

Debtor 2 _____
(Spouse, if filing) First Name   Middle Name   Last Name

United States Bankruptcy Court for the: _____ District of _____

Case number _____
(if known)

☐ Check if this is an amended filing

Official Form 122B

Chapter 11 Statement of Your Current Monthly Income

12/21

You must file this form if you are an individual and are filing for bankruptcy under Chapter 11 (other than Subchapter V). If more space is needed, attach a separate sheet to this form. Include the line number to which the additional information applies. On the top of any additional pages, write your name and case number (if known).

Part 1: Calculate Your Current Monthly Income

1. **What is your marital and filing status?** Check one only.

   ☐ **Not married.** Fill out Column A, lines 2-11.

   ☐ **Married and your spouse is filing with you.** Fill out both Columns A and B, lines 2-11.

   ☐ **Married and your spouse is NOT filing with you.** Fill out Column A, lines 2-11.

   Fill in the average monthly income that you received from all sources, derived during the 6 full months before you file this bankruptcy case. 11 U.S.C. § 101(10A). For example, if you are filing on September 15, the 6-month period would be March 1 through August 31. If the amount of your monthly income varied during the 6 months, add the income for all 6 months and divide the total by 6. Fill in the result. Do not include any income amount more than once. For example, if both spouses own the same rental property, put the income from that property in one column only. If you have nothing to report for any line, write $0 in the space.

	Column A Debtor 1	Column B Debtor 2
2. **Your gross wages, salary, tips, bonuses, overtime, and commissions** (before all payroll deductions).	$_____	$_____
3. **Alimony and maintenance payments.** Do not include payments from a spouse if Column B is filled in.	$_____	$_____
4. **All amounts from any source which are regularly paid for household expenses of you or your dependents, including child support.** Include regular contributions from an unmarried partner, members of your household, your dependents, parents, and roommates. Include regular contributions from a spouse only if Column B is not filled in. Do not include payments you listed on line 3.	$_____	$_____

5. **Net income from operating a business, profession, or farm**

	Debtor 1	Debtor 2			
Gross receipts (before all deductions)	$_____	$_____			
Ordinary and necessary operating expenses	– $_____	– $_____			
Net monthly income from a business, profession, or farm	$_____	$_____	Copy here →	$_____	$_____

6. **Net income from rental and other real property**

	Debtor 1	Debtor 2			
Gross receipts (before all deductions)	$_____	$_____			
Ordinary and necessary operating expenses	– $_____	– $_____			
Net monthly income from rental or other real property	$_____	$_____	Copy here →	$_____	$_____

Official Form 122B   Chapter 11 Statement of Your Current Monthly Income   page 1

Debtor 1 _____
     First Name   Middle Name   Last Name

Case number (if known)_____

	Column A Debtor 1	Column B Debtor 2
7. Interest, dividends, and royalties	$_____	$_____
8. Unemployment compensation	$_____	$_____

Do not enter the amount if you contend that the amount received was a benefit under the Social Security Act. Instead, list it here:............................↓

     For you .... $_____

     For your spouse... $_____

9. **Pension or retirement income.** Do not include any amount received that was a benefit under the Social Security Act. Also, except as stated in the next sentence, do not include any compensation, pension, pay, annuity, or allowance paid by the United States Government in connection with a disability, combat-related injury or disability, or death of a member of the uniformed services. If you received any retired pay paid under chapter 61 of title 10, then include that pay only to the extent that it does not exceed the amount of retired pay to which you would otherwise be entitled if retired under any provision of title 10 other than chapter 61 of that title.

     $_____ $_____

10. **Income from all other sources not listed above.** Specify the source and amount. Do not include any benefits received under the Social Security Act; payments made under the Federal law relating to the national emergency declared by the President under the National Emergencies Act (50 U.S.C. 1601 et seq.) with respect to the coronavirus disease 2019 (COVID-19); payments received as a victim of a war crime, a crime against humanity, or international or domestic terrorism; or compensation, pension, pay, annuity, or allowance paid by the United States Government in connection with a disability, combat-related injury or disability, or death of a member of the uniformed services. If necessary, list other sources on a separate page and put the total below.

     _____ $_____ $_____

     _____ $_____ $_____

     Total amounts from separate pages, if any.   + $_____   + $_____

11. **Calculate your total current monthly income.** Add lines 2 through 10 for each column. Then add the total for Column A to the total for Column B.

     [$_____] + [$_____] = [$_____]

     Total current monthly income

Part 2:   **Sign Below**

By signing here, under penalty of perjury I declare that the information on this statement and in any attachments is true and correct.

✗ _____   ✗ _____
     Signature of Debtor 1   Signature of Debtor 2

Date _____   Date _____
     MM / DD / YYYY   MM / DD / YYYY

Official Form 122B   Chapter 11 Statement of Your Current Monthly Income   page 2

Fill in this information to identify your case:

Debtor 1 _____
First Name   Middle Name   Last Name

Debtor 2 _____
(Spouse, if filing) First Name   Middle Name   Last Name

United States Bankruptcy Court for the: _____ District of _____

Case number _____
(If known)

Check as directed in lines 17 and 21:

According to the calculations required by this Statement:

☐ 1. Disposable income is not determined under 11 U.S.C. § 1325(b)(3).

☐ 2. Disposable income is determined under 11 U.S.C. § 1325(b)(3).

☐ 3. The commitment period is 3 years.

☐ 4. The commitment period is 5 years.

☐ Check if this is an amended filing

Official Form 122C–1

Chapter 13 Statement of Your Current Monthly Income and Calculation of Commitment Period

10/19

Be as complete and accurate as possible. If two married people are filing together, both are equally responsible for being accurate. If more space is needed, attach a separate sheet to this form. Include the line number to which the additional information applies. On the top of any additional pages, write your name and case number (if known).

Part 1:	Calculate Your Average Monthly Income

1. **What is your marital and filing status?** Check one only.

   ☐ **Not married.** Fill out Column A, lines 2-11.

   ☐ **Married.** Fill out both Columns A and B, lines 2-11.

Fill in the average monthly income that you received from all sources, derived during the 6 full months before you file this bankruptcy case. 11 U.S.C. § 101(10A). For example, if you are filing on September 15, the 6-month period would be March 1 through August 31. If the amount of your monthly income varied during the 6 months, add the income for all 6 months and divide the total by 6. Fill in the result. Do not include any income amount more than once. For example, if both spouses own the same rental property, put the income from that property in one column only. If you have nothing to report for any line, write $0 in the space.

| | Column A
Debtor 1 | Column B
Debtor 2 or
non-filing spouse |
| --- | --- | --- |
| 2. **Your gross wages, salary, tips, bonuses, overtime, and commissions** (before all payroll deductions). | $_____ | $_____ |
| 3. **Alimony and maintenance payments.** Do not include payments from a spouse. | $_____ | $_____ |
| 4. **All amounts from any source which are regularly paid for household expenses of you or your dependents, including child support.** Include regular contributions from an unmarried partner, members of your household, your dependents, parents, and roommates. Do not include payments from a spouse. Do not include payments you listed on line 3. | $_____ | $_____ |

5. **Net income from operating a business, profession, or farm**

	Debtor 1	Debtor 2			
Gross receipts (before all deductions)	$_____	$_____			
Ordinary and necessary operating expenses	– $_____	– $_____			
Net monthly income from a business, profession, or farm	$_____	$_____	Copy here ➔	$_____	$_____

6. **Net income from rental and other real property**

	Debtor 1	Debtor 2			
Gross receipts (before all deductions)	$_____	$_____			
Ordinary and necessary operating expenses	– $_____	– $_____			
Net monthly income from rental or other real property	$_____	$_____	Copy here ➔	$_____	$_____

Debtor 1 _____ Case number (if known) _____
First Name   Middle Name   Last Name

	Column A Debtor 1	Column B Debtor 2 or non-filing spouse
7. **Interest, dividends, and royalties**	$_____	$_____
8. **Unemployment compensation**	$_____	$_____

Do not enter the amount if you contend that the amount received was a benefit under the Social Security Act. Instead, list it here: .... ↓

For you .... $_____

For your spouse .... $_____

9. **Pension or retirement income.** Do not include any amount received that was a benefit under the Social Security Act. Also, except as stated in the next sentence, do not include any compensation, pension, pay, annuity, or allowance paid by the United States Government in connection with a disability, combat-related injury or disability, or death of a member of the uniformed services. If you received any retired pay paid under chapter 61 of title 10, then include that pay only to the extent that it does not exceed the amount of retired pay to which you would otherwise be entitled if retired under any provision of title 10 other than chapter 61 of that title.

9.	$_____	$_____

10. **Income from all other sources not listed above.** Specify the source and amount. Do not include any benefits received under the Social Security Act; payments received as a victim of a war crime, a crime against humanity, or international or domestic terrorism; or compensation, pension, pay, annuity, or allowance paid by the United States Government in connection with a disability, combat-related injury or disability, or death of a member of the uniformed services. If necessary, list other sources on a separate page and put the total below.

_____	$_____	$_____
_____	$_____	$_____
Total amounts from separate pages, if any.	+ $_____	+ $_____

11. **Calculate your total average monthly income.** Add lines 2 through 10 for each column. Then add the total for Column A to the total for Column B.

$_____ + $_____ = $_____
Total average monthly income

Part 2:   Determine How to Measure Your Deductions from Income

12. Copy your total average monthly income from line 11. .... $_____

13. **Calculate the marital adjustment.** Check one:

☐ You are not married. Fill in 0 below.

☐ You are married and your spouse is filing with you. Fill in 0 below.

☐ You are married and your spouse is not filing with you.

Fill in the amount of the income listed in line 11, Column B, that was NOT regularly paid for the household expenses of you or your dependents, such as payment of the spouse's tax liability or the spouse's support of someone other than you or your dependents.

Below, specify the basis for excluding this income and the amount of income devoted to each purpose. If necessary, list additional adjustments on a separate page.

If this adjustment does not apply, enter 0 below.

_____	$_____
_____	$_____
_____	+ $_____
Total	$_____ Copy here ➔ − _____

14. **Your current monthly income.** Subtract the total in line 13 from line 12. $_____

Debtor 1 _____   Case number *(if known)* _____
             First Name   Middle Name   Last Name

---

15. **Calculate your current monthly income for the year.** Follow these steps:

   15a. Copy line 14 here ➜ .... $ _____

   Multiply line 15a by 12 (the number of months in a year).   x 12

   15b. The result is your current monthly income for the year for this part of the form. .... $ _____

---

16. **Calculate the median family income that applies to you.** Follow these steps:

   16a. Fill in the state in which you live.   _____

   16b. Fill in the number of people in your household.   _____

   16c. Fill in the median family income for your state and size of household. .... $ _____
        To find a list of applicable median income amounts, go online using the link specified in the separate
        instructions for this form. This list may also be available at the bankruptcy clerk's office.

17. **How do the lines compare?**

   17a. ☐ Line 15b is less than or equal to line 16c. On the top of page 1 of this form, check box 1, *Disposable income is not determined under*
            11 U.S.C. § 1325(b)(3). **Go to Part 3.** Do NOT fill out *Calculation of Your Disposable Income* (Official Form 122C–2).

   17b. ☐ Line 15b is more than line 16c. On the top of page 1 of this form, check box 2, *Disposable income is determined under*
            11 U.S.C. § 1325(b)(3). **Go to Part 3 and fill out Calculation of Your Disposable Income (Official Form 122C–2).**
            On line 39 of that form, copy your current monthly income from line 14 above.

Part 3:	Calculate Your Commitment Period Under 11 U.S.C. § 1325(b)(4)

---

18. Copy your total average monthly income from line 11. .... $ _____

19. **Deduct the marital adjustment if it applies.** If you are married, your spouse is not filing with you, and you contend that
    calculating the commitment period under 11 U.S.C. § 1325(b)(4) allows you to deduct part of your spouse's income, copy
    the amount from line 13.
    19a. If the marital adjustment does not apply, fill in 0 on line 19a. .... − $ _____

   19b. **Subtract line 19a from line 18.** $ _____

20. **Calculate your current monthly income for the year.** Follow these steps:

   20a. Copy line 19b. .... $ _____

   Multiply by 12 (the number of months in a year).   x 12

   20b. The result is your current monthly income for the year for this part of the form. $ _____

   20c. Copy the median family income for your state and size of household from line 16c. .... $ _____

21. **How do the lines compare?**

   ☐ Line 20b is less than line 20c. Unless otherwise ordered by the court, on the top of page 1 of this form, check box 3,
     The commitment period is 3 years. Go to Part 4.

   ☐ Line 20b is more than or equal to line 20c. Unless otherwise ordered by the court, on the top of page 1 of this form,
     check box 4, *The commitment period is 5 years*. Go to Part 4.

Debtor 1 _____ Case number (if known)_____
         First Name   Middle Name   Last Name

Part 4:   Sign Below

By signing here, under penalty of perjury I declare that the information on this statement and in any attachments is true and correct.

✗ _____   ✗ _____
   Signature of Debtor 1   Signature of Debtor 2

Date _____   Date _____
    MM / DD / YYYY   MM / DD / YYYY

If you checked 17a, do NOT fill out or file Form 122C–2.
If you checked 17b, fill out Form 122C–2 and file it with this form. On line 39 of that form, copy your current monthly income from line 14 above.

| Print | Save As... | Add Attachment | | Reset |

SELECTED OFFICIAL FORMS

Fill in this information to identify your case:

Debtor 1 _____
First Name   Middle Name   Last Name

Debtor 2 _____
(Spouse, if filing) First Name   Middle Name   Last Name

United States Bankruptcy Court for the: _____ District of _____

Case number _____
(if known)

☐ Check if this is an amended filing

Official Form 122C-2

Chapter 13 Calculation of Your Disposable Income   04/22

To fill out this form, you will need your completed copy of *Chapter 13 Statement of Your Current Monthly Income and Calculation of Commitment Period* (Official Form 122C–1).

Be as complete and accurate as possible. If two married people are filing together, both are equally responsible for being accurate. If more space is needed, attach a separate sheet to this form. Include the line number to which the additional information applies. On the top of any additional pages, write your name and case number (if known).

Part 1:   Calculate Your Deductions from Your Income

The Internal Revenue Service (IRS) issues National and Local Standards for certain expense amounts. Use these amounts to answer the questions in lines 6-15. To find the IRS standards, go online using the link specified in the separate instructions for this form. This information may also be available at the bankruptcy clerk's office.

Deduct the expense amounts set out in lines 6-15 regardless of your actual expense. In later parts of the form, you will use some of your actual expenses if they are higher than the standards. Do not include any operating expenses that you subtracted from income in lines 5 and 6 of Form 122C–1, and do not deduct any amounts that you subtracted from your spouse's income in line 13 of Form 122C–1.

If your expenses differ from month to month, enter the average expense.

Note: Line numbers 1-4 are not used in this form. These numbers apply to information required by a similar form used in chapter 7 cases.

5. **The number of people used in determining your deductions from income**
    Fill in the number of people who could be claimed as exemptions on your federal income tax return, plus the number of any additional dependents whom you support. This number may be different from the number of people in your household.   [   ]

National Standards   You must use the IRS National Standards to answer the questions in lines 6-7.

6. **Food, clothing, and other items:** Using the number of people you entered in line 5 and the IRS National Standards, fill in the dollar amount for food, clothing, and other items. $_____

7. **Out-of-pocket health care allowance:** Using the number of people you entered in line 5 and the IRS National Standards, fill in the dollar amount for out-of-pocket health care. The number of people is split into two categories—people who are under 65 and people who are 65 or older—because older people have a higher IRS allowance for health care costs. If your actual expenses are higher than this IRS amount, you may deduct the additional amount on line 22.

Official Form 122C-2   Chapter 13 Calculation of Your Disposable Income   page 1

610

Debtor 1 _____ Case number *(if known)* _____
　　　　　First Name　　Middle Name　　　Last Name

> **People who are under 65 years of age**
>
> 7a. Out-of-pocket health care allowance per person $_____
>
> 7b. Number of people who are under 65　　　　X _____
>
> 7c. Subtotal. Multiply line 7a by line 7b.　　$_____　Copy here ➡　$_____
>
> **People who are 65 years of age or older**
>
> 7d. Out-of-pocket health care allowance per person $_____
>
> 7e. Number of people who are 65 or older　　X _____
>
> 7f. Subtotal. Multiply line 7d by line 7e.　　$_____　Copy here ➡　+ $_____

7g. **Total.** Add lines 7c and 7f. .... $_____　Copy here ➡ ....　$_____

Local Standards　You must use the IRS Local Standards to answer the questions in lines 8-15.

Based on information from the IRS, the U.S. Trustee Program has divided the IRS Local Standard for housing for bankruptcy purposes into two parts:

- Housing and utilities – Insurance and operating expenses
- Housing and utilities – Mortgage or rent expenses

To answer the questions in lines 8-9, use the U.S. Trustee Program chart. To find the chart, go online using the link specified in the separate instructions for this form. This chart may also be available at the bankruptcy clerk's office.

8. **Housing and utilities – Insurance and operating expenses:** Using the number of people you entered in line 5, fill in the dollar amount listed for your county for insurance and operating expenses.　　$_____

9. **Housing and utilities – Mortgage or rent expenses:**

　9a. Using the number of people you entered in line 5, fill in the dollar amount listed for your county for mortgage or rent expenses.　　$_____

　9b. Total average monthly payment for all mortgages and other debts secured by your home.

　　To calculate the total average monthly payment, add all amounts that are contractually due to each secured creditor in the 60 months after you file for bankruptcy. Next divide by 60.

Name of the creditor	Average monthly payment
_____	$_____
_____	$_____
_____	+ $_____

　　9b. Total average monthly payment　$_____　Copy here ➡ — $_____　Repeat this amount on line 33a.

　9c. Net mortgage or rent expense.

　　Subtract line 9b (*total average monthly payment*) from line 9a (*mortgage or rent expense*). If this number is less than $0, enter $0.　$_____　Copy here ➡ ....　$_____

10. If you claim that the U.S. Trustee Program's division of the IRS Local Standard for housing is incorrect and affects the calculation of your monthly expenses, fill in any additional amount you claim.　$_____

　　Explain why: _____

　　_____

SELECTED OFFICIAL FORMS

Debtor 1 _____   Case number _(if known)_____
First Name   Middle Name   Last Name

11. **Local transportation expenses:** Check the number of vehicles for which you claim an ownership or operating expense.

☐ 0. Go to line 14.
☐ 1. Go to line 12.
☐ 2 or more. Go to line 12.

12. **Vehicle operation expense:** Using the IRS Local Standards and the number of vehicles for which you claim the operating expenses, fill in the *Operating Costs* that apply for your Census region or metropolitan statistical area. .... $_____

13. **Vehicle ownership or lease expense:** Using the IRS Local Standards, calculate the net ownership or lease expense for each vehicle below. You may not claim the expense if you do not make any loan or lease payments on the vehicle. In addition, you may not claim the expense for more than two vehicles.

Vehicle 1   Describe Vehicle 1: _____
_____

13a. Ownership or leasing costs using IRS Local Standard...................................... $_____

13b. Average monthly payment for all debts secured by Vehicle 1.
Do not include costs for leased vehicles.

To calculate the average monthly payment here and on line 13e, add all amounts that are contractually due to each secured creditor in the 60 months after you file for bankruptcy. Then divide by 60.

Name of each creditor for Vehicle 1	Average monthly payment
_____	$_____
_____	+ $_____

Total average monthly payment $_____   Copy here ➔   — $_____   Repeat this amount on line 33b.

13c. Net Vehicle 1 ownership or lease expense
Subtract line 13b from line 13a. If this number is less than $0, enter $0. .... $_____   Copy net Vehicle 1 expense here ➔ $_____

Vehicle 2   Describe Vehicle 2: _____
_____

13d. Ownership or leasing costs using IRS Local Standard .... $_____

13e. Average monthly payment for all debts secured by Vehicle 2.
Do not include costs for leased vehicles.

Name of each creditor for Vehicle 2	Average monthly payment
_____	$_____
_____	+ $_____

Total average monthly payment $_____   Copy here ➔   — $_____   Repeat this amount on line 33c.

13f. Net Vehicle 2 ownership or lease expense
Subtract line 13e from 13d. If this number is less than $0, enter $0................ $_____   Copy net Vehicle 2 expense here ➔ $_____

14. **Public transportation expense:** If you claimed 0 vehicles in line 11, using the IRS Local Standards, fill in the *Public Transportation* expense allowance regardless of whether you use public transportation. $_____

15. **Additional public transportation expense:** If you claimed 1 or more vehicles in line 11 and if you claim that you may also deduct a public transportation expense, you may fill in what you believe is the appropriate expense, but you may not claim more than the IRS Local Standard for *Public Transportation*. $_____

Debtor 1 _____ Case number *(if known)*_____
First Name   Middle Name   Last Name

Other Necessary Expenses	In addition to the expense deductions listed above, you are allowed your monthly expenses for the following IRS categories.

16. **Taxes:** The total monthly amount that you actually pay for federal, state and local taxes, such as income taxes, self-employment taxes, social security taxes, and Medicare taxes. You may include the monthly amount withheld from your pay for these taxes. However, if you expect to receive a tax refund, you must divide the expected refund by 12 and subtract that number from the total monthly amount that is withheld to pay for taxes. Do not include real estate, sales, or use taxes.　　$_____

17. **Involuntary deductions:** The total monthly payroll deductions that your job requires, such as retirement contributions, union dues, and uniform costs.

    Do not include amounts that are not required by your job, such as voluntary 401(k) contributions or payroll savings.　　$_____

18. **Life insurance:** The total monthly premiums that you pay for your own term life insurance. If two married people are filing together, include payments that you make for your spouse's term life insurance.

    Do not include premiums for life insurance on your dependents, for a non-filing spouse's life insurance, or for any form of life insurance other than term.　　$_____

19. **Court-ordered payments:** The total monthly amount that you pay as required by the order of a court or administrative agency, such as spousal or child support payments.

    Do not include payments on past due obligations for spousal or child support. You will list these obligations in line 35.　　$_____

20. **Education:** The total monthly amount that you pay for education that is either required:
    - as a condition for your job, or
    - for your physically or mentally challenged dependent child if no public education is available for similar services.　　$_____

21. **Childcare:** The total monthly amount that you pay for childcare, such as babysitting, daycare, nursery, and preschool. Do not include payments for any elementary or secondary school education.　　$_____

22. **Additional health care expenses, excluding insurance costs:** The monthly amount that you pay for health care that is required for the health and welfare of you or your dependents and that is not reimbursed by insurance or paid by a health savings account. Include only the amount that is more than the total entered in line 7.

    Payments for health insurance or health savings accounts should be listed only in line 25.　　$_____

23. **Optional telephones and telephone services:** The total monthly amount that you pay for telecommunication services for you and your dependents, such as pagers, call waiting, caller identification, special long distance, or business cell phone service, to the extent necessary for your health and welfare or that of your dependents or for the production of income, if it is not reimbursed by your employer.　　+ $_____

    Do not include payments for basic home telephone, internet or cell phone service. Do not include self-employment expenses, such as those reported on line 5 of Form 122C-1, or any amount you previously deducted.

24. **Add all of the expenses allowed under the IRS expense allowances.** Add lines 6 through 23.　　$_____

Additional Expense Deductions	These are additional deductions allowed by the Means Test. *Note:* Do not include any expense allowances listed in lines 6-24.

25. **Health insurance, disability insurance, and health savings account expenses.** The monthly expenses for health insurance, disability insurance, and health savings accounts that are reasonably necessary for yourself, your spouse, or your dependents.

Health insurance	$_____		
Disability insurance	$_____		
Health savings account	+ $_____		
Total	$_____	Copy total here ➡	$_____

    Do you actually spend this total amount?

    ☐ No. How much do you actually spend?　　$_____

    ☐ Yes

26. **Continuing contributions to the care of household or family members.** The actual monthly expenses that you will continue to pay for the reasonable and necessary care and support of an elderly, chronically ill, or disabled member of your household or member of your immediate family who is unable to pay for such expenses. These expenses may include contributions to an account of a qualified ABLE program. 26 U.S.C. § 529A(b).　　$_____

27. **Protection against family violence.** The reasonably necessary monthly expenses that you incur to maintain the safety of you and your family under the Family Violence Prevention and Services Act or other federal laws that apply.

    By law, the court must keep the nature of these expenses confidential.　　$_____

Debtor 1 _____   Case number *(if known)*_____
         First Name   Middle Name   Last Name

28. **Additional home energy costs.** Your home energy costs are included in your insurance and operating expenses on line 8. If you believe that you have home energy costs that are more than the home energy costs included in expenses on line 8, then fill in the excess amount of home energy costs. $_____
You must give your case trustee documentation of your actual expenses, and you must show that the additional amount claimed is reasonable and necessary.

29. **Education expenses for dependent children who are younger than 18.** The monthly expenses (not more than $189.58* per child) that you pay for your dependent children who are younger than 18 years old to attend a private or public elementary or secondary school. $_____
You must give your case trustee documentation of your actual expenses, and you must explain why the amount claimed is reasonable and necessary and not already accounted for in lines 6-23.

   * Subject to adjustment on 4/01/25, and every 3 years after that for cases begun on or after the date of adjustment.

30. **Additional food and clothing expense.** The monthly amount by which your actual food and clothing expenses are higher than the combined food and clothing allowances in the IRS National Standards. That amount cannot be more than 5% of the food and clothing allowances in the IRS National Standards. $_____
To find a chart showing the maximum additional allowance, go online using the link specified in the separate instructions for this form. This chart may also be available at the bankruptcy clerk's office.
You must show that the additional amount claimed is reasonable and necessary.

31. **Continuing charitable contributions.** The amount that you will continue to contribute in the form of cash or financial instruments to a religious or charitable organization. 11 U.S.C. § 548(d)(3) and (4).   + $_____
Do not include any amount more than 15% of your gross monthly income.

32. **Add all of the additional expense deductions.** $_____
Add lines 25 through 31.

Deductions for Debt Payment

33. **For debts that are secured by an interest in property that you own, including home mortgages, vehicle loans, and other secured debt, fill in lines 33a through 33e.**

To calculate the total average monthly payment, add all amounts that are contractually due to each secured creditor in the 60 months after you file for bankruptcy. Then divide by 60.

	Average monthly payment
Mortgages on your home	
33a. Copy line 9b here .... ➔	$_____
Loans on your first two vehicles	
33b. Copy line 13b here. .... ➔	$_____
33c. Copy line 13e here. .... ➔	$_____

33d. List other secured debts:

Name of each creditor for other secured debt	Identify property that secures the debt	Does payment include taxes or insurance?	
_____	_____	☐ No ☐ Yes	$_____
_____	_____	☐ No ☐ Yes	$_____
_____	_____	☐ No ☐ Yes	+ $_____

33e. Total average monthly payment. Add lines 33a through 33d. .... $_____ Copy total here ➔ $_____

Debtor 1 _____ Case number (if known)_____
First Name   Middle Name   Last Name

34. **Are any debts that you listed in line 33 secured by your primary residence, a vehicle, or other property necessary for your support or the support of your dependents?**

☐ No. Go to line 35.
☐ Yes. State any amount that you must pay to a creditor, in addition to the payments listed in line 33, to keep possession of your property (called the *cure amount*). Next, divide by 60 and fill in the information below.

Name of the creditor	Identify property that secures the debt	Total cure amount		Monthly cure amount
_____	_____	$_____	÷ 60 =	$_____
_____	_____	$_____	÷ 60 =	$_____
_____	_____	$_____	÷ 60 = +	$_____
		Total $_____		Copy total here ➡ $_____

35. **Do you owe any priority claims—such as a priority tax, child support, or alimony—that are past due as of the filing date of your bankruptcy case? 11 U.S.C. § 507.**

☐ No. Go to line 36.
☐ Yes. Fill in the total amount of all of these priority claims. Do not include current or ongoing priority claims, such as those you listed in line 19.

Total amount of all past-due priority claims. .... $_____ ÷ 60 $_____

36. **Projected monthly Chapter 13 plan payment** $_____

Current multiplier for your district as stated on the list issued by the Administrative Office of the United States Courts (for districts in Alabama and North Carolina) or by the Executive Office for United States Trustees (for all other districts).

To find a list of district multipliers that includes your district, go online using the link specified in the separate instructions for this form. This list may also be available at the bankruptcy clerk's office.

X _____

Average monthly administrative expense $_____   Copy total here ➡ $_____

37. **Add all of the deductions for debt payment. Add lines 33e through 36.** $_____

Total Deductions from Income

38. **Add all of the allowed deductions.**

Copy line 24, *All of the expenses allowed under IRS expense allowances* .... $_____

Copy line 32, *All of the additional expense deductions*................................. $_____

Copy line 37, *All of the deductions for debt payment* ....+ $_____

Total deductions... $_____   Copy total here ➡ $_____

Debtor 1 _____   Case number *(if known)*_____
      First Name   Middle Name   Last Name

Part 2:	Determine Your Disposable Income Under 11 U.S.C. § 1325(b)(2)

39. **Copy your total current monthly income** from line 14 of Form 122C-1, *Chapter 13 Statement of Your Current Monthly Income and Calculation of Commitment Period.* .... $_____

40. **Fill in any reasonably necessary income you receive for support for dependent children.** The monthly average of any child support payments, foster care payments, or disability payments for a dependent child, reported in Part I of Form 122C-1, that you received in accordance with applicable nonbankruptcy law to the extent reasonably necessary to be expended for such child. $_____

41. **Fill in all qualified retirement deductions.** The monthly total of all amounts that your employer withheld from wages as contributions for qualified retirement plans, as specified in 11 U.S.C. § 541(b)(7) plus all required repayments of loans from retirement plans, as specified in 11 U.S.C. § 362(b)(19). $_____

42. **Total of all deductions allowed under 11 U.S.C. § 707(b)(2)(A).** Copy line 38 here .... ➔ $_____

43. **Deduction for special circumstances.** If special circumstances justify additional expenses and you have no reasonable alternative, describe the special circumstances and their expenses. You must give your case trustee a detailed explanation of the special circumstances and documentation for the expenses.

Describe the special circumstances	Amount of expense
_____	$_____
_____	$_____
_____	+ $_____
Total	$_____ Copy here ➔ + $_____

44. **Total adjustments.** Add lines 40 through 43 .... $_____   Copy here ➔   − $_____

45. **Calculate your monthly disposable income under § 1325(b)(2).** Subtract line 44 from line 39. $_____

Part 3:	Change in Income or Expenses

46. **Change in income or expenses.** If the income in Form 122C-1 or the expenses you reported in this form have changed or are virtually certain to change after the date you filed your bankruptcy petition and during the time your case will be open, fill in the information below. For example, if the wages reported increased after you filed your petition, check 122C-1 in the first column, enter line 2 in the second column, explain why the wages increased, fill in when the increase occurred, and fill in the amount of the increase.

Form	Line	Reason for change	Date of change	Increase or decrease?	Amount of change
☐ 122C-1 ☐ 122C-2	___	_____	_____	☐ Increase ☐ Decrease	$_____
☐ 122C-1 ☐ 122C-2	___	_____	_____	☐ Increase ☐ Decrease	$_____
☐ 122C-1 ☐ 122C-2	___	_____	_____	☐ Increase ☐ Decrease	$_____
☐ 122C-1 ☐ 122C-2	___	_____	_____	☐ Increase ☐ Decrease	$_____

Official Form 122C-2   Chapter 13 Calculation of Your Disposable Income   page 7

SELECTED OFFICIAL FORMS

Debtor 1 _____   Case number (if known)_____
       First Name   Middle Name   Last Name

Part 4:   **Sign Below**

By signing here, under penalty of perjury you declare that the information on this statement and in any attachments is true and correct.

✗ _____   **✗** _____
   Signature of Debtor 1   Signature of Debtor 2

   Date _____   Date _____
         MM / DD   /YYYY   MM / DD   /YYYY

Print	Save As...	Add Attachment		Reset

Fill in this information to identify the case:

United States Bankruptcy Court for the:

_____ District of _____
(State)

Case number (*if known*): _____ Chapter _____

☐ Check if this is an
amended filing

Official Form 201

Voluntary Petition for Non-Individuals Filing for Bankruptcy 06/22

If more space is needed, attach a separate sheet to this form. On the top of any additional pages, write the debtor's name and the case number (if known). For more information, a separate document, *Instructions for Bankruptcy Forms for Non-Individuals*, is available.

1. **Debtor's name**
   _____

2. **All other names debtor used in the last 8 years**
   Include any assumed names, trade names, and *doing business as* names
   _____
   _____
   _____
   _____
   _____

3. **Debtor's federal Employer Identification Number** (EIN)
   _ _ - _ _ _ _ _ _ _

4. **Debtor's address**

   Principal place of business

   _____
   Number   Street

   _____

   _____
   City   State   ZIP Code

   _____
   County

   Mailing address, if different from principal place of business

   _____
   Number   Street

   _____
   P.O. Box

   _____
   City   State   ZIP Code

   Location of principal assets, if different from principal place of business

   _____
   Number   Street

   _____

   _____
   City   State   ZIP Code

5. **Debtor's website** (URL)
   _____

| Debtor _____ | Case number *(if known)* _____ |
| Name | |

6. Type of debtor	☐ Corporation (including Limited Liability Company (LLC) and Limited Liability Partnership (LLP))
	☐ Partnership (excluding LLP)
	☐ Other. Specify: _____

7. Describe debtor's business	A. *Check one:*
	☐ Health Care Business (as defined in 11 U.S.C. § 101(27A))
	☐ Single Asset Real Estate (as defined in 11 U.S.C. § 101(51B))
	☐ Railroad (as defined in 11 U.S.C. § 101(44))
	☐ Stockbroker (as defined in 11 U.S.C. § 101(53A))
	☐ Commodity Broker (as defined in 11 U.S.C. § 101(6))
	☐ Clearing Bank (as defined in 11 U.S.C. § 781(3))
	☐ None of the above
	B. *Check all that apply:*
	☐ Tax-exempt entity (as described in 26 U.S.C. § 501)
	☐ Investment company, including hedge fund or pooled investment vehicle (as defined in 15 U.S.C. § 80a-3)
	☐ Investment advisor (as defined in 15 U.S.C. § 80b-2(a)(11))
	C. NAICS (North American Industry Classification System) 4-digit code that best describes debtor. See http://www.uscourts.gov/four-digit-national-association-naics-codes .
	__ __ __ __

| 8. Under which chapter of the Bankruptcy Code is the debtor filing?

A debtor who is a "small business debtor" must check the first sub-box. A debtor as defined in § 1182(1) who elects to proceed under subchapter V of chapter 11 (whether or not the debtor is a "small business debtor") must check the second sub-box. | *Check one:*
☐ Chapter 7
☐ Chapter 9
☐ Chapter 11. *Check all that apply:*
　☐ The debtor is a small business debtor as defined in 11 U.S.C. § 101(51D), and its aggregate noncontingent liquidated debts (excluding debts owed to insiders or affiliates) are less than $3,024,725. If this sub-box is selected, attach the most recent balance sheet, statement of operations, cash-flow statement, and federal income tax return or if any of these documents do not exist, follow the procedure in 11 U.S.C. § 1116(1)(B).
　☐ The debtor is a debtor as defined in 11 U.S.C. § 1182(1), its aggregate noncontingent liquidated debts (excluding debts owed to insiders or affiliates) are less than $7,500,000, **and it chooses to proceed under Subchapter V of Chapter 11.** If this sub-box is selected, attach the most recent balance sheet, statement of operations, cash-flow statement, and federal income tax return, or if any of these documents do not exist, follow the procedure in 11 U.S.C. § 1116(1)(B).
　☐ A plan is being filed with this petition.
　☐ Acceptances of the plan were solicited prepetition from one or more classes of creditors, in accordance with 11 U.S.C. § 1126(b).
　☐ The debtor is required to file periodic reports (for example, 10K and 10Q) with the Securities and Exchange Commission according to § 13 or 15(d) of the Securities Exchange Act of 1934. File the *Attachment to Voluntary Petition for Non-Individuals Filing for Bankruptcy under Chapter 11* (Official Form 201A) with this form.
　　☐ The debtor is a shell company as defined in the Securities Exchange Act of 1934 Rule 12b-2.
☐ Chapter 12 |

Debtor _____   Case number (if known)_____
           Name

9. Were prior bankruptcy cases filed by or against the debtor within the last 8 years?

If more than 2 cases, attach a separate list.

❑ No

❑ Yes. District _____   When _____   Case number _____
                                              MM / DD / YYYY

         District _____   When _____   Case number _____
                                              MM / DD / YYYY

10. Are any bankruptcy cases pending or being filed by a business partner or an affiliate of the debtor?

List all cases. If more than 1, attach a separate list.

❑ No

❑ Yes. Debtor _____   Relationship _____

         District _____   When _____
                                                              MM / DD / YYYY

         Case number, if known _____

11. Why is the case filed in *this* district?

Check all that apply:

❑ Debtor has had its domicile, principal place of business, or principal assets in this district for 180 days immediately preceding the date of this petition or for a longer part of such 180 days than in any other district.

❑ A bankruptcy case concerning debtor's affiliate, general partner, or partnership is pending in this district.

12. Does the debtor own or have possession of any real property or personal property that needs immediate attention?

❑ No

❑ Yes. Answer below for each property that needs immediate attention. Attach additional sheets if needed.

Why does the property need immediate attention? *(Check all that apply.)*

❑ It poses or is alleged to pose a threat of imminent and identifiable hazard to public health or safety.

What is the hazard? _____

❑ It needs to be physically secured or protected from the weather.

❑ It includes perishable goods or assets that could quickly deteriorate or lose value without attention (for example, livestock, seasonal goods, meat, dairy, produce, or securities-related assets or other options).

❑ Other _____

Where is the property?_____
                       Number   Street

_____

_____
City   State ZIP Code

Is the property insured?

❑ No

❑ Yes. Insurance agency _____

        Contact name _____

        Phone _____

Statistical and administrative information

Debtor _____   Case number *(if known)* _____
     Name

13. Debtor's estimation of available funds	*Check one:* ❑ Funds will be available for distribution to unsecured creditors. ❑ After any administrative expenses are paid, no funds will be available for distribution to unsecured creditors.

14. Estimated number of creditors	❑ 1-49 ❑ 50-99 ❑ 100-199 ❑ 200-999	❑ 1,000-5,000 ❑ 5,001-10,000 ❑ 10,001-25,000	❑ 25,001-50,000 ❑ 50,001-100,000 ❑ More than 100,000
15. Estimated assets	❑ $0-$50,000 ❑ $50,001-$100,000 ❑ $100,001-$500,000 ❑ $500,001-$1 million	❑ $1,000,001-$10 million ❑ $10,000,001-$50 million ❑ $50,000,001-$100 million ❑ $100,000,001-$500 million	❑ $500,000,001-$1 billion ❑ $1,000,000,001-$10 billion ❑ $10,000,000,001-$50 billion ❑ More than $50 billion
16. Estimated liabilities	❑ $0-$50,000 ❑ $50,001-$100,000 ❑ $100,001-$500,000 ❑ $500,001-$1 million	❑ $1,000,001-$10 million ❑ $10,000,001-$50 million ❑ $50,000,001-$100 million ❑ $100,000,001-$500 million	❑ $500,000,001-$1 billion ❑ $1,000,000,001-$10 billion ❑ $10,000,000,001-$50 billion ❑ More than $50 billion

Request for Relief, Declaration, and Signatures

WARNING -- Bankruptcy fraud is a serious crime. Making a false statement in connection with a bankruptcy case can result in fines up to $500,000 or imprisonment for up to 20 years, or both. 18 U.S.C. §§ 152, 1341, 1519, and 3571.

17. Declaration and signature of authorized representative of debtor

The debtor requests relief in accordance with the chapter of title 11, United States Code, specified in this petition.

I have been authorized to file this petition on behalf of the debtor.

I have examined the information in this petition and have a reasonable belief that the information is true and correct.

I declare under penalty of perjury that the foregoing is true and correct.

Executed on _____
       MM / DD / YYYY

✘ _____   _____
Signature of authorized representative of debtor   Printed name

Title _____

Debtor _____   Case number *(if known)*_____
             Name

18. Signature of attorney   ✖ _____   Date _____
                                      Signature of attorney for debtor   MM   / DD / YYYY

_____
Printed name

_____
Firm name

_____
Number   Street

_____   _____
City   State   ZIP Code

_____   _____
Contact phone   Email address

_____   _____
Bar number   State

SELECTED OFFICIAL FORMS

2022-06 COMMITTEE NOTE

The form is amended in response to the enactment of the Bankruptcy Threshold Adjustment and Technical Corrections Act (the "BTATC" Act), Pub. L. No. 117-151, ___ Stat. ___. The BTATC reinstates the definition of "debtor" for determining eligibility to proceed under subchapter V of chapter 11 that was in effect from March 27, 2020, through March 27, 2022, under the CARES Act, as amended (see 2020-04 Committee Note). Line 8 of the form is amended to reflect that change. This amendment will terminate two years after the date of enactment of the BTATC Act, unless extended.

2022-04 STAFF NOTATION

The CARES Act changes described in the 2020-04 Committee Note lapsed on March 27, 2022, and the form has reverted to the pre-CARES Act (February 2020) version.

In addition, the debt limit listed in line 8 of the form is adjusted effective April 1, 2022, as part of the tri-annual dollar adjustments required by 11 U.S.C. § 104.

SELECTED OFFICIAL FORMS

Fill in this information to identify the case:

Debtor name _____

United States Bankruptcy Court for the: _____ District of _____
(State)

Case number (If known): _____

☐ Check if this is an
amended filing

Official Form 204

Chapter 11 or Chapter 9 Cases: List of Creditors Who Have the 20 Largest Unsecured Claims and Are Not Insiders
12/15

A list of creditors holding the 20 largest unsecured claims must be filed in a Chapter 11 or Chapter 9 case. Include claims which the debtor disputes. Do not include claims by any person or entity who is an *insider,* as defined in 11 U.S.C. § 101(31). Also, do not include claims by secured creditors, unless the unsecured claim resulting from inadequate collateral value places the creditor among the holders of the 20 largest unsecured claims.

	Name of creditor and complete mailing address, including zip code	Name, telephone number, and email address of creditor contact	Nature of the claim (for example, trade debts, bank loans, professional services, and government contracts)	Indicate if claim is contingent, unliquidated, or disputed	Amount of unsecured claim If the claim is fully unsecured, fill in only unsecured claim amount. If claim is partially secured, fill in total claim amount and deduction for value of collateral or setoff to calculate unsecured claim.		
					Total claim, if partially secured	Deduction for value of collateral or setoff	Unsecured claim
1							
2							
3							
4							
5							
6							
7							
8							

Debtor _____   Case number (if known)_____
          Name

Name of creditor and complete mailing address, including zip code	Name, telephone number, and email address of creditor contact	Nature of the claim (for example, trade debts, bank loans, professional services, and government contracts)	Indicate if claim is contingent, unliquidated, or disputed	Amount of unsecured claim If the claim is fully unsecured, fill in only unsecured claim amount. If claim is partially secured, fill in total claim amount and deduction for value of collateral or setoff to calculate unsecured claim.		
				Total claim, if partially secured	Deduction for value of collateral or setoff	Unsecured claim
9						
10						
11						
12						
13						
14						
15						
16						
17						
18						
19						
20						

SELECTED OFFICIAL FORMS

Debtor 1 _____
         First Name   Middle Name   Last Name

Last 4 digits of Social Security number or ITIN __ __ __ __

EIN __ __ – __ __ – __ __ __ __

Debtor 2 _____
(Spouse, if filing) First Name   Middle Name   Last Name

Last 4 digits of Social Security number or ITIN __ __ __ __

EIN __ __ – __ __ – __ __ __ __

United States Bankruptcy Court for the: _____ District of _____
                                                                (State)

Case number: _____

[Date case filed for chapter 7 _____
                                MM / DD / YYYY   OR

[Date case filed in chapter _____ _____
                                MM / DD / YYYY

Date case converted to chapter 7 _____
                                MM / DD / YYYY]

Official Form 309A (For Individuals or Joint Debtors)

Notice of Chapter 7 Bankruptcy Case — No Proof of Claim Deadline   10/20

For the debtors listed above, a case has been filed under chapter 7 of the Bankruptcy Code. An order for relief has been entered.

This notice has important information about the case for creditors, debtors, and trustees, including information about the meeting of creditors and deadlines. Read both pages carefully.

The filing of the case imposed an automatic stay against most collection activities. This means that creditors generally may not take action to collect debts from the debtors or the debtors' property. For example, while the stay is in effect, creditors cannot sue, garnish wages, assert a deficiency, repossess property, or otherwise try to collect from the debtors. Creditors cannot demand repayment from debtors by mail, phone, or otherwise. Creditors who violate the stay can be required to pay actual and punitive damages and attorney's fees. Under certain circumstances, the stay may be limited to 30 days or not exist at all, although debtors can ask the court to extend or impose a stay.

The debtors are seeking a discharge. Creditors who assert that the debtors are not entitled to a discharge of any debts or who want to have a particular debt excepted from discharge may be required to file a complaint in the bankruptcy clerk's office within the deadlines specified in this notice. (See line 9 for more information.)

To protect your rights, consult an attorney. All documents filed in the case may be inspected at the bankruptcy clerk's office at the address listed below or through PACER (Public Access to Court Electronic Records at https://pacer.uscourts.gov).

The staff of the bankruptcy clerk's office cannot give legal advice.

To help creditors correctly identify debtors, debtors submit full Social Security or Individual Taxpayer Identification Numbers, which may appear on a version of this notice. However, the full numbers must not appear on any document filed with the court.

Do not file this notice with any proof of claim or other filing in the case. Do not include more than the last four digits of a Social Security or Individual Taxpayer Identification Number in any document, including attachments, that you file with the court.

	About Debtor 1:	About Debtor 2:
1. **Debtor's full name**		
2. **All other names used in the last 8 years**		
3. **Address**		If Debtor 2 lives at a different address:
4. **Debtor's attorney** Name and address		Contact phone _____ Email _____
5. **Bankruptcy trustee** Name and address		Contact phone _____ Email _____

For more information, see page 2 ▶

Official Form 309A (For Individuals or Joint Debtors)   **Notice of Chapter 7 Bankruptcy Case — No Proof of Claim Deadline**   page 1

626

Debtor		Case number (if known)
Name		

---

6. Bankruptcy clerk's office

Documents in this case may be filed at this address. You may inspect all records filed in this case at this office or online at https://pacer.uscourts.gov.

Hours open
_____

Contact phone
_____

---

7. Meeting of creditors

Debtors must attend the meeting to be questioned under oath. In a joint case, both spouses must attend.

Creditors may attend, but are not required to do so.

_____ at _____
Date   Time

The meeting may be continued or adjourned to a later date. If so, the date will be on the court docket.

Location:

---

8. Presumption of abuse

If the presumption of abuse arises, you may have the right to file a motion to dismiss the case under 11 U.S.C. § 707(b). Debtors may rebut the presumption by showing special circumstances.

[The presumption of abuse does not arise.]

[The presumption of abuse arises.]

[Insufficient information has been filed to permit the clerk to determine whether the presumption of abuse arises. If more complete information is filed and shows that the presumption has arisen, the clerk will notify creditors.]

---

9. Deadlines

The bankruptcy clerk's office must receive these documents and any required filing fee by the following deadlines.

File by the deadline to object to discharge or to challenge whether certain debts are dischargeable:

You must file a complaint:

if you assert that the debtor is not entitled to receive a discharge of any debts under any of the subdivisions of 11 U.S.C. § 727(a)(2) through (7), or

if you want to have a debt excepted from discharge under 11 U.S.C. § 523(a)(2), (4), or (6).

You must file a motion if you assert that

the discharge should be denied under § 727(a)(8) or (9).

Filing deadline: _____

Deadline to object to exemptions:

The law permits debtors to keep certain property as exempt. If you believe that the law does not authorize an exemption claimed, you may file an objection.

Filing deadline: 30 days after the *conclusion* of the meeting of creditors

---

10. Proof of claim

Please do not file a proof of claim unless you receive a notice to do so.

No property appears to be available to pay creditors. Therefore, please do not file a proof of claim now. If it later appears that assets are available to pay creditors, the clerk will send you another notice telling you that you may file a proof of claim and stating the deadline.

---

11. Creditors with a foreign address

If you are a creditor receiving a notice mailed to a foreign address, you may file a motion asking the court to extend the deadlines in this notice. Consult an attorney familiar with United States bankruptcy law if you have any questions about your rights in this case.

---

12. Exempt property

The law allows debtors to keep certain property as exempt. Fully exempt property will not be sold and distributed to creditors. Debtors must file a list of property claimed as exempt. You may inspect that list at the bankruptcy clerk's office or online at https://pacer.uscourts.gov. If you believe that the law does not authorize an exemption that the debtors claim, you may file an objection. The bankruptcy clerk's office must receive the objection by the deadline to object to exemptions in line 9.

Information to identify the case:	
Debtor 1 _____ First Name Middle Name Last Name	Last 4 digits of Social Security number or ITIN ___ ___ ___ ___ EIN ___ ___ – ___ ___ ___ ___ ___ ___
Debtor 2 (Spouse, if filing) First Name Middle Name Last Name	Last 4 digits of Social Security number or ITIN ___ ___ ___ ___ EIN ___ ___ – ___ ___ ___ ___ ___ ___
United States Bankruptcy Court for the: _____ District of _____ (State)	[Date case filed for chapter 7 _____ OR MM / DD / YYYY
Case number: _____	[Date case filed in chapter _____ _____ MM / DD / YYYY Date case converted to chapter 7 _____] MM / DD / YYYY

Official Form 309B (For Individuals or Joint Debtors)

Notice of Chapter 7 Bankruptcy Case — Proof of Claim Deadline Set   10/20

For the debtors listed above, a case has been filed under chapter 7 of the Bankruptcy Code. An order for relief has been entered.

This notice has important information about the case for creditors, debtors, and trustees, including information about the meeting of creditors and deadlines. Read both pages carefully.

The filing of the case imposed an automatic stay against most collection activities. This means that creditors generally may not take action to collect debts from the debtors or the debtors' property. For example, while the stay is in effect, creditors cannot sue, garnish wages, assert a deficiency, repossess property, or otherwise try to collect from the debtors. Creditors cannot demand repayment from debtors by mail, phone, or otherwise. Creditors who violate the stay can be required to pay actual and punitive damages and attorney's fees. Under certain circumstances, the stay may be limited to 30 days or not exist at all, although debtors can ask the court to extend or impose a stay.

The debtors are seeking a discharge. Creditors who assert that the debtors are not entitled to a discharge of any debts or who want to have a particular debt excepted from discharge may be required to file a complaint in the bankruptcy clerk's office within the deadlines specified in this notice. (See line 9 for more information.)

To protect your rights, consult an attorney. All documents filed in the case may be inspected at the bankruptcy clerk's office at the address listed below or through PACER (Public Access to Court Electronic Records at https://pacer.uscourts.gov).

The staff of the bankruptcy clerk's office cannot give legal advice.

To help creditors correctly identify debtors, debtors submit full Social Security or Individual Taxpayer Identification Numbers, which may appear on a version of this notice. However, the full numbers must not appear on any document filed with the court.

Do not file this notice with any proof of claim or other filing in the case. Do not include more than the last four digits of a Social Security or Individual Taxpayer Identification Number in any document, including attachments, that you file with the court.

	About Debtor 1:	About Debtor 2:
1. Debtor's full name		
2. All other names used in the last 8 years		
3. Address		If Debtor 2 lives at a different address:
4. Debtor's attorney Name and address		Contact phone _____ Email _____
5. Bankruptcy trustee Name and address		Contact phone _____ Email _____

For more information, see page 2 ▶

Debtor _____   Case number (if known)_____
           Name

---

6. Bankruptcy clerk's office

Documents in this case may be filed at this address. You may inspect all records filed in this case at this office or online at https://pacer.uscourts.gov.

Hours open _____

Contact phone _____

---

7. Meeting of creditors

Debtors must attend the meeting to be questioned under oath. In a joint case, both spouses must attend. Creditors may attend, but are not required to do so.

_____ at _____
Date   Time

The meeting may be continued or adjourned to a later date. If so, the date will be on the court docket.

Location:

---

8. Presumption of abuse

If the presumption of abuse arises, you may have the right to file a motion to dismiss the case under 11 U.S.C. § 707(b). Debtors may rebut the presumption by showing special circumstances.

[The presumption of abuse does not arise.]

[The presumption of abuse arises.]

[Insufficient information has been filed to permit the clerk to determine whether the presumption of abuse arises. If more complete information is filed and shows that the presumption has arisen, the clerk will notify creditors.]

---

9. Deadlines

The bankruptcy clerk's office must receive these documents and any required filing fee by the following deadlines.

File by the deadline to object to discharge or to challenge whether certain debts are dischargeable:

You must file a complaint:

- if you assert that the debtor is not entitled to receive a discharge of any debts under any of the subdivisions of 11 U.S.C. § 727(a)(2) through (7), or
- if you want to have a debt excepted from discharge under 11 U.S.C. § 523(a)(2), (4), or (6).

You must file a motion:

- if you assert that the discharge should be denied under § 727(a)(8) or (9).

Filing deadline: _____

Deadline for all creditors to file a proof of claim (except governmental units):

Filing deadline: _____

Deadline for governmental units to file a proof of claim:

Filing deadline: _____

Deadlines for filing proof of claim:

A proof of claim is a signed statement describing a creditor's claim. A proof of claim form may be obtained at www.uscourts.gov or any bankruptcy clerk's office. If you do not file a proof of claim by the deadline, you might not be paid on your claim. To be paid, you must file a proof of claim even if your claim is listed in the schedules that the debtor filed.

Secured creditors retain rights in their collateral regardless of whether they file a proof of claim. Filing a proof of claim submits the creditor to the jurisdiction of the bankruptcy court, with consequences a lawyer can explain. For example, a secured creditor who files a proof of claim may surrender important nonmonetary rights, including the right to a jury trial.

Deadline to object to exemptions:

The law permits debtors to keep certain property as exempt. If you believe that the law does not authorize an exemption claimed, you may file an objection.

Filing deadline: 30 days after the *conclusion* of the meeting of creditors

---

10. Creditors with a foreign address

If you are a creditor receiving a notice mailed to a foreign address, you may file a motion asking the court to extend the deadlines in this notice. Consult an attorney familiar with United States bankruptcy law if you have any questions about your rights in this case.

---

11. Liquidation of the debtor's property and payment of creditors' claims

The bankruptcy trustee listed on the front of this notice will collect and sell the debtor's property that is not exempt. If the trustee can collect enough money, creditors may be paid some or all of the debts owed to them in the order specified by the Bankruptcy Code. To ensure you receive any share of that money, you must file a proof of claim as described above.

---

12. Exempt property

The law allows debtors to keep certain property as exempt. Fully exempt property will not be sold and distributed to creditors. Debtors must file a list of property claimed as exempt. You may inspect that list at the bankruptcy clerk's office or online at https://pacer.uscourts.gov. If you believe that the law does not authorize an exemption that the debtors claim, you may file an objection. The bankruptcy clerk's office must receive the objection by the deadline to object to exemptions in line 9.

Official Form 309B (For Individuals or Joint Debtors) **Notice of Chapter 7 Bankruptcy Case — Proof of Claim Deadline Set**   page **2**

Information to Identify the case:	
Debtor _____ Name	EIN ___ ___ - ___ ___ ___ ___ ___
United States Bankruptcy Court for the: _____ District of _____ (State)	[Date case filed for chapter 7 _____ MM / DD / YYYY OR
Case number: _____	[Date case filed in chapter _____ _____ MM / DD / YYYY Date case converted to chapter 7 _____] MM / DD / YYYY

Official Form 309C (For Corporations or Partnerships)

Notice of Chapter 7 Bankruptcy Case — No Proof of Claim Deadline   10/20

For the debtor listed above, a case has been filed under chapter 7 of the Bankruptcy Code. An order for relief has been entered.

This notice has important information about the case for creditors, debtors, and trustees, including information about the meeting of creditors and deadlines.

The filing of the case imposed an automatic stay against most collection activities. This means that creditors generally may not take action to collect debts from the debtor or the debtor's property. For example, while the stay is in effect, creditors cannot sue, assert a deficiency, repossess property, or otherwise try to collect from the debtor. Creditors cannot demand repayment from debtors by mail, phone, or otherwise. Creditors who violate the stay can be required to pay actual and punitive damages and attorney's fees.

To protect your rights, consult an attorney. All documents filed in the case may be inspected at the bankruptcy clerk's office at the address listed below or through PACER (Public Access to Court Electronic Records at https://pacer.uscourts.gov).

The staff of the bankruptcy clerk's office cannot give legal advice.

Do not file this notice with any proof of claim or other filing in the case.

1. **Debtor's full name**		
2. **All other names used in the last 8 years**		
3. **Address**		
4. **Debtor's attorney** Name and address	Contact phone _____ Email _____	
5. **Bankruptcy trustee** Name and address	Contact phone _____ Email _____	
6. **Bankruptcy clerk's office** Documents in this case may be filed at this address. You may inspect all records filed in this case at this office or online at https://pacer.uscourts.gov.	Hours open _____ Contact phone _____	
7. **Meeting of creditors** The debtor's representative must attend the meeting to be questioned under oath. Creditors may attend, but are not required to do so.	_____ at _____ Date Time The meeting may be continued or adjourned to a later date. If so, the date will be on the court docket.	Location:
8. **Proof of claim** Please do not file a proof of claim unless you receive a notice to do so.	No property appears to be available to pay creditors. Therefore, please do not file a proof of claim now. If it later appears that assets are available to pay creditors, the clerk will send you another notice telling you that you may file a proof of claim and stating the deadline.	
9. **Creditors with a foreign address**	If you are a creditor receiving a notice mailed to a foreign address, you may file a motion asking the court to extend the deadlines in this notice. Consult an attorney familiar with United States bankruptcy law if you have any questions about your rights in this case.	

Official Form 309C (For Corporations or Partnerships)   Notice of Chapter 7 Bankruptcy Case — No Proof of Claim Deadline

SELECTED OFFICIAL FORMS

Information to identify the case:	
Debtor _____ Name	EIN __ __ - __ __ __ __ __ __
United States Bankruptcy Court for the: _____ District of _____ (State)	[Date case filed for chapter 7 _____ MM / DD / YYYY OR
Case number: _____	[Date case filed in chapter ____ _____ MM / DD / YYYY
	Date case converted to chapter 7 _____] MM / DD / YYYY

Official Form 309D (For Corporations or Partnerships)

Notice of Chapter 7 Bankruptcy Case — Proof of Claim Deadline Set 10/20

For the debtor listed above, a case has been filed under chapter 7 of the Bankruptcy Code. An order for relief has been entered.

This notice has important information about the case for creditors, debtors, and trustees, including information about the meeting of creditors and deadlines. Read both pages carefully.

The filing of the case imposed an automatic stay against most collection activities. This means that creditors generally may not take action to collect debts from the debtor or the debtor's property. For example, while the stay is in effect, creditors cannot sue, assert a deficiency, repossess property, or otherwise try to collect from the debtor. Creditors cannot demand repayment from debtors by mail, phone, or otherwise. Creditors who violate the stay can be required to pay actual and punitive damages and attorney's fees.

To protect your rights, consult an attorney. All documents filed in the case may be inspected at the bankruptcy clerk's office at the address listed below or through PACER (Public Access to Court Electronic Records at https://pacer.uscourts.gov).

The staff of the bankruptcy clerk's office cannot give legal advice.

Do not file this notice with any proof of claim or other filing in the case.

1. Debtor's full name		
2. All other names used in the last 8 years		
3. Address		
4. Debtor's attorney Name and address		Contact phone _____ Email _____
5. Bankruptcy trustee Name and address		Contact phone _____ Email _____
6. Bankruptcy clerk's office Documents in this case may be filed at this address. You may inspect all records filed in this case at this office or online at https://pacer.uscourts.gov.		Hours open _____ Contact phone _____
7. Meeting of creditors The debtor's representative must attend the meeting to be questioned under oath. Creditors may attend, but are not required to do so.	_____ at _____ Date Time The meeting may be continued or adjourned to a later date. If so, the date will be on the court docket.	Location:

For more information, see page 2 ▶

Official Form 309D (For Corporations or Partnerships) Notice of Chapter 7 Bankruptcy Case — Proof of Claim Deadline Set   page 1

631

SELECTED OFFICIAL FORMS

Debtor _____   Case number *(if known)*_____
        Name

8. Deadlines The bankruptcy clerk's office must receive proofs of claim by the following deadlines.	**Deadline for all creditors to file a proof of claim (except governmental units):** **Deadline for governmental units to file a proof of claim:**	Filing deadline: _____ Filing deadline: _____
	A proof of claim is a signed statement describing a creditor's claim. A proof of claim form may be obtained at www.uscourts.gov or any bankruptcy clerk's office. If you do not file a proof of claim by the deadline, you might not be paid on your claim. To be paid, you must file a proof of claim even if your claim is listed in the schedules that the debtor filed. Secured creditors retain rights in their collateral regardless of whether they file a proof of claim. Filing a proof of claim submits the creditor to the jurisdiction of the bankruptcy court, with consequences a lawyer can explain. For example, a secured creditor who files a proof of claim may surrender important nonmonetary rights, including the right to a jury trial.	
9. Creditors with a foreign address	If you are a creditor receiving a notice mailed to a foreign address, you may file a motion asking the court to extend the deadlines in this notice. Consult an attorney familiar with United States bankruptcy law if you have any questions about your rights in this case.	
10. Liquidation of the debtor's property and payment of creditors' claims	The bankruptcy trustee listed on the front of this notice will collect and sell the debtor's property. If the trustee can collect enough money, creditors may be paid some or all of the debts owed to them, in the order specified by the Bankruptcy Code. To ensure you receive any share of that money, you must file a proof of claim, as described above.	

Official Form 309D (For Corporations or Partnerships)   **Notice of Chapter 7 Bankruptcy Case— Proof of Claim Deadline Set**   page **2**

632

Information to identify the case:			
Debtor 1 _____			Last 4 digits of Social Security number or ITIN __ __ __ __
First Name Middle Name Last Name			EIN __ __ - __ __ __ __ __ __ __
Debtor 2 _____			Last 4 digits of Social Security number or ITIN __ __ __ __
(Spouse, if filing) First Name Middle Name Last Name			EIN __ __ - __ __ __ __ __ __ __
United States Bankruptcy Court for the: _____ District of _____ (State)			[Date case filed for chapter 11 _____ MM / DD / YYYY] OR
Case number: _____			[Date case filed in chapter _____ _____ MM / DD / YYYY
			Date case converted to chapter 11 _____] MM / DD / YYYY

Official Form 309E1 (For Individuals or Joint Debtors)

Notice of Chapter 11 Bankruptcy Case

12/22

For the debtors listed above, a case has been filed under chapter 11 of the Bankruptcy Code. An order for relief has been entered.

This notice has important information about the case for creditors and debtors, including information about the meeting of creditors and deadlines. Read both pages carefully.

The filing of the case imposed an automatic stay against most collection activities. This means that creditors generally may not take action to collect debts from the debtors or the debtors' property. For example, while the stay is in effect, creditors cannot sue, garnish wages, assert a deficiency, repossess property, or otherwise try to collect from the debtors. Creditors cannot demand repayment from debtors by mail, phone, or otherwise. Creditors who violate the stay can be required to pay actual and punitive damages and attorney's fees. Under certain circumstances, the stay may be limited to 30 days or not exist at all, although debtors can ask the court to extend or impose a stay.

Confirmation of a chapter 11 plan may result in a discharge of debt. Creditors who assert that the debtors are not entitled to a discharge of any debts or who want to have a particular debt excepted from discharge may be required to file a complaint in the bankruptcy clerk's office within the deadlines specified in this notice. (See line 10 below for more information.)

To protect your rights, consult an attorney. All documents filed in the case may be inspected at the bankruptcy clerk's office at the address listed below or through PACER (Public Access to Court Electronic Records at https://pacer.uscourts.gov).

The staff of the bankruptcy clerk's office cannot give legal advice.

To help creditors correctly identify debtors, debtors submit full Social Security or Individual Taxpayer Identification Numbers, which may appear on a version of this notice. However, the full numbers must not appear on any document filed with the court.

Do not file this notice with any proof of claim or other filing in the case. Do not include more than the last four digits of a Social Security or Individual Taxpayer Identification Number in any document, including attachments, that you file with the court.

	About Debtor 1:	About Debtor 2:
1. Debtor's full name		
2. All other names used in the last 8 years		
3. Address		If Debtor 2 lives at a different address:
4. Debtor's attorney Name and address		Contact phone _____ Email _____
5. Bankruptcy clerk's office Documents in this case may be filed at this address. You may inspect all records filed in this case at this office or online at https://pacer.uscourts.gov.		Hours open _____ Contact phone _____

For more information, see page 2 ▶

6. Meeting of creditors Debtors must attend the meeting to be questioned under oath. In a joint case, both spouses must attend. Creditors may attend, but are not required to do so.	_____ at _____ Date Time The meeting may be continued or adjourned to a later date. If so, the date will be on the court docket.	Location:

7. Deadlines The bankruptcy clerk's office must receive these documents and any required filing fee by the following deadlines.	**Deadline to file a complaint objecting to discharge or to challenge whether certain debts are dischargeable (see line 10 for more information):** ▪ if you assert that the debtor is not entitled to receive a discharge of any debts under 11 U.S.C. § 1141(d)(3), the deadline is the first date set for hearing on confirmation of the plan. The court or its designee will send you notice of that date later. ▪ if you want to have a debt excepted from discharge under 11 U.S.C. § 523(a)(2), (4), or (6), **the deadline is:**_____.
	Deadline for filing proof of claim: [Not yet set. If a deadline is set, the court will send you another notice.] or [date, if set by the court)] A proof of claim is a signed statement describing a creditor's claim. A proof of claim form may be obtained at www.uscourts.gov or any bankruptcy clerk's office. Your claim will be allowed in the amount scheduled unless: ▪ your claim is designated as *disputed, contingent,* or *unliquidated*; ▪ you file a proof of claim in a different amount; or ▪ you receive another notice. If your claim is not scheduled or if your claim is designated as *disputed, contingent,* or *unliquidated*, you must file a proof of claim or you might not be paid on your claim and you might be unable to vote on a plan. You may file a proof of claim even if your claim is scheduled. You may review the schedules at the bankruptcy clerk's office or online at https://pacer.uscourts.gov. Secured creditors retain rights in their collateral regardless of whether they file a proof of claim. Filing a proof of claim submits a creditor to the jurisdiction of the bankruptcy court, with consequences a lawyer can explain. For example, a secured creditor who files a proof of claim may surrender important nonmonetary rights, including the right to a jury trial.
	Deadline to object to exemptions: **Filing deadline:** 30 days after the The law permits debtors to keep certain property as exempt. *conclusion* of the meeting If you believe that the law does not authorize an exemption of creditors claimed, you may file an objection.

8. Creditors with a foreign address	If you are a creditor receiving mailed notice at a foreign address, you may file a motion asking the court to extend the deadlines in this notice. Consult an attorney familiar with United States bankruptcy law if you have any questions about your rights in this case.
9. Filing a Chapter 11 bankruptcy case	Chapter 11 allows debtors to reorganize or liquidate according to a plan. A plan is not effective unless the court confirms it. You may receive a copy of the plan and a disclosure statement telling you about the plan, and you may have the opportunity to vote on the plan. You will receive notice of the date of the confirmation hearing, and you may object to confirmation of the plan and attend the confirmation hearing. Unless a trustee is serving, the debtor will remain in possession of the property and may continue to operate the debtor's business.
10. Discharge of debts	Confirmation of a chapter 11 plan may result in a discharge of debts, which may include all or part of a debt. See 11 U.S.C. § 1141(d). However, unless the court orders otherwise, the debts will not be discharged until all payments under the plan are made. A discharge means that creditors may never try to collect the debt from the debtors personally except as provided in the plan. If you believe that a particular debt owed to you should be excepted from the discharge under 11 U.S.C. § 523 (a)(2), (4), or (6), you must file a complaint and pay the filing fee in the bankruptcy clerk's office by the deadline. If you believe that the debtors are not entitled to a discharge of any of their debts under 11 U.S.C. § 1141 (d)(3), you must file a complaint and pay the filing fee in the clerk's office by the first date set for the hearing on confirmation of the plan. The court will send you another notice telling you of that date.
11. Exempt property	The law allows debtors to keep certain property as exempt. Fully exempt property will not be sold and distributed to creditors, even if the case is converted to chapter 7. Debtors must file a list of property claimed as exempt. You may inspect that list at the bankruptcy clerk's office or online at https://pacer.uscourts.gov. If you believe that the law does not authorize an exemption that the debtors claim, you may file an objection. The bankruptcy clerk's office must receive the objection by the deadline to object to exemptions in line 7.

SELECTED OFFICIAL FORMS

Official Form 309 (Committee Note) (12/22)

Committee Note

Official Form 309E1, line 7 and Official Form 309E2, line 8, are amended to clarify which deadline applies for filing complaints to deny the debtor a discharge and which applies for filing complaints seeking to except a particular debt from discharge.

Debtor 1 _____
　　　　　First Name　　　　　Middle Name　　　　　Last Name

Last 4 digits of Social Security number or ITIN ___ ___ ___ ___

EIN ___ ___ – ___ ___ ___ ___ ___ ___

Debtor 2 _____
(Spouse, if filing) First Name　　　Middle Name　　　Last Name

Last 4 digits of Social Security number or ITIN ___ ___ ___ ___

EIN ___ ___ – ___ ___ ___ ___ ___ ___

United States Bankruptcy Court for the: _____ District of _____
　　　　　　　　　　　　　　　　　　　　　　　　　　　　(State)

Case number: _____

[Date case filed for chapter 11 _____
　　　　　　　　　　　　　　　　MM / DD / YYYY]　OR

[Date case filed in chapter _____ _____
　　　　　　　　　　　　　　　　MM / DD / YYYY

Date case converted to chapter 11 _____
　　　　　　　　　　　　　　　　MM / DD / YYYY]

Official Form 309E2 (For Individuals or Joint Debtors under Subchapter V)

Notice of Chapter 11 Bankruptcy Case

12/22

For the debtors listed above, a case has been filed under chapter 11 of the Bankruptcy Code. An order for relief has been entered.

This notice has important information about the case for creditors, debtors, and trustees, including information about the meeting of creditors and deadlines. Read all pages carefully.

The filing of the case imposed an automatic stay against most collection activities. This means that creditors generally may not take action to collect debts from the debtors or the debtors' property. For example, while the stay is in effect, creditors cannot sue, garnish wages, assert a deficiency, repossess property, or otherwise try to collect from the debtors. Creditors cannot demand repayment from debtors by mail, phone, or otherwise. Creditors who violate the stay can be required to pay actual and punitive damages and attorney's fees. Under certain circumstances, the stay may be limited to 30 days or not exist at all, although debtors can ask the court to extend or impose a stay.

Confirmation of a chapter 11 plan may result in a discharge of debt. Creditors who assert that the debtors are not entitled to a discharge of any debts or who want to have a particular debt excepted from discharge may be required to file a complaint in the bankruptcy clerk's office within the deadlines specified in this notice. (See line 11 below for more information.)

To protect your rights, consult an attorney. All documents filed in the case may be inspected at the bankruptcy clerk's office at the address listed below or through PACER (Public Access to Court Electronic Records at https://pacer.uscourts.gov).

The staff of the bankruptcy clerk's office cannot give legal advice.

To help creditors correctly identify debtors, debtors submit full Social Security or Individual Taxpayer Identification Numbers, which may appear on a version of this notice. However, the full numbers must not appear on any document filed with the court.

Do not file this notice with any proof of claim or other filing in the case. Do not include more than the last four digits of a Social Security or Individual Taxpayer Identification Number in any document, including attachments, that you file with the court.

	About Debtor 1:	About Debtor 2:
1. **Debtor's full name**		
2. **All other names used in the last 8 years**		
3. **Address**		If Debtor 2 lives at a different address:
4. **Debtor's attorney** Name and address		Contact phone _____ Email _____
5. **Bankruptcy trustee** Name and address		Contact phone _____ Email _____

For more information, see page 2 ▶

6. Bankruptcy clerk's office Documents in this case may be filed at this address. You may inspect all records filed in this case at this office or online at https://pacer.uscourts.gov.		Hours open _____ Contact phone _____

7. Meeting of creditors

Debtors must attend the meeting to be questioned under oath. In a joint case, both spouses must attend.

Creditors may attend, but are not required to do so.

_____ at _____   Location:
Date   Time

The meeting may be continued or adjourned to a later date. If so, the date will be on the court docket.

8. Deadlines

The bankruptcy clerk's office must receive these documents and any required filing fee by the following deadlines.

Deadline to file a complaint objecting to discharge or to challenge whether certain debts are dischargeable (see line 11 for more information):

- if you assert that the debtor is not entitled to receive a discharge of any debts under 11 U.S.C. § 1141(d)(3), the deadline is the first date set for hearing on confirmation of the plan. The court or its designee will send you notice of that date later.

- if you want to have a debt excepted from discharge under 11 U.S.C. § 523(a)(2), (4), or (6), **the deadline is:**_____.

Deadline for filing proof of claim: [Not yet set. If a deadline is set, the court will send you another notice.] or

[date, if set by the court)]

A proof of claim is a signed statement describing a creditor's claim. A proof of claim form may be obtained at www.uscourts.gov or any bankruptcy clerk's office.

Your claim will be allowed in the amount scheduled unless:

- your claim is designated as *disputed*, *contingent*, or *unliquidated*;
- you file a proof of claim in a different amount; or
- you receive another notice.

If your claim is not scheduled or if your claim is designated as *disputed*, *contingent*, or *unliquidated*, you must file a proof of claim or you might not be paid on your claim and you might be unable to vote on a plan. You may file a proof of claim even if your claim is scheduled.

You may review the schedules at the bankruptcy clerk's office or online at https://pacer.uscourts.gov.

Secured creditors retain rights in their collateral regardless of whether they file a proof of claim. Filing a proof of claim submits a creditor to the jurisdiction of the bankruptcy court, with consequences a lawyer can explain. For example, a secured creditor who files a proof of claim may surrender important nonmonetary rights, including the right to a jury trial.

Deadline to object to exemptions: **Filing deadline:** 30 days after the *conclusion* of the meeting of creditors

The law permits debtors to keep certain property as exempt.

If you believe that the law does not authorize an exemption claimed, you may file an objection.

9. Creditors with a foreign address

If you are a creditor receiving mailed notice at a foreign address, you may file a motion asking the court to extend the deadlines in this notice. Consult an attorney familiar with United States bankruptcy law if you have any questions about your rights in this case.

10. Filing a Chapter 11 bankruptcy case

Chapter 11 allows debtors to reorganize or liquidate according to a plan. A plan is not effective unless the court confirms it. You may receive a copy of the plan and a disclosure statement telling you about the plan, and you may have the opportunity to vote on the plan. You will receive notice of the date of the confirmation hearing, and you may object to confirmation of the plan and attend the confirmation hearing. The debtor will generally remain in possession of the property and may continue to operate the debtor's business.

For more information, see page 3 ▶

Official Form 309E2 (For Individuals or Joint Debtors under Subchapter V)   **Notice of Chapter 11 Bankruptcy Case**   page 2

637

SELECTED OFFICIAL FORMS

11. Discharge of debts	Confirmation of a chapter 11 plan may result in a discharge of debts, which may include all or part of a debt. See 11 U.S.C. § 1141(d). A discharge means that creditors may never try to collect the debt from the debtors personally except as provided in the plan. If you believe that a particular debt owed to you should be excepted from the discharge under 11 U.S.C. § 523 (a)(2), (4), or (6), you must file a complaint and pay the filing fee in the bankruptcy clerk's office by the deadline. If you believe that the debtors are not entitled to a discharge of any of their debts under 11 U.S.C. § 1141 (d)(3), you must file a complaint and pay the filing fee in the clerk's office by the first date set for the hearing on confirmation of the plan. The court will send you another notice telling you of that date.
12. Exempt property	The law allows debtors to keep certain property as exempt. Fully exempt property will not be sold and distributed to creditors, even if the case is converted to chapter 7. Debtors must file a list of property claimed as exempt. You may inspect that list at the bankruptcy clerk's office or online at https://pacer.uscourts.gov. If you believe that the law does not authorize an exemption that the debtors claim, you may file an objection. The bankruptcy clerk's office must receive the objection by the deadline to object to exemptions in line 8.

Official Form 309E2 (For Individuals or Joint Debtors under Subchapter V)   **Notice of Chapter 11 Bankruptcy Case**   page 3

638

SELECTED OFFICIAL FORMS

Official Form 309 (Committee Note) (12/22)

Committee Note

Official Form 309E1, line 7 and Official Form 309E2, line 8, are amended to clarify which deadline applies for filing complaints to deny the debtor a discharge and which applies for filing complaints seeking to except a particular debt from discharge.

Information to identify the case:		
Debtor _____ Name	EIN __ __ - __ __ __ __ __ __	
United States Bankruptcy Court for the: _____ District of _____ (State)	[Date case filed for chapter 11 _____ MM / DD / YYYY OR	
Case number: _____	[Date case filed in chapter _____ MM / DD / YYYY	
	Date case converted to chapter 11 _____ MM / DD / YYYY]	

Official Form 309F1 (For Corporations or Partnerships)

Notice of Chapter 11 Bankruptcy Case   10/20

For the debtor listed above, a case has been filed under chapter 11 of the Bankruptcy Code. An order for relief has been entered.

This notice has important information about the case for creditors and debtors, including information about the meeting of creditors and deadlines. Read both pages carefully.

The filing of the case imposed an automatic stay against most collection activities. This means that creditors generally may not take action to collect debts from the debtor or the debtor's property. For example, while the stay is in effect, creditors cannot sue, assert a deficiency, repossess property, or otherwise try to collect from the debtor. Creditors cannot demand repayment from the debtor by mail, phone, or otherwise. Creditors who violate the stay can be required to pay actual and punitive damages and attorney's fees.

Confirmation of a chapter 11 plan may result in a discharge of debt. A creditor who wants to have a particular debt excepted from discharge may be required to file a complaint in the bankruptcy clerk's office within the deadline specified in this notice. (See line 11 below for more information.)

To protect your rights, consult an attorney. All documents filed in the case may be inspected at the bankruptcy clerk's office at the address listed below or through PACER (Public Access to Court Electronic Records at https://pacer.uscourts.gov).

The staff of the bankruptcy clerk's office cannot give legal advice.

Do not file this notice with any proof of claim or other filing in the case.

1. **Debtor's full name**		
2. **All other names used in the last 8 years**		
3. **Address**		
4. **Debtor's attorney** Name and address	Contact phone _____ Email _____	
5. **Bankruptcy clerk's office** Documents in this case may be filed at this address. You may inspect all records filed in this case at this office or online at https://pacer.uscourts.gov.	Hours open _____ Contact phone _____	
6. **Meeting of creditors** The debtor's representative must attend the meeting to be questioned under oath. Creditors may attend, but are not required to do so.	_____ at _____ Date Time The meeting may be continued or adjourned to a later date. If so, the date will be on the court docket.	Location:

For more information, see page 2 ▶

SELECTED OFFICIAL FORMS

Debtor _____   Case number (if known)_____
       Name

7. **Proof of claim deadline**	**Deadline for filing proof of claim:**	[Not yet set. If a deadline is set, the court will send you another notice.] or
		[date, if set by the court)]
	A proof of claim is a signed statement describing a creditor's claim. A proof of claim form may be obtained at www.uscourts.gov or any bankruptcy clerk's office.	
	Your claim will be allowed in the amount scheduled unless:	
	▪ your claim is designated as *disputed, contingent,* or *unliquidated*;	
	▪ you file a proof of claim in a different amount; or	
	▪ you receive another notice.	
	If your claim is not scheduled or if your claim is designated as *disputed, contingent,* or *unliquidated*, you must file a proof of claim or you might not be paid on your claim and you might be unable to vote on a plan. You may file a proof of claim even if your claim is scheduled.	
	You may review the schedules at the bankruptcy clerk's office or online at https://pacer.uscourts.gov.	
	Secured creditors retain rights in their collateral regardless of whether they file a proof of claim. Filing a proof of claim submits a creditor to the jurisdiction of the bankruptcy court, with consequences a lawyer can explain. For example, a secured creditor who files a proof of claim may surrender important nonmonetary rights, including the right to a jury trial.	
8. **Exception to discharge deadline** The bankruptcy clerk's office must receive a complaint and any required filing fee by the following deadline.	If § 523(c) applies to your claim and you seek to have it excepted from discharge, you must start a judicial proceeding by filing a complaint by the deadline stated below. **Deadline for filing the complaint:** _____	
9. **Creditors with a foreign address**	If you are a creditor receiving notice mailed to a foreign address, you may file a motion asking the court to extend the deadlines in this notice. Consult an attorney familiar with United States bankruptcy law if you have any questions about your rights in this case.	
10. **Filing a Chapter 11 bankruptcy case**	Chapter 11 allows debtors to reorganize or liquidate according to a plan. A plan is not effective unless the court confirms it. You may receive a copy of the plan and a disclosure statement telling you about the plan, and you may have the opportunity to vote on the plan. You will receive notice of the date of the confirmation hearing, and you may object to confirmation of the plan and attend the confirmation hearing. Unless a trustee is serving, the debtor will remain in possession of the property and may continue to operate its business.	
11. **Discharge of debts**	Confirmation of a chapter 11 plan may result in a discharge of debts, which may include all or part of your debt. See 11 U.S.C. § 1141(d). A discharge means that creditors may never try to collect the debt from the debtor except as provided in the plan. If you want to have a particular debt owed to you excepted from the discharge and § 523(c) applies to your claim, you must start a judicial proceeding by filing a complaint and paying the filing fee in the bankruptcy clerk's office by the deadline.	

Information to identify the case:

Debtor _____ Name	EIN __ __ – __ __ __ __ __ __ __
United States Bankruptcy Court for the: _____ District of _____ (State)	[Date case filed for chapter 11 _____ MM / DD / YYYY OR
Case number: _____	[Date case filed in chapter _____ MM / DD / YYYY Date case converted to chapter 11 _____] MM / DD / YYYY

Official Form 309F2 (For Corporations or Partnerships under Subchapter V)

Notice of Chapter 11 Bankruptcy Case   10/20

For the debtor listed above, a case has been filed under chapter 11 of the Bankruptcy Code. An order for relief has been entered.

This notice has important information about the case for creditors, debtors, and trustees, including information about the meeting of creditors and deadlines. Read both pages carefully.

The filing of the case imposed an automatic stay against most collection activities. This means that creditors generally may not take action to collect debts from the debtor or the debtor's property. For example, while the stay is in effect, creditors cannot sue, assert a deficiency, repossess property, or otherwise try to collect from the debtor. Creditors cannot demand repayment from the debtor by mail, phone, or otherwise. Creditors who violate the stay can be required to pay actual and punitive damages and attorney's fees.

Confirmation of a chapter 11 plan may result in a discharge of debt. A creditor who wants to have a particular debt excepted from discharge may be required to file a complaint in the bankruptcy clerk's office within the deadline specified in this notice. (See line 12 below for more information.)

To protect your rights, consult an attorney. All documents filed in the case may be inspected at the bankruptcy clerk's office at the address listed below or through PACER (Public Access to Court Electronic Records at https://pacer.uscourts.gov).

The staff of the bankruptcy clerk's office cannot give legal advice.

Do not file this notice with any proof of claim or other filing in the case.

1.	**Debtor's full name**	
2.	**All other names used in the last 8 years**	
3.	**Address**	
4.	**Debtor's attorney** Name and address	Contact phone _____ Email _____
5.	**Bankruptcy trustee** Name and address	Contact phone _____ Email _____
6.	**Bankruptcy clerk's office** Documents in this case may be filed at this address. You may inspect all records filed in this case at this office or online at https://pacer.uscourts.gov.	Hours open _____ Contact phone _____

For more information, see page 2 ▶

SELECTED OFFICIAL FORMS

Debtor _____   Case number *(if known)*_____
            Name

7. Meeting of creditors The debtor's representative must attend the meeting to be questioned under oath. Creditors may attend, but are not required to do so.	_____ at _____ Location: Date Time The meeting may be continued or adjourned to a later date. If so, the date will be on the court docket.
8. Proof of claim deadline	**Deadline for filing proof of claim:** [Not yet set. If a deadline is set, the court will send you another notice.] or [date, if set by the court)] A proof of claim is a signed statement describing a creditor's claim. A proof of claim form may be obtained at www.uscourts.gov or any bankruptcy clerk's office. Your claim will be allowed in the amount scheduled unless: ▪ your claim is designated as *disputed*, *contingent*, or *unliquidated*; ▪ you file a proof of claim in a different amount; or ▪ you receive another notice. If your claim is not scheduled or if your claim is designated as *disputed*, *contingent*, or *unliquidated*, you must file a proof of claim or you might not be paid on your claim and you might be unable to vote on a plan. You may file a proof of claim even if your claim is scheduled. You may review the schedules at the bankruptcy clerk's office or online at https://pacer.uscourts.gov. Secured creditors retain rights in their collateral regardless of whether they file a proof of claim. Filing a proof of claim submits a creditor to the jurisdiction of the bankruptcy court, with consequences a lawyer can explain. For example, a secured creditor who files a proof of claim may surrender important nonmonetary rights, including the right to a jury trial.
9. Exception to discharge deadline The bankruptcy clerk's office must receive a complaint and any required filing fee by the following deadline.	If § 523(c) applies to your claim and you seek to have it excepted from discharge, you must start a judicial proceeding by filing a complaint by the deadline stated below. **Deadline for filing the complaint:** _____
10. Creditors with a foreign address	If you are a creditor receiving notice mailed to a foreign address, you may file a motion asking the court to extend the deadlines in this notice. Consult an attorney familiar with United States bankruptcy law if you have any questions about your rights in this case.
11. Filing a Chapter 11 bankruptcy case	Chapter 11 allows debtors to reorganize or liquidate according to a plan. A plan is not effective unless the court confirms it. You may receive a copy of the plan and a disclosure statement telling you about the plan, and you may have the opportunity to vote on the plan. You will receive notice of the date of the confirmation hearing, and you may object to confirmation of the plan and attend the confirmation hearing. The debtor will generally remain in possession of the property and may continue to operate the debtor's business.
12. Discharge of debts	Confirmation of a chapter 11 plan may result in a discharge of debts, which may include all or part of your debt. See 11 U.S.C. § 1141(d). A discharge means that creditors may never try to collect the debt from the debtor except as provided in the plan. If you want to have a particular debt owed to you excepted from the discharge and § 523(c) applies to your claim, you must start a judicial proceeding by filing a complaint and paying the filing fee in the bankruptcy clerk's office by the deadline.

Information to identify the case:

Debtor 1 _____
First Name   Middle Name   Last Name

Debtor 2 _____
(Spouse, if filing) First Name   Middle Name   Last Name

United States Bankruptcy Court for the: _____ District of _____
(State)

Case number: _____

Last 4 digits of Social Security number or ITIN __ __ __ __

EIN __ __ - __ __ __ __ __ __ __

Last 4 digits of Social Security number or ITIN __ __ __ __

EIN __ __ - __ __ __ __ __ __ __

[Date case filed for chapter 12 _____ MM / DD / YYYY OR

[Date case filed in chapter _____ _____ MM / DD / YYYY

Date case converted to chapter 12 _____]
MM / DD / YYYY

Official Form 309G (For Individuals or Joint Debtors)

Notice of Chapter 12 Bankruptcy Case

10/20

For the debtors listed above, a case has been filed under chapter 12 of the Bankruptcy Code. An order for relief has been entered.

This notice has important information about the case for creditors, debtors, and trustees, including information about the meeting of creditors and deadlines. Read both pages carefully.

The filing of the case imposed an automatic stay against most collection activities. This means that creditors generally may not take action to collect debts from the debtors, from the debtors' property, or from certain codebtors. For example, while the stay is in effect, creditors cannot sue, garnish wages, assert a deficiency, repossess property, or otherwise try to collect from the debtors. Creditors cannot demand repayment from debtors by mail, phone, or otherwise. Creditors who violate the stay can be required to pay actual and punitive damages and attorney's fees.

Confirmation of a chapter 12 plan may result in a discharge of debt. Creditors who want to have a particular debt excepted from discharge may be required to file a complaint in the bankruptcy clerk's office within the deadline specified in this notice. (See line 13 below for more information.)

To protect your rights, consult an attorney. All documents filed in the case may be inspected at the bankruptcy clerk's office at the address listed below or through PACER (Public Access to Court Electronic Records at https://pacer.uscourts.gov).

The staff of the bankruptcy clerk's office cannot give legal advice.

To help creditors correctly identify debtors, debtors submit full Social Security or Individual Taxpayer Identification Numbers, which may appear on a version of this notice. However, the full numbers must not appear on any document filed with the court.

Do not file this notice with any proof of claim or other filing in the case. Do not include more than the last four digits of a Social Security or Individual Taxpayer Identification Number in any document, including attachments, that you file with the court.

	About Debtor 1:	About Debtor 2:
1. Debtor's full name		
2. All other names used in the last 8 years		
3. Address		If Debtor 2 lives at a different address:
4. Debtor's attorney Name and address		Contact phone _____ Email _____
5. Bankruptcy trustee Name and address		Contact phone _____ Email _____
6. Bankruptcy clerk's office Documents in this case may be filed at this address. You may inspect all records filed in this case at this office or online at https://pacer.uscourts.gov.		Hours open _____ Contact phone _____

For more information, see page 2 ▶

SELECTED OFFICIAL FORMS

Debtor _____ Case number (if known)_____
       Name

7. Meeting of creditors Debtors must attend the meeting to be questioned under oath. In a joint case, both spouses must attend. Creditors may attend, but are not required to do so.	_____ at _____ Date Time The meeting may be continued or adjourned to a later date. If so, the date will be on the court docket.	Location:
8. Deadlines The bankruptcy clerk's office must receive these documents and any required filing fee by the following deadlines.	**Deadline to file a complaint to challenge dischargeability of certain debts:** You must start a judicial proceeding by filing a complaint if you want to have a debt excepted from discharge under 11 U.S.C. § 523(a)(2), (4), or (6).	Filing deadline: _____
	Deadline for all creditors to file a proof of claim (except governmental units):	Filing deadline: _____
	Deadline for governmental units to file a proof of claim:	Filing deadline: _____
	Deadlines for filing proof of claim: A proof of claim is a signed statement describing a creditor's claim. A proof of claim form may be obtained at www.uscourts.gov or any bankruptcy clerk's office. If you do not file a proof of claim by the deadline, you might not be paid on your claim. To be paid, you must file a proof of claim even if your claim is listed in the schedules that the debtor filed. Secured creditors retain rights in their collateral regardless of whether they file a proof of claim. Filing a proof of claim submits the creditor to the jurisdiction of the bankruptcy court, with consequences a lawyer can explain. For example, a secured creditor who files a proof of claim may surrender important nonmonetary rights, including the right to a jury trial.	
	Deadline to object to exemptions: The law permits debtors to keep certain property as exempt. If you believe that the law does not authorize an exemption claimed, you may file an objection.	**Filing deadline:** 30 days after the *conclusion* of the meeting of creditors
9. Filing of plan	[The debtor has filed a plan, which is attached. The hearing on confirmation will be held on: _____ at _____ Location:_____ Date Time] Or [The debtor has filed a plan. The plan and notice of confirmation hearing will be sent separately.] Or [The debtor has not filed a plan as of this date. A copy of the plan and a notice of the hearing on confirmation will be sent separately.]	
10. Creditors with a foreign address	If you are a creditor receiving a notice mailed to a foreign address, you may file a motion asking the court to extend the deadlines in this notice. Consult an attorney familiar with United States bankruptcy law if you have any questions about your rights in this case.	
11. Filing a Chapter 12 bankruptcy case	Chapter 12 allows family farmers and family fishermen to reorganize according to a plan. A plan is not effective unless the court confirms it. You may receive a copy of the plan. You may object to confirmation of the plan and attend the confirmation hearing. The debtor will remain in possession of the property and may continue to operate the business unless the court orders otherwise.	
12. Discharge of debts	Confirmation of a chapter 12 plan may result in a discharge of debts, which may include all or part of your debt. Unless the court orders otherwise, the discharge will not be effective until all payments under the plan are made. A discharge means that you may never try to collect the debt from the debtor except as provided in the plan. If you want to have a particular debt excepted under 11 U.S.C. § 523(a)(2), (4), or (6), you must start a judicial proceeding by filing a complaint and paying the filing fee in the clerk's office by the deadline.	
13. Exempt property	The law allows debtors to keep certain property as exempt. Fully exempt property will not be sold and distributed to creditors, even if the case is converted to chapter 7. Debtors must file a list of property claimed as exempt. You may inspect that list at the bankruptcy clerk's office. If you believe that the law does not authorize an exemption that the debtors claim, you may file an objection. The bankruptcy clerk's office must receive the objection by the deadline to object to exemptions in line 8.	

Information to identify the case:		
Debtor _____ Name	EIN __ __ - __ __ __ __ __ __	
United States Bankruptcy Court for the: _____ District of _____ (State)	[Date case filed for chapter 12	MM / DD / YYYY OR
Case number: _____	[Date case filed in chapter _____	MM / DD / YYYY
	Date case converted to chapter 12	_____] MM / DD / YYYY

Official Form 309H (For Corporations or Partnerships)

Notice of Chapter 12 Bankruptcy Case

10/20

For the debtor listed above, a case has been filed under chapter 12 of the Bankruptcy Code. An order for relief has been entered.

This notice has important information about the case for creditors, debtors, and trustees, including information about the meeting of creditors and deadlines. Read both pages carefully.

The filing of the case imposed an automatic stay against most collection activities. This means that creditors generally may not take action to collect debts from the debtor, the debtor's property, or certain codebtors. For example, while the stay is in effect, creditors cannot sue, assert a deficiency, repossess property, or otherwise try to collect from the debtor. Creditors cannot demand repayment from the debtor by mail, phone, or otherwise. Creditors who violate the stay can be required to pay actual and punitive damages and attorney's fees.

Confirmation of a chapter 12 plan may result in the discharge of debt. Creditors who want to have a particular debt excepted from discharge may be required to file a complaint in the bankruptcy clerk's office within the deadline specified in this notice. (See line 13 below for more information.)

To protect your rights, consult an attorney. All documents filed in the case may be inspected at the bankruptcy clerk's office at the address listed below or through PACER (Public Access to Court Electronic Records at https://pacer.uscourts.gov).

The staff of the bankruptcy clerk's office cannot give legal advice.

Do not file this notice with any proof of claim or other filing in the case.

1. **Debtor's full name**	
2. **All other names used in the last 8 years**	
3. **Address**	
4. **Debtor's attorney** Name and address	Contact phone _____ Email _____
5. **Bankruptcy clerk's office** Documents in this case may be filed at this address. You may inspect all records filed in this case at this office or online at https://pacer.uscourts.gov.	Hours open _____ Contact phone _____
6. **Bankruptcy trustee** Name and address	Contact phone _____ Email _____

SELECTED OFFICIAL FORMS

Debtor _____   Case number (if known) _____
                Name

For more information, see page 2 ▶

7. Meeting of creditors The debtor's representative must attend the meeting to be questioned under oath. Creditors may attend, but are not required to do so.	_____ at _____ Date Time The meeting may be continued or adjourned to a later date. If so, the date will be on the court docket.	Location:
8. Exception to discharge deadline The bankruptcy clerk's office must receive a complaint and any required filing fee by the following deadline.	You must start a judicial proceeding by filing a complaint if you want to have a debt excepted from discharge under 11 U.S.C. § 523(a)(2), (4), or (6).	Deadline for filing the complaint: _____
9. Filing of plan	[The debtor has filed a plan, which is attached. The hearing on confirmation will be held on: _____ at _____ Location:_____ Date Time] Or [The debtor has filed a plan. The plan and notice of confirmation hearing will be sent separately.] Or [The debtor has not filed a plan as of this date. A copy of the plan and a notice of the hearing on confirmation will be sent separately.]	
10. Deadlines	Deadline for all creditors to file a proof of claim (except governmental units): Deadline for governmental units to file a proof of claim: A proof of claim is a signed statement describing a creditor's claim. A proof of claim form may be obtained at www.uscourts.gov or any bankruptcy clerk's office. If you do not file a proof of claim by the deadline, you might not be paid on your claim. To be paid, you must file a proof of claim even if your claim is listed in the schedules that the debtor filed. Secured creditors retain rights in their collateral regardless of whether they file a proof of claim. Filing a proof of claim submits the creditor to the jurisdiction of the bankruptcy court, with consequences a lawyer can explain. For example, a secured creditor who files a proof of claim may surrender important nonmonetary rights, including the right to a jury trial.	Filing deadline: _____ Filing deadline: _____
11. Creditors with a foreign address	If you are a creditor receiving a notice mailed to a foreign address, you may file a motion asking the court to extend the deadlines in this notice. Consult an attorney familiar with United States bankruptcy law if you have any questions about your rights in this case.	
12. Filing a chapter 12 bankruptcy case	Chapter 12 allows family farmers and family fishermen to reorganize according to a plan. A plan is not effective unless the court confirms it. You may receive a copy of the plan. You may object to confirmation of the plan and attend the confirmation hearing. The debtor will remain in possession of the property and may continue to operate the business.	
13. Discharge of debts	Confirmation of a chapter 12 plan may result in a discharge of debts, which may include all or part of your debt. Unless the court orders otherwise, the discharge will not be effective until all payments under the plan are made. A discharge means that you may never try to collect the debt from the debtor except as provided in the plan. If you want to have a particular debt excepted from discharge under 11 U.S.C. § 523(a)(2), (4), or (6), you must start a judicial proceeding by filing a complaint and paying the filing fee in the bankruptcy clerk's office by the deadline.	

Official Form 309H (For Corporations or Partnerships)   Notice of Chapter 12 Bankruptcy Case   page 2

Information to identify the case:

Debtor 1 _____ First Name Middle Name Last Name	Last 4 digits of Social Security number or ITIN __ __ __ __ EIN __ __ – __ __ __ __ __ __ __
Debtor 2 _____ (Spouse, if filing) First Name Middle Name Last Name	Last 4 digits of Social Security number or ITIN __ __ __ __ EIN __ __ – __ __ __ __ __ __ __
United States Bankruptcy Court for the: _____ District of _____ (State)	[Date case filed for chapter 13 _____ MM / DD / YYYY OR
Case number: _____	[Date case filed in chapter _____ _____ MM / DD / YYYY Date case converted to chapter 13 _____ MM / DD / YYYY]

Official Form 309I

Notice of Chapter 13 Bankruptcy Case

10/20

For the debtors listed above, a case has been filed under chapter 13 of the Bankruptcy Code. An order for relief has been entered.

This notice has important information about the case for creditors, debtors, and trustees, including information about the meeting of creditors and deadlines. Read both pages carefully.

The filing of the case imposed an automatic stay against most collection activities. This means that creditors generally may not take action to collect debts from the debtors, the debtors' property, and certain codebtors. For example, while the stay is in effect, creditors cannot sue, garnish wages, assert a deficiency, repossess property, or otherwise try to collect from the debtors. Creditors cannot demand repayment from debtors by mail, phone, or otherwise. Creditors who violate the stay can be required to pay actual and punitive damages and attorney's fees. Under certain circumstances, the stay may be limited to 30 days or not exist at all, although debtors can ask the court to extend or impose a stay.

Confirmation of a chapter 13 plan may result in a discharge. Creditors who assert that the debtors are not entitled to a discharge under 11 U.S.C. § 1328(f) must file a motion objecting to discharge in the bankruptcy clerk's office within the deadline specified in this notice. Creditors who want to have their debt excepted from discharge may be required to file a complaint in the bankruptcy clerk's office by the same deadline. (See line 13 below for more information.)

To protect your rights, consult an attorney. All documents filed in the case may be inspected at the bankruptcy clerk's office at the address listed below or through PACER (Public Access to Court Electronic Records at https://pacer.uscourts.gov).

The staff of the bankruptcy clerk's office cannot give legal advice.

To help creditors correctly identify debtors, debtors submit full Social Security or Individual Taxpayer Identification Numbers, which may appear on a version of this notice. However, the full numbers must not appear on any document filed with the court.

Do not file this notice with any proof of claim or other filing in the case. Do not include more than the last four digits of a Social Security or Individual Taxpayer Identification Number in any document, including attachments, that you file with the court.

	About Debtor 1:	About Debtor 2:
1. **Debtor's full name**		
2. **All other names used in the last 8 years**		
3. **Address**		If Debtor 2 lives at a different address:
4. **Debtor's attorney** Name and address		Contact phone _____ Email _____
5. **Bankruptcy trustee** Name and address		Contact phone _____ Email _____
6. **Bankruptcy clerk's office** Documents in this case may be filed at this address. You may inspect all records filed in this case at this office or online at https://pacer.uscourts.gov.		Hours open _____ Contact phone _____

For more information, see page 2 ▶

Debtor _____	Case number (if known)_____
Name	

7. Meeting of creditors Debtors must attend the meeting to be questioned under oath. In a joint case, both spouses must attend. Creditors may attend, but are not required to do so.	_____ at _____ Date Time The meeting may be continued or adjourned to a later date. If so, the date will be on the court docket.	Location:

8. Deadlines
The bankruptcy clerk's office must receive these documents and any required filing fee by the following deadlines.
	Deadline to file a complaint to challenge dischargeability of certain debts:
	You must file:
	    a motion if you assert that the debtors are not entitled to receive a discharge under U.S.C. § 1328(f), or
	    a complaint if you want to have a particular debt excepted from discharge under 11 U.S.C. § 523(a)(2) or (4).
		Filing deadline: _____

	Deadline for all creditors to file a proof of claim (except governmental units):	Filing deadline: _____
	Deadline for governmental units to file a proof of claim:	Filing deadline: _____
	Deadlines for filing proof of claim: A proof of claim is a signed statement describing a creditor's claim. A proof of claim form may be obtained at www.uscourts.gov or any bankruptcy clerk's office. If you do not file a proof of claim by the deadline, you might not be paid on your claim. To be paid, you must file a proof of claim even if your claim is listed in the schedules that the debtor filed. Secured creditors retain rights in their collateral regardless of whether they file a proof of claim. Filing a proof of claim submits the creditor to the jurisdiction of the bankruptcy court, with consequences a lawyer can explain. For example, a secured creditor who files a proof of claim may surrender important nonmonetary rights, including the right to a jury trial.	
	Deadline to object to exemptions: The law permits debtors to keep certain property as exempt. If you believe that the law does not authorize an exemption claimed, you may file an objection.	Filing deadline: 30 days after the *conclusion* of the meeting of creditors
9. Filing of plan	[The debtor has filed a plan, which is attached. The hearing on confirmation will be held on: _____ at _____ Location:_____ Date Time] Or [The debtor has filed a plan. The plan and notice of confirmation hearing will be sent separately.] Or [The debtor has not filed a plan as of this date. A copy of the plan and a notice of the hearing on confirmation will be sent separately.]	
10. Creditors with a foreign address	If you are a creditor receiving a notice mailed to a foreign address, you may file a motion asking the court to extend the deadline in this notice. Consult an attorney familiar with United States bankruptcy law if you have any questions about your rights in this case.	
11. Filing a chapter 13 bankruptcy case	Chapter 13 allows an individual with regular income and debts below a specified amount to adjust debts according to a plan. A plan is not effective unless the court confirms it. You may object to confirmation of the plan and appear at the confirmation hearing. A copy of the plan [is included with this notice] or [will be sent to you later], and [the confirmation hearing will be held on the date shown in line 9 of this notice] or [the court will send you a notice of the confirmation hearing]. The debtor will remain in possession of the property and may continue to operate the business, if any, unless the court orders otherwise.	
12. Exempt property	The law allows debtors to keep certain property as exempt. Fully exempt property will not be sold and distributed to creditors, even if the case is converted to chapter 7. Debtors must file a list of property claimed as exempt. You may inspect that list at the bankruptcy clerk's office or online at https://pacer.uscourts.gov. If you believe that the law does not authorize an exemption that debtors claimed, you may file an objection by the deadline.	
13. Discharge of debts	Confirmation of a chapter 13 plan may result in a discharge of debts, which may include all or part of a debt. However, unless the court orders otherwise, the debts will not be discharged until all payments under the plan are made. A discharge means that creditors may never try to collect the debt from the debtors personally except as provided in the plan. If you want to have a particular debt excepted from discharge under 11 U.S.C. § 523(a)(2) or (4), you must file a complaint and pay the filing fee in the bankruptcy clerk's office by the deadline. If you believe that the debtors are not entitled to a discharge of any of their debts under 11 U.S.C. § 1328(f), you must file a motion by the deadline.	

Official Form 309I   Notice of Chapter 13 Bankruptcy Case   page 2

Official Form 313 (12/15)

[Caption as in 416A]

Order Approving Disclosure Statement and Fixing Time for Filing Acceptances or Rejections of Plan, Combined with Notice Thereof

A disclosure statement under chapter 11 of the Bankruptcy Code having been filed by
_____ on _____ [if
appropriate, and by _____, on _____], referring to a plan under
chapter 11 of the Code filed by _____, on _____ [if appropriate, and by
_____, on _____ respectively] [if appropriate, as modified by a
modification filed on _____]; and

It having been determined after hearing on notice that the disclosure statement [or statements] contain[s] adequate information:

IT IS ORDERED, and notice is hereby given, that:

A. The disclosure statement filed by _____ dated _____ [if appropriate,
    and by _____, dated _____] is [are] approved.

B. _____ is fixed as the last day for filing written acceptances or rejections of the
    plan [or plans] referred to above.

C. Within _____ days after the entry of this order, the plan [or plans] or a summary or summaries
    thereof approved by the court, [and [if appropriate] a summary approved by the court of its opinion, if
    any, dated _____, approving the disclosure statement [or statements]], the disclosure statement
    [or statements], and a ballot conforming to Ballot for Accepting or Rejecting Plan of Reorganization
    (Official Form 314) shall be mailed to creditors, equity security holders, and other parties in interest,
    and shall be transmitted to the United States trustee, as provided in Fed. R. Bankr. P. 3017(d).

D. If acceptances are filed for more than one plan, preferences among the plans so accepted may be
    indicated.

E. [If appropriate] _____ is fixed for the hearing on confirmation of the plan [or plans].

F. [If appropriate] _____ is fixed as the last day for filing and serving pursuant to Fed. R.
    Bankr. P. 3020(b)(1) written objections to confirmation of the plan.

_____   **By the court:** _____
MM / DD / YYYY   United States Bankruptcy Judge

[If the court directs that a copy of the opinion should be transmitted in lieu of or in addition to the summary thereof,
the appropriate change should be made in paragraph C of this order.]

Official Form 314 (02/20)

[Caption as in 416A]

Class [   ] Ballot for Accepting or Rejecting Plan of Reorganization

[Proponent] filed a plan of reorganization dated [Date] (the Plan) for the Debtor in this case. {The Court has [conditionally] approved a disclosure statement with respect to the Plan (the Disclosure Statement). The Disclosure Statement provides information to assist you in deciding how to vote your ballot. If you do not have a Disclosure Statement, you may obtain a copy from [name, address, telephone number and telecopy number of proponent/proponent's attorney.]}

{Court approval of the Disclosure Statement does not indicate approval of the Plan by the Court.}

You should review {the Disclosure Statement and} the Plan before you vote. You may wish to seek legal advice concerning the Plan and your classification and treatment under the Plan. Your [claim] [equity interest] has been placed in class [ ] under the Plan. If you hold claims or equity interests in more than one class, you will receive a ballot for each class in which you are entitled to vote.

If your ballot is not received by [name and address of proponent's attorney or other appropriate address] on or before [date], and such deadline is not extended, your vote will not count as either an acceptance or rejection of the Plan.

If the Plan is confirmed by the Bankruptcy Court, it will be binding on you whether or not you vote.

Acceptance or Rejection of the Plan

[At this point the ballot should provide for voting by the particular class of creditors or equity holders receiving the ballot using one of the following alternatives:]

[If the voter is the holder of a secured, priority, or unsecured nonpriority claim:]

The undersigned, the holder of a Class [ ] claim against the Debtor in the unpaid amount of Dollars ($)

[or, if the voter is the holder of a bond, debenture, or other debt security:]

The undersigned, the holder of a Class [ ] claim against the Debtor, consisting of Dollars ($) principal amount of [describe bond, debenture, or other debt security] of the Debtor (For purposes of this Ballot, it is not necessary and you should not adjust the principal amount for any accrued or unmatured interest.)

[or, if the voter is the holder of an equity interest:]

The undersigned, the holder of Class [ ] equity interest in the Debtor, consisting of _____ shares or other interests of [describe equity interest] in the Debtor

SELECTED OFFICIAL FORMS

[In each case, the following language should be included:]

Check one box only

❑   **Accepts the plan**

❑   **Rejects the plan**

Dated: _____

Print or type name: _____

Signature: _____ Title (if corporation or partnership) _____

Address: _____
                    _____
                    _____

Return this ballot to:

[Name and address of proponent's attorney or other appropriate address]

SELECTED OFFICIAL FORMS

2020 COMMITTEE NOTE

The form is amended in response to the enactment of the Small Business Reorganization Act of 2019, Pub. L. No. 116-54, 133 Stat. 1079. That law gives a small business debtor the option of electing to be a debtor under subchapter V of chapter 11. The first three paragraphs of the form are amended to place braces around all references to a disclosure statement. Section 1125 of the Code does not apply to subchapter V cases unless the court for cause orders otherwise. See Code § 1181(b). Thus, in most chapter V cases there will not be a disclosure statement, and the language in braces on the form should not be included on the ballot.

Official Form 315 (02/20)

[Caption as in 416A]

Order Confirming Plan

The plan under chapter 11 of the Bankruptcy Code filed by _____, on _____ [*if applicable*, as modified by a modification filed on _____,] or a summary thereof, having been transmitted to creditors and equity security holders; and

It having been determined after hearing on notice that the requirements for confirmation set forth in 11 U.S.C. § 1129(a) [or, if appropriate, 11 U.S.C. § 1129(b), 1191(a), or 1191(b)] have been satisfied;

IT IS ORDERED that:

The plan filed by _____, on _____,

[*If appropriate*, include dates and any other pertinent details of modifications to the plan] is confirmed. [*If the plan provides for an injunction against conduct not otherwise enjoined under the Code, include the information required by Rule 3020.*]

A copy of the confirmed plan is attached.

_____
MM / DD / YYYY

By the court: _____
United States Bankruptcy Judge

SELECTED OFFICIAL FORMS

2020 COMMITTEE NOTE

The form is amended in response to the enactment of the Small Business Reorganization Act of 2019, Pub. L. No. 116-54, 133 Stat. 1079. That law gives a small business debtor the option of electing to be a debtor under subchapter V of chapter 11. Citations to the statutory provisions governing confirmation in such cases are added to the form for the court to include as appropriate.

Information to identify the case:		
Debtor 1 _____ First Name Middle Name Last Name	Last 4 digits of Social Security number or ITIN _ _ _ _ EIN _ _ - _ _ _ _ _ _ _	
Debtor 2 _____ (Spouse, if filing) First Name Middle Name Last Name	Last 4 digits of Social Security number or ITIN _ _ _ _ EIN _ _ - _ _ _ _ _ _ _	
United States Bankruptcy Court for the: _____ District of _____ (State)		
Case number: _____		

Order of Discharge   12/15

IT IS ORDERED: A discharge under 11 U.S.C. § 727 is granted to:

_____   [_____]

[include all names used by each debtor, including trade names, within the 8 years prior to the filing of the petition]

_____   **By the court:** _____
MM / DD / YYYY   United States Bankruptcy Judge

Explanation of Bankruptcy Discharge in a Chapter 7 Case

This order does not close or dismiss the case, and it does not determine how much money, if any, the trustee will pay creditors.

Creditors cannot collect discharged debts

This order means that no one may make any attempt to collect a discharged debt from the debtors personally. For example, creditors cannot sue, garnish wages, assert a deficiency, or otherwise try to collect from the debtors personally on discharged debts. Creditors cannot contact the debtors by mail, phone, or otherwise in any attempt to collect the debt personally. Creditors who violate this order can be required to pay debtors damages and attorney's fees.

However, a creditor with a lien may enforce a claim against the debtors' property subject to that lien unless the lien was avoided or eliminated. For example, a creditor may have the right to foreclose a home mortgage or repossess an automobile.

This order does not prevent debtors from paying any debt voluntarily or from paying reaffirmed debts according to the reaffirmation agreement. 11 U.S.C. § 524(c), (f).

Most debts are discharged

Most debts are covered by the discharge, but not all. Generally, a discharge removes the debtors' personal liability for debts owed before the debtors' bankruptcy case was filed.

Also, if this case began under a different chapter of the Bankruptcy Code and was later converted to chapter 7, debts owed before the conversion are discharged.

In a case involving community property: Special rules protect certain community property owned by the debtor's spouse, even if that spouse did not file a bankruptcy case.

For more information, see page 2 ▶

Official Form 318   Order of Discharge   page 1

Some debts are not discharged

Examples of debts that are not discharged are:

debts that are domestic support obligations;

debts for most student loans;

debts for most taxes;

debts that the bankruptcy court has decided or will decide are not discharged in this bankruptcy case;

debts for most fines, penalties, forfeitures, or criminal restitution obligations;

some debts which the debtors did not properly list;

debts for certain types of loans owed to pension, profit sharing, stock bonus, or retirement plans; and

debts for death or personal injury caused by operating a vehicle while intoxicated.

Also, debts covered by a valid reaffirmation agreement are not discharged.

In addition, this discharge does not stop creditors from collecting from anyone else who is also liable on the debt, such as an insurance company or a person who cosigned or guaranteed a loan.

> **This information is only a general summary of the bankruptcy discharge; some exceptions exist. Because the law is complicated, you should consult an attorney to determine the exact effect of the discharge in this case.**

Fill in this information to identify the case:

Debtor 1 _____

Debtor 2 _____
(Spouse, if filing)

United States Bankruptcy Court for the: _____ District of _____

Case number _____

Official Form 410

Proof of Claim

04/22

Read the instructions before filling out this form. This form is for making a claim for payment in a bankruptcy case. Do not use this form to make a request for payment of an administrative expense. Make such a request according to 11 U.S.C. § 503.

Filers must leave out or redact information that is entitled to privacy on this form or on any attached documents. Attach redacted copies of any documents that support the claim, such as promissory notes, purchase orders, invoices, itemized statements of running accounts, contracts, judgments, mortgages, and security agreements. **Do not send original documents;** they may be destroyed after scanning. If the documents are not available, explain in an attachment.

A person who files a fraudulent claim could be fined up to $500,000, imprisoned for up to 5 years, or both. 18 U.S.C. §§ 152, 157, and 3571.

Fill in all the information about the claim as of the date the case was filed. That date is on the notice of bankruptcy (Form 309) that you received.

Part 1:	Identify the Claim

1. Who is the current creditor?

Name of the current creditor (the person or entity to be paid for this claim) _____

Other names the creditor used with the debtor _____

2. Has this claim been acquired from someone else?

☐ No
☐ Yes. From whom? _____

3. Where should notices and payments to the creditor be sent?

Federal Rule of Bankruptcy Procedure (FRBP) 2002(g)

Where should notices to the creditor be sent?

Name _____

Number   Street

City   State   ZIP Code

Contact phone _____

Contact email _____

Where should payments to the creditor be sent? (if different)

Name _____

Number   Street

City   State   ZIP Code

Contact phone _____

Contact email _____

Uniform claim identifier for electronic payments in chapter 13 (if you use one):

_ _

4. Does this claim amend one already filed?

☐ No
☐ Yes. Claim number on court claims registry (if known) _____   Filed on _____
                                                                                        MM / DD / YYYY

5. Do you know if anyone else has filed a proof of claim for this claim?

☐ No
☐ Yes. Who made the earlier filing? _____

Official Form 410   Proof of Claim   page 1

658

Part 2:	Give Information About the Claim as of the Date the Case Was Filed

6. Do you have any number you use to identify the debtor?

❑ No

❑ Yes. Last 4 digits of the debtor's account or any number you use to identify the debtor: ___ ___ ___ ___

7. How much is the claim?

$_____ . **Does this amount include interest or other charges?**

❑ No

❑ Yes. Attach statement itemizing interest, fees, expenses, or other charges required by Bankruptcy Rule 3001(c)(2)(A).

8. What is the basis of the claim?

Examples: Goods sold, money loaned, lease, services performed, personal injury or wrongful death, or credit card.

Attach redacted copies of any documents supporting the claim required by Bankruptcy Rule 3001(c).

Limit disclosing information that is entitled to privacy, such as health care information.

_____

9. Is all or part of the claim secured?

❑ No

❑ Yes. The claim is secured by a lien on property.

Nature of property:

❑ Real estate. If the claim is secured by the debtor's principal residence, file a *Mortgage Proof of Claim Attachment* (Official Form 410-A) with this *Proof of Claim*.

❑ Motor vehicle

❑ Other. Describe: _____

Basis for perfection: _____

Attach redacted copies of documents, if any, that show evidence of perfection of a security interest (for example, a mortgage, lien, certificate of title, financing statement, or other document that shows the lien has been filed or recorded.)

Value of property: $_____

Amount of the claim that is secured: $_____

Amount of the claim that is unsecured: $_____ (The sum of the secured and unsecured amounts should match the amount in line 7.)

Amount necessary to cure any default as of the date of the petition: $_____

Annual Interest Rate (when case was filed)_____%

❑ Fixed

❑ Variable

10. Is this claim based on a lease?

❑ No

❑ Yes. Amount necessary to cure any default as of the date of the petition. $_____

11. Is this claim subject to a right of setoff?

❑ No

❑ Yes. Identify the property: _____

12. Is all or part of the claim entitled to priority under 11 U.S.C. § 507(a)?	❏ No	
	❏ Yes. *Check one:*	**Amount entitled to priority**
A claim may be partly priority and partly nonpriority. For example, in some categories, the law limits the amount entitled to priority.	❏ Domestic support obligations (including alimony and child support) under 11 U.S.C. § 507(a)(1)(A) or (a)(1)(B).	$_____
	❏ Up to $3,350* of deposits toward purchase, lease, or rental of property or services for personal, family, or household use. 11 U.S.C. § 507(a)(7).	$_____
	❏ Wages, salaries, or commissions (up to $15,150*) earned within 180 days before the bankruptcy petition is filed or the debtor's business ends, whichever is earlier. 11 U.S.C. § 507(a)(4).	$_____
	❏ Taxes or penalties owed to governmental units. 11 U.S.C. § 507(a)(8).	$_____
	❏ Contributions to an employee benefit plan. 11 U.S.C. § 507(a)(5).	$_____
	❏ Other. Specify subsection of 11 U.S.C. § 507(a)(___) that applies.	$_____
	* Amounts are subject to adjustment on 4/01/25 and every 3 years after that for cases begun on or after the date of adjustment.	

Part 3: Sign Below

The person completing this proof of claim must sign and date it. FRBP 9011(b).

If you file this claim electronically, FRBP 5005(a)(2) authorizes courts to establish local rules specifying what a signature is.

A person who files a fraudulent claim could be fined up to $500,000, imprisoned for up to 5 years, or both. 18 U.S.C. §§ 152, 157, and 3571.

Check the appropriate box:

❏ I am the creditor.

❏ I am the creditor's attorney or authorized agent.

❏ I am the trustee, or the debtor, or their authorized agent. Bankruptcy Rule 3004.

❏ I am a guarantor, surety, endorser, or other codebtor. Bankruptcy Rule 3005.

I understand that an authorized signature on this *Proof of Claim* serves as an acknowledgment that when calculating the amount of the claim, the creditor gave the debtor credit for any payments received toward the debt.

I have examined the information in this *Proof of Claim* and have a reasonable belief that the information is true and correct.

I declare under penalty of perjury that the foregoing is true and correct.

Executed on date _____
MM / DD / YYYY

_____
Signature

Print the name of the person who is completing and signing this claim:

Name	_____	_____	_____
	First name	Middle name	Last name
Title	_____		
Company	_____		
	Identify the corporate servicer as the company if the authorized agent is a servicer.		
Address	_____		
	Number Street		
	City	State ZIP Code	
Contact phone	_____	Email _____	

Print	Save As...	Add Attachment		Reset

Mortgage Proof of Claim Attachment

(12/15)

If you file a claim secured by a security interest in the debtor's principal residence, you must use this form as an attachment to your proof of claim. See separate instructions.

Part 1: Mortgage and Case Information

Case number:

Debtor 1:

Debtor 2:

Last 4 digits to identify:

Creditor:

Servicer:

Fixed accrual/daily simple interest/other:

Part 2: Total Debt Calculation

Principal balance:

Interest due:

Fees, costs due:

Escrow deficiency for funds advanced:

Less total funds on hand:

Total debt:

Part 3: Arrearage as of Date of the Petition

Principal & interest due:

Prepetition fees due:

Escrow deficiency for funds advanced:

Projected escrow shortage:

Less funds on hand:

Total prepetition arrearage:

Part 4: Monthly Mortgage Payment

Principal & interest:

Monthly escrow:

Private mortgage insurance:

Total monthly payment:

Part 5: Loan Payment History from First Date of Default

	Account Activity						How Funds Were Applied/Amount Incurred					Balance After Amount Received or Incurred				
A. Date	B. Contractual payment amount	C. Funds received	D. Amount incurred	E. Description	F. Contractual due date	G. Prin, int & esc past due balance	H. Amount to principal	I. Amount to interest	J. Amount to escrow	K. Amount to fees or charges	L. Unapplied funds	M. Principal balance	N. Accrued interest balance	O. Escrow balance	P. Fees / Charges balance	Q. Unapplied funds balance

Official Form 410A   Mortgage Proof of Claim Attachment   page 1 of ___

Mortgage Proof of Claim Attachment: Additional Page (12/15)

Case number: _____

Debtor 1: _____

Part 5: Loan Payment History from First Date of Default

	Account Activity						How Funds Were Applied/Amount Incurred					Balance After Amount Received or Incurred				
A. Date	B. Contractual payment amount	C. Funds received	D. Amount incurred	E. Description	F. Contractual due date	G. Prin, int & esc past due balance	H. Amount to principal	I. Amount to interest	J. Amount to escrow	K. Amount to fees or charges	L. Unapplied funds	M. Principal balance	N. Accrued interest balance	O. Escrow balance	P. Fees / Charges balance	Q. Unapplied funds balance

Official Form 410A   Mortgage Proof of Claim Attachment   page ___ of ___

Fill in this information to identify the case:

Debtor 1 _____
　　　　First Name　　　　　Middle Name　　　　　Last Name

Debtor 2 _____
(Spouse, if filing) First Name　　Middle Name　　　Last Name

United States Bankruptcy Court for the: _____ District of _____

Case number _____
(If known)

Official Form 423

Certification About a Financial Management Course

12/15

If you are an individual, you must take an approved course about personal financial management if:

- you filed for bankruptcy under chapter 7 or 13, or
- you filed for bankruptcy under chapter 11 and § 1141 (d)(3) applies.

In a joint case, each debtor must take the course. 11 U.S.C. §§ 727(a)(11) and 1328(g).

After you finish the course, the provider will give you a certificate. The provider may notify the court that you have completed the course. If the provider does notify the court, you need not file this form. If the provider does not notify the court, then Debtor 1 and Debtor 2 must each file this form with the certificate number before your debts will be discharged.

- If you filed under chapter 7 and you need to file this form, file it within 60 days after the first date set for the meeting of creditors under § 341 of the Bankruptcy Code.

- If you filed under chapter 11 or 13 and you need to file this form, file it before you make the last payment that your plan requires or before you file a motion for a discharge under § 1141(d)(5)(B) or § 1328(b) of the Bankruptcy Code. Fed. R. Bankr. P. 1007(c).

In some cases, the court can waive the requirement to take the financial management course. To have the requirement waived, you must file a motion with the court and obtain a court order.

Part 1: Tell the Court About the Required Course

You must check one:

❑ I completed an approved course in personal financial management:

Date I took the course _____
　　　　　　　　　　　　MM / DD / YYYY

Name of approved provider _____

Certificate number _____

❑ I am not required to complete a course in personal financial management because the court has granted my motion for a waiver of the requirement based on *(check one):*

　❑ Incapacity. I have a mental illness or a mental deficiency that makes me incapable of realizing or making rational decisions about finances.

　❑ Disability. My physical disability causes me to be unable to complete a course in personal financial management in person, by phone, or through the internet, even after I reasonably tried to do so.

　❑ Active duty. I am currently on active military duty in a military combat zone.

　❑ Residence. I live in a district in which the United States trustee (or bankruptcy administrator) has determined that the approved instructional courses cannot adequately meet my needs.

Part 2: Sign Here

I certify that the information I have provided is true and correct.

_____　　_____　　Date _____
Signature of debtor named on certificate　　Printed name of debtor　　　　　　　　MM / DD / YYYY

Official Form 423　　　　　Certification About a Financial Management Course

| Print | Save As... | | Reset |

Fill in this information to identify the case:

Debtor Name _____

United States Bankruptcy Court for the:_____ District of _____
(State)

Case number: _____

❑ Check if this is an amended filing

Official Form 425A

Plan of Reorganization for Small Business Under Chapter 11   02/20

[Name of Proponent_____]'s Plan of Reorganization, Dated [Insert Date]

[If this plan is for a small business debtor under Subchapter V, 11 U.S.C. § 1190 requires that it include "(A) a brief history of the business operations of the debtor; (B) a liquidation analysis; and (C) projections with respect to the ability of the debtor to make payments under the proposed plan of reorganization." The Background section below may be used for that purpose. Otherwise, the Background section can be deleted from the form, and the Plan can start with "Article 1: Summary"]

Background for Cases Filed Under Subchapter V

A. Description and History of the Debtor's Business

The Debtor is a [corporation, partnership, etc.]. Since [insert year operations commenced], the Debtor has been in the business of _____. [Describe the Debtor's business].

B. Liquidation Analysis

To confirm the Plan, the Court must find that all creditors and equity interest holders who do not accept the Plan will receive at least as much under the Plan as such claim and equity interest holders would receive in a chapter 7 liquidation. A liquidation analysis is attached to the Plan as Exhibit____.

C. Ability to make future plan payments and operate without further reorganization

The Plan Proponent must also show that it will have enough cash over the life of the Plan to make the required Plan payments and operate the debtor's business.

The Plan Proponent has provided projected financial information as Exhibit ____.

The Plan Proponent's financial projections show that the Debtor will have projected disposable income (as defined by § 1191(d) of the Bankruptcy Code) for the period described in § 1191(c)(2) of $ _____.

The final Plan payment is expected to be paid on _____.

[Summarize the numerical projections, and highlight any assumptions that are not in accord with past experience. Explain why such assumptions should now be made.]
You should consult with your accountant or other financial advisor if you have any questions pertaining to these projections.

Debtor Name _____   Case number_____

This Plan of Reorganization (the *Plan*) under chapter 11 of the Bankruptcy Code (the *Code*) proposes to pay creditors of [insert the name of the Debtor] (the *Debtor*) from [Specify sources of payment, such as an infusion of capital, loan proceeds, sale of assets, cash flow from operations, or future income].

This Plan provides for: ☐ classes of priority claims;
☐ classes of secured claims;
☐ classes of non-priority unsecured clams; and
☐ classes of equity security holders.

Non-priority unsecured creditors holding allowed claims will receive distributions, which the proponent of this Plan has valued at approximately ☐ cents on the dollar. This Plan also provides for the payment of administrative and priority claims.

All creditors and equity security holders should refer to Articles 3 through 6 of this Plan for information regarding the precise treatment of their claim. A disclosure statement that provides more detailed information regarding this Plan and the rights of creditors and equity security holders has been circulated with this Plan. **Your rights may be affected. You should read these papers carefully and discuss them with your attorney, if you have one. (If you do not have an attorney, you may wish to consult one.)**

2.01 **Class 1** .... All allowed claims entitled to priority under § 507(a) of the Code (except administrative expense claims under § 507(a)(2), ["gap" period claims in an involuntary case under § 507(a)(3),] and priority tax claims under § 507(a)(8)).

[Add classes of priority claims, if applicable]

2.02 **Class 2** .... The claim of [_____], to the extent allowed as a secured claim under § 506 of the Code.

[Add other classes of secured creditors, if any. *Note:* Section 1129(a)(9)(D) of the Code provides that a secured tax claim which would otherwise meet the description of a priority tax claim under § 507(a)(8) of the Code is to be paid in the same manner and over the same period as prescribed in § 507(a)(8).]

2.03 **Class 3** .... All non-priority unsecured claims allowed under § 502 of the Code.

[Add other classes of unsecured claims, if any.]

2.04 **Class 4** .... Equity interests of the Debtor. [If the Debtor is an individual, change this heading to *The interests of the individual Debtor in property of the estate.*]

3.01 **Unclassified claims** Under section § 1123(a)(1), administrative expense claims, ["gap" period claims in an involuntary case allowed under § 502(f) of the Code,] and priority tax claims are not in classes.

3.02 **Administrative expense claims** Each holder of an administrative expense claim allowed under § 503 of the Code, [and a "gap" claim in an involuntary case allowed under § 502(f) of the Code,] will be paid in full on the effective date of this Plan, in cash, or upon such other terms as may be agreed upon by the holder of the claim and the Debtor.

Or

Each holder of an administrative expense claim allowed under § 503 of the Code, [and a "gap" claim in an involuntary case allowed under § 502(f) of the Code,] will be paid [specify terms of treatment, including the form, amount, and timing of distribution, consistent with section 1191(e) of the

Debtor Name _____   Case number_____

Code].

[Note: the second provision is appropriate only in a subchapter V plan that is confirmed non-consensually under section 1191(b).]

3.03	**Priority tax claims**	Each holder of a priority tax claim will be paid [Specify terms of treatment consistent with § 1129(a)(9)(C) of the Code].
3.04	**Statutory fees**	All fees required to be paid under 28 U.S.C. § 1930 that are owed on or before the effective date of this Plan have been paid or will be paid on the effective date.
3.05	**Prospective quarterly fees**	All quarterly fees required to be paid under 28 U.S.C. § 1930(a)(6) or (a)(7) will accrue and be timely paid until the case is closed, dismissed, or converted to another chapter of the Code.

Article 4: Treatment of Claims and Interests Under the Plan

4.01   Claims and interests shall be treated as follows under this Plan:

Class	Impairment	Treatment
Class 1 - Priority claims excluding those in Article 3	☐ Impaired ☐ Unimpaired	[Insert treatment of priority claims in this Class, including the form, amount and timing of distribution, if any. For example: "Class 1 is unimpaired by this Plan, and each holder of a Class 1 Priority Claim will be paid in full, in cash, upon the later of the effective date of this Plan, or the date on which such claim is allowed by a final non-appealable order. Except: [____]."] [Add classes of priority claims if applicable]
Class 2 – Secured claim of [Insert name of secured creditor.]	☐ Impaired ☐ Unimpaired	[Insert treatment of secured claim in this Class, including the form, amount and timing of distribution, if any.] [Add classes of secured claims if applicable]
Class 3 – Non-priority unsecured creditors	☐ Impaired ☐ Unimpaired	[Insert treatment of unsecured creditors in this Class, including the form, amount and timing of distribution, if any.] [Add administrative convenience class if applicable]
Class 4 - Equity security holders of the Debtor	☐ Impaired ☐ Unimpaired	[Insert treatment of equity security holders in this Class, including the form, amount and timing of distribution, if any.]

Article 5: Allowance and Disallowance of Claims

5.01	**Disputed claim**	A *disputed claim* is a claim that has not been allowed or disallowed [by a final non-appealable order], and as to which either:

(i)   a proof of claim has been filed or deemed filed, and the Debtor or another party in interest has filed an objection; or

(ii)   no proof of claim has been filed, and the Debtor has scheduled such claim as disputed, contingent, or unliquidated.

5.02	**Delay of distribution on a disputed claim**	No distribution will be made on account of a disputed claim unless such claim is allowed [by a final non-appealable order].
5.03	**Settlement of disputed claims**	The Debtor will have the power and authority to settle and compromise a disputed claim with court approval and compliance with Rule 9019 of the Federal Rules of Bankruptcy Procedure.

Article 6: Provisions for Executory Contracts and Unexpired Leases

Debtor Name _____   Case number_____

| 6.01 | **Assumed executory contracts and unexpired leases** | (a) | The Debtor assumes, and if applicable assigns, the following executory contracts and unexpired leases as of the effective date: |

[List assumed, or if applicable assigned, executory contracts and unexpired leases.]

(b) Except for executory contracts and unexpired leases that have been assumed, and if applicable assigned, before the effective date or under section 6.01(a) of this Plan, or that are the subject of a pending motion to assume, and if applicable assign, the Debtor will be conclusively deemed to have rejected all executory contracts and unexpired leases as of the effective date.

A proof of a claim arising from the rejection of an executory contract or unexpired lease under this section must be filed no later than [   ] days after the date of the order confirming this Plan.

Article 7: Means for Implementation of the Plan

[Insert here provisions regarding how the plan will be implemented as required under § 1123(a)(5) of the Code. For example, provisions may include those that set out how the plan will be funded, including any claims reserve to be established in connection with the plan, as well as who will be serving as directors, officers or voting trustees of the reorganized Debtor.]

Article 8: General Provisions

| 8.01 | **Definitions and rules of construction** | The definitions and rules of construction set forth in §§ 101 and 102 of the Code shall apply when terms defined or construed in the Code are used in this Plan, and they are supplemented by the following definitions: |

[Insert additional definitions if necessary].

| 8.02 | **Effective date** | The effective date of this Plan is the first business day following the date that is 14 days after the entry of the confirmation order. If, however, a stay of the confirmation order is in effect on that date, the effective date will be the first business day after the date on which the stay expires or is otherwise terminated. |

| 8.03 | **Severability** | If any provision in this Plan is determined to be unenforceable, the determination will in no way limit or affect the enforceability and operative effect of any other provision of this Plan. |

| 8.04 | **Binding effect** | The rights and obligations of any entity named or referred to in this Plan will be binding upon, and will inure to the benefit of the successors or assigns of such entity. |

| 8.05 | **Captions** | The headings contained in this Plan are for convenience of reference only and do not affect the meaning or interpretation of this Plan. |

| [8.06 | **Controlling effect** | Unless a rule of law or procedure is supplied by federal law (including the Code or the Federal Rules of Bankruptcy Procedure), the laws of the State of [   ] govern this Plan and any agreements, documents, and instruments executed in connection with this Plan, except as otherwise provided in this Plan.] |

| [8.07 | **Corporate governance** | [If the Debtor is a corporation include provisions required by § 1123(a)(6) of the Code.] |

Debtor Name _____   Case number _____

Language addressing the extent and the scope of the bankruptcy court's jurisdiction after the effective date of the plan.]

Article 9: Discharge

[Include the appropriate provision in the Plan]

[No Discharge -- Section 1141(d)(3) IS applicable.]

In accordance with § 1141(d)(3) of the Code, the Debtor will not receive any discharge of debt in this bankruptcy case.

[Discharge -- Section 1141(d)(3) IS NOT applicable; use one of the alternatives below]

*[The following 3 alternatives apply to cases in which a discharge is applicable and the Debtor **DID NOT** elect to proceed under Subchapter V of Chapter 11.]*

[Discharge if the Debtor is an individual and did not proceed under Subchapter V]

Confirmation of this Plan does not discharge any debt provided for in this Plan until the court grants a discharge on completion of all payments under this Plan, or as otherwise provided in § 1141(d)(5) of the Code. The Debtor will not be discharged from any debt excepted from discharge under § 523 of the Code, except as provided in Rule 4007(c) of the Federal Rules of Bankruptcy Procedure.

[Discharge if the Debtor is a partnership and did not proceed under Subchapter V]

On the effective date of this Plan, the Debtor will be discharged from any debt that arose before confirmation of this Plan, to the extent specified in § 1141(d)(1)(A) of the Code. The Debtor will not be discharged from any debt imposed by this Plan.

[Discharge if the Debtor is a corporation and did not proceed under Subchapter V]

On the effective date of this Plan, the Debtor will be discharged from any debt that arose before confirmation of this Plan, to the extent specified in § 1141(d)(1)(A) of the Code, except that the Debtor will not be discharged of any debt:
    (i) imposed by this Plan; or
    (ii) to the extent provided in § 1141(d)(6).

*[The following 3 alternatives apply to cases in which the Debtor **DID** elect to proceed under Subchapter V of Chapter 11.]*

[Discharge if the Debtor is an individual under Subchapter V]

If the Debtor's Plan is confirmed under § 1191(a), on the effective date of the Plan, the Debtor will be discharged from any debt that arose before confirmation of this Plan, to the extent specified in § 1141(d)(1)(A) of the Code. The Debtor will not be discharged from any debt:
    (i) imposed by this Plan; or
    (ii) excepted from discharge under § 523(a) of the Code, except as provided in Rule 4007(c) of the Federal Rules of Bankruptcy Procedure.

Official Form 425A   Plan of Reorganization for Small Business Under Chapter 11   page **5**

Debtor Name _____   Case number_____

If the Debtor's Plan is confirmed under § 1191(b), confirmation of the Plan does not discharge any debt provided for in this Plan until the court grants a discharge on completion of all payments due within the first 3 years of this Plan, or as otherwise provided in § 1192 of the Code. The Debtor will not be discharged from any debt:

> (i) on which the last payment is due after the first 3 years of the plan, or as otherwise provided in § 1192; or

> (ii) excepted from discharge under § 523(a) of the Code, except as provided in Rule 4007(c) of the Federal Rules of Bankruptcy Procedure.

[Discharge if the Debtor is a partnership under Subchapter V]

If the Debtor's Plan is confirmed under § 1191(a), on the effective date of the Plan, the Debtor will be discharged from any debt that arose before confirmation of this Plan, to the extent specified in § 1141(d)(1)(A) of the Code. The Debtor will not be discharged from any debt imposed by this Plan.

If the Debtor's Plan is confirmed under § 1191(b), confirmation of the Plan does not discharge any debt provided for in this Plan until the court grants a discharge on completion of all payments due within the first 3 years of this Plan, or as otherwise provided in § 1192 of the Code. The Debtor will not be discharged from any debt:

> (i) on which the last payment is due after the first 3 years of the plan, or as otherwise provided in § 1192; or

> (ii) excepted from discharge under § 523(a) of the Code, except as provided in Rule 4007(c) of the Federal Rules of Bankruptcy Procedure.

[Discharge if the Debtor is a corporation under Subchapter V]

If the Debtor's Plan is confirmed under § 1191(a), on the effective date of the Plan, the Debtor will be discharged from any debt that arose before confirmation of this Plan, to the extent specified in § 1141(d)(1)(A) of the Code, except that the Debtor will not be discharged of any debt:

> (i) imposed by this Plan; or

> (ii) to the extent provided in § 1141(d)(6).

If the Debtor's Plan is confirmed under § 1191(b), confirmation of this Plan does not discharge any debt provided for in this Plan until the court grants a discharge on completion of all payments due within the first 3 years of this Plan, or as otherwise provided in § 1192 of the Code. The Debtor will not be discharged from any debt:

> (i) on which the last payment is due after the first 3 years of the plan, or as otherwise provided in § 1192; or

> (ii) excepted from discharge under § 523(a) of the Code, except as provided in Rule 4007(c) of the Federal Rules of Bankruptcy Procedure.

Article 10: Other Provisions

[Insert other provisions, as applicable.]

Respectfully submitted,

Debtor Name _____   Case number_____

✘ _____   _____
[Signature of the Plan Proponent]   [Printed Name]

✘ _____   _____
[Signature of the Attorney for the Plan Proponent]   [Printed Name]

SELECTED OFFICIAL FORMS

2020 COMMITTEE NOTE

The form is amended in response to the enactment of the Small Business Reorganization Act of 2019, Pub. L. No. 116-54, 133 Stat. 1079. That law gives a small business debtor the option of electing to be a debtor under subchapter V of chapter 11. Because there will generally not be a disclosure statement in subchapter V cases, § 1190 of the Code provides that plans in those cases must include a brief history of the debtor's business operations, a liquidation analysis, and projections of the debtor's ability to make payments under the plan. Those provisions are added to a new Background section of the form with an indication that they are to be included in plans only in subchapter V cases.

Article 3.02 is amended to reflect a special rule for the treatment of administrative expense claims in subchapter V plans that are confirmed non-consensually. See § 1191(e).

Article 9 of the form is amended to include descriptions of the effect of a discharge in a case under subchapter V. The plan proponent is directed to include in the plan the particular provision that is appropriate for the case.

Fill in this information to identify the case:

Debtor Name _____

United States Bankruptcy Court for the:_____ District of _____
(State)

Case number: _____

☐ Check if this is an amended filing

Official Form 425B

Disclosure Statement for Small Business Under Chapter 11   12/17

[Name of Proponent   ]'s **Disclosure Statement, Dated** [Insert Date]

Table of Contents. See instructions about how to modify the table of contents if you do not have all of the sections below.

[Insert when text is finalized]

SELECTED OFFICIAL FORMS

Debtor Name _____   Case number_____

Debtor Name _____   Case number_____

I. Introduction

This is the disclosure statement (the *Disclosure Statement*) in the small business chapter 11 case of _____ (the *Debtor*). This Disclosure Statement provides information about the Debtor and the Plan filed on [insert date] (the *Plan*) to help you decide how to vote.

A copy of the Plan is attached as *Exhibit A*. **Your rights may be affected**. You should read the Plan and this Disclosure Statement carefully. You may wish to consult an attorney about your rights and your treatment under the Plan.

The proposed distributions under the Plan are discussed at pages [-] of this Disclosure Statement. [General unsecured creditors are classified in Class [ ] and will receive a distribution of [ ] % of their allowed claims, to be distributed as follows [ ].]

A. Purpose of This Document

This Disclosure Statement describes:

- The Debtor and significant events during the bankruptcy case,

- How the Plan proposes to treat claims or equity interests of the type you hold (*i.e.*, what you will receive on your claim or equity interest if the plan is confirmed),

- Who can vote on or object to the Plan,

- What factors the Bankruptcy Court (the *Court*) will consider when deciding whether to confirm the Plan,

- Why [the proponent] believes the Plan is feasible, and how the treatment of your claim or equity interest under the Plan compares to what you would receive on your claim or equity interest in liquidation, and

- The effect of confirmation of the Plan.

Be sure to read the Plan as well as the Disclosure Statement. This Disclosure Statement describes the Plan, but it is the Plan itself that will, if confirmed, establish your rights.

B. Deadlines for Voting and Objecting; Date of Plan Confirmation Hearing

The Court has not yet confirmed the Plan described in this Disclosure Statement. A separate order has been entered setting the following information:

- Time and place of the hearing to [finally approve this disclosure statement and] confirm the plan,

- Deadline for voting to accept or reject the plan, and

- Deadline for objecting to the [**adequacy of disclosure and**] confirmation of the plan.

If you want additional information about the Plan or the voting procedure, you should contact [insert name and address of representative of plan proponent].

Debtor Name _____   Case number_____

C. Disclaimer

The Court has [conditionally] approved this Disclosure Statement as containing adequate information to enable parties affected by the Plan to make an informed judgment about its terms. The Court has not yet determined whether the Plan meets the legal requirements for confirmation, and the fact that the Court has approved this Disclosure Statement does not constitute an endorsement of the Plan by the Court, or a recommendation that it be accepted.

II. Background

A. Description and History of the Debtor's Business

The Debtor is a [corporation, partnership, etc.]. Since [insert year operations commenced], the Debtor has been in the business of [_____]. [Describe the Debtor's business].

B. Insiders of the Debtor

[Insert a detailed list of the names of Debtor's insiders as defined in § 101(31) of the United States Bankruptcy Code (the Code) and their relationship to the Debtor.

For each insider, list all compensation paid by the Debtor or its affiliates to that person or entity during the 2 years prior to the commencement of the Debtor's bankruptcy case, as well as compensation paid during the pendency of this chapter 11 case.]

C. Management of the Debtor During the Bankruptcy

List the name and position of all current officers, directors, managing members, or other persons in control (collectively the *Management*) who will not have a position post-confirmation that you list in III D 2.

Name	Position

D. Events Leading to Chapter 11 Filing

[Describe the events that led to the commencement of the Debtor's bankruptcy case.]

Debtor Name _____   Case number_____

E. Significant Events During the Bankruptcy Case

[Describe significant events during the Debtor's bankruptcy case:

- Describe any asset sales outside the ordinary course of business, Debtor in Possession financing, or cash collateral orders.

- Identify the professionals approved by the court.

- Describe any adversary proceedings that have been filed or other significant litigation that has occurred (including contested claim disallowance proceedings), and any other significant legal or administrative proceedings that are pending or have been pending during the case in a forum other than the Court.

- Describe any steps taken to improve operations and profitability of the Debtor.

- Describe other events as appropriate.]

F. Projected Recovery of Avoidable Transfers

Check one box.

❑   The Debtor does not intend to pursue preference, fraudulent conveyance, or other avoidance actions.

❑   The Debtor estimates that up to $[   ] may be realized from the recovery of fraudulent, preferential or other avoidable transfers. While the results of litigation cannot be predicted with certainty and it is possible that other causes of action may be identified, the following is a summary of the preference, fraudulent conveyance and other avoidance actions filed or expected to be filed in this case:

Transaction	Defendant	Amount Claimed

❑   The Debtor has not yet completed its investigation with regard to prepetition transactions. If you received a payment or other transfer within 90 days of the bankruptcy, or other transfer avoidable under the Code, the Debtor may seek to avoid such transfer.

G. Claims Objections

Except to the extent that a claim is already allowed pursuant to a final non-appealable order, the Debtor reserves the right to object to claims. Therefore, even if your claim is allowed for voting purposes, you may not be entitled to a distribution if an objection to your claim is later upheld. Disputed claims are treated in Article 5 of the Plan.

SELECTED OFFICIAL FORMS

Debtor Name _____   Case number_____

H. Current and Historical Financial Conditions

The identity and fair market value of the estate's assets are listed in *Exhibit B*. [Identify source and basis of valuation.]

The Debtor's most recent financial statements [if any] issued before bankruptcy, each of which was filed with the Court, are set forth in *Exhibit C*.

[The most recent post-petition operating report filed since the commencement of the Debtor's bankruptcy case is set forth in *Exhibit D*.]

[A summary of the Debtor's periodic operating reports filed since the commencement of the Debtor's bankruptcy case is set forth in *Exhibit D*.]

III. Summary of the Plan of Reorganization and Treatment of Claims and Equity Interests

A. What Is the Purpose of the Plan of Reorganization?

As required by the Code, the Plan places claims and equity interests in various classes and describes the treatment each class will receive. The Plan also states whether each class of claims or equity interests is impaired or unimpaired. If the Plan is confirmed, your recovery will be limited to the amount provided by the Plan.

B. Unclassified Claims

Certain types of claims are automatically entitled to specific treatment under the Code. They are not considered impaired, and holders of such claims do not vote on the Plan. They may, however, object if, in their view, their treatment under the Plan does not comply with that required by the Code. Therefore, the Plan Proponent has *not* placed the following claims in any class:

1. Administrative expenses, involuntary gap claims, and quarterly and Court fees

Administrative expenses are costs or expenses of administering the Debtor's chapter 11 case which are allowed under § 503(b) of the Code. Administrative expenses include the value of any goods sold to the Debtor in the ordinary course of business and received within 20 days before the date of the bankruptcy petition, and compensation for services and reimbursement of expenses awarded by the court under § 330(a) of the Code. The Code requires that all administrative expenses be paid on the effective date of the Plan, unless a particular claimant agrees to a different treatment. Involuntary gap claims allowed under § 502(f) of the Code are entitled to the same treatment as administrative expense claims. The Code also requires that fees owed under section 1930 of title 28, including quarterly and court fees, have been paid or will be paid on the effective date of the Plan.

The following chart lists the Debtor's estimated administrative expenses, and quarterly and court fees, and their proposed treatment under the Plan:

Type	Estimated Amount Owed	Proposed Treatment
Administrative expenses		Paid in full on the effective date of the Plan, unless the holder of a particular claim has agreed to different treatment
Involuntary gap claims		Paid in full on the effective date of the Plan, unless the holder of a particular claim has agreed to different treatment
Statutory Court fees		Paid in full on the effective date of the Plan

Debtor Name _____   Case number_____

_____

Statutory quarterly fees   Paid in full on the effective date of the Plan

_____

Total	

2. Priority tax claims

Priority tax claims are unsecured income, employment, and other taxes described by § 507(a)(8) of the Code. Unless the holder of such a § 507(a)(8) priority tax claim agrees otherwise, it must receive the present value of such claim pursuant to 11 U.S.C. § 511, in regular installments paid over a period not exceeding 5 years from the order of relief.

The following chart lists the Debtor's estimated § 507(a)(8) priority tax claims and their proposed treatment under the Plan:

Description (Name and type of tax)	Estimated Amount Owed	Date of Assessment	Treatment		
	$		Payment interval		
			[Monthly] payment	$	
			Begin date		
			End date		
			Interest rate		%
			Total payout amount	$	
	$		Payment interval		
			[Monthly] payment	$	
			Begin date		
			End date		
			Interest rate		%
			Total payout amount	$	

C. Classes of Claims and Equity Interests

The following are the classes set forth in the Plan, and the proposed treatment that they will receive under the Plan:

1. Classes of secured claims

Allowed Secured Claims are claims secured by property of the Debtor's bankruptcy estate (or that are subject to setoff) to the extent allowed as secured claims under § 506 of the Code. If the value of the collateral or setoffs securing the creditor's claim is less than the amount of the creditor's allowed claim, the deficiency will [be classified as a general unsecured claim].

Debtor Name _____   Case number_____

The following chart lists all classes containing Debtor's secured prepetition claims and their proposed treatment under the Plan:

Class #	Description		Impairment?	Treatment	
	Secured claim of:		☐ Impaired	[Monthly] payment	$
	Name		☐ Unimpaired		
	Collateral description			Payments begin	
	Allowed secured amount	$		Payments end	
	Priority of lien			[Balloon payment]	
	Principal owed			Interest rate	%
	Pre-pet. arrearage			Treatment of lien	
	Total claim	$		[Additional payment required to cure defaults]	$
	Secured claim of:		☐ Impaired	[Monthly] payment	$
	Name		☐ Unimpaired		
	Collateral description			Payment begin	
	Allowed secured amount	$		Payments end	
	Priority of lien			[Balloon payment]	
	Principal owed			Interest rate	%
	Pre-pet. arrearage			Treatment of lien	
	Total claim	$		[Additional payment required to cure defaults]	$

2. Classes of priority unsecured claims

The Code requires that, with respect to a class of claims of a kind referred to in §§ 507(a)(1), (4), (5), (6), and (7), each holder of such a claim receive cash on the effective date of the Plan equal to the allowed amount of such claim, unless a particular claimant agrees to a different treatment or the class agrees to deferred cash payments.

Debtor Name _____   Case number_____

The following chart lists all classes containing claims under §§ 507(a)(1), (4), (5), (6), and (7) of the Code and their proposed treatment under the Plan:

Class #	Description	Impairment?	Treatment
	Priority unsecured claim pursuant to section [insert]	❑ Impaired ❑ Unimpaired	
	Total amount of claims $		
	Priority unsecured claim pursuant to section [insert]	❑ Impaired ❑ Unimpaired	
	Total amount of claims $		

3. Classes of general unsecured claims

General unsecured claims are not secured by property of the estate and are not entitled to priority under § 507(a) of the Code. [Insert description of § 1122(b) convenience class if applicable.]

The following chart identifies the Plan's proposed treatment of classes ☐ through ☐, which contain general unsecured claims against the Debtor:

Class #	Description	Impairment?	Treatment
	[1122(b) Convenience Class]	❑ Impaired ❑ Unimpaired	[Insert proposed treatment, such as "Paid in full in cash on effective date of the Plan or when due under contract or applicable nonbankruptcy law"]
	General unsecured class	❑ Impaired ❑ Unimpaired	[Monthly] payment $ Payments begin Payments end [Balloon payment] $ Interest rate from [date] % Estimated percent of claim paid %

Debtor Name _____   Case number_____

4. Classes of equity interest holders

Equity interest holders are parties who hold an ownership interest (*i.e.*, equity interest) in the Debtor. In a corporation, entities holding preferred or common stock are equity interest holders. In a partnership, equity interest holders include both general and limited partners. In a limited liability company (*LLC*), the equity interest holders are the members. Finally, with respect to an individual who is a debtor, the Debtor is the equity interest holder.

The following chart sets forth the Plan's proposed treatment of the classes of equity interest holders: [There may be more than one class of equity interests in, for example, a partnership case, or a case where the prepetition Debtor had issued multiple classes of stock.]

Class #	Description	Impairment?	Treatment
	Equity interest holders	☐ Impaired ☐ Unimpaired	

D. Means of Implementing the Plan

1. Source of payments

Payments and distributions under the Plan will be funded by the following:

[Describe the source of funds for payments under the Plan.]

2. Post-confirmation Management

The Post-Confirmation Management of the Debtor (including officers, directors, managing members, and other persons in control), and their compensation, shall be as follows:

Name	Position	Compensation

E. Risk Factors

The proposed Plan has the following risks:

[List all risk factors that might affect the Debtor's ability to make payments and other distributions required under the Plan.]

Debtor Name _____   Case number_____

F. Executory Contracts and Unexpired Leases

The Plan in Article 6 lists all executory contracts and unexpired leases that the Debtor will assume, and if applicable assign, under the Plan. *Assumption* means that the Debtor has elected to continue to perform the obligations under such contracts and unexpired leases, and to cure defaults of the type that must be cured under the Code, if any. Article 6 also lists how the Debtor will cure and compensate the other party to such contract or lease for any such defaults.

If you object to the assumption, and if applicable the assignment, of your unexpired lease or executory contract under the Plan, the proposed cure of any defaults, the adequacy of assurance of performance, you must file and serve your objection to the Plan within the deadline for objecting to the confirmation of the Plan, unless the Court has set an earlier time.

All executory contracts and unexpired leases that are not listed in Article 6 or have not previously been assumed, and if applicable assigned, or are not the subject of a pending motion to assume, and if applicable assign, will be rejected under the Plan. Consult your adviser or attorney for more specific information about particular contracts or leases.

If you object to the rejection of your contract or lease, you must file and serve your objection to the Plan within the deadline for objecting to the confirmation of the Plan.

[The deadline for filing a Proof of Claim based on a claim arising from the rejection of a lease or contract is _____.

Any claim based on the rejection of a contract or lease will be barred if the proof of claim is not timely filed, unless the Court orders otherwise.]

G. Tax Consequences of Plan

Creditors and equity interest holders concerned with how the plan may affect their tax liability should consult with their own accountants, attorneys, and/or advisors.

The following are the anticipated tax consequences of the Plan: [List the following general consequences as a minimum:

(1)   Tax consequences to the Debtor of the Plan;

(2)   General tax consequences on creditors of any discharge, and the general tax consequences of receipt of plan consideration after confirmation.]

Debtor Name _____   Case number_____

To be confirmable, the Plan must meet the requirements listed in §1129 of the Code. These include the requirements that:

— the Plan must be proposed in good faith;

— if a class of claims is impaired under the Plan, at least one impaired class of claims must accept the Plan, without counting votes of insiders;

— the Plan must distribute to each creditor and equity interest holder at least as much as the creditor or equity interest holder would receive in a chapter 7 liquidation case, unless the creditor or equity interest holder votes to accept the Plan; and

— the Plan must be feasible.

These requirements are not the only requirements listed in § 1129, and they are not the only requirements for confirmation.

A. Who May Vote or Object

Any party in interest may object to the confirmation of the Plan if the party believes that the requirements for confirmation are not met.

Many parties in interest, however, are not entitled to vote to accept or reject the Plan. Except as stated in Part IV.A.3 below, a creditor or equity interest holder has a right to vote for or against the Plan only if that creditor or equity interest holder has a claim or equity interest that is both

(1) allowed or allowed for voting purposes and

(2) impaired.

In this case, the Plan Proponent believes that classes [_____] are impaired and that holders of claims in each of these classes are therefore entitled to vote to accept or reject the Plan. The Plan Proponent believes that classes [_____] are unimpaired and that holders of claims in each of these classes, therefore, do not have the right to vote to accept or reject the Plan.

1. What is an allowed claim or an allowed equity interest?

Only a creditor or equity interest holder with an allowed claim or an allowed equity interest has the right to vote on the Plan. Generally, a claim or equity interest is allowed if either

(1) the Debtor has scheduled the claim on the Debtor's schedules, unless the claim has been scheduled as disputed, contingent, or unliquidated, or

(2) the creditor has filed a proof of claim or equity interest, unless an objection has been filed to such proof of claim or equity interest.

When a claim or equity interest is not allowed, the creditor or equity interest holder holding the claim or equity interest cannot vote unless the Court, after notice and hearing, either overrules the objection or allows the claim or equity interest for voting purposes pursuant to Rule 3018(a) of the Federal Rules of Bankruptcy Procedure.

The deadline for filing a proof of claim in this case was [_____].

[If applicable – The deadline for filing objections to claims is [_____].]

2. What is an impaired claim or impaired equity interest?

As noted above, the holder of an allowed claim or equity interest has the right to vote only if it

Debtor Name _____   Case number_____

is in a class that is *impaired* under the Plan. As provided in § 1124 of the Code, a class is considered *impaired* if the Plan alters the legal, equitable, or contractual rights of the members of that class.

3. Who is not entitled to vote

The holders of the following five types of claims and equity interests are *not* entitled to vote:

- holders of claims and equity interests that have been disallowed by an order of the Court;
- holders of other claims or equity interests that are not "allowed claims" or "allowed equity interests" (as discussed above), unless they have been "allowed" for voting purposes;
- holders of claims or equity interests in unimpaired classes;
- holders of claims entitled to priority pursuant to §§ 507(a)(2), (a)(3), and (a)(8) of the Code;
- holders of claims or equity interests in classes that do not receive or retain any value under the Plan; and
- administrative expenses.

Even if you are not entitled to vote on the plan, you have a right to object to the confirmation of the Plan [and to the adequacy of the Disclosure Statement].

4. Who can vote in more than one class

A creditor whose claim has been allowed in part as a secured claim and in part as an unsecured claim, or who otherwise hold claims in multiple classes, is entitled to accept or reject a Plan in each capacity, and should cast one ballot for each claim.

B. Votes Necessary to Confirm the Plan

If impaired classes exist, the Court cannot confirm the Plan unless:

(1) all impaired classes have voted to accept the Plan; or

(2) at least one impaired class of creditors has accepted the Plan without counting the votes of any insiders within that class, and the Plan is eligible to be confirmed by "cram down" of the non-accepting classes, as discussed later in Section B.2.

1. Votes necessary for a class to accept the plan

A class of claims accepts the Plan if both of the following occur:

(1) the holders of more than ½ of the allowed claims in the class, who vote, cast their votes to accept the Plan, and

(2) the holders of at least ⅔ in dollar amount of the allowed claims in the class, who vote, cast their votes to accept the Plan.

A class of equity interests accepts the Plan if the holders of at least ⅔ in amount of the allowed equity interests in the class, who vote, cast their votes to accept the Plan.

2. Treatment of non-accepting classes of secured claims, general unsecured claims, and interests

Even if one or more impaired classes reject the Plan, the Court may nonetheless confirm the Plan upon the request of the Plan proponent if the non-accepting classes are treated in the manner prescribed by § 1129(b) of the Code. A plan that binds non-accepting classes is commonly referred to as a *cram down* plan. The Code allows the Plan to bind non-accepting classes of claims or equity interests if it meets all the requirements for consensual confirmation except the voting requirements of § 1129(a)(8) of the Code, does not *discriminate unfairly*, and

Debtor Name _____   Case number_____

is *fair and equitable* toward each impaired class that has not voted to accept the Plan.

You should consult your own attorney if a *cram down* confirmation will affect your claim or equity interest, as the variations on this general rule are numerous and complex.

C. Liquidation Analysis

To confirm the Plan, the Court must find that all creditors and equity interest holders who do not accept the Plan will receive at least as much under the Plan as such claim and equity interest holders would receive in a chapter 7 liquidation. A liquidation analysis is attached to this Disclosure Statement as *Exhibit E.*

D. Feasibility

The Court must find that confirmation of the Plan is not likely to be followed by the liquidation, or the need for further financial reorganization, of the Debtor or any successor to the Debtor, unless such liquidation or reorganization is proposed in the Plan.

1. Ability to initially fund plan

The Plan Proponent believes that the Debtor will have enough cash on hand on the effective date of the Plan to pay all the claims and expenses that are entitled to be paid on that date. Tables showing the amount of cash on hand on the effective date of the Plan, and the sources of that cash are attached to this disclosure statement as *Exhibit F.*

2. Ability to make future plan payments and operate without further reorganization

The Plan Proponent must also show that it will have enough cash over the life of the Plan to make the required Plan payments and operate the debtor's business.
The Plan Proponent has provided projected financial information. Those projections are listed in *Exhibit G.*
The Plan Proponent's financial projections show that the Debtor will have an aggregate annual average cash flow, after paying operating expenses and post-confirmation taxes, of $ [   ].
The final Plan payment is expected to be paid on [   ].
[Summarize the numerical projections, and highlight any assumptions that are not in accord with past experience. Explain why such assumptions should now be made.]
You should consult with your accountant or other financial advisor if you have any questions pertaining to these projections.

Debtor Name _____   Case number_____

V. Effect of Confirmation of Plan

A. Discharge of Debtor

Check one box.

☐ **Discharge if the Debtor is an individual and 11 U.S.C. § 1141(d)(3) is not applicable.** Confirmation of the Plan does not discharge any debt provided for in the Plan until the court grants a discharge on completion of all payments under the Plan, or as otherwise provided in § 1141(d)(5) of the Code. Debtor will not be discharged from any debt excepted from discharge under § 523 of the Code, except as provided in Rule 4007(c) of the Federal Rules of Bankruptcy Procedure.

☐ **Discharge if the Debtor is a partnership and § 1141(d)(3) of the Code is not applicable.** On the effective date of the Plan, the Debtor shall be discharged from any debt that arose before confirmation of the Plan, subject to the occurrence of the effective date, to the extent specified in § 1141(d)(1)(A) of the Code. However, the Debtor shall not be discharged from any debt imposed by the Plan. After the effective date of the Plan your claims against the Debtor will be limited to the debts imposed by the Plan.

☐ **Discharge if the Debtor is a corporation and § 1141(d)(3) is not applicable.** On the effective date of the Plan, the Debtor shall be discharged from any debt that arose before confirmation of the Plan, subject to the occurrence of the effective date, to the extent specified in § 1141(d)(1)(A) of the Code, except that the Debtor shall not be discharged of any debt:

    (i)   imposed by the Plan, or

    (ii)   to the extent provided in 11 U.S.C. § 1141(d)(6).

☐ **No Discharge if § 1141(d)(3) is applicable.** In accordance with § 1141(d)(3) of the Code, the Debtor will not receive any discharge of debt in this bankruptcy case.

B. Modification of Plan

The Plan Proponent may modify the Plan at any time before confirmation of the Plan. However, the Court may require a new disclosure statement and/or re-voting on the Plan.

[If the Debtor is not an individual, add the following:

The Plan Proponent may also seek to modify the Plan at any time after confirmation only if

(1) the Plan has not been substantially consummated and
(2) the Court authorizes the proposed modifications after notice and a hearing.]

[If the Debtor is an individual, add the following:

Upon request of the Debtor, the United States trustee, or the holder of an allowed unsecured claim, the Plan may be modified at any time after confirmation of the Plan but before the completion of payments under the Plan, to

(1) increase or reduce the amount of payments under the Plan on claims of a particular class,
(2) extend or reduce the time period for such payments, or
(3) alter the amount of distribution to a creditor whose claim is provided for by the Plan to the extent necessary to take account of any payment of the claim made other than under the Plan.]

SELECTED OFFICIAL FORMS

Debtor Name _____   Case number_____

C. Final Decree

Once the estate has been fully administered, as provided in Rule 3022 of the Federal Rules of Bankruptcy Procedure, the Plan Proponent, or such other party as the Court shall designate in the Plan Confirmation Order, shall file a motion with the Court to obtain a final decree to close the case. Alternatively, the Court may enter such a final decree on its own motion.

VI. Other Plan Provisions

[Insert other provisions here, as necessary and appropriate.]

✗ _____   _____
[Signature of the Plan Proponent]   [Printed Name]

✗ _____   _____
[Signature of the Attorney for the Plan Proponent]   [Printed Name]

SELECTED OFFICIAL FORMS

Debtor Name _____   Case number_____

Exhibits

Exhibit A: Copy of Proposed Plan of Reorganization

Debtor Name _____   Case number_____

Exhibit B: Identity and Value of Material Assets of Debtor

SELECTED OFFICIAL FORMS

Debtor Name _____   Case number_____

Exhibit C: Prepetition Financial Statements
(to be taken from those filed with the court)

SELECTED OFFICIAL FORMS

Debtor Name _____   Case number_____

    Exhibit D: [Most Recently Filed Postpetition Operating Report]
    [Summary of Postpetition Operating Reports]

Debtor Name _____   Case number_____

Exhibit E: Liquidation Analysis

Plan Proponent's Estimated Liquidation Value of Assets

Assets		
a.	Cash on hand	$
b.	Accounts receivable	$
c.	Inventory	$
d.	Office furniture and equipment	$
e.	Machinery and equipment	$
f.	Automobiles	$
g.	Building and land	$
h.	Customer list	$
i.	Investment property (such as stocks, bonds or other financial assets)	$
j.	Lawsuits or other claims against third-parties	$
K	Other intangibles (such as avoiding powers actions)	$

Total Assets at Liquidation Value		$
Less:	Secured creditors' recoveries	− $
Less:	Chapter 7 trustee fees and expenses	− $
Less:	Chapter 11 administrative expenses	− $
Less:	Priority claims, excluding administrative expense claims	− $
[Less:	Debtor's claimed exemptions]	− $

(1) Balance for unsecured claims	$
(2) Total dollar amount of unsecured claims	$

Percentage of claims which unsecured creditors would receive or retain in a chapter 7 liquidation:	%	
Percentage of claims which unsecured creditors will receive or retain under the Plan:	%	[Divide (1) by (2)]

Debtor Name _____   Case number_____

Exhibit F: Cash on hand on the effective date of the Plan

Cash on hand on effective date of plan		$
Less: Amount of administrative expenses payable on effective date of the Plan	–	$
Less: Amount of statutory costs and charges	–	$
Less: Amount of cure payments for executory contracts	–	$
Less: Other Plan payments due on effective date of the Plan	–	$
Balance after paying these amounts		$

The sources of the cash Debtor will have on hand by the effective date of the Plan are estimated as follows:

Cash in Debtor's bank account now	$
Net earnings between now and effective date of the Plan [State the basis for such projections]	$
Borrowing [Separately state terms of repayment]	$
Capital contributions	$
Other	$
Total (This number should match "cash on hand" figure noted above)	$

SELECTED OFFICIAL FORMS

Debtor Name _____   Case number_____

Exhibit G: Projections of Cash Flow for Post-Confirmation Period

Fill in this information to identify your case:

Debtor 1 _____
        First Name   Middle Name   Last Name

Debtor 2 _____
(Spouse, if filing) First Name   Middle Name   Last Name

United States Bankruptcy Court for the: _____ District of _____

Case number _____
(If known)

Official Form 427

Cover Sheet for Reaffirmation Agreement   12/15

Anyone who is a party to a reaffirmation agreement may fill out and file this form. Fill it out completely, attach it to the reaffirmation agreement, and file the documents within the time set under Bankruptcy Rule 4008.

Part 1:	Explain the Repayment Terms of the Reaffirmation Agreement

1. Who is the creditor?

_____
Name of the creditor

2. How much is the debt?

On the date that the bankruptcy case is filed $_____

To be paid under the reaffirmation agreement $_____

$_____ per month for _____ months (if fixed interest rate)

3. What is the Annual Percentage Rate (APR) of interest? (See Bankruptcy Code § 524(k)(3)(E).)

Before the bankruptcy case was filed _____%

Under the reaffirmation agreement _____% ☐ Fixed rate
                                                     ☐ Adjustable rate

4. Does collateral secure the debt?

☐ No
☐ Yes. Describe the collateral. _____

      Current market value $_____

5. Does the creditor assert that the debt is nondischargeable?

☐ No
☐ Yes. Attach an explanation of the nature of the debt and the basis for contending that the debt is nondischargeable.

6. Using information from Schedule I: Your Income (Official Form 106I) and Schedule J: Your Expenses (Official Form 106J), fill in the amounts.

Income and expenses reported on Schedules I and J	Income and expenses stated on the reaffirmation agreement
6a. Combined monthly income from line 12 of Schedule I $ _____	6e. Monthly income from all sources after payroll deductions $ _____
6b. Monthly expenses from line 22c of Schedule J — $ _____	6f. Monthly expenses — $ _____
6c. Monthly payments on all reaffirmed debts not listed on Schedule J — $ _____	6g. Monthly payments on all reaffirmed debts not included in monthly expenses — $ _____
6d. Scheduled net monthly income $ _____ Subtract lines 6b and 6c from 6a. If the total is less than 0, put the number in brackets.	6h. Present net monthly income $ _____ Subtract lines 6f and 6g from 6e. If the total is less than 0, put the number in brackets.

Official Form 427   Cover Sheet for Reaffirmation Agreement   page 1

Debtor 1 _____ Case number _(if known)_____
First Name   Middle Name   Last Name

---

7. **Are the income amounts on lines 6a and 6e different?**

☐ No
☐ Yes. Explain why they are different and complete line 10._____

_____

8. **Are the expense amounts on lines 6b and 6f different?**

☐ No
☐ Yes. Explain why they are different and complete line 10._____

_____

9. **Is the net monthly income in line 6h less than 0?**

☐ No
☐ Yes. A presumption of hardship arises (unless the creditor is a credit union).
Explain how the debtor will make monthly payments on the reaffirmed debt and pay other living expenses. Complete line 10.

_____

_____

10. **Debtor's certification about lines 7-9**

If any answer on lines 7-9 is *Yes*, the debtor must sign here.

If all the answers on lines 7-9 are *No*, go to line 11.

I certify that each explanation on lines 7-9 is true and correct.

✗ _____   ✗ _____
Signature of Debtor 1   Signature of Debtor 2 (Spouse Only in a Joint Case)

11. **Did an attorney represent the debtor in negotiating the reaffirmation agreement?**

☐ No
☐ Yes. Has the attorney executed a declaration or an affidavit to support the reaffirmation agreement?
   ☐ No
   ☐ Yes

Part 2:   **Sign Here**

Whoever fills out this form must sign here.

I certify that the attached agreement is a true and correct copy of the reaffirmation agreement between the parties identified on this *Cover Sheet for Reaffirmation Agreement.*

✗ _____   Date _____
Signature   MM / DD / YYYY

_____
Printed Name

Check one:

☐ Debtor or Debtor's Attorney
☐ Creditor or Creditor's Attorney

Official Form 427   Cover Sheet for Reaffirmation Agreement   page 2

| Print | Save As... | Add Attachment | | Reset |

SELECTED OFFICIAL FORMS

B2000 (Form 2000) (02/20)

UNITED STATES BANKRUPTCY COURT
REQUIRED LISTS, SCHEDULES, STATEMENTS, AND FEES
Voluntary Chapter 7 Case

☐   **Filing Fee of $245.** If the fee is to be paid in installments or the debtor requests a waiver of the fee, the debtor must be an individual and must file a signed application for court approval. Official Form 103A or 103B and Fed.R.Bankr.P. 1006(b), (c).

☐   **Administrative fee of $75 and trustee surcharge of $15.** If the debtor is an individual and the court grants the debtor's request, these fees are payable in installments or may be waived.

☐   **Voluntary Petition for Individuals Filing for Bankruptcy** (Official Form 101) or **Voluntary Petition for Non-Individuals Filing for Bankruptcy** (Official Form 201); **Names and addresses of all creditors** of the debtor. Must be filed WITH the petition. Fed.R.Bankr.P. 1007(a)(1).

☐   **Notice to Individual Debtor with Primarily Consumer Debts** under 11 U.S.C. § 342(b) (Director's Form 2010), if applicable. Required if the debtor is an individual with primarily consumer debts. The notice must be GIVEN to the debtor before the petition is filed. Certification that the notice has been given must be FILED with the petition or within 15 days. 11 U.S.C. §§ 342(b), 521(a)(1)(B)(iii), 707(a)(3). Official Form 101 contains spaces for the certification.

☐   **Bankruptcy Petition Preparer's Notice, Declaration, and Signature** (Official Form 119). Required if a "bankruptcy petition preparer" prepares the petition. Must be submitted WITH the petition. 11 U.S.C. § 110(b)(2).

☐   **Statement About Your Social Security Numbers** (Official Form 121). Required if the debtor is an individual. Must be submitted WITH the petition. Fed.R.Bankr.P. 1007(f).

☐   **Credit Counseling Requirement** (Official Form 101); **Certificate of Credit Counseling and Debt Repayment Plan,** if applicable; **Section 109(h)(3) certification or § 109(h)(4) request,** if applicable. If applicable, the Certificate of Credit Counseling and Debt Repayment Plan must be filed with the petition or within 14 days. If applicable, the § 109(h)(3) certification or the § 109(h)(4) request must be filed WITH the petition. Fed.R.Bankr.P. 1007(b)(3), (c).

☐   **Statement disclosing compensation paid or to be paid to a "bankruptcy petition preparer"** (Director's Form 2800). Required if a "bankruptcy petition preparer" prepares the petition. Must be submitted WITH the petition. 11 U.S.C. §110(h)(2).

☐   **Statement of Your Current Monthly Income** (Official Form 122A). Required if the debtor is an individual. Must be filed with the petition or within 14 days. Fed.R.Bankr.P. 1007(b), (c).

☐   **Schedules of assets and liabilities** (Official Forms 106 or 206). Must be filed with the petition or within 14 days. Fed.R.Bankr.P. 1007(b),(c).

☐   **Schedule of Executory Contracts and Unexpired Leases** (Schedule G of Official Form 106 or 206). Must be filed with the petition or within 14 days. Fed.R.Bankr.P. 1007(b), (c).

☐   **Schedules of Your Income and Your Expenses** (Schedules I and J of Official Form 106). If the debtor is an individual, Schedules I and J of Official Form 106 must be filed with the petition or within 14 days. 11 U.S.C. § 521(1) and Fed.R.Bankr.P. 1007(b), (c).

☐   **Statement of financial affairs** (Official Form 107 or 207). Must be filed with the petition or within 14 days. Fed.R.Bankr.P. 1007(b), (c).

☐   **Copies of all payment advices or other evidence of payment** received by the debtor from any employer within 60 days before the filing of the petition. Required if the debtor is an individual. Must be filed with the petition or within 14 days. Fed.R.Bankr.P. 1007(b), (c).

☐   **Statement of Intention for Individuals Filing Under Chapter 7** (Official Form 108). Required ONLY if the debtor is an individual and the schedules of assets and liabilities contain debts secured by property of the estate or personal property subject to an unexpired lease. Must be filed within 30 days or by the date set for the Section 341 meeting of creditors, whichever is earlier. 11 U.S.C. §§ 362(h) and 521(a)(2).

☐   **Statement disclosing compensation paid or to be paid to the attorney** for the debtor (Director's Form 2030). Required if the debtor is represented by an attorney. Must be filed within 14 days or any other date set by the court. 11 U.S.C. § 329 and Fed.R.Bankr.P. 2016(b).

☐   **Certification About a Financial Management Course** (Official Form 423), if applicable. Required if the debtor is an individual, unless the course provider has notified the court that the debtor has completed the course. Must be filed within 60 days of the first date set for the meeting of creditors. 11 U.S.C. § 727(a)(11) and Fed.R.Bankr.P. 1007(b)(7), (c).

SELECTED OFFICIAL FORMS

B2000 (Form 2000) (02/20)

REQUIRED LISTS, SCHEDULES, STATEMENTS, AND FEES
Voluntary Chapter 11 Case

☐   **Filing fee of $1,167.** If the fee is to be paid in installments, the debtor must be an individual and must file a signed application for court approval. Official Form 103A and Fed.R.Bankr.P. 1006(b).

☐   **Administrative fee of $550.** If the debtor is an individual and the court grants the debtor's request, this fee is payable in installments.

☐   **United States Trustee quarterly fee.** The debtor, or trustee if one is appointed, is required also to pay a fee to the United States trustee at the conclusion of each calendar quarter until the case is dismissed or converted to another chapter. The calculation of the amount to be paid is set out in 28 U.S.C. § 1930(a)(6). As authorized by 28 U.S.C. § 1930(a)(7), the quarterly fee is paid to the clerk of court in chapter 11 cases in Alabama and North Carolina.

☐   **Voluntary Petition for Individuals Filing for Bankruptcy** (Official Form 101) or **Voluntary Petition for Non-Individuals Filing for Bankruptcy** (Official Form 201); **Names and addresses of all creditors** of the debtor. Must be filed WITH the petition. Fed.R.Bankr.P. 1007(a)(1).

☐   **Notice to Individual Debtor with Primarily Consumer Debts** under 11 U.S.C. § 342(b) (Director's Form 2010), if applicable. Required if the debtor is an individual with primarily consumer debts. The notice must be GIVEN to the debtor before the petition is filed. Certification that the notice has been given must be FILED with the petition or within 15 days. 11 U.S.C. §§ 342(b), 521(a)(1)(B)(iii), 1112(e). Official Form 101 contains spaces for the certification.

☐   **Bankruptcy Petition Preparer's Notice, Declaration, and Signature** (Official Form 119). Required if a "bankruptcy petition preparer" prepares the petition. Must be submitted WITH the petition. 11 U.S.C. § 110(b)(2).

☐   **Statement About Your Social Security Numbers** (Official Form 121). Required if the debtor is an individual. Must be submitted WITH the petition. Fed.R.Bankr.P. 1007(f).

☐   **Credit Counseling Requirement** (Official Form 101); **Certificate of Credit Counseling and Debt Repayment Plan,** if applicable; **Section 109(h)(3) certification or § 109(h)(4) request,** if applicable. If applicable, the Certificate of Credit Counseling and Debt Repayment Plan must be filed with the petition or within 14 days. If applicable, the § 109(h)(3) certification or the § 109(h)(4) request must be filed WITH the petition. Fed.R.Bankr.P. 1007(b)(3), (c).

☐   **Statement disclosing compensation paid or to be paid to a "bankruptcy petition preparer"** (Director's Form 2800). Required if a "bankruptcy petition preparer" prepares the petition. Must be submitted WITH the petition. 11 U.S.C. §110(h)(2).

☐   **Statement of Your Current Monthly Income** (Official Form 122B). Required if the debtor is an individual unless the case is filed under subchapter V. Must be filed with the petition or within 14 days. Fed.R.Bankr.P. 1007(b), (c).

☐   **For Individual Chapter 11 Cases: List of Creditors Who Have the 20 Largest Unsecured Claims Against You and Are Not Insiders** (Official Form 104) or **Chapter 11 or Chapter 9 Cases: List of Creditors Who Have the 20 Largest Unsecured Claims and Are Not Insiders** (Official Form 204). Must be filed WITH the petition. Fed.R.Bankr.P. 1007(d).

☐   **Names and addresses of equity security holders of the debtor.** Must be filed with the petition or within 14 days, unless the court orders otherwise. Fed.R.Bankr.P. 1007(a)(3).

☐   **Schedules of Assets and Liabilities** (Official Form 106 or 206). Must be filed with the petition or within 14 days. Fed.R.Bankr.P. 1007(b), (c).

☐   **Schedule of Executory Contracts and Unexpired Leases** (Schedule G of Official Form 106 or 206). Must be filed with the petition or within 14 days. Fed.R.Bankr.P. 1007(b), (c).

☐   **Schedules of Current Income and Expenditures.** If the debtor is an individual, Schedules I and J of Official Form 106 must be used for this purpose. Must be filed with the petition or within 14 days. 11 U.S.C. § 521(1) and Fed.R.Bankr.P. 1007(b), (c).

☐   **Statement of Financial Affairs** (Official Form 107 or 207). Must be filed with the petition or within 14 days. Fed.R.Bankr.P. 1007(b), (c).

☐   **Copies of all payment advices or other evidence of payment received by debtor from any employer within 60 days before the filing of the petition.** Required if the debtor is an individual. Must be filed WITH the petition or within 14 days. Fed.R.Bankr.P. 1007(b), (c).

☐   **Statement disclosing compensation paid or to be paid to the attorney for the debtor** (Director's Form 2030), if applicable. Required if the debtor is represented by an attorney. Must be filed within 14 days or any other date set by the court. 11 U.S.C. § 329 and Fed.R.Bankr.P. 2016(b).

☐   **Certification About a Financial Management Course** (Official Form 423), if applicable. Required if the debtor is an individual and § 1141(d)(3) applies, unless the course provider has notified the court that the debtor has completed the course. Must be filed no later than the date of the last payment under the plan or the filing of a motion for a discharge under § 1141(d)(5)(B). 11 U.S.C. § 1141(d)(3) and Fed.R.Bankr.P. 1007(b)(7), (c).

☐   **Statement concerning pending proceedings of the kind described in § 522(q)(1),** if applicable. Required if the debtor is an individual and has claimed exemptions under state or local law as described in § 522(b)(3) in excess of $170,350*. Must be filed no later than the date of the last payment made under the plan or the date of the filing of a motion for a discharge under § 1141(d)(5)(B). 11 U.S.C. § 1141(d)(5)(C) and Fed.R.Bankr.P. 1007(b)(8), (c).

* Amount subject to adjustment on 4/01/22, and every three years thereafter with respect to cases commenced on or after the date of adjustment.

SELECTED OFFICIAL FORMS

B2000 (Form 2000) (02/20)

REQUIRED LISTS, SCHEDULES, STATEMENTS, AND FEES
Chapter 12 Case

☐   **Filing Fee of $200.** If the fee is to be paid in installments, the debtor must be an individual and must file a signed application for court approval. Official Form 103A and Fed.R.Bankr.P. 1006(b).

☐   **Administrative fee of $75.** If the debtor is an individual and the court grants the debtor's request, this fee is payable in installments.

☐   **Voluntary Petition for Individuals Filing for Bankruptcy** (Official Form 101) or **Voluntary Petition for Non-Individuals Filing for Bankruptcy** (Official Form 201). **Names and addresses of all creditors** of the debtor. Must be filed WITH the petition. Fed.R.Bankr.P. 1007(a)(1).

☐   **Notice to Individual Debtor with Primarily Consumer Debts** under 11 U.S.C. § 342(b) (Director's Form 2010), if applicable. Required if the debtor is an individual with primarily consumer debts. The notice must be GIVEN to the debtor before the petition is filed. Certification that the notice has been given must be FILED with the court in a timely manner. 11 U.S.C. §§ 342(b), 521(a)(1)(B)(iii). Official Form 101 contains spaces for the certification.

☐   **Bankruptcy Petition Preparer's Notice, Declaration, and Signature** (Official Form 119). Required if a "bankruptcy petition preparer" prepares the petition. Must be submitted WITH the petition. 11 U.S.C. § 110(b)(2).

☐   **Statement of Your Social Security Numbers** (Official Form 121). Required if the debtor is an individual. Must be submitted WITH the petition. Fed.R.Bankr.P. 1007(f).

☐   **Credit Counseling Requirement** (Official Form 101); **Certificate of Credit Counseling and Debt Repayment Plan**, if applicable; **Section 109(h)(3) certification or § 109(h)(4) request**, if applicable. If applicable, the Certificate of Credit Counseling and Debt Repayment Plan must be filed with the petition or within 14 days. If applicable, the § 109(h)(3) certification or the § 109(h)(4) request must be filed WITH the petition. Fed.R.Bankr.P. 1007(b)(3), (c).

☐   **Statement disclosing compensation paid or to be paid to a "bankruptcy petition preparer"** (Director's Form 2800). Required if a "bankruptcy petition preparer" prepares the petition. Must be submitted WITH the petition. 11 U.S.C. §110(h)(2).

☐   **Schedules of Assets and Liabilities** (Official Form 106 or 206). Must be filed with the petition or within 14 days. Fed.R.Bankr.P. 1007(b), (c).

☐   **Schedule of Executory Contracts and Unexpired Leases** (Schedule G of Official Form 106 or 206). Must be filed with the petition or within 14 days. Fed.R.Bankr.P. 1007(b), (c).

☐   **Schedules of Current Income and Expenditures.** If the debtor is an individual, Schedule I and J of Official Form 106 must be used for this purpose. Must be filed with the petition or within 14 days. 11 U.S.C. § 521(1) and Fed.R.Bankr.P. 1007(b), (c).

☐   **Statement of Financial Affairs** (Official Form 107 or 207). Must be filed with the petition or within 14 days. Fed.R.Bankr.P. 1007(b), (c).

☐   **Copies of all payment advices** or other evidence of payment received by the debtor from any employer within 60 days before the filing of the petition if the debtor is an individual. Must be filed with the petition or within 14 days. Fed.R.Bankr.P. 1007(b), (c).

☐   **Statement disclosing compensation paid or to be paid to the attorney** for the debtor (Director's Form 2030), if applicable. Must be filed within 14 days or any other date set by the court. 11 U.S.C. § 329 and Fed.R.Bankr.P. 2016(b).

☐   **Chapter 12 Plan.** Must be filed within 90 days. 11 U.S.C. § 1221.

☐   **Statement concerning pending proceedings of the kind described in § 522(q)(1)**, if applicable. Required if the debtor is an individual and has claimed exemptions under state or local law as described in §522(b)(3) in excess of $170,350*. Must be filed no later than the date of the last payment made under the plan or the date of the filing of a motion for a discharge under § 1228(b). 11 U.S.C. § 1228(f) and Fed.R.Bankr.P. 1007(b)(8), (c).

---

* Amount subject to adjustment on 4/01/22, and every three years thereafter with respect to cases commenced on or after the date of adjustment.

SELECTED OFFICIAL FORMS

B2000 (Form 2000) (02/20)

REQUIRED LISTS, SCHEDULES, STATEMENTS, AND FEES
Chapter 13 Case

☐   **Filing fee of $235.** If the fee is to be paid in installments, the debtor must file a signed application for court approval. Official Form 103A and Fed.R.Bankr.P. 1006(b).

☐   **Administrative fee of $75.** If the court grants the debtor's request, this fee is payable in installments.

☐   **Voluntary Petition for Individuals Filing for Bankruptcy** (Official Form 101). **Names and addresses of all creditors** of the debtor. Must be filed WITH the petition. Fed.R.Bankr.P. 1007(a)(1).

☐   **Notice to Individual Debtor with Primarily Consumer Debts** under 11 U.S.C. § 342(b) (Director's Form 2010), if applicable. Required if the debtor is an individual with primarily consumer debts. The notice must be GIVEN to the debtor before the petition is filed. Certification that the notice has been given must be FILED with the petition or within 15 days. 11 U.S.C. §§ 342(b), 521(a)(1)(B)(iii), 1307(c)(9). Official Form 101 contains spaces for the certification.

☐   **Bankruptcy Petition Preparer's Notice, Declaration, and Signature** (Official Form 119). Required if a "bankruptcy petition preparer" prepares the petition. Must be submitted WITH the petition. 11 U.S.C. § 110(b)(2).

☐   **Statement of Social Security Number** (Official Form 121). Must be submitted WITH the petition. Fed.R.Bankr.P. 1007(f).

☐   **Credit Counseling Requirement** (Official Form 101); **Certificate of Credit Counseling and Debt Repayment Plan**, if applicable; **Section 109(h)(3) certification or § 109(h)(4) request**, if applicable. If applicable, the Certificate of Credit Counseling and Debt Repayment Plan must be filed with the petition or within 14 days. If applicable, the § 109(h)(3) certification or the § 109(h)(4) request must be filed WITH the petition. Fed.R.Bankr.P. 1007(b)(3), (c).

☐   **Statement disclosing compensation paid or to be paid to a "bankruptcy petition preparer"** (Director's Form 2800). Required if a "bankruptcy petition preparer" prepares the petition. Must be submitted WITH the petition. 11 U.S.C. §110(h)(2).

☐   **Statement of Your Current Monthly Income** (Official Form 122C). Must be filed with the petition or within 14 days. Fed.R.Bankr.P. 1007.

☐   **Schedules of Assets and Liabilities** (Official Form 106). Must be filed with the petition or within 14 days. Fed.R.Bankr.P. 1007(b), (c).

☐   **Schedule of Executory Contracts and Unexpired Leases** (Schedule G of Official Form 106). Must be filed with the petition or within 14 days. Fed.R.Bankr.P. 1007(b), (c).

☐   **Schedules of Current Income and Expenditures** (Schedules I and J of Official Form 106). Must be filed with the petition or within 14 days. 11 U.S.C. § 521(1) and Fed.R.Bankr.P. 1007(b), (c).

☐   **Statement of Financial Affairs** (Official Form 107). Must be filed with the petition or within 14 days. Fed.R.Bankr.P. 1007(b), (c).

☐   **Copies of all payment advices or other evidence of payment** received by the debtor from any employer within 60 days before the filing of the petition. Must be filed with the petition or within 14 days. Fed.R.Bankr.P. 1007(b), (c).

☐   **Chapter 13 Plan.** (Official Form 113), or local form plan (check with your local court for required plan version). Fed.R.Bankr.P 3015.1. Must be filed with the petition or within 14 days. Fed.R.Bankr.P. 3015.

☐   **Statement disclosing compensation paid or to be paid to the attorney** for the debtor (Director's Form 2030), if applicable. Must be filed within 14 days or any other date set by the court. 11 U.S.C. § 329 and Fed.R.Bankr.P. 2016(b).

☐   **Certification About a Financial Management Course** (Official Form 423), if applicable. Must be filed no later than the date of the last payment made under the plan or the date of the filing of a motion for a discharge under § 1328(b), unless the course provider has notified the court that the debtor has completed the course. 11 U.S.C. § 1328(g)(1) and Fed.R.Bankr.P. 1007(b)(7), (c).

☐   **Statement concerning pending proceedings of the kind described in § 522(q)(1),** if applicable. Required if the debtor has claimed exemptions under state or local law as described in §522(b)(3) in excess of $170,350*. Must be filed no later than the date of the last payment made under the plan or the date of the filing of a motion for a discharge under § 1328(b). 11 U.S.C. § 1328(h) and Fed.R.Bankr.P. 1007(b)(8), (c).

---

* Amount subject to adjustment on 4/01/22, and every three years thereafter with respect to cases commenced on or after the date of adjustment.

Notice Required by 11 U.S.C. § 342(b) for Individuals Filing for Bankruptcy (Form 2010)

This notice is for you if:

> You are an individual filing for bankruptcy, and
>
> Your debts are primarily consumer debts. *Consumer debts* are defined in 11 U.S.C. § 101(8) as "incurred by an individual primarily for a personal, family, or household purpose."

The types of bankruptcy that are available to individuals

Individuals who meet the qualifications may file under one of four different chapters of the Bankruptcy Code:

- Chapter 7 — Liquidation

- Chapter 11— Reorganization

- Chapter 12— Voluntary repayment plan for family farmers or fishermen

- Chapter 13— Voluntary repayment plan for individuals with regular income

You should have an attorney review your decision to file for bankruptcy and the choice of chapter.

Chapter 7:   Liquidation

	$245	filing fee
	$78	administrative fee
+	$15	trustee surcharge
	$338	total fee

Chapter 7 is for individuals who have financial difficulty preventing them from paying their debts and who are willing to allow their non-exempt property to be used to pay their creditors. The primary purpose of filing under chapter 7 is to have your debts discharged. The bankruptcy discharge relieves you after bankruptcy from having to pay many of your pre-bankruptcy debts. Exceptions exist for particular debts, and liens on property may still be enforced after discharge. For example, a creditor may have the right to foreclose a home mortgage or repossess an automobile.

However, if the court finds that you have committed certain kinds of improper conduct described in the Bankruptcy Code, the court may deny your discharge.

You should know that even if you file chapter 7 and you receive a discharge, some debts are not discharged under the law. Therefore, you may still be responsible to pay:

- most taxes;

- most student loans;

- domestic support and property settlement obligations;

- most fines, penalties, forfeitures, and criminal restitution obligations; and
- certain debts that are not listed in your bankruptcy papers.

You may also be required to pay debts arising from:

- fraud or theft;
- fraud or defalcation while acting in breach of fiduciary capacity;
- intentional injuries that you inflicted; and
- death or personal injury caused by operating a motor vehicle, vessel, or aircraft while intoxicated from alcohol or drugs.

If your debts are primarily consumer debts, the court can dismiss your chapter 7 case if it finds that you have enough income to repay creditors a certain amount. You must file *Chapter 7 Statement of Your Current Monthly Income* (Official Form 122A–1) if you are an individual filing for bankruptcy under chapter 7. This form will determine your current monthly income and compare whether your income is more than the median income that applies in your state.

If your income is not above the median for your state, you will not have to complete the other chapter 7 form, the *Chapter 7 Means Test Calculation* (Official Form 122A–2).

If your income is above the median for your state, you must file a second form —the *Chapter 7 Means Test Calculation* (Official Form 122A–2). The calculations on the form—sometimes called the *Means Test*—deduct from your income living expenses and payments on certain debts to determine any amount available to pay unsecured creditors. If

your income is more than the median income for your state of residence and family size, depending on the results of the *Means Test*, the U.S. trustee, bankruptcy administrator, or creditors can file a motion to dismiss your case under § 707(b) of the Bankruptcy Code. If a motion is filed, the court will decide if your case should be dismissed. To avoid dismissal, you may choose to proceed under another chapter of the Bankruptcy Code.

If you are an individual filing for chapter 7 bankruptcy, the trustee may sell your property to pay your debts, subject to your right to exempt the property or a portion of the proceeds from the sale of the property. The property, and the proceeds from property that your bankruptcy trustee sells or liquidates that you are entitled to, is called *exempt property*. Exemptions may enable you to keep your home, a car, clothing, and household items or to receive some of the proceeds if the property is sold.

Exemptions are not automatic. To exempt property, you must list it on *Schedule C: The Property You Claim as Exempt* (Official Form 106C). If you do not list the property, the trustee may sell it and pay all of the proceeds to your creditors.

Chapter 11: Reorganization

	$1,167	filing fee
+	$571	administrative fee
	$1,738	total fee

Chapter 11 is often used for reorganizing a business, but is also available to individuals. The provisions of chapter 11 are too complicated to summarize briefly.

SELECTED OFFICIAL FORMS

Chapter 12: Repayment plan for family farmers or fishermen

	$200	filing fee
+	$78	administrative fee
	$278	total fee

Similar to chapter 13, chapter 12 permits family farmers and fishermen to repay their debts over a period of time using future earnings and to discharge some debts that are not paid.

Chapter 13: Repayment plan for individuals with regular income

	$235	filing fee
+	$78	administrative fee
	$313	total fee

Chapter 13 is for individuals who have regular income and would like to pay all or part of their debts in installments over a period of time and to discharge some debts that are not paid. You are eligible for chapter 13 only if your debts are not more than certain dollar amounts set forth in 11 U.S.C. § 109.

Under chapter 13, you must file with the court a plan to repay your creditors all or part of the money that you owe them, usually using your future earnings. If the court approves your plan, the court will allow you to repay your debts, as adjusted by the plan, within 3 years or 5 years, depending on your income and other factors.

After you make all the payments under your plan, many of your debts are discharged. The debts that are not discharged and that you may still be responsible to pay include:

- domestic support obligations,
- most student loans,
- certain taxes,
- debts for fraud or theft,
- debts for fraud or defalcation while acting in a fiduciary capacity,
- most criminal fines and restitution obligations,
- certain debts that are not listed in your bankruptcy papers,
- certain debts for acts that caused death or personal injury, and
- certain long-term secured debts.

Bankruptcy crimes have serious consequences

- If you knowingly and fraudulently conceal assets or make a false oath or statement under penalty of perjury—either orally or in writing—in connection with a bankruptcy case, you may be fined, imprisoned, or both.

- All information you supply in connection with a bankruptcy case is subject to examination by the Attorney General acting through the Office of the U.S. Trustee, the Office of the U.S. Attorney, and other offices and employees of the U.S. Department of Justice.

Make sure the court has your mailing address

The bankruptcy court sends notices to the mailing address you list on *Voluntary Petition for Individuals Filing for Bankruptcy* (Official Form 101). To ensure that you receive information about your case, Bankruptcy Rule 4002 requires that you notify the court of any changes in your address.

A married couple may file a bankruptcy case together—called a *joint case*. If you file a joint case and each spouse lists the same mailing address on the bankruptcy petition, the bankruptcy court generally will mail you and your spouse one copy of each notice, unless you file a statement with the court asking that each spouse receive separate copies.

Understand which services you could receive from credit counseling agencies

The law generally requires that you receive a credit counseling briefing from an approved credit counseling agency. 11 U.S.C. § 109(h). If you are filing a joint case, both spouses must receive the briefing. With limited exceptions, you must receive it within the 180 days *before* you file your bankruptcy petition. This briefing is usually conducted by telephone or on the Internet.

In addition, after filing a bankruptcy case, you generally must complete a financial management instructional course before you can receive a discharge. If you are filing a joint case, both spouses must complete the course.

You can obtain the list of agencies approved to provide both the briefing and the instructional course from: http://www.uscourts.gov/services-forms/bankruptcy/credit-counseling-and-debtor-education-courses.

In Alabama and North Carolina, go to: http://www.uscourts.gov/services-forms/bankruptcy/credit-counseling-and-debtor-education-courses.

If you do not have access to a computer, the clerk of the bankruptcy court may be able to help you obtain the list.

Notice Required by 11 U.S.C. § 342(b) for Individuals Filing for Bankruptcy (Form 2010)   page 4

B2030 (Form 2030) (12/15)

United States Bankruptcy Court

_____ District Of _____

In re

Case No. _____

Debtor

Chapter _____

DISCLOSURE OF COMPENSATION OF ATTORNEY FOR DEBTOR

1. Pursuant to 11 U.S.C. § 329(a) and Fed. Bankr. P. 2016(b), I certify that I am the attorney for the above named debtor(s) and that compensation paid to me within one year before the filing of the petition in bankruptcy, or agreed to be paid to me, for services rendered or to be rendered on behalf of the debtor(s) in contemplation of or in connection with the bankruptcy case is as follows:

    For legal services, I have agreed to accept . . . . $_____

    Prior to the filing of this statement I have received . . . . $_____

    Balance Due . . . . $_____

2. The source of the compensation paid to me was:

    ☐ Debtor   ☐ Other (specify)

3. The source of compensation to be paid to me is:

    ☐ Debtor   ☐ Other (specify)

4.   ☐ I have not agreed to share the above-disclosed compensation with any other person unless they are members and associates of my law firm.

        ☐ I have agreed to share the above-disclosed compensation with a other person or persons who are not members or associates of my law firm. A copy of the agreement, together with a list of the names of the people sharing in the compensation, is attached.

5. In return for the above-disclosed fee, I have agreed to render legal service for all aspects of the bankruptcy case, including:

    a. Analysis of the debtor's financial situation, and rendering advice to the debtor in determining whether to file a petition in bankruptcy;

    b. Preparation and filing of any petition, schedules, statements of affairs and plan which may be required;

    c. Representation of the debtor at the meeting of creditors and confirmation hearing, and any adjourned hearings thereof;

B2030 (Form 2030) (12/15)

    d.   Representation of the debtor in adversary proceedings and other contested bankruptcy matters;

    e.   [Other provisions as needed]

6.   By agreement with the debtor(s), the above-disclosed fee does not include the following services:

CERTIFICATION

    I certify that the foregoing is a complete statement of any agreement or arrangement for payment to me for representation of the debtor(s) in this bankruptcy proceeding.

_____   _____
Date   *Signature of Attorney*

                               _____
                               Name of law firm

B2300A (Form 2300A) (12/15)

United States Bankruptcy Court

_____ District Of _____

In re _____
         Debtor*

Case No. _____

Address: _____

Chapter 12

Last four digits of Social-Security or Individual Taxpayer-
Identification (ITIN) No(s).,(if any):
Employer Tax-Identification (EIN) No(s).(if any):

ORDER CONFIRMING CHAPTER 12 PLAN

The debtor's plan was filed on _____ (date), and was modified on _____
(date). The plan or a summary of the plan was transmitted to creditors pursuant to Bankruptcy Rule 3015.
The court finds that the plan meets the requirements of 11 U.S.C. § 1225.

IT IS ORDERED THAT:

The debtor's chapter 12 plan is confirmed, with the following provisions:

1. Payments:
Amount of each payment: $_____

Due date of each payment: the   ☐ _____ day of each month, or
                                ☐ _____

Period of payments: ☐ _____ months,
                                ☐ until a _____ % dividend is paid to creditors holding
                                allowed unsecured claims, or
                                ☐ _____
Payable to:
_____ Standing Trustee
_____
_____

2. Attorney's Fees:
The debtor's attorney is awarded a fee in the amount of $_____, of which
$_____ is due and payable from the estate.

3. [Other provisions as needed] _____

_____

_____Date_____   _____Bankruptcy Judge_____

*_Set forth all names, including trade names, used by the debtor(s) within the last 8 years. For joint debtors, set
forth the last four digits of both social-security numbers or individual taxpayer-identification numbers._

B2300B (Form 2300B) (12/15)

United States Bankruptcy Court

_____ District Of _____

In re _____   Case No. _____
              Debtor*

Address: _____   Chapter 13

Last four digits of Social-Security or Individual Taxpayer-
Identification (ITIN) No(s).,(if any):
Employer Tax-Identification (EIN) No(s).(if any):

ORDER CONFIRMING CHAPTER 13 PLAN

       The debtor's plan was filed on _____ (date), and was modified on _____ (date).
The plan or a summary of the plan was transmitted to creditors pursuant to Bankruptcy Rule 3015. The court finds
that the plan meets the requirements of 11 U.S.C. § 1325.

IT IS ORDERED THAT:

The debtor's chapter 13 plan is confirmed, with the following provisions:

      1. Payments:
      Amount of each payment: $_____

      Due date of each payment: the   ☐ _____day of each month, or
                                          ☐ _____

      Period of payments: ☐ _____ months,
                                    ☐ until a _____% dividend is paid to creditors holding
      allowed unsecured claims, or
                                    ☐ _____
      Payable to:
      _____ Standing Trustee
      _____
      _____

      2. Attorney's Fees:
      The debtor's attorney is awarded a fee in the amount of $_____, of which $_____ is
      due and payable from the estate.

      3. [Other provisions as needed] _____

_____   _____
           Date   _Bankruptcy Judge_

* Set forth all names, including trade names, used by the debtor(s) within the last 8 years. For joint debtors, set
forth the last four digits of both social-security numbers or individual taxpayer-identification numbers.

B2310A (Form 2310A) (12/15)

United States Bankruptcy Court
_____ District Of _____

In re

Debtor*

Case No. _____

Address:

Chapter _____

Last four digits of Social-Security or Individual Taxpayer-
Identification (ITIN) No(s).,(if any):
Employer Tax-Identification (EIN) No(s).(if any):

ORDER FIXING TIME TO OBJECT TO PROPOSED MODIFICATION
OF CONFIRMED CHAPTER 12 PLAN

To the debtor, trustee, and creditors:

_____filed a proposed modification of the confirmed
plan on _____ (date). A copy of the proposed modification is
attached.

IT IS ORDERED AND NOTICE IS GIVEN THAT:

    1.   The last day for filing a written objection to the proposed
        modification is:

Date:

    2.   The proponent of the proposed modification is directed to
        serve a copy or summary of the proposed modification of the
        plan, together with a copy of this order, on the debtor, the
        trustee, the United States trustee, and all creditors no
        later than 21 days before the date set forth above.

    3.   Any objection to the proposed modification shall be filed
        and served on the debtor, the trustee, the United States
        trustee, and all creditors.

4.   If an objection is filed, a hearing to consider the proposed
     modification will be held at:

Address	Room
	Date and Time

If no objection is filed, the court may not hold a hearing.

Date: _____   BY THE COURT

                                        _____
                                        United States Bankruptcy Judge

* Set forth all names, including trade names, used by the debtor(s) within the
last 8 years. For joint debtors, set forth the last four digits of both
social-security numbers or individual taxpayer-identification numbers.

B2310B (Form 2310B) (12/15)

United States Bankruptcy Court
_____ District Of _____

In re

          Debtor*

Address:

Case No. _____

Chapter _____

Last four digits of Social-Security or Individual Taxpayer-
Identification (ITIN) No(s).,(if any):
Employer Tax-Identification (EIN) No(s).(if any):

ORDER FIXING TIME TO OBJECT TO PROPOSED MODIFICATION
OF CONFIRMED CHAPTER 13 PLAN

To the debtor, trustee, and creditors:

               _____filed a proposed modification of the confirmed
plan on _____ (date). A copy of the proposed modification is
attached.

IT IS ORDERED AND NOTICE IS GIVEN THAT:

    1.   The last day for filing a written objection to the proposed
          modification is:

Date:

    2.   The proponent of the proposed modification is directed to
          serve a copy or summary of the proposed modification of the
          plan, together with a copy of this order, on the debtor, the
          trustee, the United States trustee, and all creditors no
          later than 21 days before the date set forth above.

    3.   Any objection to the proposed modification shall be filed
          and served on the debtor, the trustee, the United States
          trustee, and all creditors.

4. If an objection is filed, a hearing to consider the proposed modification will be held at:

Address	Room
	Date and Time

If no objection is filed, the court may not hold a hearing.

Date: _____   BY THE COURT

                                             _____
                                             United States Bankruptcy Judge

---

* Set forth all names, including trade names, used by the debtor(s) within the last 8 years. For joint debtors, set forth the last four digits of both social-security numbers or individual taxpayer-identification numbers.

Information to identify the case:

Debtor 1 _____ Last 4 digits of Social Security number or ITIN _ _ _ _
            First Name   Middle Name   Last Name
                                                          EIN   _ _ - _ _ _ _ _ _ _

Debtor 2 _____ Last 4 digits of Social Security number or ITIN _ _ _ _
(Spouse, if filing) First Name   Middle Name   Last Name
                                                          EIN   _ _ - _ _ _ _ _ _ _

United States Bankruptcy Court for the: _____ District of _____
                                                              (State)

Case number: _____

Order of Discharge

IT IS ORDERED: A discharge under 11 U.S.C. § 1228(a) is granted to:

_____   [_____]

[include all names used by each debtor, including trade names, within the 8 years prior to the filing of the petition]

_____   **By the court:** _____
MM / DD / YYYY   United States Bankruptcy Judge

Explanation of Bankruptcy Discharge in a Chapter 12 Case

This order does not close or dismiss the case.

Creditors cannot collect discharged debts

This order means that no one may make any attempt to collect a discharged debt from the debtors personally. For example, creditors cannot sue, garnish wages, assert a deficiency, or otherwise try to collect from the debtors personally on discharged debts. Creditors cannot contact the debtors by mail, phone, or otherwise in any attempt to collect the debt personally. Creditors who violate this order can be required to pay debtors damages and attorney's fees.

However, a creditor with a lien may enforce a claim against the debtors' property subject to that lien unless the lien was avoided or eliminated. For example, a creditor may have the right to foreclose a home mortgage or repossess an automobile.

This order does not prevent debtors from paying any debt voluntarily. 11 U.S.C. § 524(f).

Most debts are discharged

Most debts are covered by the discharge, but not all. Generally, a discharge removes the debtors' personal liability for debts provided for by the chapter 12 plan.

In a case involving community property: Special rules protect certain community property owned by the debtor's spouse, even if that spouse did not file a bankruptcy case.

Some debts are not discharged

Examples of debts that are not discharged are:

■ debts that are domestic support obligations;

■ debts for most student loans;

■ debts for most taxes;

■ debts that the bankruptcy court has decided or will decide are not discharged in this bankruptcy case;

For more information, see page 2 ▶

Form 3180F   **Chapter 12 Discharge**   page **1**

- debts for most fines, penalties, forfeitures, or criminal restitution obligations;

- some debts which the debtors did not properly list;

- debts for certain types of loans owed to pension, profit sharing, stock bonus, or retirement plans;

- debts provided for under 11 U.S.C. § 1222(b)(5) or (b)(9) and on which the last payment or other transfer is due after the date on which the final payment under the plan was due; and

- debts for death or personal injury caused by operating a vehicle while intoxicated.

In addition, this discharge does not stop creditors from collecting from anyone else who is also liable on the debt, such as an insurance company or a person who cosigned or guaranteed a loan.

> **This information is only a general summary of a chapter 12 discharge; some exceptions exist. Because the law is complicated, you should consult an attorney to determine the exact effect of the discharge in this case.**

Information to identify the case:

Debtor 1 _____
First Name   Middle Name   Last Name

Last 4 digits of Social Security number or ITIN _ _ _ _

EIN _ _ - _ _ _ _ _ _ _

Debtor 2 _____
(Spouse, if filing) First Name   Middle Name   Last Name

Last 4 digits of Social Security number or ITIN _ _ _ _

EIN _ _ - _ _ _ _ _ _ _

United States Bankruptcy Court for the: _____ District of _____
(State)

Case number: _____

Order of Discharge

IT IS ORDERED: A discharge under 11 U.S.C. § 1228(b) is granted to:

_____   [_____]

[include all names used by each debtor, including trade names, within the 8 years prior to the filing of the petition]

_____
MM / DD / YYYY

By the court: _____
United States Bankruptcy Judge

Explanation of Bankruptcy Discharge Before Completion of a Chapter 12 Plan

The court has determined that the debtors are entitled to a discharge pursuant to 11 U.S.C. § 1228(b) without completing all of the requirements under the chapter 12 plan. A discharge pursuant to § 1228(b) is referred to as a "hardship discharge."

This order does not close or dismiss the case.

Creditors cannot collect discharged debts

This order means that no one may make any attempt to collect a discharged debt from the debtors personally. For example, creditors cannot sue, garnish wages, assert a deficiency, or otherwise try to collect from the debtors personally on discharged debts. Creditors cannot contact the debtors by mail, phone, or otherwise in any attempt to collect the debt personally. Creditors who violate this order can be required to pay debtors damages and attorney's fees.

However, a creditor with a lien may enforce a claim against the debtors' property subject to that lien unless the lien was avoided or eliminated. For example, a creditor may have the right to foreclose a home mortgage or repossess an automobile.

This order does not prevent debtors from paying any debt voluntarily. 11 U.S.C. § 524(f).

Most debts are discharged

Most debts are covered by the discharge, but not all. Generally, a discharge removes the debtors' personal liability for debts provided for by the chapter 12 plan.

In a case involving community property: Special rules protect certain community property owned by the debtor's spouse, even if that spouse did not file a bankruptcy case.

Some debts are not discharged

Examples of debts that are not discharged are:

- debts that are domestic support obligations;

- debts for most student loans;

- debts for most taxes;

For more information, see page 2 ▶

Form 3180FH   **Chapter 12 Hardship Discharge**   page **1**

■ debts that the bankruptcy court has decided or will decide are not discharged in this bankruptcy case;

■ debts for most fines, penalties, forfeitures, or criminal restitution obligations;

■ some debts which the debtors did not properly list;

■ debts for certain types of loans owed to pension, profit sharing, stock bonus, or retirement plans;

■ debts provided for under 11 U.S.C. § 1222(b)(5) or (b)(9) and on which the last payment or other transfer is due after the date on which the final payment under the plan was due; and

■ debts for death or personal injury caused by operating a vehicle while intoxicated.

In addition, this discharge does not stop creditors from collecting from anyone else who is also liable on the debt, such as an insurance company or a person who cosigned or guaranteed a loan.

> **This information is only a general summary of a chapter 12 hardship discharge; some exceptions exist. Because the law is complicated, you should consult an attorney to determine the exact effect of the discharge in this case.**

Information to identify the case:

Debtor 1 _____   Last 4 digits of Social Security number or ITIN _ _ _ _
           First Name   Middle Name   Last Name
                                                                   EIN   _ _ - _ _ _ _ _ _ _

Debtor 2 _____   Last 4 digits of Social Security number or ITIN _ _ _ _
(Spouse, if filing) First Name   Middle Name   Last Name
                                                                   EIN   _ _ - _ _ _ _ _ _ _

United States Bankruptcy Court for the: _____ District of _____
                                                           (State)

Case number: _____

Order of Discharge

IT IS ORDERED: A discharge under 11 U.S.C. § 1141(d)(5) is granted to:

_____   [_____]

[include all names used by each debtor, including trade names, within the 8 years prior to the filing of the petition]

_____   **By the court:** _____
MM / DD / YYYY   United States Bankruptcy Judge

Explanation of Bankruptcy Discharge in an Individual Chapter 11 Case

This order does not close or dismiss the case.

Creditors cannot collect discharged debts

This order means that no one may make any attempt to collect a discharged debt from the debtors personally. For example, creditors cannot sue, garnish wages, assert a deficiency, or otherwise try to collect from the debtors personally on discharged debts. Creditors cannot contact the debtors by mail, phone, or otherwise in any attempt to collect the debt personally. Creditors who violate this order can be required to pay debtors damages and attorney's fees.

However, a creditor with a lien may enforce a claim against the debtors' property subject to that lien unless the lien was avoided or eliminated. For example, a creditor may have the right to foreclose a home mortgage or repossess an automobile.

This order does not prevent debtors from paying any debt voluntarily. 11 U.S.C. § 524(f).

Most debts are discharged

Most debts are covered by the discharge, but not all. Generally, a discharge removes the debtors' personal liability for debts provided for by the chapter 11 plan.

In a case involving community property: Special rules protect certain community property owned by the debtor's spouse, even if that spouse did not file a bankruptcy case.

Some debts are not discharged

Examples of debts that are not discharged are:

- debts that are domestic support obligations;

- debts for most student loans;

- debts for most taxes;

- debts that the bankruptcy court has decided or will decide are not discharged in this bankruptcy case;

For more information, see page 2 ▶

Form 3180RI   **Individual Chapter 11 Discharge**   page **1**

■ debts for most fines, penalties, forfeitures, or criminal restitution obligations;

■ some debts which the debtors did not properly list;

■ debts for certain types of loans owed to pension, profit sharing, stock bonus, or retirement plans; and

■ debts for death or personal injury caused by operating a vehicle while intoxicated.

In addition, this discharge does not stop creditors from collecting from anyone else who is also liable on the debt, such as an insurance company or a person who cosigned or guaranteed a loan.

This information is only a general summary of an individual chapter 11 discharge; some exceptions exist. Because the law is complicated, you should consult an attorney to determine the exact effect of the discharge in this case.

Information to identify the case:

Debtor 1 _____   Last 4 digits of Social Security number or ITIN _ _ _ _
         First Name   Middle Name   Last Name
                                                  EIN _ _ - _ _ _ _ _ _ _

Debtor 2 _____   Last 4 digits of Social Security number or ITIN _ _ _ _
(Spouse, if filing) First Name Middle Name Last Name
                                                  EIN _ _ - _ _ _ _ _ _ _

United States Bankruptcy Court for the: _____ District of _____
                                                              (State)

Case number: _____

Order of Discharge
04/20

IT IS ORDERED: A discharge under 11 U.S.C. § 1141(d) is granted to:

_____   [_____]

[include all names used by each debtor, including trade names, within the 8 years prior to the filing of the petition]

_____   **By the court:** _____
MM / DD / YYYY   United States Bankruptcy Judge

Explanation of Bankruptcy Discharge under § 1141(d) in an Individual's Case under Subchapter V of Chapter 11

This order does not close or dismiss the case.

Creditors cannot collect discharged debts

This order means that no one may make any attempt to collect a discharged debt from the debtor personally. For example, creditors cannot sue, garnish wages, assert a deficiency, or otherwise try to collect from the debtor personally on discharged debts. Creditors cannot contact the debtor by mail, phone, or otherwise in any attempt to collect the debt personally. Creditors who violate this order can be required to pay debtor's damages and attorney's fees.

However, a creditor with a lien may enforce a claim against the debtors' property subject to that lien unless the lien was avoided or eliminated. For example, a creditor may have the right to foreclose a home mortgage or repossess an automobile.

This order does not prevent debtors from paying any debt voluntarily. 11 U.S.C. § 524(f).

Most debts are discharged

Most debts are covered by the discharge, but not all. Generally, a discharge removes the debtor's personal liability for debts that arose before confirmation of the plan.

In a case involving community property: Special rules protect certain community property owned by the debtor's spouse, even if that spouse did not file a bankruptcy case.

Some debts are not discharged

Examples of debts that are not discharged are:

- debts that are domestic support obligations;

- debts for most student loans;

- debts for most taxes;

- debts that the bankruptcy court has decided or will decide are not discharged in this bankruptcy case;

For more information, see page 2 ▶

Form 3180RV1   **Chapter 11 Discharge for Individual Whose Plan was Confirmed under § 1191(a)**   page 1

- debts for most fines, penalties, forfeitures, or criminal restitution obligations;

- some debts which the debtors did not properly list;

- debts for certain types of loans owed to pension, profit sharing, stock bonus, or retirement plans; and

- debts for death or personal injury caused by operating a vehicle while intoxicated.

In addition, this discharge does not stop creditors from collecting from anyone else who is also liable on the debt, such as an insurance company or a person who cosigned or guaranteed a loan.

> **This information is only a general summary of subchapter V discharge; some exceptions exist. Because the law is complicated, you should consult an attorney to determine the exact effect of the discharge in this case.**

Information to identify the case:

Debtor 1 _____   Last 4 digits of Social Security number or ITIN _ _ _ _

First Name   Middle Name   Last Name

EIN _ _ - _ _ _ _ _ _ _

Debtor 2 _____   Last 4 digits of Social Security number or ITIN _ _ _ _

(Spouse, if filing) First Name   Middle Name   Last Name

EIN _ _ - _ _ _ _ _ _ _

United States Bankruptcy Court for the: _____ District of _____

(State)

Case number: _____

Order of Discharge

04/20

IT IS ORDERED: A discharge under 11 U.S.C. § 1192 is granted to:

_____   [_____]

[include all names used by each debtor, including trade names, within the 8 years prior to the filing of the petition]

_____   **By the court:** _____

MM / DD / YYYY   United States Bankruptcy Judge

Explanation of Bankruptcy Discharge in an Individual's Case under § 1192 of Chapter 11, Subchapter V

This order does not close or dismiss the case.

Creditors cannot collect discharged debts

This order means that no one may make any attempt to collect a discharged debt from the debtor personally. For example, creditors cannot sue, garnish wages, assert a deficiency, or otherwise try to collect from the debtor personally on discharged debts. Creditors cannot contact the debtor by mail, phone, or otherwise in any attempt to collect the debt personally. Creditors who violate this order can be required to pay debtor's damages and attorney's fees.

However, a creditor with a lien may enforce a claim against the debtors' property subject to that lien unless the lien was avoided or eliminated. For example, a creditor may have the right to foreclose a home mortgage or repossess an automobile.

This order does not prevent debtors from paying any debt voluntarily. 11 U.S.C. § 524(f).

Most debts are discharged

Most debts are covered by the discharge, but not all. Generally, a discharge removes the debtor's personal liability for debts that arose before confirmation of the plan and for administrative expenses provided for in the plan.

In a case involving community property: Special rules protect certain community property owned by the debtor's spouse, even if that spouse did not file a bankruptcy case.

Some debts are not discharged

Examples of debts that are not discharged are:

- debts that are domestic support obligations;

- debts for most student loans;

- debts for most taxes;

- debts that the bankruptcy court has decided or will decide are not discharged in this bankruptcy case;

For more information, see page 2 ▶

Form 3180RV2   **Chapter 11 Discharge for Individual Whose Plan was Confirmed under § 1191(b)**   page 1

- debts for most fines, penalties, forfeitures, or criminal restitution obligations;

- some debts which the debtors did not properly list;

- debts for certain types of loans owed to pension, profit sharing, stock bonus, or retirement plans;

- debts for death or personal injury caused by operating a vehicle while intoxicated; and

- debts described by 11 U.S.C. § 1192(1): those on which the last payment is due after the first 3 years of the plan, or such other time not to exceed 5 years fixed by the court.

In addition, this discharge does not stop creditors from collecting from anyone else who is also liable on the debt, such as an insurance company or a person who cosigned or guaranteed a loan.

> **This information is only a general summary of subchapter V discharge; some exceptions exist. Because the law is complicated, you should consult an attorney to determine the exact effect of the discharge in this case.**

Fill in this information to identify the case:

Debtor name _____

United States Bankruptcy Court for the:_____ District of _____
(State)

Case number : _____

Order of Discharge

04/20

IT IS ORDERED: A discharge under 11 U.S.C. § 1192 is granted to:

_____   [_____]

[include all names used by each debtor, including trade names, within the 8 years prior to the filing of the petition]

_____
MM / DD / YYYY

By the court: _____
United States Bankruptcy Judge

Explanation of Bankruptcy Discharge in a Corporation or Partnership Case under § 1192 of Chapter 11, Subchapter V

This order does not close or dismiss the case.

Creditors cannot collect discharged debts

This order means that no one may make any attempt to collect a discharged debt from the debtor as a personal liability. For example, creditors cannot sue, assert a deficiency, or otherwise try to collect from the debtor on discharged debts. Creditors cannot contact the debtor by mail, phone, or otherwise in any attempt to collect the debt. Creditors who violate this order can be required to pay debtor's damages and attorney's fees.

However, a creditor with a lien may enforce a claim against the debtors' property subject to that lien unless the lien was avoided or eliminated. For example, a creditor may have the right to foreclose a mortgage or repossess an automobile.

This order does not prevent debtors from paying any debt voluntarily. 11 U.S.C. § 524(f).

Most debts are discharged

Most debts are covered by the discharge, but not all.

Generally, a discharge removes the debtor's personal liability for debts that arose before confirmation of the plan and for administrative expenses provided for in the plan.

Some debts are not discharged

Debts not discharged are the following:

- debts that the bankruptcy court has decided or will decide are not discharged in this bankruptcy case; and

- debts described by 11 U.S.C. § 1192(1): those on which the last payment is due after the first 3 years of the plan, or such other time not to exceed 5 years fixed by the court.

In addition, this discharge does not stop creditors from collecting from anyone else who is also liable on the debt, such as an insurance company or a person who cosigned or guaranteed a loan.

> **This information is only a general summary of subchapter V discharge; some exceptions exist. Because the law is complicated, you should consult an attorney to determine the exact effect of the discharge in this case.**

Form 3180RV3   **For Corporation or Partnership Whose Plan was Confirmed under § 1191(b)**

Information to identify the case:

Debtor 1 _____	Last 4 digits of Social Security number or ITIN _ _ _ _
First Name Middle Name Last Name	EIN _ _ - _ _ _ _ _ _ _
Debtor 2 _____	Last 4 digits of Social Security number or ITIN _ _ _ _
(Spouse, if filing) First Name Middle Name Last Name	EIN _ _ - _ _ _ _ _ _ _

United States Bankruptcy Court for the: _____ District of _____
(State)

Case number: _____

Order of Discharge   12/18

IT IS ORDERED: A discharge under 11 U.S.C. § 1328(a) is granted to:

_____   [_____]

[include all names used by each debtor, including trade names, within the 8 years prior to the filing of the petition]

_____   **By the court:** _____
MM / DD / YYYY   United States Bankruptcy Judge

Explanation of Bankruptcy Discharge in a Chapter 13 Case

This order does not close or dismiss the case.

Creditors cannot collect discharged debts

This order means that no one may make any attempt to collect a discharged debt from the debtors personally. For example, creditors cannot sue, garnish wages, assert a deficiency, or otherwise try to collect from the debtors personally on discharged debts. Creditors cannot contact the debtors by mail, phone, or otherwise in any attempt to collect the debt personally. Creditors who violate this order can be required to pay debtors damages and attorney's fees.

However, a creditor with a lien may enforce a claim against the debtors' property subject to that lien unless the lien was avoided or eliminated. For example, a creditor may have the right to foreclose a home mortgage or repossess an automobile.

This order does not prevent debtors from paying any debt voluntarily. 11 U.S.C. § 524(f).

Most debts are discharged

Most debts are covered by the discharge, but not all. Generally, a discharge removes the debtors' personal liability for debts provided for by the chapter 13 plan.

In a case involving community property: Special rules protect certain community property owned by the debtor's spouse, even if that spouse did not file a bankruptcy case.

Some debts are not discharged

Examples of debts that are not discharged are:

- debts that are domestic support obligations;

- debts for most student loans;

- debts for certain types of taxes specified in 11 U.S.C. §§ 507(a)(8)(C), 523(a)(1)(B), or 523(a)(1)(C) to the extent not paid in full under the plan;

For more information, see page 2 ▶

Form 3180W   **Chapter 13 Discharge**   page 1

- debts that the bankruptcy court has decided or will decide are not discharged in this bankruptcy case;

- debts for restitution, or a criminal fine, included in a sentence on debtor's criminal conviction;

- some debts which the debtors did not properly list;

- debts provided for under 11 U.S.C. § 1322(b)(5) and on which the last payment or other transfer is due after the date on which the final payment under the plan was due;

- debts for certain consumer purchases made after the bankruptcy case was filed if obtaining the trustee's prior approval of incurring the debt was practicable but was not obtained;

- debts for restitution, or damages, awarded in a civil action against the debtor as a result of malicious or willful injury by the debtor that caused personal injury to an individual or the death of an individual; and

- debts for death or personal injury caused by operating a vehicle while intoxicated.

In addition, this discharge does not stop creditors from collecting from anyone else who is also liable on the debt, such as an insurance company or a person who cosigned or guaranteed a loan.

This information is only a general summary of a chapter 13 discharge; some exceptions exist. Because the law is complicated, you should consult an attorney to determine the exact effect of the discharge in this case.

Information to identify the case:

Debtor 1 _____ Last 4 digits of Social Security number or ITIN _ _ _ _
　　　　　First Name　　　Middle Name　　　Last Name
　　　　　　　　　　　　　　　　　　　　　　　　　　　　EIN　_ _ - _ _ _ _ _ _ _

Debtor 2 _____ Last 4 digits of Social Security number or ITIN _ _ _ _
(Spouse, if filing) First Name　Middle Name　　Last Name
　　　　　　　　　　　　　　　　　　　　　　　　　　　　EIN　_ _ - _ _ _ _ _ _ _

United States Bankruptcy Court for the: _____ District of _____
　　　　　　　　　　　　　　　　　　　　　　　　　　(State)

Case number: _____

Order of Discharge

IT IS ORDERED: A discharge under 11 U.S.C. § 1328(b) is granted to:

_____　　[_____]

[include all names used by each debtor, including trade names, within the 8 years prior to the filing of the petition]

_____　　　　　　　　　**By the court:** _____
MM / DD / YYYY　　　　　　　　　　　　　　　　　United States Bankruptcy Judge

---

Explanation of Bankruptcy Discharge Before Completion of a Chapter 13 Plan

The court has determined that the debtors are entitled to a discharge pursuant to 11 U.S.C. § 1328(b) without completing all of the requirements under the chapter 13 plan. A discharge pursuant to § 1328(b) is referred to as a "hardship discharge."

This order does not close or dismiss the case.

Creditors cannot collect discharged debts

This order means that no one may make any attempt to collect a discharged debt from the debtors personally. For example, creditors cannot sue, garnish wages, assert a deficiency, or otherwise try to collect from the debtors personally on discharged debts. Creditors cannot contact the debtors by mail, phone, or otherwise in any attempt to collect the debt personally. Creditors who violate this order can be required to pay debtors damages and attorney's fees.

However, a creditor with a lien may enforce a claim against the debtors' property subject to that lien unless the lien was avoided or eliminated. For example, a creditor may have the right to foreclose a home mortgage or repossess an automobile.

This order does not prevent debtors from paying any debt voluntarily. 11 U.S.C. § 524(f).

Most debts are discharged

Most debts are covered by the discharge, but not all. Generally, a discharge removes the debtors' personal liability for debts provided for by the chapter 13 plan.

In a case involving community property: Special rules protect certain community property owned by the debtor's spouse, even if that spouse did not file a bankruptcy case.

Some debts are not discharged

Examples of debts that are not discharged are:

　　debts that are domestic support obligations;

　　debts for most student loans;

For more information, see page 2 ▶

Form 3180WH　　　　　　**Chapter 13 Hardship Discharge**　　　　　page **2** debts for most taxes;

debts that the bankruptcy court has decided or will decide are not discharged in this bankruptcy case;

debts for most fines, penalties, forfeitures, or criminal restitution obligations;

some debts which the debtors did not properly list;

debts for certain types of loans owed to pension, profit sharing, stock bonus, or retirement plans;

debts provided for under 11 U.S.C. § 1322(b)(5) and on which the last payment or other transfer is due after the date on which the final payment under the plan was due;

debts for certain consumer purchases made after the bankruptcy case was filed if obtaining the trustee's prior approval of incurring the debt was practicable but was not obtained; and

debts for death or personal injury caused by operating a vehicle while intoxicated.

In addition, this discharge does not stop creditors from collecting from anyone else who is also liable on the debt, such as an insurance company or a person who cosigned or guaranteed a loan.

> **This information is only a general summary of a chapter 13 hardship discharge; some exceptions exist. Because the law is complicated, you should consult an attorney to determine the exact effect of the discharge in this case.**

RELATED UNIFORM LAWS

Uniform Voidable Transactions Act.

Uniform Fraudulent Transfer Act.

Uniform Commercial Code (Selected Sections).

UNIFORM VOIDABLE TRANSACTIONS ACT*

Formerly Uniform Fraudulent Transfer Act
As amended in 2014

§ 1.   Definitions

As used in this [Act]:

(1) "Affiliate" means:

(i) a person that directly or indirectly owns, controls, or holds with power to vote, 20 percent or more of the outstanding voting securities of the debtor, other than a person that holds the securities:

(A) as a fiduciary or agent without sole discretionary power to vote the securities; or

---

(B) solely to secure a debt, if the person has not in fact exercised the power to vote;

(ii) a corporation **20** percent or more of whose outstanding voting securities are directly or indirectly owned, controlled, or held with power to vote, by the debtor or a person that directly or indirectly owns, controls, or holds, with power to vote, **20** percent or more of the outstanding voting securities of the debtor, other than a person that holds the securities:

(A) as a fiduciary or agent without sole discretionary power to vote the securities; or

(B) solely to secure a debt, if the person has not in fact exercised the power to vote;

(iii) a person whose business is operated by the debtor under a lease or other agreement, or a person substantially all of whose assets are controlled by the debtor; or

(iv) a person that operates the debtor's business under a lease or other agreement or controls substantially all of the debtor's assets.

(2) "Asset" means property of a debtor, but the term does not include:

(i) property to the extent it is encumbered by a valid lien;

(ii) property to the extent it is generally exempt under nonbankruptcy law; or

(iii) an interest in property held in tenancy by the entireties to the extent it is not subject to process by a creditor holding a claim against only one tenant.

(3) "Claim", except as used in "claim for relief", means a right to payment, whether or not the right is reduced to judgment, liquidated, unliquidated, fixed, contingent, matured, unmatured, disputed, undisputed, legal, equitable, secured, or unsecured.

(4) "Creditor" means a person that has a claim.

(5) "Debt" means liability on a claim.

(6) "Debtor" means a person that is liable on a claim.

(7) "Electronic" means relating to technology having electrical, digital, magnetic, wireless, optical, electromagnetic, or similar capabilities.

(8) "Insider" includes:

(i) if the debtor is an individual:

(A) a relative of the debtor or of a general partner of the debtor;

(B) a partnership in which the debtor is a general partner;

(C) a general partner in a partnership described in clause (B); or

(D) a corporation of which the debtor is a director, officer, or person in control;

(ii) if the debtor is a corporation:

(A) a director of the debtor;

(B) an officer of the debtor;

(C) a person in control of the debtor;

(D) a partnership in which the debtor is a general partner;

(E) a general partner in a partnership described in clause (D); or

(F) a relative of a general partner, director, officer, or person in control of the debtor;

(iii) if the debtor is a partnership:

(A) a general partner in the debtor;

(B) a relative of a general partner in, a general partner of, or a person in control of the debtor;

(C) another partnership in which the debtor is a general partner;

(D) a general partner in a partnership described in clause (C); or

(E) a person in control of the debtor;

(iv) an affiliate, or an insider of an affiliate as if the affiliate were the debtor; and

(v) a managing agent of the debtor.

(9) "Lien" means a charge against or an interest in property to secure payment of a debt or performance of an obligation, and includes a security interest created by agreement, a judicial lien obtained by legal or equitable process or proceedings, a common-law lien, or a statutory lien.

(10) "Organization" means a person other than an individual.

(11) "Person" means an individual, estate, business or nonprofit entity, public corporation, government or governmental subdivision, agency, or instrumentality, or other legal entity.

(12) "Property" means anything that may be the subject of ownership.

(13) "Record" means information that is inscribed on a tangible medium or that is stored in an electronic or other medium and is retrievable in perceivable form.

(14) "Relative" means an individual related by consanguinity within the third degree as determined by the common law, a spouse, or an individual related to a spouse within the third degree as so determined, and includes an individual in an adoptive relationship within the third degree.

(15) "Sign" means, with present intent to authenticate or adopt a record:

(i) to execute or adopt a tangible symbol; or

(ii) to attach to or logically associate with the record an electronic symbol, sound, or process.

(16) "Transfer" means every mode, direct or indirect, absolute or conditional, voluntary or involuntary, of disposing of or parting with an asset or an interest in an asset, and includes payment of money, release, lease, license, and creation of a lien or other encumbrance.

(17) "Valid lien" means a lien that is effective against the holder of a judicial lien subsequently obtained by legal or equitable process or proceedings.

§ 2. Insolvency

(a) A debtor is insolvent if, at a fair valuation, the sum of the debtor's debts is greater than the sum of the debtor's assets.

(b) A debtor that is generally not paying the debtor's debts as they become due other than as a result of a bona fide dispute is presumed to be insolvent. The presumption imposes on the party against which the presumption is directed the burden of proving that the nonexistence of insolvency is more probable than its existence.

(c) Assets under this section do not include property that has been transferred, concealed, or removed with intent to hinder, delay, or defraud creditors or that has been transferred in a manner making the transfer voidable under this [Act].

(d) Debts under this section do not include an obligation to the extent it is secured by a valid lien on property of the debtor not included as an asset.

§ 3. Value

(a) Value is given for a transfer or an obligation if, in exchange for the transfer or obligation, property is transferred or an antecedent debt is secured or satisfied, but value does not include an unperformed promise made otherwise than in the ordinary course of the promisor's business to furnish support to the debtor or another person.

(b)   For the purposes of Section 4(a)(2) and Section 5, a person gives a reasonably equivalent value if the person acquires an interest of the debtor in an asset pursuant to a regularly conducted, noncollusive foreclosure sale or execution of a power of sale for the acquisition or disposition of the interest of the debtor upon default under a mortgage, deed of trust, or security agreement.

(c)   A transfer is made for present value if the exchange between the debtor and the transferee is intended by them to be contemporaneous and is in fact substantially contemporaneous.

§ 4.   Transfer or Obligation Voidable as to Present or Future Creditor

(a)   A transfer made or obligation incurred by a debtor is voidable as to a creditor, whether the creditor's claim arose before or after the transfer was made or the obligation was incurred, if the debtor made the transfer or incurred the obligation:

(1)   with actual intent to hinder, delay, or defraud any creditor of the debtor; or

(2)   without receiving a reasonably equivalent value in exchange for the transfer or obligation, and the debtor:

(i)   was engaged or was about to engage in a business or a transaction for which the remaining assets of the debtor were unreasonably small in relation to the business or transaction; or

(ii)   intended to incur, or believed or reasonably should have believed that the debtor would incur, debts beyond the debtor's ability to pay as they became due.

(b)   In determining actual intent under subsection (a)(1), consideration may be given, among other factors, to whether:

(1)   the transfer or obligation was to an insider;

(2)   the debtor retained possession or control of the property transferred after the transfer;

(3)   the transfer or obligation was disclosed or concealed;

(4)   before the transfer was made or obligation was incurred, the debtor had been sued or threatened with suit;

(5)   the transfer was of substantially all the debtor's assets;

(6)   the debtor absconded;

(7)   the debtor removed or concealed assets;

(8)   the value of the consideration received by the debtor was reasonably equivalent to the value of the asset transferred or the amount of the obligation incurred;

(9)   the debtor was insolvent or became insolvent shortly after the transfer was made or the obligation was incurred;

(10)   the transfer occurred shortly before or shortly after a substantial debt was incurred; and

(11)   the debtor transferred the essential assets of the business to a lienor that transferred the assets to an insider of the debtor.

(c)   A creditor making a claim for relief under subsection (a) has the burden of proving the elements of the claim for relief by a preponderance of the evidence.

§ 5. Transfer or Obligation Voidable as to Present Creditor

(a)   A transfer made or obligation incurred by a debtor is voidable as to a creditor whose claim arose before the transfer was made or the obligation was incurred if the debtor made the transfer or incurred the obligation without receiving a reasonably equivalent value in exchange for the transfer or obligation and the debtor was insolvent at that time or the debtor became insolvent as a result of the transfer or obligation.

(b)   A transfer made by a debtor is voidable as to a creditor whose claim arose before the transfer was made if the transfer was made to an insider for an antecedent debt, the debtor was insolvent at that time, and the insider had reasonable cause to believe that the debtor was insolvent.

(c)   Subject to Section 2(b), a creditor making a claim for relief under subsection (a) or (b) has the burden of proving the elements of the claim for relief by a preponderance of the evidence.

§ 6. When Transfer is Made or Obligation is Incurred

For the purposes of this [Act]:

(1)   a transfer is made:

(i)   with respect to an asset that is real property other than a fixture, but including the interest of a seller or purchaser under a contract for the sale of the asset, when the transfer is so far perfected that a good-faith purchaser of the asset from the debtor against which applicable law permits the transfer to be perfected cannot acquire an interest in the asset that is superior to the interest of the transferee; and

(ii)   with respect to an asset that is not real property or that is a fixture, when the transfer is so far perfected that a creditor on a simple contract cannot acquire a judicial lien otherwise than under this [Act] that is superior to the interest of the transferee;

(2)   if applicable law permits the transfer to be perfected as provided in paragraph (1) and the transfer is not so perfected before the commencement of an action for relief under this [Act], the transfer is deemed made immediately before the commencement of the action;

(3)   if applicable law does not permit the transfer to be perfected as provided in paragraph (1), the transfer is made when it becomes effective between the debtor and the transferee;

(4)   a transfer is not made until the debtor has acquired rights in the asset transferred; and

(5)   an obligation is incurred:

(i)   if oral, when it becomes effective between the parties; or

(ii)   if evidenced by a record, when the record signed by the obligor is delivered to or for the benefit of the obligee.

§ 7. Remedies of Creditor

(a)   In an action for relief against a transfer or obligation under this [Act], a creditor, subject to the limitations in Section 8, may obtain:

(1)   avoidance of the transfer or obligation to the extent necessary to satisfy the creditor's claim;

(2)   an attachment or other provisional remedy against the asset transferred or other property of the transferee if available under applicable law; and

(3)   subject to applicable principles of equity and in accordance with applicable rules of civil procedure:

(i)   an injunction against further disposition by the debtor or a transferee, or both, of the asset transferred or of other property;

(ii) appointment of a receiver to take charge of the asset transferred or of other property of the transferee; or

(iii) any other relief the circumstances may require.

(b) If a creditor has obtained a judgment on a claim against the debtor, the creditor, if the court so orders, may levy execution on the asset transferred or its proceeds.

§ 8.   Defenses, Liability, and Protection of Transferee or Obligee

(a) A transfer or obligation is not voidable under Section 4(a)(1) against a person that took in good faith and for a reasonably equivalent value given the debtor or against any subsequent transferee or obligee.

(b) To the extent a transfer is avoidable in an action by a creditor under Section 7(a)(1), the following rules apply:

(1) Except as otherwise provided in this section, the creditor may recover judgment for the value of the asset transferred, as adjusted under subsection (c), or the amount necessary to satisfy the creditor's claim, whichever is less. The judgment may be entered against:

(i) the first transferee of the asset or the person for whose benefit the transfer was made; or

(ii) an immediate or mediate transferee of the first transferee, other than:

(A) a good-faith transferee that took for value; or

(B) an immediate or mediate good-faith transferee of a person described in clause (A).

(2) Recovery pursuant to Section 7(a)(1) or (b) of or from the asset transferred or its proceeds, by levy or otherwise, is available only against a person described in paragraph (1)(i) or (ii).

(c) If the judgment under subsection (b) is based upon the value of the asset transferred, the judgment must be for an amount equal to the value of the asset at the time of the transfer, subject to adjustment as the equities may require.

(d) Notwithstanding voidability of a transfer or an obligation under this [Act], a good-faith transferee or obligee is entitled, to the extent of the value given the debtor for the transfer or obligation, to:

(1) a lien on or a right to retain an interest in the asset transferred;

(2) enforcement of an obligation incurred; or

(3) a reduction in the amount of the liability on the judgment.

(e) A transfer is not voidable under Section 4(a)(2) or Section 5 if the transfer results from:

(1) termination of a lease upon default by the debtor when the termination is pursuant to the lease and applicable law; or

(2) enforcement of a security interest in compliance with Article 9 of the Uniform Commercial Code, other than acceptance of collateral in full or partial satisfaction of the obligation it secures.

(f) A transfer is not voidable under Section 5(b):

(1) to the extent the insider gave new value to or for the benefit of the debtor after the transfer was made, except to the extent the new value was secured by a valid lien;

(2) if made in the ordinary course of business or financial affairs of the debtor and the insider; or

(3)   if made pursuant to a good-faith effort to rehabilitate the debtor and the transfer secured present value given for that purpose as well as an antecedent debt of the debtor.

(g)   The following rules determine the burden of proving matters referred to in this section:

(1)   A party that seeks to invoke subsection (a), (d), (e), or (f) has the burden of proving the applicability of that subsection.

(2)   Except as otherwise provided in paragraphs (3) and (4), the creditor has the burden of proving each applicable element of subsection (b) or (c).

(3)   The transferee has the burden of proving the applicability to the transferee of subsection (b)(1)(ii)(A) or (B).

(4)   A party that seeks adjustment under subsection (c) has the burden of proving the adjustment.

(h)   The standard of proof required to establish matters referred to in this section is preponderance of the evidence.

§ 9.   Extinguishment of Claim for Relief

A claim for relief with respect to a transfer or obligation under this [Act] is extinguished unless action is brought:

(a)   under Section 4(a)(1), not later than four years after the transfer was made or the obligation was incurred or, if later, not later than one year after the transfer or obligation was or could reasonably have been discovered by the claimant;

(b)   under Section 4(a)(2) or 5(a), not later than four years after the transfer was made or the obligation was incurred; or

(c)   under Section 5(b), not later than one year after the transfer was made.

§ 10.   Governing Law

(a)   In this section, the following rules determine a debtor's location:

(1)   A debtor who is an individual is located at the individual's principal residence.

(2)   A debtor that is an organization and has only one place of business is located at its place of business.

(3)   A debtor that is an organization and has more than one place of business is located at its chief executive office.

(b)   A claim for relief in the nature of a claim for relief under this [Act] is governed by the local law of the jurisdiction in which the debtor is located when the transfer is made or the obligation is incurred.

§ 11.   Application to Series Organization

(a)   In this section:

(1)   "Protected series" means an arrangement, however denominated, created by a series organization that, pursuant to the law under which the series organization is organized, has the characteristics set forth in paragraph (2).

(2)   "Series organization" means an organization that, pursuant to the law under which it is organized, has the following characteristics:

(i)   The organic record of the organization provides for creation by the organization of one or more protected series, however denominated, with respect to specified property of the organization, and for records to be maintained for each protected series that identify the property of or associated with the protected series.

(ii) Debt incurred or existing with respect to the activities of, or property of or associated with, a particular protected series is enforceable against the property of or associated with the protected series only, and not against the property of or associated with the organization or other protected series of the organization.

(iii) Debt incurred or existing with respect to the activities or property of the organization is enforceable against the property of the organization only, and not against the property of or associated with a protected series of the organization.

(b)   A series organization and each protected series of the organization is a separate person for purposes of this [Act], even if for other purposes a protected series is not a person separate from the organization or other protected series of the organization.

Legislative Note: This section should be enacted even if the enacting jurisdiction does not itself have legislation enabling the creation of protected series. For example, in such an enacting jurisdiction this section will apply if a protected series of a series organization organized under the law of a different jurisdiction makes a transfer to another protected series of that organization and, under applicable choice of law rules, the voidability of the transfer is governed by the law of the enacting jurisdiction.

§ 12.   Supplementary Provisions

Unless displaced by the provisions of this [Act], the principles of law and equity, including the law merchant and the law relating to principal and agent, estoppel, laches, fraud, misrepresentation, duress, coercion, mistake, insolvency, or other validating or invalidating cause, supplement its provisions.

§ 13.   Uniformity of Application and Construction

This [Act] shall be applied and construed to effectuate its general purpose to make uniform the law with respect to the subject of this [Act] among states enacting it.

§ 14.   Relation to Electronic Signatures in Global and National Commerce Act

This [Act] modifies, limits, or supersedes the Electronic Signatures in Global and National Commerce Act, 15 U.S.C. Section 7001 et seq., but does not modify, limit, or supersede Section 101(c) of that act, 15 U.S.C. Section 7001(c), or authorize electronic delivery of any of the notices described in Section 103(b) of that act, 15 U.S.C. Section 7003(b).

§ 15.   Short Title

This [Act], which was formerly cited as the Uniform Fraudulent Transfer Act, may be cited as the Uniform Voidable Transactions Act.

§ 16.   Repeals; Conforming Amendments

(a)   . . . .

(b)   . . . .

(c)   . . . .

Legislative Note: The legislation enacting the 2014 amendments in a jurisdiction in which the act is already in force should provide as follows: (i) the amendments apply to a transfer made or obligation incurred on or after the effective date of the enacting legislation, (ii) the amendments do not apply to a transfer made or obligation incurred before the effective date of the enacting legislation, (iii) the amendments do not apply to a right of action that has accrued before the effective date of the enacting legislation, and (iv) for the foregoing purposes a transfer is made and an obligation is incurred at the time provided in Section 6 of the act. In addition, the enacting legislation should revise any reference to the act by its former title in other permanent legislation of the enacting jurisdiction.

UNIFORM FRAUDULENT TRANSFER ACT*

Amended in 2014 and renamed the Uniform Voidable Transactions Act
See also the Uniform Fraudulent Conveyance Act, to which the UFTA is the successor.

---

§ 1.   Definitions

As used in this [Act]:

(1) "Affiliate" means:

(i)   a person who directly or indirectly owns, controls, or holds with power to vote, 20 percent or more of the outstanding voting securities of the debtor, other than a person who holds the securities,

(A) as a fiduciary or agent without sole discretionary power to vote the securities; or

(B) solely to secure a debt, if the person has not exercised the power to vote;

(ii) a corporation 20 percent or more of whose outstanding voting securities are directly or indirectly owned, controlled, or held with power to vote, by the debtor or a person who directly or indirectly owns, controls, or holds, with power to vote, 20 percent or more of the outstanding voting securities of the debtor, other than a person who holds the securities,

(A) as a fiduciary or agent without sole power to vote the securities; or

(B) solely to secure a debt, if the person has not in fact exercised the power to vote;

(iii) a person whose business is operated by the debtor under a lease or other agreement, or a person substantially all of whose assets are controlled by the debtor; or

(iv) a person who operates the debtor's business under a lease or other agreement or controls substantially all of the debtor's assets.

---

(2)   "Asset" means property of a debtor, but the term does not include:

    (i)   property to the extent it is encumbered by a valid lien;

    (ii)   property to the extent it is generally exempt under nonbankruptcy law; or

    (iii)   an interest in property held in tenancy by the entireties to the extent it is not subject to process by a creditor holding a claim against only one tenant.

(3)   "Claim" means a right to payment, whether or not the right is reduced to judgment, liquidated, unliquidated, fixed, contingent, matured, unmatured, disputed, undisputed, legal, equitable, secured, or unsecured.

(4)   "Creditor" means a person who has a claim.

(5)   "Debt" means liability on a claim.

(6)   "Debtor" means a person who is liable on a claim.

(7)   "Insider" includes:

    (i)   if the debtor is an individual,

        (A)   a relative of the debtor or of a general partner of the debtor;

        (B)   a partnership in which the debtor is a general partner;

        (C)   a general partner in a partnership described in clause (B); or

        (D)   a corporation of which the debtor is a director, officer, or person in control;

    (ii)   if the debtor is a corporation,

        (A)   a director of the debtor;

        (B)   an officer of the debtor;

        (C)   a person in control of the debtor;

        (D)   a partnership in which the debtor is a general partner;

        (E)   a general partner in a partnership described in clause (D); or

        (F)   a relative of a general partner, director, officer, or person in control of the debtor;

    (iii)   if the debtor is a partnership,

        (A)   a general partner in the debtor;

        (B)   a relative of a general partner in, a general partner of, or a person in control of the debtor;

        (C)   another partnership in which the debtor is a general partner;

        (D)   a general partner in a partnership described in clause (C); or

        (E)   a person in control of the debtor;

    (iv)   an affiliate, or an insider of an affiliate as if the affiliate were the debtor; and

    (v)   a managing agent of the debtor.

(8)   "Lien" means a charge against or an interest in property to secure payment of a debt or performance of an obligation, and includes a security interest created by agreement, a judicial lien obtained by legal or equitable process or proceedings, a common-law lien, or a statutory lien.

(9)   "Person" means an individual, partnership, corporation, association, organization, government or governmental subdivision or agency, business trust, estate, trust, or any other legal or commercial entity.

(10) "Property" means anything that may be the subject of ownership.

(11) "Relative" means an individual related by consanguinity within the third degree as determined by the common law, a spouse, or an individual related to a spouse within the third degree as so determined, and includes an individual in an adoptive relationship within the third degree.

(12) "Transfer" means every mode, direct or indirect, absolute or conditional, voluntary or involuntary, of disposing of or parting with an asset or an interest in an asset, and includes payment of money, release, lease, and creation of a lien or other encumbrance.

(13) "Valid lien" means a lien that is effective against the holder of a judicial lien subsequently obtained by legal or equitable process or proceedings.

§ 2. Insolvency

(a) A debtor is insolvent if the sum of the debtor's debts is greater than all of the debtor's assets at a fair valuation.

(b) A debtor who is generally not paying his [or her] debts as they become due is presumed to be insolvent.

(c) A partnership is insolvent under subsection (a) if the sum of the partnership's debts is greater than the aggregate, at a fair valuation, of all of the partnership's assets and the sum of the excess of the value of each general partner's nonpartnership assets over the partner's nonpartnership debts.

(d) Assets under this section do not include property that has been transferred, concealed, or removed with intent to hinder, delay, or defraud creditors or that has been transferred in a manner making the transfer voidable under this [Act].

(e) Debts under this section do not include an obligation to the extent it is secured by a valid lien on property of the debtor not included as an asset.

§ 3. Value

(a) Value is given for a transfer or an obligation if, in exchange for the transfer or obligation, property is transferred or an antecedent debt is secured or satisfied, but value does not include an unperformed promise made otherwise than in the ordinary course of the promisor's business to furnish support to the debtor or another person.

(b) For the purposes of Sections 4(a)(2) and 5, a person gives a reasonably equivalent value if the person acquires an interest of the debtor in an asset pursuant to a regularly conducted, noncollusive foreclosure sale or execution of a power of sale for the acquisition or disposition of the interest of the debtor upon default under a mortgage, deed of trust, or security agreement.

(c) A transfer is made for present value if the exchange between the debtor and the transferee is intended by them to be contemporaneous and is in fact substantially contemporaneous.

§ 4. Transfers Fraudulent as to Present and Future Creditors

(a) A transfer made or obligation incurred by a debtor is fraudulent as to a creditor, whether the creditor's claim arose before or after the transfer was made or the obligation was incurred, if the debtor made the transfer or incurred the obligation:

(1) with actual intent to hinder, delay, or defraud any creditor of the debtor; or

(2) without receiving a reasonably equivalent value in exchange for the transfer or obligation, and the debtor:

(i)   was engaged or was about to engage in a business or a transaction for which the remaining assets of the debtor were unreasonably small in relation to the business or transaction; or

(ii)   intended to incur, or believed or reasonably should have believed that he [or she] would incur, debts beyond his [or her] ability to pay as they became due.

(b)   In determining actual intent under subsection (a)(1), consideration may be given, among other factors, to whether:

(1)   the transfer or obligation was to an insider;

(2)   the debtor retained possession or control of the property transferred after the transfer;

(3)   the transfer or obligation was disclosed or concealed;

(4)   before the transfer was made or obligation was incurred, the debtor had been sued or threatened with suit;

(5)   the transfer was of substantially all the debtor's assets;

(6)   the debtor absconded;

(7)   the debtor removed or concealed assets;

(8)   the value of the consideration received by the debtor was reasonably equivalent to the value of the asset transferred or the amount of the obligation incurred;

(9)   the debtor was insolvent or became insolvent shortly after the transfer was made or the obligation was incurred;

(10)   the transfer occurred shortly before or shortly after a substantial debt was incurred; and

(11)   the debtor transferred the essential assets of the business to a lienor who transferred the assets to an insider of the debtor.

§ 5.   Transfers Fraudulent as to Present Creditors

(a)   A transfer made or obligation incurred by a debtor is fraudulent as to a creditor whose claim arose before the transfer was made or the obligation was incurred if the debtor made the transfer or incurred the obligation without receiving a reasonably equivalent value in exchange for the transfer or obligation and the debtor was insolvent at that time or the debtor became insolvent as a result of the transfer or obligation.

(b)   A transfer made by a debtor is fraudulent as to a creditor whose claim arose before the transfer was made if the transfer was made to an insider for an antecedent debt, the debtor was insolvent at that time, and the insider had reasonable cause to believe that the debtor was insolvent.

§ 6.   When Transfer is Made or Obligation is Incurred

For the purposes of this [Act]:

(1)   a transfer is made:

(i)   with respect to an asset that is real property other than a fixture, but including the interest of a seller or purchaser under a contract for the sale of the asset, when the transfer is so far perfected that a good-faith purchaser of the asset from the debtor against whom applicable law permits the transfer to be perfected cannot acquire an interest in the asset that is superior to the interest of the transferee; and

(ii)   with respect to an asset that is not real property or that is a fixture, when the transfer is so far perfected that a creditor on a simple contract cannot acquire a judicial lien otherwise than under this [Act] that is superior to the interest of the transferee;

(2) if applicable law permits the transfer to be perfected as provided in paragraph (1) and the transfer is not so perfected before the commencement of an action for relief under this [Act], the transfer is deemed made immediately before the commencement of the action;

(3) if applicable law does not permit the transfer to be perfected as provided in paragraph (1), the transfer is made when it becomes effective between the debtor and the transferee;

(4) a transfer is not made until the debtor has acquired rights in the asset transferred;

(5) an obligation is incurred:

(i) if oral, when it becomes effective between the parties; or

(ii) if evidenced by a writing, when the writing executed by the obligor is delivered to or for the benefit of the obligee.

§ 7.   Remedies of Creditors

(a) In an action for relief against a transfer or obligation under this [Act], a creditor, subject to the limitations in Section 8, may obtain:

(1) avoidance of the transfer or obligation to the extent necessary to satisfy the creditor's claim;

[(2) an attachment or other provisional remedy against the asset transferred or other property of the transferee in accordance with the procedure prescribed by [ ];]

(3) subject to applicable principles of equity and in accordance with applicable rules of civil procedure,

(i) an injunction against further disposition by the debtor or a transferee, or both, of the asset transferred or of other property;

(ii) appointment of a receiver to take charge of the asset transferred or of other property of the transferee; or

(iii) any other relief the circumstances may require.

(b) If a creditor has obtained a judgment on a claim against the debtor, the creditor, if the court so orders, may levy execution on the asset transferred or its proceeds.

§ 8.   Defenses, Liability, and Protection of Transferee

(a) A transfer or obligation is not voidable under Section 4(a)(1) against a person who took in good faith and for a reasonably equivalent value or against any subsequent transferee or obligee.

(b) Except as otherwise provided in this section, to the extent a transfer is voidable in an action by a creditor under Section 7(a)(1), the creditor may recover judgment for the value of the asset transferred, as adjusted under subsection (c), or the amount necessary to satisfy the creditor's claim, whichever is less. The judgment may be entered against:

(1) the first transferee of the asset or the person for whose benefit the transfer was made; or

(2) any subsequent transferee other than a good faith transferee who took for value or from any subsequent transferee.

(c) If the judgment under subsection (b) is based upon the value of the asset transferred, the judgment must be for an amount equal to the value of the asset at the time of the transfer, subject to adjustment as the equities may require.

(d) Notwithstanding voidability of a transfer or an obligation under this [Act], a good-faith transferee or obligee is entitled, to the extent of the value given the debtor for the transfer or obligation, to

    (1)   a lien on or a right to retain any interest in the asset transferred;

    (2)   enforcement of any obligation incurred; or

    (3)   a reduction in the amount of the liability on the judgment.

 (e)   A transfer is not voidable under Section 4(a)(2) or Section 5 if the transfer results from:

    (1)   termination of a lease upon default by the debtor when the termination is pursuant to the lease and applicable law; or

    (2)   enforcement of a security interest in compliance with Article 9 of the Uniform Commercial Code.

 (f)   A transfer is not voidable under Section 5(b):

    (1)   to the extent the insider gave new value to or for the benefit of the debtor after the transfer was made unless the new value was secured by a valid lien;

    (2)   if made in the ordinary course of business or financial affairs of the debtor and the insider; or

    (3)   if made pursuant to a good-faith effort to rehabilitate the debtor and the transfer secured present value given for that purpose as well as an antecedent debt of the debtor.

§ 9.   Extinguishment of [Claim for Relief] [Cause of Action]

A [claim for relief] [cause of action] with respect to a fraudulent transfer or obligation under this [Act] is extinguished unless action is brought:

    (a)   under Section 4(a)(1), within 4 years after the transfer was made or the obligation was incurred or, if later, within one year after the transfer or obligation was or could reasonably have been discovered by the claimant;

    (b)   under Section 4(a)(2) or 5(a), within 4 years after the transfer was made or the obligation was incurred; or

    (c)   under Section 5(b), within one year after the transfer was made or the obligation was incurred.

§ 10.   Supplementary Provisions

Unless displaced by the provisions of this [Act], the principles of law and equity, including the law merchant and the law relating to principal and agent, estoppel, laches, fraud, misrepresentation, duress, coercion, mistake, insolvency, or other validating or invalidating cause, supplement its provisions.

§ 11.   Uniformity of Application and Construction

This [Act] shall be applied and construed to effectuate its general purpose to make uniform the law with respect to the subject of this [Act] among states enacting it.

§ 12.   Short Title

This [Act] may be cited as the Uniform Fraudulent Transfer Act.

§ 13.   Repeal

The following acts and all other acts and parts of acts inconsistent herewith are hereby repealed:

UNIFORM COMMERCIAL CODE*

Selected Sections

2022 Amendments appear in ~~strikeout~~/<u>underline</u> *format.*

For information on enactment of the 2022 Amendments, *see https://www.uniformlaws.org/*

Article 1

General Provisions

Part 2. General Definitions And Principles Of Interpretation

§ 1–201.   General Definitions

* * *

(b)   Subject to definitions contained in other articles of [the Uniform Commercial Code] that apply to particular articles or parts thereof:

* * *

(3)   "Agreement", as distinguished from "contract", means the bargain of the parties in fact, as found in their language or inferred from other circumstances, including course of performance, course of dealing, or usage of trade as provided in Section 1–303.

* * *

(9)   "Buyer in ordinary course of business" means a person that buys goods in good faith, without knowledge that the sale violates the rights of another person in the goods, and in the ordinary course from a person, other than a pawnbroker, in the business of selling goods of that kind. * * *

* * *

(11) "Consumer" means an individual who enters into a transaction primarily for personal, family, or household purposes

* * *

(13) "Creditor" includes a general creditor, a secured creditor, a lien creditor, and any representative of creditors, including an assignee for the benefit of creditors, a trustee in bankruptcy, a receiver in equity, and an executor or administrator of an insolvent debtor's or assignor's estate.

* * *

(16A) <u>"Electronic" means relating to technology having electrical, digital, magnetic, wireless, optical, electromagnetic, or similar capabilities.</u>

* * *

(20) "Good faith," except as otherwise provided in Article 5, means honesty in fact and the observance of reasonable commercial standards of fair dealing.

* * *

(29) "Purchase" means taking by sale, lease, discount, negotiation, mortgage, pledge, lien, security interest, issue or reissue, gift, or any other voluntary transaction creating an interest in property.

---

*   Reprinted by permission of the National Conference of Commissioners on Uniform State Laws.

(30) "Purchaser" means a person that takes by purchase.

(31) "Record" means information that is inscribed on a tangible medium or that is stored in an electronic or other medium and is retrievable in perceivable form.

* * *

(35) "Security interest" means an interest in personal property or fixtures which secures payment or performance of an obligation. "Security interest" includes any interest of a consignor and a buyer of accounts, chattel paper, a payment intangible, or a promissory note in a transaction that is subject to Article 9. "Security interest" does not include the special property interest of a buyer of goods on identification of those goods to a contract for sale under Section 2–401, but a buyer may also acquire a "security interest" by complying with Article 9. Except as otherwise provided in Section 2–505, the right of a seller or lessor of goods under Article 2 or 2A to retain or acquire possession of the goods is not a "security interest", but a seller or lessor may also acquire a "security interest" by complying with Article 9. The retention or reservation of title by a seller of goods notwithstanding shipment or delivery to the buyer under Section 2–401 is limited in effect to a reservation of a "security interest." Whether a transaction in the form of a lease creates a "security interest" is determined pursuant to Section 1–203.

* * *

(37) ~~"Signed" includes using any symbol executed or adopted with present intention to adopt or accept a writing.~~ "Sign" means, with present intent to authenticate or adopt a record:

(A) execute or adopt a tangible symbol; or

(B) attach to or logically associate with the record an electronic symbol, sound, or process.

"Signed", "signing", and "signature" have corresponding meanings.

* * *

As amended in 2003 and 2022.

Article 2

Sales

Part 7. Remedies

§ 2-702.   Seller's Remedies On Discovery Of Buyer's Insolvency

(1)   Where the seller discovers the buyer to be insolvent he may refuse delivery except for cash including payment for all goods theretofore delivered under the contract, and stop delivery under this Article (Section 2–705).

(2)   Where the seller discovers that the buyer has received goods on credit while insolvent he may reclaim the goods upon demand made within ten days after the receipt, but if misrepresentation of solvency has been made to the particular seller in writing within three months before delivery the ten day limitation does not apply. Except as provided in this subsection, the seller may not base a right to reclaim goods on the buyer's fraudulent or innocent misrepresentation of solvency or of intent to pay.

(3)   The seller's right to reclaim under subsection (2) is subject to the rights of a buyer in ordinary course or other good faith purchaser under this Article (Section 2–403). Successful reclamation of goods excludes all other remedies with respect to them.

As amended in 1966.

Article 9

Secured Transactions

Part 1. General Provisions

[Subpart 1. Short Title, Definitions, And General Concepts]

§ 9–102.   Definitions And Index Of Definitions

(a)   [Article 9 definitions.] In this article:

* * *

(3)   "Account debtor" means a person obligated on an account, chattel paper, or general intangible. The term does not include persons obligated to pay a negotiable instrument, even if the negotiable instrument evidences ~~constitutes part of~~ chattel paper.

* * *

(7)   ~~"Authenticate" means:~~

~~(A)   to sign; or~~

~~(B)   with present intent to adopt or accept a record, to attach to or logically associate with the record an electronic sound, symbol, or process.~~ [Reserved.]

* * *

(9)   "Cash proceeds" means proceeds that are money, checks, deposit accounts, or the like.

* * *

(12)   "Collateral" means the property subject to a security interest or agricultural lien. The term includes:

(A)   proceeds to which a security interest attaches;

(B)   accounts, chattel paper, payment intangibles, and promissory notes that have been sold; and

(C)   goods that are the subject of a consignment.

(13)   "Commercial tort claim" means a claim arising in tort with respect to which:

(A)   the claimant is an organization; or

(B)   the claimant is an individual and the claim:

(i)   arose in the course of the claimant's business or profession; and

(ii)   does not include damages arising out of personal injury to or the death of an individual.

* * *

(23)   "Consumer goods" means goods that are used or bought for use primarily for personal, family, or household purposes.

* * *

(27A)   "Controllable account" means an account evidenced by a controllable electronic record that provides that the account debtor undertakes to pay the person that has control under Section 12–105 of the controllable electronic record.

(27B) "Controllable payment intangible" means a payment intangible evidenced by a controllable electronic record that provides that the account debtor undertakes to pay the person that has control under Section 12–105 of the controllable electronic record.

(28) "Debtor" means:

(A)   a person having an interest, other than a security interest or other lien, in the collateral, whether or not the person is an obligor;

(B)   a seller of accounts, chattel paper, payment intangibles, or promissory notes; or

(C)   a consignee.

* * *

(31A) "Electronic money" means money in an electronic form.

* * *

(33) "Equipment" means goods other than inventory, farm products, or consumer goods.

(34) "Farm products" means goods, other than standing timber, with respect to which the debtor is engaged in a farming operation and which are:

(A)   crops grown, growing, or to be grown, including:

(i)   crops produced on trees, vines, and bushes; and

(ii)   aquatic goods produced in aquacultural operations;

(B)   livestock, born or unborn, including aquatic goods produced in aquacultural operations;

(C)   supplies used or produced in a farming operation; or

(D)   products of crops or livestock in their unmanufactured states.

* * *

(43) [Reserved.] ["Good faith" means honesty in fact and the observance of reasonable commercial standards of fair dealing.]

(44) "Goods" means all things that are movable when a security interest attaches. The term includes (i) fixtures, (ii) standing timber that is to be cut and removed under a conveyance or contract for sale, (iii) the unborn young of animals, (iv) crops grown, growing, or to be grown, even if the crops are produced on trees, vines, or bushes, and (v) manufactured homes. The term also includes a computer program embedded in goods and any supporting information provided in connection with a transaction relating to the program if (i) the program is associated with the goods in such a manner that it customarily is considered part of the goods, or (ii) by becoming the owner of the goods, a person acquires a right to use the program in connection with the goods. The term does not include a computer program embedded in goods that consist solely of the medium in which the program is embedded. The term also does not include accounts, chattel paper, commercial tort claims, deposit accounts, documents, general intangibles, instruments, investment property, letter-of-credit rights, letters of credit, money, or oil, gas, or other minerals before extraction.

* * *

(48) "Inventory" means goods, other than farm products, which:

(A)   are leased by a person as lessor;

(B)   are held by a person for sale or lease or to be furnished under a contract of service;

(C)   are furnished by a person under a contract of service; or

(D)   consist of raw materials, work in process, or materials used or consumed in a business.

(49) "Investment property" means a security, whether certificated or uncertificated, security entitlement, securities account, commodity contract, or commodity account.

* * *

(52) "Lien creditor" means:

(A)   a creditor that has acquired a lien on the property involved by attachment, levy, or the like;

(B)   an assignee for benefit of creditors from the time of assignment;

(C)   a trustee in bankruptcy from the date of the filing of the petition; or

(D)   a receiver in equity from the time of appointment.

* * *

(57) "New value" means (i) money, (ii) money's worth in property, services, or new credit, or (iii) release by a transferee of an interest in property previously transferred to the transferee. The term does not include an obligation substituted for another obligation.

* * *

(61) "Payment intangible" means a general intangible under which the account debtor's principal obligation is a monetary obligation. The term includes a controllable payment intangible.

* * *

(64) "Proceeds", except as used in Section 9–609(b), means the following property:

(A)   whatever is acquired upon the sale, lease, license, exchange, or other disposition of collateral;

(B)   whatever is collected on, or distributed on account of, collateral;

(C)   rights arising out of collateral;

(D)   to the extent of the value of collateral, claims arising out of the loss, nonconformity, or interference with the use of, defects or infringement of rights in, or damage to, the collateral; or

(E)   to the extent of the value of collateral and to the extent payable to the debtor or the secured party, insurance payable by reason of the loss or nonconformity of, defects or infringement of rights in, or damage to, the collateral.

* * *

(70) "Record", except as used in "for record", "of record", "record or legal title", and "record owner", means information that is inscribed on a tangible medium or which is stored in an electronic or other medium and is retrievable in perceivable form.

* * *

(73) "Secured party" means:

(A)   a person in whose favor a security interest is created or provided for under a security agreement, whether or not any obligation to be secured is outstanding;

(B)   a person that holds an agricultural lien;

(C)   a consignor;

(D)   a person to which accounts, chattel paper, payment intangibles, or promissory notes have been sold;

(E)   a trustee, indenture trustee, agent, collateral agent, or other representative in whose favor a security interest or agricultural lien is created or provided for; or

(F)   a person that holds a security interest arising under Section 2–401, 2–505, 2–711(3), 2A–508(5), 4–210, or 5–118.

(74) "Security agreement" means an agreement that creates or provides for a security interest.

* * *

(79A) "Tangible money" means money in a tangible form.

* * *

As amended in 1999, 2000, 2001, 2003, 2010, and 2022.

Legislative Note: *The definition of "good faith" in subsection (a)(43) was deleted from subsection (a) pursuant to a conforming amendment accompanying the 2001 amendments of Article 1. However, any jurisdiction that has not adopted the revised definition of "good faith" in Section 1–201(b)(20) should retain the definition of "good faith" in subsection (a)(43).*

[Subpart 2. Applicability Of Article]

§ 9–109.   Scope

(a)   [General scope of article.] Except as otherwise provided in subsections (c) and (d), this article applies to:

(1)   a transaction, regardless of its form, that creates a security interest in personal property or fixtures by contract;

(2)   an agricultural lien;

(3)   a sale of accounts, chattel paper, payment intangibles, or promissory notes;

(4)   a consignment;

(5)   a security interest arising under Section 2–401, 2–505, 2–711(3), or 2A–508(5), as provided in Section 9–110; and

(6)   a security interest arising under Section 4–210 or 5–118.

* * *

Part 2. Effectiveness Of Security Agreement; Attachment Of Security Interest; Rights Of Parties To Security Agreement

[Subpart 1. Effectiveness And Attachment]

§ 9–201.   General Effectiveness Of Security Agreement

(a)   [General effectiveness.] Except as otherwise provided in [the Uniform Commercial Code], a security agreement is effective according to its terms between the parties, against purchasers of the collateral, and against creditors.

* * *

§ 9–203.   Attachment And Enforceability Of Security Interest; Proceeds; Supporting Obligations; Formal Requisites

(a)   [Attachment.] A security interest attaches to collateral when it becomes enforceable against the debtor with respect to the collateral, unless an agreement expressly postpones the time of attachment.

(b)   [Enforceability.] Except as otherwise provided in subsections (c) through (i), a security interest is enforceable against the debtor and third parties with respect to the collateral only if:

(1)   value has been given;

(2) the debtor has rights in the collateral or the power to transfer rights in the collateral to a secured party; and

(3) one of the following conditions is met:

(A) the debtor has ~~authenticated~~ signed a security agreement that provides a description of the collateral and, if the security interest covers timber to be cut, a description of the land concerned;

(B) the collateral is not a certificated security and is in the possession of the secured party under Section 9–313 pursuant to the debtor's security agreement;

(C) the collateral is a certificated security in registered form and the security certificate has been delivered to the secured party under Section 8–301 pursuant to the debtor's security agreement; ~~or~~

(D) the collateral is controllable accounts, controllable electronic records, controllable payment intangibles, deposit accounts, ~~electronic chattel paper~~, electronic documents, electronic money, investment property, or letter-of-credit rights, ~~or electronic documents,~~ and the secured party has control under Section 7–106, 9–104, ~~9–105,~~ 9–105A, 9–106, ~~or~~ 9–107, or 9–107A pursuant to the debtor's security agreement; or

(E) the collateral is chattel paper and the secured party has possession and control under Section 9–314A pursuant to the debtor's security agreement.

* * *

As amended in 2003 and 2022.

§ 9–204. After-Acquired Property; Future Advances

(a) [After-acquired collateral.] Except as otherwise provided in subsection (b), a security agreement may create or provide for a security interest in after-acquired collateral.

(b) [When after-acquired property clause not effective.] Subject to subsection (b.1), a security interest does not attach under a term constituting an after-acquired property clause to:

(1) consumer goods, other than an accession when given as additional security, unless the debtor acquires rights in them within 10 days after the secured party gives value; or

(2) a commercial tort claim.

(b.1) [Limitation on subsection (b).] Subsection (b) does not prevent a security interest from attaching:

(1) to consumer goods as proceeds under Section 9–315(a) or commingled goods under Section 9–336(c);

(2) to a commercial tort claim as proceeds under Section 9–315(a); or

(3) under an after-acquired property clause to property that is proceeds of consumer goods or a commercial tort claim.

(c) [Future advances and other value.] A security agreement may provide that collateral secures, or that accounts, chattel paper, payment intangibles, or promissory notes are sold in connection with, future advances or other value, whether or not the advances or value are given pursuant to commitment.

As amended in 2022.

Part 3. Perfection And Priority

[Subpart 1. Law Governing Perfection And Priority]

§ 9–301.   Law Governing Perfection And Priority Of Security Interests

Except as otherwise provided in Sections 9–303 through ~~9–306~~ 9–306B, the following rules determine the law governing perfection, the effect of perfection or nonperfection, and the priority of a security interest in collateral:

(1)   Except as otherwise provided in this section, while a debtor is located in a jurisdiction, the local law of that jurisdiction governs perfection, the effect of perfection or nonperfection, and the priority of a security interest in collateral.

(2)   While collateral is located in a jurisdiction, the local law of that jurisdiction governs perfection, the effect of perfection or nonperfection, and the priority of a possessory security interest in that collateral.

* * *

As amended in 2003 and 2022.

§ 9–307.   Location Of Debtor

(a)   ["Place of business."] In this section, "place of business" means a place where a debtor conducts its affairs.

(b)   [Debtor's location: general rules.] Except as otherwise provided in this section, the following rules determine a debtor's location:

(1)   A debtor who is an individual is located at the individual's principal residence.

(2)   A debtor that is an organization and has only one place of business is located at its place of business.

(3)   A debtor that is an organization and has more than one place of business is located at its chief executive office.

* * *

As amended in 2010.

[Subpart 2. Perfection]

§ 9–308.   When Security Interest Or Agricultural Lien Is Perfected; Continuity Of Perfection

(a)   [Perfection of security interest.] Except as otherwise provided in this section and Section 9–309, a security interest is perfected if it has attached and all of the applicable requirements for perfection in Sections 9–310 through 9–316 have been satisfied. A security interest is perfected when it attaches if the applicable requirements are satisfied before the security interest attaches.

* * *

§ 9–309.   Security Interest Perfected Upon Attachment

The following security interests are perfected when they attach:

(1)   a purchase-money security interest in consumer goods, except as otherwise provided in Section 9–311(b) with respect to consumer goods that are subject to a statute or treaty described in Section 9–311(a);

(2)   an assignment of accounts or payment intangibles which does not by itself or in conjunction with other assignments to the same assignee transfer a significant part of the assignor's outstanding accounts or payment intangibles;

* * *

§ 9–310.   When Filing Required To Perfect Security Interest Or Agricultural Lien; Security Interests And Agricultural Liens To Which Filing Provisions Do Not Apply

(a)   [General rule: perfection by filing.] Except as otherwise provided in subsection (b) and Section 9–312(b), a financing statement must be filed to perfect all security interests and agricultural liens.

(b)   [Exceptions: filing not necessary.] The filing of a financing statement is not necessary to perfect a security interest:

* * *

(8)   in <u>controllable accounts, controllable electronic records, controllable payment intangibles,</u> deposit accounts, ~~electronic chattel paper,~~ electronic documents, investment property, or letter-of-credit rights which is perfected by control under Section 9–314;

* * *

As amended in 2003 and 2022.

§ 9–313.   When Possession By Or Delivery To Secured Party Perfects Security Interest Without Filing

(a)   [Perfection by possession or delivery.] Except as otherwise provided in subsection (b), a secured party may perfect a security interest in ~~tangible negotiable documents,~~ goods, instruments, <u>negotiable tangible documents or tangible</u> money~~, or tangible chattel paper~~ by taking possession of the collateral. A secured party may perfect a security interest in certificated securities by taking delivery of the certificated securities under Section 8–301.

* * *

As amended in 2003 and 2022.

§ 9–315.   Secured Party's Rights On Disposition Of Collateral And In Proceeds

(a)   [Disposition of collateral: continuation of security interest or agricultural lien; proceeds.] Except as otherwise provided in this article and in Section 2–403(2):

(1)   a security interest or agricultural lien continues in collateral notwithstanding sale, lease, license, exchange, or other disposition thereof unless the secured party authorized the disposition free of the security interest or agricultural lien; and

(2)   a security interest attaches to any identifiable proceeds of collateral.

* * *

(c)   [Perfection of security interest in proceeds.] A security interest in proceeds is a perfected security interest if the security interest in the original collateral was perfected.

(d)   [Continuation of perfection.] A perfected security interest in proceeds becomes unperfected on the 21st day after the security interest attaches to the proceeds unless:

(1)   the following conditions are satisfied:

(A)   a filed financing statement covers the original collateral;

(B)   the proceeds are collateral in which a security interest may be perfected by filing in the office in which the financing statement has been filed; and

(C)   the proceeds are not acquired with cash proceeds;

(2)   the proceeds are identifiable cash proceeds; or

(3)   the security interest in the proceeds is perfected other than under subsection (c) when the security interest attaches to the proceeds or within 20 days thereafter.

(e)   [When perfected security interest in proceeds becomes unperfected.] If a filed financing statement covers the original collateral, a security interest in proceeds which remains perfected under subsection (d)(1) becomes unperfected at the later of:

(1)   when the effectiveness of the filed financing statement lapses under Section 9–515 or is terminated under Section 9–513; or

(2)   the 21st day after the security interest attaches to the proceeds.

[Subpart 3. Priority]

§ 9–317.   Interests That Take Priority Over Or Take Free Of Security Interest Or Agricultural Lien

(a)   [Conflicting security interests and rights of lien creditors.] A security interest or agricultural lien is subordinate to the rights of:

(1)   a person entitled to priority under Section 9–322; and

(2)   except as otherwise provided in subsection (e), a person that becomes a lien creditor before the earlier of the time:

(A)   the security interest or agricultural lien is perfected; or

(B)   one of the conditions specified in Section 9–203(b)(3) is met and a financing statement covering the collateral is filed.

(b)   [Buyers that receive delivery.] Except as otherwise provided in subsection (e), a buyer, other than a secured party, of tangible chattel paper, tangible documents, of goods, instruments, tangible documents, or a certificated security takes free of a security interest or agricultural lien if the buyer gives value and receives delivery of the collateral without knowledge of the security interest or agricultural lien and before it is perfected.

* * *

(e)   [Purchase-money security interest.] Except as otherwise provided in Sections 9–320 and 9–321, if a person files a financing statement with respect to a purchase-money security interest before or within 20 days after the debtor receives delivery of the collateral, the security interest takes priority over the rights of a buyer, lessee, or lien creditor which arise between the time the security interest attaches and the time of filing.

* * *

(g)   [Buyers of electronic documents.] A buyer of an electronic document takes free of a security interest if, without knowledge of the security interest and before it is perfected, the buyer gives value and, if each authoritative electronic copy of the document can be subjected to control under Section 7–106, obtains control of each authoritative electronic copy.

(h)   [Buyers of controllable electronic records.] A buyer of a controllable electronic record takes free of a security interest if, without knowledge of the security interest and before it is perfected, the buyer gives value and obtains control of the controllable electronic record.

(i)   [Buyers of controllable accounts and controllable payment intangibles.] A buyer, other than a secured party, of a controllable account or a controllable payment intangible takes free of a security interest if, without knowledge of the security interest and before it is perfected, the buyer gives value and obtains control of the controllable account or controllable payment intangible.

As amended in 2000, 2003, 2010, and 2022.

§ 9–320.   Buyer Of Goods

(a)   [Buyer in ordinary course of business.] Except as otherwise provided in subsection (e), a buyer in ordinary course of business, other than a person buying farm products from a person engaged in farming operations, takes free of a security interest created by the buyer's seller, even if the security interest is perfected and the buyer knows of its existence.

(b)   [Buyer of consumer goods.] Except as otherwise provided in subsection (e), a buyer of goods from a person who used or bought the goods for use primarily for personal, family, or household purposes takes free of a security interest, even if perfected, if the buyer buys:

(1)   without knowledge of the security interest;

(2)   for value;

(3)   primarily for the buyer's personal, family, or household purposes; and

(4)   before the filing of a financing statement covering the goods.

* * *

(e)   [Possessory security interest not affected.] Subsections (a) and (b) do not affect a security interest in goods in the possession of the secured party under Section 9–313.

§ 9–322.   Priorities Among Conflicting Security Interests In And Agricultural Liens On Same Collateral

(a)   [General priority rules.] Except as otherwise provided in this section, priority among conflicting security interests and agricultural liens in the same collateral is determined according to the following rules:

(1)   Conflicting perfected security interests and agricultural liens rank according to priority in time of filing or perfection. Priority dates from the earlier of the time a filing covering the collateral is first made or the security interest or agricultural lien is first perfected, if there is no period thereafter when there is neither filing nor perfection.

(2)   A perfected security interest or agricultural lien has priority over, a conflicting unperfected security interest or agricultural lien.

(3)   The first security interest or agricultural lien to attach or become effective has priority if conflicting security interests and agricultural liens are unperfected.

(b)   [Time of perfection: proceeds and supporting obligations.] For the purposes of subsection (a)(1):

(1)   the time of filing or perfection as to a security interest in collateral is also the time of filing or perfection as to a security interest in proceeds; and

(2)   the time of filing or perfection as to a security interest in collateral supported by a supporting obligation is also the time of filing or perfection as to a security interest in the supporting obligation.

* * *

§ 9–323.   Future Advances

* * *

(b) [Lien creditor.] Except as otherwise provided in subsection (c), a security interest is subordinate to the rights of a person that becomes a lien creditor to the extent that the security interest secures an advance made more than 45 days after the person becomes a lien creditor unless the advance is made:

(1)   without knowledge of the lien; or

(2)   pursuant to a commitment entered into without knowledge of the lien.

* * *

(d) [Buyer of goods.] Except as otherwise provided in subsection (e), a buyer of goods ~~other than a buyer in ordinary course of business~~ takes free of a security interest to the extent that it secures advances made after the earlier of:

(1)   the time the secured party acquires knowledge of the buyer's purchase; or

(2)   45 days after the purchase.

(e) [Advances made pursuant to commitment: priority of buyer of goods.] Subsection (d) does not apply if the advance is made pursuant to a commitment entered into without knowledge of the buyer's purchase and before the expiration of the 45-day period.

* * *

As amended in 1999 and 2022.

§ 9–324.   Priority Of Purchase-Money Security Interests

(a) [General rule: purchase-money priority.] Except as otherwise provided in subsection (g), a perfected purchase-money security interest in goods other than inventory or livestock has priority over a conflicting security interest in the same goods, and, except as otherwise provided in Section 9–327, a perfected security interest in its identifiable proceeds also has priority, if the purchase-money security interest is perfected when the debtor receives possession of the collateral or within 20 days thereafter.

(b) [Inventory purchase-money priority.] Subject to subsection (c) and except as otherwise provided in subsection (g), a perfected purchase-money security interest in inventory has priority over a conflicting security interest in the same inventory, has priority over a conflicting security interest in chattel paper or an instrument constituting proceeds of the inventory and in proceeds of the chattel paper, if so provided in Section 9–330, and, except as otherwise provided in Section 9–327, also has priority in identifiable cash proceeds of the inventory to the extent the identifiable cash proceeds are received on or before the delivery of the inventory to a buyer, if:

(1)   the purchase-money security interest is perfected when the debtor receives possession of the inventory;

(2)   the purchase-money secured party sends ~~an authenticated~~ a signed notification to the holder of the conflicting security interest;

(3)   the holder of the conflicting security interest receives the notification within five years before the debtor receives possession of the inventory; and

(4)   the notification states that the person sending the notification has or expects to acquire a purchase-money security interest in inventory of the debtor and describes the inventory.

(c) [Holders of conflicting inventory security interests to be notified.] Subsections (b)(2) through (4) apply only if the holder of the conflicting security interest had filed a financing statement covering the same types of inventory:

    (1)   if the purchase-money security interest is perfected by filing, before the date of the filing; or

    (2)   if the purchase-money security interest is temporarily perfected without filing or possession under Section 9–312(f), before the beginning of the 20-day period thereunder.

* * *

    (g)   [Conflicting purchase-money security interests.] If more than one security interest qualifies for priority in the same collateral under subsection (a), (b), (d), or (f):

    (1)   a security interest securing an obligation incurred as all or part of the price of the collateral has priority over a security interest securing an obligation incurred for value given to enable the debtor to acquire rights in or the use of collateral; and

    (2)   in all other cases, Section 9–322(a) applies to the qualifying security interests.

As amended in 2022.

§ 9–332.   Transfer Of Money; Transfer Of Funds From Deposit Account

    (a)   [Transferee of tangible money.] A transferee of tangible money takes the money free of a security interest ~~unless the transferee acts~~ if the transferee receives possession of the money without acting in collusion with the debtor in violating the rights of the secured party.

    (b)   [Transferee of funds from deposit account.] A transferee of funds from a deposit account takes the funds free of a security interest in the deposit account ~~unless the transferee acts~~ if the transferee receives the funds without acting in collusion with the debtor in violating the rights of the secured party.

    (c)   [Transferee of electronic money.] A transferee of electronic money takes the money free of a security interest if the transferee obtains control of the money without acting in collusion with the debtor in violating the rights of the secured party.

As amended in 2022.

§ 9–333.   Priority Of Certain Liens Arising By Operation Of Law

    (a)   ["Possessory lien."] In this section, "possessory lien" means an interest, other than a security interest or an agricultural lien:

    (1)   which secures payment or performance of an obligation for services or materials furnished with respect to goods by a person in the ordinary course of the person's business;

    (2)   which is created by statute or rule of law in favor of the person; and

    (3)   whose effectiveness depends on the person's possession of the goods.

    (b)   [Priority of possessory lien.] A possessory lien on goods has priority over a security interest in the goods unless the lien is created by a statute that expressly provides otherwise.

§ 9–339.   Priority Subject To Subordination

This article does not preclude subordination by agreement by a person entitled to priority.

[Subpart 4. Rights of Bank]

§ 9–340.   Effectiveness Of Right Of Recoupment Or Set-Off Against Deposit Account

    (a)   [Exercise of recoupment or set-off.] Except as otherwise provided in subsection (c), a bank with which a deposit account is maintained may exercise any right of recoupment or set-off against a secured party that holds a security interest in the deposit account.

(b) [Recoupment or set-off not affected by security interest.] Except as otherwise provided in subsection (c), the application of this article to a security interest in a deposit account does not affect a right of recoupment or set-off of the secured party as to a deposit account maintained with the secured party.

(c) [When set-off ineffective.] The exercise by a bank of a set-off against a deposit account is ineffective against a secured party that holds a security interest in the deposit account which is perfected by control under Section 9–104(a)(3), if the set-off is based on a claim against the debtor.

Part 4. Rights Of Third Parties

§ 9–401.   Alienability Of Debtor's Rights

(a) [Other law governs alienability; exceptions.] Except as otherwise provided in subsection (b) and Sections 9–406, 9–407, 9–408, and 9–409, whether a debtor's rights in collateral may be voluntarily or involuntarily transferred is governed by law other than this article.

(b) [Agreement does not prevent transfer.] An agreement between the debtor and secured party which prohibits a transfer of the debtor's rights in collateral or makes the transfer a default does not prevent the transfer from taking effect.

§ 9–407.   Restrictions On Creation Or Enforcement Of Security Interest In Leasehold Interest Or In Lessor's Residual Interest

(a) Term restricting assignment generally ineffective.] Except as otherwise provided in subsection (b), a term in a lease agreement is ineffective to the extent that it:

(1) prohibits, restricts, or requires the consent of a party to the lease to the assignment or transfer of, or the creation, attachment, perfection, or enforcement of a security interest in an interest of a party under the lease contract or in the lessor's residual interest in the goods; or

(2) provides that the assignment or transfer or the creation, attachment, perfection, or enforcement of the security interest may give rise to a default, breach, right of recoupment, claim, defense, termination, right of termination, or remedy under the lease.

(b) [Effectiveness of certain terms.] Except as otherwise provided in Section 2A–303(7), a term described in subsection (a)(2) is effective to the extent that there is:

(1) a transfer by the lessee of the lessee's right of possession or use of the goods in violation of the term; or

(2) a delegation of a material performance of either party to the lease contract in violation of the term.

* * *

As amended in 1999.

Part 5. Filing

[Subpart 1. Filing Office; Contents And Effectiveness Of Financing Statement]

§ 9–501.   Filing Office

(a) [Filing offices.] Except as otherwise provided in subsection (b), if the local law of this State governs perfection of a security interest or agricultural lien, the office in which to file a financing statement to perfect the security interest or agricultural lien is:

(1) the office designated for the filing or recording of a record of a mortgage on the related real property, if:

(A)   the collateral is as-extracted collateral or timber to be cut; or

(B)   the financing statement is filed as a fixture filing and the collateral is goods that are or are to become fixtures; or

(2)   the office of [ ] [or any office duly authorized by [ ]], in all other cases, including a case in which the collateral is goods that are or are to become fixtures and the financing statement is not filed as a fixture filing.

* * *

Legislative Note: *The State should designate the filing office where the brackets appear. The filing office may be that of a governmental official (e.g., the Secretary of State) or a private party that maintains the State's filing system.*

§ 9–502.   Contents Of Financing Statement; Record Of Mortgage As Financing Statement; Time Of Filing Financing Statement

(a)   [Sufficiency of financing statement.] Subject to subsection (b), a financing statement is sufficient only if it:

(1)   provides the name of the debtor;

(2)   provides the name of the secured party or a representative of the secured party; and

(3)   indicates the collateral covered by the financing statement.

* * *

(d)   [Filing before security agreement or attachment.] A financing statement may be filed before a security agreement is made or a security interest otherwise attaches.

As amended in 2010.

§ 9–515.   Duration And Effectiveness Of Financing Statement; Effect Of Lapsed Financing Statement

(a)   [Five-year effectiveness.] Except as otherwise provided in subsections (b), (e), (f), and (g), a filed financing statement is effective for a period of five years after the date of filing.

* * *

(c)   [Lapse and continuation of financing statement.] The effectiveness of a filed financing statement lapses on the expiration of the period of its effectiveness unless before the lapse a continuation statement is filed pursuant to subsection (d). Upon lapse, a financing statement ceases to be effective and any security interest or agricultural lien that was perfected by the financing statement becomes unperfected, unless the security interest is perfected otherwise. If the security interest or agricultural lien becomes unperfected upon lapse, it is deemed never to have been perfected as against a purchaser of the collateral for value.

(d)   [When continuation statement may be filed.] A continuation statement may be filed only within six months before the expiration of the five-year period specified in subsection (a) or the 30-year period specified in subsection (b), whichever is applicable.

(e)   [Effect of filing continuation statement.] Except as otherwise provided in Section 9–510, upon timely filing of a continuation statement, the effectiveness of the initial financing statement continues for a period of five years commencing on the day on which the financing statement would have become ineffective in the absence of the filing. Upon the expiration of the five-year period, the financing statement lapses in the same manner as provided in subsection (c), unless, before the lapse, another continuation statement is filed pursuant to subsection (d). Succeeding continuation statements may be filed in the same manner to continue the effectiveness of the initial financing statement.

* * *

As amended in 2010.

§ 9–516.   What Constitutes Filing; Effectiveness Of Filing

(a)   [What constitutes filing.] Except as otherwise provided in subsection (b), communication of a record to a filing office and tender of the filing fee or acceptance of the record by the filing office constitutes filing.

* * *

As amended in 2010.

Part 6. Default

[Subpart 1. Default And Enforcement Of Security Interest]

§ 9–601.   Rights After Default; Judicial Enforcement; Consignor Or Buyer Of Accounts, Chattel Paper, Payment Intangibles, Or Promissory Notes

(a)   [Rights of secured party after default.] After default, a secured party has the rights provided in this part and, except as otherwise provided in Section 9–602, those provided by agreement of the parties. A secured party:

(1)   may reduce a claim to judgment, foreclose, or otherwise enforce the claim, security interest, or agricultural lien by any available judicial procedure; and

(2)   if the collateral is documents, may proceed either as to the documents or as to the goods they cover.

* * *

As amended in 2003 and 2022.

§ 9–607.   Collection And Enforcement By Secured Party

(a)   [Collection and enforcement generally.] If so agreed, and in any event after default, a secured party:

(1)   may notify an account debtor or other person obligated on collateral to make payment or otherwise render performance to or for the benefit of the secured party;

(2)   may take any proceeds to which the secured party is entitled under Section 9–315;

(3)   may enforce the obligations of an account debtor or other person obligated on collateral and exercise the rights of the debtor with respect to the obligation of the account debtor or other person obligated on collateral to make payment or otherwise render performance to the debtor, and with respect to any property that secures the obligations of the account debtor or other person obligated on the collateral;

(4)   if it holds a security interest in a deposit account perfected by control under Section 9–104(a)(1), may apply the balance of the deposit account to the obligation secured by the deposit account; and

(5)   if it holds a security interest in a deposit account perfected by control under Section 9–104(a)(2) or (3), may instruct the bank to pay the balance of the deposit account to or for the benefit of the secured party.

* * *

As amended in 2010.

§ 9–609. Secured Party's Right To Take Possession After Default

(a) [Possession; rendering equipment unusable; disposition on debtor's premises.] After default, a secured party:

(1) may take possession of the collateral; and

(2) without removal, may render equipment unusable and dispose of collateral on a debtor's premises under Section 9–610.

(b) [Judicial and nonjudicial process.] A secured party may proceed under subsection (a):

(1) pursuant to judicial process; or

(2) without judicial process, if it proceeds without breach of the peace.

(c) [Assembly of collateral.] If so agreed, and in any event after default, a secured party may require the debtor to assemble the collateral and make it available to the secured party at a place to be designated by the secured party which is reasonably convenient to both parties.

§ 9–610. Disposition Of Collateral After Default

(a) [Disposition after default.] After default, a secured party may sell, lease, license, or otherwise dispose of any or all of the collateral in its present condition or following any commercially reasonable preparation or processing.

(b) [Commercially reasonable disposition.] Every aspect of a disposition of collateral, including the method, manner, time, place, and other terms, must be commercially reasonable. If commercially reasonable, a secured party may dispose of collateral by public or private proceedings, by one or more contracts, as a unit or in parcels, and at any time and place and on any terms.

* * *

§ 9–611. Notification Before Disposition Of Collateral

* * *

(b) [Notification of disposition required.] Except as otherwise provided in subsection (d), a secured party that disposes of collateral under Section 9–610 shall send to the persons specified in subsection (c) a reasonable ~~authenticated~~ signed notification of disposition.

(c) [Persons to be notified.] To comply with subsection (b), the secured party shall send ~~an authenticated~~ a signed notification of disposition to:

(1) the debtor;

(2) any secondary obligor; and

(3) if the collateral is other than consumer goods:

(A) any other person from which the secured party has received, before the notification date, ~~an authenticated~~ a signed notification of a claim of an interest in the collateral;

(B) any other secured party or lienholder that, 10 days before the notification date, held a security interest in or other lien on the collateral perfected by the filing of a financing statement that:

(i) identified the collateral;

(ii) was indexed under the debtor's name as of that date; and

(iii) was filed in the office in which to file a financing statement against the debtor covering the collateral as of that date; and

(C)   any other secured party that, 10 days before the notification date, held a security interest in the collateral perfected by compliance with a statute, regulation, or treaty described in Section 9–311(a).

* * *

As amended in 2022.

§ 9–612.   Timeliness Of Notification Before Disposition Of Collateral

(a)   [Reasonable time is question of fact.] Except as otherwise provided in subsection (b), whether a notification is sent within a reasonable time is a question of fact.

(b)   [10-day period sufficient in non-consumer transaction.] In a transaction other than a consumer transaction, a notification of disposition sent after default and 10 days or more before the earliest time of disposition set forth in the notification is sent within a reasonable time before the disposition.

§ 9–615.   Application Of Proceeds Of Disposition; Liability For Deficiency And Right To Surplus

(a)   [Application of proceeds.] A secured party shall apply or pay over for application the cash proceeds of disposition under Section 9–610 in the following order to:

(1)   the reasonable expenses of retaking, holding, preparing for disposition, processing, and disposing, and, to the extent provided for by agreement and not prohibited by law, reasonable attorney's fees and legal expenses incurred by the secured party;

(2)   the satisfaction of obligations secured by the security interest or agricultural lien under which the disposition is made;

(3)   the satisfaction of obligations secured by any subordinate security interest in or other subordinate lien on the collateral if:

(A)   the secured party receives from the holder of the subordinate security interest or other lien ~~an authenticated~~ a signed demand for proceeds before distribution of the proceeds is completed;

* * *

As amended in 2000 and 2022.

§ 9–620.   Acceptance Of Collateral In Full Or Partial Satisfaction Of Obligation; Compulsory Disposition Of Collateral

(a)   [Conditions to acceptance in satisfaction.] Except as otherwise provided in subsection (g), a secured party may accept collateral in full or partial satisfaction of the obligation it secures only if:

(1)   the debtor consents to the acceptance under subsection (c);

(2)   the secured party does not receive, within the time set forth in subsection (d), a notification of objection to the proposal ~~authenticated~~ signed by:

(A)   a person to which the secured party was required to send a proposal under Section 9–621; or

(B)   any other person, other than the debtor, holding an interest in the collateral subordinate to the security interest that is the subject of the proposal;

(3)   if the collateral is consumer goods, the collateral is not in the possession of the debtor when the debtor consents to the acceptance; and

(4) subsection (e) does not require the secured party to dispose of the collateral or the debtor waives the requirement pursuant to Section 9–624.

* * *

(e) [Mandatory disposition of consumer goods.] A secured party that has taken possession of collateral shall dispose of the collateral pursuant to Section 9–610 within the time specified in subsection (f) if:

(1) 60 percent of the cash price has been paid in the case of a purchase-money security interest in consumer goods; or

(2) 60 percent of the principal amount of the obligation secured has been paid in the case of a non-purchase-money security interest in consumer goods.

* * *

(g) [No partial satisfaction in consumer transaction.] In a consumer transaction, a secured party may not accept collateral in partial satisfaction of the obligation it secures.

As amended in 2022.

§ 9-622. Effect Of Acceptance Of Collateral

(a) [Effect of acceptance.] A secured party's acceptance of collateral in full or partial satisfaction of the obligation it secures:

(1) discharges the obligation to the extent consented to by the debtor;

(2) transfers to the secured party all of a debtor's rights in the collateral;

(3) discharges the security interest or agricultural lien that is the subject of the debtor's consent and any subordinate security interest or other subordinate lien; and

(4) terminates any other subordinate interest.

(b) [Discharge of subordinate interest notwithstanding noncompliance.] A subordinate interest is discharged or terminated under subsection (a), even if the secured party fails to comply with this article.

§ 9-623. Right To Redeem Collateral

(a) [Persons that may redeem.] A debtor, any secondary obligor, or any other secured party or lienholder may redeem collateral.

(b) [Requirements for redemption.] To redeem collateral, a person shall tender:

(1) fulfillment of all obligations secured by the collateral; and

(2) the reasonable expenses and attorney's fees described in Section 9–615(a)(1).

(c) [When redemption may occur.] A redemption may occur at any time before a secured party:

(1) has collected collateral under Section 9–607;

(2) has disposed of collateral or entered into a contract for its disposition under Section 9–610; or

(3) has accepted collateral in full or partial satisfaction of the obligation it secures under Section 9–622.

[Subpart 2. Noncompliance With Article]

§ 9–625.   Remedies For Secured Party's Failure To Comply With Article

* * *

(b)   [Damages for noncompliance.] Subject to subsections (c), (d), and (f), a person is liable for damages in the amount of any loss caused by a failure to comply with this article. Loss caused by a failure to comply may include loss resulting from the debtor's inability to obtain, or increased costs of, alternative financing.

* * *

As amended in 2000 and 2010.

Article 12

Controllable Electronic Records

Added in 2022

§ 12–102.   Definitions.

(a)   [Article 12 definitions.]

In this article:

(1)   "Controllable electronic record" means a record stored in an electronic medium that can be subjected to control under Section 12–105. The term does not include a controllable account, a controllable payment intangible, a deposit account, an electronic copy of a record evidencing chattel paper, an electronic document of title, electronic money, investment property, or a transferable record.

* * *

(b)   [Definitions in Article 9.] The definitions in Article 9 of "account debtor", "controllable account", "controllable payment intangible", "chattel paper", "deposit account", "electronic money", and "investment property" apply to this article.

(c)   [Article 1 definitions and principles.] Article 1 contains general definitions and principles of construction and interpretation applicable throughout this article.

§ 12–103.   Relation to Article 9 and Consumer Laws.

[Article 9 governs in case of conflict.] If there is conflict between this article and Article 9, Article 9 governs.

* * *

§ 12–105.   Control of Controllable Electronic Record.

(a)   [General rule: control of controllable electronic record.] A person has control of a controllable electronic record if the electronic record, a record attached to or logically associated with the electronic record, or a system in which the electronic record is recorded:

(1)   gives the person:

(A)   power to avail itself of substantially all the benefit from the electronic record; and

(B)   exclusive power, subject to subsection (b), to:

(i)   prevent others from availing themselves of substantially all the benefit from the electronic record; and

        (ii)   transfer control of the electronic record to another person or cause another person to obtain control of another controllable electronic record as a result of the transfer of the electronic record; and

    (2)   enables the person readily to identify itself in any way, including by name, identifying number, cryptographic key, office, or account number, as having the powers specified in paragraph (1).

(b)   [Meaning of exclusive.] Subject to subsection (c), a power is exclusive under subsection (a)(1)(B)(i) and (ii) even if:

    (1)   the controllable electronic record, a record attached to or logically associated with the electronic record, or a system in which the electronic record is recorded limits the use of the electronic record or has a protocol programmed to cause a change, including a transfer or loss of control or a modification of benefits afforded by the electronic record; or

    (2)   the power is shared with another person.

(c)   [When power not shared with another person.] A power of a person is not shared with another person under subsection (b)(2) and the person's power is not exclusive if:

    (1)   the person can exercise the power only if the power also is exercised by the other person; and

    (2)   the other person:

        (A)   can exercise the power without exercise of the power by the person; or

        (B)   is the transferor to the person of an interest in the controllable electronic record or a controllable account or controllable payment intangible evidenced by the controllable electronic record.

(d)   [Presumption of exclusivity of certain powers.] If a person has the powers specified in subsection (a)(1)(B)(i) and (ii), the powers are presumed to be exclusive.

(e)   [Control through another person.] A person has control of a controllable electronic record if another person, other than the transferor to the person of an interest in the controllable electronic record or a controllable account or controllable payment intangible evidenced by the controllable electronic record:

    (1)   has control of the electronic record and acknowledges that it has control on behalf of the person; or

    (2)   obtains control of the electronic record after having acknowledged that it will obtain control of the electronic record on behalf of the person.

(f)   [No requirement to acknowledge.] A person that has control under this section is not required to acknowledge that it has control on behalf of another person.

(g)   [No duties or confirmation.] If a person acknowledges that it has or will obtain control on behalf of another person, unless the person otherwise agrees or law other than this article or Article 9 otherwise provides, the person does not owe any duty to the other person and is not required to confirm the acknowledgment to any other person.

Article A

Transitional Provisions for Uniform Commercial Code Amendments (2022)

Added in 2022

Legislative Note: *A state should codify Parts 1, 2 and 3 of this article as a part of the state's [Uniform Commercial Code].*

In its codification of this article a state should provide a title that is conducive to its usual methods of codification, which is likely to ensure that it is called to the attention of users of the state's [Uniform Commercial Code], and which will avoid misunderstandings as to the relationship of this article to the other provisions of the state's [Uniform Commercial Code]. The designation of "Article" indicates that this article is a part of the state's [Uniform Commercial Code] as are the other articles. A state that uses a designation other than "article" may adopt for this article that other designation (such as "division"). Alternatively, a state may wish to adopt for this article a distinctive designation," such as "annex," which would distinguish its focus on transitional provisions from the content of other articles.

Part 1. General Provisions and Definitions

§ A–101.   Short Title.

This article may be cited as Transitional Provisions for Uniform Commercial Code Amendments (2022).

§ A–102.   Definitions.

(a)   [Article A Definitions.] In this article:

(1)   "Adjustment date" means July 1, 2025, or the date that is one year after [the effective date of this [act]], whichever is later.

(2)   "Article 12" means Article 12 of [the Uniform Commercial Code].

(3)   "Article 12 property" means a controllable account, controllable electronic record, or controllable payment intangible.

(b)   [Definitions in other articles.] The following definitions in other articles of [the Uniform Commercial Code] apply to this article.

"Controllable account". Section 9–102.

"Controllable electronic record". Section 12–102.

"Controllable payment intangible". Section 9–102.

"Electronic money". Section 9–102.

"Financing statement". Section 9–102.

(c)   [Article 1 definitions and principles.] Article 1 contains general definitions and principles of construction and interpretation applicable throughout this article.

Part 2. General Transitional Provision

§ A–201.   Saving Clause.

Except as provided in Part 3, a transaction validly entered into before [the effective date of this [act]] and the rights, duties, and interests flowing from the transaction remain valid thereafter and may be terminated, completed, consummated, or enforced as required or permitted by law other than [the Uniform Commercial Code] or, if applicable, [the Uniform Commercial Code], as though this [act] had not taken effect.

Part 3. Transitional Provisions for Articles 9 and 12

§ A–301.   Saving Clause.

(a)   [Pre-effective-date transaction, lien, or interest.] Except as provided in this part, Article 9 as amended by this [act] and Article 12 apply to a transaction, lien, or other interest in property, even if the transaction, lien, or interest was entered into, created, or acquired before [the effective date of this [act]].

(b) [Continuing validity.] Except as provided in subsection (c) and Sections A–302 through A–306:

(1) a transaction, lien, or interest in property that was validly entered into, created, or transferred before [the effective date of this [act]] and was not governed by [the Uniform Commercial Code], but would be subject to Article 9 as amended by this [act] or Article 12 if it had been entered into, created, or transferred on or after [the effective date of this [act]], including the rights, duties, and interests flowing from the transaction, lien, or interest, remains valid on and after [the effective date of this [act]]; and

(2) the transaction, lien, or interest may be terminated, completed, consummated, and enforced as required or permitted by this [act] or by the law that would apply if this [act] had not taken effect.

(c) [Pre-effective-date proceeding.] This [act] does not affect an action, case, or proceeding commenced before [the effective date of this [act]].

§ A–302. Security Interest Perfected Before Effective Date.

(a) [Continuing perfection: perfection requirements satisfied.] A security interest that is enforceable and perfected immediately before [the effective date of this [act]] is a perfected security interest under this [act] if, on [the effective date of this [act]], the requirements for enforceability and perfection under this [act] are satisfied without further action.

(b) [Continuing perfection: enforceability or perfection requirements not satisfied.] If a security interest is enforceable and perfected immediately before [the effective date of this [act]], but the requirements for enforceability or perfection under this [act] are not satisfied on [the effective date of this [act]], the security interest:

(1) is a perfected security interest until the earlier of the time perfection would have ceased under the law in effect immediately before [the effective date of this [act]] or the adjustment date;

(2) remains enforceable thereafter only if the security interest satisfies the requirements for enforceability under Section 9–203, as amended by this [act], before the adjustment date; and

(3) remains perfected thereafter only if the requirements for perfection under this [act] are satisfied before the time specified in paragraph (1).

§ A–303. Security Interest Unperfected Before Effective Date.

A security interest that is enforceable immediately before [the effective date of this [act]] but is unperfected at that time:

(1) remains an enforceable security interest until the adjustment date;

(2) remains enforceable thereafter if the security interest becomes enforceable under Section 9–203, as amended by this [act], on [the effective date of this [act]] or before the adjustment date; and

(3) becomes perfected:

(A) without further action, on [the effective date of this [act]] if the requirements for perfection under this [act] are satisfied before or at that time; or

(B) when the requirements for perfection are satisfied if the requirements are satisfied after that time.

§ A–304.   Effectiveness of Actions Taken Before Effective Date.

(a)   [Pre-effective-date action; attachment and perfection before adjustment date.] If action, other than the filing of a financing statement, is taken before [the effective date of this [act]] and the action would have resulted in perfection of the security interest had the security interest become enforceable before [the effective date of this [act]], the action is effective to perfect a security interest that attaches under this [act] before the adjustment date. An attached security interest becomes unperfected on the adjustment date unless the security interest becomes a perfected security interest under this [act] before the adjustment date.

(b)   [Pre-effective-date filing.] The filing of a financing statement before [the effective date of this [act]] is effective to perfect a security interest on [the effective date of this [act]] to the extent the filing would satisfy the requirements for perfection under this [act].

(c)   [Pre-effective-date enforceability action.] The taking of an action before [the effective date of this [act]] is sufficient for the enforceability of a security interest on [the effective date of this [act]] if the action would satisfy the requirements for enforceability under this [act].

§ A–305.   Priority.

(a)   [Determination of priority.] Subject to subsections (b) and (c), this [act] determines the priority of conflicting claims to collateral.

(b)   [Established priorities.] Subject to subsection (c), if the priorities of claims to collateral were established before [the effective date of this [act]], Article 9 as in effect before [the effective date of this [act]] determines priority.

(c)   [Determination of certain priorities on adjustment date.] On the adjustment date, to the extent the priorities determined by Article 9 as amended by this [act] modify the priorities established before [the effective date of this [act]], the priorities of claims to Article 12 property and electronic money established before [the effective date of this [act]] cease to apply.

§ A–306.   Priority of Claims When Priority Rules of Article 9 Do Not Apply.

(a)   [Determination of priority.] Subject to subsections (b) and (c), Article 12 determines the priority of conflicting claims to Article 12 property when the priority rules of Article 9 as amended by this [act] do not apply.

(b)   [Established priorities.] Subject to subsection (c), when the priority rules of Article 9 as amended by this [act] do not apply and the priorities of claims to Article 12 property were established before [the effective date of this [act]], law other than Article 12 determines priority.

(c)   [Determination of certain priorities on adjustment date.] When the priority rules of Article 9 as amended by this [act] do not apply, to the extent the priorities determined by this [act] modify the priorities established before [the effective date of this [act]], the priorities of claims to Article 12 property established before [the effective date of this [act]] cease to apply on the adjustment date.

Part 4. Effective Date

§ A–401.   Effective Date

This [act] takes effect on . . .

FEDERAL TAX LIEN STATUTE— INTERNAL REVENUE CODE

Selected Sections

Current through June 30, 2023; Pub. L. 118–7

TITLE 26—INTERNAL REVENUE CODE

SUBCHAPTER F. PROCEDURE AND ADMINISTRATION

Chapter 64. Collection

Subchapter C. Lien for Taxes

Part II. Liens

---

§ 6321. Lien for taxes

If any person liable to pay any tax neglects or refuses to pay the same after demand, the amount (including any interest, additional amount, addition to tax, or assessable penalty, together with any costs that may accrue in addition thereto) shall be a lien in favor of the United States upon all property and rights to property, whether real or personal, belonging to such person.

CROSS REFERENCES

Action to enforce lien or to subject property to payment of tax, see 26 USCA § 7403.

Liability of operators for repayments to Mine Safety and Health Fund, see 30 USCA § 934.

Lien for liability, Employee Retirement Income Security Program, see 29 USCA § 1368.

§ 6322. Period of lien

Unless another date is specifically fixed by law, the lien imposed by section 6321 shall arise at the time the assessment is made and shall continue until the liability for the amount so assessed (or a judgment against the taxpayer arising out of such liability) is satisfied or becomes unenforceable by reason of lapse of time.

§ 6323. Validity and priority against certain persons

(a) Purchasers, holders of security interests, mechanic's lienors, and judgment lien creditors. The lien imposed by section 6321 shall not be valid as against any purchaser, holder of a security interest, mechanic's lienor, or judgment lien creditor until notice thereof which meets the requirements of subsection (f) has been filed by the Secretary.

(b) Protection for certain interests even though notice filed.—Even though notice of a lien imposed by section 6321 has been filed, such lien shall not be valid—

   (1) Securities.—With respect to a security (as defined in subsection (h)(4))—

      (A) as against a purchaser of such security who at the time of purchase did not have actual notice or knowledge of the existence of such lien; and

      (B) as against a holder of a security interest in such security who, at the time such interest came into existence, did not have actual notice or knowledge of the existence of such lien.

   (2) Motor vehicles.—With respect to a motor vehicle (as defined in subsection (h)(3)), as against a purchaser of such motor vehicle, if—

      (A) at the time of the purchase such purchaser did not have actual notice or knowledge of the existence of such lien, and

      (B) before the purchaser obtains such notice or knowledge, he has acquired possession of such motor vehicle and has not thereafter relinquished possession of such motor vehicle to the seller or his agent.

   (3) Personal property purchased at retail.—With respect to tangible personal property purchased at retail, as against a purchaser in the ordinary course of the seller's trade or business, unless at the time of such purchase such purchaser intends such purchase to (or knows such purchase will) hinder, evade, or defeat the collection of any tax under this title.

   (4) Personal property purchased in casual sale.—With respect to household goods, personal effects, or other tangible personal property described in section 6334(a) purchased (not for resale) in a casual sale for less than $1,000, as against the purchaser, but only if such purchaser does not have actual notice or knowledge (A) of the existence of such lien, or (B) that this sale is one of a series of sales.

   (5) Personal property subject to possessory lien.—With respect to tangible personal property subject to a lien under local law securing the reasonable price of the repair or improvement of such property, as against a holder of such a lien, if such holder is, and has been, continuously in possession of such property from the time such lien arose.

   (6) Real property tax and special assessment liens.—With respect to real property, as against a holder of a lien upon such property, if such lien is entitled under local law to priority over security interests in such property which are prior in time, and such lien secures payment of—

      (A) a tax of general application levied by any taxing authority based upon the value of such property;

      (B) a special assessment imposed directly upon such property by any taxing authority, if such assessment is imposed for the purpose of defraying the cost of any public improvement; or

      (C) charges for utilities or public services furnished to such property by the United States, a State or political subdivision thereof, or an instrumentality of any one or more of the foregoing.

   (7) Residential property subject to a mechanic's lien for certain repairs and improvements.—With respect to real property subject to a lien for repair or improvement of a personal residence (containing not more than four dwelling units) occupied by the owner of such residence, as against a mechanic's lienor, but only if the contract price on the contract with the owner is not more than $5,000.

   (8) Attorneys' liens.—With respect to a judgment or other amount in settlement of a claim or of a cause of action, as against an attorney who, under local law, holds a lien upon or a contract enforceable against such judgment or amount, to the extent of his reasonable compensation for obtaining such judgment or procuring such settlement, except that this paragraph shall not apply to any judgment or amount in settlement of a claim or of a cause of action against the United States to the extent that the United States offsets such judgment or amount against any liability of the taxpayer to the United States.

(9) Certain insurance contracts.—With respect to a life insurance, endowment, or annuity contract, as against the organization which is the insurer under such contract, at any time—

(A) before such organization had actual notice or knowledge of the existence of such lien;

(B) after such organization had such notice or knowledge, with respect to advances required to be made automatically to maintain such contract in force under an agreement entered into before such organization had such notice or knowledge; or

(C) after satisfaction of a levy pursuant to section 6332(b), unless and until the Secretary delivers to such organization a notice, executed after the date of such satisfaction, of the existence of such lien.

(10) Deposit-secured loans.—With respect to a savings deposit, share, or other account, with an institution described in section 581 or 591, to the extent of any loan made by such institution without actual notice or knowledge of the existence of such lien, as against such institution, if such loan is secured by such account.

(c) Protection for certain commercial transactions financing agreements, etc.—

(1) In general.—To the extent provided in this subsection, even though notice of a lien imposed by section 6321 has been filed, such lien shall not be valid with respect to a security interest which came into existence after tax lien filing but which—

(A) is in qualified property covered by the terms of a written agreement entered into before tax lien filing and constituting—

(i) a commercial transactions financing agreement,

(ii) a real property construction or improvement financing agreement, or

(iii) an obligatory disbursement agreement, and

(B) is protected under local law against a judgment lien arising, as of the time of tax lien filing, out of an unsecured obligation.

(2) Commercial transactions financing agreement.—For purposes of this subsection—

(A) Definition.—The term "commercial transactions financing agreement" means an agreement (entered into by a person in the course of his trade or business)—

(i) to make loans to the taxpayer to be secured by commercial financing security acquired by the taxpayer in the ordinary course of his trade or business, or

(ii) to purchase commercial financing security (other than inventory) acquired by the taxpayer in the ordinary course of his trade or business;

but such an agreement shall be treated as coming within the term only to the extent that such loan or purchase is made before the 46th day after the date of tax lien filing or (if earlier) before the lender or purchaser had actual notice or knowledge of such tax lien filing.

(B) Limitation on qualified property.—The term "qualified property", when used with respect to a commercial transactions financing agreement, includes only commercial financing security acquired by the taxpayer before the 46th day after the date of tax lien filing.

(C) Commercial financing security defined.—The term "commercial financing security" means (i) paper of a kind ordinarily arising in commercial transactions, (ii) accounts receivable, (iii) mortgages on real property, and (iv) inventory.

(D) Purchaser treated as acquiring security interest.—A person who satisfies subparagraph (A) by reason of clause (ii) thereof shall be treated as having acquired a security interest in commercial financing security.

(3) Real property construction or improvement financing agreement.—For purposes of this subsection—

(A) Definition.—The term "real property construction or improvement financing agreement" means an agreement to make cash disbursements to finance—

    (i) the construction or improvement of real property,

    (ii) a contract to construct or improve real property, or

    (iii) the raising or harvesting of a farm crop or the raising of livestock or other animals.

For purposes of clause (iii), the furnishing of goods and services shall be treated as the disbursement of cash.

(B) Limitation on qualified property.—The term "qualified property", when used with respect to a real property construction or improvement financing agreement, includes only—

    (i) in the case of subparagraph (A)(i), the real property with respect to which the construction or improvement has been or is to be made,

    (ii) in the case of subparagraph (A)(ii), the proceeds of the contract described therein, and

    (iii) in the case of subparagraph (A)(iii), property subject to the lien imposed by section 6321 at the time of tax lien filing and the crop or the livestock or other animals referred to in subparagraph (A)(iii).

(4) Obligatory disbursement agreement.—For purposes of this subsection—

(A) Definition.—The term "obligatory disbursement agreement" means an agreement (entered into by a person in the course of his trade or business) to make disbursements, but such an agreement shall be treated as coming within the term only to the extent of disbursements which are required to be made by reason of the intervention of the rights of a person other than the taxpayer.

(B) Limitation on qualified property.—The term "qualified property", when used with respect to an obligatory disbursement agreement, means property subject to the lien imposed by section 6321 at the time of tax lien filing and (to the extent that the acquisition is directly traceable to the disbursements referred to in subparagraph (A)) property acquired by the taxpayer after tax lien filing.

(C) Special rules for surety agreements.—Where the obligatory disbursement agreement is an agreement ensuring the performance of a contract between the taxpayer and another person—

    (i) the term "qualified property" shall be treated as also including the proceeds of the contract the performance of which was ensured, and

(ii) if the contract the performance of which was ensured was a contract to construct or improve real property, to produce goods, or to furnish services, the term "qualified property" shall be treated as also including any tangible personal property used by the taxpayer in the performance of such ensured contract.

(d) 45-day period for making disbursements.—Even though notice of a lien imposed by section 6321 has been filed, such lien shall not be valid with respect to a security interest which came into existence after tax lien filing by reason of disbursements made before the 46th day after the date of tax lien filing, or (if earlier) before the person making such disbursements had actual notice or knowledge of tax lien filing, but only if such security interest—

(1) is in property (A) subject, at the time of tax lien filing, to the lien imposed by section 6321, and (B) covered by the terms of a written agreement entered into before tax lien filing, and

(2) is protected under local law against a judgment lien arising, as of the time of tax lien filing, out of an unsecured obligation.

(e) Priority of interest and expenses.—If the lien imposed by section 6321 is not valid as against a lien or security interest, the priority of such lien or security interest shall extend to—

(1) any interest or carrying charges upon the obligation secured,

(2) the reasonable charges and expenses of an indenture trustee or agent holding the security interest for the benefit of the holder of the security interest,

(3) the reasonable expenses, including reasonable compensation for attorneys, actually incurred in collecting or enforcing the obligation secured,

(4) the reasonable costs of insuring, preserving, or repairing the property to which the lien or security interest relates,

(5) the reasonable costs of insuring payment of the obligation secured, and

(6) amounts paid to satisfy any lien on the property to which the lien or security interest relates, but only if the lien so satisfied is entitled to priority over the lien imposed by section 6321,

to the extent that, under local law, any such item has the same priority as the lien or security interest to which it relates.

(f) Place for filing notice; form.—

(1) Place for filing.—The notice referred to in subsection (a) shall be filed—

(A) Under State laws.—

(i) Real property.—In the case of real property, in one office within the State (or the county, or other governmental subdivision), as designated by the laws of such State, in which the property subject to the lien is situated; and

(ii) Personal property.—In the case of personal property, whether tangible or intangible, in one office within the State (or the county, or other governmental subdivision), as designated by the laws of such State, in which the property subject to the lien is situated, except that State law merely conforming to or reenacting Federal law establishing a national filing system does not constitute a second office for filing as designated by the laws of such State; or

(B) With clerk of district court.—In the office of the clerk of the United States district court for the judicial district in which the property subject to the lien is situated, whenever the State has not by law designated one office which meets the requirements of subparagraph (A); or

(C) With Recorder of Deeds of the District of Columbia.—In the office of the Recorder of Deeds of the District of Columbia, if the property subject to the lien is situated in the District of Columbia.

(2) Situs of property subject to lien.—For purposes of paragraphs (1) and (4), property shall be deemed to be situated—

(A) Real property.—In the case of real property, at its physical location; or

(B) Personal property.—In the case of personal property, whether tangible or intangible, at the residence of the taxpayer at the time the notice of lien is filed.

For purposes of paragraph (2)(B), the residence of a corporation or partnership shall be deemed to be the place at which the principal executive office of the business is located, and the residence of a taxpayer whose residence is without the United States shall be deemed to be in the District of Columbia.

(3) Form.—The form and content of the notice referred to in subsection (a) shall be prescribed by the Secretary. Such notice shall be valid notwithstanding any other provision of law regarding the form or content of a notice of lien.

(4) Indexing required with respect to certain real property.—In the case of real property, if—

(A) under the laws of the State in which the real property is located, a deed is not valid as against a purchaser of the property who (at the time of purchase) does not have actual notice or knowledge of the existence of such deed unless the fact of filing of such deed has been entered and recorded in a public index at the place of filing in such a manner that a reasonable inspection of the index will reveal the existence of the deed, and

(B) there is maintained (at the applicable office under paragraph (1)) an adequate system for the public indexing of Federal tax liens,

then the notice of lien referred to in subsection (a) shall not be treated as meeting the filing requirements under paragraph (1) unless the fact of filing is entered and recorded in the index referred to in subparagraph (B) in such a manner that a reasonable inspection of the index will reveal the existence of the lien.

(5) National filing systems.—The filing of a notice of lien shall be governed solely by this title and shall not be subject to any other Federal law establishing a place or places for the filing of liens or encumbrances under a national filing system.

(g) Refiling of notice.—For purposes of this section—

(1) General rule.—Unless notice of lien is refiled in the manner prescribed in paragraph (2) during the required refiling period, such notice of lien shall be treated as filed on the date on which it is filed (in accordance with subsection (f)) after the expiration of such refiling period.

(2) Place for filing.—A notice of lien refiled during the required refiling period shall be effective only—

(A) if—

(i) such notice of lien is refiled in the office in which the prior notice of lien was filed, and

(ii) in the case of real property, the fact of refiling is entered and recorded in an index to the extent required by subsection (f)(4); and

(B) in any case in which, 90 days or more prior to the date of a refiling of notice of lien under subparagraph (A), the Secretary received written information (in the manner prescribed in regulations issued by the Secretary) concerning a change in the taxpayer's residence, if a notice of such lien is also filed in accordance with subsection (f) in the State in which such residence is located.

(3) Required refiling period.—In the case of any notice of lien, the term "required refiling period" means—

(A) the one-year period ending 30 days after the expiration of 10 years after the date of the assessment of the tax, and

(B) the one-year period ending with the expiration of 10 years after the close of the preceding required refiling period for such notice of lien.

(4) Transitional rule.—Notwithstanding paragraph (3), if the assessment of the tax was made before January 1, 1962, the first required refiling period shall be the calendar year 1967.

(h) Definitions.—For purposes of this section and section 6324—

(1) Security interest.—The term "security interest" means any interest in property acquired by contract for the purpose of securing payment or performance of an obligation or indemnifying against loss or liability. A security interest exists at any time (A) if, at such time, the property is in existence and the interest has become protected under local law against a subsequent judgment lien arising out of an unsecured obligation, and (B) to the extent that, at such time, the holder has parted with money or money's worth.

(2) Mechanic's lienor.—The term "mechanic's lienor" means any person who under local law has a lien on real property (or on the proceeds of a contract relating to real property) for services, labor, or materials furnished in connection with the construction or improvement of such property. For purposes of the preceding sentence, a person has a lien on the earliest date such lien becomes valid under local law against subsequent purchasers without actual notice, but not before he begins to furnish the services, labor, or materials.

(3) Motor vehicle.—The term "motor vehicle" means a self-propelled vehicle which is registered for highway use under the laws of any State or foreign country.

(4) Security.—The term "security" means any bond, debenture, note, or certificate or other evidence of indebtedness, issued by a corporation or a government or political subdivision thereof, with interest coupons or in registered form, share of stock, voting trust certificate, or any certificate of interest or participation in, certificate of deposit or receipt for, temporary or interim certificate for, or warrant or right to subscribe to or purchase, any of the foregoing; negotiable instrument; or money.

(5) Tax lien filing.—The term "tax lien filing" means the filing of notice (referred to in subsection (a)) of the lien imposed by section 6321.

(6) Purchaser.—The term "purchaser" means a person who, for adequate and full consideration in money or money's worth, acquires an interest (other than a lien or security interest) in property which is valid under local law against subsequent purchasers without actual notice. In applying the preceding sentence for purposes of subsection (a) of this section, and for purposes of section 6324—

(A) a lease of property,

(B) a written executory contract to purchase or lease property,

(C) an option to purchase or lease property or any interest therein, or

(D) an option to renew or extend a lease of property,

which is not a lien or security interest shall be treated as an interest in property.

(i) Special rules.—

(1) Actual notice or knowledge.—For purposes of this subchapter, an organization shall be deemed for purposes of a particular transaction to have actual notice or knowledge of any fact from the time such fact is brought to the attention of the individual conducting such transaction, and in any event from the time such fact would have been brought to such individual's attention if the organization had exercised due diligence. An organization exercises due diligence if it maintains reasonable routines for communicating significant information to the person conducting the transaction and there is reasonable compliance with the routine. Due diligence does not require an individual acting for the organization to communicate information unless such communication is part of his regular duties or unless he has reason to know of the transaction and that the transaction would be materially affected by the information.

(2) Subrogation.—Where, under local law, one person is subrogated to the rights of another with respect to a lien or interest, such person shall be subrogated to such rights for purposes of any lien imposed by section 6321 or 6324.

(3) Forfeitures.—For purposes of this subchapter, a forfeiture under local law of property seized by a law enforcement agency of a State, county, or other local governmental subdivision shall relate back to the time of seizure, except that this paragraph shall not apply to the extent that under local law the holder of an intervening claim or interest would have priority over the interest of the State, county, or other local governmental subdivision in the property.

(4) Cost-of-living adjustment.—In the case of notices of liens imposed by section 6321 which are filed in any calendar year after 1998, each of the dollar amounts under paragraph (4) or (7) of subsection (b) shall be increased by an amount equal to.—

(A) such dollar amount, multiplied by

(B) the cost-of-living adjustment determined under section 1(f)(3) for the calendar year, determined by substituting "calendar year 1996" for "calendar year 2016" in subparagraph (A)(ii) thereof.

If any amount as adjusted under the preceding sentence is not a multiple of $10, such amount shall be rounded to the nearest multiple of $10.

(j)　Withdrawal of notice in certain circumstances.—

(1)　In general.—The Secretary may withdraw a notice of a lien filed under this section and this chapter shall be applied as if the withdrawn notice had not been filed, if the Secretary determines that—

(A) the filing of such notice was premature or otherwise not in accordance with administrative procedures of the Secretary,

(B) the taxpayer has entered into an agreement under section 6159 to satisfy the tax liability for which the lien was imposed by means of installment payments, unless such agreement provides otherwise,

(C) the withdrawal of such notice will facilitate the collection of the tax liability, or

(D) with the consent of the taxpayer or the National Taxpayer Advocate, the withdrawal of such notice would be in the best interests of the taxpayer (as determined by the National Taxpayer Advocate) and the United States.

Any such withdrawal shall be made by filing notice at the same office as the withdrawn notice. A copy of such notice of withdrawal shall be provided to the taxpayer.

(2)　Notice to credit agencies, etc.—Upon written request by the taxpayer with respect to whom a notice of a lien was withdrawn under paragraph (1), the Secretary shall promptly make reasonable efforts to notify credit reporting agencies, and any financial institution or creditor whose name and address is specified in such request, of the withdrawal of such notice. Any such request shall be in such form as the Secretary may prescribe.

CROSS REFERENCES

Hazardous substances releases, liability, see 42 USCA § 9607.

Liability of operators for repayments to Mine Safety and Health Fund, see 30 USCA § 934.

Treatment of certain liens in liquidation, see 11 USCA § 724.

INDEX

References are to sections of the United States Code (titles 11, 18, and 28), the Uniform Commercial Code (UCC), the Uniform Voidable Transactions Act (UVTA), the Uniform Fraudulent Transfer Act (UFTA), the Bankruptcy Rules (BKR), and the Bankruptcy Forms (BKR Form)

INDEX

CHAPTER 9 PROCEEDINGS

CHAPTER 11 PROCEEDINGS

INDEX

INDEX

INDEX

INDEX

INDEX

INDEX

INDEX

INDEX